Routledge
Encyclopedia
Narrative Theory

Routledge Encyclopedia of Narrative Theory

Edited by David Herman,
Manfred Jahn and
Marie-Laure Ryan

Routledge
Taylor & Francis Group

LONDON AND NEW YORK

First published 2005
by Routledge
2 Park Square, Milton Park, Abingdon, Oxon, OX14 4RN

Simultaneously published in the USA and Canada
by Routledge
711 Third Ave, New York, NY 10017, USA

First published in paperback 2008

Routledge is an imprint of the Taylor & Francis Group, an informa business

© 2005, 2008 Routledge Ltd

Typeset in Times New Roman by
Newgen Imaging Systems (P) Ltd, India

Printed and bound in Great Britain by
CPI Antony Rowe, Chippenham, Wiltshire

British Library Cataloguing in Publication Data
A catalogue record for this book is available from the British Library

Library of Congress Cataloging in Publication Data
Routledge encyclopedia of narrative theory/edited by
David Herman, Manfred Jahn and
Marie-Laure Ryan.
p. cm.
Includes bibliographical references and index.
1. Narration (Rhetoric)–Encyclopedias.
I. Herman, David, 1962– II. Jahn, Manfred, 1943–
III. Ryan, Marie-Laure, 1946–

PN212.R68 2004
808′.003–dc22   2004051269

ISBN10: 0–415–28259–4 (hbk)
ISBN10: 0–415–77512–4 (pbk)
ISBN10: 0–203–93289–7 (ebk)

ISBN13: 978–0–415–28259–8 (hbk)
ISBN13: 978–0–415–77512–0 (pbk)
ISBN13: 978–0–203–93289–6 (ebk)

Contents

How to use this book

The following system for cross-referencing was used: in the body of each entry, asterisks (*) mark words or phrases constituting titles of other entries to be found in the volume; when needed, additional entry titles are indicated by means of parenthetical 'see X' pointers. The 'see also' cross-references listed at the end of entries are meant to direct the reader to further relevant items in the Encyclopedia.

There are also a number of short-definition entries that, while providing a brief sketch of terms and concepts (e.g., 'homodiegetic narration', 'secondary orality', 'sjuzhet'), are mainly intended to supplement the volume's index by pointing readers to more substantial treatments of these items elsewhere in the Encyclopedia. Thus, whereas the thumbnail definitions contain cross-references to longer entries, they are not themselves cross-referenced.

Introduction

The past several decades have seen an explosion of interest in narrative, with this multifaceted object of inquiry becoming a central concern in a wide range of disciplinary fields and research contexts. The 'narrative turn' gained impetus from the development of structuralist theories of narrative in France in the mid to late 1960s. Tzvetan Todorov coined the term 'la narratologie' in 1969 to designate what he and other Francophone structuralists (e.g., Roland Barthes, Claude Bremond, Gérard Genette, and A. J. Greimas) conceived of as a science of narrative modelled after the 'pilot-science' of Saussure's structural linguistics. Noting that narratives can be presented in a wide variety of formats, media, and genres, structuralists such as Barthes argued explicitly for a cross-disciplinary approach to the analysis of stories – an approach in which stories can be viewed as supporting a variety of cognitive and communicative activities, from spontaneous conversations and courtroom testimony to visual art, dance, and virtually hundreds of mythic and literary traditions.

Only after the heyday of structuralism, however, did Barthes's call for an interdisciplinary approach to narrative begin to be answered. As accounts of what happened to particular people in particular circumstances and with specific consequences, stories have come to be viewed as a basic human strategy for coming to terms with time, process, and change – a strategy that contrasts with, but is in no way inferior to, 'scientific' modes of explanation that characterise phenomena as instances of general covering laws. A cognitive schema and discourse type manifested in both literary and non-literary forms of expression, narrative now falls within the purview of many social-scientific, humanistic, and other disciplines, ranging from sociolinguistics, discourse analysis, communication studies, literary theory, and philosophy, to cognitive and social psychology, ethnography, sociology, media studies, Artificial Intelligence, and the study of organisations, medicine, jurisprudence, and history.

The result has been an exponential growth of research and teaching activity centring around narrative. International in scope, this activity has also spawned interdisciplinary book series (e.g., *Studies in Narrative*, published by John Benjamins, *Theory and Interpretation of Narrative*, published by the Ohio State University Press, *Narratologia*, published by Walter de Gruyter, and *Frontiers of Narrative*, published by the University of Nebraska Press). Scholarship in the field has given rise, as well, to a number of internationally recognised journals in which articles about narrative figure importantly (e.g., *Image (&) Narrative, Journal of Narrative Theory, Language and Literature, Narrative, Narrative Inquiry, New Literary History, Poetics, Poetics Today*, and *Style*). Another manifestation of cross-disciplinary interest in narrative is Columbia University's Program in Narrative Medicine (http://www.narrativemedicine.org/), inaugurated in 1996. Participants in this program, which aims 'to fortify medicine with ways of knowing about singular persons available through a study of humanities, especially literary studies and creative writing', have published their work in the journal *Literature and Medicine*, among other venues.

Equally symptomatic is a spate of recent conferences exploring the potential of narrative to bridge disciplines by fostering dialogue about concerns shared by diverse fields of inquiry. For example, the symposium on 'Narrative Intelligence' sponsored in November, 1999, by the American Association of Artificial Intelligence assembled computer scientists, designers of computer games, philosophers, linguists, and theorists of literary narrative. Likewise, a U.S. conference on 'Contemporary Narrative Theory: The State of the Field', held at Ohio State University in October, 2003, brought together a wide range of perspectives on (the study of) stories. So did the two interdisciplinary conferences on 'Narrative Matters' sponsored by St. Thomas University and the University of New Brunswick in Canada in 2002 and 2004; these conferences were explicitly designed to bridge humanistic and social-scientific approaches to narrative inquiry. Other venues testifying to the emergence of interdisciplinary narrative theory as an international focus of interest include the annual conferences organised by the Society for the Study of Narrative Literature (http://www.narrativesociety.org); the colloquia sponsored by the Narratology Research Group at the University of Hamburg in 2002 and 2003, dedicated to 'What is Narratology?' and 'Narratology beyond Literary Criticism', respectively (http://www.narratology.net); recent symposia associated with the Center for Narratological Studies based at the University of Southern Denmark (http://www.humaniora.sdu.dk/narratologi/index.html), along with similar initiatives sponsored by the Centre for Narrative Research at the University of East London (http://www.uel.ac.uk/cnr/forthcom.htm); a colloquium on 'The Revival of Narrative' held in 2004 at the University of Århus in Denmark and designed for scholars and students in the field of business and management; and the 2004 interdisciplinary symposium on 'The Travelling Concept of Narrative' held at the University of Helsinki. And this list is by no means exhaustive.

However, the very predominance of narrative as a focus of interest across multiple disciplines makes it imperative for scholars, teachers, and students to have access to a comprehensive reference resource – one that cuts across disciplinary specialisations to provide information about the core concepts, categories, distinctions, and technical nomenclatures that have grown up around the study of narrative in all of its guises. The present volume aims to be just this kind of universal reference tool, providing a comprehensive resource for students and researchers in the many disciplines drawing on concepts of storytelling and using methods of narrative analysis. Thus, while providing ample coverage of structuralist models and of the frameworks developed for the study of literary narratives, beyond this the Encyclopedia seeks to give a broad overview of paradigms for analysing stories across a variety of media and genres – from film, television, opera, and digital environments, to gossip, sports broadcasts, comics and graphic novels, and obituaries, to mention only a few.

Structure and organisation of the volume

The entries contained in the volume cover the history of the field, key terms and concepts developed by theorists of narrative, various schools and approaches, important debates, and a wide range of disciplinary contexts in which narrative figures prominently. The emphasis of the encyclopedia is on ideas, and there are consequently no entries devoted to individual theorists, but the volume's detailed index will enable readers to trace important contributions by ancient as well as recent and contemporary scholars of narrative.

The main body of the Encyclopedia is made up of five types of entries, arranged in a standard A–Z format: 3000 word mini-essays devoted to major topics, concepts, and approaches; 1000 word entries devoted to important concepts and forms of narrative; 500 and 200 word entries devoted to particular genres, technical terms, and key ideas; and thumbnail definitions providing a quick sketch of such notions as 'autodigetic narration' and 'narrating-I' and supplying cross-references to entries where more substantial discussions of those ideas may be found. Entries include cross-references to other items in the volume and a list of suggestions for further reading, enhancing the pedagogical value of the Encyclopedia for students and making it possible for advanced researchers to turn directly to state-of-the-art scholarship on a given topic.

The Encyclopedia also features three navigational aids included as front matter. One is an A–Z listing of all the entries in the volume; the list is coded to indicate the length of each entry (**bold type** for 3,000 and 1,000 word entries, normal type for 500 and 200 word entries, *italics* for thumbnail definitions). Placed after the A–Z list is a thematically organised reader's guide. Grouping the entries into three broad categories – 'key terms and concepts', 'approaches and disciplinary orientations', and 'genres, media, and regional forms' – the guide is meant to chart several paths that readers might take through the Encyclopedia. (Newcomers to the field, in particular, may wish to consult the guide before using the volume.) Note that many of the entries could be assigned to more than one of the categories included in the guide. However, though they may be provisional and partly overlapping, the guide's categories do afford at least a rough-and-ready heuristic that readers can use to orient themselves as they make their way through the volume. Finally, a list of contributors follows the reader's guide. This list provides an inventory of all the entries contributed by each author.

List of entries

In the following list, **bolded titles** denote long entries (1,000 to 3,000 words), while normal titles denote short entries (200 to 500 words). *Italicised titles* denote thumbnail definitions.

actant
action theory
adaptation
address
addresser and addressee
adolescent narrative
advertisements
African narrative
agency
allegory
alteration
alterity
anachrony
analepsis
ancient theories of narrative (non-Western)
ancient theories of narrative (Western)
anecdote
animated film
annals
anti-narrative
apology
archetypal patterns
architext
Artificial Intelligence and narrative
atomic and molecular narratives
attributive discourse
audience
Australian Aboriginal narrative

authentication
author
authorial narrative situation
autobiography
autodiegetic narration
autofiction
backstory
ballad
Biblical narrative
Bildungsroman
biography
biological foundations of narrative
blog (weblog)
catachresis
catharsis
causality
character
Chicago School, the
children's stories (narratives written for children)
children's storytelling
Chinese narrative
chronicle
chronotope
cinéroman
closure
codes for reading
cognitive narratology
coincidence

Reader's guide

In the following lists, **bolded titles** denote long entries (1,000 to 3,000 words), while normal titles denote short entries (200 to 500 words). *Italicised titles* denote thumbnail definitions.

Key terms and concepts

actant
address
addresser and addressee
agency
allegory
alteration
alterity
anachrony
analepsis
archetypal patterns
architext
atomic and molecular narratives
attributive discourse
audience
authentication
author
authorial narrative situation
autodiegetic narration
backstory
catachresis
catharsis
causality
character
chronotope
closure
codes for reading
coincidence

commentary
concretisation
conflict
defamiliarisation
deixis
denarration
description
desire
dialogism
dialogue in the novel
diegesis
disnarrated, the
distance
dramatic irony
dramatic situations
dual-voice hypothesis
ekphrasis
embedding
emic and etic
emplotment
epiphany
episode
events and event-types
existent
experiencing-I
experientiality
exposition

Approaches and disciplinary orientations

medicine and narrative
memory
metahistory
narrative as argument
narrative as cognitive instrument
narrative comprehension
narrative disorders
narrative, games, and play
narrative intelligence
narrative psychology
narrative semantics
narrative therapy
narrative turn in the humanities
natural narratology
Neo-Aristotelianism
no-narrator theory
oral-formulaic theory
organisations and narrative
phenomenology of narrative
philosophy and narrative
pictorial narrativity
possible-worlds theory
postclassical narratology
post-colonialism and narrative
poststructuralist approaches to narrative
pragmatics
psychoanalysis and narrative

psychological approaches to narrative
queer theory
quotation theory
reader-response theory
realism, theories of
reception theory
rhetorical approaches to narrative
Russian Formalism
science and narrative
semiotics
simulation and narrative
sociolinguistic approaches to narrative
sociological approaches to literary narrative
sociology and narrative
space in narrative
speech act theory
speech representation
story grammars
structuralist narratology
Tel Aviv School of narrative poetics
Tel Quel
text-type approach to narrative
text-world approach to narrative
thematic approaches to narrative
theology and narrative
trauma theory
visual narrativity

Genres, media, and regional forms

adaptation
adolescent narrative
advertisements
African narrative
anecdote
animated film
annals
anti-narrative
apology
Australian Aboriginal narrative
autobiography
autofiction
ballad
Biblical narrative
Bildungsroman
biography
blog (weblog)
children's stories (narratives
   written for children)
children's story-telling
Chinese narrative

chronicle
cinéroman
comics and graphic novel
coming-out story
composite novel
computer games and narrative
confessional narrative
conversational story-telling
counterfactual history
courtroom narrative
cyberpunk fiction
dance and narrative
detective fiction
diary
didactic narrative
digital narrative
drama and narrative
dramatic monologue
dream narrative
dystopian fiction
eco-narratives

écriture féminine
encyclopedic novel
epic
epistolary novel
ergodic literature
fable
fairy tale
family chronicle
fantastic, the
fantasy
film narrative
folklore
folktale
genre fiction
gossip
Gothic novel
hagiography
historical novel
historiographic metafiction
historiography
Holocaust narrative
horror narrative
hybrid genres
hypertext
institutional narrative
interactive fiction
Japanese narrative
joke
journalism
legend
letters as narrative
life story
magical realism
medieval narrative
metafiction
modernist narrative
multi-path narrative
multi-plot narrative
music and narrative
myth: thematic approaches
myth: theoretical approaches
narrative in poetry
Native American narrative
non-fiction novel
nouveau roman
novel, the
novella
nursery rhyme

obituary
opera
oral history
Oulipo
parable
parody
participatory narrative
pastiche
philosophical novel
photographs
picaresque novel
pornographic narrative
postmodern narrative
postmodern rewrites
prison narratives
psychological novel
Quixotic novel
radio narrative
realist novel
riddle
roman à clef
roman à thèse
romance
romance novel
Sanskrit narrative
satiric narrative
science fiction
screenplay
serial form
sermon
short story
skaz
slash fiction
slave narrative
soap opera
spectacle
sports broadcast
surfiction
surrealist narrative
tabloid narrative
tall tale
television
testimonio
thriller
transgressive fictions
travel narrative
urban legend
utopian and dystopian fiction

Editorial board

Contributors

Espen Aarseth	ergodic literature; multi-path narrative
H. Porter Abbott	closure; diary; narration
Richard Aczel	horizon of expectations; polyphony; voice
Jan Alber	narrativisation; natural narratology
Marshall Alcorn	psychoanalysis and narrative
Chadwick Allen	radio narrative
Gaby Allrath and Marion Gymnich	gender studies
Frank Ankersmit	contextualism (in historiography); Figura (Auerbach); hermeneutics; historicism; historiography; micro-storie; narrative explanation
Salvatore Attardo	humour studies and narrative
Jan Baetens	cinéroman; image and narrative
Mieke Bal	interdisciplinary approaches to narrative; visual narrativity
Michael Bamberg	agency; master narrative; positioning
Ann Banfield	no-narrator theory; skaz; tense and narrative
Richard Bauman	anecdote; performance; tall tale
Thomas O. Beebee	epistolary novel
Matthew Bell	performativity; queer theory
Reda Bensmaia	reality effect; readerly text, writerly text (Barthes)
	short definition: writerly text
Francis Berthelot	fantastic, the; transgressive fictions
Ilze Bezuidenhout-Raath	advertisements
S. Elizabeth Bird	tabloid narrative
M. Keith Booker	dystopian fiction; utopian and dystopian fiction
Charles L. Briggs	ethnographic approaches to narrative
Peter Brooks	confessional narrative
Sabine Buchholz and Manfred Jahn	dramatic monologue; space in narrative
Mike Cadden	children's stories (narratives written for children)
Philippe Carrard	annals; chronicle; sports broadcast
Paul Cobley	thriller
Jenny Cook-Gumperz and Amy Kyratzis	children's storytelling
Anja Cornils	theology and narrative
Martin Cortazzi	didactic narrative; education and narrative
Michele L. Crossley	narrative psychology
Jonathan Culler	logic of narrative

Hilary P. Dannenberg	counterfactual history; plot; plot types
	short definition: coincidence
Robert Dardenne	journalism
Marc Davis	narrative intelligence
Irene J.F. de Jong	ancient theories of narrative (Western); epic; in medias res
Nilli Diengott	narratee
Bernard Duyfhuizen	framed narrative; narrative transmission
Amy J. Elias	historiographic narratology
Kamilla Elliott	adaptation
Catherine Emmott	narrative comprehension
Astrid Erll	cultural-studies approaches to narrative
Ellen Esrock	visualisation
Jeanne C. Ewert	comics and graphic novel
Wendy Faris	magical realism
Monika Fludernik	composite novel; experientiality; hybridity; letters as narrative; naturalisation; speech representation; time in narrative
Susan Leigh Foster	dance and narrative
William Frawley and David Herman	narrative semantics
Esther Fritsch	gossip, slave narrative
Christin Galster	hybrid genres
Lori Ann Garner	oral-formulaic theory; ring-composition
Harry Garuba	African narrative; oral cultures and narrative
Joanna Gavins	mental mapping of narrative; scripts and schemata; text-world approach to narrative
Adam Gearey	law and narrative
Alexandra Georgakopoulou	sociolinguistic approaches to narrative; text-type approach to narrative
Richard J. Gerrig	memory; psychological approaches to narrative
Raymond W. Gibbs Jr	intentionality
Paul Goetsch	orality
Peter Goodrich	apology; catachresis; legal fiction; narrative as argument
David Gorman	architext; fiction, theories of; paratext; truth
Leger Grindon	genre theory in film studies
Torben Grodal	evolution of narrative forms; film narrative; thought and consciousness representation (film)
Richard Grusin	remediation
	short definition: repurposing
Andrea Gutenberg	coming-out story; écriture féminine
Virpi Hämeen-Anttila	Sanskrit narrative
William F. Hanks	deixis
Terry Harpold	digital narrative
Kathleen C. Haspel	communication studies and narrative
Ursula K. Heise	eco-narratives
David Herman	actant; action theory; atomic and molecular narratives; conflict; events and event-types; existent; genealogy; linguistic approaches to narrative; mytheme; narrative as cognitive instrument; storyworlds; structuralist narratology
	short definitions: backstory; dramatic irony; episode; extradiegetic narrator; fabula; intradiegetic narrator; molecular narratives; Neo-Aristotelianism; parody; pastiche; reader address; Russian Formalism; schemata; sjuzhet
Luc Herman	encyclopedic novel
Luc Herman and Bart Vervaeck	deconstructive approaches to narrative; postclassical narratology; poststructuralist approaches to narrative
Patrick Colm Hogan	archetypal patterns; narrative universals
Patrick Colm Hogan and Lalita Pandit	ancient theories of narrative (non-Western)
Anna M. Horatschek	alterity

Richard Humphrey	family chronicle; historical novel
Linda Hutcheon	reflexivity
Linda and Michael Hutcheon	opera
Lars-Christer Hydén	medicine and narrative
Ken Ireland	temporal ordering
David Schnasa Jacobsen	sermon
Manfred Jahn	alteration; cognitive narratology; dream narrative; epiphany; focalization; Freytag's triangle; mediacy; narrative situations; quotation theory
	short definitions: anachrony; analepsis; attributive discourse; authorial narrative situation; autodiegetic narration; experiencing-I; figural narration; first-person narration; frequency; heterodiegetic narration; historical present; homodiegetic narration; hypertext and hypotext (Genette); hypodiegetic narrative; interior monologue; narrating-I; narrative speed; palimpsest; paralepsis and paralipsis; point of attack; prolepsis; prospective narration; psychonarration; reflector; retrospective narration; second-person narration; simultaneous narration; syllepsis; third-person narration; transfocalization and transvocalisation; unreliable narration
Fotis Jannidis	author
Henry Jenkins	computer games and narrative
Joergen Dines Johansen	semiotics
Barbara Johnstone	discourse analysis (linguistics)
Sara Gwenllian Jones	fantasy; serial form; slash fiction; television
	short definition: soap opera
Irene Kacandes	address; trauma theory
Emma Kafalenos	indeterminacy; photographs
Madeleine Kasten	allegory
Michael Kearns	codes for reading; genre theory in narrative studies
Patrick Keating	montage; point of view (cinematic); shot
Bart Keunen	sociological approaches to literary narrative
Tom Kindt	biography
Mario Klarer	ekphrasis
Barbara Korte	travel narrative
Liesbeth Korthals Altes	ethical turn; irony; roman à thèse; Tel Quel
Sarah Kozloff	voice-over narration
Martin Kreiswirth	narrative turn in the humanities
Jerrold Levinson	soundtrack
Charlotte Linde	institutional narrative; life story
	short definition: organisations and narrative
Martin Löschnigg	autobiography; summary and scene
Susan Lohafer	short story
Peter Lunenfeld	story arc
Howard Mancing	biological foundations of narrative; novel, the; picaresque novel; Quixotic novel
Uri Margolin	authentication; character; formalism; naming in narrative; person; reference
Alastair Matthews	medieval narrative
Sigrid Mayer	simple forms
Maggie McCarthy	Bildungsroman; novella
William McGregor	Australian Aboriginal narrative; gesture
Brian McHale	dual-voice hypothesis; free indirect discourse; function (Jakobson); genre fiction; narrative in poetry; postmodern narrative; realeme; surfiction; verisimilitude
Brian McHale and Moshe Ron	Tel Aviv School of narrative poetics
Alison McMahan	animated film; simulation and narrative
Jan Christoph Meister	minimal narrative; narrative units; computational approaches to narrative

Elizabeth Mertz and Jonathan Yovel	courtroom narrative
Jacob L. Mey	pragmatics
Peter Michelson	pornographic narrative
David J. Mickelsen	spatial form
Dean A. Miller	hero
Linda Mills	narrative therapy
Nick Montfort	Artificial Intelligence and narrative; interactive fiction
Christian Moraru	intertextuality; narrative versions; postmodern rewrites
Linda J. Morrison	sociology and narrative
Warren Motte	Oulipo
Eva Müller-Zettelmann	nursery rhyme
Harold Neemann	fairy tale
William Nelles	embedding; function (Propp); mise en abyme
	short definition: narrative levels
Michael Newman	mindscreen
Michael Newman and David Herman	scene (cinematic)
Göran Nieragden	emic and etic
John D. Niles	ballad
Alleen Pace Nilsen	adolescent narrative
Neal Norrick	conversational storytelling; joke
Ansgar Nünning	commentary; historiographic metafiction; implied author; metanarrative comment; reliability
Patricia O'Connor	prison narratives
Patrick O'Donnell	metafiction
Patrick O'Neill	exposition; narrative structure
Alan Palmer	philosophical novel; psychological novel; realist novel; stream of consciousness and interior monologue; thought and consciousness representation (literature)
Louis Panier	narrative transformation
Torsten Pflugmacher	description
James Phelan	distance; narrative progression; rhetorical approaches to narrative
James Phelan and Wayne C. Booth	narrative techniques; narrator
John Pier	chronotope; metalepsis; isotopy
Arkady Plotnitsky	philosophy and narrative; science and narrative
Cathy Lynn Preston	urban legend
Gerald Prince	disnarrated, the; narrativity; point of view (literary); nouveau roman
Richard C. Prust	phenomenology of narrative
Heta Pyrhönen	detective fiction; retardatory devices; suspense and surprise; thematic approaches to narrative; thematisation
Peter J. Rabinowitz	audience; showing versus telling; speech act theory
Josef Hermann Real	satiric narrative
Luis Fernando Restrepo	testimonio
Brian Richardson	anti-narrative; causality; denarration; narrative dynamics
David H. Richter	Biblical narrative; Chicago School, the
Donald A. Ritchie	oral history
Andreea Deciu Ritivoi	identity and narrative
Ruth Ronen	realism, theories of
Georges Roque	graphic presentation as expressive device
Marie-Laure Ryan	catharsis; dramatic situations; media and narrative; mode; narrative; narrative, games, and play; panfictionality; possible-worlds theory; story grammars; tellability; virtuality
	short definitions: grand récit; hagiography; hypertext; interactivity; multi-plot narrative; participatory narrative; point; riddle; secondary orality; trebling/triplication
Mary Ellen Ryder	romance novel

Richard Saint-Gelais	transfictionality
Jean-Marie Schaeffer and Ioana Vultur	immersion; mimesis
Wolf Schmid	defamiliarisation
Ralf Schneider	emotion and narrative; reader constructs; reader-response theory; reception theory
	short definitions: concretisation; Constance School; implied reader
Steven Jay Schneider	horror narrative
Daniel R. Schwarz	Holocaust narrative
Robert A. Segal	myth: theoretical approaches
Dan Shen	diegesis; mind-style; mood (Genette); narrating (Genette); story-discourse distinction
Amy Shuman	folklore
Jack Sidnell	communication in narrative
	short definition: addresser and addressee
Roberto Simanowski	spectacle
Paul Simpson	modality
Michael Sinding	foregrounding
Roy Sommer	drama and narrative
Ellen Spolsky	gapping
Nigel Starck	obituary
Sue P. Starke	romance
Gerard Steen	metonymy; metaphor; parable
Nancy L. Stein and Valerie I. Kissel	story schemata and causal structure
Claudia Sternberg	screenplay
Randall Stevenson	modernist narrative
Philip Stewart	roman à clef
Peter Stockwell	science fiction; surrealist narrative
Carola Surkamp	perspective
Edina Szalay	Gothic novel
Aaron Tate	fable; folktale; legend
Lisa Tatonetti	Native American narratives
Bronwen Thomas	dialogue in the novel
Jill Walker	blog (weblog); cyberpunk fiction
Steven F. Walker	myth: thematic approaches
Robyn Warhol	feminist narratology; gaze; unnarratable, the
Michael G. Watson	Japanese narrative
Hayden White	emplotment; metahistory
Patrick Williams	dialogism; heteroglossia; ideology and narrative; Marxist approaches to narrative; post-colonialism and narrative
Susan Winnett	desire
Ruth Wodak	discourse analysis (Foucault)
Werner Wolf	intermediality; leitmotif; music and narrative; pictorial narrativity
Timothy C. Wong	Chinese narrative
Natascha Würzbach	motif
Katharine Young	frame theory
Kay Young and Jeffrey Saver	narrative disorders
Frank Zipfel	autofiction; non-fiction novel
Rolf A. Zwaan	situation model

A

ACTANT

One of the first projects of *structuralist narratology was the attempt to create a systematic framework for describing how *characters participate in the narrated action. Echoing Aristotle's subordination of character to action or *plot, Vladimir Propp (1968 [1928]) provided the basis for structuralist accounts of actants, which found their fullest expression in the work of A.J. Greimas (1983 [1966], 1987 [1973]). Conceived as 'fundamental role[s] at the level of narrative deep structure' (Prince 1987: 1), '*actants* are general categories [of behaviour or doing] underlying all narratives (and not only narratives) while [*actors*] are invested with specific qualities in different narratives' (Rimmon-Kenan 1983: 34).

Propp's groundbreaking analysis of the 'functions' performed by characters in Russian *folktales furnished a precedent for this structuralist conception of actants (*see* FUNCTION (PROPP)). Construing the function as 'an act of character, defined from the point of view of its significance for the course of the action' (1968 [1928]: 21), Propp argued that many seemingly diverse functions join together to create a few, typifiable 'spheres of action'. He developed a typology of seven general roles (the villain, the donor, the helper, the sought-for-person and her father, the dispatcher, the *hero, and the false hero) that correspond to the ways in which characters can participate in the plot structures found in the *genre of the folktale (Propp 1968 [1928]: 79–80).

Greimas drew on the syntactic theories of Lucien Tesnière (1976 [1959]) to re-characterise Propp's 'spheres of action' as actants. Associating actants with 'narrative syntax' (Greimas 1987 [1973]: 106), Greimas further argued that whereas

'an articulation of actors constitutes a particular *tale*; a structure of actants constitutes a *genre*' (1983 [1966]: 200). Working to refine Propp's typology of general roles, Greimas initially identified a total of six actants to which he thought all particularised narrative actors could be reduced: Subject, Object, Sender, Receiver, Helper, and Opponent. He explicated this scheme as follows: '[i]ts simplicity lies in the fact that it is entirely centred on the object of desire aimed at by the subject and situated, as object of communication, between the sender and the receiver – the desire of the subject being, in its part, modulated in projections from the helper and opponent' (1983 [1966]: 207).

In later work, however, Greimas demoted Helpers and Opponents to positive and negative 'auxiliants', thereby raising questions about the internal coherence and modelling adequacy of the actantial framework (Herman 2002: 128–33). At issue is the appropriate number and kinds of actants for all narrative genres and sub-genres, as well as the procedure for matching general actantial roles with particularised actors. A further issue is scalability, or the extent to which sentence-level units and structures can be used to analyse units and structures at the level of narrative discourse.

SEE ALSO: dramatic situations

References and further reading

Greimas, Algirdas Julien (1983 [1966]) *Structural Semantics: An Attempt at a Method*, trans. Danielle McDowell, Ronald Schleifer, and Alan Velie, Lincoln: University of Nebraska Press.
—— (1987 [1973]) 'Actants, Actors, and Figures', in Paul J. Perron and Frank H. Collins (trans.) *On*

Meaning: Selected Writings in Semiotic Theory, Minneapolis: University of Minnesota Press.

Herman, David (2002) *Story Logic: Problems and Possibilities of Narrative*, Lincoln: University of Nebraska Press.

Prince, Gerald (1987) *A Dictionary of Narratology*, Lincoln: University of Nebraska Press.

Propp, Vladimir (1968 [1928]) *Morphology of the Folktale*, trans. Laurence Scott, revised by Louis A. Wagner, Austin: University of Texas Press.

Rimmon-Kenan, Shlomith (1983) *Narrative Fiction: Contemporary Poetics*, London: Methuen.

Tesnière, Lucien (1976 [1959]) *Eléments de syntaxe structurale*, Paris: Klinksieck.

DAVID HERMAN

ACTION THEORY

Action theory, a subdomain of analytic *philosophy pioneered by scholars such as Rescher (1966) and von Wright (1966, 1983), explores ontological as well as epistemological dimensions of (human) action. It seeks to specify the minimal conditions for and distinguishing features of actions, which are construed as deliberate, planned behaviours within a larger context that also includes unplanned *events or happenings; more or less durative processes that may have been triggered by an agent, but that then continue to unfold over time; and actual as well as possible states or conditions in the world, i.e., ways the world is before, after, or as a result of the performance (or non-performance) of an action. Narrative analysts such as van Dijk (1976), Doležel (1998), Margolin (1986), Ryan (1991), and Herman (2002) have explored applications of action theory for the study of stories, focusing on story structure (*see* STORY-DISCOURSE DISTINCTION), *plot, *character, and the overall configuration of *storyworld. Conversely, narrative theory may help illuminate what an action really is.

Davidson (1980) poses questions that are central for any theory of action: 'What events in the life of a person reveal agency; what are his deeds and his doings in contrast to mere happenings in history; what is the mark that distinguishes his actions?' (43). Significantly, telling a narrative entails trying to forestall questions of just this sort, and action theorists have themselves drawn parallels between analysing actions and telling stories about what agents have done. Thus, von Wright (1983) suggests that '[t]o understand behaviour as

intentional ... is to fit it into a "story" about an agent' (42). Narratives, then, rely implicitly on conceptual frameworks that action theorists strive to make explicit. But more than this, action theory brings into focus key properties of narrative itself.

In his pathbreaking work on the logic of action, von Wright (1966) defines acting as intentionally bringing about or preventing a change in the world. In turn, change occurs when some state of affairs either ceases to be or comes to be. Thus a complete description of an action encompasses three components: (i) the *initial state*, or the state in which the world is at the moment when action is initiated; (ii) the *end-state*, or the state in which the world is when the action has been completed; and (iii) the state in which the world would have been had it not been for the action in question. Especially consequential for narrative theory is von Wright's emphasis on the importance of item (iii) for action representation. Whereas the end-state is simply the *result* of the action, von Wright calls the comparison of the initial state and the end-state (a comparison that yields item iii) the *acting-situation* or, alternatively, the *opportunity* of action (124). Grasping an acting-situation or opportunity for action is thus tantamount to being able to formulate a counterfactual conditional statement about what would have happened had it not been for what an agent did on a given occasion. So to build a logic for action sentences, one must model not only 'sentences describing results of action but also ... sentences describing states which are, or are not, transformed through the action' (von Wright 1983: 111).

At least since Bremond (1973), narrative theorists have likewise stressed that narratives unfold against a backdrop consisting of what might have happened but did not. In von Wright's terms, this work suggests that it is part of the nature of narrative to indicate, in a more or less explicit and sustained way, that the actions being recounted are embedded in acting-situations. Negative sentences in a narrative, for example, serve to foreground opportunities for action, indicating how paths chosen by storyworld participants acquire their significance from the place they occupy within a network of paths *not* chosen. As Labov (1972) puts it in his account of mechanisms of evaluation in oral narratives, '[n]egative sentences ... provide a way of evaluating events by placing them against the background of other events which might have happened, but did not' (381; cf. Prince 1988).

Meanwhile, Ryan (1991: 148–74) has drawn on *possible-worlds theory to argue that the number of virtual or unactualised states, events, and actions in a narrative increases in proportion with its *tellability. A story in which many things might have gone wrong is inherently more tellable than one involving characters who, as they act, are subject to little or no risk. Herman (2002) argues that *genre-based preferences determine the extent to which acting-situations will be foregrounded over results (or vice versa) in a given narrative. *Obituaries foreground results, i.e., the achievements of the deceased. By contrast, exploring characters' motives, dispositions, and attitudes, *psychological novels like those of Henry James show a preference for acting-situations.

Just as action theory helps illuminate core properties of narrative, research on narrative may in turn clarify just what an action is. A central problem of action theory concerns how many actions should be identified as such within a given stretch of behaviour, with various scholars outlining austere, moderate, and prolific accounts (Davis 1979: 30ff.). Arguably, however, actions could not be mentally projected at all in the absence of narrative-based norms for act individuation (Herman 2002: 69–73). Protocols are needed to distinguish a range of discrete, more or less richly profiled acts – acts located in a storyworld – from an undifferentiated mass or agglomeration of behaviours. In this construal, narrative furnishes a heuristic for marking off regions of purposive action within the general field of activity. The scope of the actions thus demarcated, and the level of granularity with which they are represented, is crucially related to the kind of story being told.

SEE ALSO: agency; atomic and molecular narratives; character; counterfactual history; disnarrated, the; modality; narrative explanation; possible-worlds theory

References and further reading

Bremond, Claude (1973) Logique du récit, Paris: Seuil.
Davidson, Donald (1980) Essays on Actions and Events, Oxford: Clarendon Press.
Davis, Lawrence H. (1979) Theory of Action, Englewood Cliffs, NJ: Prentice-Hall, Inc.
van Dijk, Teun A. (1976) 'Philosophy of Action and Theory of Narrative', Poetics, 5, 287–338.
Doležel, Lubomír (1998) Heterocosmica: Fiction and Possible Worlds, Baltimore: Johns Hopkins University Press.
Herman, David (2002) Story Logic: Problems and Possibilities of Narrative, Lincoln: University of Nebraska Press.
Labov, William (1972) 'The Transformation of Experience in Narrative Syntax', in Language in the Inner City, Philadelphia: University of Pennsylvania Press.
Margolin, Uri (1986) 'The Doer and the Deed: Action Basis for Characterization in Narrative', Poetics Today, 7, 205–26.
Prince, Gerald (1988) 'The Disnarrated', Style, 22, 1–8.
Rescher, Nicholas (1966) 'Aspects of Action', in Nicholas Rescher (ed.) The Logic of Decision and Action, Pittsburgh: University of Pittsburgh Press.
Ryan, Marie-Laure (1991) Possible Worlds, Artificial Intelligence, and Narrative Theory, Bloomington: Indiana University Press.
von Wright, Georg Henrik (1966) 'The Logic of Action – A Sketch', in Nicholas Rescher (ed.) The Logic of Decision and Action, Pittsburgh: University of Pittsburgh Press.
——(1983) Practical Reason, Ithaca: Cornell University Press.

DAVID HERMAN

ADAPTATION

Adaptation refers to the representation of a work in another medium (see REMEDIATION), as when a play is adapted to a ballet, or within the same medium, as when a *novel adapts another novel (Genette 1997). Adaptation can occur within or between any *media. It engages many aspects of media and their contexts and has been studied through a wide spectrum of critical lenses. Meisel (1983) documents pervasive nineteenth-century adaptations among the *visual, literary, and dramatic arts. Subsequently, adaptations have been made among written texts, painting (see PICTORIAL NARRATIVITY), sculpture, *comics, *photography, *music, *dance, theater (see DRAMA AND NARRATIVE), *film, *television, new media (see DIGITAL NARRATIVE), and more.

Critical approaches to adaptation are equally diverse. *Semiotic, *formalist, narratological, *structuralist, and genre-oriented critics tend to approach adaptation as translation, focusing on categorical differentiations and comparative relations between media, on processes of adaptation, and on tensions between fidelity of the second work to the first and fidelity of the second work to its own medium (McFarlane 1996). Other critics reject translation models as aesthetically and interpretively limiting. Wagner (1975) favours *transposition*, in which the first work provides only a seed of inspiration for the adaptation. Bruhn (2000) prefers *transmedialisation*, a term that emphasises *intermediality, over terms like *transmutation*, which figures adaptation as the displacement of one form by the other, and *transfiguration* and *transformation*, which present adaptation as an unduly hierarchical or vaguely mystical affair. Elliott (2003) characterises some adaptations as figural operations: for example, an operation in which a film adaptation of prose fiction works *metaphorically, like a vehicle transforming a tenor, precluding any simple return to the novel as origin, so that adaptation emerges as a mutually transforming rather than as a one-way process.

Numerous scholars construct adaptation as interpretation, whether aesthetic or critical (Wagner 1975). Interpretive adaptations take many forms: imitation, appreciation, criticism, parody or 'blank parody' (emptied of *satiric edge and didactic message), dialectic, *deconstruction, *psychoanalysis, *cultural study, pastiche, or cannibalisation (resulting in an empty commodification) (Wagner 1975; Jameson 1991; Cardwell 2002; Elliott 2003). Many interpretivists are concerned less with the semiotics, media, and *genres of adaptation than with how a work adapts to a new social context or *audience, especially when an adaptation entails intercultural, international, or transhistorical shifts, or when it occurs between differently valued media, like high and low art forms. Contexts may be mythological, ideological, *psychological, phenomenological, *cognitive, canonical, pedagogical, historical, national, political, *identity-based, *sociological, economical, technological, or otherwise related to the production, reception, and consumption of particular adaptations (Cardwell 2002; Elliott 2003). To date, adaptation studies have tended to divide along formal and contextual lines, but the process of adaptation so manifestly engages both formal and contextual elements that the field offers strong potential for integrating these concerns with applications to humanities criticism more generally.

SEE ALSO: cinéroman; ekphrasis; ideology and narrative; intertextuality; myth: thematic approaches; narrative versions; postmodern rewrites

References and further reading

Bruhn, Siglind (2000) *Musical Ekphrasis: Composers Responding to Poetry and Painting*, Hillsdale, NY: Pendragon.

Cardwell, Sarah (2002) *Adaptation Revisited: Television and the Classic Novel*, Manchester: Manchester University Press.

Elliott, Kamilla (2003) *Rethinking the Novel/Film Debate*, Cambridge: Cambridge University Press.

Genette, Gérard (1997) *Palimpsests: Literature in the Second Degree*, trans. Channa Newman and Claude Doubinsky, Lincoln: University of Nebraska Press.

Jameson, Fredric (1991) *Postmodernism, or, the Cultural Logic of Late Capitalism*, Durham: Duke University Press.

McFarlane, Brian (1996) *Novel to Film: An Introduction to the Theory of Adaptation*, Oxford: Clarendon.

Meisel, Martin (1983) *Realizations: Narrative, Pictorial, and Theatrical Arts in Nineteenth-Century England*, Princeton: Princeton University Press.

Wagner, Geoffrey (1975) *The Novel and the Cinema*, Rutherford, NJ: Farleigh Dickinson University Press.

KAMILLA ELLIOTT

ADDRESS

In literary contexts, the term 'address' refers to vocative formulations that identify the reader directly, hence also the term 'reader address'; 'you' and 'dear reader' are the most common appellations in English prose fiction (*see* NOVEL, THE). In Romance and many other languages and literatures, the pronouns of address can be singular or plural (sometimes dual), and formal or informal. The third-person can also serve as a form of address when the point is to emphasise unequal status between speaker and addressee, for instance, to show respect or scorn (as when Barth's (1968) *narrator curses: 'The reader!').

Address in narrative is usually interpreted as a strategy to get the reader more involved. Lausberg (1998: 339) writes, for instance, that 'it ... snatches the reader concerned away from the anonymous mass of readers'. Robyn Warhol, however, has shown that narrators can use reader address either to engage or to distance (1989). Gerald Prince's concept of the *narratee as recipient of the *narration (1971) paved the way for analyses like Brian McHale's of so-called 'second-person fiction' (1987), in which entire texts are narrated in address form (*see* PERSON).

From within their respective disciplines, the philosopher Martin Buber and the linguist

Emile Benveniste explicated the acknowledgement of subjectivity and creation of interrelationship effected by the pair I/you. Ann Banfield calls 'you' the 'pre-eminent sign of interaction' (1982: 120). Similarly, in her analysis of the figure of apostrophe in lyric poetry, Barbara Johnson remarks on the 'ineradicable tendency of language to animate whatever it addresses' (1987: 191). Putting these insights into dialogue with conversation analysis – which distinguishes among 'addressees' (those who are addressed), 'hearers' (those who can physically hear the address), and 'recipients' (those who orient toward the address in anticipation of replying) (Goodwin and Heritage 1990: 291–92) – suggests that individual readers of address in fiction can occupy all three positions when they choose to become addressees by (hearing)-reading the address and (receiving)-interpreting it as an utterance meant for them. Irene Kacandes documents actual reader-response to instances of address in fiction, concluding that 'even when "you" has a name and a specific story, the second-person pronoun wields power to move readers, evidently causing most of them to feel themselves individually addressed and/or to feel strong emotions about the experience of reading the address that creates an unusual relationship between the narrator and narratee' (2001: 162).

SEE ALSO: audience; communication in narrative; deixis; reader constructs; reader-response theory; rhetorical approaches to narrative

References and further reading

Banfield, Ann (1982) *Unspeakable Sentences: Narration and Representation in the Language of Fiction*, London: Routledge & Kegan Paul.

Barth, John (1968) *Lost in the Funhouse*, New York: Doubleday.

Benveniste, Emile (1971) *Problems in General Linguistics*, vol. 1, trans. Mary Elizabeth Meek, Coral Gables: University of Miami Press.

Buber, Martin (1955 [1923]) *Ich und Du*, Cologne: Hegner.

Goodwin, Charles, and John Heritage (1990) 'Conversation Analysis', *Annual Review of Anthropology*, 19, 283–307.

Johnson, Barbara (1987) *A World of Difference*, Baltimore: Johns Hopkins University Press.

Kacandes, Irene (2001) *Talk Fiction: Literature and the Talk Explosion*, Lincoln: University of Nebraska Press.

Lausberg, Heinrich (1998) *Handbook of Literary Rhetoric: A Foundation for Literary Study*, trans. Matthew T. Bliss, Annemiek Jansen, and David E.

Orton, eds. David E. Orton and R. Dean Anderson, Leiden, Netherlands: Brill.

McHale, Brian (1987) *Postmodernist Fiction*, London: Methuen.

Prince, Gerald (1971) 'Notes toward a Categorization of Fictional "Narratees"', *Genre*, 4, 100–05.

Warhol, Robyn (1989) *Gendered Interventions: Narrative Discourse in the Victorian Novel*, New Brunswick: Rutgers University Press.

IRENE KACANDES

ADDRESSER AND ADDRESSEE

Terms used to refer to speech act participants variously realised in concrete communicative situations as 'speaker and hearer' or 'writer and reader'. Literary texts are sometimes said to embody a 'structure of address' through which they *position the reader or recipient (as a member of a group, as a confidant, as a subordinate etc.). *See* COMMUNICATION IN NARRATIVE; FUNCTION (JAKOBSON).

ADOLESCENT NARRATIVE

As part of popular culture, books for teenagers are strongly influenced by movies, *television, and now the Internet and video games (*see* COMPUTER GAMES AND NARRATIVE; DIGITAL NARRATIVE; FILM NARRATIVE). They make for an interesting contrast with *postmodern texts for adults, because even the most deconstructed teenage books respect the basic principles of *tellability. They have an orientation, a complicating action, an evaluation, and a resolution (Labov 1972) (*see* DISCOURSE ANALYSIS (LINGUISTICS)). Even in poetry and information books, young readers demand that 'something happen'.

Critics unfamiliar with the wealth of high quality literature produced for today's teenagers tend to assume that adolescent literature is exclusively about the physical and emotional challenges connected to puberty. Certainly, such topics are included, but defining young adult or adolescent literature on the basis of such limited subject matter is inaccurate and leads to the question of whether adolescent literature is really a *genre. If it is, how then does it relate to other genres such as *science fiction, *fantasy, *biographies, murder mysteries (*see* DETECTIVE FICTION), adventure tales, self-help books, and informative non-fiction? All of these genres are published for teenagers and taught in classes in adolescent literature.

Narrative theory may help answer these questions by providing insights into what these various types of literature have in common when targeting a particular age group. Conversely, looking at this range of material through narratological concepts may help scholars refine their theoretical positions. A serious study of adolescent narrative would bring the additional benefit of helping critics understand the direction in which our culture is moving. Publishers, teachers, and librarians are so eager to get books into the hands of young readers that books for this *audience, when compared to those for a general adult audience, are more likely to reflect current trends.

Dresang (1999) claims that critics need new ways to examine the changing forms and formats of the books written for young people. Points of interest include the changing perspectives concerning what is appropriate for and accessible to young readers. One of the new ways to approach adolescent narratives is to read them against the background of cyber-culture. Discussing the 'edgy' fiction that is making literature 'cool' again, Spitz (1999) writes that teen fiction may 'be the first literary genre born of the Internet'. He believes that these fast-paced narratives have a kinship with MTV and the Internet in that they take advantage of the ease with which kids process information in unconventional formats. The books that Spitz used as examples include a book that blends a boy's journal with a movie script he is writing while he waits to go on trial, a book written entirely through *letters to 'Dear Friend', a book with chapters alternating between the 1800s and today, and a book in which a thirteen-year-old girl rejects the social worker's report and writes her own account of an affair she had with her mother's lover which ended in a murder and a suicide.

The unusual formats of these books are tied to the stories they tell and to teenagers' resistance to pages and pages of 'plain old type'. Lewis Carroll's Alice was a forerunner of today's young readers when she asked, 'And what is the use of a book without pictures or conversation?' Perhaps the most distinctive aspect of today's young adult novels is their conversational style. They sound as if one teenager is writing directly to another. The protagonists are in their teens, or perhaps their twenties. When, and if, the books feature adults, the viewpoint is still likely to be that of a young person and the problems will be the kinds of challenges that young adults face such as establishing their independence, discovering their sexuality, learning how to get along with cohorts and adults, and developing the moral codes they will rely on throughout life.

These subjects make interesting stories, especially when seen through fresh eyes, which is one reason that so many films and television sitcoms feature teenagers or young adults not yet weighed down with family responsibilities. These protagonists are portrayed as smart young people who can solve problems without sentimentality and without falling back on adults for help. Many of the books are told in the first-person, which makes it easier for the readers to forget that the story was actually written by an adult. And even when authors do not use first-person *narration, they fill their stories with *dialogue so that the characters can speak for themselves.

One of the problems of a first-person narrative is that only one person's viewpoint can be represented (*see* FOCALIZATION; PERSON; PERSPECTIVE). *Authors sometimes get around this restriction by having different *characters narrate different chapters. Another technique is to have an unreliable *narrator reveal information in such a way that the reader figures things out faster or more clearly than does the narrator (*see* RELIABILITY). Still another technique is for an author to write as an adult, but to tell a story from the youth of the narrator. This allows the writer to use 'adult' language and words that would sound false or pretentious if they came from the mouth of a teenaged character.

Within the last decade, much of what young people read has been written by other teenagers. The wide availability of the Internet and the relative ease with which websites can be created, together with the creation of special programs in writing clubs, libraries, and schools, have encouraged young adults to put together their own websites where young people's writing can be published. These websites are in many ways taking the place of the *zines* (special interest magazines produced through desktop publishing) which were popular in the 1990s.

Encouraged by the interest that young people are showing in the writings of other teenagers, several mass-produced magazines have been created with the purpose of publishing teen writing, along with teen-produced *photography and art.

In one magazine that Nilsen and Donelson (2000) looked at, 90% of the pieces were written in the first-person. In another, which included more news-like articles and reviews, about 75% of the writing consisted of first-person stories. Poetry slams, and theater evenings in which students present their own monologues rather than the traditional school play, are other channels through which young adults are given opportunities to appreciate each other's literary works.

SEE ALSO: children's stories (narratives written for children); image and narrative; narrative situations

References and further reading

Dresang, Eliza T. (1999) *Radical Change: Books for Youth in a Digital Age*, New York: H. W. Wilson.

Labov, William (1972) 'The Transformation of Experience in Narrative Syntax', in *Language in the Inner City*, Philadelphia: University of Pennsylvania Press.

Nilsen, Alleen Pace, and Kenneth L. Donelson (2000) *Literature for Today's Young Adults*, New York: Addison Wesley and Longman.

Rosenblatt, Louise (1983) *Literature as Exploration*, New York: Modern Language Association.

Spitz, David (1999) 'Reads Like Teen Spirit', *Time*, July 19.

ALLEEN PACE NILSEN

ADVERTISEMENTS

Advertisements are any paid form of non-personal presentation and promotion of ideas, goods, or services by an identified sponsor. They consist of text and *image(s), organised in a manner which strengthens the interplay between the verbal and the non-verbal elements. Narrative advertising relies on a sender (teller), a message (tale), and an addressee (*see* FUNCTION (JAKOBSON)). Advertisement texts pose a particular challenge for analysis, as there are hundreds of discourse types 'which merge into each other and defy exact definition' (Cook 1992: 4). Advertisements can either be commercial (e.g., consumer, trade, or corporate advertising) or non-commercial (e.g., government or charity advertising). They appear in various *media, such as *radio, *television, print, the Internet, mobile technology, etc. They influence policies and the appearance of media as they advance and perpetuate ideas and values, and create needs that are indispensable to a specific economy.

Narrative advertisements are an important object of analysis because they have to raise the product's selling point within the limits of a temporally and spatially restricted storyline. Because of these restrictions many aspects of the narrative message can often only be implied or suggested (*see* GAPPING). Nevertheless, the most basic functions of advertisements are to inform, persuade, or do both. Advertisements generally share three basic action patterns which, following Greimas (1983 [1966]), occur in all narrative, namely, (1) *desire, search, or aim (involving a subject and an object); (2) communication (involving a sender and a receiver); and (3) auxiliary support or hindrance (involving a helper and/or an opponent) (*see* ACTANT).

Often it is the medium that dictates whether an advertisement has a *narrative structure or not. Radio and television clearly lend themselves to narrative by presenting a *storyworld mimetically. It seems that advertisers prefer using a narrative structure in advertisements for utilitarian products such as beer, cereals, laundry detergent, etc. This structure provides the opportunity to show a change of state (a 'before' and 'after' effect) and how the product brings this about. Advertisements for luxury products (designer clothes, cars, jewellery) tend to be more descriptive (*see* DESCRIPTION), and the emphasis is on the product and no longer on *narrators or *characters. A synecdochic or *metonymic relation operates 'where the product is represented as an intrinsic part of the chic and elegant lifestyle that the advertisement typically portrays' (Toolan 2001: 84).

Advertising is often criticised because it creates false needs, aspirations, and wants, which could lead to anti-social behaviour and a breakdown of social structures – for instance, an advertisement showing an idealised American way of life could have a detrimental effect on a traditional African society. More generally, advertisements reflect the essence of the social structure and cultural *identity of a country or specific society (*see* CULTURAL STUDIES APPROACHES TO NARRATIVE).

SEE ALSO: communication studies and narrative; sociology and narrative

References and further reading

Cook, Guy (1992) *The Discourse of Advertising*, London: Routledge.

Greimas, Algirdas Julien (1983 [1966]) *Structural Semantics: An Attempt at a Method*, trans. Danielle McDowell, Ronald Schleifer, and Alan Velie, Lincoln: University of Nebraska Press.

Hermerén, Lars (1999) *English for Sale: A Study of the Language of Advertising*, Lund: Lund University Press.

Selden, Raman, and Peter Widdowson (1993) *A Reader's Guide to Contemporary Literary Theory*, Hertfordshire: Harvester Wheatsheaf.

Toolan, Michael (2001) *Narrative: A Critical Linguistic Introduction*, London: Routledge.

Vestergaard, Torben, and Kim Schroeder (1985) *The Language of Advertising*, Oxford: Blackwell.

ILZE BEZUIDENHOUT-RAATH

AFRICAN NARRATIVE

Narrative in Africa is as old as human habitation on the continent. The complexity created by this time scale is further compounded by the hundreds of languages spoken on the continent that all have their own narrative traditions and histories. To speak of African narrative therefore is to refer to a subject so vast and varied that systematic coverage of it needs to be addressed via the approaches that claim to have developed a conceptual grasp of the material.

Perhaps the most significant descriptive and analytical division in the field arising from the foregrounding of the medium through which the narrative is presented is a conceptual distinction between oral and written narratives (see ORAL CULTURES AND NARRATIVE; ORALITY). The differences between them are regularly highlighted and used as a contrastive framework for understanding the specific nature of written narratives in Africa. Orality is so often said to be fundamental to African narrative that even when written narratives are the subject of analysis the focus is usually on identifying the oral essence underlying the writing. There is no doubt that oral narratives are dynamically present in contemporary African societies, and that they do, to a large extent, influence the styles and structures of written narratives. Indeed, within the same community, it is not unusual to find age-old oral tales thriving in a coeval coexistence with the most recent *postmodern narrative experimentation conducted in writing.

During the long history of storytelling in Africa, storytellers and their *audiences developed their own conventions and categories for the production and reception of oral narratives. Various local *genres and idioms were constructed for structuring *performance and for guiding participation and critique. Among the Yorùbá of south western Nigeria alone, the proliferation of names for various narrative forms indicates a highly developed generic consciousness and a critical awareness of the formal conventions. Yoruba terms such as the *ìjálá, ewì, odù ifá*, and *oríkì* refer to poetic forms governed by specific generic conventions and idioms known to both artist and audience. The vocabulary of narrative terms is equally rich in virtually all the ethnic communities and language groups in the continent. Some genres such as the praise poem, funeral dirge, proverb, trickster tale, riddle, dilemma tale, etc. are virtually ubiquitous and often have identifiable sub-genres in some communities. Unfortunately, however, this strong generic consciousness displayed at local community levels was not matched by the concepts deployed in early scholarship on oral narratives.

When serious scholarly attention began to be paid to African oral narratives in the nineteenth-century, researchers adopted the dominant academic trend of the time, rather than building on local understanding. These trends were largely based on evolutionist and diffusionist theories of culture (see ETHNOGRAPHIC APPROACHES TO NARRATIVE). Evolutionist approaches under the guidance of Edward Burnet Tylor (1832–1917) and James George Frazer (1854–1941) regarded African oral narratives as survivals of an earlier age, remnants from the infancy of humankind. These narratives were seen as representing earlier stages in the linear progress of human history; and the overriding concern was understanding the evolution of human culture. Diffusionists, on the other hand, were concerned about the point of origin of specific tales and the paths of their diffusion to various regions of the world. Diffusionist scholars led by the Grimm brothers, Antti Aarne, and Stith Thompson produced extensive *motif indices in the quest for the archetypal tale (see FOLKTALE).

This concern with culture was later to be displaced by a rising interest in society and social structures inspired largely by the anthropologists Malinowsky and Radcliff-Brown, who by the 1930s began to insist on the importance of empirical studies of so-called 'primitive' societies. The new emphasis on ethnographies and the concerns of the structural-functional anthropologists carried into the study of oral narrative. Function was now the operative concept and tales were read in terms of their function in maintaining the social structure and stabilising society. According to Isidore Okpewho (1992), the academic interests that influenced the study of African oral narratives can be broadly classified as the ethnological (governed by an interest in culture), the cognitionist (characterised by a focus on the mind), and the taxonomic (engaged with dissecting the morphology of the tale, to appropriate the telling title of Vladimir Propp's book) (see NARRATIVE UNITS; STRUCTURALIST NARRATOLOGY). Though the perspectives adopted may not neatly and exclusively fall into one or the other of these categories, it is fairly safe to say that the evolutionists and functionalists (tales as carriers of culture) fall within the first ethnological camp while those concerned with the mentalities of 'primitive' peoples fall within the second, and the formalists in the third (see FORMALISM). But structuralists, at least those of a Lévi-Straussian persuasion, often straddle all three.

Most of these approaches were often tied to specific disciplines and their methodologies, usually anthropology, psychology, *sociology, and literary studies. Contemporary approaches tend to be more *interdisciplinary, emphasising performance and creativity together with the dynamics of social and cultural context, the importance of various publics and power relations, and the *agency of performers themselves (Barber and Moraes Farias 1989; Brown 1999; Furniss and Gunner 1995). In a sense, it can be said that the scholarly approaches by a long tortuous route have finally come to what the storytellers and their communities always knew or took for granted: that any understanding of African narrative must be grounded, literally and metaphorically, in the conventions and idioms created by the people themselves and their own understanding of the meanings of these narratives. It is only after this that meaningful theoretical and comparative work can begin.

It is probably necessary to ask at this point where the unique 'Africanness' of African narrative lies. The history of colonialism, the dominance of Western categories of knowledge, and the consequent quest to establish an African *identity and perspective have made this a regular question in academic inquiry (see POST-COLONIALISM AND NARRATIVE). And the question is often posed in these terms: is there a unique, ontological essence that marks African narrative as African? The answer quite simply is no. The 'Africanness' of African narrative resides only in the specific contexts of the cultures and histories of the production of narrative in Africa.

SEE ALSO: Australian Aboriginal narrative; Chinese narrative; Japanese Narrative; Native American narrative; Sanskrit narrative

References and further reading

Barber, Karin, and P. F. de Moraes Farias (eds) (1989) *Discourse and its Disguises: The Interpretation of African Oral Texts*, Birmingham: Birmingham University Press.

Brown, Duncan (ed.) (1999) *Oral Literature and Performance in Southern Africa*, Oxford: James Currey.

Finnegan, Ruth (1970) *Oral Literature in Africa*, Oxford: Oxford University Press.

Furniss, Graham, and Liz Gunner (eds) (1995) *Power, Marginality and African Oral Literature*, Cambridge: Cambridge University Press.

Julien, Eileen (1992) *African Novels and the Question of Orality*, Bloomington: Indiana University Press.

Okpewho, Isidore (1992) *African Oral Literature: Backgrounds, Character, and Continuity*, Bloomington: Indiana University Press.

HARRY GARUBA

AGENCY

Central to agency are the questions: what is an action (versus an *'event', a 'happening' or a 'state') (see ACTION THEORY)? Whose action is it (including who can be held responsible for it)? Is it meaningful and morally 'good' or 'bad'? Three aspects of agency, all equally relevant for narrative theorising (though from different perspectives), can be singled out as especially important: (1) agency as an epistemic issue (for the use of narratives in the social sciences); (2) linguistic agency (for the analysis of *character representations in the *storyworld); and (3) agency in narrating a storied world (pertaining to the author-narrator-audience relationship) (see AUDIENCE; AUTHOR; NARRATOR).

(1) The question of (human) agency is central to the study of self, *identity, and personhood.

Agency can be located according to two contrasting views: it is either a 'subject position' that is determined by dominant discourses and *master narratives (*see* POSITIONING), or it embodies the self-creating (if not self-inventing) subject. From the first perspective (a world-to-subject direction of fit), the subject's actions are given to the subject by social, historical and/or biological forces, subjecting the subject and determining its action potential. From the second perspective (a subject-to-world direction of fit), the human subject creates itself; it is based on consciousness and free will, capable of making decisions, and agentively engaged in both world- and self-making, particularly in narrative self-constructions (Bruner 1990). All attempts to position the subject (dialectically) in some middle-ground between these two extreme points of departure start with some form of socio-cultural grounding within which the subject can agentively position itself; such models situate the subject in levels of responsibility and commitment, the negotiation of which results in the becoming of a moral person.

(2) 'Linguistic agency' (also called 'agentivity' or 'animacy') refers to the linguistic marking of different *perspectives in which represented characters are viewed as relating to objects and to other characters in the (represented) world (*see* EXISTENT). Languages typologically offer different lexical and grammatical choices for character and event construction, and by making such choices speakers signal different perspectives (and position selves and others) in terms of more versus less agency, dynamism, and affectedness. In this way, speakers can downplay or foreground characters' (as well as their own) involvement in narrated events and event sequences, and also create evaluations and stances with regard to who is morally right or at fault.

(3) Singling out and ordering events in terms of their *tellability (and thus as relevant to the listener and to the speech situation) – and marking them as told from a particular *point of view – constitute important stepping stones in the construction of what Mills (1940) termed the 'grammar of motives'. That grammar in turn regulates social relationships at the cultural as well as situated level of interactions, thereby contributing to narrative sense-making as well as the interpretation of narratives. Besides the issue of the degree of agentivity ascribed to characters, a question that is central for narrative analysis is whether

the overall order is created by the agency of the author, by the agency of the *implied author, or by the position of a narrator, or whether 'agency' itself lies within the consciousness of reader or audience in the reception and perception process (*see* READER-RESPONSE THEORY).

SEE ALSO: ethical turn

References and further reading

Bruner, Jerome (1990) *Acts of Meaning*, Cambridge, Mass.: Harvard University Press.
Budwig, Nancy (1995) *A Developmental-Functionalist Approach to Child Language*, Mahwah: Lawrence Erlbaum.
Mills, C. Wright (1940) 'Situated Actions and Vocabularies of Motive', *American Sociological Review*, 5, 904–13.
Quigley, Jean (2000) *The Grammar of Autobiography: A Developmental Account*, Mahwah: Lawrence Erlbaum.

MICHAEL BAMBERG

ALLEGORY

Derived from Greek *allos* (other) and *agoreuo* (to speak publicly, in the *agora* or marketplace), allegory may be broadly defined as the art of 'speaking other', that is, of conveying a multiple meaning. Conceived as a *rhetorical figure, allegory achieves this effect through the use of sustained *metaphor. Within allegorical narrative, we find the difference between 'public' and 'private' meaning characteristically internalised and thematised as a quest for perfect referentiality (*see* REFERENCE). In addition to these two distinct though related uses the term is understood to cover the sense of allegorical interpretation or *allegoresis*, which involves the search for deeper meaning in an existing, often authoritative text.

As a *narrative technique, allegory occurs in literature as well as in *film and visual art (*see* IMAGE AND NARRATIVE; INTERMEDIALITY; MEDIA AND NARRATIVE; PICTORIAL NARRATIVITY; VISUAL NARRATIVITY). What distinguishes an allegorical narrative from its interpretative counterpart is that it dramatises the practice of *allegoresis*. More specifically, the story unfolds as a *commentary on a – usually textual – system of meaning, e.g., the Bible (*see* BIBLICAL NARRATIVE). Thus the entire action in the fourteenth century *Pearl* is taken up by an encounter between the protagonist and his dead daughter, who instructs him in Christian doctrine and shows him the heavenly Jerusalem. Narrative allegory flourished in the Middle Ages, when it proved singularly adaptable to the genre of the dream poem (*see* DREAM NARRATIVE; MEDIEVAL NARRATIVE). After the seventeenth century it lost its dominant position in the west; yet the work of *postmodern writers such as Thomas Pynchon, Paul Auster, and Salman Rushdie testifies to its lasting appeal.

Allegory has its roots in three different traditions. The oldest of these is the interpretative tradition, which originated in ancient Greece (*see* ANCIENT THEORIES OF NARRATIVE (WESTERN)). Prompted by the need to justify Homer's prominent place in Greek culture, interpreters in the sixth century BC began to construe certain 'immoral' episodes in his work symbolically. This practice of looking for hidden meanings or *hyponoiai* was elaborated by the Stoics as well as by Jewish and Christian exegetes, who, though generally true to the sacred letter, undertook to explain scriptural meaning both literally *and* allegorically (*see* THEOLOGY AND NARRATIVE). Thus Augustine taught that *truth, in obscure or morally questionable passages, appears as it were shrouded in a figurative garment – a divine stratagem which, apart from sharpening the reader's intellect, prevents the gem thus concealed from being cheapened by too ready accessibility.

The notion of allegory as combining a figurative surface with a deeper meaning was preserved in the relatively recent rhetorical tradition. Cicero, in his *Orator* (46 BC), observes that a succession of metaphors produces a wholly different style of speech, which the Greeks call *allegoria*. Over a century later, Quintilian defines allegory as a trope expressing one thing in words and another in meaning. This definition may still be seen to inform the late twentieth century 'reinvention' of allegory by Fredric Jameson and other cultural critics who have invoked the figure's radically discontinuous structure to characterise the postmodern experience. On the other hand the deconstructivist critic Paul de Man has argued that it is impossible to distinguish between referential and tropological language in any text, if only because the narrating *voice is itself the tropological product of a grammatical system (*see* DECONSTRUCTIVE APPROACHES TO NARRATIVE). De Man demonstrates how some self-reflexive narratives enact this

predicament by providing so-called allegories of their unreadability, as happens when a *narrator casts doubt on the status of his own text (de Man 1979) (*see* REFLEXIVITY).

Within the tradition of allegorical narrative, whose beginnings are closely interwoven with *genres such as the *fable and the *parable, two different types may be distinguished. The first is personification allegory, where abstractions (e.g., reason), equipped with a 'physical' mask or *prosopon*, are made to act in a story that is itself the externalised representation of a spiritual *conflict or quest. A prototypical example is the battle between personified vices and virtues in Prudentius' late fourth century *Psychomachia*. Since the semantic relationship between a personified *character's name and the quality it embodies need not in itself be ambiguous, one might wonder what, in this type of allegory, constitutes the *allos* of meaning. The answer is that even the 'timeless' abstraction is usually a mouthpiece of *historically* rooted doctrine; a circumstance that explains the liability of personified characters to undermine the expectations raised by their names (cf. Paxson 1994). The *authors of various medieval *artes poeticae* may have been aware of the problem since, following the classical *Rhetorica ad Herennium*, they discuss the animation of abstract nouns under the figure of *metonymy. Here, we find the figurative transaction governed by perceptions not of similarity, as with metaphor, but of contiguity.

If personification allegory does not escape its entanglement in history, the second type relies on the temporal connection for its very construction principle. This type, known as historical or political allegory, establishes a self-conscious relationship with an authoritative narrative or historical event which precedes it, and which provides its interpretative frame or 'pretext' (Quilligan 1979) (*see* HISTORIOGRAPHY; INTERTEXTUALITY). Examples are John Dryden's *Absalom and Achitophel* (1681), which employs biblical characters and episodes to satirise a contemporary political intrigue, and George Orwell's *Animal Farm* (1945), an adaptation of the ancient beast fable.

Walter Benjamin, in his study of early modern German *drama, designates the temporal dimension as precisely that which distinguishes allegory from symbolism. Both allegory and the symbol operate through natural imagery. Yet where the 'momentary' symbol aims at showing things under their eternal aspect, allegory's structure as a succession of metaphors – that is, a projection of the spatial image into *time – inevitably subjects it to the effects of temporality (cf. de Man 1983). Thus Benjamin notes how, in German baroque allegory, history inscribes itself into nature as decay: a discovery leading him to observe that allegories are, in the realm of thought, what ruins are in the realm of things.

SEE ALSO: dream narrative; Figura (Auerbach); indeterminacy; metafiction

References and further reading

Benjamin, Walter (1977) *The Origin of German Tragic Drama*, trans. John Osborne, London: NLB.
Fineman, Joel (1981) 'The Structure of Allegorical Desire', in Stephen Greenblatt (ed.) *Allegory and Representation*, Baltimore: Johns Hopkins University Press.
de Lubac, Henri, S. J. (1998) *The Four Senses of Scripture: Medieval Exegesis*, vol. 1, trans. Marc Sebanc, Grand Rapids: Eerdmans and T&T Clark.
Madsen, Deborah L. (1994) *Rereading Allegory: A Narrative Approach to Genre*, New York: St. Martin's Press.
de Man, Paul (1979) *Allegories of Reading: Figural Language in Rousseau, Nietzsche, Rilke, and Proust*, New Haven: Yale University Press.
—— (1983) 'The Rhetoric of Temporality', *Blindness and Insight: Essays in the Rhetoric of Contemporary Criticism*, Minneapolis: University of Minnesota Press.
Paxson, James J. (1994) *The Poetics of Personification*, Cambridge: Cambridge University Press.
Quilligan, Maureen (1979) *The Language of Allegory: Defining the Genre*, Ithaca: Cornell University Press.
Teskey, Gordon (1996) *Allegory and Violence*, Ithaca: Cornell University Press.

MADELEINE KASTEN

ALTERATION

Narratologists use the term 'alteration' to refer to a momentary radical violation or 'infraction' of the code which governs a narrative discourse (Genette 1980: 194). An alteration subverts a crucial expectation established by either the maxims of cooperative storytelling (*see* PRAGMATICS) or a specific *narrator-*narratee contract (*see* AUTO-BIOGRAPHY). Genette distinguishes two main types: (1) 'paralepsis' is an infraction caused by 'saying too much' – e.g., a historiographer narrating what happened when no witness was present;

(2) 'paralipsis' is an infraction caused by 'saying too little', by withholding crucial information – e.g., an *authorial narrator pretending to be subject to ordinary human knowledge restrictions (*see* NARRATIVE SITUATIONS; GAPPING). (A useful mnemonic for keeping the terms distinct is to pair the rhetorical figure of ellipsis [omission] with paralipsis.) An alteration produces a jarring effect on a reader and requires cognitive emergency measures such as (1) naturalising it to conform to current expectations (*see* NATURALISATION), (2) explaining it as a motivated exception, (3) accepting it as an intentional 'alienation' (*see* DEFAMILIARISATION), or (4) treating it as an unintentional oversight, error, or 'goof' (*see* INTENTIONALITY).

References and further reading

Edmiston, William F. (1991) *Hindsight and Insight*, University Park: Pennsylvania State University Press.
Genette, Gérard (1980 [1972]) *Narrative Discourse*, trans. J. E. Lewin, Oxford: Blackwell.

MANFRED JAHN

ALTERITY

Although Hegel in his master-slave *allegory was the first to establish alterity – i.e., 'otherness' – as a condition of *identity, it was his view that it only served as a transitory phase in the dialectical identity formation of the absolute spirit. It is mainly through modernist art and *psychoanalysis that alterity attained its status as a subversive and emancipatory force against the hegemony of bourgeois subject models (*see* MODERNIST NARRATIVE). Indeed, with the advent of modernism, alterity has become a central focus in *philosophy and literary theory as a counterterm for identity and subjectivity. Taking Derrida's deconstruction or Lacan's rewriting of Freud's psychoanalytic model as a starting point, feminist and postcolonial theorists have used the term 'alterity' to denote the *position of persons or groups who are used as differentiating foils in dominant identity discourses (*see* DECONSTRUCTIVE APPROACHES TO NARRATIVE; FEMINIST NARRATOLOGY; GENDER STUDIES; MASTER NARRATIVE; POST-COLONIALISM AND NARRATIVE). In turn, in the field of narrative theory, scholars such as Henry Louis Gates, Jr., Abdul R. JanMohamed, Mary Louise Pratt,

Eve Kosofsky Sedgwick, Marianna Torgovnick, Patrick Brantlinger, and Patrick McGee have highlighted epistemological, psychological, and sociological dimensions of alterity, suggesting how narratives representing various kinds of otherness open up space for a critique of the status quo. However, although narrative representations of alterity in texts like the 'international novels' of E.M. Forster and D.H. Lawrence can have an emancipatory potential as a critical corrective for dominant power structures, as Edward Said points out, portrayals of otherness can also be enmeshed in ideological constructs bound up with the notion of reinforced identity (*see* IDEOLOGY AND NARRATIVE) – as suggested by texts like Joseph Conrad's *Heart of Darkness* or Rudyard Kipling's *Kim*.

In literary theory generally as well as in narrative theory specifically, recent debates increasingly tend to consider ethics as the genuine locus for the discussion of alterity (*see* ETHICAL TURN). The Jewish phenomenologist Emmanuel Levinas can be considered the father of a philosophy of alterity. For him the ultimate Other (*Autrui*, with a capital A) is the sheer phenomenological fact of being, the terrifying 'there is' which defies the ego and all personal forms of the symbolic and thus undermines any *closure. In his ethics irreducible alterity is met in the face of the other person (*autrui*, with a lower-case 'a'). Levinas influenced philosophers and critics from Sartre, Derrida, and Lyotard, to Cixous, Kristeva, and Irigaray. Drawing on the Levinasian paradigm in the context of narrative theory Adam Zachary Newton holds that any narrative discourse already implies an ethics if narrative is perceived as an intersubjective *performance or act. Focusing on the Saying rather than the Said, Zachary analyses and evaluates narrative openness and closure in texts like Joseph Conrad's *Lord Jim*, Richard Wright's *Native Son*, and Kazuo Ishiguro's *The Remains of the Day* with regard to their ability to make 'the invisible visible' as a gap or rupture in their depiction of selves and communicative intersubjectivity.

Also relevant for the study of alterity in narrative contexts are ethnological and imagological studies. These studies compare different cultures or cultural artefacts as well as the *images cultures form of their own identities (autostereotypes) in contradistinction to other cultures (heterostereotypes) (*see* ETHNOGRAPHIC APPROACHES TO NARRATIVE). In such studies, alterity traditionally points towards obvious differences of cultural

practices like rituals or institutional procedures from the perspective of the observer. With the incorporation of discourse-analytic, *deconstructive, and psychoanalytic models as analytical tools of *cultural studies, the focus of 'deep hermeneutical approaches' (Habermas) shifted from surface phenomena to culturally and historically specific deep structures which unconsciously encode the perception and value systems not only of all individuals socialised under their regime, but also of scientific disciplines like philosophy, philology, *theology, biology, and psychology (*see* DISCOURSE ANALYSIS (FOUCAULT)). Applied most extensively in gender and post-colonial studies, deep hermeneutical readings by critics like Said, Bhabha, McGee, Kristeva, and Spivak uncover general 'imaginary' (JanMohamed 1983) principles of 'othering' employed in contexts as different as race, nation, or gender-based differentiation and stigmatisation. From this perspective a colonial novel like Conrad's *Heart of Darkness*, despite its explicit criticism of imperialist practices, implicitly measures any claim to subjectivity or identity against the normative image of 'the White Man' (Spivak). That image is depicted in Marlow, who represents the intellectual and moral counterpoint to the ideologically naive white women as well as to the body-centred, mute, and pre-civilised Africans of the text. In a similar way Dickens' *David Copperfield* employs class and gender differences to 'naturalise' as norms the identity of the white bourgeois male and its female counterpart, the angel in the house. In order to universalise and fix their cultural codes and privileged world models, both novels transfer scripts and frames pertaining to nature to cultural categories like race and gender (*see* SCRIPTS AND SCHEMATA). However, deep-hermeneutical readings based on psychoanalytical or *Marxist hypotheses uncover these universalising strategies of othering as historically and culturally specific attempts to stabilise a potentially endangered worldview by projecting and thereby externalising threatening phenomena of reality onto the 'other'.

The tendency to universalise culturally specific concepts is frequently also imputed to *structuralist narratology itself, whose models arguably imply and perpetuate culturally specific values and worldviews and offer only a limited range of possibilities to capture innovative narrative representations of reality. In addition to taking metanarrative and metalinguistic concerns thematised in deep hermeneutics into account, narrative theorists would do well to rethink notions of *character in terms of Heidu's 'semiotic square of alterity', which differentiates between ipseity (identity), alterity, non-alterity, and non-ipseity in order to point toward an otherness which cannot be accommodated within the reference system undergirding a *narrator's discourse (*see* REFERENCE). By the same token, *postclassical narratology can benefit from a rapprochement with feminist and post-colonial attempts to construct non-oppositional concepts of identity and alterity. Novels by Salman Rushdie or Hanif Kureishi, whose characters can be analysed in terms of *hybridity (Said, Bhabha) or *performativity (Butler), try to evade the dichotomy of alterity and identity and thereby transcend the horizon of the binary logic attributed to and demanded of the occidental subject in Western epistemology.

SEE ALSO: hermeneutics; psychological approaches to narrative; sociology and narrative

References and further reading

Brinker-Gabler, Gisela (ed.) (1995) *Encountering the Other(s): Studies in Literature, History and Culture*, Albany: State University of New York Press.
Gates, Henry L. Jr. (ed.) (1986) '*Race', Writing, and Difference*, Chicago: Westview Press.
Heidu, Peter (1990) 'The Semiotics of Alterity: A Comparison with Hermeneutics', *New Literary History*, 21, 671–91.
Horatschek, Anna M. (1998) *Alterität und Stereotyp: Die Funktion des Fremden in den 'International Novels' von E. M. Forster und D. H. Lawrence*, Tübingen: Narr.
JanMohamed, Abdul R. (1983) *Manichean Aesthetics: The Politics of Literature in Colonial Africa*, Amherst: University of Massachusetts Press.
Lanser, Susan Sniader (1981) *Fictions of Authority: Woman Writers and Narrative Voice*, Ithaca: Cornell University Press.
McGee, Patrick (1992) *Telling the Other: The Question of Value in Modern and Post-colonial Writing*, Ithaca: Cornell University Press.
Newton, Adam Zachary (1995) *Narrative Ethics*, Cambridge, Mass.: Harvard University Press.
Perkus, Aaron (1995) 'The Instincts of "Race" and "Text"', in Gisela Brinker-Gabler (ed.) *Encountering the Other(s): Studies in Literature, History and Culture*, Albany: State University of New York Press.

ANNA-M. HORATSCHEK

ANACHRONY

A deviation from strictly chronological storytelling, as in a flashback or a flashforward. *See* TEMPORAL ORDERING.

ANALEPSIS

Going backwards in *time to cover an earlier episode, a flashback. *See* TEMPORAL ORDERING.

ANCIENT THEORIES OF NARRATIVE (NON-WESTERN)

For centuries – sometimes millennia – before the advent of modern, globalised culture, traditions of literary theory developed in India, China, the Arab world, and Japan. Works in these traditions do not always closely resemble what most Euro-American theorists see as prototypical cases of narrative theory. However, that only increases their value for contemporary readers since it suggests the limitations of currently dominant views of narrative. Narrative theory may focus on the production, *reception, or structure of literary works (*see* NARRATIVE STRUCTURE; READER-RESPONSE THEORY). Moreover, it may be primarily normative or descriptive. Narrative theory today is largely descriptive and focused on structure. Non-Western theories did treat structure and description; however, they often focused on *authors or readers rather than texts, and they were frequently normative, either aesthetically or ethically, as were Western theories before the twentieth century.

India

South Asian writers systematically theorised about narrative over several hundred years of an unbroken tradition. The overarching framework, *rasadhvani* theory, combines the idea of *rasa* (empathic emotion) with *dhvani* (suggestion). A crucial presupposition of the *rasadhvani* theory is that each plotted work is organised by internal and external goals. Internally, the *characters have specific purposes. Externally, the author strives to produce an emotional effect in the *audience. The two types of goals are closely inter-related. Both the characters and the readers engage in an ongoing appraisal of the fulfilment or non-fulfilment of the characters' goals. This gives rise to emotions in both characters and readers (*see* EMOTION AND NARRATIVE).

Ideally, each work is structured by one dominant *rasa*, though works include many subordinate emotions as well. Most importantly, these subordinate emotions include a set of what are now called 'junctural emotions' (Hogan 2003), emotions that arise at critical moments of appraisal in the narrative sequence. These occur as a result of the narrative 'determinants' (what contemporary cognitivists call 'eliciting conditions') and lead to narrative 'consequents' (or actional and expressive outcomes), inflecting the 'permanent states' of characters and altering their 'transitory conditions'. By this account, the interarticulation of emotion and *plot structure is thoroughgoing. When successful, it creates an enhanced potential for triggering a reader's emotional memories of his/her own real-life appraisals. According to Abhinavagupta (tenth century), that triggering of a reader's personal memories is what fosters his/her emotional response to a story.

The details of narrative structure are elaborated in several influential works (*see* NARRATIVE STRUCTURE). In the *Daśarūpa*, Dhanaṃjaya (924–996 CE) identifies five stages of action: the beginning, effort, anticipation of success, certainty of success, and obtainment, or non-obtainment, of the fruit (*see* ACTION THEORY). There are five *sandhis* or junctures as well, related to these stages, stressing moments of transition: *mukha* (face), *pratimukha* (obverse face), *garbha* (womb), *avamarṣa* (doubt or pause), and *nirvahaṇa* a (final resolution). There is a mirroring relation between *mukha* and *pratimukha*, suggesting an initial turn that sets the pursuit in motion. The *garbha* implies invisibility, indecipherability, an initial moment from which we cannot predict outcomes, but from which the story grows organically. *Nirvahana* is clearly the end; the term connotes both resolution and dissolution. Perhaps the most crucial of these is the 'pause', an explicit point of appraisal. In combination, the stages of action and the *sandhis* define narrative structure along the following lines. There is an initial change in situation that spurs a character's pursuit of some goal and there is a final resolution that puts an end to that pursuit. In the middle, the character first engages in effortful action, then hesitates or pauses due to uncertainty about the possibility of success. After this pause, the character takes up the action again with

renewed effort. This effort crucially involves an attempt to control distracting emotions and overcome self-doubt. It may be followed by another pause, then a further renewal of effort, or by the resolution.

The stages of action and the *sandhis* are bound up with the typology of *rasas*. The traditional eight *rasas* are set out in the *Nāṭyaśāstra* (attributed to Bharatamuni, but composed by various writers between the second century BCE and the sixth century CE). These *rasas*, along with their corresponding ego-centred emotions, are as follows: the heroic/valour, the furious/anger, the terrible/fear, the pathetic/sorrow, the erotic/love, the comic/mirth, the odious/disgust, the marvellous or the fantastic/astonishment. These are necessarily worked out in the course of the appraisals which occur at points of juncture. The dominant emotion bears primarily on the initial change in situation. The ancillary emotions bear on subsequent junctures, especially the pause. In this way, *rasas*, stages of action, and *sandhis* join to define narrative *genres.

A ninth *rasa*, peace, was added by Abhinavagupta, following his idea that all the *rasas* and associated emotions of a work should resolve in peace. This is, of course, a narrative-related point, for Abhinavagupta is referring to the final juncture of the plot, when the action ceases. In Abhinavagupta's view, the sense of resolution that completes a narrative must give the audience a feeling of emotional calm; it must end the *desire for further pursuit of the goal (*see* CLOSURE). The idea is not unrelated to Aristotle's notion of *catharsis. The two theories are different, but share a common point about the specifically emotive and audience-centred evaluation of narrative completion.

China

In Chinese, the general term for literary art is *wen* or 'pattern' (*see* CHINESE NARRATIVE). As this suggests, the crucial characteristic of literature, including narrative, is pattern. A common view – expounded, for example, by Liu Xie (465–522 CE) – is that *wen* derives from *Tao*, the 'Way', the ultimate, what should be followed as the deepest nature of all things. One could think of *Tao* as the unmanifest or implicit universal principle, while the various patterns (*wen*) of the universe (in narrative, government, or whatever) are manifestations of the *Tao*. However, not all such manifestations are equally direct or full. Many Chinese theorists share the view that the classics are the fundamental literary manifestation of the *Tao*, mediating between the *Tao* and subsequent literary works (e.g., in defining genres).

Of course, the manifestation of the Tao is not confined to the classics. The ultimate is manifest in people individually, in societies, and in nature as well. After the classics, literary *wen* results from all these manifestations collectively. In this way, literature is a sort of interference pattern. It is produced by the interaction of patterns from literary tradition (the classics), the author, society, and nature. Any given theorist emphasises one or another. Strict traditionalists stress the classics. Revolutionary non-conformists stress the author. Political critics stress society. The most influential theorists, such as Lu Ji (261–303 CE) and Liu, tend to adopt a more balanced view. One of the most important ideas in this combined approach is that of 'flexible adaptability'. The classics are important, but they do not provide rigid rules. They are part of variable manifestations of the Tao and thus must be modified in accordance with current circumstances.

But how does an author create literature, including narrative, that brings together these manifestations without producing a chaos of conflicting patterns? This is where Chinese theory becomes very concrete and practical. For example, Lu Ji (Lu Chi) sets out a series of precepts that follow directly from the idea of *wen*. The writer must begin by reading the classics and experiencing both nature and society. Having done this, however, he/she sets aside the books and enters into solitude. At this point, he/she jots down whatever comes to his/her mind – what is now called 'free writing' but, in this context, may be understood as adding the individual's inner way to those of the classics, society, and nature. Lu goes on to discuss processes of selection, organisation, revision for coherence and so on – all necessary to make the implicit pattern of the work fully manifest.

Liu Xie (Liu Hsieh) makes similar points, with fuller elaboration, treating such issues as paragraphing and the use of summary phrases. Perhaps most significantly, Liu stresses the importance of discipline. It is not easy to manifest the Tao in *wen*. In consequence, Liu adds the moral and physical training of the author to the list of necessary procedures. Here as elsewhere, the claim is not one that applies to narrative uniquely. But it

necessarily holds for narrative. Given the classical principles of *wen*, the physical well-being of the author is necessarily part of a normative and author-oriented theory of narrative – an idea quite at odds with contemporary views of narrative theory in the west.

Centuries later, theorists such as Chin Sheng-t'an (1608–1661 CE) addressed narrative more directly (Rolston 1990). Unsurprisingly, one particular concern of these writers was patterned unity. They tended to focus on two issues in this regard. One concerned temporal sequence, especially the ways in which an author might treat transitions from one episode to another (e.g., striving for a feeling of continuity or one of abrupt change) (*see* TEMPORAL ORDERING). This analysis is broader than, say, Aristotle's treatment of reversal. But, rather than opposing one another, the two theories seem complementary and mutually illuminating. The second issue concerned parallels across episodes. *Events, *characters, *images, etc., could be repeated at intervals with some variation, either to establish similarity or to indicate opposition. For example, two characters may be set in parallel situations to show some common trait or to contrast their attitudes and actions. When applied to events, this analysis recalls the sorts of unity suggested by Aristotle under the title of 'design', again suggesting the complementary nature of these traditions.

The Middle East

Deeply influenced by Plato and Aristotle, a number of important Arabic theorists developed an account of the ethical impact of literature, including, prominently, literary narrative (*see* ETHICAL TURN). In this account, our actions are either spontaneous or the result of deliberation. In deliberative action, we reason from general principles to particulars and base our action on this reasoning. In spontaneous action, we do not deliberate, but base our action on emotion. Thus we might be immediately drawn to a certain sort of object or activity, and immediately repulsed by another. The function of stories is to modify our spontaneous likes and dislikes. We follow through the events of a story and these lead us to have feelings for the characters and for their acts. We then go out into the world and, when we are faced with similar characters or situations, we transfer our feelings from the literary work to the world.

Consider a very simple example. Perhaps in ordinary life, I am repulsed by beggars and never give them money. I read a story that develops my sympathy for beggars or perhaps my disgust with people who do not give money to beggars. I then see a beggar and immediately transfer the sympathy to the beggar, or I transfer the disgust to myself as I initially ignore his/her request. In consequence, I give money to the beggar. I do this without considering any general ethical precepts and without drawing inferences about what is ethically proper in this case. My act is the result of a practical transferral of emotional response from one instance (in a literary work) to another, comparable instance (in the world). It proceeds without the intervention of abstract, ethical reasoning.

Arabic theorists also considered just what emotions a story should cultivate. Though they drew in part on Aristotle's account of pity and fear, they seem to have primarily concerned themselves with Islamic legal practice. In Muslim law, there are two axes of obligation. The first is one's obligation to Allāh– fundamentally, submission. The second is one's obligation to other people. This includes, for example, giving alms to the poor (one of the five pillars of Islam). In keeping with this, the Arabic theorists isolated two primary emotions that should be cultivated through stories – *taqwā* and *raḥmah*, piety and compassion.

Piety may be cultivated by narratives in which the good are rewarded and the evil punished, as in the paradigmatic Qur'ānic stories that serve as 'warnings' (*see* DIDACTIC NARRATIVE). But piety is not a simple matter of encouraging spiritual prudence. The crucial factors in the literary cultivation of piety are our feelings about a story's characters and their acts. We should find ourselves repulsed by impious acts and drawn to pious acts. In some cases, these feelings may be developed more effectively by not punishing the impious or by not rewarding the pious (as in stories of martyrs). Moreover, piety may be fostered by stories that do not depict pious or impious acts at all, but instead aim to produce a more direct sense of awe before God, as in stories treating the wondrous 'signs' of Allāh's manifestation in the created world.

Raḥmah, the feeling of compassion, is triggered, first of all, by a character's undeserved suffering – often tragic suffering in roughly the Aristotelian sense. In the latter case, the character for whom we feel compassion is not evil. Rather, he/she has made some mistake. The recognition that the mistake produced this suffering helps lead us toward piety and the avoidance of sin. But it also fosters in us a sense of *raḥmah* toward those who suffer, even when they are at fault, as long as they are not wholly evil. (Of course, it fosters the same emotion, even more strongly, when the individuals in question are not at fault at all.) Finally, *raḥmah* may be cultivated more indirectly by stories that depict acts of compassion in appealing ways.

Japan

Monogatari, the general term used in Japanese to refer to a wide variety of literary narratives, literally means 'talk of things'. The different things or topics that one may talk about, and the manners in which one may talk about them, lead logically to an organisation of genres and sub-genres. Thus, a mass of narrative literature may be divided into *denki monogatari* (concerning the supernatural), *rekishi monogatari* (concerning history), and so forth—or, considering manner rather than topic, *utamonogatari* (emphasising poetry) and *tsukurimonogatari* (emphasising prose).

The division between *denki* and *rekishi monogatari* (concerning the supernatural and history), and the general opposition between *monogatari* and *nikki*, or *diary (see Miner, Odagiri, and Morrell 1985: 290), raise the question of the relation between reality and fiction. The 'truth' or veracity of fiction is a cross-culturally recurrent issue (*see* FICTION, THEORIES OF). It is given significant treatment by Japanese literary theorists. In Lady Murasaki's tenth century *Genji Monogatari*, the topic is broached in the famous 'Glowworm' chapter. Genji chides Tamakatsuro for being so absorbed in reading fiction. She claims that when she reads a story, she always accepts it as treating something that actually occurred. At first glance, Tamakatsuro's idea might bear resemblance to Coleridge's notion of the 'suspension of disbelief'. However, Murasaki relates this to the Buddhist concept of *upāya*, or 'adapted truth' (Murasaki 1960: 503; *see* TRUTH). The basic idea of *upāya* is that not everyone is capable of reaching absolute truth, and no one can be experiencing absolute truth all the time. Thus fictions are sometimes necessary to aid our advancement toward enlightenment. These fictions are no less real than anything else we take to be real due to our limited and relative knowledge. Indeed, the fictions are, in a sense, more real than the world of experience, since they lead us toward absolute truth. Murasaki develops this idea of *upāya* beyond narrowly religious concepts, such as heaven, and uses it to analyse literary narrative.

In his response to Tamakatsuro, Genji offers two other perspectives that are central to Japanese narrative theory. The first refers to emotive expressivism. Genji thinks narrative is a way of 'talking about things' by an author who has felt so strongly about a sequence of events that he/she cannot keep it shut inside, unspoken. The second goes beyond this personalistic approach to social and temporal issues. The temporal aspect is particularly important, for it manifests the concern for *time and loss through time that is in many ways the most distinctive feature of Japanese aesthetic theory. Specifically, Genji says that an author tells a story because he/she cannot bear to think that there will be a time when these people and events are forgotten (*see* MEMORY). Though still expressivist, the emphasis here is on preservation of what has happened, a sort of struggle against time, rather than on romantic self-absorption.

A closely related focus on time and evanescence may be found in the important concept of *aware* or *mono no aware*, which is to say, sensitivity to things, a sensitivity that necessarily involves melancholic feelings brought on by the inevitable passing of beauty. The idea has a long history in Japanese aesthetics. It was developed most famously by Norinaga (1730–1801), who stressed its importance both in theory and in practical criticism (e.g., in his influential analysis of *Genji Mongatari*).

Probably the best known Japanese narrative theory is found in the great Nō dramatist, Zeami (c. 1364–1443). His analyses too are bound up with a deep awareness of time, its passage and rhythms. In his theory of *plot, Zeami draws a fundamental distinction between *jo*, *ha*, and *kyū* or beginning, middle, and end. This may sound like Aristotle's famous division, but the ideas are not identical. Zeami particularly emphasises, not the causal rigor, but the pacing of the three sections of a well-made plot. The *jo* is slow and fluid; the *ha*, literally 'breaking', is restless; the *kyū* is fast paced, but ends with a resolution. The nature of this resolution is important. It should give a sense of fulfilment to the audience. This sense of fulfilment, Zeami explains, comes about precisely through the communication of *aware* (Zeami 1984: 138).

Non-European theories today

Though they have yet to make their way into anthologies of narrative theory, non-Western narrative theories continue to influence the production and evaluation of literature in many parts of the world. A range of Indian and Japanese arts are informed by these theories, and Muslim critics continue to address the issues taken up by the Arabic Aristotelians. The rise of post-colonial studies has spurred interest in some of these ideas as well (*see* POST-COLONIALISM AND NARRATIVE). Finally, writers such as Hogan and Oatley have drawn on non-European theories in the context of cognitive science. In short, though still relatively little known in western narratology, these theories remain a vital part of ongoing projects, both artistic and critical.

SEE ALSO: ancient theories of narrative (Western); Chinese narrative; Japanese narrative; Sanskrit narrative

References and further reading

Abhinavagupta (1968) *The Aesthetic Experience According to Abhinavagupta*, trans. and ed. Raniero Gnoli, Varanasi: Chowkhamba Sanskrit Series Office.

Bharatamuni (n.d.) *The Nāṭyā Śastra* Delhi: Sri Satguru Publications.

Dhanamjaya (1965) *The Daśarūpa: A Treatise on Hindu Dramaturgy*, trans. George Haas, New York: AMS Press.

Hisamatsu, Sen'ichi (1963) *The Vocabulary of Japanese Aesthetics*, Tokyo: Centre for East Asian Cultural Studies.

Hogan, Patrick Colm (2003) *The Mind and Its Stories: Narrative Universals and Human Emotion*, Cambridge: Cambridge University Press.

—— and Lalita Pandit (eds) (1996) *College Literature*, 23 (special issue on 'Comparative Poetics: Non-Western Traditions of Literary Theory').

Ibn Rushd (Averroes) (1986) *Averroes' Middle Commentary on Aristotle's Poetics*, trans. and ed. Charles Butterworth, Princeton: Princeton University Press.

Ibn Sina (Avicenna) (1974) *Avicenna's Commentary on the Poetics of Aristotle: A Critical Study with an Annotated Translation of the Text*, trans. and ed. Ismail Dahiyat, Leiden: E.J. Brill.

Liu Hsieh (1959) *The Literary Mind and the Carving of Dragons*, trans. and ed. Vincent Yu-chung Shih, New York: Columbia University Press.

Lu Chi (1966) 'Rhymeprose on Literature: The *Wên-Fu* of Lu Chi (A.D. 261–303)', trans. and ed. Achilles Fang, in John Bishop (ed.) *Studies in Chinese Literature*, Cambridge, Mass.: Harvard University Press.

Miner, Earl, Hiroko Odagiri, and Robert E. Morrell (1985) *The Princeton Companion to Classical Japanese Literature*, Princeton, NJ: Princeton University Press.

Murasaki, Lady (1960) *The Tale of Genji*, trans. Arthur Waley, New York: Modern Library.

Oatley, Keith (2002) 'Emotions and the Story Worlds of Fiction', in Melanie Green, Jeffrey Strange, and Timothy Brock (eds.) *Narrative Impact: Social and Cognitive Foundations*, Mahwah, NJ: Erlbaum.

Rolston, David L. (ed.) (1990) *How to Read the Chinese Novel*, Princeton: Princeton University Press.

Zeami (1984) *On the Art of the Nō Drama: The Major Treatises of Zeami*, trans. and ed. J. Thomas Rimer and Yamazaki Masakazu, Princeton, NJ: Princeton University Press.

PATRICK COLM HOGAN AND LALITA PANDIT

ANCIENT THEORIES OF NARRATIVE (WESTERN)

Many narratological concepts have their roots in classical antiquity, but the ancients did not develop comprehensive or systematic theories of *narrative. Reflections on storytelling must be culled from diverse places: the narrative texts themselves, philosophical discussions, *rhetorical treatises, philological scholarship, and the mixed bag of the marginal comments or scholia (Kennedy 1989; Meijering 1987) (*see* PHILOSOPHY AND NARRATIVE).

The oldest ancient narrative, the Homeric *epic, sets the tone for all subsequent reflection on the functions of storytelling: though primarily a form of entertainment, which gives delight (e.g., *Odyssey* 8.91–2), stories may also provide examples of how, or how not, to behave (e.g., *Iliad* 1.259–74; cf. Horace's *Ars Poetica*, lines 333–34: 'poets aim either to benefit, or to amuse, or to utter words at once both pleasing and helpful to life'). Historians likewise considered their works to be profitable, since *events which had happened were likely to happen again (cf. Thucydides, *History of the Peloponnesian War* 1.22). This focus on the *didactic function of storytelling informs many of the ancient ideas about narrative.

Reflections on form

The first major ancient discussion of the form of narrative derives from Plato (429–347 BC). In the third Book of his *Republic* he discusses the *education of the Guardians, the rulers of the ideal state sketched in this work. In order to show the detrimental influence of literature – and hence prepare for his eventual banishment of most literature from his state – Plato's spokesman Socrates explains that all narratives consist of two parts: the speeches (Greek *mimesis) and the parts between the speeches (Gr. *dihegesis haple*): in the diegetic parts the poet speaks as himself, whereas in the mimetic parts he speaks 'as if being someone else' (one of the characters) (*see* DIEGESIS; SPEECH REPRESENTATION). It is against the mimetic parts of narratives that Plato levels most of his critical arrows. His first point is philosophical: since the world around us is already only a copy of the ideal Forms, the *mimesis* in literary texts is a copy of a copy, and hence even further removed from philosophical reality. His second point is moralistic: since most characters in literature (in Plato's eyes) say objectionable things, *mimesis* is a dangerous device, in that it might infect readers with the baseness of the literary figures. Though his intention was practical rather than theoretical, Plato thus introduced one of the major issues in narratology – namely, that of *mode (Genette 1980).

It has become customary in narratological scholarship to equate Lubbock's famous opposition of *'showing vs. telling' with Plato's *mimesis* vs. *diegesis*. This is incorrect on two counts: showing can encompass more than the use of speech, whereas diegesis need not be a form of telling; indeed, the diegesis in the Homeric epic, Plato's prime example, is a typical instance of showing rather than telling, the narrator abstaining from all explicit comment.

The second major discussion of narrative is found in the *Poetics* of Aristotle (384–322 BC), a treatise which can be seen as an answer to Plato (who was Aristotle's teacher) and a defence of literature. For Aristotle, to engage in *mimesis*, i.e., in imitative behaviour and artistic image-making, is an instinct of human beings. Precisely because mimetic literature is not reality itself but a representation of reality, it is 'more philosophical and serious' than *historiography, in that it deals with general *truths rather than particulars. Aristotle differs from Plato, in considering narratives *as a whole* mimetic (on his concept of *mimesis*, see Halliwell 2002); yet, in chapter 3 he comes up with the same distinction between the poet speaking as himself or as one of the characters.

Both in Plato and in Aristotle the distinction between 'narrating while remaining oneself' vs. 'speaking while becoming someone else' is used not only to distinguish the parts *within* a narrative (*see* NARRATIVE UNITS), but also to define *genres: epic combines diegetic and mimetic parts, *drama is purely mimetic, and dithyrambs are purely diegetic. This distinction will remain in use throughout antiquity.

It is a matter of debate whether Aristotle may be credited with the invention of the notion of the *narrator as an agent who is to be distinguished from the historical *author, one of the basic principles of modern narratology. In chapter 24 of the *Poetics* he claims that poets should speak as little as possible themselves, and then continues to praise Homer, who 'after a brief proem at once brings on stage a man or woman'. Since the poet in the Homeric epics in fact speaks a great deal (45% of the *Iliad* consists of diegesis, and 34% of the *Odyssey*), this could imply that for Aristotle the poet after the proem no longer speaks as himself but assumes a role or persona, that of narrator (de Jong 1987). Others take this passage to mean that Aristotle, for a moment abandoning his own definition of *mimesis*, returns to the more restricted Platonic definition and here praises Homer for his abundant use of direct speech (Halliwell 2002).

Reflections on plot

We owe to Aristotle the notion of *plot: mimetic poetry represents men in action in the form of a plot (Gr. *muthos*), which is the arrangement (Gr. *sunthesis*) of the actions (*Poetics* chapter 6). Aristotle considers plot to be the most important principle in mimetic poetry, more important than *character. Whereas in reality incidents follow each other chronologically and often randomly, the incidents of a well-constructed plot should form a unified whole, having a beginning, middle, and end (chapter 7). Some narratologists see in Aristotle's concept of the plot a forerunner of the *Russian formalist distinction of *fabula vs. *sjuzhet, but as Lowe (2000) has pointed out, Aristotle is interested less in the process of selecting, ordering, and colouring incidents so as to transform a fabula into a plot, than in the causal connection between incidents (*see* CAUSALITY; STORY-DISCOURSE DISTINCTION; TEMPORAL ORDERING). He demands a plot which tells what could happen probably or necessarily. Moreover, the plot should generate fear and pity in the recipients (*see* CATHARSIS).

The effective order of the elements of a story is a central point of interest in later criticism too, where it is known as *taxis* or *oikonomia* (Meijering 1987). It is in this context that the scholia speak of *proanaphonesis* or *prolepsis* (anticipation or foreshadowing), seed (hint or advance mention), and *paraleipsis* (leaving out of details to be told at a later, more effective moment), terms which will become part and parcel of modern narratology (*see* ALTERATION).

Reflections on fictionality

It is a matter of debate when the ancients adopted the notion of fiction (*see* FICTION, THEORIES OF). For one thing, there is no one term corresponding to the modern-day conception of fiction, but rather a number of terms which refer to more or less related phenomena: *fabula, plasma, mimesis, muthos, figmentum*. Ancient critics were more interested in fiction as the invention of new stories versus the traditional ones than in fiction as the opposite of historical truth. Indeed, antiquity hardly had a notion of literature in the sense of *belles lettres:* (1) literary texts until the invention of the novel in Hellenistic times (300 BC) formed part of social life, in that they were not consumed privately but publicly; (2) conversely, what we call scholarly, historiographical, or rhetorical texts were not principally separated from literature; and (3) the subject matter of most literature, the traditional stories or *myths as we call them, was considered an early stage of history. Nevertheless, there was an understanding, expressed in the earliest narrative texts themselves, that stories can consist of a combination of truthful elements and 'lies resembling truth' (Hesiod *Theogony* 27–28). According to some scholars, the idea of fiction only originated at the moment when oral literature came to be replaced by written literature (Rösler 1980) or when from a matter of inspiration writing literature became a craft (Gr. *techne*) (Finkelberg 1998; Gill and Wiseman 1993) (*see* NARRATIVE TECHNIQUES; ORAL CULTURES AND NARRATIVE).

Reflections on narratees

Though the notion of the *narratee is absent from ancient theory, it did show great awareness of the fact that literature (in the broad sense defined above) is always aimed at a recipient (*see* READER CONSTRUCTS; READER-RESPONSE THEORY). After all, ancient literature for most of its life was oral or at least aural. As a result, we find occasional remarks in rhetorical treatises on devices which are aimed at what we would nowadays call the narratee; the ensuing examples are collected from Lausberg (1998): (1) vividness (Gr. *enargeia*, Latin *evidentia*): to narrate vividly and graphically and thereby turn the recipient into an eyewitness of the *events recounted is an ideal which is advocated by both poets (cf. e.g., *Odyssey* 8.488) and critics ('Longinus', *On the sublime* 15; Quintilian, *Institutio Oratoria* 8.3.61–73). (2) The use of the present tense (historical present): 'if you introduce events in past time as happening at the present moment, the passage will be transformed from a narrative into a vivid actuality' ('Longinus', *On the sublime* 25; cf. Quintilian, *I.O.* 9.2.41) (*see* TENSE AND NARRATIVE). (3) Apostrophe: turning away from your actual *audience to another one, which in the case of a narrative text means the narrator addressing not his or her narratee but one of the characters in his or her story (Quintilian, *I.O.* 9.2.38). (4) Directly addressing your recipient: 'change of person [from third into second] gives an equally vivid effect, and often makes the audience feel themselves set in the thick of the danger' (Longinus, *On the sublime* 26) (*see* NARRATION; PERSON). (5) *Gapping: 'not all possible points should be punctiliously and tediously elaborated, but some should be left to the comprehension and inference of the hearer, who when he perceives what you have left unsaid becomes not only your hearer but your witness' (Demetrius, *On Style*, 4.222).

Ancient historiography as a form of narrative

The nature of ancient historiography is largely determined by its first specimen, Herodotus' *Histories* of the fifth century BC (see Fornara 1983 and Grant 1995 for overviews). Though deriving his historical method from his contemporaries, the Ionian natural physicists (Thomas 2000), Herodotus chose the Homeric epics as his literary model. This explains the narrative form (as opposed to the argumentative form of the physicists), the insertion of speeches, and the presentation by an external, largely omniscient narrator (Strasburger 1966). The habit of inserting long speeches by historical characters will remain a characteristic of almost all ancient historiography. Since there existed no tape recordings and hardly any archives yet, ancient historians generally wrote these speeches themselves. This license is reflected on explicitly by Thucydides (ca. 460–400 BC), who

in chapter 1.22 of his *History of the Peloponnesian War* writes that 'the speeches are given in the language in which, as it seemed to me, the several speakers would express, on the subjects under consideration, sentiments most befitting the occasion, though at the same time I have adhered as closely as possible to the general sense of what was actually said'.

Apart from the free inclusion of pseudo-original speeches, ancient historians were in general more liberal in their use of literary devices than is customary nowadays. It was not enough to offer the facts; they had to be presented in an accomplished way. Thus a famous passage on ancient historiography in the *De Oratore* (2.15) of Cicero runs as follows: 'The nature of the subject needs chronological arrangement and geographical representation: and since, in reading of important affairs worth recording, the plans of campaign, the executive actions and the results are successively looked for, it calls also, as regards such plans, for some intimation of what the writer approves, and, in the narrative of achievement, not only for a statement of what was done and said, but also of the manner of doing or saying it; and, in the estimate of consequences, for an exposition of all contributory causes, whether originating in accident, discretion, or foolhardiness; and, as for the individual actors, besides an account of their exploits, it demands particulars of the lives and characters of such as are outstanding in renown and dignity'. Faced with the task of fulfilling this list of demands, ancient historians did not eschew *auxesis* or *amplificatio*, the embroidering of the facts with invented details. For some scholars the rhetoric of ancient historiography seriously impairs its *reliability as a historical source (Woodman 1988). Ancient historians did have, however, an arsenal of devices by which to increase their authority (Marincola 1997): stress on their impartiality and expertise, polemic with other historians, critical discussion of sources, claims of autopsy (*see* AUTHENTICATION; REALITY EFFECT).

Another consequence of the close affinity between Homeric epics and ancient historiography is the latter's focus on the achievements of the happy few and on military exploits. Ancient historiography is also more interested in the *anecdotal than in the analysis of larger social or economic factors. A matter of great interest was motivation and causation – i.e., the forces responsible for making history develop as it did.

Here gods, chance, fate, or the personality of the men involved were decisive factors.

SEE ALSO: ancient theories of narrative (non-Western); formalism; structuralist narratology

References and further reading
Finkelberg, Margalit (1998) *The Birth of Literary Fiction in Ancient Greece*, Oxford: Clarendon Press.

Fornara, Charles W. (1983) *The Nature of History in Ancient Greece and Rome*, Berkeley: University of California Press.

Genette, Gérard (1980) *Narrative Discourse*, trans. Jane E. Lewin, Ithaca: Cornell University Press.

Gill, Chris, and Timothy P. Wiseman (1993) *Lies and Fiction in the Ancient World*, Exeter: University of Exeter Press.

Grant, Michael (1995) *Greek and Roman Historians: Information and Misinformation*, London: Routledge.

Halliwell, Stephen (2002) *The Aesthetics of Mimesis: Ancient Texts and Modern Problems*, Princeton: Princeton University Press.

de Jong, Irene J. F. (1987) *Narrators and Focalizers: The Presentation of the Story in The Iliad*, Amsterdam: John Benjamins.

——(2001) *A Narratological Commentary on the Odyssey*, Cambridge: Cambridge University Press.

Kennedy, George (ed.) (1989) *The Cambridge History of Literary Criticism*, vol. 1, Cambridge: Cambridge University Press.

Lausberg, H. (1998) *Handbook of Literary Rhetoric: A Foundation for Literary Study*, Leiden: Brill.

Lowe, Nick (2000) *The Classical Plot and the Invention of Western Narrative*, Cambridge: Cambridge University Press.

Marincola, John (1997) *Authority and Tradition in Ancient Historiography*, Cambridge: Cambridge University Press.

Meijering, Roos (1987) *Literary and Rhetorical Theories in Greek Scholia*, Groningen: Forsten.

Rösler, Wolfgang (1980) 'Die Entdeckung der Fiktionalität in der Antike', *Poetica*, 12, 283–319.

Strasburger, Herman (1966) *Die Wesenbestimmung der Geschichte durch die antike Geschichtsschreibung*, Wiesbaden: Steiner.

Thomas, Rosalind (2000) *Herodotus in Context: Ethnography, Science and the Art of Persuasion*, Cambridge: Cambridge University Press.

Woodman, Antony J. (1988) *The Rhetoric of Ancient Historiography: Four Studies*, London: Croom Helm.

IRENE J.F. DE JONG

ANECDOTE

An anecdote is a short, humorous narrative, purporting to recount a true incident involving real people. Etymologically, 'anecdote' derives from classical antecedents (Greek *anekdotos*, Latin *anecdota*) referring to things unpublished, suggesting the importance of oral transmission, but anecdotes have also served as a popular literary resource since classical antiquity. The characteristic formal features of the *genre include a focus on a single scene and a tendency to limit attention to two actors, generally a named principal and an interlocutor. Anecdotes tend to be heavily dialogic in construction, often culminating in a punch line rendered in direct discourse (*see* SPEECH REPRESENTATION). Anecdotes also tend to attach themselves to individuals known for their quick wit and verbal dexterity, often celebrities, intellectuals, and local or family characters.

SEE ALSO: humour studies and narrative; joke; legend; orality; simple forms

References and further reading
Bauman, Richard (1986) *Story, Performance, and Event: Contextual Studies of Oral Narrative*, Cambridge: Cambridge University Press.

Brownlow, Louis (1960) *The Anatomy of the Anecdote*, Chicago: Chicago University Press.

Osborn, James M. (1966) 'Ana and Anecdotes as Literary Genre', in Joseph Spence, *Observations, Anecdotes, and Characters of Books and Men*, ed. James M. Osborn, Oxford: Clarendon Press.

Taylor, Archer (1970) 'The Anecdote: A Neglected Genre', in Jerome Mandel and Bruce A. Rosenberg (eds) *Medieval Literature and Folklore Studies*, New Brunswick: Rutgers University Press.

RICHARD BAUMAN

ANIMATED FILM

Our understanding of animated *film, those serial drawings that are endowed with life when they are filmed and projected, is currently undergoing a seismic shift. Animated films always represented camera moves and changes in *perspective in the layers of drawing and they way they were shot. The increased use of digitised special effects and computer-generated graphics often makes it impossible to tell animation from live-action film. Much special-effects work that would have been done with stop-motion and animatronics is now done with computer-generated graphics. Two high-profile cases, *Jurassic Park* (1993) (Buckland 1999) and *Mars Attacks!* (1996) (McMahan 2004), are indicative of an industry-wide shift from full stop-motion films (such as *Nightmare Before Christmas* and *Chicken Run*) to 3-D computer-generated (CG) graphics in films such as *Final Fantasy* (2001). There has also been a shift from drawing 2-D animation to creating it digitally, as in Disney's *Beauty and the Beast* (1991). This film integrates hand-drawn cells and CG animation, mostly in backgrounds – a combination first attempted in Disney's the *Black Cauldron* and *The Great Mouse Detective*.

In light of the changes evidenced in these films, it becomes clear that defining animation as 'not live action cinema' is insufficient and that the paradigm for making animation a subset of live-action cinema is no longer workable. In fact, the reverse appears to be true.

Live-action cinema and animated film share their origins in motion studies. Both were born out of the drive to mechanisation, the drive to capture, store, and replay motion at will. The mechanisation of cinema in the twentieth century and the digitisation of cinema in the twenty-first century are related drives. Early filmmakers such as Emil Reynaud developed systems for motion capture, digitisation (taking analogue material, cutting it up to reduce it to units of information, changing the image by colouring and other alterations, and putting it all back together to form a new whole), and rotoscoping (basing an animation on live-action footage usually through some form of tracing), all before 1901. Trick films, such as those of Georges Méliès, have always highlighted the border between animation and live-action cinema. The production of animation itself gradually became more mechanised. At first artists like Emile Cohl, who began making animated films for Gaumont and Lux in 1908–1909, and his U.S. counterpart, Windsor McCay, had produced every drawing for an animated film by hand.

In 1910, however, the philosophy of Taylorism, or scientific management, became popularised in the U.S. Frederick Taylor had proposed a 'science of systems' or work efficiency for factories in the 1880s, which Louis Brandeis had applied to the railroads in 1910. Bray patented a *system* of scientific management for animation studios. The idea was to automate the process so that a maximum number of unskilled labourers could be used for smaller tasks, while the more skilled labourers could be exploited in the most efficient way possible. (Two-dimensional animation suffered in Europe during World War I, although some animators such as Lortac, who brought Taylorism to European animation, managed to survive by producing commercials and public service films) (Crafton 1982). Walt Disney was the foremost producer of cartoons (short animated films primarily aimed at young children), as we know them, and produced what was probably the first animated feature film with *Snow White* in 1934. The Disney animated features have become the standards against which other animated films are defined, though the company suffered after Disney's death in 1967. Its fortunes were turned around when the scripts were given more attention and when the company started using their Computer Animation Production System (CAPS), in which images were drawn by hand but then scanned, animated, and coloured in the computer. This led to immense improvements in the look of Disney animation in general and made possible films like *Who Framed Roger Rabbit?* (1988) that presented a combination of live-action and animation reminiscent of the blending of the two in the films of Emil Cohl and Windsor McCay. The difference was the means to achieve it: in 1908 the means was mechanical; from 1988 on the means are increasingly digital.

The overlap between animation and live-action is highlighted by the appearance of *synthespians* – a combination of human actor plus digital character, beginning with the stained glass knight in Barry Levinson's *Young Sherlock Holmes* (1985) and continuing with Luxo, Jr., the titular character of the 1986 short by John Lasseter, the first fully computer-animated film. Luxo features the same technology that led to Pixar's *Toy Story* and *A Bug's Life*. Cameron's *The Abyss* (1989) and *Terminator 2: Judgment Day* (1991) made character morphing into a household word. Synthespians achieved leading roles in films like *Dragonheart* (1996), *Antz* (1998), and *The Phantom Menace* (1999); in the first two the actors that were the sources for the characters were still recognisable. But Jar-Jar Binks from *Phantom Menace* and Gollum in *The Lord of the Rings: The Two Towers* (2002) only use their human progenitors as sources of motion capture.

Usually live-action cinema is seen as the dominant film paradigm with animation as a sub-genres. However, this analysis of the role of mechanisation and then digitisation shows that it may be more productive to see animation as the dominant paradigm, with live-action, trick and stop-motion films, and special effects as subsets of Animated Film.

SEE ALSO: children's storytelling; comics and graphic novel; digital narrative; pictorial narrativity

References and further reading

Buckland, Warren (1999) 'Between Science Fact and Science Fiction: Spielberg's Digital Dinosaurs, Possible Worlds, and the New Aesthetic Realism', *Screen*, 40.2, 177–92.

Crafton, Donald (1993 [1982]) *Before Mickey: The Animated Film 1898–1928*, Chicago: University of Chicago Press.

Lutz, E. G. (1998 [1920]) *Animated Cartoons: How They Are Made, Their Origin, and Development*, Bedford, Mass.: Applewood Books.

McMahan, Alison (2002) *Alice Guy Blaché, Lost Cinematic Visionary*, New York: Continuum.

—— (2004) *Tim Burton, Animator*, New York: Continuum.

Sobchack, Vivian (ed.) (2000) *Meta-morphing: Visual Transformation and the Culture of Quick Change*, Minneapolis: University of Minnesota Press.

Talbot, Frederick A. (1970 [1912]) *Moving Pictures*, New York: Arno Press.

ALISON McMAHAN

ANNALS

In historiographic contexts, the term 'annals' refers to the record of real, noteworthy events arranged chronologically according to solar years. In Antiquity and the Middle Ages, annals (e.g., the Roman *Annales maximi*, the Carolingian *Annals of Fulda*) were mere lists devoid of *narrativity; they had no central subject, offered no causal explanation linking one event to the next, and simply terminated without concluding (*see* CAUSALITY). Though still consisting of lists, modern annals (e.g., *Annals of English Drama*) are organised around a single, homogeneous topic, and aim at comprehensiveness. The term 'annals' is also found today in the names of numerous scholarly journals (e.g., *Annals of Science*), denoting the project of circulating recent research worthy of notice. For specialists of earlier periods, annals are valuable because they offer 'precise, factual, and reliable' information about a certain era (van Caenegem 1997: 50). From the standpoint of historiographic theory, annals are also useful because they show that there are 'alternatives' to the well-made plots

of current historical discourse (White 1987: 5), thus helping to expose the constructedness of that discourse.

SEE ALSO: chronicle; historiography

References and further reading

van Caenegem, R. C. (1997) *Introduction aux sources de l'histoire médiévale*, Turnhout: Brepols.

White, Hayden (1987) *The Content of Form: Narrative Discourse and Historical Representation*, Baltimore: Johns Hopkins University Press.

PHILIPPE CARRARD

ANTI-NARRATIVE

The term 'anti-narrative' designates narratives that ignore or defy the conventions of natural narrative. It is thus a more rigorous and less inclusive term than *anti-novel*, commonly used in the 1960s and 1970s to refer to any work of fiction that is self-conscious of its status as *fiction (*see* NOVEL, THE). More precisely, *anti-narrative* denotes a narrative that depicts crucial *events or relations that are impossible in the real world (excluding, that is, events intended to be read as allegorical or supernatural). The most prominent of these include a contradictory chronology in the story world, ontological framebreaking, and multiple, irreducibly incompatible versions of basic events (*see* NARRATIVE VERSIONS). Though the term 'anti-narrative' is not widely discussed *per se*, the concept is perhaps implicit in the notion of *natural narrative, the conventions of which it abrogates; its practice is prominent and widespread.

In the identification of anti-narratives, issues of degree are important. Numerous narratives, including most of the plays of Shakespeare, contain chronological oddities, confusions, or contradictions, few of which are noticeable to the casual reader or playgoer. An anti-narrative by contrast will have obvious, sustained, and irreconcilable contradictions at more than one major point in the narrative, and it will not be possible to explain these contradictions away by appeal to the unreliability or incompetence of any narrator or an unusual feature of the fictional world. In an anti-narrative, narrative chronology may be completely contradictory or several different storylines occupying different temporal zones may 'leak' into each other. Anti-narratives frequently make use of *metalepsis, as characters may escape from novels to threaten their *authors or a reader may be murdered by the fictive figures he reads about. Another common feature of anti-narratives is the varied repetition of unrepeatable events, such as the death of the protagonist depicted more than once in different manners with no way to determine which death is more 'real' or definitive. Some anti-narratives employ *denarration, in which portions of the fictional world are negated or 'erased'. Conventional characterisation is another element often abandoned by this mode, as radically mutable constructions supplant conventional stable, human-like personalities, though in some anti-narratives, such as Robbe-Grillet's *La Jalousie*, the characterisations are relatively consistent the better to foreground the contradictions elsewhere in the text (*see* CHARACTER).

The quintessential anti-narrative is generally thought to be Alain Robbe-Grillet's *La Jalousie*. The first one is arguably Diderot's *Jacques le fataliste*. Other authors associated with anti-narrative include Vladimir Nabokov, Natalie Sarraute, Samuel Beckett, and Raymond Queneau, all of whom were once regularly referred to as anti-novelists. Other practioners include Gertrude Stein, John Barthes, G. Cabrera Infante, Philippe Sollers, and Italo Calvino. It is generally associated with the *nouveau roman*, the *Tel Quel* novel, and *postmodernist narrative.

SEE ALSO: metafiction; narrative

References and further reading

Fludernik, Monika (1996) 'Games with Tellers, Telling and Told', in *Toward a Natural Narratology*, London: Routledge.
McHale, Brian (1987) *Postmodernist Fiction*, London: Methuen.
Orr, Leonard (1991) *Problems and Poetics of the Non-aristotelian Novel*, Lewisburg PA: Bucknell University Press.
Richardson, Brian (2000) 'Narrative Poetics and Post-modern Transgression: Theorizing the Collapse of Time, Voice, and Frame', *Narrative*, 8.1, 23–42.

BRIAN RICHARDSON

APOLOGY

Apology refers to the rhetorical *genre of defence, from the classical theological defence of the faith or apologetics (*see* THEOLOGY AND NARRATIVE). The apology presents the true narrative of the creed, faith, or discipline that has suffered attack (Vickers 1988). A frequent title during the Reformation, apology is defined as the genre 'which signifies defence, not with arms, but with reason, answer in defence, excuse, purgation or clearing of that of which one is charged' (Harding, 1565 sig 1r). The apology takes the form of trial and judgment and is in consequence argumentative or technically agonistic in style: 'In every Apology or excuse, three things meet together, the plaintiff or accuser, the defendant, the crime objected'. The most influential apology was probably John Jewel's *Apologie* which argues that the Church of England simply restores to uninterrupted usage a faith that preceded the Roman (1564, fol G1b). Jewel later counterposes the true faith, the first or original dogma in the form of an already extant faith – 'we have planted no new religion, but only renewed the old'– to the false, namely 'your new fantasies, which you have painted with the colour of antiquity' but which are, needless to say, 'vain and naught' (1564, 491). Cognate with the apology were its refutations in the form of works against (*adversus*) the heretical, and similarly treatises of denunciation (*deballacyon*), confutation, antirrhetic (against false images), and salvo or counterblast (*irenicum*).

Sharing its root with *legend or *fable (*apologus*), the apology in essence tells the story of the one true faith and uses that story to justify the creed, the dogmas, and constitutions of the Church. Apology thus has a strongly legal connotation and although its roots are in theology, the secular juridical tradition borrowed the form and rhetorical tools of the apology in establishing the narrative and the dogmatic tradition of civil law (Goodrich, 1995, ch. 3). Any foundational treatise, that is to say any institutional or dogmatic statement of the articles of a tradition or discipline, will tend to use the form of the apology (*see* INSTITUTIONAL NARRATIVE). The foundational work will establish the legitimate origin, the singular narrative or lineage of the discipline while simultaneously discounting false histories, alternative narratives, plural or other truths. The apology is the form of the statement of orthodoxy and particularly in disciplines such as theology and law, the exposition of orthodoxy still comes in the narrative form of the exegesis or exposition of a singular *truth most usually captured in a sacred text, a classic, or *corpus iuris*. The rhetorical style of the apology is generally demonstrative and univocal: there are unitary principles and right answers that can be expressed best in a logical form that purports to eschew all ornament or figurative speech. The denial of rhetoric is a principal figure of the apology and evidences that the most effective rhetoric is that which appears the least rhetorical. Medieval rhetoric had a term for the rhetoric of truth, namely *rectorica*, a combination of rule and rhetoric, right and speech, which ironically became the preferred form of foundational treatise or modern apology.

SEE ALSO: law and narrative; narrative as argument; rhetorical approaches to narrative

References and further reading

Goodrich, Peter (1995) *Oedipus Lex. Psychoanalysis, History, Law*, Berkeley: University of California Press.
Harding, Thomas (1565) *A Confutation of a Booke Intituled an Apologie of the Church of England*, Antwerp: Ihon Laet.
Jewel, John (1564) *An Apologie or Answere in Defence of the Churche of Englande*, London: n.p.
—— (1567) *A Defence of the Apologie of the Churche of Englande*, London: Fleetstreet.
More, Thomas (1533) *The Apologye*, London: W. Rastell.
Vickers, Brian (1988) *In Defence of Rhetoric*, Oxford: Oxford University Press.

PETER GOODRICH

ARCHETYPAL PATTERNS

Archetypal patterns are complexes of properties found across a wide range of literary works, extending back to ancient poems, stories, *myths, and rituals. Archetypes are a central concept in the *psychological theories of C.G. Jung and the literary theories of Northrop Frye. For both, an archetype is a shared symbol. For Jung, it is a symbol shared by all humanity. (For more on Jung, *see* NARRATIVE UNIVERSALS.) For Frye, it is a symbol shared by those within a particular tradition.

In *Anatomy of Criticism* (1957), Frye articulated an influential theory of literature that includes a range of principles, but focuses particularly on archetypes. Frye first identifies symbols as any isolable unit of a literary work (*see* NARRATIVE UNITS). We may distinguish two sorts of symbols. First, symbols may be units of meaning or *reference. Symbols of this sort include standard *images, such as submersion in water (often, though not invariably, a representation of rebirth). The second sort of symbol is more commonly termed a *structure*. It places units of meaning or reference in complex relations with one another. Standard narrative patterns form symbols of this (structural) sort (*see* NARRATIVE STRUCTURE).

Frye isolates four levels of symbols. First, there are symbols of language – words, names, etc. Literary study of symbols at this level includes historical/referential criticism. Second, there are symbols that are internal to a literary work. These include the image patterns that were the focus of analysis in New Criticism. Third, there are symbols that pervade a given tradition. Frye refers to these as archetypes. Frye's final level of symbolism is the 'anagogic', which is the universal level and is largely fused with the archetypal level in practical criticism.

Frye organised archetypes into four large categories: comedy, *romance, tragedy, and *irony/ *satire. These involve common patterns of imagery, often associated with seasons. They also include standard narrative sequences and character types. Thus comedies typically present us with lovers who are initially prevented from marrying, but subsequently manage to be united, despite parental or other resistance. Romance is most often a quest. (In this, Frye's work parallels that of some earlier writers, such as Vladimir Propp (1968 [1928]) and Joseph Campbell (1968).)

Frye tacitly divides characters into those that serve the *plot and those that serve the mood. In each category, he makes a further division into characters that facilitate and those that obstruct (*see* ACTANT). Thus the *hero and the hero's helper are characters who facilitate advancement toward resolution of the plot. Rivals and enemies are 'blocking' characters who obstruct that advancement. Finally, Frye adds to this organisation a further division of characters who present themselves as greater than they are ('alazons') and characters who present themselves as less than they are ('eirons').

Subsequent critics have worked on archetypal patterns, developing, disputing, and extending the ideas of Jung, Frye, and others. This work has often combined archetypal criticism (or 'myth criticism', as it is sometimes called) with more recent critical approaches, as in Annis Pratt's (1981) feminist archetypal criticism.

References and further reading

Campbell, Joseph (1968) *The Hero with a Thousand Faces*, Princeton: Princeton University Press.

Frye, Northrop (1957) *Anatomy of Criticism: Four Essays*, Princeton: Princeton University Press.

Pratt, Annis (1981) *Archetypal Patterns in Women's Fiction*, Bloomington: Indiana University Press.

Propp, Vladimir (1968 [1928]) *Morphology of the Folktale*, trans. Laurence Scott, revised by Louis A. Wagner, Austin: University of Texas Press.

PATRICK COLM HOGAN

ARCHITEXT

Genette coined this term to designate an umbrella category under which that of *genre would be subsumed. The need for a broader term follows from his demonstration, in *The Architext* (1992 [1979]), of the extraordinarily confused, heterogeneous state of the received notion of genre. The fact that a given work can be identified generically as a *Gothic novel, for example, is one kind of generalisation about it; the fact that it is a *narrative, or that it is written in prose, belong to distinct kinds of generalisation. In *Palimpsests* Genette provided a clarification, as follows: if a genre is one abstract category under which particular literary works may be grouped according to various formal or *thematic features they exhibit, the architext would be the totality of all such general categories, of which genre is only one (1997: 1, 4). Although it has yet to find much resonance in literary studies, the architext remains an extremely suggestive concept.

References and further reading

Genette, Gérard (1992 [1979]) *The Architext: An Introduction*, trans. Jane E. Lewin, Berkeley: University of California Press.

—— (1997 [1982]) *Palimpsests: Literature in the Second Degree*, trans. Channa Newman and Claude Doubinsky, Lincoln: University of Nebraska Press.

DAVID GORMAN

ARTIFICIAL INTELLIGENCE AND NARRATIVE

Artificial intelligence (AI) attempts to understand intelligence and to implement computer systems that can learn, reason, and make intelligent decisions. *Philosophy, *linguistics, and psychology are all involved in AI; computer science has had a central role. AI has dealt with narrative almost from the beginning. The production and understanding of narrative are interesting types of intelligent behaviour, since organising experience into narrative may be essential to human cognition (Schank 1990). (This topic forms the concern of scholars of *narrative intelligence; *see* NARRATIVE AS COGNITIVE INSTRUMENT.) The first two types of narrative projects undertaken by artificial intelligence researchers were dialogue systems involving conversational *characters and story-generation systems. The latter include both programs that simulate an environment and narrate the events that happens in it, and programs that select which events will occur on the basis of pre-established models of *plot or character (*see* COMPUTATIONAL APPROACHES TO NARRATIVE). Some of what has been learned in these systems has been employed in interactive systems, including systems that provide an interactive dramatic experience.

The term 'artificial intelligence' itself was coined in 1955. Arthur Samuel had already written a program that played checkers against itself and learned to play at the championship level; *computer games have remained important to AI research and applications. One early and perhaps archetypal AI system in a different domain was the General Problem Solver (GPS) developed by Alan Newell and Herbert Simon in the late 1950s to prove mathematical theorems. (Russell and Norvig [2003] has more on the history of AI and introduces its essential mathematical and computational techniques.)

ELIZA (Weizenbaum 1966) was the first conversational character. The system communicated in text and simulated a Rogerian psychotherapist. Although it simply matched patterns in the user's input and looked up responses, the system created the sense of a character and often elicited narratives from users; some found it compelling for psychotherapeutic, literary, or dramatic reasons (Murray 1997: 214–47). Its successors included the simulated schizophrenic PARRY (1971), an academic project by Ken Colby, and the commercial program Racter (1984) by William Chamberlain. A book of poems, *The Policeman's Beard is Half Constructed*, was attributed to Racter.

SHRDLU (Winograd 1972) used text and graphics to simulate a robot that could rearrange blocks. The system could answer questions about what had happened and could narrate the actions that had resulted in the current configuration; it was an important ancestor of interactive fiction such as *Adventure* (1975–1976) and *Zork* (1977–1978). Several later systems had the generation and *narration of stories as their main goal. The first of these was TALE-SPIN (Meehan 1976), which used planning to generate *fables about animals with simple drives and goals. The system's memorable, amusing errors revealed how difficult it is to automatically generate interesting stories. Michael Lebowitz's UNIVERSE (1984) refined this approach and enhanced the representation of characters (embellishing certain stereotypes) to generate soap-opera narratives. MINSTREL (Turner 1994) was a similar system designed to generate Arthurian tales; it was able to get 'bored' and move on to other topics. A recent automatic storyteller is BRUTUS (Bringsjord and Ferrucci 2000), a system that uses a formal model of betrayal and has sophisticated abilities as a *narrator. These story-generating systems do not accept user input as they narrate, but they show how AI can be deeply involved with *digital narrative even in non-interactive systems.

In the early 1990s, Carnegie Mellon University's Oz Project developed interactive narrative systems that used AI techniques. Graphical and all-text projects considered how parsing natural language, generating surface texts, and representing the emotional states of characters could be handled in a dramatic framework. One thread of this project led to the work of Joe Bates's company Zoesis, while Michael Mateas continued the Oz Project's work at CMU, completing a graphical, Aristotelian, interactive *drama, *Façade*, in collaboration with Andrew Stern (Mateas 2002). *Façade* does not have an all-powerful 'director' or completely autonomous characters; it allows the characters in the drama to cooperate (even when they are fighting with one another) to attain common goals (e.g., 'effectively portray an argument and make the user uncomfortable').

Almost all of the systems mentioned above use techniques associated with rule-based or symbolic AI, also called 'good old-fashioned AI' (GOFAI), and represent story elements and ways of narrating explicitly. Since the 1990s much AI work has been done in a different framework, successfully employing statistical methods and connectionist principles. Such approaches, although effective, are often unable to provide an explicit, human-understandable representation of the system's knowledge or an explanation for its actions, which some see as a disadvantage for work with narrative. Statistical systems have been used to generate poetry (e.g., Jon Trowbridge's freely available system Gnoetry) and in some work involving narrative and cognition (e.g., the computational neuroscience project Shruti at Berkeley), but hidden Markov models, Bayesian methods, neural networks, machine-learning techniques, and similar approaches have been largely restricted to such non-narrative tasks as poetry generation and lower-level text understanding. Whether GOFAI will continue to be favoured for creative narrative work or whether more recent AI techniques will be used in these endeavours as well remains to be seen.

SEE ALSO: cognitive narratology; interactive fiction; psychological approaches to narrative

References and further reading

Bringsjord, Selmer, and David A. Ferrucci (2000) *Artificial Intelligence and Literary Creativity: Inside the Mind of BRUTUS, a Storytelling Machine*, Hillsdale, NJ: Lawrence Erlbaum.

Gnoetry, http://www.beardofbees.com/gnoetry.html

Mateas, Michael (2002) *Interactive Drama, Art, and Artificial Intelligence*, Ph.D. Thesis (Technical Report CMU-CS-02-206), School of Computer Science, Carnegie Mellon University.

Meehan, James (1976) *The Metanovel: Writing Stories by Computer*, Ph.D. Thesis, Yale University.

Murray, Janet (1997) *Hamlet on the Holodeck: The Future of Narrative in Cyberspace*, New York: Free Press.

Russell, Stuart, and Peter Norvig (2003) *Artificial Intelligence: A Modern Approach*, Englewood Cliffs, NJ: Prentice Hall.

Ryan, Marie-Laure (1991) *Possible Worlds, Artificial Intelligence, and Narrative Theory*, Bloomington: Indiana University Press.

Schank, Roger C. (1990) *Tell Me a Story: A New Look at Real and Artificial Memory*, New York: Charles Scribner.

Shruti, http://www.icsi.berkeley.edu/~shastri/shruti/index.html

Turner, Scott R. (1994) *The Creative Process: A Computer Model of Storytelling and Creativity*, Hillsdale, NJ: Lawrence Erlbaum.

Weizenbaum, Joseph (1966) 'Eliza – a Computer Program for the Study of Natural Language

Communication between Man and Machine', *Communications of the ACM*, 9, 36–45.

Winograd, Terry (1972) *Understanding Natural Language*, New York: Academic Press.

NICK MONTFORT

ATOMIC AND MOLECULAR NARRATIVES

Arthur Danto (1985) proposed the distinction between atomic and molecular narratives as part of his attempt to integrate *action theory and models of historical explanation developed within analytic *philosophy (*see* HISTORIOGRAPHY; NARRATIVE EXPLANATION). Construing actions as a byproduct of narrative explanations of *events, Danto equated singular or basic actions with *atomic narratives*, which he graphically represented as follows:

F G

/. /

The slash marks represent the termini of an event, i.e., a change in the world, with F and G standing for states or conditions that obtain at each terminus. The dot represents the action that gets narratively constructed as producing the change in question.

As Danto notes, there can be *sequences* of changes that no single action or cause serves to explain. For such sequences Danto suggested the term 'molecular narratives'. Thus, although the fall of the Roman empire can be conceived as a chain of atomic narratives, there is no single causal principle whose scope ranges over every atomic narrative in the chain. Such macro-sequences can be represented as:

F G H I

/. /. /. /

where the three successive changes are F→G, G → H, and H → I. The action that precipitated the change H → I, at which point Rome's rule officially reached an end, does not suffice to explain F → I. The molecular narrative required to account for this larger change cannot be viewed, therefore, as simply an end-to-end series of atomic narratives. In other words, molecular narratives exhibit gestalt properties, being more than just the product of the atomic narratives that they contain.

References and further reading

Danto, Arthur C. (1985) *Narration and Knowledge*, New York: Columbia University Press.

DAVID HERMAN

ATTRIBUTIVE DISCOURSE

Also referred to as a 'tag', attributive discourse is a phrase identifying the agent and the activity of a mental process or a *speech act. Attributive tags are constructions involving *verba dicendi* or *inquits* (she said, asked, replied, announced etc.), *verba cogitandi* or c*ogitats* (she thought, realised, felt, etc.), or *verba sentiendi/percipiendi* or *percepits* (she saw, heard, remembered, etc.). *See* QUOTATION THEORY (also: SPEECH REPRESENTATION; THOUGHT AND CONSCIOUSNESS REPRESENTATION (LITERATURE)).

AUDIENCE

Audience is a general term that covers any receiver of a text, be it a reader, a viewer, or a listener. Although study of audiences goes back to Aristotle and Plato, audience was generally ignored by the *formalists (especially the New Critics) most influential in Anglo-American criticism of the 1940s and 1950s. Acting according to principles most powerfully formulated in Wimsatt and Beardsley's *The Affective Fallacy*, these formalists valued the work itself (considered as a formal object) more highly than any effects it may have (*see* CHICAGO SCHOOL, THE). But a variety of forces in the 1960s and early 1970s, both political and literary, brought audiences (especially readers) centre stage. Booth's analysis of rhetoric in *The Rhetoric of Fiction* paid significant attention to the role of the reader in the act of communication, and judged the quality of the text largely in terms of author/reader communion. Even more radical was Fish's early notion of 'Affective Stylistics', which argued that texts are events, rather than objects, and that the critic's job is to ask what texts do to readers (*see* READER-RESPONSE THEORY). Norman Holland, in *Dynamics of Literary Response*, used Freudian psychology to explore how readers transform the fantasies underlying literary texts. Roland Barthes declared the 'death of the author' so that the reader could be born. In the years since, the question has no longer been whether or not the reader was relevant to analysis. Rather, the question has become, 'which reader?'. For reader critics work with so many different notions of the reader that they hardly constitute a single theoretical school.

Some theorists focus on actual rather than abstract readers, although differences in disciplinary interests produce radical differences in ways of thinking about those readers. Mailloux's concerns, for instance, are primarily historical, as he explores interpretive controversies through the history of the cultural practices that have constituted particular texts for readers. Radway looks at readers (specifically, readers of popular romances) and their interpretive strategies from a sociological perspective that pays particular attention to *gender and class (see ROMANCE NOVEL; SOCIOLOGICAL APPROACHES TO LITERARY NARRATIVE). Holland, in *5 Readers Reading*, concretises his earlier generalisations by looking at a group of actual readers from a *psychological perspective, arguing that their interpretations stem from their individual psychological makeups. Bleich, in his influential *Readings and Feelings*, looks at reading primarily from a pedagogical perspective, exploring the ways that students' individual personalities marked classroom discussion.

Other critics, especially those influenced by classical narratology (see STRUCTURALIST NARRATOLOGY), are primarily concerned with various idealisations and abstractions – implied readers, intended readers, and postulated readers of various sorts. The distinctions are fuzzy, but important. Implied readers can be determined on the basis of textual features alone. Intended readers, because they are hypothesised by the author, can often be established only by a study of the text in its biographical and historical context. Postulated readers, like Fish's 'informed reader' or his influential notion of 'interpretive community' (a group of readers who share interpretive practices), are independent of the text. In fact, they precede the text and serve as a *hermeneutic device for deciphering it. Different interpretive communities will read the 'same' text in radically different ways. Jauss locates his postulated reader in history, arguing that different historical contexts produce different *horizons of expectations that, in turn, provide different parameters for interpretation (see RECEPTION THEORY).

In narrative *fiction, the variety of readers escalates further: just as the simultaneous existence of multiple speakers (primarily *author and

*narrator) complicates the nature of the discourse, so the simultaneous existence of their multiple audiences complicates the act of reception. Prince popularised the notion of the *narratee, the audience to whom the narrator is addressing the narration. Rabinowitz distinguishes between the authorial audience (the audience assumed by the author as he or she makes rhetorical choices, an audience that recognises that the work is a work of fiction) and the narrative audience (an imaginary audience that takes the narrator as 'real'). While the narratee and narrative audience seem similar, there is a significant difference between them, stemming in part from the differences between the narratological tradition in which Prince is working and the rhetorical tradition in which Rabinowitz participates: while the narratee is a figure, either implied or explicit, in the text, the narrative audience is a role that the real audience pretends to play.

Despite these differences in theoretical perspective, the elevation of the reader to a status equal to that of the author has simultaneously given both urgency and nuance to questions about how literary meaning is made, how interpretations are grounded, and how literary quality is judged. It has also forced reconsideration or replacement of once-familiar concepts: because Phelan's notion of *narrative progression, for instance, takes reader experience into account, it allows interpretive nuances unavailable to critics working with purely textual notions of plot and form. At the same time, as the feminist reader criticism of Fetterley and Barlowe demonstrates, exploration of the variety of readers connected to any text has led to renewed interest in the *ideology of literature – not simply the ideology contained 'in texts', but also the ideology implied in interpretive practices themselves.

SEE ALSO: communication in narrative; feminist narratology; reader constructs; rhetorical approaches to narrative

References and further reading

Barlowe, Jamie (2000) *The Scarlet Mob of Scribblers: Rereading Hester Prynn*, Carbondale: Southern Illinois University Press.

Barthes, Roland (1977 [1968]) 'The Death of the Author', in *Image–Music–Text*, trans. Stephen Heath, New York: Hill and Wang.

Bleich, David (1975) *Readings and Feelings: An Introduction to Subjective Criticism*, Urbana, Illinois: National Council of Teachers of English.

Booth, Wayne C. (1983 [1961]) *The Rhetoric of Fiction*, Chicago: University of Chicago Press.

Fetterley, Judith (1978) *The Resisting Reader: A Feminist Approach to American Fiction*, Bloomington: Indiana University Press.

Fish, Stanley (1980) *Is There a Text in This Class?: The Authority of Interpretive Communities*, Cambridge, Mass.: Harvard University Press.

Holland, Norman N. (1975) *5 Readers Reading*, New Haven: Yale University Press.

Jauss, Hans Robert (1982) *Toward an Aesthetic of Reception*, trans. Timothy Bahti, Minneapolis: University of Minnesota Press.

Mailloux, Steven (1989) *Rhetorical Power*, Ithaca: Cornell University Press.

Phelan, James (1996) *Narrative as Rhetoric: Technique, Audiences, Ethics, Ideology*, Columbus: Ohio State University Press.

Prince, Gerald (1980 [1973]) 'Introduction to the Study of the Narratee', in Jane Tompkins (ed.) *Reader-Response Criticism*, Baltimore: Johns Hopkins University Press.

Rabinowitz Peter J. (1998 [1987]) *Before Reading: Narrative Conventions and the Politics of Interpretation*, Columbus: Ohio State University Press.

Radway, Janice (1984) *Reading the Romance: Women, Patriarchy, and Popular Literature*, Chapel Hill: University of North Carolina Press.

PETER J. RABINOWITZ

AUSTRALIAN ABORIGINAL NARRATIVE

Narrative holds a primary place in Australian Aboriginal societies, traditional and post-contact. Storytelling is highly valued, good *narrators are held in high esteem, and narratives are valuable as items of exchange; moreover, the narrative mode of thought has a fundamental role in comprehending and codifying knowledge about the world. Significantly, narrative is construed as fact, not *fiction; traditionally, fiction was not recognised as a narrative *genre distinct from non-fiction.

Writing was traditionally unknown, and Australian Aboriginal narratives (AANs) were orally performed (see Hercus and Sutton 1986, Koch 1993, and Merlan 1996, for samples) (*see* ORAL CULTURES AND NARRATIVE; ORALITY). Recent years have witnessed the emergence of written narratives in both traditional and post-contact languages, authored by Aboriginal people (e.g.,

Morgan 1987). This entry focuses on the traditional, oral types of narrative.

A widespread and notable stylistic feature of spoken AANs is the use of pausing; narratives are typically delivered in short segments of speech bounded by pauses. Following the ethnopoetical tradition (e.g., Tedlock 1983), some investigators liken oral narratives to poetry, and take pauses to define lines (e.g., Muecke 1982), as illustrated by 1–3, translated from a Gooniyandi *myth about fire. (Figures in brackets indicate length of pause in seconds.)

1   lots of old men were sitting around together (2.28)
2   they were sitting (2.40)
3   in the very cold time rain came to them (3.32)

Place is fundamental to ANN and worldview; indeed, landscape apparently serves as a mnemonic system, places evoking memories of events associated with them (*see* SPACE IN NARRATIVE). Place-to-place movement constitutes a backbone for ANNs of all types; myths are generally tied to named places, and serve as charters for land ownership.

Narratives recount sequences of spatio-temporally related *events and event-types. McGregor proposes that narratives in Gooniyandi are constituted by sequences of episodes containing minimal narratives, sequences made up of an initial state, an active event, and a final state, typically the inverse of the initial state (Prince 1973) (*see* MINIMAL NARRATIVE; NARRATIVE UNITS). 1–3 begin the first episode, which continues:

1   it was cold no blankets
2   no matches
3   no tents people just had nothing
4   before in the Dreamtime
5   at that time they sat
6   outside
7   rain hit them
8   all
9   it made them cold

1 and 2 represent the initial state, 3 an event; 4–9 elaborate on the circumstances of the people. 10–11 recalls the event of 3, and 12 recounts entry to the final state, the inverse of the presumed initial state of the people, before the arrival of rain.

Episode boundaries tend to be associated with initial scene-changing adverbials and full noun-phrase (rather than pronominal) reference; pauses tend to be longer than usual. Episode structures have also been proposed for narratives

in Gunwinjgu (Carroll 1996), Pitjantjatjara/
Yankuntjatjara (Klapproth Muazzin 2001), and
Aboriginal English (Muecke 1982), although each
of these investigators employs different criteria for
identifying episodes.

More speculatively, McGregor suggests that
Gooniyandi narratives typically also show a ternary Complication – Turning-Point – Resolution
structure. For instance, in the fire myth, the Complication arises when someone steals fire from the
people; the Turning Point comes when the people
find this person in a cave with it; and the Resolution
is their presumed repossession of the fire.

These elements are not always apparent, for
instance in stories relating everyday activities like
fishing and hunting and gathering, where nothing
extraordinary happens. Should such stories be
excluded from the genre of narrative, or has the
investigator failed to appreciate the Complication –
Turning-Point – Resolution structure, apparent to
members of the culture? Klapproth Muazzin suggests other cross-cultural differences in the construal
of these elements, arguing that personal problem
solving, though crucial to Western narratives, is
irrelevant in Pitjantjatjara/Yankuntjatjara narratives: complications are not constituted in those
narratives as problems confronting persons –
problems that must be resolved through their individual efforts, as part of their personal development.

Stories are narrated in interactions, and are
dialogic, not monologic; they are constructive
both interactionally and cognitively (Klapproth
Muazzin 2001), and involve interactants in an
interpersonal act of joint construction of a
*storyworld. Narrators are responsible for telling
the story, and thus for the major linguistic input;
*audiences minimally acknowledge receipt and
understanding of the message with backchannel
utterances such as *mm*, and *nhn*, but may also
contribute more significantly, e.g., by making
suggestions, asking questions, and the like. Audiences are not expected to be captive, and a listener
might go to sleep or walk away. Sometimes two or
more individuals jointly take on the role of narrating; one might serve as primary narrator, the
other might be a respondent who draws out the
narrative. In interaction with Europeans, some
narrators demand the presence of other knowledgeable persons to 'witness' the veracity of their
*performance.

AANs share many features with narratives in
other cultures; differences lie more in details and

emphases than kind. In-depth investigations are
few, and many issues remain unresolved, including: the generality of the above characteristics;
appropriate modes of representing and translating orally delivered narratives; how narrative is
acquired; the uses of repetition and quotation; the
role of grammar in the construction of storyworld;
and the emergence of new narrative genres.

SEE ALSO: communication in narrative; conversational storytelling; discourse analysis (linguistics);
ethnographic approaches to narrative; folklore;
gesture; Japanese narrative; narrative universals;
sociolinguistic approaches to narrative

References and further reading

Carroll, Peter (1996) *The Old People Told Us: Verbal Art
    in Western Arnhem Land*, PhD thesis, University of
    Queensland.
Clunies Ross, Margaret (1986) 'Australian Aboriginal
    Oral Traditions', *Oral Tradition*, 1, 231–71.
Hercus, Luise, and Peter Sutton (1986) *This Is What Hap-
    pened: Historical Narratives by Aborigines*, Canberra:
    Australian Institute of Aboriginal Studies.
Klapproth Muazzin, Danièle (2001) *Holding the World in
    Place: Narrative as Social Practice in Anglo-Western
    and in a Central Australian Aboriginal Culture*, PhD
    thesis, University of Bern.
Koch, Grace (ed.) (1993) *Kaytetye Country: an Aboriginal
    History of the Barrow Creek Area*, Alice Springs:
    Institute for Aboriginal Development.
McGregor, William (1987) 'The Structure of Gooniyandi
    Narratives', *Australian Aboriginal Studies*, 20–28.
Merlan, Francesca (ed.) (1996) *Big River Country: Stories
    from Elsey Station*, Alice Springs: Institute for
    Aboriginal Development.
Morgan, Sally (1987) *My Place*, Fremantle: Fremantle
    Arts Centre Press.
Muecke, Stephen (1982) *The Structure of Australian
    Aboriginal Narratives in English: A Study in Dis-
    course Analysis*, PhD thesis, University of Western
    Australia.
Prince, Gerald (1973) *A Grammar of Stories: An Intro-
    duction*, The Hague: Mouton.
Tedlock, Dennis (1983) *The Spoken Word and the
    Work of Interpretation*, Philadelphia: University of
    Pennsylvania Press.

WILLIAM McGREGOR

AUTHENTICATION

The term 'authentication' (or, alternatively, 'authentication function') was coined by Lubomír Doležel
to designate those narrational features that determine the ontological status of entities within

a fictional world (*see* EXISTENT; STORYWORLD). A constitutive convention of literary narrative stipulates that 'entities introduced in the discourse of the anonymous third-person narrator are *eo ipso* authenticated as fictional facts, while those introduced in the discourses of the fictional persons are not' (Doležel 1998: 149) (*see* NARRATOR; PERSON).

Third-person narratorial discourse thus establishes the fictional world and defines what is the case in it, while claims made in the *characters' discourses are true in this world only if they conform with the narratorial ones. Subjective third-person *narration creates an intermediary zone of relatively authenticated fictional facts. In first-person or homodiegetic narration, the narrator is personalised and his or her claims cannot therefore possess absolute authenticating force. Furthermore, different kinds of claims made by such a narrator (for example, specific or general) may be assigned different degrees of narrative authority. In some forms of narrative the authenticating force of the narrator's discourse is completely undermined, and the existence of fictional facts of any kind becomes questionable (*see* RELIABILITY). Examples are narratorial self-irony in *skaz* and *metafictional play, which lay bare the possibilities and procedures of textual-world creation, thus blocking the activity of world-creation itself.

SEE ALSO: fiction, theories of; irony; reflexivity; truth

References and further reading

Doležel, Lubomír (1980) 'Truth and Authenticity in Narrative', *Poetics Today*, 1.3, 7–25.
—— (1998) *Hetrocosmica: Fiction and Possible Worlds*, Baltimore: Johns Hopkins University Press.

URI MARGOLIN

AUTHOR

The term 'author' is usually understood to refer to the person who created a text. Intense theoretical discussions from the 1940s onwards have shown that apart from unproblematically referring to the creator of a text, the concept of author is also used to determine the meaning of a text, to relate it to other texts by the same person or to historical contexts, and to establish a dimension of norms and values, style, and thematic unity. Moreover, it is generally understood today that in specific historical and cultural situations the concept of 'author' is crucial for many cultural practices involving texts. The use of this concept is embedded in theories of creativity (e.g., the author as 'genius'), textuality (e.g., the author as the intersection of multiple discourses), and communication (e.g., the literary work as expression of an author's feelings and emotions). Assumptions such as these determine which uses of the concept of 'author' are possible or even necessary in literary criticism. Often the *agency of an 'author' is used to invoke a sense of stylistic and thematic identity, and many well-established routines of literary criticism and editing depend on it for publishing texts as 'collected works'. The concept is also important for the historical understanding of a text because the author is the main link between a text and its historical and pragmatic contexts, especially language, fields of knowledge, and cultural practices.

However, while the 'author' is evidently a crucial component in the overall framework of a narrative text's elements and relations, its status in narrative theory has remained highly controversial. Contemporary models of narrative communication distinguish between author, *implied author, and *narrator. The latter two concepts refer to entities constructed on the basis of textual features, while 'author' refers to some real world agent (*see* NO-NARRATOR THEORY). Even if most theories of narrative communication stress the essential difference between author, narrator, and implied author, often to such an extent as to exclude the author from narratological analysis, most readers use the text as a basis for inferential processes which simultaneously construct narrator, implied author, and author images. The image of the author (such as the common concept of 'the ironical Thomas Mann') is constructed not only on the basis of text-internal clues, but also on the basis of knowledge derived from *paratexts and other sources.

In classical *hermeneutics the process of understanding a text was viewed as an attempt to reconstruct an author's *intention. The critique of such naive uses of the notion of author developed in two waves. Wimsatt and Beardsley formulated the first attack in their influential essay on 'The Intentional Fallacy' (1954 [1946]). Basing their stance on the premise that a literary text is self-contained and that its meaning is solely determined by textual clues, they considered authorial intention external information and therefore irrelevant for understanding the text. Equally important were the attacks launched in two essays written in the 1960s – Barthes's 'The Death of the Author' (1977 [1967]) and Foucault's 'What Is an Author?' (1979 [1969]). Barthes's essay describes a development in modern literature which replaces the sacralised author with the figure of the humble writer who is merely a medium for the multiple meanings bound up in the language of the text. On this view, it is the act of reading rather than the act of writing which is instrumental in creating a text's meaning. Building on Barthes's account, Foucault's 'What Is an Author?' describes four major aspects that characterise the reach of the 'author-function': (1) Texts produced, read, and distributed in discourses tied to a firmly established author-function are legally owned by their authors. (2) The author-function can be subject to a variety of limitations: some discourses have no author-function at all, some have an author-function today but did not have one in the past, and some had an author-function in the past but do not have one now. Thus, in the Middle Ages, literary texts were distributed without any reference to their authors while scientific texts received their authority through their author's name. (3) The author concept enables a reader to construct common features across texts based on shared systems of values, similar style, and historical or theoretical unity or development. (4) In such texts, the first-person personal pronoun usually ceases to refer to the actual writer of the text (see PERSON).

In popular usage, the formula 'the death of the author' implies that texts can and should be understood without any reference to the historical author and his or her intentions, and that the meaning of a text is the product of its interaction with a potentially infinite number of pretexts (see INTERTEXTUALITY). While Foucault actually acknowledged that the author function was of crucial importance for many contemporary texts, he also envisioned a utopian world created by radical social changes (seemingly imminent in the 1960s) in which the author-function would be obsolete. Yet even though the general theoretical discourse from the 1980s onward was dominated by the death-of-the-author slogan, literary criticism remained remarkably unaffected by it and freely continued to employ terms like 'author' and 'work'. As a matter of fact, this practice is supported both by empirical observation

and theoretical argument. For instance, empirical research has isolated quantifiable features unequivocally distinguishing the texts of one author from those of another, hence falsifying the hypothesis that unity of style is just a readerly projection (Burrows 1995). Moreover, recent research into the historical distribution and development of the author-function has shown that Foucault's hypotheses – especially his claim that literary discourse in the Middle Ages was not constrained by the author-function – were largely inaccurate. Evidently, Foucault also paid insufficient attention to the type of authorial agency which manifests itself in the selection and arrangement of textual material.

References and further reading

Barthes, Roland (1977 [1967]) 'The Death of the Author', in *Image/Music/Text*, New York: Hill and Wang.

Burke, Seán (ed.) (1995) *Authorship: From Plato to the Postmodern*, Edinburgh: Edinburgh University Press.

Burrows, John F. (1995) 'Computers and the Idea of Authorship', in Deryck M. Schreuder (ed.) *Celebrating the Humanities: Jubilee Essays*, Canberra: Australian Academy of the Humanities.

Foucault, Michel (1979 [1969]) 'What Is an Author?', in Josué V. Harari (ed.) *Textual Strategies: Perspectives in Post-Structuralist Criticism*, London: Methuen.

Iseminger, Gary (ed.) (1992) *Intention and interpretation*, Philadelphia: Temple University Press.

Wimsatt, William K., and Monroe C. Beardsley (1954) 'The Intentional Fallacy', in Wimsatt and Beardsley (eds) *The Verbal Icon: Studies in the Meaning of Poetry*, Lexington: Kentucky University Press.

FOTIS JANNIDIS

AUTHORIAL NARRATIVE SITUATION

One of the three narrative situations proposed by Franz Stanzel: a third-person narrative told by an intrusive and (usually) omniscient *narrator. *See* NARRATIVE SITUATIONS; PERSON.

AUTOBIOGRAPHY

The term 'autobiography' is a composite of the Greek *autós* ('self'), *bios* ('life'), and *gráphein* ('write'). While in a wider sense all fictional writing is autobiographical, autobiography as a *genre may be defined as a comprehensive non-fictional narrative in prose in which the *author renders the facts of her/his own life, usually in first-person form (*see* FICTION, THEORIES OF; NARRATIVE SITUATIONS; PERSON). Autobiographical discourse is retrospective as the author surveys her/his past life from her/his present point of view and attempts to explain the development of her/his personality (*see* TIME IN NARRATIVE; NARRATION). The focus on inner life distinguishes autobiography from the memoir, which emphasises the author's public role among well-known contemporaries.

As opposed to *biography, where the author renders someone else's *life story, autobiography is necessarily incomplete and (theoretically) open to constant rewriting. Structurally, the temporal distance between experiencing-I and narrating-I is the pivotal point in autobiographical narration, enabling the author to adopt a variety of attitudes, from sympathy to ironic distance, toward her/his earlier self (*see* IRONY). Deviations from the standard first-person form have been more frequent since the beginning of the twentieth century (Henry Adams, *The Education of Henry Adams*, 1918; Gertrude Stein, *The Autobiography of Alice B. Toklas*, 1933), using first-person/third-person shifts in order to express a sense of the fragmentation of individual *identity (cf. Ronald Fraser, *In Search of a Past*, 1984).

Although there have been representations of the self since late antiquity (St. Augustine's *Confessiones* [AD 397–398] being a cornerstone in the history of the form), autobiography has only been recognised as a distinct literary genre since the late eighteenth-century. By that time, the confessional pattern of religious autobiography (John Bunyan, *Grace Abounding*, 1666) had given way to an emphasis on subjectivity and individual development (Jean-Jacques Rousseau, *Les Confessions*, 1782–1789), and the rendering of childhood experiences became increasingly important. Autobiography proliferated in the nineteenth-century, when individuals felt the need to ascertain their identities in the face of a rapidly changing environment, and works by Goethe, Mill, Newman, and others represent some of the highlights of the Western autobiographical tradition. In the twentieth century, tendencies towards the fragmentary (Virginia Woolf, *Moments of Being*, 1976), attempts at blurring the boundaries between fact and fiction (Christine Brooke-Rose, *Remake*, 1996), and an epistemological scepticism which calls into doubt not only the concept of 'identity', but also the role of narrative in creating coherence

and meaning (Sartre, Michel Leiris) are prominent especially in writers' autobiographies. At the same time, particularly since the 1960s, there have been ideologically motivated autobiographies by members of marginalised groups as well as innumerable run-of-the-mill autobiographies ghostwritten, more often than not, for film stars and other celebrities.

Theoretical positions on autobiography have overcome an earlier, essentialist understanding of the genre as the representation of an autonomous and homogeneous self. Roy Pascal's emphasis on 'inner truth' may still be indebted to such a view, yet his observation that autobiography imposes patterns on lives clearly supersedes simple models of unitary selfhood, putting the narrative construction of the autobiographical subject into the foreground. Such a conception of the autobiographical act as a creative rather than a mimetic process raises profound questions about the generic status of autobiography (*see* MIMESIS; REFLEXIVITY). Although it is basically a nonfictional genre, the dynamics of memory as well as selection and narrative structuring provide it with an element of fictionality (*see* FICTION, THEORIES OF). There has also been, in addition to autobiography, a prominent tradition of fictional narratives imitating its form, and *postmodernist writing has produced *autofictions which straddle generic boundaries. As there are no textual features upon which a distinction between factual and fictional autobiography can be based, Philippe Lejeune proposed the idea of an 'autobiographical contract' which guarantees the reader that the discourse is non-fictional. According to Lejeune, this contract is confirmed by the signature of the author, i.e., by her/his identity in name with the narrator, as opposed to their non-identity in fiction (cf. Cohn 1999).

After the late 1970s, *poststructuralist (including *feminist) theories of autobiography eliminated notions of 'subject', 'self', and author as independent sovereignties. With Jacques Derrida, Paul de Man, and others, the theory of autobiography entered its deconstructionist phase (*see* DECONSTRUCTIVE APPROACHES TO NARRATIVE). Because the deconstructionists denied all linguistic *reference, there could be no representation of self in language, but only an illusion of self generated by a purely textual subject. Since the late 1980s, however, the concept of autobiographical reference has reappeared. But now the referent is no longer a pre-existing self, but rather a time-bound human experience corresponding with the temporality of narrative. Indeed, experience as such may be conceived in narrative categories, which makes the text of an autobiography a duplex structure, i.e., a narrative rendering of what was already experienced as narratively organised (*see* EXPERIENTIALITY; NARRATIVISATION). This position also conforms with the *'narrative turn' in the human sciences, when historians, sociologists, and psychologists such as Jerome Bruner began to investigate the framing of our experience in the form of narrative(s) (*see* NARRATIVE AS COGNITIVE INSTRUMENT). According to the 'narrativist' view, the self is the product of her/his stories, and autobiography therefore is a psychological process of creating an identity rather than a literary form *per se*. Further interest in autobiography has focused particularly on aspects of *gender and ethnicity, revising the canon of 'classical' autobiographies and their concept of the self.

SEE ALSO: narrative psychology

References and further reading

Anderson, Linda (2001) *Autobiography*, London: Routledge.

Bruner, Jerome (1990) *Acts of Meaning*, Cambridge, Mass.: Harvard University Press.

Cohn, Dorrit (1999) *The Distinction of Fiction*, Baltimore: Johns Hopkins University Press.

Eakin, Paul John (1992) *Touching the World: Reference in Autobiography*, Princeton: Princeton University Press.

—— (1999) *How Our Lives Become Stories: Making Selves*, Ithaca: Cornell University Press.

Egan, Susanna (1999) *Mirror Talk: Genres of Crisis in Contemporary Autobiography*, Chapel Hill: The University of North Carolina Press.

Freeman, Mark (1993) *Rewriting the Self: History, Memory, Narrative*, London: Routledge.

Lejeune, Philippe (1989) *On Autobiography*, trans. Katherine Leary, ed. Paul John Eakin, Minneapolis: University of Minnesota Press.

Marcus, Laura (1994) *Auto/biographical Discourse: Theory, Criticism, Practice*, Manchester: Manchester University Press.

Olney, James (1972) *Metaphors of Self: The Meaning of Autobiography*, Princeton: Princeton University Press.

Pascal, Roy (1960) *Design and Truth in Autobiography*, London: Routledge & Kegan Paul.

MARTIN LÖSCHNIGG

AUTODIEGETIC NARRATION

In Genettean narratology, a first-person *narration in which the *narrator is the story's protagonist. *See* PERSON.

AUTOFICTION

Autofiction is a homodiegetic narrative that declares itself to be *fiction – by being called *'novel' on the front page, for example – but actually relates *events of the *author's own life and identifies the *author in the text by his or her real name (*see* NARRATION; PARATEXT). The term was coined in 1977 by the French author and critic Serge Doubrovsky in the preface to his first 'novel' *Fils*, and has led to much debate in France, especially in regard to Doubrovsky's controversial *Le livre brisé* (1989), whose manuscript version allegedly contributed to the suicide of the author's wife. Autofiction was later connected to American fictional *autobiographies such as Frederick Exley's *A Fan's Note* (1966) and Ronald Sukenick's *Up* (1968), as well as to predecessors such as Gertrude Stein's *The Autobiography of Alice B. Toklas* (1933) and *Roland Barthes by Roland Barthes* (1975).

Three interpretations of autofiction can be distinguished. (1) Unlike traditional autobiography, Doubrovsky claims, autofiction displays an achronological and *rhetorical arrangement of events based on methods of *psychoanalysis (*see* TEMPORAL ORDERING). Critics have described Doubrovsky's own work as a special kind of autobiographical narrative that uses the devices of fiction and *metafiction in order to achieve self-reconfiguration but still respects the so-called autobiographical contract. (2) More broadly, the term 'autofiction' is used by Genette and others to describe any fictional text in which the homodiegetic *narrator bears the name of the author. This includes *realist novels, *fantastic stories like Borges's 'The Aleph' (1949) and 'The Other' (1972), and texts in which the *identity of the author and the *narrator remains indeterminate because only the first name is used (e.g., Marcel in Proust's *Remembrance of Things Past* [1913–1927]). (3) The most specific definition is that of a *genre of its own characterised by a double author-reader contract: the autobiographical contract demanding the author to tell the *truth about his life, and the fictional contract allowing fabulation and invention.

The specificity of autofiction lies in the unresolvable paradox of these contradictory reading instructions (Darrieussecq 1996; Hughes 2002).

In a *poststructuralist context autofiction highlights the constructed, creative, and fictional character of all (autobiographical) narration, the eradication of the difference between fact and fiction, the questioning of the common distinction between art and life, and the collapse of the concept of a homogenous, autonomous subject identity. Some critics have argued that a great number of authors who write autofictional narratives are members of so-called social minorities – Doubrovsky and Ronald Sukenick are Jewish, Hervé Guibert and Christophe Donner are gay – and they suggest that it is precisely this paradoxical genre that allows for the creative reconfiguration of minority identities.

SEE ALSO: hybrid genres; panfictionality; postmodern narrative; reflexivity

References and further reading

Cohn, Dorrit (1999) *The Distinction of Fiction*, Baltimore: Johns Hopkins University Press.

Darrieussecq, Marie (1996) 'L'autofiction, un genre pas sérieux', *Poétique*, 27, 367–80.

Doubrovsky, Serge, Jacques Lecarme, and Philippe Lejeune (eds) (1993) *Autofictions & Cie*, Paris: Université de Paris.

Genette, Gérard (1993) *Fiction and Diction*, trans. Catherine Porter, Ithaca: Cornell University Press.

Hornung, Alfred, and Ernstpeter Ruhe (eds) (1992) *Autobiographie & Avant-garde*, Tübingen: Narr.

Hughes, Alex (2002) 'Recycling and Repetition in Recent French Autofiction: Marc Weitzmann's Doubrovskian Borrowings', *Modern Language Review*, 97.3, 566–76.

Ireland, John (ed.) (1993) *Genre*, 26.1 (Special issue dedicated to Doubrovsky).

Lejeune, Philippe (1989) *On Autobiography*, trans. Katherine Leary, ed. Paul John Eakin, Minneapolis: University of Minnesota Press.

FRANK ZIPFEL

B

BACKSTORY

A type of *exposition often involving analepsis or flashback; a filling in of the circumstances and *events that have led to the present moment in a *storyworld, and that illuminate the larger implications of actual or potential behaviours by *characters occupying a particular narrative 'now'. *Narrative techniques such as beginning a story *in medias res require that backstory be given analeptically, whereas in other cases (e.g., in many *realist novels) the backstory is provided at the outset. *See* TEMPORAL ORDERING.

BALLAD

In critical terminology as opposed to popular usage, a ballad is a relatively short narrative poem or song composed in stanzas. What has been called 'the ballad of tradition' (Gerould 1957) is customarily distinguished from sophisticated literary ballads as well as from parlour songs and from street ballads turned out by the broadside press. The ballad *genre emerged during the Middle Ages out of a coalescing of other narrative and lyric forms (*see* HYBRID GENRES). Traditional ballads are of anonymous authorship and are subject to musical and textual variation, hence their appeal to specialists in *folklore. Ballads often feature romantic, tragic, horrific, or quasi-historical themes and show a fondness for supernatural elements such as revenants, witchcraft, enchantments, and the devil. Many English-language ballads have continental European counterparts with the difference that some European ballads are stichic in form (proceeding line by line rather

than in stanzas) and thus resemble *epic songs. Stylistically, traditional ballads are marked by impersonal third-person *narration, formulaic diction, incremental repetition, trebling of elements, extreme contrasts, frequent use of a refrain, substantial formalised *dialogue, action beginning *in medias res, and a stylised pacing that has been called 'leaping and lingering' (*see* NARRATIVE SITUATIONS; PERSON). As has been discussed by Toelken (1995), ballads often encode erotic meanings through *metaphor. Although Buchan (1972) has argued that ballads were formerly composed by the *oral-formulaic method, most scholars agree that they are normally memorised.

Francis James Child (1882–1898) did much to advance the comparative and historical study of individual ballads and to establish a ballad canon, and older ballads are therefore known by their 'Child number'. During World War I, Cecil J. Sharp showed that English ballad tradition still continued strong in the Southern Appalachians. Field collections of folksongs and ballads have subsequently been made in many regions and are archived in such centres as the American Folklife Center at the Library of Congress and the School of Scottish Studies, Edinburgh. Bronson (1959–1972) assembled a vast collection of tunes with texts, many of them dating from twentieth-century tradition.

Many authors since Thomas Percy and William Wordsworth have composed sophisticated poems in a manner reminiscent of popular balladry. With author-collectors such as Robert Burns and Walter Scott, it is sometimes difficult to distinguish traditional elements from original ones. Although some scholars now regard the ballad genre as an artificial category and favour the more inclusive term 'narrative folksong', that term, too, has its drawbacks, for it directs attention to musical *performance to the exclusion of texts that are recited or meant for the printed page.

SEE ALSO: narrative in poetry; oral cultures and narrative

References and further reading

Bronson, Bertrand Harris (ed.) (1959–1972) *The Traditional Tunes of the Child Ballads*, 4 vols., Princeton: Princeton University Press.
Buchan, David (1972) *The Ballad and the Folk*, London: Routledge.
Child, Francis James (ed.) (1882–1898) *The English and Scottish Popular Ballads*, 5 vols., Boston: Houghton Mifflin.
Gerould, Gordon Hall (1957) *The Ballad of Tradition*, New York: Oxford University Press.
Toelken, Barre (1995) *Morning Dew and Roses: Nuance, Metaphor, and Meaning in Folksongs*, Urbana: University of Illinois Press.

JOHN D. NILES

BIBLICAL NARRATIVE

The Bible (from Greek *ta biblia* — 'the books') is, uniquely among major literary works, an anthology originally consisting of inscribed scrolls containing a variety of narrative forms, including *myths, *legends, *folktales, *fables, satires, histories, and apocalyptic prophecies of the end of time (*see* HISTORIOGRAPHY; SATIRIC NARRATIVE). The particular texts anthologised and their order varies among religious denominations. Jews accept as inspired only the Hebrew Bible, Protestants only the canonised Christian writings ('New Testament') along with the Hebrew Bible (by Christians called the 'Old Testament'). Roman Catholics include in addition a set of late Jewish writings excluded from the Hebrew Bible, called the Apocrypha.

The books of the Hebrew Bible were first written down in Hebrew and Aramaic over a long period between around 930 BC and 165 BC. None was written expressly to be part of a set of 'scriptures', because the very notion of scripture began to take shape long after most of the texts were written. In the decades after the destruction in 70 AD of the Temple in Jerusalem, survivors shaped the Hebrew Bible as part of an effort to recast the Jewish religion into a portable form for synagogue worship. Similarly, most of the Christian writings included in the New Testament were written in Greek between 70 and 115 AD, as sacred writings bearing witness to the history and significance of Jesus of Nazareth to readers who could no longer meet him or those who had known him.

The Bible is one of the few major literary works whose authorship is essentially unknown (*see* AUTHOR). Apart from several epistles by Paul, we cannot be certain of the name of the author of any of the texts comprising the Bible, since in the light of historical-philological study, the traditional ascriptions (e.g., that Moses wrote the five books from Genesis through Deuteronomy) cannot be sustained. The authors of the gospels of Matthew and John could not, given the date of the texts, have been the Matthew or John mentioned among the disciples of Jesus. Most books of the Bible, even the shortest, are layered texts, redacted from several different sources, often with editorial interpolations to guide interpretation and reference. The book of Revelation appears to have originated as an apocalypse by Jewish followers of John the Baptist, but was adapted to the New Testament by the addition of a Christian introduction and epilogue.

Different editorial practices dominated the Old and New Testaments. The New Testament includes alternate witnesses to the same events, whose discrepancies may require reconciliation. For example, the gospels of Matthew, Mark, and Luke record that Simon of Cyrene carried the cross of Jesus to Calvary, while John records that Jesus carried it himself. What might seem a contradiction was resolved by hypothesising an event mentioned in none of the gospels: that carrying the cross, Jesus fell under its weight, after which Simon was drafted to bear the burden. (Such a narrative, created to reconcile contradictions in the text, solve puzzles, or make its morality more edifying, is called a *midrash*; *see* GAPPING; PRAGMATICS.)

In the Old Testament, alternate versions of stories are often edited into a coherent whole rather than presented as separate testimonies (*see* NARRATIVE VERSIONS). In the Noah story (Genesis 5:31 to 9:17), two different accounts have been interleaved so cleverly that it is difficult to see the joins, which appear only when one asks whether the flood lasted 40 days or 150, whether there were just two of each animal or fourteen of some and two of others, and whether the name of the enraged deity who causes the flood is God (*Elohim* in Hebrew) or the LORD (*YHWH*). These characteristics of Biblical narrative inspired a 'source criticism' parsing Biblical texts into their presumed constituents and exploring their differing assumptions, agendas, and *ideologies. At the same time, a 'redaction criticism' attempted to understand the *intentions and effects ascribable to the various editors who compiled, combined, and attempted to reconcile these sources.

Contemporary narrative theory on the Bible begins with the observation of Erich Auerbach (1946) that Biblical narratives are presented with a powerful sense of tacit background. The account of Abraham's near-sacrifice of Isaac in Genesis 22 is spare, without decorative detail, insisting through its silences that the reader interpret God's demand and Abraham's unquestioning compliance in the context of the covenant scenes that preceded it, and the fulfilment of that covenant long afterwards. The masterly *rhetorical analyses of Biblical texts by Meir Sternberg (1985) take off from Auerbach in exposing other peculiar traits and conventions of Biblical narrative, such as the way narrative pattern generates expectations, often for the purpose of surprising the reader by frustrating those expectations, or the way descriptive adjectives, uncommon in Biblical prose, often become hooks on which shifts in the *plot are hung.

Jan Fokkelman (1975) exposed the fine structural patterns in biblical narratives at the level of the episode, the word, even at times that of the phoneme. In a very different way, Robert Alter (1981) has applied close reading associated with the New Criticism to Biblical texts, often in the interest of restoring a higher unity to narratives that might otherwise be considered discontinuous or abrupt. Mieke Bal's combination of narratological and *feminist analysis insightfully related the stories about 'lethal women' to those about passive female victims in the book of Judges (1988). As one might expect, the Bible in the 1980s and 1990s was also deconstructed, viewed as a social text, and explored through the lenses of *post-colonialism and *gender theory (*see* DECONSTRUCTIVE APPROACHES TO NARRATIVE). It generally survived those regimes better than the manipulations of magisterial critics such as Northrop Frye (1982) and Harold Bloom (1991) who, hamstrung by ignorance of Biblical Hebrew, forced the text to yield easy certainties about its archetypes and its authors (*see* ARCHETYPAL PATTERNS). Missing from the panoply of narratological

methods thus far is one that can deal responsibly with *narrative structures larger than the episode.

SEE ALSO: ancient theories of narrative (non-Western)

References and further reading

Alter, Robert (1981) *The Art of Biblical Narrative*, New York: Basic Books.
Auerbach, Erich (1946) *Mimesis: Dargestellte Wirklichkeit in der abendländischen Literatur*, Bern: A. Francke.
Bal, Mieke (1988) *Death and Dissymmetry: The Politics of Coherence in the Book of Judges*, Chicago: University of Chicago Press.
Bloom, Harold and David Rosenberg (1991) *The Book of J*, New York: Grove Weidenfeld.
Fokkelman, J. P. (1975) *Narrative Art in Genesis: Specimens of Stylistic and Structural Analysis*, Assen: Van Gorcum.
Frye, Northrop (1982). *The Great Code: The Bible and Literature*, New York: Harcourt, Brace and Jovanovich.
Sternberg, Meir (1985) *The Poetics of Biblical Narrative*, Bloomington: Indiana University Press.

DAVID H. RICHTER

BILDUNGSROMAN

Arguably Germany's best-known literary *genre, the Bildungsroman (*novel of formation) often retains its German name in other languages. Traditionally, it depicts a young man abandoning provincial roots for an urban environment to explore his intellectual, emotional, moral, and spiritual capacities. Whether nurturing or inimical, this new environment proffers the possibility of attaining wisdom and maturity. Johann Wolfgang von Goethe's *Wilhelm Meisters Lehrjahre* (*Wilhelm Meister's Apprentice Years*) (1794–1796) is usually credited with being the first example of the genre, and it still serves as the standard against which other Bildungsromane are measured.

Promoted in the eighteenth-century by Herder, Goethe, Schiller, and Humboldt, *Bildung* had become a humanist ideal of organic growth and fulfilment of human potential through active engagement with the world. In practice, it was only available to educated, middle-class men. Most generally, *Bildung* is a process of cultivating inner talents and becoming integrated within a larger community. *Conflict usually arises between an ideal of self-determination and the demands of socialisation, making *Bildung* a complicated mix of individual *action inseparable from social or cultural influence. Close affinities therefore obtain between the Bildungsroman, the *Erziehungsroman* (novel of *education), the *Entwicklungsroman* (novel of development), and the story of initiation. Precursors to the Bildungsroman were religious *autobiographies and the *picaresque novel.

First recognised as a new genre in Christian Friedrich von Blanckenburg's *Essay on the Novel* (1774), the Bildungsroman received its name from Karl Morgenstern in 1803. Hegel made fun of it in an oft-quoted passage from *Phenomenology of the Spirit* (1807), claiming its prototypical protagonist to be ultimately a 'Philistine like everybody else'. Wilhelm Dilthey formally defined the Bildungsroman in his 1870 *biography of Friedrich Schleiermacher, linking the genre firmly to *Wilhelm Meister* as its prototype. Classic examples of the genre are Gottfried Keller's *Der grüne Heinrich* (1854–1855; 1879–1880), Adalbert Stifter's *Der Nachsommer* (1857), Marcel Proust's *A la recherche du temps perdu* (1913–1927), James Joyce's *Portrait of the Artist as a Young Man* (1914), Dorothy Richardson's *Pilgrimage* (1915–1946), Thomas Mann's *Der Zauberberg* (1924), Günter Grass's *Die Blechtrommel* (1959), and William Golding's *Rites of Passage* (1980).

The term 'Bildungsroman' was not widely used until the late twentieth century when critics began devoting much attention to the genre, with many critics (among them Martin Swales, Jeffrey Sammons, Franco Moretti, and Todd Kontje) interrogating and often questioning its basic axioms. More recently, however, scholars such as Gilles Deleuze, Félix Guattari, and Susan Fraiman have re-examined the concept of *Bildung* within the contexts of *gender and race, specifically addressing the narrative possibilities of the female, the black, and the post-colonial Bildungsroman, examples of which include Virginia Woolf's *The Voyage Out* (1915), Carson McCullers's *The Member of the Wedding* (1946), Toni Morrison's *Sula* (1973), and Hanif Kureishi's *The Black Album* (1995).

SEE ALSO: feminist narratology; post-colonialism and narrative

References and further reading
Buchanan, Ian, and Claire Colebrook (eds) (2000) *Deleuze and Feminist Theory*, Edinburgh: Edinburgh University Press.
Fraiman, Susan (1993) *Unbecoming Women: British Women Writers and the Novel of Development*, New York: Columbia University Press.
Kontje, Todd (1993) *The German Bildungsroman: History of a National Genre*, Columbia, SC: Camden House.
Moretti, Franco (1987) *The Way of the World: The Bildungsroman in European Culture*, London: Verso.
Sammons, Jeffrey L. (1981) 'The Mystery of the Missing Bildungsroman, or: What Happened to Wilhelm Meister's Legacy?', *Genre*, 14, 229–46.
Swales, Martin (1978) *The German Bildungsroman from Wieland to Hesse*, Princeton: Princeton University Press.

MARGARET McCARTHY

BIOGRAPHY

Biography is a *genre of *historiography concerned with representing the lives of individual people. The genre developed during the fourth century BC, but the term 'biographia' (from Greek *bios* 'life' and *graphein* 'write') is not found prior to the sixth century AD; the word is used with its modern meaning for the first time in John Dryden's *Life of Plutarch* (1683).

Since the eighteenth-century, all definitions of biography have come to depend on a set of three core criteria. A biography (1) consists of a written text; (2) represents the life of a real person; and (3) does so in the mode of factual speech, that is, it is to be understood as true (*see* FICTION, THEORIES OF; TRUTH). The various definitions of the concept also agree that, in general, biographies are narrative texts that approach their subject retrospectively and organise their content by giving it a coherent causal structure (*see* CAUSALITY; NARRATION). Some definitions are extended to distinguish biography from *autobiography – i.e. biographical works in which the *author is identical with the represented subject.

Since classical times, critical reflection on biography has focused on identifying its exact position in the field of historiographical genres. Because of their claim to provide fact-based reconstructions of past *events, biographies can be classified as a form of historical writing. At the same time, both their evaluative statements and their presentation of historical material typically draw on literary strategies and techniques to a degree greater than that normally expected in the context of historiography. This observation has, in the wake of the linguistic and *narrative turn witnessed by the humanities in the twentieth century, frequently led to the thesis that biographies produce rather than reconstruct *life stories. That supposition, however, overlooks the distinction between the narrative form and the fictional status of a text. The fact that biographies can borrow from the methods of the *epic on the one hand, and that *novels like Wolfgang Hildesheimer's *Marbot* adopt the style of a balanced biographical account on the other, merely shows that formal characteristics alone do not normally provide sufficient evidence for determining the fictionality or factuality of a biographical account. In most cases, the formal aspect must be supplemented by an investigation of the author's intention and a study of how the text reworks the facts it relates (*see* INTENTIONALITY).

Passages dedicated to the lives of individual people can be found in even the oldest texts known to us – those left by the advanced cultures of China, the ancient East, and ancient Egypt (*see* CHINESE NARRATIVE; SANSKRIT NARRATIVE) – but biography did not develop into a distinct form of historical writing until the fourth century BC. To quote the title of an anthology of biographies written by Cornelius Nepos in the first century BC, the earliest texts in the genre were typically concerned with the *Life of Eminent Men*. Classical biographers such as Theophrastus, Tacitus, and Plutarch were primarily concerned with the lives of statesmen, military leaders, poets, and philosophers, and were more interested in composing *character studies with a claim to exemplary status than in retelling the stories of individual lives.

Similar principles underlie hagiography, the type of biography that emerged as the dominant form of the genre during the conversion of Europe to Christianity. Accounts of the lives of saints, drawing on the gospels of Matthew, Mark, and Luke, began to appear in the second century and flourished in the Middle Ages (*see* BIBLICAL NARRATIVE; MEDIEVAL NARRATIVE). The intention to morally educate the recipients is considerably more pronounced in them than in classical biographical texts (*see* DIDACTIC NARRATIVE).

The original nature of the biographical genre changed fundamentally as new concepts of individuality began to emerge. The biographical accounts of the Italian Renaissance laid the foundations for the development of biography as we know it today. While the biographies of the fourteenth and fifteenth centuries, which dealt above all with the lives of artists, did not depart fully from the tradition of classical biographical texts, the gradual awakening of interest in the individual meant that typical human qualities were increasingly accompanied by idiosyncratic features in biographical works.

The genre underwent a far more radical transformation in the wake of the social and cultural upheaval that swept the western world in the eighteenth-century and replaced the old and strictly hierarchical class structure with the new order of bourgeois society. In the course of this process, we can see the traditional concept of the individual as a static construct consisting of class, character, and temperament being displaced by a dynamic concept of human value that associated individuals with their unique life stories. This radical change in the concept of individuality had two main consequences for the genre of biography. First, it was now theoretically possible for any human being to become the subject of a biographical text. Second, the focus of biography shifted from the systematic study of characters to the narrative presentation of life stories.

The development of biography after 1800 is again part of a larger trend – namely, attempts by modern European nation-states to harness various forms of cultural production and exploit them for political purposes. As with historical writing in general, the genre of biography took on a scientific character in the nineteenth-century. At the same time, it became an indispensable tool in official efforts to foster and communicate national *identity – from 1835, multivolume biographical anthologies about figures of national importance began to appear in many European countries.

During the last hundred years, the genre has repeatedly found itself the target of intense criticism. The underlying theme of all such attacks is that biography is based on an understanding of the individual that has become hopelessly obsolete in the wake of the psychological and philosophical findings that have undermined the traditional concept of the subject since the end of the nineteenth-century. This argument goes on to claim that, rather than representing the life of an individual with greater or lesser success, a biographical text produces it with literary means. On the one hand, this kind of analysis has led to calls to abandon biography for good; on the other, it has stimulated writers such as Virginia Woolf and Jean-Paul Sartre in their attempts to revitalise the genre.

However, the debates among scholars concerning the nature and theoretical structure of biography have had little effect on the popularity enjoyed by the genre among readers. Nor have theories of biography had a substantial impact on the concept behind most of the biographies that continue to appear in great quantity and enjoy widespread distribution year after year.

SEE ALSO: agency; autofiction; character; narrative techniques

References and further reading

Biography: An Interdisciplinary Quarterly, (1978ff.) Hawaii: The University Press of Hawaii.

Cohn, Dorrit (1999) *The Distinction of Fiction*, Baltimore: Johns Hopkins University Press.

France, Peter, and William St Clair (eds) (2002) *Mapping Lives: The Uses of Biography*, Oxford: Oxford University Press.

Klein, Christian (ed.) (2002) *Grundlagen der Biographik: Theorie und Praxis biographischen Schreibens*, Stuttgart: Metzler.

Parke, Catherine N. (2002) *Biography: Writing Lives*, London: Routledge.

Sonnabend, Holger (2003) *Geschichte der antiken Biographie: Von Isokrates bis zur Historia Augusta*, Darmstadt: Wissenschaftliche Buchgesellschaft.

TOM KINDT

BIOLOGICAL FOUNDATIONS OF NARRATIVE

A fundamental function of the human brain is to understand, interpret, and explain the world to itself. A growing number of neuroscientists, biologists, cognitive psychologists, and philosophers have stressed that the human mind/brain is less a computer than a storyteller. Neuroscientist Michael S. Gazzaniga has written of the brain's 'interpreter', while philosopher William H. Calvin discusses the role of the brain's *'narrator'. Further, for Calvin, the brain operates like a 'Darwin Machine': it has the ability to evolve anticipated scenarios in milliseconds in a virtual (rather than real) environment (*see* VIRTUALITY). Philosopher Daniel C. Dennett sees the mind/brain as a 'virtual machine' that creates a 'centre of narrative gravity', running 'multiple drafts', not in a 'Cartesian Theatre', but simultaneously throughout the brain. We have the sensation of 'seeing' (imagining) images in the virtual machine of our brain, but these images are not to be found in any specific place (*see* VISUALISATION). The brain narratively

creates the virtual reality it perceives out of its own emergent imaginative powers.

Psychologist Merlin Donald argues that other animals at best live in an 'episodic' culture, one bound to the here-and-now and dominated by perception, whereas our uniquely human consciousness frees our species from the bonds of the episodic and permits it to roam freely throughout the past, the future, and the imagined (*see* TIME IN NARRATIVE). The first phase of human development beyond the episodic stage is the 'mimetic' stage, a pre-linguistic, gesture-based mode of communication (*see* GESTURE; MIMESIS). From this developed the 'mythic' or storytelling, phase of human development, a stage which is still very much with us today (*see* MYTH: THEORETICAL APPROACHES). According to Donald, our 'linguistic controller' has given us a whole new system for representing reality employing narrative models.

In other words, our brain tells us stories all the time in order both to anticipate the future and to understand itself, the world, and, of course, literary texts. In fact, literary theorist Mark Turner (1996) has argued that the single most fundamental human cognitive process is narrative: the basic principle of mind is story or parable, which we project onto other situations in order to understand them (*see* METAPHOR). We cannot help trying to find meaning in everything that forms part of our lives, and the human animal's primary mode of epistemology is narrative, which is more basic and more powerful than abstract or paradigmatic logic. We are narrative animals – in the words of sociologist Walter R. Fisher, *homo narrans*.

SEE ALSO: cognitive narratology; narrative as cognitive instrument; narrative disorders; psychological approaches to narrative; science and narrative; thought and consciousness representation (literature)

References and further reading

Calvin, William H. (1990) *The Cerebral Symphony: Seashore Reflections on the Structure of Consciousness*, New York: Bantam.

Dennett, Daniel C. (1991) *Consciousness Explained*, Boston: Little, Brown.

Donald, Merlin (1991) *The Origins of the Modern Mind: Three Stages in the Evolution of Culture and Cognition*, Cambridge, Mass.: Harvard University Press.

Fisher, Walter R. (1987) *Human Communication as Narration: Toward a Philosophy of Reason, Value, and*

Action, Columbia: University of South Carolina Press.

Gazzaniga, Michael S. (1992) *Nature's Mind: The Biological Roots of Thinking, Emotions, Sexuality, Language, and Intelligence*, New York: Basic Books.

Turner, Mark (1996) *The Literary Mind*, New York: Oxford University Press.

Young, Kay, and Jeffrey L. Saver (2001) 'The Neurology of Narrative', *Sub-Stance*, 30.1–2, 72–84.

HOWARD MANCING

BLOG (WEBLOG)

A weblog, or blog, is a frequently updated website consisting of dated entries arranged in reverse chronological order so the most recent post appears first (*see* TEMPORAL ORDERING). Typically, weblogs are published by individuals and their style is personal and informal. Weblogs first appeared in the mid-1990s, becoming popular as simple and free publishing tools became available towards the turn of the century. Since anybody with an Internet connection can publish his or her own weblog, there is great variety in the quality, content, and ambition of weblogs, and a weblog may have anywhere from a handful to tens of thousands of daily readers.

Examples of the *genre exist on a continuum from *confessional, online *diaries to logs tracking specific topics or activities through links and commentary. Though weblogs are primarily textual, experimentation with sound, *images, and videos has resulted in related genres such as photoblogs, videoblogs, and audioblogs (*see* INTERMEDIALITY; MEDIA AND NARRATIVE).

Most weblogs use links generously, allowing readers to follow conversations between weblogs by following links between entries on related topics. Readers may start at any point of a weblog, seeing the most recent entry first, or arriving at an older post via a search engine or a link from another site, often another weblog. Once at a weblog, readers can read on in various orders: chronologically, thematically, by following links between entries or by searching for keywords. Weblogs also generally include a blogroll, which is a list of links to other weblogs the author recommends. Many weblogs allow readers to enter their own comments to individual posts.

Weblogs are *serial and cumulative, and readers tend to read small amounts at a time, returning hours, days, or weeks later to read entries written since their last visit. This serial or episodic structure is similar to that found in *epistolary novels or diaries, but unlike these a weblog is open-ended, finishing only when the writer tires of writing (*see* NARRATIVE STRUCTURE).

Many weblog entries are shaped as brief, independent narratives, and some are explicitly or implicitly fictional, though the standard genre expectation is non-fiction (*see* FICTION, THEORIES OF). Some weblogs create a larger frame for the micro-narratives of individual posts by using a consistent rule to constrain their structure or themes (*see* OULIPO); thus, Francis Strand connects his stories of life in Sweden by ending each with a Swedish word and its translation. Other weblogs connect frequent but dissimilar entries by making a larger narrative explicit: *Flight Risk* is about an heiress's escape from her family, *The Date Project* documents a young man's search for a girlfriend, and Julie Powell narrates her life as she works her way through Julia Child's cookbook.

SEE ALSO: digital narrative; life story; thematic approaches to narrative

References and further reading

Anonymous (2002) *The Date Project*, http://thedateproject. blogspot.com/

Isabella, V. (2003) *She's a Flight Risk*, http://shes. aflightrisk.org

Lejeune, Philippe (2000) *"Cher écra..." Journal personnel, ordinateur, Internet*, Paris: Seuil.

Powell, Julie (2003) *The Julie/Julia Project*, http:// blogs.salon.com/0001399/

Strand, Francis (2003) *How to Learn Swedish in 1000 Difficult Lessons*, http://francisstrand.blogspot.com/ (websites accessed August 2003)

JILL WALKER

C

CATACHRESIS

Classically defined as the trope of misapplication or abuse, catachresis (*abusio*) refers to the internal narrative or changes in the meaning of a word, defined classically as the extension of a word to a novel or improper meaning. Thus, for example, the word *foot*, whose original reference is to a limb, is used to refer to the foot of a hill; *leaf* is extended to refer to leaves of paper or pastry. Catachresis can be divided into two types. First, we have those usages that emerge by association or *metalepsis, where the novel use extends an original meaning, as with animadversion, whose primary meaning is to turn the mind towards, but which came to mean criticism. Second, we have usages emerging by similarity or *metaphor, where the novel meaning is based upon likeness, as with tongue of a shoe or, to use an example of Puttenham's: 'I lent my love to loss, and gaged my life in vaine', where lending is understood originally to have referred to money (1869 [1589]).

Catachresis encodes the social history of language and marks the trajectory or narrative of linguistic development at a lexical level. It is for this reason that Renaissance *rhetorical handbooks term catachresis the most free and powerful of the tropes (Lamy, 1676 [1675]). It is the source of invention of arguments and the expression of imagination (*see* NARRATIVE AS ARGUMENT), it codifies custom and can equally be termed the record of *sociolinguistic and political struggles over meaning, as most obviously in the modern era with the use of gay to mean homosexual. According to Du Marsais (1757), catachresis is the general form of all invention and thus 'it reigns over all the other figures', by which he means that any alteration in use marks a deviation from the accepted or proper signification. Catachresis is in this sense the exemplary source of linguistic novelty because it is the most extreme form of metaphor or altered use.

References and further reading

Du Marsais, Chesneau (1757) *Des Tropes*, Paris: Carez.
Lamy, Bernard (1676 [1675]) *The Art of Speaking*, London: Godbid.
Puttenham, George (1869 [1589]) *The Arte of English Poesie*, London: Murray.

PETER GOODRICH

CATHARSIS

Through the notion of *catharsis* (purification), Aristotle describes the effect of tragedy on the spectator: tragedy is an 'imitation of action ... effecting through pity and fear the purification of such emotions'. In its attribution of a therapeutic value to tragedy, a value inherited from the origin of Greek *drama in ritual, the concept of *catharsis* seems self-explanatory, but its precise interpretation remains controversial. How can one explain that by eliciting terror and pity, tragedy will free the spectator from the negative effect of these *emotions? Is tragedy a sacrifice, and the tragic *hero a scapegoat whose downfall purifies the community from harmful feelings, or is Aristotle proposing a kind of homeopathic cure for existential anguish: experience a little dose of terror and pity in the fictional world, and you will be relieved of these feelings in the real world? Through the concept of catharsis, Aristotle may be attempting to deal with the scandalous fact that experiencing terror and pity for fictional individuals is a source of pleasure – the 'purification' of these feelings denoting in this interpretation their aesthetic sublimation. No matter how we resolve these questions, however, *catharsis* presents tragedy as the instrument of a deeply transforming spiritual event, and the pleasure taken in the suffering of the hero as a morally pure experience.

SEE ALSO: ancient theories of narrative (Western)

Reference and further reading

Aristotle (1996) *Poetics*, trans. Malcolm Heath, London: Penguin.

MARIE-LAURE RYAN

CAUSALITY

A cause in narrative literature is an *action or *event that directly or obliquely produces a transformation (*see* NARRATIVE TRANSFORMATION). Causality is one of the most fundamental aspects of narrative and is present at a number of different textual levels. Its effects will be discussed in the following order: concepts of causality, causality and the actions of *characters, causal relations between successive events and episodes in the story, twentieth-century critical concerns about causality in *fiction, causality and the definition of *narrative, the causal laws that govern fictional worlds, and finally the causal relations among distinct storylines.

Concepts of causality

Causality has been a significant subject in the history of *philosophy. Aristotle, drawing on earlier traditions, identified four types of cause: efficient cause, that which initiates the change; formal cause, that into which a thing is changed; material cause, that in which a change is made; and final cause, or the purpose for which the change was made (*see* CHICAGO SCHOOL, THE). Boethius provided a very powerful framework for several centuries' discussion of the more global issues of fortune, providence, and necessity: synthesising Greek and Christian traditions, he averred that apparent fortune is illusory and is itself ruled and arranged by fate. Fate in turn is subject to providence, which is the way that God disposes everything to the good. These concepts were foundational for the cosmologies of the Middle Ages, Renaissance, and seventeenth century.

Among modern philosophers who have dealt with causality, Hume is by far the most important, having called the very notion of cause into question. Hume pointed out that however many times we may observe one event followed by another, we can never observe any power or necessity that makes the effect follow from the cause. In the end, we have only two events, one of which is repeatedly observed to follow the other. Hume's stance is the basis for most later thinking on causation, including contemporary probabilistic approaches, according to which we say one event causes another when there is an extremely high probability that the second event will follow the first. Though central to the history of ideas, these and subsequent philosophical concepts usually had a fairly limited effect on narrative practice.

Causality and the actions of characters

Causal relations between characters in narrative are central to questions about their psychology, motivations, and interactions within the framework of the *plot; occasionally they also involve metaphysical issues as well. Troilus' final soliloquy in Chaucer's *Troilus and Criseyde* fully conforms to Boethian doctrine, and Edgar Allan Poe's sceptical protagonist in 'The Angel of the Odd' painfully learns the important role of the unusual and accidental in human experience. André Breton dramatises a world of 'objective chance' in *Nadja*, and the man determined to commit an unmotivated, 'gratuitous act' in Gide's *Lafcadio's Adventures* thereby attempts to make a statement about metaphysical freedom. In 'Tlön, Uqbar, Orbis Tertius', Jorge Luis Borges creates an entire world whose inhabitants are unable to conceive of causal relations: for them, the perception of a cloud of dark smoke on the horizon and then of the burning field and then of the still smoldering cigarette that produced the fire would merely be considered an example of the association of ideas. In Beckett's *Molloy*, causal doctrines of Descartes and other Rationalists are parodied in the Moran section, while the figure of Molloy acts out a Humean denial of connection between causes and effects.

Causal connections among events

Much more significant is the relation between events. Causal connection between successive events in the story has been the most widely discussed aspect of causality in narrative, though there is still considerable disagreement as to just where it exists and how far it extends. E. M. Forster's famous distinction between what he called 'story' and 'plot' hinged on the presence or absence of causal connection. In Forster's example, 'The king died, and then the queen died', the events are merely connected by their place in a temporal sequence, while in 'The king died, and then the queen died of grief', the time-sequence is preserved, but the sense of causality overshadows it (1927: 86) (*see* TEMPORAL ORDERING). This formulation was widely accepted for many years; in 1978, however, Seymour Chatman pointed out that because of the purposive character of speech, readers will assume that even in the first example the queen's death has something to do with the king's; though not explicitly stated, the connection is nevertheless implicitly present (1978: 46). A very different result appears if one is faced with propositions about events that are widely separated in *space or *time. 'A politician is assassinated in Portugal, then a bridge collapsed in Aden, and the next day a tsunami hit Fiji' will not usually be thought to constitute a narrative unless some causal network can be invoked to show that they are part of the same story. Noël Carroll discusses such possible 'miniature narratives' in his attempt to characterise what precisely constitutes a causal connection among events.

Causal connection among narrative units

A similar situation arises in the critical work surrounding the causal connection between larger *narrative units. Since Aristotle, critics have differentiated between stories whose events are mutually entailing and constitute a 'unity of action' as opposed to episodic narratives that contain narrative units that may be removed or rearranged without affecting the work as a whole. It makes all the difference whether an event comes after or is caused by that which precedes it, Aristotle affirmed (*Poetics*, section X). But it does not follow that there is no causal connection holding together the more episodic stories. For example, at the end of a *picaresque tale, the picaro has invariably been altered by some of his otherwise random experiences. The effects may be faint or widely dispersed, and not all the episodes may have been necessary to produce the final transformation, but a causal matrix can nevertheless be readily discerned. Not every event needs to be linked in a single causal

chain; some may be necessary but not sufficient conditions of what follows in the story, many may be relatively adventitious, and still others will be able to be removed without affecting the story. Despite the fact that few narratives are as compulsively entailing as the plays of Corneille or the novels of Jane Austen, in which all the major events are part of a single causal chain, it may nevertheless be concluded that causal connection is inevitably present in narrative. A causal connection is usually present, if only in oblique or attenuated form, among most or all substantial story sequences (though not every single scene or event) in a narrative.

Twentieth-century critical concerns about causality in narrative

In the last third of the twentieth century, attempts were made to elide or deconstruct causal connection altogether. Roland Barthes affirmed that 'the mainspring of narrative is precisely the confusion of consequetion [that is, consecutiveness] and consequence, what comes *after* being read in narrative as what is *caused by*; in which case narrative would be the systematic application of the logical fallacy denounced by Scholasticism in the formula, *post hoc, ergo propter hoc* – a good motto for destiny' (1977: 44). But Barthes' formulation posits as a deceptively seamless whole the very issues Aristotle complained were often too obviously disjoined. As Mieke Bal would later clarify, it is a frequent misconception that chronological and causal sequences are always interrelated. It is true, of course, that one can only kill one's father after having been engendered; one may even do so because one is engendered by one's father; but there may also be entirely different reasons for committing patricide (1985: 42). Some *deconstructive theorists have suggested that certain texts can invert the ordinary sequence of first cause, then effect. Jonathan Culler, discussing the events in *Oedipus Rex* and *Daniel Deronda* in the light of Paul de Man's speculations on cause and effect, argues that some of the key effects of these works actually *produce* their own causes, as the temporal direction of causation is reversed (*see* LOGIC OF NARRATIVE). Although in theory the deed ought to be the cause of Oedipus' guilt, the play makes possible an alternative reading in which cause and effect are reversed and guilt is what produces the deed. Culler's conclusions have been vigorously contested by Jon-K. Adams (1989) and others, who argue that Culler is guilty of conflating the play's *fabula with the *characters' eventual knowledge of that fabula; thus no causal anomalies arise (*see* STORY-DISCOURSE DISTINCTION).

Causal connection among events has frequently been presupposed in a number of plot grammars (including Barthes'), though only on rare occasions is it identified as such (see Ryan 1991). Meanwhile, cognitive science has drawn new attention to causality in narrative (*see* COGNITIVE NARRATOLOGY; PSYCHOLOGICAL APPROACHES TO NARRATIVE). Empirical research has produced some suggestive results, showing, for example, that subjects remember events better when they form part of a causal chain. Bortolussi and Dixon (2003) caution, however, that an essential difficulty with any such analysis of causal chains and character plans is that one cannot count on this information being in the text; instead, it must be inferred by the reader, and any such reconstructions will vary from one reader to another (113–16) (*see* READER-RESPONSE THEORY). This is particularly the case for *modernist works that toy with causality and obscure or attenuate its force.

Like more conventional works, non- and anti-realist texts also contain connections between successive events, and these often ignore or subvert assumptions derived from ordinary experience (*see* REALISM, THEORIES OF). Roy Jay Nelson refers to some of these as 'nonrectilinear causal strategies', and includes under this rubric repetitions of mythic patterns (*see* MYTH: THEMATIC APPROACHES), Proustian textual amplification and expansion, causally fragmented fabulas, and mental representations of unfolding events. David Hayman explores still more unconventional orderings, such as textual self-generation and repetition, echoes, and interlocking patterns in the *nouveau roman* and other experimental work. In some of these texts, causal ties are supplemented, parodied, or even intermittently replaced by other forms of connection.

Meanwhile, a number of feminist theorists (e.g., Tobin 1978: 7–12) have expressed suspicion over causal accounts in general and many more have attacked those that imply or demand specific teleologies. In the same vein, feminists have argued that critical notions of probability, realism, and *verisimilitude are often misapplied in the case of women's fiction. Nancy K. Miller (1981) notes that for centuries, women writers have veered away from anticipated or approved conclusions for their female protagonists and were then accused of violating the conventions of *realism or creating poor plots whose swervings were inadequately motivated. These attacks assumed women writers could not or would not obey traditional conceptions of plausibility and propriety. Instead, Miller argues, the writers should be seen as trying to expand the parameters of what might be plausible events for female agents. Dissenting women writers contest limitations of representation by resisting culturally sanctioned endings and by offering in their place differently motivated acts, events, and connections (*see* AGENCY; FEMINIST NARRATOLOGY; GENDER STUDIES; IDEOLOGY AND NARRATIVE).

Causality and the definition of narrative

It is not clear that causality can be entirely supplanted in a work that remains a narrative (*see* ANTI-NARRATIVE). Some theorists argue in fact that causal connection is a necessary condition of any narrative. While many definitions of narrative limit themselves to representations of two or more events in a time sequence, others argue for the necessity of some kind of causal connection (discussed in Richardson 1997: 89–96). One of the most compelling examples in this debate has been set forth by *film theorists David Bordwell and Kristin Thompson. Trying to identify the difference between narrative and non-narrative cinema, they postulate the following sequence: 'A man tosses and turns, unable to sleep. A mirror breaks. A telephone rings.' As it stands, this sequence is merely a group of independent images that do not constitute a narrative (*see* GAPPING). If, on the other hand, cause and effect relationship occurring in time can be established between the events, then the film is a narrative. This would be the case in the following scenario: 'A man has a fight with his boss; he tosses and turns during the night, unable to sleep. In the morning he is still so angry that he smashes the mirror while shaving. Then his telephone rings, his boss has called to apologize' (1990: 55). In either case, the images may form an interesting totality, thus satisfying Grice's observations on the purposive nature of human discourse (*see* PRAGMATICS); only in the latter case, however, is it a narrative sequence.

'Causal settings' of fictional worlds

Causality not only manifests itself in connections among the events of the story but also is a key aspect of the *storyworld presented via narrative texts. Every fictional universe has distinctive ontological features (see Ryan 1991: 31–47) and each operates under a set of causal laws (*see* POSSIBLE-WORLDS THEORY; TEXT-WORLD APPROACHES TO NARRATIVE). The system of causation that governs a narrative is as central an element of its setting as are the related components of space and time. A work's 'causal setting', or the canon of probability that orders its fictional world, is usually one of four basic types: supernatural, naturalistic, chance, or *metafictional.

In a supernatural causal setting, extra-natural forces such as gods, fairies, and magicians have power to shape and direct events. Examples of this kind of text include *Oedipus Rex*, *Macbeth*, *Paradise Lost*, and *Faust*. In a fictional world governed by a naturalistic causal system, all transformations are caused by natural laws and recognisable human traits and actions. Here, the probable and the verisimilar rule, and authors attempt to reproduce the causal parameters of everyday life. Works in this mode include Terence's *The Brothers*, Thackeray's *Vanity Fair*, and Zola's *Germinal*. In chance worlds, ordinary or probable causal progressions are interrupted or absent (*see* NARRATIVE PROGRESSION). Coincidences proliferate implausibly, familiar causes fail to produce their invariable effects, and statistically unlikely events abound. Other unusual, contingent orderings of events, as found in oneiric, absurdist, or *magical realist texts, may also be grouped here. Chance worlds are found in *Ulysses*, Conrad's *Chance*, and Angela Carter's *Wise Children*. Metafictional orderings are present when the events of the fictional world are explicitly altered by its creator in an act of *metalepsis, as when an actor portraying the *author comes on stage at the end of John Gay's *The Beggar's Opera* to declare that the impending tragic ending is wrong and must be altered. Metafictional causation is present in works like Diderot's *Jacques the Fatalist*, Rushdie's *Midnight's Children*, and Beckett's texts, like *Worstward Ho*, that employ *denarration.

Since these causal settings are mutually exclusive when applied to the world we inhabit (it is either supernatural or naturalistic, but not both), it is often the case that different explanatory worldviews are tested in a given work. In *Oedipus Rex*, the supernatural power of fate as affirmed by Teiresias triumphs over other characters' beliefs that it does not exist or its power can be eluded. By contrast, many nineteenth-century *realist novels and plays took pains to show that no supernatural claim had any support in the world represented in the text (*see* DRAMA AND NARRATIVE). What Todorov calls the *'fantastic' tale is that of a narrative world the causal setting of which is suspended between supernatural and naturalistic positions until the ending. When the causal setting of a narrative is unclear or in doubt, it is often the case that the reader is made to experience the same causal uncertainty that the characters do (*see* INDETERMINACY). Other texts, like Hawthorne's *The House of the Seven Gables*, allow different, competing causal frameworks to seem validated by the narrative; readers may perceive that world as they please. At the end of *Jonathan Wild*, Henry Fielding does something different by attempting to perfectly fuse providential design, poetic justice, and the demands of probability: as the innocent Mr Heartfree finds himself with a noose around his neck, the *narrator, spurning the example of John Gay, announces he would rather have suffered half of mankind to be hanged than have saved one contrary to the strictest rules of writing and probability (needless to say, justice does triumph in this case).

The establishment of causal laws within fictional discourse comes with its own oddities, and the notion of chance has proven quite challenging since the ancient Greek playwright Agathon noted that it is only likely that many unlikely things occur. Strictly speaking, chance is not possible in a world governed by fate, providence, destiny, or a rigorous determinism. In other conceptions, its role is significant; by the 1880s, novelists began to recognise that they had to include a certain number of chance events in the name of realism (*see* REALITY EFFECT), but the precise status of such events has provoked utterly opposed theoretical accounts. Kavanagh has asserted that the chance event is recalcitrant to narrative (1993: 113); Derrida affirms the importance of the *clinamen*, or causal swerve; Monk argues that the phrase 'chance in narrative' is oxymoronic, since the disruptions occasioned by chance events are always recuperated by some sense of formal design (1993: 7–10); and Richardson postulates a paradox of chance in fictional representation: its absence suggests a dubiously deterministic causalism, while its presence invariably indicates authorial intervention, since chance in fiction is never a chance occurrence (1997: 166–68).

Connections among storylines

In a narrative, the events in one storyline may be rather tightly connected causally and then juxtaposed to another such storyline with which it, the first storyline, has few points of direct contact. Since the Renaissance, authors have juxtaposed multiple loosely joined storylines together in the same work. Many modern authors have experimented further with this situation, creating ever more disjoined, tangential, and non-intersecting storylines. In her essay on 'Modern Fiction', Virginia Woolf identified the air of probability embalming the whole work as one of the antiquated notions that contemporary writers needed to transcend. Modernist classics like *Ulysses* and *Mrs Dalloway* keep direct causal connection among key storylines to a minimum: it is unclear whether the storylines involving Stephen Dedalus and Leopold Bloom are substantially causally interconnected, while the Clarissa Dalloway and Septimus Smith storylines hardly touch. Later texts like Beckett's *Molloy* and Faulkner's *The Wild Palms* dilute or remove causal connection still further. Finally, certain *postmodern works (Severo Sarduy's *Cobra* and Calvino's *If on a winter's night a traveller*) seem to dissolve most connections among storylines.

SEE ALSO: story schemata and causal structure

References and further reading

Adams, Jon-K. (1989) 'Causality and Narrative', *Journal of Literary Semantics*, 18, 149–62.

Bal, Mieke (1985) *Narratology: Introduction to the Theory of Narrative*, Toronto: University of Toronto Press.

Barthes, Roland (1977) 'Introduction to the Structural Analysis of Narrative', in *Image-Music-Text*, New York: Hill and Wang.

Bordwell, David, and Kristin Thompson (1990) *Film Art*, 3rd ed, New York: McGraw Hill.

Bortolussi, Marisa, and Peter Dixon (2003) *Psychonarratology: Foundations for the Empirical Study of Literary Response*, Cambridge: Cambridge University Press.

Carroll, Noël (2001) 'On the Narrative Connection', in Willie van Peer and Seymour Chatman (eds) *New Perspectives on Narrative Perspective*, Albany: University of New York Press.

Chatman, Seymour (1978) *Story and Discourse: Narrative Structure in Fiction and Film: Narrative Structure in Fiction and Film*, Ithaca: Cornell University Press.

Culler, Jonathan (1980) 'Fabula and Sjuzhet in the Analysis of Narrative', *Poetics Today*, 1.3, 27–37.

Forster, E. M. (1927) *Aspects of the Novel*, London: Harcourt, Brace and World.

Hayman, David (1987) *Re-Forming the Narrative: Toward a Mechanics of Modernist Fiction*, Ithaca: Cornell University Press.

Kavanagh, Thomas M. (1993) *Enlightenment and the Shadows of Chance: The Novel and the Culture of Gambling in Eighteenth-Century France*, Baltimore: Johns Hopkins University Press.

Miller, Nancy K. (1981) 'Emphasis Added: Plots and Plausibilities in Women's Fiction', *PMLA*, 96, 36–48.

Monk, Leland (1993) *Standard Deviations: Chance and the Modern British Novel*, Stanford: Stanford University Press.

Nelson, Roy Jay (1990) *Causality and Narrative in French Fiction from Zola to Robbe-Grillet*, Columbus OH: Ohio State University Press.

Richardson, Brian (1997) *Causality and the Nature of Modern Narrative*, Newark, DE: University of Delaware Press.

Ryan, Marie-Laure (1991) *Possible Worlds, Artificial Intelligence and Narrative Theory*, Bloomington: Indiana University Press.

Tobin, Patricia (1978) *Time and the Novel: The Genealogical Imperative*, Princeton: Princeton University Press.

BRIAN RICHARDSON

CHARACTER

As a narratological term, *character* (French *personnage*, German *Figur*), refers to a *storyworld participant, i.e., any individual or unified group occurring in a *drama or work of narrative *fiction. In a narrower sense, the term is restricted to participants in the narrated domain, to the exclusion of the *narrator and *narratee. Meanwhile, in everyday usage the term 'character' is often used to refer to someone's personality, that is, an individual's enduring traits and dispositions. The homonymy of the technical and ordinary terms has sometimes led to the exclusive concentration on the *psychological aspects of literary figures. All theoretical models of character divide into mimetic or representational (first formulated by Aristotle), treating character as a human or human-like entity, and non-mimetic (e.g., Roland Barthes's model), reducing it to a text-grammatical, lexical, *thematic, or compositional unit. The major theoretical paradigms currently available for the *mimetic study of character are the semantic (*possible-worlds theory), *cognitive (readers' mental models), and communicative (the process of narrative mediation; *see* FUNCTION (JAKOBSON); NARRATIVE TRANSMISSION). While the three approaches are different in their points of departure, they reveal significant complementarity, and sometimes even convergence, providing jointly a fairly rich theory of character.

Semantic theories

In possible-worlds semantics character is modelled as an individual who is a member of some non-actual state of affairs. Such an individual is created by *semiotic means and designated by a referring expression of some kind (*see* REFERENCE). Inside the non-actual domain the individual is located in *space and *time and prototypically assigned human-like properties: physical or external, actantial (including communicative), social, and mental or internal (cognitive, emotive, volitional and perceptual) (*see* ACTANT). The individual may also be ascribed enduring personality traits and dispositions, knowledge and belief sets, intentions, wishes, attitudes, *desires and *emotions, and, of course, internal states and actions (*see* INTENTIONALITY). Minimally, it must possess an agential capacity (*see* AGENCY). Unlike actual individuals, all the information about characters is limited to the text that calls them into existence, so they are radically incomplete in some respects. Many predications about them hence get an indeterminate truth value (*see* GAPPING; INDETERMINACY). Conversely, they need not conform to any ontological regularity of actuality, and may even be inconsistent or possess incompatible properties. Characters are presented textually as a discontinuous series of states, and their continuity is world-dependent. By a constitutive narrative convention, it is possible in some fictional worlds to have unrestricted mental access to such individuals, and thus obtain certain knowledge about their interiority (*see* THOUGHT AND CONSCIOUSNESS REPRESENTATION (LITERATURE)).

Since non-actual individuals are semiotically created, one can ask about the minimal constitutive conditions under which they can be introduced and sustained. Firstly, the referring expressions by which such an individual is designated should be used referentially, to pick out an entity in a domain, not just played with as pure signifiers. Beyond bare existence, it should be possible to assign at least one property to the individual for every state in which it exists. Further conditions fulfilled by most narratives include uniqueness, that is, that an individual should be distinguishable in each state of affairs in which it exists from all other coexisting individuals, and coherence of features, which means that they form a definable pattern or intelligible structure. Still another condition would be temporal continuity or *identity in spite of all changes undergone. The problematisation or non-fulfilment of any one of these conditions is always thematically foregrounded, and when none of them is fulfilled one encounters the death of character or its reduction to pure verbal expressions.

Individuals in storyworlds may have any kind of modal status. They may thus exist in the textual-actual world, that is, in the fact domain of this world, but also in any of its sub-worlds such as the hypothetical or counterfactual (Ryan 1991; Werth 1999; *see* VIRTUALITY). Or they may exist merely in the belief, wish, intention, or imagination sphere of another character or characters, such as the gardener Putois in Anatole France's story of the same title. The modal status of a character may be undecided or disputed for much of a story: does N. N. exist or is s/he just a mental construct in the belief or imagination world of one or more other characters? By the same token, widely different versions of the same individual – whose existence and properties in the factual domain of the storyworld are confirmed by an authoritative narrating instance – may be entertained by different coagents (*see* NARRATOR). In the absence of such an instance, however, the *truth value of any version may remain in dispute.

While the dimensions for the characterisation of storyworld participants are universal (physical, mental, behavioural), the number and nature of the properties any individual possesses with respect to a particular dimension may vary enormously – depending on the individual's role in the story, the type of storyworld portrayed and what is necessary, possible, or probable in it (*see* MODALITY), and the aesthetics of the *author or literary school. In stories with dual-world ontologies, such as human and divine, individuals belonging to different zones may be radically different as regards the most basic types of properties (bodily shape, mental ability). Individuals designated by the same proper name sometimes occur in storyworlds generated by different texts written by the same or different authors, such as the numerous Don Quixotes or Don Juans throughout the centuries. The question of the 'sameness' of these individuals immediately arises, and also the legitimacy of transferring information about the same named individual from one storyworld to another, leading at the limit to their fusion (*see* TRANSFICTIONALITY). Is it the same individual, different versions of one and the same figure, or distinct and separate individuals? Opinions vary, but the most convincing view would regard the relation between the original individual and his or her namesake in another storyworld created later as one of counterparthood, not sameness, this relation being a matter of degree, with no clearly agreed upon minimal conditions (*see* NAMING IN NARRATIVE).

A similar problem involves actuality variants in fictional worlds, such as individuals bearing the names of historical figures, for example Napoleon, interacting with fictional ones. How much of the historical information about such individuals may one thus introduce into the storyworld, and how much of the historical features need be preserved so we can claim that this is a version of the original individual? Is an ex-emperor named Napoleon, living in exile in New Orleans a version of the original one? And how about a sheep farmer called Sherlock Holmes? As for the relation between fictional individuals and actuality in general, one can distinguish three kinds. A fictional individual may be just semiotically motivated with respect to pre-existent literary codes and stereotypes. It may in addition be considered verisimilar if its property structure is such that it could be instantiated in actuality according to one's version of actuality (*see* VERISIMILITUDE). A character is realistic if it is verisimilar according to the prevailing world model of nineteenth-century western culture (*see* REALISM, THEORIES OF).

Fictional individuals, no less than actual ones, are often endowed with a rich mental life. A recent development within fictional-world semantics is the utilisation of cognitive-science concepts and theories to produce a disciplined description of characters' mental functioning, from perception to metacognition. The basic model is that of information processing: its acquisition, mental representation, storage and retrieval, and production of new information.

Cognitive theories

Traditional, pre-theoretical discussions of character have introduced some distinctions which have become standard in critical practice. Depending on the number and variety of mental features attributed to a character it can be termed flat or round. It has been said that flat characters cannot surprise us while round ones can. In the course of the action, characters may remain psychologically unchanged, hence static, or the may undergo mental change such as development or decline, and hence be dynamic. Employing one or another kind of folk cum literary psychology, characters can be classified in numerous ways into character types.

But how do readers construct any image of a character to begin with? A tentative answer to this fundamental question is provided by the cognitive approach as elaborated in the last few years by Culpeper, Jannidis, and Schneider. In this paradigm, character is seen as a mental model of a storyworld participant, constructed by the reader incrementally in the course of reading (text comprehension) on the basis of constant interplay between specific textual data and general knowledge structures stored in the reader's long-term *memory (*see* NARRATIVE COMPREHENSION; PSYCHOLOGICAL APPROACHES TO NARRATIVE). The construction of the mental model is initiated by the identification of a referring expression in the text as designating a discourse entity and a recognition that occurrences of other tokens of the same expression in the discourse (or other expressions) pick out the same entity. The reader then establishes a distinct entity in his or her mental map to which features are ascribed on the basis of textual data and around which a minimal situational frame is constructed, consisting of this individual, time, place, and state or *event (*see* SITUATION MODEL).

The conceptual unit that readers intuitively label 'character' is thus mentally generated in response to textual clues. As one reads on, guided by the 'read for character' control system, one gathers textual cues which characterise the mental entity in focus. This is bottom-up or data-driven processing, involving both explicit property ascription and character-related information which could serve as basis for such ascription. Once a certain number of properties have been gathered, they often activate a knowledge structure stored in long-term memory under which these properties can be subsumed and integrated into a character model. Information gathering and the search for a category under which it may be subsumed may well be running concurrently. The knowledge structures in question include scripts, schemas, and stereotypes (*see* SCRIPTS AND SCHEMATA), and may encompass the psychological, social, communicative, and physical dimensions. They may originate in world knowledge, but also in knowledge of literary *genres and conventions and in specific literary texts, including generalisations about character made in the text currently being read. Actual world models and literary ones often diverge, and the question then arises as to which of them should predominate in a given case. While the model reader and professional literati will give the literary ones precedence, ordinary readers tend to give precedence to entrenched actual-world models. The same issue arises when the actual-world models of the text's original *audience are very different from those held by current readers. Once a fit between data and category is established, *categorisation* takes place, and readers may then proceed top down, integrate all the information currently available, fill in or complete their mental model of the individual, formulate expectations about further textual information about it, and explain previous information.

Inference drawing, based on character-related information beyond explicit property ascription, is crucial in mental model building, especially when the mental properties of characters are concerned, since these are often implied by non-mental data, e.g., about a character's actions. Such inference drawing is abductive (logically incomplete) and probabilistic with respect to both the antecedent/conclusion relation and the norm or maxim guiding it. Such norms are based both on world knowledge, for example folk psychology, and on literary knowledge.

Several basic assumptions specific to inferencing in literary contexts are that since all textual information is deliberately created and displayed by an author, all of it is potentially significant for character portrayal; that formal patterns of character grouping, parallels or oppositions may also be relevant here; and that information varies in *reliability depending on its origin (ranging from an omniscient narrating voice to the individual in question). A fairly complex computation is hence involved in such inferencing operations. Additional information about a categorised character may fall into the established pattern or it may require a modification of the mental image of this character which does not involve abandoning the initial category. In such a case one can speak of schema refreshment, subcategorisation, or *individuation*. But the incoming information may contrast directly with the defining features of the selected category, causing schema disruption, *decategorisation* of the character, the invalidation of previous inferences, and the focused search for a new, more adequate category. Schema disruption leads to deautomatisation of perception and may draw the reader's attention to the very nature of the cognitive operations involved (*see* DEFAMILIARISATION; FOREGROUNDING). Since characters exist in temporal frames, a category may sometimes apply to one phase of their existence, with a new one required for a later phase, and a second-order category required to integrate the two. Either because of failed re-categorisation or from the very beginning, a reader may not be able to find a suitable stereotype in his or her knowledge base for categorising a given character. Or the reader may be interested in character features other than category membership. In such cases the formation of mental models proceeds bottom-up and piecemeal, slowing processing and heightening awareness. It may also have to tolerate incongruent category features and defer integration and *closure, and could be named *personalisation*.

Communicative theories

In classical narratology a character is an occupant of one or more constitutive roles in the two-levelled process of narrative transmission, being either a narrative agent, a focalizer (*see* FOCALIZATION), a narrator, or a narratee. Because of the possibility of narrative *embedding, these four positions may likewise occur on any embedded level as well. The three key questions for any communicatively oriented model of character are: where does information about the individual occupying any of these positions come from? What are its nature and scope? What is its truth-functional status or reliability?

The most obvious source of information about the properties – physical, mental, or social – of the occupant of any position are explicit characterisation statements, that is, statements that directly ascribe a trait or property to an individual. A narrative agent can be characterised by himself, his co-agents, and a narrator who stands on a higher communicative and sometimes also epistemic level (except in first-person present-tense *narration) (*see* NARRATIVE SITUATIONS; PERSON). Any act of characterisation involves its originator, topic entity, and addressee and, according to the identity or difference between them, eight configurations are possible in the case of narrative agents. Focalizers cannot self-characterise, but inferences about their mental dimension can be drawn from the nature of the information they take in and the ways they process it. A global narrator qua narrator can only self-characterise, while a narratee can always be characterised by the narrator, or have his self-characterisation quoted by the narrator.

The reliability of any characterisation statement made by a narrative agent is the subject of a complex computation involving both general factors (intelligence, knowledge, honesty) and specific contextual ones (who characterises whom, for whom, in what situation, and with what intention). Narrators can be reliable or not with respect to both the information they provide on any subject and their evaluation or judgement of it, and this holds for any self-characterisations or characterisations of others that they might make. The basic rule seems to be that any characterisation statement made by a narrative agent, narratee, or personalised narrator needs always to be assessed by the reader and placed on a gradient ranging from total acceptance to total rejection. But the maker of a characterisation statement always gets himself characterised implicitly on the basis of the matter and manner of her characterisation and the relation between the two. By narrative convention, characterisation statements made by an omniscient impersonal narrating voice are true and serve as a yardstick for assessing the validity of such statements made by all others (*see* AUTHENTICATION). The only exception seems to be narratorial *irony, which is a matter of interpretation. Explicit characterisation of a storyworld participant by a global narrator can be given all at once, usually when the character is first introduced, in which case it is termed block characterisation. Or it may given piecemeal throughout the text. Finally, like all other statements, characterisation statements too can be modalised as merely quoted, probable, hypothetical, counterfactual, wishful, and so on.

As already mentioned, much of the textual information that serves to ascribe properties to storyworld participants is implicit or indirect.

Often, therefore, a certain item of textual information is identified on the basis of a semantic trigger as a signifier for the properties of a given individual. In the case of narrative agents, this trigger is provided by a genre convention which defines what information is significant for the characterisation of an individual in this or that kind of storyworld (Jannidis 2001). The next step consists of employing an inference rule to extract the relevant properties, an activity already discussed in the previous section. While individual items are text-specific, there are three major sources of information for inferring a narrative agent's properties, especially mental ones. (1) Dynamic elements: a character's physical and verbal actions or behaviour, their content, manner, and context. (2) Static elements: a character's appearance, natural setting and man-made milieu, assuming that contiguity implies similarity between physical and mental, the physical serving as signifier for the mental. (3) Formal compositional patterns of character-grouping by way of similarity and contrast, assuming that forms of organisation reflect forms of content. In contrast, a narrator qua narrator can only be characterised on the basis of the verbal action of narration, and narrators and narratees in general may in some cases be amenable to only very minimal characterisation beyond their structural communicative capabilities.

Non-mimetic theories

All mimetic theories of character assume a non-verbal situation, extension, or domain of reference with individuals, time, place, states, and events evoked by the narrative text, the individuals in question being fictional human or human–like entities. Non-mimetic theories, in contrast, refuse to go beyond the textual, intensional, or semiotic profile of the narrative discourse. Character is thus viewed as a topic entity of a connected discourse, a name to which distinctive lexical features are attached, a role in a case grammar (agent, patient, etc.), a device for achieving an aesthetic effect (laughter, horror), an element in an architectonic pattern (parallels and contrasts), or a functional piece in *plot conceived as a set of formal moves (agent, foil). On the thematic level, character has been viewed as an ideological position, point of intersection of *motifs or themes, and as an exemplification of an issue, problem, attitude, value, or idea (*see* IDEOLOGY AND NARRATIVE).

But are the mimetic and non-mimetic views of character mutually exclusive? Starting from a functional view of narrative, which recognises the narratological usefulness of both approaches, James Phelan has suggested an integrative model of character, distinguishing in it three basic 'components': the mimetic (character as person), thematic (character as idea), and synthetic (character as artificial construct). He goes on to point out that all functions exist in every character occurrence, and it is the relation among them (which one is foregrounded and which de-emphasised) which varies from one narrative to another.

SEE ALSO: reader-response theory

References and further reading

Bortolussi, Marisa, and Peter Dixon (2003) *Psychonarratology*, Cambridge: Cambridge University Press.
Culpeper, Jonathan (2001) *Language and Characterisation*, Harlow: Longman.
Emmott, Catherine (1997) *Narrative Comprehension: A Discourse Perspective*, Oxford: Clarendon Press.
Garvey, James (1978) 'Characterization in Narrative', *Poetics*, 7, 63–78.
Glaudes, Pierre, and Yves Reuter (1998) *Le Personnage*, Paris: PUF.
Grabes, Herbert (1978) 'Wie aus Sätzen Personen werden', *Poetica*, 10, 405–28.
Jannidis, Fotis (2001) *Figur und Person*, unpublished Habilitationsschrift.
Knapp, John (ed.) (1990) 'Literary Character', *Style*, 24.3 (special issue).
Koch, Thomas (1991) *Literarische Menschendarstellung*, Tuebingen: Stauffenberg.
Margolin, Uri (1987) 'Introducing and Sustaining Characters in Literary Narrative', *Style*, 21.1, 107–24.
—— (1989) 'Structuralist Approaches to Character in Narrative: The State of the Art', *Semiotica*, 75.1–2, 1–24.
—— (1996) 'Characters and their Versions', in Calin-Andrei Mihailescu and Walid Hamarneh (eds) *Fiction Updated*, Toronto: University of Toronto Press.
Palmer, Alan (2004) *Fictional Minds*, Lincoln: University of Nebraska Press.
Phelan, James (1989) *Reading People, Reading Plots*, Chicago: University of Chicago Press.
Ryan, Marie-Laure (1991) *Possible Worlds, Artificial Intelligence, and Narrative Theory*, Bloomington: Indiana University Press.
Schneider, Ralf (2000) *Grundriss zur kognitiven Theorie der Figurenrezeption*, Tübingen: Stauffenberg.
—— (2001) 'Towards a Cognitive Theory of Literary Character', *Style*, 35.4, 607–40.
Werth, Paul (1999) *Text Worlds*, London: Longman.

URI MARGOLIN

CHICAGO SCHOOL, THE

The Chicago School of formalist criticism (also known as the 'Neo-Aristotelians') began in the 1940s, when Ronald Salmon Crane and a group of kindred spirits began to develop a rhetorical poetics of literature, including narrative literature (*see* FORMALISM; RHETORICAL APPROACHES TO NARRATIVE). Crane's group, which included Elder Olson, Norman Maclean, and Richard McKeon, cultivated their opposition to the more popular formalism of their day, the 'New Criticism' centred in the South and subsequently at Yale. Where the New Critics viewed literature in terms of tropes, the Chicago School viewed literature through Aristotle's concepts of *eidos* (shaping form) and *synolon* (formed matter). Poetic works of art are syntheses in which *plot, *character, and thought (the formal cause) give shape to language (the material cause), using various techniques or devices of disclosure (the efficient cause), in order to create an object with the power to affect readers in determinate ways (the final cause) (*see* CAUSALITY). This determinate power of literary texts was associated with the ends of traditional literary genres, so that in 'The Concept of Plot and the Plot of *Tom Jones*' Crane presents Fielding's text as a unique realisation of comic form. But however well this method worked with masterpieces like *Tom Jones*, it faltered with less coherent works and generic hybrids (*see* HYBRID GENRES). Later reformulators of this poetics, such as Sheldon Sacks and Ralph Rader of the second generation of the Chicago School, were to explore how Crane's notion of architectonic form could be reconciled with the multifarious *intentions of *authors and the institutional shapes that culture bequeaths to literature.

While Crane's complex poetics inspired more respect than imitation, his student Wayne C. Booth (1961) indelibly influenced the way scholars talk about narrative by creating not a poetics but a rhetoric of fiction, an attempt to discover how authors shape the narrative text to create the appropriate readerly response (*see* READER-RESPONSE THEORY). Many of Booth's terms became standard issue, including *'implied author', for the formal location of authorial values within a text, and 'unreliable narrator', for any *narration (personified or not within the text) whose values, intellectual, aesthetic, or *ethical, depart from those of the implied author (*see* RELIABILITY).

Booth may also have influenced the sorts of narrative literary scholars wanted to talk about. At a time when New Critical fashion favoured 'dramatic' *narrative techniques that avoided authorial *commentary and other overt signals of the teller behind the tale, Booth argued that all choices of how to tell a story were rhetorical decisions, chosen to maximise the impact of the story. Thus the 'omniscient' techniques of Fielding or Thackeray, with their chatty addresses to the reader, were not intrinsically inferior to the seemingly objective techniques favoured by James or Hemingway. Booth's warning against building narrative theory around modernism (*see* MODERNIST NARRATIVE) came to the attention of readers precisely when the modernist project was being challenged by *postmodern texts by Barth and Butor, Kundera and Calvino, which insistently called the reader's attention to fictional artifice.

James Phelan (1981; 1989) and Peter Rabinowitz (1987) represent a third generation of the Chicago School. If Booth had moved away from the poetics of Crane toward a more explicitly rhetorical view of texts embodying complex, even contradictory authorial intentions, Booth's students have moved away from the controlling principle of the text toward a view of literary meaning as determined by (as Phelan has put it) 'recursive relationships among authorial agency, textual phenomena, and reader-response'.

Rabinowitz has focused thus far on reader-response. For Rabinowitz a narrative generates two virtual *audiences: an authorial audience (the social/interpretive community for whom the author wrote the text) and a narrative audience (the community to whom the *narrator speaks and for whom the fictional world is real). Rabinowitz argues that the fact that skilled readers can interpret texts at all is largely owing to four sets of conventions that constitute an implicit 'contract' between authors and readers within a given social/interpretive community: (1) rules of *notice* that determine which details within a text have claims on the reader's attention; (2) rules of *signification* that determine how the reader may draw meanings from noticed details; (3) rules of *configuration* that allow readers to infer the probable shape or form of a text because of their familiarity with a repertory of *genres; (4) rules of *coherence* that allow readers to repair textual disjunctures and inconsistencies. Rabinowitz's project has involved understanding these rules and their interactions.

Whereas Rabinowitz has worked on the obverse of Booth's problem – what the reader has to know how to do in order to get shaped by authorial rhetoric – Phelan has attempted to extend Booth's project in three distinct directions. His first book (Phelan 1981) attacked the problem of language and style, an area generally neglected by the Chicago School, to see how rhetorical narratology might work at the level of the sentence. In his second (Phelan 1989) he proposed a revision of the understanding of both plot (in terms of a somewhat more supple architectonic principle he terms 'progression') and character. Instead of flat and round characters, as theorised by Forster, Phelan views fictional agents in terms of their *mimetic, thematic, and synthetic characteristics, and associated functions within the progression. Another study (Phelan 1996) was devoted to elucidating problems of narrative *voice and *focalization. It is probably no accident that this grand-pupil of Crane has been working successively on aspects of the material, the formal, and the efficient causes of narrative literature.

Other notable members of the third generation of the Chicago School who have written on aspects of narrative theory include Barbara Foley, Elizabeth Langland, David Richter, and Harry Shaw.

References and further reading

Booth, Wayne C. (1961) *The Rhetoric of Fiction*, Chicago: University of Chicago Press.
Crane, Ronald S. (1952) 'The Concept of Plot and the Plot of *Tom Jones*', *Critics and Criticism: Ancient and Modern*, Chicago: University of Chicago Press.
Foley, Barbara (1986) *Telling the Truth: Theory and Practice of Documentary Fiction*, Ithaca: Cornell University Press.
Forster, E. M. (1927) *Aspects of the Novel*, New York: Harcourt Brace.
Langland, Elizabeth (1984) *Society in the Novel*, Chapel Hill: University of North Carolina Press.
Phelan, James (1981) *Worlds from Words*, Chicago: University of Chicago Press.
——(1989) *Reading People, Reading Plots*, Chicago: University of Chicago Press.
——(1996) *Narrative as Rhetoric*, Columbus: Ohio State University Press.
Rabinowitz, Peter (1987) *Before Reading*, Ithaca: Cornell University Press.
Rader, Ralph (1973) 'Defoe, Richardson, Joyce and the Concept of Form in the Novel', in *Autobiography, Biography and the Novel*, Los Angeles: William Andrews Clark Memorial Library.
Richter, David H. (1974) *Fable's End*, Chicago: University of Chicago Press.

Sacks, Sheldon (1964) *Fiction and the Shape of Belief*, Berkeley: University of California Press.

Shaw, Harry E. (1983) *The Forms of Historical Fiction*, Ithaca: Cornell University Press.

DAVID H. RICHTER

CHILDREN'S STORIES (NARRATIVES WRITTEN FOR CHILDREN)

A fundamental question for scholars of children's literature is how this type of literature is constituted as a distinct *genre. How is children's fiction different than literature for adults? Is *Alice's Adventures in Wonderland* a children's book or a book about a child for adults? Discussions about the genre as a whole have tended to characterise children's stories as distinct from adult literature either by degree or kind. Those who have it that children's literature is characterised by nothing more than greater simplicity in all areas of *narrative structure often argue that the genre is no less elegant or artistic for that simplicity – 'simple' doesn't imply 'simplistic'. Those who regard children's literature as characterised by unique features and elements have concentrated on a number of areas: picture books, narrative *voice, the *implied author and reader (*see* READER CONSTRUCTS), *character, and *plot types.

The study of picture books has been an important area for identifying the unique characteristics of children's books. Perry Nodelman employs linguistic theories and frameworks for studying visual art to make the case that there are distinct narrative relationships between words and pictures in picture books written for children (*see* IMAGE AND NARRATIVE; PICTORIAL NARRATIVITY; VISUAL NARRATIVITY). Each of the two *media handles story, chronology, objectivity/subjectivity, deductive/inductive decoding, and *description differently, and the juxtaposition of picture and word can be either complementary or ironic (*see* IRONY).

The question of implied readership is important in the study of children's narratives since, along with young adult literature, it is distinct from other genres by virtue of being named for an *audience. Barbara Wall's study of the mechanisms of *address in children's chapter books shows us that a story can contain single address (children only), double address (children and adults in alternative moments in the narrative), or dual address (both age-based audiences addressed simultaneously). Indeed, many have theorised that locating the 'child in the book', as Aidan Chambers characterised it, is the most important issue in defining a children's narrative. The distinction between a book being about children and it being for them is vital. The examination of the voice of the child in the narrative, and the degree to which it is considered authentic, is a central concern of a great many critical discussions, and the relationship between the implied author, *narrator, *narratee, and implied child audience bears importantly on the determination of the appropriateness of a narrative for children. Does the narrator pander to the reader? Is there a tension between didacticism and report (*see* DIDACTIC NARRATIVE)? To what extent does the implied author provide *ethical and moral guidance? Is the narratee a child or does the narrator – whether child or adult – speak to an identifiable narratee?

Character construction in children's literature often involves anthropomorphism, or personification. The frequency of this narrative feature explains why there have been numerous studies on the subject. At one end of the continuum of personification there are what we might call people in fur – those characters who are animal in name only, such as those found in *The Wind in the Willows* – while at the other end there are animals realistically portrayed but for the fact that their consciousness has been cast in human speech – such as is found in *Black Beauty* (*see* THOUGHT AND CONSCIOUSNESS REPRESENTATION (LITERATURE)). Animal characters or toy objects (such as dolls) personified as human serve almost as a code for 'children's book', though often readers of *Watership Down* and *Animal Farm* are surprised to find themselves confronting adult literature. Anthropomorphic representations can be used to mask differences in class, race, and ethnicity as well as to appeal to children through *fantasy. The most insightful in-depth study of character in children's fiction is Nikolajeva (2002).

The story patterns most often discussed in children's fiction involve a movement away from and return to home. Scholars have tried to distinguish children's from adult stories by means of asking whether or not the child protagonist returns home or whether he or she, as in Huck Finn's case, lights out for the territories. While initial arguments tended to create an either/or case (children's stories feature return; *adolescent and adult stories feature departure at the end), the growing plot complexity of children's novels has made any such easy reduction impossible.

SEE ALSO: Bildungsroman; children's storytelling; comics and graphic novel; fable; fairy tale; nursery rhyme

References and further reading

Blount, Margaret (1974) *Animal Land: The Creatures of Children's Fiction*, London: Hutchinson & Co.

Chambers, Aidan (1985) 'The Reader in the Book', in *Booktalk: Occasional Writing on Literature and Children*, New York: Harper & Row Publishers.

Children's Literature Association Quarterly, 15 (2).

Children's Literature Association Quarterly, 28 (1).

Higonnet, Margaret R. (1987) 'Narrative Fractures and Fragments', *Children's Literature*, 15, 37–54.

McGillis, Rod (1991) 'The Embrace: Narrative Voice and Children's Books', *Canadian Children's Literature*, 63, 24–40.

Mills, Claudia (1998) 'The Ethics of the Author/Audience Relationship in Children's Fiction', *Children's Literature Association Quarterly*, 22.4, 181–87.

Nikolajeva, Maria (2000) *From Mythic to Linear: Time in Children's Literature*, Lanham, MD: Scarecrow Press.

—— (2002) *The Rhetoric of Character in Children's Fiction*, Lanham, MD: Scarecrow Press.

Nodelman, Perry (1985) *Words About Pictures: The Narrative Art of Children's Picture Books*, Athens: University of Georgia Press.

Otten, Charlotte, and Gary D. Schmidt (eds) (1989) *The Voice of the Narrator in Children's Literature: Insights from Writers and Critics*, New York: Greenwood Press.

Shavit, Zohar (1986) *The Poetics of Children's Literature*, Athens, GA: University of Georgia Press.

Studies in the Literary Imagination, 18 (2).

Wall, Barbara (1991) *The Narrator's Voice: The Dilemma of Children's Fiction*, New York, NY: St. Martin's Press.

Wyile, Andrea Schwenke (1999) 'Expanding the View of First-Person Narration', *Children's Literature in Education*, 30.3, 185–202.

MIKE CADDEN

CHILDREN'S STORYTELLING

Whether the narrative is a bedtime story or a dinner table account of the day's *events, children tell stories to others about events or other personal *anecdotes. They retell their *memories or provide an ongoing explanation of present actions in narrative form. Recent work has questioned earlier assumptions that written stories read or told to children constitute the main models of children's narrative experience, by showing that children's sense of story or *narrative as *genre is greatly influenced by all manner of oral and visual accounts of past events (Cook-Gumperz 1995; *see* CHILDREN'S STORIES (NARRATIVES WRITTEN FOR CHILDREN)). Whether children are the storytellers or *audience, they learn to recognise the typical characteristics of narrative as a distinct mode of discourse organisation (*see* DISCOURSE ANALYSIS (LINGUISTICS)).

There is a progression in the development of the ability to understand and tell stories. Younger children's narratives report routine events but lack a high point, either omitting an instigating problem event or omitting how the story is resolved. Evaluative material, including codas and outcomes, are only added later (Peterson and McCabe 1983). It is important to note, however, that the idealised story structure is itself subject to cultural variation. In contrast to European-American children's elaborated stories of single experiences, Japanese children tell brief stories about collections of experiences. Collaborative storytelling practices socialise children to 'count on others' filling out parts of stories' as part of the culturally valued 'notion of rapport and empathy' (Minami and McCabe 1995: 443). Cultural beliefs about what constitutes tellable events worthy of *narration (*see* TELLABILITY) vary greatly across cultures and are reflected in the story structures that children display at school (Blum-Kulka 1997; Heath 1983; *see* EDUCATION AND NARRATIVE; SOCIOLINGUISTIC APPROACHES TO NARRATIVE).

A recent focus of narrative research is children's oral narrative practices. White middle-class children are read to, and children of many cultures are told stories, but what are the storytelling events in which children participate themselves? An early form of oral narrative that white middle-class children engage in with parents, but mainly with peers, is dramatic narratives of pretence (Heath 1984). Narratives produced during pretend play have different *voices with distinctive marking (Cook-Gumperz 1995; Kyratzis 1999; Wolf and Hicks 1989). The narrative voice describes what is happening in the play and is indicated by various 'pretend' markers as well as a profusion of connectives including 'because'. In addition to the narrative voice, there are two others: the voice of enactment, through which children play the role of characters, and the voice of stage-managing, through which children negotiate background details, speaking in their own voice. Tense-aspectual marking options in narrative, including the simple present and -ing durative ending, afford various *perspectives to be taken on the story action (*see* TENSE AND NARRATIVE). Narrative devices such as these allow narrative to be used for moral *positioning.

How narratives are conversationally occasioned has been another major focus of research on children's stories (*see* COMMUNICATION IN NARRATIVE; CONVERSATIONAL STORYTELLING). African-American working class children, particularly girls, were observed by Goodwin (1990) to engage in pretend play, but not all children engage in this practice. When we consider cultures other than white middle-class American culture, conversationally occasioned stories that children participate in are found in dispute sequences (Goodwin 1990) and as parts of displays of skill among peers in school and in the community (Ervin-Tripp and Kuntay 1997; Heath 1983).

Children's gender identity concerns are also reflected in story structure (*see* GENDER STUDIES; IDENTITY AND NARRATIVE). Kyratzis (1999) found that preschoolers positioned themselves with respect to various qualities associated with gender identities in their collaborative narratives of pretence. Girls told stories where they depicted selves as nurturant and lovable while boys depicted characters who were rough and conquest-oriented. Nicolopoulou (2002) observed that preschoolers, over time with their nursery school classroom peers, developed story themes that embodied issues of gender identity; differential *storyworlds were reflected in different structures in girls' and boys' stories.

Another influence on story structure is children's purposes for telling stories. Children's social goals can be built upon in developing narrative skills. When children are asked to dictate stories to the teacher that are later to be acted out by the peer group as a play, this practice 'brings home to the child in a vivid way what is required for a narrative scenario to be effectively complete, self-contextualising, and satisfying' (Nicolopoulou 2002: 139) and is effective in building school-related skills. Narratives evolve over time in a context. As shown by Green and Dixon (1993), children's written classroom journal entries reflected oral themes that the class had discussed over the year as a group. These findings underscore the importance of *intertextuality in the joint construction of narratives produced in classroom life.

Children's narratives develop in social and cultural contexts. Only by understanding cultural beliefs and practices can educators validate children's community experiences and bridge gaps between school and community ways of learning and telling stories.

SEE ALSO: orality; psychological approaches to narrative; sociology and narrative

References and further reading

Blum-Kulka, Shoshana (1997) *Dinner Talk: Cultural Patterns of Sociality and Socialization in Family Discourse*, Mahwah, NJ: Lawrence Erlbaum.

Cook-Gumperz, Jenny (1995) 'Reproducing the Discourse of Mothering: How Gendered Talk Makes Gendered Lives', in Kira Hall (ed.) *Gender Articulated*, London: Routledge.

Ervin-Tripp, Susan M., and Aylin Kuntay (1997) 'The Occasioning and Structure of Conversational Narratives', in Talmy Givón (ed.) *Conversation: Cognitive, Communicative, and Social Perspectives*, Amsterdam: John Benjamins.

Goodwin, Marjorie H. (1990) *He-Said-She-Said: Talk as Social Organization among Black Children*, Bloomington: Indiana University Press.

Green, Judith L., and Carol Dixon (1993) 'Talking Knowledge into Being: Discursive and Social Practices in Classrooms', *Linguistics and Education*, 5, 231–40.

Heath, Shirley B. (1983) *Language, Life, and Work in Communities and Classrooms*, Cambridge: Cambridge University Press.

—— (1984) 'Taking a Cross-cultural Look at Narrative', *Topics in Language Disorders*, 7, 84–94.

Kyratzis, Amy (1999) 'Narrative Identity: Preschoolers' Self-construction through Narrative in Same-sex Friendship Group Dramatic Play', *Narrative Inquiry*, 9, 427–55.

Minami, Masahiko, and Alyssa McCabe (1995) 'Rice Balls and Bear Hunts: Japanese and North American Family Narrative Patterns', *Journal of Child Language*, 22, 423–45.

Nicolopoulou, Ageliki (2002) 'Peer Group Culture and Narrative Development', in Shoshan Blum-Kulka and Catherine Snow (eds) *Talking to Adults: The Contribution of Multiparty Discourse to Language Acquisition*, Mahwah, NJ: Erlbaum.

Peterson, Carole, and Allyssa McCabe (1983) *Developmental Psycholinguistics: Three Ways of Looking at a Child's Narrative*, New York: Plenum Press.

Wolf, Dennie, and Deborah Hicks (1989) 'The Voices within Narratives: The Development of Intertextuality in Young Children's Stories', *Discourse Processes*, 12, 329–53.

JENNY COOK-GUMPERZ AND AMY KYRATZIS

CHINESE NARRATIVE

The narrative tradition in China unfolded in a manner opposite to its counterpart in the West that led from *epic to *romance and from romance to the *novel. In contrast, Chinese narrative began as a product of a very dominant literate culture before taking on oral characteristics, most probably under the influence of both the philosophy and the practice of Buddhist preachers from India. Even as *orality provided a certain leavening to the written narratives, however, literate characteristics, based on a separate written language that was all but sacrosanct, remained the ideal until the early decades of the twentieth century, when the written vernacular took its place as part of the country's efforts to modernise.

The cultural influence of the writing system, which is based on imagistic graphs rather than on a phonetic alphabet, cannot be overstated. Begun as a means to transcribe court rituals around 1200 BCE, the *wenyan* (literary language) written with these graphs 'never came close to reflecting any contemporary living variety of Sinitic speech' (Mair 1994: 708). The situation exaggerated the contrast between orality and literacy that exists in all literate cultures. Where speech tended to be repetitive and exhaustive, for example, *wenyan* was exceedingly terse and elliptical; and where speech was fleeting and evanescent, *wenyan* was revered precisely for providing a kind of permanence that extended human mortality. In practice, *wenyan* was more widely employed for lyrical poetry or discursive essays, which flourished throughout Chinese history, than for narrative, whether in poetry or prose.

Quite in keeping with its ritualistic beginnings, this literary language was the medium of the first true narrative in Chinese history, the *Zuo Commentary* (*Zuo zhuan*, attributed to Zuo Qiuming, third century BCE), which fleshed out the laconic chronological listing of events in the feudal states from 722 to 481 BCE in the *Spring and Autumn Annals*, a part of the Confucian classical canon (*see* ANNALS; CHRONICLE; HISTORIOGRAPHY). While providing narrative interest, the *Zuo Commentary* advances didactically the concept of *li* (ritual propriety), instrumental in the creation of the literary language itself. *Li* is considered to be 'the constant principle of Heaven, the righteousness of earth, and the proper action of mankind' (Duke Zhao, twenty-fifth year, trans. Watson 1962: 45), and anyone acting without a sense of *li* is doomed to certain failure, just as acting according to *li* guarantees success.

The tradition of historical narrative begun in the *Zuo Commentary* thus subordinates narrative particulars to general moral principle, a procedure the *Records of the Grand Historian* Sima Qian (ca. 145-ca. 85 BCE) follows, even as he sharply questions the blind faith in success going to those practicing the moral good. The *Records'* core, the seventy chapters on *biographies of outstanding individuals, is directed to demonstrating the opposite, so that written history itself becomes an instrument to right what amounts to cosmic injustice.

As narrative, the *Records* livens up its serious moral concerns with genuine passion, and overcomes the naturally laconic terseness of its language with dramatic detail and an eye for the sensationalised fact as well as for *legend. Its sustained influence on Chinese historiography, and indeed all of China's narrative culture, can be traced in large measure to its readability. With the *Records*, Chinese narrative took a huge step in the direction of fictionalisation, even as the vast majority of its readers respected it as history, as both literary and literal *truth in keeping with the *wenyan* it employs.

The reverence for written historical narrative, on the other hand, helps account for the traditional relegation of oral storytelling *performances to the entertainment category. But it was in such performances, which surely began well before the descriptions of them in the twelfth century urban centres of the Song dynasty, that fact was extended into fiction to heighten interest, rather than to bring out or emphasise moral truth. The relatively recent discovery of the semi-vernacular *bianwen* (Transformation Texts) from the Tang dynasty (AD 618–907) confirms the role of Buddhism in freeing the narrative imagination from the restrictions of factuality and in developing the written vernacular. When this language and its dominant oral residues became the medium for the collected stories of outlaws who gathered together in the marshlands of Shandong province (*Shuihu zhuan* or *Water Margin*; first known text, fourteenth century), the work was categorised as *xiaoshuo*, or a minor narrative, and kept very much apart from truthful history for its evident flights of fancy commonly found in oral storytelling.

The same label, originally given to relatively abbreviated accounts of morally inconsequential phenomena or events in literary prose, was applied to the many vernacular narrative texts dating to the Ming dynasty (1368–1644). A small number of these texts inevitably took on the serious concerns of their literati editors or *authors who infused social or philosophical concerns into the presentation of extraordinary facts or events designed primarily to heighten the interest of the reader. The result was the introduction into *xiaoshuo* of a kind of seriousness that makes it easier for later scholars to identify it with novelistic fiction in Europe and America. The outstanding example of this is the eighteenth-century *Honglou meng* (*A Dream of Red Mansions*, by Cao Xueqin, ca.1715–ca.1763), which makes *fiction itself a part of its thematic exploration of illusion and reality in human life.

In general, however, vernacular narratives did not rise from their lesser status in China's literary hierarchy until the twentieth century, when they were equated with modern *novels by native scholars who saw them as models for making vernacular Chinese the official language for all writing. The price for becoming a tool for modern reform, however, was the loss of their historical identity, something scholarship, whether native or foreign, has yet to restore.

SEE ALSO: African narrative; ancient theories of narrative (non-Western); Australian Aboriginal narrative; Japanese Narrative; Native American narrative; oral cultures and narrative; Sanskrit narrative

References and further reading

Mair, Victor H. (1994) 'Buddhism and the Rise of the Written Vernacular in East Asia: The Making of National Languages', *The Journal of Asian Studies*, 53.3, 707–51.

Ong, Walter J. (1982) *Orality and Literacy: The Technologizing of the Word*, London: Methuen.

Plaks, Andrew H. (1977) 'Towards a Critical Theory of Chinese Narrative', in Andrew H. Plaks (ed.) *Chinese Narrative: Critical and Theoretical Essays*, Princeton: Princeton University Press.

Watson, Burton (1962) *Early Chinese Literature*, New York: Columbia University Press.

TIMOTHY C. WONG

CHRONICLE

In historiographic contexts, the term 'chronicle' refers to a record of noteworthy *events arranged chronologically. Chronicles may concern the whole world (e.g., Ekkehard of Aurach's *Universal Chronicle*), as well as more restricted subjects like a city (e.g., Villani's *Florentine Chronicles*), a country (e.g., Walsingham's *Chronicle of England*), or an endeavour (e.g., Joinville's *Chronicle of the Crusade of St. Louis*). The border between *annals and chronicle is unstable in Antiquity and the Middle Ages (*see* MEDIEVAL NARRATIVE). In some cases, 'chronicle' refers to a mere list and is synonymous with 'annals'; in others, it designates a continuous text that combines the 'records contained in several annals', obtaining a 'more complete and comprehensive story' (Barnes 1963: 65). Modern chronicles usually consist of data organised chronologically around a single, homogeneous topic (e.g., *Chronicle of the First World War*) (*see* TEMPORAL ORDERING). The term 'chronicle' is also found today in the names of periodicals (e.g., *The Chronicle of Higher Education*), as well as in the titles of fictional and historical works (e.g., Rice's *Chronicles of the Vampires*, or Ophüls's documentary film *The Sorrow and the Pity: Chronicle of a French City under the Occupation*).

Theorists and philosophers have discussed the issue of whether chronicles are *narratives and, if so, of what variety. Walsh distinguishes between 'plain' and 'significant' narrative, i.e., between the account of past events and the explanation of those events; he regards 'chronicle' as a member of the first category, 'history proper' as a member of the second (Walsh 1967: 32–33). Rejecting that dichotomy, Danto argues that 'plain' and 'significant' narratives have in fact the same structure and fulfil the same function; both 'explain what happened', whether they simply 'relate' events or 'spell out' the connections among them (Danto 1985: 138). Danto also maintains that chronicles (in the sense of 'lists of events reported at the time of their occurrence') cannot be narratives; their *authors do not know 'how things came out' (356), and thus can neither decide which events are worth selecting, nor characterise those events using such terms as 'crisis', 'climax', and 'turning point' (354). White establishes a similar distinction. Chronicles, according to him, may have a central subject and appear to unfold as a narrative; but they do not so much 'conclude' as merely 'terminate', stopping 'in medias res' without completing the story they seemed to be telling (White 1987: 17). In this respect, White argues, chronicles are more 'realistic', i.e., more faithful to the 'ways that reality offers itself to perception', than the narratives of modern historiography (25); for the world does not come to us in the form of well-made plots, but as mere 'sequences' that never begin nor conclude (24).

SEE ALSO: emplotment; historiography; metahistory

References and further reading

Barnes, Harry E. (1963) *A History of Historical Writing*, New York: Dover.
Danto, Arthur C. (1985) *Narration and Knowledge*, New York: Columbia University Press.
Walsh, William H. (1967) *Philosophy of History: An Introduction*, New York: Harper.
White, Hayden (1987) *The Content of Form: Narrative Discourse and Historical Representation*, Baltimore: Johns Hopkins University Press.

PHILIPPE CARRARD

CHRONOTOPE

The term 'chronotope', touchstone of one of Mikhail Bakhtin's treatments of the *novel (*see* HETEROGLOSSIA; POLYPHONY), is a multifaceted concept that escapes sharp definition. Unlike narrative theorists who divide *time and *space into separate categories, Bakhtin insists on their 'intrinsic connectedness': through the 'thickening' or 'materialising' of time in space, narrative *events become representable. The chronotopicity of literary images was identified by Lessing (objects in space can be described only in temporal sequences), but chronotopes also go back to the Kantian conception of time and space (although they are not transcendental, but rooted in immediate reality), to the theory of relativity (which posits objects and events in terms of spatio-temporal relations), and to Russian research in the 1920s on the ordering of physiological systems in response to specific situations. In individual works, chronotopes form

a bridge between formal elements of texts and the time/space of their production/reception.

A way of understanding experience, of modelling the world, chronotopes provide a 'ground' for representation out of which narrative events emerge, a series of temporal markers conjoined with spatial features which, together, define specific historical, biographical, and social relations. Chronotope also extends to *genre; Bakhtin, however, distinguishes not between *epic, dramatic, and lyric, but between epic, which portrays an 'absolute past' cut off from the present, and novel, where the representation of events occurs at a temporal level and within a scheme of cultural values implicating both *author and reader.

Chronotopes also form the basis for a historical poetics of the novel. Bakhtin identifies three chronotopes in the Greek adventure novel (second–fifth centuries AD) that extend to modern times: in these texts, time is not biographical, and as the *characters undergo ordeals without changing, the order of events is immaterial (see BIOGRAPHY; TEMPORAL ORDERING); similarly, space remains abstract, interchangeable, and historically undetermined. Some of these novels, however (e.g., *Satyricon*), portray the transformation of character (leading to Christian narratives of temptation/rebirth). With Rabelais, the chronotope connecting man with his actions reaches a high point, while the nineteenth-century *Bildungsroman emphasises the *hero, located in historical time, in the process of becoming. Other chronotopes – the road (*picaresque novels), the threshold (crisis time), etc. – resemble *motifs, involving what might be termed 'congealed events' (the Gothic castle, imbued with an aura of historicity). Such classes of chronotopes can be correlated with particular sub-genres of narrative.

A genre-making concept based on spatio-temporal relations, chronotope has inspired such over-extensions as chronotopes of *memory, of the *Holocaust, etc. It has also been criticised for vacillating between transhistorical universals and historically-bound genres (Todorov 1984) and for being too general for narratological analysis (Riffaterre 1996) (see NARRATIVE UNIVERSALS). Nevertheless, Riffaterre himself has integrated the concept into *diegesis, and another theorist (Dentith 1997) has redefined it as a matrix comprising *sjuzhet and *fabula. Morson and Emerson (1990) have sought to extrapolate from chronotope and other Bakhtinian principles a 'prosaics' of narrative.

SEE ALSO: dialogism; heteroglossia; Marxist approaches to narrative

References and further reading

Bakhtin, Michael (1981) *The Dialogic Imagination: Four Essays*, ed. Michael Holquist, trans. Michael Holquist and Caryl Emerson, Austin: University of Texas Press.

Clark, Katerina, and Michael Holquist (1984) *Mikhail Bakhtin*, Cambridge, Mass.: Harvard University Press.

Dentith, Simon (1997) *Bakhtinian Thought: An Introductory Reader*, London: Routledge.

Holquist, Michael (1990) *Dialogism: Bakhtin and His World*, London: Routledge.

Morson, Gary Saul, and Caryl Emerson (1990) *Mikhail Bakhtin: Creation of a Prosaics*, Stanford: Stanford University Press.

Riffaterre, Michael (1996) 'Chronotopes in Diegesis', in Calin-Andrei Mihailescu and Walid Hamarneh (eds) *Fiction Updated: Theories of Fictionality*, Toronto: University of Toronto Press.

Todorov, Tzvetan (1984) *Mikhail Bakhtin: The Dialogic Principle*, trans. Wlad Godzich, Minneapolis: University of Minnesota Press.

JOHN PIER

CINÉROMAN

The cinéroman (literally: film-novel) is a literary *genre offering the illustrated book-version of a movie. Typically, it presents a large series either of *photographs taken on the set or of screen-shots of the finished movie accompanying the complete *dialogues of the *film. Although it may resemble at first sight the published version of a script, the cinéroman normally does not provide the technical parameters contained in the script. Moreover, it offers a more fluent and homogenised version of the script's storyline and dialogues. Finally, it is important to stress the differences between the cinéroman and three other sub-genres: first, the illustrated reprint of the *novel on which the film script was based (*see* ADAPTATION); second, the novelisation of the movie (which is the reworking of the script as completely new novel); third, the photonovella, which is generally based on an original script. With the film script, the cinéroman shares some of its forms and practices, so that in actuality it is not always easy to distinguish between these two genres.

The history of the cinéroman is as old as that of film itself, and the genre is one of the major direct examples of the interaction between cinema and literature. The concrete forms of this collaboration between word and *image, however, have shifted dramatically since the very first experiments with the cinéroman around 1900. In the beginning, the cinéroman was used to promote the new medium of film: the very existence of a printed equivalent endowed the movies with a form of cultural prestige (in the case of the first feature films), while at the same time the cinéroman was used as a teaser for upcoming sequels (in the case of the single-reel stories based on the adventures of popular characters) (*see* SERIAL FORM). Later, the cinéroman was elevated to the status of an autonomous work of literary art, and several periods and *authors have demonstrated a particular interest in the genre (the best known example being the cinéromans by Alain Robbe-Grillet).

It is widely accepted that the cinéroman has never been an artistic success. A bimedial work, it has always suffered from a lack of balance between the verbal and the visual (*see* INTERMEDIALITY). Indeed, the cinéroman relies heavily upon the dominant position of the printed word, mainly the dialogues, and does not seem able to compensate or question this domination by visual means. In this respect, it simply repeats the flaws of most photonovellas, whose artistic failure has become axiomatic. The visual aspects of movies in print are often better served by scholarly editions of scripts than by autonomous cinéromans. A good example of such a scholarly treatment is Bruce Mau's reinterpretation of *La Jetée*, a famous avant-garde film by Chris Marker (1964).

SEE ALSO: media and narrative

References and further reading

Mau, Bruce, and Chris Marker (1992) *La Jetée/The Jetty*, New York: Zone Books.

Robbe-Grillet, Alain (1959) *L'Année dernière à Marienbad*, Paris: Minuit.

Virmaux, Alain, and Claudette Virmaux (1982) *Le cinéroman*, Paris: Edilig.

JAN BAETENS

CLOSURE

Often associated with ending, epilogue, or dénouement, *closure* should not be confused with these terms (*see* NARRATIVE UNITS). Rather, closure refers to the satisfaction of expectations and the answering of questions raised over the course of any narrative.

Narratives may end without closure; indeed, much discussion of *modernist and *postmodernist narrative has stressed its 'anti-closural' (Smith 1968) or 'open-ended' character. Rabinowitz (1989) distinguishes 'inertial' from 'non-inertial' endings, the one arriving according to expectations, the other not, yet neither necessarily yielding nor failing to yield closure. Narratives are often described as either having or not having closure. For example, in an Aristotlean analysis of tragedy, closure is what allows the successful work to be seen as an entity complete in itself; similarly, in Smith's analysis of poetic closure, it is what allows the reader to be 'satisfied by the failure of continuation' (Smith 1968: 34). Nonetheless, most narratives of any complexity fail to close in some respects, however strong the sense of overall closure may be.

In critical practice, definitions of closure vary. In his study of 'rhetorical fictions' (including the *fable and the apologue), Richter distinguishes between closure as largely the fulfilment of generic expectations (see GENRE THEORY IN NARRATIVE STUDIES) and 'completeness' as the full and adequate development of what a work sets out to do. By contrast, in her study of closure in the novel, Torgovnick (1981) adopts a definition of closure that is almost identical to Richter's completeness.

In later twentieth century literary theory, focus on closure has shifted from formal qualities in the text to attitudes brought to the text by readers (see READER-RESPONSE THEORY). Thus, *audiences bred to be sceptical of closure will find openness in nineteenth-century canonical texts where the original audiences found closure. In much *poststructuralist theory, all closure is imposed since language itself is a vehicle not of meaning but its deferral. Kermode, in a landmark study of 'the sense of an ending', argues that endings marked by narrative closure arise out of the mind's natural inclination to convert the raw contingency of *events into a shape that conveys order and meaning. White similarly argues that history as practised in modern western culture is a narrative art in which closure plays a key role of imposing 'moral meaning' on events.

SEE ALSO: emplotment; indeterminacy; narrativity; reader constructs

References and further reading

Kermode, Frank (1967) *The Sense of an Ending: Studies in the Theory of Fiction*, London: Oxford University Press.

Rabinowitz, Peter (1989) 'End Sinister: Neat Closure as Disruptive Force', in James Phelan (ed.) *Reading Narrative: Form, Ethics, Ideology*, Columbus: Ohio State University Press.

Richter, David H. (1974) *Fable's End: Completeness and Closure in Rhetorical Fiction*, Chicago: University of Chicago Press.

Schlueter, June (1995) *Dramatic Closure: Reading the End*, London: Associated University Presses.

Smith, Barbara Herrnstein (1968) *Poetic Closure*, Chicago: University of Chicago Press.

Torgovnick, Marianna (1981) *Closure in the Novel*, Princeton: Princeton University Press.

Welsh, Alexander (ed.) (1979) *Narrative Endings*, Berkeley: University of California Press.

White, Hayden (1980) 'The Value of Narrativity in the Representation of Reality', in W. J. T. Mitchell (ed.) *On Narrative*, Chicago: University of Chicago Press.

H. PORTER ABBOTT

CODES FOR READING

Codes enable communication by establishing a common ground on which the producer and the receiver of an utterance can meet; they have been compared to other human systems such as the rules of a game and the conventions of etiquette. A code for the reading of narrative can be understood as a loose set of rules by which a person identifies and interprets the essential components of a narrative text (*narrator, *actants, *narrative progression, etc.). This sense of the term 'code', a sense deriving from structuralism, differs from the ordinary use of the term in expressions such as 'Morse code', in which there is a precise and unvarying correlation between a signal and its meaning.

In his pioneering study of codes, Barthes (1974) specifies how five codes can shape a reader's movement through a text. Initially recognising the text as a narrative, a reader will then apply the proairetic code to organise the text's actions, the referential code to connect the text's world to accepted bodies of knowledge, the semic code to organise its *characters and characterising details, the symbolic code to connect the text to larger structures of signification, and the *hermeneutic code to follow the text's development of narrative suspense. Chatman (1979) adds a sixth, the metacodic code, by which the text signals, the reader infers, and the culture suggests which codes are appropriate for a given text. *Paratextual materials (e.g., titles, bookstore sections) and *mode of presentation (*film, homily, billboard, etc.) function in this metacodic way.

The study of codes belongs to the field of discourse *pragmatics, which also concerns itself with schemata, scripts, frames, and plans (*see* DISCOURSE ANALYSIS (LINGUISTICS); FRAME THEORY; SCRIPTS AND SCHEMATA). Schema, script, and plan are typically used to describe how people order their actions. Code and frame make possible the interpretation of texts. One of the most important questions for the study of codes is this: Are all human experiences understood by means of codes that have been shaped by culture and that reinforce a governing *ideology, or do some codes reflect structures (e.g., physical, biological) existing independent of culture (*see* BIOLOGICAL FOUNDATIONS OF NARRATIVE; NARRATIVE UNIVERSALS)? While the term 'code' has a wide range of applications, from describing the processing of single sentences to describing group rituals to describing how ideology may influence individual cognition and behaviour, current narrative theory most often uses the term to refer to the institutionalised semiotic structures that allow *authors and readers to communicate through texts.

SEE ALSO: communication in narrative; communication studies and narrative; function (Jakobson); reader-response theory; semiotics; structuralist narratology

References and further reading

Barthes, Roland (1974) *S/Z*, trans. Richard Miller, New York: Hill and Wang.

Chatman, Seymour (1979) 'The Styles of Narrative Codes', in Berel Lang (ed.) *The Concept of Style*, Philadelphia: University of Pennsylvania Press.

Culler, Jonathan (1975) *Structuralist Poetics: Structuralism, Linguistics, and the Study of Literature*, Ithaca: Cornell University Press.

Givón, Talmy (1989) *Mind, Code and Context: Essays in Pragmatics*, Hillsdale, NJ: Lawrence Erlbaum.

Rabinowitz, Peter (1987) *Before Reading: Narrative Conventions and the Politics of Interpretation*, Ithaca: Cornell University Press.

Scholes, Robert, Nancy Comley, and Gregory Ulmer (1995) *Text/Book: An Introduction to Literary Language*, New York: St. Martin's Press.

MICHAEL KEARNS

COGNITIVE NARRATOLOGY

Cognitive theory investigates the relations between perception, language, knowledge, *memory, and the world; cognitive narratology is interested in the roles of stories within the ranges and intersections of these phenomena.

From a cognitive vantage, many of the common sense positions of 'classical' narratology have to be approached with due scepticism. Classical narratology tended to place an arbitrary focus on a restricted set of core *genres, treated narratives as self-sufficient products rather than as texts to be reconstructed in an ongoing and revisable readerly process, and ignored the forces and desires of psychological, social, cultural, and historic contexts (*see* CULTURAL STUDIES APPROACHES TO NARRATIVE). However, even in the heyday of structuralist dissection of texts, theories of 'reception' had begun to suggest a counterbalance: Wolfgang Iser postulated the concept of the 'implied reader', Stanley Fish cast his vote for an 'affective stylistics', Paul Grice laid down the rules of the 'Cooperative Principle' (*see* PRAGMATICS), and Roland Barthes allowed readers to co-construct writerly texts (*see* READERLY TEXT, WRITERLY TEXT (BARTHES)). All of these moves signalled a cognitive turn, and many of the *'postclassical' narratological approaches have pursued a cognitivist orientation since (*see*, e.g., NATURAL NARRATOLOGY; PSYCHOLOGICAL APPROACHES TO NARRATIVE; RHETORICAL APPROACHES TO NARRATIVE). At the same time – though more by fortuitous coincidence than by systematic exchange or exploration – the cognitive sciences themselves have begun to recognise the 'storied' nature of perception, sense-making, memory, and *identity formation.

The following survey begins by sketching the investigator's problem of observing cognitive processes directly and introduces the formula 'seeing X as Y' as a foundational axiom. The impact of this axiom is illustrated by primary and secondary effects triggered in the process of reading, while higher-order mental representations can be described as functions of 'frames', 'scripts', and 'preference rules'. Finally, the entry briefly discusses the position of cognitive narratology within a network of disciplines which have a special interest in stories and storytelling (*see* INTERDISCIPLINARY APPROACHES TO NARRATIVE; NARRATIVE TURN IN THE HUMANITIES).

Seeing X as Y: the constructivist basis of cognitive research

One of the basic difficulties in any cognitive exploration is that the working of cognition cannot be observed directly. We may believe we know how our minds work and we may be able to explain what caused one to arrive at particular decisions about perceived facts, but both introspection and conscious metareflection can virtually only see the tip of the iceberg, whereas the automatic processes that prepare the ground for reflection are not themselves open to inspection or rational explanation. The problem, as Gilles Fauconnier puts it, is that 'the investigator is no longer a mere spectator. He or she is one of the actors, part of the phenomenon under study. The thinking and talking that need to be demystified are also the thinking and talking used to carry out the demystification' (1994: xvii). Fauconnier uses the word 'mystification' advisedly because when one stops to consider what happens in ordinary perception one realises that cognition performs incredible feats – channelling a flood of external stimuli, correlating and evaluating new data on the basis of what is already known and understood, and condensing information in such a manner as to allow split-second decisions if necessary. Some of these decisions are based on internal narratives that provide participant roles, functions, and causal rationale for online experience, addressing questions such as 'What is my role in this ongoing story – am I (going to be) *hero, villain, victim, or witness, and what is required of me to fulfil these roles?' (*see* ACTANT; NARRATIVE AS COGNITIVE INSTRUMENT).

Precisely because cognition can only be described by epithets such as 'mystery' and 'miracle', neither deductive thinking nor educated guessing get the researcher very far. In order to approach and, from an *artificial intelligence (AI) perspective, replicate the art and achievement of cognition, researchers usually make a deliberate attempt to wipe the slate clean. Ray Jackendoff (1987) does this by sharply distinguishing between (1) the *real world* ('R-world') as it exists before perception and language, and (2) the *phenomenal world* ('P-world') as it is intuitively perceived and described in ordinary language terms. Because the R-world is posited to exist before perception and language the investigator will merely gesture towards it, or at best characterise it as a 'a flux', 'a chaos', 'a pattern of sensory stimuli', a 'succession of noises and marks', 'black marks on paper', and so on. (Radical constructivists are even prepared to accept that P-world and R-world are mental projections of basically the same kind (Fauconnier 1994: 14)). On this basis, all *story arcs of cognitive explanation – to use a narrative metaphor – boil down to the formula of 'seeing X as Y', or, more specifically, 'seeing an R-world X as a P-world Y'.

While the clean-slate approach may look like an academic abstraction, it has a real enough analogue in cognitive AI. The cognitive AI programmer can take nothing for granted and has to implement all heuristics explicitly. To the machine, all input is inherently indeterminate and even when it comes in the form of letters, words, and sentences each element may still be open-endedly ambiguous. In narratology, Meir Sternberg's 'Proteus Principle' – the many-to-many correspondences between linguistic form and representational function – presents a similar clean-slate assumption whose practical advantage becomes obvious when one uses it to reanalyse seemingly familiar phenomena such as *narrative situations, *description, and *free indirect discourse (see Jahn 1997). Significantly, the true magnitude of natural language ambiguity was only recognised when AI researchers began to design programs for parsing natural language sentences in the early 1970s. While it turned out that it was not too difficult for a computer to generate all possible parsings of a sentence it was, and still is, almost impossibly difficult to replicate the human cogniser's ability to see only whichever most likely reading is relevant in a given context. One intuitively plausible theory had it that human cognisers work on predetermined preferences and never consider all options (see the discussion of preference rules below). Yet, in a number of remarkable experiments conducted in the late 1970s, David Swinney and his collaborators presented striking evidence that in the initial phases of sentence recognition human cognisers do indeed test a wide array of options before committing themselves to the single reading that ultimately reaches conscious awareness.

Reading and cognition

Because the physical process of reading is situated at the interface between narrative text and narrative understanding (or *narrativisation) theories of readers and reading have been at the heart of reception-oriented narrative theory (*see* READER

CONSTRUCTS; READER-RESPONSE THEORY; RECEPTION THEORY). However, the lower-level cognitive processes are equally as interesting.

In Jackendoff's (1987) model of the reading process, the perceptual input of written text goes bottom up through a number of perception modules accomplishing letter recognition as well as phonological and syntactic analysis before it is understood in a top-level frame of 'conceptual representation'. Processing need not and generally does not stop at this stage; in fact, the processes *following* the primary generation of conceptual representation are crucial for any theory of imaginative reading. Redirected to the lingual and motor faculties, conceptual representations may trigger motor actions such as laughing, crying, or – when reading a musical score – conducting an imaginary orchestra. Conceptual representation can also filter back into the mind's language faculty and enable one to 'sound' the words spoken by *narrator and/or *characters as internal speech ('imaginary audition'), and, if required, to produce physical output like reading out loud. Likewise, conceptual information may flow back into the mind's vision module and generate 'imaginary vision' ('visual imagery') in the absence of a corresponding image on the retinal screen – hence the primary visual input of the single word *duck* may be sufficient to get someone to draw a picture of a duck without actually seeing one.

It is precisely this secondary activation of auditory and visual faculties that explains why and how texts can 'evoke' the *voices of characters and narrators (Fludernik 1996) and how readers can let themselves be imaginatively transported into the world of action (Gerrig 1993; *see* IMMERSION). Further evidence on the triggering of such narrative effects is presented in Duchan and her collaborators' (1995) account of what they call 'deictic shift theory' (*see* DEIXIS). The cognitive agent in deictic shift theory is a mobile 'deictic centre' ('focalizer', in *focalization theory), which registers *space and *time coordinates as well as actors, *action sequence, and events. One of the main concerns of deictic shift theory is to track the moment-to-moment changes of states of information both in the deictic centre and in the reader.

Frames, scripts, and preference rules

As AI cognitivists recognised, in order to resolve ambiguity and to integrate local information into larger conceptual frameworks, the human processor accesses a store of situational and contextual knowledge. To replicate this ability, AI theorists such as Marvin Minsky, Roger C. Schank, and Robert P. Abelson made a highly influential attempt to replace the concept of context by more explicit and detailed constructs which they called 'frames' and 'scripts' (*see* SCRIPTS AND SCHEMATA). Both concepts aim at reproducing a human cogniser's knowledge and expectations about standard *events and situations. Frames basically deal with situations such as seeing a room or making a promise while scripts cover standard action sequences such as playing a game of football, going to a birthday party, or eating in a restaurant. Frames and scripts specify 'defaults' to encode expectations, 'nodes and relations' to capture categories and hierarchies, and 'terminals' and 'slots' to provide data integration points whose goodness of fit is regulated by sets of necessary, probabilistic, and typicality conditions.

Specifically taking up the cue offered by frame and script theories, Jackendoff (1987) has suggested treating a frame's or a script's conditions as 'preference rules'. A preference rule is usually cast in the form *Prefer to see A as B given a set of conditions C*, and it describes a discrete cognitive decision based on inductive clues, graded judgements, and typicality characteristics (its set of conditions). A 'preference rule system' is an ordered set of primary and secondary preference rules all clamouring to contribute to the cognitive decision currently required. In fact it is this competition within the system which allows alternative decisions and ultimately determines whether a phenomenon is perceived as 'standard, stereotypical, new, unusual, indeterminate or persistently ambiguous' (Jackendoff 1987: 252). In the case of textual data, frames and scripts supply the defaults that fill gaps (*see* GAPPING) and provide the presuppositions that enable one to understand what the text is about. Many higher-level communication and comprehension strategies discussed in the literature – especially the speaker/hearer assumptions and felicity conditions of *speech acts (Searle), the 'implicatures' of cooperative communication (Grice), the mental modelling of narrative situations (Jahn 1997), and the heuristics of reading a text as a token of a particular narrative genre (Herman 2002) – lend themselves to being formulated as hearer/reader-oriented preference rule systems.

Frames of real-life experience, narrative mediation, and narrative genres are also used as hierarchically ordered cognitive modules in Fludernik's (1996) pathbreaking design of a *natural narratology. Discussing the *aesthetic* (non-deceptive) illusionism of narrative texts, Fludernik contrasts (a) a level of theoretical abstraction which considers the materiality of the text and carefully notes the presence of cognitive signals, cues, and triggers, and (b) a level of natural interpretation on which ordinary (but competent) readers construct naturalised or narrativised readings (*see* NATURALISATION). Thus natural narratology is able to explain how readers are likely to understand a text and at the same time to indicate which P-world description is likely to be used in an articulation of that understanding. To maintain this twofold aim, the theorist must strongly resist the temptation to duplicate the moves of natural interpretation on the theoretical level. Consequently, natural narratology views many standard narratological terms, including narrators, voice, and narrative conceptions of time and space as P-world entities.

Cognitive failure and cognitive dynamics

Although the cognitive correlatives of frames and scripts are highly efficient inference engines, they are not fail-safe devices. In fact, cognitive slip-ups are an important source of evidence, and a particularly notorious type of cognitive failure is known as the 'garden-path effect'. The example commonly cited is the sentence 'The horse raced past the barn fell', a construction which traps the reader/hearer in a processing error from which it is hard if not impossible to recover. (The sentence's subject is not, as everybody spontaneously thinks, 'the horse' but 'the horse (that was) raced past the barn' – which means that the sentence is just as well-formed and meaningful as, for instance, 'The horse ridden past the barn fell', which presents no processing difficulty at all.) What garden-path cases demonstrate is that cognition can get tripped up by following a strong first preference – such as to read 'raced' as a past-tense verb rather than a past participle. What makes the garden-path effect particularly relevant within the framework of narratological analysis is that 'garden pathing' can be shown to occur in many types of narratives including short and seemingly *simple forms such as jokes and riddles, where they are in fact instrumental in creating a central

effect. One of the most famous literary garden-path narratives is Ambrose Bierce's 'An Occurrence at Owl Creek Bridge', in which the wholly unexpected death of the protagonist at the end of the story requires a radical reinterpretation of the preceding passages.

In a major essay on 'literary dynamics' in Faulkner's 'A Rose for Emily', Menakhem Perry (1979) presents an analysis of the cognitive frames that are used (and sometimes discarded) in the process of reading a narrative text. In Perry's use of the concept, a frame captures a reader's current knowledge representation vis-à-vis questions like 'What is happening? What is the state of affairs? What is the situation? Where is this happening? What are the motives? What is the purpose? What is the speaker's position?'. Drawing on findings of studies in visual cognition and character-attribution, Perry is particularly interested in frame-replacement heuristics, including the relevance of discarded readings and the impact of first and second readings. Conducting a similar inquiry into literary dynamics, Meir Sternberg has pointed out that many narrative texts employ strategic cues that trigger analogues of the 'primacy' and 'recency' effects found in cognitive laboratory experiments. As Sternberg points out, works of fiction frequently manipulate the reader's appreciation of characters, especially when intentionally misleading 'first impressions' have to be revised as the narrative progresses.

High-level literary dynamics are also at issue when readers construct mental representations of *storyworlds, as Herman (2002) shows in great detail. According to Herman, the key to the logic of stories and storytelling lies in the preference rules and processing strategies of cognitive (re)construction, simultaneously facilitating *narrative comprehension and the creation of intelligent world models (*see* NARRATIVE INTELLIGENCE).

This is not the place to review the more general cognitive-psychological issues of storytelling, but for standard introductions to what is now usually identified as *narrative psychology, Sarbin (1986) is a much-cited reference text, while Vincent Hevern provides an excellent Internet resource guide, and Dixon and Bortolussi (2003) have staked out a claim for a field called 'psychonarratology'. Jerome Bruner, one of the major forces behind the cognitive turn in the humanities, is rightly famous for his explorations into narrative self-conceptions and 'narrative identities'. Focusing on mechanisms such as 'indexing' and 'reminding', Roger Schank (1995) has investigated the social and psychological issues of intelligent reciprocal storytelling. Culling evidence from narrative texts as well as neuro-scientific research, Mark Turner (1996) argues that cognitive processes are of an essentially literary character and that humans are unique in their ability to blend concepts and stories in order to access ever more complex frames and scripts.

Interdisciplinary communication

Situated at a point where the narrative and cognitive turns meet, cognitive narratology provides a meeting ground for many disciplines, including literature, history, linguistics, pragmatics, *philosophy, and psychology. If cognitive narratology is to succeed as an interdisciplinary project, the participant disciplines must be encouraged to look over their respective fences, but they must also be allowed to pursue their special interpretive strategies. As in many other social scenarios, it is the cognitive strategies themselves that can be brought to bear on the situation. The principle of 'seeing X as Y' that informs the constructivist approach to cognitive investigation, combined with the theories of *possible worlds (Ryan) and mental spaces (Fauconnier 1994), is in fact eminently suited for encouraging interdisciplinary communication. Already, notable synergetic effects are beginning to emerge. As the essays collected in Herman (2003) show, theorists have begun to develop integrational rather than local models; the empirical and technical camps have become receivers as well as suppliers of testable hypotheses; and fictional as well as factual narratives have come to be recognised as treasure-troves of cognitive exploration.

SEE ALSO: mimesis; situation model

References and further reading

Marisa Bortolussi, and Dixon, Peter (2003) *Psychonarratology*, Cambridge: Cambridge University Press.
Duchan, Judith F., Gail A. Bruder, and Lynne E. Hewitt (eds) (1995) *Deixis in Narrative: A Cognitive Science Perspective*, Hillsdale: Erlbaum.
Fauconnier, Gilles (1994) *Mental Spaces: Aspects of Meaning Construction in Natural Language*, Cambridge: Cambridge University Press.
Fludernik, Monika (1996) *Towards a 'Natural' Narratology*, London: Routledge.
Gerrig, Richard J (1993) *Experiencing Narrative Worlds: On the Psychological Activities of Reading*, New Haven: Yale University Press.
Herman, David (2002) *Story Logic: Problems and Possibilities of Narrative*, Lincoln: University of Nebraska Press.
—— (ed.) (2003) *Narrative Theory and the Cognitive Sciences*, Stanford: CSLI Publications.
Jackendoff, Ray (1983) *Semantics and Cognition*, London: MIT Press.
—— (1987) *Consciousness and the Computational Mind*, London: MIT Press.
Jahn, Manfred (1997) 'Frames, Preferences, and the Reading of Third-person Narratives: Towards a Cognitive Narratology', *Poetics Today*, 18.4, 441–68.
—— (1999) '"Speak, friend, and enter": Garden Paths, Artificial Intelligence, and Cognitive Narratology', in David Herman (ed.) (1999) *Narratologies: New Perspectives on Narrative Analysis*, Columbus: Ohio State University Press.
—— (2004) 'Foundational Issues in Teaching Cognitive Narratology', *EJES*, 8.1, 105–27.
Margolin, Uri (2003) 'Cognitive Science, the Thinking Mind, and Literary Narrative', in David Herman (ed.) *Narrative Theory and the Cognitive Sciences*, Stanford: CSLI Publications.
Perry, Menakhem (1979) 'Literary Dynamics: How the Order of a Text Creates Its Meanings', *Poetics Today*, 1–2, 35–64; 311–61.
Sarbin, T. R. (ed.) (1986) *Narrative Psychology: The Storied Nature of Human Conduct*, New York: Praeger.
Schank, Roger C. (1995) *Tell Me a Story: Narrative and Intelligence*, Evanston: Northwestern University Press.
Sternberg, Meir (1993) *Expositional Modes and Temporal Ordering in Fiction*, Bloomington: Indiana University Press.
Turner, Mark (1996) *The Literary Mind*, Oxford: Oxford University Press.

MANFRED JAHN

COINCIDENCE

In the coincidence *plot, the paths of *characters with a previous connection intersect in the *time and *space of the *storyworld, in apparently random circumstances. In the most powerful form the connection is one of kinship, leading to scenes of recognition which can be catastrophic (*Oedipus Rex*) or euphoric (*Jane Eyre*). See PLOT TYPES.

COMICS AND GRAPHIC NOVEL

The use of graphic forms to present narrative dates back to earliest human times. *Media resembling what we today call comics have existed at least since the invention of the printing press and were first used extensively in gallows broadsheets in the seventeenth century. The Victorian era saw the first flowering of the 'comic strip' – a short (one page or less) graphic narrative printed in newspapers or magazines. In the first decade of the twentieth century dramatic experimentation with the form established comic strips as a serious artistic concern (see, for example, Winsor McCay's *Little Nemo in Slumberland*). The 'comic book' followed in the 1920s. This was most often a multipage booklet with a longer narrative, or several narratives, marketed directly to children and teenagers (see CHILDREN'S STORIES (NARRATIVES WRITTEN FOR CHILDREN)). The graphic novel, an extended narrative geared towards adult readers and incorporating both text and *images, has gained followers since the 1980s. The term 'comix' is often applied to graphic narratives intended for adult audiences, signalling that these works are not necessarily 'comic' in their intent. Sabin (1996) provides a comprehensive history of the development of these narrative *genres.

A narratological method specific to comics and the graphic novel must take into account both textual and graphic elements in the panels, a challenge for critics habituated to text-based narrative. Images must contain details that propel the story forward, saving (literal) page space that would otherwise be required for textual *exposition. Transitional elements which move the narrative from one scene to the next, visual elements which condense or elide textual or verbal elements, and framing devices which negotiate between the temporalities of the verbal/textual *narration, all contribute to a complex narrative method (see PICTORIAL NARRATIVITY; SUMMARY AND SCENE; TIME IN NARRATIVE).

Eisner (1990 [1985]) wrote the first book-length study of the mechanics of graphic narratives and did so in graphic form. Already famous for his 'Spirit' series of graphic novels, Eisner deploys his skills to demonstrate how the passage of time, the establishment of setting (see SPACE IN NARRATIVE), and the tone of the narration translate from spoken or written language to image. He then establishes a theory of panel size and style relative to narrative. For instance, long, stretched-out panels slow the pace of the narrative; small, successive ones speed it up. Eisner also analyses in detail the use of panel framing to establish *point of view and mood.

McCloud (1996), another comic artist, also presents his theories in graphic form. McCloud builds on Eisner's account to elaborate a theory of comics based on both visual symbols (the 'vocabulary' of comics) and on 'closure', which he defines as the reader's ability to imagine the actions which are not drawn, but which must take place between the drawn panels (see GAPPING; READER-RESPONSE THEORY). Note, however, that this definition is unrelated to that offered by narrative theorists for *closure in print narratives. McCloud argues that the reader closes the gap when she 'draws' for herself those actions which take place in the spaces between the panels (the 'gutter'). For McCloud, the gutter takes on both typographical and phenomenological significance; he calls closure the 'grammar' of comics. Like Eisner, McCloud emphasises the ways in which comics substitute visual space for time, by relying on relative size and shape of successive panels (see VISUAL NARRATIVITY). Also like Eisner he investigates stylistic issues, including line width and type as used to convey *emotion and the lettering styles used to capture the essence of sound.

Harvey (1996) takes issue with McCloud's emphasis on sequence as the essential character of the medium. Harvey himself insists on the importance of the relationship of the verbal to the visual in comics, and also applies the term 'closure'– not to the reader's completion of missing information in a sequence, but rather to an undefined semantic association made between word and image. *The Art of the Comic Book* provides close studies of the narrative experimentation of artists from the 1930s to the 1990s and devotes a chapter to the relationship between *film and comics, a subject Eisner (1996) also takes up in his second work devoted to the analysis of the genre.

Perhaps the first comprehensive 'reading' of a graphic narrative focused on those techniques which translate from print narratives is Spiegelman (1999 [1968]). An analysis of Bernard Krigstein's short graphic fiction, 'Master Race', Spiegelman's article was published well in advance of major theoretical approaches to comic narrative. In it, Spiegelman analyses panel size and shape, the use of strong, repeating horizontal and vertical elements to create mood and represent motion, the problems of limited panel space, the blending of flashbacks and foreshadowing (see TEMPORAL ORDERING), and the iconic reduction of visual signs. Many of the techniques he pinpoints here would be deployed later in his own critically acclaimed graphic narratives, including *Maus*.

Several literary critics have addressed the narratology of comics as part of a larger investigation into *narrative structure. Chatman (1978), like McCloud, analyses the reader's response to the events taking place between the panels in comic strips – in a discussion of the reader's ability to infer abstract narrative statements. O'Neill (1994) uses the newspaper strip *Calvin and Hobbes*, by Ben Watterson, to illustrate the complexities of *focalization, and Gary Larson's *The Far Side* to demonstrate the ludic effects of *metalepsis.

SEE ALSO: cinéroman; graphic presentation as expressive device; novel, the

References and further reading

Chatman, Seymour (1978) *Story and Discourse: Narrative Structure in Fiction and Film*, Ithaca: Cornell University Press.
Eisner, Will (1990 [1985]) *Comics and Sequential Art*, Tamarac: Poorhouse Press.
—— (1996) *Graphic Storytelling and Visual Narrative*, Tamarac: Poorhouse Press.
Harvey, Robert C. (1996) *The Art of the Comic Book: An Aesthetic History*, Jackson: University Press of Mississippi.
McCay, Winsor (1989) *The Complete Little Nemo in Slumberland*, vol. 1: 1905–1907, New York: Fantagraphics Press.
McCloud, Scott (1996) *Understanding Comics: The Invisible Art*, New York: Harper Perennial.
O'Neill, Patrick (1994) *Fictions of Discourse: Reading Narrative Theory*, Toronto: University of Toronto Press.
Sabin, Roger (1996) *Comics, Comix & Graphic Novels: A History of Comic Art*, London: Phaidon.
Spiegelman, Art (1999 [1968]) '"Master Race": The Graphic Story as an Art Form', in *Comics, Essays, Graphics and Scraps*, Rome: Centrale dell'Arte.

JEANNE C. EWERT

COMING-OUT STORY

Frequently found in short stories and novels of the 1970s and 1980s, the coming-out story centres on the formation of a protagonist's homosexual *identity and his or her self-disclosure to other *characters. Because of its affiliation with gay and lesbian identity politics it tends to promote the notion of a stable self and the ideal of a unified, uncontradicted community. Both in *autobiographical texts and in real life two dimensions of coming-out can be distinguished: an interior process of self-recognition and an exterior process of making one's sexual orientation public. The coming-out story resembles the *Bildungsroman and the initiation story in that it involves a quest, a mentor figure, and a journey; but it also deviates from these generic models by portraying the protagonist's entry into a subculture rather than his or her integration into heteronormative society (*see* GENRE THEORY IN NARRATIVE STUDIES).

The narrative *telos* of paradigmatic coming-out novels such as Rita Mae Brown's *Rubyfruit Jungle* (1973) or David Leavitt's *The Lost Language of Cranes* (1986) lies in the reassessment of the protagonist's identity and the recognition of the acceptability of same-sex relationships. Strategies of inversion are used to turn conventional value systems upside down so that homosexuality is seen to correlate with 'nature' and 'authenticity'. The central concept of a hidden, authentic self which needs to be liberated goes back to Radclyffe Hall's *The Well of Loneliness* (1928). Contrary to the Bildungsroman *hero, the coming-out protagonist has to make an effort to 'unlearn' gender-specific norms of behaviour in order to survive in a homophobic culture. The coming-out story typically either ends in rebellion and escape, as in Elizabeth Riley's *All that False Instruction* (1975), or generates a tragic ending in exile and suicide, as in Andrew Holleran's *Dancer from the Dance* (1978). With their emphasis on dialogue and colloquial style, written coming-out stories often mimic oral storytelling (Martin 1988; *see* CONVERSATIONAL STORYTELLING; ORALITY).

As 'narratives of identification' (Roof 1996) addressed to a potentially gay or lesbian readership (*see* AUDIENCE), coming-out stories are eminently political. Within the lesbian-feminist subculture of the 1970s, the telling of coming-out stories was considered a *rite de passage* leading to the formation of a collective identity (Zimmerman 1990). From the 1980s on, coming-out stories have been increasingly criticised for their ethnic and racial exclusions and for their sole focus on young protagonists. With the rise of *queer theory, the 1970s model of the coming-out story went out of fashion. *Fantasy and *magical realism are increasingly used to queer the textual world or provide imaginative retreats (as in Jeanette Winterson's *Oranges Are Not the Only Fruit*, 1985, or Paul Magrs's *Could It Be Magic?*, 1997), and AIDS stories have begun to explore new and far more dangerous sites of knowledge and secrecy (as in Dominique Fernandez's *Gloire de Paria*, 1987).

SEE ALSO: adolescent narrative; gender studies; life story

References and further reading

Martin, Biddy (1988) 'Lesbian Identity and Autobiographical Difference[s]', in Bella Brodzki and Celeste Schenck (eds) *Life/Lines: Theorizing Women's Autobiography*, Ithaca: Cornell University Press.
Roof, Judith (1996) *Come As You Are: Sexuality and Narrative*, New York: Columbia University Press.
Zimmerman, Bonnie (1990) *The Safe Sea of Women: Lesbian Fiction 1969–1989*, Boston: Beacon.

ANDREA GUTENBERG

COMMENTARY

Commentary is a general category designating those speech acts (*see* SPEECH ACT THEORY) by a *narrator that go beyond providing the facts of the fictional world and the recounting of *events. (For this reason they are also occasionally identified as 'authorial intrusions' or 'interventions'.) Belonging to the static modes of a narrative (Bonheim 1982), comments by a narrator can be distinguished from *description, the dynamic modes of a narrative (especially report or *narration proper), summary, *speech representation, and reader *address. Although comments have been attacked in the name of objectivity and are usually set off from 'pure' narrative modes such as report, scene, and summary (*see* SUMMARY AND SCENE), they form an integral part of the 'rhetoric of fiction' (Booth 1961; *see* RHETORICAL APPROACHES TO NARRATIVE). Comments are typically made by overt and omniscient narrators (*see* NARRATIVE SITUATIONS), but they can also occur in the context of homodiegetic and autodiegetic narration as well as in *voice-over narration in *film (Chatman 1990).

The wide umbrella of 'commentary' actually subsumes utterances which refer to different elements of a narrative and fulfil different functions (Nünning 1989). Following Chatman's *story-discourse distinction, two basic kinds of comments can be distinguished: commentary on the story and commentary on the discourse (Chatman 1978). The former can be subdivided into explanatory, evaluative, and generalising comments, while the latter refers to the act of narration rather than to the represented world of the characters. In commentary on the story, a narrator can explain or interpret an event, a character's motivation, or the significance of a narrative element (interpretation), express his or her personal values and moral opinions (judgement), or express 'gnomic' and philosophical statements (generalisation). Commentary on the discourse includes self-reflexive and self-conscious references to the act or process of narration (*see* METANARRATIVE COMMENT; REFLEXIVITY). All types of commentary can either be explicit or implicit (*see* IRONY; RELIABILITY). Commentary can fulfil a variety of functions: it can be merely ornamental, but it can also serve important rhetorical or ideological purposes (Nünning 1989; *see* IDEOLOGY AND NARRATIVE). Since it conveys a narrator's *voice, values, and norms more distinctly than any other feature of a narrative, commentary can project an image of the narrator as honest, insincere, or morally untrustworthy (Lanser 1981). *Feminist narratologists have pointed out that narratorial interventions can either function as a distancing device or as one which engages the reader's sympathy (Warhol 1989).

References and further reading

Bonheim, Helmut (1982) *The Narrative Modes*, Cambridge: Brewer.
Booth, Wayne C. (1983 [1961]) *The Rhetoric of Fiction*, Chicago: University of Chicago Press.
Chatman, Seymour (1978) *Story and Discourse: Narrative Structure in Fiction and Film*, Ithaca: Cornell University Press.
—— (1990) *Coming to Terms*, Ithaca: Cornell University Press.
Lanser, Susan Sniader (1981) *The Narrative Act: Point of View in Prose Fiction*, Princeton: Princeton University Press.
Nünning, Ansgar (1989) *Grundzüge eines kommunikationstheoretischen Modells der erzählerischen Vermittlung*, Trier: WVT.
Warhol, Robyn R. (1989) *Gendered Interventions: Narrative Discourse in the Victorian Novel*, New Brunswick, NJ: Rutgers University Press.

ANSGAR NÜNNING

COMMUNICATION IN NARRATIVE

Anthropologists, linguists, and folklorists often isolate narratives from the processes of interaction within which they emerge before submitting them to analysis. Indeed, by eliciting narratives through the use of interview questions, the researcher effectively treats as inconsequential the interactional context within which such narratives are situated. In contrast, contemporary work in both conversation analysis and linguistic anthropology treats narratives not as isolable, self-contained objects but as stories embedded both within larger frameworks of activity and within a sequentially organised series of turns-at-talk (see Goodwin 1990; Ochs 1997). For conversational participants narratives are accountably occasioned within particular communicative events. This can be seen through a consideration of the manner in which such stories are initiated and, in particular, through an examination of a specific practice, called a story preface, routinely used by tellers to begin stories in conversation.

The following example is taken from a recording of a dinner-time conversation. The participants are three siblings, Virginia, Wes, and Beth, their mother, and Wes's girlfriend Prudence ('she' = Beth). (A note on the transcription. Parentheses are used to indicate the onset and termination of simultaneous talk in contiguous lines. Numbers (e.g., 0.4) are used to indicate the length, in seconds, of pauses. Colons indicate lengthening of the sound they follow. 'h' indicates aspiration as an outbreath and sometimes as laughter within a word (e.g., *porkc(h)ho(h)ps*). '°h' indicates inbreath).

37.	PRU: →	You know what she said one ti:me?
38.		(.)
39.		((dog bark))
40.		(0.4)
41.	PRU: →	One [night we were talki- we had porkchops fer dinner an' =
42.	VIR:	[( )
43.	PRU:	= thuh next mornin' I went tuh wake her u(huh)p °hm! an' she
44.		was in thuh bed goin' (1.1) they're porkchops. They're all:
45.		porkchops. People are porkc(h)-ho(h)ps sih hih high heh
46.	WES:	heh heh heh
47.		(.)
48.	PRU:	hhhh uhh! A(h)ll thuh p(h)eop-(h)le a(h)re p(h)orkcha(h)
49.		hh uh h[hh

In ordinary conversation such as we are considering here the organisation of speaking turns is locally managed on a turn-by-turn basis. As Sacks *et al.* (1974) demonstrated, participants anticipate points where the current turn will be complete. Such projected points of possible completion

constitute 'discrete places in the developing course of a speaker's talk (. . .) at which ending the turn or continuing it, transfer of the turn or its retention become relevant (Schegloff 1992: 116). These points are, then, transition-relevant. Story prefaces, such as Prudence's 'You know what she said one time?' solve a problem generated by this system. In telling a story, a speaker often reaches completion of a turn-unit (e.g., 'we had porkchops for dinner') without thereby completing the story. In such cases, in order to allow for the telling of a story in its entirety, the usual association of turn completion and transition relevance must be suspended. A story preface allows recipients to see that points of possible turn completion which fall within the scope of the preface are not transition-relevant and do not constitute opportunities for another speaker to take a turn.

Story-prefaces are also addressed to a related problem of how the turn-by-turn organisation of talk is to be resumed at story's completion. Thus, a preface provides recipients with clues regarding what the story will consist of and what it will take for the story to be over. So, in the example given, recipients can monitor Prudence's telling to locate 'something that Beth said' and, upon hearing such a thing, will have reason to expect the completion of the telling is imminent. Tellers – if not in the preface then elsewhere in the telling – also typically provide recipients with resources with which to determine what kind of a response is due at story's completion. Prudence, for instance, punctuates the final lines of her story with laugh tokens (e.g., line 45's 'porkc(h)ho(h)ps'), thereby marking this as something funny and the story as a whole as 'humorous' (*see* HUMOUR STUDIES AND NARRATIVE; JOKE).

Story prefaces do more than simply carve out a place for a story within an unfolding course of talk. Consider the following example from the same occasion. Here Wes and Virginia discuss Beth's excessive drinking.

32.	VIR: →	pt! You know the other weeken' [when she went downta =
33.	PR?:	[˙uhh
34.	VIR:	= Charleston?
35.	WES: →	She tried tuh quit smokin', I know that. B't she couldn'
36.		do that.
37.		(0.3)
38.	VIR: →	(Well,) (.) she wen' downta Charleston the other

39.	weeken' with Paul?
40.	(0.9)
41. VIR: →	An' Paul s[aid ( )
42. BET: →	[(They were) down there, stu:pid.
43.	(0.4)
44. PRU: →	An' wha'd Paul say?
45. VIR: →	Paul said she was laughin' 'er head
	off an' she was so:
46.	bombed.
47.	(0.2)
48. PRU: →	eh huh huh [huh

According to Sacks, the principle of 'recipient design' entails that a speaker should not tell his or her 'recipient what they already know' (1995: 438) (*see* PRAGMATICS). In aligning participants as story-recipients then, tellers are concerned to determine whether the story they propose to tell is 'news' for the recipient(s) – that it is not already known to them. In the second example, the participants' orientation to this aspect of recipient design is displayed with particular clarity. Thus, at line 42, Beth attempts to arrest and block Virginia's telling by suggesting that it violates the rule of recipient design: according to Beth, Virginia is telling Wes and Prudence what they already know ('They were down there, stupid'.). Beth's effort to block the telling appears successful and the story is only resumed after Prudence asks 'What did Paul say?', thereby suggesting that she is uninformed with respect to at least this component of the story. It is thus apparent that issues of newsworthiness are crucially implicated not only in the initiation of a story but also across the course of its production (*see* TELLABILITY).

Schegloff (1997: 97) notes that people generally tell stories to do something – 'to complain, to boast, to inform, to alert, to tease, to explain or excuse or justify, or to provide for an interactional environment in whose course or context or interstices such actions and interactional inflections can be accomplished'. Recipients of stories are then oriented not only to the story as a recognisable unit of talk distinguished by a variety of formal features, but also to *what is being accomplished* through its telling. In order to explicate this aspect of conversational storytelling it is necessary to situate stories within the particular sequences in which they are encountered by the participants. It is this location that provides the participants with the resources needed to discern what action is being performed through the story.

SEE ALSO: communication studies and narrative; conversational storytelling; discourse analysis (linguistics); ethnographic approaches to narrative; sociolinguistic approaches to narrative

Reference and further reading

Goodwin, Marjorie Harness (1990) *He-Said-She-Said: Talk as Social Organization among Black Children*, Bloomington: Indiana University Press.
Ochs, Elinor (1997) 'Narrative', in Teun A. van Dijk (ed.) *Discourse as Structure and Process*, London: Sage.
Sacks, Harvey (1995) *Lectures on Conversation*, vol. 2, Oxford: Blackwell.
——, Emanuel A. Schegloff, and Gail Jefferson (1974) 'A Simplest Systematics for the Organization of Turn-taking in Conversation', *Language*, 50.4, 696–735.
Schegloff, Emanuel A. (1992) 'To Searle on Conversation: A Note in Return', in John R. Searle *et al.* (eds) *(On) Searle on Conversation*, Amsterdam: John Benjamins.
——, (1997) '"Narrative Analysis" Thirty Years Later', *Journal of Narrative and Life History*, 7.1–4, 97–106.

JACK SIDNELL

COMMUNICATION STUDIES AND NARRATIVE

Narrative is so essential to the way humans speak, think, and act that communication scholars refer to homo sapiens as 'homo narrans' (Fisher 1987). From a communication perspective, narrative is an ongoing process of creating, using, and arranging symbols that organise human experience in sequential and consequential ways, as units of discourse and ways of seeing, behaving, and being (Fisher 1987: 63; Sunwolf and Frey 2001: 121). Narrative communication entails more than imitating life and enlightening or moving *audiences, as *ancient theories of narrative claim (Lucaites and Condit in Gerbner 1985); it is constitutive of every sphere of human activity, from *identity and relationship development, to the socialisation of individuals into institutions and cultures, to the invitation of audiences to identify with and participate in larger social, political, and public narratives (Gerbner 1985; Mumby 1993) (*see* INSTITUTIONAL NARRATIVE; SOCIOLOGY AND NARRATIVE).

Communication research on narrative emerged as an outgrowth of paradigm shifts within the field of communication and related disciplines. In the mid-twentieth century, communication research generally explored either the production of messages and what they represented, or perceptions of them and their effects. In the 1960s, social constructionist and symbolic interactionist theories contributed more systemic and dialectical conceptions of communication to research in the field. In the ensuing decades, research began to link the effects of messages with features of their design (e.g., Gerbner's research highlights the 'cultivating' effects of *television storytelling (Morgan 2002)). Inspired by Kuhn's treatise on scientific paradigms, communication scholars in the 1970s sought their own universal model to explain human communication behaviour. In 1984, Fisher introduced the 'narrative paradigm' as a metaphor for entire processes of producing and perceiving messages. In addition to message design and effects, communication researchers now consider narrative to be central to the construction of culture, identity, relationships, and social movements.

The narrative paradigm offers conceptions of narrative as more than a specific literary *genre or an element of *rhetorical discourse (Fisher 1987: 59). For Fisher, narrative is a mode of reasoning that directs rhetorical inquiry, invites moral evaluation, and guides human behaviour through various recounting and accounting practices (Fisher 1987: 62) (see NARRATIVE AS COGNITIVE INSTRUMENT). While its assertion that all human communication constitutes *narration has been challenged (Gerbner 1985; Mandelbaum 2003), Fisher's paradigm has been embraced by communication studies as a humanistic and democratising alternative to elite scientific paradigms for explaining human behaviour (see SCIENCE AND NARRATIVE). The narrative paradigm claims that audiences participate in the construction and assessment of communication messages through their evaluation of 'narrative fidelity' (whether and how narratives 'ring true') and 'narrative probability' (whether and how narratives cohere) (Fisher 1987: 47–48). Defining communication as an intersubjective and accessible process, Fisher's theory marks a shift away from normative theories of communication that are concerned with efficacy to constitutive theories of communication that are concerned with human epistemology, ontology, and motivation.

Despite its focus on specific forms of narrative ('recounting' and 'accounting for') and communication (literary texts and public discourse), the narrative paradigm has spawned far-reaching explorations of narrative in communication studies.

Narrative communication is examined in interpersonal, organisational, public, and mediated contexts. Using methods derived from *sociolinguistics (Labov 1972), conversation analysis (Sacks 1992), *semiotics, *poststructuralist approaches to narrative, and *Artificial Intelligence research, communication researchers analyse the many forms narrative communication takes in interviews, interactions, institutional procedures, public address, *performances, and media productions, including *anecdotes, accounts, complaints, *jokes, *myths, stories, and reports. The features of narrative they analyse include participants' methods of evaluating narrative to convey the point of its telling (Labov 1972), replaying experience and orienting it to various recipients (Goffman 1974), and engaging others to collaborate in storytelling and related activities (Sacks 1992). Applying concepts from Burke's (1945) theories of symbolic action, Goffman's (1974) theories of social interaction (including *frame theory), and *speech act theories to their structural analyses of narrative, communication scholars build explanations of communication problems, practices, and phenomena that emerge from humans' efforts to achieve mutual understanding and accomplish social action.

Communication theories of narrative include explanations of (a) media representations as vehicles of myth and *ideology (Hall 1997), (b) narrative discourse used by members of institutions such as families, organisations, and the media to socialise, legitimise, and exercise social control (Langellier, Witten, and Zelizer in Mumby 1993), and (c) narrative practices used in interaction to manage 'dispreferred' activities such as complaining, blaming, criticising, and delivering bad news (Mandelbaum 2003).

SEE ALSO: communication in narrative; conversational storytelling; discourse analysis (linguistics); ethnographic approaches to narrative; media and narrative; narrative turn in the humanities

References and further reading

Berger, Arthur Asa (1997) Narratives in Popular Culture, Media, and Everyday Life, Thousand Oaks, CA: Sage.
Burke, Kenneth (1945) A Grammar of Motives, New York: Prentice-Hall.
Fisher, Walter R. (1987) Human Communication as Narration: Toward a Philosophy of Reason, Value, and Action, Columbia, SC: University of South Carolina Press.

Gerbner, George (ed.) (1985) 'Homo Narrans: Story-Telling in Mass Culture and Everyday Life: A Symposium', *Journal of Communication*, 35, 73–171.

Goffman, Erving (1974) *Frame Analysis: An Essay on the Organization of Experience*, New York: Harper and Row.

Hall, Stuart (ed.) (1997) *Representation: Cultural Representations and Signifying Practices*, London: Sage.

Labov, William (1972) 'The Transformation of Experience in Narrative Syntax', in *Language in the Inner City: Studies in the Black English Vernacular*, Philadelphia: University of Pennsylvania Press.

Langellier, Kristin M. (1989) 'Personal Narratives: Perspectives on Theory and Research', *Text and Performance Quarterly*, 9, 243–76.

Mandelbaum, Jenny (2003) 'How to "Do Things" with Narrative: A Communication Perspective on Narrative Skill', in John O. Greene and Brant R. Burleson (eds) *Handbook of Communication and Social Interaction skills*, Mahwah, NJ: Erlbaum.

Morgan, Michael (ed.) (2002) *Against the Mainstream: The Selected Works of George Gerbner*, New York: Lang.

Mumby, Dennis (ed.) (1993) *Narrative and Social Control: Sage Annual Review of Communication Research*, 21, Newbury Park, CA: Sage.

Sacks, Harvey (1992) *Lectures on Conversation*, vol. 2, Gail Jefferson (ed.), Oxford: Blackwell.

Sunwolf and Lawrence R. Frey (2001) 'Storytelling: The Power of Narrative Communication and Interpretation', in W. Peter Robinson and Howard Giles (eds) *The New Handbook of Language and Social Psychology*, Chichester: Wiley.

KATHLEEN C. HASPEL

COMPOSITE NOVEL

The term 'composite novel', coined by Maggie Dunn and Ann Morris in 1995, refers to the short story cycle, that is to say to collections of *short stories which share common settings and *characters. Such texts therefore display some overall *thematic and structural features, allowing readers to follow the development of one or more characters through the sequence of tales. Prominent modernist examples of the *genre are James Joyce's *Dubliners* (1914), Sherwood Anderson's *Winesburg, Ohio* (1919), and Ernest Hemingway's *In Our Time* (1923), as well as William Faulkner's *The Unvanquished* (1938) and *Go Down Moses* (1942). Despite some possible antecedents in Kipling's tales from the 1890s in which the locale remains constant and at least one major character called Strickland is featured in a number of texts, the genre has thrived almost exclusively in the United States (Hamlin Garland, Tama Janowitz, Sarah Orne Jewett, Garrison Keillor, William Saroyan, Joyce Carol Oates, John Updike, and Eudora Welty) as well as in (expatriate) Indian fiction in English, e.g., Shauna Singh Baldwin, Chitra Banerjee Divakaruni, Gita Mehta, Rohinton Mistry, Raja Rao, Robbie Clipper Sethi, Sara Suleri, and M. G. Vassanji. The connection between stories in the cycle can be sporadic and superficial, with the emphasis on the individual tales (Janowitz, Mistry), but some composite novels use the form to portray the life of a community (Welty, Anderson) or to trace the development of one major character in a manner reminiscent of the *Bildungsroman (George in *Winesburg, Ohio*).

The short story cycle should be linked to forms of multiperspectivism since it frequently serves to portray the diversity of life in a given community, presenting a spectrum of views and philosophies of life found among its members (*see* PERSPECTIVE). Although some short story cycles are actually set in large cities, the genre overwhelmingly features small towns, villages, and rural or ethnic communities. Common themes are the boredom of provincial life or the deadening conformity affecting villagers.

Narratologically speaking, composite novels often alternate between homo- and heterodiegetic *narration, and external and internal *focalization. In addition, many collections deploy the first-person plural pronoun in *reference to the villagers and thus adumbrate versions of we-narrative (*see* PERSON). Finally, the composite novel bears comparison with novel series like Faulkner's Yoknapatawpha County novels or Balzac's *La Comédie Humaine* which also have a common setting and share a number of recurring characters.

SEE ALSO: novel, the; serial form

References and further reading

Dunn, Maggie and Ann Morris (1995) *The Composite Novel: The Short Story Cycle in Transition*, New York: Twayne.

Kennedy, J. Gerald (1995) *Modern American Short Story Sequences*, Cambridge: Cambridge University Press.

MONIKA FLUDERNIK

COMPUTATIONAL APPROACHES TO NARRATIVE

All computational approaches to narrative involve an encounter between technology and culture. However, these approaches can differ significantly with regard to the 'how' and the 'why' motivating their individual practices, and more fundamentally in their understanding of what a computer and a narrative actually are. In order to make this diversity transparent the present overview will consider two defining characteristics: methodology and objectives.

Computational approaches to narrative range from those which are *computer-aided* to those which are, at least in theory, fully *computerised*. Computer-aided approaches use computers as tools which may aid or augment the application of human intelligence to narratives; computerised approaches, by contrast, attempt to emulate and automate what some researchers refer to as a specifically human *'narrative intelligence' (Mateas and Senger 2003). Computational approaches to (textual) narrative can pursue three different goals: (1) the production or (2) the analysis of concrete narratives and (3) the modelling of narrative intelligence. The modelling of narrative intelligence may focus either on the processes by which humans understand narrative representations, or else on the processes by which they generate them.

1. Authoring tools: The computer-aided production of narratives is the purpose of writing or editing tools, such as *WritePro FictionMaster*. Whereas most programs amount to little more than an electronic creative writing seminar, some are indeed based on fairly elaborate theories of *plot and *character design implemented in their algorithms, as in the case of *Dramatica Pro*. Typically, these tools prompt the user to define initial parameters, such as *genre and characters, and will then use this input to generate storyline and character templates which the writer must subsequently expand into natural language text. Design principles and program algorithms generally try to enforce adherence to conventions believed to be crucial to a commercially successful mainstream narrative.

2. Analytical tools: Compared with authoring tools, tools developed for the computational analysis of narrative are more directly related to narrative theory and narratology. Narratological theories typically focus on high-level concepts such as temporal structure, plot, character, genre etc. (*see* TIME IN NARRATIVE). Interestingly enough, though textual analysis is one of the primary concerns of humanities computing, hardly any software tools dedicated to the computational analysis of narratives in terms of these high-level concepts have been developed to date. Why?

Typically, the features that set narratives apart from other kinds of textual representations cannot be identified solely on the basis of words. For example, in order to identify a prolepsis (a flash-forward) in a narrative, we must normally interpret the meaning of words holistically on the level of sentence and then relate that interpretation to the information contained in other sentences (see Stoicheff *et al.*, 2003) (*see* DISCOURSE ANALYSIS (LINGUISTICS); TEMPORAL ORDERING). This is beyond the capability of algorithms designed to identify and interpret linguistic phenomena up to the sentence level. Indeed, even the algorithmic identification of an individual word's meaning will succeed only if the word is used in a standardised (in most cases: its literal) sense. *Metaphors, analogies, and allusions pose serious problems to machine intelligence (see McCarty 2003).

Since the 1970s computational linguists have slowly begun to bridge the gap between the processing of basic linguistic features and that of high-level semantic and *hermeneutic concepts (examples include work in computational stylometry, corpus analysis, authorship attribution, theme and content analysis, and the analysis of text coherence) (*see* AUTHOR; THEMATIC APPROACHES TO NARRATIVE). Yet for the time being the many-layered and inference-based semantics of a narrative will be fully accessible to a computer only if the text is available in machine-readable format and is either accompanied by an extensive dictionary or a formal representation of its meaning (*see* NARRATIVE SEMANTICS). The development of mark-up languages such as *Standardized General Markup Language* (SGML) and mark-up conventions as set down by the *Text Encoding Initiative* (TEI) have therefore received particular attention since the late 1980s. Text encoding makes explicit formal as well as semantic features by inserting machine-readable descriptors (tags) into the text. Once these are present we can run algorithms that will analyse a text for specific tags and tag constellations. Text encoding of some features – for example, proper names as indicators for characters – can be partially automated by using parsers that look up words in a dictionary or check predefined syntax patterns (*see* NAMING IN NARRATIVE). However, the bulk of more challenging interpretive encoding still has to be done manually.

3. Modelling narrative intelligence: Understanding the processes by which humans interpret, react to, and generate narrative representations was historically the first objective of literary and aesthetic reflection. From Aristotle's *Poetics* to present-day narratology, this functional perspective on storytelling remains one of the dominant topics in theories of narrative. However, computational approaches to modelling narrative intelligence actually originated outside this tradition. They are mostly based on two modern methodologies which only developed in the latter half of the twentieth century: cognitive science and *Artifical Intelligence (AI).

Cognitivist theories and principles commonly inform the computational modelling of how humans understand narratives as narratives – for example, how they identify an action in a narrative representation (Meister 2003). AI-related approaches, on the other hand, try to conceptualise algorithms that can produce natural-language narratives, sometimes drawing on *story grammars. However, even the most advanced storytelling machines can at best produce domain-specific concrete narratives (Bringsjord and Ferrucci 2000), while the integration of narratological and computational models of narrative and the field of *digital narrative have already resulted in challenging new ways of conceptualising narrative in general (Ryan 1991, 2001). This suggests that the most important contribution which computational approaches can make to our understanding of narrative may well be of a theoretical rather than of a practical nature.

SEE ALSO: cognitive narratology

References and further reading

Bringsjord, Selmer, and David Ferrucci (2000) *Artificial Intelligence and Literary Creativity: Inside the Mind of BRUTUS, a Storytelling Machine*, Mahwah, NJ: Erlbaum.
Mateas, Michael, and Phoebe Senger (eds) (2003) *Narrative Intelligence*, Amsterdam: John Benjamins.
McCarty, Willard (2003) *Depth, Markup and Modelling*, http://www.kcl.ac.uk/humanities/cch/wlm/essays/depth/Depth.html
Meister, Jan Christoph (2003) *Computing Action: A Narratological Approach*, New York: de Gruyter.
Ryan, Marie-Laure (1991) *Possible Worlds, Artificial Intelligence, And Narrative Theory*, Bloomington: Indiana University Press.
—— (2001) *Narrative as Virtual Reality: Immersion and Interactivity in Literature and Electronic Media*, Baltimore: Johns Hopkins University Press.
Stoicheff, R. P., Allison Muri, Joel Deshaye, *et al.* (2003) *The Sound and the Fury: a Hypertext Edition*, University of Saskatchewan, http://www.usask.ca/english/faulkner
TAPoR (ongoing) *Textual Analysis Portal for Research*, http://tapor.ualberta.ca/
TEI (ongoing) Text Encoding Initiative, http://www.tei-c.org/

JAN CHRISTOPH MEISTER

COMPUTER GAMES AND NARRATIVE

Game designer and theorist Brenda Laurel has described 'interactive stories' as 'an elusive unicorn we can imagine but have yet to capture' (*see* INTERACTIVE FICTION). The relationship between games and stories provokes disagreements among game theorists and critics, designers, and players. Several factors make this debate difficult to resolve: first, the computer game is an emergent form undergoing rapid technological change and aesthetic experimentation; second, the computer game is a hybrid medium, which combines traits of several different cultural traditions, including improvisational theatre, games, and stories (*see* HYBRID GENRES; INTERMEDIALITY; MEDIA AND NARRATIVE); and third, the category of computer games is enormously expansive, describing all forms of playful engagement with computers, and thus no one model can fully account for the range of experiences which get labelled as games.

Among game designers and players, the debate often centres on questions of structure and freedom. Game designer Greg Costikyan argues that there is an 'immediate conflict' between stories and games: too tightly structured, too little freedom for the player. Although many games represent abstract puzzles or remediate traditional sports and games, some games do aspire towards balancing the competing aesthetic demands of storytelling and gameplay, building upon *genre conventions from cinema or pulp literature (*see* FILM NARRATIVE; REMEDIATION).

To date, 'cut scenes', i.e., pre-rendered non-playable segments, have become the central means of *exposition in games. Game designer Chris Crawford challenges whether such works can be called interactive stories, since there is such a clear separation between storytelling and interactivity. Some have argued that the cut scene/play scene distinction could be deployed to artistic effect almost as a form of Greek tragedy – where players struggle against their fates – but few games have actually assigned thematic values to this distinction (*see* DRAMA AND NARRATIVE).

Game designers distinguish between games which have 'hard-rails' (which set limits on player choice in order to render a pre-structured experience) and those which have 'soft rails' (which allow greater freedom for player innovations to shape the outcome). More recently, games such as *Grand Theft Auto 3* have embraced an even more open-ended structure; these games create highly responsive environments for players to explore, allowing them to set and pursue their own goals, though they also often offer optional missions which follow a tighter narrative logic. Players bring different expectations to the medium with the result that games at both ends of this continuum rank among the all time top-selling titles.

Some scholars have analysed games in terms of their relationship to cinema and literature. Janet Murray, for example, has argued that games represent a significant but still primitive step along a process of media evolution towards her ideal – a fully immersive, fully responsive virtual reality environment which has the narrative complexity and psychological depth of Shakespeare (*see* IMMERSION; VIRTUALITY). Murray is interested in games as a model for what she calls 'procedural authorship', seeing the act of creating rules as setting the preconditions for the player's narrative experience. Espen Aarseth, on the other hand, argues that games, like hypertexts, are better understood as cybernetic systems rather than as storytelling systems, coining the term *'ergodic literature' to describe works whose shape and structure are highly dependent on the intervention of their readers.

Over the past few years, a strong critique of narrative-based theories of computer games has emerged from a movement of self-identified ludologists. The term, ludology, refers to the study of games. The ludologists argue for the importance of linking digital games to their predigital counterparts, seeing games as 'at least as medium-independent as stories' (Eskelinen 2001) and culturally valuable on their own terms, demanding their own analytic categories. They stress the importance of analysing

gameplay mechanics and rule systems rather than *narrative structures and *plot devices.

Games, Jesper Juul argues, are not narratives, since technically speaking, they are not narrated – that is, the player experiences the *events in real time with varied outcomes whereas stories follow a predetermined structure and often get recounted after the fact (*see* NARRATION; NARRATIVE TECHNIQUES). In this formulation, we may tell stories about our experience of game playing but games are not stories *per se*. While some games may rely on narrative pretexts to help orientate players to their goals, our experience of these works is more often about competing against a cybernetic system or another player, solving puzzles, overcoming obstacles, and navigating through *space.

More recently, Gonzalo Frasca (2003) has argued for a distinction between representation (which he sees as the central building block of narrative) and *simulation (which he sees as the most valuable contribution of computer games). Representation and simulation may draw on many of the same building blocks (characters, settings, events), which is why they are so often conflated. Representations depict worlds; simulations model their underlying logic.

Building upon Michel de Certeau's concept of 'spatial stories', Henry Jenkins contends that theorists need to draw on tools from narrative, *performance, architectural, and game theory in order to fully understand games. Spatial stories, according to de Certeau, enact our struggles to possess, traverse, or access spaces. Such works may be loosely structured, depending less on character development or narrative logic than on the exploration of compelling worlds. Game design, according to this formulation, represents a form of 'narrative architecture', more similar to amusement park design than to, say, filmmaking. Game designers don't tell stories; they design worlds, selecting features which they think are ripe with narrative possibilities, shaping the player's movement through space, and controlling the flow of information needed to make sense of the story situations they encounter along the route. Game spaces may contain enactments of narrative events or embed story information as clues; they may evoke memories of previously encountered narratives or provide, in game designer Will Wright's terms, 'dollhouses' where they may construct their own stories.

These debates within game studies make valuable contributions to narrative theory by pushing against its outer limits, consistently raising questions about where the category of stories ends and where other kinds of aesthetic experiences begin.

SEE ALSO: Artificial Intelligence and narrative; computational approaches to narrative; digital narrative; multi-path narrative; narrative, games, and play; narrative intelligence

References and further reading

Aarseth, Espen (1997) *Cybertext: Perspectives on Ergodic Literature*, Baltimore: Johns Hopkins University Press.
de Certeau, Michel (1988) *The Practice of Everyday Life*, trans. Steven F. Rendall, Berkeley: University of California Press.
Costikyan, Greg (2000) 'Where Stories End and Games Begin', *Game Developer*, 44–53.
Crawford, Chris (1984) *The Art of Computer Game Design*, Berkeley: McGraw Hill.
Eskelinen, Markku (2001), 'The Gaming Situation', *Game Studies*, 1.1, htttp://cmc.uib.no/gamestudies/0101/eskelinen
Frasca, Gonzalo (2003) 'Simulation Versus Narrative: Introduction to Ludology', in Mark J. P. Wolf and Bernard Perron (eds) *The Video Game Theory Reader*, New York: Routledge.
Jenkins, Henry (2003) 'Games as Narrative Architecture', in Pat Harrington and Noah Frup-Waldrop (eds) *First Person*, Cambridge: MIT Press.
Juul, Jesper (2001) 'Games Telling Stories?', *Game Studies*, 1.1, http://cmc.uib.no/gamestudies/0101/juul-gts
Laurel, Brenda (2001) *Utopian Entrepreneur*, Cambridge: MIT Press.
Murray, Janet (1997) *Hamlet on the Holodeck: The Future of Narrative in Cyberspace*, Cambridge: MIT Press.

HENRY JENKINS

CONCRETISATION

The mental process of filling a text's gaps, also referred to as blanks, lacunae, *indeterminacies, and *Leerstellen. See GAPPING; READER-RESPONSE THEORY (also: VIRTUALITY).

CONFESSIONAL NARRATIVE

Confessional narrative gets its main impetus from Jean-Jacques Rousseau's *Confessions*, though there was religious confessional literature long before Rousseau (Saint Augustine, for example), and more or less intimate first-person narratives,

whether as memoirs, *letters, *diaries, or foot-of-the gallows confessions of crime. But the posthumous publication of Rousseau's *Confessions* (starting in 1782) coincides with and contributes to a new interest in and valuation of the individual that stands at the inception of our modern conceptions of selfhood and introspection (*see* IDENTITY AND NARRATIVE). 'Confession' – as opposed to the memoir, for instance – implies that the speaker or writer wishes or even needs to reveal something that is hidden, possibly shameful, and difficult to articulate. The confessional tradition in *autobiographical writing (Rousseau's case) will rest its claim to authenticity and importance on its revelatory quality, which may be self-accusatory or self-exculpatory, and is usually both. The confessional tradition in fictional narrative often dramatises a *narrator who tells us something that he or she might in normal social circumstances prefer to keep hidden – and has perhaps hitherto kept hidden. Examples, among very many others, would be Benjamin Constant's *Adolphe* (1816), a novel of self-loathing and, at same time, narcissistic self-preoccupation; and Ivan Turgenev's *Spring Torrents* (1872), characterised more by nostalgia and regret. The confessional narrator may be self-deceptive in ways detectable by the reader, as in Henry James's *The Aspern Papers* (1888) and André Gide's *The Immoralist* (1902): the rhetoric of the *genre may involve a kind of hide-and-seek, where the reader finds that what is confessed by the narrator is not the whole or the pertinent *truth (*see* RELIABILITY).

Confession is predicated on self-awareness and the search for self-knowledge. Yet can we ever be certain of finding the ultimate truth about the self? Fyodor Dostoevsky is the master of the possibly unending dialectics of confession. This may be most evident in *Notes from Underground* (1864), but *Crime and Punishment* (1866) and *The Brothers Karamazov* (1879–1880) also turn crucially on confessions made and not made. The work of Sigmund Freud, perhaps especially his case-histories, confirms the lessons of fictional and autobiographical confessions: that the self is not wholly transparent to itself, that the explanatory stories it tells about its condition and self-definition can be lies as well as truths (*see* PSYCHOANALYSIS AND NARRATIVE).

Modern literature, from Romanticism on, accords the greatest importance to confessional narrative, and most major novelists at some point practice it in some form: see, for some interesting variations on the genre, Mary Shelley, *Frankenstein* (1818); Thomas DeQuincey, *Confessions of an English Opium Eater* (1822); James Hogg, *The Private Memoirs and Confessions of a Justified Sinner* (1824); Charles Dickens, *David Copperfield* (1850); Marcel Proust, *In Search of Lost Time* (1913–1927); Italo Svevo, *The Confessions of Zeno* (1923); Philip Roth, *The Counterlife* (1986). Such a rich and disparate list suggests that confessional narrative lies somewhere close to the heart of the modern novelistic project and its desire to know what it is like to be a particular human being.

SEE ALSO: novel, the

References and further reading

Brooks, Peter (2000) *Troubling Confessions*, Chicago: University of Chicago Press.
Coetzee, J. M. (1992 [1985]) 'Confession and Double Thoughts: Tolstoy, Rousseau, Dostoevsky', in David Atwell (ed.) *Doubling the Point: Essays and Interviews*, Cambridge, Mass.: Harvard University Press.

PETER BROOKS

CONFLICT

For some analysts, a minimal condition for narrative is the thwarting of intended actions by unplanned *events, which may or may not be the effect of other *characters' intended actions (*see* ACTION THEORY). This is another way of expressing the intuition that stories prototypically involve *conflict*, or some sort of (noteworthy, *tellable) disruption of an initial state of equilibrium by an unanticipated and often untoward event or chain of events. Propp (1968 [1928]) argued that in the corpus of Russian *folktales that he studied, all such disruptive, conflict-inducing occurrences could be characterised as variants of the single *function 'act of villainy'. Todorov (1968) extrapolated from Propp's findings to suggest that *every* narrative prototypically follows a trajectory leading from an initial state of equilibrium, through a phase of disequilibrium, to an endpoint at which equilibrium is restored (on a different footing) because of intermediary events – though not all narratives trace the entirety of this path (Bremond 1973; Kafalenos 1995).

Analogously, in the Anglo-American tradition, Brooks and Warren (1959) characterise conflict as an essential component of narrative *fiction. They suggest that fictional narratives can be broken down into plot-stages (*exposition, complication, climax, and denouement) tracing the experiences of *storyworld participants who are faced with some sort of conflict, whether external or internal. Hence, for Brooks and Warren, conflict is what links *plot with character (1959: 172).

In the model outlined more recently by Herman (2002), narratives can be decomposed into sequences of states, events, and actions that involve an identifiable participant or set of participants equipped with certain beliefs about the world and seeking to accomplish goal-directed plans. The conflicts that participants encounter in trying to actualise these plans – whether because of unpredicted obstacles, conflicting plans hatched by other participants, or other difficulties – confer on sequences the noteworthiness or tellability distinguishing a story from a stereotype (*see* SCRIPTS AND SCHEMATA). From this perspective, conflict is constitutive of narrative, though its source, manifestations, and relative pervasiveness will vary from story to story.

References and further reading

Bremond, Claude (1973) *Logique du récit*, Paris: Seuil.
Brooks, Cleanth, and Robert Penn Warren (1959 [1943]), *Understanding Fiction*, New York: Appleton-Century-Crofts.
Herman, David (2002) *Story Logic: Problems and Possibilities of Narrative*, Lincoln: University of Nebraska Press.
Kafalenos, Emma (1995) 'Lingering along the Narrative Path: Extended Functions in Kafka and Henry James', *Narrative*, 3, 117–38.
Propp, Vladimir (1968 [1928]) *Morphology of the Folktale*, trans. Laurence Scott, revised by Louis A. Wagner. Austin: University of Texas Press.
Todorov, Tzvetan (1968) 'La Grammaire du récit', *Languages*, 12, 94–102.

DAVID HERMAN

CONSTANCE SCHOOL

A school of reader-oriented criticism originating in the early 1970s and represented most prominently by Hans-Robert Jauss and Wolfgang Iser of Constance University, Germany. The work of both theorists was instrumental in drawing attention to the meaning-generating activities of the reception process and in overcoming purely text-centred approaches. *See* READER-RESPONSE THEORY; RECEPTION THEORY.

CONTEXTUALISM (IN HISTORIOGRAPHY)

Contextualism requires the historian to understand texts (or human action) by situating them in or relating them to the 'right' historical context. As such it is to be contrasted with textualism – as exemplified by e.g., the New Criticism or deconstruction – for which there is nothing outside the text (though it might be argued that in deconstruction the text functions as its own context). Contextualists disagree about the relationship between text and context. Some argue that the text is a simple reflection of its context. This position is defended by orthodox Marxists and by some practitioners of the history of ideas. Quentin Skinner thus claims that the historian could 'read off' a speaker's or writer's intentions from the context of his utterances while John Pocock maintains that political vocabularies function as the context determining textual meaning. Other contextualists propose a more 'dialogical', or dialectical, model for the relationship between text and context, leaving ample room for (textual) meaning that is not reducible to context. For example, Foucault uses the metaphor of struggle, and even of 'war and battle', for characterising the relationship between text and context. This is in agreement with the practice of *historicism and *hermeneutics, though practice in these disciplines is rarely supported by theoretical argument.

SEE ALSO: deconstructive approaches to narrative; dialogism; Marxist approaches to narrative

References and further reading

Bevir, Mark (1999) *The Logic of the History of Ideas*, Cambridge: Cambridge University Press.

FRANK ANKERSMIT

CONVERSATIONAL STORYTELLING

In everyday conversation, participants engage in storytelling for a range of purposes. Generally, one conversationalist becomes the storyteller, while the others become listeners. The teller introduces the story so as to secure listener interest, gain control of the floor and ensure understanding. Then the teller must shape information from *memory into a verbal *performance designed for the current context. This may include interruptions and comments from listeners; indeed, recipients may seek to redirect the storyline, to reformulate its point or even to become full-fledged co-tellers of the story. In any case, story recipients obviously understand and evaluate the story they hear rapidly enough to respond appropriately to it, perhaps with matching stories of their own.

Response stories adopt themes and *perspectives from foregoing stories, and thereby co-determine their final interpretation. Conversationalists may also manipulate stories in progress as well as topical talk to segue into stories of their own. Tellers employ prefaces and abstracts for their stories, not only in order to gain the floor but also to signal what sort of participation and response are expected. Prefaces establish the *tellability of stories on the basis of originality, topical relevance, relation to current *events or familiarity and humour (these last three features enhance the opportunity for co-narration). Once a story is underway, listeners may join in, contributing funny comments, invented details, and constructed *dialogue, even in unfamiliar stories.

Storytelling in conversation serves to convey interpersonal information and values, to align and realign group members, to demonstrate parallel experiences, enhance rapport, and entertain listeners. Tellers may employ stories in argumentation or to illustrate a point (*see* NARRATIVE AS ARGUMENT), to inform one another of events and to express their feelings about them. We also find diffuse stories with bits and pieces scattered through a section of conversation. Narrative-like sequences emerge from and recede back into turn-by-turn talk, blurring the boundaries. Accounts of recurrent experiences reconstruct remembered events just as true narratives do. Collaborative fantasies illustrate the negotiation of storyline and perspective in narrative fashion as well.

Labov and Waletzky (1967) awakened interest in spoken narrative and showed the potential for a systematic analysis of content. Work in this vein usually centres on interview data and stories elicited on specific topics (such as 'Were you ever in a situation where you were in serious danger of being killed?') rather than the contextually appropriate performance of narrative characteristic of polyphonic conversation (*see* POLYPHONY). Labov and Waletzky were primarily interested in establishing for each narrative a sequence of clauses matching remembered events and assigning clauses to six function elements (abstract, orientation, complication, evaluation, resolution, and coda), but they also concerned themselves with tellability and the importance of evaluation in securing listener interest and response, and with telling rights, based on knowledge of the events reported.

In the early 1970s, Sacks, Jefferson, and others began to analyse conversational stories, including response stories and families of stories in greater detail. Conversation Analysis viewed stories as extended turns within the turn-taking system, and raised apposite questions about how tellers gain the floor for long turns, how they preface and close stories, how hearers respond, how stories in sequence are related, etc. By the late 1970s, Tannen, Polanyi, Chafe, Schiffrin, and others were reporting observations on framing, tellability, *tense variation, co-telling, repetition and formulaicity in conversational *narration. They utilised *frame theory to describe strategies for recalling, organising, and verbalising stories. Frames (also called schemas and scripts) capture both relations between narrative units and overarching narrative patterns (*see* NARRATIVE UNITS; SCRIPTS AND SCHEMATA). Repetition and formulaicity signal openings, transitions and closings, as well as providing the principal image for developing a narrative, with consequences for the organisation, recall, and later verbalisation of stories.

Examination of storytelling in real conversational contexts, especially polyphonic conversational performance, retelling and less canonical forms of narration, e.g., by C. Goodwin, Ochs *et al.*, Blum-Kulka, and Norrick, revealed complex relations between context, tellability, and participation rights. The tellability of stories depends more on the dynamics of the narrative event itself than on any specifically newsworthy content, as witness children telling familiar stories at the request of their parents and co-narration of familiar stories among friends or family. Co-narration allows group members to work as a team and to present a joint personality. Group retelling stabilises story content and form, and it helps coalesce group perspectives and values.

Retellings provide a special perspective on conversational narrative, because they highlight the distinctions between a basic story and those aspects of the narration tied immediately to the local context. Comparison of two renditions of a story in separate contexts reveals the range of permutations and paraphrases a teller may produce to match the story with diverse topics and *audience responses. Close similarities in phrasing often appear among the non-narrative clauses of evaluation and background information, as well as in dialogue. The virtual identity of certain phrases from one telling to the next suggests significant nearly verbatim recall of whole chunks or a consistent use of specific narrative techniques at crucial points in a story. Frequent retelling leads tellers to crystallise and recycle stories as fairly complete units, sometimes with moveable subsections, tailoring them as necessary to fit the current context.

SEE ALSO: communication in narrative; discourse analysis (linguistics); sociolinguistic approaches to narrative

References and further reading

Bamberg, Michael (ed.) (1997) *Oral Versions of Personal Experience: Three Decades of Narrative Analysis* (Special Issue of the *Journal of Narrative and Life History*, 7).

Blum-Kulka, Shoshana (1993) '"You Gotta Know How to Tell a Story": Telling, Tales, and Tellers in American and Israeli Narrative Events at Dinner', *Language in Society*, 22, 361–402.

Chafe, Wallace (1980) 'The Development of Consciousness in the Production of a Narrative', in Wallace Chafe (ed.) *The Pear Stories*, Norwood: Ablex.

Goodwin, Charles (1986) 'Audience Diversity, Participation and Interpretation', *Text*, 6, 283–316.

Jefferson, Gail (1978) 'Sequential Aspects of Storytelling in Conversation', in Jim Schenkein (ed.) *Studies in the Organization of Conversational Interaction*, New York: Academic Press.

Labov, William, and Joshua Waletzky (1967) 'Narrative Analysis: Oral Versions of Personal Experience', in June Helm (ed.) *Essays on the Verbal and Visual Arts*, Seattle: University of Washington Press.

Norrick, Neal R. (1997) 'Twice-Told Tales: Collaborative Narration of Familiar Stories', *Language in Society*, 26, 199–220.

—— (2000) *Conversational Narrative*, Amsterdam: John Benjamins.

Ochs, Elinor, Ruth Smith, and Carolyn Taylor (1989) 'Detective Stories at Dinner-Time: Problem Solving through Co-Narration', *Cultural Dynamics*, 2, 238–57.

Polanyi, Livia (1985) *Telling the American Story*, Norwood: Ablex.

Sacks, Harvey (1972) 'On the Analyzability of Stories by Children', in John J. Gumperz and Dell Hymes (eds) *Directions in Sociolinguistics*, New York: Holt, Rinehart and Winston.

Sacks, Harvey (1992) *Lectures on Conversation*, 2 vols., in G. Jefferson (ed.), Oxford: Blackwell.

Schiffrin, Deborah (1981) 'Tense Variation in Narrative', *Language*, 57, 45–62.

Shuman, Amy (1986) *Storytelling Rights*, New York: Cambridge University Press.

Tannen, Deborah (1978) 'The Effect of Expectations on Conversation', *Discourse Processes*, 1, 203–09.

NEAL NORRICK

COUNTERFACTUAL HISTORY

A counterfactual hypothetically alters an *event in the past, creating a new outcome: e.g., 'if Gorbachev had lost the succession struggle in 1985 the Soviet Union would not have disintegrated before 1992' (Fearon 1996: 52). Counterfactual thought experiments are fundamental to the way human beings think (Roese and Olson 1995; Fauconnier and Turner 2002); they occur in many narrative forms and on varying scales, ranging from philosophical speculation (Lewis 1973), through the *natural narratives individuals formulate in responding to sudden tragic events or reviewing their *life stories (Roese and Olson 1995), to counterfactuals which remodel history (*see* HISTORIOGRAPHY; PHILOSOPHY AND NARRATIVE).

Counterfactual history occurs in several discourse forms: as an analytical method in the political and social sciences (Tetlock and Belkin 1996), in the counterfactual historical essay (Squire 1932 [1931], Ferguson 1997), and in the fictional *genre of alternate history (Alkon 1994), also known as the 'parahistorical novel' (Helbig 1988).

Historical counterfactuals focus on turning points in history, such as the failed invasion of the Spanish Armada in 1588 or the Allied victory in 1945. Historians, like most counterfactual theorists, see counterfactuals as fundamentally causal propositions and tend to prefer monocausal arguments to butterfly-effect causal reasoning (*see* CAUSALITY). Only plausible scenarios are valid for historical theorists; thus a counterfactual like 'if Napoleon had had Stealth bombers at Waterloo, he would not have been defeated' (Fearon 1996: 55) is causally sound, but historically implausible.

In contrast with historical research, fictional narratives that depict counterfactual historical scenarios, like Philip K. Dick's *The Man in the High Castle*, do not necessarily foreground counterfactual reasoning. Primarily a detailed creation of the social and cultural texture of a world in which the Axis powers won World War II, Dick's novel casually introduces the historical antecedent in a conversation between two characters. Some fictional forms often only loosely link antecedent and consequent. Keith Robert's *Pavane* depicts a twentieth-century English society which is the outcome of the assassination of Elizabeth I in 1588. In *science fiction *plots, time travellers interfere in past events to create counterfactual history. By contrast, the genre of *historiographic metafiction sometimes rewrites the *biography of a historical figure, such as Peter Ackroyd's *Milton in America*. The historical relativism of this genre also suppresses the hierarchy of fact versus counterfact underlying historical counterfactuals, suggesting instead that history itself is a textual construct.

References and further reading

Alkon, Paul (1994) 'Alternate History and Postmodern Temporality', in Thomas R. Cleary (ed.) *Time, Literature and the Arts: Essays in Honor of Samuel L. Macey*, Victoria, BC: University of Victoria Press.

Fauconnier, Gilles, and Mark Turner (2002) *The Way We Think: Conceptual Blending and the Mind's Hidden Complexities*, New York: Basic Books.

Fearon, James D (1996) 'Causes and Counterfactuals in Social Science: Exploring an Analogy between Cellular Automata and Historical Processes', in Tetlock and Belkin (1996).

Ferguson, Niall (ed.) (1997) *Virtual History: Alternatives and Counterfactuals*, London: Picador.

Helbig, Jörg (1988) *Der parahistorische Roman*, Frankfurt: Lang.

Lewis, David (1973) *Counterfactuals*, Oxford: Blackwell.

Roese, Neal J., and James M. Olson (eds) (1995) *What Might Have Been: The Social Psychology of Counterfactual Thinking*, Mahwah, NJ: Lawrence Erlbaum.

Squire, J. C. (ed.) (1932 [1931]) *If It Had Happened Otherwise: Lapses into Imaginary History*, London: Longmans, Green and Co.

Tetlock, Philip E., and Aaron Belkin (eds) (1996) *Counterfactual Thought Experiments in World Politics: Logical, Methodological, and Psychological Perspectives*, Princeton, NJ: Princeton University Press.

HILARY P. DANNENBERG

COURTROOM NARRATIVE

Research on courtroom narrative has shed light on the intricate relationship between social structure and power, on the one hand, and linguistic patterning and use, on the other. In addition, analysis of courtroom discourse has contributed to a deeper understanding of the complex facets of narrative, examining many discursive and *sociolinguistic aspects together (*see* DISCOURSE ANALYSIS (LINGUISTICS)).

Before reaching the courtroom, legal narratives typically undergo transformation from the less constrained format of speakers' spontaneous troubles-telling, through conversations in lawyers' offices and mediation settings, to formulation of court filings and discussions with court personnel, and finally to accounts rendered in courtrooms – ranging from more informal settings such as small claims courts through plea bargains and motions, to full-blown trials in more formal courtrooms (Conley and O'Barr 1998). The imposition of legal frames moves litigant narratives away from more emotional and relational stories toward accounts organised around theories of cause-and-effect and responsibility that respond to the requirements of legal rules (*see* CAUSALITY; NARRATIVE EXPLANATION). Relational narratives follow more everyday storytelling conventions (*see* CONVERSATIONAL STORYTELLING), and are more typical of less socially powerful speakers in legal settings (lay as opposed to professional, female as opposed to male, etc.). Some potentially valid legal claims may be dismissed and silenced if they are expressed by litigants in these kinds of disapproved linguistic forms – whether in informal courts or in court-ordered mediation settings (Fineman 1991). However, if the case does reach formal litigation, a mix of narrative conventions comes into play and *emotion can be accepted into the story – as long as it is presented within careful discursive constraints by trained attorneys.

One obvious constraint on narratives in formal courtrooms in many countries is the frequent framing of accounts within question-answer sequences – with the notable exceptions of the less-constrained stories told by attorneys at the beginnings and ends of trials (Atkinson and Drew 1979). In the course of these co-constructed narratives, attorneys' and judges' framing may import political values into the metalinguistic and pragmatic structuring of courtroom narration (*see* PRAGMATICS). For example, Matoesian has traced the ways in which legal frames distort rape narratives in court, revealing a patriarchal logic embedded in the discursive structure of these stories. In examining the structure of the courtroom language surrounding guilty pleas, Philips demonstrates

how conservative vs. liberal ideologies of judges affect the differential framing of defendants' narratives – although shared professional ideologies also produce some striking similarities as well (*see* IDEOLOGY AND NARRATIVE). Hirsch's work on courtroom narratives in Kenyan Islamic courts provides a complex analysis of the 'possibilities and limitations of creative reworkings of social relations' through narrative. In particular, she demonstrates that women use narrative in making claims while men use other kinds of language and metalanguage. As is the case with relational versus rule-oriented narratives, these divergent and gendered discursive choices will have differentially powerful effects in court (*see* GENDER STUDIES). Some research has explored the relationship between written legal narratives and the 'recontextualisation' (i.e., enactment or translation) of these texts in court (Philips 1998; Hirsch 1998).

Legal clinicians have examined how attorneys serve as translators who shape client narratives, sometimes missing what clients view as the central point of their stories (Cunningham 1992). Narrative analysis reveals a difficult dilemma: at times there is a choice between narratives or other discursive forms that will be effective in a courtroom, on the one hand, and narratives that are true to clients' experiences, on the other hand. More optimistically, some have approached the stories told to and by jurors as a vehicle for achieving a felicitous mix of legal and lay wisdom, in the service of doing justice (Burns 1999).

Lawyers and other courtroom actors constantly engage in communicative events using both institutional and non-institutional poetic conventions that in turn – as an institutional requirement – pretend to correspond to extra-legal fabulas (*see* INSTITUTIONAL NARRATIVE; STORY-DISCOURSE DISTINCTION). Traditionally, legal persuasion was considered in terms of Aristotelian 'decision-making', as syllogisms based on probabilistic calculi of the plausibility of occurrences; from this perspective, the 'facts' are wholly distinct from the substantive rules that would later apply to them. The narrative critique points to the blurring of the line between law and fact that occurs in legal reality-reconstruction. Critiques examine the *rhetorical force of courtroom narration in terms of structure, *performance, and effect (*see* NARRATIVE STRUCTURE).

Pennington and Hastie, for example, have criticised the standard view, under which factual reconstruction is purportedly guided by jurors' assessment of the probability that a set of discrete *events occurred, as required by the pertinent legal tests (for example, how likely was it that Jones stabbed Smith, and/or that Jones was drunk at the time, and/or that Smith threatened Jones prior to the killing). Instead, Pennington and Hastie demonstrate that 'story models' underlie jurors' cognitive processes – and thus trials' outcomes (*see* COGNITIVE NARRATOLOGY). This insight undermines the law's focus on the admissibility of discrete 'information bytes' and shifts attention to their meaning – i.e., to narrative relations and poetic characteristics. Indeed, according to Jackson, courts' bias in favour of narrative coherence is a primary principle for organising and manipulating factual reconstructions of events under dispute. Narrative invocation of familiar interpretative contexts determines a legal narrative's plausibility no less than traditional questions of evidence admissibility. Such contexts are typically manipulable through appeals to ideological background knowledge. Thus lawyers' arguments invoke the stories found in shared cultural *myths and other narrative patterns, both when attorneys engage in factual reconstruction and when they inform legal agents about their institutional obligations (Amsterdam and Hertz 1992). However, critics warn against the romanticisation of courtroom narratives, noting opportunities for the abuse of stories and for the alienation of both tellers and interpreters (Brooks 1996). White, for his part, emphasises the communicative potential of courtroom *narration, viewed as a context for dialogue, translation, and exchange (*see* DIALOGISM).

SEE ALSO: communication studies and narrative; discourse analysis (Foucault); law and narrative; narrative as cognitive instrument

References and further reading

Amsterdam, Anthony G., and Randy Hertz (1992) 'An Analysis of Closing Arguments to a Jury', *New York Law School Law Review*, 37, 55–122.

Atkinson, J. Maxwell, and Paul Drew (1979) *Order in Court: The Organization of Verbal Interaction in Judicial Settings*, Atlantic Highlands, N.J.: Humanities Press.

Brooks, Peter (1996) 'The Law as Narrative and Rhetoric', in Peter Brooks and Paul Gewirtz (eds) *Law's Stories: Narrative and Rhetoric in the Law*, New Haven: Yale University Press.

Burns, Robert (1999) *A Theory of the Trial*, Princeton: Princeton University Press.

Conley, John, and William M. O'Barr (1998) *Just Words: Law, Language and Power*, Chicago: University of Chicago Press.

Cunningham, Clark (1992) 'The Lawyer as Translator, Representation as Text: Towards an Ethnography of Legal Discourse', *Cornell Law Review*, 77, 1298–387.

Fineman, Martha (1991) *The Illusion of Equality: The Rhetoric and Reality of Divorce Reform*, Chicago: University of Chicago Press.

Hirsch, Susan (1998) *Pronouncing and Persevering: Gender and the Discourses of Disputing in an African Islamic Court*, Chicago: University of Chicago Press.

Jackson, Bernard (1988) *Law, Fact and Narrative Coherence*, Merseyside, UK: Deborah Charles Publications.

Matoesian, Gregory (2001) *Law and the Language of Identity: Discourse in the William Kennedy Smith Rape Trial*, Oxford: Oxford University Press.

Pennington, Nancy, and Reid Hastie (1991) 'A Cognitive Theory of Juror Decision Making: The Story Model?' *Cardozo Law Review*, 13, 519–57.

Philips, Susan (1998) *Ideology in the Language of Judges: How Judges Practice Law, Politics, and Courtroom Control*, Oxford: Oxford University Press.

White, James Boyd (1990) *Justice as Translation: An Essay in Cultural and Legal Criticism*, Chicago: University of Chicago Press.

ELIZABETH MERTZ AND JONATHAN YOVEL

CULTURAL STUDIES APPROACHES TO NARRATIVE

The ubiquity of narrative in culture and the socio-historical dimension of narrative forms are focal points of interest for cultural studies approaches to narrative. Their main aim is probably best described as 'anthropologise narrative!' (adapting a phrase from Paul Rabinow, in Clifford and Marcus 1986: 241). An intensified dialogue between cultural studies and narrative theory has led those disciplines which are concerned with social practices (e.g., history, ethnology, and psychology) to acknowledge the importance of narrative in cultural processes. Conversely, literary studies (including narratology) have opened up towards the specific cultural and historical contexts in which narrative forms are produced and received. This contextualisation of literary narrative has been going on since the mid-1980s. Its greatest challenge is the conception of the intricate relation between (literary) text and (cultural) context. Cultural studies approaches to narrative have not formed a single, monolithic school, but instead produced different theories and methods, subsumed under terms like 'cultural analysis', 'diachronisation', or 'cultural and historical narratology'.

History and theory of an interdisciplinary approach

Since the early 1970s the acknowledgement of the omnipresence of narrative in culture has led to a *narrative turn in the humanities. Most significantly, the interrelations between cultural practices and narrative forms were elucidated by (1) Hayden White's metahistorical investigation of *plot structures in nineteenth-century *historiography and his conclusions about their ideological implications (*see* EMPLOTMENT; IDEOLOGY AND NARRATIVE; METAHISTORY); (2) by *psychological approaches to narrative, especially the studies of Jerome Bruner, who has shown that we organise autobiographic *memory mainly in the form of narrative (*see* AUTOBIOGRAPHY; NARRATIVE PSYCHOLOGY); and (3) by *ethnographic approaches to narrative, e.g., the concept of 'writing culture' (Clifford and Marcus 1986). The latter approach follows Clifford Geertz's metaphor of 'culture as text' but focuses on the narrative forms and epistemological problems connected with the production of ethnographic texts. What all three approaches have in common is that they make use of narratological concepts and models originally developed for the study of literary texts in order to grasp and evaluate specifically cultural phenomena. The narrative turn in the humanities has shown that the basic cultural function of narrative is the construction of meaningful temporal processes (*see* TIME IN NARRATIVE), be it on the individual or collective level, and be it in the framework of literary, mythical, or historical symbolic systems (*see* MYTH: THEORETICAL APPROACHES). Narrative is thus not confined to the literary realm but rather appears as a basic cultural tool used to make sense of experience (*see* NARRATIVE AS COGNITIVE INSTRUMENT).

From the mid-1980s onwards, on the other hand, more and more narratologists have become interested in the various manifestations of contextual factors in narratives. Thus, converging moves have taken place: a narrative turn in the disciplines investigating social and cultural processes and a cultural turn in narratology – each having profited from insights gained in the other, complementary area of research. The development of a narratology sensitive to cultural processes must be understood in the context of recent developments within literary studies: as a critical reaction to the practice of text-centred interpretation (e.g., New Criticism and Deconstructivism; *see* DECONSTRUCTIVE APPROACHES TO NARRATIVE), various approaches have emerged which try to re-historise and recontextualise literature. Movements which had significant influence not only on literary studies in general but also on narratology include (1) Cultural Materialism, developed at the Birmingham Centre for Contemporary Cultural Studies as early as the 1960s (esp. by Raymond Williams and Stuart Hall) and based on concepts of Marxist philosophy and sociology (*see* MARXIST APPROACHES TO NARRATIVE; SOCIOLOGICAL APPROACHES TO LITERARY NARRATIVE); and (2) New Historicism, a combination of the former approach with ideas deriving from ethnology and discourse analysis in its Foucauldian guise, theorised and practised (esp. by Stephen Greenblatt and Louis Montrose) mainly in the late 1980s (*see* DISCOURSE ANALYSIS (FOUCAULT)).

Approaches within literary studies which merge narratological models with concepts derived from cultural studies have to be located within *postclassical narratology. They are a part of the more general move away from strict taxonomies, seemingly universal grammars of narrative (*see* STORY GRAMMARS), and text-centred, ahistorical, acontextual analyses done by classical narratology – and towards a host of contextual factors subsumed under the heading 'culture': discourses and symbolic forms, collective memory, invented traditions and imagined communities, concepts of *identity and *alterity, ritual and social conventions, to name but a few areas of research. One example of the possible gains of such an enterprise are recent studies of unreliable narration: since Wayne Booth's introduction of the term in the 1960s narratologists have tried to tackle the phenomenon by using text-centred approaches and by aiming at universal definitions (*see* RELIABILITY). A narratology sensitive to cultural processes, however, insists that unreliability is a culturally and historically variable phenomenon not to be located within the literary system alone. Rather, it emerges – and must thus be studied and classified – in changing networks of philosophical, psychological, and social discourses (cf. Zerweck 2001; *see* PHILOSOPHY AND NARRATIVE).

Concepts of culture have been developed within a wide range of disciplines (e.g., philosophy, *sociology, ethnology), involve different methodologies (e.g., *hermeneutic interpretation, discourse analysis), and follow diverse ideological assumptions and political purposes (*see* FEMINIST NARRATOLOGY; GENDER STUDIES; POST-COLONIALISM AND NARRATIVE). 'Culture' as envisaged by cultural studies approaches to narrative is neither restricted to art and high culture, nor does it only point to popular or minority culture. Instead, a broad semiotic understanding of culture (*see* SEMIOTICS), operating within a socio-constructivist framework, is best suited to encompass the wide variety of research fields which are opened up by approaches to the narratives of culture. Conceived accordingly, 'culture' is the result of the collective construction of reality. Culture-generating constructive processes take effect in different semiotic dimensions: the social dimension (i.e., social institutions), the mental dimension (i.e., ideas, values, conventions), and the material dimension (i.e., 'texts' in a broad sense, meaning man-made 'objects') (Posner 1989). A 'cultural formation' is a geographically, ethnically, and historically distinct actualisation of human semiosis including all of its specific social, mental, and material aspects. As an artefact, the narrative text must be primarily located within the material dimension of a cultural formation. It is, however, inherently connected with social processes and mental phenomena such as collective values, concepts of identity, and cognitive schemata (*see* COGNITIVE NARRATOLOGY; SCRIPTS AND SCHEMATA).

Cultural studies approaches to narrative open up two basic directions of research (cf. Bal 1990): (1) the analysis of *narrative structures in symbolic forms and cultural practices other than literary texts (e.g., non-fictional texts, painting, and ritual; *see* LAW AND NARRATIVE; MEDICINE AND NARRATIVE; MYTH: THEMATIC APPROACHES; MEDIA AND NARRATIVE; PICTORIAL NARRATIVITY). This project involves a close dialogue between narratology and the respective 'target discipline' as well as an 'exporting' of narratological methods (e.g., close reading and structural analysis) and concepts (e.g., *plot and *focalization) to other areas of research; (2) the analysis of how literary texts are interwoven with cultural contexts. This project, which will be outlined below, involves 'importing' methods, concepts, and knowledge of cultural theory and history, and investigating the specific intersections

between literary narrative and culturally relevant topics. In both cases, however, interdisciplinarity is of paramount importance (*see* INTERDISCIPLINARY APPROACHES TO NARRATIVE).

Text and context

One of the major challenges of cultural studies approaches to literary narrative is the conceptualisation of the relation between text and context. It is now generally accepted that literary works do not mimetically mirror cultural constellations, i.e., that they are not documents or transparent media which easily give access to an underlying (past) reality. But neither does literature seem to be a realm separated from reality. What complicates the matter even more is the fact that a 'con*text*' is not the sum of given data, as suggested in positivist ('*old* historicist') accounts, but a 'text', too. For the cultural and literary historian, the context is thus not a 'datum' but another 'interpretandum', just like the literary text itself.

Most influentially, New Historicism (later dubbed the 'Poetics of Culture') has located the literary text within cultural contexts. One basic assumption of neo-historicist studies is – to quote a famous chiasm by Montrose – the 'historicity of texts and the textuality of history' (see Veeser 1989: 20). According to New Historicism, collective beliefs and experiences are generated in synchronic cultural systems. They are the result of a 'circulation of social energy', a 'negotiation' and 'exchange' of language, stories, and aesthetic forms across symbolic forms and cultural practices (such as *travel writing, religious tracts, literature, ritual, and theatre). In this perspective, literary texts play an important role in the discursive networks of a given culture, from which they derive their 'energy' and which they in turn actively shape. Although New Historicism has contributed to a heightened sensitivity of literary studies towards cultural and historical processes, it has also been widely criticised for its tendency to relate text and context in a selective, associative, and often seemingly arbitrary way.

Within narrative theory, two basic conceptions of the text/context relation have proved highly influential: Paul Ricoeur's model of a 'threefold mimesis' and Fredric Jameson's notion of 'ideology of form'. Ricoeur (1984–1986) conceives of Aristotelian *mimesis as a circle in which narrative text and cultural context intersect. He distinguishes three stages of a dynamic mimetic process: mimesis I (prefiguration), mimesis II (configuration) and mimesis III (refiguration). A narrative text is (1) prefigured by its cultural context with its specific symbolic order. It (2) configures (or: emplots) extra-literary elements (the 'real' and the 'imaginary') into an exemplary temporal and causal order (*see* CAUSALITY). In the act of reading, finally, the narrative composition is actualised. It becomes part of the symbolic order of a cultural formation, which is thereby (3) refigured and – here the circle closes – functions in turn as the source of narrative pre-understanding on the level of mimesis I. While Ricoeur's first and third levels are intersections between narrative text and cultural context, only mimesis II, the configuration of textual elements, is observable to the narratologist and literary historian. It is here that Jameson's (1989) 'ideology of form' comes into play: if one considers narrative forms not as containers of content and meaning, but as meaningful cultural phenomena themselves, the narratological analysis of the level of configuration allows assumptions to be made about the interrelation of text and context: The specific forms of narrative *voice, *focalization, and plot hint at pre-existing cultural constellations as well as at possible effects and social functions of the fictional narrative (cf. Fluck 1996).

From the point of view of cultural studies approaches, the literary text is not to be conceived as outside, above, or below, but rather as an integral part of its cultural context. Literary narrative can not only articulate collective experience, values, and concepts of identity, but also restructure the symbolic order of a given cultural formation. Narrative forms are 'forms of expression' in specific cultures; they are solutions (or 'answers') provided to challenges (or 'questions') arising in specific cultural contexts. Like all properties of culture, narrative forms are neither trans-historical nor trans-cultural entities, but mutable forms of human expression. In contrast to the methods developed within classical narratology, therefore, the relations among narrative forms on the one hand and their semantic dimensions or cultural functions on the other cannot be presented within a fixed taxonomy. Instead, the cultural and historical variability and the polyfunctionality of narrative forms require detailed studies of 'form-in-context' (cf. Herman 1999).

Proceeding from these theoretical premises, cultural studies approaches to narrative can fulfil a mediating function between a treatment of literature as historical documents on the one hand and context-free formal analysis on the other. In the cultural field of memory, for instance, narrative plays a major role. Its forms are part of a cultural tradition and with their capacity to explain temporal processes powerful agents in memorial practices. A combination of cultural history, theories of memory, and categories of narratology can further our understanding of fictional narrative as a medium which not only stages but actively shapes cultural memory (cf the impact of *Holocaust narrative). The aim of such an integrated approach should not be the mapping of aesthetic forms to social functions (cf. the controversy between Dorrit Cohn, John Bender, and Mark Seltzer in *New Literary History*, 1995), but rather a careful analysis of how narrative forms are put to use in literature and in other symbolic systems (e.g., myth, law, history) in order to create versions of a shared past. With their ideologically loaded forms, literary narratives are able to exert considerable influence on and even reconfigure the narratives underlying existent collective memories.

Options: 'cultural analysis' and 'cultural and historical narratology'

As far as the writing of literary and cultural history is concerned, combinations of narratological and cultural studies approaches have been put to use since the early 1980s (Armstrong 1987; Bender 1987). In the realm of narrative theory, the idea of a 'cultural narratology' was explicitly put forth a decade later (Onega and Landa 1996; Currie 1998); however, it was hardly ever developed in depth. So far, there are two branches of narratological research which have produced full-fledged cultural studies approaches to narrative – termed 'cultural analysis' on the one hand, and 'diachronic', 'cultural', or 'cultural and historical' narratology on the other.

1. Judging from the sheer amount and variety of her investigations into the relation of culture and narrative, the depth and intensity of inter-disciplinary dialogue, and the level of theoretical reflection, Mieke Bal's 'cultural analysis' approach appears to be the most important synthesis of cultural studies and narrative theory. Bal, who has published books on such seemingly diverse topics as *structuralist narratology, art history, and Bible studies (*see* BIBLICAL NARRATIVE), is one of the

first theorists to have recognised that the 'point of narratology' (Bal 1990) depends on its establishing a closer dialogue with cultural studies. She understands narrative not as a *genre, but as a *mode, and an active force within culture. Narrative, according to Bal, is moreover a transdisciplinary concept, the study of which must be and has been from the beginning an interdisciplinary project. Her choice of the term 'cultural analysis' (rather than 'cultural studies') has implications with regard to areas of research and method. First, Bal's focus is not primarily on cultural processes, but on objects (texts, paintings, etc.), which are viewed as part of culture. Second, 'analysis' points to her careful 'close reading' of the objects' formal properties.

Bal often draws on categories derived from classical narratology, yet understands them as 'travelling concepts' (Bal 2001) to be further developed in the framework of an interdisciplinary approach. For example, since the early 1980s Bal has understood focalization not so much in Genette's formalist terms (zero-focalization is impossible according to Bal), but in socio-cultural terms as the relation between the subject and the object of perception. As such, focalization is always ideologically charged – and thus a concept of cultural analysis. Bal's analyses of the forms and meanings of focalization in cultural objects are neither confined to the narratological method nor to literary works as objects. Combining narratology, feminist concerns, and visual studies, Bal analyses Proust and the Book of Judges as well as Rembrandt's paintings and art exhibitions.

2. From the mid-1990s onwards, a number of German and Austrian projects (chiefly to be seen in the specific context of German *Kulturwissenschaften*) have focused on integrating narratological models into the analysis of synchronic cultural systems and diachronic processes. An historical perspective on narrative categories was already anticipated by Franz Stanzel, whose differentiation of the typical *narrative situations is the result of a historio-synthetic approach (quite unlike the analytic taxonomy provided by Genette). Monika Fludernik (1996; 2003), one of Stanzel's students, has further emphasised the historical dimension of narrative forms (*see* NATURAL NARRATOLOGY). Her detailed and comprehensive reconstruction of the development of narrative forms from *medieval to *postmodern literature shows that narrative devices are not trans-historical phenomena but have developed over long periods and in close relation to cognitive schemata shared among the historical readership. Fludernik thus promotes a 'diachronisation' and (as a result) a de-essentialisation of narratological categories.

Ansgar Nünning (2000) presents the case for a combined cultural and historical narratology, and the project has been put to the test in a number of studies of the relations between historiographic and fictional narrative, of unreliable narration and multiperspectivity, of *feminist narratology, and of forms and functions of national stereotyping. Explicitly underlining the heuristic value of narratological analysis, Nünning engages in a dialogue with New Cultural History and consistently historicises and contextualises fictional narrative. Gabriele Helms (2003) likewise contributes to what she calls a 'cultural narratology' by using Bakhtin's concept of *dialogism in order to show how *narrative techniques in the contemporary Canadian *novel actively contribute to or impede a text's challenges to hegemonic discourses and social injustices. Both Nünning and Helms show that analysis of such 'semantisations' of narrative forms lead to wide-ranging insights into historical mentalities and social constellations.

What both 'cultural analysis' and 'cultural and historical narratology' as prominent cultural studies approaches to narrative demonstrate, is that narrative and its forms are an active and formative part of historical cultures. The contextualisation and 'diachronisation' of narrative forms can make an important contribution to literary and cultural history and at the same time challenge and fine-tune narratology's traditional categories.

References and further reading

Armstrong, Nancy (1987) *Desire and Domestic Fiction: A Political History of the Novel*, New York: Oxford University Press.

Bal, Mieke (1990) 'The Point of Narratology', *Poetics Today*, 11.4, 727–53.

——(2001) *Travelling Concepts in the Humanities. A Rough Guide*, Toronto: University of Toronto Press.

Bender, John (1987) *Imagining the Penitentiary: Fiction and the Architecture of Mind in Eighteenth-Century England*, Chicago: University of Chicago Press.

Clifford, James, and George E. Marcus (eds) (1986) *Writing Culture. The Poetics and Politics of Ethnography*, Berkeley: University of California Press.

Currie, Mark (1998) *Postmodern Narrative Theory*, London: Macmillan.

Fluck, Winfried (1996) 'The American Romance and the Changing Functions of the Imaginary', *New Literary History*, 27.3, 415–57.

Fludernik, Monika (1996) *Towards a 'Natural' Narratology*, London: Routledge.

—— (2003) 'The Diachronization of Narratology', *Narrative*, 11.3, 331–48.

Helms, Gaby (2003) *Challenging Canada: Dialogism and Narrative Techniques in Canadian Novels*, Montreal: McGill-Queen's University Press.

Herman, David (ed.) (1999) *Narratologies: New Perspectives on Narrative Analysis*, Columbus, OH: Ohio State University Press.

Jameson, Fredric (1981) *The Political Unconscious: Narrative as a Socially Symbolic Act*, London: Methuen.

Nünning, Ansgar (2000) 'Towards a Cultural and Historical Narratology: A Survey of Diachronic Approaches, Concepts, and Research Projects', in Bernhard Reitz and Sigrid Rieuwerts (eds) *Anglistentag 1999 Mainz: Proceedings*, Trier: WVT.

Onega, Susana, and José Angel García Landa (eds) (1996) *Narratology: An Introduction*, London: Longman.

Posner, Roland (1989) 'What is Culture? Toward a Semiotic Explication of Anthropological Concepts', in W. A. Koch (ed.) *The Nature of Culture*, Bochum: Brockmeyer.

Ricoeur, Paul (1984–1988) *Time and Narrative*, 3 vols, trans. Kathleen McLaughlin and Paul Pellauer, Chicago: University of Chicago Press.

Veeser, H. Aram (ed.) *The New Historicism*, London: Routledge.

Zerweck, Bruno (2001) 'Historicizing Unreliable Narration: Unreliability and Cultural Discourse in Narrative Fiction', *Style*, 35.1, 151–78.

ASTRID ERLL

CYBERPUNK FICTION

Cyberpunk fiction is a sub-genre of *science fiction set in a near future where the world is saturated with technology. The first *novels and *films in the *genre appeared in the early 1980s. The term 'cyberpunk' was introduced as the title of a story by Bruce Bethke in 1983, and was first used to describe a genre in 1984, by Gardener Dozois. The prefix 'cyber-' comes from cybernetics, indicating the genre's concern with today's information technology, and the '-punk' refers to the subversive outcasts and street kids the genre usually casts as its protagonists.

Cyberpunk typically portrays dystopic worlds where civilisation has been shattered by environmental or political catastrophes (*see* DYSTOPIAN FICTION). The environment is often unstable or hostile, nation-states tend to be extinct, and land and people are divided between corporations, sects, racial, or ideological groupings. The protagonists are often poor and outsiders to existing power structures; nevertheless, they are far from powerless because they are skilled manipulators of the technology that controls most other citizens of the world. These *heroes combine the streetwise subversion of punks with a love of technology: they are wired, wear enhanced reality glasses, and are brilliant hackers, often with a moral cause. Often a portion of the narrative in cyberpunk fiction takes place in a virtual or technologically enhanced environment.

William Gibson's 1984 novel *Neuromancer* is one of the first cyberpunk novels, and besides introducing the word *cyberspace*, it has had great influence in defining the genre. Ridley Scott's 1982 film *Bladerunner* (based on Philip K. Dick's 1968 novel *Do Androids Dream of Electric Sheep?*) is also an important landmark. Bruce Sterling has been another important author, and his introduction to the anthology *Mirrorshades* is seen as a manifesto for cyberpunk fiction. Despite the repeated announcement of the death of cyberpunk, new authors further developed the genre in the 1990s, led by Neal Stephenson (*Snowcrash*, *Diamond Age*). By the turn of the century the *Matrix* movies had definitively brought cyberpunk themes and motifs into the mainstream.

Cyberpunk is particularly influenced by the New Wave of 1950s science fiction, where authors such as Brian Aldiss and J. G. Ballard wrote books that drew upon present problems rather than dreaming of distant planets, time travel, or technological utopias. Catastrophe has already happened in these novels, as in cyberpunk, and the nature of the disaster is close to the writer's contemporary problems with the environment, politics, and technological change. Cyberpunk is also influenced by American hard-boiled *detective fiction of the 1920s and 30s, developing both its themes of urban violence and corruption and the outsider hero, as well as by *postmodern narrative, which in turn has been influenced by cyberpunk.

References and further reading

Cavallaro, Dani (2000) *Cyberpunk and Cyber-culture: Science Fiction and the Work of William Gibson*, London: The Athlone Press.

McCaffery, Larry (ed.) (1991) *Storming the Reality Studio: A Casebook of Cyberpunk and Postmodern Science Fiction*, Durham: Duke University Press.

Sterling, Bruce (ed.) (1988) *Mirrorshades: The Cyberpunk Anthology*, New York: Ace Books.

JILL WALKER

D

DANCE AND NARRATIVE

The dancer carves a sweeping arc through space, turns abruptly away, sinks to the floor, and after a long stillness, spirals through standing to a daring balance. Or the dancer walks onstage, greets the *audience, and proceeds to illustrate the story she is about to dance by explaining the *gestures that connote specific people, places, and actions of the tale she will dance. Yet the *performance that follows includes not only these gestural sequences, but also long phrases of rapid, rhythmic foot patterns that punctuate the story with virtuoso physical dexterity. Or the dancer swivels into a frozen posture, eerily familiar, but displaced at lightning speed by a second, third, and fourth pose, all ganged together so as to sequence images from popular culture in relation to a complex and driving musical accompaniment. Are these bodies telling stories? What do their movements mean? How do we as viewers know what they are saying?

For most of the twentieth century, the answers to these questions derived from a distinction between the abstract and the representational. Whether they address American modern dance, south Indian classical Barata Natyam, or hip-hop, the three examples described above, both choreographers and scholars have generally presumed an oppositionality between the world of words, in which stories are told, and a world of physicality within which can be crafted a kind of expression that defies or escapes verbal description. According to this opposition, the kinds of dancing that tell stories utilise repertoires of gestures such as the romantic ballets' use of pantomime or the Barata Natyam's use of mudras as described above. The rest of dancing offers something other – ephemeral, intangible,

and unspeakable. Thus the founding figure of the modern dance tradition, Isadora Duncan, was reputed to have observed: 'If I could say it, I wouldn't have to dance it'. Philosopher Susanne Langer rationalised this observation by theorising dance as a symbolic endeavour that functions to convey the dynamism of aliveness. Choreographer George Balanchine insisted that ballet manifests pure beauty, and equally, a rendering of music's architecture into physical form.

This desire to locate dance outside of representation (*see* MIMESIS) constitutes one of the principal aesthetic features of modernism. Eighteenth-century choreographers, in contrast, wanted nothing more than to see their ballets as stories. Drawing on the ancient Roman experiments in pantomime conducted by Pylades and Bathyllus, choreographers such as Marie Sallé and Jean Georges Noverre developed a new kind of danced spectacle that relied entirely on movement and gesture to narrate a story (*see* NARRATION). Their experiments resulted in the establishment of dance as an independent *genre, entirely separate from *opera, that plotted danced *characters to follow a narrative arc from beginning through middle to end (*see* STORY ARC). Even these ballets, however, alternated between scenes that resembled spoken *dialogue and those that displayed the virtuoso mastery of complex and intricate sequences of steps (*see* SUMMARY AND SCENE). The most successful ballets were those that devised a reason for such displays, either in the form of a festival or ball, or through the invention of a supernatural creature, e.g., a sylph or fairy, whose manner of moving might reasonably be dancing (Foster 1996).

Recent expansion of narrative theory, however, to include non-verbal texts such as painting (see PICTORIAL NARRATIVITY), music (see MUSIC AND NARRATIVE) or the routines of daily life (see LIFE STORY) holds new applicability as a framework that could illuminate the workings of dance as a mode of communication. At the same time, a proliferation of new choreographic experimentation and new ways of analysing dance suggest that dance can, in turn, contribute new insights to the study of narrative. When viewed as the matter out of which narrative can be constructed, the dancing body, no longer natural or unspeakable, can be assessed as a culturally constructed, historically specific physicality capable of reproducing and also creating cultural values and meanings (Novack 1990). Choreography theorises corporeal, individual, and social *identity by placing bodies in dynamic rapport, one with another, that suggests an unfolding of their relations that inevitably charts a narrative trajectory. Whether tragic or comic, *satiric or mythic, *antinarrative or *metanarrative, this *narrative structure implies a political and ideological intent (see IDEOLOGY AND NARRATIVE). Whether the dancing body is valorised or celebrated, transcended in order to make evident the workings of the soul, or simply asked to state something about its disposition, its aesthetics are its politics (Franko 1993; Manning 1993; Savigliano 1995; Tomko 1999).

Narrative theory encourages an analysis of the dance's choreography, and also the full apparatus that surrounds and supports dance production, including the training process of learning to dance, the occasion and context of presentation, and the audience's reception. As a system of representational *codes and conventions that is shared by choreographers and viewers, a dance performance yields up multiple interpretations that account variously for its choices of vocabulary, style, and syntax (Foster 1986). It may offer a principal form and manner of address; however, viewers might choose to read against or past that intended response.

If narrative theory frames these kinds of considerations for dance, dance, in turn, asks how narrative might be defined as embodied motion. It asks narrative theory to consider how authorial voice takes space and weight within the text, and how a text creates momentum, dynamism, gravity, or a sense of rhythm (Goellner and Shea Murphy 1995). Even more crucial, dance, by calling into sharp relief the incommensurability between verbal *description and the object of that description, encourages a reflexive scrutiny of the process through which the creation and telling of a story occur.

SEE ALSO: media and narrative

References and further reading

Foster, Susan Leigh (1986) Reading Dancing, Berkeley: University of California Press.
—— (1996) Choreography and Narrative, Bloomington: Indiana University Press.
Franko, Mark (1993) Dance as Text, Cambridge: Cambridge University Press.
Goellner, Ellen, and Jacqueline Shea Murphy (eds) (1995) Bodies of the Text, New Brunswick: Rutgers University Press.
Langer, Susanne (1953) Feeling and Form, New York: Charles Scribner's Sons.
Manning, Susan (1993) Ecstasy and the Demon, Berkeley: University of California Press.
Novack, Cynthia (1990) Sharing the Dance, Madison: University of Wisconsin Press.
Noverre, Jean Georges (1966) Letters on Dancing and Ballets, trans. C. Beaumont, Brooklyn: Dance Horizons.
Savigliano, Marta (1995) Tango and the Political Economy of Passion, Boulder: Westview Press.
Tomko, Linda (1999) Dancing Class, Bloomington: Indiana University Press.

SUSAN LEIGH FOSTER

DECONSTRUCTIVE APPROACHES TO NARRATIVE

Deconstruction finds its origin in the early works of the French *poststructuralist Jacques Derrida and in the *rhetorical analyses of the Yale school (Harold Bloom, Paul de Man, Geoffrey Hartman, J. Hillis Miller). Together these five critics published a sort of manifesto (1979). Although Derrida went to great lengths to point out that there can be no deconstructivist method or theory – since deconstruction is inherent in language and as such simply happens all the time – there are some distinguishing features of the deconstructivist approach to narrative texts: the focus on the text's materiality; the analysis of *narrative as a trope unfolding its own deconstruction; the unavoidability of misreadings (see INDETERMINACY); and the blurring of the boundaries between literature and criticism. All of these characteristics are related to Derrida's concept of différance, indicating that meaning arises from differences between terms, which can thus never be defined in their own right. Terms are endlessly linked to each other, and 'contaminate' one another, very often on the basis of their material (written or acoustic) form.

For the purposes of narrative textual analysis, this means that deconstruction will pay great attention to word-plays, anagrams, sound-associations, and all forms of material links that are thought to inform the dynamic evolution of the text (*see* NARRATIVE DYNAMICS). Thus Derrida reads literary texts as a play on the name of the *author, focusing e.g., on words like '*éponge*' in the works of the French author Ponge.

Deconstructive approaches to narrative also thematise the point that analyses cannot grasp the text itself, since one can only speak of text A in terms of texts B, C, and so forth. This thematisation is especially obvious in the *intertextuality of deconstructive analyses. Such analyses typically examine the text under perspectives afforded by their confrontation with other literary and non-literary texts.

Even without this emphasis on other texts, the deconstructive analysis of a specific narrative pays tribute to the principle of *différance*. Any narrative element can only be defined in terms of other elements. This means that any definition or *description is always a figure of speech, a *metaphor talking about a term via another term. The idea that all language is figurative and metaphorical not only informs Derrida's famous 1971 essay on 'white mythology' (1982), but also highlights the basic concern of the Yale approach to narrative. Fiction is studied as tropological narrative. Thus de Man (1979: 205) claims that 'the paradigm for all texts consists of a figure (or a system of figures) and its deconstruction'. Narrative posits metaphors and in unfolding those it deconstructs them.

Reading narrative requires unfolding the process of tropes presenting and undermining themselves. Since no term or trope can be grasped in its own right, any reading is a necessary deviation of the tropological narrative – a metaphor of a metaphor, that is, an *allegory of reading. If de Man (1979) talks about the necessity of misreading, if Miller (in Bloom *et al.* 1979) makes claims about the impossibility of reading, and if Bloom (1973) states that 'misprision' of texts forms the core of all literary and critical writing, this is not to discard the possibility of critical or narratological interpretations, but to show the unavoidable *différance* that takes place in any interpretation. Interpretation never reaches the final meaning or *truth of a text; it is not a totalising and finite project but an endless and self-contradictory

attempt that finds itself deviating from the text it approaches. As such, all true criticism is crisis, according to de Man.

Only in misreadings can narratives survive. Deconstructive readings are not merely parasitical, however; they also function as host for the text. More generally, such readings are always double or dialogical, involving both approach and deviation, construction as well as deconstruction (*see* DIALOGISM). In this in-between status, criticism and literature meet: there is no narrative or narratology 'in its own right'; narrative texts and narrative theories exist only in a persistent dialogue. As a result, the distinctions between text and theory are blurred. In the words of Hartman (1980: 201), 'literary commentary may cross the line and become as demanding as literature'. Conversely, literature is read as theory, *fiction as *metafiction. Barbara Johnson (1980), for example, analyses the characters of Melville's novella, *Billy Budd, Sailor*, as representative of different types of readerly attitudes.

In their concrete narrative interpretations, deconstructivists focus on the figures and places in the narrative where the text turns against itself, i.e., where it contradicts itself or where traces can be found of other literary and non-literary texts. Special attention is paid to dualisms that are posited by the narrative and that always involve a hierarchy (e.g., male above female). The critic stresses the undervalued term in the dualism – as happens in *gender studies and *post-colonial approaches to narrative – and from that angle deconstructs the hierarchy and *ideology installed by the text. He or she opens up the narrative by confronting it with its *paratext and with other texts, some of them quite marginal or unexpected. All types of boundary transgression, including *metalepsis and paralepsis (*see* ALTERATION), are treated as essential to the narrative and not as marginal by-products.

SEE ALSO: philosophy and narrative; postclassical narratology

References and further reading

Bloom, Harold (1973) *The Anxiety of Influence: A Theory of Poetry*, New York: Oxford University Press.
——, Paul de Man, Jacques Derrida, Geoffrey Hartman, and, J. Hillis Miller (1979) *Deconstruction and Criticism*, New York: Continuum.

Derrida, Jacques (1976) *Of Grammatology*, trans. Gayatri Chakravorty Spivak, Baltimore: Johns Hopkins University Press.

—— (1982) *Margins of Philosophy*, trans. Alan Bass, Chicago: University of Chicago Press.

Hartman, Geoffrey (1980) *Criticism in the Wilderness*, New Haven: Yale University Press.

Johnson, Barbara (1980) *The Critical Difference: Essays in the Contemporary Rhetoric of Reading*, Baltimore: Johns Hopkins University Press.

de Man, Paul (1979) *Allegories of Reading: Figural Language in Rousseau, Nietzsche, Rilke, and Proust*, New Haven: Yale University Press.

Punday, Daniel (2003) *Narrative after Deconstruction*, Albany: University of New York State Press.

LUC HERMAN AND BART VERVAECK

DEFAMILIARISATION

Viktor Shklovskii coined 'defamiliarisation' (Russian *ostranenie*, 'making strange') as the key term of *Russian Formalism in his essay *Art as Technique* (1917) (*see* FORMALISM). The device of defamiliarisation provides the formalist basis of the concept of deviation, which rejects the ideas of imitation, reproduction, and *mimesis. According to deviation theory, the function of art lies not in representing content and transmitting messages but rather in defamiliarising both its subject matter and the devices with which that subject matter is presented.

In Shklovskii's examples, defamiliarisation has three increasingly specific senses: (1) deviation from conventionalised forms of representation; (2) disruption of automated patterns of representation; (3) alienation of familiar objects, concepts, and forms. The intended effect of artful defamiliarisation is to increase the effort and duration of perception because, Shklovskii claims, the process of perception is an end in itself in art and must be prolonged accordingly. There are two effects of artful disruption of perception: (1) a conscious 'seeing' of the represented object (the opposite of automated recognition) which grasps the essence of the object and thereby prevents the perceiving subject from losing both its sense of reality and consequently its life; (2) the stimulation of a feel for perception itself, which makes the subject aware of the making of a thing. Shklovskii's examples illustrate the defamiliarisation of several different kinds of object: (1) objects of extralinguistic reality (defamiliarised, for example, by way of *metaphors, riddles, and all non-conventional *naming practices); (2) social institutions, whose true nature is obscured by conventionalised representation and reception (examples of this kind of defamiliarisation are found in Tolstoy's portrayal of the institutions of property, *opera, war, marriage, and corporal punishment, from the point of view of outsiders); (3) language (poetic language as a disruption of 'practical' language); and (4) the artistic device itself (in defamiliarisation in the sense of making strange, a conventionalised method which has lost its perceptibility is made palpable again by being laid bare).

The concept of defamiliarisation underlies all subtheories of formalism (the theories of verse, of the fabula and the sjuzhet, of the construction of the sjuzhet, and of the *skaz) (*see* STORY-DISCOURSE DISTINCTION). Approaches to defamiliarisation have focused on either the aesthetic or the *ethical aspect of this multifaceted concept. Brecht became acquainted with it during his trips to Russia in 1932 and 1935, and was stimulated by it to develop his theory of the alienation effect (*Verfremdungs-Effekt*), in which the ethical aspect predominates. Defamiliarisation also gave rise to the immanentist idea of literary evolution as the result of cycles of automatisation and deautomatisation. As Shklovskii himself pointed out, defamiliarisation is particularly prominent in Laurence Sterne's *Tristram Shandy*, whose metanarrative excursions lay bare the device of conventional storytelling (*see* METANARRATIVE COMMENT), and in the innumerable *metalepses used in Cervantes's *Don Quixote*. More generally, defamiliarisation informs all anti-realist and playful *narrative techniques, especially those used in *metafictions and in *postmodern rewrites (*see* REALISM, THEORIES OF).

References and further reading

Erlich, Victor (1955) *Russian Formalism: History – Doctrine*, The Hague: Mouton.

Hansen-Löve, Aage A. (1978) *Der russische Formalismus*, Vienna: Österreichische Akademie der Wissenschaften.

Lachmann, Renate (1970) 'Die "Verfremdung" und das "Neue Sehen" bei Viktor Sklovskij', *Poetica*, 3, 226–49.

Shklovskii, Victor (1917) 'Art as Technique', in *Russian Formalist Criticism*, trans. Lee T. Lemon and Marion J. Reis, Lincoln: University of Nebraska Press.

Striedter, Iurii (1969) 'Zur formalistischen Theorie der Prosa und der literarischen Evolution', in Iurii Striedter (ed.) *Texte der russischen Formalisten*, vol. 1, Munich: Fink.

WOLF SCHMID

DEIXIS

Along with proper names and definite descriptions (e.g., the poet from Chile), 'deictics' are linguistic expressions whose prototypical function is to contribute to acts of definite *reference (*see* NAMING IN NARRATIVE). They are found in all human languages, corresponding roughly to English *this, these, that, those, here, there, now, then* and the so called 'pronouns' (*I, you, we, he, she, they*). The term 'deixis' (deictic) derives from the Greek 'to show directly' and such expressions have in common that they usually point at or demonstrate their object. Variously called indexicals (Morris 1946; Peirce 1955 [1940]; Husserl 1978 [1939]; Benveniste 1974 [1965]), indicator expressions (Sacks 1992) or shifters (Jesperson 1965 [1934]; Jakobson 1971 [1957]), deictics have a number of distinctive features relevant to both ordinary speech and narrative practices. The first is that they are used to individuate objects in terms of their accessibility in the discourse context (*see* EXISTENT). Hence 'this' usually refers to objects immediate to the situation in which it is uttered, 'here' to the place in which it is uttered, 'I' to whoever utters 'I' and so forth. The second is that they achieve reference not by describing their object, but by directing attention to it, often by means of accompanying *gestures. The third is that the referential scope of deictics is variable, as in 'here' used to point to a spot on the speaker's body, the setting of talk, the region, country, or broader space of reference (*see* DESCRIPTION; SPACE IN NARRATIVE). The combined result of these features is that such expressions seem to refer without in any way characterising their object, and it is impossible to state the usage conditions on deictics by enumerating properties that must be displayed by the objects to which they refer. Rather, in order to establish reference, the deictic must be understood relative to the utterance or narrative field in which it occurs.

This relativity is especially evident when deictics occur in quoted or indirect discourse (*see* SPEECH REPRESENTATION). Hence if on Monday Eric tells Brian 'I'll see you here this afternoon' and Brian reports the exchange to Mia later in the week, he can say 'Eric said he would see me there that afternoon', in which case 'I, you, here, this' have been shifted to 'he, me, there, that' without altering the references. If on the other hand Brian uses direct quotation, he can say 'Eric said "I'll meet you here this afternoon"'". In this case the original form of Eric's utterance has been retained, but the deictics have been transposed, since in using Eric's words, Brian has uttered deictics whose meaning must be understood relative the original context, not the context in which he produces the quotation. Therefore, in Brian's utterance 'I' refers not to himself, but to Eric, and 'you' refers not to Mia (his addressee) but to himself (Eric's original addressee). Stepping back from the technical details illustrated by such facts, it can be seen that deictics in any language are a resource by which speakers, *authors and *narrators position themselves and their *characters relative to the settings in which they produce discourse. In a narrative work, the use of such expressions plays a central role in anchoring description to *perspective and also co-articulating multiple perspectives (*see* FOCALIZATION). Such phenomena are notoriously subtle and difficult to learn in a foreign language, yet they are so familiar and automatic as to be nearly invisible to native speakers. The difficulty is due to the fact that whereas deixis is a universal feature of languages, the inventory of deictics, the precise distinctions they mark and the pragmatics of proper usage all vary cross-linguistically.

From a linguistic perspective, the deictic field (Bühler 1990 [1934]) consists of the combined dimensions of space, *time, *person, perception, discourse, and perspective which jointly define the immediate setting in which utterances are produced. At the centre of this field is the indexical ground or *origo* relative to which relations of proximity, temporality, perceptual access, givenness in discourse, and prospection and retrospection are arrayed. This field is the elementary frame of reference, itself embedded in a broader setting by way of contextual or textual elements. Through embedding, the positions that make up the deictic field are invested with values and further relations that go far beyond deixis *per se*: persons and characters who occupy the positions of Speaker, Addressee are individuals with their own features, just as the objects referred to in actual speech are endowed with qualities. The result of embedding is to subordinate the deictic field to an emerging frame of relevance, which may be an activity, a narrative unfolding, taken for granted, or in dispute among the parties. In each case, deixis is a point of articulation between language structure, expressive *voice, perspective, and the overall field in which subjects, objects, and their involvements emerge.

Given its specific features, deixis plays a key role in narrative. From the viewpoint of textual cohesion deictic forms maintain reference to persons, places, and objects within a text as it unfolds. For the same reason, shifts in the deictic grounding of description may help mark the boundaries between episodes and other *narrative units, just as they position characters and narrators relative to storylines. First-person narrative, *dialogue, relations of simultaneity, flashback, foreshadowing, the historical present, and the boundaries between what Bakhtin (1986) called *'chronotopes' all depend for their coherence upon deictic relations (see TENSE AND NARRATIVE). Similarly, the relations between direct discourse, quotation, indirect discourse and *'free indirect discourse' rely for their definition upon deixis. Textual *genres are often characterised by distinctive configurations of deictic elements, as in first-person narrative, the interpetation of evidential and person references in testimonial narrative (see TESTIMONIO), and temporal deixis in historical narrative (see HISTORIOGRAPHY). Similarly, the structure of *address, voice, perspective and deictic transposition all use deixis as a resource for positioning the reader/hearer in relation to the narrative.

SEE ALSO: discourse analysis (linguistics); pragmatics; speech act theory

References and further reading

Bakhtin, M. M. (1986) *Speech Genres and Other Late Essays*, (eds) Caryl Emerson and Michael Holquist, trans. Vern W. McGee, Austin: University of Texas Press.
Benveniste, Émile (1974 [1965]) 'Le langage et l'experience humaine', in *Problèmes de liguistique générale*, vol. 2, Paris: Gallimard.
Bühler, Karl (1990 [1934]) *Theory of Language: The Representational Function of Language*, trans. Donald Fraser Goodwin, Amsterdam: John Benjamins.
Duchan, Judith F., Gail A. Bruder, Lynne E. Hewitt (eds) (1995) *Deixis in Narrative: a Cognitive Science Perspective*, Hillsdale, NJ: Lawrence Erlbaum.
Hanks, William F. (1996) *Language and Communiciative Practice*, Boulder, CO: Westview.
—— (2000) *Intertexts: Writings on Language, Utterance and Context*, Lanham MD: Rowman and Littlefield Publishers, Inc.
Husserl, Edmund (1978 [1939]) 'Origin of Geometry', in *Phenomenology and Sociology: Selected Readings*, ed. Thomas Luckmann, trans. David Carr, New York: Penguin.
Jakobson, Roman (1971 [1957]) 'Shifters, Verbal Categories, and the Russian Verb', in *Selected Writings of Roman Jakobson*, vol. 2, The Hague: Mouton.
Jespersen, Otto (1965 [1934]) *The Philosophy of Grammar*, New York: W. W. Norton.
Margolin, Uri (1984) 'Narrative and Indexicality', *Journal of Literary Semantics*, 13, 181–204.
Morris, Charles (1946) *Signs, Language, and Behavior*, New York: George Braziller.
Peirce, C. S. (1955 [1940]) 'Logic as Semiotic: The Theory of Signs', in Justus Buchler (ed.) *Philosophical Writings of Peirce*, New York: Dover.
Sacks, Harvey (1992) *Lectures on Conversation*, ed. Gail Jefferson, Oxford: Blackwell.

WILLIAM F. HANKS

DENARRATION

The term 'denarration' is currently used in two distinct senses: 'ontological' denarration is the unresolvable denial of previously established story *events, and 'existential' denarration denotes the loss of *identity in *postmodern culture and society.

Ontological denarration occurs when a *narrator denies or negates events or *descriptions that had until that point been part of the *storyworld. The following pair of statements constitutes an act of denarration: 'that day it rained non-stop in Deauville' followed by 'that day the sun shone uninterruptedly in Deauville'. By contrast, the *disnarrated, as defined by Gerald Prince, refers to narrative possibilities that are mentioned in the text but not actualised. Contradictory statements are common in fiction, but most of the time they can be attributed to conventional causes like an unreliable *narrator, different accounts of the same events made by different perceivers, an author-character assaying different possibilities before determining on a particular depiction, or even the rare case in which an *author inadvertently contradicts himself or herself (see FOCALIZATION; RELIABILITY). Denarration is different, and involves the alteration of the fictional world. When an omniscient and authoritative narrator says that a fictional space is all black, then all white, then all grey, he or she is creating and then negating and recreating the fictional world and there is no way that statement can be denied or refuted unless the narrator himself or herself goes on to do so.

The practice of ontological denarration extends at least as far back as Denis Diderot's *Jacques the Fatalist* (1796). Authors like Samuel Beckett and Alain Robbe-Grillet have explored some of the furthest reaches of this practice. Beckett's *Molloy* includes of a series of statements that negate each other without any obvious method of resolving such contradictions; it concludes with the duplicitous narrator admitting that the words he used to begin his *narration were false. Still more extreme is Beckett's *Worstword Ho*, which comes into being by postulating, negating, and then postulating still other possible narrative elements and entities and which ends in sustained series of such erasures. In such extreme cases, the story becomes irretrievable and all one is left with is the narrative's discourse (*see* STORY-DISCOURSE DISTINCTION).

Existential denarration, by contrast, describes a person's loss of *life story, a state particularly notable in the case of celebrities, where destruction of narrative identity is usually caused by the type of haphazard information disseminated in extended media coverage (*see* IDENTITY AND NARRATIVE). As Coupland (1996: 179) puts it, a denarrated person feels 'lost, dangerous, out of control and susceptible to the forces of randomness'. Discussing Coupland's test cases, Berressem (2002) argues that the oscillation between identity-preserving narrative *closure and catastrophic denarration is a typical end-of-millenium phenomenon.

SEE ALSO: unnarratable

References and further reading

Berressem, Hanjo (2002) 'DeNarration: Literature at the End of the Millenium', in Gerhard Hoffmann and Alfred Hornung (eds) *Postmodernism and the 'Fin de Siècle'*, Heidelberg: Winter.
Coupland, Douglas (1996) *Polaroids from the Dead*, London: Flamingo.
McHale, Brian (1987) *Postmodernist Fiction*, New York: Methuen.
Richardson, Brian (2001) 'Denarration in Fiction: Erasing the Story in Beckett and Others', *Narrative*, 9, 168–75.

BRIAN RICHARDSON

DESCRIPTION

Description is a *text-type which identifies the properties of places, objects, or persons (*see* EXISTENT). Classical narratology defines description as a narrative pause interrupting the presentation of the chain of *events (*see* TEMPORAL ORDERING; TIME IN NARRATIVE). From a structural point of view, descriptions specify themes and subthemes (e.g., 'house', 'doors', 'windows') and link them to a range of complements including stative verbs ('be', 'have'), adjectives, similes, and *metaphors. Since it is not always easy to identify the principle organising the individual themes, special textual markers indicating spatial oppositions (near/far, up/down, left/right) or ordering links (enumeration, from least to most important, etc.) are often used to achieve descriptive coherence (*see* SPACE IN NARRATIVE).

Description follows a metonymic logic in which the individual themes are related by what Jakobson has called the principle of contiguity (*see* METONYMY). The principle of contiguity invokes the reader's knowledge of thematic relations given in reality, culture, or aesthetic convention. Ruth Ronen claims that descriptive elements and their relations 'are not part of the reality but are taken in fact from a purely ideological set of models destined to organise a historical-social space' (Ronen 1997: 277). Hence a closer discourse analysis may be called for in order to investigate the full function and impact of description in specific texts (*see* DISCOURSE ANALYSIS (FOUCAULT)).

Is description possible in the visual *media? 'Tacit description' seems to be the standard mode of assertion in *photography, whereas 'explicit description' in *film is not uncommon in scenes where the storyline has not yet begun or is obviously interrupted. Despite the fact that filmic description 'cannot be vague', as Chatman (1990: 41) puts it, it is up to the viewer to establish specific links, values, and properties.

Recent narratological studies have shown that description is not merely an ornamental way of establishing setting or *character. Instead, it is emphasised that 'narration can just as easily function at the service of description as vice versa' (Chatman: 1990: 2). By distinguishing a surface level and a deep-structural (functional) level, theorists have found it useful to refer to both 'narratized descriptions' and 'descriptized narrations' (Mosher 1991: 426). For instance, a descriptive passage acquires a narrative quality if it is motivated by a speaking or perceiving character in the story. Conversely, a passage that looks as if it were pure *narration may function as a description if it is not part of the storyline or the text's narrative logic of 'choice, risk, consequence [or] irreversibility' (Chatman 1990: 32).

SEE ALSO: ekphrasis; events and event-types; narrative

References and further reading

Bal, Mieke (1981) 'On Meanings and Descriptions', *Studies in Twentieth Century Literature*, 6.1–2, 100–48.

Chatman, Seymour (1990) *Coming to Terms: The Rhetoric of Narrative in Fiction and Film*, Ithaca: Cornell University Press.

Hamon, Philippe (1982) 'What is a Description?', in Tvzetan Todorov (ed.) *French Literary Theory Today*, Cambridge: Cambridge University Press.

—— (1993) *Du descriptif*, Paris: Hachette.

Kittay, Jeffrey (ed.) (1981) *Yale French Studies*, 61. (Special Issue: "Towards a Theory of Description").

Lopes, José Manuel (1995) *Foregrounded Description in Prose Fiction*, Toronto: University of Toronto Press.

Mosher, Harold F., Jr (1991) 'Towards a Poetics of Descriptized Narration', *Poetics Today*, 3, 425–45.

Ronen, Ruth (1997) 'Description, Narrative, and Representation', *Narrative*, 3, 274–86.

TORSTEN PFLUGMACHER

DESIRE

A psychoanalytically inflected notion of desire has been variously invoked to explain issues of dynamics, motivation, and *reception not adequately accounted for in *formalist and *structuralist studies of narrative (*see* NARRATIVE DYNAMICS; PSYCHOANALYSIS AND NARRATIVE). In psychoanalytic discourse, desire's hallmark is less its relation to any real object than its essential unrealisability. Always in excess of its ostensible object, desire manifests and perpetuates itself in language along a chain of metonymic substitutions (*see* METONYMY). Because desire can be understood formally in relation to the category of metonymy and dynamically in terms thematised in narrative, it has become central to postformalist narratologies that examine the relation between *narrative structure and its *psychological, social, historical, and ideological concerns (*see* IDEOLOGY AND NARRATIVE; POSTCLASSICAL NARRATOLOGY).

Ross Chambers calls desire 'the force that can change things' (253), yet there is little consensus about either the status of this force or the change it initiates. Brooks locates desire in both Story and Discourse, since narratives not only tell stories of desire but also arouse and deploy readers' and characters' desire for meaning (*see* STORY-DISCOURSE DISTINCTION). He terms desire 'the motor force of narrative'; the *plots it generates seek consummations that exhaust and resolve the energies it has mobilised within both the text and the reader. Although Brooks allows for the ultimate illusoriness of such totalising *closure, he argues that the power of the desire for closure enforces this illusion and constitutes the compulsion to 'read for the plot'. Bersani sees desire as denying the narrative closure that Brooks sees as its goal. Whereas Brooks would see Elizabeth Bennett's marriage to Mr Darcy in *Pride and Prejudice* as the appropriate consummation of desires that have, through narrative, discovered their proper objects, Bersani would see the narrative that culminates in Elizabeth's and Darcy's union as a 'repressive discourse' that 'submerges and legitimates' (16) desires that are by definition anathema to and in excess of the social systems that would tame them. For Bersani, desire is thus not in the service of signification and closure, but is rather the primary-process drive that would undo them and that narrative combats and resists with all its force.

*Feminist readings of desire in narrative call for a scrutiny of the *gender ideologies of both psychoanalysis and narratology. Whereas De Lauretis shows desire in narrative to be oedipally prescripted and 'still at work ... in contemporary epistemologies and social technologies' (125), Winnett calls for readings that foreground narratives' own resistances to the theoretical paradigms that would predetermine the gender and hence the trajectory of desire.

References and further reading

Bersani, Leo (1986) *The Freudian Body: Psychoanalysis and Art*, New York: Columbia University Press.

Brooks, Peter (1984) *Reading for the Plot*, New York: Knopf.

Chambers, Ross (1991) *Reading (the) Oppositional (in) Narrative*, Chicago and London: University of Chicago Press.

Clayton, Jay (1989) 'Narrative and Theories of Desire', *Critical Inquiry*, 16.1, 33–53.

De Lauretis, Teresa (1982) *Alice Doesn't: Feminism, Semiotics, Cinema*, Bloomington: Indiana University Press.

Deleuze, Gilles, and Félix Guattari (1983) *Anti-Oedipus: Capitalism and Schizophrenia*, trans. Robert Hurley, Mark Seem, and Helen R. Lane, Minneapolis: University of Minnesota Press.

Lacan, Jacques (1968) *The Language of the Self: The Function of Language in Psychoanalysis*, trans. Anthony Wilden, New York: Delta.

Winnett, Susan (1991) 'Coming Unstrung: Women, Men, Narrative, and Principles of Pleasure', *PMLA*, 105.3, 505–18.

SUSAN WINNETT

DETECTIVE FICTION

As a generic term, detective fiction refers to a narrative whose principal action concerns the attempt by an investigator to solve a crime and to bring a criminal to justice, whether the crime involves a theft, or one or more murders. The treatment of crime and detection is grounded in a relationship of complicity between *authors and readers that resembles a game played according to a set of rules (*see* CODES FOR READING; GENRE THEORY IN NARRATIVE STUDIES; READER-RESPONSE THEORY). The fundamental formal rules of this game are comprised by the questions 'Whodunit?' and 'Who is guilty?' Usually the consequences of a crime are revealed well before the *events that led up to it become known. This situation structures detective fiction – but backwards: the *plot aims at establishing a linear, chronological sequence of events that will eventually explain its own baffling starting point (*see* TEMPORAL ORDERING). The detective's reconstruction of the past includes the analysis of the human interactions leading to the crime. In order to determine 'whodunit?' detectives assess how moral responsibility is to be allotted among the suspects. This evaluation arises from the difference between the judicial and the moral codes, which may, but need not, overlap, for an agent may be both legally and morally responsible (i.e., guilty) or one but not the other. The question 'Whodunit?' is thus not identical with the question 'Who is guilty?' because the investigation shows guilt to be a more universal phenomenon than crime.

Fictional detectives represent law and order, but they often resort to illegal methods, for which reason their professional skills resemble the skills of criminals. In the figure of the detective the legal and moral codes of law enforcement intersect with those of the criminal order. Therefore, the investigation is just as much a probing into an investigator's moral principles as it is a scrutiny of the suspects and their social context. The final arbitration on moral issues belongs thus to authors and readers.

The sub-genres of mainstream detective fiction treat crime and detection differently. *Classical detective fiction* presents crime as a puzzle to be solved through a 'who-why-how-when-where' chain of questions that the detective poses. Writing and reading this form is supposedly governed by rules that include giving the reader a chance of solving the puzzle before the detective does. Ideally, the solution produces insight, the perception of an interlocking pattern governing the author's crafting and solving of the enigma (e.g., Agatha Christie). *Hard-boiled detective fiction* depicts the battle of an investigator against criminal forces infesting those structures that ought to uphold society, emphasising the protagonist's heroism, perseverance, and moral choices. The reader follows an exciting quest rather than trying to solve an enigma (e.g., Raymond Chandler). In the *police procedural* the plot moves between the criminal's planning and committing of crimes and the technical and specialised process of police investigation, with emphasis on procedure and collective *agency (e.g., Patricia Cornwell). *Feminist detective fiction* uses generic conventions in order to investigate and criticise social conditions under patriarchy (e.g., Sara Paretsky) (*see* FEMINIST NARRATOLOGY; GENDER STUDIES). The *metaphysical or postmodern detective story* accentuates the generic features of its mainstream counterpart by presenting the text itself as the mystery to be solved. The plot manipulates temporal and causal relations without establishing the ground from which to organise the pieces narrated into a coherent whole (*see* CAUSALITY). It parodies the notion of solution as *closure, either by supplying inconclusive solutions or by refusing to provide one. It uses the conventions and settings of mainstream detective fiction in order to textualise reality, highlighting its constructed nature. Through these measures it calls on readers to act as the co-creators of the text, for our reading and interpretation are the major means of lending coherence to the narrative (e.g., Paul Auster).

Detective fiction invariably includes an overt preoccupation with its own formal and *thematic characteristics. Characters, for example, discuss the crime at hand by comparing it to cases from detective fiction. This self-reflexivity (*see* REFLEXIVITY) has invited literary theorists to use the genre in order to illustrate how detective fiction encapsulates the basic principles of *narrativity. The generic framework highlights the models from which detective fiction borrows and from which it knowingly departs, drawing attention to the operations of *intertextuality. The backward construction of plot depends on a narrative presentation in which the story of the investigation embeds the story of a crime that has supposedly taken place prior to the beginning of the investigation. The story of the investigation is itself, in turn, often embedded in a story told, for example, by a 'Watson' figure, highlighting the fictitious writing of the text itself. These three stories are located at different narrative levels, illustrating the hierarchical organisation of narrative and creating a sense of *time (see EMBEDDING). The *desire to find out 'whodunit' combined with the suspension of the answer act together as the structuring force of plot. The ambiguously fragmented presence of the crime story causes detective and reader to order and interpret clues and events in the light of the questions they are trying to answer. Thus the preoccupation with narrative is mirrored in a related feature: the reading and interpreting of stories. The detective acts as a figure for the reader so that methods of detection have been examined in the light of theories of reading and interpretation (Hühn 1987; Pyrhönen 1999). By emphasising narrative sequence, suspense, and closure; by making the hierarchical organisation of narrative levels visible; by illustrating the operations of intertextuality; and by reflecting reading, writing, and interpretation, detective fiction represents narrativity in its basic form.

SEE ALSO: narrative structure; suspense and surprise

References and further reading

Bennett, Donna (1979) 'The Detective Story: Towards a Definition of Genre', *PTL*, 4, 233–66.
Hühn, Peter (1987) 'The Detective as Reader: Narrativity and Reading Concepts in Detective Fiction', *Modern Fiction Studies*, 33.3, 451–66.
Merivale, Patricia, and Susan Sweeney (eds) (1999) *Detecting Texts: The Metaphysical Detective Story from Poe to Postmodernism*, Philadelphia: University of Pennsylvania Press.
Most, Glenn W., and William W. Stowe (eds) (1983) *The Poetics of Murder: Detective Fiction and Literary Theory*, New York: Harcourt Brace Jovanovich.
Porter, Dennis (1981) *The Pursuit of Crime: Art and Ideology in Detective Fiction*, New Haven: Yale University Press.
Pyrhönen, Heta (1994) *Murder from an Academic Angle: An Introduction to the Study of the Detective Narrative*, Columbia, S.C.: Camden House.
—— (1999) *Mayhem and Murder: Narrative and Moral Problems in the Detective Story*, Toronto: University of Toronto Press.
Walker, Ronald G., and June M. Frazer (eds) (1990) *The Cunning Craft: Original Essays on Detective Fiction and Literary Theory*, Macomb: Western Illinois University Press.

HETA PYRHÖNEN

DIALOGISM

Although it might appear to be no more than a neo-logistic version of *dialogue, Bakhtin's term *dialogism* is far richer and more complex. In his view, the speakerly exchange or interaction of dialogue is in fact no more than the embodiment of the dialogic nature of all discourse, the fact that language (even that which performs as monologue) is oriented towards the discourse (word, *voice, or utterance) which has preceded it, and that which it anticipates (however hypothetically) (see INTERTEXTUALITY; POLYPHONY). This layering and multivoicing both downgrades the individual subject as intentional source of meaning, and emphasises the socially located and constructed nature of meaning (see INTENTIONALITY). Insofar as dialogism represents the social reality of languages (as opposed, for instance, to the abstract or formalised linguistic system), it inevitably has a political dimension. So instead of the egalitarian give and take of (ideal) dialogue, dialogism highlights the contending forces in society and their unequal nature (see SOCIOLINGUISTIC APPROACHES TO NARRATIVE).

Bakhtin's preference for narrative in the shape of the *novel over poetry or *drama is due to the former's 'double-voiced' nature (see DUAL-VOICE HYPOTHESIS; NARRATIVE IN POETRY), its ability both to instantiate and foreground dialogism, to formally embody it, and to represent it in terms of social reality, its contradictions, inequalities, struggles. The novel's narrative antithesis – the *epic – is rejected by Bakhtin on the grounds of its closed, distanced, determined-once-and-for-all nature. Against the epic's relative monologism, historical distance, and *closure at all levels, all these being traits that derive from its reliance on 'a single, unitary authorial discourse', Bakhtin champions the openness, the *indeterminacy, the 'unresolved contemporaneity' of the novel. The fact that the novel inscribes dialogism at the level both of form and content means that it is unlikely to suffer the fate of the epic – 'completely finished, a congealed and half moribund genre' – since its dialogic openness means that it is the one *genre which embraces and embodies change.

The dialogic contemporaneity of the novel is grounded in 'experience, knowledge and practice (the future)'. That dimension of future-oriented praxis is in turn a measure of the political importance of dialogic narrative. The fact that the novel represents the future of literature as far as Bakhtin can see is not the least of its political implications. As well as being the genre which best embodies dialogism, the novel also has an effect on other genres, insofar as they are not absolutely closed off like the epic. The transformative, relativising nature of novelistic discourse impacts on drama or poetry, 'novelising' them, opening them up to dialogism, to all those social languages which for Bakhtin they typically deny, repress, or exclude. Such a process may only be partial, but from a Bakhtinian perspective it can also only be beneficial.

SEE ALSO: heteroglossia; Marxism and narrative

References and further reading

Bakhtin, Mikhail (1981) *The Dialogic Imagination*, ed. Michael Holquist, trans. Caryl Emerson and Michael Holquist, Austin: University of Texas Press.
Gardiner, Michael (1992) *The Dialogics of Critique*, London: Routledge.
Hirschkop Ken, and David Shepherd (eds) (1989) *Bakhtin and Cultural Theory*, Manchester: Manchester University Press.

PATRICK WILLIAMS

DIALOGUE IN THE NOVEL

Novelistic or 'fictional' dialogue (Toolan 1985) refers to the direct representation of *characters' speech whereby some sense of interaction or exchange of views is created. Dialogue fulfils the important narrative functions of characterisation and advancing the *plot. Dialogue novels (e.g., the works of Ivy Compton-Burnett or Manuel Puig's *Kiss of the Spider Woman*) foreground speech and keep narrative input to a minimum. However, dialogue in the *novel is usually framed by the

*narrator's use of speech tags such as 'he said', 'she said'. These often serve the function of 'stage directions' (Page 1973), providing paralinguistic and prosodic information (e.g., 'she whispered', 'he rattled on, moving closer to her'). They may also provide an evaluation of the dialogue and/or the characters (e.g., 'she confessed', 'he said, unsure of himself'). The term 'suspended quotation' (Lambert 1981) refers to instances where the same character's utterances is interrupted by the narrator's discourse, often for the purposes of *irony.

Critical debates centre on the extent to which novelistic dialogue is, or should be, mimetic of naturally occurring speech (*see* MIMESIS). Dialogue in the novel is often deliberately stylised and artificial, and even where it purports to be a realistic or accurate representation, this is always tidied up or edited (Leech and Short 1981). Further, stylisticians have studied fictional dialogue in order to evaluate the limits of applicability of models of naturally occurring conversation, such as Grice's Co-operative Principle or Conversation Analysis. For their part, cultural theorists have argued that our notions of what constitutes effective dialogue change over time, and that literary representations play a crucial role in defining prevailing ideas and ideals. Davis (1987) has argued that novelistic representations are biased against group talk and privilege the individual, so that what Kennedy (1983) calls the 'duologue of personal encounter' comes to represent the norm or ideal. However, instances of multiparty talk have been identified in the novel, and Thomas (2002) argues that these radically challenge our notions of what constitutes the norm or ideal of dialogue. Another source of debate is the extent to which dialogue in the novel may be *dialogic, providing the reader with competing *voices where no one voice has the final say, or whether ultimately dialogue is subsumed by the discourse of the *narrator. Dialogue also plays an important part in creating the effects of *heteroglossia and *polyphony which Bakhtin identifies as crucial to the novel form.

SEE ALSO: dual-voice hypothesis; free indirect discourse; speech representation; quotation theory

References and further reading

Davis, Lennard J. (1987) *Resisting Novels: Ideology and Fiction*, London: Methuen.
Fludernik, Monika (1993) *The Fictions of Language and the Languages of Fiction*, London: Routledge.

Kennedy, Andrew (1983) *Dramatic Dialogue: the Duologue of Personal Encounter*, Cambridge: Cambridge University Press.

Lambert, Mark (1981) *Dickens and the Suspended Quotation*, New Haven: Yale University Press.

Leech, Geoffrey, and Michael H. Short (1981) *Style in Fiction: A Linguistic Introduction to English Fictional Prose*, London: Longman.

Page, Norman (1973) *Speech in the English Novel*, London: Longman.

Thomas, Bronwen E. (2002) 'Multiparty Talk in the Novel: The Distribution of Tea and Talk in a Scene from Evelyn Waugh's *Black Mischief*', *Poetics Today*, 23.4, 657–84.

Toolan, Michael (1985) 'Analysing Fictional Dialogue', *Language and Communication*, 5.3, 193–206.

BRONWEN THOMAS

DIARY

A diary or journal is a record, kept intermittently, of thoughts, feelings, or *events (*see* THOUGHT AND CONSCIOUSNESS REPRESENTATION (LITERATURE)). Entries may be dated or undated. Personal diaries, like the Puritan diary or the *journal intime*, are characteristically private and inward-looking. As a log or record of accounts, the diary is an ancient form, and can be found on codices and cuneiform tablets. The chief defining characteristic of a narrative diary is its intercalated mode of composition, where the writing process is situated between the events of an ongoing story (*see* TEMPORAL ORDERING; TIME IN NARRATIVE). Diaries are also almost invariably single-author texts. Despite the high frequency of present-tense reflection addressed by the diarist to herself or himself, diaries can and do accommodate the entire range of narrative *tenses, often include long stretches of retrospective *narration, and have been addressed to readers other than the diarist, ranging from confidantes to the general public (*see* AUDIENCE).

Though the diary, because of its unplanned and incondite manner of production, has long been considered the least literary of forms, both it and its fictional counterparts have, since the 1960s, been given increasing critical and theoretical attention as literary *genres in their own right. Indeed, Lejeune, in reaction to this trend, has sought to restore priority to the non-fictional diary as a private practice rather than as a set of published artefacts. Work on both fictional and non-fictional diaries, particularly in the widening field of women's diaries (Bunkers and Huff 1996),

has seen in the diary's cloistered character, its amenability to composition under the pressure of immediate feeling, and its freedom from formal constraint a compatibility with ideas of the self as multiple, improvisatory, and unbounded (*see* GENDER STUDIES; IDENTITY AND NARRATIVE). Critical studies of the use of the diary form in fictional work have focused special attention on issues of narratorial *reliability (Martens 1985), including the potential of the form's intercalated mode of production to give the writing itself a causal agency in the unfolding story (Abbott 1984). Other work on the diary novel (Field 1989, Martens 1985, Prince 1975) has stressed the genre's fluid status and the difficulty of distinguishing it from forms like the *epistolary novel, the first-person novel, and even the non-fictional diary.

SEE ALSO: novel, the; person

References and further reading

Abbott, H. Porter (1984) *Diary Fiction: Writing as Action*, Ithaca, NY: Cornell University Press.

Bunkers, Suzanne L., and Cynthia A. Huff (1996) *Inscribing the Daily: Critical Essays on Women's Diaries*, Amherst: University of Massachusetts Press.

Canetti, Elias (1979) 'Dialogue of the Cruel Partner', in *The Conscience of Words*, trans. Joachim Neugroschel, New York: Seabury Press.

Field, Trevor (1989) *Form and Function in the Diary Novel*, Totowa, NJ: Barnes & Noble.

Fothergill, Robert A. (1974) *Private Chronicles: A Study of English Diaries*, London: Oxford University Press.

Lejeune, Philippe (1999) 'The Practice of the Private Journal: Chronicle of an Investigation (1986–1998)', in Rachel Langford and Russell West (eds) *Marginal Voices, Marginal Forms: Diaries in European Literature and History*, Amsterdam: Rodopi.

Martens, Lorna (1985) *The Diary Novel*, Cambridge: Cambridge University Press.

Prince, Gerald (1975) 'The Diary Novel: Notes for the Definition of a Sub-Genre', *Neophilologus*, 59, 477–81.

H. PORTER ABBOTT

DIDACTIC NARRATIVE

Didactic narrative, such as short *fiction, brief *anecdotes, *fables, or *parables, is used to instruct learners, in either formal or informal contexts (*see* SHORT STORY; SIMPLE FORMS). Its main purposes are moral education and the transmission of particular kinds of knowledge, often combined with the teaching of literacy skills. The pedagogic use of narrative has a venerable history in indigenous oral traditions and in religious writing worldwide (*see* ORAL CULTURES AND NARRATIVE). It is found in the *Chinese philosophical anecdotes of Confucius and Mencius; in Hindu, Buddhist, and Christian parables and teaching stories (*see* SANSKRIT NARRATIVE; SERMON); in the humorous animal fables of Aesop or La Fontaine; in the witty stories of the Persian poet Sa'di; and in the Mathnavi tales of the mystical Islamic poet Rumi (*see* ANCIENT THEORIES OF NARRATIVE (NON-WESTERN); NARRATIVE IN POETRY).

Didactic narrative is generally characterised by: (1) apparent simplicity and accessible meanings, though often with more profound layers of interpretation; (2) memorable content; (3) highlighted language using formulaic phrases, *metaphors, proverbs, or verse; (4) wide applicability of the teaching point through analogy. In Western *education, didactic narratives fell into disfavour in the twentieth century because they were seen as glib moralising or as classroom preaching. But the emphasis in current education on multicultural contexts has led to a renaissance of didactic narrative. It is no longer seen as a means to impose moral obligations, but rather as a source of multiple readings which provide an opportunity for the open discussion of moral and philosophical issues (*see* INDETERMINACY).

SEE ALSO: children's stories (narratives written for children)

References and further reading

Arberry, A. (1961) *Tales from the Mathnavi*, London: George Allen & Unwin.
Sa'di, M. A. (1964) *The Gulistan or Rose Garden of Sa'di*, trans. E. Rehatsek, London: George Allen & Unwin.

MARTIN CORTAZZI

DIEGESIS

Diegesis in modern narrative theory has two different senses, both originating from ancient Greek. On the one hand, it refers to story, typically in a *film, a sense that came into English in the early nineteenth-century from the Greek word diegesis (*The New Oxford Dictionary of English*). In *Narrative Discourse*, Genette borrowed this term from

film theory and, in distinguishing narrative levels, used it as a substitute for *story* (*see* EMBEDDING; STORY-DISCOURSE DISTINCTION; STORYWORLD). In Genette's classification, the extradiegetic level, for instance, is the level above the (primary) story, and the intradiegetic level is inside the story. Since Genette's classification of narrative levels has gained popularity among narratologists, this sense of diegesis has found its way into many works of narrative theory.

Another usage of diegesis is concerned with the manner of *narration. It originated in the third book of Plato's *Republic*, where Socrates draws a distinction between *mimesis and diegesis as two contrasting ways of narrating the speeches of the characters (*see* SPEECH REPRESENTATION). In simplest terms, mimesis is dramatic imitation, and diegesis is indirect presentation. This distinction has been widely referred to by narrative theorists when discussing written narration. But Socrates, in making the distinction, is concerned with oral narration, as indicated by his explicit references to *'voice' and *'gesture' (Plato 1992: 26; see also Shen 2001: 128). While mimesis is a matter of the poet's assuming the voice and gesture of the *character in representing the character's words verbatim, diegesis, by contrast, is a mode where the poet speaks in his or her own voice and renders the character's words summarily. This distinction is somewhat neutralised in Aristotle's *Poetics*: 'the poet may imitate by narration – in which case he can either take another personality as Homer does, or speak in his own person, unchanged' (Aristotle 1992: 51). Aristotle, that is to say, treats mimesis and diegesis as two alternative modes of 'imitation', which encompasses the representation of both speech and action. The distinction between mimesis and diegesis resurfaced in the opposition of *showing* (direct scenic representation of events and speech) versus *telling* (indirect presentation and summary) articulated by Anglo-American critics at the turn of the twentieth century and is now more or less widely embraced by narrative theorists, even though there is a general tendency to treat the two terms as polar points on a gradual scale (*see* SHOWING VS. TELLING; SUMMARY AND SCENE).

Significantly, the two senses of diegesis outlined above belong to two different dimensions of narrative. Within the framework of the story-discourse distinction, the first sense belongs to the level of story, and the second to the level of discourse.

SEE ALSO: mood; narrative techniques; thought and consciousness representation (literature)

References and further reading

Aristotle (1992) 'Poetics', in H. Adams (ed.) *Critical Theory Since Plato*, Orlando: Harcourt Brace Jovanovich.

Genette, Gérard (1980) *Narrative Discourse*, trans. J. E. Lewin, Ithaca: Cornell University Press.

Pearsall, Judy (ed.) (1998) *The New Oxford Dictionary of English*, Oxford University Press.

Plato (1992) 'Republic', in H. Adams (ed.) *Critical Theory Since Plato*, Orlando: Harcourt Brace Jovanovich.

Shen, Dan (2001) 'Narrative, Reality, and Narrator as Construct: Reflections on Genette's "Narrating"', *Narrative* 9.2, 123–29.

DAN SHEN

DIGITAL NARRATIVE

Critical and theoretical study of digital narrative (henceforth DN) has been encumbered by the difficulty attending a discipline oriented by a moving target: as the technical framework of digital texts has evolved, so have narrative procedures of those texts changed. Vastly increased computer processing speed and storage capacity, improved portability of computing devices (a shift from slow and expensive time-share systems to networked personal desktop, laptop, and now 'palmtop' computers); new computer operating systems (most importantly, the rise of graphical user interfaces [GUIs], in which objects on the screen are manipulated by keyboard, mouse, or game controller); and the growth of high-speed, broadband telecommunications networks (the Internet and World Wide Web), have fostered practices of DN which were not possible two or three decades ago.

Nevertheless, formal and procedural continuities are traceable between the earliest and the most recent DNs. Simulation techniques of text-based *computer games of the 1960s and 1970s are discernible in the interactions of contemporary animated, real-time single- and multiplayer games. Narrative devices typical of *interactive fiction of the mid-1970s (including *embedding and *metalepsis) strongly resemble devices of hypertext fiction of the 1980s and 1990s, without the graphic depiction of those devices common in GUI-based hypertexts (*see* MULTI-PATH NARRATIVE).

Visual-spatial tropes of narrative progress in early computer console games ('Hunt the Wumpus' [1972], 'ADVENT' [mid-1970s], 'Zork' [late 1970s], etc.) are repeated in more refined forms in recent games such as Robyn and Rand Miller's *Myst* trilogy (1993–2003), id Software's *Quake* (1996) and the many games based on its gaming engine, and Jordan Mechner's *The Last Express* (1997). Similarly, a mapping of *narrative progression onto finely-rendered depictions of *space is a basic element of virtual reality systems celebrated by critics such as Murray as the future of DN. But it must be noted that DN is presently in what may be termed the era of its Incunabula; the specific contributions of DN to practices of narrative remain unclear.

Hypertext: 'everything is deeply intertwingled'

Digital computers are general-purpose recombinatorial devices. Because tools for creating, editing, and publishing them permit or even enforce these traits, digital texts are often robustly non-serial and recursive. From the earliest experiments in DN, authors have frequently chosen to aestheticise and thematise narrative digression and discontinuity; breaks in serial structure are commonplace in DNs, and are widely assumed to represent its most distinctive characteristic.

The example of digital hypertext is instructive in this regard. ('Hypertext': a system of 'linked' textual units of varying size and kind, often computer-based, permitting the *author and reader to traverse the linked units without regard to their serial structure; *see* NARRATIVE UNITS.) Nelson, who coined the term 'hypertext' in the early 1960s, has famously described the whole of the textual field as 'deeply intertwingled', bound up in ramifying and interdependent constellations that transgress conventions of *media, *genre, and discipline. Many hypertext theorists writing in the 1990s adopted Nelson's vision of 'Xanadu' – his name for a distributed global network in which all texts are open to linkage and 'transclusion' – as an ideal model of hypertextual form.

This concept of an absolutely extended and saturated textual field raises obvious difficulties with regard to narrative aspects of such a virtual entity, a problem familiar to students of *intertextuality. Nonetheless, its utopian appeal has contributed to theorists' enthusiasm for 'freedoms' permitted by ever-expanding constellations of the link. In their view, (digital) hypertexts are *a priori* less textually and narratively constrained than print and *film, because these forms will always be tightly bound to the Procrustean beds of the page and the reel. Hypertexts are freed of such confines, they propose; their fluid structures permit the author and reader to construct textual and narrative sequences that analogue media cannot support. Consequently, these theorists have argued, hypertexts subvert the very distinction between author and reader (hypertext readers find their own way in the text, and are thus authors in their own right; *see* READER-RESPONSE THEORY); and refuse formal operations of *closure (hypertexts foreground the susceptibility of language to unfettered connotation; cf. Landow; Murray).

A notable weakness of these claims is that they are based on impoverished descriptions of how readers and viewers engage with print and still and moving *images; those engagements are more contingent and inconsistent than has been generally acknowledged. Novice and seasoned readers alike treat print's rules of engagement with equal impertinence: they begin and end where they please; they may easily – and often do – read against conventions of order or integrity (Barthes 1975; Harpold 2003; McGann 2001). Rules for deriving narrative meaning from still images are flexible and idiomatic with respect to cultural and historical context and viewer competence. Conditions of reception of the moving image may be short-circuited by accident, intention, or competing interests: film reels may be shown out of order; *television narratives may be interrupted by unrelated mini-narratives in the form of commercials or public announcements; the fast-forward button is always at hand, etc. Some theorists have argued that the textual and narrative freedoms of digital media may be more quantitative than qualitative. The increased flexibility with which digital texts may be recombined, repurposed, and manipulated by the reader or viewer, they observe, calls attention to this dimension of their reception, which may be less evident or practicable in recombinations of comparably 'chunky' analogue media (Bolter and Grusin 1999; Manovich 2001).

A favourite proposition of hypertext scholarship of the early 1990s is that digital texts, especially hypertexts, represent a practical laboratory for testing arguments of a wide range of postmodern literary and narrative theories (Landow 1997; *see* INDETERMINACY; POSTMODERN NARRATIVE). However, this alignment of hypertextual practice with postmodern theories of textual production has been criticised for conflating distinct *semiotic and narrative paradigms of those theories – for example, Derridean 'undecidability' and Barthesian 'plurality' – or for misconstruing the contexts of their application. A related proposition, that digital hypertexts extend operations of printed texts in which multiple, non-serial sequences are a prominent feature (Cortázar's *Hopscotch* [1966], Pavič's *Dictionary of the Khazars* [1988], Queneau's *Cent mille milliards de poèmes* [1961], Saporta's *Composition no. 1* [1962], etc.), similarly oversimplifies the resemblance of digital texts to their print precursors. This analogy of digital and print operations neglects the role in the printed texts of the reader's material engagement in its operations (shuffling, folding, page-turning, etc.) – a dimension of reading that must be phenomenologically distinct in the case of digital texts (*see* INTERMEDIALITY).

Algorithms and procedures in digital narratives

DNs are produced in relation to deterministic, algorithmic systems having a finite number of states. Algorithms, the series of instructions regarding computation, storage, retrieval, and recombination of data, constitute the 'intelligence' of modern computer programs and operating systems. They determine what these devices may do with data they capture or hold in computer memory, how the computer responds to the user's contributions to its operations, and the scope and range of myriad functions of hardware and software of which the user many never become aware. These algorithmic structures determine the form of the user's responses, as he or she adapts the derivation of the meaning of the interaction to the syntax and semiotics of the computing framework. Thus, for example, a specific signal from a program may present the user with a range of actions, or confirm or otherwise mark the meaning of a prior action. Many such signals typically arrive and require responses at the same time; the user may not be aware of all them or their significance. The effect of his or her responses will be shaped by the program's designation of appropriate or inappropriate user behaviours – that is, their fit with rules of the interaction.

As early students of narrative *formalism recognised, operations of many narratives may be represented by algorithmic schemata constituting a finite set of generative rules defining narrative production and interpretation (*see* FUNCTION (PROPP); STORY SCHEMATA AND CAUSAL STRUCTURE; STRUCTURALIST NARRATOLOGY). The resemblance of such formal representations of narrative to the programmed operations of digital texts is suggestive of critical approaches to narrative that may have particular application to DNs. (Ryan proposes several algorithmic models of narrative based on computing paradigms, though she does not apply them to DNs.)

Of special importance in the reception of DN is the overlap of generative rules of narrative with the idioms and methods of human-computer interaction. Many fictional DNs are read with applications designed with little attention to practices of fiction; very different textual and narrative genres may be read within the frameworks of a single application (a web browser or hypertext reader), with a common set of features and navigational tropes. The same may be said, of course, of the different textual and narrative genres published within the common framework of the modern codex. However, an important difference between digital and print conditions in this context is the support in the former for such 'features' as full-text searching and (in GUI applications) the mapping of narrative structure onto interface objects such as buttons, menus, and dialogues. These constitute alternative systems of reading; they will produce alternative aesthetic and narrative effects, which may or may not be consistent with the aims of the author (*see* INTENTIONALITY).

Divergences between the technical framework of digital texts and the narrative aims of the author are likely to decrease – at least for texts composed with digital reading in mind – as software and hardware are increasingly applied to varied authorial practices and authors become more conversant with programming methods and are thus better able to control the presentation and responses of their texts. Increasingly, digital texts are playing a central role in the hybridisation of 'old' and 'new' media forms (a back-and-forth borrowing of formal conventions Bolter and Grusin term *'remediation'). This is one result of a progressive merging of tools used in the creation of media: many of the same programs are now used in the design of (print) magazines, books, and interactive websites; animation tools and video editing software created for computer *simulations or videogame design are used in the production of a film for theatrical release (*see* HYBRID GENRES). Texts crafted with one medium in mind are consumed in another (e.g., 'e-books', digital versions of printed texts reworked to fit the design of screen-based reading programs), or they are created with multiple media in mind (e.g., a magazine article appearing in print and on a website).

The interface: ergodics and digital anti-narrativity

Not all digital texts signify narratively. Not all elements of those that do contribute to the production and reception of narrative. Digital texts are, of course, not unique in this regard, and the significance of *paratextual elements of narrative forms are an important area of inquiry with relevance beyond DN. However, the function of paratexts of DN would seem to be distinguished by the degree of their performative contribution to narrative signification (*see* PERFORMATIVITY). On-screen 'widgets' (windows, icons, menus, buttons, scrollbars, and the like; manipulable controls and objects of the depicted gameworld) by which means the reader of a GUI DN traverses narrative sequences may delimit structures of those sequences – this region of the simulated space of a game leads to other regions; this node of a hypertext is joined to another node, and thence to a third, etc., – but they also frequently determine which sequences are available to the reader and what meaning might be derived from them. Activating one element shown on the screen and not another, or choosing one of several possible options presented as alternatives, will in many DNs block access to narrative sequences that were previously available. Laurel's study of the mimetic function of 'metanarrative' elements of digital texts was an early and influential analysis of these effects (*see* METANARRATIVE COMMENT; MIMESIS).

Often, the consequences of such turns in a DN are not signalled in advance; a reader will be unaware that he or she has effected a narrative branching, or will only discover this when the active sequence concludes without a resolution anticipated by an earlier prolepsis, or when a subsequent reading discovers 'new' sequences previously undisclosed (*see* TEMPORAL ORDERING). This distinctive contingency of narrative production poses important difficulties for the description of DN: elements of the story expressed by a given traversal of the text may be directly contradicted by successive traversals. Because contradictory *motifs may not be presented as open alternatives – an individual reader or reading may never disclose the existence of a contradiction – it may be impossible to discern which story is the 'correct' one, except at the level of a single reading (*see* STORY-DISCOURSE DISTINCTION). The invisibility of narrative branching and its results is cited by some critics of DN as a suspect trait: readers are, they complain, held hostage to arbitrary machinations of the text which are never revealed or justified, and whose significance can only be guessed at.

An important direction of investigation of these effects has been opened by the investigation of literary ergodics, first described by Aarseth. *Ergodic texts (from *ergon* and *hodos*, Greek words for 'work' and 'path') are those requiring a 'non-trivial effort' on the part of the reader, by which means different semiotic sequences are generated in each reading. Students of ergodics are content to leave undefined the kind and degree of this readerly expenditure. Of greater significance, they propose, is that a wide range of such expenditures is discernible among print and digital texts, and that the variability of results of such expenditures marks the dynamic and generative character of these texts. Ergodics, they contend, offers a more fruitful approach to analysis of such variable texts than ill-defined terms like 'non-linearity' and 'interactivity'.

The focus of ergodic analysis on the generative labour of meaning production has inclined advocates of this model to discard the *hermeneutic emphasis of 1990s new media criticism, and to foreground features of digital texts that resist in some way hermeneutic decoding: *montage/collage techniques, aleatory recombinations of textual units, intelligent agents, and methods of simulation and *immersion. (Manovich's analysis of the influence on new media of early avant-garde cinema is an important contribution to the study of these features. Mateas and Senger's collection comprises recent research on narrative and intelligent agents. Wolf and Perron's collection includes several essays on the role of simulation and immersion in gameplay.) Some proponents of the ergodic model have argued that analysis of narrative operations is particularly inappropriate in the study of computer games. These are, they claim,

largely or entirely non-narrative texts, enacted by contingent player choices which may generate unforeseen, even unprecedented, results having no narrative effect or consequence. Games are played, not narrated; they happen, they are not recounted.

This is an extreme claim. The role of *performance in readers' engagements with print or digital texts may be in some circumstances narratively significant – this is one assumption of procedural narrative traditions such as those developed by members of the *Oulipo – though the contribution of performance to narrative is often unclear. It seems doubtful that the unfolding of gameplay in real time is not grasped by many players as a species of narrative, marked by a beginning and end of play, a series of *conflicts and obstacles and their resolution or overcoming, even when no 'story' is thus related by an identifiable *narrator to a *narratee. (This projection of narrative meaning into the structure of gameplay will be more tentative and inconsistent in the case of simulation games in which the player's direction of gameplay is severely limited.) Moreover, extra-narrative signification of some elements of a narrative text is not, as McGann has cogently observed, a new feature of digital media. The 'old' media have always been subject to performative conditions of their reading and viewing; reading is a multiform and generative process, not just the representation of a found semiotic structure. The visible and material language of the page will extend beyond serial procedures of the letter and the line, to include responses or effects those procedures activate but do not limit. Some of them may be narratively meaningful; others would seem to pertain only to textual mimesis, or to the cultural and institutional standing of the text.

A weaker version of this emphasis on digital non-narrativity merits, however, careful consideration. Representation and simulation need not be unconditionally differentiated with respect to genre or media. Digital texts may signal, by dint of their possibly greater performativity, a breakdown of this distinction in programmable and aleatory textual forms and the consequent need for more flexible distinctions between *narration and performance than predigital media may have required. In this context, the 'event' of gameplay or narrative branching in a digital text might be understood in terms of an active reworking or transgression – a performance – of diegetic limits, such that the player or reader functions as a pseudo-actant or -focalizer, spanning intra- and extra-narrative fields (*see* ACTANT; DIEGESIS; FOCALIZATION). Paratextual and visual-spatial attributes of the on-screen presentation of the digital text may also signify in ways that are not strictly narrative, but which must inflect the reception of the narrative meaning of a digital text. Rosenberg's influential essay on performative values of spatial and typographic structures of electronic poetry and hypertext marks an important opening of this line of inquiry.

Manovich has proposed that the human-computer interface is rapidly becoming a shared 'cultural interface' for the creation and reception of symbolic objects of all kinds. The narrative toolbox of the twenty-first century reader is likely to comprise basic, if critically unexamined, familiarity with the idioms of the interface and its procedures, and with computationally and algorithmically generated narrative sequences. Narratology will no doubt adapt to resulting changes in the structure, method, and conditions of reception of its object. This may require, however, a revision of basic assumptions concerning the domain and range of narrative.

SEE ALSO: Artificial Intelligence and narrative; computational approaches to narrative; computer games and narrative; modernist narrative; narrative intelligence; semiotics

References and further reading

Aarseth, Espen J. (1997) *Cybertext: Perspectives on Ergodic Literature*, Baltimore: Johns Hopkins University Press.

Barthes, R. (1975) *The Pleasure of the Text*, Hill and Wang, New York.

Bolter, Jay David, and Richard Grusin (1999) *Remediation: Understanding New Media*, Cambridge, Mass.: MIT Press.

Harpold, Terry (2003) 'Hypertext', in Julian Wolfreys (ed.) *Glossalalia*, Edinburgh: Edinburgh University Press.

Joyce, Michael (1995) *Of Two Minds: Hypertext Pedagogy and Poetics*, Ann Arbor, MI: University of Michigan Press.

Landow, George P. (1997) *Hypertext 2.0: The Convergence of Contemporary Critical Theory and Technology*, Baltimore: Johns Hopkins University Press.

Laurel, Brenda (1993) *Computers as Theatre*, Reading, MA: Addison-Wesley.

Manovich, Lev (2001) *The Language of New Media*, Cambridge, Mass.: MIT Press.

Mateas, Michael, and Phoebe Senger (eds) (2003) *Narrative Intelligence*, Amsterdam: John Benjamins.

McGann, Jerome (2001) *Radiant Textuality: Literature after the World Wide Web*, New York: Palgrave.

Murray, Janet H. (1997) *Hamlet on the Holodeck: The Future of Narrative in Cyberspace*, Cambridge, Mass.: MIT Press.

Nelson, Theodor Holm (1990) *Literary Machines 90.1*, Sausalito, CA: Mindful Press.

Rosenberg, Jim (1996) 'The Structure of Hypertext Activity', in *Hypertext 1996*, Bethesda, MD: Association for Computing Machinery.

Ryan, Marie-Laure (1991) *Possible Worlds, Artificial Intelligence, and Narrative Theory*, Indiana University Press, Bloomington, IN.

Wolf, Mark J. P., and Bernard Perron (eds) (2003) *The Video Game Theory Reader*, Routledge, New York.

TERRY HARPOLD

DISCOURSE ANALYSIS (FOUCAULT)

In recent years, many notions of 'discourse' have been used in a variety of disciplines. This is partly due to the 'linguistic turn' in the social and cultural sciences, and partly due to a sociology-oriented linguistics which emerged simultaneously with the Chomskyan paradigm (Rabinow 1998: 3) (*see* SOCIOLINGUISTIC APPROACHES TO NARRATIVE). Michel Foucault and his work play a decisive role in discourse and literary studies as well as in narrative theory, often under the heading of Critical Discourse Analysis (Fohrmann and Müller 1988; Wodak 1996, 2003; *see also* DISCOURSE ANALYSIS (LINGUISTICS)). Foucauldian thought bears importantly on many aspects of narrative theory, including the definition of *narrativity and *narrative itself, the constitution of narrative sense, the constraints determining the production and circulation of narrative discourses, and the role of narrative discourses in the maintainance of order and power structures (Seltzer 1984; Bender 1987; see Cohn 1999, ch. 10, for a narratological discussion and Viehöver 2001 for an extensive overview).

Foucault's lecture on 'Orders of Discourse', held at the *Collège de France* in 1970, helps explain why the philosopher's ideas have had such a major impact on domains that include cultural, linguistic, and narrative studies. In this lecture, Foucault lays down a number of crucial axioms about the nature and contexts of 'discursive events' (*énoncés*):

> I make the assumption that the production of discourse is at once controlled, selected, organized and canalized in every society – and that

this is done by way of certain procedures whose task it is to subdue the powers and dangers of discourse, to evade its heavy and threatening materiality.

(Foucault 1984: 10–11)

Although Foucault refers to many definitions of 'discourse' in his lecture, it is equally important to note what 'discourse' is *not* supposed to mean, specifically, that it is neither defined thematically nor by a strict system of concepts, and that it is not an object but rather a set of relationships existing between discursive events. These stipulations open the door to a dedicated functional approach, enabling the cultural critic to identify static and dynamic relationships between discursive events and to address the causes and consequences of historical change. While discursive events are always based on and ordered through the current system of rules, norms, social conventions, *institutions, etc., incessant power struggles continually undermine and revise such conventions, creating new orders and new 'discursive formations'. Because the power relation is integral to discourse – indeed, without the power relation there would be total disorder – communication is never free of power and its mostly detrimental side effects.

Telling stories, in Foucault's view, is a strategy for ordering the world's 'flow of discourse'. According to theories that conceive of narrative as an archetype of communicative action (Somers 1994), *narrativity informs 'almost any verbal utterance . . . ranging from fragmentary reports and abortive anecdotes to those . . . that we are inclined to call "tales" or "stories" ' (Herrnstein Smith 1981: 228), a definition which sidesteps the linguistic atomism implicit in many linguistic and sociolinguistic approaches to narrative (*see* COMMUNICATION STUDIES AND NARRATIVE). Processes of ordering regulate all aspects of discourse including the basic constitution of sense and meaning in social interaction and, more specifically, in every narrative. Constitution of sense is one of four major processes which to a considerable extent are determined by principles of exclusion and reduction (Viehöver 2001: 181–82). Indeed, basic conventions of discourse rest on what Foucault calls 'prohibitions', such as the fact that no one is allowed to speak about everything on every occasion. In addition to various types of prohibitions Foucault also distinguishes a range of 'internal' ordering procedures involving classification and arrangement,

the selection and distribution of narrated *events, and the role of chance. Naturally the speaking subject itself is also constrained by the educational capital at his or her disposal and by restriction of access to certain *modes and *genres of discourse (*see* AGENCY).

Two major phenomena which result from such processes of ordering and restriction are 'discipline' and 'confession' (Foucault 1981) (*see* CONFESSIONAL NARRATIVE). Discipline produces conforming people or 'docile bodies' by isolating the individual from the group and subjecting him or her to procedures of normalisation. Confession, on the other hand, subjectifies human beings, seemingly allowing them to freely talk about themselves and their own needs and promoting the illusion that emancipation and liberation are possible options. In reality, however, argues Foucault, confession is just another way of reinforcing and submitting to power, most obviously to the authority of the confessor. A large body of research on a variety of related narrative *genres has been developed on the basis of these theoretical perspectives (see Weiss and Wodak 2003 and Keller *et al.* 2001 for an overview).

SEE ALSO: confessional narrative; ideology and narrative; Marxist approaches to narrative; master narrative; sociology and narrative

References and further reading

Bender, John (1987) *Imagining the Penitentiary*, Chicago: University of Chicago Press.
Cohn, Dorrit (1999) *The Distinction of Fiction*, Baltimore: Johns Hopkins University Press.
Fohrmann, Jürgen, and Harry Müller (1988) *Diskurstheorien und Literaturwissenschaft*, Frankfurt: Suhrkamp.
Foucault, Michel (1981) *History of Sexuality*, trans. R. Hurley, London: Penguin.
—— (1984) 'The Order of Discourse', in Michael Shapiro (ed.) *Language and Politics*, Oxford: Blackwell.
Herrnstein Smith, Barbara (1981) 'Narrative Versions, Narrative Theory', in W. J. T. Mitchell (ed.) *On Narrative*, Chicago: University of Chicago Press.
Keller, Rainer, Andreas Hirseland, and Werner Schneider (eds) (2001) *Handbuch Sozialwissenschaftliche Diskursanalyse*, Opladen: Leske and Budrich.
Rabinow, Paul (ed.) (1998) *The Foucault Reader*, New York: Pantheon.
Reisigl, Martin, and Ruth Wodak (2001) *Discourse and Discrimination*, London: Routledge.
Seltzer, Mark (1984) *Henry James and the Art of the Novel*, Ithaca: Cornell University Press.

Somers, Margaret R. (1994) 'The Narrative Constitution of Identity', *Theory and Society*, 23, 605–49.

Viehöver, Willy (2001) 'Diskurse als Narrationen', in Keller, Hirseland, and Schneider (eds) *Handbuch Sozialwissenschaftliche Diskursanalyse*, Opladen: Leske and Budrich.

Weiss, Gilbert, and Ruth Wodak (eds) (2003) *Critical Discourse Analysis: Theory and Interdisciplinarity*, London: Palgrave.

Wodak, Ruth (1996) *Disorders in Discourse*, London: Longman.

—— (2003) 'Critical Discourse Analysis – Theory and Methodology', in Clive Seale (ed.) *Qualitative Research Practice*, London: Sage.

RUTH WODAK

DISCOURSE ANALYSIS (LINGUISTICS)

Linguists who refer to themselves as discourse analysts explore what can be learned about language and about speakers by studying language in use (*see* PRAGMATICS). Unlike generative linguists, they examine written texts or transcripts of spoken or manually signed discourse rather than relying on intuitions about grammar. They are interested in the structure and function of pieces of talk or text that are larger than a single sentence, and in how the structure of sentences is influenced by how they function in the linguistic and social contexts in which they are deployed. By 'discourse', they mean actual instances of talk, writing, or linguistic communication in some other medium. Some explicitly try to link features of discourse in this sense with aspects of what scholars in the Foucauldian tradition call 'discourses': circulating sets of ideas and social practices that may include ways of talking (*see* DISCOURSE ANALYSIS (FOUCAULT)). Other discourse analysts have other agendas. Some are interested in the kinds of questions linguists have always asked: questions about how language is represented in the mind, how the production and interpretation of discourse can best be modelled, how languages change, how language is acquired, and so on. Others explore the linkages between discursive and social phenomena in a wide variety of contexts, including institutional communication (*see* INSTITUTIONAL NARRATIVE), the discursive construction of *identity and *memory, political discourse, organisational behaviour, communication in families, and so on.

Narrative discourse has always been a source of data and an object of study for discourse analysts. Interest in narrative arose in the context of other research agendas, but, with time, linguists have come to see narrative as important in its own right, and discourse analysts' work on narrative has become increasingly interdisciplinary (*see* INTER-DISCIPLINARY APPROACHES TO NARRATIVE). What typically distinguishes linguists' approaches to discourse from those of rhetoricians, critical theorists, historians, and others is attention to the finest-grained details of language in use. Discourse analysts are interested in how and why smaller pieces of language like sounds, words, phrases, sentences, and paragraphs combine into larger ones and in how large-scale referential, interpersonal, and expressive effects result from small-scale choices of words and structures. In what follows, I first trace the history of discourse analysis (DA), then sketch some of the most influential research by linguists on the structure and functions of narrative.

Historical overview

Contemporary linguistics has historical roots in nineteenth-century philology, diachronic (historical) language study aimed at the exegesis of texts. Following Saussure's call to refocus language study on synchronic structure, dominant approaches for most of the twentieth century attended to sounds, phrases, and clauses rather than connected discourse. Beginning in the 1960s, however, linguists working in several intellectual traditions began to converge on two related ideas about discourse: (1) the idea that the structure of phrases and sentences is shaped in part by how they function in conversations and texts, and (2) the idea that texts and conversations are shaped, just as sentences are, by repeatable patterns of structure, that could be called 'grammar'. In the UK, M. A. K. Halliday, building on work by J. R. Firth, began to develop 'systemic-functional grammar' and to ask about how sentences cohere with others in texts. In the U.S., Kenneth Pike and other linguists associated with the Summer Institute of Linguistics developed a similarly function-based way of understanding sentence and discourse structure called tagmemic grammar. At the same time, the emergence of variationist sociolinguistics, Conversation Analysis, and interactional sociolinguistics, and the ethnography of communication brought discourse into the purview of students of language change, *sociology of language, and anthropological linguistics, respectively (*see* SOCIOLINGUISTIC APPROACHES TO NARRATIVE).

In France, Marxist linguists began to explore how *ideology is constructed in and revealed through discourse (Pêcheux 1969). Somewhat later, British linguists influenced by Birmingham-school social theory brought a similarly critical approach to discourse to Anglophone attention, proposing that, since discourse analysis could never be simply descriptive, its goal should be to uncover how power circulates, usually invisibly, in discourse (Fairclough 1992). Although this approach, usually called Critical Discourse Analysis, remains influential, current work is more eclectic, drawing on pragmatics, *sociolinguistics, and interactional linguistics and on various strands of sociological, *rhetorical, literary, and anthropological theory. Many discourse analysts, particularly those whose disciplinary homes are in linguistics, continue to be interested primarily in questions about language, but the use of DA, however defined, as a systematic, grounded method of analysis has become increasingly interdisciplinary. Textbooks no longer presuppose that all discourse analysts are linguists; instruction in DA is offered, sometimes in the context of programs in 'discourse studies', in various academic specialities and journals such as *Discourse Studies*, *Discourse in Society*, and *Text* publish the work of people with a variety of disciplinary affiliations.

Linguistic approaches to narrative discourse

Interest in narrative first arose in the context of two lines of work in linguistics: functional grammar and variationist sociolinguistics. Some of the earliest work on how the function of utterances affected their form used narrative as a source of data, in part because narratives long enough for identifying patterns of form-function co-variation were available in many languages. The development of large digital corpora of written texts and transcribed speech in many genres, along with software tools for their analysis, has meant that functionalist linguists now pay less exclusive attention to narrative.

Meanwhile, William Labov's work on the structure of oral personal experience narrative (PEN) began in the context of research about

linguistic variation (why not everyone talks alike, or talks the same way all the time) and language change. In order to elicit unselfconscious, 'vernacular' speech, Labov had people tell stories about themselves, often about dangerous or embarrassing experiences. Such stories formed the basis for what has probably been the most influential contribution to the study of narrative from the field of linguistics, an article first published in 1967 called 'Narrative Analysis: Oral Versions of Personal Experience' (Labov and Waletzky 1997 [1967]). Labov and Waletzky's goal was to describe the invariable semantic deep structure of PEN, with an eye to correlating surface differences with the 'social characteristics' of *narrators. Labov's project was similar to that of the proto-structuralist Vladimir Propp (*see* FUNCTION (PROPP)) in its attempt to lay out the underlying syntagmatic structure of *plot elements in narrative (*see* STRUCTURALIST NARRATOLOGY). However, whereas Propp's model did not specify in advance what size or type of discourse unit might carry plot-relevance in a story, Labov and Waletzky focused primarily on the functions of individual clauses. According to Labov and Waletzky, a clause in PEN can serve one of two functions, referential or evaluative. Referential clauses have to do with what the story is about: *events, *characters, setting (*see* SPACE IN NARRATIVE). Evaluative clauses (and evaluative aspects of referential clauses) have to do with why the narrator is telling the story and why the *audience should listen to it: evaluative material states or highlights the point of the story (*see* TELLABILITY). The Labov and Waletzky article concentrates on *reference in narrative, especially reference to events. A later book chapter (Labov 1972) concentrates on evaluation. I summarise both accounts together here, focusing mainly on the parts of each that have been most influential.

Any narrative, by definition, includes at least two 'narrative clauses'. A narrative clause is a clause that cannot be moved without changing the order in which events must be taken to have occurred (*see* TEMPORAL ORDERING). If two narrative clauses are reversed, they represent a different chronology: 'I punched this boy / and he punched me' implies a different sequence of events than 'This boy punched me / and I punched him'. Although *'minimal narratives' like these consist of just two narrative clauses, a 'fully developed' narrative may include more narrative clauses as well as 'free' clauses that serve other functions.

Each functional element serves a double purpose, making reference to events, characters, feelings, and so on that are understood to have happened or existed outside of the ongoing interaction (*see* STORYWORLD), and at the same time structuring the interaction in which the story is being told by guiding the teller and the audience through the related events and insuring that they are comprehensible and worth recounting.

Narrators typically begin by *abstracting* the story, often with a clause or two at the beginning of a narrative summarising the story to come. In response to Labov's 'danger-of-death' question ('Have you ever been in a situation where you thought you were in serious danger of getting killed?'), for example, one person began, 'I talked a man out of – Old Doc Simon I talked him out of pulling the trigger', then elaborated with a narrative. (Examples are Labov's.) The *abstract* announces that the narrator has a story to tell and makes a bid for the right to tell it, a bid supported by the suggestion that it will be a good story, worth the audience's time and the speaking rights the audience will temporarily relinquish.

Elements of the narrative associated with *orientation* introduce characters, temporal and physical setting, and situation: 'It was on a Sunday, and we didn't have nothin' to do after I – after we came from church'; 'I had a dog – he was a wonderful retriever, but as I say he could do everything but talk'. Orientation often occurs near the beginning, but it may be interjected at other points, when needed. The characteristic orientation *tense in English is the past progressive: '*I was sittin'* on the corner an' shit, smokin' my cigarette, you know'; '*We was doing* the 50-yard dash'.

Complicating action is represented in narrative clauses that recapitulate a sequence of events leading up to their climax, the point of maximum *suspense. These clauses refer to events in the world of the story and, in the world of the telling, they create tension that keeps auditors listening. The *result or resolution* releases the tension and tells what finally happened.

Throughout the narrative, in particular just before the result or resolution, narrators include *evaluative* elements. These are words, phrases, or structural choices that state or highlight what is interesting or unusual about the story, why the audience should keep listening and allow the teller to keep talking. Evaluation may occur in free clauses in which the narrator comments on the story, stepping outside it: 'And it was the strangest feeling'; 'But it was really quite terrific'. Alternatively, it may occur in clauses that attribute evaluative commentary to characters in the story: 'I just closed my eyes/I said, "O my God, here it is!"' Or evaluation can be embedded in the narrative, in the form of extra detail about characters ('I was shakin' like a leaf'), suspension of the action via paraphrase or repetition (*see* RETARDATORY DEVICES); 'intensifiers' such as *gesture or quantifiers ('I knocked him *all* out in the street'); elements that compare what did happen with what didn't or could have or might happen (*see* DISNARRATED, THE); 'correlatives' that tell what was occurring simultaneously; and 'explicatives' that are appended to narrative or evaluative clauses.

At the end of the story, the teller may announce via a *coda* that the story is over, 'sometimes providing a short *summary of it or connecting the world of the story with the present ('And that was that'; 'He's a detective in Union City/And I see him every now and again').

Two aspects of Labov's work have caused recurrent confusion. One of these has to do with the meaning of the term *'narrative'. For Labov, a 'narrative' was a sequence of clauses with at least one temporal juncture, but a 'complete' or 'fully-formed' narrative included such things as orientation and evaluation as well. 'Personal-experience narrative' included both 'minimal' and more elaborate types. Many subsequent researchers continued to use the same term – *narrative* – both for any talk representing a sequence of past events and for talk specifically meant to get and keep someone interested in listening to a recounting of events. (The difference at issue surfaces in the distinction between, on the one hand, the way witnesses have to talk about the past in a police report or courtroom ['just the facts'] and, on the other hand, the way casual conversationalists have to talk about the past when people are competing for the floor and have to make their contributions *tellable.) This conflation has resulted in confusion both in the design and in the reporting of narrative research, since the two uses of *narrative* refer to two levels of analysis, 'narrative' in the first sense being a necessary part of 'narrative' in the second sense. Some discourse analysts (e.g., Livia Polanyi) have accordingly found it helpful to substitute another term, such as *story*, for the second sense.

A second source of confusion has been the normative sound of some of Labov's terminology, and, partly in consequence, the normative way in which his analysis can be read. Labov's claim to be describing 'the normal structure of narrative' or characterising 'fully developed' or 'complete' narratives has led some to suppose that Labov was making more universal and/or more judgmental claims than may have been intended. It has been observed, for example, that not all stories have abstracts or codas and that PEN is often less monologic than were the stories Labov analysed. It has been easy to forget that the PEN Labov characterised was collected in research interviews with relative strangers, and that the fact that stories arising in different contexts turn out to be different actually does more to support Labov's claims about the connection between narrative form and contextual function than to debunk them.

Labov was not alone in his interest in generalising about the underlying formal and semantic structure of narratives (see NARRATIVE SEMANTICS). Another influential approach to the organisation of oral narrative was that of the anthropologist Dell Hymes (1981) (see ETHNOGRAPHIC APPROACHES TO NARRATIVE; ORAL CULTURES AND NARRATIVE), who showed that Native American myth, which earlier ethnographers had transcribed in paragraphs and treated as prose, was actually performed in poetic lines and stanzas marked by grammatical parallelism, recurring words or particles such as see, I say, or lo, and repeated numerical patterns of phrases (see MYTH: THEORETICAL APPROACHES; NATIVE AMERICAN NARRATIVE). Line-based transcription systems arising from the observation that oral discourse is not produced in paragraphs have been widely adopted in narrative research. Meanwhile, cognitive-science research (see ARTIFICIAL INTELLIGENCE AND NARRATIVE; COGNITIVE NARRATOLOGY) aimed at producing completely explicit models for how narrative is produced and comprehended includes work by Kintsch and van Dijk (1978), which sought to describe semantic 'macrostructures' and the 'macrorules' that model how stories are understood, as well as work on *'story grammars' (de Beaugrande 1982).

Turning from macro- to microstructure, linguists have also explored a number of grammatical constructions characteristic of narrative. The use of the English simple present tense in narrative in place of the past, traditionally referred to as the Historical Present, has been connected with the marking of evaluative high points and the

characterisation of social relations (Wolfson 1982). Tannen (1986) examines how and why storytellers 'construct' *dialogue for characters in their stories, sometimes giving them words they could not possibly have said or which the narrator could not possibly have heard. Ferrara and Bell (1995) discuss the history of quotatives, the verbs such as say, go, ask, and so on with which narrators introduce constructed dialogue, focusing particularly on the emergence in English of the new quotative be like (see QUOTATION THEORY; SPEECH REPRESENTATION).

Narrative in interaction

Much recent work on the linguistics of narrative looks beyond the abstract functional requirements of monologic storytelling, exploring how the structure of a narrative is affected by its embedding in its particular interactional context (see COMMUNICATION IN NARRATIVE). Research in this framework examines how the structure of stories reflects the fact that stories perform social actions and studies how audiences are involved, directly or indirectly, in their *performance and construction. Attention to the interactive co-construction of narrative has also led to increased attention to the kinds of minimal and fragmentary narratives that are created in settings such as legal testimony (see COURTROOM NARRATIVE; LAW AND NARRATIVE) and online chat. In keeping with the move towards interdisciplinarity in DA, discourse analysts are also paying increasing attention to the functions of narrative in larger social practices and processes such as identity formation and the discursive construction of evidence, morality, community, temporality, and place.

SEE ALSO: communication studies and narrative; conversational storytelling; identity and narrative; life story; linguistic approaches to narrative; story schemata and causal structure

References and further reading

Bamberg, Michael G. W. (ed.) (1997) *Journal of Narrative and Life History*, vol. 7. (Special issue on *Oral Versions of Personal Experience: Three Decades of Narrative Analysis*.)
de Beaugrande, Robert. A. (1982) 'The Story of Grammars and the Grammar of Stories', *Pragmatics*, 6, 383–422.
van Dijk, Teun A. (ed.) (1997) *Discourse Studies: A Multidisciplinary Introduction*, 2 vols., Thousand Oaks, CA: Sage.

Fairclough, Norman (1992) *Discourse and Social Change*, Cambridge, UK: Polity.

Ferrara, Kathleen, and Barbara Bell (1995) 'Sociolinguistic Variation and Discourse Function of Constructed Dialogue Introducers: The Case of *Be +* *Like*', *American Speech*, 70, 265–90.

Hymes, Dell (1981) *In Vain I Tried to Tell You: Essays in Native American Ethnopoetics*, Philadelphia: University of Pennsylvania Press.

Johnstone, Barbara (2002) *Discourse Analysis*, Malden, MA: Blackwell.

Kintsch, Walter, and Teun A. van Dijk (1978) 'Toward a Model of Text Comprehension and Production', *Psychological Review*, 85.5, 363–94.

Labov, William (1972) 'The Transformation of Experience in Narrative Syntax', *Language in the Inner City*, Philadelphia: University of Pennsylvania Press.

——, and Joshua Waletzky (1997 [1967]) 'Narrative Analysis: Oral Versions of Personal Experience', *Journal of Narrative and Life History*, 7, 3–38.

Pêcheux, Michel (1969) *Analyse Automatique du Discours*, Paris: Dunod.

Polanyi, Livia (1985) *Telling the American Story: A Structural and Cultural Analysis of Conversational Storytelling*, Norwood, NJ: Ablex.

Schiffrin, Deborah (1994) *Approaches to Discourse*, Cambridge, Mass.: Blackwell,

——, and Heidi E. Hamilton (eds) (2001) *The Handbook of Discourse Analysis*, Malden, MA: Blackwell.

Tannen, Deborah (1986) 'Introducing Constructed Dialogue in Greek and American Conversational Narrative', in Florian Coulmas (ed.) *Direct and Indirect Speech*, New York: Mouton de Gruyter.

Wolfson, Nessa (1982) *CHP: The Conversational Historical Present in American English Narrative*, Dordrecht: Foris.

BARBARA JOHNSTONE

DISNARRATED, THE

As delineated by Prince, the disnarrated comprises those elements in a narrative which explicitly consider and refer to what does *not* take place (but could have). It can pertain to a *character's unrealised imaginings (incorrect beliefs, crushed hopes, false calculations, erroneous suppositions), to a path not followed by the *events recounted, or to a narrative strategy not exploited. Consider, for instance, 'Jane thought that she'd get one very easily but it proved impossible', 'John should have foreseen that Mary wouldn't agree but John was not very swift', 'The game could have gone on but it didn't', or 'I could easily claim that they had many adventures but I won't'.

Since it expresses that which does not occur, the disnarrated is the antithesis of the non-narrated or unnarrated, the ellipses underlined by a *narrator,

indicated through a retroactive filling in, or inferable from significant lacunae in the chronology of events (*see* GAPPING; TEMPORAL ORDERING). The disnarrated also differs from the *unnarratable, that which cannot be narrated or is not worth narrating because it violates (formal, generic, authorial, social) conventions and laws, because it defies the powers of the narrator, or simply because, being insufficiently interesting, it falls below the threshold of narratability or *tellability. Moreover, the disnarrated must be distinguished from *denarration (the narrator's denial or negation of an event or state of affairs that had earlier been affirmed).

Though not essential to narrative, the disnarrated can fulfil many significant functions. It can, for example, serve as a rhythmic instrument by regularly slowing down the presentation of what does take place (*see* RETARDATORY DEVICES). Through the depiction of foolish desires and flawed ponderings, what might be but is not, it can act as a characterisation device, contribute to the elaboration of a theme (illusion and reality, appearance and being, imagination and perception), or help to depict the relation between narrator and *narratee. Furthermore, it can help to make explicit the logic whereby every narrative progresses by following certain directions instead of others, by discounting as much as recounting or accounting: the disnarrated or choices not made, roads not taken, goals not reached. Indeed, the most important function of the disnarrated is usually a *rhetorical one. By pointing to unactualised possibilities and unexploited lines of development, by refusing this norm or rejecting that convention, the disnarrated underscores the tellability of the narrative ('This narrative is worth telling because it *could have been* otherwise, because it normally *is* otherwise, because it *was not* otherwise') and affects its *narrativity.

SEE ALSO: virtuality

References and further reading

Prince, Gerald (1988) 'The Disnarrated', *Style*, 22, 1–8.

—— (1992) *Narrative as Theme: Studies in French Fiction*, Lincoln: University of Nebraska Press.

Ryan, Marie-Laure (1991) *Possible Worlds, Artificial Intelligence and Narrative Theory*, Bloomington: Indiana University Press.

GERALD PRINCE

DISTANCE

Distance refers to the similarities and differences between any two agents involved in narrative communication along one or more axes of measurement. The agents are *author, *narrator, *character, and *audience, including *narratee, narrative audience, authorial audience (or *implied reader), and actual audience. The most common axes are spatial, temporal, intellectual, emotional, physical, psychological, and ethical. Thus, author and narrator may be intellectually close but ethically distant; narrator and character may be emotionally close but temporally distant; narratee and actual audience may be psychologically close but physically distant. Booth (1961) first gave the concept prominent attention and, while pointing out multiple kinds of distance, he gave particular emphasis to that between *implied author and narrator, the basis, in Booth's view, for unreliable narration (*see* RELIABILITY). Other theorists have focused upon other kinds of distance: Prince (1973), in developing the concept of narratee, on that between this figure and the implied reader; Rabinowitz (1977), in developing his schema of audiences, on that between the narrative audience and the authorial audience and that between each of those and the actual audience.

Since Booth's discussion of distance, the concept has remained central to work on unreliable narration. Where Booth identified two main kinds of unreliability, about facts and about values, later theorists such as Phelan and Martin (1999), Cohn (2000), and Olson (2003) have noted the importance of distance between a narrator's intellectual comprehension of events and that of the implied author and/or reader. Even among theorists who have debated whether unreliability should be located in the relation between implied author and narrator or in that between the narrator and the reader (Nünning 1997), distance has remained linked to unreliability. Distance also can be relevant to the understanding of *narrative progression, since changes in distance between an implied author and a character-narrator or between a narrator and an audience are often crucial to a narrative's development.

Although one may chart the multiple combinations of agents and axes in any particular narrative, some combinations will be more salient than others. In *Lolita*, the most salient combinations are that of the author and the narrator and that of the narrator and narratee along the ethical axis: Nabokov needs to establish his ethical distance from Humbert Humbert's paedophilia even as Humbert initially tries to seduce the narratee into condoning it. In *The French Lieutenant's Woman*, the most significant combination is the temporal distance between the author and narrator, on the one hand, and the characters, on the other. Fowles locates the author and narrator (and thus, the narratee and the authorial audience) in the 1960s and the characters in the 1860s as part of his project of explaining the cultural shift from the Victorian era to the modern one. In narratives that involve a character narrator speaking (rather than writing) to an identified narratee, spatial and temporal distances between these two agents are minimal and other kinds of distance such as the ethical relation between the narrator and the authorial audience become most important.

SEE ALSO: ethical turn; narrative techniques; rhetorical approaches to narrative

References and further reading

Booth, Wayne C. (1961) *The Rhetoric of Fiction*, Chicago: University of Chicago Press.
Cohn, Dorrit (2000) 'Discordant Narration', *Style*, 34, 307–16.
Nünning, Ansgar (1997) 'Deconstructing and Reconceptualizing the Implied Author: The Implied Author – Still a Subject of Debate', *Anglistik: Mitteilungen des Verbandes deutscher Anglisten*, 8.2, 95–116.
Olson, Greta (2003) 'Reconsidering Unreliability: Unreliable, Fallible, and Untrustworthy Narrators', *Narrative*, 11.1, 93–109.
Phelan, James, and Mary Patricia, Martin (1999) 'The Lessons of Weymouth: Homodiegesis, Unreliability and Ethics in *The Remains of the Day*', in David Herman (ed.) *Narratologies: New Perspectives on Narrative Analysis*, Columbus: Ohio State University Press.
Prince, Gerald (1973) 'Introduction à l'étude du narrataire', *Poétique*, 14, 178–96.
Rabinowitz, Peter J. (1977) 'Truth in Fiction: A Reexamination of Audiences', *Critical Inquiry*, 4, 121–41.

JAMES PHELAN

DRAMA AND NARRATIVE

Storytelling can be regarded as the default case of dramatic or filmic entertainment: the history of drama is also a history of communicating narratives to live *audiences (*see* FILM NARRATIVE).

Long before the emergence of the *novel as the prototypical narrative *genre, narrative experiments were a central feature of stage plays. Diegetic elements (i.e., elements of verbal storytelling) catered to the need for effective *exposition and helped to overcome limitations of *time and setting imposed by the pressure of normative poetics, by social and political conventions, and by the restrictions of stage design. Heavily relying on narrative, the medieval mystery plays (the annual Cycles performed in major towns such as York, Chester, Wakefield, and Coventry) aimed to show, in the course of one to three days, the whole history of the universe from the creation of Heaven and Earth to Doomsday (*see* MEDIEVAL NARRATIVE; SERIAL FORM). More recently, both the emergence of narrative stage genres such as the memory play and the continuing development of narrative visual *media such as film, *television, and *computer games have focused attention on drama as a medium for fictional storytelling (*see* FICTION, THEORIES OF).

But is there really no difference between the visual representation of action on a theatre stage or movie screen on the one hand and the account of an action as given by a fictional *narrator in a novel on the other? Can the specific communicative situations typical of drama and the novel (see Pfister 1988) as well as *pragmatic aspects (e.g., contexts of *reception) be neglected in favour of transgeneric and transmedial approaches to storytelling (*see* INTERMEDIALITY)? The answer to these questions largely depends on the underlying definitions of *narrative and *narrativity. These will be discussed in the following section. This is followed by a short differentiation of the two main dramatic genres, tragedy and comedy, and a survey of diegetic elements in drama. The remaining sections introduce the latest efforts to develop a fully-fledged 'narratology of drama' which pay special attention to narratorial discourse – a key question within the ongoing debate concerning drama and narrative.

'Narrative' in narratology

From a narratological point of view, narrative has been defined as the recounting of at least two real or fictive *events, neither of which logically presupposes or entails the other (Gerald Prince; Shlomith Rimmon-Kenan), as a series of statements that deal with a causally related sequence of events that concern human (or human-like) beings (Dorrit Cohn), as a representation of a series of causal events or situations *not* limited to human agents or anthropomorphic entities (Brian Richardson), as *verbal* (as opposed to visual or performative) transmissions of narrative content (Gérard Genette), or, from a cognitive point of view, as a mode of naturalising a text or *performance in the reception process (Monika Fludernik) (*see* CAUSALITY; COGNITIVE NARRATOLOGY; NATURAL NARRATOLOGY; NATURALISATION; VISUAL NARRATIVITY). Answers to the question about the specificity of narrative can be either text-oriented, defining narrativity as 'the set of properties characterising narrative and distinguishing it from non-narrative' (Prince 2003: 64), or reception-oriented, defining narrativity in cognitive terms as 'a function of narrative texts' which 'centres on experientiality of an anthropomorphic nature' (Fludernik 1996: 26). The latter reconceptualisation of narrativity allows for a more inclusive concept of narrative which is not restricted to prose and *epic verse but also includes drama, film, and narrative poems (*see* NARRATIVE IN POETRY). Thus narrative can be reduced neither to formal properties of a narrative discourse (narratorial mediation in the traditional sense) nor to its representation in a special medium (the written fictional text), but also includes performances as long as they inspire interpretation through narrative frames (*see* FRAME THEORY).

Dramatic narratives: tragedy and comedy

The conventional generic distinction between dramatic narratives, which imitate speech and actions (*mimesis), and epic narratives, which recount actions and events (*poiesis*), goes back to Plato's *Politeia* and also forms the core of Aristotle's *Poetics* (*see* ANCIENT THEORIES OF NARRATIVE (WESTERN)). Here, epic narrative is differentiated from drama with its two formal types, tragedy and comedy, a distinction whose heuristic and didactic value is still widely acknowledged in contemporary literary theory. Definitions of comedy and tragedy usually point to themes (everyday vs. monumental), endings (happy ending vs. catastrophe), *characters (common vs. exceptional), and the overall tone of a play (humorous vs. serious).

Apart from this, the two dramatic genres can be distinguished by the respective roles of their protagonists, their *plot structures (*see* FREYTAG'S TRIANGLE; PLOT TYPES), and the pragmatic functions ascribed to them (by normative theories of drama in the tradition of Aristotle). Tragedy is usually characterised by (1) a series of fatal errors and wrong decisions made by the protagonist himself/herself (either due to the Gods' interference, as in ancient Greek drama, e.g., Sophocles' *King Oedipus*, or to flaws in the *hero's own personality, as in Shakespeare's *Hamlet*) which lead to his/her demise; (2) external obstacles which mirror and explain the hero's internal development from happiness to misery and, by convention, death (*see* CONFLICT); and (3) the social function of *catharsis, which 'purifies' the spectators' *emotions and encourages them to avoid tragic mistakes by letting them witness the fate of a tragic hero with whom they can identify. Comedy is characterised by the opposite qualities: (1) the villain's actions, not the errors of the protagonist himself or herself, form the main obstacles he or she has to overcome; (2) the hero's journey starts with a series of fundamental problems which in the course of the plot can be solved by the hero so that he or she can be rewarded by the conventional happy ending (usually marriage); and (3) the social function of providing entertainment, although comedies may also convey social criticism or political satire (*see* SATIRIC NARRATIVE).

Of course, this traditional juxtaposition of tragedy vs. comedy as the two main forms of drama is one of ideal types which represent opposite ends on a scale. This scale also accommodates a variety of hybrid forms such as tragicomedy, black humour, farce, theatre of the absurd, and so on (*see* HYBRID GENRES). As a matter of fact, the categorical distinction between tragedy and comedy has always presented all sorts of theoretical difficulties. Both tragic and comic drama are clearly plot-oriented genres mainly concerned with telling morally and didactically motivated or sometimes merely amusing stories – stories of the rise and fall of prototypical heroes and their antagonists (*see* DIDACTIC NARRATIVE). These functional characters form and inhabit complex and meaningful fictional *storyworld. From the point of view of plot-oriented narratologies such as the approaches chosen by Etienne Souriau (1950) or Thomas Pavel (1985), the functional roles played by characters (conceived of as

*actants as suggested by Greimas), fictional events, teleological developments, and semantically charged *closures allow not only for a systematic analysis of narrative situations in dramatic texts but also for a narrative grammar of drama (*see* DRAMATIC SITUATIONS; STORY GRAMMARS).

Diegetic elements in drama

Sequences of events and functional characters are by no means the only regular elements of drama which can be classified as 'narrative'. As a matter of fact, there is a large number of narrative strategies that are frequently used in dramatic texts. Among these are various forms of *metalepsis (i.e., transgressions of the boundaries between diegetic levels by characters or narrators), direct audience *address (prologue, epilogue, asides, summaries, soliloquies, and parabasis, i.e., an opening song performed by the classical Chorus, attacking members of the *audience), choric speeches, and messenger reports in Greek drama as well as modern narrator figures such as the stage manager in Thornton Wilder's *Our Town*, verbal *descriptions of offstage action, the play within the play, *mise en abyme*, narratives embedded within dramatic action (*see* EMBEDDING), all kinds of *metanarrative comments, stage directions, choric figures, and narrating characters (*see* SPEECH REPRESENTATION). This list of diegetic elements in drama can be expanded by transgeneric narrative strategies and storytelling techniques which can be used by both playwrights and novelists. As Jan Mukařovský and Jiří Veltruský have demonstrated, a *structuralist analysis of *dialogue in a play allows for a differentiation of three fundamental communicative situations which can be used for devising a typology of dramatic narratives. Other examples of transgeneric strategies include *montage techniques (scenic narration) and reversals of chronology (*see* SUMMARY AND SCENE; TEMPORAL ORDERING).

As these examples show, narration in drama is not restricted to mimesis (i.e., imitation in the Aristotelian sense, or in narratological terminology, the 'showing' of an action), but can also make use of the diegetic mode of narration (i.e., narratorial mediation, or 'telling'). Traditionally, diegetic elements in drama have either been labelled as 'un-dramatic' exceptions to the (mimetic) rule or else closely linked to specific *rhetorical functions such as exposition or communicating events that cannot be shown because of temporal or spatial and practical restrictions (narrative is used to provide backstory, explain chronological *gaps, represent armies, landscapes, seasons, and other elements which cannot be represented directly) (*see* SPACE IN NARRATIVE). Another way of naturalising dramatic narrative was opened up by Brecht, who explicitly linked the diegetic strategies used in his plays to specific ideological effects and purposes such as *defamiliarisation and anti-illusionist theatre (*see* IDEOLOGY AND NARRATIVE). In general, however, narrative theory stuck to the assumption that the events in narrative texts are recounted by a narrator, while dramatic presentation relies on a mimetic portrayal of fictional events, normally lacking any form of narratorial mediation.

Despite this tradition of separating drama and narrative, the last two decades have seen numerous attempts to bridge the gap between the two. On the one hand, the close relationship between dramatic (mimetic) and narrative (diegetic) storytelling is also emphasised by the transgeneric use of critical terminology: key terms and core concepts like scene, character, protagonist, antagonist, dramatic *irony, *suspense, comic relief, *point of view, *perspective structure, monologue, dialogue, exposition, plot and subplot, poetic justice, ending, and closure, to name but a few, are used in the analysis of both novels and plays. This clearly suggests that there are overlaps and interplays between different modes of storytelling (Hart 1991). On the other hand, a number of theorists have also made proposals for a 'narratology of drama' (Jahn 2001). This could not only provide a theoretical and terminological framework for the narratological analysis of both mimetic and diegetic storytelling in drama and film, but also prepare the ground for a systematic transgeneric and transmedial narrative theory.

Toward a narratology of drama

Genette's groundbreaking work on narrative did not prove helpful for narratologists interested in drama, film, or painting (*see* PICTORIAL NARRATIVITY). Narrative, Genette insists, has to be viewed as a specific way of representing events rather than as a quality of texts belonging to different genres. Its characteristic feature, Genette claims, is the *verbal* transmission of fictional stories. If one follows Genette, neither the dramatic representation of stories on the stage nor their transmission by what he terms extranarrative media (film, comic strip, etc.) can be termed 'narrative', and neither are genuinely interesting to narratology or, more specifically, to discourse-oriented narratology (*see* COMICS AND GRAPHIC NOVEL; STORY-DISCOURSE DISTINCTION). Genette's definition deviates from the transgeneric and intermedial tradition of narratology, which in the mid-twentieth century focused on storytelling regardless of the medium or *mode in which it became manifest. In order to account for this, Genette suggests a division of narratology into two approaches, a *thematic approach (concentrating on the story as the narrative content) and a formal, discourse-oriented approach (the analysis of narrative representation). In Genette's system, thematic approaches to storytelling might well include drama, film, and painting, whereas the formal analysis of narrative is restricted to narrative fiction.

Chatman favours a more liberal point of view. He argues that all fictional texts devoted to storytelling share narrative features such as a temporal structure, a set of characters, and a setting. Therefore, structural similarities between plays and novels are more important than the different ways in which these stories are told (*diegesis) or shown (mimesis): the difference between diegetic and mimetic storytelling is secondary to the distinction between narrative and non-narrative *text-types. Equally important is Chatman's theoretical assumption of the existence of narrating instances in (seemingly) narratorless narratives (e.g., novels without an overt narrator) including films and plays. This systematic inclusion of narrators as structural elements (ranging from overt narrators to mere arranger functions) into a theory of narrative paves the way for a post-Genettian, plot- *and* discourse-oriented theory of narrative as recently outlined by Jahn.

Following a discussion of the shortcomings of both Genette's definition of narrative and his argument regarding the communicative structure of dramatic texts, Jahn highlights some crucial areas such as the (diegetic) status of stage directions (which constitute narrative pauses and thus can be ascribed to a narratorial discourse organising the temporal structure of the story in a play) (*see* NARRATION); the possibility of multiple levels of communication within dramatic texts resembling the multilevelled *narrative structures of novels with embedded narratorial acts; and functional genre correspondences such as crossover techniques of dramatisation and epicalisation. He then proceeds to modify Chatman's well-known taxonomy of text-types (1) by introducing a 'playscript mode' that can be found not only in plays but also in novels, just as plays and performances can make use of epic narrative modes, (2) by replacing Chatman's subdivisions 'diegetic' and 'mimetic' by the more pragmatic categories 'written/printed' vs. 'performed', and (3) by including separate categories for both the scripts and the performances of plays, films, and *operas which allow for a precise conceptualisation of the interactions between these various forms of representation *within* the overall model of genres and modes of narration.

Jahn's modifications of Chatman's model and Richardson's essays addressing various facets of narrativity in drama, such as the categories of order, frequency, duration, point of view, narrative *voice, and narration, constitute a theoretical framework that can bring the narratology of drama into relation with other systematic approaches, such as communicational drama theory (Pfister 1988) and theatre *semiotics (Elam 2002). A narratology of drama is one important building block of a genuinely transgeneric and intermedial theory of narrative as outlined in the essays in Nünning and Nünning. Another central issue to be addressed in this context concerns the *functions* of narrative in drama (see Hart 1991). Besides its four primary functions (i.e., exposition, suggestion, compression, and address), narrative adds to the playwright's creative tools, facilitates interdiscursive experimentation, and encourages self-reflexivity by the disruption of dramatic action (*see* REFLEXIVITY). Historically, dramatic narrative has also been used by playwrights seeking to observe the principles of *verisimilitude and decorum. In Renaissance drama, for instance, violent action had to be narrated rather than shown on stage in order to maintain public order. A systematic approach to the history of drama and narrative would also have to take into account generic issues, as the same narrative elements can fulfil quite different functions in comedy and tragedy.

Areas for further research

There are several areas in which the emerging narratology of drama could initiate further research. (1) Following Jahn's modifications of Chatman's model of text-types and narrative modes, the (generic) distinction between mimetic and diegetic narrative needs to be replaced by an integrative model which allows for an analysis of diegesis in plays, movies, cartoons etc. (2) This model should be correlated with the communicative model of fictional storytelling (see Pfister 1988) in order to provide the broad theoretical framework which is required to keep up with recent developments in fictional storytelling. For instance, *computer games continuously explore new ways of accessing fictional worlds which are neither epic nor dramatic in the traditional sense but combine mimetic and diegetic narrative in a variety of ways. (3) Another field of research for a narratology of drama is the systematic analysis of the various functions of diegesis and mimesis: diegetic features such as a narrator figure are used differently in comedy and serious forms of drama respectively. (4) Closely related to this generic approach is a diachronic survey of the occurrence and functions of diegetic elements in dramatic narrative, preparing the ground for an alternative history of drama. (5) Finally, one of the most interesting aspects of a narratology of drama is that it reveals blind spots of novel-centred narrative poetics. As the majority of existing narratological models were developed on the basis of and for the analysis of fiction, some areas such as the nature and potential of *performance time* have been neglected. 'Metatemporal' dramatic narratives with contradictory story times such as Shakespeare's *Midsummer Night's Dream* (Richardson 1987); radical antinomies/asymmetries between text time and stage time; and implicit or explicit metatheatrical reflections on the conventions of temporal representation, as in Tom Stoppard's *Travesties*, all pose new challenges to narrative theory and require a systematic evaluation and modification of existing models of temporal structure.

References and further reading

Chatman, Seymour (1990) *Coming to Terms: The Rhetoric of Narrative in Fiction and Film*, Ithaca: Cornell University Press.

Doty, Kathleen (1989) 'Dialogue, Deixis and Narration in a Dramatic Adaptation', *Poetica*, 31, 42–59.

Elam, Keir (2002) *The Semiotics of Theatre and Drama*, London: Routledge.

Fludernik, Monika (1996) *Towards a 'Natural' Narratology*, London: Routledge.

Genette, Gérard (1988 [1983]) *Narrative Discourse Revisited*, trans. Jane E. Lewin, Ithaca: Cornell University Press.

Hart, Jonathan (1991) 'Introduction: Narrative, Narrative Theory, Drama: the Renaissance', *Canadian Review of Comparative Literature*, 18, 117–65.

Jahn, Manfred (2001) 'Narrative Voice and Agency in Drama: Aspects of a Narratology of Drama', *New Literary History*, 32, 659–79.

Nünning, Ansgar, and Vera Nünning (eds) (2002) *Erzähltheorie transgenerisch, intermedial, interdisziplinär*, Trier: WVT.

Pavel, Thomas G. (1985) *The Poetics of Plot: The Case of the English Rennaisance Drama*, Manchester: Manchester University Press.

Pfister, Manfred (1988) *The Theory and Analysis of Drama*, trans. J. Holiday, Cambridge: Cambridge University Press.

Prince, Gerald (2003) *A Dictionary of Narratology*, Lincoln: University of Nebraska Press.

Richardson, Brian (1987) "Time is out of Joint": Narrative Models and the Temporality of Drama', *Poetics Today*, 8.2, 299–309.

—— (1988) 'Point of View in Drama: Diegetic Monologue, Unreliable Narrators, and the Author's Voice on Stage', *Comparative Drama*, 22.3, 193–214.

—— (2001) 'Voice and Narration in Postmodern Drama', *New Literary History*, 32.3, 681–94.

Souriau, Etienne (1950) *Les Deux cent mille situations dramatiques*, Paris: Flammarion.

ROY SOMMER

DRAMATIC IRONY

A mode of *irony in which the *audience knows more than the *characters, often leading to complex types of *reader-response, in which readers both identify with and *distance themselves from characters' plights. Dramatic irony is often contrasted with situational irony, in which *events result in unexpected consequences, and verbal irony, in which a character or *narrator says one thing but means another. *See* NARRATIVE TECHNIQUES.

DRAMATIC MONOLOGUE

Although closely related to a monologue or soliloquy in drama, the term 'dramatic monologue' is mainly used to refer to a short written form, often a poem, displaying the extended *speech of a single *character who is a participant in a developing *plot. While precursors can be traced back to Old-English poems and popular *ballads, the form acquires autonomous status in the work of Robert Browning (1812–1889), whose *My Last*

Duchess (1842) is generally cited as the prototypical example.

Four major subtypes of the dramatic monologue can be distinguished: (1) the 'dialogic' dramatic monologue, a form in which a conversation is edited by a higher-order narratorial agent in such a manner that only the turns of one of the speakers are represented (*My Last Duchess* belongs to this type); (2) the 'interior' dramatic monologue, which expresses the character's intimate thoughts and deliberations; (3) the 'oration' dramatic monologue (public speeches, pleas, etc.); and (4) the 'narration' dramatic monologue, showing the character in the process of telling a story of personal experience (*confession, eye-witness report, etc.). All four subtypes are equally represented in Browning's monologue cycle *The Ring and the Book* (1868–1869), an account of a seventeenth century murder trial which anticipates many features associated with twentieth century *modernist fiction – the 'dramatisation' called for by Henry James, *voices projecting from written texts, the interior monologue, and multiple *focalization (*see* STREAM OF CONSCIOUSNESS AND INTERIOR MONOLOGUE).

Because the dramatic monologue throws a focal spotlight on the speaking character, the form is excellently suited to creating character studies. Typically, in an act of involuntary self-characterisation, monologists give away crucial information about themselves. In *My Last Duchess*, for instance, it becomes clear not only that the Duke of Ferrara's current marital aspirations are based on greed, but also that he is responsible for the disappearance and probable death of his first wife. As is to be expected, it is the unreliable voices of minds clouded by ignorance, vanity, envy, and obsession that are featured more prominently than the dull voices of unassailable virtue (*see* RELIABILITY).

Situated at a point where 'drama meets poetry' and 'fiction meets drama' (Cohn 1978: 255), the dramatic monologue is a *hybrid genre *par excellence* and continues to be used across *media and *genres both autonomously and as a form of embedded speech. Emancipated from its poetic roots in Browning's work it can be seen to appear in prose fiction such as Edgar Allan Poe's 'mad monologist' stories, Franz Kafka's 'A Report to an Academy' (1919), the 'Cyclops' chapter in James Joyce's *Ulysses* (1922), and Elizabeth Bowen's *Oh, Madam ...* (1941). The form returns to drama in

Karl Kraus's *The Last Days of Mankind* (1918) and is masterfully redeployed in Alan Bennett's *Talking Heads* television monologues (1988). The 'dialogic' subtype in particular continues to thrive in popular forms such as the stand-up comedian's telephone sketch.

SEE ALSO: drama and narrative; narrative in poetry; orality; skaz

References and further reading

Chatman, Seymour (1978) *Story and Discourse: Narrative Structure in Fiction and Film*, London: Cornell University Press.
Cohn, Dorrit (1978) *Transparent Minds*, Princeton: Princeton University Press.
Howe, Elisabeth A. (1996) *The Dramatic Monologue*, New York: Twayne.
Langbaum, Robert (1957) *The Poetry of Experience: The Dramatic Monologue in Modern Literary Tradition*, London: Chatto.
Loehndorf, Esther (1997) *The Master's Voice: Robert Browning, the Dramatic Monologue, and Modern Poetry*, Tübingen: Francke.
Rader, Ralph (1976) 'The Dramatic Monologue and Related Lyric Forms', *Critical Inquiry*, 3, 131–51.

SABINE BUCHHOLZ AND MANFRED JAHN

DRAMATIC SITUATIONS

Proto-structuralism and structuralism approached the phenomenon of story by proposing generative models which produced *narrative structures through the combination of a finite number of elements (*see* NARRATIVE UNITS; STORY-DISCOURSE DISTINCTION; STRUCTURALIST NARRATOLOGY). The best-known of these models is Vladimir Propp's analysis of Russian *folktales into thirty-one 'functions' (*event types defined in terms of their significance for the story as a whole) and seven roles for participants (*hero, villain, donor, etc.) (*see* FUNCTIONS (PROPP)). The order of Propp's functions was fixed, so that variants could only be obtained by making some functions optional. In 1950, Etienne Souriau proposed a system of dramatic situations with far greater combinatorial power. Though Souriau's system was designed for the theatre, where action takes a particularly concentrated form, its range of applicability extends to all plot-centred, archetypal narrative *genres. The model limits itself to the description of the strategic relations between characters, and does not outline

a diachronic *plot skeleton, as does Propp's sequence of functions.

Souriau's use of the term 'function' corresponds to Propp's roles rather than to Propp's functions. Borrowing his nomenclature from astrology, he distinguishes six dramatic functions: the Lion, or agent, whose *desire initiates the action; Mars, the opponent, whose desire competes with the will of the Lion; the Sun, or desired object; the Earth, or intended recipient; the Balance, or arbiter, and the Moon, or helper. The moon can combine with any of the other five functions, depending on who is being helped. Functions are embodied by the *characters in the plot, but several functions can be fulfilled by the same character, or several characters can fulfil the same function. Different dramatic situations are generated by varying the number of characters, or by distributing the functions differently among the characters. For instance, in a love story, where Peter is the agent, Paul the opponent, and Mary the desired object, Peter can woo Mary for himself, in which case he is the recipient, or for somebody else; the arbiter of Mary's fate can be either Peter, Paul, Mary herself, or an additional character; the helper can represent Peter's, Mary's, or Paul's interests. The system expresses alliances between characters by attributing to a character a helper function oriented toward another character: Mary for instance can be on the side of Peter, if she loves him, on the side of Paul, or on the side of neither. Following this system, a three-character love story can generate thirty-six different dramatic situations. In addition to strategic functions, Souriau's model includes a *point of view function, whose purpose is to select one of the characters as the focus of the spectator's emotional investment. This character can vary during the action; but since the agent and opponent functions are symmetrical, a shift of point of view from agent to opponent results in the opponent being regarded as the agent.

The possibility inherent in Souriau's system of attributing several functions to the same character anticipates Greimas' distinction between actors and *actants. Souriau's taxonomy of functions also foresees later attempts by linguists, such as Charles Fillmore, to model sentences in terms of a predicate surrounded by a constellation of arguments fulfilling various semantic roles. A combination of the kinds of models proposed by Propp, Souriau, and Greimas with Fillmore's so-called 'case grammar' would attribute roles to characters on the macro-level, but would allow these roles to vary on the micro-level.

SEE ALSO: drama and narrative; narrative situations; narrative transformation; plot types; semiotics; story grammars

References and further reading

Fillmore, Charles (1968) 'The Case for Case', in Emmon Bach and Robert T. Harms (eds) *Universals of Linguistic Theory*, New York: Holt, Rhinehart and Wilson.

Propp, Vladimir (1968 [1928]) *Morphology of the Folktale*, 2nd edition, trans. Laurence Scott, revised by Louis A. Wagner, Austin: University of Texas Press.

Scholes, Robert (1974) *Structuralism in Literature*, New Haven: Yale University Press.

Souriau, Etienne (1950) *Les Deux cent mille situations dramatiques*, Paris: Flammarion.

MARIE-LAURE RYAN

DREAM NARRATIVE

Dreaming is a hallucinatory state based on perception, sensation, and other types of mental action. Modern dream theory has been shaped by two major events: the publication of Freud's *Interpretation of Dreams* in 1900 and Aserinsky and Kleitman's discovery of REM-sleep in 1953. While Aserinsky and Kleitman provided much-needed laboratory evidence related to the frequency and duration of dream phases, it is Freud's earlier speculative account that continues to dominate discussion in the humanities. According to Freud, dreams are like rebuses (picture riddles), seemingly unfathomable yet based on meaningful messages and causes (see CAUSALITY). In Eric Berne's concise Freudian definition, a dream is 'an attempt to gain satisfaction of an Id tension by hallucinating a wish-fulfilment'. Because an Id-wish is a sex- or aggression-oriented primitive impulse at odds with the belief system of the civilised Ego, it needs to be camouflaged through a series of 'dreamwork' transformations such as symbolic translation, displacement, and condensation.

Dream matter in narrative texts either takes the form of framed 'oneiric inserts' (Carroll's *Alice in Wonderland*) or it comes as an autonomous narrative that never transcends the world of the dream (Kafka's *The Trial*, Joyce's *Finnegans Wake*). All *genres and *media have found ways of depicting dreams, hence representations of dreams can be found in poems (Coleridge, *Kubla Khan*), *radio plays (Eich, *Dreams*), theatrical plays (Strindberg, *A Dream Play*), and *film (Kubrick, *Eyes Wide Shut*, based on Schnitzler's *Dream Novella*) (see DRAMA AND NARRATIVE). In *myth and *folklore, orally transmitted dream narratives often occupy a position of high cultural privilege (see AFRICAN NARRATIVE; AUSTRALIAN ABORIGINAL NARRATIVE).

Dream action is typically characterised by bizarre *events and *existents, sudden breaks in continuity, reduced motor activity of the dreamer-agent as well as lack of coherence and *closure. Yet, as Bertrand Russell noted, dreamlikeness is not a necessary condition for dreaming, nor is absence of dreamlikeness proof of non-dreaming. The philosopher's dilemma recurs in two dream-narrative gambits, one involving a character who is tricked into believing that something that really happened was only a dream (Calderon's *Life Is a Dream*), the other playing a trick on the reader by suggesting that the events presented are real when in fact they are a character's hallucination (as in Bierce's 'An Occurrence at Owl Creek Bridge').

'Is a dream (a) narrative?', narratologist Gerald Prince has pointedly asked (*Style*, 34, 2000, p. 317), suggesting the answer is No because hallucinatory perception, like real perception, cannot be (a) narrative. However, if Freud is right and dreams are the product of a fiction-creating 'dreamwork' device, then they are based on a multimedial mode of composition much like that of film, whose specific techniques – *montage, dissolve, slow motion, etc. – clearly provide a powerful set of dream-effect analogies (Metz 1982). With the spread of trans-medial and intermedial narratological projects, both the *narrativity of dreams and the dream-film analogy are key subjects demanding further investigation.

SEE ALSO: intermediality; psychoanalysis and narrative

References and further reading

Brook, Stephen (1983) *The Oxford Book of Dreams*, Oxford: Oxford University Press.

Canovas, Frédéric (1994) 'This is Not a Dream: Drawing the Line Between Dream and Text', *Journal of Narrative Technique*, 24.2, 114–26.

Freud, Sigmund (1953 [1900]) *The Interpretation of Dreams*, London: Hogarth Press.

Metz, Christian (1982) *The Imaginary Signifier: Psycho-analysis and the Cinema*, trans. Celia Britton *et al.*, Bloomington: Indiana University Press.

States, Bert O. (1993) *Dreaming and Storytelling*, Ithaca: Cornell University Press.

MANFRED JAHN

DUAL-VOICE HYPOTHESIS

The dual-voice hypothesis states that sentences of *free indirect discourse and related phenomena combine the *voice of a *character with that of the *narrator, or superimpose one on the other. (The possibility of superimposing two characters' voices in the same sentence has been mooted, but examples are rare, if they exist at all.) Such 'combined discourse' (as this phenomenon is called in *Tel Aviv poetics) is especially pronounced in cases of narratorial *irony at the character's expense. Examples:

1   Nothing need be said; nothing could be said. There it was, all around them. It partook, she felt, carefully helping Mr Bankes to a specially tender piece, of eternity. . . . (Woolf)
2   Uncle Charles repaired to the outhouse. (Joyce)

In (1), a passage of free indirect discourse, the narratorial interpolation 'carefully helping Mr Bankes' etc. insinuates an ironic doubleness of tone into the entire passage; in (2), the narrator's discourse is coloured by Uncle Charles' characteristic usage, 'repaired'.

The classic statement of the dual-voice hypothesis is Pascal's (1977), anticipated by Voloshinov (1986 [1929]), whose dual-voice account of free indirect discourse underwrites and corroborates Bakhtin's (1981 [1934–1935]) theory of the polyphonic novel (*see* DIALOGISM; POLYPHONY). A powerful counter-argument was mounted by Banfield (1982), who challenged the communication model, which assumes that, even in the absence of a first-person narrator, every sentence is expressed by a narrator and addressed to a *narratee, except those quoted directly from a character's speech (*see* NO-NARRATOR THEORY). By her account, free indirect sentences are narratorless, indeed speakerless, representing the character's consciousness without expressing either the narrator's or the character's 'voices'. Fludernik (1993, 2001), building on Stanzel's model, partly endorses Banfield's refutation of the dual-voice hypothesis,

but grants that readers *naturalise sentences like 1–2 by constructing personae, including that of the narrator, to whom stylistic features could be attributed. That is, readers reframe such sentences as acts of communication, sometimes 'combined' acts.

The dual-voice hypothesis remains controversial, but it seems clear that the effect of dual-voice varies from period to period, and that nineteenth-century *realist novels (from which Pascal drew his examples) yield a much stronger sense of 'duality' than *modernist novels (from which Banfield drew hers).

SEE ALSO: narration; quotation theory; speech representation; thought and consciousness representation (literature)

References and further reading

Bakhtin, Mikhail (1981 [1934–1935]) 'Discourse in the Novel', in Michael Holqist and Caryl Emerson *The Dialogic Imagination: Four Essays*, trans. Caryl Emerson and Michael Holquist, Austin: University of Texas Press.

Banfield, Ann (1982) *Unspeakable Sentences: Narration and Representation in the Language of Fiction*, Boston: Routledge and Kegan Paul.

Fludernik, Monika (1993) *The Fictions of Language and the Languages of Fiction: The Linguistic Representation of Speech and Consciousness*, London: Routledge.

—— (2001) 'New Wine in Old Bottles? Voice, Focalization and New Writing', *New Literary History*, 32.3, 619–38.

Pascal, Roy (1977) *The Dual Voice: Free Indirect Speech and its Functioning in the Nineteenth-Century European Novel*, Manchester: Manchester University Press.

Voloshinov, V. N. (1986 [1929]) *Marxism and the Philosophy of Language*, trans. Ladislaw Matejka and I. R. Titunik, Cambridge, Mass.: Harvard University Press.

BRIAN McHALE

DYSTOPIAN FICTION

If a utopia is an imaginary ideal society that dreams of a world in which the social, political, and economic problems of the real present have been solved, then a dystopia is an imagined world in which the dream has become a nightmare. Also known as anti-utopias, dystopias are often designed to critique the potential negative implications of certain forms of utopian thought. However, dystopian *fiction tends to have a strong satirical dimension that is designed to warn against the possible consequences of certain tendencies in the real world of the present (*see* SATIRIC NARRA-TIVE). The three crucial twentieth century dystopian fictions are Yevgeny Zamyatin's *We* (1924), Aldous Huxley's *Brave New World* (1932), and George Orwell's *Nineteen Eighty-Four* (1949).

SEE ALSO: utopian and dystopian fiction; science fiction

References and further reading

Booker, M. Keith (1994) *The Dystopian Impulse in Modern Literature: Fiction as Social Criticism*, Westport, CT: Greenwood Press.
—— (1994) *Dystopian Literature: A Theory and Research Guide*, Westport, CT: Greenwood Press.
Kumar, Krishan (1987) *Utopia and Anti-Utopia in Modern Times*, Oxford: Blackwell.

M. KEITH BOOKER

E

ECO-NARRATIVES

Eco-criticism, an area of research that has established itself principally in American Studies since the early 1990s, focuses on the ways in which cultural communities at different historical moments define nature, how they envision the connection between humans and their natural environment, and what cultural functions they attribute to the natural. Such implicit and explicit concepts of nature manifest themselves across a wide range of cultural practices and artefacts, among which storytelling figures prominently. From mythological creation stories to *science fiction novels and filmed nature documentaries, cultural concepts of the natural world underlie a variety of *narrative structures (see CULTURAL STUDIES APPROACHES TO NARRATIVE; MYTH: THEORETICAL APPROACHES). Along this spectrum of narratives about nature, ecological or environmentalist stories often stand out through their sense that the natural world is threatened and requires protection from human impacts. In the analysis of such narratives, questions of *genre, viewpoint, and *realism have attracted particular attention in eco-criticism.

Ecological storytelling frequently relies on and transforms traditional literary genres. In the 1960s and 1970s, when environmental crises first entered public awareness in Western societies, apocalyptic narrative played an important role in conveying the possible future consequences of contemporary social practices. Influential books such as Rachel Carson's *Silent Spring* and Paul Ehrlich's *The Population Bomb* deploy millennial images of blight, famine, and devastation to drive home the urgency of their call for change. In much more attenuated form, apocalyptic narrative continues to function as a component of ecological discourse today (see DISCOURSE ANALYSIS (FOUCAULT)). Pastoral, as a genre that foregrounds the peaceful and harmonious life of rural communities, has provided another important template for environmental storytelling. The contrast between the pure and authentic life of the country and the corrupt culture of the city or the court in traditional pastoral can be mobilised, in a context of perceived threat to the environment, as a way of understanding either the functioning of nature without human intervention, or the difference between sustainable and non-sustainable forms of living in the natural world. More intermittently, generic forms such as *epic, tragedy, the *Gothic novel, the *Bildungsroman, and the *detective story also appear in ecological narrative. Beyond such specific genre templates, narrative conventions make themselves felt more indirectly in assumptions about the typical behaviour of, for example, political collectives or families that are transferred from the human to the animal realm in texts, *films, or museum displays, as insect communities are imagined to function like monarchies, or animal dioramas are arranged in such a way as to suggest nuclear families. While such transfers can be powerful means of making the natural world come alive for the human observer, scientists and environmentalists have often expressed concern that the application of culturally specific notions of, for instance, social hierarchy or gender relations can lead to profound misapprehensions of non-human behaviour.

A different approach to the question of genre in ecological narrative was proposed in the 1970s by Joseph Meeker in his book *The Comedy of Survival*, which analyses and criticises conventional genre templates in terms of their inbuilt assumptions about humans' relation to nature. Tragedy, Meeker argues, is based on a deeply anthropocentric perspective in which an individual human's decline or death is viewed as a transcendental crisis. In contrast, comedy, with its emphasis on cyclical recurrence and on the passage from one generation to another, reflects a worldview more in tune with an ecological perspective. Such an ideological critique of narrative genres from an environmentalist angle has yet to be developed further in ecocriticism.

The question of anthropocentrism also emerges in relation to narrative viewpoint (*see* FOCALIZATION; PERSPECTIVE; POINT OF VIEW (LITERARY)). Some eco-critics have asked whether a medium such as literature, which relies entirely on human language, can possibly reflect anything other than a deeply anthropocentric view of nature. What might a representation of the natural look like that would not privilege the human over other species? Asking such questions leads to an analysis of who (or what) can function as a narrative agent who sees or speaks and relays *plot events to the audience (*see* AGENCY). In premodern forms of narrative, such as indigenous orature or the ancient and medieval European genre of the *fable, not only humans but all sorts of animals appear as full-fledged characters who act and speak; in modern Western narrative, such characters tend to appear mostly in children's literature and cartoons, while they have largely vanished from 'serious' fiction (*see* CHILDREN'S STORIES (NARRATIVES WRITTEN FOR CHILDREN)). Some twentieth-century writers (e.g. Ursula K. Le Guin), however, have adopted non-human narrators as a means of relativising modern, human-centred perspectives. Such experiments with viewpoint force readers to approach familiar situations from a thoroughly alien perspective, and thereby to reconsider humans' relation to the non-human world.

These experiments also raise the question whether it is necessary or desirable for ecologically oriented literature to rely on realist modes of narration. Much nature writing in the American and European traditions clearly takes a more or less mimetic approach to the question of representation, often basing itself on the acts of looking at or walking through natural landscapes (*see* MIMESIS). Yet it has been argued that a more comprehensive understanding of nature must have recourse either to stylised representations of types (such as are common in guides to birds, mushrooms, or butterflies) or to abstract modelling (such as that of hydrological or climatological systems), and that this kind of approach to the representation of nature would subvert conventional realist modes of *narration (*see* REALIST NOVEL). While no descriptive nature writing has yet emerged that responds to these challenges with literary experiment, ecologically oriented *novels and *short stories have appeared that push the boundaries of narrative realism through elements of science fiction, *fantasy, and *magical realism. Indeed, science fiction has turned into one of the literary genres in which ecological themes are most insistently explored. Some works of science fiction foreground in particular the new challenge that confronts ecological realism at the turn of the millennium: namely, developing modes of narration that convey a sense of ecosystems not only in their local and regional manifestations, but also in their global reach.

References and further reading

Buell, Lawrence (1995) *The Environmental Imagination: Thoreau, Nature Writing, and the Formation of American Culture*, Cambridge, Mass.: Harvard University Press.
—— (2001) *Writing for an Endangered World: Literature, Culture and Environment in the U.S. and Beyond*, Cambridge, Mass.: Harvard University Press.
Glotfelty, Cheryll, and Harold Fromm (eds) (1996) *The Ecocriticism Reader: Landmarks in Literary Ecology*, Athens, GA: University of Georgia Press.
Killingsworth, M. Jimmie, and Jacqueline S. Palmer (1996) 'Millennial Ecology: The Apocalyptic Narrative from *Silent Spring* to Global Warming', in Carl G. Hendl and Stuart C. Brown (eds) *Green Culture: Environmental Rhetoric in Contemporary America*, Madison: University of Wisconsin Press.
Meeker, Joseph W. (1972) *The Comedy of Survival: Studies in Literary Ecology*, New York: Scribner's.
Phillips, Dana (1999) 'Ecocriticism, Literary Theory, and the Truth of Ecology', *New Literary History*, 30, 577–602.

URSULA K. HEISE

ÉCRITURE FÉMININE

Écriture féminine (EF) is a term coined by Hélène Cixous to denote both an avant-garde theory and a writing practice developed in the 1970s. Its main representatives, Cixous herself, Luce Irigaray, and

Julia Kristeva, were all influenced by the French women's movement (*see* GENDER STUDIES), post-structuralism, Derridean deconstructionism, and Lacanian *psychoanalysis (*see* DECONSTRUCTIVE APPROACHES TO NARRATIVE; POSTSTRUCTURALIST APPROACHES TO NARRATIVE). EF searches for a femininity marginalised within the symbolic order and tries to express it through female-body oriented writings that subvert the rules of Western logo-centrism and phallocentrism. Although they conceive of textual structures and the body as strictly interdependent, especially Cixous and Irigaray have repeatedly been criticised for biological essentialism (Moi 1985; Weber 1994).

EF texts are never purely analytical but transform basic theoretical tenets into narratives containing strongly lyrical elements and inscriptions of corporeality which are aimed at breaking up the body-mind dichotomy. For instance, Irigaray's *parler femme* takes its creative power from female, non-unified autoeroticism and the central image of the female labia constantly touching each other, thus illustrating the multiplicity, excess, and endlessness of woman's *jouissance*, a concept also explored by Kristeva and Cixous. In order to disrupt patriarchal discourse, Irigaray practises a theatrical, exaggerated mimicry of masculine specular logic, which has always assigned to woman the role of the negative Other (*see* ALTERITY; DISCOURSE ANALYSIS (FOUCAULT)). *Jouissance* also provides a positive alternative to Freud's notion of masochistic female penis envy and the psychoanalytical definition of woman via lack. Especially in Cixous's theory, the uncritically glorified figure of the mother, of her non-narcissistic, nurturing qualities and her empathy, take the place of Lacan's law of the father and the phallus. Her difficult texts focus on women's bodily experience and translate the utopia of motherliness into symbiotic reworkings of intertexts (*see* INTERTEXTUALITY).

Generally, EF texts foreground the materiality of language by focusing on rhythm and sound, they privilege *voice as a form of presymbolic communication and conceive of writing as a libidinal act. EF resists all unifying generic categorisations, prefers dialogic to monologic *narrative structures (*see* DIALOGISM), openness to *closure, and employs an elliptic, associative, and metaphorical style (*see* METAPHOR). Examples of EF put into narrative practice include Monique Wittig's *Les Guérillères* (1969) and Cixous' *Le rire de la*

Méduse (1975) and *La jeune née* (1975), the latter written with Catherine Clément. Interestingly, Kristeva developed her influential poetological concept of the feminine semiotic – a predominantly suppressed pre-oedipal realm of ungendered libidinous energies, rhythmic pulses, and primary drives – on the model of *modernist avant-garde writing by experimental male authors such as Lautréamont, Mallarmé, Joyce, and Artaud. While every act of signification is a bipolar process of the semiotic subverting the assumptions of the symbolic, the semiotic flowers especially in poetic language and non-rational, marginal discourses. Moreover, for Kristeva, gender is situated in the linguistic domain and largely unconnected to biology so that the practice of EF is open to authors of both sexes.

SEE ALSO: feminist narratology; semiotics

References and further reading

Jones, Ann Rosalind (1981) 'Writing the Body: Toward an Understanding of "Écriture féminine"', *Feminist Studies*, 7.2, 247–63.

Marks, Elaine, and Isabelle de Courtivron (eds) (1980) *New French Feminisms*, Amherst: University of Massachusetts Press.

Moi, Toril (1985) *Sexual/Textual Politics: Feminist Literary Theory*, London: Methuen.

Sellers, Susan (1991) *Language and Sexual Difference*, New York: St. Martin's.

Weber, Ingeborg (ed.) (1994) *Weiblichkeit und weibliches Schreiben*, Darmstadt: WBG.

ANDREA GUTENBERG

EDUCATION AND NARRATIVE

Recent scholarship on education and narrative focuses on developing narrative approaches to classroom learning and understanding educational experiences. It also examines the experiences of teachers, their professional *biographies and institutional lives (*see* INSTITUTIONAL NARRATIVE). This is done through: (1) applying theories of psychological, linguistic, social, and cultural practices of learning through storytelling and using *didactic narrative in classrooms; (2) conducting theoretical and applied research which examines the social construction of learning and teaching experiences; (3) educational development committed to raising awareness of the achievement of professionals; and (4) the identification through narrative analysis of the role of humane and poetic aspects of education.

Storytelling in the classroom has a long tradition of being used for language development and moral education. In the West, this approach had become dominated by written narrative but it has recently been complemented by a revival of *performance practices in which teachers creatively adapt stories and encourage learners to tell them. Oral storytelling is seen as developing narrative competence so that learners come to appreciate chronology, causation, *plot, dilemmas, and *emotions (see CAUSALITY; TEMPORAL ORDERING). In retelling their own personal experiences, learners come to understand them and, hence, themselves. Egan advocates the development of the imagination and the learning of knowledge in school through stories. Classroom narrative mediates the acquisition of knowledge in any curriculum subject and narrative activities socialise children into imaginative worlds and, arguably, into their own narrative *identity. There is, however, increasing recognition of the cultural diversity of narrative practices among young people. Awareness of this diversity may help solve a problem: narratives by students from minority groups can be wrongly assessed by teachers, resulting in what Hymes terms 'narrative inequality' in teachers' perceptions of learners' educational abilities and their voices or social identities (see SOCIO-LINGUISTIC APPROACHES TO NARRATIVE).

Much productive research has been done looking at teachers' work through an examination of their narratives about classroom experience. This research shows that, as told in teachers' stories, there are archetypes or schemata of recurring classroom *events and pedagogic dilemmas which are a feature of teachers' professional culture (see ARCHETYPAL PATTERNS; SCRIPTS AND SCHEMATA). The analysis of teachers' narratives also reveals a profound sense of professional identity and dilemmas between the personal and professional self in contexts of institutional change. Getting teachers to produce their personal narrative accounts of teaching and then reflect critically on their meanings and contexts is increasingly used in teacher development. Through narrative inquiry, novices reflect on and evaluate their own or others' teaching practices and beliefs. However, this narrative reflection can be extended to include an extra dimension – one suggesting that through the recalling and reconstructing of narrative events, learning itself is reconstructed and reflexively

evaluated. Narratives therefore not only reflect past learning events but narrating them is itself continued learning. This double concept of narrative learning has been found by Cortazzi et al. to include chains of learning transmission and narrative networks in which student-to-student *narration is vicarious cascaded learning; i.e., as one student's personal learning is progressively recounted to others through informal social networks, they also learn from the first student's experience.

Studies of teachers' *life stories, career biographies, and longer term professional development have emphasised *agency, power, and change, the sources of professional knowledge in social and historical contexts, and the formation of political or cultural meaning, including reading educational lives as texts which establish career coherence. Some of this narrative research in education is designed to 'name silenced lives', as McLaughlin and Tierney put it, to bring out the personal identity or political voice of minorities or *feminist perspectives. A problem now recognised is a dilemma familiar to ethnographers: how to distinguish the roles (or biases) of the researcher, the research, and the researched when researchers also have their own educational narratives of which the research is a part. Some researchers tell the story of researching the stories and explicate their own theoretical or methodological presuppositions. A few, like Clough, have followed one *ethnographic trend in presenting experienced insights: they have taken narrative research data and fictionalised them into stories (see FICTION, THEORIES OF), deliberately weaving social and educational research reports with literature.

Many of the current developments in narrative and education have an underlying theme of restoring or developing the personal, humane, and poetic dimensions of learning and teaching. This is sometimes in opposition to technocratic approaches to the curriculum or utilitarian approaches to improving educational institutions. Teachers' stories often reveal the mystery and magic of learning, their sense of vocation, and such qualities as *humour, integrity, or persistence in difficult circumstances. They are told with style but researchers often ignore the performance and on-the-spot dramatic functions of storytelling, even when the researchers, as teachers, may use heightened performance in their own stories told to children. With so much current attention being paid to teachers' stories, it is important to devote equal attention to investigations into learners' narrative accounts of their learning and how they develop educational voices and identities. This learner-centred educational narrative research will, one hopes, continue to reveal more of the human dimension of education.

SEE ALSO: children's storytelling; master narrative

References and further reading

Clough, Peter (2002) *Narratives and Fictions in Educational Research*, Buckingham: Open University Press.

Cortazzi, Martin (1993) *Narrative Analysis*, London: Falmer Press.

——, Lixian Jin, Debbie Wall, and Sue Cavendish (2001) 'Sharing Learning through Narrative Communication', *International Journal of Language and Communication Disorders*, 36, 252–57.

Egan, Kieran (1989) *Teaching as Storytelling: An Alternative Approach to Curriculum in the Elementary School*, Chicago: University of Chicago Press.

Erben, Michael (ed.) (1998) *Biography and Education: A Reader*, London: Falmer Press.

Hymes, Dell (1996) *Ethnography, Linguistics, Narrative Inequality: Towards an Understanding of Voice*, London: Taylor & Francis.

Jalongo, Mary, Joan Isenberg, and Gloria Gerbracht (1995) *Teachers' Stories: From Personal Narrative to Professional Insight*, San Francisco: Jossy-Bass.

McEwan, Hunter, and Kieran Egan (eds) (1995) *Narrative in Teaching, Learning, and Research*, New York: Teachers College Press.

McLaughlin, Daniel, and William Tierney (eds) (1993) *Naming Silenced Lives: Personal Narratives and Processes of Educational Change*, New York: Routledge.

Trimmer, Joseph (ed.) (1997) *Narration as Knowledge: Tales of the Teaching Life*, Portsmouth, NH: Boynton/Cook.

MARTIN CORTAZZI

EKPHRASIS

According to the rhetorical handbooks of late Antiquity, the term 'ekphrasis' (lat. *descriptio*) subsumed any verbal *description of visual phenomena, including depictions of battles, plagues, fortifications, funerals, and artefacts. In his third century AD *Progymnasmata*, Theon states that ekphrasis brings 'what is illustrated vividly before one's sight' and that its virtues are 'clarity and vividness, such that one can almost see what is narrated' (Spengel 1883–1886: 2.118–19; trans. Bartsch 1989). In contrast to classical usage, contemporary word and image scholarship defines the term as a literary description of real or imagined pieces of visual art, as for example, 'The Shield of Achilles' in the *Iliad*, the murals in Virgil's *Aeneid*, the bas-reliefs in Dante's 'Purgatorio', and the tapestry in Shakespeare's 'Rape of Lucrece', as well as shorter texts such as Keats' 'Ode on a Grecian Urn', or Ashbery's 'Self-Portrait' in a Convex Mirror (Klarer 1999; Webb 1999).

The most recent attempts to define ekphrasis foreground the notion of a double representation. W. J. T. Mitchell, for example, sees ekphrasis as a 'verbal representation of visual representation' (1992: 696), and James Heffernan postulates that 'what *ekphrasis* represents in words, therefore, must itself be '*representational*'' (1993: 4). Most modern scholars tend to bracket the original features of classical ekphrasis and primarily focus on the representational issue. The reasons for this lie partly in the current theoretical climate and partly in the nature of the examples adduced.

Literary allusions to pieces of visual art necessarily carry, in their very structure, a highly charged self-reflexive potential. By verbally describing a piece of visual art, ekphrasis touches on two questions: (1) Where are the limits of word and image? (2) Where are the respective limits of art and nature? Literary references to pieces of visual art inevitably construct a distinction between verbal and visual media. By evoking an object rendered in visual art, *ekphrases* implicitly differentiate between art and nature, i.e., distinguish between representation and non-representation. Hence, ekphrasis highlights the dichotomies of art vs. nature and word vs. image which lie at the heart of representational theorising. The degrees of difference between these oppositions vary in each period and culture, thus offering an indirect look at central mimetic concepts of the time (*see* MIMESIS). The study of ekphrasis is therefore particularly suited to reconstructing the representational climate of a historical period as well as shedding light on the historicity of its *media (Klarer 2001).

SEE ALSO: image and narrative; intermediality; pictorial narrativity; reflexivity; visual narrativity

References and further reading

Bartsch, Shadi (1989) *Decoding the Ancient Novel: The Reader and the Role of Description in Heliodorus and Achilles Tatius*, Princeton: Princeton University Press.

Heffernan, James A. W. (1993) *Museum of Words: The Poetics of Ekphrasis from Homer to Ashbery*, Chicago: University of Chicago Press.

Hollander, John (1995) *The Gazer's Spirit: Poems Speaking to Silent Works of Art*, Chicago: University of Chicago Press.

Klarer, Mario (1999) 'Introduction', *Word & Image*, 15.1, 1–4. (Special issue on 'Ekphrasis'.)

—— (2001) *Ekphrasis: Bildbeschreibung als Repräsentationstheorie bei Spenser, Sidney, Lyly und Shakespeare*, Tübingen: Niemeyer.

Krieger, Murray (1992) *Ekphrasis: The Illusion of the Natural Sign*, Baltimore: Johns Hopkins University Press.

Mitchell, W. J. T. (1992) '*Ekphrasis* and the Other', *South Atlantic Quarterly*, 91.3, 695–719.

Spengel, Leonard (ed.) (1883–1886) *Rhetores Graeci*, 3 vols., Leipzig: Teubner.

Webb, Ruth (1999) 'Ekphrasis Ancient and Modern: The Invention of a Genre', *Word & Image*, 15.1, 5–33.

MARIO KLARER

EMBEDDING

The most widely accepted use of the term 'embedding' in the context of narrative theory is to designate the literary device of the 'story within a story', the structure by which a *character in a narrative text becomes the *narrator of a second narrative text framed by the first one. While this might seem a rather specialised topic, examination of almost any body of texts reveals that the structure of embedded narrative is ubiquitous in the literature of all cultures and periods. The relationship between the embedding and embedded stories inevitably entails significant interpretive consequences, as the reader can hardly fail to speculate about the dramatic and thematic connections between the two distinct yet conjoined stories. In addition to this strictly discourse-centred model of embedding, many critics use the term more broadly, to designate such analogous forms as the painting that depicts a painting, or the *film within which a character makes a movie. Still broader uses extend the term beyond such formal applications to include *cultural studies approaches, seeing texts as embedded within networks of material practices, or writing as a form of human behaviour embedded within systems of forces that direct human nature. In the analysis of narratives, however, most theorists follow the discourse-centred model, in which one narrator's discourse embeds that of another narrator's at a subordinate narrative level.

Common sense suffices to loosely divide embedded narratives into two types by their size or extent. In some narratives, such as Chaucer's *Canterbury Tales*, a relatively slender 'frame' story sets up a dramatic situation within which characters narrate a series of tales that make up the bulk of the work. In others, a sustained primary narrative is interrupted by a much shorter story told by one character to another, as the parable 'Before the Law' is embedded within Kafka's *The Trial*. But efforts to describe and analyse the forms and functions of embedded narrative tended to remain *ad hoc* discussions of individual examples until the dissemination of *structuralism in the latter part of the twentieth century. Genette's model for the analysis of narrative levels has become the standard starting point for virtually all contemporary discussions of narrative embedding. In his system, the flesh and blood *author and reader are considered to function outside of the narrating situation proper. The outermost narrative level is thus that of the extradiegetic narrator, an imaginary agent constructed by the reader from textual cues, whose voice is conventionally credited with the narrating of the entire story, and whose audience, the extradiegetic *narratee, is a similarly abstract entity. A character within this *diegesis, or narrative world (*see* STORYWORLD), who tells a story is an intradiegetic narrator, and the character to whom he or she narrates this story is an intradiegetic narratee. A character within one of these intradiegetic narratives may in turn tell a story, which occurs at the metadiegetic level, followed by the tetradiegetic, pentadiegetic, and so on. The 'inner' intradiegetic or metadiegetic level is embedded within the 'outer' extradiegetic or intradiegetic level. Narrators may also be characters in the worlds of the stories they narrate (homodiegetic) or exist outside that world (heterodiegetic). The precision of Genette's scheme ameliorates the forbidding nature of the terminology – critics adopting the model can discuss even the most complexly embedded texts with a common vocabulary.

While Genette's model remains the *lingua franca* for discussions of embedding, other theorists have developed influential refinements to his basic descriptive model. Bal has suggested that *point of view, or *'focalization', may itself be considered as susceptible to embedding – just as one narrator's discourse may be embedded within that of another, so too may one character's focalization be embedded within another's. Nelles has suggested distinctions between embedding by shifts in narrative level, which he labels vertical embedding, and horizontal embedding, with a shift in narrator but not narrative level. Grouping these two cases under the rubric of verbal embedding, he then isolates a different form that he calls modal embedding, as in a *dream narrative, where there is no shift of narrator or narrative level, but rather a shift in the 'reality' of the fictional world depicted.

The end of these attempts at description is of course to facilitate literary analysis. The interpretive consequences of narrative embedding are themselves varied and complex, but Barth, Genette, and Nelles have all proposed categories for classifying the primary types of effects produced by the structure. The models of Barth and Genette are broadly similar, identifying three primary functions: dramatic or explanatory, in an embedded narrative explaining or influencing the course of the embedding narrative; thematic, exploiting contrasts or analogies between the two narratives; and mechanical or gratuitous, entailing little significant relation between the narratives. Nelles argues that virtually all embedded narratives entail dramatic and thematic functions, and dismisses the notion of gratuitous embedding. He proposes that embedded narratives be analysed by considering the degree to which they foreground three primary codes: hermeneutic, relating to enigma and interpretation; proairetic, relating to *action, motivation, and *reference; and formal, highlighting structural boundaries within the text. In marked contrast to the practice of these narrative theorists, who have been content to modify and adapt Genette's proposals, Ryan has developed an independent model of narrative boundaries based on the metaphor of the stack, which is derived from computing and widely used in models of discourse associated with research in *Artificial Intelligence. Her system dispenses with Genette's terminology, but still covers many of the distinctions that later critics have grafted onto his model, including those between verbal and modal embedding, which she defines in terms of illocutionary and ontological boundaries, and between real and fictional narrative worlds, a distinction not always consistently observed in Genettian models.

SEE ALSO: frame theory; framed narrative; metalepsis; mise en abyme; narration; quotation theory

References and further reading

Bal, Mieke (1981) 'Notes on Narrative Embedding', *Poetics Today*, 2, 41–59.

Barth, John (1981) 'Tales Within Tales Within Tales', *Antaeus*, 43, 45–63.

Dällenbach, Lucien (1989) *The Mirror in the Text*, trans. Jeremy Whiteley and Emma Hughes, Chicago: University of Chicago Press.

Füredy, Viveca (1989) 'A Structural Model of Phenomena with Embedding in Literature and Other Arts', *Poetics Today*, 10, 745–69.

Genette, Gérard (1980) *Narrative Discourse*, trans. Jane E. Lewin, Ithaca: Cornell University Press.

McHale, Brian (1987) 'Chinese-Box Worlds', in *Postmodern Fiction*, Cambridge: Methuen.

Nelles, William (1997) *Frameworks*, New York: Peter Lang.

Paxson, James (2001) 'Revisiting the Deconstruction of Narratology: Master Tropes of Narrative Embedding and Symmetry', *Style*, 35, 126–50.

Ricardou, Jean (1981) 'The Story Within the Story', trans. Joseph Kestner, *James Joyce Quarterly*, 18, 323–38.

Ryan, Marie-Laure (2002) 'Stacks, Frames, and Boundaries', in Brian Richardson (ed.) *Narrative Dynamics: Essays on Time, Plot, Closure, and Frames*, Columbus: Ohio State University Press.

WILLIAM NELLES

EMIC AND ETIC

Originally formulated by Pike (1954) in analogy with the linguistic distinction between phonemic and phonetic analysis, the emic-etic dichotomy has been adopted by narratologists to distinguish an 'internal' approach to narrative texts from an 'external' one. In this way, narratologists have adhered to a crucial tenet of structuralism (*see* STRUCTURALIST NARRATOLOGY). While the etic approach uses extrinsic criteria for classifying stories, the emic approach uses intrinsic ones which build on common knowledge structures and familiarity. In *ethnographic approaches, the etic perspective involves a researcher's detached, 'alien' attitude, while the emic perspective adopts an insider's 'domestic' understanding of objects and events. Narrative theorists have used the opposition to distinguish between emic and etic story beginnings (Stanzel 1984). In a more special sense, the term 'etic' is sometimes used to refer to purely classificatory categories, or to elements which exist outside the world of fiction, such as historic locations, personalities, and events (*see* REALEME; FICTION, THEORIES OF).

References and further reading

Headland, Thomas N., Kenneth L. Pike, and Marvin Harris (eds) (1990) *EMICS and ETICS: The Insider/ Outsider Debate*, London: Sage.

Pike, Kenneth L. (1954) *Language in Relation to a Unified Theory of the Structure of Human Behaviour*, Glendale, CA: Summer Institute of Linguistics.

Stanzel, Franz K. (1984) *A Theory of Narrative*, transl. Charlotte Goedsche, Cambridge: Cambridge University Press.

GÖRAN NIERAGDEN

EMOTION AND NARRATIVE

Understanding narrative, just like understanding in general, is never purely cognitive. It is one of the major attractions of narratives, whether presented in *novels, plays, or *films, that they elicit emotional responses in their *audiences (*see* DRAMA AND NARRATIVE). The affective impact of narrative derives from various sources. First of all, we react to the *events and *existents within the story, but we may also respond to the features of the discourse, and we can generally enjoy or dislike the formal characteristics of a work (*see* STORY-DISCOURSE DISTINCTION). Many narratives create emotional response by manipulating information. Thus, plot-relevant information may be presented or withheld in ways that create surprise, uncertainty, and suspense as to what will happen, or – if the outcome of a story or an episode is already known or can be guessed at – how things happen (*see* SUSPENSE AND SURPRISE). Even such straightforward mechanisms as surprise, uncertainty, and suspense depend upon whether the reader, viewer, or listener relates emotionally to the agents in a fictional world, is interested in their fate, and prefers certain outcomes of stories to others (cf. Gerrig 1993: 65–96; *see* IMMERSION). Interest is a crucial aspect of narrative understanding also insofar as it focuses attention on certain aspects of the narrative.

Since the proposal of a psychobiological theory of aesthetic emotion in the 1970s, which correlated aesthetic enjoyment with the level of physiological arousal caused by complex and unfamiliar stimuli (Berlyne 1974), researchers have corroborated that aesthetic appreciation of a work crucially depends on the recipient's previous training and his or her individual level of tolerance for complexity. For instance, when readers encounter incoherence in texts, emotions are triggered which activate search strategies that help to match textual information

with superordinate schemata of understanding (Miall 1989; Miall and Kuiken 1994; *see* SCRIPTS AND SCHEMATA). Readers will experience the greatest enjoyment when confronted with what they perceive as manageable levels of complexity and novelty. Experienced readers will consequently derive greater enjoyment from texts regarded as difficult than unskilled readers.

In descriptions of recipients' emotional reactions to fictional *characters, the term 'identification' has traditionally been very popular. However, even in *psychoanalysis, the field from which it originates, it is a metaphorical concept at best and had perhaps better be avoided altogether. Thus, for the reader of a novel to relate emotionally to a character's hopes, joys, fears, plights, etc., it is not necessary that he or she share any traits with that character at all. Also, real identification, in the sense of a change of personality traits over longer periods of time, is unlikely to happen in relation to more than one character. This leaves reactions to all other characters crowding a fictional world unaccounted for. Cognitive-psychological investigations of emotion have shown that 'empathy' is the more adequate term, since it captures a person's ability to mentally represent another person's situation as well as to evaluate the relevance and desirability of that situation and its potential outcomes (Zillmann 1991). While many narratives invite the recipient to share sets of assumptions about the world, the evaluative stance taken in reception ultimately depends on the reader's own attitudes, values, and beliefs as shaped, at least in part, by cultural contexts. Although attempts to conceptualise the range of human emotions in systematic fashion tend to yield frustratingly little agreement, it seems that joy, hope, relief, fear, pity, disappointment, and anger are the major types of empathic emotion activated in response to characters in a narrative (Hogan 2003). What kind of emotion results from empathy and how intense it is in each case depends on the recipient's attitude towards a character, which is turn influenced by his or her value system in general, so that reaction to a character's situation and evaluation continually interact.

Many cognitive-psychological investigations of emotional response to narrative have focused on film (cf. Smith 1995; Tan 1996; Zillmann 1991), but emotions also occur in the reception of print narratives. It is important to note that differences in narrative mediation engender different kinds of response. In film viewing, much affective response is triggered by automatic (i.e. non-conscious) reactions to the characters' emotions as signalled by their facial expressions – an impact that is considerably heightened by the speed and dynamics of film viewing. In contrast, reading offers greater opportunity for conscious reflection. Readers are frequently invited to consider a character's motivations in detail and to share that character's *perspective, and they may interrupt the reception process at will. If the reader gets access to the character's plans, hopes, wishes, etc., a mode of access which is achieved mostly by techniques of presenting the character's consciousness, this will have especially powerful effects.

SEE ALSO: focalization; media and narrative; narrative comprehension; reader-response theory; storyworld; thought and consciousness representation (film); thought and consciousness representation (literature)

References and further reading

Berlyne, Daniel E. (1974) *Aesthetics and Psychobiology*, New York: Appleton-Century-Crofts.
Cupchik, Gerald C. (1994) 'Emotion in Aesthetics: Reactive and Reflective Models', *Poetics*, 23, 177–88.
Frijda, Nico, and Dick Schram (eds) (1995) *Poetics*, 23. 1–2 (special issue on 'Emotions and Cultural Products').
Gerrig, Richard J. (1993) *Experiencing Narrative Worlds: On the Psychological Activities of Reading*, New Haven: Yale University Press.
Hjort, Mette, and Sue Laver (eds) (1997) *Emotion and the Arts*, New York: Oxford University Press.
Hogan, Patrick Colm (2003) *The Mind and Its Stories: Narrative Universals and Human Emotion*, Cambridge: Cambridge University Press.
Kneepkens, E. W. E. M., and Rolf Zwaan (1994) 'Emotions and Literary Text Comprehension', *Poetics*, 23.1–2, 125–38.
Miall, David S. (1989) 'Affect and Narrative: A Model of Response to Stories', *Poetics*, 17, 259–72.
——, and Don Kuiken (1994) 'Foregrounding, Defamiliarization, and Affect: Response to Literary Stories', *Poetics*, 22.5, 389–407.
Nell, Victor (1988) *Lost in a Book: The Psychology of Reading for Pleasure*, New Haven: Yale University Press.
Smith, Murray (1995) *Engaging Characters: Fiction, Emotion, and the Cinema*, Oxford: Clarendon Press.
Tan, E. S. (1996) *Emotion and the Structure of Narrative Film: Film as an Emotion Machine*, Mahwah, NJ: Erlbaum.
Zillmann, Dolf (1991) 'Empathy: Affect from Bearing Witness to the Emotions of Others', in Jennings Bryant and Dolf Zillmann (eds) *Responding to the Screen: Reception and Reaction Processes*, Hillsdale, NJ: Erlbaum.

RALF SCHNEIDER

EMPLOTMENT

The term 'emplotment' refers to the transformation of a set of historical *events (a *chronicle) into a sequence endowed with the structure of the *plot types of *myths or literary *genres. Historical events, in Hayden White's theory, do not come to mental perception in the form and with the structure of stories. By emplotment, sets of events can be transformed into stories with beginnings, middles, and ends and thereby provided with positive or negative moral or ideological valences. A partial list of the kinds of emplotment used by historians includes tragic, comic, *epic, and farcical. Paul Ricoeur utilised the notion of emplotment (*mise en intrigue*) to characterise the *narrativity of historical temporality. The conventional view is that historical events are narratable because historical reality is made up of lived stories. On this view, emplotment is less a construction than a discovery.

SEE ALSO: historiography; metahistory; narrativisation; plot

References and further reading

Ricoeur, Paul (1984–88) *Time and Narrative*, 3 vols, trans. Katherine Blamey and David Pallauer, Chicago: University of Chicago Press.
White, Hayden (1973) *Metahistory: The Historical Imagination in Nineteenth-century Europe*, Baltimore: Johns Hopkins University Press.

HAYDEN WHITE

ENCYCLOPEDIC NOVEL

In the essay on *genre contained in his *Anatomy of Criticism* (originally published in 1957), Northrop Frye saw the encyclopedic impulse of Menippean satire as the basis for later 'encyclopedic forms' such as Sterne's *Tristram Shandy* (1759–1767) (*see* SATIRIC NARRATIVE). However, the terms *encyclopedic novel* and *encyclopedic narrative* did not really become popular in criticism until the publication of Edward Mendelson's two groundbreaking articles in 1976. Mendelson's discussion brings together Pynchon's *Gravity's Rainbow* (1973), Joyce's *Ulysses* (1922), Melville's *Moby-Dick* (1851), Goethe's *Faust* (1810/1833), and even Dante's *Divine Comedy* (written between 1314 and 1321), suggesting that these texts 'all attempt to render the full range of knowledge and beliefs of a national culture, while identifying the ideological perspectives from which that culture shapes and interprets its knowledge' (Mendelson 1976a: 1269) (*see* IDEOLOGY AND NARRATIVE).

The emphasis on the genre's orientation towards a national culture and the suggestion that encyclopedic narrative originates at the edge of that culture limit the applicability of Mendelson's definition. This problem can be solved by considering the genre with reference to its effect on the *audience. By processing an enormous amount of information from a variety of fields, quite a few big novels produce the illusion on the part of the reader that they have encyclopedic proportions and perhaps even manage to impose some form of order on the wealth of material. Following this broader definition, novels such as *The Gold Bug Variations* (1991), by Richard Powers, and *The Last Samurai* (2001), by Helen Dewitt, would also qualify as encyclopedic novels.

The fact that the reader is left with an illusion implies failure. Both Hillary Clark (1992) and Jed Rasula (1999) have suggested that the encyclopedic novel narrativises the inherent limits of the encyclopedic undertaking itself (*see* NARRATIVISATION). The reader is meant to experience these limitations simultaneously with the idea that the book he or she is reading represents the totality of knowledge. The emphasis on illusion aligns the broad definition of the encyclopedic novel with a sophisticated understanding of the encyclopedia itself. Although the market value of the encyclopedia as a genre still hinges on the suggestion that its buyers will acquire or at least get in touch with the totality of knowledge, Diderot already indicated in the eighteenth-century that the encyclopedia was essentially an open form. Oscar Kenshur and Wilda Anderson have shown that, while cross-references were originally put in as a compensation for the arbitrary order of the alphabet, Diderot considered them as stimuli for the audience, resulting in the juxtaposition of different views and thus undermining the idea of a neat and definitive body of knowledge. The more often readers consulted the encyclopedia, the more they would come to notice the illusion on which the entire genre was built.

The encyclopedic novel, too, serves to highlight the illusory basis of 'total knowledge', even as it manifests the totalising impulse also associated with the project of encyclopedias.

SEE ALSO: novel, the

References and further reading

Anderson, Wilda (1986) 'Encyclopedic Topologies', *Modern Language Notes*, 101, 912–29.

Clark, Hillary (1992) 'Encyclopedic Discourse', *SubStance*, 21.1, 95–110.

Frye, Northrop (1971) *Anatomy of Criticism*, Princeton: Princeton University Press.

Kenshur, Oscar (1986) *Open Form and the Shape of Ideas: Literary Structures as Representations of Philosophical Concepts in the Seventeenth and Eighteenth-Centuries*, Lewisburg: Bucknell University Press.

Mendelson, Edward (1976a) 'Encyclopedic Narrative: From Dante to Pynchon', *Modern Language Notes*, 91, 1267–75.

—— (1976b) 'Gravity's Encyclopedia', in George Levine and David Leverenz (eds) *Mindful Pleasures: Essays on Thomas Pynchon*, Boston: Little, Brown.

Rasula, Jed (1999) 'Textual Indigence in the Archive', *Postmodern Culture*, available via http://www.iath.virginia.edu/framesindex.html

LUC HERMAN

EPIC

An epic (from the Greek *epos*: 'word', 'discourse') is a long narrative poem about *heroes performing impressive deeds usually in interaction with gods (Hainsworth 1991; *see* NARRATIVE IN POETRY). As one of the oldest, most widespread, and longest-lasting narrative *genres, epic has given rise to a large variety of sub-genres: we have heroic epic (Babylonian *Gilgamesh*; Sanskrit *Mahabharata*; Homer's *Iliad* and *Odyssey*); romantic epic (Apollonius Rhodius's *Argonautica*); national epic (Virgil's *Aeneid*); historical epic (Silius Italicus's *Punica*); chivalric epic (*Beowulf*, *Nibelungenlied*, *Poemio de mio Cid*, *Chanson de Roland*); Christian epic (Dante's *Divina Commedia*, Milton's *Paradise Lost*); allegorical epic (Spenser's *Faerie Queene*); and satiric epic (Ariosto's *Orlando Furioso*) (*see* ALLEGORY; ROMANCE; SATIRIC NARRATIVE).

The origin of the epic genre in heroic poetry (Bowra 1952) explains its characteristic tone and themes. Heroic poetry preserves the memory of glorious deeds of the past performed by superior beings who sought and deserved honour. It usually develops at a time of general decline and tends towards idealisation: warriors are strong and courageous, women beautiful, palaces luxurious, and even the singers depicted within the poems hold an honoured position which need not necessarily correspond to reality. *Heroes show their mettle in battles, against human foes, monsters, or powers of nature. They win admiration primarily because they possess praiseworthy qualities to a higher degree than ordinary people: they are strong, swift, enduring, resourceful, and eloquent.

In most ancient epics the gods play a prominent role (Feeney 1991). This divine 'machinery' is a sign of the special status of the heroes, who are judged by the gods to be worthy of their help or opposition. The gods also function as a convenient narrative device, in that the *narrator may employ them to bring about forceful changes in his *plot; in this respect they anticipate the *deus ex machina* of later Attic *drama.

For the development of the Western European epic, the Homeric epics have been the most influential. This model provides a set of formal devices which have become characteristic of the genre.

(1) The Muse-invocation: in the proem, the opening section of his song, and sometimes in the course of the story, the singer-narrator calls on the Muses to provide him with information (not inspiration; this is a later development of the figure of the Muse). Such invocations do no not turn the poet into a mere mouthpiece, but rather are a sign of his professional status and authority. The function of the Muses will change over time (Spentzou and Fowler 2002).

(2) The beginning *in medias res: the Homeric narrator concentrates on a particular phase of the Trojan war and of Odysseus' adventures, while evoking the rest in scenes which mirror the beginning and end of the war (*Iliad*) or having it recounted by the hero himself in a sustained analepsis or flashback comprising four books (*Odyssey*) (*see* SUMMARY AND SCENE; TEMPORAL ORDERING).

(3) The simile: a passage of two to twenty lines which describes a phenomenon from nature or daily life and which is attached to an element of the story: a warrior is compared to a lion or an army to waves crashing on a shore. Characteristic of the Homeric simile is its length: the image develops into a small narrative of its own. Similes primarily serve as an illustration: a lion suggests courage and power, waves a noisy mass, stars glittering armour

and martial spirit. But they may also have a structural or *thematic function (Moulton 1977) (*see* METAPHOR).

(4) High incidence of direct speech (*see* SPEECH REPRESENTATION). According to Aristotle (*Poetics* 24), Homer was unique in his tendency to make his *characters speak. Indeed, 45% of the *Iliad* and 66% of the *Odyssey* consists of direct speech. The abundance of speeches reflects the importance of the spoken word in the heroic world, where a hero is supposed to be 'a speaker of words and doer of deeds' (*Iliad* 9.443) (Martin 1989). In later ancient epics, too, long speeches remain the rule, often betraying the influence of oratory (for Vergil, see Highet 1972).

(5) Catalogues, especially of warriors and troops: in the second book of the *Iliad* the narrator inserts a catalogue of the Greek and Trojan contingents. Such lists, which consist of recurrent elements of identical structure, become a stock-element of epics (see the famous catalogue of Argonauts in Argonautica, book 2, for another example) (*see* NARRATIVE STRUCTURE).

(6) *Ekphrasis: the detailed *description of an object or scenery (*see* EXISTENT; SPACE IN NARRATIVE). The pace of epic narrative style in general is slow, and at times the Homeric narrator takes his time to describe at leisure a location (e.g., Alcinous's palace and garden in *Odyssey* 5) or a piece of armour (most famously, the Shield of Achilles in *Iliad* 18). These descriptions are usually dynamic, in that we either hear of the history of the object in question or see it being fabricated 'before our eyes'.

(7) On a more general level, the Homeric epics, the culmination of a long tradition of anonymous storytelling, and the foundation of much of ancient literature, offer a narratological goldmine, in that they exemplify countless narrative devices (prolepsis, analepsis, misdirection, *gapping, *suspense, etc.), which via drama, *historiography, and the ancient *novel will become part and parcel of our modern novel (de Jong 2001) (*see* NARRATIVE TECHNIQUES).

The Homeric epics display all the characteristics of oral poetry, though scholars are still divided as to how they actually came about: was Homer's original oral version transmitted during several generations until it was written down; did Homer dictate his own song; or did he perhaps himself already make use of writing? The oral characteristics include: standard epithets ('swift-footed Achilles', 'much-enduring Odysseus'), typical scenes (sacrifice, meal, embarking, arming), recurrent lines ('and thus he spoke the winged words'), and traditional themes (withdrawal from battle, divine council, delayed recognition) (see ORAL CULTURES AND NARRATIVE; ORAL-FORMULAIC THEORY; ORALITY; cf. Parry 1971 and Edwards 1987). Even though later epics were written from the start, they retained these elements, which were considered typical of the grandeur of the epic genre.

References and further reading

Bowra, Cecil M. (1952) *Heroic Poetry*, New York: St. Martin's Press.

Edwards, Mark W. (1987) *Homer. Poet of the Iliad*, Baltimore: Johns Hopkins University Press.

Feeney, Dennis C. (1991) *The Gods in Epic: Poets and Critics of the Classical Tradition*, Oxford: Oxford University Press.

Hainsworth, Bryan (1991) *The Idea of Epic*, Berkeley: University of California Press.

Highet, Gilbert (1972) *The Speeches in Vergil's Aeneid*, Princeton: Princeton University Press.

De Jong, Irene J. F. (2001) *A Narratological Commentary on the Odyssey*, Cambridge: Cambridge University Press.

Martin, Richard P. (1989) *The Language of Heroes: Speech and Performance in the Iliad*, Ithaca: Cornell University Press.

Moulton, Carroll (1977) *Similes in the Homeric Epics*, Göttingen: Vandenhoeck & Ruprecht.

Parry, Adam (ed.) (1971) *The Making of Homeric Verse: The Collected Papers of Milman Parry*, Oxford: Oxford University Press.

Spentzou, Effi, and Don Fowler (eds) (2002) *Cultivating the Muse: Struggles for Poet and Inspiration in Classical Literature*, Oxford: Oxford University Press.

IRENE J.F. DE JONG

EPIPHANY

In standard usage, *epiphany* refers to a revelation of divine power, specifically, to the manifestation of Christ. The term was appropriated by James Joyce in *Stephen Hero* (1905) to denote a sudden moment of insight, not necessarily of a religious nature. (In the novel, the artist-protagonist makes it a point to record these 'most delicate and evanescent of moments' conscientiously.) The concept is closely related to what other modernist authors such as Conrad, Woolf, and Mansfield term 'moment of vision', 'moment of being', or 'glimpse'; indeed Woolf usefully contrasts 'moments of being' to the barren 'moments of non-being' of ordinary, non-reflective consciousness. Epiphanies gain structural weight in narratives that focus on the stories unrolling within a character's consciousness (see THOUGHT AND CONSCIOUSNESS REPRESENTATION (LITERATURE)), especially in *genres such as the *Bildungsroman, the story of initiation, and the story of recognition. 'Epiphanic endings' have become a standard form of *closure, and the structural potential of the device is strengthened by the inclusion of deceptive or false epiphanies (see Mansfield's 'Bliss' for a particularly striking example).

SEE ALSO: focalization; modernist narrative

References and further reading

Beja, Morris (1971) *Epiphany in the Modern Novel*, London: Peter Owen.

Nichols, Ashton (1987) *The Poetics of Epiphany*, Tuscaloosa: The University of Alabama Press.

Woolf, Virginia (1976) *Moments of Being: Unpublished Autobiographical Writings*, ed. Jeanne Schulkind, London: Grafton.

MANFRED JAHN

EPISODE

A bounded, internally coherent sequence of situations and *events that can be chained together with other such *narrative units to form larger *narrative structures. *Story grammars decompose episodes into an initiating event, internal reaction by one or more characters, and outcome of the characters' resulting goal-directed behaviour, with possibilities for recursive *embedding of additional episodes (e.g., the initiating event can itself be an episode). *See* FORMALISM.

EPISTOLARY NOVEL

Epistolary novels (or 'letter novels') are *novels narrated wholly or in large part through letters written by the characters (see LETTERS AS NARRATIVE). Epistolary novels frequently account for their own origins and textual disposition by including paratextual information as to how the letters were collected, exchanged, edited, and published (see PARATEXT). Epistolary fiction saw its heyday in the late seventeenth, eighteenth, and early nineteenth-centuries, when its formal disposition towards conveying varied and often contradictory *perspectives became fundamental to the production of the modern novel.

The form can be traced back as far as the Roman author Ovid and the late Hellenic author Alciphron. What we today identify as the epistolary novel began as a unique love story between individuated, realistic *characters. In this sense, Juan de Segura's *Processo de Cartas* (1548; *Exchange of Love Letters*) may be called the 'first epistolary novel'. Subsequently, important *authors, such as Samuel Richardson, Jean-Jacques Rousseau, J.W. von Goethe, and Ugo Foscolo used the form. Many nineteenth-century novelists, from Jane Austen to Fyodor Dostoevsky, also experimented with epistolarity before turning to the device of the omniscient *narrator. A number of fictions use a mixed mode, in which letters carry much but not all of the narrative. Besides letters, Amos Oz's *Kufsah shekhorah* (1987; *Black Box*) contains telegrams, the report of a private investigator, selected notecards by a political scientist on the subject of religious fanaticism, and reviews of the resultant book. Many Renaissance fictions include letters on nearly every page, but embed these within a third-person narrative. An inverse structure occurs when an entire narrative begins as a letter (e.g., with a salutation, 'Dear So-And-So'), but is not subdivided into individual letters and shows none of the further dialogic signs of epistolarity (*see* DIALOGISM). In the late twentieth century the form found particular favour among women authors from all parts of the globe.

Arguably, the early modern period preferred the epistolary form because its preoccupation with the creation of meaning and with questioning the received order was best conveyed in pluralistic, fragmented textual forms, such as encyclopedias, *dialogues, and letters. Much of epistolary fiction's power derived from the letter's instrumentality in legal, economic, and political institutions, and its use as a source of news. Epistolary fiction therefore lent a seriousness and a moral context to fiction which the novel had been said to lack. Transformed in the twenty-first century into phenomena such as the 'e-mail novel', epistolary fiction provides a unique bridge across centuries of narrative experimentation, from classical to contemporary.

SEE ALSO: narration; person

References and further reading

Altman, Janet (1982) *Epistolarity*, Columbus: Ohio State University Press.

Beebee, Thomas (1999) *Epistolary Fiction in Europe 1500–1850*, New York: Cambridge University Press.

Day, Robert Adams (1966) *Told in Letters: Epistolary Fiction Before Richardson*, Ann Arbor: University of Michigan Press.

Favret, Mary (1993) *Romantic Correspondence*, Cambridge: Cambridge University Press.

Kauffman, Linda (1992) *Special Delivery: Epistolary Modes in Modern Fiction*, Chicago: University of Chicago Press.

MacArthur, Elizabeth (1990) *Extravagant Narratives*, Princeton: Princeton University Press.

Perry, Ruth (1980) *Women, Letters, and the Novel*, New York: AMS.

Watson, Nicola (1994) *Revolution and the Form of the British Novel, 1790–1825*, New York: Oxford University Press.

THOMAS O. BEEBEE

ERGODIC LITERATURE

In literary theory the term '*ergodic*' ('work-path' from the Greek *ergon + hodos*) has been used to denominate literature that produces a semiotic sequence which may differ from reading to reading (Aarseth 1997). One of the first well-known ergodic texts is the ancient Chinese book of oracular wisdom, the *I Ching* (c. 1000 BC), which consists of 64 text fragments that are read according to a randomly produced number.

Among other forms of ergodic literature are hypertext fictions, text-based adventure games, and automatic story and poetry generators. Ergodic literature is not a literary *genre, but a perspective focusing on the structural aspects and differences of literary *media that go beyond the standard and dominant sequential structure of the codex book. An ergodic text may contain its own machine for manipulating itself (e.g. a computer program), or it may contain instructions for the reader to do so, as in the case of Raymond Queneau's *Cent Mille Milliards de Poèmes*, a printed book that contains 140 sonnet lines that can be flipped to combine into no less than 10^{14} sonnets.

SEE ALSO: computational approaches to narrative; computer games and narrative; digital narrative; narrative, games, and play

References and further reading

Aarseth, Espen (1997) *Cybertext: Perspectives on Ergodic Literature*, Baltimore: Johns Hopkins University Press.
Queneau, Raymond (1961) *Cent Mille Milliards de Poèmes*, Paris: Gallimard.

ESPEN AARSETH

ETHICAL TURN

What has been, since the 1980s, labelled the *ethical turn* in narrative theory refers to several, partly overlapping developments: a pointed interest in *narrativity and narrative literature from the side of moral philosophy (*see* PHILOSOPHY AND NAR-RATIVE); an increased reflection, from within narratology itself, on the relation between ethics and the *novel; and the corresponding growth of criticism focussing on ethical issues in narrative fiction, such as the encounter with otherness, self-fashioning, values, responsibility, and violence. Criticism of the latter sort often involves the explicit personal ethical engagement of the critic.

Although philosophers like Derrida and Levinas wrote incisively on the ethical workings of poetry, as did Nussbaum on *drama, ethical criticism tends to concentrate on the novel. Usually this is justified with the argument that the novel through its form and its thematic material represents precisely what ethics is about, namely: a reflection on human *action and *character; conflicting drives, *desires, and choices evolving in time, offered for the reader's appreciation or judgement from different *perspectives (*see* CON-FLICT). In the explosive growth of ethical criticisms, with so many conceptions of ethics around, the following main tendencies can be distinguished (interestingly, ethical criticism is most popular in Britain and the U.S., where the moral strand in the humanities is traditionally strong).

(1) In continuity with the humanist tradition of reading for wisdom, and relying on an Aristotelian, pragmatic, and flexible notion of ethics, a number of theorists have argued (most forcefully, Nussbaum) that reading narrative fiction offers a valuable complement to moral philosophy: it provides a kind of experiential learning, suggests alternatives for 'how to live the good life', and exercises moral awareness and flexibility. In a kindred spirit, but more interested in the formal aspects of literary communication, rhetorical narratology (Booth 1988; Phelan 1996) studies the devices through which narrative texts construct value-effects and elicit the reader's ethical engagement (*see* RHETORICAL APPROACHES TO NARRATIVE). These approaches share their confidence in *common sense* ('our' sense of life), in language as a reliable vehicle of meanings, and in texts as the expression of an ethos that can be reconstructed (Booth goes as far as to personify books as friends).

(2) Precisely these and related 'humanistic' notions come under fire both in Levinas' ethics of *alterity and in the *deconstructive ethics developed by Derrida, Blanchot, Lyotard, and Paul de Man. Narrative-pertinent models inspired by these philosophers locate the ethical insight literature has to offer in the experience of the radical strangeness of the other, the self, and the world, and in the final undecidability of meaning and values.

(3) Finally, critics focusing on the representation of race, *gender, class, and multiculturalism, tend to share the deconstructive suspicion of 'humanistic' ethics, considered complicitous with patriarchal and colonial Western oppression. 'Undecidability' as the ultimate ethics of the novel, however, is frequently traded for more polemically formulated alternatives, such as feminist (Irigaray, Cornell, Armstrong) or post-colonial ethics (Bhabha, Spivak) (*see* FEMINIST NARRATOLOGY; POST-COLONIALISM AND NARRATIVE).

Narrative fiction between ethics and aesthetics

Since Plato's *Republic*, verbal *mimesis of character and action has been experienced by some as a threat to morality and social order; to which Aristotle's *Poetics* offers the counter-argument that literary mimesis provides its own kind of learning and *truth (*see* ANCIENT THEORIES OF NARRATIVE (WESTERN)). From the eighteenth-century on, the autonomy of the aesthetic, linked to freedom of expression and democracy, was progressively institutionalised, while Kant gave it its philosophical legitimisation: art serves no practical – social, moral, or economic – interests. Thus the novel could become a laboratory for testing social norms and values. In practice, while novelists and readers discover the thrills of transgression, the horizon of morality remains very present, and much fiction criticism and *reception still tends to be moralistic. At worst, this leads to censorship. At best, moral transgression is recuperated in terms of a higher ethics of art (Georges Bataille) or related to art's critical, utopian function (Adorno).

During the twentieth century, the development of literary studies into an autonomous academic discipline went hand in hand with the evacuation of the traditionally prominent concern for ethical issues. Especially in *structuralist narratology, the striving towards scientific objectivity required the separation between subject and object of research, which made a 'committed' ethical approach toward narrative fiction inappropriate for epistemological reasons. Moreover, since the 1970s, with the intensifying critique of Western culture, the notion of ethics itself had become suspect. Newly emancipated groups – from feminists and queers to ethnic minorities – denounced the notion of universal ethics as the instrument and legitimisation of structures of power and oppression (see QUEER THEORY). Foucault, Derrida, Deleuze, Lacan, Said, and others, having read their Marx, Nietzsche, and Freud, questioned the traditional basic ethical ('metaphysical') concepts, such as the autonomous subject, value, meaning, and truth.

Ironically, however, while literary scholars carefully avoided the question of ethics, moral philosophers, dissatisfied with Kantian deontology as well as with utilitarian ethics, suddenly (re)discovered literature, and especially the novel. MacIntyre's pathbreaking *After Virtue* (1981) was soon followed by other philosophic contributions arguing the importance of narrativity for a theory of ethics (Nussbaum 1990; Taylor 1989; Rorty 1989; Ricoeur 1990). Narrativity – a feature not limited to literature, but prominently present in the novel – was described as a fundamental to ethics in various senses: mainly in the construction of personal *identity (MacIntyre 1981; Ricoeur 1990), and in the exemplification, clarification, or subversion of values and 'world visions' through *plot (Nussbaum 1990; Ricoeur 1990). Although in some cases this meant a rehabilitation of the autonomous subject (Nussbaum 1990), in others there clearly is an endeavour to think what ethics and responsibility can mean in the era of 'split' subjects, overdetermined by the discourses that speak (through) them. Even those thinkers who had most fiercely criticised 'humanism', like Foucault, Derrida, and Lyotard, started to reflect explicitly on their own – postmodern – ethics. Interestingly, they transfer to ethics some crucial

characteristics of the aesthetic: ambivalence, plurality, and the idea of the constructedness of personal existence, as in Foucault's 'aesthetics of life' or Rorty's ironic play with multiple vocabularies. This has been interpreted as an overtaking of ethics by aesthetics, but the reverse can be argued as well.

Main tendencies

In the current explosion of ethical criticism, three main tendencies can be distinguished: (1) pragmatist and rhetorical ethics; (2) ethics of alterity; (3) political approaches to ethics.

(1) Working within the American pragmatic tradition, Nussbaum, Booth, Parker, and Phelan argue that narrative fiction can play an important role in the moral development of readers by modelling their *emotions, self-conception, and view of life. This kind of criticism does not merely discuss the moral standpoints explicitly thematised in a work; what is more, it claims to trace the *ethos* implied in the whole composition. Re-actualising Aristotelian ethics, Nussbaum argues that narrative fiction is an indispensable complement to moral philosophy: the latter is bound to abstract language and concerned with universals, whereas moral disposition and action require flexibility, imagination, and the capacity to adapt to concrete situations, to which universals usually do not apply in any obvious way. By engaging us in situations of value-conflicts, narrative exercises our practical moral sense, allowing for vicarious experiential learning. Nussbaum and Parker focus mainly on the development of moral awareness in characters. Nussbaum interestingly calls attention to the meanings and values conveyed through the representation of emotions, an interest shared by ancient rhetoric: Aristotle already distinguished the persuasive effects of *pathos* besides those of *ethos* (concerning the *reliability of the speaker) and *logos* (referring to the argumentation). Booth's and, more recently, Phelan's contribution lies in their analysis of the rhetorical devices responsible for the contradictory pattern of desires which narratives impose upon their readers – devices such as *point of view, *distance, reliability of the teller, *voice, or *tense. Crucial in this kind of narrative criticism is the discussion within oneself or with others triggered by the 'encounter of a storyteller's ethos with that of the reader or the listener', a process Booth calls 'co-duction' (Booth 1988: 70–75).

Although devoted to a pluralist, pragmatic, and open conception of ethics, Nussbaum, Parker, and Booth do not always avoid the pitfall of moralism: they tend to value in literature its potential for moral elevation rather than its aesthetic and/or ethical complexity, which often involves ambiguity. Nussbaum reads for 'moral guidance', 'practical wisdom', coloured by a strong civic sense. The novels she considers essential for moral learning are novels of deliberation, combining 'attention to particulars' and 'richness of feeling', such as can be found in Henry James's works. Proust, though greatly admired, is ultimately criticised by her as too solipsistic, while Beckett appears as too nihilistic, engaged in a (socially) unproductive search for silence (Nussbaum 1990: 308–9, passim). Despite his openness, Booth, too, considers those books most valuable which offer ultimately unambiguous 'friendships of virtue', as the Classics do. However, the careful rhetorical approach that he and, after him, Phelan develop, can lead to a fruitful approach to the ethical dimension of aesthetic form; it does not necessarily lead to prefabricated moralistic judgements, though it will always involve the critic's individual moral response.

(2) Where Nussbaum and Booth build on common sense, virtues, shared values, and vocabularies, this striving towards 'sameness' is precisely what Levinas and deconstructive philosophers like Derrida and Lyotard unmask as an attempted appropriation of the other by the self or the same. For Levinas, ethics means to place myself under the absolute command of the Other. The ethical relation always occurs in the face-to-face relation with the other. This explains why Levinas values the *Saying* over the *Said*. Compared to the concrete, unique, and relational act of Saying, involving an I and a You at a specific moment, the Said always means a concession to a 'truth' which in its generality betrays the specificity of the moment and of the relationship. Not surprisingly Levinas in most of his works displays a rather negative conception of literature, as reading offers no direct face-to-face contact between reader and text or author. However, critics such as Gibson and Newton have shown the relevance of Levinas' ethics for the analysis of narrative fiction. They argue that modern fiction – from Conrad and Rhys to Beckett – can be shown to stage the act of Saying and to problematise the Said. Such fiction invites the reader to join in the event of the utterance (or the act of writing), which can thus become an ethical experience. In conformity with Levinas' distrust of the possessiveness of the Self and the Same, reading should be envisaged not as the appropriation of a work, but as a double 'undoing': as a reader, one must agree to lose oneself in the submission to the call of the text as Other, and to lose the work as a graspable, coherent whole.

Interestingly close to Levinas in many ways (especially in its respect for otherness), deconstructivist narrative ethics at first seems a contradiction in terms: the subversion by deconstructive philosophy of the traditional pillars of ethics – the notion of an autonomous subject, meaning, truth – seems to make any ethics obsolete, if not impossible. The animosity against this philosophical and textual approach, which dared to challenge common sense and Western 'humanism', was widespread. Information about Heidegger's attitude during Nazism and the discovery that one of the major deconstructionists, Paul de Man, wrote for a Nazi-controlled paper in his early twenties, of course quickly fuelled the critiques. J. Hillis Miller was among the first to claim that ethics, understood as reflection on and respect for alterity, had always been at the heart of deconstructive thinking. In his programmatic work, *The Ethics of Reading*, he argues that far from being 'free textual play', deconstructive reading is ethical in its attention to the ways in which texts both undermine and defer/differ from (in the sense of Derrida's *différance*) their own meanings and intentions (*see* INTENTIONALITY). This kind of reading shows how texts undermine the reader's expectations and his or her desire for totality and *closure. Literature is the place where morality, understood as deontological, is exposed in its rigidity and partiality, and set off against the disruptive power of imagination and ambivalence. In privileging undecidability, this reading tries itself to avoid petrification into moral judgements.

In a similarly radical manner, Blanchot and Lyotard locate the ethical dimension of fiction and modern art in their capacity to bring forward the unrepresentable in presentation itself – what has been called the negative sublime (Lyotard) – and to reveal the emptiness which haunts the world of things (Blanchot). Deconstructive narrative criticism will value precisely those texts which are problematic for Nussbaum or Booth: self-referential, obscure, undecidable works such as

Joyce's and Beckett's, or postmodern experimental novels (*see* POSTMODERN NARRATIVE). However, criticism inspired by an ethics of literature as radical undecidability, linked to the textual mechanism of *différance*, also runs the risk of discovering the same in all texts, thus reducing ethics to something very abstract and general. This is especially the case in Hillis Miller's readings. In dialogue with Levinas, Derrida works out a conception of ethics which attempts to articulate the suspension of judgement with the necessity, in concrete situations, to judge (see Critchley's (1992) interesting discussion of this tension within deconstruction).

(3) Not all critics claiming an affiliation with deconstruction are devoted to 'undecidability' and abstraction. Some commentators, trained in deconstructive reading of faultlines and contradictions in discourse, have used their skills to analyse how art bears witness to history, especially to traumatic history, with the Holocaust as the main point of reference (*see* HOLOCAUST NARRATIVE; TRAUMA THEORY). Focusing on how art deals with experiences that defy representation, this criticism itself claims to bear witness to the victims (see Felman and Laub 1992, who analyse the 'crisis of witnessing' in the Holocaust in Camus' and Celan's work, and also in the personal testimonies represented in Lanzmann's film *Shoah*). Also relevant in this context is the moral engagement in feminist, queer, and post-colonial criticism, which in various degrees claim to be deconstructive. Most theorists working in these areas share a rejection of traditional Western, 'phallogocentric' oppressive ethics, setting forward alternatives which claim to cultivate an ethics more respectful of alterity, of the right to difference – understood quite concretely as cultural or sexual difference. Feminist ethics tends to cultivate sensibility and affect, as opposed to a 'patriarchal' ethics privileging norm, reason, and domination. Wary, however, of a new essentialising of gender roles, both Cornell and Irigaray stress that such an ethics is both critical and utopian: new relations between man and woman, or between self and other have to be invented, a process which requires the full disruptive power of imagination. This is where narrative fiction comes in, analysed as representation of the oppression of women as the other, but also as the invention of new gender roles. From the post-colonial angle, Homi Bhabha and Gayatri Spivak explore in narrative fiction what *hybridity

can offer to ethics: an encounter of otherness within the self, and the questioning of (cultural) identities as fixed 'locations of culture'. Spivak practices a double 'ethical resistance' from her position as a woman and as an ex-colonised subject. All these explicitly committed ethical approaches to narrative tend to defend conceptions of ethics that promote specific emancipatory political agendas. In their normativity, they are in fact closer to traditional morality than to a Derridean 'undecidability'.

Open questions

In all these approaches, some convictions appear to be widely shared, namely (1) that narrative fiction and criticism are not inconsequential 'free play', and (2) that criticism is a singular and particular event which engages the responsibility of the critic and of the text as well as its *author. But beyond this agreement, dissension reigns. What definition of ethics appears most fruitful for analysing narrative as a specific cultural practice? It can be argued that any approach is reductive when, in defining the ethical dimension of narrative (literature), it privileges language as simply transitive and literature as offering a clear moral guidance (Nussbaum 1990); but it is just as reductive to consider language as radically intransitive and literature as the experience of strangeness, absence of meaning, and the evanescence of the self. It seems more productive to analyse how narrative fiction broaches issues located on a spectrum stretching between the two extremes: how – through what devices – narrative texts, written and read in specific contexts, thematise, problematise, or consolidate specific moral values and norms; and how their ethical value can lie in the questioning of morality itself. A systematic empirical investigation of the actual effects of different kinds of readings, of different kinds of works, in specific settings (for instance in school) would be a useful complement to these often normative hermeneutic approaches (*see* HERMENEUTICS). Another open question is that of the epistemological and ethical status of the critic's discourse. There is no such thing as 'the' ethics of a text, only various ethical readings. The dangers of using a literary work as a vehicle for promoting pre-set ethical ideas are obvious. However, a careful rhetorical and narratological analysis at least provides a textual basis for an ethically fruitful discussion of interpretations. Ethical reading, if it is to take literature seriously, requires sophisticated skills in aesthetic (narratological and rhetorical) analysis.

SEE ALSO: cultural studies approaches to narrative; fiction, theories of

References and further reading

Bhabha, Homi (1994) *The Location of Culture*, London: Routledge.

Booth, Wayne (1988) *The Company We Keep. An Ethics of Fiction*, Berkeley, CA: University of California Press.

Critchley, Simon (1992) *The Ethics of Deconstruction: Derrida and Levinas*, Oxford: Blackwell.

Cornell, Drucilla (1991) *Beyond Accommodation: Ethical Feminism, Deconstruction and the Law*, London: Routledge.

Derrida, Jacques (1992) *Acts of Literature*, ed. Derek Attridge, London: Routledge.

Felman, Shoshana, and Dori Laub (1992) *Testimony: Crises of Witnessing in Literature, Psychoanalysis and History*, London: Routledge.

Gibson, Andrew (1999) *Postmodernity, Ethics, and The Novel: From Leavis to Levinas*, London: Routledge.

Hillis Miller, J. (1987) *The Ethics of Reading: Kant, de Man, Eliot, Trollope, James, and Benjamin*, New York: Columbia University Press.

Levinas, Emmanuel (1981) *Otherwise than Being*, trans. Alphonso Lingis, The Hague: Martinus Nijhoff.

MacIntyre, Alisdair (1981) *After Virtue: A Study in Moral Theory*, Notre Dame, IN: University of Notre Dame Press.

Newton, Adam Z. (1995) *Narrative Ethics*, Cambridge, Mass.: Harvard University Press.

Nussbaum, Martha (1990) *Love's Knowledge: Essays on Philosophy and Literature*, Oxford: Oxford University Press.

Phelan, James (1996) *Narrative as Rhetoric: Technique, Audiences, Ethics, Ideology*, Columbus, OH: Ohio State University Press.

Ricoeur, Paul (1984–88) *Soi-même comme un autre*, Paris: Seuil.

Rorty, Richard (1989) *Contingency, Irony, and Solidarity*, Cambridge: Cambridge University Press.

Spivak, Gayatri Chakraworty (1996) 'Echo', in Donna Landry and Gerald MacLean (eds) *The Spivak Reader*, London: Routledge.

Taylor, Charles (1989) *Sources of the Self: The Making of Modern Identity*, Cambridge, Mass: Harvard University Press.

LIESBETH KORTHALS ALTES

ETHNOGRAPHIC APPROACHES TO NARRATIVE

Exploring the many ways that ethnographic inquiry and the study of narratives intersect has provided an important stimulus for producing theoretical and methodological innovations in both of these research areas. This entry focuses primarily on how researchers have documented narratives ethnographically, but it also addresses recent attempts to examine the sorts of narratives that ethnographers tell in representing their inquiries.

Franz Boas connected ethnography and narrative intimately in the way he laid out American anthropology in the early twentieth century. In the 1960s and 1970s, the ethnography of speaking focused attention on the documentation of both formal and interactive features of narratives, studying *genres that ranged from *myth, *legend, and *fairy tale to personal narratives, rumour, and *gossip. Work undertaken during this period under the aegis of conversation analysis similarly stressed interactive dimensions (*see* COMMUNICATION IN NARRATIVE; DISCOURSE ANALYSIS (LINGUISTICS)). An emphasis on *performance prompted scholars to examine the culturally constitutive features that structured aesthetically elaborated forms of intercourse between performers and *audiences. Ethnopoetics sparked innovation in the way that transcriptions and translations were presented and how scholars analysed relationships between forms and meanings. In the 1980s and 1990s, scholars became interested in how narratives get detached from the contexts in which they are enacted, focusing on how narratives are linked to prior settings and discourses at the same time that *narrators anticipate future recontextualisations. Further, theorists began to examine the standardised narratives told by ethnographers, revealing how anthropologists construct images of exotic cultures through *rhetorical strategies and complex relations of power. These critiques prompted experiments in how ethnographies are written and read.

While it would be difficult to locate a single dominant ethnographic perspective on narrative at present, many scholars have turned to documenting how narratives are produced in and circulate through institutions (*see* INSTITUTIONAL NARRATIVE), thereby constituting forms of authority and social inequality within nation-states and transnational forms of governmentality.

From Boas to the ethnography of speaking

Franz Boas was a German immigrant of Jewish descent who became one of the most influential anthropologists in the U.S. Noting that features of narrative content 'give us a picture' of 'the mode of life and the chief interests of the people' (1927: 329), Boas presented collecting narratives in 'native' languages as a crucial component of ethnography. He deemed narratives to embody authentic voices and express what most interests a people, thus constituting a sort of collective *autobiography that is less susceptible to distortion by the cultural biases of the ethnographer. A great deal of Boas's vast narrative corpus was written by multilingual culture brokers who created texts that encoded this notion of authenticity. For example, his most important collaborator, George Hunt, was the son of a Englishman who worked for the Hudson Bay Company and a Tlingit (Native American woman); nevertheless, Hunt produced volumes of material on the Kwakwaka'wakw ('Kwakiutl') communities in which he was raised. Boas generally stripped the narratives he published of details that drew attention to the complex social and discursive processes through which they were produced, thereby projecting them as the unfolding of what he sometimes referred to as 'the mind of the American native' rather than as the result of complex multicultural and multilingual mediations.

Boas viewed traditional narratives, particularly myths, as shaping everyday thoughts and actions, especially in 'primitive' groups (see ORAL CULTURES AND NARRATIVE). Rather than interpreting stories as constructions of collective experience, Boas viewed narratives as artistic forms that involved a play of imagination with social forms that distorted everyday life and history. Narratives thus do not map social life but constitute secondary explanations that operate unconsciously. Boas accordingly argued that narratives can provide accurate means of documenting culture and history only when read analytically by anthropologists. Boas's interest in the role of narrative in rationalising ideologies and practices overlaps with the work of Bronislaw Malinowski, who played an influential role in moving British anthropologists toward an ethnographic focus. Malinowski deemed myth to be a social charter that provided a basis for shaping and naturalising ideologies and modes of conduct (see IDEOLOGY AND NARRATIVE). For both Boas and Malinowski, interest in narrative intersected with a concern for language and its social context.

Another major figure in ethnographic approaches to narrative was Claude Lévi-Strauss. Unlike Boas and Malinowski, Lévi-Strauss conducted little ethnography himself. Narratives collected by ethnographers working around the world, particularly in the Americas, were the focus of his theoretically elaborated analyses. Lévi-Strauss privileged narratives as key ethnographic sources due to what he deemed to be their central locus as sites in which societies creatively and collectively posed the epistemological questions that they confronted in daily life. His approach was deeply ethnographic in its concern with linking the symbols and binary oppositions that he found in narratives, particularly myths, to a range of other dimensions of social life, such as plastic arts, bodily decorations, ritual, and kinship. Nevertheless, he was largely unconcerned with the need to collect narratives in their ethnographic contexts; he considered texts, including translations that were obtained under quite contrived conditions and subject to significant modification (such as summarisation) to be suitable objects of analysis. Lévi-Strauss thus sacrificed concern with formal patterns and with how tellings were woven into daily life in favour of an emphasis on narrative content.

From the time of its emergence in the 1960s in the work of Hymes (1974), the *ethnography of speaking* transformed the relationship between narrative and ethnography in a number of crucial ways. First, rather than considering narratives to be a crucial object of analysis *a priori*, as did Boas, Lévi-Strauss, and Malinowski, practitioners aligned with this approach viewed the collection of narratives as part of the job of documenting the full range of speech genres evident in a particular 'speech community' (see TEXT-TYPE APPROACH TO NARRATIVE). Second, ethnographers of speaking explored multiple communicative functions beyond the referential, incorporating the Austinian view of speech as possessing a performative capacity, that is, as not just referring to but constituting social action (see PERFORMATIVITY; PRAGMATICS; REFERENCE; SPEECH ACT THEORY). Third, questions of narrative style loomed much larger than they had for Lévi-Straussian structuralists (see STRUCTURALIST NARRATOLOGY), leading practitioners to detail the features of particular narrative genres as well as the elements that distinguished narratives from other speech forms. Unlike many literary approaches, ethnographers of speaking viewed style not from the perspective of a Kantian aesthetics (that separates out formal patterns from cognition and social/political effects) but ethnographically as a part of communicative events and patterns. Fourth, ethnographers of speaking sought to document narratives *in use*, as they emerged both within the course of both daily life and as part of ritual or other special settings. The goal was thus not to isolate a narrative as an aesthetic or cultural object but to grasp how it was indexically located in the historical, social, and cultural setting in which it emerged. Thus, just as issues of rhetoric and *voice provided new means of deriving ethnographic insights from narratives, the ethnographic study of narratives generated heightened requirements for documentation. To be sure, the epistemological and methodological underpinnings of the ethnography of speaking were quite distinct from those associated with conversation analysis, as classically articulated by Sacks. Nevertheless, both fields converged during the 1970s in prompting many students of narrative to record stories in their contexts of use and to draw attention to the interactional organisation of narratives (*see* SOCIOLINGUISTIC APPROACHES TO NARRATIVE).

Performance and ethnopoetics

A new organising framework for the ethnographic study of narrative emerged in the mid-1970s through the work of Bauman and Hymes under the aegis of *performance*. Like the ethnography of speaking, concern with performance sparked fruitful convergences between anthropologists, folklorists, linguists, and literary scholars (*see* FOLKLORE). In essence, emphasising performance brought formal features into a stronger relationship with dimensions of social interaction and social organisation. This analytic frame focused attention on the emergence of narratives and other performances through the interaction between performers and audiences. Performances are thus distinguished from everyday communicative interaction, even ones that constitute brief *epiphanies in the mist of daily life. Bauman characterised this relationship as a heightened responsibility assumed by the performer for a display of communicative virtuosity that involves special types of communicative competence and is subject to evaluation by audience members. Performances are keyed by special framing devices (such as opening and closing formulae), special registers (including ritual or archaic languages),

such formal features as parallelism and metrical patterning, formulaic dialogic exchanges between participants (*see* ORAL-FORMULAIC THEORY), and figurative forms, such as simile and *metaphor.

Hymes stresses the transformative or 'breakthrough' dimension of performance, as participants shift to heightened forms of communicative interaction that open up special forms of creativity. Performance was viewed as highly metadiscursive, as exposing expressive forms and their communicative effects to *reflexivity in the form of scrutiny, evaluation, and contestation and to the simultaneous unfolding of a variety of communicative functions. Bauman, Hymes, and other scholars deemed features of the patterning and social organisation of performance to be specific to particular genres and speech communities, thereby underlining the need for their systematic ethnographic documentation. Briggs suggested that different performative genres involve contrastive degrees of openness to the penetration of emergent features of interaction, thereby commenting in different ways on a wide range of dimensions of social life. He argued that narrative performances relate to political economy both as they are shaped by the constraints that restrict access to hegemonic communicative forms – particularly in situations dominated by racial, class, or sexual oppression – and also as they performatively reveal, extend, challenge, or transform inequalities. The study of narrative and political economy has been influenced by Bourdieu's work. Specifically, Bourdieu reveals the interconnections between (1) access to narratives (and their value as forms of 'symbolic capital'), and (2) access to institutions (particularly educational) in which 'communicative competence' is bestowed (*see* EDUCATION AND NARRATIVE; SOCIOLOGICAL APPROACHES TO LITERARY NARRATIVE).

The 1970s and 1980s also witnessed a range of experiments with the transcription and translation of narratives, as guided by ethnographic criteria, under the guise of *ethnopoetics*. Tedlock proposed a format that attempted to convey the acoustic dimensions of performances. If the formal features of narratives provide important clues to meaning and social interaction, then such elements as pauses, volume, and special vocal effects should be marked explicitly in texts. Hymes contrastively argued that texts should be organised around systematic relationships between form and function, as revealed by what he referred to as verse analysis, rather than acoustic form alone. Although their visions of what matters in the analysis and transcription of narratives differed widely, both sought to turn transcriptions into documents that could be of greater value in studying narratives ethnographically.

Beyond 'context': intertextuality and recontextualisation

Ironically, a Russian literary scholar, Bakhtin, has exerted one of the greatest influences on the ethnographic study of narrative, particularly after his works became more widely available in English in the 1970s and 1980s. Bakhtin and other members of his circle illuminated the dynamics of a central facet of narratives – reported speech (*see* SPEECH REPRESENTATION) – demonstrating how the complex pragmatics associated with different forms of reported speech enabled narrators to place elements of their narrative in complex and shifting relationships to themselves, *characters, and audiences. Bakhtin's *Dialogic Imagination* and other writings pushed scholars to re-examine the emphasis they had placed on how narratives were wedded to the social and discursive contexts of performances. He rather viewed speech as deeply shaped by *intertextuality, drawing attention to how the form, meaning, and effect of any utterance constructs relationships with prior texts and contexts at the same time that it anticipates future enactments. Bakhtin similarly pointed to the question of how texts construct their own authority, in part, by situating themselves and the parties seen as producing, speaking, circulating, and receiving them in relation to other voices, styles, texts, and roles (*see* DIALOGISM).

Bauman and Briggs build on Bakhtin's approach in developing a framework for analysing the pragmatics of narrative performances and the way they construct ideologies of language and social action. They suggest that narratives involve a process of *entextualising* discourse in such a way as to enable it to be separated in varying degrees from its discursive and social surroundings, which they refer to as *decontextualisation*. An opposing process of *recontextualisation* draws attention both to the way that a text is seen as an iteration of a prior discourse – thereby drawing audiences into other discursive realms – and how narratives point (implicitly or explicitly) to anticipated future recontextualisations (*see* NARRATIVE VERSIONS).

Silverstein points to the 'pragmatic calibration' that narrators use in constructing complex relations between narrated events and the narrative events associated with performances or inscriptions, particularly through the use of *verba dicendi*, *deixis, *tense, and poetic patterning. Traditionalisation, framing a narrative as a recontextualisation of a collective realm that is socially constructed as prior to the present, involves an ideological invocation of ties to prior texts and contexts. By contrast, gossip narratives are often oriented toward structuring future retellings and shaping which parties will be 'entitled' (Sacks 1995) to tell and hear stories. Briggs and Bauman argue that narrators and audiences can emphasise the *links* that exist between texts and other sites of recontextualisation; alternatively, they foreground the *gaps* that can separate them. By discursively positioning themselves vis-à-vis these intertextual links and gaps – and thereby ideologically constructing the pasts, presents, and futures to which they are seen as connected – writers and narrators invoke powerful tools for constructing ideologies and imbuing social relations with power. Nevertheless, as Bakhtin's work reminds us, the effectiveness of such strategies is contingent on the active assimilation of speech by audiences, who can recontextualise even authoritative discourse through parody or satire (*see* SATIRIC NARRATIVE), thereby opening cavernous intertextual gaps.

Rhetorical criticism of ethnographic narratives

During the 1980s, rhetorical criticism brought connections between ethnography and narrative into scholarly prominence in another way: published ethnographies were critically scrutinised with a view to identifying the types of narratives that ethnographers themselves produce in representing social worlds. (Unfortunately, potential connections between such critical approaches to the narrative construction of ethnography, on the one hand, and the ethnographic perspectives on narrative reviewed earlier in this essay, on the other hand, have not been systematically explored.) Clifford examined ethnographies published in the twentieth century with respect to the standardised tropes that they use in creating their own authority. Professional ethnographers presented themselves as the voices of experience, as revealing the *truth of cultures that were constructed as timeless, local, static, exotic, and Other. Clifford and other critics used literary and rhetorical analysis to expose the standardised metaphors, introductory formulae, theoretical abstractions, monologicality, and hierarchical arrangements of multiple discourses (including the voices of 'informants') that constituted the ethnographic monograph as a genre. Notions of culture and difference, along with the sense of detached objectivity projected by ethnographers, were characterised as effects of particular *narrative techniques that changed over generations. These narrative techniques are used to write crucial details 'out of the story': the partiality of ethnographers' perspectives, the fragmented nature of ethnographic knowledge, and the strategies of representation and power relations that enabled ethnographers to speak for Others. These critiques exacerbated the post-colonial crisis of ethnographic authority (*see* POST-COLONIALISM AND NARRATIVE).

Some ethnographers reacted to these critiques by drawing on a wide range of *modernist and *postmodern literary techniques in experimenting with ethnographic narrative. Some ethnographies were presented in novelistic form, with fictionalised characters and settings, and some writers presented themselves in the guise of multiple characters. Others attempted to construct texts dialogically, deliberately giving up some control over the final product and thereby sharing authority (to quite varying degrees) with 'natives' and other collaborators. Rejecting attempts to structure ethnographies around notions of unified subjects and coherent *narrative structures that presupposed what Clifford refers to as a controlling mode of authority (1988: 54), some ethnographers have drawn attention to power inequalities, opening up contestations for authority among multiple voices and creating texts that embrace fragmentary, multiple points of view in openly confronting questions of power, rhetoric, history, and language.

Narratives, institutions, globalisation and power

Rather than witnessing the emergence of a single dominant framework guiding ethnographic approaches to narrative, the period that began in the 1990s has been characterised by hybridisations of familiar techniques in mapping new social realities and processes. Interest in the ethnographic

study of narratives and in narratives that sustain relations of power and domination converged on both sides of the Atlantic in research on the production and circulation of narratives in institutions of the nation-state and other dominant sectors. Ethnographers have studied the importance of narratives in shaping everyday practices and forms of authority, sparking interest in the role of narratives in *law, *medicine, education, public assistance, and other types of institutions. The social roles that are constructed in institutional narratives and the differential rights of professionals and clients in producing, circulating, and interpreting these stories help sustain power inequalities. Scholars have collected personal and institutional narratives as means of studying how these roles are constructed, naturalised, and challenged. Literary scholars, historians, and ethnographers have all focused on foundational narratives that are presented as providing a legitimising *genealogy for nations and states. Narrative analysis similarly enters into the study of globalisation as scholars track the transnational circulation of stories that shape neo-liberal forms of surveillance and control, new economic regimes, and social movements centred on human rights, sexuality, ecology, anti-globalisation, women's rights, and indigenous peoples (*see* ECO-NARRATIVES; GENDER STUDIES).

In short, interest in ethnography and in narrative has intersected in intimate, shifting, and often contested ways for more than a hundred years. Exploring these connections continues to yield important insights into social worlds and the complex theoretical, methodological, and political issues involved in representing them. Whatever forms it may take, it seems clear that the interface between narrative and ethnography will continue to generate important sites for creatively reconfiguring the study of both ethnography and narrative for future generations of scholars.

SEE ALSO: conversational storytelling; cultural studies approaches to narrative; tellability

References and further reading

Bakhtin, M. M. (1981) *The Dialogic Imagination: Four Essays*, ed. Michael Holquist, trans. Caryl Emerson and Michael Holquist, Austin: University of Texas Press.

Bauman, Richard (1977) *Verbal Art as Performance*, Prospect Heights, IL: Waveland.

Bauman, Richard, and Charles L. Briggs (1990) 'Poetics and Performance as Critical Perspectives on Language and Social Life', *Annual Review of Anthropology*, 19, 59–88.

Boas, Franz (1927) *Primitive Art*, Oslo: H. Aschehoug.

Bourdieu, Pierre (1991) *Language and Symbolic Power*, trans. Gino Raymond and Matthew Adamson, Cambridge, Mass.: Harvard University Press.

Briggs, Charles L. (1988) *Competence in Performance: The Creativity of Tradition in Mexicano Verbal Art*, Philadelphia: University of Pennsylvania Press.

——, and Richard Bauman (1992) 'Genre, Intertextuality, and Social Power', *Journal of Linguistic Anthropology*, 2, 131–72.

Clifford, James (1988) *The Predicament of Culture: Twentieth-Century Ethnography, Literature, and Art*, Cambridge, Mass.: Harvard University Press.

——, and George E. Macus (eds) (1986) *Writing Culture: The Poetics and Politics of Ethnography*, Berkeley: University of California Press.

Hymes, Dell H. (1974) *Foundations in Sociolinguistics: An Ethnographic Approach*, Philadelphia: University of Pennsylvania Press.

—— (1981) *'In Vain I Tried to Tell You': Essays in Native American Ethnopoetics*, Philadelphia: University of Pennsylvania Press.

Lévi-Strauss, Claude (1963 [1958]) *Structural Anthropology*, trans. Claire Jacobson and Brooke Grundfest Schoepf, New York: Basic Books.

Malinowski, Bronislaw (1926) *Myth in Primitive Psychology*, London: K. Paul, Trench, Trubner & Co.

Sacks, Harvey (1995) *Lectures on Conversation*, ed. Gail Jefferson, Oxford: Blackwell.

Silverstein, Michael (1993) 'Metapragmatic Discourse and Metapragmatic Function', in John A. Lucy (ed.) *Reflexive Language: Reported Speech and Metapragmatics*, Cambridge: Cambridge University Press.

Tedlock, Dennis (1983) *The Spoken Word and the Work of Interpretation*, Philadelphia: University of Pennsylvania Press.

CHARLES L. BRIGGS

EVENTS AND EVENT-TYPES

In their attempts to define what stories are, theorists have attributed to narrative the core property of representing events, or changes of state. Although there is ample evidence that events are indeed an essential component of narrative, recent work in narrative theory suggests the need for analysing or decomposing the notions 'event' and 'state' into a cluster of more finely grained concepts. The term 'event-types' refers to the output of this reanalysis, which has been informed by developments in neighbouring fields such as *action theory, *Artificial Intelligence, *linguistics, and the philosophy of language.

The saliency of events for narratives can be highlighted by comparing stories with other *text-types. In the case of the proposition expressed as (1), for example, the proposition does not convey a narrative because, rather than representing an event, it merely ascribes a property.

(1) Water is H_2O.

As a *description, (1) expresses a stative proposition rather than an event. Inductive generalisations such as (2) do not qualify as narratives either.

(2) Water freezes at 0 degrees centigrade.

In (2), the freezing of the water is a proposition about the physical behaviour of water in general, not an event indexed to a particular place and time. Expressions of 'covering laws' of this sort should be contrasted with narratives such as (3), which tells about a particular fluctuation in the temperature and the consequences thereof.

(3) The temperature dropped to 0 last week and the pond behind my house froze.

Events, conceived as time- and place-specific transitions from some source state S (pond unfrozen) to a target state S' (pond frozen), are thus a prerequisite for narrative.

As Prince (1973) noted, however, events are a necessary but not a sufficient condition for stories. What distinguishes (4) from (5) – what makes (5) a narrative instead of a mere agglomeration of unrelated elements, as in (4) – is the structure into which states and events are slotted in the second case but not the first.

(4) The pond was frozen. The pond was unfrozen. The temperature dropped.

(5) The pond was unfrozen. Then the temperature dropped. In consequence, the pond was frozen.

In (4) two states and an event are presented additively, but in (5) the target state is an inversion of the source state, and moreover the inversion in question is caused by the event that intervenes between the source and target states (*see* CAUSALITY). Todorov (1968) imposed an even more restrictive condition on how states and events have to be distributed for narrative to obtain. For Todorov, narratives prototypically follow a trajectory leading from an initial state of equilibrium, through a phase of disequilibrium, to an endpoint at which equilibrium is restored (on a different footing) because of intermediary events – though not every narrative traces the entirety of this path (cf. Bremond 1973; Kafalenos 1995).

Omitted thus far is any account of the difference between events such as the temperature's dropping and, say, my going ice skating on the frozen pond. This is the sort of difference that the concept of event-types seeks to capture. Ryan (1991), for example, reanalyses events by drawing a threefold distinction between *happenings*, *actions*, and *moves*, with moves being a specific type of action. Whereas actions are deliberately targeted toward a goal and have a voluntary human or human-like agent, happenings occur accidentally, having a patient but not an animated agent. Moves, meanwhile, are conflict-solving actions designed to accomplish high-priority goals and marked by a high risk of failure. In Ryan's scheme, moves bear the focus of narrative interest and should be distinguished from incidental or habitual doings. Hence, in Kafka's *The Metamorphosis*, Gregor Samsa's insectoid transformation is coded as a happening. An example of an action would be Gregor's using his mouth to open the bedroom door, and Gregor's (failed) attempt to communicate with the Office Manager constitutes a move.

Parallel research in linguistic semantics also reveals the importance of event-types in narrative. Depending on the semantic model adopted, states linked by types of events can be analysed into permanent and temporary conditions, and events themselves can be subdivided into causes, motions, and actions that may in turn be temporally bounded or unbounded. However, information about the relative boundedness of events is contained in the aspect of the verbs denoting those events; hence, whereas event-types pertain to the realm of story, the coding of happenings and actions as completed or ongoing pertains to narrative discourse (*see* STORY-DISCOURSE DISTINCTION). (6) and (7), for example, code the same basic action as unbounded and bounded, respectively.

(6) Smith was working to pay off his debts.
(7) Smith had worked to pay off his debts.

There are also, in addition to material events, mental events of the kind reported in (8), which actually embeds a material event within a mental one:

(8) Jones believed that Smith had worked to pay off his debts.

The point to emphasise is that none of these event-types or coding strategies is alien to narrative, given its flexibility as framework for thinking and communicating.

Arguably, though, different *genres of narrative display preferences for different distributions and combinations of event-types. Bounded actions regularly occur in *epics; the imperative to celebrate and memorialise *acts* of heroism results in a dispreference for unbounded events. The *psychological novel, by contrast, displays a distinct preference for combining unbounded actions with both permanent and temporary states, particularly states of mind and processes of reflection. For example, Henry James' characters are constantly negotiating and mulling over the complexity of human affairs. Study of event-types might thus afford the basis for a typology of narrative genres.

SEE ALSO: historiography; narrative; narrative semantics; narrative units; plot; story grammars

References and further reading

Bremond, Claude (1973) *Logique du récit*, Paris: Seuil.
Frawley, William (1992) *Linguistic Semantics*, Hillsdale, NJ: Lawrence Erlbaum.
Herman, David (2002) *Story Logic: Problems and Possibilities of Narrative*, Lincoln: University of Nebraska Press.
Kafalenos, Emma (1995) 'Lingering along the Narrative Path: Extended Functions in Kafka and Henry James', *Narrative*, 3, 117–38.
Prince, Gerald (1973) *A Grammar of Stories*, The Hague: Mouton.
Ryan, Marie-Laure (1991) *Possible Worlds, Artificial Intelligence, and Narrative Theory*, Bloomington: Indiana University Press.
Todorov, Tzvetan (1968) 'La Grammaire du récit', *Langages*, 12, 94–102.

DAVID HERMAN

EVOLUTION OF NARRATIVE FORMS

A widespread conception of the origin of narrative locates its earliest manifestations in oral language, arguably the first communicative medium developed by humans (*see* CONVERSATIONAL STORY-TELLING; NATURAL NARRATOLOGY). *Media have indeed had a decisive impact on the evolution of narrative forms, as this entry will show. We may however speculate that the media forms are elaborations of mental mechanisms that precede the development of media. The basic mental task for living beings consists of controlling motion through *space in accordance with those preferences that survival and fitness dictate. The nervous system is constructed to provide a flow of information leading from perception to *emotion and cognition, and from these to motor action. The competence for story-making and story-comprehension (as well as for basic metaphoric thinking) has evolved as a tool for the superior control of this flow and thus for the control of action (see METAPHOR; NARRATIVE COMPREHENSION). What is more, neurologists have located those brain structures that centrally support story-construction (Young and Saver 2001).

The basic mental narrative mechanisms involve the following operations: (1) constructing a space, a 'scene', out of the incoming sensory data from different sense modalities (see SUMMARY AND SCENE); (2) representing the story-experiencing being's location and interests/emotions within that space (see EXPERIENTIALITY); and (3) working toward the fulfilment of these interests by building and executing plans, an activity that requires the ability to imagine alternative future scenarios. This entry calls 'story' the product of these operations, whether it is textualised or remains a purely mental construct. Canonical stories are driven either by external causes or by inner goals. In a story driven by an external cause, certain types of perceptions lead to emotions (such as feelings of danger or loss), which trigger in turn an action sequence, such as escaping from or fighting a lion. In a story driven by an inner goal, action sequences are triggered by intents, such as wanting to get food or a mate. The inner story will keep track of the past (lion is close), of the emotional evaluation, and of the future goal (shoot). Due to the survival value of reasoning about *causality, story-producing mental structures have a strong bias for establishing causal links.

The mental capabilities required to experience stories existed long before language was invented (maybe only 50,000 years ago), and they exist in different degrees of sophistication in higher animals. According to the neurologist Damasio, our basic consciousness consists of an ongoing wordless filmlike narrative that creates order out of the incoming sensory data and internal emotions, cognitions, and goals. When remembering stories, the different perceptual, cognitive, emotional, and

pre-motor brain functions are activated 'offline' – that is, without being in actual perceptual contact with the exterior world. Life for humanoids became increasingly social, and the social environment became very prominent. Via so-called mirror-neurons (in the pre-motor and the somatosensory cortex), humans (and monkeys) would simulate ('mirror') the experiences of other humans and eventually have empathic emotions. This would allow them to experience stories that they had only seen performed by other people. To experience stories is thus prior to the telling of stories, and the archetypal stories are therefore first-person online experiences and *memories thereof. The invention of media, from language onwards, has allowed representations of different aspects of the mental story, according to the different capabilities of different media, but external media have also enhanced our ability to construct complex stories.

Spoken language is the first story medium, except for proto-theatrical forms based on non-verbal language and acting (see DRAMA AND NARRATIVE). Language stabilises experiences and makes them intersubjective and easier to recall, order, and manipulate, but its abstractions lack the rich resolution of perceptions. Since language activates only the pre-motor planning centres, heard stories lack the full motor dimension of basic story experience. Language also has the capacity to refocus the story experience from a first-person to a third-person *perspective (see NARRATION; PERSON). It enhances that perspective, and might thereby facilitate third-person empathic emotions. The development of the faculty of imagination is linked to those survival-enhancing mechanisms that make it possible to imagine different possible future actions. Language removed all constraints on the veracity of stories by making it possible to suspend the online indexicality of direct perceptual experiences (see DEIXIS). Stories about religious and supernatural phenomena therefore probably came into existence at the same time as language in the big cultural explosion around 50,000 years ago.

Even higher animals perform rudimentary non-verbal acting, but the cultural explosion may have also boosted proto-theatrical performances. The dramatic form of stories possesses online perceptual qualities and a third-person perspective, the distanced spectator position. Physical constraints on dramatic performances make some stories more suitable to the stage than other stories. Verbal narratives have no difficulty representing movement through vast spaces, chronicling complicated actions, or creating a quick temporal progression. Drama is much more spatially constrained, and limited to representations of a few contiguous temporal scenes. But it is well-suited to representing personal interaction based on strongly emotion-evoking events, from courting to tragic death. Theatre has prompted a series of ancillary techniques, from the art of making sets to the art of structuring *events and *characters.

The invention of written stories surpassed the memory constraints of oral stories, and thus supports complex narratives, including chronological rearrangements (*see* TEMPORAL ORDERING). Writing and printing made it possible to store, retrieve, and communicate narrative experiences and skills.

In some respects, the invention of *film returned viewers to pre-linguistic narrative experiences by directly simulating them by audiovisual means, thereby giving an intersubjective dimension to these experiences. Although narrative films are partly based on theatrical techniques, films are able to simulate a first-person perceptual experience and attention in a here-and-now form and can, as in literary narrative, move freely through *time and space. The 'pre-linguistic' massive display of 'raw' perceptual information provides it with emotional impact, but it also makes communication of highly abstract messages difficult.

The latest narrative medium is video games and similar interactive media (*see* COMPUTER GAMES AND NARRATIVE; INTERACTIVE FICTION). The 'motor dimension' is finally integrated with that of perception so that visual and acoustic information affords motor actions that in turn create new perceptions. Even more than film, video-game stories are close to pre-linguistic experience, especially those that simulate motion, (man)hunting, or gathering as in first-person shooter games. Through this ability to simulate perception and motor action, and also to create a world that can be inhabited by players (*see* STORYWORLD), computer games open up the possibility of quite new narrative forms and narrative experiences.

SEE ALSO: biological foundations of narrative; narrative as cognitive instrument; simulation and narrative

References and further reading

Damasio, Antonio R. (1999) *The Feeling of What Happens. Body and Emotion in the Making of Consciousness*, New York: Harcourt Brace.

Fauconnier, Gilles and Mark Turner (2002) *The Way We Think. Conceptual Blending and the Mind*, New York: Basic Books.

Grodal, Torben (1997) *Moving Pictures. A New Theory of Film Genre, Feelings, and Cognition*, Oxford: Clarendon/Oxford University Press.

—— (2003) 'Stories for Eyes, Ears, and Muscles. Video Games, Media, and Embodied Experiences', in Mark J. P. Wolf and Bernard Perron (eds) *Video Game Theory Reader*, London: Routledge.

Young, Kay, and Jeffrey L. Saver (2001) 'The Neurology of Narrative', *SubStance*, 30.1/2, 72–84.

TORBEN GRODAL

EXISTENT

Chatman (1978) defines *existents* as 'the objects contained in story-space [as opposed to discourse-space] . . . namely character and setting' (107) (*see* STORY-DISCOURSE DISTINCTION). Prince (1987) follows Chatman in making existents and *events the two fundamental constituents of story.

Herman (2002: 115–69) works toward a more granular account, drawing on work in linguistic semantics and functional grammar to subdivide existents into *storyworld participants and non-participants. The model, which rescales sentence-level semantic or 'thematic' roles to accommodate discourse-level phenomena such as *character and setting, identifies a range of participant and non-participant roles – e.g., agents, patients, experiencers, instruments, and locations. In this scheme, the terms *participants* and *non-participants* refer to two general categories of thematic roles (cf. Frawley 1992: 201–28). Participants encompass roles played by entities or individuals that are projected as being centrally or obligatorily involved in *events in the storyworld; non-participants encompass roles played by entities or individuals that are projected as being only peripherally and optionally involved.

SEE ALSO: actant; narrative semantics

References and further reading

Chatman, Seymour (1978) *Story and Discourse: Narrative Structure in Fiction and Film*, Ithaca: Cornell University Press.

Frawley, William (1992) *Linguistic Semantics*, Hillsdale, NJ: Lawrence Erlbaum.

Herman, David (2002) *Story Logic: Problems and Possibilities of Narrative*, Lincoln: University of Nebraska Press.

Prince, Gerald (1987) *A Dictionary of Narratology*, Lincoln: University of Nebraska Press.

DAVID HERMAN

EXPERIENCING-I

The first-person reference character in a first-person narrative; specifically, in retrospective first-person narration, the earlier self who underwent the experiences recounted by the older 'narrating-I'. *See* NARRATIVE SITUATIONS.

EXPERIENTIALITY

In Fludernik (1996) the term 'experientiality' is defined as the 'quasi-mimetic evocation of "real-life" experience' which invokes actantial frames, correlates with the evocation of consciousness or of a speaker role, and relies on the cognitive schema of human embodiedness' (12–13; *see* ACTANT). Embodiment correlates with the specificity of the protagonists' spatial and temporal location. In *conversational storytelling, experientiality emerges from the dialectics of *tellability and point (Labov 1972; Fludernik 1991, 1996: 28–30). Stories convey, for instance, the excitement, anguish, or surprise of the narrated experience and at the same time retrospectively evaluate it and endow it with significance.

The introduction of the concept of experientiality serves the purpose of displacing *plot as the defining element of *narrativity; plot is treated as one major but not the only manifestation of experientiality. This allows Fludernik to integrate interior monologue *novels and many *postmodern texts with the narrative *genre – a move that in standard plot-oriented definitions of narrativity was problematic.

SEE ALSO: cognitive narratology; natural narratology; scripts and schemata; stream of consciousness and interior monologue; thought and consciousness representation (literature)

References and further reading

Fludernik, Monika (1991) 'The Historical Present Tense Yet Again', *Text*, 11.3, 365–98.

—— (1996) *Towards a 'Natural' Narratology*, London: Routledge.

Labov, William (1972) *Language in the Inner City: Studies in the Black English Vernacular*, Philadelphia: University of Pennsylvania Press.

MONIKA FLUDERNIK

EXPOSITION

The term 'exposition' refers to the scene-setting presentation of circumstances preceding the primary narrative action. For the ancients, *expositio* (Latin 'setting forth') was the third part of the seven-part classical oration, its task being to define terms and state the issues to be proved. It was thus also known as *explicatio*, and it was in this sense that the term also came to denote material, frequently preliminary, 'explaining' the contexts of the dramatic action to be presented on stage (*see* DRAMA AND NARRATIVE).

In Gustav Freytag's well-known pyramid diagram illustrating the structure of a tragedy (*see* FREYTAG'S TRIANGLE), *exposition* is the first of five phases: *exposition, complication, climax, reversal*, and *catastrophe* (1908 [1863]: 114–15). In the most authoritative contemporary model, to some extent developing observations by Tomashevskii, Meir Sternberg classifies narrative expositions, in descriptive and functional terms, according to three interactive presentational criteria (1993 [1978]: 236). Expositions may be preliminary or delayed; they may be concentrated or distributed; and they may appear in narratives that present their story either *ab ovo* or with an initial plunge *in medias res. An exposition may thus be preliminary and concentrated (as in Balzac's *Père Goriot*, where some thirty pages of scene-setting information precede the beginning of the story proper); or it may be delayed and concentrated (as in Faulkner's *Light in August*, where the opening chapters present the protagonist in a highly negative light and several subsequent expository chapters provide a very different view of his actions and motives). Alternatively, an exposition may be delayed and distributed (as in many *detective fictions, where expository information is typically released piecemeal throughout the narrative, frequently as late as its concluding scenes); or it may be preliminary and distributed (as in Ford's *The Good Soldier*, whose opening pages contain references to both subsequent and antecedent events). Any one of these four possibilities, furthermore, may occur in a narrative where the order of story-events and their discursive presentation is the same (narration *ab ovo*); or it may occur in the more complex context of a narrative beginning in medias res (such as *The Odyssey* or *The Aeneid*) (*see* TEMPORAL ORDERING).

The common aim of all expositional strategies is to arouse and/or maintain readers' interest in the action presented by creating anticipation of future events while satisfying curiosity about the past circumstances leading to the story told. The most straightforward form of exposition – extensively used by nineteenth-century writers, notably including Scott, Balzac, and Trollope – is preliminary and concentrated. Its major advantage, when used successfully, is its comfortably expansive character, only gradually arousing the reader's interest in the anticipated action in the course of providing an explanatory context for it; its major disadvantage, when used less successfully, is the risk it runs of losing the reader's interest before that action has even begun. The other, less straightforward expositional forms constitute different strategies for balancing those potential gains and risks, frequently involving the use of 'expositional gaps' (Sternberg 1993 [1978]: 52) resulting from the delayed release of information.

SEE ALSO: description; gapping; narration; narrative techniques; narrative units

References and further reading

Freytag, Gustav (1908 [1863]) *Technique of the Drama*, trans. Elias J. McEwan, Chicago: Scott.
Sternberg, Meir (1993 [1978]) *Expositional Modes and Temporal Ordering in Fiction*, Bloomington: Indiana University Press.
Tomashevskii, Boris (1965) 'Thematics', *Russian Formalist Criticism: Four Essays*, trans. Lee T. Lemon and Marion J. Reis, Lincoln: University of Nebraska Press.

PATRICK O'NEILL

EXTRADIEGETIC NARRATOR

A *narrator who is not part of any surrounding diegetic frame. Extradiegetic narrators are to be distinguished from intradiegetic narrators (i.e., character-narrators) who occupy a place in a *storyworld and tell narratives evoking another, embedded storyworld. Thus, in a text like Conrad's *Heart of Darkness*, the extradiegetic narrator produces the framing narrative about Marlow's storytelling acts in the narrative 'now', whereas Marlow himself functions as an intradiegetic narrator, producing a *framed tale about Kurtz that transports his *narratees back to an earlier time-frame. *See* DIEGESIS; VOICE (also: EMBEDDING).

F

FABLE

A fable is a brief narrative told in order to provide moral instruction or to transmit an *ethical point of view. Often the fable is an animal tale in which protagonists behave as humans and represent stock traits, faults, or tendencies in human behaviour. At the same time the fable's protagonists also frequently maintain certain animal characteristics, which function as associative links between the human and animal spheres. Gods, humans, and inanimate objects also appear as active agents. Some scholars believe that the fable developed directly from the animal tale, which is itself considered a sub-type of the *folktale. Formally speaking, the fable's narrative typically presents the moral crux of the story, while a pithy or proverbial statement of the didactic point is (frequently, but not always) added at the end.

Tradition assigns the earliest Greek form of the fable to Aesop (6th BCE), while the Jatakas, or lives of the Buddha, are an equally important source, as is the Sanskrit story collection, the Panchtantra (300–500 CE), which spread widely and influenced Persian, Arabic, and European collections through oral and written transmission.

SEE ALSO: didactic narrative; Sanskrit narrative

References and further reading

Edgerton, Franklin (1924) *The Panchatantra Reconstructed*, New Haven: American Oriental Society.
Hertel, Johannes (1914) *Das Pancatantra, seine Geschichte und seine Verbreitung*, Leipzig and Berlin: Teubner.
Perry, B.E. (1959) 'Fable', *Studium Generale*, XII (1), 17–37.

AARON TATE

FABULA

A term used by *Russian Formalists to denote the chronological sequence of situations and *events that can be reconstructed on the basis of cues provided in a narrative text. In the account developed in Seymour Chatman's influential book *Story and Discourse* (1978), the fabula is the 'story' level of narrative, i.e., the 'what'. Such narrative content can be presented in a variety of ways at the 'discourse' level of narrative, i.e., the 'how' that *formalist terminology called the *sjuzhet. *See* STORY-DISCOURSE DISTINCTION (also: STRUCTURALIST NARRATOLOGY; TEMPORAL ORDERING).

FAIRY TALE

The fairy tale is a hybrid narrative *genre consisting of folkloric and literary elements, characterised by the effect the marvellous has on its structure (*see* FOLKLORE; HYBRID GENRES). A fairy tale typically combines the following three features: (1) a correction of a misdeed or lack (*see* FUNCTION (PROPP)); (2) a demonstration of the characters' exemplary destiny according to a moral system clearly divided into good and evil; and (3) a fairy tale microcosm serving as a self-sufficient system of *reference. Comprising a structure that is both permanent and flexible, fairy tales allow for different adaptations while remaining recognisably self-identical. Capable of transforming themselves by incorporating historically changing cultural themes, they have conserved the freedom of oral narrative with its accommodating structure (*see* CONVERSATIONAL STORYTELLING). Open in their determinations and dimensions, fairy tales exploit the supernatural as a decisive force at play in resolving the protagonists' fate.

Fairy tales present themselves from the outset as fictional narratives (see FICTION, THEORIES OF). While endowed with ordinary human qualities, fairy tale protagonists generally lack any psychological depth. They define themselves by means of their actions instead of their psychology. The perception of humans conveyed in fairy tales is timeless in that their *characters represent types rather than individuals. The fairy tale universe does not necessarily exclude the real-world. The imaginary simply takes hold of everyday reality. Since the principle of contradiction seems to be cancelled out, everything becomes possible as if by magic. The marvellous becomes commonplace; supernatural operations occur without any explanation at all.

Fairy tales derive much of their meaning from their psychological context, i.e., the patterns organising the symbols and the forces underlying their creation. The narratives often deal with psychosexual themes based on the ego-syntonic quality of libidinal aspirations, i.e., the quality that makes such aspirations compatible with an individual's total personality (see DESIRE). The wishful nature of fairy tales informs the predominantly sexual symbolism, which Freudian scholars analyse as identical to *dreams (see PSYCHOANALYSIS AND NARRATIVE). Governed by dynamics similar to the ways in which the dreamwork operates a transition between latent and manifest contents, a fairy tale transforms a limited number of fantasies into a narrative. These transformational processes include dramatisation, displacement, condensation or dissociation, and symbolisation.

According to Bettelheim, fairy tales simultaneously appeal to the conscious, preconscious, and unconscious levels of human personality. A fairy tale allows for fitting unconscious content into conscious fantasies, thus giving a coherent shape and presence to the tensions of the Id while suggesting solutions that are in harmony with the demands of the ego and superego. For Jungians, on the other hand, the characters and *events portrayed in fairy tales represent *archetypal phenomena. All fairy tales describe one and the same psychological process defined as individuation, or process of differentiation, structured by the collective unconscious. Each fairy tale emphasises a particular aspect of the self, i.e., the model ego complex resulting from a psychological balance acquired through integrating unconscious archetypes. Hence, all fairy tales tell the story of acquiring a self.

SEE ALSO: fable; simple forms

References and further reading

Bettelheim, Bruno (1977) *The Uses of Enchantment*, New York: Random House.

Holbek, Bengt (1987) *Interpretation of Fairy Tales*, Helsinki: Academia Scientarium Fennica.

Flahaut, François (1988) *L'Interprétation des contes*, Paris: Denoël.

von Franz, Marie-Louise (1970) *An Introduction to the Interpretation of Fairy Tales*, New York: Spring Publications.

——(1977) *Individuation in Fairy Tales*, New York: Spring Publications.

Propp, Vladimir (1968 [1928]) *Morphology of the Folktale*, trans. Laurence Scott, revised by Louis A. Wagner, Austin: University of Texas Press.

Robert, Raymonde (1982) *Le Conte de fées littéraire en France de la fin du XVIIe à la fin du XVIIIe siècle*, Nancy: Presses Universitaires de Nancy.

HAROLD NEEMANN

FAMILY CHRONICLE

The family *chronicle, family saga, or generational *novel, which emerges in early *realism with Edgeworth's *Castle Rackrent* (1800) and Galt's *The Entail* (1822) and has since *modernism been a much-practised *genre on both high and popular planes, is marked by a time-frame spanning usually three or four generations, and a cast drawn primarily, if not exclusively, from one family or house. Its dual thematic focus is the dissection of the family as institution, as in Saltykov's *The Golovlevs* (1880), Butler's *The Way of All Flesh* (1902), or Ba Jin's *The Family* (1937), and the travails of a family as a synecdoche for the development of a class or nation, as in Martin du Gard's *Les Thibault* (1922–1940), Joseph Roth's *Radetzkymarsch* (1932), or Updike's *In the Beauty of the Lilies* (1996).

Other generic features are the largely housebound setting; a structure of temporal islands centring on the foci of family *time – births, christenings, meal-times, festivities, gatherings, burials, testaments; family cults of *memory, from portrait to heirloom; the chronicle within the chronicle; the incursion into the family of the 'other' – often art or beauty; the decline, sale, or literal destruction of the house; the revelatory family law-suit; a contrasting family as foil to the protagonists; marked *intertextuality, notably in references to the Pentateuch; and a vested interest in long durations and their endowment with pattern. The genre is thus to be distinguished from day-by-day accounts of family life as practised by Yonge in *The Daisy Chain* (1857), and also from the sub-genre called the 'aga-saga', named after a brand of cooker commonly owned by British families of a particular class and type.

The family chronicle is the form often taken by the on-running, consecutive *roman-fleuve* but is narratologically more varied. *Castle Rackrent* is an early example of unreliable narration (*see* RELIABILITY), Aksakov's *Family Chronicle* (1856) of pre-reminiscence. Although from Zola to Lawrence the genre is largely authorial in stance (*see* NARRATIVE SITUATIONS), it burgeons in modernism into the impressionism of G.B. Stern, the post-impressionism of Woolf, the intricate 'unamaze' of Faulkner, and the cubism of Stein (*see* MODERNIST NARRATIVE). Postmodernism brings the spoofs and romps of Nabokov's *Ada or Ardour* (1969) and Rushdie's *The Moor's Last Sigh* (1995) (*see* POSTMODERNIST NARRATIVE), *magical realism the allusive flights of Marquez and Allende.

Ideologically, the genre anticipates and reflects the emergence, crisis, and transformations of the modern family (*see* IDEOLOGY AND NARRATIVE). Naturalism, with its emphasis on heredity and social Darwinism, informs the Goncourts, Verga, and especially Zola's *Rougon-Macquart* (1871–1893) and Mann's *Buddenbrooks* (1901). Nationalism (Freytag, Walpole) and fascism (Ponten, Stehr) leave their stamp as well. In modernism, with its anti-Victorian stance, Galsworthy's *Forsyte Saga* (1907–1953), hinging on marital rape, is the inspiration. Fairbairns' feminist *Stand We at Last* (1983) is the first saga to end in a commune.

The family chronicle, a site of memory concerned with one of the central institutions of memory itself, has the longest time-span of any modern genre and increasingly highlights memory's uses and forms. As such it is the apt annalist and accountant of discontinuity and disruption, prominent in *post-colonial, Shoa, and American-Jewish literatures (*see* ANNALS; HOLOCAUST NARRATIVE).

References and further reading

Humphrey, Richard (forthcoming) *The Caravan in the Desert: The Family Chrincle as Genre from Edgeworth to Foer.*

Ru, Yi-Ling (1992) *The Family Novel: Toward a Generic Definition*, New York: Peter Lang.

Tobin, Patricia (1978) *Time and the Novel: The Genealogical Imperative*, Princeton: Princeton University Press.

RICHARD HUMPHREY

FANTASTIC, THE

The fantastic emerges from the twilight areas of Christianity: the mystery of death and the afterlife, the ambiguity between good and evil. It is associated with the dark figures of the Devil and his creatures: witches, vampires, ghosts, the living dead. It arose with the Inquisition in the fifteenth century, but came into its own as a literary *genre toward the end of the eighteenth-century. As Todorov points out, the distinctive feature of the fantastic as genre is uncertainty about the presence of supernatural events. This features distinguishes the fantastic from 'the marvellous', where the existence of the supernatural (connected to the magic and pagan world) is regarded as an established fact.

The more characteristic manifestations of the fantastic belong to late eighteenth- and nineteenth-centuries. The Gothic period began in 1765 with *The Castle of Otranto* by Walpole, followed by the novels of Radcliffe (*The Mysteries of Udolpho*, 1794), Lewis (*The Monk*, 1796), Maturin (*Melmoth the Wanderer*, 1826) and much later Stoker (*Dracula*, 1897) (*see* GOTHIC NOVEL). During the nineteenth-century, the fantastic developed along two lines: the properly fantastic, linked to religious and metaphysical questions; and the *science fiction branch, inspired by technological progress. Two novels were prominent in this evolution: *Frankenstein* (1818), by Shelley, and *Dr. Jekyll and Mr. Hyde* (1886), by Stevenson, where the theme of the double is connected to scientific research.

The nineteenth-century remains the high point of the fantastic. This period includes authors as varied as Hoffmann (*Nachtstücke*, 1817), who introduced extraordinary elements into daily life; Poe (*Tales of the Grotesque and Arabesque*, 1817), whose fictional worlds combine sarcasm and a deep sense of anxiety in the face of death; Maupassant (*Le Horla*, 1887), who explored the supernatural as a symptom of mental disease; and James (*The Turn of the Screw*, 1898), who develops aspects of the genre that are fit for psychoanalytic investigation (*see* PSYCHOANALYSIS AND NARRATIVE).

During the twentieth century, the fantastic developed a variety of cultural dimensions. The Anglo-Saxon school includes such authors as Lovecraft (*The Charles Dexter Ward Case*, 1927), Rice (*Interview with the Vampire*, 1976) and King (*The Shining*, 1977), who continue in the tradition of terror and *suspense. German-speaking authors, such as Kafka (*Die Verwandlung*, 1916), emphasise the social aspects of the fantastic introduced by Hoffmann. The French fantastic is influenced by surrealism (*see* SURREALIST NARRATIVE), for instance in Vian's *L'Ecume des jours* (1976). And finally, Latin-American authors such as Borges (*Ficciones*, 1956) develop a type of fantastic based on paradoxes and narrative distortions. But these non-Anglo-Saxon varieties of the fantastic may better be described as examples of *magic realism or *transgressive fictions.

SEE ALSO: fantasy

References and further reading

Goimard, Jacques (2003) *Critique du fantastique et de l'insolite*, Paris: Pocket.
King, Stephen (1981) *Stephen King's Danse Macabre*, New York: Everest House.
—— (2000) *On Writing*, New York: Scribner.
Marcel, Patrick (2002) *Atlas des brumes et des ombres*, Paris: Gallimard.
Todorov, Tzvetan (1975 [1970] *The Fantastic: A Structural Approach to a Literary Genre*, Trans. Richard Howard, Ithaca and New York: Cornell University Press.

FRANCIS BERTHELOT

FANTASY

The terms *fantasy* and *the *fantastic* are often used interchangeably to describe a metagenre of disparate works characterised by a degree of explicit anti-realism and embracing *horror, high fantasy, dark fantasy, *science fiction, *cyberpunk, futurism, *Gothic fiction, ghost stories, *magical realism, *counterfactual histories, *myths, *folklore and *fairy tales (*see* REALISM, THEORIES OF). The origins of modern fantasy lie in eighteenth-century Romanticism and its fascination with nature and pastoral fantasy, the heroic, the mythic, and the exotic (*see* HERO). During the nineteenth-century it became a force in British literature with the publication of *novels such as Mary Shelley's *Frankenstein*, Lewis Carroll's *Alice in Wonderland*, and Bram Stoker's *Dracula*, written within the context of growing public interest in supernatural phenomena, esotericism, *dreams, and madness. By the early twentieth century, the fantastic was firmly established as a literary *genre and was spreading into the new medium of cinema in *films such as *The Cabinet of Dr. Caligari* and *Metropolis*. Its characteristic diversity is evident in the variety of works that fall within its compass, including H.P. Lovecraft's bizarre *Cthulhu* novels, Mervyn Peake's Gothic *Gormenghast* trilogy, J.R.R. Tolkien's mythic *The Lord of the Rings*, and, more recently, Phillip Pullman's multidimensional *His Dark Materials* trilogy.

This diversity makes fantasy an unusually difficult genre to define. It has no set conventions apart from anti-realism and its subject matter may be wizardry, or a fictional application of quantum theory, or the Celtic twilight, or a Californian town besieged by vampires. Roger Caillois defined the fantastic simply as 'the impression of irreducible strangeness', a description considered by the *structuralist Todorov to be too woolly and subjective. Todorov distinguishes the fantastic from the uncanny and the marvellous, arguing that it exists only in a poised indecision between the natural and the supernatural. His narrow and precise definition of the fantastic sees it as the product of the hesitation of an individual confronted by a phenomenon that disobeys the natural laws of actuality. However, the narrowness of Todorov's definition gives it only limited usefulness. It excludes, for example, works which construct worlds in which the fantastic itself is constituted as the natural law rather than as a disruption of it. Subsequent theorists, such as Rosemary Jackson and James Donald, develop broader interpretations of fantasy and the fantastic than does Todorov. Drawing upon psychoanalytical theory (*see* PSYCHOANALYSIS AND NARRATIVE), Jackson considers fantasy as primarily an imaginative genre of *desire and rebellion, through which the forbidden and the repressed are expressed, boundaries are transgressed and 'subversive' ideas explored through *metaphors of monsters, magic, aliens, and other fantastical elements.

Scholars and aficionados frequently stress a distinction between fantasy and science fiction, arguing that science fiction is predicated upon scientific possibilities while fantasy is predicated upon scientific impossibilities (most notably, magic and the supernatural). Here, as elsewhere, fantasy is identified in terms of its disregard for the natural laws of material reality, but this is not to say that it has no realist elements (*see* REALIST NOVEL). Characters' motivations, actions, and reactions are generally realist, even if the situations they exist in and confront are not. Societies have order, economies, politics, values, even though their citizens may have magical powers and share their world with fantastical creatures. Stories often focus on heroic struggles between the forces of good and evil, played out among exotic cultures in worlds or universes controlled by logics different than those of our world.

Construction of a detailed fictional world is a key feature of most fantasy fiction (*see* STORY-WORLD). Often, quests or other journeys function to structure the narrative as a series of encounters and *conflicts that allow exploration of the fictional world as well as advancing the *plot. The world in a work of fantasy may be our own world, rendered strange by the presence of certain fantastical phenomena; or it may be a wholly separate world; or it may involve movements between, or the perception of, different realities existing simultaneously (*see* POSSIBLE-WORLDS THEORY). Tolkien's *The Lord of the Rings* – arguably the most influential and most imitated work of literary fantasy – devotes hundreds of pages to fleshing out the world of Middle Earth, with detailed descriptions of its landscapes, cultures, histories, and mythologies, and two fully developed elvish languages. J. K. Rowling's *Harry Potter* books centre upon the enclosed setting of Hogwarts School for Witchcraft and Wizardry, a realm filled with eccentric characters whose motivations and actions span the moral spectrum and where dramas of cosmic consequence unfold. Whether they are vast or localised, the worlds of fantasy works are always richly constructed in ways that continually extend their novelty.

The combination of novelty, semantic density, and freedom from many of the restraints of realism that characterises fantasy fictional worlds also furnishes them with unlimited storytelling possibilities. This, in turn, makes fantasy particularly suited to the processes of *remediation and extension that have increasingly dominated commercial culture since the 1960s. A popular work of fantasy may originate in one medium and then be remediated in several others. *The Lord of the Rings* and *Harry Potter* began as novels but have become multimedia cultural phenomena that also include *films, *computer games, guidebooks and analyses, maps, toys, and a range of other merchandise. The same process has occurred around fantastic genre *television series such as *Star Trek*, *Xena: Warrior Princess*, and *Buffy the Vampire Slayer*; films such as *Star Wars*; comic books such as *Batman* and *The X-Men* (*see* COMICS AND GRAPHIC NOVEL); and computer games such as *Mortal Kombat* and *Tomb Raider*. Their brandnamed fictional worlds function as almost inexhaustible storytelling resources in an industry that is today worth billions.

SEE ALSO: media and narrative

References and further reading

Caillois, Roger (1966) *Images, images . . . : Essais sur le role et les pouvoirs de l'imagination*, Paris: José Corti.
Donald, James (ed.) (1989) *Fantasy and the Cinema*, London: British Film Institute.
Jackson, Rosemary (1981) *Fantasy: the Literature of Subversion*, London: Routledge.
Jones, Sara Gwenllian, and Roberta E. Pearson (eds) (2004) *Cult Television*, Minneapolis: University of Minnesota Press.
Tzvetan Todorov (1975) [1970] *The Fantastic: A Structural Approach to a Literary Genre*, trans. Richard Howard, Ithaca, NY: Cornell University Press.

SARA GWENLLIAN JONES

FEMINIST NARRATOLOGY

Feminist narratology systematically studies story and discourse with an eye to differences of gender (*see* GENDER STUDIES; STORY-DISCOURSE DISTINCTION). Depending on the approach, the feminist narratologist may focus on the gender of *authors, authorial (intended) *audiences, actual readers, *characters, *narrators, and/or *narratees (*see* READER CONSTRUCTS; READER-RESPONSE THEORY). Feminist narratology comprises theory and practice, intervening in gender-neutral models of narrative as well as producing gender-conscious readings of individual narrative texts.

Poststructuralist feminism raised challenges to classical narratology in the 1980s, arguing that the categorical binarism of structuralist models formed an inadequate framework for thinking through differences of race, class, gender, nationality, and sexuality (*see* POSTSTRUCTURALIST APPROACHES TO

NARRATIVE; STRUCTURALIST NARRATOLOGY). While many feminist critics avoided narratology in favour of less schematic approaches, others argued that narratology's clarity and specificity could provide a vocabulary for identifying marks of gender in narrative. Feminist narratology made an important departure from one of structuralism's fundamental tenets, however. Whereas classical narratology made universalising claims for describing all narratives produced in any culture, feminist narratology insisted on placing narratives in their historical and cultural contexts. Having taken that step, feminist narratologists soon pointed out that structuralist narratologists almost always based their taxonomies on examples taken from male-authored texts.

Feminist narratologists have not proposed comprehensive models of narrative that would contradict or supplant those which have developed in the larger field of narratology. Instead, they have noted exceptions to general tenets as well as putting forward new categories – or new understandings of already established categories. Given their emphasis on culture and history, feminist narratologists tend most often to combine the insights of feminism and of narratological analysis in developing gender-centred interpretations of individual texts. In this respect, their practice departs from the more generalised poetics of their structuralist predecessors.

Susan Sniader Lanser coined the movement's name in her foundational essay, 'Toward a Feminist Narratology' in 1986, but other feminist critics had been practising the approach since the late 1970s. At first feminist narratology concentrated on the patterns formed by female characters' experiences within narrative *plots. Nancy K. Miller, for instance, argued in *The Heroine's Text* (1980) that eighteenth-century 'feminocentric' French and English *novels offer only two possible fates to the female characters at their centres: they can get married or they can die. Other precursors to feminist narratology focused less on story than on narrative discourse, looking at the effect an author's or narrator's gender might have on how a story gets told. An influential example of this approach is Rachel Blau DuPlessis's *Writing Beyond the Ending* (1985), a study of gendered disruptions of traditional narrative *closure in novels. Essays collected by Elizabeth Abel, Marianne Hirsch, and Elizabeth Langland (1983) drew connections between women writers'

gendered experience and their handling of *narrative structures, as did Molly Hite's 1989 book on narrative forms in contemporary feminist writing.

Lanser's 1986 essay, which grounded her 1992 *Fictions of Authority*, revises the narratological category of *voice to include feminine modes of discourse that had been overlooked in narratology's original formulations. Lanser focused on the 'grammatical gender' of narrators, showing that a female narrator's voice can both subvert and accommodate the authority implicit in *narration. Lanser's most memorable example is an 1832 text purporting to be a letter from a happy bride to her best friend, a text which carries a completely different meaning if the reader skips every other line. The second meaning contradicts the first, as the bride complains bitterly of her fate. Lanser points out that the language of the 'surface text' is traditionally 'feminine', while the style of the 'subtext' is forceful, powerful, and authoritative, i.e., 'masculine'. Her feminist formulation of 'voice' requires an attention to the doubleness inherent in the woman writer's discourse, absent from classical narratology. Lanser's proposal to elevate the gender of the narrator to the same analytic status as the diegetic and *person categories met with strong resistance from narratologist Nilli Diengott, who argued that Lanser's project was too concerned with interpretation to qualify as theoretical poetics, the subject presumed to be proper to narratology. Gerald Prince was among those structuralist narratologists who, in the aftermath of Diengott's attack, defended feminist narratology's efforts to look beyond narrative's general principles and comment on its functioning.

Robyn R. Warhol (1989) builds on Lanser's example, comparing masculine and feminine modes of authorial *address to the narratee in Victorian novels. Whereas Lanser's study focuses exclusively on female authors, Warhol detaches narrators' gender from their authors' sex. Committed to anti-essentialist definitions of gender, both theorists emphasise the culturally constructed status of 'feminine' and 'masculine' narrative discourse. Their example is strongly followed by Sally Robinson in her 1991 study of contemporary women novelists, which treats gender not as a prior category, but as an effect produced within and by narrative.

Though Warhol's later work (2003) carries feminist narratology into the analysis of popular-cultural forms including *film and *television, feminist narratology chiefly concentrates on studies of literary texts written by women. Kathy Mezei's 1996 edited collection gives special emphasis to studies of Jane Austen and Virginia Woolf among other British novelists. Feminist narratology in the past decade has continued to concentrate more on narrative discourse than on story, with insightful studies on closure by Alison Booth (1993), on narration by Alison Case (1999), and on narrative voice by Joan D. Peters (2002).

References and further reading

Abel, Elizabeth, Marianne Hirsch, and Elizabeth Langland (eds) (1983) *The Voyage In: Fictions of Female Development*, Hanover: University Press of New England.

Booth, Alison (1993) *Famous Last Words: Changes in Gender and Narrative Closure*, Charlottesville: University Press of Virginia.

Case, Alison (1999) *Plotting Women: Gender and Narration in the Eighteenth- and Nineteenth-Century British Novel*, Charlottesville: University Press of Virginia.

Diengott, Nilli (1988) 'Narratology and Feminism', *Style*, 22, 42–51.

DuPlessis, Rachel Blau (1985) *Writing Beyond the Ending: Narrative Strategies of 20th-century Women Writers*, Bloomington: Indiana University Press.

Hite, Molly (1989) *The Other Side of the Story: Structures and Strategies of Contemporary Feminist Narrative*, Ithaca: Cornell University Press.

Lanser, Susan S. (1986) 'Toward a Feminist Narratology', *Style*, 20, 341–63.

—— (1992) *Fictions of Authority: Women Writers and Narrative Voice*, Ithaca: Cornell University Press.

Mezei, Kathy (ed.) (1996) *Ambiguous Discourse: Feminist Narratology and British Women Writers*, Chapel Hill: University of North Carolina Press.

Miller, Nancy K. (1980) *The Heroine's Text: Readings in the French and English Novel, 1722–1782*, New York: Columbia University Press.

Peters, Joan D. (2002) *Feminist Metafiction and the Evolution of the British Novel*, Gainesville: University Press of Florida.

Prince, Gerald (1996) 'Narratology, Narratological Criticism, and Gender', in Calin-Andrei Mihailescu and Walid Hamarneh (eds) *Fiction Updated: Theories of Fictionality, Narratology, and Poetics*, Toronto: University of Toronto Press.

Robinson, Sally (1991) *Engendering the Subject: Gender and Self-Representation in Contemporary Women's Fiction*, New York: State University of New York Press.

Warhol, Robyn R. (1989) *Gendered Interventions: Narrative Discourse in the Victorian Novel*, New Brunswick: Rutgers University Press.

—— (2003) *Having a Good Cry: Effeminate Feelings and Narrative Forms*, Columbus: Ohio State University Press.

ROBYN WARHOL

FICTION, THEORIES OF

Throughout the history of literary study, the overwhelming majority of narratives of interest to critics have been fictional; indeed, the terms *fiction* and **narrative* seem often to be used as synonyms. Yet the concept of fiction, when it has been a topic of reflection at all, has remained a puzzle; during the past century, theories differing widely both in details and broad orientation have been proposed to explain it. Moreover, since some narratives are non-fictional, it is clear that the synonymous usage of the terms is loose at best and confused at worst. In any case, a related problem that has recently attracted attention is that of the symptoms or signposts of fictionality.

Theories of what?

It is very easy to recognise fiction, but very hard to explain it. Let us begin halfway between recognition and explanation, with a definition: fiction is one kind of intendedly but non-deceptively untrue discourse (*see* INTENTIONALITY). Each element of this definition could do with some unpacking, and some qualification.

Fiction must consist of 'intendedly untrue' statements because otherwise there would be no way to recognise it, or to distinguish it from factual discourse. (There are theorists who do not accept such a distinction; and, if the **panfictionality* thesis is correct, this entry is superfluous.) Fictional statements need not actually be untrue because it would not make any difference to a work's fictional status whether any of the statements made in it turned out to be true by coincidence – hence the disclaimer familiar to film-goers about the possibility of accidental resemblances between the persons or **events* represented to actual persons or events (*see* ROMAN À CLEF). Likewise factual discourse is intended to be true, although it may not be: mistaken statements are still factual ones.

The falsity of fictional discourse must be 'non-deceptive', if only to distinguish fiction from lying (and again there have been those who would deny the distinction, as far back as Plato). Lying is another type of factual discourse; if the deceptive intention behind a lie were recognised, it would fail. Likewise if someone failed to recognise the non-deceptive intention motivating fictional discourse, then what we might call the fictional transaction would fail. Therein lies the humour in

Don Quixote's reaction to the puppet-show (Part 2, ch. 26), when he storms the stage and beheads puppets that he takes to be villainous Moors.

Finally, fiction is 'one kind' of at least partly untrue discourse produced without intention to deceive because there are other kinds – perhaps the most important being figures of speech such as *metaphor or *irony (New 1999). What distinguishes fiction from tropes in particular is, first, that whereas it is individual sentences that are figurative, fictional discourse must present a *narrative, which typically involves a series of sentences. A deeper distinction may lie, as Aristotle recognised, in the subject-matter of fictional narrative: 'persons engaged in action' (*Poetics* 1448a). On this criterion, even a one-sentence narrative can be differentiated from a sentence that features a trope.

These clarifications leave open a few other frequently asked preliminary questions. Here are three, with brief responses. (1) The definition given is limited to fiction in the linguistic medium: does it make sense to talk about fiction in, e.g., visual media (*see* PICTORIAL NARRATIVITY; VISUAL NARRATIVITY)? Although a number of recent theorists – notably Kendall Walton – have attempted to develop an account of fiction that cuts across *media, the scope of the present discussion will be limited to verbal fictions, and indeed to those that are recounted; even *drama will be left aside. (2) The definition seems to assume an absolute fact/fiction distinction, as if 'factual' were synonymous with 'non-fictional': can there not be borderline or hybrid cases? Although some of the material in the final section of this entry may be pertinent to this question, the rest of it will be limited to clear-cut cases of fiction. This has been the practice of most theorists, who assume that a good explanation of the fact/fiction distinction can be extended to account for such border phenomena as historical fiction (*see* HISTORICAL NOVEL), the new *journalism, and the various hybrid forms sometimes labelled 'faction' (*see* HYBRID GENRES). Some theorists put *myth or *autobiography into this category, although both assignments are controversial. Finally, a non-issue: (3) cannot the boundary between fiction and non-fiction fluctuate? There is virtually no theorist of fiction who would deny that a text once regarded as factual can be read as fiction in a later period; the significant question concerns the theoretical significance of such fluctuation.

Theories of fiction usually approach the question of what fiction is and how it can be understood either through *pragmatics or semantics (*see* NARRATIVE SEMANTICS). Semantic approaches look for something distinctive in the content of fictional discourse, such as the use of proper names (*see* NAMING IN NARRATIVE), the role (if any) of *reference or *truth in fiction, and the nature of fictional entities (*see* EXISTENT). Pragmatic approaches focus on the production and *reception of fiction – that is, on the activity of fiction-making, including the intentions and conventions involved, and the social role that fiction plays. Historically, most theorists have pursued one approach or the other; the relationship between the two kinds of theories deserves more attention. It is arguable that they are complementary, semantic theories dealing with what is inside (as we might put it) of a piece of fictional discourse, and pragmatic theories with what happens on the exterior.

Approaches through pragmatics

It was Sir Philip Sidney who gave the first distinctively pragmatic account of fiction: 'Now, for the poet, he nothing affirms, and therefore never lieth'. While the best-known of the modern pragmatic analyses, by John Searle, cannot be reduced to an aphorism, the core thesis seems much the same, rewritten in the terminology of *speech act theory: 'the pretended illocutions that constitute a work of fiction are made possible by the existence of a set of conventions which suspend the normal operation of the rules relating illocutionary acts and the world' (1979 [1974–1975]: 67). Since fiction involves statements, it is this kind of illocutionary action that Searle has primarily in mind. On his account, the rules relating the world to this illocutionary act require of a statement-maker (a) a commitment to the truth of what has been stated, (b) an obligation to provide evidence for that truth if the statement is challenged, and (c) the intention to be recognised as conforming to rules (a) and (b) in making the statement. When these rules are suspended by the conventions of fictional discourse, a speaker can no longer be held responsible for any of these things. In short, the fiction-writer does not perform the illocutionary act of stating, and thus is not accountable for the possible falsehood of what he or she says.

There is an obvious limitation to this account: it is entirely negative. A theory of fiction must explain what the fiction-maker actually does.

Searle prefaces the analysis just quoted with a general description of how novelists and other fiction-writers pretend to perform illocutionary acts, but it remains undeveloped. There is a further problem with the analysis in terms of pretence: even if it is correct to say that the fiction-maker is pretending to do something (e.g., to make serious statements), the author/performer cannot do so in isolation (*see* AUTHOR). An adequate account must recognise that there is an *audience involved, and include it in a complete explanation of the phenomenon of fiction. Searle's achievement has been to offer an initial formulation of the pretence hypothesis. His treatment has inspired a number of alternative proposals, which follow his in explaining fiction primarily in pragmatic terms, but which also aim to address the shortcomings of the pretence hypothesis.

Gregory Currie's account elaborates on the thought that fiction-making is a kind of communicative action. 'Fictive utterance' – telling a fictional story – is not a pretence of (non-fictional) assertion, but instead a parallel activity. Just as the intention of someone making an assertion is that his or her listeners will take it to be true, someone uttering a fictional statement intends that the audience will make-believe that it is true. Thus the concept of pretence drops out of this account as superfluous. An objection to Currie's theory is that, in severing fictional statements from factual ones so completely, it leaves fictional utterance undefined. The discourse of fiction seems on the face of it to include statements, not some completely different kind of speech act; it is a virtue of the pretence hypothesis to recognise this point.

The notion of make-believe invoked by Currie in his account of fiction shows the influence of Walton, who develops the theme of make-believe much more fully. Like Currie, Walton downplays the relevance of pretence, partly because the term suggests a unilateral action on the part of the fiction-maker. Fiction is essentially a shared activity, involving the audience of a narrative as well as its maker, an activity that Walton finds it more appropriate to call make-believe. He also rejects Searle's assumption that fiction is a matter of linguistic pretence: for a sign in any medium, 'to be fictional is [...] to possess the function of a prop in a game of make-believe' (1990: 106). While few theorists have followed Walton in his effort to locate and explain the phenomenon

of fiction across all the representational arts, the major obstacle to accepting his version of the pragmatic account, even when limited to the verbal medium, is that notions of play and make-believe simply seem too vague, too thin, or too amorphous to explain an activity as specific and robust as that involved in the fictional transaction. If anything, it seems that the order of explanation should run the other way, with play explained as an elementary form of fiction-making (*see* CHILDREN'S STORYTELLING; NARRATIVE, GAMES, AND PLAY).

In the most detailed formulation of a pragmatic account yet offered, Peter Lamarque and Stein Olsen describe fiction as a social practice, governed by rules or conventions, in which stories are told that their audiences treat as consisting of assertions and other standard illocutionary acts, while knowing that they are not. Although Lamarque and Olsen prefer to call this make-believe rather than pretence, they provide the fullest analysis of the notion first invoked by Searle.

Approaches through semantics

Reversing the usual order of presentation, pragmatic accounts of fiction have been surveyed here before semantic ones, in recognition of the fact that content alone is neither a necessary nor a sufficient condition of fictionality. Nevertheless, many theorists of fiction have felt that there is something distinctive or otherwise characteristic in the subject-matter of fictional discourse, beginning with Aristotle. In *Poetics* 9, he utilises his logical terminology to draw a famous distinction between history, the subject-matter of which is 'particulars', and poetry, which deals in 'universals' (1451b) – despite appearances to the contrary (*see* ANCIENT THEORIES OF NARRATIVE (WESTERN); HISTORIOGRAPHY).

The philosophers who developed modern logic around 1900 began by replacing Aristotelian categories like universal and particular with an apparatus that includes singular terms (such as names), which serve to denote objects, and predicates, which express properties. Given these categories, fiction can be explained semantically as discourse involving sentences that are false because they contain singular terms that are 'empty' – that fail to denote anything. This became the standard account of fiction among analytic philosophers, although a variant developed among philosophers who preferred to call sentences with empty names not false, but lacking in truth value (neither true nor false). In any case, the basic principle of semantic theories as initially formulated is that fiction does not share factual discourse's aim of being true (see Beardsley 1981 for an overview). The problem with this thesis is that it leaves the specificity and variety of fiction unexplained: obviously, a sentence can fail to be true in many, many different ways – otherwise literary fiction would not teem with all the *characters and events with which it does. To analyse fiction as a general use of false sentences does nothing to explain its specificity.

One way of addressing this problem using the resources of modern logic is to reinterpret the discourse of fiction so as to replace the 'empty' singular terms that occur in it with a concatenation of predicates. Thus the name 'Sherlock Holmes' would be re-construed as an individuating description of the character ('a nineteenth-century British amateur detective who . . . '). This analysis, the best-known version of which may be Nelson Goodman's, has the advantage of allowing for the distinct content of each fictional narrative without surrendering the claim that some of the expressions that appear in these narratives do not denote anything. Its shortcoming is that it fails to account for statements in a narrative that contain a mix of denoting and non-denoting expressions ('The letter reached Gatsby while he was still at Oxford').

Another approach adapts the theory of *possible worlds developed by modal logicians. David Lewis has offered the most suggestive philosophical account thus far of the usefulness of the concept in dealing with fiction: if we think of a fictional narrative being told 'as known fact rather than fiction', surely we are thinking of a possible world. Meanwhile, a number of literary theorists have pursued the general program of analysing the familiar but vague notion of fictional worlds in terms of possible worlds: prominent figures include Lubomír Doležel, Thomas Pavel, and Marie-Laure Ryan. The greatest virtue of this kind of approach is that it restores legitimacy to talk about truth and falsity within fictional discourse. There has been some dispute among interested theorists over the way (or ways) in which the conception of possible worlds applies to the study of fictional narrative, but no strong objections to the program have yet emerged. Its failure to gain universal acceptance

thus far may have something to do with the elaborate metaphysical apparatus it involves – the theoretical question is whether the concept of possible worlds offers the simplest way to explain fictionality.

The nature and relevance of possible worlds has been one topic among several extensively discussed by semantically oriented theorists; others include the ontological status of fictional beings and the cognitive value of fiction. Such issues may belong more to metaphysics or epistemology than to literary or aesthetic theory. What they have in common is that they pertain to *reference; but while this has been almost the exclusive focus of semantic theories of fiction, a topic equally important in semantic theory, inference, has remained untouched (one exception is Lewis 1978, which raises the question of how to draw valid conclusions from premises that include factual truths and statements true only in some fictional work). Since inference and reference are complementary matters, it seems likely that, once theorists turn their attention to the logical connections between statements within a narrative (as well as their connection to statements about the narrative), it should have a major effect on the referential issues that dominate the current scene.

Signposts of fictionality

A recent development in the theory of fiction has been an interest in the question of whether there can be markers in a stretch of discourse that identify it as fictional. In part this has been a reaction to a claim made in passing in Searle's analysis of fiction: no purely linguistic or textual property of a narrative can serve as a criterion of it fictionality (1979: 65, 68). Most philosophers of language would likely agree with Searle's generalisation; but literary theorists more sensitive to the specifics of literary discourse have questioned it. Dorrit Cohn and Gérard Genette, for example, both cite the work of Käte Hamburger, who in the 1950s undertook to develop a poetics of literature based on the *phenomenology of language (1973). In the course of her investigation, Hamburger observed that there are linguistic forms unique to fictional discourse, but she did not systematically pursue the suggestion, which was in any case only a byproduct of her research. Following

Cohn's, Genette's, and others' elaborations of Hamburger's ideas, a list of possible identifying criteria (or signposts) for fiction would include the following:

- omniscient *narration or unrestricted *focalization;
- extensive use of *dialogue, *free indirect discourse, or interior monologue (*see* STREAM OF CONSCIOUSNESS AND INTERIOR MONOLOGUE);
- anaphoric use of pronouns lacking antecedents;
- detemporalised use of verb tenses and temporal adverbs, to indicate internal chronology only (e.g., 'Now was the time'; *see* TENSE AND NARRATIVE);
- use of deictics and spatial adverbs to indicate frame-internal reference only ('There on the left was Ellis Island') (*see* DEIXIS; SPACE IN NARRATIVE);
- distinguishability of *narrator from *author;
- use of *metalepsis;
- paratextual markers (e.g., *Smith: A Novel*).

There is no consensus as to whether any of these linguistic usages or literary devices can serve as universal indicators of fictionality, thus refuting Searle's claim. This remains an area for investigation and discussion. (Philosophers like Searle may well be influenced by the correct idea that there can be no indicators of factual discourse, since if one was proposed, it would immediately become a challenge to fiction-writers to co-opt: hence the frequency of the fictional imitation of non-fiction.)

A further motivation for theoretical caution concerning the signpost question lies in the uncertain status of theorising about fiction. This entry started by distinguishing between a definition of fiction and an explanation of it – and the devices just listed have been proposed as something else again, namely qualities that a work or passage exhibits as a consequence of being fictional. The problem is that many elements of our definition – non-deceptive untruth for example – could also be classified as markers of fiction; and likewise items in the list of markers – say, the author/narrator distinction – might plausibly be used in an explanation of the concept, or else in a definition. A resolution to the signpost question depends upon sorting out these matters.

The significance – indeed the urgency – of the signpost question comes from what, for theorists of fiction, has been far and away the most important development in recent narrative theory: the dawning realisation (first articulated by Cohn and Genette) that narratology, despite its pretensions to generality, has so far been confined to fictional narrative. Extending the concepts and categories of what has become 'classical' narratology to non-fiction is not a straightforward matter. The restricting factor appears to be the poorly understood nature of factual discourse. If so, then the way to a truly universal narrative theory appears to run through the theory of fiction.

SEE ALSO: non-fiction novel; philosophy and narrative; text-world approach to narrative

References and further reading

Beardsley, Monroe (1981 [1958]) *Aesthetics: Problems in the Philosophy of Criticism*, Indianapolis: Hackett.

Cohn, Dorrit (1999) *The Distinction of Fiction*, Baltimore: Johns Hopkins University Press.

Currie, Gregory (1989) *The Nature of Fiction*, Cambridge: Cambridge University Press.

Genette, Gérard (1993 [1991]) *Fiction and Diction*, trans. Catherine Porter, Ithaca, NY: Cornell University Press.

Goodman, Nelson (1968) *Languages of Art: An Approach to the Theory of Symbols*, Indianapolis: Bobbs-Merrill.

Hamburger, Käte (1973 [1957]) *The Logic of Literature*, trans. Marilynn J. Rose, Indianapolis: Indiana University Press.

Lamarque, Peter, and Stein Haugom Olsen (1994) *Truth, Fiction and Literature*, Oxford: Clarendon.

Lewis, David (1983 [1978]) 'Truth in Fiction', in *Philosophical Papers*, vol. 1, Oxford: Oxford University Press.

Mihailescu, Calin-Andrei, and Walid Hamarneh (eds) (1996) *Fiction Updated: Theories of Fictionality, Narratology, and Poetics*, Toronto: University of Toronto Press.

New, Christopher (1999) *Philosophy of Literature: An Introduction*, New York: Routledge.

Pavel, Thomas (1986) *Fictional Worlds*, Cambridge, Mass.: Harvard University Press.

Ryan, Marie-Laure (1991) *Possible Worlds, Artificial Intelligence and Narrative Theory*, Bloomington: Indiana University Press.

Searle, John (1979 [1974–1975]) 'The Logical Status of Fictional Discourse', in *Expression and Meaning: Studies in the Theory of Speech Acts*, Cambridge: Cambridge University Press.

Walton, Kendall (1990) *Mimesis as Make-Believe: On the Foundations of the Representational Arts*, Cambridge, Mass.: Harvard University Press.

DAVID GORMAN

FIGURA (AUERBACH)

The concept of 'figura' (literally, 'prefiguration') is related to the Greek word *typos* and the Latin *forma* and acquired a technical meaning with the Fathers of the Church. For example, in his *Adversus Marcionem* Tertullianus (b. AD 160) uses the story of Moses's twelve spies exploring Canaan as a prefiguration of Christ's coming and of the acts of the twelve apostles. In his *Divina commedia* Dante used the notion to characterise the relationship between this world and the next. The history and meaning(s) of the notion have most carefully been explored by Erich Auerbach, whose definition of the term was based on three prototypical conditions: (1) *figura* ties together two *events or persons separated from each other in place and time; (2) the events or persons in question are typically, though not always, situated in historical *time; and (3) the first event or person is an anticipation of the latter and the latter the fulfilment of the former. Other contemporary theorists of *figura* have been Walter Benjamin and, more recently, Hayden White.

Reference and further reading

Auerbach, Erich (1968) *Mimesis: The Representation of Reality in Western Literature*, trans. Willard R. Trask, Princeton: Princeton University Press.

FRANK ANKERSMIT

FIGURAL NARRATION

One of the three narrative situations proposed by Franz Stanzel: a third-person narrative in which the *events of the story are seen through they eyes of a 'reflector' character. *See* NARRATIVE SITUATIONS (also: FOCALIZATION).

FILM NARRATIVE

Film has aesthetics of its own, linked to the ability to show moving pictures. Thanks in part to the incorporation of a *soundtrack into movies in the late 1920s, film is also a medium for a *Gesamtkunstwerk* (total work of art), a medium that integrates most other arts in its representation, from *music, architecture, and acting to literature and poetry (*see* INTERMEDIALITY; MEDIA AND NARRATIVE).

The basic features of film *narration were developed in the twenty years that followed the invention of the medium in 1895. These features were inspired partly by literary and partly by dramatic narrative (*see* DRAMA AND NARRATIVE). Like *novels, but unlike theatrical drama, film may easily present narratives that comprise many *spaces and change of *time or location. Like theater, film provides direct perceptual access to space and *characters, and the typical duration of film narratives is comparable to that of theatrical drama.

In its first few years, film was not used for narrative purposes, but soon the production of narrative movies became the main commercial use of the film recording technique. In several respects film is the medium that provides the closest 'realistic' match to our unmediated sensory perception of the world. Realist aestheticians like André Bazin have recommended that film reproduce reality in such a way as to minimise the traces of a narrating agency (*see* NARRATOR; REALISM, THEORIES OF). Siegfried Kracauer went so far as to claim that the story most suited for the medium is the story 'found' in reality. But from the very beginning trick film used the medium for non-realist purposes, and some formalist theoreticians such as Rudolf Arnheim have stated that film art resides in formal deviations from real life experiences (*see* FORMALISM).

The phenomenology of film narration

Whereas drama is experienced from a fixed position (the spectator's seat in the theater), the film may be presented from all possible positions. These positions often mimic to some extent the situation of characters within the fictional world, or diegetic world, as it is called in film studies (*see* DIEGESIS; STORYWORLD). This feature may be similar to literary modes of presentation, except that 'point of view' in film is not only a *metaphor, but often also a concrete perceptual fact linked to the camera position (*see* POINT OF VIEW (CINEMATIC)).

Although narration in film is often described with the help of a terminology borrowed from literary theory, several film scholars have argued that this is misleading, because filmmakers have a different status in the minds of viewers than *authors in the minds of readers (*see* AUDIENCE; READER CONSTRUCTS; READER-RESPONSE THEORY). Whereas humans often experience verbal narratives as a communication from a storyteller in everyday life and have innate dispositions to do so, there is no such experience in relation to visual information. Therefore, when film shows spaces, persons, and *events our natural attitude will be to perceive them in the same way as we look at the 'untold' world, a world in which the only storytellers are human beings. The ordinary viewer of a mainstream film will rarely know the name of the director, and may experience the film as a (fictional) simulation of real character experiences.

Critics of the notion of film as storytelling by a narrator have suggested several alternatives that emphasise how film is a kind of direct story-experience. One suggestion consists of saying that film cues viewers to simulate the events of the film (Currie 1995; Grodal 1997; see SIMULATION AND NARRATIVE); another suggestion is that the film is a kind of anonymous trigger for the viewer's construction of a story (Bordwell 1985). However, there are certain types of film, especially art films and comedies, which highlight the fact that they are communications from a director to viewers. Films are often made by a large group of people, such as producer, director, camera operators, actors, and sound experts, and a filmic narration controlled by a single person is the exception rather than the rule. When this happens – usually in art films – the description of who narrates becomes more similar to that of literary narration.

Compared to written narratives, film (like theater) may provide a wide variety of data simultaneously. A multi-soundtrack widescreen film is able to present at the same time thousands of objects, aspects, sounds, and movements. It is therefore impossible to isolate discrete signifiers that correspond to words (see SEMIOTICS). The screen may even be subdivided into two or more windows, and the soundtrack may provide information that originates in another time and/ or space than the time and space of the screen image. This happens for instance when the soundtrack is used as a channel for a narrator in *voice-over narration. Sound and image may even convey different messages, as is the case in the counterpoint use of a Strauss waltz in Stanley Kubrick's *2001 – A Space Odyssey*. In contrast to the reader of a novel, the spectator of a film has no influence on the viewing speed, a situation which may lead to cognitive-perceptual overload in the viewer. To alleviate this problem,

filmmakers may try to organise the data hierarchically, for instance by choosing a camera angle, a focus, and a distance from events that foreground certain phenomena, or by mixing sounds in such a way as to make some of them more salient than others.

VHS and DVD have made it possible for spectators to view a film in a more individualised way, enabling them to stop the film, to play it backwards, to go through it in slow motion, or to view it frame by frame. These techniques make the reception of films much more similar to reading written texts than when they are viewed in a movie theater.

A description of film narration may take its point of departure in the process of film production. To the extent that the camera reproduces the ways in which the eyes and the brain attend to real-world events, the technical description of the shooting process provides important clues to the film experience. Film highlights the cognitive schemata and mechanisms that support our perceptual comprehension of the world, and central aspects of film aesthetics rely on playing with perceptual and cognitive mechanisms (see SCRIPTS AND SCHEMATA; PSYCHOLOGICAL APPROACHES TO NARRATIVE).

Film production

Film production is often divided into four components: *Mise-en-scène*, cinematography, editing, and sound. *Mise-en-scène* comprises all those activities that take place in front of the camera, such as arranging set elements, controlling the lighting, designing the costumes and appearance of the actors, and monitoring their behaviour. Lighting may cue attention, define relations between texture and object structure, and mood. Classical Hollywood mainly used three-point lighting: a directed so-called key light on the main characters, a diffuse so-called fill light to soften shadows, and a back light on the background. Noir films often only used key light that created expressive shadows and hard contours; romantic films excel in soft 'fill' light. Film acting differs from drama acting because the visual closeness often demands a more naturalistic style than theater, although silent movies compensated for the lack of verbal information with expressiveness.

Cinematography consists of those elements that relate to the camera. One element is the time in which the camera runs without interruption (the *shot). The duration of shots may range from a fraction of a second to the entire duration of the film. Another element is the distance between the viewer's construction of the point of observation and the objects portrayed, often described in relation to the representation of humans. The basic shot distance is the medium shot, which provides a view of the head and upper part of the body. Shots that significantly exceed that distance are called long shots, whereas the shots that are taken from a shorter distance are called close-ups. The combination of camera angle and distance provides the framing of the screen picture, its delimitation. The focal length of the camera lens also influences the experience: telephoto lenses decrease depth cues whereas lenses with a short focal length enhance the sense of depth. A third component of cinematography is camera movements, such as moving the camera up and down (tilt), side to side (pan), and around its axis (roll), and a fourth resides in the movement of the camera through space (by dolly, crane, or some other platform). A fifth element, point of view shots (POV), mimics the vision of a live observer (*see* FOCALIZATION).

Editing consists of all those processes that take place after the film has been shot. Its most important aspect is the combination of shots into scenes by cutting the shot to a suitable length and splicing it together with another shot (*see* SCENE (CINEMATIC)). (The point of splicing is called the cut.) Another function of editing is to combine scenes into larger units such as sequences and acts (*see* NARRATIVE UNITS), to mix sound and *images, and occasionally to modify lighting and colour tone. Editing may thus modify *mise-en-scène*.

Since the shooting involves several cameras and provides all the necessary materials for the editing process, the editor can choose between several renditions of the same scene. The classical way of editing is called continuity editing or analytical *montage, also known as 'The Classical Hollywood Style'. Its main principle is to make transitions from shot to shot as easily comprehensible as possible. A common strategy for easing transitions consists of providing an adequate spatial orientation, for instance by means of a long shot that provides general information about space. This is known as an 'establishing shot'. Another common technique is adherence to the so-called 180-degree rule: never let the camera cross the line of action. If, for example, a car was first shot from the left side of a road and then from the right, viewers would think that it had turned 180 degrees. Editing further picks up the strategic points in space, and selects angle and framing to guide the viewer's attention toward the most important narrative elements.

The presentation often cuts or reduces actions so that only samples of the trajectory of an object or movement of a person are shown, and the eye establishes continuity by means of motion-schemas. Dialogue is generally presented by shot-reverse-shot: the two speakers are shown by an alternation of shots that focus on the current speaker, but that also include the shoulder of the listener. If two spaces are narratively connected (such as the respective locations of a pursuing and a pursued character separated by a significant distance) they are shown by crosscutting, i.e., by alternating between shots of the two spaces. Editing may facilitate the parsing of the film into distinct structural units by fading to black after important scenes, although recent films use this device sparingly.

The basic building block of film is a shot that represents events in real time and only shows one time-space at a time. But editing may change that, especially when its purpose is to represent deviant mental states (*see* THOUGHT AND CONSCIOUSNESS REPRESENTATION (FILM)). Time may be stretched in slow motion, and it may even stop, in stills. Time may also be compressed in fast-motion. Such changes are the most salient when they take place inside a single shot. But when a scene is represented by a series of shots, the cutter can still speed up or slow down time by deleting events or by showing the same event from different angles. By using various kinds of double exposure (mixing two images), films may fuse different times and/or different spaces. Manipulating the relations between the soundtrack and the visual display can represent even more complex worlds and states.

Styles of film narration

André Bazin advocated a special kind of filmmaking. He recommended that shots should be very long (long takes) in order to provide the phenomenological 'feel' of the duration of time and processes, even if this means presenting periods in which nothing happens. Furthermore, the space should not be a fragmented mosaic of shots, but should be rendered instead through 'deep focus', that is to say, through long shots captured by lenses that make the foreground, middle ground, and background equally sharp, so as to confer phenomenal unity on the interactions between different persons. This style may be seen as a variation of continuity editing, because it emphasises continuity of time, space, objects, and action. But in contrast to continuity editing, which pre-forms and guides the viewer's attention, it locates realism in a certain way of representing the world, and not in guiding the viewer's attention through framing techniques.

Continuity editing is not the only editing philosophy. The Russian director and film theoretician Sergei Eisenstein advocated for instance a dialectic editing style, in which two adjacent shots contrast with each other in order to create a new meaning. The contrast could be formal and perceptual (e.g., difference in line orientation) as well as related to content, such as good vs. evil. He also used metaphorical links, as when he juxtaposed a shot of workers being gunned down with a shot of a bull being slaughtered. Such montage effects are often found in art film, music videos, and commercials (see TELEVISION). In mainstream films, by contrast, they are mostly used sparingly, mainly to spice up an editing based on continuity or to describe subjective phenomena such as *dreams and hallucinations, although some newer mainstream films use more complex editing.

Sound has accompanied moving pictures from almost the beginning of cinema, in the form of music, sound effects, or narration, but it was only in the late 1920s that sound and image were technically integrated in the form of a soundtrack located on the film. An important factor in the use of sound is the technology, which ranges from the early rather low-resolution mono sound to the latest stereo or multitrack sound with high digital resolution. Sound may be diegetic, i.e., derive from the fictitious world, or non-diegetic. Music, the most important non-diegetic sound-type, enhances the mood of a given scene and supports the narrative tempo. Many filmmakers and critics feel that sound, even the non-diegetic type, is a crucial enhancement of a film's *reality effect because it suppresses the 'ghostly' qualities of the silver screen.

Film as story

Film may also be described in terms of its storytelling capacities. The basic story type, also known as *canonical story*, is typical of *genres such as action, adventure, and comedy. It takes place in progressing time, it is focused on one or a few characters, and it is motivated by their plans and goals. The canonical story format is not particular to film; rather, it corresponds to a basic verbal story format and probably relies on an elementary neurological-mental pattern that links perceptions of events with *emotions that motivate goal-directed actions. Psychologists have argued that films are the closest representation of our basic consciousness. In filmic action, as in consciousness, perceptions elicit concern-motivated emotions; these emotions lead in turn to a cognitive strategy that is successfully or unsuccessfully implemented through a (motor-based) action sequence. Eventually, the initial perception may be replaced with emotion-setting and goal-setting inner motives in the main character(s).

Since events in real life take place in a forward-directed time, the events of a film will be easier to remember if they are presented in the same way we experience real events, namely as chains of causes and effects (see CAUSALITY; MEMORY; STORY SCHEMATA AND CAUSAL STRUCTURE). The build up of emotions, both in film and in life, also depends on a temporal progression, since emotions are first caused by events and then motivate actions that can satisfy the preferences expressed in these emotions (see NARRATIVE PROGRESSION). Temporal rearrangements will impede or block the simulation of the chronological flow from emotional cause to releasing actions and will therefore create a build up of feelings that have no release conditions. Such 'saturated' feelings are typical of lyrical presentations, e.g., music videos. The viewer may furthermore have difficulties in understanding major temporal rearrangements, due to time pressure during viewing. In mainstream films the violations of canonical temporal progression reside mainly in short flashbacks, for instance in images of the characters' childhood experiences (see TEMPORAL ORDERING). Some types of tragic melodrama will use flashforward at the beginning of the film to prepare viewers for the tragic outcome, to direct their curiosity toward how- (as opposed to why-) questions and to create the sense of an inevitable and fatal undertow.

In earlier days, flashbacks were often marked visually, for instance by zooming in on or tracking toward the eyes of the remembering character. Other ways to indicate visually that a scene is situated in the past include the use of another colour tone, a cruder image resolution, or an image that is out of focus.

The typical mainstream film will have a double plot line, one romantic and the other action oriented (*see* PLOT TYPES). In *Raiders of the Lost Ark*, for instance, the search for the ark is combined with a love story. The *plot will typically be organised in four acts that Kristin Thompson calls 'Set-Up', encompassing Complicating Actions, Developments, Climax, and Epilogue. Each act leads to a turning point that prepares for the next act. For pragmatic reasons, such as the length of the typical mainstream film (90 to 120 minutes), this structure presents strong similarities with classical theater dramaturgy, first described by Aristotle (*see* FREYTAG'S TRIANGLE).

The simplest type of narrative presents the story in accordance with the main characters' understanding of the diegetic world. Once viewers are persuaded to share this understanding and its supporting values, they will simulate the story from a *perspective that emulates that of the character. But the story may also be shown from a deviant perspective. This deviation may be caused by discrepancies in knowledge, as when an omniscient filmmaker provides the viewer with more or less information than the character possesses.

In contrast to mainstream film, art film narration is often uncanonical. Art films frequently present major temporal rearrangements (cf. *Memento*), and it may be impossible to recover the *fabula from the discourse, as in Alan Resnais's classic *L'année dernière à Marienbad*. Lyrical and descriptive elements may dominate (*see* DESCRIPTION). Basic emotions supporting active coping, i.e., emotions that are supported by the sympathetic nervous system ('fight and flight'-emotions) are supplanted with parasympathetic 'feed and copulation'-emotions or with negative emotions like melancholia. Art film also evokes emotions related to higher cognitive functions such as those involved in establishing a personal *identity.

Film often provides seemingly unmediated perceptual information from a point of view that is close to that of the main characters. This experience is enhanced by the fact that special so-called mirror neurons in the brain tend to mimic the action and body experiences of characters. Some theoreticians, as well as some ordinary viewers, may therefore describe the viewer's experience as a simulation of the experience of the main characters, or even as a kind of identification. As we have seen, however, some types of films trigger viewer experiences that differ to varying degrees from the values and perspectives of the main character. This is especially true of comedies and of *metafictional works based on alienation effects (*see* DEFAMILIARISATION). An important part of film narration consists therefore in varying the degree to which viewers identify with characters, with partial fusion as one pole and total estrangement as the other. Variation in the distance between viewer and character is created through techniques that either break or reinforce the mimetic illusion.

SEE ALSO: cognitive narratology; evolution of narrative forms; mimesis; mindscreen; narrative structure; narrative techniques

References and further reading

Andrew, Dudley (1976) *The Major Film Theories*, New York: Oxford University Press.

Bazin, André (1967, 1972) *What is Cinema? I–II*, Berkeley: University of California Press.

Bordwell, David (1985) *Narration in the Fiction Film*, Madison: University of Wisconsin Press.

——, and Kristin Thompson (2001 [1979]) *Film Art: An Introduction*, New York: McGraw-Hill.

Branigan, Edward (1992) *Narrative Comprehension and Film*, London: Routledge.

Currie, Gregory (1995) *Image and Mind: Film, Philosophy and Cognitive Science*, Cambridge: Cambridge University Press.

Grodal, Torben (1997) *Moving Pictures: A New Theory of Film Genres, Feelings, and Cognition*, Oxford: Clarendon/Oxford University Press.

Kozloff, Sarah (1988) *Invisible Storytellers: Voice-Over Narration in American Fiction Film*, Berkeley: University of California Press.

Kracauer, Siegfried (1960) *Theory of Film: The Redemption of Physical Reality*, New York: Oxford University Press.

Stam, Robert, Robert Burgoyne, and Sandra Flitterman-Lewis (1992) *New Vocabularies in Film Semiotics: Structuralism, Post-Structuralism and Beyond*, London: Routledge.

Thompson, Kristin, and David Bordwell (2003 [1994]) *Film History: An Introduction*, New York: McGraw-Hill.

TORBEN GRODAL

FIRST-PERSON NARRATION

A narrative in which the *narrator tells a story of personal experience referring to himself or herself in the first-person. *See* NARRATIVE SITUATIONS (also: AUTOBIOGRAPHY; CONFESSIONAL NARRATIVE; DISCOURSE ANALYSIS (LINGUISTICS); PERSON).

FOCALIZATION

According to Gérard Genette (1980 [1972]), the field of narratology is divided into three parts termed Tense, Mood, and Voice. *Tense theory treats the possibilities of temporal arrangement and presentation (Order, Speed, and Frequency) (*see* TEMPORAL ORDERING; TIME IN NARRATIVE); *Voice theory addresses *narrators, narrative *embedding (*framed narrative), and the choice of grammatical *person; *Mood theory analyses 'the regulation of narrative information' (1988 [1983]: 41), subsuming (a) modes of presenting action, speech, and thought (*see* SPEECH REPRESENTATION; THOUGHT AND CONSCIOUSNESS REPRESENTATION (LITERATURE)), and (b) modes of selection and restriction of the information conveyed by a narrative. Mood theory part (b) is what Genette calls focalization, promoting an already existing word (both in French and English) to a theoretical term. Focalization denotes the perspectival restriction and orientation of narrative information relative to somebody's (usually, a *character's) perception, imagination, knowledge, or *point of view (*see* PERSPECTIVE). Hence, focalization theory covers the various means of regulating, selecting, and channelling narrative information, particularly of seeing *events from somebody's point of view, no matter how subjective or fallible this point of view might turn out to be (*see* RELIABILITY).

Genette begins his account of focalization by acknowledging the valuable insights offered in the work of mainly six earlier critics – Cleanth Brooks and Robert Penn Warren, Jean Pouillon, Georges Blin, Norman Friedman, and Tzvetan Todorov. Brooks and Warren built their account on the question 'Who sees the story?'; Pouillon distinguished three vision modes, *vision avec* ('vision with', i.e., from within a character's mind), *vision par derrière* ('vision from behind', or from an omniscient narratorial vantage), and *vision du dehors* ('vision from outside', a camera-like view); Blin analysed Stendhal's strategic use of subjectively restricted fields of perception (*restrictions de champs*); Friedman proposed a system covering seven types of narrative points of view, and Todorov focused on whether the narrator knows more than, as much as, or less than the characters.

Although Genette's appropriation of these earlier models comes in the modest guise of a 'reformulation', it offers considerable improvements. First, Genette introduces a systematic distinction by setting the question 'who sees?' (identifying a subject of focalization) against the question 'who speaks?' (identifying the subject of *narration, i.e., the *narrator). Second, he defines focalization by combining and adjusting the five proto-narratological accounts listed above. And third, he details a typology comprising three major focalization types (zero, internal, and external), roughly equivalent to the triadic models of Pouillon's vision and Todorov's knowledge approach.

Concepts and categories of focalization

Genette's model basically arranges types and techniques of focalization in an order of increasing degrees of restrictions of narrative information. The main types A, B, and C apply at both local and global levels of analysis, whereas the subtypes of B obtain globally (across whole texts) only.

(A) In *non-focalization/zero-focalization*, events are narrated from a wholly unrestricted or omniscient point of view (as in Fielding's *Tom Jones* and many Victorian novels). Here is an example from the voice-over narrative of Billy Wilder's *The Apartment*: 'On November first, 1959, the population of New York City was 8,042,783. If you laid all these people end to end... they would reach from Times Square to the outskirts of Karachi, Pakistan'.

(B) In *internal focalization*, the presentation of events is restricted to the point of view, perception, and cognition of a *focal character*, as in the 'impressionistic' beginning of Manfield's *Miss Brill*: 'Although it was so brilliantly fine – the blue sky powdered with gold and great spots of light like white wine splashed over the Jardins Publiques – Miss Brill was glad that she had decided on her fur'. The filmic equivalent of internal focalization is the 'point of view shot' (*see* POINT OF VIEW (CINEMATIC)).

Globally, across a whole text, internal focalization can be arranged in any of the following patterns: (1) *fixed focalization* denotes the presentation of events from the point of view of a single focal character (standard example, Joyce's *Portrait of the Artist as a Young Man*); (2) *variable focalization* presents different story episodes through the eyes of different focal characters (for instance, in Woolf's *Mrs. Dalloway* events are variously seen through the eyes of Clarissa Dalloway, Richard Dalloway, Peter Walsh, Septimus Warren Smith, Rezia Smith, and other characters; (3) *multiple focalization* presents an episode more than once, each time seen through the eyes of a different focal character (as in White's *The Solid Mandala*).

(C) *External focalization* is a presentation restricted to behaviourist report and outside views, basically reporting what would be visible to a camera. The standard example is Hemingway's 'The Killers' – 'He wore a derby hat and a black overcoat buttoned across the chest. His face was small and white and he had tight lips'.

Of the three main types, B (internal focalization) is of major importance not only because it captures the natural restrictions inherent in ordinary situated perception but also because it circumscribes a mode of presentation characteristic of much of twentieth century *modernist narrative. Narratives making extensive use of focal characters are also identified as 'figural texts' (Stanzel; *see* NARRATIVE SITUATIONS), or 'reflector-mode' narratives (Fludernik); the focal character has also been labelled 'centre of consciousness', 'reflector' (Henry James), 'refractor' (Brooks and Warren), 'figural medium' (Stanzel), 'filter' (Chatman), 'internal focalizer' (Bal), or 'SELF' (Banfield).

While the question 'who sees?' is still widely used as a shorthand formula, Genette (1988 [1983]) acknowledges that it is too specifically vision-oriented and had better be replaced by 'Who perceives?'. Nelles (1997: ch. 3) accordingly conjugates focalization through the five modes of perception, obtaining 'ocularisation' (sight), 'auricularisation' (sound), 'gustativisation' (taste), 'olfactivisation' (smell), and 'tactivilisation' (touch). The following excerpt from the closing pages of D. H. Lawrence's short story 'England, My England' shows these submodes of focalization in action:

Before him, below, was the highroad, running between high banks of grass and gorse. He saw the whitish, muddy tracks and deep scores in the road, where the part of the regiment had retired. Now all was still. Sounds that came, came from the outside. The place where he stood was still silent, chill, serene.

As is quite typical of internally focalized passages staging a focal character's perception, the text easily slips from ocularisation to auricularisation to focalized representation of bodily sensation (chillness), inviting the reader both to witness and to co-experience the situation as it is perceived by the focal character. The terms 'ocularisation' and 'auricularisation' have also been used by Jost (1989) for perspectivised information transmitted via the visual and auditory channels of filmic composition.

Post-Genettean focalization theory has been strongly influenced by Bal's critique of Genette's model and her introduction of various new terms and definitions. Basically, Bal proposes five major modifications. First, she throws out Genette's tripartite typology (types A, B, and C above), arguing that focalization is a necessary rather than an optional feature of narrative texts. Specifically, she points out that the concept of 'external' focalization is vague about who sees, what is seen, and how it is seen. Second, she redefines external focalization as a technique that orients the text around the perception and point of view of the narrator (acting as 'external' or 'narrator-focalizer'). Third, she replaces Genette's 'focal character' by the term 'internal focalizer', thus enabling a systematic opposition between internal and external focalizers/focalizations. Fourth, she distinguishes between perceptible and imperceptible 'focalizeds' (objects of focalization) – things visible in the real-world as opposed to things visible only in a character's consciousness or imagination. Fifth, as a consequence of admitting focalizers of unequal status and textual power (specifically, narrators vs. characters), she inquires into the mechanics and hierarchies of presenting other minds' perceptions, of adopting somebody's point of view, of 'delegating' textual focalization to a subordinate focalizer, and of chaining or embedding focalizations – a character-focalizer remembering > remembering something, or a narrator-focalizer seeing > what an internal focalizer remembers > having seen > in a dream, etc. Many of these complex scenarios invite close analysis of multi-perspectival narration, reliable vs. fallible perception, concordant vs. discordant focalization, and so on.

Approaching focalization from a cognitivist position (see COGNITIVE NARRATOLOGY), Jahn (1996; 1999) has argued that focalization is a means of opening an imaginary 'window' onto the narrative world (see STORYWORLD), enabling readers to see events and *existents through the perceptual screen provided by a focalizer functioning as a story-external or story-internal medium. A full picture of focalized and focalizing narration includes the narrator who, talking about what he or she imaginatively perceives, enables the reader to transpose to fictional points of view and to enter into a state of *immersion. Focalization, on this view, is a matter of creating and managing windows into the narrative world and of regulating – guiding, but also manipulating – readers' imaginary perception. Conceived of as a primary trigger for *authors, narrators, and readers alike, focalization is here seen as a foundational process both in storytelling and in story-understanding, not, as in its classical conception, as a secondary filter restricting the representation of already existing narrative facts.

For a finer scale of focalizations, Jahn (1999) distinguishes between 'strict focalization' (views originating from a determinate spatio-temporal position), 'ambient focalization' (story events and existents seen from more than one angle as in mobile, summary, or communal views), 'weak focalization' (an object seen from an unspecific spatio-temporal position), and 'zero focalization' (a wholly aperspectival view). Despite its metaphorical basis, the 'window' notion lends itself to a number of extrapolations, especially ones derived from the 'windows' of the movie and the computer screen – configurations comprising actual and virtual windows, open and closed windows, successor and continuator windows, merging and splitting windows, and so on (these technical terms are introduced by Ryan 1987 in the context of segmenting a storyline into *'montage' units). Complex shifts in focalization can be described using these concepts, and recurrent patterns of window-shifting can be found in narratives across many *media, including literary, theatrical, and *film narratives (see DRAMA AND NARRATIVE).

Using a different kind of imaginary perception as a foundational criterion of focalization, Herman's (2002: ch. 8) model of 'hypothetical focalization' addresses 'hypotheses framed by narrator or character about what might be or might have been seen or perceived – if only there were someone who could have adopted the requisite perspective'. Hypothetical focalization comes in many guises, among which the stock device of the virtual or floating observer is best known ('The eye of an observer might have discovered . . .'). Herman also distinguishes whether passages of hypothetical focalization involve an explicit appeal to a witness (yielding 'direct hypothetical focalization'), as in the example above, or whether it is constituted implicitly as in the case of counterfactual conditionals ('If it hadn't been raining, she would have noticed that . . .'), creating an instance of 'indirect hypothetical focalization'. Hypothetical focalizations abound in fiction and it is clearly not sufficient to classify them as mere instantiations of 'empty deictic centres' (Banfield) or as variants of narratorial focalization. Rather, as Herman points out, both hypothetical and ordinary (nonhypothetical) focalization encode epistemic modalities ranging from certainty to *virtuality to radical uncertainty. Herman specifically relates the epistemic semantics of focalization to the *possible-worlds semantics of narrative and narrative *genres.

Re-tracing the foundational assumptions of Genettean Focalization theory, Niederhoff (2001) offers an interesting argument for retaining 'focalization' and perspective as complementary theoretical terms. Both concepts, Niederhoff argues, describe restrictions of information: perspectival restriction is anchored in the standpoint of the focal character, and focalization presents filtered information about a focalized object. But on the analogy of the camera the two types of restriction do not necessarily amount to the same thing: while the camera's position determines its perspectival orientation, perspective alone is not exhaustively indicative of what the picture shows. Obviously, the object in focus can be anything within the camera's angle of vision, and identical objects can be seen from a variety of positions. In a narrative text, two different focalizers, observing a scene from an identical position might not see (or recognise) the same things, just as two focalizers placed in different positions might well see the same thing. Hence textual passages may be based on identical focalizations but different perspectives or on identical perspectives but different focalizations – it is this latter configuration that obtains in Joyce's 'Two Gallants', the test case discussed by Niederhoff. The downside to Niederhoff's account is that few narratologists will be willing to reintroduce a new (old) category – perspective – outside focalization. In keeping with the syncretistic origins of the concept, it would seem more natural to differentiate between perspectival and filtering factors of focalization.

Debates on the scope of focalization

One of the questions that every narratologist has to decide for himself or herself is whether to adopt Genette's or Bal's terms, or possibly use a mixed model such as Nieragden's (2002). It is prudent to bear in mind that there are three points that argue in favour of Genette's classical model: it establishes and strengthens the distinction between 'who speaks' and 'who sees'; it avoids the category error (famously perpetrated by Booth and others) of confusing focal characters with narrators; and it allows full combinatorial freedom in the sense that all types and features of focalization are allowed to co-occur (at least in principle) with all other aspects of narration. Nevertheless, many commentators have stressed the gains of Bal's model, particularly the stipulation that focalization is always present in one form or another, the notion of external and internal focalizers, and the possibility of *mise en abymes* of embedded focalizations.

A rather unhappy side-effect of competing models and overlapping terminologies is that the non-specialist reader is often confronted with intractable ambiguities even in the writings of individual narratologists. While external focalization, according to Genette, refers to a narrative style presenting what is visible to a camera recording the external surfaces of people and things, Bal's external focalization is something else entirely – a mode of presentation anchored in narratorial imaginary perception. These categories do not mix well, even though alternate terms such as external focalization (Genette) vs. narrator-focalization (Bal) are freely available in theory. Unfortunately, this option of a clean terminological distinction is not accepted universally, mainly, it seems, because, in the absence of a copyright on theoretical terms, theorists are keen on appropriating the attractive external-internal dichotomy.

On the level of heuristic efficiency, Bal's account often enables insightful analysis which is unavailable from within the Genettean framework. For instance, a passage such as D. H. Lawrence's 'All this Gudrun knew in her subconsciousness, not in her mind' (an item reported by Dorrit Cohn) can be analysed as 'narratorial focalization of imperceptible objects', a phrasing which grasps the narrator's present evaluation of the character's unconscious or semi-conscious sense data. Hemingway's 'The Killers', another notorious test case, is plain external focalization in Genette's model, whereas in the framework of Bal's terms it is 'internal focalization of purely perceptible objects', a description which seems somewhat closer to the text's behaviourist report of events seen through the (seemingly) neutral camera of a character's eyes. Less problematic, it would seem, is the extension of Genettean fixed, variable, and multiple focalization patterns to cases of Balian external focalization. On this basis, texts like Fowles's *The Collector*, Faulkner's *The Sound and the Fury*, and Browning's *The Ring and the Book* can be grasped as cases of multiple narratorial focalization.

As was noted above, Genette himself suggested expanding the original focalization formula 'who sees?' into 'who perceives?'. Other commentators, such as Rimmon-Kenan, (1983) have pointed out that the full range of 'facets' of focalization includes not only perceptual processes but also psychological and ideological orientations (*see* IDEOLOGY AND NARRATIVE). While it is obvious that psychologically and ideologically coloured expressions of *emotion, voice, belief, evaluative stance, and so on are strong markers of focalization it is also clear that these indicators apply equally to focal characters and to narrators, severely challenging the distinction between speaking narrators and perceiving characters. This is the reason why Chatman, staunchly defending the story-discourse divide as an essential narratological axiom, opposes not only Rimmon-Kenan's expansive definition of focalization but the term 'focalization' itself. What virtually all conceptions of focalization fail to account for, he claims, are 'the quite different mental process of characters and narrators' (1990: 145). Consequently, he proposes the term 'slant' for the narrator's mindset and attitudes and the term 'filter' for the reflector character's mental processes (1990: 143). Although the terms are enlightening in isolation, they fail to discriminate as intended, especially if one considers the role of imaginary perception noted above. It seems that the difference between narrators and characters is more appropriately seen as a matter of hierarchy, function, and representational authority, not of different mental processes. In any event, Chatman's spirited argument did not succeed in replacing focalization as a technical concept.

Also pursuing the goal of maximum theoretical transparency, Prince (2001) has suggested that internal focalization – in his opinion, the only type of focalization really worth bothering about – be reduced to the condition of perceptual filtering alone. On this basis, a focal character shown in an act of perception amounts to a story-level event, emancipated from (thus freely combinable with) any feature of narrative discourse. Against this it has been argued, notably by James Phelan, along with other contributors in Chatman and van Peer (2001), that all emotive and perceptual aspects of focalization can and indeed must be brought to bear on an appreciation of the narrator's own psychological and ideological orientations, the factors that determine his or her perceptions, beliefs, and emotions. This view clearly reasserts Bal's major point, namely that there is no narration without focalization, just as there is no focalization without narration.

SEE ALSO: story-discourse distinction

References and further reading

Bal, Mieke (1985) *Narratology*, trans. Christine van Boheemen, Toronto: Toronto University Press.

Chatman, Seymour (1990) *Coming to Terms: The Rhetoric of Narrative in Fiction and Film*, Ithaca: Cornell University Press.

Edmiston, William F. (1991) *Hindsight and Insight*, University Park: Pennsylvania State University Press.

Füger, Wilhelm (1993) 'Stimmbrüche: Varianten und Spielräume narrativer Fokalisation', in Herbert Foltinek, Wolfgang Riehle, and Waldemar Zacharasiewicz (eds) *Tales and 'their telling difference': Zur Theorie und Geschichte der Narrativik*, Heidelberg: Winter.

Genette, Gérard (1980 [1972]) *Narrative Discourse*, trans. Jane E. Lewin, Oxford: Blackwell.

—— (1988 [1983]) *Narrative Discourse Revisited*, trans. Jane E. Lewin, Ithaca: Cornell University Press.

Herman, David (2002) *Story Logic: Problems and Possibilities of Narrative*, Lincoln: University of Nebraska Press.

Jahn, Manfred (1996) 'Windows of Focalization: Deconstructing and Reconstructing a Narratological Concept', *Style*, 30.2, 241–67.

—— (1999) 'The Mechanics of Focalization: Extending the Narratological Toolbox', *GRAAT*, 21, 85–110.

Jost, François (1989) *L'oeil-Caméra: Entre film et roman*, Lyon: Presses Universitaires.

Nelles, William (1997) *Frameworks: Narrative Levels and Embedded Narrative*, Frankfurt: Lang.

Niederhoff, Burkhard (2001) 'Fokalisation und Perspektive', *Poetica*, 33.1, 1–21.

Nieragden, Göran (2002) 'Focalization and Narration: Theoretical and Terminological Refinements', *Poetics Today*, 23.4, 685–97.

Phelan, James (2001) 'Why Narrators Can Be Focalizers – and Why It Matters', in Willie van Peer and Seymour Chatman (eds) *New Perspectives on Narrative Perspective*, Albany: State University of New York Press.

Prince, Gerald (2001) 'A Point of View on Point of View or Refocusing Focalization', in Willie van Peer and Seymour Chatman (eds) *New Perspectives on Narrative Perspective*, Albany: State University of New York Press.

Rimmon-Kenan, Shlomith (1983) *Narrative Fiction: Contemporary Poetics*, London: Methuen.

Ryan, Marie-Laure (1987) 'On the Window Structure of Narrative Discourse', *Semiotica*, 64.1/2, 59–81.

Sanders, José, and Gisela Redeker (1996) 'Perspective and the Representation of Speech and Thought in Narrative Discourse', in Gilles Fauconnier and Eve Sweetser (eds) *Spaces, Worlds, and Grammar*, Chicago: University of Chicago Press.

MANFRED JAHN

FOLKLORE

Folklorists study both the formal, stylistic, and *thematic dimensions of texts (including *genre, repertoire, and language) and the conditions of cultural textual production (including *performance, repertoire, community aesthetics, conceptions of *memory, and the identities of participants both within a narrative and in a performance situation) (*see* IDENTITY AND NARRATIVE).

'Folklore' as a category describing vernacular, traditional, face-to-face, cultural expressions passed orally from one generation to the next is an invention of modernity (*see* ORAL CULTURES AND NARRATIVE). Indeed folklore could be seen as modernity's other, designed to differentiate between the contemporary and the past, the industrial urban mechanical world, and the urban peasant artisan world. Distinctions among folk, elite, high, popular, traditional, and modern cultural expressions are best understood in this context, as strategies for granting status or legitimising categories. Eighteenth- and nineteenth-century philologists, antiquarians, and folklorists categorised and compared textual variations in an endeavour to preserve the past and validate nationalist identity (Abrahams 1993). Twentieth-century classification systems, such as Stith Thompson's ambitious *Motif Index of Folk Literature* (1966), created global taxonomies based on collections of *folktales from around the world. Beginning in the 1960s, the discipline of folklore studies experienced a paradigm shift from textual comparison to *ethnographic observations of folklore in performance, focused on understanding folklore as a dimension of local character and culture (*see* CULTURAL STUDIES APPROACHES TO NARRATIVE).

The study of folklore today combines ethnographic research on performance with critical reflection on the romantic legacies of the discipline. The romantic inheritance is attributed to the eighteenth-century theologian, philosopher, and collector of folksongs, Johann Gottfried von Herder, who articulated the idea of folklore as the authentic voice of the people, a concept fundamental to the development of nationalism (*see* IDEOLOGY AND NARRATIVE). The Brothers Grimm adopted these ideas in their collection of folk tales. As a site for observing how the present imagines, memorialises, constructs, reconfigures, and invents the past, folklore today is recognised as a constructed reality involving the production of nostalgia (Stewart 1991), heritage (Kirshenblatt-Gimblett 1998), and authenticity claims (Bendix 1997; Stewart 1998).

Folk narrative research regards texts as cultural artefacts that have been extracted from performances. The production of texts always involves processes of decontextualisation – in which texts are removed from one cultural context and recontextualised in another – as well as [of] entextualisation – in which a selection of communication is extracted and identified as a unit of meaning (Bauman and Briggs, 1990; Shuman, 1986) (*see* NARRATIVE UNITS). In other words, for folklorists, a text is always a fragment of both a larger cultural repertoire and a situated performance. Vladimir Propp's foundational study, *The Morphology of the Folktale*, and Alan Dundes's application of this model to *Native American collections provided models for identifying the formal characteristics of repertoire in culturally based collections of texts.

Studies of narrative in communicative contexts focus on the repertoires of individual performers, on the social uses of narrative, on interactions among participants, and on cultural aesthetics (*see* COMMUNICATION STUDIES AND NARRATIVE). Building upon Dell Hymes' concept of the ethnography of communication, this performance approach considers narrative as a speech event in relationship to the norms and conventions of larger speech community and addresses formal features of style and genre. Beyond the immediate context of performance, research addresses the uses of narrative and the modes of transmission to new tellers and new contexts. The distinction between 'active bearers of tradition', who perform narratives, and passive bearers, who know narrative repertoires that they do not perform, is not fixed. Not only do narrative performances follow the conventions of speech communities; speech communities also are constituted by shared narratives, which can become a vehicle for recognising community in shared experience (*see* INSTITUTIONAL NARRATIVE).

As folklore research shifted to the study of performance, the field of inquiry broadened to include not only *epic, *fable, *fairy tale, folktale, *legend, and *myth but also genres of *conversational storytelling. Research on folk narrative in context addresses both the stability and dynamics of narrative production. The singularity of each performance points to the dynamic dimension of folklore, with no fixed or authentic text existing apart from those performances. At the same time, performances depend upon cultural norms and conventions – upon *audience expectations as well as conventions for style and genre so that texts and their performances can be relatively stable across time and with different tellers (Ben-Amos 1993). The study of performance dynamics is not limited to observation of actual performances, however, and several scholars have proposed models for examining what John Foley calls 'the rhetorical persistence of traditional forms' (1995: 60–98), the traces of oral performances in collections of written texts (Albert Lord; Dell Hymes; Richard Bauman; Charles Briggs) (*see* ORALITY).

Studies of folk narrative began with collections of texts and only later, beginning in the 1960s, did the study of performance become a dominant paradigm of research. Since that time, research has tended to focus on dynamics rather than stability in texts. Peter Seitel has developed a model for understanding what he calls 'finalization', i.e., the use of generic conventions of *plot and style to create textual coherence.

In its attention to the contextual dimensions of performance, the formal features of genre, and the classification of narrative as 'traditional' or 'folk', folk narrative research encompasses the politics as well as the poetics of textual production.

SEE ALSO: ballad; oral-formulaic theory; oral history; simple forms; tall tale

References and further reading

Abrahams, Roger (1993) 'Phantoms of Romantic Nationalism in Folkloristics', *Journal of American Folklore*, 106, 3–37.

Bauman, Richard, and Charles Briggs (1990) 'Poetics and Performance as Critical Perspectives on Language and Social Life', *Annual Review of Anthropology*, 19, 59–88.

Ben-Amos, Dan (1993) ' "Context" in Context', *Western Folklore*, 52, 209–26.

Bendix, Regina (1997) *In Search of Authenticity: The Formation of Folklore Studies*, Madison: University of Wisconsin Press.

Foley, John Miles (1995) *The Singer of Tales in Performance*, Bloomington: Indiana University Press.

Hymes, Dell (1972) 'Models of the Interaction of Language and Social Life', in John J. Gumperz and Dell Hymes (eds) *Directions in Sociolinguistics: The Ethnography of Communication*, New York: Holt, Rinehart and Winston.

Kirshenblatt-Gimblett, Barbara (1998) *Destination Culture: Tourism, Museums, and Heritage*, Berkeley: University of California Press.

Propp, Vladimir (1968 [1928]) *Morphology of the Folktale*, trans. Laurence Scott, revised by Louis A. Wagner, Austin: University of Texas Press.

Seitel, Peter (1999) *The Powers of Genre: Interpreting Haya Oral Literature*, Oxford: Oxford University Press.

Shuman, Amy (1986) *Storytelling Rights: The Use of Oral and Written Texts by Urban Adolescents*, Cambridge: Cambridge University Press.

Stewart, Susan (1984) *On Longing: Narratives of the Miniature, the Gigantic, the Souvenir, the Collection*, Baltimore: Johns Hopkins University Press.

—— (1991) *Crimes of Writing: Problems in the Containment of Representation*, Oxford: Oxford University Press.

Thompson, Stith (1966) *Motif-Index of Folk-Literature; a Classification of Narrative Elements in Folktales, Ballads, Myths, Fables, Medieval Romances, Exempla, Fabliaux, Jest-Books, and Local Legends*, Bloomington: Indiana University Press.

Young, Katharine (1987) *Taleworlds and Storyrealms: the Phenomenology of Narrative*, Dordrecht: Nijhoff.

AMY SHUMAN

FOLKTALE

The term 'folktale' designates a traditional narrative, *author unknown, whose form and content are transmitted in prose, primarily through oral *performance but also through copied or printed collections, and whose sequence and details vary according to the skill, interest, and demands of teller and *audience. A broader definition is sometimes found, whereby the folktale is treated simply as a prose narrative on a traditional theme, transmitted orally – and so can function as a cover term for *genres as various as *legend, *fairy tale, *tall tales, humorous *anecdotes, and others. But since boundaries between oral genres can be permeable in living transmission, specialists tend to separate the folktale from other narrative genres for purposes of analytical specificity and classification.

In order to differentiate folktales from legends, for example, the fictive element of the tale is treated as fundamental and for this reason comprises an important classificatory criterion for assigning a narrative to the category of folktale – though any decision regarding the degree to which ancient and medieval folktales were considered fictions by their contemporary audiences remains largely speculative (*see* ANCIENT THEORIES OF NARRATIVE (WESTERN); FICTION, THEORIES OF; MEDIEVAL NARRATIVE). Fieldwork has confirmed that elements of entertainment and didactic functionality are essential to the folktale (*see* DIDACTIC NARRATIVE). Variation in performance and its meaning for audiences and researchers will always depend upon local variables, including the conventions and expectations of the particular tradition, the skill and lifeworld of the storyteller, the particular audience present at the hearing, and the occasion of performance.

A folktale may be based on a single *motif or many, upon a single episode or many, and an established pattern frequently emerges, which scholars call a 'tale-type'. Much labour has gone into the identification and classification of folktale tale-types and their constitutive motifs, the fruits of which include the indexes compiled by Antti Aarne, *The Types of the Folktale*, revised and twice enlarged by Stith Thompson, and *The Motif-Index of Folk-Literature*, compiled by Thompson. Motifs and episodes thus are identifiable components of the folktale, and can be compared both tradition-internally and cross-culturally, though any comparative investigation must always confront the problem that similarities arise for multiple reasons, be they by cultural contact, genetically diachronic transmission, polygenetic origination, or a combination of these and related factors. The practice of composing and transmitting folk narratives is probably as old as human sociability, and for that reason the question of a tale's origin is usually beyond empirical grasp.

Vladimir Propp's (1968 [1928]) pioneering analysis of the structure of Russian fairy tales was an important development in the study of folk (and other) narratives, and subsequently became an essential work in *structuralist narratology and *semiotics. For the last century, the Folklore Fellows' Communication monograph series (1910–) has been an important venue for the publication of many indispensable motif and tale-type indexes, among other works dedicated to folktale and folkloristic research.

SEE ALSO: fairy tale; folklore; function (Propp); oral cultures and narrative; orality

References and further reading

Aarne, Antti, and Stith Thompson (1961) *The Types of the Folktale*, Helsinki: Academia Scientiarum Fennica.
Leena-Siikila, Anna, (ed.) (1910–) *Folklore Fellows' Communications Monograph Series* (280 volumes to date), Helsinki: Academia Scientiarum Fennica.
Propp, Vladimir (1968 [1928]) *Morphology of the Folktale*, trans. Laurence Scott, revised by Louis A Wagner, Austin: Texas University Press.
Thompson, Stith (1955–1958) *Motif-Index of Folk Literature* (6 vols), Bloomington: Indiana University Press.

AARON TATE

FOREGROUNDING

The term 'foregrounding' refers to how deviations from some background norm of expectations enter the attentional foreground, producing cognitive 'deautomatisation' (*see* SCRIPTS AND SCHEMATA). Language may deviate by regularity (e.g., rhyme, fixed meter) or irregularity (e.g., breaking meter or syntax). Prague structuralist Jan Mukařovský saw systematic foregrounding ('*aktualisace*') as defining poetic language. *Russian Formalist Shklovskii earlier explored the analogous concept of *'defamiliarisation'. Jakobson saw formal 'parallelisms' defining poetic language by foregrounding linguistic form. Later developments (see van Peer 1986) recognise types of foregrounding violating various norms (e.g., of ordinary language, literary convention, individual text); degrees of foregrounding; and various constraints on its relevance. *Reader-response studies confirm that foregrounding increases 'strikingness', interpretive salience, and emotional effect.

SEE ALSO: emotion and narrative; formalism; psychological approaches to narrative; semiotics

References and further reading

Jakobson, Roman (1960) 'Closing Statement: Linguistics and Poetics', in Thomas A. Sebeok (ed.) *Style in Language*, Cambridge: MIT Press.
Mukařovský, Jan (1964 [1932]) 'Standard Language and Poetic Language', in Paul L. Garvin (ed.) *A Prague School Reader on Esthetics, Literary Structure, and Style*, Washington, DC: Georgetown University Press.
van Peer, Willie (1986) *Stylistics and Psychology: Investigations of Foregrounding*, London: Croom Helm.
Shklovskii, Viktor (1965 [1917]) 'Art as Technique', in Lee T. Lemon and Marion J. Reis (eds and trans.) *Russian Formalist Criticism: Four Essays*, Lincoln, NE: University of Nebraska Press.

MICHAEL SINDING

FORMALISM

Formalism is sometimes misleadingly equated with Russian Formalism, a literary-critical school which was active between roughly 1914–1929, and which, according to many, is a major originator of modern literary theory in general. But as a general approach to literature and narrative, formalism is much wider and older. An approach to literature (or literary narrative) may be termed formalist if it is informed by the following claims and assumptions.

1   It is possible to distinguish conceptually two basic aspects of the literary work, variously referred to as content and form, the what and the how, material and device (Shklovskii 1990 [1929]), matter and manner (technique), *Gehalt* and *Gestalt* (Walzel 1923). In narrative studies, alternate terms include story and discourse, narrated and *narration, fabula and sjuzhet (*see* STORY-DISCOURSE DISTINCTION).

2   While the contents of literary works manifest infinite variety, their forms consist of a limited number of invariant elements which can be described in an explicit and systematic way.

3   A literary work is a piece of verbal art, a product of deliberate crafting, shaping, or making by its *author (poiesis). Since a work of literature is a man-made object, the basic question of the formal approach is: 'how is it made' (Eikhenbaum 1974). Hence literary analysis in general and narrative studies in particular should be concerned with the 'how' side. Indeed, the artistic value of a work of literature is defined by its form and technique, primarily or exclusively.

Major emphasis on questions of form and of making is as old as literary theory itself.

Aristotle's *Poetics*, for example, declares at the very outset its intention to discuss problems concerned with 'the art of poetic composition in general and its various species...; how plots should be constructed...; [and] how many other component elements are involved in the process' (*Poetics* 1447a8). In its concentration on the how side of narrative and in its quest for invariants, patterns, and typologies, most of classical or *structuralist narratology is formalist in its approach, as any cursory examination of the standard textbooks in the field will indicate (*see* POSTCLASSICAL NARRATOLOGY). But not entirely the formal side is dominant here, but not exclusive, and different versions of classical narratology vary as regards the amount of non-formal aspects they include. It is in fact impossible to provide an exclusively formalist model of narrative, since the mimetic vs. formal separation is purely notional and methodological (*see* MIMESIS).

In actuality, narrative content (story stuff, fabula) can only exist and be encountered as shaped or discoursed (sjuzhet), while narrative form and method of presentation always involve some content element. Pure formalism can be viewed as the desire to abstract the formal components, aspects, or patterns of the work from any semantic content. But this can be achieved only with respect to some very elementary architectonic patterns such as parallelism, gradation, or loop (see below). Most formal elements, however, maintain some semantic load. Thus, abstract plot models can refrain from specifying kinds of *action, but not from speaking of equilibrium, disturbance, and *conflict. *Focalization is indeed a relation between observer, object observed, and resultant vision, but it involves essentially cognition and information processing, both richly semantic. The represented domain can be abstracted into 'static' and 'dynamic' *motifs (Tomashevskii 1965), but both terms inescapably imply state and state change.

If the hallmark of formalist approaches consists in their near exclusive focusing on issues of form, one ought to be able to provide some definition of this key concept itself. Form is indeed notoriously difficult to define, but one can use as the widest working definition a recent proposal according to which the form of verbal art means those non-representational properties of a text's sign sequence and of its communicative content which

are significant from a literary (that is, artistic) point of view (Pettersson 2000: 256).

Two main senses of form are usually distinguished in aesthetic theory.

1 Form as structure, or the total set of relations between the elements of a work as a whole and between the whole and its parts.
2 Form as style or manner of doing something.

In narrative, form as structure can be specified, following Pettersson's distinction between communicative content and sign sequence, as (1.1) form(s) of content – content consisting of a narrative's action, *characters, locations and themes or ideas – and as (1.2) form(s) of expression, that is, of language as manifested in the styles and utterances occurring in a work and in their interrelations. Form as manner (German: *Darstellungsweise*; Russian: *metoda izobrazhenie*) consists of providing answers to the question: what techniques, methods, and procedures are employed to present or portray (and ultimately to invoke verbally) some representational element. *Summary and scene, *showing and telling are thus two different ways of verbally presenting an *event (*see* NARRATIVE TECHNIQUES).

The two senses of form are clearly not restricted to verbal art, and are in fact general aesthetic categories, as is stipulated by the formal(ist) approach itself. Basic issues of literary form are hence discussed in most general theories of art, where the aim is first to establish categories which apply to several/all arts and then define in their terms the major specific features of each. The classical example in American aesthetics is Monroe Beardsley's *Aesthetics* (1958). Fruitful insights can sometimes be gained from perusing such aesthetic theories, and the rise of formalist approaches to narrative in Germany and Russia between 1900–1920 was in fact motivated by contemporary aesthetic theories (Doležel 1990). In fact, any self-aware literary-formalist approach in the twentieth century has presented itself as rooted in some explicit aesthetic theory or doctrine. In and by themselves, though, such theories operate at a high level of abstraction and, trying to establish universal categories, they often miss the specifics of verbal narrative. For better or worse, none of these theories forms the basis of current, as contrasted with early twentieth-century, narrative theory. In what follows I shall focus on aspects of form in the (proto) narratological theories of Russian

Formalism, whose insights have largely been taken up and integrated into current narrative theories.

Form as structure of content

Form as structure has variously been designated by a whole range of terms, including composition, organisation, arrangement, design, pattern, articulation, architectonics, ordering, morphology, construction, or disposition. Underlying all of these terms is the model of an ordered whole, defined by a grid of interrelations. Analysis can commence with the whole and proceed to its constituent parts, or, conversely, ask how the parts or units are interrelated to constitute one whole object (*see* NARRATIVE UNITS).

When speaking of forms or structures of content in narrative, one ought to distinguish further between (1.1.1) simultaneous patterns and (1.1.2) successive or sequential ones. Simultaneous or 'spatial' patterns, for example parallelism or contrast, may be formed by any two or more mimetic elements of any size: *events, ideas, themes, locations, or characters, and are perceivable when these elements are viewed simultaneously. Sequential patterns concern the transitions or linkages between adjacent segments of a series or a sequence, especially scenes or events, or between series of the same kind. Both types of patterns defined thus far are first-order, as they involve only one level of patterning. A huge range of second-order patterns (1.1.3) is opened up as soon as one considers the relations between the 'natural' (logical, temporal, and causal) order and connections of mimetic elements, especially states and events (the narrated), and the order and connections of their textual presentation, i.e., their narration (*see* CAUSALITY; TEMPORAL ORDERING). While first-order patterns constitute a relation between two or more elements present in the text, second-order patterns involve a relation between a textually present sequence (story as discoursed) and a textually absent one (story material in its chronological and causal order) which needs to be reconstructed from it. All three kinds of patterns have been distinguished and illustrated in the work of Russian Formalists. Let us now examine each of them in greater detail, and with reference to some of the scholars who have provided the relevant major insights.

Two or more mimetic (representational) elements of the same kind, when perceived simultaneously – and irrespective of their scope or how far apart in the text they are – may reveal a pattern of complete or partial *repetition*, with partial repetition in its turn representing a set of variations on a core element or a graduated series (intensification, staircase construction) like the three wishes or the three attempts in the *folktale. An additional pattern of the same kind is that of positive and negative *parallelism* (or similarity and contrast) of situations, ideas, or character features. *Analogy* is simply a case of correspondence between members of sets: the role of A in his group is equivalent to that of B in the other group, event A in one *plot line is equivalent to event B in the other. Other simultaneous patterns are defined by the relative position of their members. To this group belong *symmetry*, counterpoint, and balancing relations, as well as regular *alternation* (switching) between elements belonging to two parallel plot lines, or alternation between characters, tones, attitudes, locations and the like. Such patterns can also be regarded as defining a regularity of distribution of some information item along the text sequence, a regularity which may on occasion be governed by a complex geometric formula.

One can in fact distinguish at this point in a general way between two major modes of linking narrative scenes: juxtaposing and unfolding, or spatial (simultaneous) and sequential (*see* SPATIAL FORM). Another important pattern in this context is the *mirror image* relation between action sequences, or between first and last scene, chapter or book of an *epic (*see* RING-COMPOSITION). Examples are rising and then falling action, and Aristotle's tying and untying of the plot (*desis* and *lysis*). Yet another pattern of simultaneous relations is provided by part-whole, macro-micro reflections or homology, currently referred to as fractals. In all such cases, the same pattern, say rising and falling action, governs a text segment, such as one scene, as well as the text as a whole. This formal part-whole correspondence is one particular variety of the part-whole relation referred to as *mise en abyme*.

Once again, let us recall that the formal patterns we have seen so far are of various sizes and are manifested by all major mimetic elements, thereby forming universals of narrative crafting. This was precisely the point made by Viktor Shklovskii, one of the leading figures of Russian Formalism, in his book *Theory of Prose* (1929). The book presents primarily an enumeration and wide exemplification of the patterns listed above, which the author refers to as 'constructional devices'. He goes on to claim that the same set of such devices can be found on the level of rhetorical figures and on that of plot construction, and that these devices are small in number and universal in distribution, covering all cultures, periods, and *genres. In his view they constitute the invariants of narrative, or its universal grammar, independent of any specific content, and provide a set of moulds into which any narrative content must be poured. True to his formalist aesthetics, Shklovskii maintains that the content aspect of artistic narrative is a mere excuse for deploying formal patterns, and that the most artistic narrative is one in which they are unmotivated, being played off for their own sake. This obviously flies in the face of the common belief that form should be functional.

Sequential patterns begin with the modes of transition and connection between adjacent units of a series, especially scenes or episodes. Boris Tomashevskii, another leading Russian Formalist, employed the term 'motivation' to designate the reason or justification for the introduction of an element into a narrative sequence, and distinguished between realistic, that is, mimetic, and artistic or compositional kinds of motivation (*see* REALISM, THEORIES OF). The modes of transition between scenes or episodes are of exactly the same two kinds. Mimetic modes vary greatly in terms of their 'tightness' and complexity (*see* PLOT TYPES). The simplest is *montage, or juxtaposition of scenes (or scene fragments) unrelated in *time, place or participants, and lacking in any apparent motivation for their selection or order (*see* SPACE IN NARRATIVE). Next is simple addition or concatenation, a stringing together of episodes, the Aristotelian 'simple plot'. The motivation here is temporal order, with or without sameness of participants. A much tighter linkage between adjacent scenes exists when they are related causally or in terms of some finality, including agents' intentions (*see* INTENTIONALITY). E.M. Forster illustrated the difference between the last two modes in the following two phrases: 'The king died, and then the queen died' as opposed to 'The king died and then the queen died of grief'.

Following Roman Jakobson (and David Lodge later on), one can distinguish two basic kinds of artistic composition or motivation in narrative: the metonymic and the metaphoric, based respectively on the relations of contiguity and similarity between adjacent units (*see* METAPHOR; METONYMY). Moving from a *description of a person to that of his house would exemplify contiguity, while having a description of a storm at sea follow a scene of an emotional outburst illustrates similarity. At this point questions of composition begin to blend into issues of artistic method and style, of the basic techniques of evoking a narrated domain.

Whole narrative sequences, no less than individual scenes, can be related to each other in various ways. The Russian Formalists studied the ever-increasing complexity involved in the transition and expansion from *anecdote to *short story, collection of short stories (*see* COMPOSITE NOVEL), and finally *novel. They also examined the various relations between a containing framework story and its contained or inset stories as in Boccaccio's *Decameron* (*see* EMBEDDING; FRAMED NARRATIVE), and examined the relations between a pre-existent narrative sequence and a larger one into which it is incorporated. Such relations turn out to vary from subordination and integration to mere insertion with clear preservation of former boundaries. Finally, when viewing what Tolstoi called the total 'labyrinth of interconnections' of various sizes, both simultaneous and successive, defining a given narrative, one can distinguish in a global fashion between simple and complex, loose and tight modes of organisation, and characterise a narrative as formally integrated or dissociated, unified or fragmentary, open or closed.

Issues concerning the textual order of presentation of the narrated and the resultant configurations constitute the next area of forms of content. Temporal ordering is amenable to quantitative consideration and to abstraction from semantic factors, and clearly falls under form as composition, arrangement, or disposition of parts. The Russian Formalists were the first to distinguish between the natural (temporal, causal, logical) order of events and its particular textual sequencing, and to insist that distortions of the natural order of events, such as omission, transposition, digression, and disproportion between the duration of a narrated event and the length of text devoted to it, constituted a major part of the artfulness of telling. According to the Formalists, the more contrived and perceptible the form as such, and the more it dominates over the content, the better the art. In one of the most extreme formulations, proposed by Shklovskii, the subject matter is a mere excuse or carrier for displaying formal virtuosity. Shklovskii also felt one could classify and describe such procedures systematically, but it was not until Genette's landmark study that the task was accomplished.

Form as structure of expression

Having spoken at length about forms of content, I turn now to a striking example of formalism vis-à-vis forms of expression – namely, the work of Bakhtin, a Russian scholar who was a contemporary of the Formalists, and whose study of Dostoevskii, for example, arose in the formalist context. Bakhtin rebuked the formalists for failing to develop an adequate theory of forms of expression in narrative, analogous to the one they did formulate for lyric poetry. Whereas in poetry the basic unit of expression is indeed the word or line, as the formalists claimed, Bakhtin suggested that in narrative it is the utterance. Thus, for Bakhtin, narrative *fiction represents not a domain consisting of states, events, and agents but rather a linguistic activity or the interplay of *voices and their utterances. The form of a narrative is thus defined by the logico-semantic relations between the utterances of the different characters, and between their utterances and those of the *narrator. The dynamics of a narrative is accordingly defined not by actions, but by the changing interrelations between these utterances (*see* NARRATIVE DYNAMICS).

In his book on Dostoevskii, Bakhtin proposed a typology of the basic kinds of relations between utterances, which abstracts from any specific contents or themes (*see* DIALOGISM). He also distinguished between traditional narrative, where the narrator's utterances dominate those of the characters' and serve as the text's linguistic and ideological yardstick, and Dostoevskii's novels, in which the plurality of characters' voices is not encompassed in the narrator's superordinate one (*see* IDEOLOGY AND NARRATIVE; POLYPHONY).

Form as manner of representation

When dealing with any mimetic element, a formalist approach would be concerned not with its make up, but rather with how it is (re)presented, that is, with the technique or method used for its portrayal. The underlying assumption here is that in verbal art, no less than in pictorial art, a wide spectrum of options is available for this purpose (*see* PICTORIAL NARRATIVITY). A method of portrayal is defined by the particular selection of information items provided for a given mimetic element – say, a person's physical appearance, their proportion, and the manner of their combination.

On a higher level of abstraction, one can try to generalise from the techniques used for portraying individual items to some universal representational options, such as schematic or detailed, fragmentary or unified, illusionist or anti-illusionist, realistic or grotesque, and many dozens more, with most if not all of these terms being applicable to visual art as well. Such high-level characterisations can then be further associated with given periods or movements or regarded as timeless possibilities. On the highest level of generalisation, the Russian Formalists introduced *defamiliarisation as a general aesthetic and cognitive procedure manifested to one degree or another in all narrative methods of portrayal from antiquity to the present. Since defamiliarisation consists of making us aware of the 'artfulness' or constructedness of any mimetic element in artistic narrative, the formalists valued it highly, going sometimes so far as to proclaim it the essence of artistic method as a whole. The Formalists celebrated other, similar methods of (non) portrayal, e.g., introducing formal devices without any realistic motivation, and having a narrative expose its nature as formal game. Both procedures are widely employed in twentieth century experimental art, both visual and verbal, and find their culmination in the *postmodernist pursuit of form for its own sake.

References and further reading

Bakhtin, Mikhail (1984) *Problems of Dostoevsky's Poetics*, trans. Caryl Emerson, Minneapolis: University of Minnesota Press.
Beardsley, Monroe (1958) *Aesthetics*, New York: Harcourt, Brace & World.
Doležel, Lubomír (1990) *Occidental Poetics*, Lincoln: University of Nebraska Press.
Eikhenbaum, Boris (1974) 'How Gogol's "Overcoat" is Made', in Robert Maguire (ed.) *Gogol from the Twentieth Century*, Princeton: Princeton University Press.
Genette, Gérard (1980) *Narrative Discourse*, trans. Jane E. Lewin, Ithaca: Cornell University Press.
Jakobson, Roman (1987) 'Two Aspects of Language and Two Types of Aphasic Disturbances', in *Language in Literature*, Cambridge, Mass.: Harvard University Press.
Lodge, David (1977) *The Modes of Modern Writing*, London: Arnold.

Pettersson, Anders (2000) *Verbal Art*, Montreal: McGill-Queens University Press.

S., Viktor (1970 [1928]) *Material i stil' v romane L. N. Tolstogo Vojna i mir*, The Hague: Mouton.

—— (1990 [1929]) *Theory of Prose*, trans. Benjamin Sher, Elmwood Park: Dalkey Archive.

Tomashevskii, Boris (1965) 'Thematics', in Lee T. Lemon and Marion J. Reis (eds) *Russian Formalist Criticism*, Lincoln: University of Nebraska Press.

Walzel, Oskar (1923) *Gehalt und Gestalt im dichterischen Kunstwerk*, Berlin: Babelsberg.

URI MARGOLIN

FRAME THEORY

Conversational narratives are set off from their surround by frames. These frames may do other work in the story or the conversation but whatever else they do, they define the limits of *narrative. Books have frames, too, in the form, for instance, of their covers, but these frames are made of a different material than what they frame, while in conversational narrative, both the frame and the narrative are made of spoken language. Frames of written narrative like tables of contents or chapter headings work more like their conversational counterparts, from which they are probably derived (Tannen 1993). The framing of stories in conversation has been studied by scholars interested in conversation analysis, *sociolinguistics, narratology, and the theory of small group interaction (*see* COMMUNICATION STUDIES AND NARRATIVE; DISCOURSE ANALYSIS (LINGUISTICS)). These various approaches are assembled here under the aegis of *frame analysis*.

The term 'frame analysis' is Erving Goffman's, for whom the frame analysis of talk is a specific instance of our capacity to distinguish between 'the content of a current perception and the reality status we give to what is thus enclosed or bracketed within perception' (1974: 3). The 'brackets' he calls frames. Goffman explicitly takes the notion of bracketing or framing from *phenomenology. Frame theories taken from *Artificial Intelligence have also influenced narrative analysis (*see* COGNITIVE NARRATOLOGY; SCRIPTS AND SCHEMATA). Goffman was specifically interested in the frame analysis of 'strips' of activity, by which he meant assemblages of *events presented or taken as unitary phenomena by a perceiver (1974: 8). Part of the business of everyday life in general and of talk in particular is to put forward strips of doings or sayings as events of a certain ontological status.

How such acts and utterances get framed up is the subject of his analysis.

Much of talk consists of what Goffman called 'replays', representations of events in a narrative mode. Hearers of replays echo its double constitution by at some times immersing themselves in the realm of events the story is about *as if* that realm were real – crying when a *character dies, for instance, or being curious about what happened next (*see* IMMERSION; SUSPENSE AND SURPRISE) – and at other times attending to the narrative as discourse – evaluating the *performance or being sceptical about its claims to *truth. Thus the frame analysis of narrative involves the analysis not only of strips of discourse but also of the strips of activities to which the discourse refers (*see* STORY-DISCOURSE DISTINCTION).

The story frames strips of activities in the world of the tale, called variously the taleworld (Young 1986) or the *storyworld, by cutting out from an implicitly complete reality a sequence of events to be told. The narrative discourse that reports the story, called storyrealm by Young, is framed off from the conversation either by exhibiting its differences at its edges as a boundary or by locating indicators of its ontological status elsewhere. The conversation is framed as a 'subuniverse', in William James' term, in the realm of the ordinary (1950: 283–324). Events in the taleworld are thus framed by the storyrealm, which is framed by the conversation.

The frame analysis of conversational narrative focuses on the relationship between the story and the events it is about, on one side, and the story and the conversation in which it is told, on the other. Eight types of frames set stories off from their conversational surround on the pattern:

Conversation[Preface[Opening[Orientation [Beginning[Story]End]Closing]Evaluation]Coda] Conversation.

The innermost pair of frames, beginnings and ends, mark the edges of the strip of activities in the taleworld that is to be narrated. These are so consequentially related that, as narratologist Paul Ricoeur points out, beginnings could be said to entail ends (1980: 180). Thus beginnings and ends frame events for stories by imputing to events a consequentiality they may not natively possess (*see* CAUSALITY).

Just as beginnings and ends frame events for stories, so openings and closings frame stories for conversations. They consist of locutions, sometimes formulaic, that mark a shift of discourse from conversation to narrative. In so doing, they may also indicate narrative *genre. 'Once upon a time' and 'The end', for instance, frame stories as *folktales. Openings and closings such as 'I like the story about' and 'That's what I wanted to tell you' frame stories as conversational *anecdotes.

Whereas beginnings and ends are part of the taleworld, and openings and closings part of the storyrealm, prefaces and codas are part of the realm of conversation. Prefaces solicit permission to suspend turntaking in order to tell a story. Prefaces like 'I've got a great story for you' can also serve as what conversation analyst Harvey Sacks calls 'interest arousers' (Sacks 1992: 226). Codas reinstitute turntaking. According to Labov, they consist of descriptions of the aftermath of the events in the story (1972: 366). Codas like 'You can still see the remnants down in the wood' bring hearers back to the moment in the conversation at which they entered the narrative. Prefaces and codas thus create an enclosure in conversation for stories.

The orientation sections that typically precede stories provide hearers with information they will need in order to follow the story. In so doing, they direct hearers' attention from the conversation or the storytelling to the realm of events the story is about, framing that realm as a taleworld. Evaluations like 'Great story' or 'You must have felt terrible', which hearers produce at the end of a story, not only offer some sort of emotional response (Labov 1972: 366) but also frame the storyrealm or the taleworld as aesthetic object available for assessment.

Goffman's footing in interactional studies extended the analysis of conversational narratives beyond a special focus of discourse analysis to an aspect of the phenomenology of everyday life. Frame theory proposes that we inhabit 'multiple realities', in philosopher Alfred Schutz's phrase (1973: 245). We cross the threshold between one layer of reality and another with a little bump or shock (Schutz 1972: 254). These bumps are here characterised as frames. Some realities are looped inside others as enclaves in the ordinary, as stories are in conversations. Others hook the past and pull it into the present, as stories pull events into conversations. Frames are not only bumps in the topography of the real; they are also 'meta-communications', as Bateson puts it, about the ontological status of our experience of strips of activities or strips of discourse as stories.

SEE ALSO: communication in narrative; conversational storytelling; framed narrative; narrative transmission; sociolinguistic approaches to narrative

References and further reading

Bateson, Gregory (1972) *Steps to an Ecology of Mind*, New York: Ballantine Books.
Goffman, Erving (1974) *Frame Analysis*, New York: Harper Colophon.
James, William (1950) *Principles of Psychology*, vol. 2, New York: Dover.
Labov, William (1972) *Language in the Inner City*, Philadelphia: University of Pennsylvania Press.
Ricoeur, Paul (1984–88) 'Narrative Time', *Critical Inquiry*, 7.1, 169–90.
Sacks, Harvey (1992) *Lectures on Conversation*, ed. Gail Jefferson, Oxford: Blackwell.
Schutz, Alfred (1973) *On Phenomenology and Social Relations*, trans. Helmut R. Wagner, Chicago: University of Chicago Press.
Tannen, Deborah (ed.) (1993) *Framing in Discourse*, New York: Oxford University Press.
Young, Katharine (1986) *Taleworlds and Storyrealms: The Phenomenology of Narrative*, Dordrecht, The Netherlands: Martinus Nijhoff.

KATHARINE YOUNG

FRAMED NARRATIVE

Framed narratives occur in *narrative situations when *events are narrated by a *character other than the primary *narrator or when a character tells a tale that, although unrelated to the main story, contains a moral message for the listener in the text (see NARRATEE). The 'frame' metaphor likens its narrative effect to the aesthetic effect of the frame surrounding a painting (see FRAME THEORY), and complex instances are likened to 'Chinese Boxes' (story within story within story); however, a narrative frame usually functions transactively with the framed story, and spatial descriptions of framed narratives only partially represent the dynamic narrative transaction that occurs (see NARRATIVE DYNAMICS).

Commonly, framing occurs with simple *embedding or else the 'intercalating' of one narrative within another. Embedding refers to the narrative situation in which part of the main narrative or a significant *plot detail is displaced atemporally (see TEMPORAL ORDERING) to another location in the narration. Thus, flashbacks and other analeptic narratives are framed by the current moment of the narrative in which they are embedded. Intercalation occurs when the inset narrative is not directly related to the main narrative. Although intercalated narratives need to bear some *thematic relevance to the main narrative, these digressions defer the central plot line. A special case obtains for 'digressive intercalated apologues': narratives told by a character to provide the protagonist with a moral tale that will establish the context for a change in behaviour.

In *novels, framed narrative often occurs when an oral narrative is transcribed for the purpose of textual transmission (*see* ORALITY). However, despite transcriber promises of faithfulness to the original, the logical gap between oral *narration and its transcription within the framing narrative opens interpretive space for the reader to ask 'What has been left out of the transcription?', or 'What may have been changed?' The presence of an 'Editor' or character involved with the transmission of a framed text recontextualises that text (*see* NARRATIVE TRANSMISSION). Since framed texts are not usually written for the narratee identified by the framing 'narrative of transmission', such recontextualisation contributes to the aesthetic effect of the framed narrative by providing more than one layer of reception that the reader must negotiate, thereby defamiliarising the narrative act.

Narrative framing relates to the concept of diegetic levels (*see* DIEGESIS; NARRATIVE STRUCTURE). As each narrating act contains another narrating act, the diegetic level shifts from the initial extradiegetic level to an intradiegetic level of narration, to a metadiegetic level of narration, and beyond. The limit of diegetic narrative framing is set by the conditions of containment obtaining among the different narrations – as is illustrated in the case of Mary Shelley's *Frankenstein* in the diagram below.

In *Frankenstein*, Robert Walton narrates at an extradiegetic level in his journal, in which he transcribes the intradiegetic oral narration of Victor Frankenstein, who, in turn quotes the metadiegetic oral narration of the Creature he created (*see* QUOTATION THEORY). The Creature's narration frames yet another narrative level when he tells the history of the De Lacey family. The Creature's reporting of the De Lacey family history represents a virtual crossing of the narrating frame since, although based on the oral and epistolary narrations of the De Laceys, the narrative instance continues to obtain with the Creature. Spatially, these different narrations and narratives can be related as a series of embedded boxes.

A spatial representation of this sort, however, cannot account either for the finer details of embedding or for frame violations such as the Creature's meeting with Walton over Frankenstein's dead body (*see* METALEPSIS) or the Creature's copies of Safie's letters (which he gives to Victor to 'prove the truth' of his tale and which Victor, in turn, shows to Walton). Moreover, a simplified spatial representation cannot account adequately for temporal issues that accompany the narrating situations or the embedded narratives.

In *Frankenstein* the framing device also indicates a narrative contract between the teller and the listener. Stories are told in exchange for something else: in *Frankenstein*, a promise of revenge. This logic of exchange further connects the frame novel to the narrative of *desire, and the frame structure is particularly suited for the narrative of desire because, as Brooks (1984) observed, it resembles the psychoanalytic scene of the 'talking cure' (*see* PSYCHOANALYSIS AND NARRATIVE). The extradiegetic narrator plays the 'analyst', listening to the intradiegetic narrator's

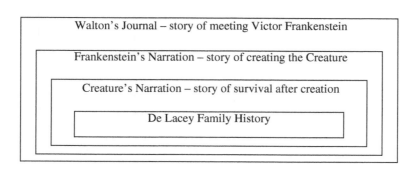

*life story – a telling that forces the 'patient' to re-examine his or her life, to reveal the repressed *trauma that can only be 'cured' by the patient confronting the traumatic event, now framed in narrative, and finally acknowledging that it is past (*see* IDENTITY AND NARRATIVE; NARRATIVE PSYCHOLOGY).

Framed novels of the sort described require a fully characterised extradiegetic narrator. Although this extradiegetic narrator might only minimally be a character in his or her own right, the role is critical as listener/transcriber/reader of the intradiegetic narration. Usually this extradiegetic narrator participates in a narrative of transmission that deconstructs the convention of suspended disbelief accompanying novels that claim some prior condition of textuality or *narrativity, as in fictions of a 'found manuscript' which now must be made public. The fiction of the manuscript is a thinly veiled *authenticating device that requires the Editor to provide a variety of framing *paratexts such as prefaces, notes, and afterwords designed to tell the story of discovery and to legitimise the text. *Epistolary, *diary, and many memoir novels – which stage the narrative discourse of a 'narrating self' framing the 'experiencing self' into a *post hoc* narrative – inevitably require an Editor to be inferred (even if only as an abstract agent) for a plausible logic of *narrative transmission. The private nature of *letters, diaries, and some memoirs necessitates an intermediary, who is always a part of the novel's narrating instance and whose paratexts must be interpreted as a part of the overall fiction of the text.

More problematic are 'historiodiegetic' paratexts (Duyfhuizen 1992): extrafictional frames placed by the author as an attempt to overdetermine the reader's experience of the text by insisting that the narrative is not *autobiographical but only a *fiction. Paradoxically, historiodiegetic paratexts that promote a text's fictionality undermine the various modes of narrative framing that seek to authenticate the framed narrative. Such frame violations reveal the device of framing to be a self-deconstructing play with the 'fiction of authenticity' the frame is deployed to establish. This double play also affects 'hybrid' narratives, constructed of multiple documents – letters, diaries, transcribed testimony, memoirs, even inset novels – that an extradiegetic narrator must piece together to frame a coherent narrative. Using narrative

framing both to authenticate and to put into question narrative transmission has been a novelistic feature at least since *Don Quixote* (*see* QUIXOTIC NOVEL).

SEE ALSO: communication in narrative

References and further reading

Bakhtin, Mikhail (1981) *The Dialogic Imagination*, trans. Caryl Emerson and Michael Holquist, ed. Michael Holquist, Austin: University of Texas Press.

Brooks, Peter (1984) *Reading for the Plot: Design and Intention in Narrative*, New York: Knopf.

Caws, Mary Ann (1985) *Reading Frames in Modern Fiction*, Princeton: Princeton University Press.

Chatman, Seymour (1978) *Story and Discourse: Narrative Structure in Fiction and Film*, Ithaca: Cornell University Press.

Duyfhuizen, Bernard (1992) *Narratives of Transmission*, Rutherford, NJ: Fairleigh Dickinson University Press.

Genette, Gérard (1980 [1972]) *Narrative Discourse: An Essay in Method*, trans. Jane Lewin, Ithaca: Cornell University Press.

—— (1997 [1987]) *Paratexts: Thresholds of Interpretation*, trans. Jane Lewin, Cambridge: Cambridge University Press.

Kestner, Joseph A. (1978) *The Spatiality of the Novel*, Detroit: Wayne State University Press.

Lanser, Susan (1981) *The Narrative Act: Point of View in Prose Fiction*, Princeton: Princeton University Press.

Newman, Beth (1986) 'Narratives of Seduction and the Seductions of Narrative: The Frame Structure in *Frankenstein*', *ELH*, 53, 141–63.

Ryan, Marie-Laure (2002 [1990]) 'Stacks, Frames, and Boundaries', in Brian Richardson (ed.) *Narrative Dynamics: Essays on Time, Plot, Closure, and Frames*, Columbus: Ohio State University Press.

BERNARD DUYFHUIZEN

FREE INDIRECT DISCOURSE

Free indirect discourse (FID) is a much-discussed form for representing *characters' speech or thought, known in French as *style indirect libre*, in German as *erlebte Rede*, and in English by a number of alternative names, including 'narrated monologue' (Cohn 1978). Intuition suggests that FID is related to direct and indirect forms of reporting speech and thought, though whether it can be derived in any rigorous way from these other forms is controversial. This relation is reflected in the following examples, based on a sentence from Joyce.

1   Direct discourse: He said, 'I will retire to the outhouse'.
2   Indirect discourse: He said that he would retire to the outhouse.
3   FID: He would retire to the outhouse.

FID is 'indirect' because it conforms in *person and *tense to the template of indirect discourse, but 'free' because it is not subordinated grammatically to a verb of saying or thinking ('He said that' etc.). Nothing about FID is uncontroversial, from its history and distribution to its putative function as a vehicle of *dual-voice discourse. In particular, it remains unclear whether FID is best characterised in terms of linguistic markers (aggressively argued by Banfield, 1982) or as readers' hypotheses about textual anomalies (as suggested by Ron, 1981); presumably both are involved.

SEE ALSO: speech representation; thought and consciousness representation (literature)

References and further reading

Banfield, Ann (1982) *Unspeakable Sentences: Narration and Representation in the Language of Fiction*, Boston: Routledge and Kegan Paul.
Cohn, Dorrit (1978) *Transparent Minds: Narrative Modes for Presenting Consciousness in Fiction*, Princeton: Princeton University Press.
Fludernik, Monika (1993) *The Fictions of Language and the Languages of Fiction: The Linguistic Representation of Speech and Consciousness*, London and New York: Routledge.
Ron, Moshe (1981) 'Free Indirect Discourse, Mimetic Language Games and the Subject of Fiction', *Poetics Today*, 2.2, 17--39.

BRIAN McHALE

FREQUENCY

Part of Genettean 'tense' theory, frequency analysis investigates the relationship between the number of times *events are inferred to have happened in the *storyworld and the number of times that they are narrated. There are three basic possibilities: events can be recounted 'singulatively' (telling once what happened once), 'repetitively' (telling several times what happened once) or 'iteratively' (telling once what happened many times). *See* TIME IN NARRATIVE.

FREYTAG'S TRIANGLE

Freytag's triangle (also known as 'Freytag's pyramid') is a simple *plot diagram which represents the action and *suspense structure of classical five-act tragedy (*see* DRAMA AND NARRATIVE). Originally proposed by the German playwright and critic Gustav Freytag (1816–1895) in a strongly normative study entitled *Die Technik des Dramas* (1863), the three points of a triangle are used to represent a play's introduction (A), climax (B), and catastrophe (C):

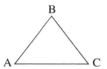

The introduction or *exposition (A) introduces characters, settings, and the initial state of affairs. The 'rising action' (AB) covers the protagonist's attempts to realise his or her goals and ambitions in the face of complications and obstacles (*see* CONFLICT). The climax or turning point (B) marks the highpoint of the protagonist's career and the beginning of his or her downfall. The falling action (BC), often accompanied by a strengthening of opposing forces, represents the protagonist's declining fortune and culminates in the catastrophe (C) of his or her death.

The schema is easily exemplified by Shakespeare's *Richard III*, a play famous for its symmetrical structure. Most of the exposition is accomplished in Richard's initial soliloquy (I.1). The stations of the rising action are marked by a series of intrigues that clear the protagonist's way to the throne. Richard's career reaches its climax when he is crowned king at the end of Act III. The falling action is heralded by the news of Richmond's rebel force, and the protagonist's catastrophe comes in the battle of Bosworth (Act V), where he is slain.

Refining this general schema, Freytag adds three 'moments': the 'inciting moment' that gets the rising action going (in *Richard III*, Richard's decision 'to prove a villain'), the 'tragic moment', anticipating the reversal (the defection of his ally, Buckingham, in IV.2), and 'the moment of final suspense' (not present in *Richard III*, but elsewhere an incident momentarily stopping the protagonist's fall and promising a happy ending). In his discussion of individual plays, Freytag freely redistributes points and moments along the action lines, draws overlapping triangles to represent multistrand plots, and adds local climaxes. Subsequent theorists have found it advisable to distinguish 'turning-point climaxes' (such as B) from 'high-emotion' or 'suspense climaxes' occurring anywhere along the axes. It is obvious that only a few modifications – particularly, reconceptualising the rising action as 'complication' and the falling action as 'resolution', plus replacing 'catastrophe' by *closure – suffice to turn Freytag's triangle into a general model of *narrative progression identifying a *narrative universal across cultures, *media, and *genres. Variations of the model include *story grammar definitions of episode structure and *'story arc' and 'character arc' conceptions. Other theorists, recognising the triangle's masculinist *ideology, have argued the case for emancipatory narrative forms foregrounding open-ended and climax-deferring structures like those found in the work of dramatist Caryl Churchill or in *écriture féminine; they have also stressed the need for developing narratological concepts capable of registering these structures (cf. Winnett 1990 and see FEMINIST NARRATOLOGY).

References and further reading

Freytag, Gustav (1983 [1863]) *Die Technik des Dramas*, Stuttgart: Reclam.

Pfister, Manfred (1988) *The Theory and Analysis of Drama*, Cambridge: Cambridge University Press.

Winnett, Susan (1990) 'Coming Unstrung: Women, Men, Narrative, and Principles of Pleasure', *PMLA*, 105.3, 505–18.

MANFRED JAHN

FUNCTION (JAKOBSON)

Six functions of language were identified by the Russian-born American linguist Roman Jakobson (1896–1982), each corresponding to one of the six factors of verbal communication. The six factors are the addresser, the addressee, the context (or 'world of reference') (*see* REFERENCE), the code in which the message is encoded, the channel of contact between addresser and addressee, and the message itself. Corresponding to the addresser is the 'expressive' function; to the addressee, the 'conative' function; to the context, the 'referential'

function; to the code, the 'metalingual' function; to the channel, the 'phatic' function; and to the message itself, the 'poetic' function. All six functions are performed by every communicative act, but in each case one of the six dominates, transforming the others and orienting them in a characteristic way. For example, expletives are dominated by the expressive function, imperatives by the conative function, factual texts by the referential function, glosses and clarifications by the metalingual function, casual greetings by the phatic function, and verbal art by the poetic function. Texts dominated by the poetic function continue to express, address, refer, etc., but all these other functions are subordinated to the text's 'focus on the message for its own sake'.

Jakobson's notion of the functional 'dominant' provides the basis for a typology of *genres in terms of functional hierarchy, e.g., in a classic *realist novel, the referential function ranks second after the poetic function, but in a novel of social protest the conative function ranks second, while in a *metafiction it is the metalingual function. It also captures the dynamics of literary-historical change from one period to the next, which rarely involves the disappearance of one set of elements and their replacement by new ones, but more typically arises from a reshuffling of the hierarchy of functions, i.e., a shift of dominant, as in the transition from *modernist to *postmodernist narrative (McHale 1987).

Reservations have sometimes been voiced concerning the authoritarian and coercive implications of Jakobson's concept of the dominant (Jefferson 1990). These may be partly answered by pointing to Jakobson's pluralistic understanding of this concept. Evidently the same text may be characterised in terms of different dominants depending upon the level, scope, and focus of the analysis. As a work of verbal art, it may be characterised by the poetic dominant; as an example of verse by one of the historically variable dominants of verse (meter, rhyme, intonation); as a text belonging to a particular period by its period's dominant; etc.

Moreover, nothing prevents one's reading a text 'against the grain' of its functional hierarchy. With the passage of time, many referential, expressive, conative, and metalingual texts (histories, memoirs, *letters, speeches, philosophical texts) have come to be read as literary, i.e., dominated by the poetic function. Conversely, a literary text can be read as a historical, biographical or psychological document, or in terms of its *reception, i.e., referentially, expressively, or conatively.

References and further reading

Jakobson, Roman (1960) 'Closing Statement: Linguistics and Poetics', in Thomas Sebeok (ed.) *Style in Language*, Cambridge, MA: MIT Press.
—— (1987 [1935]) 'The Dominant', in *Language and Literature*, Cambridge, Mass.: Harvard University Press.
Jefferson, Ann (1990) 'Literariness, Dominance and Violence in Formalist Aesthetics', in Peter Collier and Helga Geyer-Ryan (eds) *Literary Theory Today*, Ithaca: Cornell University Press.
McHale, Brian (1987) 'From Modernist to Postmodern Fiction: Change of Dominant', in *Postmodernist Fiction*, New York and London: Methuen.

BRIAN McHALE

FUNCTION (PROPP)

A function is defined by Propp as 'an act of a character, defined from the point of view of its significance for the course of the action' in a narrative (*see* CHARACTER). The concept is developed in Propp's 1928 book *Morphology of the Folktale*, in which he analyses a series of 100 Russian *fairy tales and determines that all fairy tales share a single structure. Examples of functions are 'an interdiction is addressed to the hero', 'the hero reacts to the actions of the future donor', or 'the villain is punished'. Within functions, characters play seven types of role: hero, villain, donor, helper, dispatcher, sought-for person, and false hero. The system allows a restricted accumulation of roles by the same character; the sought-for person will for instance act as donor if she gives a magical agent to the hero. Propp isolates thirty-one core functions that constitute the fundamental components common to every fairy tale. Further, Propp concludes that the sequence of functions has its own laws and always follows in the same order: 'Theft cannot take place before the door is forced'. While not every function occurs in every tale, 'the absence of certain functions does not change the order of the rest'.

Propp's brilliant and original assertion that the multiplicity of a hundred fairy tales can be reduced to a single structure is widely recognised as a key moment in the development of structuralism (*see* STRUCTURALIST NARRATOLOGY). Few subsequent theorists have accepted all of Propp's conclusions literally, however, and Bremond and Verrier have shown in detailed analyses of examples from his corpus of fairy tales that Propp's theory does not satisfactorily account for the very texts he set out to explain. Several critics have noted that the sequence of functions appears to be more flexible than Propp believed, and many have contested the number of core functions. Several attempts have been made to refine his model and to extend it to other *genres and periods. Kafalenos, for example, proposes a more abstract eleven-function model that represents 'the fundamental stages of the narrative sequence, from the disruption of an equilibrium to the establishment of a new equilibrium'. Greimas's influential revision of Propp bundles a reduced set of functions together and assigns them to six *actants. But despite recent scepticism about Propp's applications of his method, his concepts of functions and sequences have proven of durable value and continue to generate considerable theoretical interest.

SEE ALSO: dramatic situations; folktale

References and further reading

Barthes, Roland (1977) 'Introduction to the Structural Analysis of Narrative', *Image-Music-Text*, trans. Stephen Heath, New York: Hill and Wang.
Bremond, Claude (1980) 'The Logic of Narrative Possibilities', *New Literary History*, 11, 387–411.
——, and Jean Verrier (1984) 'Afanasiev and Propp', trans. Thomas G. Pavel and Marylin Randall, *Style*, 18, 177–95.
Greimas, Algirdas Julien (1983) *Structural Semantics: An Attempt at a Method*, trans. Daniele McDowell, Ronald Schleifer, and Alan Velie, Lincoln: University of Nebraska Press.
Kafalenos, Emma (1997) 'Functions after Propp: Words to Talk about How We Read Narrative', *Poetics Today*, 18, 469–94.
Propp, Vladimir (1968 [1928]) *Morphology of the Folktale*, trans. Laurence Scott, revised by Louis A. Wagner, Austin: University of Texas Press.
—— (2002 [1928]) 'Fairy tale Transformations', trans. C.H. Severens, in Brian Richardson (ed.) *Narrative Dynamics: Essays on Time, Plot, Closure, and Frames*, Columbus: The Ohio State University Press.

WILLIAM NELLES

G

GAPPING

Texts do not supply all the information needed for their interpretation. Furthermore, the more widely agreed upon any specific information is, the more likely it is to go without saying (Perelman and Olbrechts-Tyteca 1969: 8). As a series of philosophers, literary theorists, and cognitive scientists have shown, a satisfying interpretation of a narrative sequence emerges from the interactions or joint work of a text and an *audience (*see* READER-RESPONSE THEORY). In the presence of a gappy text (and all texts are gappy), if there is no evidence to the contrary, audiences assume that a communication is intended. Culler called this assumption the rule of signification (1975: 115); Grice, the cooperative principle (1975: 45); Simon Baron-Cohen, the Theory of Mind. On the strength of this assumption audiences mobilise a variety of cognitive abilities in combination with a large amount of linguistic, social, and cultural information, allowing them to complete perceived patterns, making sense of them in context (*see* SCRIPTS AND SCHE-MATA). Although it is generally assumed that it is the text that evokes this pattern, the reader merely completing it, it has not been easy to assess the balance of power between the text and the audience: who has the last word? If a text's generativity is in principle unlimited, can an individual's understanding of a text or the extent of its influence ever be fully articulated? These questions remain open. (See the work of Jacques Derrida, Ray Jackendoff, and Stanley Cavell).

Ever since the phenomenologist Roman Ingarden (1973 [1937]) argued that literary texts require their audiences to provide information to disambiguate and fill in the text's points of *indeterminacy, literary theorists, philosophers, and cognitive scientists have been interested in this joint activity of meaning making. Wolfgang Iser was among the first literary theorists to perceive the productivity of this dynamic approach to literary study. Throughout the 1970s and 80s, critics worked to describe what information or systems of rules (grammars) readers activate in response to literary texts (Stanley Fish, Jonathan Culler, Ellen Schauber and Ellen Spolsky), and what might prompt appropriate information to be brought forth (H. R. Jauss, Wolfgang Iser, Paul Grice, John Searle, Mary Louise Pratt, and Norman Holland). Some of these studies were particularly concerned to recognise not only what Bleich had earlier on called the 'communal negotiation of knowledge' (1978: 102), but also the balances or imbalances of power within specific historical contexts, especially as these ideological forces influence the interpretive field (Harold Bloom, Hayden White, Meir Sternberg, Stephen Orgel, Stephen Greenblatt, Sacvan Bercovitch, and Myra Jehlen). In the last decade of the twentieth century, cognitive scientists and cognitive literary theorists began to investigate what brain mechanisms might underlie the ability to complete the patterns a narrative adumbrates in a way that provides a satisfying interpretation (Mark Turner, Raymond Gibbs, Jr.), and how those evolved brain mechanisms do their work within the local constraints of culture (Andy Clark, Ellen Spolsky, Alan Richardson, Mary Thomas Crane).

SEE ALSO: cognitive narratology; narrative comprehension; pragmatics; psychological approaches to narrative; reader constructs; situation model

References and further reading

Bleich, David (1978) *Subjective Criticism*, Baltimore: Johns Hopkins University Press.

Clark, Andy (1997) *Being There: Putting Brain, Body, and World Together Again*, Cambridge: MIT Press.

Culler, Jonathan (1975) *Structuralist Poetics: Structuralism, Linguistics and the Study of Literature*, Ithaca, NY: Cornell University Press.

Grice, H. Paul (1975) 'Logic and Conversation', in Peter Cole and Jerry L. Morgan (eds) *Syntax and Semantics*, Vol III: Speech Acts, New York: Academic Press.

Ingarden, Roman (1973 [1937]) *The Cognition of the Literary Work of Art*, trans. Ruth Ann Crowly and Kenneth R. Olsen, Evanston: Northwestern University Press.

Iser, Wolfgang (1978) *The Act of Reading: A Theory of Aesthetic Response*, Baltimore: Johns Hopkins University Press.

Perelman, Chaim, and Lucie Olbrechts-Tyteca (1969) *The New Rhetoric: A Treatise on Argumentation*, trans. John Wilkinson and Purcell Weaver, Notre Dame: University of Notre Dame Press.

Schauber, Ellen, and Ellen Spolsky (1986) *The Bounds of Interpretation: Linguistic Theory and Literary Text*, Stanford: Stanford University Press.

Spolsky, Ellen (1993) *Gaps in Nature: Literary Interpretation and the Modular Mind*, Albany: SUNY Press.

ELLEN SPOLSKY

GAZE

'The gaze' refers to the representation of the act of looking. Originating in *psychoanalysis, the gaze came into narrative theory through feminist film criticism. Grounded in the *perspective of the consciousness through which a narrative's *point of view is focused, the gaze frames the object of *narration. A technical equivalent is *focalization, but the gaze carries connotations of *gender.

The study of the gaze began as an investigation of the ways women are objectified in narrative. In 1975, Laura Mulvey subversively adapted Freudian thinking about castration to show how the camera in classical Hollywood film figuratively mutilates and fetishises women's bodies. Feminist narratologists have drawn upon Mulvey's model, often to show how female *authors grant subjectivity to women *characters and *narrators. For example, Beth Newman (1990) demonstrates how *Wuthering Heights* puts female characters in a position to return the male gaze; Elizabeth Meese (1992) considers the exchange of gazes between lesbians in narrative. Sometimes called the glance,

the 'female gaze' revises the form and the function of its 'male' counterpart.

SEE ALSO: feminist narratology; film narrative

References and further reading

Meese, Elizabeth (1992) 'When Virginia Looked at Vita, What Did She See', *Feminist Studies*, 18, 99–117.

Mulvey, Laura (1975) 'Visual Pleasure and Narrative Cinema', *Screen*, 16, 6–18.

Newman, Beth (1990) 'The Situation of the Looker-On: Gender, Narration, and Gaze in *Wuthering Heights*', *PMLA*, 105, 1029–41.

ROBYN WARHOL

GENDER STUDIES

Although the study of formal and structural aspects of narratives has never been one of the principal aims of gender studies (*see* FORMALISM; NARRATIVE STRUCTURES), there are a number of gender-conscious approaches to narrative theory which have contributed to a 'gendering' of literary analyses. Proceeding from the assumption that gender is a highly relevant category for any study of narrative, feminist literary critics of diverse theoretical affiliations as well as critics working in the broader field of gender studies have suggested ways of combining formal and structural analyses with a focus on gender-related issues. The various gender-conscious approaches to narrative, which differ in terms of their conceptualisation of gender (as well as sex and sexuality), have shown that there is no aspect of narrative that can be conceived of as gender-neutral: not only do the production and reception of texts intersect with issues of gender (*see* READER-RESPONSE THEORY), narrative strategies and narrative agents are also influenced by gender and may even be said to produce gender (*see* AGENCY; NARRATIVE TECHNIQUES).

Gender studies vs. women's studies

As an *interdisciplinary project rather than a discipline in its own right, gender studies explore the meanings of gender across diverse segments of culture. This approach, which emerged in the course of the 1980s and has since become highly influential, especially in the Anglo-American academic context, is in many respects indebted to the older interdisciplinary field of women's studies.

There has always been a considerable degree of overlap between gender studies and women's studies, since these areas of research share a number of concerns as well as the basic assumption that gender is an organising principle of culture and society (*see* CULTURAL STUDIES APPROACHES TO NARRATIVE). Yet, though the boundary between the two fields is undeniably blurred in many individual publications, gender studies and women's studies still differ significantly both in terms of their scope and with respect to some of their theoretical premises. In contrast to women's studies and feminism, which prioritise the female point of view in order to correct the traditional neglect of women's concerns, gender studies strive for a broader approach to the relation between culture and gender (*see* ETHNOGRAPHIC APPROACHES TO NARRATIVE). This tendency has, for example, led to the rise of the study of masculinities as a prolific branch of gender studies. In particular, gender studies seek to overcome the limited perspective associated with strands of feminism that maintain the significance of binary gender differences or propagate gynocentric views such as the emphasis on supposedly feminine values and ethics (*see* ETHICAL TURN). Traditionally, women's studies and feminism have, moreover, tended to postulate a given and comparatively unified female subject that is at the centre of a political agenda, while gender studies, adhering to a strictly anti-essentialist stance, focus on the conceptualisation of gender as a culturally and socially constructed and thus historically variable category (*see* DISCOURSE ANALYSIS (FOUCAULT); IDEOLOGY AND NARRATIVE).

Central categories of analysis

Since their beginnings, gender studies have witnessed some major reconceptualisations. The term 'gender' was originally borrowed from grammar to distinguish biological differences between male and female bodies (sex) from socio-culturally constructed attributions of meaning to sexed bodies and the behavioural expectations resulting from those ascriptions (gender). Gender studies are thus based on the central assumption that the differences between masculinity and femininity are not causally linked to biological characteristics.

While gender has accordingly been conceived of as subject to cultural and historical change, sex continued to be treated as a given. Since the early 1990s, however, the stability of the category 'sex', which was previously taken for granted, has also been questioned. In particular, Judith Butler's influential writings have challenged previous conceptions of sex, claiming that sex is also a socially, discursively produced construct rather than a pre-discursive fact, in other words, 'a gendered category' itself (Butler 1990: 7). According to Butler and other theoreticians in the field, neither sex nor gender is ever produced once and for all; rather, they are constantly created anew in ongoing performative acts (*see* PERFORMATIVITY). Another factor that has increasingly been taken into account by gender studies is sexuality. Sexuality relates to both psychological and material phenomena, i.e. to erotic *desires and to a person's sexed being (Bristow 1997), and intersects with the categories sex and gender in the process of the construction of subjectivity and identity (*see* IDENTITY AND NARRATIVE; QUEER THEORY). Within gender studies the three central categories gender, sex, and sexuality are further complicated by the enterprise of conceptualising them in terms of their interaction with factors such as class, race, and ethnicity. The investigation of the manifold ways in which the power relations in a society are determined by these interrelating factors has opened up a fruitful dialogue between gender studies and post-colonial studies (*see* POST-COLONIALISM AND NARRATIVE).

Given the fact that narratives – both literary and non-literary – are among the prime sites of the cultural construction of gender, sex, and sexuality, it follows that gender studies encompass a number of approaches which focus specifically on the relationship between narratives and gender-related issues. What these different approaches have in common is that they link texts with social practices and ideologies, thus exploring the influence of cultural, social, and historical factors associated with gender, sex, and sexuality on formal aspects of narrative. Since the mid-1990s, gender studies have made significant forays into what used to be the domain of feminist literary criticism. In many respects, the branch of gender studies that is dedicated to the study of narratives draws upon and continues earlier feminist work whilst at the same time striving to transcend and question the more limited outlook characteristic of feminist criticism (*see* FEMINIST NARRATOLOGY). In order to gain a synoptic perspective on gender-oriented approaches to narrative, however, one must begin by situating attempts to establish a gendered poetics of narrative in the wider context of feminist literary studies.

Early (feminist) gender-conscious approaches to narrative

Although feminist literary criticism in general has tended to focus more on matters of content than on structural or formal aspects of narrative texts, a number of works within feminist studies have made a significant contribution to a gender-conscious narrative theory. Up to the mid-1980s the structural features that were critically reassessed from a feminist point of view were invariably elements of the story level (*see* STORY-DISCOURSE DISTINCTION). *Plot patterns in particular have been examined by a number of feminist critics. The groundbreaking studies falling into this category, which include Molly Hite's *The Other Side of the Story* (1989) and Nancy K. Miller's *The Heroine's Text* (1980), seek to show that women's writing is characterised not only by its content, but also by how these stories are narrated. In *Writing Beyond the Ending* (1985) Rachel Blau DuPlessis contends that up to the beginning of the twentieth century, feminocentric stories could end only in one of two events – either the female *character's marriage or her death. Feminist *modernist and *postmodernist writers, however, developed a number of alternative endings for their female characters (*see* CLOSURE), thus circumventing the limitations inherent in traditional plot patterns (*see* PLOT TYPES). Studies of women's *autobiographies also claim that gender is an important factor in the analysis of narrative structures. Such studies conceptualise narrative strategies in women's autobiographies as attempts to find a female *voice and to define women's identity. Relating autobiographical *narrativisations of identity to the writer's gender, they argue that narrative structures tend to correspond to an opposition between female and male identities. Thus, a range of fragmented, disjunctive narrative structures is seen as reflecting female identity, which is considered to be generally more fragmentary and more discontinuous than the male self as a result of the specific socio-cultural coordinates of women's lives.

A close link between gender and narrative structures is also postulated by those approaches that are usually subsumed under the label of 'French feminism'. In contrast to Anglo-American feminism, which has always tended to pay particular attention to social and historical contexts, French feminism, influenced by poststructuralism, focuses on textual structures (*see* POSTSTRUCTURALIST APPROACHES TO NARRATIVE). Concepts like Hélène Cixous's *écriture féminine or Luce Irigaray's *parler femme* are based on the assumption that feminine identity can be expressed, explored, even unleashed in a type of writing that defies androcentric constraints by opting for strategies such as non-linearity, non-teleology, and the fragmentation of narratives or deviation from grammatical rules. Although French feminism has frequently been accused of propagating essentialist positions, *écriture féminine* is in fact a concept that is not limited to female writers. Cixous cites a number of male-authored texts as prime examples of feminine writing, thus conceptualising narrative structures as gendered but not as inherently linked to sex.

Gender and reading

The relationship between the reception of texts (*see* RECEPTION THEORY) and gender has been one of the major concerns of feminist and gender-centred approaches in literary criticism since the onset of second-wave feminism. In her study *The Resisting Reader* (1978) Judith Fetterley, for example, examines how androcentric texts in the American literary canon encourage female readers to identify with the privileged masculine point of view. To avoid this identification, an act of resistance on the part of the female reader is required. This already indicates that the conceptualisation of reading as a gendered activity is complicated by the insight that women raised in patriarchal societies have traditionally been taught to read 'as men', which contradicts the assumption that differences in the reception process can be straightforwardly attributed to the recipient's gender. Whereas Jonathan Culler has used a poststructuralism-inspired argument about the always-deferred nature of experience to question the very idea of 'reading as a woman', critics such as Elaine Showalter assign a greater role to gender-specific experience. According to Showalter, the problematic link between femaleness and a given position can be resolved by replacing the phrase 'reading as a woman' by 'reading as a feminist' (*see* READER-RESPONSE THEORY).

Gendered narratology

The most concerted attempt to establish gender as a central category of analysis in narrative theory has become known as feminist narratology. In contrast to the study of autobiography and theories of reading, which have developed independently of classical narratology, the origin of this theory is directly linked to a critical reassessment of *structuralist narratology (*see* POST-CLASSICAL NARRATOLOGY). Indeed, the focus of feminist narratology is consciously transgressive in that this theory has sought to take into account the very different premises, methodologies, and concerns of feminist literary theory and traditional narratology. The designation 'feminist narratology', which was coined by Susan S. Lanser in her pathbreaking article 'Toward a Feminist Narratology' (1986), does not do full justice to the orientation toward a gendered view of narratology that has become particularly pronounced since the late 1990s (even though the tendency was already present *in nuce* in a number of earlier studies). In fact, feminist narratologists themselves have often used terms such as 'gendered poetics' (Lanser), 'the engendering of narratology' (Lanser), or 'the genderization of narrative' (Fludernik) to refer to their branch of narrative theory, thus highlighting the centrality of gender rather than a specifically feminist perspective. By means of an extensive critique of the gender-blindness of structuralist narrative theory, feminist narratology has shown that, far from generating 'objective' analyses of texts, the disregard for questions of gender in fact promotes a privileged attention to narrative strategies employed by male writers. Rejecting a supposedly gender-neutral approach, feminist narratology emphasises that gender is a decisive aspect not only of the story but also of the discourse; that is to say, gender is important not only for the 'what' but also for the 'how' of *narration.

One of the central insights provided by a gender-conscious narratology is the observation that readers almost invariably attribute sex and gender to *narrators. A number of studies (Schabert 1992; Lanser 1999; Fludernik 1999) have shown how the sex and gender of narrators – and, more recently, of *narratees (*see* AUDIENCE) – whose sex is not indicated explicitly in the text are constructed on the basis of textual markers, cultural clues, and readers' knowledge about the *author's sex his/her previously published texts, and so on (*see* PARATEXT).

Even supposedly gender-neutral heterodiegetic narrators are thus routinely gendered by readers. The endeavour of gendered narratology is not limited to establishing gender as a narratological category, however, but also includes the consideration of what consequences a gendered interpretation of narrative agents might have for the overall meaning attributed to the text.

In addition to gendering the instances involved in the process of narrative mediation, feminist narratologists have adopted the concept of gender to describe specific narrative strategies. Within feminist narratology, there are two distinct ways of using the term 'gendered narrative strategy': (1) Robyn Warhol's (1989) differentiation between distancing and engaging narratorial interventions in Victorian *novels, which links the 'gender' of the narrative strategies of heterodiegetic narrators to the sex of their authors, and (2) Alison Case's (1999) notion of feminine narration, i.e., the illusion created in eighteenth- and nineteenth-century novels that homodiegetic female narrators' activities are limited to an unformed rendering of their own experience, which ties the gender of the narrative strategy to the sex of the narrator, irrespective of the author's sex. These two contrastive uses of the concept of a gendered narrative strategy can be accounted for by taking into consideration the difference in the default gender markings of heterodiegetic and homodiegetic narrators, with the former being normatively unmarked for sex and the latter being usually both sexed and gendered (cf. Lanser 1999).

From the late 1990s onwards: recent development

Since the late 1990s feminist narratology has increasingly opted for a more inclusive gender-conscious orientation. This shift has made itself felt in a number of ways. (1) While earlier feminist narratological studies generally focused on literary texts by women writers, publications since the late 1990s have begun to call for an exploration of the dynamics of gender construction in both male-authored and female-authored texts. (2) Some gender-oriented approaches to narrative theory move beyond literary narratives and include narratives in other *media, such as the *soap opera (Warhol 1999) or *film (Lanser 1999) – a tendency that correlates with the broader cultural orientation of gender studies as opposed to the more limited scope of traditional feminist narratology. (3) Since the late 1990s, studies in feminist/gender narratology increasingly emphasise the dynamic construction of gender provoked by narratives and take into account both textual strategies and variables of the reception process. Warhol (1999, 2001), for example, conceptualises gender as a 'textual effect' rather than as a pre-existing condition of the reception process. (4) Gender-oriented narratological studies are venturing more and more beyond the focus on the category gender to include sex and sexuality, thus seeking to align themselves with the ongoing diversification of coordinates considered relevant within the broader field of gender studies. In a number of publications, most clearly perhaps in 'Sexing Narratology: Toward a Gendered Poetics of Narrative Voice' (1999), Lanser suggests that feminist narrative theory tends to lag behind state-of-the-art feminist theory and gender studies. In particular, she advocates the integration of sex as a formal category into a poetics of narrative (Lanser 1999: 168). The development of gender-conscious approaches to narratology since the late 1990s has shown that the task of combining narrative theory and gender studies is still an ongoing project. Thus, for the foreseeable future, it seems likely that narrative theory will continue to be influenced by the evolving concerns of gender theory and feminist theory.

References and further reading

Allrath, Gaby (2000) 'A Survey of the Theory, History, and New Areas of Research of Feminist Narratology', *Literatur in Wissenschaft und Unterricht*, 33.4, 387–410.

Bristow, Joseph (1997) *Sexuality*, London: Routledge.

Butler, Judith (1990) *Gender Trouble: Feminism and the Subversion of Identity*, London: Routledge.

Case, Alison (1999) *Plotting Women: Gender and Narration in the Eighteenth and Nineteenth Century British Novel*, Charlottesville: University Press of Virginia.

DuPlessis, Rachel Blau (1985) *Writing beyond the Ending: Narrative Strategies of Twentieth-Century Women Writers*, Bloomington, IN: Indiana University Press.

Fetterley, Judith (1978) *The Resisting Reader: A Feminist Approach to American Fiction*, Bloomington, IN: Indiana University Press.

Fludernik, Monika (1999) 'The Genderization of Narrative', *GRAAT*, 21, 153–75.

Hite, Molly (1989) *The Other Side of the Story: Structures and Strategies of Contemporary Feminist Narrative*, Ithaca, NY: Cornell University Press.

Lanser, Susan (1986) 'Toward a Feminist Narratology', *Style*, 20.1, 341–63.

——(1999) 'Sexing Narratology: Toward a Gendered Poetics of Narrative Voice', in Walter Grünzweig and Andreas Solbach (eds) *Grenzüberschreitungen: Narratologie im Kontext/Transcending Boundaries: Narratology in Context*, Tübingen: Narr.

Miller, Nancy K. (1980) *The Heroine's Text: Readings in the French and English Novel, 1722–1782*, New York: Columbia University Press.

Schabert, Ina (1992) 'The Authorial Mind and the Question of Gender', in Elmar Lehmann and Bernd Lenz (eds) *Telling Stories: Studies in Honour of Ulrich Broich on the Occasion of his 60th Birthday*, Amsterdam: Grüner.

Warhol, Robyn R. (1989) *Gendered Interventions: Narrative Discourse in the Victorian Novel*, New Brunswick: Rutgers University Press.

——(1999) 'Guilty Cravings: What Feminist Narratology Can Do for Cultural Studies', in David Herman (ed.) *Narratologies: New Perspectives on Narrative Analysis*, Columbus: Ohio State University Press.

——(2001) 'How Narration Produces Gender: Femininity as Affect and Effect in Alice Walker's *The Colour Purple*', *Narrative*, 9.2, 182–87.

GABY ALLRATH AND MARION GYMNICH

GENEALOGY

In his 1887 book *Zur Genealogie der Moral* (*On the Genealogy of Morals*), Friedrich Nietzsche used the term 'genealogy' to designate a mode of historico-philosophical inquiry, which was later reinvigorated by Michel Foucault in such works as 'Nietzsche, Genealogy, History' (1984 [1971]). In this usage, genealogy is a mode of investigation that works to uncover forgotten interconnections, re-establish obscured or unacknowledged lines of descent, and expose family resemblances between institutions, belief-systems, practices, and discourses that might otherwise be viewed as wholly distinct. By the same token, countering interpretations which appeal to structures, norms, or practices that stand above nature and history, the genealogist aims to show that those norms and practices are in fact the expression of someone's pragmatic interest (Hill 1998), and are grounded in the particularities of human *conflict. Hence, the project of the genealogist is to frame a narrative about how modes of thought and conduct, assumed to be timelessly valid or 'objective' and hence unaffected by specific human endeavours, have in fact served to promote the interests of one group over another. In this way, genealogy seeks to denaturalise 'the contingent [social, institutional, discursive, or other] structures we mistakenly consider given, solid, and extending without change into the future as well as into the past' (Nehamas 1986: 110).

References and further reading

Foucault, Michel (1984 [1971]) 'Nietzsche, Genealogy, History', in Paul Rabinow (ed.) *The Foucault Reader*, New York: Pantheon Books.

Hill, R. Kevin (1998) 'Genealogy', in Edward Craig (ed.) *The Routledge Encyclopedia of Philosophy*, vol. 4, London: Routledge.

Nehamas, Alexander (1986) *Nietzsche: Life as Literature*, Cambridge, Mass.: Harvard University Press.

Nietzsche, Friedrich (1968 [1887]) *On the Genealogy of Morals*, trans. Walter Kaufmann, in Walter Kaufmann (ed.) *Basic Writings of Nietzsche*, New York: The Modern Library.

DAVID HERMAN

GENRE FICTION

This is a term for mass-market entertainment fiction, formerly published in inexpensive pulp-paper magazines (hence the synonym 'pulp fiction'), but now typically marketed in paperback format; it is also called 'formula fiction' and *Trivialliteratur*. *Genre fiction* is actually a misnomer insofar as it implies that some varieties of fiction are bound by genre formulas, but not others. In a sense, all fiction is genre fiction; nevertheless, some varieties do depend more heavily than others on shared conventions, and cater more openly to the expectations of readers familiar with these conventions.

A rough indicator of current genre categories is the labelling system of bookstore shelves: mystery, *science fiction and *fantasy, *horror, *romance, occasionally Westerns and erotica (see PORNO-GRAPHIC NARRATIVE), rarely *historical fiction (which typically is shelved with general fiction). Each of these umbrella categories actually subsumes a number of distinguishable genres or sub-genres; thus, for example, 'mystery' includes mystery fiction as such, but also *detective fiction and crime fiction, which in turn includes the sub-genre of police procedural fiction, and so on (Malmgren 2001). Sub-genres proliferate, largely in response to the market's hunger for novelty, but also partly as an unfolding of a genre's internal logic or in response to changing historical circumstances (or

all three at once). For example, the spy novel, which arose between the World Wars and thrived during the Cold War, is largely moribund today, its niche occupied by the techno-thriller.

Different genres tend to foreground different aspects of narrative poetics, and thus to engage different areas of narrative theory. Science fiction, for example, foregrounds world-building, so its distinctive features are perhaps best captured through a *possible-worlds approach to narrative (Malmgren 1991). By contrast, mystery and detective fiction foreground the displacement of discourse (sjuzhet) relative to story (fabula) and the opening and filling of narrative gaps (see GAPPING), and so are best approached by way of the *story-discourse distinction. Romance is distinguished by its construction of a mainly female readership, and in the uses that its readers make of the genre in their everyday lives, aspects which have been approached successfully from the perspective of *reader-response theory (Radway 1984).

Genre fiction plays a crucial role in literary evolution, as the *Russian Formalist critics recognised when they identified the phenomenon of the 'elevation of the cadet branch', that is, the recycling of 'low' genres as 'high' literature (Tynyanov 2000 [1924]), a process that has regularly refreshed mainstream fiction with 'pulp' motifs and conventions. Genre fiction is also of great relevance to *media theorists because of its affiliation with the dominant genres of movie, *television, *comics, and video-game narratives (see COMPUTER GAMES AND NARRATIVE; FILM NARRATIVE).

SEE ALSO: genre theory in film studies; genre theory in narrative studies

References and further reading

Cawelti, John G. (1975) *Adventure, Mystery and Romance*, Chicago: University of Chicago Press.

Malmgren, Carl D. (1991) *Worlds Apart: Narratology of Science Fiction*, Bloomington: Indiana University Press.

—— (2001) *Anatomy of Murder: Mystery, Detective, and Crime Fiction*, Bowling Green, OH: Bowling Green State University Popular Press.

Radway, Janice A. (1984) *Reading the Romance: Women, Patriarchy, and Popular Literature*, Chapel Hill: University of North Carolina Press.

Tynyanov, Yury (2000 [1924]) 'The Literary Fact', trans. Ann Shukman, in David Duff (ed.) *Modern Genre Theory*, Harlow: Longman.

BRIAN McHALE

GENRE THEORY IN FILM STUDIES

Classical Hollywood cinema has been described as a cinema of stars and genres. A film genre is a flexible and shifting category based upon a body of conventions including narrative conventions intuitively shared by the *audience and filmmakers. Film theorists appeal to various narrative models in characterising the popular story formulas shaping film production. David Bordwell has emphasised a linear structure that features a tight causal linkage motivating the action from one scene to the next at an accelerating pace; this structure is typical of action-adventure films (*see* CAUSALITY). Rick Altman, in contrast, argues for multifocalization of the genre narrative, by focusing on competing couples, parallel plot lines, or pauses in development for *spectacle events, qualities that are evident in the musical.

For their part, Bordwell and Kristin Thompson highlight generic motivation in film narrative generally. Particular films often motivate action merely from the expectations generated by genre convention: for example, breaking into song and dance in the musical or the sudden appearance of an alien in *science fiction film. No doubt the intertextual conventions of genres allow filmmakers to build narratives around patterns that have satisfied audiences in the past (*see* INTERTEXTUALITY).

The central narrative concept of genre theory in film studies is the master *plot, a series of typical events linked into a causal progression that establishes the conventions of a particular genre's story. The master plot will be larger than most fictions in the genre, and individual films will select from, vary, or add to the routine formula, but the master plot incorporates the general story expectations of the spectator and often supplies background information assumed by any particular film (*see* READER-RESPONSE THEORY; SCRIPTS AND SCHEMATA). There are frequently a few prominent master-plot patterns within a genre. For example, Rick Altman identifies the *'fairy tale', the 'show', and the 'folk' as three plot variations marking the musical film; Noël Carroll posits the discovery, the complex discovery, and the overreacher plots for *horror; others have identified the rise and fall pattern of the gangster tale (*see* PLOT TYPES).

Following Vladimir Propp's study of the *folktale, analysts frequently break the genre's master plot into a series of moves detailing development.

Susan Sontag breaks down the 1950s science fiction film into five basic steps; Leger Grindon posits ten events that characterise the boxing film. Carroll finds four basic functions in the horror film – onset, discovery, confirmation, and confrontation – and offers over a dozen variations on these primary functions.

The underlying causes driving the genre narratives are conflicts that arise from the unresolved problems marking the society that produces them. Following Claude Lévi-Strauss and his study of myths, commentators argue that the repetition characterising film genres is similar to retelling myths in the oral tradition (*see* MYTH: THEORETICAL APPROACHES; ORALITY). Each genre portrays a persistent social problem as a dramatic *conflict and each retelling presents the opportunity for an imaginative resolution from a fresh perspective. Though the resolution may offer only temporary relief from anxiety provoked by this problem, the persistence and depth of the conflict guarantee that more films will offer additional solutions, and an audience will continue to be attracted to the subject because it portrays a compelling and widely shared experience. The resolution of this conflict, or its decline in the social consciousness, will likely contribute to the fading of a genre's popularity. For example, the conflicts between freedom in nature versus the constraints of settlement in the Western do not seem as pressing for the contemporary audience as the conflict between technological power and personal identity found in the science fiction film.

Two perspectives have arisen in regard to the myth model that finds a compelling social problem underlying the master plot of a genre: the ritual and the ideological approach. The ritual approach (Schatz 1981) emphasises the experience of confronting the conflict and successfully bringing it to a resolution, however unconvincing, as a means of allaying the anxiety of the audience. This approach identifies audience satisfaction as the root cause of genres' popularity, suggesting that audiences desire to deal with the social conflict motivating the genre. It also assumes that film genres are based on an earnest intent to address the motivating conflict. On the other hand, the ideological approach (Wood 1979) finds in the designs of the film industry, or other agents of social domination, an attempt to subdue the audience by distorting the nature and causes of the prevailing social conflict and deceiving the audience into believing in a simplistic and ineffective resolution of the problem. From this perspective film genres function as a means of social control. Altman has suggested that stable, long-standing genres may enjoy an extended popularity when the audience desire for ritual satisfaction intersects with the ideological drive for social control.

Altman's concept of the 'generic crossroads' illustrates how both factors, ritual and ideology, can function in the same film. The generic crossroads arises throughout the plot when the protagonist must choose between a culturally sanctioned option and the alternative that produces generic pleasure. Usually the protagonist will choose the subversive option, guaranteeing generic pleasure until the conclusion, when prevailing values are reinforced and the audience is eased back into familiar social values. For example, in *The Godfather*, Michael Corleone must decide whether he is going to remain the respectable member of his family or participate in avenging the attack on his father. Michael chooses vengeance and murders Solozzo and McClusky. The gangster's typical choice of violence and its rewards gives the audience generic pleasure – until the conclusion, during which the gangster's downfall returns the audience to a reassuring sense of culturally sanctioned values. So at the end of *The Godfather*, Michael dominates the underworld, but has destroyed the family he was fighting to preserve. The generic crossroads allows the audience to enjoy the ritual satisfaction of overcoming social problems (in the case of *The Godfather*, that of assuring personal justice in a corrupt society), while at the same time reinforcing traditional family values that support the prevailing ideology. Furthermore, the generic pleasure offered by the film may not provide the viewers with a viable solution to the underlying problem, but only an elusive source of satisfaction that distracts the audience from thinking through the conflict in a more effective manner.

SEE ALSO: film narrative; genre theory in narrative studies; horizon of expectation; ideology and narrative

References and further reading

Altman, Rick (1999) *Film/Genre*, London: British Film Institute.
Bordwell, David (1985) *Narration in the Fiction Film*, Madison: University of Wisconsin Press.
Carroll, Noël (1990) *The Philosophy of Horror*, London: Routledge.
Neale, Steve (2000) *Genre and Hollywood*, London: Routledge.
Schatz, Thomas (1981) *Hollywood Genres*, New York: Random House.
Wood, Robin (1979) 'An Introduction to the American Horror Film', in Andrew Britton, Richard Lippe, Tony Williams, and Robin Wood (eds) *The American Nightmare: Essays on the Horror Film*, Toronto: Festival of Festivals.

LEGER GRINDON

GENRE THEORY IN NARRATIVE STUDIES

Genre theory reflects one of the fundamental realities of human cognition and communication: we understand and refer to phenomena by comparing them to existing categories and if necessary by modifying the categories or creating new ones. This theory studies the kinds of texts: their defining features, their production (by individuals, groups, institutions, and cultures), their processing (by individuals and *audiences), and their *reception (as a social, cultural, ideological, and historical phenomenon). To place a text in a genre category is immediately to interpret the category in terms of a theory about genre; it is to make assumptions about a text's production, processing, or reception, or some combination of these, and it reflects and reinforces a range of interpretive practices, from the normally unconscious (such as applying the language's rules of syntax or perceiving experience through ideological screens) to the most highly conscious (such as evaluating the text's quality and purpose). The key assumption of the genre theorist is that these practices both depend on and influence the type of text that is produced and the various categories to which a text may be assigned. To approach a text as *narrative is to implement expectations about point, *narrative progression or transformation, *actants, and *narrator (*see* NARRATIVITY; TELLABILITY); in fact, any text containing a sequence of *events invites these expectations.

History of genre theory

Genre theory began with Aristotle, who built on Plato's distinction between imitation and description and thus went far beyond the Greek practice of classifying poetry mainly by its metrical form. Defining imitation as the fundamental characteristic of all art, Aristotle distinguished three literary types – *epic, lyric, and dramatic (*see* DRAMA AND NARRATIVE) – according to the means of imitation (melody, language, rhythm), the objects imitated (humans idealised, parodied, or rendered naturalistically), and the manner of imitation (*narration or dramatic presentation). Imitation, according to Aristotle, is a natural human instinct, as is the susceptibility to rhythm and melody.

While Aristotle was mainly interested in scientifically describing the range of possible literary types, later genre theorists, influenced by Horace, added a strong prescriptive element, especially in the debate over the relative value of literature and non-literature and of types within the category of literature. Through the Renaissance and into the nineteenth-century, the study of genre followed Aristotle's focus on literary genres, distinguishing among these genres and describing the generic antecedents of individual works by noting formal features (e.g., verb *tense, verse form), occasion, and degree of *mimesis. Literary narrative, like all other art forms, was understood to be defined by its quality of imitation (that is, it was fictional rather than historically true), with human action, represented through *characters and *plot, being the object imitated (*see* FICTION, THEORIES OF). The nineteenth-century distinction between *novel and *romance was essentially the Aristotelian distinction between humans rendered naturalistically and humans idealised.

In the seventeenth and eighteenth centuries, however, the actual practice of writers began to call into question the classificatory and genealogical activities of the Aristotelian tradition and the prescriptivism of the Horatian. By parodying and blending (or hybridising) genres (*see* HYBRID GENRES), especially by incorporating forms such as the *letter and the *diary that were not traditionally thought of as fulfilling the Aristotelian criterion of imitation, novelists problematised the use of mimesis and formal features to distinguish among genres. By claiming to present *truths, they undermined another long-standing distinction, that between entertainment and moral edification. The Aristotelian tracing of genealogies among texts or types was also made more difficult by the explosion of the publishing industry, which put writers more in the service of market demands and

to a certain extent decreased the power of the conservative, genre-focused literary establishment. In fact the rise of the novel both as a recognised, although ill-defined, literary type and as a significant player in the publishing economy also contributed to the blurring of the fundamental Aristotelian criterion of imitation as the chief characteristic of a work of art.

Genre theory in the twentieth century

In the twentieth century, partly to deal with this much more complex literary universe and partly to accommodate the argument of linguists and structuralists that the distinction between literature and non-literature cannot be defended on formal grounds, genre theorists moved beyond the formalist, taxonomic approach and developed a functionalist approach, which includes all naturally occurring forms (usually termed speech genres or discourse modes) and the various functions they serve for individuals, groups, and societies (*see* DISCOURSE ANALYSIS (LINGUISTICS); FORMALISM; FUNCTION (JAKOBSON)). This approach has some claim to being more inclusive and more fundamental than that derived from Aristotle, because it incorporates the discourse forms found in spontaneous, everyday language use as well as those used in other non-literary contexts such as instruction manuals, news reports, directories, and textbooks. On the other hand, the formalist approach to genre in the twentieth century actually provided additional tools for describing the textual differences among forms and for identifying possible but highly unusual or non-existent forms, such as a narrative cast in future tense. These benefits significantly complement the functionalist approach.

One such benefit has been to refine the term 'genre'. Genette (1992) provides a distinction, especially helpful for narrative studies, between 'linguistic modes' or 'natural forms', whose study belongs to *pragmatics, and 'genres' as 'properly literary categories' (64). According to this distinction, narrative discourse is best characterised as a linguistic *mode that can be used in any literary genre (71). The distinction is complemented by the 'law of genre' expressed by Derrida: 'Every text participates in one or several genres, there is no genreless text; there is always a genre and genres, yet such participation never amounts to belonging. And not because of an abundant overflowing or a free, anarchic and unclassifiable productivity, but because of the *trait* of participation itself, because of the effect of the code and of the generic mark' (1980: 230; *see* CODES FOR READING). Derrida is making two points with this law. First, to participate in a genre is at the same time to imply or evoke the boundaries between this genre and others, boundaries that are established in the very act of participation itself; the result of participation is never a state of belonging that leaves behind the act of participation. Second, texts do not participate in genres within a vacuum but are placed in them by humans applying codes and reading for genre marks. The law of genre holds equally for natural forms and literary forms, although it probably tends to function more on an automatic or preconscious level for the former.

Genette's and Derrida's points are well illustrated by Manuel Puig's *El beso de la mujer arana* (*The Kiss of the Spiderwoman*) (1976). This book-length prose fiction is marketed (and taught) as a novel; however, most of the text is set up as narrator-less *dialogue, so that formally it has more similarity with a play. Genette would say that to term the text 'a narrative' could obscure the various ways that narrative actually functions within the text. Similarly, Derrida's law requires that a careful reader recognise the several genres in which the text participates as well as the reader's own role in establishing that participation. The more complex understanding of genre articulated by Genette, Derrida, Todorov (1990), and Fowler (1982), among other recent theorists, is consistent with narratologists' broadening of their investigative focus to include all possible instances of narrative and the shaping of these instances by economics, culture, and *ideology. This new focus frees the narratologist studying Puig's text to explore how a reader might construct a narrative from the dialogue, how narratives function both within and outside of the dialogue, and how the politics of *gender influence and are in turn influenced by the novel's narrative elements.

The hermeneutic circle, genre theory, and narrative studies

Implicit in Derrida's law and prominent in much twentieth-century genre theory is the hermeneutic circle of interpretation, by which a whole is understood in terms of its parts while the parts are understood in terms of the whole. For genre theory, the circle encompasses typologies and the examples which both illustrate and shape those typologies. *Hermeneutics, as both theory and method, disallows the privileging of any one perspective: not functions, not sociological or psychological laws, not even the basic components of a language, are allowed wholly to govern analysis. For genre theory, this means that distinctions among types can never be absolute and will always reflect a specific theoretical orientation.

At least three claims have been made for according to narrative a special status as an object of study, although none of these claims violates hermeneutics' proscription against foundationalist methods. First, narrative serves certain essential functions for human beings, such as organising a set of events according to chronology and tell-ability in order to facilitate the understanding of those events (*see* TEMPORAL ORDERING). We experience these functions because they manifest themselves through types of texts whose members resemble one another as do family members – comic book, *autobiography, film noir, classic western, and so forth (*see* COMICS AND GRAPHIC NOVEL). Second, the narrative discourse mode (like some other speech genres and some literary genres, rhyming verse, for example) is learned at the same time and probably in the same way as a first language is learned, which means that language users display the same innate competence in using narrative as they display in using their native tongue's lexicon, syntax, and semantics. Third, cultures have historically privileged some literary genres, and these privileged genres in turn tend to support the dominant culture and ideology; narrative is probably the most powerful and most prominent component of the *myths, *legends, national *epics and so forth playing this role. The novel, for example, a literary genre, became popular in England at the same time the middle-class was becoming powerful and was originally a significant medium for transmitting the middle-class ideology of materialism.

The more complex, nuanced, and flexible understanding of genres that has resulted from the functionalist approach, from the theorising of the hermeneutic circle, and from the definition of genre itself parallels and reinforces a similar enrichment of narrative studies. Instead of differentiating types in absolute terms by formal features, theorists are now more likely to arrange them along various continua, both formal and functional, frequently placing specific literary and non-literary types closer to each other than to other types from the same general category. This recognition of family resemblance across the (now problematised) boundary between literature and non-literature especially applies to the many types which make use of narrative. A conventional prose autobiography might be formally indistinguishable from a fictional homodiegetic narrative in prose, whereas the latter differs formally and experientially from a fictional narrative in blank verse, such as Robert Browning's *The Ring and the Book* (1868), and from a *film with *voice-over narration such as *American Beauty* (1999).

Genre theory and the production, processing, and reception of narrative

The relationship between genre theory and narrative studies plays out in the vectors of production, processing, and reception, which can be isolated, albeit artificially, for purposes of analysis. Within the production vector, a practical understanding of how individuals use language would dictate that genres guide and constrain but do not wholly shape expression. A genre's conventions constitute a range of choices for the language user, including the choice to parody, ironise, or evade the choices themselves (*see* IRONY). Two important constraints on choice have been articulated within narrative studies. From the cognitivist perspective, insofar as narrative constituents, structures, and functions are grounded in universal human experience or cognitive processes, they are more difficult to control than are the components of a literary genre. (Some cognitivists would go so far as to say that the constituents are 'hard wired' into the human brain and thus cannot be controlled.) From a *cultural studies perspective, a culture's *master narratives and myths, because they constitute part of the basic equipment with which producers of texts view the world, are seen as especially likely to appear within and even to control texts containing narrative. Ideology also influences the relationship between gender and genre within the production vector. The patriarchal publishing industry in England and America was served for several centuries by social strictures against women's coming before a reading public in their own persons, rather than as personae, and by the legal and social impediments to women's owning the products of their labour. The relatively high market value of the genres making use of narrative motivated the industry to control writers and their products.

Genre theory generally insists that conventions dominate the processing vector – how an individual interacts with a text. Some of this processing will tend to occur automatically, but a variety of conditions including textual features, a particular reader's predilections, and the immediate context may cause a reader to pay more conscious attention to the conventions of genre. The target audience of mass-market classic westerns will draw fairly automatically on expectations, strategies, and rules having to do with the essential components of narrative, with the conventions of the genre (such as historical setting), and with elements of the culture's ideology that the genre reinforces (such as crime punished, virtue rewarded, heterosexual love valued). However, readers of Doctorow's novel *Welcome to Hard Times* (1960) will experience a challenge to and thus will be made more aware of conventions such as the showdown between good and evil. The same can be said of any readers of Robbe-Grillet's *Les gommes* (1953) whose expectations have been shaped by mass-market *detective fiction. Narrative theorists must rely on generic or modal categorisations in order to study this shifting boundary between automatic and reflective processing. It would be impossible to analyse the processing of a text without entering the hermeneutic circle, because humans understand phenomena by comparing types.

The same can be said for the vector of reception – a text's interaction with the culture in which it is produced or is being purveyed. As codes, genres contribute to the institutional, ideological, and cultural factors influencing reception. The principle of genre as it manifests itself in a cultural context – that certain behaviours and attitudes are expected in the presence of certain text-types – is transmitted by a society's institutions. The marketing of books offers a good example of how reception is now understood: the category within which a new book is marketed is probably second only to the author's name in determining how that book will be talked about and read, and for an *author whose name is not already a commodity, clear generic identity is essential to commercial success. Generic identity is established within a context of conventions that precedes but may be altered by the advent of the text. However, many narrative theorists argue that narrative is the most wide-reaching and powerful type of discourse: it is the most effective tool by which an ideology preserves and strengthens itself as well as the most effective component of a revolution against an ideology. This argument is based on the principle that a culture's ideology is most effectively organised and transmitted through narratives. The commercial success of recent popular studies such as Hawking's *A Brief History of Time* (1988) and Greene's *The Elegant Universe* (1999) is almost certainly due in part to their *narrative structure and more particularly to the master narrative of progress that both reinforce.

Future directions for genre theory in narrative studies

The same elements that influence reception – ideology, economics, contextualisation cues, inferences, and so forth – are of course also important in the production and processing of texts. A writer's production of a text may be shaped by his/her awareness that the text will be received by publishers with certain expectations about the commercial viability of its genre; these expectations probably reflect the culture's ideology and probably are based on a conservative sense of generic conventions, whether or not the publishers accept or are willing to challenge ideology and conventions. Because of narrative's importance to the transmission and reinforcement of ideology and because the processing of narrative has been so carefully studied, narrative may constitute the richest field for developing and testing a poetics of genre, and this poetics in turn will continue to contribute to narratology. That narrative functions as a mode (a natural type) has been fairly well established, but the details of that function remain to be worked out for the many genres (literary and everyday) in which it participates. Much work also remains to be done in applying to the teaching of narrative the key insight of recent genre theory: that narrative, rather than being just another name for literary types such as 'short story', 'romance', and 'novel', should instead be understood both as a natural way of using language in order to achieve certain ends and as a component of many genres.

SEE ALSO: genre fiction; genre theory in film studies; sociological approaches to literary narrative; text-type approach to narrative

References and further reading

Culler, Jonathan (1975) *Structuralist Poetics: Structuralism, Linguistics, and the Study of Literature*, London: Routledge and Kegan Paul.
Derrida, Jacques (1980) 'The Law of Genre', trans. Avital Ronell, *Glyph*, 7, 202–32.
Duff, David (ed.) (2000) *Modern Genre Theory*, Harlow, England: Longman.
Fowler, Alastair (1982) *Kinds of Literature: An Introduction to the Theory of Genres and Modes*, Cambridge, Mass.: Harvard University Press.
Genette, Gérard (1992) *The Architext: An Introduction*, trans. Jane E. Lewin, Berkeley: University of California Press.
Glyph 7 (1980): special issue on genre.
Hirsch, E. D., Jr. (1967) *Validity in Interpretation*, New Haven and London: Yale University Press.
Jauss, Hans Robert (1982) *Toward an Aesthetic of Reception*, trans. Timothy Bahti, Minneapolis: University of Minnesota Press.
Perloff, Marjorie (ed.) (1989) *Postmodern Genres*, Norman: University of Oklahoma Press.
Poetics 10 (1981), nos. 2 and 3: special issues on genre theory, ed. Marie-Laure Ryan.
Todorov, Tzvetan (1990) *Genres in Discourse*, trans. Catherine Porter, Cambridge: Cambridge University Press.

MICHAEL KEARNS

GESTURE

The term 'gesture', as used here, refers to the visible bodily actions – especially of the hands and arms, but also of the face and head – that humans use expressively in face-to-face interactions, accompanying speech, including narrative *speech acts. Gestures are co-produced with, and are co-expressive with, speech; they serve as partners with speaking in communicative performance, strategically deployed in the construction and conveyance of meaning (Kendon 2001). (Other types of gesture exist, including pantomime and emblems (e.g., the OK sign); these are not necessarily associated with speech, and are excluded from the present discussion.)

Gestures play important roles in spoken narratives, providing expressive means for denoting aspects of the *storyworld that may be difficult or impossible to convey in words (Kendon 2001). They can be frequent: McNeill suggests a general rule of one gesture per clause; however, their frequency varies enormously according to *narrator, narrative, *narrative situation, and culture. Gestures tend to coincide with unexpected information, at peaks of communicative dynamism, e.g., with the introduction of new *characters (McNeill 1992; Levy and Fowler 2000). While gestures are typically produced by narrators, *audiences can also be active gesturers; gestures thus play a role in the collaborative enterprise of jointly constructing narrative (Gullberg 2003; Kendon 2001; *see* COMMUNICATION IN NARRATIVE).

McNeill proposes a correlation between gesture types and three levels or frames (*see* FRAME ANALYSIS): narrative, metanarrative, and paranarrative. (These types are contentious (Kendon 2001), as are McNeill's assignment of clauses and gestures to frames.) The narrative frame is constituted by expressions representing the storyworld. Associated gestures are iconic or deictic (*see* DEIXIS). Iconic gestures depict some aspect of the described *event or some entity in it (*see* EXISTENT) – e.g., a person swinging on a rope could be represented by a gesture tracing out an arc with one hand. Deictic (pointing) gestures have a referential function: the linguistic expression introducing a character into a narrative might be accompanied by a deictic gesture localising the referent in interactive space (*see* REFERENCE; SPACE IN NARRATIVE). The referent can subsequently be invoked by a deictic gesture indexing that location (McNeill 1992; McNeill, Cassell, and Levy 1993; Gullberg 2003).

The metanarrative frame concerns the organisation of the narrative as a text, including the narrator's means of identifying parts of its structure. Accompanying gestures are deictic (e.g., pointing to places in the space in front of the speaker associated with aspects of the *plot) or metaphoric, representing an image of (a part of) the narrative as an abstract entity (*see* METAPHOR). The following fragment, quoted in McNeill (1992: 198), includes a metaphoric gesture given in narrating a Sylvester and Tweety cartoon; it represents the narrator as conveyor of an object, the upcoming narrative episode, simultaneously denoted by the accompanying words.

and ... of course the next development in the plot is

[Metaphoric gesture, timed with utterance of 'develop-': both hands present object to listener]

Also associated with the metanarrative frame are beats, small baton-like rhythmic movements of the hand or fingers. Beats index the accompanying word or phrase as particularly significant semantically and narratologically; for instance, beats often mark the beginning of new episodes (*see* NARRATIVE UNITS).

The paranarrative frame concerns the construal of the narrative interaction itself as an interpersonal event, and is constituted by the projection by narrators of their own *voice to the audience. Gestures associated with this frame are more restricted – metaphoric and iconic gestures never (or rarely) occur – and include just beats and deictic gestures pointing to a speech interactant; *gaze also plays a prominent role (Goodwin and Goodwin 1992).

*Time is crucial to event development in narrative; space is just as central, and gesture is an important *semiotic resource deployed by narrators in constructing spatial relations. The shared interactive space between the narrator and addressees is typically used to stand for storyworld space, and gestures relating to this shared space represent storyworld spatial relations. In English, narrators often represent spatial configurations such as 'in (to)' and 'out (of)' by gestures depicting movement into or out of the shared interactive space (Özyürek 2000).

In many *Australian Aboriginal cultures both iconic and deictic gestures in narratives are absolutely rather than relativistically oriented, preserving the cardinal orientations of the storyworld. Thus, Haviland reports how a Guugu Yimithirr narrator oriented absolutely an iconic gesture depicting a boat capsizing in an east-west direction; this orientation was maintained over narrations separated by several years, even though the speaker was facing in different cardinal directions. The narrator shortly afterwards performed a deictic gesture indicating the location of the coast, some 3.5 miles away from the capsized boat, by indicating a direction to the south-west from the current location of the narrator. Both gestures involve a shift of deictic centre: storyworld space is represented as though shifted to the deictic centre of interactive space. Haviland also documents how a Zinacantec Tzotzil narrator employed absolutely oriented gestures, even though explicit directional terms are rarely used in that language, and the spoken narrative contained hardly any references to cardinal directions.

Not only do gestures serve communicative functions, but they have important cognitive functions as well, such as facilitating the organisation of information in a way suitable for linguistic expression (Kita 2000; see also McNeill 1992: 245). A narrative interaction conducted in the absence of visual contact between the interlocutors, e.g., over the telephone, would normally be accompanied by gestures, the primary motivation for which would be cognitive. More interestingly, Gullberg argues that both cognitive and communicative considerations underlie over-use of certain types of deictic gesture in the narratives of second language learners.

Research in a wider variety of languages and cultures is required before we can be certain of the extent to which the correlations between gesture types and narrative frames obtains, and the extent to which gestures can differ in nature, function, and the use they make of interactive space (see Kita, Danziger, and Stolz 2001).

SEE ALSO: discourse analysis (linguistics), ethnographic approaches to narrative; pragmatics; psychological approaches to narrative

References and further reading

Goodwin, Charles, and Marjorie Goodwin (1992) 'Context, Activity and Participation', in Peter Auer and Aldo di Luzo (eds) *The Contextualization of Language*, Amsterdam: Benjamins.

Gullberg, Marianne (2003) 'Gestures, Referents, and Anaphoric Linkage in Learner Varieties', in Christine Dimroth and Marianne Starren (eds) *Information Structure, Linguistic Structure and the Dynamics of Language Acquisition*, Amsterdam: Benjamins.

Haviland, John (2000) 'Pointing, Gesture Spaces, and Mental Maps', in David McNeill (ed.) *Language and Gesture*, Cambridge: Cambridge University Press.

Kendon, Adam (2001) 'Gesture as Communication Strategy', *Semiotica*, 135, 191–209.

Kita, Sotaro (2000) 'How Representational Gestures Help Speaking', in David McNeill (ed.) *Language and Gesture*, Cambridge: Cambridge University Press.

——, Eve Danziger, and Christel Stolz (2001) 'Cultural Specificity of Spatial Schemas, as Manifested in Spontaneous Gestures', in Merideth Gattis (ed.) *Spatial Schemas and Abstract Thought*, Cambridge, Mass.: MIT Press.

Levy, Elena, and Carol Fowler (2000) 'The Role of Gestures and other Graded Language Forms in the Grounding of Reference in Perception', in David McNeill (ed.) *Language and Gesture*, Cambridge: Cambridge University Press.

McNeill, David (1992) *Hand and Mind: What Gestures Reveal about Thought*, Chicago: Chicago University Press.

——, Justine Cassell, and Elena Levy (1993) 'Abstract Deixis', *Semiotica*, 95, 5–19.

Özyürek, Asli (2000) 'The Influence of Addressee Location on Spatial Language and Representational Gestures of Direction', in David McNeill (ed.) *Language and Gesture*, Cambridge: Cambridge University Press.

WILLIAM McGREGOR

GOSSIP

Gossip is a communicative practice widely engaged in, but often discounted as idle, trivial, or immoral. It is a label for informal, personal talk that, occurring among people who know each other fairly well, concerns other people not present, and insists on its own frivolity. The narrative quality of gossip arises from the way gossipers interpret fragmentary knowledge about people and *events and project it in the form of tellable stories (Spacks 1985) (*see* NARRATIVITY; TELLABILITY). Moreover, it is characterised by a reduction of complex issues, motivations and behaviour, an uncertain *truth status, and rich use of telling detail.

Historically, gossip referred to a person who can become a godparent (OE *god-sib*), then to a drinking companion. Over time it became associated with women's speech, referring to women present at a birth and, starting in the nineteenth-century, to idle talk especially among women, acquiring a pejorative meaning in the process. The themes of gossip are mostly transgressions of social norms, making gossip a site where these norms are maintained and negotiated and participation in it becomes a sign of social membership. Its manifold motivations as entertainment, information, and influence (Rosnow and Fine 1976) serve individual as well as community needs (e.g., information and impression management, the projection and venting of aggression, social control, and maintenance of social boundaries). The distinction between gossip and rumour is a gradual one, gossip having a smaller scope and a more personal nature. Some feminist scholars attribute gossip to a female, domestic sphere, rumour to a male, public sphere. Ultimately, it is the conjunction of context, theme, and speaker's attitude which determines whether talk is considered gossip.

Creating stories from fragments of people's lives is pleasurable, entertaining, and empowering and at the same time a violation of trust and potentially harmful to the targets of gossip. This ambiguity marks it as 'discreet indiscretion' (Bergmann 1993 [1987]) because private confidential information is passed on selectively. Since gossip both conforms to social norms and subverts them through its vicarious enjoyment of transgressions, it is highly ambivalent. Literary uses of gossip (e.g., by Sterne, Austen, Hawthorne, Morrison, Erdrich) draw on this ambivalence and use it thematically and formally. In fiction, gossip can serve as a signifier of social *realism, similar to the use of dialect (*see* SPEECH REPRESENTATION). Writers use its association with oral culture and with women's speech, its unreliability (particularly in the case of gossipy *narrators), its status as a discourse of familiarity on the one hand or as illegitimate discourse on the other. Since gossip is largely made up of words of others (repeating what others said), it can be used as a tool for multiperspectival *narration (*see* PERSPECTIVE). Some feminist scholars have attempted to positively re-evaluate gossip as female speech (a form of 'genderlect') and alternative epistemology, and in organisation theory gossip has been re-evaluated as a discourse that builds skill and solidarity.

SEE ALSO: conversational storytelling; dialogism; gender studies; orality; reliability

References and further reading

Bergmann, Jörg (1993 [1987]) *Discreet Indiscretions: The Social Organization of Gossip*, trans. J. Bednarz, New York: de Gruyter.
Goodman, Robert, and Aaron Ben Ze'ev (eds) (1994) *Good Gossip*, Lawrence, KS: University of Kansas Press.
Goodwin, Marjorie Harness (1990) *He-Said-She-Said: Talk as Social Organization among Black Children*, Bloomington: Indiana University Press.
Rosnow, Ralph L., and Gary Alan Fine (1976) *Rumor and Gossip: The Social Psychology of Hearsay*, New York: Elsevier.
Spacks, Patricia (1985) *Gossip*, New York: Knopf.
Tebutt, Melanie (1995) *Woman's Talk? A Social History of Gossip in Working-Class Neighbourhoods, 1880–1960*, Aldershot/Hants: Scolar Press.

ESTHER FRITSCH

GOTHIC NOVEL

The Gothic *novel is a literary *genre that flourished in the late eighteenth- and early nineteenth-centuries. The Gothic, however, is also a mode of writing stretching through centuries, cultures, and geographical locations. In both forms, it is a literature of fear and nightmare which shows special interest in the underside of humanity: the evil within the psyche and the disintegration of subjectivity.

The term 'Gothic' was originally used in a derogative sense to emphasise the genre's spiritual links with the barbarism, superstition, and irrationality associated with the Middle Ages. Horace Walpole's *The Castle of Otranto: A Gothic Story* (1764), the first specimen of the genre, draws on predecessors like the sentimental novel and graveyard poetry of the eighteenth-century. It challenges the neoclassical ideals of unity, coherence, and order – ideals cherished by the Enlightenment in general. Walpole's story of revenge establishes the most characteristic conventions of the genre; these conventions pertain to setting (haunted castle), *character (monomaniac villain, heroine-in-distress), and *plot (curse, transgression of taboos, significance of supernatural phenomena).

The Gothic achieves its peak of popularity in the 1790s with the publication of works as diverse as William Godwin's political *Caleb Williams* (1794), Matthew Gregory Lewis's *pornographic *The Monk* (1796), Mary Wollstonecraft's feminist *Maria and the Wrongs of Woman* (1798), and, especially, Ann Radcliffe's *romances. In *The Mysteries of Udolpho* (1794) and her other novels, Radcliffe launches the Female Gothic, an alternative tradition to Walpole's Male Gothic. Radcliffe innovates on the genre by proposing rational explanations of supernatural events, by providing elaborate descriptions of sublime landscapes, and by focusing on the struggles of the heroine-in-flight.

In the nineteenth-century, the Gothic responds to the contemporary anxieties surrounding the fast-developing natural sciences with the introduction of characters like the mad scientist (Mary Shelley's *Frankenstein, or, the Modern Prometheus*, 1818), vampires (Bram Stoker's *Dracula*, 1897), alter egos and doubles (Edgar Allan Poe's tales of terror; Oscar Wilde's *The Picture of Dorian Gray*, 1891; Henry James's *The Turn of the Screw*, 1898). While earlier works isolated good and bad qualities in separate characters, now the battlefield between opposing poles is relocated within a single character, thus reflecting on the confusingly heterogeneous and unfathomable nature of the self in the face of scientific rationality. This is how the genre can explore issues like the assimilation of socio-cultural anxieties, the transgression of socially sanctioned norms of race, class, and *gender, and the effect of ever-present repressed human forces jeopardising the status quo. Adaptability and versatility continue to uphold the unwavering popularity of the Gothic novel. Fear and violence being its key interests, the genre has been used to depict diverse ages, places, and experiences – from the racist American South (William Faulkner's *Absalom, Absalom!*, 1936; Toni Morrison's *Beloved*, 1987), through feminist concerns with the female condition (Margaret Atwood's *Lady Oracle*, 1976), to the threatening megalomania and fragmentation of contemporary society (Angela Carter, Joyce Carol Oates, Stephen King).

SEE ALSO: horror narrative; thriller

References and further reading

Botting, Fred (1996) *Gothic*, London: Routledge.
Hogle, Jerrold E. (2002) *The Cambridge Companion to Gothic Fiction*, Cambridge: Cambridge University Press.
Punter, David (1996) *The Literature of Terror: A History of Gothic Fictions from 1765 to the Present Day*, London: Longman.

EDINA SZALAY

GRAND RÉCIT

A concept proposed by Jean-François Lyotard, *grand récit* (literally translated as 'grand narrative' but sometimes also referred to as 'metanarrative' or 'master narrative') is a global explanatory scheme that legitimises *institutions (such as the practice of *science) by representing them as necessary to the historical self-realisation of an abstract or collective entity, such as Reason, Freedom, the State, or the Human Spirit. According to Lyotard, the epistemological crisis of postmodernism stems from a loss of faith in *grand récits*. See MASTER NARRATIVE; POSTMODERN NARRATIVE.

GRAPHIC PRESENTATION AS EXPRESSIVE DEVICE

The graphic presentation of a text consists of its visual aspect: typography, page setting, layout, creative use of marks (dots, asterisks, brackets, etc.), blanks as well as use of figures, *images,

figurative or abstract designs, as in Sterne's highly innovative *Tristram Shandy* (De Voogt 1988). Despite the efforts of Symbolist writers like Mallarmé to employ these devices (as in *Un coup de dés jamais n'abolira le hasard*), their importance for the meaning of texts, both poetic and narrative, has long been overlooked.

According to Saussure, linguistic signs are arbitrary: the graphic value of letters is purely negative and functions in opposition to other letters, so that the way a *t*, for example, is handwritten doesn't matter. The only thing that counts is to avoid any confusion with similar letters, like *l* or *d*. This view denies the importance of graphic signs, since their only role is that of conveying the signified. In a Saussurean framework, then, typography must be as transparent as possible: the main function of fonts is to make reading easier. Consequently, graphic signs should be *legible* and not *visible*. However, this opposition has been questioned by the creative way Italian Futurists, Russian Futurists, and Dadaists used typography. Since the 1980s, much more attention has been given to the graphic qualities of texts. This emphasis on visual features has been called *grammatextuality* (Lapacherie 1984).

Yet, if we are to take into account the graphic presentation of a text, characterisation of grammatexts as 'expressive' is not sufficient, since their use of graphic features might be merely decorative. We must consider whether typography is arbitrary or has a narrow relationship to the meaning of the printed text. The most satisfactory approach is arguably a *semiotic one: from this standpoint, a graphic signifier is not the mere signifier of a linguistic signified, but a sign as such, a visual sign (Groupe μ 1992) having its own signified, which usually corresponds to the signified of the written words (as when the thickness of a type is used to signify the importance of the contents of a sentence), but is sometimes semantically opposed to it.

Long restricted to poetry, graphic effects have recently played an increasing role in narrative. Alternation between fonts has been used to distinguish narrative strands and *times (Calvino, *Invisible Cities*), *narrators (Danielewski, *House of Leaves*), or focalizers (italics as a means to express *stream of consciousness) (*see* FOCALIZATION; THOUGHT AND CONSCIOUSNESS REPRESENTATION (LITERATURE)). Semi-blank pages appeal to the reader's imagination (Butor, *Où*); crossed-out passages place text under erasure (Danielewski); and text divided into columns or boxes questions the linearity of reading or the chronology of events (Arno Schmidt, *Evening Edged in Gold*) (*see* TEMPORAL ORDERING). Under the influence of the Internet, experimental narrative tends more and more to take the form of a 'hypermediated display' (*see* REMEDIATION) made of distinct text windows.

SEE ALSO: image and narrative; visual narrativity

References and further reading

Baetens, Jan (1988) 'Le transcripturaire', *Poétique*, 73, 51–70.

Christ, Anne-Marie (1979) 'Rhétorique et typographie, la lettre et le sens', *Revue d'esthétique*, 1–2, 297–323.

De Voogd, Peter J. (1988) '*Tristram Shandy* as Aesthetic Object', *Word and Image*, 1.4, 383–92.

Graphies (1977) *Catalog Exhibit*, Brussels, Musées Royaux des Beaux-Arts de Belgique.

Groupe μ (1992) *Traité du signe visuel: Pour une rhétorique de l'image*, Paris: Seuil.

Lapacherie, Jean-Gérard (1984) 'De la grammatextualité', *Poétique*, 59, 283–94.

—— (1994) 'Typographic Characters: Tensions between Text and Drawing', in Reid (1994).

Reid, Martine (ed.) (1994) *Yale French Studies*, 84 (special issue on *Boundaries: Writing and Drawing*).

GEORGES ROQUE

H

HAGIOGRAPHY

A medieval *genre of *biography permeated with marvellous elements that recounts the legendary lives of saints as a model of *ethical and religious life for the reader to imitate. *See* LEGEND; MEDIEVAL NARRATIVE.

HERMENEUTICS

Hermeneutics is a theory of interpretation. The term is derived from the Greek hermèneus ('interpreter'), or hermèneia ('interpretation'). The etymology of the term suggests that interpretation can be meaningfully compared to translating a foreign-language text into one's own and that there is a world of meaning that is shared by both the interpreter and his or her object of interpretation. Moreover, this shared world of meaning is seen as the bridge between the two of them, enabling interpreters to get access to their object of investigation. This is where the humanities, i.e., the domain of hermeneutic understanding, differ from the sciences. The difference stems from the nature of the object of investigation: in the humanities it is the human mind (in a broad sense), in *science things not necessarily human or even animate. This difference is codified in the opposition between *Verstehen* (hermeneutic understanding) and *Erklären* (scientific explanation).

But in hermeneutics this shared world of meaning is both a given and a problem. It is a given since only thanks to this shared world of meaning can interpreters get access to their object of investigation; it is a problem since the subject and the object of hermeneutic understanding experience this shared world *differently*. The main problem of hermeneutic understanding is how to transcend

precisely *this* difference. The answer to the problem is the so-called 'hermeneutic circle' (Dilthey). Interpreters take their own world of meaning as their initial model for understanding the past and then observe where this model fails to do justice to the past. They correct this model accordingly and then observe where even the corrected model fails, and so on *ad infinitum*. In this way the interpreter will come ever closer to the past's world of meaning, without ever completely accessing it. This is why hermeneuticists often (though not always) question the reconstruction of authorial intention as the historian's self-evident goal (*see* INTENTIONALITY).

One should clearly distinguish between German and Anglo-Saxon hermeneutics. German hermeneuticists such as F. E. D. Schleiermacher, W. Dilthey, and H. G. Gadamer focus on the interpretation of texts, whereas Anglo-Saxon hermeneuticists such as R. G. Collingwood, W. Dray, and G. H. von Wright are mainly interested in the explanation of human action. Dilthey's hermeneutics moves between the three notions of *Erlebnis*, *Ausdruck* and *Verstehen*: understanding a text's meaning (*Verstehen*) is achieved by reconstructing the experience of the world (*Erlebnis*) that is expressed (*Ausdruck*) in the text or a work of art. According to Gadamer the interpreter should aim at 'a fusion of his own horizon' of experience and meaning with that of his object of interpretation (*Horizontverschmelzung*) (*see* HORIZON OF EXPECTATIONS). Nevertheless, the Gadamerian hermeneuticist must be aware of the fact that (1) the effort can never be completely successful, and (2) that this is not to be regretted since the past only manifests itself in this gap between the historian's 'horizon' and that of the text's *author. Collingwood, Dray, and von Wright argue that the action of the historical agent should be explained by reconstructing why, in situation S, the agent opted for a certain action A in order to realise intention or 'telos' I. This explanatory model is therefore also described as 'intentionalist' or 'teleological'.

SEE ALSO: action theory; historicism; historiography; narrative explanation

References and further reading

Szondi, Peter (1995) *Introduction to Literary Hermeneutics*, Cambridge: Cambridge University Press.
Weinsheimer, Joel C. (1991) *Philosophical Hermeneutics and Literary Theory*, New Haven: Yale University Press.

FRANK ANKERSMIT

HERO

Derived from ancient Greek, the word 'hero' covers a multidimensional concept. Its complexity stems from the history and typology of notions of the hero, as well as from their expression in a variety of contexts, mythological, literary, and other. In historical perspective, hero-tales were part of the cultural thesaurus of the Græco-Roman educated (and popular) cultural cosmos; this inheritance was passed on to the East Roman/Byzantine thought world, while certain 'iconic' hero-figures (drawn from the Homeric *epics) were known and even imitated in the medieval West. The West's medieval era was also marked by a tradition of orally transmitted 'knightly' heroic narratives (*see* MEDIEVAL NARRATIVE; ORAL CULTURES AND NARRATIVE). Further, intellectual developments connected to the European Renaissance gave 'classical' heroic sources new importance by seeking out, collecting, and editing the texts that could be recovered from the past.

The so-called Romantic movement of the late eighteenth to the early nineteenth-century opened up a new set of narrative choices and possibilities. First, the ancient hero is connected to a cult of *fictive* individualism: a heroic (often tragic, fatal) life is invented in both poetry and prose. Second, the ancient texts are re-examined and re-edited, with a view to establishing near-perfect authenticity (coherent with an 'original'). Third, cultural attention focuses on how a new sense of a national-cultural-linguistic *past* was revealed in particular heroic (epic) narratives, narratives

originally catering to medieval warrior-aristocratic elites and their stylised self-images. Hence the renewed interest in the Spanish *Poema el Mio Cid*, the Byzantine Greek *Digenes Akritas*, the German *Nibelungenlied*, and others, including the Norse sagas. Finally, the hero is taken as a new model or historical exemplum of exceptional, potent character, as we see in Carlyle's 'Great Man' notion (Carlyle 1968 [1841]).

The new theories of analytic psychology make the hero a focus of deep human currents: Otto Rank provides a key text here (Rank 1964 [1914]), though everyone remembers Freud and the hero-king Oedipus (*see* MYTH: THEORETICAL APPROACHES; PSYCHOANALYSIS AND NARRATIVE). Another social science, anthropology, widened the scope of investigation to interrogate non-Western (usually pre-literate) cultures; new and exotic kinds of heroes were found, encased in a variety of myths, *legends, and tales (*see* ETHNOGRAPHIC APPROACHES TO NARRATIVE).

The mid-to-late twentieth century saw the publication of numerous studies dealing with the nature of the hero. These studies increasingly emphasised narrative shaping and content. Lord Raglan (Raglan 1936) took a collection of hero-tales and parsed them according to his own formula (Raglan was a member of the Myth and Ritual school, where all myths were built from existing rituals). Another typological exploration involved a probe of the heroic quest, defined as a key event made up of 'stable, constant elements in folktales' (Propp 1968 [1928]) (*see* FOLKTALE). Yet another facet to the problem of the hero, one springing from the *performative* side, was explored by scholars concerned with how a 'bard' created his hero-tales: the original Homeric epic was dissected to recover compositional techniques, and modern exemplars and parallels were discovered (cf. Lord 1960; *see* ORAL-FORMULAIC THEORY; PERFORMANCE; RING-COMPOSITION).

More recently, the hero (especially in myth) has been typed according to a semi-Jungian formula by Joseph Campbell (Campbell 1949). The *biography and the multiform adventures of the hero have been drawn into a treatment emphasising the polarities of his character, as he is simultaneously semi-animal and nearly divine, valuable to a society and potentially dangerous, a life force and a death-seeker (Miller 2000).

SEE ALSO: actant; character

References and further reading

Campbell, Joseph (1949) *The Hero With a Thousand Faces*, Princeton: Princeton University Press.
Carlyle, Thomas (1968 [1841]) *Hero-Worship and the Heroic in History*, London: Oxford University Press.
Lord, Albert (1968) *The Singer of Tales*, New York: Athenaeum.
Miller, Dean (2000) *The Epic Hero*, Baltimore, MD: Johns Hopkins University Press.
Propp, Vladimir (1968 [1928]) *Morphology of the Folktale*, trans. Laurence Scott, revised by Louis A. Wagner, Austin: University of Texas Press.
Raglan, Lord (F. R. Somerset) (1936) *The Hero, A Study in Tradition, Myth and Drama*, London: Methuen.
Rank, Otto (1964 [1914]) *The Myth of the Birth of the Hero*, New York: Random House.

DEAN A. MILLER

HETERODIEGETIC NARRATION

In Genettean narratology, a narrative whose *narrator does not belong to the set of characters inhabiting the *storyworld. *See* NARRATION; PERSON.

HETEROGLOSSIA

As theorised by Bakhtin, heteroglossia is a condition of more modern societies, in contrast to the monoglossia or polyglossia which characterised earlier forms of society. Heteroglossia is marked by the recognition of difference, multiplicity, or stratification both within and between languages. As such, it is a powerful rejection of the unifying, dominative claims of monoglossia, whether these are 'merely' discursive or substantively political.

In relation to narrative, heteroglossia stands as the appearance in real life of that plurality of languages of class, *gender, region, or *ideology which enter the *novel in the form of *dialogism, resulting – in Bakhtin's most praised *authors such as Dostoevsky – in a polyphonic narrative. Ironically, this desired *polyphony involves a downgrading or sidelining of the very narrative which embraces it, given that in polyphonic novels 'the plot is subordinated to the task of coordinating and exposing languages to each other'. However, Bakhtin prescriptively declares that the novel 'must be a microcosm of heteroglossia', suggesting that the more the novel incorporates social heteroglossia, the better.

SEE ALSO: Marxist approaches to narrative; plot

References and further reading

Bakhtin, Mikhail (1981) *The Dialogic Imagination*, trans. Caryl Emerson and Michael Holquist, Austin: University of Texas Press.
Hirschkop, Ken, and David Shepherd (eds) (1989) *Bakhtin and Cultural Theory*, Manchester: Manchester University Press.

PATRICK WILLIAMS

HISTORICAL NOVEL

The historical *novel, which emerged in the grand re-division of mnemonic labour around 1800, swiftly became and has since remained literature's pre-eminent venue for narrative *memory. Its broad narrative scope and minutely discriminated time-scale made it literature's best-stocked verbal museum (*see* TIME IN NARRATIVE). Its concern for the quiddity of the past made it a force in the development of narrative *realism. Its vested interest in versions of the past made it both literature's dominant report on reporting and its metanarrative on narrative history (*see* HISTORIOGRAPHIC METAFICTION; MASTER NARRATIVE). Its highlighting of a broadly social, rather than predominantly martial, past made it an important corrective to *historiography itself. As literature's well-briefed, quizzical attorney at the tribunal on the past, the *genre was the natural successor to, and supplanter of, the *epic and *ballad, on whose shortcomings as histories it often remarked.

The chief narrative features of the genre are perhaps best brought out in comparison with two genres coeval with it: the *family chronicle (Edgeworth, Galt) and the historical *novella (Kleist, Balzac). Whereas the family chronicle offers a longitudinal, supra-generational survey of past decades, the historical novel's narrative is latitudinal, offering a detailed cross-section of a single period in the past. And whereas the historical *Novelle* focuses on an isolated, often untoward *event, with a limited cast and a *causality often fate-bound or chance-ridden, the historical novel tends to unfold a many-stranded, richly sub-plotted canvas of its portrayed age, its large cast and ambit offering a more enlightened view of causation (*see* PLOT). In all three genres, however, verified material is narrated alongside unverified, the historical novel being particularly known for placing, and so re-evaluating, an historical personage within its broader play of forces.

The genre, as it develops from Scott's *Waverley* (1814) to his first eminent successors, Cooper, Manzoni, Balzac, Pushkin, and Stendhal, must be distinguished from the countless earlier novels set in the past – as far back as Mme. de Lafayette (some would say, Xenophon). For with the acceleration of society and its manifold reflection in European Romanticism comes a new sense for the pastness of the past, for the differentiate between past and present. Social change and the evaluation of change become central *thematic concerns. *Plots often hinge on the tension between knowledge then and knowledge now, and thus on the two lives lived by *characters – the confused, unwitting lives they live forwards and the meaningful lives subsequently retrodicted, a topos which leads ultimately to the wide-ranging reflections on free will, determinism, and historical necessity in Tolstoy's *War and Peace* (1865–1869).

The social acceleration which engendered this set of themes fostered also the genre's sense for the simultaneity of the non-simultaneous. Many early historical novels from Scott to Tieck centre on a temporal *conflict, between a backward and an advanced culture; the topos is apt for historical novels of the emergent nation-state and returns in the *post-colonial work of, say, Achebe and Ngugi. Similarly prominent are conflicts between contrasting concepts of time – in Cooper's *The Pioneers* (1823) the conflict is given an ecological, in Manzoni's *The Betrothed* (1827) a theological turn (*see* ECO-NARRATIVES; THEOLOGY AND NARRATIVE).

In order to achieve the above themes, the genre develops several narrative ploys – the journey to the backward, and often far-flung, culture; the cultured traveller figure; the go-between – often a spy, double-agent, or turncoat – who introduces us to both camps, cultures, ages, or stages; and the civilian on the battlefield, a topos subsequently taken over by the war novel (*see* MOTIF).

Narratologically, the nineteenth-century historical novel relied largely on the authorial narrative stance (*see* NARRATIVE SITUATIONS), although Scott's *Redgauntlet* (1824) turns early to the *epistolary form. From *Waverley* and *The Heart of Midlothian* (1818) on, however, the genre embodies an early form of multiperspectivity, the plot hinging on competing versions of the past, at times adjudicated on in a court scene (*see* NARRATIVE VERSIONS; PERSPECTIVE). This sense is compounded by the frequent historian figure in the historical novel, a topos common after *The Antiquary* (1816) and proliferating in the crisis of *historicism up to Fontane.

In modernism, in Faulkner's *Absalom! Absalom!* (1936) or Woolf's *Between the Acts* (1941), the shaping, re-constructing, re-membering act of the historian comes to the fore (*see* MODERNIST NARRATIVE). And as modernism shades into postmodernism, so the historians in the genre become more numerous, prominent, reflective, perplexed (*see* POSTMODERNIST NARRATIVE; REFLEXIVITY). In Barth and Pynchon, Swift and Barnes, *historiographic metafiction, implicit in the genre from the outset, becomes its explicit burden. Historiography is picked over and probed, now epistemologically, now poetologically, now ideologically, now politically (*see* IDEOLOGY AND NARRATIVE).

If the above description of the historical novel is valid, then it follows that many a definition of the genre is awry. It is not helpful to stipulate that the genre must take place x years ago, since the social acceleration which gave rise to the genre has itself accelerated, calling for historical re-enactment at ever shorter intervals. Nor is it helpful to postulate that the historical novel must contain 'major' historical individuals, since the thrust of the genre is to reinvestigate just what personages deserve that label. The historical novel is better characterised as a work which contains enough of the above-listed family resemblances for it to make sense to view it as a member of the family.

Like all generic families, the historical novel has produced highly diverse progeny. Much popular historical fiction uses the past largely as a stock-room of exotic props and backdrops, a cue for stirring narrative, a theater for derring-do. At its finest, however, the genre is literature's riposte to 'Great Man' or drum-and-trumpet history, its re-enactment of historiography's re-enactments, its standing committee on historical over-simplification. And significantly, the genre has endured. New genres emerge when there is work to be done on society's grand narratives; they continue as long as that work remains incomplete.

References and further reading

Fleishman, Avrom (1971) *The English Historical Novel: Walter Scott to Virginia Woolf*, Baltimore: Johns Hopkins University Press.

Humphrey, Richard (1986) *The Historical Novel as Philosophy of History*, London: Institute of Germanic Studies.

Lukács, Georg (1962) *The Historical Novel*, trans. Hanna and Stanley Mitchell, Harmondsworth: Penguin.

Nünning, Ansgar (1995) *Von historischer Fiktion zu historioraphischer Metafiktion*, 2 vols., Trier: WVT.

Shaw, Harry E. (1983) *The Forms of Historical Fiction: Sir Walter Scott and His Successors*, Ithaca: Cornell University Press.

RICHARD HUMPHREY

HISTORICAL PRESENT

The temporary use of the present tense in a predominantly past-tense narrative, usually serving the function of highlighting a crucial moment. *See* NARRATION (also: TENSE AND NARRATIVE; TIME IN NARRATIVE).

HISTORICISM

In the most general sense historicism asks us to look at the world from a historical perspective afforded by the study of the past. Five meanings of the term should be discerned:

(1) Historicism requires the historian to understand the past on its own terms, to avoid anachronisms and, especially to avoid projecting on the past the historian's own *ethical and political norms. This is the variant of historicism that is ordinarily associated with Leopold von Ranke, who is regarded as the founder of historicism as the scientific study of the past. As Ranke famously put it: 'it is not the historian's task to judge the past or to learn lessons from the past that may be of use for the present and the future, but merely to show what happened' ('... bloss zu zeigen wie es eigentlich gewesen').

(2) The former notion of historicism is radicalised into the claim that in order to understand the past historians should project themselves into the past, whether the investigated past is a historical agent or the *author of a text to be interpreted. The demand to avoid anachronism that is part of the previous definition is then narrowed down to the demand that the historian should see the past as it was seen by historical agents themselves. This notion of historicism is roughly identical with that of *hermeneutics.

(3) In a third conception of historicism, the term is analogous to those of e.g., scientism, sociologism, and psychologism. Historicism then means that we should see the world from the perspective of history (see 1 above), or that the essence or the *identity of something (whether it be an individual, a state, an institution etc.) is to be found in its *history*. This is the conception of historicism that revolutionised the Western worldview in the transition from the Enlightenment to Romanticism (and beyond): it meant the exchange of a static for a dynamic conception of the world and of what it contains (Karl Mannheim). It is not easy to see how one can do history at all without embracing this variant of historicism.

(4) The term 'historicism' has been used by Karl Popper to refer to so-called speculative philosophies of history. In this usage, (a) some pattern is discerned in all of human history; (b) a mechanism is identified that pushes history from one phase in the pattern to the next one; and (c) predictions are made about the future course of history (think of, e.g., Fichte, Hegel, Marx, Spengler or Toynbee). This conception of historicism is incompatible with those mentioned in items 1 and 2 above. In fact, historicists like Ranke or Burckhardt are among the fiercest opponents of speculative philosophies of history.

(5) In 1982 Stephen Greenblatt, a literary historian, introduced the notion of 'the New Historicism'. This approach to the past (in Greenblatt's case the literature and culture of Elizabethan England) remains closer to historicism as defined under (1) and (3) than its advocates often realise; but contemporary theorists such as Althusser, Macherey, de Certeau and, above all, Foucault have also importantly contributed to Greenblatt's conception of (the new) historicism.

SEE ALSO: discourse analysis (Foucault); historiography

References and further reading

Aram, Veeser H. (ed.) (1994) *The New Historicism Reader*, New York: Routledge.

Rüsen, Jörn (1993) *Konfigurationen des Historismus*, Frankfurt: Suhrkamp.

FRANK ANKERSMIT

HISTORIOGRAPHIC METAFICTION

The term 'historiographic *metafiction' was introduced by Linda Hutcheon (1988; 1989) as an umbrella category for postmodernist forms of art and literature that combine documentary historical actuality with formalist self-reflexivity and parody (*see* REFLEXIVITY). More specifically, the term designates a new kind of *historical novel and a distinct sub-genre of *postmodern narrative, viz. novels which are intensely self-reflexive, while also referring to historical events and personages (e.g., Salman Rushdie's *Midnight's Children*, 1981; Graham Swift's *Waterland*, 1983; Julian Barnes' *Flaubert's Parrot*, 1984). Undermining the borders between *historiography and *fiction, historiographic metafiction self-consciously explores the status and function of narrative as an ideological construct shaping history and forging *identity rather than merely representing the past (*see* IDEOLOGY AND NARRATIVE).

Hutcheon, whose definition is influenced by postmodern theories of architecture, argues that the self-conscious reworking of documentary material in contemporary fiction is one of the defining characteristics of the postmodern. Valuable though Hutcheon's argument is, her claim that historiographic metafiction 'defines postmodernism' (1988: 52) may go too far. Critics have pointed out that the questioning of the *truth status of historiography is not confined to postmodern scepticism and relativism, but is instead a reflection of a persistent inquiry into the limits of historical knowledge that can be traced back both to eighteenth-century philosophers and to American short-story writers (Engler and Scheiding 1998). Similarly, the emergence of historiographic metafiction coincides with the rise of the historical novel as a literary *genre (Engler and Müller 1994).

Blurring the different generic conventions of fiction and historiography, historiographic metafiction prompts reflection on its own mimetic engagement with the past by exploring the narrative construction of reality and foregrounding the epistemological problems involved. It thus differs substantially from the use of history in the traditional historical novel, which does not question that history can be represented as it 'really was'. Just like other types of *metafiction, historiographic metafiction may either be 'explicit' (using the devices of metafiction to thematise the epistemological, methodological, and linguistic problems involved in any attempt to construct a coherent account of the past) or 'implicit' (incorporating its metahistoriographic concerns in formal structural features of the text) (*see* NARRATIVE STRUCTURES). In either case, historiographic metafiction deals not so much with historical events, personages, and facts as with the reconstruction of the past from the point of view of the present, often reflecting the insights of modern theories of history – theories focusing on the epistemological and narratological problems that beset historiography. Historiographic metafiction reminds the reader that history, while it exists as a continuous collective process, is accessible only as a narrative produced by human beings who remember, interpret, and represent events from a particular point of view. The radical destabilisation of historical representation in historiographic metafiction is thus intricately linked with moral and *ethical concerns (Kotte 2001).

SEE ALSO: metahistory; emplotment

References and further reading

Engler, Bernd, and Kurt Müller (eds) (1994) *Historiographic Metafiction in Modern American and Canadian Literature*, Paderborn: Schöningh.
—— and Oliver Scheiding (eds) (1998) *Re-Visioning the Past*, Trier: WVT.
Hutcheon, Linda (1988) *A Poetics of Postmodernism*, London: Routledge.
—— (1989) *The Politics of Postmodernism*, London: Routledge.
Kotte, Christina (2001) *Ethical Dimensions in British Historiographic Metafiction*, Trier: WVT.
Nünning, Ansgar (1995) *Von historischer Fiktion zu historiographischer Metafiktion*, Trier: WVT.
Onega, Susana (ed.) (1995) *Telling Histories: Narrativizing History, Historicizing Literature*, Amsterdam: Rodopi.

ANSGAR NÜNNING

HISTORIOGRAPHIC NARRATOLOGY

Aristotle's distinction between the poet and historian is probably the first divide between *fiction and history. 'Historiographic narratology', a discipline inaugurated by Cohn (1999: ch. 7), attempts to distinguish techniques within fictional narratives from those within *non-fiction historical narrative or *historiography (*see* NARRATIVE TECHNIQUES). Historiographic narratology asks whether fiction and historical non-fiction share narratological categories and whether narratological analysis is capable of distinguishing fictional from non-fictional historical narrative solely on the basis of 'signposts' or textual markers of fictionality. Building on the work of Gerald Prince and Tzvetan Todorov, Cohn claims that narratology usually assumes two levels of narration in fiction (story and discourse) but historical narrative creates a tri-level model consisting of reference/story/discourse (*see* STORY-DISCOURSE DISTINCTION). Cohn thus reassesses the status of *reference within narratology and claims that historical narrative may be distinguished from fictional narrative by the former's unique terms of external reference.

Cohn notes that following the Aristotelian call for unity of *plot and before the advent of *metahistory (White 1973), differences at the level of story were usually considered sufficient for distinguishing history from fiction. But since Hayden White and others began to clarify the importance of plot in historical narratives, narrative theories distinguishing historical from fictional narratives on the basis of story-level differences have come to be viewed as inadequate. According to Cohn, the difference between historical narration and fiction must be based on signposts that exist at the level of discourse. Unlike fiction, historical narrative (1) constructs a modal system that forbids the author/narrator to present undocumented first-person *characters' thoughts or third-person characters' thoughts (although it may use the 'must-have-thought' style of inferred psychologies; *see* POSSIBLE-WORLDS THEORY); (2) focuses more on mentalities than on individual minds and thereby produces both distinctive discursive conventions (such as prevalence of *summary over scene) and the need to rethink *focalization; and (3) is based on a relation of homonymy between *author and *narrator (a historical narrative will always assert that its narrator is identical to the author on the book's title page).

In other disciplines there also have been attempts to define the narrative properties of historical accounts and their impact on historical *truth claims. The narratological debate is closely related to that in historiography in the work of, among others, Hayden White, Walter Benjamin, Paul Ricoeur, and Hans Kellner.

References and further reading

Ankersmit, Frank R. (1983) *Narrative Logic: A Semantic Analysis of the Historian's Language*, The Hague: Martinus Nijhoff.
Benjamin, Walter (1968) 'Theses on the Philosophy of History', in Hannah Arendt (ed.) *Illuminations*, trans. Harry Zohn, New York: Schocken Books.
Cohn, Dorrit (1999) *The Distinction of Fiction*, Baltimore: Johns Hopkins University Press.
Dray, W. H. (1971) 'On the Nature and Role of Narrative in Historiography', *History and Theory*, 10.2, 153–71.
Kellner, Hans (1989) *Language and Historical Representation: Getting the Story Crooked*, Madison: University of Wisconsin Press.
Mink, Louis O. (1987) 'History and Fiction as Modes of Comprehension', in Brian Fay, Eugene O. Golob, and Richard T. Vann (eds) *Historical Understanding*, Ithaca: Cornell University Press.
Ricoeur, Paul (1965) *History and Truth*, trans. Charles A. Kelbley, Evanston: Northwestern University Press.
White, Hayden (1973) *Metahistory: The Historical Imagination in Nineteenth-Century Europe*, Baltimore: Johns Hopkins University Press.
—— (1987) *The Content of the Form: Narrative Discourse and Historical Representation*, Baltimore: Johns Hopkins University Press.

AMY J. ELIAS

HISTORIOGRAPHY

Historiography is the writing of history. Three levels can be discerned in the writing of history, each of them corresponding (1) to a separate stage in 'the history of the writing of history' (sometimes also referred to as *historiography*) and (2) to the central themes in the theoretical reflection on the nature of historical writing. The most simple variant of historical writing (to be found in the early Middle Ages) is the *'chronicle', which consists of a mere enumeration of important *events on a yearly basis. At a second stage, roughly since the thirteenth and fourteenth centuries, the temporal order of chronicle is retained but the historian now also aims at an explanation of the events recounted in the chronicle (*see* NARRATIVE EXPLANATION). This is called 'annalistics' (*see* ANNALS). In a third phase, finally, the historian's narrative is meant to establish a coherent presentation of all the events mentioned in his or her text. This coherence expresses the 'image' or 'picture' the historian proposes to the reader of a certain part or aspect of the past. This results in what has been regarded since the end of the eighteenth-century (and especially since the birth of *historicism) as 'the scientific writing of history'. This tripartition will be retained below when dealing with the main issues in contemporary historical theory.

Chronicle

The chronicle raises the problem of how individual statements about the past are related to the past. In turn, this raises the epistemological problem of historical *truth. In order to avoid excessive overlap with the philosophical issue of truth, the problem of historical truth can be narrowed down to the question of how true statements are possible about an object – i.e., the past – that no longer exists. For this is where the problem of truth differs most conspicuously in history as opposed to other disciplines where the object of investigation is available here and now. The theory most successfully dealing with the problem is constructivism. Constructivists, such as Michael Oakeshott, Jack Meiland, and Leon Goldstein, argue that though the past is not available to the historian, historical evidence is. So what the historian can do is to collect all the relevant evidence, closely investigate and analyse it and, finally, use this for a conjecture of what the past *may* well have been like. But crucial to the constructivist's argument is that these conjectures can never be compared to the past itself – once again, for the simple reason that the past no longer exists. Therefore the historian can only give us constructions and never *re*-constructions of the past. Constructivism has been criticised for confusing 'verification' (i.e., conclusions about the past based on available evidence) with *'reference' (i.e., what these conclusions are believed to be true of); but constructivists might reply by saying that distinguishing between verification and reference begs precisely the question that is under dispute.

Accepting constructivism will invite the historical theorist to embrace the 'coherence' theory of truth rather than the 'correspondence' theory. For since the past is no longer available the historian can never ascertain whether his or her conjectures do 'correspond' to actual historical fact. What 'coheres' best with available evidence and with accepted views about the past is therefore the most realistic criterion of historical truth.

Annalistics

Annalistics raises the question of how historians explain the past. Three theories should be discerned: (a) causalism, (b) Anglo-Saxon *hermeneutics, and (c) narrativism. Since narrativism conceives the object of historical explanation differently than causalism and Anglo-Saxon hermeneutics, it will receive separate treatment in the next section.

(A) CAUSALISM

With regard to causalism one should distinguish between what makes us ask for causes and what requirements have to be satisfied for a causal explanation to be acceptable (*see* CAUSALITY). The former question is answered by so-called 'abnormalism'. Abnormalists, such as e.g., Robin Collingwood, Robert McIver, and Herbert Hart, argue that we only ask for causes when something unusual happens, hence something 'abnormal' deviating from what we consider to be the 'normal' course of things (*see* SCRIPTS AND SCHEMATA). For example, we don't ask for causes as long as a train remains neatly on the rails, but only when we suddenly find it in the meadows between the cows. And then again something 'abnormal', such as rock on the rails or the presence of a truck on a level-crossing, will be found to have been the cause. This will inevitably bring into play the historian's moral and political values since these will partly determine what will strike the historians as 'abnormal' (or not). A Machiavellian historian will be provoked to ask for causes at different occasions than the historian accepting a Kantian ethical stance. However, it should be added that this problem does not necessarily interfere with the intersubjective acceptability of the causes that are given by the historian.

The best-known and most widely discussed theory concerning what requirements (historical) explanation has to satisfy is the so-called 'covering law model' (CLM). According to the CLM the explanation of event E (the *explanandum*) requires (1) a general law stating that if an event of type C takes place, an event of type E will also take place and (2) an event of type C has been observed. The premises (1) and (2) *together* are called the *explanans*, and premise (2) the *cause* of event E. Premise (1) is an empirical law to be (dis-)confirmed by empirical evidence; the deduction of E from its *explanans* is not empirical but in agreement with the logical *modus ponens* rule. Lastly, the general law of premise (1) 'covers', so to speak, cause and effect; hence the model's name.

The CLM was first advocated by Carl Hempel in 1942 (though its roots go back to David Hume) and has been severely criticised ever since. A first problem is that history seems to know no general laws. This problem was met by allowing an explanation of E by means of statistical laws stating that events of type C are followed with probability P by events of type E. Event C is then with probability P the cause of the E. The weakness of the statistical variant of the CLM is that it leaves us unable to explain *individual* events of type E, since the occurrence of both E and not-E is in agreement when it comes to the statistical law.

Another proposal for circumventing the problem of the absence of general laws in history has been formulated by Arthur Danto. Danto begins by insisting that the CLM always explains *types* of events, hence events *under a certain description* of them. He then goes on to argue that if the event E is re-described in a different, more general way, a reliable general law explaining E under this more general *description will in all likelihood be available. But this has the disadvantage of widening the distance between the concrete historical event itself and the description in terms of which it is explained. So this confronts a follower of the CLM with the unpleasant dilemma of either explaining E in its historical concreteness (but then no reliable general laws will be available to support the explanation) or explaining E in terms of a description that is miles apart from its historical concreteness. Morton White advocated a final, heroic move when he recommended reducing the *explanans* of E to its cause (i.e., the second premise of the *explanans* as defined in the original CLM). The covering law would then merely offer a stronger or weaker support (depending on the degree of its empirical confirmation) to the causal claim made by the explanation. Though this move may look nice from a logical point of view, it obviously did little to remove the practical inadequacies of the CLM.

Though the CLM has never recovered from these criticisms and has, since then, been abandoned by the vast majority of historical theorists, it went on to live a kind of shadow-existence in comparativist historical explanation. Comparativists often rely on John Stuart Mill's methods of agreement and of difference. If you have two comparable evolutions both resulting in an event of type E, those events that the two comparable evolutions have in common are said to have been E's cause. This is the method of agreement. If you have two comparable evolutions with one resulting in E and the other in not-E, the events that are *not* shared by both evolutions are said to be the causes of, respectively, E and not-E. This is the method of difference. Comparativists then go on to insist that they did not rely upon any laws, either general or statistical, in the procedure. But this is disputable. For, obviously, if there were no law connecting the events selected with the help of Mill's two methods to their consequences (either E or not-E), the explanation would fail to hold. So comparativism and Mill's two methods presuppose an acceptance of the CLM – and one can say that Mill's methods have a merely heuristic role to play here.

(B) ANGLO-SAXON HERMENEUTICS

In view of these problems with the CLM, theorists turned to hermeneutics. Hermeneutics as an explanatory model has its *locus classicus* in the writings by Robin Collingwood. Collingwood deflected traditional nineteenth-century German hermeneutics (with its emphasis on the interpretation of texts) toward a hermeneutics focusing on the explanation of human action. Anglo-Saxon (explanatory) hermeneutics has here its origins. The idea is that when having to explain a historical agent's action A, the historian should project himself into the agent's situation S and attempt to understand why doing A made sense in that situation (*see* ACTION THEORY). 'The historian must re-enact the past in his own mind' – thus Collingwood – and this means that the historian understands or explains the past by 're-enacting' in his own mind exactly the same thought-processes that made the historical agent perform a certain action.

There are two problems with explanatory hermeneutics as proposed by Collingwood and developed by others such as William Dray. In the first place, as Adam Ferguson already observed in 1767: 'nations stumble upon establishments, which are indeed the result of human *action*, but not the execution of any human *design*'. Think of the crash of 1929: everybody became poorer, but this surely was nobody's intention (*see* INTENTIONALITY). So 're-enactment' is helpless when confronted with the unintended results of intentional human action. And it may well be argued that precisely this is the natural object of historical investigation.

A second problem is the question whether Anglo-Saxon hermeneutics can avoid an appeal to (a variant of the) CLM. Anglo-Saxon hermeneuticists themselves insists that no such appeal should be necessary since the logical heart of their argument is a *factual* observation. At issue is the historian's *factual* observation that under the relevant circumstances he or she would have thought and done exactly the same as the historical agent. Be this as it may, 're-enactment' would be unreliable if its application yielded different results for different historians. So if 're-enactment' is to work, it will need the support of some kind of general statement of the form: 'each rational person (or historian) would have decided that performing action A is the thing to do in situation S'. But this would reduce the 're-enactment' theory to the regularity thesis of the CLM.

Later theorists, such as Alan Donagan, Georg Henrik von Wright, and Rex Martin tried to vitiate the argument by closely investigating the nature of the relationship between (1) the situation S in which the historical agent finds himself or herself, (2) the intentions I provoked by his or her awareness of S, and (3) his or her choice for action A in order to achieve I. The conclusion of this investigation is that the relationship between S, I, and A is logical rather than empirical (as is argued by the follower of the CLM). For example, it is part of the *meaning* of one's having intention I that one will be prepared to perform A: if the agent did not perform A, he or she can never have had intention I. However, even if the argument did hold (which is questionable), it does not seem to be particularly helpful. For what difference does it make, in the end, whether the regularity thesis associated with the CLM is expressed by an empirical or a logical rule?

The scientific writing of history

This brings us to (*c*) *narrativism*, which is nowadays the most widely held theory of history. Narrativists emphasise that historians always write texts (narratives) about the past and that no theory of history can be persuasive that fails to take this into account (*see* METAHISTORY). For what the historian has to say about the past should primarily be related to the *whole* of the text and not to its separate *components*. This may also explain why narrativism has no pretension to be an alternative to the views discussed above, but is, instead, the exploration of new territory. One may, for example, be a follower of the CLM with regard to the text's components and, at the same time, a narrativist with regard to its whole.

The origins of narrativism, though, can be traced back to nineteenth-century historicism and the historicists' notion of the 'historical idea' (Wilhelm von Humboldt). The historical idea could best be described as a quasi-Aristiotelian entelechy of historical periods, nations, cultures, social movements, etc. determining that these should manifest in due course of time all the features that they happened to have. And they do so just as the 'entelechy' of an acorn will cause the acorn to develop into a huge and impressive oak. The historical idea gives us both the essence of and what is unique to a historical period etc.; and by getting hold of it the historian will succeed in *explaining* it in the way historians are expected to explain the past. Lastly, we should note that the historical idea is not to be found in the parts but only in the *whole* of a period, as such it has its textual counterpart not in the historical text's *components* but only in the *whole* of the historian's text.

The most influential contemporary historical narrativist is Hayden White. White made use of literary theory in order to clarify the nature of the historical text. White starts with the observation that the historical text always is a selection from the manifold of the past. No historical narrative renders the past in all its complexity. White then argues that one of the four tropes of *metaphor, synecdoche, *metonymy, or *irony will always guide the historian in this selection procedure. Synecdoche reduces the complexity of the past by looking for its essence (think of the synecdoche 'he is all heart'); metaphor does so by relating the essence to something that is not part of the past itself (think of the metaphor 'my love is a rose'); metonymy organises knowledge of the past by fitting it within a certain structure as is done in the *sciences; and irony questions each proposal for selection. Furthermore, to the set of the four tropes corresponds a set of modes of *emplotment (comic, romantic, tragic, and *satirical), of argument (organicist, formist, mechanistic, and contextualist), and of ideological implication (conservative, anarchist, radical, and liberal; *see* IDEOLOGY AND NARRATIVE). Tropes, modes of emplotment, and modes of argument and of ideological implication organise together the whole of the historian's narrative.

White's claim that his four tropes determine the nature of the historian's text has been of decisive significance for contemporary historical theory because the issue of the historical text (as a whole) could now no longer be disregarded. Moreover, the tropological model inspired a new and challenging research program focusing on the historical text *as* text; in this way a wholly new way of doing the history of historical writing came into being and this is a gain that will never be lost again. But the model also has its weaknesses. The structuralism of the model does not do sufficient justice to how the historical text organises (knowledge of) the past by suggesting that there are only four ways of doing so, whereas it may be argued that each historical text is the result of a selection procedure that is specific for *this* text's historical object. Formulated in White's own technical terminology, one might say that there are (or should be) not just four 'tropes' but exactly as many 'tropes' as there are historical topics. But if this objection is accepted, the model can no longer pretend to provide the historian with an answer to the question how he or she should select. For the tropes have then lost their theoretical *a priori* status.

This problem can be overcome with the help of Louis O. Mink's notion of 'configurational comprehension', which Mink elucidated as follows: 'but in the configurational comprehension of a story which one has *followed*, the end is connected with the promise of the beginning as well as the beginning with the promise of the end, and the necessity of the backward reference cancels out, so to speak, the contingency of the forward references. To comprehend temporal succession means to think of it in both directions at once, and then time is no longer the river which bears us along but the river in aerial view, upstream and downstream seen in a single survey' (*Historical Understanding* 1987: 56, 57). Mink argues here that the historian should always aim at achieving so much coherence in his or her text that what is separate in the past itself is transformed into a textual unity. And when doing so *time is, so to speak, transcended or annulled by the historian's narrative. Historical writing is the undoing of the dispersion by historical time.

Two comments are in order. In the first place, this is a return to the historicist notion of the historical idea with the important qualification that unity is no longer situated in *the past itself* (i.e., in the historical idea), but rather presented as a product of *the historical text*. Secondly, Mink's emphasis that coherence is exclusively a property of the historian's text, but never of the past itself, also implies that there will be an unbridgeable gap between the past and the historical text, between

the past as it was lived by the people from the past, on the one hand, and (the historian's) narrative, on the other. As Mink put it: 'stories are not lived, but told'. This is where narrativists such as Mink, Danto, and White differ from narrativists like Paul Ricoeur and David Carr. For the latter there is no such radical discontinuity between life and story; and this is why for them the historian's narrative can be a textual expression of the Truth of life and of the past. But for Mink, Danto and White the gap between life and story can never be bridged.

The most promising approach to historiography may be a combination of White's and Mink's views; in this model, the individual historical narrative will be seen (with White) as a metaphor carefully constructed by the historian in order to achieve (with Mink) a textual unity in terms of which the past can be understood. Accordingly, in historiographic contexts, metaphor can be viewed as being a relationship not between textual elements, as ordinarily is the case with metaphor, but between the historian's text (as a whole) and the part of the past that the text is about.

References and further reading

Ankersmit, Frank R. (2001) *Historical Representation*, Stanford: Stanford University Press.
Mink, Louis (1987) 'Narrative Form as a Cognitive Instrument', *Historical Understanding*, eds. B. Fay, E. O. Golob, and R. T. Vann, Ithaca: Cornell University Press.
Munslow, Alun (1997) *Deconstructing History*, London: Routledge.
Stanford, Michael (1998) *An Introduction to the Philosophy of History*, Oxford: Blackwell.
White, Hayden (1973) *Metahistory: The Historical Imagination in Nineteenth-century Europe*, Baltimore: Johns Hopkins University Press.

FRANK ANKERSMIT

HOLOCAUST NARRATIVE

The Holocaust is a term used to describe the Nazi's systematic campaign to eliminate the Jewish population of Europe in what Hitler and his followers called the Final Solution. It included death camps such as Auschwitz where millions were gassed as well as roving bands of military assassins called *Einsatzgruppen*. While Hitler's racial laws discriminating against the Jews began in 1933, mass extermination did not begin until 1941, lasting until

Hitler's defeat in 1945. It is estimated that 6 million Jews were killed.

Holocaust narratives, fictional and non-fictional (see FICTION, THEORIES OF), transmute facts in the crucible of art and have become a prominent part of how the collective *memory of the Holocaust is shaped and survives. As the Holocaust Museum in Washington, D.C., shows us, it is when Holocaust history is personalised and dramatised, when abstractions and numbers give way to human drama, that the distance between us and Holocaust victims closes. Wrestling with trauma (see TRAUMA THEORY), survivors rely on memory and narrative to give shape to their lives. They strive to re-establish a lineage to which the self has a link and to wrench themselves from history even while acknowledging history. In a sense, Holocaust narratives rescue language from its perversion in such terms as 'Final Solution' or 'Arbeit Macht Frei' ('Work will make you free') – the sign on the Auschwitz gates that falsely suggested that the purpose of the concentration camp was to reform inmates who would earn their freedom.

Holocaust narratives enable readers to enter into the subjective world of victims and to respond to historical *events from their *perspective. If the Nazis succeeded in turning words into charred bones and flesh as well as skeletons that survived in terror, bodies almost completely deprived of their materiality – writing about the Holocaust paradoxically restores the imaginative to its proper place and breathes new life into victims and survivors. Were the victims who survived to remain numb and mute, they would in some way remain *material* without soul as well as participants in an amnesia that protected the culprits.

Holocaust memoirs of Eli Wiesel and Primo Levi render the horrors of living through the Nazi era and trace the process by which they were transformed from respectable members of European communities into concentration camp victims (see AUTOBIOGRAPHY). Written during her adolescence in Holland and published posthumously after she perished in the camps, Anne Frank's diary renders in first-person terms what it was like for Jews to live in hiding (see NARRATION; PERSON).

Wiesel's *Night*, Levi's *Survival at Auschwitz*, and *The Diary of Anne Frank* demonstrate that in the most effective memoir – and Anne rewrote her original *diary so it is something of a memoir – the

artist shapes his or her vision into a coherent form, highlighting some episodes that have value in terms of his or her vision, while discarding or giving minimal attention to others. This shaping is what differentiates the most compelling Holocaust memoirs from the thousands that have been published in the wake of renewed interest in the Holocaust.

Early fictional Holocaust narratives tended to be realistic and to rely on factual material (see REALIST NOVEL). Using the narrative device of an editor editing the discovered documents of survivors, John Hersey's *The Wall* depicts the day-to-day life in the Warsaw ghetto culminating in the heroic Warsaw Ghetto uprising. In *This Way to the Gas Chambers, Ladies and Gentleman*, Tadeusz Borowski shows through a collection of his first-person *short stories what it was like to be a privileged non-Jewish Polish prisoner at Auschwitz. For example, when the *narrator is on the squad meeting the arriving transports, he realises with mixed emotions that he is himself participating in victimisiation of Jews.

Other writers believed that the intelligibility of history, even the place of evil in history, depends on reconfiguring it in imaginative and aesthetic terms (see HISTORIOGRAPHY; METAHISTORY). As 1945 became more distant in time less realistic narratives became as effective as purportedly objective forms of fiction in presenting events that seem to defy understanding. As early as 1959, André Schwarz-Bart's *The Last of the Just* combined a mythic and *epic overview with a kind of apocalyptic vision and oscillated between heightened and realistic language (see MYTH: THEMATIC APPROACHES). Broadening the scope and context of Holocaust narrative, he placed the Holocaust in the context of Jewish persecution in Europe dating back to the Middle Ages. While Thomas Keneally's *Schindler's List* is in the *genre of Holocaust documentary realism, Stephen Spielberg's epic film transforms Keneally's story about a Nazi industrialist who saves Jews into an epic that visualises the Holocaust in the form of a black and white documentary and includes major Holocaust topoi, from deprivation of human rights and deportation to slave labour and death camps.

Aharon Appelfeld's *Badenheim 1939* (and other of his novels such as *The Age of Wonders* and *The Retreat*), Leslie Epstein's *King of the Jews*, and Art Spiegelman's *Maus* books demonstrate the potential of mythic and metaphoric rendering of the

Holocaust (*see* METAPHOR). These writers draw upon a strand of hyperbole that looks back immediately to prior Jewish writers Franz Kafka and Bruno Schulz, and, earlier, to a Jewish tradition which emphasised *parable and *folktale – as in the work of Sholem Aleichem – to illustrate cultural, religious, and *ethical values.

While *The Diary of Anne Frank, Night*, and *Survival at Auschwitz* established the high seriousness and intense attention to the actual facts that we expect if not require of Holocaust narratives, Appelfeld's mocking *fables, Spiegelman's *comics, Epstein's caricatures and dreamscapes, and Schwarz-Bart's use of myth and *legend to structure his narrative are all departures from traditional naturalism and realism. Yet paradoxically their very efforts to depart from *mimesis break down and show how the searing reality of the Holocaust resists these innovative forms. It is precisely this tension between putative formal solutions and inchoate resistance to allowing form to dominate that is at the very centre of the artistic accomplishment of a great many Holocaust narratives. These more experimental *authors acknowledge that representations – like all narrative representations – are illuminating distortions rather than facsimiles of what really happened. But paradoxically, their reversion to documentary techniques – for example, the unexpected *photographs in *Maus* and specific detailed testimony of the death camps – demonstrates an inner resistance to aesthetic decisions that undermine realism or solemnity (*see* REALISM, THEORIES OF). As they depart from realism, these authors may fear – perhaps unconsciously – that such aesthetic decisions risk dishonouring the dead and trivialising the Holocaust.

Holocaust narratives – both fictional and non-fictional – share a number of features. Many of them depict catastrophe without resorting to apocalyptic visions. Writers as diverse as Primo Levi, Elie Wiesel, Anne Frank, Aharon Appelfeld, Tadeusz Borowski, André Schwarz-Bart, John Hersey, and Cynthia Ozick all realise that the Holocaust questions the possibility of a moral universe. All of these writers understand how we domesticate the implausible and unthinkable into experiences within our ken. Recurring qualities are brevity, a spare style, a childlike vision of the adult world, an ingenuousness through which horrors are realised, a desire to humanise an experience without losing its mythic quality, and a structural principle – in

part derived from biblical forms and rabbinic parables (*see* BIBLICAL NARRATIVE) – which ostentatiously highlights and foregrounds some episodes at the expense of others. Each traces the gradual devolution of an organic community in the face of Nazi obsession with their war against the Jews. Indeed, most Holocaust texts begin in a pedestrian world of apparent normalcy within a seemingly stable culture. What follows is usually a progressive narrative of disruption and deterioration, a teleology of unweaving of the strands of individual and cultural constructions, until Jews are faced with unspeakable horrors of hunger, starvation, deportation, disease, crematoriums, and death marches.

References and further reading

Appelfeld, Aharon (1988) 'After the Holocaust', in Berel Lang (ed.) *Writing and the Holocaust*, New York: Holmes & Meier.

Bauman, Zygmunt (1989) *Modernity and the Holocaust*, Ithaca: Cornell University Press.

Dawidowicz, Lucy (1975) *The War Against the Jews, 1933–1945*, New York: Holt, Rinehart and Winston.

Des Pres, Terence (1970) *The Survivor: An Anatomy of Life in the Death Camps*, New York: Oxford University Press.

Dresden, Sem (1995) *Persecution, Extermination, Literature*, trans. Henry G. Schoax, Toronto: University of Toronto Press.

Ezrahi, Sidra DeKoven (1980) *By Words Alone: The Holocaust in Literature*, Chicago: University of Chicago Press.

Gilbert, Martin (1986) *The Holocaust: The Jewish Tragedy*, London: Collins.

Hilberg, Raul (1967) *The Destruction of the European Jews*, Chicago: University of Chicago Press.

Lacapra, Dominick (1994) *Representing the Holocaust: History, Theory, Trauma*, Ithaca: Cornell University Press.

Langer, Lawrence L. (1975) *The Holocaust and the Literary Imagination*, New Haven: Yale University Press.

—— (1991) *Holocaust Testimonies: The Ruins of Memory*, New Haven: Yale University Press.

Schwarz, Daniel R (1999) *Imagining the Holocaust*, New York: St. Martin's Press.

DANIEL R. SCHWARZ

HOMODIEGETIC NARRATION

In Genettean narratology, a narrative in which the *narrator is also one of the characters inhabiting the *storyworld. *See* NARRATION; PERSON.

HORIZON OF EXPECTATIONS

The term 'horizon of expectations' refers to the set of expectations and shared assumptions held by readers in any given period according to which they understand, interpret, and judge literary texts. The term was introduced into literary theory by Hans Robert Jauss, the leading member of the Constance School of literary *reception theory, in his *Literary History as a Challenge to Literary Theory* (1967; see Jauss 1982: 3–45). Horizons of expectation are in perpetual flux; as they change, so does our understanding and evaluation of literary texts. For Jauss, the meaning and value of a literary work is not fixed and timeless, but unfolds in the history of its reception. The process of reception is seen as an ongoing dialogue between historically situated readers and texts. The task of literary history is, on the one hand, to reconstruct the horizon of expectations that gave life to a historical work, and, on the other, to reveal the critical expectations of the historian's own moment. It is precisely in the encounter with the historical text, as a product of expectations different from our own, that our own horizon of expectations is most concretely revealed to us.

Literary works do not, however, merely reflect the horizon of expectations of their own historical moment. They may also challenge (and by challenging foreground) these historical expectations. For Jauss, the 'aesthetic distance' of any new text from the horizon of expectations characteristic of its own age is a measure of its literary value. The greater the aesthetic distance, the higher the literary value.

Jauss takes his concept of the horizon primarily from the *hermeneutics of Martin Heidegger and Hans-Georg Gadamer, Jauss's teacher. Heidegger had pointed out that the Greek term *horizein* (literally, 'to delimit') had undergone a change of meaning to include both the limits of what is seen and the limits of the act of seeing (Jauss 1989: 199). Gadamer had figured the task of historical understanding as a fusion of horizons (*Horizontverschmelzung*) resulting from a dialogue between interpreter and interpreted (Gadamer 1975: 306–07). The dialogic encounter with the *alterity of the historical other forces us to objectify our own subjective position as itself a historically situated otherness (see DIALOGISM). Although Jauss saw this notion of a fusion of horizons as naive, Gadamer himself never meant it to suggest an objective meeting and reconciliation of past and present; rather, Gadamer held, any projection of the past's alterity will always remain a historically situated projection from the present.

Similarly problematic is Jauss's use of the horizon of expectations in assessing aesthetic value. The idea that 'aesthetic distance' from expected norms is a measure of value *per se* is itself the product of a historically specific horizon of expectations. Originality and experimentation have not always been the key criteria for aesthetic value.

References and further reading

Gadamer, Hans-Georg (1975), *Truth and Method*, trans. Joel Weinsheimer and Donald G. Marshall, London: Sheen and Ward.
Jauss, Hans Robert (1982) *Towards an Aesthetic of Reception*, trans. Timothy Bahti, Minneapolis: University of Minnesota Press.
—— (1989) *Question and Answer: Forms of Dialogic Understanding*, trans. Michael Hays, Minneapolis: University of Minnesota Press.

RICHARD ACZEL

HORROR NARRATIVE

Horror as a narrative mode can be traced back to the origins of representational art. Cave paintings depicting terrifying creatures wreaking havoc on defenceless humans find contemporary analogues in the monster movies playing to packed houses in theaters across the globe. The timeless popularity of horror as a cross-medium *genre appealing primarily to young men and women – perhaps as an adolescent rite of passage, or as a practice ground for the display of socially-sanctioned gender roles – is well-established, and the primitive human need to consume fictional tales of horror is indisputable (*see* FICTION, THEORIES OF; GENDER STUDIES).

When theorising horror, three questions frequently arise: (1) What is the main affect that horror narratives seek to engender in *audiences? (2) Why is it that people are so often frightened by what they know isn't real? And (3) why do so many of us take pleasure from threatening beings and scenarios that would truly horrify if encountered in real life?

There are several different schools of thought concerning the first question above. Sigmund

Freud (1990) characterised the 'uncanny' as that which arouses dread and horror: 'something which is familiar and old-established in the mind and which has become alienated from it only through the process of repression'. In contrast, Noël Carroll (1990) invokes the work of anthropologist Mary Douglas, who attributes feelings of disgust and aversion to apparent transgressions or violations of a particular culture's accepted norms and values (*see* ETHNOGRAPHIC APPROACHES TO NARRATIVE). For Carroll, horror narratives produce an admixture of fear and disgust in audiences through the dangerous, unnatural figure of the monster. Tzvetan Todorov, meanwhile, distinguishes between the *fantastic, the uncanny, and the marvellous in literature, all of which find a place within the horror genre. The fantastic is that hesitation experienced by someone familiar only with the laws of nature, confronting a seemingly supernatural *event. The uncanny for Todorov ultimately offers a resolution governed by natural laws, while the marvellous offers a resolution governed by supernatural laws.

With respect to the question of why we are so often frightened by what we know isn't real, one influential theory (elaborated by Carroll and others) holds that, when people consume horror fictions, the only thing required is that they entertain the *thought* of the frightening entities and events in question – a belief in the monster's existence is not necessary for feelings of horror to result. As for the seemingly perverse pleasures often produced by fictional horror narratives, a popular view has it that consuming such fictions is akin to riding a roller coaster: although we get the adrenaline rush that comes with feeling momentarily unprotected and out of control, we know that ultimately no harm will come to us. As Isabel Pinedo (1997) puts it, fictional horror allows for a 'bounded experience' of fear.

SEE ALSO: catharsis; emotion and narrative; Gothic novel; psychoanalysis and narrative

References and further reading

Carroll, Noël (1990) *The Philosophy of Horror; or, Paradoxes of the Heart*, New York: Routledge.
Freud, Sigmund (1990 [1919]) 'The "Uncanny"'', in James Strachey (ed.) *The Penguin Freud Library, Volume 14: Art and Literature*, London: Penguin.
King, Stephen (1983) *Danse Macabre*, New York: Berkley Books.
Pinedo, Isabel (1997) *Recreational Terror: Women and the Pleasures of Horror Film Viewing*, Albany: SUNY Press.
Schneider, Steven Jay (ed.) (2004) *The Horror Film and Psychoanalysis: Freud's Worst Nightmares*, New York: Cambridge University Press.
Todorov, Tzvetan (1970) *The Fantastic: A Structural Approach to a Literary Genre*, Cornell: Cornell University Press.

STEVEN JAY SCHNEIDER

HUMOUR STUDIES AND NARRATIVE

The study of humour has a long and distinguished tradition, going back to the Greeks. Three main theories have been developed: the incongruity theory (of which the frame/script models below are an instance), the aggression theory, and the relief theory (which claims that humour 'releases' mental 'forces'). The tripartite metatheoretical analysis was introduced in Raskin (1985). The interplay of humour studies and narrative has taken two main directions: the analysis of short humorous narratives (i.e., *jokes) in terms of Proppian *functions and the analysis of the humorous aspect of texts of any length or complexity. Started by an influential article by Morin (1966) the function-based analysis of jokes gained some currency among scholars in Europe, especially in France, Germany, and Italy. Although several analyses were given, all of which differed from a strictly Proppian analysis, the three functions were usually presented as follows: a first function sets up the narrative, a second function introduces a complication, which is resolved (by the punch line) in the third function. However, further work showed that this sequence is in fact common to all narratives (cf. Bremond's elementary sequence in his account of the *logic of narrative). Thus the analysis which purported to be specific to jokes was in fact common to all narratives. Interest in this approach has waned since the 1990s. A detailed account of these issues, with bibliography, can be found in Attardo (1994: 85–91).

A specific analysis of jokes was developed in the frame/script approach to linguistic semantics (Raskin 1985) (*see* FRAME THEORY; SCRIPTS AND SCHEMATA). This approach finds two necessary and sufficient conditions for a text to be funny: the text must be compatible with two distinct scripts and these must be semantically opposite. However, Raskin's model was deliberately limited to short texts which ended in punch lines. In fact, Oring (1989) claimed that the presence of a final punch line is the distinguishing feature between jokes and *anecdotes. Beginning in the mid-1990s, an application of the frame/script-based models of humour to long narrative texts was developed. One of its chief tenets is that instances of humour may occur anywhere in the text (i.e., not just in final position, as in jokes). The neologism 'jab line' was introduced to differentiate freely occurring humour instances from punch lines. Semantically both are analysed in the same way, but punch lines disrupt the narrative, effectively ending it, whereas jab lines do not disrupt the narrative and in fact in some cases are part of its development.

Another important aspect of the broadening of the semantic humour theory is the plotting of the distribution of the jab and punch lines along the linear development of the text. The frequency of occurrence of instances of humour shows interesting patterns that vary from work to work, although no large-scale studies have been yet made to ascertain the gamut of variation. However, the presence in a given text of high humour frequency areas, in which as many as one instance of humour every 18 words is found, and low frequency areas, in which no humour is found ('serious relief'), shows clearly that the distribution of the humour is not random, at least in some texts. Another way of analysing the distribution of humour in a text is by highlighting all jab and punch lines that are related either formally or semantically, thus establishing 'strands', i.e., formally and thematically ordered sets of instances of humour. This technique allows in-depth analysis of connections between *characters and certain kinds of jokes.

Significantly, the existence of specifically humorous narratives has been established. It had been claimed that all humorous narratives are in fact non-humorous stories in which some (or many) jab and punch lines have been inserted. It is possible to provide a non-humorous complete summary of such a narrative. However, there are at least three kinds of narratives that are humorous in and of themselves (no non-humorous complete summary can be provided of these).

The first type uses a non-humorous plot, ending in a punch line. Texts of this type are structurally similar to a joke: they consist of a (usually long) set-up phase, followed by a final punch line that leads to a reinterpretation of the story (examples are Katherine Mansfield's *Feuille D'Album* and Edgar Allan Poe's *The System of Dr. Tarr and Dr. Fethers*). The second type has a humorous plot with metanarrative disruption (*see* METANARRATIVE COMMENT). This is a kind of text that contains one or more disruptions of the narrative conventions of its genre and these disruptions have a humorous nature (mere disruption is not necessarily humorous, as Pirandello's plays show). Examples of this kind of humorous text are Mel Brooks' *Spaceballs*, and Sterne's *Tristram Shandy*, probably the greatest example of the *genre. The third type turns on a *plot in which the central complication of the story is itself humorous (examples are Wilde's *Lord Arthur Savile's Crime* and Labiche's *Un chapeau de paille d'Italie*).

Attardo (2001) provides an in-depth analysis of extended humorous texts. A related approach with a stronger emphasis on *characters is found in Chlopicki's work, which revolves around the idea of character frames that are developed as readers process the text.

SEE ALSO: irony

References and further reading

Attardo, Salvatore (1994) *Linguistic Theories of Humour*, Berlin: Mouton de Gruyter.
—— (2001) *Humorous Texts: A Semantic and Pragmatic Analysis*, Berlin: Mouton de Gruyter.
Chlopicki, Wladyslaw (2001) 'Humorous and Non-humorous Stories: Are There Differences in Frame-based Reception?', *Stylistika*, 10, 59–78.
Hay, Jennifer (2001) 'The Pragmatics of Humour Support', *HUMOUR: International Journal of Humour Research*, 14.1, 55–82.
Morin, Violette (1966) 'L'histoire drôle', *Communications*, 8, 102–19.
Oring, Elliott (1989) 'Between Jokes and Tales: On the Nature of Punch Lines', *HUMOUR: International Journal of Humour Research*, 2.4, 349–64.
Raskin, Victor. (1985) *Semantic Mechanisms of Humour*, Dordrecht: Reidel.

SALVATORE ATTARDO

HYBRID GENRES

Derived from the Latin word *hybrid* ('having a mixed character, based on heterogeneous or incongruous sources'), the term 'hybrid genre' is used to designate works of art which transgress genre boundaries by combining characteristic traits and elements of diverse literary and non-literary *genres. A precondition for this is a thorough examination and transformation of established genre conventions. Although hybrid genres are highly innovative and contribute significantly to the development of novel forms of art, little sustained effort has been made to discuss the impact of generic crossings or to systematise their recent proliferation.

In the field of narrative, the most remarkable instances of hybrid genres are found in the areas of *television, *film, and narrative literature. On TV, performative documentaries such as Ken Loach's *Hidden Agenda* (1990) deliberately blur the boundaries between 'classic' documentaries and fiction films by interpolating documentary film material and authentic interviews with fictional scenes and *dialogues, mixing the conventions of e.g., documentary, *thriller, and spy movie. Likewise, avant-garde filmmakers such as Peter Greenaway not only transgress the boundaries between different filmic genres, but freely incorporate material from pictorial, literary, and graphic arts (*see* PICTORIAL NARRATIVITY). The same is true of hybrid literature: From its very beginning, narrative *fiction has drawn widely from literary and non-literary discourses, adapting them to its specific historical and formal needs and often importing them unchanged into its own *narrative structure (*see* DISCOURSE ANALYSIS (FOUCAULT); HETEROGLOSSIA).

Indeed, the history of the *novel can be read in terms of *hybridity and homogeneity, with decidedly hybrid beginnings in the seventeenth and eighteenth-centuries, a strong move towards homogenisation in the nineteenth-century, and a similarly strong move towards hybridisation in the late twentieth century. Famous examples of hybrid narrative fiction include Francis Kirkman's *The Counterfeit Lady Unveiled* (1673), Lawrence Sterne's *Tristram Shandy* (1759–1767), James Joyce's *Ulysses* (1922), George Perec's *La Vie mode d'emploi* (1978), Leslie Marmon Silko's *Storyteller* (1981), Ntozake Shange's *Sassafrass, Cyprus and Indigo* (1987), Adam Thorpe's *Ulverton* (1992), and Laura Esquivel's *La ley del amor* (1995). Hybrid novels such as the ones just listed combine, transform, and subvert the conventions of several narrative sub-genres; break down the boundaries between fiction, poetry, and *drama;

import non-literary discourses and text-types; and employ narrative strategies that strive to imitate the organising principles of painting, *music, and film. Hybrid narratives can be interspersed with *short stories or *fairy tales, poetry or drama; they confront the reader with scientific treatises, courtroom testimonies, film scripts, or cooking recipes. By transgressing genre boundaries, hybrid genres aim at distancing themselves from the homogeneous, one-voiced, and 'one-discoursed' worldview conventional narratives seem to suggest, a notion which is closely related to Bakthin's concept of the *dialogic imagination. Moreover, hybrid genres are intricately linked to the notion of a hybrid *identity, which is fluid, unstable, incessantly in search of and transforming itself. Due to their complex *gestalt*, hybrid genres are best approached with the help of theories of genre, *hybridity, *intermediality, and *intertextuality.

SEE ALSO: cinéroman; narrative in poetry

References and further reading

Galster, Christin (2001) *Hybrides Erzählen* und hybride Identität im britischen Roman der Gegenwart, Frankfurt: Lang.

Geertz, Clifford (1980) 'Blurred Genres: The Refiguration of Social Thought', *The American Scholar*, 49, 165–79.

Joseph, May, and Jennifer Natalya Fink (eds) (1999) *Performing Hybridity*, Minneapolis: University of Minnesota Press.

Krewani, Angela (2001) *Hybride Formen: New British Cinema – Television Drama – Hypermedia*, Trier: WVT.

Nünning, Ansgar (1997) 'Crossing Borders and Blurring Genres', *EJES*, 1, 217–38.

CHRISTIN GALSTER

HYBRIDITY

In the nineteenth-century, the term 'hybridity' was applied mainly to the offspring of mixed breeding in both human and non-human contexts (Young 1995). In narrative study, the term 'hybrid texts' is used to refer to *novels in which Western and post-colonial (native) writing traditions creatively interact, as in the work of Salman Rushdie. In literature, the term was first employed by Mikhail Bakhtin to characterise the novel as an inherently *hybrid genre. The 'artistic hybrid' (1981: 360) employs three strategies: hybridisation (the 'mixture of two social languages within the limits of a single utterance' (358)), stylisation, and the use of *dialogue (*see* HETEROGLOSSIA). Hybridity came into its own in the late 1980s and 1990s when it was appropriated by post-colonial literary theory, especially by Homi Bhabha (1994) as well as Stuart Hall, Paul Gilroy, Henry Louis Gates, Kobena Mercer, and others. From a negative evaluation of hybridity as bastardy, miscegenation, and genetic contamination, post-colonial critics have reinterpreted the concept, converting it into a positive label of multiculturalist racial intermixing, syncretism, and transnationality (Nederveen Pieterse 2001).

Three stages of hybridisation can be observed: (a) a mere mixing or merging of cultures or ethnicities (e.g., the ideals of a pluralist society in which different cultures coexist according to the ethics of multiculturalism); (b) a more dynamic reading of hybridity in terms of Bhabha's concept of *mimicry* (the two cultural *identities tend to adopt features one of the other); and (c) a refunctionalisation of *alterities within one's own cultural horizon (Fludernik 1998: 261). Bhabha's concept of mimicry can best be illustrated by the figure of Aziz in E. M. Forster's *A Passage to India* (1924), in which the Indian doctor attempts to become British, but is never perceived by the British to achieve perfect Englishness. Conversely, British subjects in India could slide into native habits, 'go native' (see the figure of Strickland in Kipling's short stories). At stage three, refunctionalisation, aspects of the foreign culture are integrated into one's own moral and cultural universe and redeployed for new purposes. Thus, in a story by the Canadian author Shauna Singh Baldwin, *Montreal 1962*, the wife of a Sikh immigrant to Canada goes out to work in order to safeguard her husband's honour (*izzat*) since he would have to take off his turban to find work and feed the family. The wife transforms an activity which would be disreputable in her home country into a positive action (saving the husband's honour); she does not try to emancipate herself (which would be the Canadian reading of her taking a job). Similarly, the British redeployment of native forms of audience (*darshana*) during the Raj is an instance of using an alien cultural item and integrating it with one's own politics of imperial appeasement.

Within the discourse of multiculturalism, hybridity has frequently been equated with creolisation (Gates 1992; Hall 1993), syncretism, and – most recently – diasporism. In the late 1990s, celebrations of hybridity were designed to liberate the subject from cultural constraints, encouraging a free appropriation of cultural markers by a process of *bricolage*. The recent shift towards diaspora, cultural rights theory, and cultural confrontation in the wake of 9/11 has tended to emphasise the limitations of hybridity.

Currently, the term hybridity is being extended to cover hybrid genres, hybrid technologies, and hypertext (Grassian) (*see* DIGITAL NARRATIVE).

SEE ALSO: cultural studies approaches to narrative; post-colonialism and narrative

References and further reading

Bakhtin, Mikhail (1981) *The Dialogic Imagination: Four Essays*, trans. Caryl Emerson and Michael Holquist, Austin, TX: University of Texas Press.
Bhabha, Homi K. (1994) *The Location of Culture*, London: Routledge.
Fludernik, Monika (ed.) (1998) *Hybridity and Postcolonialism: Twentieth-Century Indian Literature*, Tübingen: Stauffenburg.
Gates, Henry Louis Jr. (1992) 'Hybridity Happens: Black Brit Bricolage Brings the Noise', *Village Voice Literary Supplement*, 109, 26–27.
Grassian, Daniel (2003) *Hybrid Fictions: American Literature and Generation X*, London: McFarland.
Hall, Stuart (1993 [1990]) 'Cultural Identity and Diaspora', in Patrick Williams and Laura Christman (eds) *Colonial Discourse and Post-colonial Theory: A Reader*, New York: Harvester Wheatsheaf.
Nederveen Pieterse, Jan (2001) 'Hybridity, So What?', *Theory, Culture & Society*, 18, 219–45.
Young, Robert J. C. (1995) *Colonial Desire: Hybridity in Theory, Culture and Race*, London: Routledge.

MONIKA FLUDERNIK

HYPERTEXT

A collection of texts or text fragments interconnected by links that afford a choice of reading orders. Primarily a mode of organisation of documents within an electronic database, hypertext is the basic structure of Internet sites, but the concept has also been exploited in literary narrative. *See* DIGITAL NARRATIVE (also: ERGODIC LITERATURE; MULTI-PATH NARRATIVE).

HYPERTEXT AND HYPOTEXT (GENETTE)

In Genettean poetics, a hypertext is a text that builds on or contains traces of an earlier text, the hypotext. Alternate terms used in intertextuality theory are 'intertext' and 'pretext', respectively. *See* NARRATIVE VERSIONS (also: INTERTEXTUALITY).

HYPODIEGETIC NARRATIVE

Coined by narratologist Mieke Bal and preferred by many narratologists over the Genettean 'metadiegetic narrative', the term denotes a story within a story, a narrative embedded within a framing narrative. *See* EMBEDDING; FRAMED NARRATIVE.

IDENTITY AND NARRATIVE

The question of personal identity has puzzled philosophers for a long time, and various approaches proposed in the Western tradition have constantly run into the difficulty of reckoning with the fact that change is built into the biological condition of the human being. To define identity as sameness or preservation of some essential quality of a person, then, seemed counter-intuitive. Yet the very meaning of the term 'identity' is predicated on constancy, on the absence of change. To escape this dilemma, some philosophers attempted to define personal identity as continuity of situations featuring the person, and shifted the emphasis from identifying a person through characteristics to finding patterns that hold together the actions committed and *events experienced by that person (see ACTION THEORY). The transition was facilitated by the recognition that human beings are historical agents whose lives have temporal duration, with beginnings, middles, and endings, and it benefited from the insights revealed in a major debate that took place in the 1960s in the philosophy of history, on the nature and role of narrative in the study of history (see AGENCY; HISTORIOGRAPHY).

The result of this debate was an increased reliance on the explanatory and descriptive power of narratives in the presentation of historical accounts. Do narratives have a similar power when it comes to understanding a person's life history? Scholars who believe so usually fall in two categories: those who use narrative as a cognitive instrument, and maintain that when we tell our *life stories we impose order on chaotic events, structuring amorphous, lived experience (Bruner, Mink, Dennett; see NARRATIVE AS COGNITIVE INSTRUMENT), and those for whom narrative has ontological value, i.e., those for whom the ordered narrative of a life reflects the narrative order of experience (Ricoeur, MacIntyre). As a compromise between these two positions, narrative can be deemed a heuristic that allows us to study how the act of recounting lived experience, regardless whether this act is independent from the actual experience, and can create a coherent identity for the individual whose story is recounted. In more empirically oriented disciplines (*sociolinguistics, *discourse analysis (linguistics), *ethnography), the heuristic function of narratives has produced important studies of how a consistent identity is shaped in everyday interactions (see COMMUNICATION IN NARRATIVE).

From action to character

In the 1980s, Paul Ricoeur introduced the idea that the complexity of a human life, with its many transformations brought about by the sheer passage of *time, can become more palatable to our understanding if it is put in a narrative format. A decade later, taking his lead from Wilhelm Dilthey, who deemed life a series of interconnected events, Ricoeur argued that we make sense of our own and of others' *biographies the same way we understand stories: by following a *plot and the protagonist featured in it. In narrative terms, then, the identity of a person is the identity of a *character. Ricoeur's view of narrative was largely based on Aristotle's *Poetics*, from which he borrowed the notion of characters being shaped by their actions and experiences. What makes characters recognisable to the audience is the ordered series of events in which they are featured. While lived experience can be 'messy' and hard to explain or categorise, stories have plots that mediate between disparate components of action – chance occurrences, unfulfilled intentions, unknown causes, unexpected effects – and the temporal unity of the story recounted (*see* CAUSALITY; INTENTIONALITY). The function of the plot is to detect concordance within dispersal by making connections even between seemingly disjoined episodes of a story. *Emplotment – structuring the story into a coherent sequence of actions and events – is also a process by which the effect of contingency, as unpredictability and randomness, is converted into the effect of necessity or probability exerted by the configuring act of the storyline (*see* LOGIC OF NARRATIVE).

From the perspective of a narrative understanding of identity, the focus is on what happens in a person's life rather than on some inherent, essential quality that defines that person. From a narrative standpoint, then, a person is fundamentally an agent, insofar as his or her identity is shaped by his or her actions. But the difficulty posed by this view is that equating people with characters of their life stories, rather than with the *narrators or perhaps even the *authors of these stories, limits the amount of self-reflection, self-awareness, or self-control we are willing to grant individuals. Ricoeur himself pondered the dilemma of whether to place the self in the character-, narrator-, or author-position, and further complicated it by pointing out the inevitable incompleteness of one's life story for as long as one is alive. Yet without knowledge of how the narrative ends, how to make sense of the plot (*see* CLOSURE)?

Narrative theories of identity posit a past self, retrospectively defined from the vantage of the present, but fail to shed much light on the present self, which remains systematically elusive, as philosophers had complained all along. Ricoeur finds a partial response to such difficulties in the philosophy of history. When recounting historical events, historians use a model of comprehension based on the interpenetration of our experience of the past and our intentions for and anticipations of the future. As we bring to life an event that happened in the past, we endow it with meaning that combines experience with expectation. Similarly, identity defined in narrative terms is not the story of a past self, told from the privileged perspective of a present self that remains nevertheless invisible, unknown. Instead, the story is continuously adjusted to accommodate and reconcile, if necessary, the self whose actions have already been committed with the self who makes plans for future action. Such a revised understanding of the narrative view also addresses Ricoeur's observation that a life story can be recounted in several possible ways, that there is a multitude of potential scenarios that can account for the actions and experiences of an individual, rather than one single *master narrative.

The social and ethical configurations of life stories

Ricoeur's narrative theory of identity is based on moderate ontological assumptions about the narrative nature of reality itself. Where Ricoeur leaves some room for the possibility that the stories shaping our identity are constructed rather than extracted from the inherently narrative structure of experience, MacIntyre rejects altogether the notion of a non-narrative reality. Also influenced by Aristotle, but by his ethics rather than his poetics, MacIntyre sees human life as a quest for an ultimate good, and narrative as the ideal medium for the implicit *telos*, or goal-orientation, of life thus conceived (*see* ETHICAL TURN). In his view, people are 'storytelling animals', because it is only in the context of a containing narrative that isolated actions and words become instances of meaningful and purposive behaviour. MacIntyre's narrative view of identity is coloured, as in the case of Ricoeur, by his Aristotelian allegiances. His ideas are inextricably connected to assumptions about the moral and ethical make-up of an individual: to be the character of your life story, according to MacIntyre, is to be accountable for the actions that can be imputed to you. In response to philosophers who require strict psychological continuity as the criterion of identity, MacIntyre argues that a person identified as A under one *description is the same as the person identified as B under a different description if she can give an intelligible narrative account that explains what A and B have in common, or how they could represent, perhaps at different times and places, representations of the same individual. Personal identity, therefore, does not stem from any kind of psychological continuity but from the unity of character and action required by the unity of narrative. Beyond identification through *reference (names or descriptions; *see* NAMING IN NARRATIVE), stories establish the identity of a character by creating chains of events and offering causal explanations when change is involved. The listener comes to know the characters of a story by understanding the sequence of actions in which they are involved.

But individuals are not only accountable for their actions. In their turn, they can also hold others accountable, and each life story is part of an interlocking set of narratives. Unlike Ricoeur's, MacIntyre's theory also has a distinct communitarian streak: for him, the fact that a person's life can be variously narrated is a consequence of the embeddedness of individual lives in the existence of a community: the life stories of others shape ours variously (*see* SOCIOLOGY AND NARRATIVE). This communitarian streak can also be found in Bruner's narrative theory of identity. Investigating the *genre of *autobiography, Bruner claims that individuals make sense of their personal experience by articulating it along the lines of consecrated literary genres – *Bildungsroman, black comedy, and others. Such genres provide a foundation for our sense of identity, while at the same time making us members of the community that created them. Bruner, however, views narrative as an epistemic structure that makes reality intelligible to us, rather than as an ontological carrier of an already narrativised reality. Similarly, for Mink, stories are never 'lived', but always 'told', in the sense that we cannot differentiate 'raw' events from their narrated representations. We gain access to events through a story, and what might seem to be sheer description is another narrative. Mink contends that life has no beginnings, middles, or ends. As storytellers, we provide a beginning, middle, and it is only in a retrospective narrative that we can speak of hopes being fulfilled or unfulfilled, goals accomplished or not, decisions sound or mistaken.

For his part, Dennett maintains that we develop a sense of self-identity by fostering the illusion of a 'Central Headquarters' where our decisions are made, because we assume that responsibility for our actions and intentions is only possible if it can be traced to a sort of central authority that oversees our behaviour. Also committed to the ethical and social significance of agency, but sceptical with regards to the possibility of 'pinning down' the self, Dennett argues that identity is a *myth created in response to our need to understand the actions of individuals, including our own. On this account, identity is a theoretical construct that plays a role

similar to that of the centre of gravity in physics. Unidentifiable by colour, mass, or any other physical properties, the centre of gravity is an abstraction designed to convey information about an object, to explain its behaviour in the present, and anticipate it in the future. Similarly, it is important to assume that individuals have an identity represented as the centre of narrative gravity because such a centre gives coherence and meaning to all of our experiences and actions. Dennett found confirmation for his theory in the medical research conducted by neuroscientists on individuals with brain impairment. Such research has shown that patients with serious brain injuries that should have made it impossible for them, according to medical criteria, to have a unified field of consciousness and a coherent perception of their own experience were still able to find strategic ways to maintain psychological unity. From the perspective of neuroscience and cognitive science, such unity is the mark of a normal psychological life, but it is not an actual feature as much as a cognitive illusion that shapes our perceptions and evaluations of who we are and what we do. This illusion represents our desire to make our experience cohere into the story that represents our autobiography.

Identity and narrative in everyday communication

The connection established by philosophers between narrative and identity has been fruitfully exploited in various social sciences, such as anthropology, sociology, psychology, and linguistics. The ontological status of this connection plays a less important role in these fields, especially in those which, under phenomenological auspices, bracket the question of the real, choosing instead to focus on the everyday practices by which members of a community develop a sense of themselves and their environment. Holstein and Gubrium, for example, claim that the formation of identity is anchored in narrative practice, defined as a form of interpretive activity that includes the process of storytelling, the resources used to tell stories, and the circumstances of *narration. Storytelling is both constrained by cultural and social conventions and actively shaped by individuals. Resources for narrating range from brief recollections of specific events to an extended account of virtually a lifetime of experience.

An important theoretical and analytical concept developed in these fields is that of a personal narrative or life story, which represents a type of oral, autobiographical communication often resulting from the interaction between an interviewer and the respondent (*see* ORAL HISTORY). Ethnographers and sociolinguists are interested in how individuals recounting personal narratives use language in order to create a logical and temporal order among lived events (*see* TEMPORAL ORDERING). They view narrative as both a genre and an activity, paying attention to specific verbal constructions as well as to the social transactions and negotiations such constructions permit. The *orality of life stories could constitute a source of incoherence or randomness in the articulation of events and actions: given the nature of this communicative situation, with the turn-taking in asking questions and formulating answers, it is inevitable that the narrators would digress, improvise, leave out information, or try to present themselves in a certain light. But Linde has shown that despite such opportunity for incoherence, storytellers usually manage to articulate a coherent story by resorting to various 'coherence structures' that enable them to take stock and make sense of their experiences. Coherence structures consist of themes and plots along which the individual can articulate a systematic sense of self. Reflecting upon the activity of narrating a life story, Bertaux characterises it as an effort to totalise subjectively one's past experiences by binding them together into the plot, but more importantly, by also providing retrospective evaluations of those experiences and thus linking the past to the present. Life stories aspire to *verisimilitude rather than *truth: they do not recapture the past but engage in its active reconstruction from the standpoint of the present. Thus, individuals recounting their life stories have access to 'narrative editing', as they can and do 'step out of their stories' to re-adjust the perspective or to focus on how their account is received by the *audience (Riessman 1990).

While much narrative scholarship focuses on the coherence of personal stories, Ochs and Capps argue that sometimes, in order to understand how narratives shape identity, we must also attend to the less coherent accounts, the 'works in progress' that allow their tellers to cope with problematic, unresolved life experiences. The narratives that lack coherence display a different kind of plot, which draws from multiple *perspectives and is often designed in collaboration with the listener. Through such co-authoring, life stories connect individuals to existing communities, or create new communities. Gergen and Gergen question the possibility of narrative self-construction to ever be an entirely private matter, as long as in order to convey a private experience one needs to incorporate it in a system of meaning shared by others. For Ochs and Capps, too, interaction is central to the narrative process that shapes identity. They contend that once an experience has been related, it enters public discourse and multiple participants in the discourse determine the meaning it acquires. But the authority of others in shaping the story of an individual can also become oppressive, and sometimes individuals have to 'reclaim' their stories as a way of empowering themselves and overcoming dependency on hegemonic discursive practices. Thus, feminists recognise that stories are inevitably rooted in culture, but they suggest that an individual can selectively use resources existing in culture and social discursive practices in order to create the story that best defines who he or she is. Instead of simply assimilating the ideological messages encapsulated in the stories that compose their cultural environment, individuals can critically assess and alter discourse and thus, reconstruct their identity through reflective practice (*see* IDEOLOGY AND NARRATIVE; GENDER STUDIES).

If certain standpoints from which identity is narrated become essentialised or too homogenised, the resulting identities are forced to conform to stereotypes, be they racial, gendered, or ethnic. Post-colonial theorists are devoting much effort to recuperating the authentic narratives of historically disenfranchised ethnic groups, rather than reading their identity through the lens of the master narratives developed by the colonisers, which impose their representation of reality, often figuring the 'native' as primitive, irrational, evil (*see* POST-COLONIALISM AND NARRATIVE). But postmodernist scholars have questioned the very notion of any 'authentic', singular identity narrative, and have proposed instead that several plots corresponding to the multifaceted world in which we live shape us. Trinh Minh-ha maintains that identity is located at the intersection of multiple narrative scenarios, and that instead of asking 'who' we are we should be concerned with 'where', 'when', and 'how' we are, and allow for the possibility that the answers may not necessarily cohere into a single plot. The stress on biographical coherence has been criticised by Pierre Bourdieu, as the intrusion of the analyst who tries to impose a certain pattern on narrated experience. Scholars of different persuasions, however, such as cognitive philosophers, philosophers of history, conversational analysts, and ethnographers, define coherence not as a formal structure but rather as a cognitive strategy, or as an effort to find meaning and stability in the lived experience of an individual. Thus defined, narrative coherence is an important theoretical and analytical concept that incorporates the rupture and continuity characteristic of most people's lives. The narrative perspective on identity, regardless of its disciplinary context, recognises the need to account for both the transformation and stability of individuals, and uses stories as the ideal medium for reconciling change with sameness (*see* NARRATIVISATION).

SEE ALSO: narrative psychology; positioning

References and further reading

Bertaux, Daniel (1997) *Les récits de vie*, Paris: Nathan.
Bourdieu, Pierre (1986) 'L'illusion biographique', *Actes de la Recherche en Sciences Sociales*, 62/63, 69–72.
Bruner, Jerome (1987) 'Life as Narrative', *Social Research*, 54, 11–32.
Dennett, Daniel (1996). *Elbow Room: Varieties of Free Will Worth Wanting*, Cambridge: MIT.
Gergen, Kenneth J., and Mary M. Gergen (1997) 'Narratives of the Self', in Lewis P. Hinchman and Sandra K. Hinchman (eds) *Memory, Identity, Community*, Albany, NY: State University of New York Press.
Holstein, James A., and Jaber F. Gubrium (2000) *The Self We Live By: Narrative Identity in a Postmodern World*, Oxford: Oxford University Press.
Linde, Charlotte (1993) *Life Stories: The Creation of Coherence*, New York: Oxford University Press.
MacIntyre, Alasdair (1985) *After Virtue: A Study in Moral Theory*, Notre Dame: Notre Dame University Press.
Mink, Louis (1987) 'Narrative Form as a Cognitive Instrument', *Historical Understanding*, eds. B. Fay, E. O. Golob, and R. T. Vann, Ithaca: Cornell University Press.
Ochs, Elinor, and Lisa Capps (2001) *Living Narrative: Creating Lives in Everyday Storytelling*, Cambridge, Mass.: Harvard University Press.
Ricoeur, Paul (1984–1988) *Time and Narrative*, trans. Kathleen McLaughlin and David Pellauer, Chicago: University of Chicago Press.
——— (1992) *Oneself as Another*, trans. Kathleen Blamey, Chicago: University of Chicago Press.
Riessman, Catherine Kohler (1993) *Narrative Analysis*, Thousand Oaks: Sage.
Trinh Minh-ha (1992) *Framer Framed*, New York: Routledge.

ANDREEA DECIU RITIVOI

IDEOLOGY AND NARRATIVE

How the relationship between narrative and ideology is understood depends at least in part on which theoretical model of ideology is being utilised. Marxist *Ideologiekritik* has the longest tradition of analysing ideology in relation to narrative, but within Marxism both positive and negative models of ideology have been current at different times – or even at the same time. As a result of this variability, Raymond Williams and others have ruled out the idea of establishing a single 'correct' Marxist model of ideology.

Between the poles of, on the one hand, a traditionalist view which would see literature – because it is 'art' – as able to transcend the constraints of ideology, and, on the other, a reflection theory of literature which would see the text as unable to do more than represent the dominant ideologies of the period, Marxist critics articulate more complex understandings. Even for someone like Lukács, whose view of literature is broadly reflectionist, narrative does much more than merely repeat or reflect ideologies. For example, Lukács suggests that narrative can provide, at the level of the aesthetic, a resolution for those real (apparently insoluble) contradictions which constitute class-based society. At the same time, for Lukács, the accurate *narration of, for example, periods of social change or crisis can enable writers – sometimes unwittingly – to get beyond their own ideological affiliations.

For Gramsci, forms of cultural production – especially narrative – play an important role in convincing people of the *truth of a certain preferred view of the world, thereby securing their consent to being ruled by the group or class whose particular preferred *perspective the text represents. While the strategy may be limited (in the context of colonialism, for example, where most of the colonised could not read such narratives), it may nevertheless be crucial. Thus, in that same colonial context, the members of the colonised culture who *could* read and who needed to be won over were precisely the educated members of the middle or upper classes who were essential as intermediaries, facilitating as far as possible the consent of the colonised community at large.

The colonial context also points to the important ways in which the ideological critique of narrative has moved beyond its class-based origins to areas such as *gender and race. For instance, a significant element in earlier feminist analysis consisted of the identification of patriarchal attitudes or sexist ideologies inscribed in texts (*see* FEMINIST NARRATOLOGY). These could be linked to issues of class and capitalism, but were clearly not circumscribed by them. In a similar way, one of the first stages of the post-colonial critique was the identification and rejection of ideologies of racial or cultural superiority so powerfully articulated in the *novels of empire (*see* POST-COLONIALISM AND NARRATIVE).

Although concepts of ideology may have moved increasingly towards the neutral or non-judgemental, the critique of ideology in narrative remains most compelling when it addresses those ideological formations which are decidedly *not* neutral, and which legitimate continuing modes of domination or exploitation.

SEE ALSO: cultural studies approaches to narrative; Marxist approaches to narrative; sociological approaches to literary narrative

References and further reading

Eagleton, Terry (1976) *Criticism and Ideology*, London: Verso.
—— (1991) *Ideology*, London: Verso.
Jameson, Fredric (1982) *The Political Unconscious*, London: Methuen.
Williams, Raymond (1977) *Marxism and Literature*, Oxford: Oxford University Press.

PATRICK WILLIAMS

IMAGE AND NARRATIVE

The success of classic theories about the expressive power of words versus images (see, e.g., Lessing's *Laokoon* (1776)) explains why fixed images have long been considered incompatible with narrative devices and storytelling. Emphasising the differences between word and image, i.e., between *time and *space, Lessing attacked the idea that literature was 'painting with words' and painting 'narration with colour'. He saw the two *media as predisposed to the representation of different meanings: *description for painting, *narration for language, and he was sceptical of attempts by one medium to invade the territory of the other. His ideas, which remained influential until the mid-twentieth century, were questioned by the emergence of mass-media as well as by the avant-garde, both of which refused the strict separation of words and images. During the heyday of the *novel (stretching between its 'rise' in the second half of the eighteenth-century and the post-modernist critique of the *genre), the tension between word and images was strongly felt; during this phase the presence of visual material in verbal storytelling was reduced to a merely illustrative function and thus excluded from the core of the literary system. The suspicion toward images resulted from the encounter of two types of arguments, which have always been very closely intertwined.

The first one was *ideological*, and had to do with the distinction between high and low art: the image was seen as more 'female' than 'male'; visual literacy was seemingly easier to achieve than verbal literacy; and industrial evolutions in print technology demonstrated a clear link between the increased role of the image on the one hand and mass communication on the other. These factors led to the dismissal of the use of illustrations by 'serious' novelists, who viewed illustrations as compromising the high-art ambition of their work. The most famous example of this rejection was Gustave Flaubert. Despite the example of the merger of word and image in the high-art 'artist book' (whose beginnings can be traced back to the 1870s, but whose scope was limited to poetry), the use of images in narrative works was excluded from the field of 'serious' production, but allowed in other, less prestigious genres (for instance children's literature or the popular novel) and in alternative ways of publishing (for instance the prepublication of the novel in instalments in highly commercial journals or popular reprints in cheap editions) (*see* CHILDREN'S STORIES (NARRATIVES WRITTEN FOR CHILDREN)).

The second argument underwriting the suspicion toward images was *mediological*, and had to do with the distinction between the fictional character of storytelling and the non-fictional character of a certain type of picture, namely, the *photograph. If the difficult encounter of storytelling and (non-photographic) images was a matter of competition between the arts, the use of photographs in novels seemed a real menace to the ontological specificity of *fiction. It is for instance not coincidental that the photographs in the collaboration between Henry James and Alvin Langdon Coburn were very 'pictorialist' (and thus more 'artful' than 'straight' photographs). The effect of the pictures was to suggest an atmosphere, rather than to contribute to the construction of the fictional world (*see* STORYWORLD).

The shifting attitudes towards the use of images as part of the story must to be situated at the intersection of ideological and mediological considerations. The avant-garde critique of the hierarchy of high art and low art forms has undoubtedly fostered a wider use of images in storytelling. Meanwhile, the critique of the assumption that artistic storytelling is necessarily fictional has taken away the basis for the discrimination against photographic images. Thus the *Surrealists' experiments with new ways of documentary storytelling, exemplarily in André Breton's *Nadja* (1928), were both a rejection of the bourgeois novel as gratuitous and formulaic fiction and an attempt to include photographic material in ways that were no longer simply illustrative. Images in this practice become full-fledged narrative elements. A further step is taken when pictures not only replace the descriptive parts of the novel, but also provide information crucial for understanding the narrative itself, as in the collage-novels invented by Man Ray, or when sequences of photographs create 'mute' narratives (as in the work of Duane Michals, or Marie-Françoise Plissart). Since the 1920s, book-object artists have tried to engender narratives by merging word and images in ways that made the two media almost indistinguishable. A well-know example is Tom Philips's *A Humument*.

The importance of ideological and mediological issues can also be detected in more contemporary forms of word-and-image storytelling. *Postmodern writers such as W. G. Sebald (who includes photographic illustrations in all of his novels) or Douglas Coupland (who authored *Polaroids from the Dead*) use pictures in ways that are clearly more systematic and diverse than in the work of their forerunners. At the same time, however, they criticise the mainstream conception of photography and its role in the contemporary society of the spectacle. Sebald's pictures are 'tricked', in the sense that the referential backing of his images is no longer guaranteed (*see* REFERENCE). Photographs lose their referentiality,

their testimonial value, while at the same time they increase dramatically their potential as vehicles of fictional narrative. Coupland's images, mostly nostalgic pop-artefacts of the 1960s, are freely inserted in a text which can be read as a critique of postmodern consumer society in the age of *television.

The emerging experiments with e-narrative, the latest form of multimedia storytelling, seem to re-enact the difficulties of blending words and images encountered during the nineteenth-century. Except for the specific case of *computer games and virtual reality (which for authors such as Janet Murray represent the real future of digital storytelling), most examples of fictional narratives continue to emphasise the dominant position of the word, reducing images once again to their classic role of more or less dispensable illustrations, even though they reinforce the visual dimensions of the words themselves.

SEE ALSO: comics and graphic novel; digital narrative; graphic presentation as expressive device; ideology and narrative; intermediality; pictorial narrativity; visual narrativity

References and further reading

Breton, André (1960) *Nadja*, New York: Grove.
Coupland, Douglas (1996) *Polaroids from the Dead*, London: Flamingo.
Debray, Régis (1991) *Cours de médiologie générale*, Paris: Gallimard.
Hunter, Jefferson (1987) *Image and Word: The Interaction of Twentieth-Century Photographs and Texts*, Cambridge, Mass.: Harvard University Press.
Michals, Duane (1976) *Real Dreams*, Danbury, NH: Addison House.
Murray, Janet (1997) *Hamlet on the Holodeck*, New York: The Free Press.
Phillips, Tom (1980) *A Humument*, London: Thames and Hudson.
Plissart, Marie-Françoise (1985) *Droit de regards*, Paris: Minuit.
Sebald, W. G. (1992) *Die Ausgewanderten*, Frankfurt: Eichborn.

JAN BAETENS

IMMERSION

The term 'immersion' is most commonly encountered in theoretical contexts related to multimedia environments, *computer games, and other implementations of virtual reality. This leads sometimes to the erroneous belief that only modern technological devices have the capability to produce states or processes of immersion. In fact, immersion is central to mental simulation in general and to mimetic art in particular (*see* MIMESIS; SIMULATION AND NARRATIVE). The last point has been recognised in Western Culture at least since Plato, whose analysis in *The Republic* (esp. Bks III and X) highlights some of the central features of immersion.

In its most general sense, immersion refers to any state of absorption in some action, condition, or interest. As such the term has been used and continues to be used in various contexts, notably in anthropology (where it refers to an emphatic kind of communication with the divine) and language learning. In narrative theory, immersion is normally used in a narrower sense. It retains the idea of absorption but specifies its nature, its vehicle, and its target domain as follows:

- narrative immersion is a simulative process, more precisely a specific form of the pervasive phenomenon of mental simulation (Currie and Ravenscroft 2002);
- narrative immersion is induced by props (Walton 1990) or mimetic primers, which may be verbal, visual, visual-acoustic, or even visual-acoustic-tactile;
- the functioning of these primers is at least in part cognitively impenetrable (Dokic and Proust 2002: viii) or pre-attentional;
- the target domain of narrative immersion is a mentally projected world, i.e., a holistic set of mental representations foregrounding phenomenological and spatial properties perspectively organised (Dokic and Proust 2002; *see* PERSPECTIVE; SPACE IN NARRATIVE; STORYWORLD).

Given that adopting the stance of immersion implies being absorbed in the mentally represented content in such a way as to treat it – up to a point – as if it were the actual object or situation, the process of immersion has often been related to illusion, most famously by Plato. He particularly emphasised the 'getting carried away' phenomenon which is constitutive of immersive experiences induced by mimetic devices (in Plato's time, painting and *drama; *see* PICTORIAL NARRATIVITY), and which appears to be due to the effectiveness of pre-attentional mimetic 'baits'. He concluded that immersion, being inaccessible to analytical thought, was dangerous and epistemically void.

Admittedly, the psychological and representational features of the state of imaginative immersion are still very poorly understood. Nevertheless, Plato's view of immersion as an illusionist device that fools the senses and the mind seems to be misguided. In fact, Walton maintains that in the course of the immersion process, the reader, spectator, etc. always remains conscious of the fact that he or she is indulging in a 'game of make-believe' (Walton 1990), retaining an awareness of the distinction between the imagined situation induced by the mimetic primers and his or her real-world surroundings. Immersion appears to be a dual-plane mental state (Lotman 1977) in which the pre-attentional mimetic primers induce a real-world treatment of at least some elements of the representational stimuli. But as soon as they enter consciousness, their real-world pretension is bracketed by the knowledge of the actual (simulative) causal nexus having led to their formation. So, in some way the mental dynamics of immersion are related to that of perceptual illusions which present the same combination of pre-attentional 'errors' being bracketed – but not destroyed! – by conscious control.

For immersion to be effective, the priming stimulus must of course be able to elicit an imaginary counterpart of an object or situation in the real world (*see* EXISTENT; SITUATION MODEL). This would explain why mimetic representations in the technical sense, e.g. representations such as *photographs, which resemble the objects and situations they represent (or more precisely the stimuli which are or would be induced by an encounter with the actual objects or situations mirrored by the simulation), seem to be especially strong immersion-inducing vehicles. Yet, verbal narratives also are known to have very powerful immersion-inducing capabilities. Therefore it seems that a semiotic vehicle which is based on an arbitrary relationship between sign and represented content can also induce an immersive response (*see* SEMIOTICS). This in turn would seem to suggest that the existence of a mimetic primer is not a necessary condition for immersion.

One could be tempted to argue against the foregoing by introducing the notion of pretence (as Searle and Genette have done) and by claiming that the central mimetic dimension of verbal narrative fiction stems from the fact that, taking the linguistic appearance of truth-claiming speech acts, it resembles and imitates the assertive stance of factual *narration (*see* SPEECH ACT THEORY; TRUTH). Now, it is true that fictional narratives imitate to varying degrees factual narratives, and this would seem to imply that they operate through mimetic primers. But as Marie-Laure Ryan (2001: 93) has convincingly shown, both fictional *and* non-fictional narrative texts invite the readers to imagine a world, though non-fictional narrative presents as a whole no mimetic dimension. A parallelism of the same kind, although operating primarily on the plane of perception, holds true for cinematographic representation: both fictional and documentary movies induce perceptual immersion (*see* FILM NARRATIVE). Of course, contrary to referentially oriented representations, fictional devices are generally (but not always, and not necessarily) constructed so as to maximise their immersion-inducing power. Nevertheless, immersion is not limited to fictional representations.

So how are we to account for the immersion-inducing nature of verbal narratives, be they fictional or factual? As Paul Ricoeur has suggested, it could well be that mimesis defines narration as such. This would imply that the decisive plane of the mimetic dimension (and consequently of the immersion-producing power) of verbal narratives is not that of the microstructural (linguistic) level, but that of the macrostructural level of the inferential logic of action. If the logic of narrative (be it fictional or factual) mirrors – imitates – the implicit inferential logic of action guiding our real-world experiences, then all narratives are mimetic, a fact which could explain why even factual stories function as immersion-producing devices.

SEE ALSO: action theory; digital narrative; fiction, theories of

References and further reading

Currie, Gregory, and Ian Ravenscroft (2002) *Recreative Minds*, Oxford: Oxford University Press.
Dokic, Jérôme, and Joëlle Proust (eds) (2002) *Simulation and Knowledge of Action*, Amsterdam: John Benjamins.
Gerrig, Richard (1993) *Experiencing Narrative Worlds: On the Psychological Activities of Reading*, New Haven: Yale University Press.
Lotman, Iurii (1977) *The Structure of the Artistic Text*, Ann Arbor: University of Michigan Press.
Plato (1993) *The Republic*, trans. A. D. Lindsay, New York: Knopf.
Ricoeur, Paul (1984–88) *Time and Narrative*, vols 1–3, trans. Kathleen Blamey and David Pellauer, Chicago: University of Chicago Press.
Ryan, Marie-Laure (2001) *Narrative as Virtual Reality: Immersion and Interactivity in Literature and Electronic Media*, Baltimore: Johns Hopkins University Press.
Walton, Kendall (1990) *Mimesis as Make-Believe: On the Foundations of the Representational Arts*, Cambridge, Mass.: Harvard University Press.
Wolf, Werner (2003) *Ästhetische Illusion und Illusionsdurchbrechung in der Erzählkunst*, Tübingen: Niemeyer.

JEAN-MARIE SCHAEFFER AND IOANA VULTUR

IMPLIED AUTHOR

The term 'implied author', which was introduced by Wayne C. Booth (1983 [1961]) in the context of the neo-Aristotelianism of the *Chicago School as a response to both the New Critical stance against authorial intention (*see* INTENTIONALITY) and the aesthetic ideal of impersonality, has become a household word in the critical discourse on narrative fiction. There is, however, no widespread agreement about what the term actually designates. Booth describes the implied author as the real *author's 'second self', 'an implied version of "himself" that is different from the implied authors we meet in other men's work', and 'as an ideal, literary, created version of the real man' (1983 [1961]: 70–1; 75). According to Booth, the implied author also embodies the text's 'core of norms and choices' (74) and satisfies 'the reader's need to know where, in the world of values, he stands – that is, to know where the author *wants* him to stand' (73). The implied author is thus not a technical or formal device, but the source of the beliefs, norms, and purposes of the text, the origin of its meaning, the embodiment of 'the moral and emotional content of each bit of action and suffering of all the characters. It includes, in short, the intuitive apprehension of a completed artistic whole' (73). Through the narrative resources which Booth subsumes under the umbrella of 'the rhetoric of fiction', an (implied) author imposes his or her (or rather its) intention, beliefs, and norms and values on the *implied reader (*see* AUDIENCE), which most theorists assume to be 'the mirror image' (Chatman 1990: 75) of the implied author.

Ever since Booth proposed the implied author the usefulness of the concept has been the subject of intense debate. While critics and theorists working within the tradition of *rhetorical approaches to narrative (e.g. Booth, Chatman, Nelles,

Phelan, Rabinowitz) consider it to be an indispensable element of textual analysis, *structuralist narratologists (e.g. Bal, Genette, Rimmon-Kenan, Diengott) have complained about the anything-goes nature of its many definitions. Although Chatman, one of the most prominent defenders of the implied author, rejects no less than four of the five explanations provided by Booth, he still considers Booth's 'core of norms and choices' as 'essential to narratology and to text theory in general' (Chatman 1990: 83). Following Booth and Chatman, Phelan (2004) argues that the notion of the implied author is necessary in order to account for such phenomena as *irony, hoaxes, ghost-written books, and the manipulations of unreliable narrators, because the implied author provides the otherwise elusive standard against which to gauge the *reliability of a narrator's statements.

Most objections raised against the implied author concern potential theoretical contradictions in Booth's formulation of the concept. For example, it seems to be a contradiction in terms to define the implied author as the structure of the text's norms and thus to conflate it with the text as a whole, and at the same time cast it in the role of the addresser in the communication model of narrative (Nünning 1997) (see FUNCTION (JAKOBSON)). About the only thing that seems uncontroversial is that the implied author can be distinguished from the *narrator and the *characters, both of which are identifiable as textual speakers with clearly delimited speech segments. However, the notion of the implied author refers to a 'voiceless' and depersonified phenomenon (Diengott 1993: 73), which is neither speaker, *voice, subject, nor participant in the narrative communication situation.

In yet another reconceptualisation, the implied author has been seen as the 'reader's idea of the author', i.e. as 'a construct inferred and assembled by the reader from all the components of the text' (Rimmon-Kenan 2002 [1983]: 87; cf. Chatman 1990: 77). Similarly, rejecting both the reader-response version of an 'inferred author' and the conflation of the implied author with the text, Phelan (2004) stresses the continuity that pertains between the real author and his or her implied counterpart, defining the latter as 'a streamlined version of the real author, an actual or purported subset of the real author's capacities, traits, attitudes, beliefs, values, and other properties

that play an active role in the construction of the particular text'. Other narratologists (e.g., Nünning 1997; Kindt and Müller 1999) have suggested the need to abandon the concept in favour of terms like 'narrative strategy' or 'text intent' because these are less likely to be construed as anthropomorphised entities situated in a communicative setting. Whether narratology is well served by such a problematic concept as the implied author, be it of the personalised or depersonified, or the textual or reader-response variety, remains an open question which continues to generate controversial debate.

SEE ALSO: narrative techniques

References and further reading

Booth, Wayne C. (1983 [1961]) *The Rhetoric of Fiction*, Chicago: University of Chicago Press.

Chatman, Seymour (1990) *Coming to Terms: The Rhetoric of Narrative in Fiction and Film*, Ithaca: Cornell University Press.

Diengott, Nilli (1993) 'The Implied Author Once Again', *Journal of Literary Semantics*, 22, 68–75.

Kindt, Tom, and Hans-Harald Müller (1999) 'Der "implizite Autor": Zur Explikation und Verwendung eines umstrittenen Begriffs', in Fotis Jannidis, Gerhard Lauer, Matias Martinez, and Simone Winko (eds) *Rückkehr des Autors: Zur Erneuerung eines umstrittenen Begriffs*, Tübingen: Niemeyer.

Nünning, Ansgar (1997) 'Deconstructing and Reconceptualizing the "implied Author": The Resurrection of an Anthropomorphicized Passepartout or the Obituary of a Critical Phantom?', *Anglistik*, 8.2, 95–116.

Phelan, James (2004) 'The Implied Author and the Location of Unreliability', in *Living to Tell about It: A Rhetoric and Ethics of Character Narration*, Ithaca: Cornell University Press.

Rimmon-Kenan, Shlomith (2002 [1983]) *Narrative Fiction: Contemporary Poetics*, London: Methuen.

ANSGAR NÜNNING

IMPLIED READER

Probably the most influential of all *reader constructs, the term was invented by Wolfgang Iser and construed as the communicational counterpart of the implied author. Although the concept is usually taken to cover the whole range of reading effects, it is inferred on the basis of textual evidence rather than on an analysis of real reader responses. *See* IMPLIED AUTHOR; READER-RESPONSE THEORY.

INDETERMINACY

Indeterminacy in linguistic communication has been established through the well-known accounts of Roman Ingarden, who argues that the impossibility of describing an object in its entirety makes areas of indeterminacy in literary texts unavoidable, and Jacques Derrida, who demonstrates the slippage in the relation between the signifier and the signified from addresser to addressee and among addressees (*see* FUNCTION (JAKOBSON); NARRATIVE TRANSMISSION; SEMIOTICS). Other *media in which narratives are represented also introduce indeterminacy, either through their polysemy (visual representation of an isolated moment or a series of moments, *dance, and by some theorists' accounts instrumental *music) or through contradictions between two or more tracks of information (*film, conjoined verbal-visual and verbal-musical objects). Narratives share the indeterminacies that are the effect of medium with other modes of communication. Indeterminacies specific to narrative pertain to who does what, when, how often, at what ontological level or *modality, and to what effect, in the narrative world that perceivers/readers (re)construct (*see* STORYWORLD). These too, like the indeterminacies specific to media, are an effect of the discourse (*see* STORY-DISCOURSE DISTINCTION): the quantity of information it supplies (both omissions and contradictions matter), the sequence in which given information is meted out, and the quality of the lens through which information is proffered.

Gaps in the discourse leave gaps in the narrative world; some of these gaps are judged less important by *narrators and/or readers – Sternberg's (1985) 'blanks', Prince's 'unnarratable' – than others (*see* GAPPING). Sternberg distinguishes between permanent gaps in the discourse (which create permanent gaps – an obvious source of indeterminacy – in the narrative world) and temporary gaps in the discourse, which affect readers' (re)construction of the narrative world during the process of reading, first at the point in the telling/reading at which the omitted data occur and then again at the later point where the omitted data are revealed (Sternberg 1978). Readers' temporary misconstructions of the narrative world during the process of reading, in response to temporary gaps, can be the source of misinterpretations of *characters or *events that arguably endure even after the omitted information is known, leaving contradictory – and thus indeterminate – narrative worlds in readers' memories (Kafalenos 1999). Prince draws another pertinent distinction: between gaps in information to which narrators call attention in the discourse (the 'unnarrated' – a practice that ensures readers' awareness of an indeterminate element in the narrative world), and, in contrast, events that narrators include in the discourse but describe as not having occurred in the narrative world (the *'disnarrated'). The effects of the 'disnarrated' would seem to resemble those McHale associates with *postmodern narratives in which a narrator first posits then places *sous rature* (erases) or *denarrates (Richardson 2001) an event or character: 'the "erased" state of affairs still persists, if only as a kind of optical afterimage' (1987: 99). These instances in which the discourse offers an account it declares invalid, like the more blatant instances in *postmodern narratives in which two or more contradictory accounts are offered as equally authoritative, are sources of indeterminacy in the narrative world.

While the narrator of a fictional account is considered responsible for determining what is withheld and what sequence information is given in, the lens or focalizer (the character whose perceptions and conceptions about the narrative world the reader is permitted to know; *see* FOCALIZATION) controls how much information is available to be told and how it is coloured. The many studies analysing *reliability – whether of narrators, focalizers, or *implied authors – demonstrate the importance accorded by readers (including theorists) to finding ways to discriminate between what is and is not accurate in any given account. Doubt about the quality of the lens – the accuracy of a focalizer's perceptions or conceptions or of a narrator's report – introduces indeterminacy in the narrative world. In addition, in some postmodern narratives the problem of determining the accuracy of the lens is heightened by the impossibility of determining the identity of the focalizer, whether temporary (the retrospective shift in focalization that Ricardou describes) or permanent (Kafalenos 1992). Further, *free indirect discourse can blur information about whose vocabulary the reported words reflect. *Speech representations fusing a narrator's with a character's *voice sometimes lead to verbal productions whose source remains indeterminate.

A more recently recognised source of indeterminacy in the narrative world arises when readers are left to determine the boundaries of the discourse. Readers' choices about what to consider as included in a 'discourse' affect the narrative world they reconstruct. Narratives that are published unbound or that resemble in format an encyclopedia require readers to decide – as installations in the visual arts require viewers to decide – not only in what sequence to read or view but when to consider their reading/viewing completed, at least for that occasion. For readers of *biographies, *autobiographies, and other narrative accounts of events in our world, further information is always potentially available (Ryan 1997), and as a result our (re)constructions of our world are always subject to change. Fictional narratives incorporate various strategies that offer readers the parallel (although more limited) experience of deciding how much information to take into consideration in (re)constructing a narrative world. These strategies include sequels and prequels, narratives that offer multiple endings, series of narratives in which apparently the same character recurs (James Bond), narratives into which characters familiar from other narratives seem to have migrated (see POSTMODERN REWRITES), interactive hypertexts (see DIGITAL NARRATIVES), and transformations from one medium to another (*films made from *novels, novels developed from films) (see ADAPTATION; CINÉROMAN; INTERMEDIALITY).

SEE ALSO: image and narrative; multi-path narrative; photographs; reader-response theory; temporal ordering; transfictionality

References and further reading

Kafalenos, Emma (1992) 'Toward a Typology of Indeterminacy in Postmodern Narrative', *Comparative Literature*, 44.4, 380–408.
—— (1999) 'Not (Yet) Knowing: Epistemological Effects of Deferred and Suppressed Information in Narrative', in David Herman (ed.) *Narratologies: New Perspectives on Narrative Analysis*, Columbus: Ohio State University Press.
McHale, Brian (1987) *Postmodernist Fiction*, London: Routledge.
Prince, Gerald (1992) 'The Disnarrated', in *Narrative as Theme: Studies in French Fiction*, Lincoln: University of Nebraska Press.
Ryan, Marie-Laure (1997) 'Postmodernism and the Doctrine of Panfictionality', *Narrative*, 5.2, 165–87.
Sternberg, Meir (1978) *Expositional Modes and Temporal Ordering in Fiction*, Bloomington: Indiana University Press.
—— (1985) *The Poetics of Biblical Narrative: Ideological Literature and the Drama of Reading*, Bloomington: Indiana University Press.
Ricardou, Jean (1971) *Pour une théorie du nouveau roman*, Paris: Seuil.
Richardson, Brian (2001) 'Denarration in Fiction: Erasing the Story in Beckett and Others', *Narrative*, 9.2, 168–75.

EMMA KAFALENOS

IN MEDIAS RES

From Latin 'into the middle of things', in medias res is a device used to begin the story at a crucial point in the middle, usually close to the end of the fabula (see STORY-DISCOURSE DISTINCTION). The phrase derives from Horace's remark that 'ever he [the poet] hastens to the issue, and hurries his hearer into the middle of things, as if already known, and what he despairs of treating effectively he abandons' (*Ars Poetica* 147–48). Two features are combined here: (1) an *author should not treat everything but concentrate on a single action (cf. Aristotle, *Poetics* 8) and (2) he or she should start at the end (possibly including earlier phases of the fabula in the form of analepses or flashbacks). The prime examples of beginning in medias res are the Homeric *Iliad* (which treats some 50 days of the tenth year of the Trojan war) and the *Odyssey* (which concentrates on 40 days of the tenth year of the protagonist's wanderings).

The origin of the device lies in the traditional nature of early Greek literature: the *audience was familiar with the stories and the singers could therefore start at whatever point they thought most effective (see ORAL CULTURES AND NARRATIVE). As Horace's formula 'as if they were known' reveals, by his time the device has already become generalised, so as to include newly invented stories which dispense with an *exposition. This type of opening became standard procedure for *epic texts. Of course it is also used in a great number of modern *novels and *short stories.

SEE ALSO: temporal ordering

IRENE J. F. DE JONG

INSTITUTIONAL NARRATIVE

Most institutions exist and reproduce themselves within a rich field of narratives. It is important to understand the use of narrative within institutions, since institutional constraints have an important effect on the structure of the narratives told within them, and reciprocally, the telling of stories is one major way that institutions create and reproduce their structure, and the power relations that exist within them (see IDEOLOGY AND NARRATIVE).

The term 'institution' is used here rather than 'organisation', although both terms are employed, in different disciplines, for the types of social group examined here. *Institution*, in common use, is a broader term than organisation. It is used here to represent any social group that has a continued existence over time, whatever its degree of reification or formal status may be. Thus, an institution may be a nation, a corporation, the practice of medicine, a regular Tuesday night poker game, or the class of '75. An organisation is a formally defined group, with defined membership, boundaries, and legal responsibilities. Thus, American business is an institution, whereas IBM or General Motors are organisations. Additionally, the term 'institutional memory' is in wide (though undefined) general use, and narrative is an important component of institutional *memory.

Narratives in institutions are used to accomplish two distinguishable results. The first function involves the continuation of the life of the institution itself. Narrative is used to reproduce the institution, continue or challenge its power structures, induct new members, create the identity of the institution and its members, adapt to change, and deal with contested or contradictory versions of the past (see IDENTITY AND NARRATIVE). These are ways an institution uses narrative to create and reproduce its identity by the creation and maintenance of an institutional memory. The second type of function that narrative performs in institutions is the use of narrative to carry out the daily work of the institution. This includes the telling of stories by members of the institution to carry on their own work (see CONVERSATIONAL STORY-TELLING). It also includes the attempts of non-members to use narrative in institutional settings such as legal or medical situations, where professionals require the use of specialised, privileged, non-narrative forms of discourse (see LAW AND NARRATIVE; MEDICINE AND NARRATIVE).

Narrative and institutional reproduction

One of the major functions of narrative within institutions is to accomplish the work of reproducing, maintaining, changing, or contesting the institution's self-representation and the power relations of the parties within it. Just as individuals maintain *life stories, institutions also have stories which represent who 'We' are.

Within institutions, many stories are told daily. To understand the creation of institutional identity, it is important to distinguish between immediate and long-term stories, and between the personal stories of members of the institution, and the stories of the institution which can be told by any member. Many ephemeral narratives are told in institutions: stories about today's computer problem, the flu that's going around, or news about a co-worker or manager. While they contribute to the creation of membership and identity, institutions are more affected by those narratives that are repeatable for a long period of *time by many tellers. This class is the non-participant narrative (NPN): a narrative told by a speaker who was not a participant or witness to the *events narrated, but heard them from someone else. The NPN is type of third-person narrative told by a *narrator who was not present even as a minor actor or witness (see NARRATION; NARRATIVE SITUATIONS; PERSON). The analytic importance of the NPN is that we know that these are the narratives that have an extended life in the institution, since their very form assures us that they have been retold at least once (see NARRATIVE VERSIONS). Thus, they have an important function within institutions in constituting the way that institutions remember their past and use those acts of remembering to create current identities for both the institution and its members.

The ways in which an institution can represent its past to create a strong identity for itself and its members has been directly studied in a large American insurance company (Linde 2000; 2001). The company invokes its past on many occasions, most frequently through narratives. Many of these narratives focus on the life of the founder. This company, like many, has a charismatic founder, and tells many stories about him over fifty years after his death, using his actions and virtues as a model for current members of the company. (Narratives of founders are one of the most common kinds of stories told within institutions.)

There is an authorised history of the company in circulation, framed as the *biography of the founder. This biography is frequently consulted by managers for stories to use in speeches. A monthly newsletter retells *anecdotes about the founder, and the company's history. Speeches at national, regional and local meetings provide occasions for storytelling. The past is invoked either to arouse pride in the members, or to show that although times are hard, the company has weathered hard times before without sacrificing its essential character and principles.

Part of the training of new employees includes stories of the founder and the history of the company, used to induct new members into the culture of the institution. Such narrative induction is an important method for socialising new members, and for new members to develop their identity within the institution. Narrative induction is the process by which people take on an existing set of stories as relevant to their own story. Again, it is the non-participant narrative that is used to reproduce collective memory of the institution and to induct new participants into being carriers of this memory.

There are three parts to this process. The first is that a person comes to take key stories within the institution as relevant to his or her own. These are usually tales of the founder, or of another person whose career is presented as normative. New members come to recognise these stories, accept them as meaningful, and most importantly, retell them. The second part is that new members learn to tell their own stories in a way shaped by these normative stories, framing them, as having similar events or evaluative meanings. This is an important way that institutional values are reproduced. (For example, many religious conversion stories are formed in this way.) Finally, some peoples' stories may be as an instance of a normative pattern. These stories are different from a story of a heroic founder. Rather, institutions have career tracks – local models for success – and stories of individuals are told to exemplify a life available to any motivated member of the institution: a story of ordinary rather than extraordinary success. (The steps from undergraduate student to tenured professor represent an academic example of such an institutional trajectory.)

Beginning in the 1990s, a number of popular management books described for managers the desirability of creating storytelling practices in their institutions to improve employee participation and interaction. Additionally, as corporations lose members through downsizing or retirement, there has come to be a concern about loss of the knowledge of these departing workers. One solution currently being attempted is capturing their knowledge through exit interviews, and the creation of databases of stories. Because the process of eliciting narratives and storing them in databases almost entirely eliminates the context of these stories, such efforts have as yet produced few if any useful results.

Narrative and the work of institutions

Narratives facilitate the daily work of institutions, but as yet, there have been few detailed studies of this process. One exception is Orr's analysis of narrative in the work of copier repair technicians (Orr 1996). Although the work of repairing copiers appears to be primarily a mechanical rather than a linguistic and social matter, Orr demonstrates that narrative forms an important part of copier repair. These technicians could not accomplish their jobs without participating in a community which continuously tells stories about copiers, clients, and repair technicians, maintaining an ongoing community memory of difficult problems, unexpected and undocumented solutions, and heroic diagnoses. It might appear that the need for a community store of narratives is created by inadequate official documentation of how the machines should be repaired. But in fact, personal experience of any form of technology documentation, as well as analysis of the problem of describing complex physical structures, suggests that decontextualised documentation will always need to be supplemented with stories of particular cases (see NARRATIVE EXPLANATION).

One problem in the use of narrative to accomplish work has to do with the institutional position of the narrators. These repair technicians have informal social arrangements, such as breakfast meetings, which allow them to exchange the stories carrying knowledge about particular machines and clients, and errors in particular documentation. But there are no mechanisms allowing this knowledge about machines or documentation to move to the groups in the institutions which design copiers, or write manuals. This is a widespread problem. Technical information about the details of the work is narrated within the group that does the work, but these narratives do not generally travel to other groups in the institution.

Narrative across the boundaries of institutions

When individuals deal with professional institutions such as law or medicine, they are frequently required to provide personal information in a linguistic form dictated by that institution. There have been many studies of what happens to the structure of narrative (and to the narrators) when one of the parties in a conversation is able to officially require another party to tell his or her story in a specified form. This can happen in medical interviews, social service offices, schools, and encounters between citizens and the legal system, to name just a few (see EDUCATION AND NARRATIVE). People needing to tell their stories often find that their preferred conversational narratives are unacceptable when they must be told in a formal situation to someone representing a powerful institution.

Indeed, this mismatch of discourse types has been proposed as a central characteristic of discourse at institutional boundaries, produced when 'one person – a citizen of a modern nation/state – comes into contact with another – a representative of one of its institutions' (Agar 1985: 147). In studies of medical and legal discourse, Agar proposes a three-part framework for institutional discourse which typically consists of a face-to-face meeting, usually a series of question-answer pairs to diagnose the client's problem; directives for action, given by an institutional representative either to the client or to the institution; and a report made by the institutional representative of the diagnosis and directives.

This framework suggests why it is often difficult for someone to tell his or her story to an institutional representative. Much of the work of the institutional representative is to categorise the client's problem within the institution's system. However, such categorisation is frequently the disputed issue across the institutional boundary. Further, this is not a simple difference of opinion, but is rather the beginning of the production of an institutional record which has serious ongoing consequences. In most such encounters, there is a marked difference in power: the institutional representative almost always has much more power than the member of the public to determine

the final form of the record, and the form of the record can have long-term consequences which are unknown to the member of the public. Situations like this have been studied in the domains of medicine, law, and education.

In medical interviews, there is an implicit conflict between patients' and doctors' preferred discourse genres. Patients prefer to describe their condition by telling a story, while physicians prefer a question-answer form (see COMMUNICATION IN NARRATIVE; DISCOURSE ANALYSIS (LINGUISTICS)). The question-answer form matches the records which physicians must create, and the diagnosis tree for determining the medical problem. Additionally, production pressure affects medical discourse, since physicians are often required to keep patient interviews short (often to a specified number of minutes). They fear that allowing patients to control the interview by telling their stories will produce an unfocused discourse which will not provide the needed information within the allotted time. Physicians often attempt to diagnose the main problem by pursuing the complaint that the patient first mentions. Yet empirical studies show that patients do not always begin with the health issue which concerns them most. Recent attempts to improve this situation have led the Accreditation Council for Graduate Medical Education to include in its proposed competencies for medical residents interpersonal and communicative skills. Future research will assess the effectiveness of this change in medical training.

Legal settings also produce a conflict between people's desire to frame their experience as a narrative, and the question-answer format necessary for institutional documentation. For example, when people on the witness stand try to tell stories, which by their structure require personal judgement in their evaluation of events, they are confined by the questions and directions of lawyers and judges to tell just the facts (see COURTROOM NARRATIVE). Studies of the work of public safety dispatchers (911 operators), paralegal interviewers eliciting accounts of spousal abuse, and police officers gathering reports from crime victims show a conflict between the question-answer format required to get the information needed to fill out the necessary form, and the witness's or victim's need to tell the story of what happened as a narrative.

Conflicts like this arise because the two (or more) parties in the conversation do not share knowledge and agreement of what facts are relevant, what kinds of statement are permitted, and what form, if any, a narrative may take in that institutional context. Witnesses do not normally know the legal rules governing admissible testimony. A witness or victim of a crime does not know what form the operator must fill out, nor that the computer requires the operator to fill out its fields in order, rather than being able to sieve out the information needed as it comes up in the victim's narrative.

Similarly, studies of discourse in school settings show that schools require students to produce forms of spoken discourse shaped by the conventions of expository written texts. These conventions require decontextualisation of information, a discourse addressed to a generalised *audience rather than those particular persons present, a focus on a single topic, and explicit marking of topic shifts. This kind of 'spoken-written' discourse is quite different from the vernacular forms that students normally use for narration (*see* ORALITY). A number of works argue that while white middle-class children are trained in such decontextualisation skills even before entering kindergarten, children of other ethnic groups may not understand these discourse norms, and hence may produce narratives which are not acceptable in a classroom (*see* SOCIOLINGUISTIC APPROACHES TO NARRATIVE).

Narratives and institutional power

Both within institutions and across institutional boundaries, the use of narrative raises the question of power relations and storytelling rights: who has rights to tell what kinds of stories, who may speak officially for the institution, and what kinds of stories may not be told, officially or unofficially. Positional power grants storytelling rights, as does long tenure within an institution. Access to institutional power also means access to communication channels, which allow for the promulgation of some stories and the suppression of others. While institutions are able to maintain control of official narratives, oppositional stories can be maintained unofficially within institutions. Individuals may tell them informally, but they are most stably carried on by counter-institutions. Thus, a labour union within a corporation may maintain for its members stories about events which differ from the official accounts. While some counter-stories preserve the memory of different events from those in the official story, others may use the same past

events to provide a different interpretation of present happenings. Thus, an oppositional group may agree to the official account of the founding values of a corporation, but then use that account to argue that management's current actions represent the opposite of those values.

SEE ALSO: communication studies and narrative; master narrative

References and further reading

Agar, Michael (1985) 'Institutional Discourse', *Text*, 5.3, 147–68.
Bamberg, Michael (2000) *Narrative Inquiry*, Volume 12.1 (Special issue on 'Counter Narratives').
Conley, John, and William O'Barr (1996) 'Rules versus Relationships in Small Claims Disputes', in Allen D. Grimshaw (ed.) *Conflict Talk: Sociolinguistic Investigations of Arguments in Conversations*, Cambridge: Cambridge University Press.
Frankel, Richard (1983) 'The Laying on of Hands: Aspects of the Organization of Gaze, Touch and Talk in a Medical Encounter', in Susan Fisher and Alexandra Todd (eds) *The Social Organization of Doctor-Patient Communication*, Washington DC: Centre for Applied Linguistics.
Gunnarsson, Britt-Louise, Per Linnell, and Bengt Nordberg (eds) (1996) *The Construction of Professional Discourse*, New York: Longman House.
Linde, Charlotte (2000) 'The Acquisition of a Speaker by a Story: How History Becomes Memory and Identity', *Ethos*, 28.4, 608–32.
—— (2001a) 'Narrative and Tacit Knowledge Exchange', *Journal of Knowledge Management*, 5.2, 160–71.
—— (2001b) 'Narrative in Institutions', in Heidi Hamilton, Deborah Schiffrin and Deborah Tannen (eds) *Handbook of Discourse Analysis*, Oxford: Basil Blackwell.
Martin, Joanne, Sim Sitkin, and Michael Boehm (1985) 'Founders and the Elusiveness of a Cultural Legacy', in P. J. Frost, Larry F. Moore, Meryl Reis, Craig C. Lundberg, and Joanne Martin (eds) *Organizational Culture*, Beverly Hills: Sage Publications.
Orr, Julian (1996) *Talking about Machines*, Ithaca: ILR Press.
Scollon, Ron, and Suzanne B. K. Scollon (1981) 'The Literate Two-year-old: The Fictionalization of Self', in Ron Scollon and Suzanne Scollon (eds) *Narrative, Literacy and Face in Interethnic Communications*, Norwood NJ: Ablex.
Shuman, Amy (1986) *Storytelling Rights: The Uses of Oral and Written Texts by Urban Adolescents*, Cambridge: Cambridge University Press.
Tulviste, Peeter, and James V. Wetsch (1995) 'Official and Unofficial History: The Case of Estonia', *Journal of Narrative and Life History*, 4.4, 311–31.
Watson, Rubie (1994) *Memory, History and Opposition Under State Socialism*, Santa Fe, New Mexico: School of American Research Press.

Whelan, Jack (1995) 'A Technology of Order Production: Computer-aided Dispatch in Public Safety Communications', in Paul ten Have and George Psathas (eds) *Situated Order: Studies in the Social Organization of Talk and Embodied Activities*, Washington, D.C.: University of America Press.

CHARLOTTE LINDE

INTENTIONALITY

Intentions generally refer to private mental acts that precede, and are the originating cause of, human action (*see* ACTION THEORY; CAUSALITY). For instance, a writer usually has some specific idea in mind that motivates him or her to write a particular sequence of words in creating a narrative. Within narrative theory, literary theorists and philosophers vigorously debate whether readers' assumptions about authorial intentions should play a role in how narratives are interpreted (*see* AUTHOR). Over the past 60 years, scholars have provided a variety of responses to this question about 'intentionalism', each of which entails different methods of reading, and interpreting, narratives. These responses are reviewed below. Many of these arguments originally arose in debates about the proper treatment of literary texts in general. But in recent decades, similar claims about intentionality have been made in regard to how types of narratives should be read, including narratives produced in religious, legal, and scientific contexts.

Subjective intentionalism and the formalist response

'Subjective intentionalism' is a long-standing approach to narrative interpretation that often focuses on the *biographies of authors who create texts. This view maintains that an author's successfully realised intentions determine a text's meaning. Authorial intentions, if successfully executed, are publicly manifest in the work. The meaning of a text can be ambiguous or multilayered, but this is usually because the author purposefully intended the narrative to be read in this way (*see* NARRATOR; RELIABILITY). The intentions behind a narrative need not have been be consciously present in the author's mind when he or she wrote the text. Moreover, an author might have difficulty articulating a work's main intentions, if asked, just as people often have difficulty in describing what they did in performing a familiar, yet complex, action.

It is almost impossible for authors to write in such a way that all of their intentions will be transparent to all readers. At the same time, authors don't necessarily intend to communicate only unambiguous meanings in their texts. Many authors also intend to achieve various aesthetic goals some of which are best met by leaving certain messages unclear. Moreover, it is not always reasonable to ascribe a single intention to the author of a text, especially a literary work. Longer narrative works are generally produced over a period of time, and it is unlikely that the complex structure of goals and intentions that motivates the final text will remain perfectly consistent throughout the writing process. For these reasons, the New Critics in the 1930s through 1960s rejected subjective intentionalism as both impractical and misguided. They argued for a fundamental separation of subject and object (reader and text), rendering the text separate from both its historical context and its readers (*see* FORMALISM). The 'Intentional Fallacy' (Wimsatt and Beardsley 1946) suggested that the original 'design or intention of the author' is not the appropriate standard either for judging the aesthetic merits of a text or for determining anything about its formal characteristics. Intentions may be relevant to what a writer was trying to do, but they are not always indicative of what the author has actually done in making a work. Authors can even be mistaken in the interpretations they offer, and they may have more difficulty in reporting their intentions clearly than they had expressing their intentions in the work. Readers need not consider authors' intentions, because they can restrict their interpretations of what textual segments mean by appealing to the contexts in which such segments appear.

Postformalist and poststructuralist approaches

In the 1960s a significant backlash emerged against the strict views of New Criticism. E. D. Hirsch argued that a text has to represent someone's meaning and that no adequate proposal exists for judging the validity of an interpretation unless the author's narrative intentions are taken into account. A word sequence means nothing in particular unless either somebody means something by it, or else someone understands something from reading it. Hirsch acknowledged that in searching for authorial intentions, readers should not seek the actual explicit thoughts of the real author while composing the text. Authorial intentions must be tied to public, shareable meanings as evident in the text itself. Readers should begin by positing a *genre for a particular work (e.g. scientific prose, lyric poetry, a *novel, an *epic narrative, or a play) and use this as a general framework for interpreting the author's typical meanings. Even though authorial intentions are not the only possible norm of interpretation, they provide the only practical norm for a cognitive discipline of interpretation. Without consideration of authorial intentions, there is simply too much *indeterminacy and instability in the public linguistic conventions governing meaning and no stable object for narrative analysis. Once critics have correctly reproduced the author's verbal meaning, they are free to relate that meaning to whatever contexts they want or think will be relevant to their *audience.

From the late 1960s through the early 1990s, a number of philosophers and literary critics developed arguments that provided independent support for Wimsatt and Beardsley's notion of the intentional fallacy. *Poststructuralists such as Roland Barthes announced the 'death of the author' as a precondition for the desired 'birth of the reader' in literary criticism (see READER-RESPONSE THEORY). For deconstructionist critics, there is a break that 'intervenes from the moment that there is a mark' on the paper, a mark that, once there, achieves meaning independent of authorial intentions through its 'iterability', or its place in the web of all texts past and present (Derrida 1982; see DECONSTRUCTIVE APPROACHES TO NARRATIVE). Though authors may think they know what they intend, their thought and language are at the mercy of socio-economic, psychological, and historical forces that cause them to say something other than what they actually intended. This blindness makes authors' intentions far less interesting than the operation of these external forces as revealed in their work.

Poststructuralist arguments concerning the death of the author in textual criticism go beyond the *hermeneutic claim that a text can acquire new meanings once it has been freed from authorial control. More specifically, deconstructionists such as Jacques Derrida argue that a text must from the very beginning be free from an author's intentions.

Deconstruction doesn't demand a complete disregard for authorial intentions. For instance, in his reading of Rousseau's texts, Derrida (1976) appears to construct interpretations that Rousseau 'himself could scarcely have been brought to entertain'. Yet Derrida is not ignoring Rousseau's intentions as much as arguing that understanding of what a text can mean often requires seeing how it says something other than its specified intent. Derrida doesn't deny that language possesses intentional meaning. Instead, Derrida emphatically rejects the idea that *philosophy can specify the rules for explaining how any text can mean.

Finding middle ground: hypothetical intentionalism

It is now a central theme of much contemporary criticism that a literary text is a complex entity composed of different meanings, presented not as alternatives and not successively, but as mutually interacting and simultaneous. One proposal from the 1990s attempts to reconcile the openness of the literary text with consideration of intentionality. According to this proposal, what a work means is expressed by a 'hypothetical intention' (i.e., a complex intention that a member of the intended or an ideal audience would be most justified in ascribing to the work) (Levinson 1992). A narrative's meaning is established by hypothesising intentions authors might have had, given the context of creation, rather than relying on, or trying to seek out, the author's subjective intentions (see IMPLIED AUTHOR). Readers' interpretations of narratives depend on their inferences about a hypothetical author founded in the linguistic conventions and artistic practices at the time the author wrote the work, as well as in publicly available knowledge of how the text was created. A work might display a multiplicity of meanings given the large set of intentions readers can hypothesise about an author and the conditions under which a work was written. This multiplicity of meanings is perfectly appropriate to propose even if the actual author intended only a single interpretation for a text.

This broader concept of authors' hypothesised intended meanings can show how some meanings are justified with respect to a given historical period, because they are rooted abstractly in the consciousness of the historically constructed author, even if they may not be ascribable to the actual author. Most generally, understanding the meaning of a text, especially in cases where several equally reasonable interpretations are available, is not (and should not be) limited by what the author personally intended. But an audience can construct its best contextually informed hypothesis of authorial intentions for a given text in light of what is known about the author, the author's background, and the historical and cultural conditions under which the work was created.

Eco's model reader and beyond

For his part, Umberto Eco has argued for the importance of limiting the range of admissible interpretations of narratives so that some readings can be widely recognised, and rejected, as 'over-interpretations'. People can often recognise over-interpretations of a text without necessarily being able to prove that one interpretation is the right one, or that it must be the only defeasible reading. Critics might say that any interpretation of a text is a bad one, because different public criteria can and should be brought to bear in making such a determination. According to Eco, the aim of narratives is to produce the 'model reader' – that is, the reader who interprets a text as it was designed to be read (and this includes the possibility of the text being read with multiple interpretations) (see READER CONSTRUCTS). The 'empirical reader' is a reader who makes conjectures about the kind of 'model reader' postulated by the text. Readers interpreting empirical authors do not speculate about the author's intentions, but restrict their understandings to the text's intentions. Eco provides no specific rules for limiting interpretation, but he advances the idea that certain interpretations of texts prove themselves over time to the satisfaction of a relevant community.

The intentionalism debates have focused primarily on whether appeal to an author's real or hypothetical intentions should be used in justifying specific interpretations of narratives. Yet many anti-intentionalists, such as the New Critics and deconstructionists, confuse the activity of self-consciously arguing about intentions with the activity of assuming intentions – not a specific one, but just the unavoidable fact of one. This is a very important point. Too many of these debates assume that readers have a choice in acknowledging or rejecting consideration of an author's

intentions in determining a text's meaning. But critics of intentionalism ignore the possibility that readers tacitly assume that meaning is the product of some sort of intentional agent, an assumption that shapes, to some extent, how texts are presumed to be understood and appreciated. No theory can eliminate the cognitive impulse to assume that *someone* wrote a narrative for *some intentional purpose*, which, at the very least, constrains fast, unconscious reading processes, similar to those that occur in understanding spoken language.

SEE ALSO: pragmatics; psychological approaches to narrative

References and further reading

Barthes, Roland (1977) 'The Death of the Author', in *Image-Music-Text*, trans. Stephen Heath, New York: Hill and Wang.
Derrida, Jacques (1976) *Of Grammatology*, trans. Gayatri Chakravorty Spivak, Baltimore: Johns Hopkins University Press.
—— (1982) 'Signature Event Context', in *Margins of Philosophy*, trans. Alan Bass, Chicago: University of Chicago Press.
Eco, Umberto (1992) *Interpretation and Overinterpretation*, ed. Stefan Collini, New York: Cambridge University Press.
Fish, Stanley (1980) *Is There a Text in This Class?*, Baltimore: Johns Hopkins University Press.
Gibbs, Raymond (1999) *Intentions in the Experience of Meaning*, New York: Cambridge University Press.
Hirsch, Edward D. (1967) *The Aims of Interpretation*, Chicago: University of Chicago Press.
Knapp, Steven, and Walter Benn Michaels (1982) 'Against Theory', *Critical Inquiry*, 8, 723–42.
Levinson, Jerrold (1992) 'Intention and Interpretation: A Last Look', in Gary Iseminger (ed.) *Intention and Interpretation*, Philadelphia: Temple University Press.
Tompkins, Jane (ed.) (1980) *Reader-response Criticism: From Formalism to Post-structuralism*, Baltimore: Johns Hopkins University Press.
Wimsatt, William, Jr., and Monroe C. Beardsley (1946) 'The Intentional Fallacy', *Sewanee Review*, 54, 468–88.

RAYMOND W. GIBBS, JR.

INTERACTIVE FICTION

In interactive fiction (IF), a form of *digital narrative and *computer game, the computer system narrates *events in a simulated world in which the user commands a *character (see NARRATION). This world, IF's content plane, is analogous to the *storyworld, but a program simulates it interactively, allowing different events to occur after different commands. Input and output are often entirely textual, with typed commands such as 'look through the window', 'attack the dragon', and 'ask the librarian about the freeway' being understood. IF originated with *Adventure* (Will Crowther and Don Woods, 1975–1976) and became very popular in the home-computing era. Often authored by an individual or small group, it was developed by companies including Level 9, Magnetic Scrolls, and Infocom (which sold *Zork I–III*, based on the minicomputer IF *Zork* developed at MIT). After the 1980s commercial boom ended, individuals continued to play and discuss IF, and to develop it using free systems, including Inform and TADS. The annual IF Competition began in 1995; the IF Archive provides hundreds of free IF works.

References and further reading

Baf's Guide to the IF Archive, http://wurb.com/if/
IF Competition, http://ifcomp.org
Jerz, Dennis G. 'An Annotated Bibliography Of Inter-active Fiction Scholarship', http://jerz.setonhill.edu/if/bibliography/
Montfort, Nick (2003) *Twisty Little Passages: An Approach to Interactive Fiction*, Cambridge: MIT Press.

NICK MONTFORT

INTERACTIVITY

A feed-back loop through which user input affects the behaviour of a text, especially regarding the choice of information to be displayed. A feature found mainly in *digital narratives, interactivity may be either selective (clicking on links) or productive (contributing text, performing actions), and it may result in the real-time creation of a story. *See* COMPUTER GAMES AND NARRATIVE; COMPUTATIONAL APPROACHES TO NARRATIVE.

INTERDISCIPLINARY APPROACHES TO NARRATIVE

Relations between disciplines can be multidisciplinary, when several disciplines work together on a common problem, e.g., a period study; they can be transdisciplinary, when the difference between disciplines and the *media they each study is

suspended in favour of the study of a common theme, e.g. representations of martyrdom; or they can be interdisciplinary, when several disciplines reflectively deploy methods from other disciplines, either because the object requires it, or because the approach is more productive when not confined to disciplinary traditions (Bal 1988).

Within the narrower question of strictly interdisciplinary work – a question involving methodological issues above all – relationships between disciplines vary. Some scholars consider narrative an inherently interdisciplinary field, because in its traditional appearances in *novels and other forms of storytelling it consists of language, deploys rhetorical figures, is processed psychically – mentally as well as affectively – and thus involves cognition. Thus, narrative analysis bridges narratology and, respectively, linguistics, psychology, and cognitive science. In other cases, the study of a single-discipline object such as literary narrative often invokes other disciplinary methods as 'helpers' in order to 'thicken' the analysis, or specialise in a particular kind of interpretation. Thus, psychoanalytic criticism places narrative within the field of affect, *memory, and personal experience (*see* PSYCHOANALYSIS AND NARRATIVE). *Sociological approaches can analyse *dialogues or otherwise represented utterances in terms of group-bound speech *genres (*see* SPEECH REPRESENTATION); they can also study events such as the salon gatherings in Proust's *Remembrance* as class-based sketches or parodies. Meanwhile, anthropological study of particular narrative forms, such as oral narratives, praise songs, or rituals, will focus on the cultural conventions underlying the deployment of narrative form (*see* ETHNOGRAPHIC APPROACHES TO NARRATIVE). Finally, narrative as an object of study occurs within the object domain of a variety of disciplines. *Film and *television studies, art history, and even musicology cannot avoid the question of the *narrativity of its objects (*see* MUSIC AND NARRATIVE; PICTORIAL NARRATIVITY; VISUAL NARRATIVITY).

The example of what has been called 'psycho-narratology' can help understand these different relationships and assess their merit. This interdiscipline comprises both psychoanalytic and *psychological work. Felman (1977) proposes to re-examine the meaning of the seemingly neutral 'and' that connects the two disciplines involved, and the different forms of subordination it obscures. Narrative, psychoanalytic criticism's favourite literary mode, is sometimes subjected to a psychoanalytic search for hidden motives such as Oedipal desires (De Lauretis 1983) or for other psychoanalytic preoccupations. It can also be studied as a trigger of psychoanalytically relevant response, such as projection (Felman 1977). Peter Brooks sees in *narrative structure itself a psychoanalytic impulse (*see* DESIRE). On the other hand, narrative theory has been brought to bear on psychoanalytic theory and its deployment of storytelling as a mode of theorising (Felman 1977). In yet a different interdisciplinary relation, psychoanalysis and narrative have been seen as analogously structured on the basis of temporality (Schleifer 1983; *see* TIME IN NARRATIVE).

When literature is subjected to a psychoanalytic gaze, subtle and refined interpretations enrich the narrative object seen as emerging from an individual human psyche compelled to tell stories that somehow 'carry' that psyche's unconscious burden. Whatever the merit of such interpretations, they remain anchored in the assumption that a text is relevantly linked to the woman or man who wrote it, an assumption in tension with the text-based nature of other trends in narrative theory. Such interpretations can also be banal, as in searches for Oedipal complexes in any number of texts from the tradition of the novel. On the other hand, the analysis of projection and transference in the acts of reading that Felman performs on criticism of specific narratives – e.g. by Camus, Poe, or Henry James – links the psychoanalytic concern with texts, not authors, as triggers of those responses. Here, the text is not subjected to the 'other' theory but demonstrates the latter's relevance for an understanding of the text's effectivity.

The narratological analysis of Freud's case studies constitutes a different mode of interdisciplinary inquiry. Here, possibly, the mode of inquiry with which narrative theory engages is turned into a patchwork of textual genres, among which narrative is prominent. Some scholars contend that the property of fictionality, easily assumed for narrative, cannot be attributed to texts who use context does not accommodate such interpretations without discomfort (cf. Cohn 1999; *see* FICTION, THEORIES OF). Nevertheless, the narratological analysis of the Oedipus story (Felman 1977) provides important new insights into how the psychoanalytic theory needed, or in its own terms, 'desired' that story. And the famous dossier on Freud's *Dora* contributes to our understanding of narrative's social life (Marcus).

Brooks' theory, which is ultimately anthropological, explains such narrative phenomena as delay, plotting, transformation, and repetition within a conception of narrative that is psychoanalytically motivated. Thus, he probes the connections between the 'how' and the 'why' of *narrativisation as a cultural mode of behaviour. Here, neither theory – anthropology or narratology – predominates; both are set off against larger questions of culture. In the same vein are attempts to connect narrative aspects such as *focalization to cinematic suture (Silverman 1983) or to visual narrative. These are instances of interdisciplinary inflections of one discipline through another without using either one as 'theory' to be 'applied' to the other.

Yet another relationship between (empirical) psychology and narratology appears when the admittedly speculative models of narrative theory are tested, by means of questionnaires, on actual readers. The term 'psychonarratology' has been proposed for such an empirical-psychological theory of narrative (Bortolussi and Dixon 2003). The authors claim that humanistic narratologists shun psychological theory because the latter's scientific bent appears 'difficult'. Some readers, however, may be unpersuaded by Bortolussi and Dixon's attempts to formulate empirical tests for narratological hypotheses; the tests arguably require excessive narrowing of the investigative field, and thus a marginalisation of the challenges faced by readers of complex, 'real-world' narratives. More generally, it remains to be seen if such tests will ever manage to incorporate the interpretive nature of reading itself.

Others have attempted to reformulate narratological problematics and concepts in the frameworks of other disciplines. Most frequently, linguistics and cognitive science provide the revised terminology (Herman 2002). This reframing may lead to revision or even extension of categorisations. At the very least, reframing within linguistic frameworks helps narrative theorists to consider non-literary narratives such as those created in everyday speech (*see* CONVERSATIONAL STORYTELLING).

There is hardly a cultural practice where some form and degree of narrativity does not play a part. Legal practice is just one example; the anthropological study of cultures, another (Fabian 2001).

Although it is not always visible to narratologists who work exclusively in literary fields, the inter-disciplinary status of narratology becomes obvious when narrative theorists engage in various modes of dialogue with social and natural scientists, film scholars, musicologists, and art historians.

SEE ALSO: cognitive narratology; intermediality; law and narrative; linguistic approaches to narrative; media and narrative; narrative; science and narrative; structuralist narratology

References and further reading

Bal, Mieke (1988) *Murder and Difference: Gender, Genre and Scholarship on Sisera's Death*, trans. Matthew Gumpert, Bloomington: Indiana University Press.

Bortolussi, Marisa, and Peter Dixon (2003) *Psycho-narratology: Foundations for the Empirical Study of Literary Response*, Cambridge: Cambridge University Press.

Brooks, Peter (1977) 'Freud's Masterplot: Questions of Narrative', in Shoshana Felman (ed.) *Literature and Psychoanalysis: The Question of Reading Otherwise*, Baltimore: Johns Hopkins University Press.

Cohn, Dorrit (1999) *The Distinction of Fiction*, Baltimore: Johns Hopkins University Press.

De Lauretis, Teresa (1983) 'Desire in Narrative', in *Alice Doesn't: Feminism, Semiotics, Cinema*, London: Macmillan.

Fabian, Johannes (2001) 'Time, Narration, and the Exploration of Africa', in *Anthropology with an Attitude*, Stanford, CA: Stanford University Press.

Felman, Shoshana (1977) *Literature and Psychoanalysis: The Question of Reading Otherwise*, Baltimore: Johns Hopkins University Press.

Fludernik, Monika (1996) *Towards a 'Natural' Narratology*, London: Routledge.

Herman, David (2002) *Story Logic: Problems and Possibilities of Narrative*, Lincoln: University of Nebraska Press.

Schleiffer Ronald (1983) 'The Space and Dialogue of Desire: Lacan, Greimas, and Narrative Temporality', in *Lacan and Narration: The Psychoanalytic Difference in Narrative Theory*, Baltimore: Johns Hopkins University Press.

Silverman, Kaja (1983) *The Subject of Semiotics*, New York: Oxford University Press.

MIEKE BAL

INTERIOR MONOLOGUE

A representation of a character's silent inner speech; an extended and direct *quotation of thoughts. The form was 'invented' by Edouard Dujardin in 1887, became famous when James Joyce used it in the concluding chapter of *Ulysses* (1922), and is a staple narrative technique today. *See* STREAM OF CONSCIOUSNESS AND INTERIOR MONOLOGUE (also: NARRATION; THOUGHT AND CONSCIOUSNESS REPRESENTATION (LITERATURE)).

INTERMEDIALITY

The term 'intermediality' was coined in 1983 by the German scholar Aage A. Hansen-Löve in analogy with *'intertextuality' in order to capture relations between literature and the visual arts (and to some extent also *music) in Russian symbolism. The notion first spread in research published in German but has by now become internationally recognised, although it is still sometimes confused with 'intertextuality', especially if 'text' is used as an umbrella term covering all semiotic systems (*see* SEMIOTICS). If, however, 'text' is used more narrowly, referring to verbal texts only, the distinction between intertextuality and intermediality is straightforward. Thus understood, intertextuality is a variant of 'intramediality' and refers exclusively to 'homomedial' relations between verbal texts or text systems. Intermediality, in contrast, applies in its broadest sense to any transgression of boundaries between *media and thus is concerned with 'heteromedial' relations between different semiotic complexes or between different parts of a semiotic complex. 'Interart relations' is also a formerly much used synonym of 'intermediality'. However, this collocation is often felt to be problematic since its connotation of 'high art' might lead to the exclusion of artefacts, *performances, and new media whose status as art is doubtful.

The emerging preference for 'intermediality' over rival terms such as 'interart relations' and 'intertextuality' indicates the increasingly *interdisciplinary profile of the research being conducted in this domain. Although the term 'intermediality' originated in a literature-centred milieu and is still used mostly in relation to literature, it has far transcended the boundaries of the literary field. This is also why, strictly speaking, the objects that are linked or characterised by intermediality should be called 'semiotic complexes or entities', a designation that includes not only various *genres and groups of texts but also artefacts, performances, installations, and so on. Yet for brevity's sake imprecise terms such as 'work' or 'composition' continue to be employed and will be used in this entry.

Problems of definition and typology

Curiously, problems of definition and typology have not hindered intermediality research. The most obvious among these is the problem of defining the term 'medium' itself. A plethora of meanings has been connected with this notion, ranging from a very narrow conception as a technical channel for transmitting information to an extremely wide definition in which 'medium' designates all 'extensions of man', be it of the body or the consciousness (McLuhan 1964: 3). Neither of these extremes is helpful, as intermediality research is not usually concerned with, e.g., the differences between a print version and an electronic version of the same *novel (*see* ADAPTATION), nor with means of transportation as extensions of the human body. Rather, intermediality deals with media as conventionally distinct means of communicating cultural contents. Media in this sense are specified principally by the nature of their underlying semiotic systems (involving verbal language, pictorial signs, music, etc., or, in cases of 'composite media' such as *film, a combination of several semiotic systems), and only in the second place by technical or institutional channels. Still, this compromise notion of medium, which is usually employed in intermediality research, leaves it open for discussion whether, for instance, the transposition of a novel into a *drama is an intramedial phenomenon (remaining inside literature as a culturally recognised semiotic system) or an intermedial one (involving different conventions and channels of transmission).

Another problem affecting the term 'intermediality' is the question of its extension. Some scholars have restricted it to phenomena that can be documented within a given 'work', that is, to a direct or indirect participation of more than one medium in the signification and/or structure of a given semiotic entity; others have gone beyond this narrow definition and have also included 'extracompositional' forms which result from relations or comparisons between medially different semiotic entities. With a view to such frequent cases as filmic adaptations of novels it is certainly desirable to extend the scope of intermediality to cover such extracompositional cases.

However, while the narrow, 'intracompositional' sense seems to focus on more 'tangible' transgressions of boundaries between media, these being 'givens' of the semiotic entities under scrutiny, one must be aware of the fact that the objects of extracompositional intermediality are often merely products of the critic's interdisciplinary approach and his or her conception of similarities and differences.

Forms

The dependence of intermediality on the critic's perspective is perhaps most obvious in the extracompositional variant that has been termed 'transmediality' (Rajewsky 2002: 12). Transmedial phenomena are phenomena that are non-specific to individual media. Since they appear in more than one medium, they point to palpable similarities between heteromedial semiotic entities. Transmediality appears, for instance, on the level of ahistorical formal devices and ways of organising semiotic complexes, such as repetition of *motifs and *thematic variation (e.g., in music and literature), *metalepsis (in *fiction, film, painting, etc.), and *narrativity. Narrativity in particular cannot be restricted to verbal narratives alone but also informs *opera, film, ballet (*see* DANCE AND NARRATIVE), the visual arts and, as some have argued, to some degree even instrumental music (*see* NARRATIVE; NARRATIVE TURN IN THE HUMANITIES; PICTORIAL NARRATIVITY; VISUAL NARRATIVITY). Other instances of transmediality concern characteristic historical traits that are common to either the form or the content level of several media in given periods, such as the pathetic expressivity which is characteristic of eighteenth-century sensibility and which can be found in drama, fiction, poetry, opera, instrumental music, and the visual arts (*see* NARRATIVE IN POETRY). Finally, transmediality can equally appear on the content level alone. This is, for example, the case in certain *archetypal subjects and 'themes' such as the unfolding of romantic love or the *conflicts between generations and genders (*see* GENDER STUDIES). Again, all of these subjects are equally treated in verbal texts, the visual arts, film, opera, etc.

There are also cases in which discernibly similar contents or formal aspects appear in heteromedial entities but where it is clear – or desirable to emphasise – that one medium acted as an origin in a process of medial transfer. This second type of extracompositional intermediality is therefore not an occurrence of 'transmediality' but of an 'intermedial transposition'. As with all forms of intermediality, this variant can apply to parts or to the entirety of individual semiotic entities and also to larger units such as genres. In addition, in intermedial transposition, this range of possibilities applies to both the 'source' and the 'target' medium. An instance of partial intermedial transposition in the field of formal devices would be the employment of a *narrator – originally a component of verbal narratives – in film (in the form of *voice-over narration) or in drama (as an *'epic' presenter). The most common variant of intermedial transposition in contemporary culture applies to entire semiotic complexes, as happens in adaptations of novels into film, film into novels, drama into opera, etc. Sometimes the intermedial transposition affects an entire genre, as when the structure of *detective fiction, originally a genre of verbal fiction, is mapped onto comic strips or films (see COMICS AND GRAPHIC NOVEL; REMEDIATION).

Extracompositional intermediality as such does not necessarily affect the meaning or outer appearance of particular works or performances, while intracompositional intermediality does. Like extracompositional intermediality the intracompositional variant can occur in two main forms. The most obvious of these forms is 'multimediality' or 'plurimediality'. Plurimediality can, for instance, be observed in operatic performances, which regularly involve dramatic text, music, and visual signs, but also in novels that contain illustrations or musical scores. Plurimediality occurs, in short, whenever two or more media are overtly present in a given semiotic entity at least in one instance. This co-presence implies that the components of the medial mixture are discernible on the level of the signifiers without being semiotically dependent on each other (as a verbal text would be that is reproduced as a part of a picture). Such discernibility can be assumed as given even when the medial components are not 'quotable' separately (as would be the case in humming the melody of a song as opposed to reciting its text; see QUOTATION THEORY). The combination of media, e.g., in ballet (a synthesis of dance, non-verbal drama, and music), in comic strips (combinations of words and images), or in *radio plays (composites of sound, music, and verbal language), shows not only that plurimediality creates medial hybrids but also that the regular use of such hybrids may result in the emergence of new, syncretistic media. So, once again, intermediality is at least as much a 'reading' effect as a fact of the phenomena under consideration (see HYBRID GENRES).

As opposed to plurimediality, which spans many variants – from the juxtaposition of relatively separate media to complex syntheses of medial components – the second variant of intracompositional intermediality, 'intermedial reference', suggests neither medial hybridity nor semiotic heterogeneity since it does not imply the incorporation of signifiers of other media. Rather, works and performances in which intermediality is present as a *reference seem to be medially and semiotically homogeneous, for the involvement of another medium here takes place only covertly or indirectly: through signifiers and sometimes also signifieds pointing to it. In contrast with plurimediality, the other medium enters as a conceptual rather than a physical presence, and the base medium retains the character of a homomedial semiotic complex. Intermedial reference can indicate another medium in general or address an entire heteromedial genre – in which case it is a parallel to what in intertextuality theory is called 'system reference' (Broich and Pfister 1985: 52); alternatively, intermedial reference can also gesture towards an individual heteromedial work – in which case the term 'individual reference', which also derives from intertextuality theory (Broich and Pfister 1985: 48), is appropriate. In addition, as with other variants of intermediality, the units affected by intermedial references can vary from individual parts to entire works, performances, etc. (see NARRATIVE UNITS).

In both system reference and individual reference the following subforms can be distinguished. The first is 'explicit reference' or 'intermedial thematisation', a term which is typically used in the context of verbal media (see THEMATISATION). Here the heteromedial reference resides in the signifieds of the referring semiotic complex, while its signifiers are employed in their usual way and do not contribute to heteromedial imitation. In verbal media, such explicit reference is easiest to identify; it is present, for instance, whenever another medium (or a work produced in another medium) is mentioned or discussed in a text. Explicit reference can also appear in the form of representatives of other media, such as painters and musicians as characters in novels. In non-verbal media, which arguably can only 'thematise' other media in a metaphorical sense, explicit reference is nevertheless possible in certain cases of heteromedial representation and allusion. Thus, music or literature may explicitly be referred to in a painting by depicting a musician playing an instrument or a person reading a book.

Since music cannot unambiguously refer to a reality outside itself, let alone to an abstract concept such as a different medium, explicit reference, strictly speaking, does not have a musical equivalent. However, music can point to another medium by a partial quotation or 'reproduction', provided this other medium is a composite and comprises music itself. Thus, an instrumental composition may refer to an opera by 'quoting' a melody from it: as a result, the entire heteromedial work (here, the opera quoted from) may be suggested to the listener. Similarly, a novel may quote the text of a well-known song, thereby presenting the entire song (including the music) to the reader's inner ear.

As reference by partial reproduction implies an extreme case of heteromedial *mimesis, it constitutes one of three subforms of 'implicit intermedial reference' (see Rajewsky 2002: 114). In all of these forms the intermedial signification is the effect of some kind of imitation of another medium or a heteromedial artefact and leads to an imaginative representation of it in the recipient's mind.

The second variant of implicit reference is 'evocation'. Evocation imitates the effects of another medium or heteromedial artefact by monomedial means (without, however, involving heteromedial quotation). It appeals to the recipient's imagination and therefore goes beyond explicit reference, which points to another medium in a non-imaginative, denotative or 'technical' way. Thus, novels can evoke a painting in the reader's mind through ekphrastic description (see EKPHRASIS), and they can evoke a specific musical composition in one's inner ear by describing its effect on certain characters. However, the evocation of images as such (e.g., of a landscape) is also a general effect of aesthetic illusion (see IMMERSION), hence does not require reference to another medium. In contradistinction to such general effects (but also to intermedial transposition), intermedial evocations are usually combined with some explicit marking (notably intermedial thematisation), or else the intermedial reference would be lost as a part of the signification of the respective work or performance.

The necessity of marking intermediality in some explicit way also applies to 'formal intermedial imitation', the third subtype of implicit reference. This is a particularly interesting phenomenon because the intermedial signification in this case is the effect of a salient iconic use of signs. In fact, the characteristic feature of formal imitation consists in the attempt to shape the material of the semiotic complex in question (its signifiers, in some cases also its signifieds) in such a manner that it acquires a formal resemblance to typical features or structures of another medium. Examples of formal imitation, which can again be observed both in entire semiotic units and in segments, include instances of 'literarisation' of music (as in programme music), the 'musicalisation of fiction' (Wolf 1999), the 'filmicisation' of novels (Rajewsky 2002) and the 'musicalisation' of painting (as attempted by Klee and Kandinsky). Similar intermedial effects were also aimed at in 'pictorialised' *realist novels, notably through a descriptive procedure that transcends ordinary ekphrasis and imitates perceptual structures which are triggered by the contemplation of a specific picture (see DESCRIPTION). Of course, in all of these cases the intermedial '-isation' process can only remain a mere approximation (or a critical *metaphor), because it is factually impossible, e.g., for a painting to 'turn into' a musical composition.

It is easy to criticise the 'poverty' or 'as-if' quality of such formal intermedial imitations and evocations or even the entire enterprise of classifying intermedial forms. Indeed, such a typology can never be more than an attempt at charting the vast field of possible intermedial relations. As in all classifications there are borderline cases and multiple labellings of one and the same phenomenon (thus, the 'quotation' of well-known film-music in a radio play accompanying a verbal *dialogue may be seen as both an instance of plurimediality and a case of intermedial reference by partial reproduction). However, what is more important than emphasising the problematics of 'intermediality' and its theory is to have conceptual and terminological tools that transcend mere ad hoc descriptions and impressions, to become aware of intermedial phenomena (even if they remain in a state of adumbration), and to be able to use these tools and this awareness profitably for the analysis of (literary) narratives and other cultural artefacts.

The relevance of intermediality

Intermediality is in fact an important notion for the comparison and analysis of the arts and media as well as their cultural contexts, both from a systematic and a historical perspective. From a historical point of view it can, for instance, be said that plurimediality has been relevant since time immemorial, that is, since the very beginnings of vocal music, dramatic art, and the joint use of painting and architecture. There are, however, periods in which specific cross-relations between certain media are particularly numerous. This applies in particular to implicit references, whose emergence is of a relatively recent date. For instance, addressing and imitating the condition of music in another medium is a phenomenon originating in the nineteenth-century. Such phenomena can provide important insights into the history of aesthetics (e.g., the Romantic privileging of music as an imaginative, non-mimetic art) but also into the development of individual media (e.g., non-mimetic tendencies in literature and the visual arts). As for possible benefits that can be reaped from the concept of intermediality for a systematic view of the arts and media, one may for instance point out that being alerted to the 'transmedial' features of narrativity can shed a new light on the possibilities, as well as the limits, of individual media when it comes to adopting *narrative structures.

Of particular importance is, of course, the functional analysis of intermediality for individual works, performances, *authors, genres, and periods. Thus, the manifold references to painting in nineteenth-century realist fiction are not only an interesting symptom of the 'visual turn' that took place in Western cultural history; these references also enhance the aesthetic illusion of individual texts as a vital means of their ideological and *didactic persuasiveness (see IDEOLOGY AND NARRATIVE). However, in literature, implicit intermedial references in the mode of formal imitation can also be indicative of an anti-illusionist, self-reflexive, or meta-aesthetic turn (see METAFICTION; REFLEXIVITY), as can be seen in postmodernist experimental fiction (see POSTMODERN NARRATIVE). Yet the increasing incidence of intermediality in fiction is just one facet of what could be called the 'intermedial turn' in Western culture since modernism (see MODERNIST NARRATIVE). This intermedial turn manifests itself in manifold experimentations in twentieth century art and culminates in today's attempts at creating maximally believable virtual realities as an apogee of multimedial practice (see IMMERSION).

References and further reading

Barricelli, Jean-Pierre, and Joseph Gibaldi (eds) (1982) *Interrelations of Literature*, New York: MLA.
Broich, Ulrich, and Manfred Pfister (eds) (1985) *Intertextualität: Formen, Funktionen, anglistische Fallbeispiele*, Tübingen: Niemeyer.
Clüver, Claus (1989) 'On Intersemiotic Transposition', *Poetics Today*, 10.1, 55–90.
Hansen-Löve, Aage A. (1983) 'Intermedialität und Intertextualität: Probleme der Korrelation von Wort- und Bildkunst: Am Beispiel der russischen Moderne', in Wolf Schmid and Wolf-Dieter Stempel (eds) *Dialog der Texte: Hamburger Kolloquium zur Intertextualität*, Vienna: Gesellschaft zur Förderung slawistischer Studien.
Hedling, Erik, and Ulla-Britta Lagerroth (eds) (2002) *Cultural Functions of Intermedial Exploration*, Amsterdam: Rodopi.
Helbig, Jörg (ed.) (1998) *Intermedialität: Theorie und Praxis eines interdisziplinären Forschungsgebiets*, Berlin: Schmidt.
Konstantinovic, Zoran, *et al.* (eds) (1981) *Literature and the Other Arts: Proceedings of the IXth Congress of the ICLA*, Innsbruck: Amoe.
Lagerroth, Ulla-Britta, Hans Lund, and Erik Hedling (eds) (1997) *Interart Poetics: Essays on the Interrelations of the Arts and Media*, Amsterdam: Rodopi.
McFarlane, Brian (1996) *Novel To Film: An Introduction to the Theory of Adaptation*, Oxford: Clarendon.
McLuhan, Marshall (1964) *Understanding Media: The Extensions of Man*, New York: McGraw-Hill.
Rajewsky, Irina O. (2002) *Intermedialität*, Tübingen: Francke.
Wagner, Peter (ed.) (1996) *Icons – Texts – Iconotexts: Essays on Ekphrasis and Intermediality*, Berlin: de Gruyter.
Wolf, Werner (1999) *The Musicalization of Fiction: A Study in the Theory and History of Intermediality*, Amsterdam: Rodopi.
Zima, Peter V. (ed.) (1995) *Literatur intermedial: Musik – Malerei – Photographie – Film*, Darmstadt: Wissenschaftliche Buchgesellschaft.

WERNER WOLF

INTERTEXTUALITY

Intertextuality refers to the presence of a text A in a text B. A is the 'intertext' if one stresses the textual precursor, the 'pretext' absorbed by a later text. Or, one could call B the intertext if one lays emphasis on the text incorporating a previous text and thereby becoming intertextual. Alternatively,

Doležel argues that A and B are intertexually bound if they share 'semantic traces' regardless of chronology. Further, critics that Doležel labels 'absolute intertextualists' posit intertextuality as an intrinsic, universal attribute of texts, for Kristeva, Barthes, Derrida, Sollers, and Riffaterre, all texts are inherently intertextual. Finding this 'universalist' view unhelpful, other scholars restrict intertextuality to the interplay of identifiable (Genette) or 'traceable' texts (Doležel).

The discussion that follows has two parts. The first provides an overview of 'universal' narrative intertextuality. The second deals with the 'limited' type, where intertextuality involves short stories, novels, and other narratives that rework particular texts. Further, this part covers primarily 'inter-narrative' exchanges, which entail the integration of a narrative A (rather than an essay or a cartoon) into a narrative B. Also, whereas one can define narrative broadly (as in 'the Enlightenment narrative') and thus locate 'narratives' and their intertextual ties almost everywhere, I examine here chiefly fictional narrative intertextuality, that is, intertextual modes where at least B (if not both A and B) is *fiction.

Universalist foundations: structural linguistics and narrative grammar

The universalist approach to intertextuality draws from Saussurean linguistics and its counterpart, *Russian Formalism; from Bakhtin's critique of both theoretical paradigms; and, finally, from Kristeva's recovery of Bakhtin. Saussure's structural principles, especially the 'differential' value of the linguistic system's components and the paradigm/syntagm dynamic, have influenced narrative poetics, and so has Propp's 'morphology' (*see* STRUCTURALIST NARRATOLOGY). Saussure, Propp, Jakobson, Tomashevskii, and other formalists helped Greimas, Bremond, Todorov, and Barthes describe narrative as consisting of basic units like actions, *motifs, and *characters organised into classes and selected in a specific way by particular narratives, which subject (combinations of) those units to certain generative-transformative rules (*see* NARRATIVE UNITS; STORY GRAMMARS). As Todorov notes, Propp analysed one hundred *fairy tales, isolating thirty-one 'functions' or recurrent structural elements (*see* FUNCTION (PROPP)). While there are far more than a hundred Russian (and other) narratives of this sort, Propp's

model predicts that they will all share, albeit without direct reference to one another, the same functions.

Similarly, drawing explicitly from Saussure's distinction between *langue* and *parole*, Lévi-Strauss observes that the 'savage mind' spins mythic narratives that combine pre-existent 'constituent units' or *'mythemes'. *Myths, Lévi-Strauss writes in *Structural Anthropology*, tell stories; to understand these stories, one must isolate the classes of sentences (or 'gross constituent units') constituting them. Lévi-Strauss looked at a much larger narrative corpus than Propp's, and one that was cross-cultural, but his argument about the structural kinship of myths and *legends does not differ from the Russian scholar's: all narratives can be said to be somehow related, i.e., intertextual – in the sense that they all use the same 'grammar', are 'formulaic'.

Bakhtin's legacy: cultural and ideological analyses of narrative intertextuality

Unlike Saussure, Bakhtin dwells primarily upon *parole* (utterance), which he views as a social, 'dialogic' act fraught with 'others' words' (1986: 89). The *dialogism of the utterance and of the 'text as utterance' (104) renders all major Bakhtinian concepts such as 'answerability', 'double-voicedness', the carnivalesque, and *'heteroglossia' variations on the intertextual theme. Indeed, with help from Bakhtin and his circle, Kristeva was the first to coin the term 'intertextuality', insisting that 'the text is *productivity*', 'a permutation of texts, an intertextuality: in a text's space several enunciations, lifted from other texts, intersect and neutralize one another' (1976: 12). This famous quote belongs to *Le Texte du roman*, and it is noteworthy that in *The Dialogic Imagination* and elsewhere Bakhtin maintains that the *novel is the most 'heteroglossic' *genre, that, in fact, heteroglossia is 'the prerequisite for authentic novelistic discourse'. Also of Bakhtinian (or Bakhtinian/Medvedevian) inspiration is Kristeva's use of the notion 'ideologeme', which considers the text's intertextual position within the broader text of society and history (Kristeva 1980: 36–37) (*see* IDEOLOGY AND NARRATIVE). Thus, the dialogism of a given *speech act, the heteroglossia of a Dostoevskii novel, etc., alert us not only to the linguistic 'otherness' or heterogeneity of the utterance and narrative but also to their cultural and ideological complexity.

Once society, history, and culture are seen as 'texts', intertextuality becomes central to New Historicism, *cultural studies and *identity studies, post-colonial scholarship, debates around globalised 'network society', the Internet, and hypertext (*see* DIGITAL NARRATIVE; HISTORIOGRAPHY; POST-COLONIALISM AND NARRATIVE). Conversely – and concurrently – the 'cultural turn' in literary theory and discourse studies impacts the study of narrative intertextuality (*see* DISCOURSE ANALYSIS (FOUCAULT)). Both shifts encourage us to place narratives not only at the crossroads of other verbal or written, primarily literary texts, but equally within the larger 'texts' of race, *gender, sex, class, or empire. Regarding *The Great Gatsby*, for instance, 'cultural intertextualists' recommend that we look in the novel not only for references and allusions to works by Benjamin Franklin and Horatio Alger, but for the broader discourse of 'social Darwinism' prior as well as contemporary to Fitzgerald's book: *autobiographical accounts and speeches of well-known tycoons, self-reliance handbooks, and newspaper articles. Furthermore, we are encouraged to see *Gatsby* at the intersection of various discourses of the 'roaring twenties', discourses that have objects as diverse as the Prohibition underworld, advertising, *gender, race, homosociality, and homosexuality (*see* ADVERTISEMENTS; QUEER THEORY).

Poststructuralism and telling as retelling

Kroeber suggests that stories are 'intended' to be retold as much as they are meant to be told (*see* INTENTIONALITY). This holds true particularly in oral literature because *audiences have always already heard this or that *folktale and thus identify it as a version of a previous narrative (*see* NARRATIVE VERSIONS; ORAL CULTURES AND NARRATIVE). In other words, a myth or *anecdote is *a priori* intertextual, in the sense of repeating prior tellings. Like J. Hillis Miller in *Fiction and Repetition*, Kroeber posits that repetition is embedded in the 'principles of narrativity' (1992: 3) (*see* NARRATIVITY). Miller (1992) returns to repetition to show how the putative referentiality and 'straightforward linearity' of Victorian narrative is 'troubled' by intertextuality (*see* REFERENCE; TEMPORAL ORDERING). One usually seizes a Dickens novel, the critic contends, as an undeviating,

forward-moving story driven by narrative teleology. Yet the reader realises before long that the Dickensian *line* is not *linear* but a thread affected by all sorts of repetitions: 'returnings', 'knottings', 'recrossings', 'crinklings to and fro', 'suspensions, interruptions', etc. (Miller 1992: 17) (*see* SUSPENSE AND SURPRISE; RETARDATORY DEVICES). Resulting is a narrative labyrinth quite opposite to 'logocentric' and 'monologic' narrative lines. Dickens's readers, and readers generally, may assume that reading, meaning making, inheres in 'identifying' the 'true meaning of the word', the 'original presence' rendered absent by its (written) mark. But as soon as we open *Great Expectations* we are thrown into a linguistic maze, for 'each word inheres in a labyrinth of branching interverbal relationships going back not to a referential source but to something already, at the beginning, a figurative transfer' (Miller 1992: 19) (*see* MULTIPATH NARRATIVE).

Miller mentions Rousseau and Condillac as sources of his figurative theory of narrative intertextuality, but Nietzsche has been the better-known 'tropologist' ever since de Man's *Allegories of Reading*. In fact, Miller follows de Man's *'allegory' to designate what in narrative complicates linearity, transparence, conformity to a scheme. In brief, allegory 'expresses the impossibility of expressing unequivocally' (Miller 1992: 21), of making (keeping) straight, simple, referential that which has always been non-linear, complex, impure, tied into, and derived from, larger systems. 'The language of narrative', Miller contends, 'is always displaced, borrowed. Therefore any single thread leads everywhere, like a labyrinth made of a single line or corridor crinkled to and fro' (24). Every 'origin' turns out a fork in the road, much like the passage in Elizabeth Gaskell's *Cranford* that talks about origins, generation, and procreation (*see* FAMILY CHRONICLE), but whose own *genealogy cannot be established since the text's multiply quotational language has no single, identifiable source (Miller 1992: 26). The novel's vocabulary is 'on loan' from other texts.

Like other members of the Yale School, Hartman and Barbara Johnson in particular, Miller has been influenced by Derrida's and Barthes's generalised or universalist model of intertextuality. *Of Grammatology*'s *il n'ya pas de hors-texte* – 'there is no outside-text'– should be mentioned here alongside Barthesian pieces such as 'The Death of the Author', 'From Work to Text', *The Pleasure of the Text*, *S/Z*, and others, where the text is defined as a 'network' or 'tissue of quotations'. Heeding such formulations of texts' inherently intertextual condition, *poststructuralists deploy intertextuality as an alternative to 'influence' by, and 'imitation' of, 'nature', 'culture', or 'sources' such as *authors, works, *motifs, and styles. Enlisting intertextuality in a general critique of 'referentiality' and its 'transcendental' presuppositions, they seek to cut a number of conceptual Gordian knots: aesthetic autonomy, originality, priority, invention, authorship, talent (or 'genius'), intention, *agency, the human(ist) subject.

From universal to limited intertextuality: narrative intertextuality and literary history

Among the Yale School members, Bloom is perhaps best known for his work on intertextuality. On the one hand, his understanding of intertextuality is 'radically' universalist. All texts – poems, in Bloom's case – are intertexts, 'inter-poems' (Broich 1997: 251), which renders textuality and intertextuality synomymous. Following Freud and the Kabbalah's 'ontologised' intertextuality, Bloom reconstructs literary history as a narrative of 'misreading'. New poets, Bloom claims, 'misread' their precursors; more importantly, the new poets' writings reflect, *write* this very 'misprision'. Accordingly, poetic writing obtains intertextually; i.e., it is *re*writing. But on the other hand, Bloom examines the misreading/miswriting exchange between a precursor and an ephebe, providing a counterweight to his 'intrinsic' or 'generalised' intertextuality. Hence the scene of intertextuality is always played out in a localised setting, itself subject to narrative representation, with particularised (writing) agents locked in agonistic struggle with other such agents from the past, whom they 'defeat' through more or less unconscious acts of misreading.

This double-bind also informs Henry Louis Gates, Jr.'s 'Signifyin(g)', which, in essence, does for the history of African American narrative what Bloom has done for the history of modern poetry. Gates quotes Bloom several times and, also like Bloom, shows how a writer interpellates his or her predecessor. No reading of Alice Walker's *The Colour Purple*, Gates maintains, can afford to ignore Walker's revision of Zora Neale Hurston's *Their Eyes Were Watching God*. *The Colour Purple*

does not mark a 'beginning', an initiation of a narrative starting *ex nihilo*, but rather a segment in an 'extended ebony chain of discourse'. Consequently, African American storytellers – biographical authors as well as fictional *narrators – are determined as Signifiers; to tell their stories, they actually retell stories, rework topoi, tropes, and styles, i.e., repeat with a difference. Gates's theory thus resembles Kroeber's, but overall the African American scholar underscores the differential effects of repetition rather than the repetitive undergirdings of new stories. Noteworthy, too, is Gates's cultural approach, for he studies not only how Ishmael Reed's novel *Mumbo Jumbo* plays upon Ralph Ellison's *Invisible Man*, but also how Reed's text inscribes itself in the 'text' of blackness.

Negotiating 'general' and 'particular' modes of narrative intertextuality

Todorov himself suggests that the universalist view of narrative as intrinsically intertextual is also that theory's weakness. In brief, the 'morphology of functions', the 'grammar of motifs', the 'logic of actions', etc. do not deal with an intertextuality of texts *per se*, but rather with an abstract combinatory system involving 'predicates' and related categories. Or, as Allen writes apropos of Barthes, these structural components would simply point to the presence of a *code in the text (Allen 2000: 183). However, to work out a compromise between an absolute – and thus theoretically 'useless' (Doležel) – model of intertextuality and an untheorised drawing of intertextual parallels between this or that story, one must, where narrative intertextuality is concerned, go farther than Todorov's taxonomy of transformations, which is still a sort of 'universal grammar'.

Thus, one could look for a certain narrative text that appears to body forth exemplarily a certain combination of functions, to instantiate a pattern, scheme, motif, or genre so effectively as to come to symbolise or stand for those, and provide an intertextual resource or template to future narratives working with that pattern, scheme, motif, or genre. To illustrate, the 'rags-to-riches' narrative, present in many oral and written cultures, presupposes a predicate sequence that can be described in general terms. In American literature in particular, this scheme has been memorably embodied ('encoded') by a particular 'Ur-text', Franklin's *Autobiography*. Hence, in the case of

The Great Gatsby, the novel does build broadly on the general 'rags-to-riches' narrative matrix; but, more specifically, Fitzgerald's novel sets itself up in an explicit intertextual dialogue with a pre-existing 'self-made-man' text, Franklin's, as demonstrated by Jay Gatsby's 'general resolves' list and other intertextual moments of the novel.

Michel Tournier's novel *Le Roi des aulnes* (translated as *The Ogre*) lays bare this very problem. Its narrating protagonist, Abel Tiffauges, asks himself whether Albuquerque, hero of an anecdote in Montaigne's *Essays*, purportedly re-enacts a specific scene from Saint Christopher's life as narrated in Jacques de Voragine's *La Légende dorée*, or whether Albuquerque and the Christian martyr just happen to perform independently the same symbolic act transparent in the saint's name (*Christopher* means 'Christ-bearer').

Embedding as 'limited' narrative intertextuality

Tournier's solution to this dilemma is worth mentioning. True, Tiffauges seems to uphold the 'generalist', 'archetypal' view according to which no direct, explicit intertextual reference is involved in Montaigne. But as a text, *Le Roi des aulnes* goes in the opposite direction. Not only does Tournier's novel reference *La Légende dorée*; Tiffauges and his friend Nestor also re-enact the Saint Christopher-Jesus Christ episode barely a few pages before the Montaigne-Voragine connection is brought up. Several things occur because of this re-enactment. First, and most obviously, intertextuality itself becomes foregrounded, even though the reader decodes it retroactively, by a feedback loop provided through the Albuquerque episode. Second, the text constitutes a blasphemous parody of sorts, for Tiffauges – the 'ogre' – is anything but a Christ figure. Furthermore, parodic intertextuality works here as a critique of the moral, cultural, and religious values of Saint Christopher College, where Tiffauges and Nestor are enrolled and where they reproduce, in the intertextual and performative sense (*see* PERFORMATIVITY), the Christ-bearing scene from Voragine. One witnesses, in other words, a case of narrative *embedding, or multiple embedding to be more precise, with Voragine's story lodged inside Montaigne's, which in turn lies inside Tournier's. In some fiction writers, this Russian-dolls or Chinese-box type of embedded narrative may amount to, or may suggest, 'infinite

regress', as Broich notes (*see* FRAMED NARRATIVE; MISE EN ABYME; REFLEXIVITY).

Todorov holds up the *Arabian Nights* as an example where the embedded stories do not belong to different texts ('Scheherazade tells that Jaafer tells that the tailor tells that...') (1977 [1971]: 70–72). But critics like Mieke Bal have discussed under 'embedding' instances of *intertextual* embedding, where a given narrative A is 'nested' inside – and 'interpolates', as it were – another narrative B, which furnishes the framework within which A is reproduced, altered, or somehow used. In this situation embedding and 'limited' intertextuality become synonymous.

Limited intertextuality, postmodernism, and the postmodern rewrite

Genette's taxonomy helps classify all possible relations between texts A and B as allusion, commentary, parody, pastiche, plagiarism, *irony, paraphrase, travesty, *quotation, etc. and the various degrees and kinds of textual transformation involved. The latter may amount to nothing more than a 'benign', isolated quotation or may entail more substantial plays upon, and alterations of, narrative A. It is worth remembering that the modern narrative form par excellence, the novel, arises intertextually in the 'limited' sense in which *Don Quixote* revamps parodically chivalric *romances (*see* QUIXOTIC NOVEL). But equally important is defining narrative intertextuality historically, showing, that is, how different moments and trends in the history of fiction define themselves with respect to the varying roles assigned to the intertextual devices inventoried by Genette and others.

On this account, one could also break up critics of intertextuality into two groups: those who deem intertextuality, including 'limited' intertextuality, a universal, perennial discursive staple, as present in Montaigne as in Tournier; and those who believe that writers like Tournier illustrate a new, characteristically *postmodern brand of intertextuality and, conversely, that intertextuality can help us understand what is unique about postmodernism. The former include classical scholars, 'universalists' and reading theorists like Riffaterre (1983), traditional critics like Hermerén (1990: 84), and even Broich, who sometimes tend to assimilate limited intertextuality to an ahistorical notion of 'imitation' and 'influence' (Broich 1997: 249–50).

The latter insist that postmodernism foregrounds, more extensively and more conspicuously than classicism or modernism, intertextuality as the condition of all textuality, speaking to a post-structuralist philosophy of textuality (*see* MODERNIST NARRATIVE). What is more, the same critics also specify that a) postmodern narrative makes limited intertextuality its foremost genetic principle; b) such narrative thematises, reveals as its 'structural metaphor' (Ricardou 1967), places *en abyme* (Dällenbach 1989), and otherwise lays bare, quite self-consciously, this principle, in passages that have been variously identified as 'self-apparent' (Klinkowitz 1984), metalinguistic, meta-literary, *metanarrative – or 'typically' postmodern.

In sum, postmodern narrative can be defined as a fictional form in which 'limited', self-acknowledged intertextuality tends to become dominant practice. Further, as Broich notes, postmodern intertextuality is 'generally' *deconstructive rather than constructive, which is to say, it critiques the 'pretext' and its ideology instead of 'imitating' them. Exceptions aside, the remarkable proliferation of *postmodern rewrites warrants the definition above. An extreme case of 'limited' narrative intertextuality, the postmodern rewrite is arguably the most elaborated intertextual form, obtaining through full-blown renarrativisation or narrative parallel. This often subjects the rewritten narrative to a thorough, formally flaunted and ideologically motivated reworking, as in Alice Randall's *The Wind Done Gone*. Rewriting Margaret Mitchell's *Gone with the Wind* from the perspective of a mulatto woman, Cynara, *The Wind Done Gone* renders central to the story a black voice and worldview whose absence in Mitchell's text led to one-dimensional African American characters and racial clichés.

References and further reading

Allen, Graham (2000) *Intertextuality*, London: Routledge.

Bakhtin, M. M. (1986) *Speech Genres and Other Late Essays*, eds. Caryl Emerson and Michael Holquist, trans. Vern W. McGee, Austin: University of Texas Press.

Bloom, Harold (1973) *The Anxiety of Influence: A Theory of Poetry*, New York: Oxford University Press.

Broich, Ulrich (1997) 'Intertextuality', in Hans Bertens and Douwe Fokkema (eds) *International Postmodernism: Theory and Literary Practice*, Amsterdam: John Benjamins.

Dällenbach, Lucien (1989) *The Mirror in the Text*, trans. Jeremy Whiteley with Emma Hughes, Chicago: University of Chicago Press.

Gates, Henry Louis, Jr. (1988) *The Signifying Monkey: A Theory of African-American Literary Criticism*, New York: Oxford University Press.

Genette, Gérard (1997 [1982] *Palimpsests: Literature in the Second Degree*, trans. Channa Newman and Claude Doubinsky, Lincoln: University of Nebraska Press.

Hermerén, Göran (1991) *Art, Reason, and Tradition: On the Role of Rationality in Interpretation and Explanation of Works of Art*, Lund: Bloms Boktryckeri.

Klinkowitz, Jerome (1984) *The Self-Apparent Word: Fiction as Language/Language as Fiction*, Carbondale: Southern Illinois University Press.

Kristeva, Julia (1976) *Le Texte du roman: Approche sémiologique d'une structure transformationelle*, The Hague: Mouton.

—— (1980) *Desire in Language: A Semiotic Approach to Literature and Art*, ed. Leon S. Roudiez, trans. Thomas Gora, Alice Jardine, and Leon S. Roudiez, New York: Columbia University Press.

Kroeber, Karl (1992) *Retelling/Rereading: The Fate of Storytelling in Modern Times*, New Brunswick: Rutgers University Press.

Miller, J. Hillis (1992) *Ariadne's Thread: Story Lines*, New Haven: Yale University Press.

Morgan, Thaïs (1989) 'The Space of Intertextuality', in Patrick O'Donnell and Robert Con Davis (eds) *Intertextuality and Contemporary American Fiction*, Baltimore: Johns Hopkins University Press.

Plett, Heinrich (ed.) (1991) *Intertextuality*, Berlin: De Gruyter.

Ricardou, Jean (1967) *Problèmes du nouveau roman*, Paris: Seuil.

Riffaterre, Michel. (1983) *Text Production*, trans. Térèse Lyons, New York: Columbia University Press.

Todorov, Tzvetan (1977 [1971]) *The Poetics of Prose*, trans. Richard Howard, Ithaca: Cornell University Press.

CHRISTIAN MORARU

INTRADIEGETIC NARRATOR

A *character-narrator who, embedded in a higher-order narrative, is the teller of a story within a story. For example, in Joseph Conrad's *Heart of Darkness*, Marlow is a *character in the *story-world whose narratorial acts evoke another, embedded storyworld when he recounts his journey into the Belgian Congo, his encounter with Kurtz, and so on. See DIEGESIS; VOICE (also: EMBEDDING; FRAMED NARRATIVE).

IRONY

Irony, in its broadest sense, inextricably involves all major elements of a communicative situation: a speaker and his/her intention, the utterance itself, and the interpretive strategies of the recipient (*see* COMMUNICATION IN NARRATIVE; INTENTIONALITY). Most contemporary theories recognise four forms of the phenomenon: (1) irony as a verbal strategy, (2) dramatic or situational irony, (3) irony as a structural principle, and (4) irony as a general attitude to life and art.

(1) The verbal strategy of irony has been described as both a semantic and a pragmatic rhetorical figure (*see* PRAGMATICS; RHETORICAL APPROACHES TO NARRATIVE). Quintilian and Cicero defined irony *as saying the opposite* of what one means, communicating an intentional mockery (anti-phrasis), or as *saying something else* than is expected in the given circumstances (using euphemism, periphrase, allusion, or hyperbole). These ancient rhetoricians already followed an approach in which the communicative context as well as the ethos of speaker and *audience play a determining role. Recent research in linguistic pragmatics and rhetoric stresses that in order to be interpreted as ironic, an utterance must contain or imply a value judgement charged with *emotion (Hutcheon 1994). On this view, irony is based on a clash of argumentative values, strategically implying rather than stating the unacceptability of a certain position. As Sperber and Wilson have argued, an ironic utterance is perceived as if set between quotation marks, as the echo of an invalid or inappropriate utterance, targeting both the originator of that utterance (i.e. the victim) and the belief system that gave rise to it (*see* QUOTATION THEORY). In irony, according to Sperber and Wilson, discourse is *mentioned* and not *used*. Booth, for his part, famously distinguished between *stable* and *unstable* types of irony, depending on the accessibility of the intended meaning. Enlightenment writers and philosophers preferred stable ironies (Voltaire's *Candide*, Swift's *Modest Proposal*), whereas modernists since Flaubert have generally opted for more unstable variants (*see* MODERNIST NARRATIVE).

Ironic communication implies several participant roles, the main ones being the ironist, his or her 'confederates', and the victim. Hutcheon gives a comprehensive survey of the possible functions of irony, which range from norm-reinforcing, via playful ('ludic') to aggressive and 'aggregative' (community building) cases. Ironic communication is clearly a risky business, both for ironists and their interpreters (Hutcheon 1994; Hamon 1996). This is especially true for literary narrative, as the reader cannot rely on paraverbal markers of irony, such as winks or intonation. However, peri-textual signs may function as indicators of irony (Booth 1974); so do transgressions of expectations grounded in what Grice characterised as maxims of Quantity and Quality (demanding conciseness, relevance, and truthfulness) as in hyperbolic praise or blame, or flagrant contradictions between a judgement and its context. Production and interpretation of verbal irony requires sophisticated linguistic, literary, and ideological competences (*see* IDEOLOGY AND NARRATIVE). To 'construct' irony the reader engages in a hermeneutic calculus encompassing *perspectives, *voices, values, intentions, and *reliability (*see* HERMENEUTICS).

(2) Dramatic, or more generally, situational irony shares with verbal irony a contradiction in evaluative insight. It is the observation of a sharp *conflict between a given assessment of a state of affairs and reality ('isn't it ironic that ...'). This type of irony is much exploited in *drama, especially in tragedy (see Thirlwall's pioneering study). Oedipus's appreciation of his situation – a king well in power and happily married – appears a dramatic misjudgement for a better-informed audience. Here the ironist is variously conceived of as life, fate, or God. In literary narrative, this kind of irony requires an analysis of the strategic distribution of knowledge, and of 'discrepant awareness'.

(3) The concept of irony as a structural principle was developed by New Critics such as Cleanth Brooks. A key concept in the definition of poetry as an organic whole built on the tension of conflicting forces, it has also been applied to the close reading of literary narrative, and it survives in *deconstructive readings as the teasing out of contradictory textual forces.

(4) Irony as a general attitude to life and art occurs in historically and culturally determined forms such as the following.

Socratic irony is a verbal strategy in the service of a philosophical attitude (*see* PHILOSOPHY AND NARRATIVE). Claiming that he knew nothing, Socrates kept questioning his interlocutors, echoing their seemingly common sense beliefs in apparent candour until they were forced to derive wholly unexpected conclusions and had to revise their beliefs. The *eiron* (ironist) was variously condemned for dissimulating his own insight and escaping his public responsibility (by Demosthenes, Theophrastus), or praised as an incarnation of (ironical) wisdom (Kierkegaard).

Romantic irony is as much a philosophical as an artistic notion, developed by the early German Romantics such as Friedrich Schlegel and Karl Solger. The originary Romantic irony is the observation of the paradox of human condition: man is capable of conceiving of infinity but unable to reach it. Similarly, a work of art aims at the absolute but is limited by nature. Hence, in narrative art, the recourse to techniques which ironically foreground art's limitations and conventionality but ultimately suggest the unrepresentable totality, the mixture of *genres and styles (*see* HYBRID GENRES), the juxtaposition of the grotesque and the sublime, the use of fragments (*see* GAPPING), the interruption of *narration by untimely digressions, the self-reflexive destruction of narrative illusion (*see* MIMESIS; REFLEXIVITY) – all of these so-called *postmodern devices were already cherished by Schlegel's contemporaries.

Modernist irony refers to the subversion of any stable value-position in literary narrative, resulting for example from ambiguous modes of discourse (*see* FREE INDIRECT DISCOURSE) and/or the use of indeterminate points of view, as in the *novels of Flaubert, Musil, and Mann (*see* INDETERMINACY; POINT OF VIEW (LITERARY)). These writers implicitly question and ironically target not only the belief systems of their fallible *characters but also the very notion of the 'omniscient' *narrator, suggesting a mindset of general scepticism.

Postmodernist writers have further radicalised romantic and modernist irony so that all assertions are heard as echoes, even though the ultimate ideological stance of the speaker responsible for this effect of *intertextual recycling is irretrievable (consider the work of Michel Houellebecq and Martin Amis). For postmodernist narrative theory and its practice of disparaging seemingly outdated terms, irony continues to pose a serious challenge because investigation of the phenomenon is more than ever dependent on concepts such as voice, ethos, subject, *author, and intention.

References and further reading

Behler, Ernst (1990) *Irony and the Discourse of Modernity*, Seattle: University of Washington Press.

Booth, Wayne (1974) *A Rhetoric of Irony*, Chicago: University of Chicago Press.

Brooks, Cleanth (1971) 'Irony as a Principle of Structure', in Hazard Adams (ed.) *Critical Theory since Plato*, New York: Harcourt Brace Jovanovich.

Grice, Paul (1989) *Studies in the Way of Words*, Cambridge, Mass.: Harvard University Press.

Hamon, Philippe (1996) *L'Ironie littéraire: Essai sur les formes de l'écriture oblique*, Paris: Hachette.

Hutcheon, Linda (1994) *Irony's Edge: The Theory and Politics of Irony*, London: Routledge.

Sperber, Dan, and Deirdre Wilson (1981) 'Irony and the Use-Mention Distinction', in Peter Cole (ed.) *Radical Pragmatics*, New York: Academic Press.

Thirlwall, Connop (1833) 'On the Irony of Sophocles', *The Philological Museum*, 2, 483–537.

LIESBETH KORTHALS ALTES

ISOTOPY

In Greimas's structural semantics, *isotopy* is any set of recurrent linguistic categories (e.g., proper names, verb *tenses) along a syntagmatic chain making possible the uniform reading of a discourse and resolution of its ambiguities. In the generative process, iteration of categories includes syntactic isotopies and semantic isotopies. At the discursive level, the recurrence of semes (minimal, contrastively defined units of meaning) produces relations of equivalence, resulting in thematic isotopies (abstract, underlying structures of global meaning) and, at the surface level, figurative isotopies. Thematic isotopies include *actants (addresser, addressee, subject, object) which, through actorialisation, temporalisation, and spatialisation, appear in figurative isotopies as actors (*characters in a spatiotemporal setting). Several figurative isotopies may converge around a single thematic isotopy (works with recurrent obsessions); conversely, a single figurative isotopy may embrace several thematic isotopies (puns). Co-occurring figurative isotopies may correspond to an equal number of thematic isotopies; these 'pluri-isotopies' result in polysemy and, through connectors (e.g., *metaphor, *metonymy), in multiple readings (*see* ALLEGORY; INDETERMINACY). Isotopies bear on the deep-structure coherence as well as the surface-structure cohesion of discourse construed as utterance (*énoncé*). Recent research has also focused on their emergence through acts of enunciation.

SEE ALSO: semiotics; structuralist narratology; thematisation

References and further reading

Fontanille, Jacques (1999) *Sémiotique et littérature*, Paris: PUF.

Greimas, Algirdas Julien, and Joseph Courtès (1983 [1979]) *Semiotics and Language: An Analytical Dictionary*, trans. Larry Crist *et al.*, Bloomington: Indiana University Press.

JOHN PIER

J

JAPANESE NARRATIVE

Lyric poetry and songs were the first genres to be set down in writing in Japan. Many longer poems (*chôka*) feature a *narrativity that all but disappears in the shorter poetic forms preferred in later periods. The first major narrative work, the *Kojiki* (*Record of Ancient Matters*, 712 CE), contains creation *myths, tales of gods, *legends of the earliest Japanese sovereigns, and more factual accounts of recent emperors. Early texts were written in a cumbersome system using Chinese glyphs sometimes for phonetic value and sometimes for meaning, but by the middle of the Heian period (784–1185), the process of writing was greatly simplified by the development of a phonetic syllabary, and a high degree of literacy came to be expected of all members of the ruling classes. Not only did this syllabary facilitate the writing of personal *diaries, records of court life, *letters and *waka* poetry, it also encouraged experimentation in different forms of narrative. A few tales (*monogatari*) have exotic foreign settings, but most fictional narratives of the period are strongly grounded in the experience at court of the *authors, with few *fantastic elements. *Plots typically hinge on the relations between the sexes. Many of the known authors of tales were female members of the middle aristocracy, serving in the 'salon' of a princess or empress. Fewer male authors can be identified by name, perhaps because men were expected to restrict themselves to more formal writing in Chinese.

Hundreds of invented exchanges of *waka* poetry following the same rules as real-life poetic correspondence are included in the acknowledged masterpiece of the courtly tale *genre, Murasaki Shikibu's *Genji monogatari* (*The Tale of Genji*, ca. 1013). The work also alludes frequently to canonical poems as well as to earlier narrative works, both historical and fictional. The *narrator maintains the pretence of telling an actual story of the recent past. In a famous passage, the *hero Genji first denigrates tales as 'lies', then (speaking as a would-be lover) praises them as faithful to a higher *truth about life, and finally (speaking as a father) warns against the dangers of reading romantic fiction to impressionable young women (Tyler 2001: 461–62; *see* ROMANCE). The narrator dryly notes the contradiction. The *voice of the narrator, clearly female and a member of a particular class, is audible throughout, in the honorific verb forms distinguishing degrees of respect due to *characters and the *narratees, and in passages that translate as first-person asides (*sôshji*), commenting on the action or on the act of *narration itself (*see* COMMENTARY; METANARRATIVE COMMENT). She complains of fatigue or fallible *memory, or makes excuses for what she has revealed about the protagonist (Tyler 2001: 80, 312, 375). The popular and critical reception of *Genji monogatari* has been continuous to this day, with a voluminous history of premodern commentary. The 'modern' features of its style struck Virginia Woolf and other readers of Arthur Waley's translation (1925–1933; *see* MODERNIST NARRATIVE). Waley himself drew attention to the Proustian technique of mentioning a character as if she had already been introduced.

A number of other important narrative genres flourished in the Heian period. One of the earliest were 'poem tales' (*uta monogatari*) such as *Ise monogatari* (the *Tales of Ise*, tenth century), an episodic collection of more than one hundred short narratives based around the life of a ninth-century poet. From this example, writers learned how stories might be constructed around a figure from the imagined or actual past. *Rekishi monogatari* (historical tales) recording memorable incidents at court compare very favourably with earlier narrative histories written in Chinese, and show considerable skill in the selection of vivid detail. Several begin by having the narrator overhear two very old men recall the events of earlier reigns, a framing device found elsewhere (*see* FRAMED NARRATIVE). The first collections of anecdotal tales (*setsuwa*) were assembled as an aid for Buddhist preachers, but soon incorporated a very wide range of religious and secular stories, some set in India and China, dealing with all classes of society and ranging in tone from piety to earthy humour (*see* ANECDOTE; SERMON). The massive *Konjaku monogatarishû* (*Tales of Times Now Past*, ca. 1120) influenced modern writers like Akutagawa Ryûnosuke (1892–1927).

War tales (*gunki monogatari*), the major narrative genre of the *medieval period, raise narratological questions of authorship, genre, *reception, and the interplay between *orality and literacy. The tales are typically the work of many hands, with numerous variants for reading or recitation. In the case of *Heike monogatari* (*The Tale of the Heike*), the version for oral *performance dictated by the reciter Kakuichi in 1371 has long been admired for its language and tone, balancing lyrical and *epic elements. The influence of the *Heike* corpus on the *noh* theater and other genres is great (*see* DRAMA AND NARRATIVE), second only to *Genji monogatari*.

With the introduction of printing in the seventeenth century, earlier classics went through numerous editions, reaching wide *audiences. The variety of new narrative genres is well represented in a recent anthology (Shirane 2002). The witty 'books of a floating world' (*ukiyo-zôshi*) of the prolific Ihara Saikaku (1642–1693) teem with realistic detail in a way that has suggested comparisons with Defoe and Swift. The last major figure before the Meiji Restoration was Bakin (1767–1848), author of historical romances that borrow features of Chinese popular fiction.

During the Meiji period (1868–1912) there was much debate about what could be salvaged from earlier narrative forms in creating the new genre of *shôsetsu* or *novel. Modern Japanese writers have been greatly influenced by the techniques of Western novels and *short stories, but it is notable that many of the most distinguished modern novelists have also been deeply influenced by premodern Japanese narrative.

SEE ALSO: African narrative; Australian Aboriginal narrative; Chinese narrative; fiction, theories of; historiography; narrative in poetry; Native American narrative; Sanskrit narrative

References and further reading

Keene, Donald (1999) *Seeds in the Heart: Japanese Literature from the Earliest Time to the late Sixteenth Century*, New York: Columbia University Press. (First of a four-volume history of Japanese literature.)

Kornicki, Peter (2000) *The Book in Japan: A Cultural History from the Beginnings to the Nineteenth-Century*, Honolulu: University of Hawaii Press.

McCullough, Helen Craig (1988) *The Tale of the Heike*, Stanford: Stanford University Press.

Shirane, Haruo (2002) *Early Modern Japanese Literature: An Anthology, 1600–1900*, New York, Columbia University Press.

Tyler, Royall (2001) *The Tale of Genji*, New York: Viking.

MICHAEL G. WATSON

JOKE

In the internal organisation of narrative jokes as independent discourses, joke structure intertwines with *narrative structure. The 'build-up' comprises the body of the joke, and the 'punchline' structurally closes the joke. The punchline reverses the sense we would expect from the build-up, and forces a previously unexpected sense to our attention, according to characteristic techniques identified by Freud (1960 [1905]). The reversal evokes a clash between opposed semantic scripts (Raskin 1985); we can often recognise a 'script-switch trigger' as well, that is, a word or phrase around which the joke's dual meaning revolves. In the classic one-liner *A panhandler came up to me today and said he hadn't had a bite in weeks, so I bit him*, the phrase 'had a bite' belongs structurally to the build-up, while functioning as the script-switch trigger. In the narrative/joke structure below, the build-up coincides with the orientation and much of the complicating action (clauses A–B), and the punchline corresponds to the resolution (clause C) (*see* DISCOURSE ANALYSIS (LINGUISTICS)). Together the structures yield a narrative with a final humorous twist.

BUILD-UP	A	A panhandler came up to me today
trigger	B	and said he hadn't *had a bite* in weeks,
PUNCH	C	so I bit him

The frame in force in the build-up, namely a panhandler seeking a handout from a passer-by, vanishes in the punchline, where a previously backgrounded frame takes hold in which the victimised passer-by becomes the attacker, while the panhandler becomes the victim. By contrast, dialogic jokes like knock-knocks and riddle jokes are structured around turn-by-turn talk, and they differ accordingly (*see* COMMUNICATION IN NARRATIVE).

In the performance of jokes in discourse contexts, jokes function as preformed interactional units for *mutual revelation* (Norrick 1993). Joketelling can seem aggressive in addressing potentially offensive topics, and can indicate power in disrupting turn-by-turn talk and controlling the floor; at the same time, joketelling introduces a play frame and modulates rapport with a receptive audience, because the teller demonstrates background knowledge, attitudes, and group memberships, while giving the *audience a chance to ratify them (Sacks 1974). Thus, joketelling can affect the alignment of participants in interaction in various ways. Participants interactively negotiate joke topics, prefaces to jokes, the *performance itself and the reaction to it. Jokes develop cohesively out of serious topical talk or word play; they segue back into serious talk about the content, quality, or performance of the joke itself – or they suggest further jokes. Timing in the conversational joketelling performance is compounded of disparate elements: features of the joke text, teller strategies, standard joke prefaces, formulas and patterns, the teller's style of delivery, and audience response (Norrick 2001).

SEE ALSO: humour studies and narrative

References and further reading

Attardo, Salvatore, and Victor Raskin (1991) 'Script Theory Revis(it)ed: Joke Similarity and Joke Representation Model', *Humour*, 4, 293–347.
Freud, Sigmund (1960 [1905]) *Jokes and Their Relation to the Unconscious*, New York: Norton.
Norrick, Neal R. (1993) *Conversational Joking*, Bloomington: Indiana University Press.
—— (2001) 'On the Conversational Performance of Narrative Jokes: Toward an Account of Timing', *Humour*, 14, 255–74.
Raskin, Victor (1985) *Semantic Mechanisms of Humour*, Dordrecht: Reidel.
Sacks, Harvey (1974) 'An Analysis of the Course of a Joke's Telling', in Richard Bauman and Joel Sherzer (eds) *Explorations in the Ethnography of Speaking*, Cambridge: Cambridge University Press.

NEAL NORRICK

JOURNALISM

Conventional journalism emphasises traditional news values of timeliness, proximity, importance, *conflict, novelty, and accuracy and is defined through the spare and efficient 'inverted pyramid', which orders facts from most to least important. The form is well suited to organising, delivering, and showcasing facts in a journalistic environment that holds truth-telling and objectivity to be guiding principles (*see* TRUTH). Even though they call all articles 'stories', journalists and those studying journalism distinguish between the dryer, business-like inverted pyramid narratives of conventional journalism and the freer, more flexible forms they call 'narrative' or 'literary' journalism, which incorporates devices, structures, and sometimes themes found in literature (*see* NARRATIVE STRUCTURES; NARRATIVE TECHNIQUES).

Narrative journalism allows reporters access to subjects and people not usually considered newsworthy, thereby offering increased potential to report outside a conventional journalism of conflict, scandal, crime, and the abnormal. Springing from more inviting and natural forms than the inverted pyramid, narrative journalism broadens the appeal of news through compelling presentation. This, however, can sometimes lead to a prioritising of entertainment over news values, diminishing journalistic integrity as the major source of valid information. Narrative journalism, like the use of particularised stories in *historiography, can have the effect of making individual actions primary, thereby skewing perceptions of the world by de-emphasising social and other forces. Journalistic stories provide their own context – good when well-researched and complete, but misleading when reporters include facts because they conform to the 'story' or omit them because they do not. Because of its form, then, narrative journalism sometimes appears less objective then conventional journalism.

Some view Thucydides' accounts of the Peloponnesian War and oral and broadside *ballads as forerunners of modern narrative journalism, which provides story-like non-fiction with a beginning, middle, and end; characterisation; and *plot or theme. It often includes conventional news values, but emphasises other things, including a story well told. Stories in early American newspapers often were untrue or exaggerated, but found their 'news' value in qualities they illustrated – charity, loyalty, honesty, and courage. Newspapers published simple stories illustrating rewards of hard work and sins of sloth or intemperance. They also published true, or based-in-truth, stories of shysters, murderers, and adventurers. For decades, they published serial fiction and other stories by the likes of Sir Arthur Conan Doyle and Charles Dickens (see SERIAL FORM).

News forms changed after the 1840s, perhaps reflecting a more industrial and urban rather than rural and bucolic news attitude. That period's Penny Press showed that facts and information garnered more profit than opinion and moralising. Further, the telegraph influenced news content, form, and definitions, especially what was considered 'timely'. With daily publication and deadlines, news came to be defined as daily occurrences. The fiction-like morality tales faded after the Civil War as journalists turned to the delivering just the facts in the inverted pyramid, a practice and form that came to epitomise journalism.

In his and Edward Johnson's *The New Journalism* (1973), however, Tom Wolfe argued that this conventional journalism no longer explained or described the complex 1960s of Vietnam; the Civil Rights, gay rights, and women's movements; and the social revolution. He thought narrative journalism could replace the dying *novel as a social force. The book, still an intriguing read, featured writers such as Gay Talese, Joe Eszterhas, and Richard Goldstein, whose journalism, indeed, reads like *fiction. They used, Wolfe explained, four major fictional techniques: scene-by-scene construction (see SUMMARY AND SCENE), *dialogue rather than direct quotes (see SPEECH REPRESENTATION), varying points of view (see POINT OF VIEW (LITERARY)), and *gestures, mannerisms, and personal characteristics as cultural signposts. Even though most 'new journalists' published in books or magazines, they nonetheless influenced

a generation of newspaper journalists, who opened tradition-bound newspapers to different approaches to news and feature stories. Also, since the 1963 Kennedy assassination, *television became an important news source influencing print with '60 Minutes'-style narrative forms.

In the late 1980s and early 1990s, 'The New Journalism' re-emerged as 'Literary Journalism', featuring similar fictional devices. Norman Sims in two books on literary journalism argued that this narrative approach emphasised depth reporting and required considerable time with subjects. This may make Literary Journalism seem more responsible than New Journalism, criticised for its recreated dialogue (e.g., Truman Capote's *In Cold Blood*) and for blending fact and fiction (e.g., Hunter Thompson's two *Fear and Loathing* books). Today's narrative journalists spend months and sometimes years with subjects, infiltrating their lives to present sophisticated accounts of events, issues, and people. Leon Dash, then of *The Washington Post*, virtually lived with sources to report and write *Rosa's Story*, about the matriarch of a drug-riddled D.C. Family. Tom French of the *St. Petersburg Times* spends years reporting such stories as 'South of Heaven', which records the senior year of four or five high school students, and the Pulitzer-Prize-winning *Angels and Demons*, which recounts the fateful vacation trip by a Midwestern mother and two daughters to Florida, where they were raped and killed. These stories, now books, exemplify the best of newspaper literary journalism – fiction-like in their approaches, but impeccably reported and detailed.

Narrative's most consistent influence remains the overdone *anecdote lead ('Mary Jones sat at her kitchen table, eating spinach quiche, when she heard the crash'). But New and Literary Journalism excited journalists, promising a 'new' creative potential and opening for exploration new areas of community life. The Internet's *media convergence and spontaneous presentation formats with the merging of text, video, audio, and interactivity will likely inspire further experimentation with narrative journalism forms (see DIGITAL NARRATIVE).

Even now, narrative journalism is both dangerous and exciting. Danger comes from loss of credibility and embarrassment of clichéd and poorly done 'literary' journalism – or, worse, from stories faked by reporters pressured to entertain as well as inform. Excitement comes from new *perspectives and nuances gained from superbly written stories, accurately reflecting realities of living in today's world.

SEE ALSO: non-fiction novel

References and further reading

Franklin, Jon (1986) *Writing for Story*, New York: Atheneum.
Kerrane, Kevin, and Ben Yagoda (eds) (1997) *The Art of Fact*, New York: Scribner.
Sims, Norman (ed.) (1990) *Literary Journalism in the Twentieth Century*, New York: Oxford University Press.
——, and Mark, Kramer (eds) (1995) *Literary Journalism*, New York: Ballantine Books.
Wolfe, Tom, and Edward Johnson (eds) (1973) *The New Journalism*, New York: Harper & Row.

ROBERT DARDENNE

L

LAW AND NARRATIVE

Contemporary western legal theory and *philosophy has drawn widely on narrative. For analytical convenience the reception of narrative theory can be broadly divided into four categories. These categories are not sealed; the richness of this area of legal thought is the movement of ideas between scholars and philosophical orientations. What follows, then, is a crude set of distinctions that impose a frame on a diverse body of materials.

A first category includes those scholars who use narrative theory for the insights it offers into the adjudicative process and the construction of the trial in the courtroom (see COURTROOM NARRATIVE). This concern with forensic narrative has also extended into an engagement with the narrative elements of judicial reasoning and legal reasoning in general. A second major category of work is focused on what has come to be known as law and literature, where literary narratives are studied for their relevance to law. The third category reflects perhaps the most developed and sophisticated version of research into narrative theory. Legal scholars have drawn on philosophically inflected accounts of literary and other narratives, to provide general jurisprudential accounts of law. In particular, *postmodern legal thought has welcomed theories of narrative drawn from continental philosophy, but the conventional Anglo-American jurisprudential tradition has also drawn on narrative theory to provide support for accounts of adjudication and the structure of the common law. A fourth category gestures toward the concern with the narrative constructions of *identity in feminism (see FEMINIST NARRATOLOGY; GENDER STUDIES), critical race theory, and *post-colonial theory.

Narrative and adjudication

The work of Bernard Jackson (1988) provides a theoretically developed account of narrative in the area of adjudication. Jackson argues that narrative is an essential part of legal decision making, picking up and developing themes within schools of both positivist and realist jurisprudence. The theoretical suppositions underlying this work return to the structuralist *semiotics of A.J. Greimas, which, in turn relies on the notion of a 'semio-narrative' level in the work of Vladimir Propp (see FUNCTION (PROPP); STRUCTURALIST NARRATOLOGY). Propp's work shows that human *action is structured in a narrative fashion. Narrative is understood as a sequence that moves from the setting of goals, the performance of those goals, and the reflection on success or failure (see Bremond 1973). Within this sequence there will be figures who aid or obstruct the subject (see ACTANT).

In applying this analysis to law, we are concerned with the particular legal forms these *narrative structures take. Based on a semiotic concern with law as a form of communication, this mode of narrative analysis has the potential to develop a sophisticated understanding of the construction of legal meaning. The trial provides a focus for this research. Because analysis of the processes in a courtroom is complex, it is necessary to take an exemplary aspect: witness testimony. Testimony in court can be modelled in Greimasian terms. Imagine that the plaintiff has called a witness. The witness has a helper in the form of counsel for the plaintiff. The witness also has an opponent: counsel for the defence. Whilst counsel for the plaintiff will seek to persuade the jury of the veracity of the witness testimony, counsel for the defence will attempt to cast doubt on the version of *events that the witness has given. Of course, if there is a witness who is hostile to the plaintiff's case, counsel for the plaintiff will act as an opponent, and counsel for the defence will act as a helper.

In an outlining an analysis of this sort, Jackson is drawing attention to basic positions that can be occupied by different actors as a narrative develops about the case in the courtroom (see AGENCY; POSITIONING). At a more general level, the model can also be used to think more broadly about legal reasoning. Jackson's argument is that legal reasoning, which tends to represent itself as scientific, makes use of narrative forms (see SCIENCE AND NARRATIVE). In summary, what is important in Jackson's work is a conjunction of social psychology and narrative theory as a way of understanding both legal processes and the nature of law in general.

Albeit less orientated to structuralist modes of analysis, a concern with forensic narrative is also evident in the wider scholarship. Work to date has considered *Holocaust narratives in the courtroom, constitutional law as narrative, and the narratives that are at work in criminal trials. A wide-ranging treatment of these themes, with an emphasis on the U.S. scholarship, can be found in Brooks and Gewirtz (1996). This collection also displays a representative concern with the ways in which narrative can problematise legal reasoning. Minow's contribution to the volume opposes the power of narrative to social-science methodologies, in particular law and economics reasoning. Although narrative is linked to the ability to think in new ways (see NARRATIVE AS COGNITIVE INSTRUMENT), it is still something untrustworthy and can disrupt the categories that legal reasoning depends upon. This theme can be linked to an emerging concern with the impact of technology on courtroom narratives. Strictly separate from the interest with fictional representations of lawyers in *film studies, this work looks to the impact of *television on the forms of legal argument in the wake of cases like Rodney King and O.J. Simpson (see NARRATIVE AS ARGUMENT). Prior to the advent of televised trials, legal argument had developed in relative isolation from the wider culture. Instantaneous communications suggest that it will become more difficult to deploy arcane vocabularies to justify the outcome of a trial. Rather, courtroom narrative may have to adapt to the demands of the televisual *spectacle.

Sherwin (2000) provides a useful overview of the scholarship in this area.

Law and literature

Law-and-literature scholarship, or literary jurisprudence, has tended to dwell upon the nineteenth- and twentieth-century *realist novel, although forays have been made into the sacred texts of the Christian and Judaic traditions (see BIBLICAL NARRATIVE; NOVEL, THE). Debates in law and literature have centred on claims that fictional narratives open the reader to the question of *ethical responsibility. To help contextualise these debates, a central theme will be traced through the work of Richard Weisberg, James Boyd White, and Robin West.

For Weisberg (1984) *modernist literature is defined as a critique of legalistic proclivity, i.e., of the fetishisation of legal authority. Weisberg has studied this theme extensively with reference to the collaborationist lawyers of the Vichy regime, and to the novels of Dickens, Camus, Kafka, and Dostoevskii. A different approach to the ethics of literature can be found in the work of James Boyd White. White's work involves a literary *hermeneutics. Narrative is not a privileged category as such, but literature is relied upon as a way of reading that can show both how principled legal reasoning is possible, and how an ethical relationship with others can be understood (see ETHICAL TURN). A greater reliance on narrative is evident in a particularly intriguing work by Robin West (1993). West's study endeavoured to deploy Northrop Frye's narrative typologies to understand the different positions adopted by philosophical approaches to law. Thus, those legal philosophies that tend to treat human *conflict as inevitable, and see law as the only way in which conflict can be resolved or kept to an acceptable level, are associated with tragic narrative. Forms of liberal legal theory that see the good society as achievable are analogous with comedic narrative. West's approach could lead to a closer study of the dependence of legal philosophy on literary tropes (see EMPLOTMENT; METAHISTORY).

Other recent developments in law and literature reveal the influence of feminism. This makes for a differently composed canon of texts, and a rejection of the necessarily ethical nature of literary narrative. The work of Aristodemou (2000) is informed by Lacanian *psychoanalysis, and sees narrative as an organisation of *desire. Aristodemou valorises literature as an expression of desire against a philosophy and a law that have always claimed to speak the *truth. Literature is central because it has always told lies. Fantastical narratives of women as lawmakers (*see* FANTASTIC, THE), such as those found in Angela Carter's *fairy tales, are summoned as imaginations of orders that challenge the patriarchal obsessions of the law.

Scholars in the field of law and literature that are particularly alive to the problematic of narrative would include Melanie Williams, Wai Chi Dimock, and Karin van Marle. There are also ongoing engagements with the nature of narrative in journals such as *Law and Critique, the Yale Journal of Law and Humanities, the International Journal for the Semiotics of Law,* and *Cardozo Studies in Law and Literature.*

Narrative, philosophy and jurisprudence

Jurisprudence can be understood as the rigorous investigation of the nature of law. Narrative theory has been used extensively by scholars drawing on continental and *poststructuralist philosophies. One of the primary sites for the development of this kind of thinking has been postmodern jurisprudence. The work of Douzinas *et al.* is exemplary. They take a starting point in Kant's moral theory. Kant's ethics depend on the operation of the categorical imperative, the 'as if' which allows moral rules to be generalised. This provides the foundation for a peculiarly modernist account of law as formal and self-authorising. Douzinas and Warrington read this 'as if' as an indication that Kant's idea of the moral law depends on narrative. Elaborating this position, they present narrative as the essential link between aesthetics and ethics. This suggests that there is a need to keep stories of law and justice in circulation and to keep retelling stories, interchanging *narrators and *narratees (*see* NARRATIVE VERSIONS). One should not necessarily assume that authority is legitimate. For instance, one could imagine the judge as defendant, or the defendant as judge. Although this role of narrative must be argued for and sustained, justice ultimately remains irreducible both to narrative and to jurisprudential rules. Justice is the absolute command that comes out of the encounter with the other (*see* ALTERITY). Developed here is a rethinking of the ancient aporia of justice that comes from diverse sources, but is revisited in the

work of Derrida, Lyotard, and Levinas. Justice remains outside of, or even in excess of, positive law. Work on legal *phenomenology also finds narrative as essential to an account of legal discourse that can uncover the sufferings of those who are the subjects of law's judgements.

A key body of work in the development of postmodern jurisprudence is that of Peter Goodrich. Goodrich brings together narrative theory, rhetoric, and psychoanalysis in a particularly challenging conjugation (*see* RHETORICAL APPROACHES TO NARRATIVE). Goodrich's early work presented forensic rhetorical practice as involving a use of commonplaces (*loci communes* or *topoi*) that fit with *audience expectation and hence narrativise the legal fact pattern or argument being presented in terms familiar to the audience (*see* NARRATIVISATION). At the level of semiotics, legal doctrine is understood as the narrative of the social, telling stories of the lineage of persons and the genealogy of groups. Building on the psychoanalytical studies of the French legal historian Pierre Legendre, Goodrich (1995) traces the structures of legal *institutions, affective objects, and identificatory images in the narrative of legality or lawful sociality as such. This genealogical method does not trace a coherent line of development from the past to the present. Past contradictions are not resolved through the inexorable workings of history. *Genealogy interprets history as a series of accidents; the present is only one of a number of radically contingent possibilities (*see* COUNTERFACTUAL HISTORY). Law as an institution is blind to the possibilities that lie within it.

Beyond its role in the critique of legal institutions, narrative theory has been used by Ronald Dworkin (1986) to forward a liberal account of the law. Dworkin can be seen as a critic of a narrow positivistic philosophy of law that would see law as a science of rules, stressing the fundamental nature of principles and rights. Elaborating a theory of judicial interpretation that locates judicial activity within the wider constraints of the law, Dworkin conceived of the law developing like a chain novel. Behind this notion is an understanding of the integrity of law. Legal judgements are thought of as interpretive acts that are both backward- and forward-looking. Just as the contributor to a chain novel must make sure that her chapter is coherent with what has already been written, and can be developed coherently by those who follow, the judge must ensure the coherence of an individual judgement with the law as whole. Ultimately this theory needs to be understood in the context of the reinvention of a peculiarly Anglo-American version of liberal legal theory. Its critics would resist the notion that any great insight can be gained into law's essentially scientific and logical nature through a comparison with literary narrative. Critics of Dworkin (e.g., Douzinas *et al.* 1991) who draw on more structuralist or semiotic positions have also taken issue with his understanding of narrative.

Philosophically informed accounts of narrative and law are not restricted to jurisprudence. Hayden White's essay 'The Value of Narrative in the Representation of Reality' contains some essential insights into the centrality of law for narrative, philosophy, and history (*see* HISTORIOGRAPHY). Drawing on Hegel, White suggests that questions of legitimacy and legality constitute a prerequisite for ordered narrative. Any self-conscious, structured account of history as a realisation of narrative in a modern, sophisticated form must have as a condition of possibility structures of legitimacy and right. Ultimately, narrative and law are seen as elements in a broader account of historical being, and the very construction of a world that makes sense and can be judged.

Law, narrative, and identity

Accounts of law that draw on social, political, and cultural theory have studied narrative as a source of insights into the legal construction of identity. Sites of interest have included the narratives associated with race, belonging, and penology, as well as the manifold ways in which legal institutions are embedded in broader historical narratives. In this context, the celebrated work of Robert Cover (1992; cf. Sarat 2001) is difficult to pigeonhole but could be seen as offering particularly rich readings of constitutional law and issues of violence and narrative as it relates to the law. Cover's approach stresses that all narratives are organised into a moral teleology that attempts to shape the world that it describes. Law is always located in a social text, the material world that Cover describes as a *nomos*. Narrative figures in this work as a category of sociological importance; narrative can provide phenomenological insight into law's construction and ordering of the social world (*see* SOCIOLOGY AND NARRATIVE).

Narrative has also proved useful in post-colonial legal theory and critical race theory. Although very different endeavours, these schools share a concern with law's racism, and narrative has proved a useful way of studying the constructions and experiencing of race. Critical race literature is wide, and has from its inception appreciated the relevance of narrative to the legal construction of race (see Farley 1997). Narrative is deployed to show that 'whiteness' has to be 'created' in the same way that the social world as a whole is constructed. The creation of whiteness is predicated on the denigration of the black body. The white body is experienced as pleasure and the black body is denigrated as loathsome and ugly. Farley (1997) argues that the extent of the colourline can be further studied in the masochistic attitude of blacks towards their own bodies.

The construction of race, and narrative's role within it, is central to the work of Peter Fitzpatrick (1992), who can be seen as one of the pioneers of post-colonial theory in law. His project is concerned with the narrative dimensions of western legal order. Narrative is associated with mythology. Law and *myth are comparable in that they articulate reality and give it form. Although modern, secular law would deny its narrative or mythological dimensions, this is an element of its self-presentation as a science that allows the law to be differentiated from 'non-scientific' and non-Western modes of dispute resolution. Thus, a mythology of law is concerned with the auto-creation and justification of a mode of thought, an entire metaphysical set of suppositions that make a worldview possible and allow law to define itself as the order of the civilised. There is an elaboration of these themes in later work (cf. Young 1999) that makes use of Freud's myth of the primal horde, a primal narrative, as illustrative of a recurrent and structuring tension within modern law.

SEE ALSO: apology; legal fiction

References and further reading

Aristodemou, Maria (2000) *Law and Literature: Journeys form Her to Eternity*, Oxford: Oxford University Press.
Bremond, Claude (1973) *Logique du récit*, Paris: Seuil.
Brooks, Peter, and Paul Gewirtz, (eds) (1996) *Law's Stories: Narrative and Rhetoric in Law*, New Haven: Yale University Press.

Cover, Robert (1992) *Narrative, Violence and the Law: The Essays of Robert Cover*, Martha Minow, Michael Ryan, and Austin Sarat (eds), Ann Arbor: University of Michigan Press.

Douzinas, Costas, Ronnie Warrington, and Shaun Mc Veigh (1991) *Postmodern Jurisprudence*, London: Routledge.

Dworkin, Ronald (1986) *Law's Empire*, London: Fontana.

Farley, Anthony (1997) 'The Black Body as Fetish Object', *Oregon Law Review*, 76.3, 461–533.

Fitzpatrick, Peter (1992) *The Mythology of Modern Law*, London: Routledge.

Goodrich, Peter (1995) *Oedipus Lex*, Berkeley: University of California Press.

Jackson, Bernard (1998) *Law, Fact and Narrative Coherence*, Liverpool: Deborah Charles Publications.

Sarat, Austin (ed.) (2001) *Law, Violence and the Possibility of Justice*, Princeton: Princeton University Press.

Sherwin, Richard, K. (2000) *When Law Goes Pop*, Chicago: University of Chicago Press.

Weisberg, Richard (1984) *The Failure of the Word: The Lawyer as Protagonist in Modern Fiction*, New Haven: Yale University Press.

West, Robin (1993) *Narrative, Authority and the Law*, Ann Arbor: University of Michigan Press.

White, Hayden (1980) 'The Value of Narrativity in the Representation of Reality', *Critical Inquiry*, 7.1, 5–27.

White, James Boyd (1990) *Justice as Translation: An Essay in Cultural and Legal Criticism*, Chicago: University of Chicago Press.

Young, Robert M. (1999) 'Human Nature, Psychotherapy, and the Law: Issues of Violence and Racism', http://human-nature.com/rmyoung/papers/pap117h.html

ADAM GEAREY

LEGAL FICTION

The history of Western *law, by which is meant the narrative of legal development or change, is the history of legal fictions. Western law is a tradition of declarative statements of rules, a history of tables, codes, commandments, texts, and other permanent inscriptions of a written law. Within this tradition, law is prior to its application and simply needs to be found and declared. This generates the paradox of legal interpretation: the prior law takes the form of a general statement of a rule that cannot possibly foresee all future *events. Where the subsequent case entails a novelty or simply a set of facts not foreseen by the sovereign or legislature, the court will have to choose between adherence to the letter of the law or extension of the prior law by means of the fiction that the novel situation can be found in the text of the earlier decree. Legal fiction thus takes the form of the declaration that a novelty is the same as or can be treated 'as if' it is the same as *a prior* form.

The classical source of legal fictions lies in the laws of Twelve Tables, the earliest codification of Roman law (Goodrich 1986). The Twelve Tables prohibited judges any deviation from or alteration of the letter of the law. Bound strictly to the text, judges had to treat later novelties by means of fictions: if, for example, the law applied only to men, then women and children could in certain circumstances be treated 'as if' they were men. An event that took place in Spain, to take a later example, would be treated as if it took place in London, if the courts wanted jurisdiction. Justice could thus be done without infraction of the norm that prohibited judicial law making. The relevant maxim of law was that fiction could only be used to promote justice: *in fictione iuris semper est aequitas* (*Wilkes v The Earl of Halifax*). The later great codes of Western law, and even common law legislation which was never codified, counterposed the sovereignty of written law, the exemplary *corpus iuris* or body of law, to the ancillary and subordinate position of the interpreter. In varying forms, the fiction subsisted that the text alone was the source of law.

Critics of the common law, most famously Jeremy Bentham (1932) and most recently the critical legal studies movement, have used the pervasive employment of judicial invention to impugn the impartiality and rationality of law (Schlag 1998). In Bentham's colourful terminology, fiction was a syphilis running in the veins of the system, it was a sign of moral turpitude, it was mendacity plain and simple and stood in relation to justice as swindling to trade. If fiction is endemic to the elaboration and application of legal norms, critical legal scholars have subsequently argued, law is political. Judges invent circumstances – *narratives – to justify novel rule applications and to resolve disputes. The rule of law, therefore, is at best a general guide to decisions that are formulated for political reasons in relation to social *conflicts that haphazardly come before the courts.

SEE ALSO: fiction, theories of; narrative as argument

References and further reading

Bentham, Jeremy (1932) *Theory of Fictions*, ed. C.K. Ogden, London: Routledge.

Fuller, Lon (1967) *Legal Fictions*, Stanford: Stanford University Press.

Goodrich, Peter (1986) *Reading the Law*, Oxford: Blackwell.

Schlag, Pierre (1988) *The Enchantment of Reason*, Durham, NC: Duke University Press.

Wilkes v Earl of Halifax [1769] 2 Wils. K.B. 256, 95 ER 797.

PETER GOODRICH

References and further reading

Dégh, Linda (1976) 'Legend and Belief', in Dan Ben-Amos (ed.) *Folklore Genres*, Austin: University of Texas Press.

Honko, Lauri (1964) 'Memorates and the Study of Folk Beliefs', *Journal of the Folklore Institute*, 1.1/2, 5–19.

Lüthi, Max (1966) *Volksmärchen und Volkssage: Zwei Grundformen erzählender Dichtung*, Bern: Francke.

von Sydow, Carl W. (1978 [1948]) *Selected Papers on Folklore*, New York: Arno Press.

AARON TATE

LEGEND

The term 'legend' refers to a traditional narrative that provides an aitiology (i.e., an account of the origin or cause) of some extraordinary local detail or the narrative of a person, place, or *event as if it were based on historical actuality (*see* CAUSALITY). The teller of a legend need not be an acknowledged performer, though participation in the *narration by an active *audience will require communal access to the tradition (*see* PERFORMANCE). From the performative point of view, the telling of a legend frequently leads directly to debate or discussion between teller and audience, thus complicating narrative authority and confirming the peculiar status of the legend.

Though flourishing in settings where oral narration predominates, transmission of legends is in no way limited to oral means: examples of textual transmission abound. The Grimm brothers first used the term in 1816, though folklorists later refined its range in relation to other types of legends, such as: memorate (personal experience of a supernatural occurrence), fabulate (material reworked in oral telling), local (bound to a specific place), and migratory (a more general *fiction). Readers must differentiate between *legenda* in its medieval sense (composition and perusal of hagiographic works on the lives of saints) and the Germanic *Sage* (saga, legend). Newer technologies, such as print, *television, and the Internet, have contributed to the renewal of this form of narrative and have produced many new instances of it (*see* DIGITAL NARRATIVE; URBAN LEGENDS).

SEE ALSO: folklore; oral cultures and narrative; orality

LEITMOTIF

The musicological term 'leitmotif' (from German *Leitmotiv*) mainly denotes a device of Wagnerian *opera, a 'musical idea [...] whose purpose is to represent or symbolize a person, object, place, [or] idea' (Warrack 1980). Its 'readability' can be facilitated by a resemblance between music and extra-musical reference; primarily, however, it depends on the memorable simultaneity of music and dramatic content at the introduction of the motif. Recalling this association at subsequent occurrences is the basis for the leitmotif's 'guiding', commenting, and aesthetically unifying functions.

In literary criticism, the term is frequently reduced to denoting a recurring central *motif. However, the term can also be used more profitably to designate an associative linkage between a *narrative unit and a characteristic connotation, and it is precisely this linkage which generates the leitmotif's significance in repetition, variation, and recombination with other connotations. In his preface to *Der Zauberberg*, Thomas Mann explicitly mentions the leitmotif as a device to 'musicalise' literature (*see* MUSIC AND NARRATIVE), and its impact can be traced not only in *Der Zauberberg* but also in much of other twentieth-century fiction, including Joyce's *Ulysses*, Proust's *A la recherche du temps perdu*, and J. Roth's *Radetzkymarsch* (*see* MODERNIST NARRATIVE).

References and further reading

Warrack, John (1980) 'Leitmotiv', in Stanley Sadie (ed.) *The New Grove Dictionary of Music and Musicians*, London: Macmillan.

WERNER WOLF

LETTERS AS NARRATIVE

The popularity of the *epistolary novel tempts one to regard letter-writing as an inherently narrative *genre. Nevertheless, early collections of correspondence such as the Paston letters, the Cely Letters from the fifteenth century, or the *Original Letter Illustrative of English History* of the sixteenth century contain very few extensive narrative passages but have brief factual report clauses throughout. In early correspondence, letters served as petitions or concentrated on conveying news, asked for information, and facilitated business transactions (Nevalainen 2001: 212). Renaissance collections of fictional letters served the purpose of instructing merchants and the semi-literate. They frequently included love letters as models for imitation.

Kany (1937) locates the roots of epistolary *fiction in early antiquity, the major classical model being Ovid's *Heroides*. In the Renaissance, according to Claudio Gullién (1986: 71–73), several different types of epistolary genres existed, including both verse and prose forms. Not only did several collections include series of letters that spelt out a story, they also began to display the double *narrative structure of epistolary fiction which Genette characterised as 'intercalated narration': the *plot of epistolary narrative includes both the *events narrated in the letters and the writing of these letters – narrative experience and its narrational representation therefore occur in alternation (*see* NARRATION). From the Renaissance onward, the more extensive epistolary texts move away from the type of *novel which merely 'quotes' numerous items of the lovers' correspondence within a homodiegetic or heterodiegetic narrative frame (letters-in-the-novel, see Füger 1977), to the unmediated presentation of sequences of letters. In this new form, letters are offered to the reader without connecting narrative passages and without a *narrator figure, except for the letter writers themselves. Even before the advent of the full-fledged first-person novel in Defoe, epistolary fiction produced narratives of limited *perspective and alternated between correspondents to create a multiperspectival effect.

Aphra Behn's *Love-Letters Between a Nobleman and his Sister* (1684–1687) occupies a special place in the history of English fiction. Modelling her texts on early French and Spanish epistolary antecedents (cp. Kany 1937; Visconti 1994), Behn pioneered the epistolary novel as a literary genre in English literature and at the same time started to dissolve it in the direction of authorial narrative (*see* NARRATIVE SITUATIONS): whereas Part I of *Love Letters* contains practically only letters (protoype of the epistolary novel), Parts II and III add more and more narrative, radically reducing the letters which become mere inserts in the narrative. The genre established itself as a popular novel form in the eighteenth-century with Richardson, Smollett, and Burney. The epistolary novel, well into the twentieth century, has been a predominantly female genre, practised by women *authors and focussing on female victimisation by men (*see* FEMINIST NARRATOLOGY; GENDER STUDIES).

References and further reading

Füger, Wilhem (1977) 'Der Brief als Bau-Element des Erzählens', *DVJS*, 51, 628–58.
Gullién, Claudio (1986) 'Notes Toward the Study of the Renaissance Letter', in Barbara Kiefer Lewalski (ed.) *Renaissance Genres*, Cambridge, Mass.: Harvard University Press.
Kany, Charles E. (1937) *The Beginnings of the Epistolary Novel in France, Italy and Spain*, Berkeley: University of California Press.
Nevalainen, Terttu (2001) 'Continental Conventions in Early English Correspondence', in Hans-Jürgen Diller and Manfred Görlach (eds) *Towards a History of English as History of Genres*, Heidelberg: Winter.
Visconti, Laura (1994) 'The Beginnings of the Epistolary Novel in England', in Roy Eriksen (ed.) *Contexts of Pre-Novel Narrative*, Berlin: Gruyter.

MONIKA FLUDERNIK

LIFE STORY

The term 'life story' is used in many contexts, including *medicine, psychology, *oral history, anthropology, etc. as well as in ordinary conversation (*see* CONVERSATIONAL STORYTELLING; ETHNOGRAPHIC APPROACHES TO NARRATIVE; HISTORIOGRAPHY; PSYCHOLOGICAL APPROACHES TO NARRATIVE). In all these contexts, the term refers to a narratively organised selection, relevant to the speech situation, of the formative *events of the life of the *narrator. While certain types of life story are elicited by experts, such as doctors, police officers, psychologists, etc., in conversations the narrator chooses those events which must be known for someone to know the narrator. Family, friends, co-workers, etc., have different expectations of what kinds of knowledge should be shared. Indeed, this is a defining characteristic of the closeness of a relation: the parties expect to be updated on significant events in the life of the other. If I have not heard that my best friend has changed jobs or residence, I can assume that these things in fact have not happened (*see* PRAGMATICS).

Technically, the life story is defined as a temporally discontinuous unit consisting of all the stories told by an individual during the course of his/her lifetime satisfying the following criteria: (1) The story's primary evaluation is a point about the speaker, not a general point about the way the world is. This distinction concerns the way the story is constructed, not the choice of events. That is, I can tell a story about what happened in the hospital to show how I deal with difficult circumstances, or to show what's wrong with hospitals. Only a story of the first type would be part of my life story. (2) The stories have extended reportability: they are about the kinds of events which are tellable over the course of a long period of *time (*see* TELLABILITY). Certain types of stories conventionally have extended reportability: stories about career milestones, marriage, childbirth, divorce, major illness, religious or ideological conversions, etc. These examples are culturally defined landmark events, but they are not obligatory components of the life story. They are available for a speaker to use, but any speaker may make an idiosyncratic choice of events for those stories repeated again and again. This is a matter of individual creativity and reflects a personal understanding of the events of one's life.

Life stories change over time, and in relation to the situation of telling. New narratives are added, old ones are dropped or reframed. This changeability raises the question of whether the life story expresses a core self. Is there an essential nature of the individual carried in the life story, or are we now *postmodern selves, fragmented and created by shifting circumstances (*see* IDENTITY AND NARRATIVE; POSITIONING)? Just as the formulation of the self differs from culture to culture, so too does the life story. While it is nearly ubiquitous in Western conversational contexts, there are cultures which do not have such a discourse unit, or in which life stories are used only by exemplary individuals or for the purposes of group construction.

SEE ALSO: narrative units

References and further reading

Berman, Laine (1998) *Speaking through the Silence: Narratives, Social Conventions and Power in Java*, Oxford: Oxford University Press.
Langness, Lewis, and Gelya Frank (1981) *Lives: An Anthropological Approach to Biography*, Novato, CA: Chandler and Sharp.
Linde, Charlotte (1993) *Life Stories: The Creation of Coherence*, Oxford: Oxford University Press.

CHARLOTTE LINDE

LINGUISTIC APPROACHES TO NARRATIVE

*Narration, text, and story are foundational categories in many contemporary narratological accounts (Fowler 1977; Genette 1980 [1972]; Rimmon-Kenan 2002); these accounts treat narrative telling and *reception as communicative processes, a text as their product, and a *storyworld as that text's referential ground (*see* REFERENCE). Narrative phenomena pertaining to all three categories have been examined from perspectives afforded by linguistic research.

Work in *speech act theory and linguistic *pragmatics has thrown light on narratorial acts viewed as communicative transactions involving *authors, *narrators, and *audiences, and theories of *conversational storytelling have drawn on these same pragmatic and *discourse-analytic tools. At the level of the text, linguistic models have been brought to bear on phenomena such as *deixis, *tense usage, *speech and *thought representation, and *dialogue. Linguistic approaches to the story level, meanwhile, have resulted in theories of *actants, semantically oriented models of *event structure, and formalised *story grammars.

A more basic issue in this connection is the status of linguistic theory vis-à-vis narrative texts (Fowler and Herman 2003). For their part, narratologists working under the auspices of French structuralism typically employed linguistic theory as a model, *metaphor, or analogy, viewing linguistics as the 'pilot-science' on which a systematic account of narrative might be based. From the *structuralist perspective, narrative is a code or 'langue' whose structure is homologous with the structure of language proper; this narrative code underlies particular narrative texts just as the structure of a language underlies the specific messages (Saussure's 'parole') whose design and interpretation the linguistic system makes possible. By contrast, analysts working in the Anglo-American tradition of stylistic research (e.g., Fowler 1977; Halliday 1971; Leech and Short 1981; Banfield 1982; Fludernik 1993; Toolan 2001) have sought to apply various types of linguistic analysis directly to narrative texts, viewing the language of fiction as just that – language (in use). Perhaps because of these differences of approach, metatheoretical inquiry into the relations between linguistic models and paradigms for narrative analysis has become a basic research activity in its own right, i.e., an important subdomain of narrative theory itself (cf. Herman 2002: 2–5). At the same time, growing interest in the *semiotic and *cognitive structures supporting narrative across *media (*film, *music, *dance, etc.) has raised additional questions about the limits of applicability of linguistic frameworks for narrative-theoretical research.

SEE ALSO: agency; communication in narrative; communication studies and narrative; ethnographic approaches to narrative; function (Jakobson); life story; mind-style; narrative semantics; sociolinguistic approaches to narrative; text-type approach to narrative

References and further reading

Banfield, Ann (1982) *Unspeakable Sentences: Narration and Representation in the Language of Fiction*, Boston: Routledge and Kegan Paul.

Fludernik, Monika (1993) *The Fictions of Language and the Languages of Fiction: The Linguistic Representation of Speech and Consciousness*, London: Routledge.

Fowler, Roger (1977) *Linguistics and the Novel*, London: Methuen.

——, and David Herman (2003) 'Linguistics and Literature: Language of Prose Fiction', in William Frawley (ed.) *The Oxford International Encyclopedia of Linguistics*, vol. 2, Oxford: Oxford University Press.

Genette, Gérard (1980 [1972]) *Narrative Discourse: An Essay in Method*, trans. Jane E. Lewin, Ithaca: Cornell University Press.

Halliday, Michael A. K. (1971) 'Linguistic Function and Literary Style: An Enquiry into the Language of William Golding's "The Inheritors"', in Seymour Chatman (ed.) *Literary Style: A Symposium*, London: Oxford University Press.

Herman, David (2002) *Story Logic: Problems and Possibilities of Narrative*, Lincoln: University of Nebraska Press.

Leech, Geoffrey N., and Michael H. Short (1981) *Style in Fiction*, London: Longman.

Rimmon-Kenan, Shlomith (2002) *Narrative Fiction: Contemporary Poetics*, London: Routledge.

Toolan, Michael J. (2001) *Narrative: A Critical Linguistic Introduction*, London: Routledge.

DAVID HERMAN

LOGIC OF NARRATIVE

There are different sorts of logic at work in narratives, but the *logic of narrative* is a logic distinctive of *narrative. The logic of causation specifies that under conditions x, y will occur (*see* CAUSALITY). The logic of narrative, on the contrary, makes no claim to ineluctable necessity; it shows how one thing can or did lead to another. Philosophers of history have maintained that history exhibits the logic of narrative rather than of causation: history does not enable us to predict that x will lead to y but shows us how, in this particular case, x happened to lead to y. Later events require earlier ones for their intelligibility, and this relation, rather than predictability, is the logical continuity of narrative (Gallie 1964: 26; *see* HISTORIOGRAPHY). To understand the narrative is to follow the logic of how x led to y.

In the development of narratology, the concept of the logic of narrative was introduced by Claude Bremond to contest Vladimir Propp's notion of *function. Propp's functions are determined above all by the outcome. Bremond claimed that the logic of narrative is, on the contrary, an open one, where each moment presents multiple possibilities. His logic of narrative is thus a logic of *action rather than of *narrative structure: one *event introduces a bifurcation of subsequent possibilities, and the narrative progresses by following one of these rather than others (cp. Danto 1985; Herman 2002).

In fact, there is a double logic to narrative: at the level of actions, the *hero's triumph is explained by steps that preceded and led to it, but at the level of discourse, the demands of theme and *genre determine his triumph; this must happen or the story won't work. The demands of thematic and generic coherence, for instance, are what determine that Oedipus must have killed his father. The experienced reader of narratives internalises both logics, expecting, on the one hand, that certain sorts of events will follow from the character of the protagonist and his or her past acts, yet knowing, on the other, that certain results are necessary to make this a satisfactory story. When we say that a development in a narrative is 'too neat', we recognise the conflict between these two logics of narrative (Culler 1981).

SEE ALSO: story-discourse distinction

References and further reading

Bremond, Claude (1973) *Logique du récit*, Paris: Seuil.
—— (1980) 'The Logic of Narrative Possibilities', *New Literary History*, 11, 387–411.
Culler, Jonathan (1981) 'Story and Discourse in the Analysis of Narrative', *The Pursuit of Signs*, London: Routledge.
Danto, Arthur (1985) *Narration and Knowledge*, New York: Columbia University Press.
Gallie, W. B. (1964) *Philosophy and Historical Understanding*, London: Chatto.
Herman, David (2002) *Story Logic: Problems and Possibilities of Narrative*, Lincoln: University of Nebraska Press.

JONATHAN CULLER

M

MAGICAL REALISM

Magical realism is a *genre of contemporary *fiction in which a limited number of *fantastic elements appear within a preponderantly realistic narrative (*see* REALIST NOVEL; REALISM, THEORIES OF). The term first appears in 1925 in the German art critic Franz Roh's discussion of new realist painting as it reactivated mimetic techniques in reaction to the abstract qualities of Expressionism (*see* MIMESIS). Initially flourishing primarily in Latin America, in such texts as Alejo Carpentier's *The Kingdom of this World* (Cuba 1949), Juan Rulfo's *Pedro Páramo* (Mexico 1955), Wilson Harris's *Palace of the Peacock* (Guyana 1960), Carlos Fuentes's *Aura* (Mexico 1962), Miguel Angel Asturias's *Mulata* (Guatemala 1963), and the stories of Julio Cortázar (Argentina 1951–1956), among others, it has now spread around the world. Gabriel García Márquez's *novel *One Hundred Years of Solitude* (Columbia 1967), for which he won the Nobel Prize in 1982, is widely considered the consummate masterpiece of this genre. Two other major works that attest to its widespread distribution are Günter Grass's *The Tin Drum* (Germany 1959) and Salman Rushdie's *Midnight's Children* (India 1980). More recent examples of the genre include D. M. Thomas's *The White Hotel* (Great Britain 1981), Isabel Allende's *The House of the Spirits* (Chile 1982), Patrick Süskind's *Perfume* (Germany 1985), Fuentes's *Christopher Unborn* (Mexico 1987), Toni Morrison's *Beloved* (United States 1988), Ana Castillo's *So Far from God* (United States 1993), and those mentioned below.

Often the magical *events in magical realism are narrated in great realistic detail but without the *narrator registering surprise or commenting on their strangeness. This matter-of-fact narration of extraordinary events with no *commentary is often characterised as 'childlike' or 'naive' because it accepts non-realistic events with no sense of surprise in the same way that a child appears to accept phenomena such as fairies or Santa Claus. Amaryll Chanady terms this acceptance 'resolved antinomy', meaning that events of different orders or conflicting *codes are presented as equally accepted by the narrator, so that the reader's acceptance of them is modelled by the narrator's. She distinguishes that narrative situation from the 'unresolved antinomy' in the fantastic, in which, as Todorov has argued, the conflicting codes are presented as problematic by the narrator, so that the reader hesitates between conflicting interpretations of phenomena or events as miraculous or merely uncanny. Perhaps the best-known example of a magical event that accumulates realistic details with no narratorial commentary is the account of the famous journey of 'a trickle of blood' in chapter 7 of *One Hundred Years of Solitude*: it 'came out under the door, crossed the living room, went out into the street, continued on in a straight line across the uneven terraces, went down steps and climbed over curbs,...made a right angle at the Buendía house,...crossed through the parlor, hugging the walls so as not to stain the rugs,...' etc.

More recently, magical realism has developed a wide variety of narrative stances, and there are numerous instances of comments that could be attributed to a narratorial *voice. In book 3, chapter 2, of *Midnight's Children*, for example, the narrator implicitly calls into question Saleem Sinai and his companions becoming transparent in the forest, commenting that Saleem 'saw now that the colourlessness of insects and leeches and snakes might have more to do with the depredations worked on their insectly, leechy, snakish imaginations than with the absence of sunlight'. This account causes the initially magical physical events to verge on the mental and metaphorical, and the reader to hesitate regarding their ontological status (*see* METAPHOR; MODALITY). Furthermore, even when the narrator presents magic with no commentary, the conventions of realism employed by the text will often cause readers to hesitate when they encounter magical phenomena.

A prime difficulty in defining this genre is that it often emerges where two or more cultural and narrative traditions clash – most commonly post-Enlightenment Western empiricism and pre-Enlightenment beliefs and practices, the former generating largely realistic narratives and the latter ones including mythic tales with supernatural events (*see* HYBRID GENRES; MYTH: THEMATIC APPROACHES). Because of this hybridity, a characteristic narratological feature of magical realism is that the *focalization oscillates between these two *perspectives. In other words, focalization is problematised in magical realism because the narrator reports two different kinds of perceptions: events that are verifiable from a modern Western empirical viewpoint, as well as events that are impossible to verify by that standard, such as people flying through the air, or trails of blood climbing street curbs.

Because of that cultural hybridity magical realism is now increasingly recognised as a leading genre in post-colonial fiction, allowing for the voices and traditions of formerly colonised cultures to emerge into the global literary arena (*see* POST-COLONIALISM AND NARRATIVE). Theorising the post-colonial nature of magical realism, Stephen Slemon points out that because neither of the two conflicting codes of realism and fantasy achieves primacy in the text, the reader remains suspended between the two. This heterogeneity reflects the multicultural situation of much magical realism and the way in which the post-colonial subject is suspended between at least two cultural systems. But not all magical realism appears in intercultural or post-colonial environments. Witness Günter Grass's *The Tin Drum*, José Saramago's *The Stone Raft* (Portugal 1986), Marie Darrieussecq's *Pig Tales* (France 1998), and a number of *films (often adapted from novels),

such as *The Witches of Eastwick*, *Field of Dreams*, *Wolf*, *Thinner*, and even two TV series, *Northern Exposure* and *Allie McBeal* (*see* TELEVISION). These works are productions of metropolitan centres that include a few magical events within a predominantly realistic mode.

Thus magical realism's widespread diffusion even in spaces of relative cultural homogeneity may result from the penetration of those spaces by the mentality of the global village, in which the dominant logical positivism of the West is destabilised. Euro-American realism at first adapts *thematic and narrative elements from ancient and indigenous cultures; indigenous *authors in turn adopt realistic practices, and ultimately first-world narrators narrate their own cultural events from the perspective of the cultural other, now integrated into their own, while indigenous authors absorb and radically modify realism from the inside, making it serve their own political and cultural agendas, not the least of which is the entry into major literary marketplaces. Such is the case with recent works like Rushdie's *Midnight's Children*, Ben Okri's *The Famished Road* (Britain 1991), and Laura Esquivel's immensely popular film (and book) *Like Water for Chocolate* (Mexico 1989). According to Franco Moretti (1996), the innovative nature of magical realist narrative is the first instance in modern times of formal innovation occurring outside Europe.

References and further reading

Aizenberg, Edna (1995) 'The Famished Road: Magical Realism and the Search for Social Equity', *Yearbook of Comparative and General Literature*, 43, 25–30.

Camayd-Freixas, Erik (1998) *Realismo mágico y primitivismo: Relecturas de Carpentier, Asturias, Rulfo y García Márquez*, Lanham: University Press of America.

Chanady, Amaryll (1985) *Magical Realism and the Fantastic: Resolved versus Unresolved Antinomy*, New York: Garland.

Chiampi, Irlemar (1983) *El realismo maravilloso: Forma e ideología en la novela hispanoamericana*, trans. Agustín Martínez and Margara Russotto, Caracas: Monte Avila.

Cooper, Brenda (1998) *Magical Realism in West African Fiction: Seeing with a Third Eye*, New York: Routledge.

Durix, Jean-Pierre (1998) *Mimesis, Genres, and Post-Colonial Discourse: Deconstructing Magic Realism*, New York: St. Martin's.

Faris, Wendy B. (2004) *Ordinary Enchantments: Magical Realism and the Remystification of Narrative*, Nashville: Vanderbilt University Press.

Linguanti, Elsa, Francesco Casotti, and Carmen Concilio (eds) (1999) *Coterminous Worlds: Magical Realism and Contemporary Post-colonial Literature in English*, Amsterdam: Rodopi.

Moretti, Franco (1996) *Modern Epic: The World System from Goethe to García Márquez*, trans. Quintin Hoare, New York: Verso.

Slemon, Stephen (1995) 'Magic Realism as Post-colonial Discourse', in Lois Parkinson Zamora and Wendy Faris *Magical Realism: Theory, History, Community*, Durham: Duke University Press.

Todorov, Tzvetan (1975) *The Fantastic: A Structural Approach to a Literary Genre*, trans. Richard Howard, Ithaca: Cornell University Press.

Zamora, Lois Parkinson, and Wendy B. Faris (eds) (1995) *Magical Realism: Theory, History, Community*, Durham: Duke University Press.

WENDY FARIS

MARXIST APPROACHES TO NARRATIVE

Marxism as a body of ideas has always had a special relationship to narrative, both its production and its interpretation. In a 'negative' or oppositional sense, it is elaborated as a rejection of a range of dominant narratives in Western society concerning history and humanity (*see* MASTER NARRATIVE). In its positive mode, it is both an analytical and anticipatory narrative of progressive human self-emancipation via the transformations in the class structure of society and the modes of production. It has also more recently – and notoriously – been categorised by Lyotard in *The Postmodern Condition* as one of the 'grand narratives' of the Enlightenment which have had their day. The precise status of the narratives involved is also a matter of debate – Marx's famous 'stages' model of social development has been understood both as an infallible prophecy and as nothing more than a heuristic tool to allow him to analyse the complex nature of capitalism. Marxist concern with literary or cultural narratives is part of this wider process of social analysis but is not coterminous with it. Marx and Engels's own interest in literature was extensive, but their writings on it – though perceptive – were not systematic, and this entry will concern itself with a necessarily limited range of Marxist theorists whose attention has precisely been systematically focused on questions of narrative.

Lukács: totality and typicality

The currently out of fashion Georg Lukács was one of the major Marxist thinkers of the twentieth century, and probably the greatest advocate of the importance of narrative in the shape of the nineteenth-century novel – though, increasingly, its value for Lukács depended on whether it was a *realist novel or not. Lukács followed Hegel in regarding the *novel as 'the epic of the contemporary world', and it is the nature of the relationship between narrative and world which particularly concerns him (*see* EPIC). One of the reasons for Lukács's fall from critical favour is his connection with the 'reflection' theory of literature, unfairly deemed to be naive and overly simplistic. Lukács, however, does more than simply recycle the old idea of art holding a mirror up to nature (*see* MIMESIS): his version of reflection is more complex, more historicised, and more political. For Lukács there are better and worse reflections or representations of reality – dependent on the extent of the revelation of the nature of reality, and above all of the social totality (another unfashionable concept central to Lukács's theorising). Totality is not the harmonious whole which the word might suggest; contemporary society is above all fragmented by the effects of capitalism, its inhabitants increasingly alienated from one another and themselves. In addition to portraying these facts, narrative, for Lukács, should resist and overcome them, creating an image of individual or collective wholeness which is the deeper *truth about humanity. Narrative's ability to work on two levels in this way is also reflected in what are for Lukács the most satisfactory of the novelistic *characters, the 'typical'. 'Typical' characters are both properly individual, in the best tradition of realist fiction, embodying essential human qualities, and at the same time instantiating the social or historical forces which typify the period. The ability of the best novels (along with the best art of all types) to portray the truly important aspects of an era allows them almost to transcend the constraints of the particular, becoming 'world historical' in their scope and politically progressive in their effects (actual or potential), and that progressive aspect holds true despite the class position or political or ideological affiliation of the *author (*see* IDEOLOGY AND NARRATIVE; NOVEL, THE).

The importance of the historical dimension is one of the reasons for Lukács's pioneering study of the *historical novel as a *genre which at its best reveals the true relationship of the historically located individual to the world that he or she inhabits. Such an ability to get beyond the surface details of contemporary life is in Lukács's eyes precisely what is lacking in more recent narrative, as he sets out in his classic essay 'Narrate or Describe?'. For him, the great era of the realist novel peaks with the 1848 revolutions; prior to that, the properly realist writers such as Balzac, Tolstoy, or Dickens 'narrated' society. They were both involved in the developments of society and produced ordered, retrospective, hierarchically organised *narratives of those developments which allowed appropriate artistic (and readerly) assessment or understanding of them. Against that organised narration of social developments, writers such as Flaubert, and even more so Zola, offer *descriptions which do not penetrate beyond surface phenomena. The more modern novelists are more distanced as a result of the alienating processes of social transformation, but ironically that distance produces nothing like the all-comprehending narrative vision of the earlier realists. If Zola's naturalism was bad enough, the *modernist narratives of the early twentieth century seemed even worse, and the Brecht-Lukács polemic on the nature and relative value of *realism and modernism constitutes one of the key Marxist theoretical debates on culture. (By common consent, Brecht got rather the better of the argument, but could offer nothing of the scope of Lukács's synthesising analyses.) Nevertheless, the fact that Lukács's realism has a cognitive dimension as well as an aesthetic-representative one; the fact that his model of reflection involves rather more than passive reproduction; and the fact that realism is a profoundly political category – all of this means that his vision of narrative is not to be lightly dismissed.

Macherey: figuring ideology

One of the aspects of Lukács's theorising of narrative which seemed normal or acceptable at the time – but less so subsequently – is that it is highly evaluative. *Proper* realism, the *correct* narrative form, *accurate* reflection – the qualification of all these categories with value-laden terms puts Lukács at the opposite extreme from Pierre Macherey. Macherey reacts against normative, evaluative criticism, 'criticism as appreciation', offering instead 'criticism as explanation', providing a particular knowledge of the text – its conditions of possibility, its relationship to ideology and history – which traditional criticism never talks about. In fact, things which are spoken about or not are crucial to Macherey's theory. At the heart of his analysis of the literary text is the question of the latter's relationship to ideology, and one of the key aspects of that relationship is the notion of the *non-dit* (the 'not-said') – i.e., those things which the text does not talk about, which indeed it cannot talk about because of the structurally limiting effect of ideology. Resolutely opposed to the traditional image of the author as creator of the text, Macherey emphasises the notion of the author as producer, working with a stock of pre-given materials (literary, linguistic, or ideological) and crafting the text from them. The particular working or 'figuring' of ideology in the text involves a relationship of mutual constraint or *conflict: ideology, as mentioned, involves the avoidance or dissimulation of certain (unspeakable) facts about the world and thereby imposes a particular kind of silencing on the narrative; at the same time, the text 'puts ideology into contradiction', according to Macherey, so that its real nature can be identified and articulated by the critic. It is also the sites of textual 'stress' – silences, gaps, omissions – which allow the critic to see where and how ideology is at work in the narrative (*see* GAPPING; NARRATION).

In this, Macherey is drawing on the notion of a 'symptomatic' reading, borrowed from his fellow Marxist philosopher Louis Althusser. Influenced in turn by *psychoanalysis, symptomatic reading treats ideology as something like a textual unconscious, unconsciously incorporated, and revealed by the work of the critic and the application of his or her theoretical apparatus. Just as the production of the text by the author involves, in Althusser's terms, 'transformative labour', so does its explanation by the critic. The labour of the critic is two-fold – firstly, to analyse the text on its own terms, to establish its 'class of truth', to examine its efforts to construct coherence and unity (and the more the text works to produce coherence, the more it pressures its ideological components into incoherence); secondly, to move outside the text, to relate it to those historical and political circumstances which simultaneously constitute its conditions of possibility and the unspeakable reality which ideology will not articulate (*see* REFERENCE). Another implication of the limiting and silencing effect of ideology is that the text cannot possibly be the harmonious totality posited both by traditional literary critics and by Marxists like Lukács (organic for the former, constructed for the latter). For Macherey, the literary narrative is 'decentred', incomplete, disparate, even 'faulty' in the case of an author such as Verne, but is in no way diminished by that fact – that is simply the (real) nature of the text, as opposed to its illusory or ideological status as harmonious whole.

Bakhtin: the other voices of narrative

If Macherey marks an important step away from the idea of the novel as a coherent totality, a larger and very influential step in the same direction is represented by the work of Mikhail Bakhtin. For Bakhtin, 'the utter inadequacy of literary theory is exposed when it is forced to deal with the novel'. That this is so is in large part the result of the nature of the novel: a complex, multilayered, multivoiced form, one which is both open and – unlike other genres – still rapidly developing. Similarly, although Macherey gave more attention to the role of the language of narrative than earlier Marxists, it is the work of Bakhtin and his collaborators or pseudonymous alter egos, especially Voloshinov, which places the role of language and discourse at the centre of literary (and ideological) analysis (*see* DISCOURSE ANALYSIS (FOUCAULT)). Linguistically derived concepts such as *dialogism and *heteroglossia have been among the most influential aspects of Bakhtin's theory, though Bakhtin considered his work to be 'trans-linguistic' rather than straightforwardly linguistic.

For Bakhtin and Voloshinov, society is 'heteroglot', a space constituted by the coexistence of many languages, *voices, and discourses; importantly, these are all marked by class or regional origin, ideological affiliation, etc, and at the same time differentially located within the power relations – and power struggles – of society (*see* SOCIOLINGUISTIC APPROACHES TO NARRATIVE). This politicised diversity is precisely what the novel – unlike any other genre – can accommodate, and for Bakhtin the more that takes place, the better the resultant narrative. To Bakhtin, the creation of the 'polyphonic' novel (*polyphony being the literary form of social heteroglossia) is what makes

Dostoevskii a more satisfactory writer than Tolstoi. Polyphony is not just the replication of the variety of 'voices' in society, however; it is also a question of how characters and their speech are located in relation to the authorial voice (*see* SPEECH REPRESENTATION). For Bakhtin, Tolstoi's voice is more dominant and controlling, his characters and their speech less autonomous as a result, making his novels more monologic. In a way similar to Lukács, but for different reasons, Bakhtin argues that it is not the case that the more politically progressive writer (in this instance, Tolstoi) necessarily produces the more progressive text (however construed). The fact that the progressive authorial ideology appears to be ultimately less important than the progressive textual/narrative practice is interesting, given the pioneering work of Bakhtin and Voloshinov on ideology in relation to discourse and the way in which different linguistic tendencies and textual forms instantiate power relations in society.

Another way in which the novel can be regarded as progressive is in its potential for subversion. The novel is the inheritor of the medieval notion of the carnivalesque, which Bakhtin analyses in *Rabelais and His World* (*see* MEDIEVAL NARRATIVE). Historically, carnival is the periodic space where marginalised, dominated groups, or individuals can invert social hierarchies, openly reject the structures which oppress them, and mock those in power, while the carnivalesque as a mode of resistance divides critics over whether it is merely licensed subversion, a sanctioned letting-off of steam, or whether, in Gramscian terms, it represents the seeds of a counter-hegemony, a historic bloc of the oppressed in the process of formation. For Bakhtin, the openness of the novel form, its receptiveness to the carnivalising voices and attitudes of the marginalised Others of society, confers a particular ability to resist official discourses or ideologies. This ability to resist, in turn perhaps gives more obvious or active grounds for optimism than the Lukácsian knowledge of historical conditions produced via the typical or the world-historical, or the Machereyan critical scope for disentangling the ideologies woven into the fabric of narrative.

Jameson: the battlefield of theory

For Macherey, one thing which a Marxist approach to narrative had rigorously to avoid was any *hermeneutic aims or ambitions. In his view, there is no question of Marxism interpreting the meaning of the text. For Fredric Jameson, on the other hand, a hermeneutic approach is essential, and his most important book (Jameson 1982) opens with a 100-page chapter 'On Interpretation'. For Jameson, what is required of theory is 'some new or more adequate immanent or anti-transcendent hermeneutic model'. In fact, despite boldly flying the flag of (historically grounded) interpretation, Jameson's approach – working immanently (i.e., from within the narrative itself) but always moving beyond it – bears obvious and striking similarities to that of Macherey. (The fact that from a certain perspective the 'moving beyond' obviously invites accusations of transcendence is something of which Jameson is well aware.) For him, interpretation is 'a Homeric battlefield' where the 'strongest' theory – the one with the greatest explanatory adequacy – will prevail until supplanted by a stronger. In his view, Marxism has the greatest explanatory power because it can historicise, and thereby explain the limitations of, its opponents.

Narrative for Jameson is enormously important; it is no less than 'the central function or *instance* of the human mind', and as such its manifold forms demand to be interpreted (*see* NARRATIVE AS COGNITIVE INSTRUMENT). In approaching the hermeneutic task, Jameson is not content with merely vanquishing theoretical opponents – he also wants to enlist their best insights, taking, for example, the 'semiotic square' of linguist A. J. Greimas and both extending it (by historicising its components) and employing it to great effect as an analytical tool (*see* SEMIOTICS). The actual narratives Jameson analyses range from medieval *romances* to Conrad's novels, but like many other theorists it is the nineteenth- and early-twentieth-century texts – naturalist, realist, and modernist – which principally engage his attention. Jameson's reading of Conrad's *Lord Jim* and *Nostromo* could hardly be further from Lukács's condemnation of Modernism's 'complete dissolution of all content and all form'. For Jameson, Lukács was correct to link modernist narrative to the reification of everyday life under capitalism, but both his explanation and (ethical) judgement were unnecessarily reductive. In its place, not only does Jameson provide a bravura interpretative performance (using Greimas, Lukács, Barthes, and others), but he also offers a far more adequate historical explanation than Lukács, locating the

texts within the complex cultural shifts of the turn of the century (rather than in a narrative of seemingly irreversible literary decline), and also within the processes of the spread of capitalism and colonialism. In addition, Jameson sketches three 'horizons' or levels of analysis of narrative: firstly, the text as symbolic act within the horizon of a generalised historical or political context; secondly, within the framework of the social order, the text as subsumed 'ideologeme' within the great collective or class discourses; thirdly, the text operates as an element in 'the ideology of form', produced in the 'slow' history of the transformations of modes of production, within the horizon of human history as a whole. This sounds both hugely ambitious and worryingly vague, but Jameson works hard to instantiate his claims in his analysis of Balzac, Gissing, and Conrad.

Decolonising Marxism

Most of Jameson's work on narrative, like that of other Marxists, has been Eurocentric in focus. In an attempt to rectify that, Jameson wrote an article on 'Third World Literature in the Era of Multinational Capitalism', which as well as pointing to Western theorists' and educators' lack of attention to 'other' narratives (*see* ALTERITY), provocatively argues that all Third World narratives function as *allegories of their nations of origin. This kind of generalisation is certainly no more far-ranging than those Jameson had produced in other circumstances (cf. his three 'horizons'), but it created considerable opposition from non-Western theorists, Marxist as well as non-Marxist. Jameson's most vociferous critic was perhaps the Indian Marxist Aijaz Ahmad, who objected especially strongly to Jameson's perceived reductiveness and homogenising of very different forms of non-Western cultural production as 'Third World literature'. Indeed, although Ahmad did not phrase it in quite these terms, it is Jameson's own narrative of non-Western narrative production which is at the heart of the problem.

Despite the problems with Jameson's formulation of non-Western narrative in this essay, it does at least draw attention to the over-ready identification of narrative (as an otherwise unmarked or undifferentiated category) with Western narrative. Some of the problems of the relationship between Western and non-Western forms and norms are highlighted in the work of two other non-Western Marxists. Chidi Amuta's *The Theory of African Literature* engages with both African and Western critics and theorists in an effort to overcome 'Marxism's patronising and Eurocentric silence about Africa'. Amuta aims to construct 'a totalising, dialectical (in place of a metaphysical) perspective' – and, as the terminology indicates, is not afraid of currently unfashionable categories such as totality. In keeping with the ambitions of an earlier period, Amuta sets out a 'Dialectical Theory of African Literature' organised around categories of history, the mediating subject, and the literary artefact/event. More specifically on narrative, he offers a materialist analysis of the classic African novelists Chinua Achebe, Ousmane Sembene, and Ngugi wa Thiong'o.

Indeed, in addition to being one of the best-known African practitioners of narrative, Ngugi himself has also become an influential theorist; the title of his 1986 collection *Decolonising the Mind* has become a kind of catchphrase within certain parts of post-colonial studies. Ngugi's theories on narrative are set within the context of the politics of cultural production and consumption generally. In his own writing, Ngugi returns to narrative forms which are relevant to his intended African *audience (*see* AFRICAN NARRATIVE), above all, those narratives which are also politically enabling, in areas ranging from indigenous cultural *identity to anti-imperial resistance. The objective is to counter the mystifications and historical distortions perpetrated by the ideologies of capitalism and imperialism, and Ngugi particularly aims to recover the lost or disavowed narratives of the achievements of ordinary people in the dual context of the emergence of the nation and the rejection of colonialist domination. Here, the subtle analysis of narrative matters far less than what can be achieved by means of the narrative in the context of human self-emancipation – no bad aim for a Marxist, or indeed anyone else.

SEE ALSO: cultural studies approaches to narrative; post-colonialism and narrative; sociological approaches to literary narrative

References and further reading

Amuta, Chidi (1989) *The Theory of African Literature*, London: Zed Books.
Bakhtin, Mikhail (1968) *Rabelais and His World*, trans. Helene Iswolsky, Cambridge: MIT Press.
—— (1981) *The Dialogic Imagination*, trans. Caryl Emerson and Michael Holquist, ed. Michael Holquist, Austin: University of Texas Press.
Eagleton, Terry (1976) *Marxism and Literary Criticism*, London: Methuen.
Jameson, Fredric (1982) *The Political Unconscious*, London: Methuen.
—— (1986) 'Third World Literature in the Era of Multinational Capitalism', *Social Text*, 15, 65–88.
Lukács, Georg (1969) *The Historical Novel*, trans. Hannah and Stanley Mitchell, Harmondsworth: Penguin.
—— (1978) 'Narrate or Describe?', in *Writer and Critic: Selected Essays*, trans. and ed. Arthur Kahn, London: Merlin.
Macherey, Pierre (1978) *A Theory of Literary Production*, trans. Geoffrey Wall, London: Routledge.
Mulhern, Francis (ed.) (1992) *Contemporary Marxist Literary Criticism*, Harlow: Longman.
Ngugi wa Thiong'o (1986) *Decolonising the Mind*, London: Heinemann.
Williams, Raymond (1977) *Marxism and Literature*, Oxford: Oxford University Press.

PATRICK WILLIAMS

MASTER NARRATIVE

The term 'master narrative' typically refers to pre-existent socio-cultural forms of interpretation. They are meant to delineate and confine the local interpretation strategies and *agency constellations in individual subjects as well as in social institutions (*see* INSTITUTIONAL NARRATIVE). Lyotard originally coined the terms *grand récit* and *metanarrative* for what are nowadays commonly referred to as master narratives; he furthermore characterised the Enlightenment (the narrative of infinite progress and liberty) and *science (the triumph of pure knowledge) as the two great master narratives of Modernity. In *postmodern theorising, the era of master narratives viewed as secure knowledge systems that formed the centre of cultural epochs has come to an end, leaving us 'stranded' in the heterogeneity of performed knowledges that are competing with one another, changing the question from what is true to what knowledge is being used for (*see* TRUTH). Indeed, in late-modern and postmodern social and literary analyses the term 'master narrative' has been extended to all sorts of legitimisation strategies for the preservation of the status quo with regard to power relations and difference in general (e.g., differences related to *gender and sexuality, race, ethnicity, age, etc.).

Foucault's analyses of the discourses of the insane and imprisoned, and of homo- and heterosexuality, followed up and elaborated in the field of Critical Discourse Analysis (Fairclough 1992; *see* DISCOURSE ANALYSIS (FOUCAULT)), centre on master narratives from a 'macro' perspective, analysing the strength and coherence of such master narratives as well as their historical changes. In contrast, others have adopted a more microanalytic approach. They have studied how the (personal) stories of individuals as personal sense-making strategies (in Lyotard's terms *petit récits*) resort to and corroborate, but also resist and subvert, socio-culturally dominant master narratives (Bamberg and Andrews 2004). The questions faced by both macro- and micro-analytic approaches concern the nature or fabric of both master and counter-narratives (as ideologies, *plot constructions, storylines, and discourses), as well as the social and individual forces that cause macro-narratives to change. Of particular relevance is the problem of resources that enable the individual subject to draw up *positioning strategies that contribute and ultimately lead to (historical) change. Central to discussions around master and counter-narratives is the problem of how locally situated narrating can bring about any liberation and emancipation from dominant master narratives, or whether this hope is just a nostalgic leftover of the master narratives of the Modern, with only local 'rupturing effects' now being possible.

References and further reading

Bamberg, Michael, and Molly Andrews (eds) (2004) *Considering Counternarratives: Narrating, Resisting, Making Sense*, Amsterdam: John Benjamins.

Chouliaraki, Lilie, and Norman Fairclough (1999) *Discourse in Late Modernity: Rethinking Critical Discourse Analysis*, Edinburgh: Edinburgh University Press.

Fairclough, Norman (1992) *Discourse and Social Change*, Cambridge: Polity Press.

Foucault, Michel (1972) *The Archeology of Knowledge*, New York: Pantheon.

Lyotard, Jean-François (1984) *The Postmodern Condition: A Report on Knowledge*, trans. Geoff Bennington and Brian Massumi, Minneapolis: University of Minnesota Press.

MICHAEL BAMBERG

MEDIA AND NARRATIVE

From its earliest days on, narratology has been conceived as a project that transcends disciplines and media. In 1964, Claude Bremond suggested that stories can be transposed from one medium to another without losing their essential properties. While this suggestion overlooks the configuring action of media, we cannot ignore its implications for the definition of *narrative. If Bremond is right, narrative is not in essence a language-based artefact, but a mental construct which can be created in response to various types of signs. Sharing Bremond's belief in the medium-independent nature of narrative, Roland Barthes argued that narrative is present in written literature, oral conversation, *drama, *film, painting, *dance, and mime (*see* CONVERSATIONAL STORYTELLING; PICTORIAL NARRATIVITY; VISUAL NARRATIVITY). Only *music is omitted from this list, though the narrative dimension of music has been the object of lively and often controversial discussions within musicology.

What are media?

Neither Barthes nor Bremond proposes a definition of medium: they demonstrate the transmedial existence of narrative through an enumeration of categories which, intuitively, we regard as media. Upon closer examination, however, the definition of the concept of medium is far from evident. In media theory, as in other fields, what constitutes an object of investigation depends on the purpose of the investigator. Ask a sociologist or cultural critic to enumerate media, and he or she will answer: *television, *radio, *film, the Internet (*see* DIGITAL NARRATIVE). An art critic may list: music, painting, sculpture, literature, drama, the *opera, *photography, architecture. An artist's list would begin with clay, bronze, oil, watercolour, fabrics, and it may end with exotic items used in so-called 'mixed-media' works, such as grasses, feathers, and beer can tabs. An information theorist or historian of writing will think of sound waves, papyrus scrolls, codex books, and silicon chips. How should narratologists answer, when asked to list the media relevant to their field?

The disparity of these answers is due to the ambiguity of the concept of medium. The entry for medium in Webster's Ninth New Collegiate Dictionary (1991) includes, among other meanings of questionable relevance to the present issue, the following two definitions:

> A channel or system of communication, information, or entertainment.
> Material or technical means of artistic expression.

Let's call (1) the transmissive definition, and (2) the *semiotic definition. Transmissive media include television, radio, the Internet, the gramophone, the telephone – all distinct types of technologies –, as well as cultural channels, such as books and newspapers. Semiotic media would be language, sound, *image, or more narrowly, paper, bronze, the human body, or the electromagnetically coded signals stored in computer memory.

Transmissive conceptions

In the transmissive conception of medium, ready-made messages are encoded in a particular way, sent over the channel, and decoded on the other end. Television can for instance transmit films as well as live broadcasts, news as well as recordings of theatrical performances. Before they are encoded in the mode specific to the medium in the first sense, some of these messages are realised through a medium in the second sense. A painting must be done in oil before it can be digitised and sent over the Internet. A musical composition must be performed on instruments in order to be recorded and played on a gramophone. Transmissive media thus involves the translation of objects supported by semiotic media into a secondary code.

Some theorists, including Walter Ong, have objected to the transmissive conception of medium, arguing that it reduces them to hollow pipelines, or conduits, through which information passes without being affected by the shape of the pipe. It is almost an axiom of contemporary media theory that the materiality of the medium – what we may call its affordances – matters for the type of meanings that can be encoded. On the other hand, if we regard meaning as inextricable from its medial support, medium-free definitions of narrative become untenable. What then would entitle us to compare messages embodied in different media and to view them as manifestations of a common narrative structure?

To maintain the possibility of studying narrative across media we must find a compromise between the hollow pipe interpretation and the unconditional rejection of the conduit metaphor (which itself is a concrete visualisation of Roman Jakobson's model of communication [see FUNCTION (JAKOBSON); NARRATIVE TRANSMISSION]). This means recognising that the shape and size of the pipeline imposes conditions on what kind of stories can be transmitted, but also admitting that narrative messages possess a conceptual core which can be isolated from their material support. Because of the configuring action of the medium, however, it is not always possible to distinguish an encoded object from the act of encoding. In the live broadcasts of television, for instance, the object to be sent is created through the act of recording itself. Insofar as they present their own affordances, channel-type media can be simultaneously modes of transmission and semiotic means of expression. It is in this second capacity that they impact narrative form and meaning.

Semiotic conceptions

The precise definition of the semiotic conception of medium presents similar difficulties. Until the development of digital technology, the idea of medium as 'technical means of expression' appeared relatively straightforward: the medium of a work was both the substance out of which the work was fashioned by the artist, and the material support, or body, under which it was meant to be apprehended by the audience. But the computerisation of the production process has created the possibility of a split between these two kinds of support. A text composed on a computer can be distributed under a traditional 'old media' support. This raises the question of whether the use of digital tools doubles the number of media – each old one now possessing a new digital twin – or whether the support under which the work reaches the audience forms the decisive criterion of 'mediality', independently of the means of production. Far from forming a given, the status of digital technology as expressive medium depends on the extent to which the work takes advantage of its distinctive properties. These properties can be neutralised (for instance in the case of a print novel composed on a word processor); weakly exploited (a movie that makes use of digitally composed special effects but is projected on a standard cinema screen), or fully developed (a narrative form that can only be experienced in a digital environment, such as hypertext or *computer games). But it would be perhaps more appropriate to regard digitality as a medium family whose individual members correspond to the particular types of authoring software. A Storyspace hypertext narrative of the early nineties will significantly differ, for instance, from a Flash game or Director 'movie' produced at the beginning of the twenty-first century. The code of authoring programs is a second-order means of expression, and the various software supports should therefore be considered the submedia of digitality – just as clay tablets, papyrus scrolls, and codices are the submedia of manuscript writing.

Media and genres

Another difficult issue is the delimitation of medium with respect to *genre. Both medium and genre exercise constraints on what kinds of stories can be told, but whereas genre is defined by more or less freely adopted conventions chosen for both personal and cultural reasons, medium imposes its possibilities and limitations on the user. It is true that we choose both the genre and the medium we work in, but we select media for their affordances, and we work around their limitations, trying to overcome them or to make them irrelevant. For instance, painters introduced perspective to add a third dimension to the flat canvas. Genre by contrast purposefully uses limitations to optimise expression, to channel expectations, and to facilitate communication: tragedy must be about the downfall of a hero and use the mimetic mode of narrativity; concertos (after the Baroque era) must feature significant solos by one or two instruments; *novels must be long and *novellas medium-length, and both must possess some degree of *narrativity. These conventions are imposed as what Iurii Lotman has called a second-order semiotic system on the primary mode of signification. Genre conventions are thus genuine rules specified by humans, whereas the constraints and possibilities offered by media are dictated by their material substance and mode of encoding. But insofar as they lend themselves to many uses, media support a variety of genres. Still, it is often difficult to decide whether a given category should be classified as a genre or a medium. Hypertext, for instance, is a genre if we view it as a type of text, but it is a (sub)medium if we regard it as an electronic tool for the organisation of text.

The distinctness of genre and medium suggests that media should not be regarded as collections of properties that rigidly constrain the form of narrative, but rather as sets of virtualities which may or may not be actualised, and are actualised differently by every instance of the medium. It follows that narrative can play a variety of games with its supporting medium: it can go with the medium and fully exploit its properties; it can ignore the idiosyncrasies of the medium and use it purely as a transmission channel; or it can actively fight some of the properties of the medium for expressive purposes. A computer game in which players adopt an avatar and create its destiny through their actions represents the case of full exploitation (you cannot take the game out of the computer); a Stephen King novel posted on the Internet takes no artistic advantage whatsoever of its digital support; and a print narrative with multiple branches (*see* MULTI-PATH NARRATIVE) subverts the linear reading protocols typical of novels of its medium.

What counts as narrative medium?

In the last analysis, what counts as a medium for the narrative scholar is a type of material support for texts that truly makes a difference as to what kind of narrative content can be evoked (semantics, or story), how these contents are presented (syntax, or discourse), and how they are experienced (*pragmatics). This approach implies a standard of comparison. 'Mediality' is thus a relational rather than an absolute property. To test the thesis of the relativity of mediality with respect to narrative, let us consider the respective status of the gramophone and of daily newspapers.

From a technological point of view the gramophone stands as a prototypical medium. When it was developed at the end of the nineteenth-century, it did to sound what writing had done to language. Thanks to the new technology sound could now be recorded, and it was no longer necessary to be within earshot of its source to apprehend auditory data. From a narratological perspective, however, the purely transmissive medium of the gramophone did not make a noticeable difference. Though it could have been the support of a new narrative genre, the gramophone was primarily used for the recording of music or opera, this is to say, in a transmissive/reproductive rather than creative capacity. It wasn't until the development of wireless telegraphy that a long-distance auditory type of narrative was popularised, namely the radiophonic play (*see* RADIO NARRATIVE). Daily newspapers represent the opposite situation: historians of technology would regard them as a manifestation of the same medium as books, since they rely on roughly the same printing techniques, but narratologists would defend their medium status with respect to books by pointing out that the daily press promoted a new style of reporting real world events, which gave birth to an autonomous narrative genre. Daily newspapers also differ pragmatically from other types of communication channels in that they must be delivered regularly at 24-hour intervals. The coverage of a time-consuming crisis must therefore begin before the crisis is resolved, and the daily reports lack the completeness and retrospective perspective of other types of narrative (*see* CLOSURE). All these characteristics suggest that newspapers do indeed support a distinct kind of narrativity (*see* JOURNALISM).

For a type of information support to qualify as a narrative medium, it must not only make a difference in the areas of story, discourse, or pragmatics but also present a unique combination of features. These features can be drawn from areas such as the following.

1   Spatio-temporal extension. Media fall into three broad categories: purely temporal ones, supported by language or music exclusively; purely spatial media, such as painting and photography; and spatio-temporal media, such as the cinema, dance, image-language combinations, and digital texts. (One might argue, however, that oral storytelling and print narrative involve a visual, and consequently spatial component; this would leave only long-distance oral communication such as radio and telephone as a language-supported example of the purely temporal category [*see* SPACE IN NARRATIVE; TIME IN NARRATIVE]).

2   Kinetic properties. A spatio-temporal medium can be static (i.e., combinations of still pictures and text [*see* COMICS AND GRAPHIC NOVEL]) or dynamic (moving pictures, or media relying on the human body as means of expression, such as *dance or the theater).

3   Senses being addressed and variety of semiotic codes being used. This is the domain of what we may call 'multimedia', or more properly 'multichannel' media. The various channels of a medium can be occupied by language, a code which speaks to the mind through the conventional meaning of its signs, or by purely sensory modes of expression, such as sound or pictures, which convey meaning without relying on a fixed semantic content.

4   Priority of sensory channels. Thus the opera should be considered distinct from a theater production that makes use of music, even though the two media include the same sensory dimensions and semiotic codes, because the opera gives the sound channel higher priority than the theater.

5   Technological support and materiality of signs. Here are some examples of differences in technological support which lead to significant differences in narrative expressivity: television differs from the cinema because of its ability to broadcast narratives in real time; photography differs from painting because it is the mechanically obtained imprint of a real-life scene. Photographic narratives have, consequently, greater testimonial value than pictorial ones, even though photos can be manipulated and reality can be staged.

6   Cultural role and methods of production/distribution. This is the factor that accounts for why books and newspapers are the recipients of different kinds of narratives.

The contribution of non-verbal media to narrative meaning

The media listed above present wide differences in their storytelling abilities. Rather than placing all of its members on equal footing, narrative media theory should therefore recognise various degrees of narrative power. The top of the scale is occupied by those media that include a natural language component, because natural language is arguably the only semiotic code capable of making distinct propositions, besides the formal languages of logic and mathematics. Language is also unique in its ability to state, rather than merely suggest, the existence of causal relations between events – an essential part of *narrative semantics (*see* CAUSALITY). Music by contrast lacks the precise semantics that make it possible to articulate definite stories. As for painting and photography, they are prevented by their purely spatial nature from explicitly representing what Paul Ricoeur regards as the proper subject matter of narrative: the temporal nature of human experience. The highest narrative potential undoubtedly belongs to those media that are able to articulate a fully new and determinate story, as do oral and written narrative, drama, and the cinema. But this does not mean that media based on purely sensory channels cannot make unique contributions to the formation of narrative meaning. There are, quite simply, meanings that are better evoked through pictures, sound, or *gestures than through language, and while these meanings may be unable to create self-sufficient narrative worlds without assistance from other types of signs, they expand our ability to imagine these worlds. For instance, a musical piece such as Tchaikovsky's 1812 Overture cannot explain the fine points of military strategy, but it captures the soul of the two countries at war far more powerfully than any history book can do: Russia is represented by a majestic religious hymn introduced by the low tones of the violas and cellos, while France is signified by the strident sounds of the brass and percussion, out of which emerge a few recognisable bars from La Marseillaise. After a chaotic confrontation of these two themes punctuated by cannon shots the peaceful Russian hymn takes over, accompanied by church bells and now played by the entire orchestra.

Besides expanding the world of a known story, non-verbal media may exercise their narrative power as the outlining of a partially empty narrative script, leaving it to the appreciator to fill it with specific content. Or as Emma Kafalenos has suggested for painting and photography, they may depict what Lessing called a 'pregnant moment' in a narrative action, to be connected by the spectator to a past and a future. It is only by recognising other *modes of narrativity than telling an *audience ignorant of these facts that something happened to somebody – modes such as illustrating, retelling, evoking, and interpreting – that we can acknowledge the narrative power of media without a language track.

SEE ALSO: adaptation; intermediality; orality; remediation

References and further reading

Barthes, Roland (1977) 'Introduction to the Structural Analysis of Narrative', in *Image Music Text*, trans. Stephen Heath, New York: Hill and Wang.

Bremond, Claude (1973) *Logique du récit*, Paris: Seuil.

Jakobson, Roman (1960) 'Closing Statements: Linguistics and Poetics', in Thomas Sebeok (ed.) *Style in Language*, Cambridge, Mass.: MIT Press.

Kafalenos, Emma (1996) 'Implications of Narrative in Painting and Photography', *New Novel Review*, 3.2, 53–66.

Lessing, Gotthold Ephraim (1984) *Laocoön: An Essay on the Limits of Painting and Poetry*, trans. E. A. McCormick, Baltimore: Johns Hopkins University Press.

Lotman, Iurii (1977 [1970]) *Structure of the Literary Text*, trans. Gail Lenhoff and Ronald Vroon, Ann Arbor: University of Michigan, Department of Slavic Languages and Literatures.

Manovich, Lev (2001) *The Language of New Media*, Cambridge, Mass.: MIT Press.

Ong, Walter J. (1982) *Orality and Literacy: The Technologizing of the Word*, London: Methuen.

Ricoeur, Paul (1984–88) *Temps et récit I*, Paris: Seuil.

Ryan, Marie-Laure (ed.) (2004) *Narrative Across Media: The Languages of Storytelling*, Lincoln: University of Nebraska Press.

Worth, Sol (1981) 'Pictures Can't Say Ain't', in Larry Gross (ed.) *Studies in Visual Communication*, Philadelphia: University of Pennsylvania Press.

Wutz, Michael, and Joseph Tabbi (eds) (1997) *Reading Matters: Narrative in the New Media Ecology*, Ithaca: Cornell University Press.

MARIE-LAURE RYAN

MEDIACY

'Mediacy' (*Mittelbarkeit*) is Franz Stanzel's term for designating the indirect ('mediate') character of verbal narratives (mainly *fiction) as opposed to the 'immediate' or direct modes of presentation available in *drama and *film. A variant of Genette's 'act of narrating' and Chatman's *narrative transmission, mediacy is a quality that characterises essential features of narrative discourse, particularly *narrative situations, audibility of the narrator's *voice, temporal and causal arrangement of story events (*see* CAUSALITY; PLOT; TIME IN NARRATIVE), and arrangement of narrative information (*see* FOCALIZATION). As is recognised by all discourse narratologists (*see* STORY-DISCOURSE DISTINCTION), the mediacy continuum ranges from perspicuous foregrounding of narratorial activity (as in *metanarrative comment), via cooperative and unobtrusive storytelling to attempts to hide all traces of the narrative act (*see* NO-NARRATOR THEORY). While mediacy captures the specificity of literary (written mainstream) narrative texts, it is clearly restrictive in scope, and from the vantage of transgeneric and transmedial approaches its importance has receded behind that of more widely accepted concepts such as *experientiality and *narrativity.

References and further reading

Chatman, Seymour (1978) *Story and Discourse: Narrative Structure in Fiction and Film*, Ithaca: Cornell University Press.
Stanzel, Franz Karl (1984 [1979]) *A Theory of Narrative*, trans. Charlotte Goedsche, Cambridge: Cambridge University Press.

MANFRED JAHN

MEDICINE AND NARRATIVE

Research on the forms and functions of narrative in relation to medicine, illness, and health has expanded rapidly since the early 1980s. Its development is marked by diversity in theoretical perspectives and methods brought to bear on a variety of problems. The 'narrative and medicine' area includes not only narratives in the medical setting, but also the use of narratives in everyday non-clinical settings.

Social-scientific and humanities-oriented researchers have shown a great desire to understand how people suffering from illness are affected in their daily lives and how they see their situations 'from the inside', as opposed to understanding the illness from the perspective of the medical institution's definition of the illness. Mishler conceptualises this conflict as a struggle between the 'voice of the life world' and the 'voice of medicine'. The former tends to be suppressed in medical interviews, and there are severe limitations on the extent to which patients can present their own versions of their problems. Several researchers have tried to examine the 'voice of the life world' in more detail.

For sick people, relatives, and professionals in the care sector, narrative offers an opportunity to emphasise *events, experiences, and consequences that lack relevance in the narrower biomedical perspective on illnesses (*see* EXPERIENTIALITY). Biomedical thinking is based on the belief that illnesses will fit into the generally applicable illness theories; they are processes in sick people that can be explained with the aid of biomedically defined causes for the illnesses. The use of narratives is based on an understanding of the actual individual and his/her suffering, within the framework of his/her daily life and life history, and is built on the relationship between the person, his/her suffering, and the illness.

Three different areas can be identified as the topics and areas of interest among investigators. The first is the patient's use of narrative as a way of articulating illness and suffering in a biographical context and also in reconstituting identities that have been damaged by illness (illness narratives) (*see* IDENTITY AND NARRATIVE; LIFE STORY). The second area is the use of narrative as a way of formulating and communicating medical knowledge, primarily among health professionals (narratives *about* illness). The third area is that of narratives used in clinical settings as a way of negotiating illness and disease, to work on patient's illness narratives, and also as a way of changing medical practice (narrative as a clinical tool).

Illness narratives in a narrower sense include sick people's narratives about their own illnesses, and about the effect they have had on their own lives (Bury 1982; Frank 1995; Mishler 1984; Williams 1984). These can also include the narratives of relatives about the effects the illnesses have had on their relationships with the sick people and on their own lives. In this sense the illness narratives are related in the context of everyday conversations with family members, friends, and colleagues (*see* CONVERSATIONAL STORYTELLING). Illness narratives also appear as written *biographical or *autobiographical accounts (Couser 1997; Hawkins 1993). Both the oral and the written illness narratives help to configure and articulate experiences and events that change one's life and its prerequisites.

Narratives about illness consist mainly of the oral and written narratives that medical personnel like doctors and nurses tell about the sick people they encounter, and about their illnesses (Hunter 1991; Sacks 1985). Narratives about illness can have many different functions. One example is to summarise and communicate clinical experiences that are not told in clinical textbooks; others are to tell how illnesses affect the patient's entire life situation, or to discuss the medical personnel's work in relation to sick patients, as when a mistake is made. Narratives about illness can also play an important role in communication between different professional care groups.

The illness narrative's use as a clinical tool focuses on the way the narrative can be used in the clinical meeting between, for instance, doctor and patient, in work with brain-damaged patients, or in psychotherapeutic work with people who have serious mental illnesses (Charon 2001; Kleinman 1988; Mattingly 1998; Schafer 1980).

Illness narratives

Illnesses, especially chronic ones but also acute ones, threaten a person's habitual daily life by the fact that the functionality of the body or of one of its parts is impaired, or indeed is removed entirely. These changes can concern both the body's outer, visible shell, as well as the internal parts that are invisible to the naked eye. Illnesses can also be latent, and portend a functional change, for example in the early discovery of cell changes. This makes physical changes and illnesses stand out as threatening figures against the background of everyday life. They are often experienced as external and alien events that intrude upon the ongoing life process.

Frank (1995) points out that public health care and treatment in the western world were dominated for most of the twentieth century by a biomedically oriented practice that had as a consequence the patient's loss of his or her illness narrative; he/she was reduced to the 'bearer' or the 'host' of the illness. A 'narrative surrender' occurred here in which the narratives that make up the patient's context for understanding the nature and onset of his or her illness lose their value when confronted with the medical system. The biomedical *descriptions and understanding of the illness dominate instead. Frank states that during the latter part of the twentieth century, sick people in the western world have had increasing opportunities to take control of their own illnesses. We no longer have to let the medical system and its experts take over our illnesses and, ultimately, our own bodies. A direct consequence of this development, says Frank, is that we regain interest in illness narratives, simply because the narrative is the everyday information form that we use to understand our own illnesses, and make them comprehensible.

*Narrativisation of the illness process and event is a method of meaning making where illness events and symptoms are framed within a life-world context. This is true both for the oral narratives that are told to family, friends, or researchers, and for the written, book-length narratives intended to be read by anonymous readers who may be suffering themselves.

People who are ill weave the threads of their illnesses, their presumed origins, trajectories of problems, and their personal and social consequences into the fabric of their stories. By doing this, they strive for and sometimes attain answers to such questions as *why* this happened to them and what they can look forward to in the future. Their stories are also made public as they communicate with others in their social circles who may offer suggestions and new interpretations that may complicate or change the original story. Thus, patients' narratives enter a social discourse where personal and cultural meanings of their illnesses are discussed and negotiated, providing ways of dealing with their problems that do not rely solely on the medical framework. They may also restore a sense of personal *agency lost through the objectifying procedures of clinical care and treatment (Hydén 1997).

Most illnesses may seem to lack all connection with earlier life events, and consequently they disrupt our sense of continuity and coherence; they create a 'biographical disruption' (Bury 1982). Thus illness onsets and illnesses tend to raise moral questions about one's own life, and these demand answers. Illness narratives offer an opportunity both to reconstruct a new biographical context and to fit the illness disruption into a new storyline, and thus to provide answers to questions about the meaning of the illness. Through this 'narrative reconstruction' (Williams 1984), narratives can provide a context that encompasses both the illness event and surrounding life events, and that thus recreates a state of interrelatedness.

Frank proposes three storylines specifying relations between patients' selves, bodies, and illnesses and their expectations for the future. He calls them 'restitution', 'chaos', and 'quest' narratives (*see* PLOT TYPES). These three different storylines can all be found in patient's illness narratives to varying degrees and in various relations with one another.

The storyline of the restitution narrative positions the illness as a temporary and limited time of bodily impairment or affliction. The afflicted persons remain the same persons as before the illness, and when it passes or they are in remission they expect to be restored to their former levels of functioning. Essentially, being ill does not change the identity of the ill person. By contrast, the chaos storyline depicts life as radically disrupted; the self is submerged in the illness, chaos reigns, the severity of symptoms is unpredictable, and the future is uncertain. The final storyline, the quest narrative, expresses a sense of self that has been changed by the illness. Being ill initiates a journey toward a new identity. As witnesses to their own transformation, these individuals believe they have learned something valuable that can bring back and pass along to others – particularly to other sufferers from pain and illness.

Book-length personal accounts of illness were uncommon before 1950. Since then more and more books have been published describing how a person is afflicted with an illness. They describe the illness process, the form of treatment, whether treatment is the traditional medical one or an alternative medical one, and finally the person's eventual recovery or death. In many cases the author is the person who was ill, and wrote right up until the time he/she died. In other cases, people close to the patient have pieced together a story from fragments left by the ill person, or else they have described the illness process themselves. Biographies or autobiographies about the experience of illness (and bodily dysfunctions), treatment, and death, have been termed 'pathographies' (Hawkins 1993) and 'autopathographies' (Couser 1997).

Hawkins, applying an approach based on studies of comparative literature to written illness narratives, argues that pathographies generally are based on certain recurrent *metaphors and *myths. She states that there are four special metaphors that are occur frequently in modern pathography – battle, journey, rebirth, and 'healthy-mindedness'. Her analysis emphasises how writers may make use of established *genres and narrative strategies to reconfigure their lives and illness experiences in culturally recognisable and acceptable forms (see NARRATIVE TECHNIQUES). These various metaphors help in organising the ill person's experience of illness and his or her relation to both the illness and treatment.

One of the central metaphors discussed by Hawkins is the rebirth myth. This myth is in many respects a close parallel to Frank's quest narrative. The transformation of self through illness is central to rebirth; the patient has suffered a severe life crisis and come through it, emerging regenerated as a new human being. Typically, she says, these narratives are organised into three parts. The first is the time before the onset of illness, often viewed retrospectively as marked by an unhealthy life style that is now rejected. This leads to the second part, the crisis accompanying the onset of illness, which has become a matter of life or death. This, finally gives way to the third part, rebirth or regeneration, the resolution of the crisis, and entry into a new life with a different appreciation of the world. Hawkins suggests that this narrative genre draws upon and replaces traditional religious conversion stories – for example, that of the sinner who has met God face to face, realises and regrets his/her life of sinfulness, undergoes conversion, and begins a new God-fearing life.

Narratives about illness

Several researchers and clinicians have suggested that narrative has a central place in medicine as a means, especially for medical doctors, of assembling and integrating information from various sources, and articulating and communicating clinical knowledge (see NARRATIVE AS COGNITIVE INSTRUMENT).

The narrative is a form that is well suited for clinical case presentation in medicine, and it has been used and cultivated in that way since at least the end of the nineteenth-century. Freud, for instance, was very apt at composing narratives about his cases the same way that *novels or suspense stories are created – something that probably contributed to his case studies becoming easily accessible and widely read (Schafer 1980; see PSYCHOANALYSIS AND NARRATIVE). A modern proponent of this tradition is Oliver Sacks, whose books are about patients with various types of neurological traumas and problems. His narrative case presentations allow the reader to view the world from the injured patient's perspective, and how it is to live with dysfunctions and traumas. Although Sacks tries to convey an 'inside' *perspective rather than an 'outside' one (see FOCALIZATION), his literary case presentation still relies mainly on the medical point of view; it is the voice of the medical doctor attempting to present the perspective of the patient.

Clinical medicine can essentially be understood as an interpretative practice concerned with the identification and treatment of singular cases of illness. The abstract scientific medical knowledge has to be translated into an understanding of that particular ill individual and communicated both to the patient and other health professionals. Medical doctors, especially, use narrative forms to present cases in patient rounds, case conferences, and medical charts as a mode of communicating medical experience and knowledge to both colleagues and students (Hunter 1991). In case presentations, narratives are used in order to describe the circumstances that resulted in a patient coming to the attention of the medical system. They also describe the nature of the patient's problem or disease, what has been done, and what is planned. These narratives subordinate the chronological chain of events of the patient's life to a *plot of relevant medical goals and events.

Another type of narrative about illness consists of the *anecdotes about patients and especially unusual or deviant instances of illness signs and processes. Telling about patients in rounds and conferences in the form of a narrative makes it possible to emphasise the specific and deviant features of particular cases within the general framework of what is known about different types of illness and their typical forms of appearance. This narrative strategy makes possible a pragmatic and instrumental orientation to the treatment of patients.

Narrative as a clinical tool

Several researchers have emphasised the importance of patients' illness narratives as a means by which doctors can acquire a more detailed clinical picture of the patient. In this perspective the medical practitioner must become acquainted with the patient's narrative, not only in order to make a correct diagnosis, but also in order to propose a treatment program that is acceptable to the patient (Kleinman 1988).

The narrative does not, however, constitute a neutral instrument in the meeting between the patient and the doctor. Instead, there is a struggle to determine which narrative about the patient's illness will be the dominant one (Clark and Mishler 1992). In typical medical interviews, physicians either ignore or interrupt patients' storied everyday accounts of the problems. The traditional narrative put forward by the doctor has the form of a *chronicle in which signs and symptoms are ordered sequentially but removed from the larger context of patients' lives. Patients try to restore the everyday context of the illness, citing symptoms in their daily experiences and their impact on how they can function personally and socially. In order for the patient to be able to present these contextualised stories the physicians must relinquish or at least moderate their dominance and move toward becoming more attentive and responsive listeners, encouraging patients to tell their stories instead of imposing the medical plot of illness and cure.

Charon has argued for the development of a 'narrative medicine', emphasising the ability of the physician to absorb, interpret, and respond to patients' stories. The doctor has to learn the process of close, attentive listening to the patient in order to hear the patient's narrative questions, but also to recognise that there are often no clear answers to these questions. With conspicuous listening a relationship is created that allows the physician to arrive at a diagnosis, interpret physical findings, and involve the patient in obtaining effective care.

Narrativisation may also serve as an active component in therapeutic clinical work. Mattingly describes how health professionals in many contexts try to shape a progressive course of treatments and the process of recovery into a coherent *plot, which she refers to as 'therapeutic emplotment' (see NARRATIVE THERAPY). Placed in a narrative context, physical dysfunctions or the daily tedium of routine rehabilitation may take on new meaning and thus become endurable. This form of therapeutic *emplotment may also influence or change the patient's time horizon for the course of the illness, by establishing a link between the medical interventions and the trajectory of recovery, and engendering hope of eventual cure.

Active work with narrative plots is something that also takes place in the psychoanalytic dialogue (Schafer 1980). One way in which identity and sense of self are established is through the telling of stories. In the psychoanalytic situation the analysand tells his/her analyst about him/herself and others, past and present. The analyst comments, questions, and interprets these stories, and thereby retells the stories along psychoanalytic lines. During the psychoanalytic process the analyst's reiterations influence the analysand's telling of stories. In this way new and jointly constructed narratives emerge, giving the analysand a rebirth.

SEE ALSO: institutional narrative; trauma theory

References and further reading

Bury, Mike (1982) 'Chronic Illness as Biographical Disruption', *Sociology of Health and Illness*, 4, 167–182.

Charon, Rita (2001) 'Narrative Medicine: A Model for Empathy, Reflection, Profession, and Trust', *Journal of American Medical Association*, 286, 1897–1902.

Clark, Jack, and Elliott Mishler (1992) 'Attending Patient's Stories: Reframing the Clinical Task', *Sociology of Health and Illness*, 14, 344–371.

Couser, Thomas (1997) *Recovering Bodies: Illness, Disability, and Life Writing*, Madison: University of Wisconsin Press.

Frank, Arthur (1995) *The Wounded Storyteller: Body, Illness, and Ethics*, Chicago: University of Chicago Press.

Hawkins, Anne (1993) *Reconstructing Illness: Studies in Pathography*, West Lafayette: Purdue University Press.

Hunter, Kathryn (1991) *Doctor's Stories: The Narrative Structure of Medical Knowledge*, Princeton, N.J.: Princeton University Press.

Hydén, Lars-Christer (1997) 'Illness and Narrative', *Sociology of Health and Illness*, 19, 48–69.

Kleinman, Arthur (1988) *The Illness Narratives: Suffering, Healing, and the Human Condition*, New York: Basic Books.

Mattingly, Cheryl (1998) *Healing Dramas and Clinical Plots: The Narrative Structure of Experience*, New York: Cambridge University Press.

Mishler, Elliot (1984) *The Discourse of Medicine: Dialectics of Medical Interviews*, Norwood, N.J.: Ablex Publishing Company.

Sacks, Oliver (1985) *The Man Who Mistooke His Wife for a Hat*, London: Duckworth.

Schafer, Roy (1980) 'Narration in the Psychoanalytic Dialogue', in W. J. T. Mitchell (ed.) *On Narrative*, Chicago: University of Chicago Press.

Williams, Gareth (1984) 'The Genesis of Chronic Illness: Narrative Re-Construction', *Sociology of Health and Illness*, 6, 175–200.

LARS-CHRISTER HYDÉN

MEDIEVAL NARRATIVE

Medieval narrative belongs to a period in which literature in the vernacular, on which this discussion concentrates, made the transition from oral to written form against the background of Christian *theology (see ORAL CULTURES AND NARRATIVE; ORALITY). Modern theories may need to be modified for the purpose of analysing medieval narratives, which depend on period-specific concepts of *fiction and the *author, are based on distinctive causal and chronological structures (see CAUSALITY), represent *characters as types, and were performed aloud in a communal context (see AUDIENCE; PERFORMANCE).

The medieval narrative communication situation includes a performer as well as an author and a *narrator. *Gesture and intonation give the narrative text, which could be altered with each recital, an additional layer. The role of the narrator can be complex – religious literature, for example, uses first-person plural forms to establish a bond between narrator and *narratee inside the narrated world, where both experience the narrative of divine truth, and outside it, where they join in expressions of piety (see PERSON). The theories applicable to such narratives, however, are not always transferable to texts with oral origins (see ORAL-FORMULAIC THEORY).

The oral context of the *Nibelungenlied* led its poet to suppress references to the role of the author (Coxon 2001: 147). In German, at least, it is more common for the author-function to be represented in texts without an oral background (Coxon 2001: 220). However, while excurses and manuscript practice show that the concept of the author was recognised, narratives depended as much on references to written sources as on authors for their legitimacy, and scribes could alter the composition of a narrative to reflect different approaches – texts not only changed *horizons of expectation but could also be changed by them. Different versions of the same narrative represent one form of medieval *intertextuality (see NARRATIVE VERSIONS). A second type involves characters and *events that appear in several texts without those texts forming a clear causal or chronological sequence.

Within individual narratives, material causality has a relatively minor role. The heroic *epic is finally motivated by the *hero's inevitable downfall, *biblical narratives are geared towards the revelation of divine truth, and *historiography arranges events in order to show a finite, predetermined Christian history unfolding from type to antitype (see ALLEGORY). Even in narratives from the pre-Thomistic period that do not fall into these categories, humans are the instruments of God, who has ultimate control over what happens (Vitz 1989: 178–79). Events in a narrative can cause other events only if permitted to do so by God.

Christian thought also affected the perception of *time, which was treated as static rather than gradually progressing. This prevents time schemes from being identified in narratives such as the *Chanson de Roland* (Grunmann-Gaudet 1980). In more literate works such as *Yvain*, however, linear time can be an important element of *narrative structure (Lock 1985: ii–iii). The distinction between natural and artificial order in Latin treatises indicates a theoretical awareness of the function of *temporal ordering (Kelly 1991: 69–71), but in practice rhyme rather than logic can determine *tense usage in a text such as *Perceval* (Ollier 1980).

From a modern perspective, it might be thought that medieval narratives consist of nothing more than sequences of weakly connected elements. In fact, they can show considerable complexity. The moral of the Arthurian *romance, for example, is encoded in the bipartite structure of the *genre: the superficial stability attained in the first segment is transformed into lasting social harmony in the second. It has been argued that narrative structure, particularly in the work of Chrétien de Troyes, marks the (re)emergence of western vernacular fiction (Haug 1997: 91–106). However, as shown by narratives such as *König Rother*, bipartite structure is not specific to the Arthurian romance. Oral heroic narratives, initially based on historical events, may have become fictionalised as they became adapted to fit an abstract pattern (Haug 1971). Rather than treating such narratives as the product of a series of transformations between synchronic levels in the manner of *structuralist narratology, this theory sees them as the result of a diachronic process in which the initial events are gradually rearranged to fit a predetermined schema. The introduction of fictional events into historiographic narratives, meanwhile, involves changing the historical field prior to the subsequent processes of selection and connection described by Hayden White (*see* EMPLOTMENT; METAHISTORY).

Like the *truth of medieval narrative, its characters are measured according to *ideology, not reality. They are representative types, such as the ideal ruler, rather than individuals, although instances of character development can be found. The intensity of a character trait is more important than the nature of the trait itself (Vitz 1989: 16–17), and actions cannot always be analysed with modern models (*see* ACTION THEORY). Greimas's theory of *actants, for example, operates with future-orientated wish-fulfilment, whereas Christianity calls for *caritas*, which is open-ended because one can never finish doing God's will (Vitz 1989: 129–30). Human *desire can initiate a narrative, but a conclusion can only be provided with God's acquiescence and need not consist of satisfaction of the original wish. Rhetoric and didacticism function as alternative markers of *closure (Vitz 1989: 207).

SEE ALSO: communication in narrative; evolution of narrative forms

References and further reading

Coxon, Sebastian (2001) *The Presentation of Authorship in Medieval German Narrative Literature 1220–1290*, Oxford: Clarendon Press.

Green, D. H. (2002) *The Beginnings of Medieval Romance: Fact and Fiction, 1150–1220*, Cambridge: Cambridge University Press.

Grunmann-Gaudet, Minnette (1980) 'The Representation of Time in *La Chanson de Roland*', in Minnette Grunmann-Gaudet and Robin F. Jones (eds) *The Nature of Medieval Narrative*, Lexington, KY: French Forum.

Haug, Walter (1971) 'Die historische Dietrichsage: Zum Problem der Literarisierung geschichtlicher Fakten', *Zeitschrift für deutsches Altertum und deutsche Literatur*, 100, 43–62.

—— (1997) *Vernacular Literary Theory in the Middle Ages: The German Tradition, 800–1300, in Its European Context*, trans. Joanna M. Catling, Cambridge: Cambridge University Press.

Kelly, Douglas (1991) *The Arts of Poetry and Prose*, Turnhout: Brepols.

Lock, Richard (1985) *Aspects of Time in Medieval Literature*, New York: Garland.

Ollier, Marie-Louise (1980) 'Le Roman au douzième siècle: Vers et narrativité', in Minnette Grunmann-Gaudet and Robin F. Jones (eds) *The Nature of Medieval Narrative*, Lexington, KY: French Forum.

Smalley, Beryl (1974) *Historians in the Middle Ages*, London: Thames & Hudson.

Vitz, Evelyn Birge (1989) *Medieval Narrative and Modern Narratology: Subjects and Objects of Desire*, New York: New York University Press.

ALASTAIR MATTHEWS

MEMORY

Memory processes and memory representations play a critical role in most aspects of narrative understanding. Processes are the mental operations that enable individuals to transform perceptual input (e.g., speech or words on a page) into an elaborated experience of a narrative world (*see* STORYWORLD). Those mental processes give rise to representations, which are the products of understanding that are stored in long-term memory.

Moment-by-moment narrative processing involves working memory. Working memory is defined as a memory system that enables people to temporarily store and manipulate information. Working memory has capacity limitations, which has consequences for narrative processing because those limitations disallow the entirety of all but the most simple narratives to be processed all at once (Kintsch 1988; *see* MINIMAL NARRATIVE). The *memory-based processing* approach to narrative understanding provides an account of the changing contents of working memory as narratives unfold. According to this model, each segment of a narrative generates an automatic search of long-term memory (McKoon and Ratcliff 1992; O'Brien, Lorch, and Myers 1998). This search provides access to both schematic information and relevant information from earlier in a narrative. Suppose a narrative included the sentence 'Chris drank a Martini while he waited for Sharon to arrive at the restaurant'. A full understanding of that utterance might require that working memory include a representation of the sentence itself, schematic information about restaurant practices, and particular information about the purpose of Chris and Sharon's restaurant visit (gathered from earlier in the narrative).

Much of the research on memory relevant to narrative has focused on the role schematic information plays in the understanding and recall of narratives (*see* SCRIPTS AND SCHEMATA). For example, in his foundational study, Bartlett (1932) asked English readers to recall a North American *folktale. Bartlett found that his participants' reproductions were modified from the original stories in the direction of their own cultural experience. Bartlett's research foreshadowed contemporary accounts of the roles that schemas play in narrative circumstances. The concept of the schema is quite general: Schemas encode generalisations across individuals' experiences with categories of people, places, *events, and so on (Brewer and Nakamura 1984). When people understand narratives, schemas help structure their understanding. This is why, for example, an author can tacitly evoke an entire scenario with a sentence as simple as 'Chris drank a Martini while he waited for Sharon to arrive at the restaurant'. Because a whole scenario becomes accessible in memory, readers can understand references to other aspects of the whole (e.g., 'Chris signalled the waiter to bring him a second drink') without the author's having to expend extra effort (e.g., 'There was a waiter...'). Thus, readers use information from long-term memory to generate, for example, expectations and implications.

Theories of narrative representation suggest that people create several different types of representations as their understanding deepens. The initial representation remains close to the details of the text. However, this surface representation is ephemeral. Under most circumstances, the type of representation that endures for the long-term encodes the meaning or gist of the text rather than its surface form. This representation incorporates inferences – information culled from long-term memory that goes beyond the words themselves. An ultimate type of representation is the *situation model* – a representation of 'the state of affairs described in a text' (Zwaan and Radvansky 1998: 162). Research has focused on the various types of information – e.g., the passage of *time, *characters' movement through *space, characters' ability to accomplish their goals – that structure these situation models.

Readers are able to encode inferences and construct situation models because they access long-term memory structures as an important element of narrative understanding. However, every narrative licenses an unlimited number of inferences. For example, 'Chris' and 'Sharon' are likely to have hearts, lungs, livers, and so on but it would be the very rare reader whose situation model explicitly encoded that information (e.g., it would be unlikely that a reader would imagine that she had read the sentence, 'Chris had a heart', as part of the text). Because readers cannot encode all possible inferences, theorists have tried to determine which subset readers encode automatically. Automatic inferences are 'those that are encoded in the absence of special goals or strategies on the part of the reader, and they are constructed in the first few hundred milliseconds of processing. They therefore merit attention because they form the basic representation of a text from which other, more purposeful inferences are constructed' (McKoon and Ratcliff 1992: 441).

With respect to automatic inferences, there has been a major theoretical divide (Gerrig and Egidi 2003). On one side are *memory-based* theories that suggest that automatic inferences arise only through the normal operation of memory process (e.g., McKoon and Ratcliff 1992; O'Brien *et al.* 1998). On the other side are *explanation-based* theories that suggest that people's goals with respect to narrative understanding determine which categories of inferences are automatic (e.g., Graesser, Singer, and Trabasso 1994; Singer, Graesser, and Trabasso 1994). For memory-based theories, automatic inferences are generated through ordinary memory processes. For explanation-based theories, automatic inferences require narrative-specific processes that enable readers to explain why the narrative mentions certain actions, events, and states. However, both theories recognise that narrative understanding requires fluid integration of information from the narrative itself with information from long-term memory.

SEE ALSO: cognitive narratology; mental mapping of narrative; narrative comprehension; pragmatics; psychological approaches to narrative; reader-response theory

References and further reading

Bartlett, Frederic C. (1932) *Remembering*, Cambridge: Cambridge University Press.

Brewer, William F., and Glenn V. Nakamura (1984) 'The Nature and Function of Schemas', in Robert S. Wyer and Thomas K. Srull (eds) *Handbook of Social Cognition*, vol. 1, Hillsdale, NJ: Erlbaum.

Gerrig, Richard J. (1993) *Experiencing Narrative Worlds*, New Haven: Yale University Press.

——, and Giovanni Egidi (2003) 'Cognitive Psychological Foundations of Narrative Experiences', in David Herman (ed.) *Narrative Theory and the Cognitive Sciences*, Stanford, CA: Publications of the Centre for the Study of Language and Information.

Graesser, Arthur C., Murray Singer, and Tom Trabasso (1994) 'Constructing Inferences During Narrative Text Comprehension', *Psychological Review*, 101, 371–95.

Kintsch, Walter (1988) 'The Role of Knowledge in Discourse Comprehension: A Construction-Integration Model', *Psychological Review*, 95, 163–82.

McKoon, Gail, and Roger Ratcliff (1992) 'Inference During Reading', *Psychological Review*, 99, 440–66.

O'Brien, Edward J., Robert F. Lorch, Jr., and Jerome L. Myers (eds) (1998) *Discourse Processes*, 26 (2 and 3) (Special issue on 'Memory-based Text Processing').

Singer, Murray, Arthur C. Graesser, and Tom Trabasso (1994) 'Minimal or Global Inferences During Reading', *Journal of Memory and Language*, 33, 421–41.

Zwaan, Rolf A., and Gabriel A. Radvansky (1998) 'Situation Models in Language Comprehension and Memory', *Psychological Bulletin*, 123, 162–85.

RICHARD J. GERRIG

MENTAL MAPPING OF NARRATIVE

A considerable range of approaches to narrative are based on the notion that human beings process and understand discourse by constructing mental representations of it in their minds. The detailed mental maps that readers form of narratives, variously also called 'frames' (Emmott 1997), 'worlds' (Gerrig 1993; Werth 1999) and 'mental spaces' (Fauconnier 1994; Semino 2003), enable them, for example, to track the movements of characters and objects through *time and *space, and to experience and understand focalized narration (*see* FOCALIZATION). The majority of approaches to narrative, which focus on mental mapping, take their theoretical and methodological influences from cognitive linguistics and cognitive psychology.

SEE ALSO: cognitive narratology; deixis; narrative comprehension; possible-worlds theory; situation model; text-world approach to narrative

References and further reading

Emmott, Catherine (1997) *Narrative Comprehension: A Discourse Perspective*, Oxford: Oxford University Press.

Fauconnier, Gilles (1994) *Mental Spaces: Aspects of Meaning Construction in Natural Language*, Cambridge: Cambridge University Press.

Gerrig, Richard (1993) *Experiencing Narrative Worlds: On the Psychological Activities of Reading*, New Haven: Yale University Press.

Semino, Elena (2003) 'Possible Worlds and Mental Spaces in Hemingway's "A Very Short Story"', in Joanna Gavins and Gerard Steen (eds) *Cognitive Poetics in Practice*, London: Routledge.

Werth, Paul (1999) *Text Worlds: Representing Conceptual Space in Discourse*, London: Longman.

JOANNA GAVINS

METAFICTION

Metafiction is a term first introduced by narrative theorist and historian Robert Scholes to indicate the capacity of *fiction to reflect on its own framing and assumptions. While the term has been perceived as a primary quality of *postmodern narrative, as Robert Alter (1975) argues, across the long history of the *genre novels have often contained metafictional elements (*see* NOVEL, THE). Commenting on the self-mirroring imagery and structure of *Don Quixote* (1605) (*see* QUIXOTIC NOVEL), Alter shows the extent to which, from its earliest days, the novel has been 'self-reflexive' (*see* REFLEXIVITY). 'Metafiction' has achieved such wide currency both as a historical component of fiction and as a hallmark of postmodernism that entire works such as Linda Hutcheon's *Narcissistic Narrative* (1980) and Patricia Waugh's *Metafiction* (1984) have been devoted to it.

The conceptualisation of 'metafiction' as an aspect of narrative practice evolved from the mid-70s to the mid-80s, precisely when the 'explosion of theory' and the attempt to define postmodernism as ethos and epoch was taking place in the United States and Europe. During this time, as well, the fiction of Jorge Luis Borges was being translated into English and widely popularised as providing the foundation for postmodern literature. Borges's fiction is foundationally metafictional; it foregrounds the nature of fiction as an artifice that both mirrors and refracts reality such that it reflects back on how the language of narrative achieves the effect of referencing reality through imaginary means (*see* REALISM, THEORIES OF; REFERENCE). Borges's story, 'Pierre Menard, Author of the *Quixote*', offers a revealing example in purporting to be a biographical sketch of a modern writer who attempts to write a 'second original' of Cervantes's novel without consulting or copying from the seventeenth century 'first original' (*see* BIOGRAPHY). In portraying the techniques by which Menard successfully accomplishes the incredible and pointless feat, Borges conceives of all the examples of fiction written across time as existing simultaneously in a vast hall of mirrors, each partially reflecting and reduplicating all of the others. Yet while each reflects its common fictional ancestry in this manner, each is also located within the matrix of historical circumstances, authorial intentions (*see* INTENTIONALITY), and linguistic specificities that makes it distinctly relevant to the constructed reality in which it reflexively locates itself as an act of writing.

Borges provides another example of metafictional recognition in 'The Garden of Forking Paths', a story of assassination and conspiracy. At the conclusion of the story the *narrator, pursued by a mysterious adversary, finds himself in a garden labyrinth, and discovers at its centre a cabinet containing the 'infinite novel' of his ancestor, Ts'ui Pen. Engaging in a discussion with the keeper of this textual labyrinth within a labyrinth, the narrator hears that 'In all fictions, each time a man meets diverse alternatives, he chooses one and eliminates the others; in the work of the impossible-to-disentangle Ts'ui Pen, the character chooses – simultaneously – all of them. *He creates*, thereby, "several futures", several *times*, which themselves proliferate and fork' (Borges 1998: 125). The story's elaborate *metaphor of fiction as infinite labyrinth offers a reflexive commentary on the difference between realistic fiction and metafictional fiction (*see* REALIST NOVEL): in the former, there is a linear path leading to a singular fate; in the latter, this illusion of singularity is shattered as each specific fiction both incorporates the entirety of the fictional universe with its infinite paths and alternatives, while inevitably also following the singular path or *plot laid out in any narrative taking place in human *time (*see* MULTI-PATH NARRATIVE). Thus, 'The Garden of Forking Paths' inspires metafictional reflections on the relation between time and fiction, the work of plot, and the active role of the reader in constructing, by interpreting, a narrative (*see* READER-RESPONSE THEORY).

The capacity of fiction to be metafictional is a frequent subject of postmodern narrative, whether the energies of this movement are located historically in the late-twentieth century, or stylistically across centuries in such works as *Don Quixote*, Laurence Sterne's *Tristram Shandy* (1760–1767), or James Joyce's *Ulysses* (1922). In some hands, this capacity is stretched to the point of parody, as is the case in Gilbert Sorrentino's *Mulligan Stew* (1979), where various *characters speak to each other about their dissatisfaction over being characters in a novel, or in Vladimir Nabokov's *Pale Fire* (1962), in which a textual commentary becomes the occasion for the tale of a madman. An elaborate, encyclopedic compilation of metafictional tendencies can be found in John Barth's *LETTERS* (1979), in which characters and plots from Barth's previous novels interact to produce a narrative that is both a recycling and renovation of Barth's *oeuvre* to that point (*see* ENCYCLOPEDIC NOVEL).

Such examples have stirred much debate about the purposes of postmodern metafiction. In his twinned essays, 'The Literature of Exhaustion' and 'The Literature of Replenishment', John Barth asks whether metafiction is, merely, involuted and narcissistic, speaking only to the uselessness and exhaustion of fiction in contemporary times, or whether its very 'metafictivity' speaks to the continuous replenishment of the imagination that fiction offers in its self-conscious return to origins and reflection upon itself? In its metafictional moments, does fiction transform reality through new acts of imagination (since, for Borges, the textual universe is not 'other' to reality, but a primary component of it)? Or is fiction, in those moments, merely recognising its status as a partial reflection of reality, a fragmentary shard that mirrors a small part of the whole? Or, at the extreme, is fiction an imaginary projection utterly divorced from reality, its metafictionality serving as a sign of the alienation separating the imaginary from the real? Ultimately, both as a narrative term and fictional strategy, 'metafiction' bears our attention in that it signifies the extent to which the act of narrative delineates the intricate relationship between mind and world for which it serves as an intermediary.

SEE ALSO: historiographic metafiction; mise en abyme

References and further reading

Alter, Robert (1975) *Partial Magic: The Novel as a Self-Conscious Genre*, Berkeley: University of California Press.

Barth, John (1984) *The Friday Book: Essays and Other Nonfiction*, New York: Putnam.

Borges, Jorge Luis (1998) *Collected Fictions*, trans. Andrew Hurley, New York: Penguin.

Christensen, Inger (1981) *The Meaning of Metafiction*, Bergen: Universitetsforlaget.

Hutcheon, Linda (1980) *Narcissistic Narrative: The Metafictional Paradox*, Waterloo, Ont.: Wilfred Laurier University Press.

McCaffery, Larry (1982) *The Metafictional Muse: The Works of Robert Coover, Donald Barthelme, and William H. Gass*, Pittsburgh: University of Pittsburgh Press.

Scholes, Robert (1979) *Fabulation and Metafiction*, Urbana: University of Illinois Press.

Waugh, Patricia (1984) *Metafiction: The Theory and Practice of Self-Conscious Fiction*, New York: Methuen.

PATRICK O'DONNELL

METAHISTORY

The term 'metahistory' was originally coined to characterise 'overdetermined' historical works such as Oswald Spengler's *Decline of the West* and Arnold J. Toynbee's *A Study of History*. Hayden White used the term to refer to the presuppositions – conceptual, figurative, and metaphysical – regarding the nature of historical reality required for belief in the possibility of a distinctively historical kind of knowledge. Since the past is not directly accessible to perception and can be known only by way of traces, monuments, and documents, our knowledge of it is always partial, incomplete, tentative. Metahistory identifies the elements of *emplotment, argument, and ideological implication required to fill out the record of the past, represent it in discourse, and explain its relevance to the present (*see* IDEOLOGY AND NARRATIVE).

Historians typically organise their data in the form of a chronicle of *events. The events and agents of the chronicle are then endowed with story functions by means of emplotment and transformed thereby into a tale, with beginning, middle, and end – which provides the sequence of events with teleological meaning. As thus narrativised (*see* NARRATIVISATION), historical series are turned into stories, but stories of a specific kind or *genre. White uses the broad *plot types suggested by Northrop Frye to classify the kinds of plots by which series of events are transformed into sequences: *epic, *romance, comedy, tragedy, and *satire or farce (*see* DRAMA AND NARRATIVE).

Identifying a chain of events (chronicle), transforming it into a sequence (story), and endowing it with narrative meaning (by emplotment) is only the first step in constituting an object of study as a specifically historical entity. Modern historians must then proceed to discern the relations obtaining among the elements of the historical field, identify the causal forces that operated in the endowment of the events they have studied with the aspect of a story, and account for the way things 'came out' as they did. The explanation of an outcome of a sequence of events can take the form of an appeal to commonplaces ('What goes up must come down') or to one or another system of putatively universal laws ('Changes in the economic base will cause changes in the social relations of production'). White suggests that, unlike the physical sciences, history and the historical sciences in general utilise a wide variety of putatively universal laws of historical change: materialist, idealist, religious, mythological. However, since by definition an historical event (of whatever size or scale) is a particular, it cannot be governed by general laws. The result is that a given presentation of a given set, series, or sequence of historical events will typically feature a wide range of putative laws to explain them. This is the metahistorical aspect of any historical interpretation of reality.

SEE ALSO: causality; closure; historiographic metafiction; historiography; narrativity; plot; science and narrative

References and further reading

Frye, Northrop (1963) 'New Directions from Old', *Fables of Identity: Studies in Poetic Mythology*, New York: Harcourt, Brace, and World.
White, Hayden (1973) *Metahistory: The Historical Imagination in Nineteenth-Century Europe*, Baltimore: Johns Hopkins University Press.

HAYDEN WHITE

METALEPSIS

An operation found in various fields, the contamination of levels in a hierarchical structure as it occurs in narrative is known as metalepsis (*see* NARRATIVE STRUCTURE). The *embedding of narratives normally respects the separation between the level of *narration and that of the narrated *events, but metalepsis produces a 'short-circuiting' of levels, calling this distinction into question and having repercussions for a number of other distinctions current in narrative theory. In *structuralist narratology, metalepsis remained undertheorised, but more recent research suggests its centrality for narrative theory, placing it alongside *metaphor and *metonymy, tropes with which it shares the notions of transformation, substitution, and succession.

Originating in ancient legal discourse (*see* LAW AND NARRATIVE), metalepsis (from Greek *meta-*: in the midst of, among, between, after, according to; *lambánein*: to take) has been associated historically with both synonymy (contextually inappropriate use of a synonym, omitting the central term linking two others) and *metonymy, either simple (cause for effect or effect for cause) or extended (chain of associations or connotations). The rhetorical classification of metalepsis has never been fully resolved (figure or trope?), but shows connections on the one hand with allusion, euphemism, litotes, hypotyposis and *allegory, and on the other with temporal transfer as a form of metonymy that explains the precedent by the consequent ('a few ears of corn' for 'a few years') or the consequent by the precedent ('I have lived' for 'I am dying') (see, e.g., Du Marsais, eighteenth-century; *see* CATACHRESIS). However, the likening of metalepsis to metonymy was refused by Fontanier (nineteenth-century), who considered it a proposition substituting an indirect expression for a direct expression (Phaedra declaring she 'burns' for Theseus, although she loves Hippolyte).

Genette, reviewing these evolutions within a narratological context, describes such transfers as 'author's metalepses', as when Virgil 'has Dido die' or when Diderot contemplates 'getting the Master married and making him a cuckold' or, conversely, when in a story by Cortázar, the reader of a *novel is killed by a character in that novel. Such transgressions of narrative level constitute 'narrative metalepsis': intrusion into the *storyworld by the extradiegetic *narrator or by the *narratee (or into deeper embedded levels), or the reverse. In Balzac's 'While the venerable churchman climbs the ramps of Angoulême, it is not useless to explain...', narrative levels are nearly convergent, the *time of the *narration and that of the story coincide (*see* STORY-DISCOURSE DISTINCTION), and the narrator/narratee axis is implicitly doubled by the author/reader axis, demonstrating in a nutshell the potential of metalepsis to undermine heuristic distinctions relating to *time, level, and addresser/addressee in narrative (*see* AUTHOR; READER CONSTRUCTS). Unlike metadiegetic (or embedded) narratives that serve either an explanatory or a thematic function vis-à-vis the embedding narrative that contains them, metalepses fold narrative levels back onto the present situation of the narrating act, uprooting the boundary between the world of the telling and that of the told or even, in extreme cases, effacing the line of demarcation between *fiction and reality. For Genette, such metaleptic effects defy *verisimilitude, creating an atmosphere of 'strangeness' (BIZARRERIE) which is either comical or *fantastic or some combination thereof.

Narrative metalepsis is thus not a mere stylistic oddity, but a potentiality implicit in all embedded narratives. Occurring with the change of level, metalepsis is woven into the fabric of narrative categories, most notably those of time and place (*see* SPACE IN NARRATIVE), and must thus be seen as lying at the crossroads of various textual features. Wherever present, it deliberately transgresses the 'threshold of embedding' or even that of representation, underscoring the process of textualisation, and while the result is often to disrupt mimetic illusion, the effect can also be to heighten the fictionality of a narrative and/or the sense of *immersion, suggesting that metalepsis may serve as a figure of creative imagination (*see* MIMESIS). Thus, 'minimal' metalepses (the Balzac example), though transgressive, tend to draw the extradiegetic narratee (reader) into the picture, whereas 'authorial' metalepses (the Diderot example) may put him/her at a distance. More emphatically, 'ascending' metalepses, characterised by 'extrametaleptic' transgression (from embedded to embedding story level, as in the Cortázar example), mark a certain affinity between character and narratee. In 'descending' metalepses, by contrast, 'intrametaleptic' transgressions may result in collaboration between narrator and narratee (the narrator of *Adam Bede* inviting the extradiegetic narratee to visit the protagonist's sitting room with him) or in a breach of the narrative contract (the narrator of *Tristram Shandy* ridding himself of his *heroes in volume III so as to write his 'Author's Preface').

Violations of level also occur in theater (Pirandello, Handke) and in painting (Escher, Magritte), as well as in fields other than artistic representation (*see* DRAMA; PICTORIAL NARRATIVITY). Drawing on Hofstadter's study of logical paradoxes in mathematics, logic, computer science, etc., McHale has identified metalepsis with 'Strange Loops' or 'Tangled Hierarchies', providing a theoretical framework for 'ontological' metalepses: in the movement up or down distinct hierarchical levels, these levels collapse into one another. Escher's *Drawing Hands* illustrates this problem of abnormal recursive embedding; in narrative, a comparable violation of the Chinese-box principle is Brooke-Rose's *Thru*, where

characters and narrators invent each other, it remaining undecidable which narrative level is superior, which inferior. From this perspective, metalepsis bears on *metafiction and *metanarrative comment, with questions of metalanguage and metatextual functions lying in the background. In a fruitful distinction that marks the current state of reflection on these narrative transgressions, Marie-Laure Ryan has pointed out the existence of rhetorical and ontological varieties of metalepsis, but in the analysis of specific texts it may prove that they overlap.

SEE ALSO: mise en abyme; postmodern narrative; reflexivity; rhetorical approaches to narrative

References and further reading

Genette, Gérard (1980) *Narrative Discourse: An Essay in Method*, trans. Jane E. Lewin, Ithaca NY: Cornell University Press.
—— (1988) *Narrative Discourse Revisited*, trans. Jane E. Lewin, Ithaca NY: Cornell University Press.
—— (2003) *Métalepse: De la figure à la fiction*, Paris: Seuil.
Herman, David (1997) 'Toward a Formal Description of Narrative Metalepsis', *Journal of Literary Semantics*, 26.2, 132–52.
Malina, Debra (2002) *Breaking the Frame: Metalepsis and the Construction of the Subject*, Columbus: Ohio State University Press.
McHale, Brian (1987) *Postmodernist Fiction*, London: Routledge.
Nelles, William (1997) *Frameworks: Narrative Levels and Embedded Narrative*, New York: Lang.
Pier, John, and Jean-Marie Schaeffer (eds) (2004) *Métalepses: Entorses au pacte de représentation*, Paris: Éditions de l'EHESS.
Ryan, Marie-Laure (2004) 'Logique culturelle de la métalepse, ou la métalepse dans tous ses états', in John Pier and Jean-Marie Schaeffer (eds) *Métalepses: Entorses au pacte de représentation*, Paris: Éditions de l'EHESS.
Wagner, Frank (2002) 'Glissements et déphasages: Note sur la métalepse narrative', *Poétique*, 130, 235–53.

JOHN PIER

METANARRATIVE COMMENT

Like the term 'self-conscious narration', metanarrative comment is an umbrella term designating self-reflexive utterances which address the act or process of *narration, i.e., comments referring to the discourse rather than the story (Chatman 1978; *see* COMMENTARY; REFLEXIVITY; STORY-DISCOURSE

DISTINCTION). Although the terms 'metanarrative' and 'metafictional' are closely related and often used interchangeably, they can be distinguished. While *metafictional* comments foreground or disclose the fictionality of a narrative (e.g., 'Of course, Paul, our hero, is just a character in a novel'), *metanarrative* comments do not undercut the fabric of the fiction (*see* FICTION, THEORIES OF). Rather, they are self-reflexive narrative references to the act of storytelling or to those elements by which a narrative is constituted and communicated (e.g., 'It is almost impossible to describe what happened in those pregnant moments'; Prince 1987: 51), i.e., narrative utterances about *narrative rather than fiction about fiction.

Despite the ubiquity of metanarrative commentary in both fictional and non-fictional narratives (e.g., *anecdotes and *urban legends), metanarrative comments have long been a lacuna in narrative theory. Until recently, little attention was paid to such metanarrative phenomena as digressions and other self-reflexive narratorial interventions. Research has largely focused on self-conscious fiction, concentrating on metafictional forms of narrative self-reflexivity, whereas metanarrative comments, which do not destroy the illusion of the narrated world, have hardly received any attention. Prince (1982), who devotes a subchapter to 'Metanarrative Signs', is an exception to the rule.

A number of recent articles have redressed the balance, putting the subject of metanarrative comment back on the map of narratological enquiry (Nünning 2001; Fludernik 2003). These studies have provided a descriptive analysis of the various formal, structural, content-related, and functional types of comments as well as a survey of the changing functions they have fulfilled in *novels from the seventeenth century to the present. Metanarrative comments function as authenticating, empathy-inducing, or parodic devices (*see* AUTHENTICATION; IMMERSION). They typically occur on the discourse level of narrative transmission, but intradiegetic character-narrators on the diegetic level of the story world may also thematise metanarrative aspects (*see* DIEGESIS; EMBEDDING; THEMATISATION). Similarly, the objects of metanarrative comments can either be situated in the story, on the discourse level, or on the paratextual level (*see* PARATEXT). Fludernik (2003) suggests subdividing metanarrative statements into metadiscursive, metanarrational, and

meta-aesthetic subtypes, drawing attention to the extensiveness and historical variability of the phenomenon.

References and further reading

Chatman, Seymour (1978) *Story and Discourse: Narrative Structure in Fiction and Film*, Ithaca: Cornell University Press.
Fludernik, Monika (2003) 'Metanarrative and Metafictional Commentary: From Metadiscursivity to Metanarration and Metafiction', *Poetica*, 35, 1–39.
Genette, Gérard (1980 [1972]) *Narrative Discourse*, trans. Jane E. Lewin, Oxford: Blackwell.
Hutcheon, Linda (1996 [1989]) 'Incredulity toward Metanarrative: Negotiating Postmodernism and Feminisms', in Kathy Mezei (ed.) *Ambiguous Discourse: Feminist Narratology and British Women Writers*, Chapel Hill: University of North Carolina Press.
Nünning, Ansgar (2001) 'Metanarration als Lakune der Erzähltheorie', *Arbeiten aus Anglistik und Amerikanistik*, 26.2, 125–64.
Prince, Gerald (1982) *Narratology: The Form and Functioning of Narrative*, New York: Mouton.
——(1987) *A Dictionary of Narratology*, Lincoln: University of Nebraska Press.

ANSGAR NÜNNING

METAPHOR

Metaphor is based in a non-literal analogical relation between two concepts or conceptual domains and can be important for narrative in three ways. Its best-known manifestation is as a deliberate figure of speech on the part of the *narrator or a *character. In such contexts metaphor plays a *rhetorical* role. For instance, Bob Dylan tells the story of the falsely tried boxer Hurricane in the protest song of that title, and says that American 'justice is a game'. Deliberate metaphor can be creative or conventional, and is closely related to the second way in which metaphor can be important for narrative. For metaphor can also simply be a conventional figure of speech that is part and parcel of everyday language. Thus, we often speak of life and love as a journey, argument and politics as war, and so on (cf. Lakoff and Johnson 1980). When metaphor is used without a deliberate rhetorical purpose, it plays a more generally *linguistic* role in narrative. The language of narrators and characters or agents in stories is replete with this kind of conventional metaphor, and has been analysed as such in stylistics, for instance with reference to *mind-style. Thirdly, metaphor can be a mode of *narration, and hence play a *structural* role in narrative with respect to arrangement and organisation (*see* NARRATIVE STRUCTURE; NARRATIVE TECHNIQUES). For example, James Joyce's *Ulysses* is a *novel that is grounded in a structural metaphorical correspondence with Homer's *Odyssey*, as is signalled by its title.

In each of these three manifestations, metaphor involves understanding one thing in terms of something else. In Bob Dylan's deliberate rhetorical figure, an unfavourable, critical comparison is made between dealing justice and playing games; in our everyday language use, a generally neutral comparison is made between all kinds of concepts and other, usually more concrete concepts; and in James Joyce's narrative structure, an ironic comparison is made between the everyday doings of Mr Bloom and the heroic exploits of Odysseus (*see* IRONY). Whether it is intended critically, neutrally, or ironically, the nature of metaphor resides in the non-literal comparison between aspects of two distinct domains of thought (cf. Fauconnier and Turner 2002). In that respect, it contrasts with *metonymy, which is defined by the figurative connection between two domains of thought that are part of a larger, encompassing conceptual domain.

Even though these three manifestations of metaphor in narrative offer so many opportunities for understanding one thing in terms of something else, it is a different matter whether every individual reader or listener actually does activate two conceptual domains for every metaphorical expression or structure in a narrative. There is some psycholinguistic evidence suggesting that interpreters do indeed process conventional linguistic metaphors in this way (cf. Gibbs 1994), but the evidence is certainly not complete or representative. Evidence regarding the processing of rhetorical or structural metaphor is even scarcer.

Much of the effect of metaphor in narrative will also depend on its form and the way it is signalled. The invitation to compare one conceptual domain with another is hard to miss in the case of Joyce's famous novel, where the title clearly flags the *author's intention (*see* INTENTIONALITY). Similarly, there are specific *genres of storytelling that, *as* genres, signal a conventionally metaphorical structure requiring a similarly metaphorical mode of understanding; relevant genres include

*allegory, *parable, and pastoral (cf. Lodge 1977). However, narratives may also have internal metaphorical structures, as when one story is embedded in another story as a metaphorical sign to the reader or a character (*see* EMBEDDING; MISE EN ABYME). If a character reflects on the metaphorical relation between the stories, the metaphorical structure will have a self-evident effect on the reader.

In rhetorical and linguistic uses of metaphor, metaphor may be signalled and expressed in different ways when a non-literal analogy is expressed as an extended metaphor or, for instance, as an *A is B* metaphor, like Bob Dylan's 'justice is a game'. Similes can also be seen as expressions of metaphor, and they may be plain or extended as well. Moreover, such formal realisations of metaphor are not restricted to literary stories. Here is an example of an extended metaphor from the sports pages about the English national football team that competed in the European Cup soccer tournament of 1996:

> If success in major tournaments is largely a matter of *waking up* at the right moment, then England can be congratulated on their sense of timing. Just as *the bad dream was threatening to recur*, Terry Venables' team *received their alarm call*. They should not, however, *expect a Continental breakfast in bed*.

The italicised words can be related to the figurative source domain that is used to understand the non-figurative target domain.

Apart from the signalling strategies for and forms of metaphor, there are other factors that affect the prominence and significance of its rhetorical and linguistic use. For instance, metaphors may become more prominent and significant (but they may also be overshadowed) when they are combined with other tropes, like irony or hyperbole. Metaphors also exhibit varying degrees of conventionality, creative metaphors being more striking to the addressee than conventional ones, which are often not even accepted as truly metaphorical. The discursive properties of metaphor, too, may be important for their prominence and significance, such as their position at crucial points in the story, whether at utterance level, paragraph level, or episode level (*see* NARRATIVE UNITS).

About the distribution of structural, rhetorical, and linguistic metaphor in various types and aspects of narrative, little is known. This is because of the lack of a reliable identification procedure and because research on metaphor in literary as well as everyday narrative is typically concerned with single cases, mainly coming from literary studies and anthropology (Cameron and Low 1999; Goatly 1997).

SEE ALSO: psychological approaches to narrative

References and further reading

Cameron, Lynne, and Graham Low (eds) (1999) *Researching and Applying Metaphor*, Cambridge: Cambridge University Press.
Fauconnier, Gilles, and Mark Turner (2002) *The Way We Think: Conceptual Blending and the Mind's Hidden Complexities*, New York: Basic Books.
Gibbs, Raymond W. (1994) *The Poetics of Mind: Figurative Thought, Language, and Understanding*, Cambridge: Cambridge University Press.
——, and Gerard Steen (eds) (1999) *Metaphor in Cognitive Linguistics*, Amsterdam: Benjamins.
Goatly, Andrew (1997) *The Language of Metaphors*, London: Routledge.
Lakoff, George, and Mark Johnson (1980) *Metaphors We Live By*, Chicago: University of Chicago Press.
Lodge, David (1977) *The Modes of Modern Writing: Metaphor, Metonymy and the Typology of Modern Literature*, London: Edward Arnold.

GERARD STEEN

METONYMY

Metonymy involves understanding one thing in terms of something else that is closely related to it, such as part for whole or producer for product ('a Picasso'). Metonymy can be important for narrative in three ways. Firstly, metonymy can be a deliberate figure of speech on the part of the *narrator or a *character, and hence play a *rhetorical* role. For instance, the narrator in Salman Rushdie's *Satanic Verses* condenses a whole series of consecutive *events belonging to one scenario by using the noun phrases that have been italicised in the following passage; these noun phrases function metonymically:

> All over the city, after *telephones, motorcyclists, cops, frogmen* and *trawlers dragging the harbor for his body* had labored mightily but to no avail, epitaphs began to be spoken of the darkened star.
>
> (Rushdie 1989: 12)

The unusual coordination of the telephones (standing for the people who use them) with the three groups of rescue workers and finally the trawlers signals the deliberate and rhetorical use of the metonyms for the purpose of striking condensation. The rhetorical use of metonymy can be creative or conventional, and is therefore closely related to the second way in which metonymy has a bearing on narrative. For metonymy can also simply be a conventionalised figure of speech that is naturally used in everyday language, and hence play a *linguistic* role in narrative. Thus, we conventionally substitute producers for their products ('a Picasso'), buildings for the institution ('the White House'), and places for events ('Waterloo') (*see* Panther and Radden 1999; Barcelona 2000). The language of narrators and characters or agents is full of this kind of conventional metonymy. The third way in which metonymy is important for narrative is as a mode of *narration; then it plays a *structural* role in narrative. Thus, the chronological and causal sequencing of distinct events in a *plot has been analysed as so many metonymic moves by the narrator, taking the addressee from one situation to another, with the situations constituting contiguous parts evoking a larger whole that is left unexpressed (*see* CAUSALITY; TEMPORAL ORDERING). A similarly metonymic function has been attributed to the narrator's switching from characters to settings to events themselves (cf. Lodge 1977).

The nature of metonymy resides in the connection between aspects of two subdomains of thought that are included in a more encompassing conceptual structure. In deliberate rhetorical figures such as Rushdie's, one relatively simple linguistic expression gives access to a more encompassing schema or scenario of which it is just one part (*see* SCRIPTS AND SCHEMATA). In our everyday language use, a connection is made between all kinds of concepts and other concepts that are related in one more encompassing knowledge structure. And in *narrative structure, aspects of the plot can stand for the whole projected series of events, or aspects of a situation can stand for the complete evoked situation (*see* SITUATION MODEL).

Metonymy is to be contrasted with *metaphor, which can be defined as a non-literal analogical relation between two domains of thought. Roman Jakobson has suggested that all discourse oscillates between a metaphoric and a metonymic pole of expression, and this claim has triggered a large amount of debate (see Bohn 1984, for an overview of the structuralist phase of this debate, and Dirven and Pöring 2002, for the cognitive sequel). Attempts have also been made, both in structuralist as well as in cognitive linguistics and poetics, to reduce either figure to the other, or even to a third (synecdoche) (*see* COGNITIVE NARRATOLOGY; STRUCTURALIST NARRATOLOGY). However, it seems more fruitful to regard metonymy and metaphor as distinct and examine how they may overlap and interact with each other in use.

Even though the three manifestations of metonymy in narrative offer so many opportunities for understanding something in terms of something that is closely related to it, it is a different matter whether every individual reader or listener actually does activate the two parts of the encompassing domain and performs the required inference. There is hardly any psycholinguistic evidence that supports such an inferential view of metonymy processing, and psychological work on *gapping, *descriptions of objects, and *spaces has not been conceptualised in terms of metonymy (*see* PSYCHOLOGICAL APPROACHES TO NARRATIVE).

Much of the effect of metonymy in narrative depends on the interaction between its linguistic, rhetorical, and structural functions, on the one hand, and its form and the way it is signalled, on the other. In the case of metonymic narrative structure, the invitation to connect one conceptual domain with another, either between two parts of the story itself or between the story and the projected *storyworld, is often hard to miss. Not much signalling is required because pragmatic demands of creating text coherence encourage addressees to make the relevant connections (Emmott 1997; *see* NARRATIVE COMPREHENSION; PRAGMATICS). In rhetorical as opposed to structural uses of metonymy, the use of a series of related metonymies, as in the case of Rushdie, may have a more prominent and significant effect than a single occurrence. Moreover, when one particular aspect of a story (such as a character's clothes or one of his or her body parts) is repeatedly used in a metonymic fashion, it can turn into a symbol that acquires additional meaning throughout the story (Riffaterre 1990). Even completely conventional metonymies, such as the use of 'kiwis' for people from New Zealand, may acquire more prominence and significance when they are repeated frequently, as in sports reporting (*see* SPORTS BROADCAST).

About the distribution of rhetorical and linguistic metonymy in various types and aspects of narrative, little is known. According to Jakobson and Lodge, however, structural metonymy may be assumed to lie at the basis of almost all narrative.

SEE ALSO: novel, the

References and further reading

Barcelona, Antonio (ed.) (2000) *Metaphor and Metonymy at the Crossroads: A Cognitive Perspective*, Berlin: Mouton de Gruyter.

Bohn, Willard (1984) 'Roman Jakobson's Theory of Metaphor and Metonymy: An Annotated Bibliography', *Style*, 18, 534–50.

Dirven, René, and Ralph Pöring (eds) (2002) *Metaphor and Metonymy in Comparison and Contrast*, Berlin: Mouton de Gruyter.

Emmott, Catherine (1997) *Narrative Comprehension: A Discourse Perspective*, Oxford: Oxford University Press.

Jakobson, Roman (1956) 'Two Aspects of Language and Two Types of Aphasic Disturbances', in Roman Jakobson and Morris Halle (eds) *Fundamentals of Language*, The Hague: Mouton.

Lodge, David (1977) *The Modes of Modern Writing: Metaphor, Metonymy and the Typology of Modern Literature*, London: Edward Arnold.

Panther, Klaus-Uwe, and Günther Radden (eds) (1999) *Metonymy in Language and Thought*, Amsterdam: Benjamins.

Riffaterre, Michael (1990) *Fictional Truth*, Baltimore: Johns Hopkins University Press.

Rushdie, Salman (1989) *The Satanic Verses*, Harmondsworth: Viking.

GERARD STEEN

MICRO-STORIE

Micro-storie (the term derives from Italian, where *storie* is the plural of *storia*) focus on an apparently insignificant historical *event which is nevertheless believed to deserve a detailed historical analysis. It deserves a detailed analysis not because of the nature of the event itself but because of what it exemplifies. Specifically, what a micro-storia might exemplify is the essential tensions, frictions, or *conflicts of a period; and it does so, above all, because it happens to be situated at the intersection of a number of important features of a historical period. In sum, micro-storie are narratives of small 'anomalous' events. The intuition is that the nature of a period is revealed to us by conflict and anomaly rather than in terms of structure or system. History most clearly reveals itself to us where it is at odds with itself. Examples can be found in Foucault (1994), Ginzburg (1980), and Zemon-Davis (1983).

SEE ALSO: historiography

References and further reading

Foucault, Michel (1994) *Moi Pierre Rivière, ayant égorgé ma mère, ma soeur et mon frère . . . : un cas de parricide au XIXe siècle*, Paris: Gallimard.
Ginzburg, Carlo (1980) *The Cheese and the Worms: The Cosmos of a Sixteenth-century Miller*, London: Routledge.
Zemon-Davis, Natalie (1983) *The Return of Martin Guerre*, Cambridge, Mass.: Harvard University Press.

FRANK ANKERSMIT

MIMESIS

The concept of mimesis (meaning 'imitation' or 'representation' in Greek, and designated by the word *imitatio* in Latin) has been a central paradigm in Western art theory since Greek antiquity. As an explicit or implicit general theory of artistic representation it dominated European artistic thought until the end of the eighteenth-century.

The first important discussions of mimesis can be found in philosophical discourse, namely in Plato's Dialogues (*Republic*, Bks. III and X; *The Sophist; Laws*) and a little later in Aristotle's *Poetics*. The divergent conceptions developed by these two philosophers have structured Western attitudes toward mimesis and also toward fiction.

Plato's theory of representation is founded on a strong opposition between mimesis and *diegesis*. Speaking about the stories and *myths, he distinguishes between:

a simple story (*haple diegesis*), in which poets speak in their own name without pretending to be someone else (as in dithyrambs for example);

a story by *mimesis* (imitation), in which poets speak through their *characters (as in tragedy and comedy), which means that they pretend being someone else;

a mixed form, which combines the two previous forms (as in *epic poetry, where the diegetic narrative mode of the simple story alternates with mimetically represented *dialogue) (*see* SPEECH REPRESENTATION).

Plato prefers pure narration and he discredits representation by *mimesis*. In Book X of the *Republic*, he excludes mimetic artists from the Ideal City. Taking as a starting point the famous example of the three beds (the bed as Idea, the bed made by the joiner, and the bed painted by the painter), he argues that mimetic representation (the bed painted by the painter), being only a copy of a copy, is cut off from the only real referent, the Idea (the bed made by the joiner being itself only a copy of the bed as Idea; *see* REFERENCE). But mimesis is also dangerous: this is due to its illusionist character and to the fact that it changes people's outlook not by rational persuasion but by emotive contamination (*see* EMOTION AND NARRATIVE).

The concept of *mimesis* developed by Aristotle in his *Poetics* diverges from that of Plato on four central points:

Mimesis coincides with artistic representation as such: *epic poetry, *drama, the art of dithyrambs, of flute and lyre, painting, choreography, and religious poetry are all mimetic (*see* DANCE AND NARRATIVE; PICTORIAL NARRATIVITY). The differences between them consist only in the manner and *mode of representation.

Mimesis is an ontogenetic universal: it is an inborn gift which manifests itself in every human being, starting with childhood (*Poetics*, ch. 4) (*see* NARRATIVE UNIVERSALS).

Mimesis is a specific form of cognition, which has its own legitimacy. Mimetic representation is even considered by Aristotle superior to history, because poetry expresses the general (that which could be), while history only expresses the particular (that which has been) (ch. 9).

Mimesis is a source of pleasure: in mimetic art cognition and pleasure go hand in hand (ch. 4).

During the Middle Ages, the concept of mimesis is not very prominent because art is mostly seen as an imprint of the invisible and eternal world (*see* MEDIEVAL NARRATIVE). But it starts playing an important role again during the Renaissance. Leon Battista Alberti for example considers imitation as the most direct way to beauty. During the age of Neoclassicism, it becomes the central concept of art theory. It generally has an important normative dimension as can be seen in Charles Batteux's *Fine arts reduced to a single principle* (1746): the principle of mimesis is used by him to ground a radical distinction between mechanical arts and fine arts; only fine arts imitate the Beauty of Nature.

At the end of the eighteenth-century, the normative and analytic usefulness of mimesis becomes more and more contested. Drawing their inspiration from Kant's *Critique of Judgment*, the German Romantics reject the mimetic conception of art, replacing it with the principle of productive imagination. Although the definition of art in terms of mimesis was not entirely discarded during the nineteenth- and twentieth-centuries (*realism, naturalism, and 'socialist realism' are all founded on a mimetic view of art), many modern and contemporary ideas about art have been founded on the romantic theory of productive imagination and have often developed an openly anti-mimetic stance.

To reinstate mimesis as a heuristic concept, it is necessary to disconnect it from its normative component. Although Auerbach, Gadamer, Genette, and Ricoeur – to name only some of the prominent modern and contemporary authors using or discussing the notion – define mimesis sometimes in widely different senses, they use it in a descriptive rather than a normative way. It also seems reasonable to restrict its sense to that of representational art drawing in one way or another on effects of perceived similarity. Even then, the notion still remains complex and difficult to handle. On what level should we anchor the similarity relationship in the domain of verbal narratives for example? If, following Searle or Genette, we anchor mimesis on the level of linguistic structure, i.e., regard it as language imitating language, the concept applies only to fictional counterparts of non-fictional *genres, because the only similarity relationship that can be drawn on that level is one that relates the fictional counterpart to a non-fictional genre. A fiction can indeed be an imitation of a *biography, *autobiography (or even of a non-narrative genre), while the converse does not hold. Although epistemologically stringent, this restrictive use of the notion seems at odds with the common sense assumption (expressed in Auerbach's very fruitful use of the notion) that narrative texts imitate reality and not only other narratives (*see* REALITY EFFECT).

If, on the contrary, one follows Ricoeur, who anchors the similarity relationship on the macrostructural level of the inferential logic of action – the logic of narrative *emplotment being

supposed to mirror the implicit inferential logic of action guiding our real-world experiences (*see* ACTION THEORY; SCRIPTS AND SCHEMATA) – then all narratives can be considered as mimetic. But this solution also encounters at least one problem: if both fictional and factual narratives are mimetic, what happens to the distinction between fictional and factual narrative? One way out would be to reactivate the Aristotelian distinction between general and particular *truth. But this could well seem too high a price to pay in terms of descriptive adequacy as far as the comprehension of fictional texts is concerned. So, the only remaining possibility seems to be to distinguish fictional and factual narratives in purely functional terms, i.e., in terms of different epistemic and pragmatic uses.

SEE ALSO: ancient theories of narrative (Western); fiction, theories of; immersion

References and further reading

Aristotle (1997) *Poetics*, trans. Malcolm Heath, New York: Penguin Books.
Auerbach, Eric (1953) *Mimesis: The Representation of Reality in Western Literature*, trans. Willard R. Trask, Princeton, N. J.: Princeton University Press.
Gadamer, Hans-Georg (1987) *The Relevance of the Beautiful and Other Essays*, trans. Nicholas Walker, Cambridge: Cambridge University Press.
—— (1993) *Truth and Method*, trans. Joel C. Weinsheimer and Donald G. Marshall, New York: Continuum.
Genette, Gérard (1988) *Narrative Discourse Revisited*, trans. Jane E. Lewin, Cornell University Press.
——(1991) *Fiction et Diction*, Paris: Seuil.
Plato (2003) *The Collected Dialogues of Plato*, trans. Lane Cooper, Princeton, N.J.: Princeton University Press.
Ricoeur, Paul (1984–88) *Time and Narrative*, vols. 1–3, trans. Kathleen Blamey and David Pellauer, Chicago: University of Chicago Press.
Schaeffer, Jean-Marie (1999) *Pourquoi la fiction?*, Paris: Seuil.

JEAN-MARIE SCHAEFFER AND IOANA VULTUR

MINDSCREEN

The term 'mindscreen' refers to a mode of representing subjectivity in *film narrative. Like first-person *narration (*see* PERSON), mindscreen originates in a *character's consciousness. Unlike a point of view *shot, which presents images seen through a character's eyes, mindscreen is the dramatisation of a character's thoughts, memories, fantasies, or *dreams. Mindscreen may refer to representations of a character's verbal narration (*Rashomon*). More centrally, mindscreens may show dreams (*The Wizard of Oz*), memories of past events (*Hiroshima, mon amour*), or fantasies and visions (*Ally McBeal*). Mindscreens may also be subjective sequences of ambiguous status (*8 1/2*).

The term itself was popularised by Kawin (1978); other film theorists, such as Bordwell (1985), describe this kind of narration more simply in terms of degrees of subjectivity and objectivity.

SEE ALSO: thought and consciousness representation (film); point of view (cinematic)

References and further reading

Bordwell, David (1985) *Narration in the Fiction Film*, Madison: University of Wisconsin Press.
Branigan, Edward (1984) *Point of View in the Cinema: A Theory of Narration and Subjectivity in Classical Film*, Berlin: Mouton.
Kawin, Bruce F. (1978) *Mindscreen: Bergman, Godard, and First-Person Film*, Princeton: Princeton University Press.

MICHAEL NEWMAN

MIND-STYLE

Roger Fowler (1977: 103) coined the term *mind-style* to refer to any distinctive linguistic representation of an individual mental self, whether of a *character, *narrator, or *implied author. The impression of a mind-style is usually cumulatively conveyed through consistent linguistic choices, which together cut the narrated world to a distinctive cognitive pattern (*see* STORYWORLD). Mind-style is typically a matter of the narrator's use of language to imitate in an implicit way the structure of the character's mental self. A striking case in point is this excerpt from Chapter 5 of William Golding's *The Inheritors*:

> ... The bushes twitched again. Lok steadied by the tree and gazed. A head and a chest faced him, half-hidden.... A stick rose upright and there was a lump of bone in the middle.... The stick began to grow shorter at both ends. Then it shot out to full length again ...

Here, the modern narrator uses the protagonist Lok's primitive world-view to transmit the story. From Lok's *perspective, a man's raising a bow is perceived as 'A stick rose upright', and the man's drawing the bow as 'The stick began to grow shorter at both ends'. Significantly, Lok's mind-style as conveyed by language does not come to the reader as narrated thoughts, not even as narrated perception (compare: He saw that...), but as the world-view adopted by the narrator to transmit the story. A character's mind-style can be conveyed either through straightforward 'imitative' *narration, as in the present case, or through a combination of 'imitative' narration and free direct (or indirect) discourse as in stream-of-consciousness novels (*see* SPEECH REPRESENTATION; STREAM OF CONSCIOUSNESS AND INTERIOR MONOLOGUE).

Some scholars have taken mind-style to refer especially but not exclusively to the writer's habitual way of experiencing and interpreting things (Leech and Short 1981: 188ff.). But Fowler himself is concerned in particular with a character's mind-style in third-person narration, and most of his followers apply the term either in the same way or focus on a first-person narrator-protagonist's mind-style as revealed by his/her specific way of narrating or conceptualising (e.g., Bockting 1994; Semino 2002).

A character's mind-style in third-person narration creates a narrative space where the *story-discourse distinction cannot hold: as the mental profile of a character, it belongs to the level of story, but as a means adopted by the narrator for transmitting the story, it also belongs to the level of discourse (Shen 2002). Precisely because of the discourse function of a character's mind-style, we get from the discourse a subjective picture of the storyworld related by a third-person heterodiegetic narrator – as in the Golding example quoted above.

Strictly speaking, mind-style is a technique confined to the verbal medium, forming a subtle means of characterisation in narrative texts. Whether mind-style could also be found in non-verbal narrative *media is a question worthy of further attention.

SEE ALSO: focalization; linguistic approaches to narrative; thought and consciousness representation (literature)

References and further reading

Bockting, Ineke (1994) 'Mind Style as an Interdisciplinary Approach to Characterisation in Faulkner', *Language and Literature*, 3, 157–74.

Fowler, Roger (1977) *Linguistics and the Novel*, London: Methuen.

Halliday, M. A. K. (1971) 'Linguistic Function and Literary Style: An Inquiry into William Golding's *The Inheritors*', in S. Chatman (ed.) *Literary Style: A Symposium*, Oxford: Oxford University Press.

Leech, Geoffrey N., and Michael H. Short (1981) *Style in Fiction*. London: Longman.

Nischik, Reingard (1991) *Mentalstilistik*, Tübingen: Narr.

Semino, Elena (2002) 'A Cognitive Stylistic Approach to Mind Style in Narrative Fiction', in Elena Semino and Jonathan Culpeper (eds) *Cognitive Stylistics: Language and Cognition in Text Analysis*, Amsterdam: John Benjamins.

Shen, Dan (2002) 'Defence and Challenge: Reflections on the Relation Between Story and Discourse', *Narrative*, 10, 422–43.

DAN SHEN

MINIMAL NARRATIVE

Formal definitions (Prince 1973) conceive of the minimal narrative as a sequence of two propositions that denote identical entities occurring in temporally and qualitatively distinct states (*see* EXISTENT). State 2 can thus be read as a *narrative transformation of state 1. For example, E. M. Forster's hypothetical story 'The king died, and then the queen died of grief' contains a minimal narrative about the transformation of the happy couple (state 1) into two dead lovers (state 2).

Genette (1988 [1983]) holds that 'The king died' already denotes two states and a transformation. Likewise, semiologists (Greimas 1987) would argue that Forster's narrative actually implies a total of four propositions ('the king was alive' vs. 'the king is dead', 'the queen is alive' vs. 'the queen is dead'). Moreover, these two *events are related in a causal manner indicated by the explanatory 'of grief'. Herein resides the quintessential hermeneutic surplus value that sets the minimal narrative apart from a mere ordered sequence of logical propositions: the narrative's overall meaning.

SEE ALSO: atomic and molecular narratives; causality; hermeneutics; narrative semantics; story grammars

References and further reading

Forster, E. M. (1927) *Aspects of the Novel*, New York: Harcourt Brace.

Genette, Gérard (1988 [1983]) *Narrative Discourse Revisited*, trans. Jane E. Lewin, Ithaca: Cornell University Press.

Greimas, Algirdas Julien (1987) *On Meaning: Selected Writings in Semiotic Theory*, trans. Paul J. Perron and Frank H. Collins, Minneapolis: University of Minnesota Press.

Prince, Gerald (1973) *A Grammar of Stories*, The Hague: Mouton.

Todorov, Tzvetan (1977) 'Narrative Transformations', in *The Poetics of Prose*, trans. Richard Howard, Ithaca: Cornell University Press.

JAN CHRISTOPH MEISTER

MISE EN ABYME

Mise en abyme has become the accepted shorthand for referring to any part of a work that resembles the larger work in which it occurs. The device is easier to illustrate than to define, and several well-known examples have become canonical: in painting, Van Eyck's *Arnolfini* portrait, in which a mirror within the painting reflects the painted scene from another angle (*see* PICTORIAL NARRATIVITY); in *drama, 'The Murder of Gonzago', the play within *Hamlet*, which dramatises key actions of the main *plot of the play itself; in narrative fiction, Poe's 'The Fall of the House of Usher' in which his characters' reading of the events of *The Mad Trist* is synchronised with the occurrence of similar incidents in the house around them; in popular culture, packages that include in their design a smaller picture of the package itself.

While the device of *mise en abyme* appears to be as ancient as art itself, found as readily in *The Odyssey* and *Oedipus Rex* as in the *nouveau roman*, the concept is not explicitly formulated until Gide's 1893 journal entry in which he hits upon the 'comparison with the device of heraldry that consists in setting in the escutcheon a smaller one "*en abyme*", at the heart-point'. The complete phrase '*mise en abyme*' enters the theoretical lexicon with Magny, who specifies among the device's aesthetic effects that of creating an impression of widening and deepening a work, of opening a vertiginous abyss ('abyme') before the reader. Magny, like Ricardou, sees a paradoxically double function for the *mise en abyme*: while the label emphasises its ability to disorient and disrupt the narrative in which it appears (often by appearing to break out of its containment), it can also serve to clarify and unify the containing work, revealing themes or anticipating narrative developments. Dällenbach painstakingly analyses these two categories (which he calls paradoxical reflection and simple reflection) into subtypes, and posits a third category of infinite reflection, in which the parallelism between the part and whole is multiplied by repetition and *embedding. Despite the notable quantity and quality of the work done on *mise en abyme*, the device continues to elude precise delimitation. As Ron ruefully concedes in his own important discussion, the fundamental criterion of resemblance virtually rules out such precision, as 'anything can be said to resemble anything else in some respect'.

SEE ALSO: framed narrative; metalepsis; reflexivity

References and further reading

Dällenbach, Lucien (1989) *The Mirror in the Text*, trans. Jeremy Whiteley and Emma Hughes, Chicago: University of Chicago Press.
Gide, André (1984) *Journals 1889–1939*, trans. J. O'Brien, London: Penguin.
Jefferson, Ann (1983) '*Mise en abyme* and the Prophetic in Narrative', *Style*, 17, 196–208.
Magny, Claude-Edmonde (1950) *Histoire du roman français depuis 1918: Tome 1*, Paris: Seuil.
Ricardou, Jean (1981) 'The Story Within the Story', trans. Joseph Kestner, *James Joyce Quarterly*, 18, 323–38.
Ron, Moshe (1987) 'The Restricted Abyss: Nine Problems in the Theory of *Mise en Abyme*', *Poetics Today*, 8, 417–38.
White, John J. (2001) 'The Semiotics of the *mise-en-abyme*', in Olga Fischer and Max Nänny (eds) *The Motivated Sign: Iconicity in Language and Literature 2*, Amsterdam: John Benjamins.

WILLIAM NELLES

MODALITY

The term 'modality' refers to the judgements of belief and obligation that speakers and writers attach to utterances. It covers those expressions which relate to the *truth (or otherwise) of what is being uttered and to the proposition, situation, or *event described by an utterance. It also encompasses the speaker's or writer's assessment of the degree of permission or duty that obtains in certain kinds of *speech acts. In the study of narrative, the analysis of modal structures and systems has been conducted largely within two different scholarly traditions. In the first, modality is defined in a specifically linguistic sense, with emphasis on the *interpersonal* function it plays in language. Modality in these terms has become an important tool for the stylistic analysis of *point of view. The second tradition situates modality in a more philosophically conceived framework, placing the emphasis on its capacity to shape narrative worlds (*see* STORYWORLD; TEXT-WORLD APPROACH TO NARRATIVE) and its potential to produce stories. In this paradigm, the study of narrative modality intersects closely with work in *possible-worlds theory. The account that follows explores both of these approaches to modality.

The key linguistic work on modality and narrative is Roger Fowler's model of point of view (Fowler 1996 [1986]). Fowler draws much of the stimulus for his model – and indeed, borrows the term 'psychological point of view' – from the *semiotician Boris Uspenskii (Uspenskii 1973). Fowler's main concern, however, is to situate the rather more impressionistic terms of Uspenskii's study in an explicit framework of language structure at the heart of which sits the concept of modality. The basic premise of this framework is simple: different patterns of modality characterise different *genres of narrative fiction. Fowler proposes a four-part model comprised of two types of *internal* narrative point of view (emanating from the subjective viewpoint of a particular *character's consciousness) and two types of *external* viewpoint (where narrative events are relayed from a position *outside* the consciousness of any character-narrator) (*see* FOCALIZATION; NARRATIVE SITUATIONS; NARRATOR; THOUGHT AND CONSCIOUSNESS REPRESENTATION (LITERATURE)). The internal types are defined both by foregrounded modality and by the presence of *verba sentiendi* which, following Uspenskii's terminology, are words denoting thoughts, feelings, and perceptions. Of a number of examples of prose fiction gathered by Fowler, the opening of F. Scott Fitzgerald's *novel *The Great Gatsby* offers a particularly useful illustration of the internal type at work.

Of the two external forms, the first type is marked by an absence of authorial modality. All markers of the interpersonal function are stripped away and replaced with categorical assertions, which is why this technique serves to engender an 'objective-realist' type of narrative style, a style where impersonal physical *description dominates at the expense of psychological development and interpretation (*see* REALIST NOVEL). The second external form, by contrast, embodies a heightened modality in which a narrator struggles to make sense of the fictional world. Such narratives are characterised by 'words of estrangement', e.g., *as if*, *it seemed*, and *it appeared to be*, which indicate a narrator's reliance on external signals and appearances to sustain a description. According to Fowler, pre-eminent exponents of the first style of external viewpoint are Gustave Flaubert and Ernest Hemingway, while the second type of pattern dominates much of the writing of Franz Kafka and Mervyn Peake.

The Fowler-Uspenskii model of point of view has proved attractive to stylisticians largely because it offers accessible and principled linguistic criteria with which to explore a variety of styles of writing. However, the model is not without theoretical limitations. It does not, for example, separate sufficiently the modal profile of a text from its mode of *narration and nor does it make any distinction between different *types* of modality. Missing from the model is the crucial distinction in the modal system between *epistemic* and *deontic* modality, where epistemic modality is expressed through linguistic constructions which refer to belief, knowledge, and perception, and deontic modality through references to the degree of obligation or permission that attaches to an utterance. These and other issues prompted Simpson to develop an expansion of the Fowler-Uspenskii model (Simpson 1993). He proposes three different types of *modal shading*, which distinguish between epistemic, deontic, and other less common types of modality. Broadly put, certain narrative styles can be delineated through regularly co-occurring patterns of modality. For example, the genre of *Gothic fiction is in part epitomised by extensive use of epistemic modality.

Moving now to philosophically grounded studies of modality and narrative, the pioneering work in this area is Lubomír Doležel's study of fictionality and possible worlds (Doležel 1976, 1998). Doležel argues that narrative worlds are partly organised through different modal systems, and in the formation of particular fictional worlds, certain modal systems can be arranged or manipulated in different ways. He identifies four such systems for the analysis of narrative: deontic,

epistemic, alethic, axiological. The deontic modal structure of a fictional world is formed by the concepts of permission, prohibition, and obligation. Thus, a story in which a deontic modality predominates is one that concerns moral and legal constraints and involves narrative action which is stimulated by the triadic progression of punishment, test, and predicament. A pre-eminent example of this category is Dostoevsky's *Crime and Punishment*, whose central character, Raskolnikov, 'deontically alienates' himself from the natural world's legal and moral prohibitions. The epistemic modal system, on the other hand, is predicated upon the concepts of knowledge, ignorance, and belief. The modal base of the epistemic narrative is the mystery or secret, from which develops the transformation of ignorance into enlightenment. More explicitly, an epistemic narrative works through an imbalance of knowledge, where certain events that have happened in the fictional world remain unknown to some or all of its characters. That imbalance is what activates the epistemic search to solve the secret or mystery. *Detective stories are obvious examples of this category, although works such as Conrad's *Heart of Darkness* and Dickens's *Little Dorrit* have strongly epistemic profiles also.

Meanwhile, the *alethic* system of modality is shaped by the concepts of possibility, impossibility, and necessity. Stories in which the alethic system is foregrounded often explore alternative possible worlds in which narrative agents impossible in the real world (gods, spirits, and so on) are assigned properties and perform actions in the fictional world (*see* ACTION THEORY; AGENCY). Often, what is impossible in the natural world becomes possible in its counterpart world, and agents from one narrative world may intervene in the events of another world. Lewis Carroll's *Alice's Adventures in Wonderland* provides a paradigm case of this type of story. Finally, the *axiological* system is constituted by the concepts of goodness, badness, and indifference. In stories where the axiological system is paramount, characters desire certain values and are consequently prompted into initiating action that will lead to an attainment of those values. The underlying structure of the most popular type of story with this axiological structure is the quest, which provides the modal base for a host of narratives, ranging from the expedition of the argonauts to typical love narratives. Doležel singles out Sinclair Lewis's *Babbitt* and Michail

Lermontov *A Hero of our Time* as examples of stories structured through the axiological system.

The study of modality as it relates to narrative analysis continues to develop mainly within the distinct traditions of analysis introduced above. There is no doubt that both approaches, the linguistic-stylistic and the philosophical, offer insightful models of analysis in their own terms, although exploring the common ground between the two remains a task for further research. Undoubtedly, a future synthesis of the two approaches will lead to yet more refined and subtle distinctions in the modal typography of narrative texts.

References and further reading

Doležel, Lubomír (1976) 'Narrative Modalities', *Journal of Literary Semantics*, 5, 5–14.
——(1998) *Heterocosmica: Fiction and Possible Worlds*, Baltimore, MD: Johns Hopkins University Press.
Fowler, Roger (1996 [1986]) *Linguistic Criticism*, Oxford: Oxford University Press.
Simpson, Paul (1993) *Language, Ideology and Point of View*, London: Routledge.
Uspenskii, Boris (1973) *A Poetics of Composition*, trans. Z. Zavarin and S. Wittig, Berkeley: University of California Press.

PAUL SIMPSON

MODE

As a narratological and literary concept, mode is an umbrella term that means different things to different theorists. Its usages represent two broad types: the local and the global. In the local use, mode refers to different types of discourse or representation within a narrative text. An example of the local conception is Genette's use of the French word *mode* as a section title in *Figures III* (usually translated as *mood* in English). Here the term covers phenomena such as frequency (*see* TIME AND NARRATIVE), direct and indirect discourse (*see* SPEECH REPRESENTATION), *perspective, and *focalization. For Helmut Bonheim, similarly, 'narrative modes' are represented by local phenomena, such as 'speech', 'report', *'description', and 'comment' (*see* COMMENTARY). In the global usage, mode is a label that describes entire categories of texts. In *genre theory, under the influence of Northrop Frye, 'mode' occasionally refers to macro-genres, such as what Goethe called the three 'natural kinds' of poetry: the Aristotelian triad of the lyric, *epic, and dramatic (de Bruyn 1993) (*see*

DRAMA AND NARRATIVE). These types encompass many culture-specific, conventionally defined genres. Genette (1992) invokes a similar opposition of mode to particular genres when he describes narrative itself as a 'natural form' or 'mode'.

The most influential interpretation of mode comes from Aristotle's *Poetics*. After defining poetry as an imitation, Aristotle writes in section 2 that imitations can be differentiated according to three criteria: medium (literally: imitating *in different things*), object (imitating *different things*) and mode (imitating *by different ways*). His concept of mode develops Plato's distinction, in book III of *The Republic*, between *mimesis and *diegesis. In the mimetic mode, according to Plato, the poet imitates the speech of characters, while in the diegetic mode, he speaks as himself (or as a *narrator, as contemporary narratology describes the case of narrative *fiction). Plato regards epic poetry as a combination of the mimetic and diegetic modes, and tragedy as a type of poetry obtained by removing all of the poets' words. For Aristotle, the two basic poetic modes become imitation by means of *narration, and imitation through the activity of agents – in other words, through dramatic enactment.

Whereas Plato's distinction between diegetic and mimetic representation is compatible with an interpretation that regards these categories as local *narrative* modes (since both are found in epic poetry), Aristotle's treatment suggests a global conception that presents narrative and drama as distinct modes within the larger set of poetry. In this model, the mimetic/dramatic is *not* a narrative mode. Contemporary narrative theory is still split between these two positions: some narratologists (Genette) restrict narrative to the speech act of a narrator reporting events, i.e., to the diegetic mode, while others (Chatman), conceiving of narrative as a medium-free cognitive construct, regard dramatic enactment and verbal representation as different modes of realisation of this construct.

If mimesis and diegesis are distinct narrative modes, one may ask whether the catalogue of modes stops there, or whether it includes other categories. Ryan (2004) suggests that if narratology is to expand into a transmedial field of study capable of accounting for musical and *visual as well as literary forms (*see* MUSIC AND NARRATIVE; PICTORIAL NARRATIVITY), or for *computer games and improve theater as well as for drama and movies (*see* FILM NARRATIVE), it must recognise a wider variety of global modes. The cognitive construct that defines narrativity can be brought to mind in the following ways (this list is a tentative one, and makes no claim to being exhaustive):

Textual (or external) vs. internal mode: In the textual mode, narrative meaning is encoded in material signs. In the internal mode, it is 'stored in memory and performed in the mental theater of recollection, imagination, and dream' (Jahn 2003). The internal mode does not presuppose a textualisation: we can tell ourselves stories in the privacy of our minds.

Autonomous vs. illustrative (or ancillary): In the autonomous mode, the text transmits a story that is new to the receiver. In the illustrative mode, the text retells and completes a story, relying on the receiver's previous knowledge of the plot. The illustrative mode is typical of pictorial narratives.

Receptive vs. participatory: In the receptive mode the recipient plays no active role in the events presented by the text. In the participatory mode the plot is not completely prescripted. The recipient becomes an active character in the story, and through this agency he or she contributes to the dynamic creation of the plot in the real time of the performance. The participatory mode describes computer games and improve theater (*see* DIGITAL NARRATIVE; INTERACTIVE FICTION).

Determinate vs. indeterminate: In the determinate mode the text specifies a sufficient number of points on the narrative trajectory to project a reasonably definite script. In the indeterminate mode, only one or two points are specified, and it is up to the interpreter to imagine one (or more) of the virtual curves that traverse these coordinates (*see* INDETERMINACY). The indeterminate mode is found in narrative paintings that tell original stories through the representation of what Lessing calls a 'pregnant moment'.

Literal vs. metaphorical: Whereas literal narration fully satisfies the definition of narrative, the metaphorical mode uses only some of its features (*see* METAPHOR). Recognising a metaphorical mode enables the theorist to acknowledge many of the contemporary extensions of the term 'narrative' without sacrificing the precision of its definition. The metaphorical mode is illustrated by musical narrative, or by narratives about non-individuated, abstract entities. (Cf. the 'narratives of race, class and gender' of cultural studies.)

SEE ALSO: ancient theories of narrative (Western); cognitive narratology; media and narrative; showing vs. telling

References and further reading

Aristotle (1996) *Poetics*, trans. Malcolm Heath, London: Penguin.
Bonheim, Helmut (1982) *The Narrative Modes*, Cambridge: Brewer.
de Bruyn, Frans (1993) 'Genre Criticism', in Irena R. Makaryk (ed.) *Encyclopedia of Contemporary Literary Theory*, Toronto: University of Toronto Press.
Chatman, Seymour (1990) *Coming to Terms: The Rhetoric of Narrative in Fiction and Film*, Ithaca: Cornell University Press.
Frye, Northrop (1957) *Anatomy of Criticism*, Princeton: Princeton University Press.
Genette, Gérard (1972) *Figures III*, Paris: Seuil.
—— (1992) *The Architext: An Introduction*, trans. Jane E. Lewin, Berkeley: University of California Press.
Jahn, Manfred (2003) ' "Awake! Open your Eyes!" The Cognitive Logic of External and Internal Stories', in David Herman (ed.) *Narrative Theory and the Cognitive Sciences*, Stanford, CA: CSLI Publications.
Lessing, Gotthold Ephraim (1984) *Laocoön: An Essay on the Limits of Painting and Poetry*, trans. Edward Allen McCormick, Baltimore: Johns Hopkins University Press.
Lubbock, Percy (1965) *The Craft of Fiction*, London: Jonathan Cape.
Plato (1963) *The Republic*, Vol I, trans. Paul Shorey, Cambridge, Mass.: Harvard University Press.
Ryan, Marie-Laure (2004) 'Introduction', in Marie-Laure Ryan (ed.) *Narrative Across Media: The Languages of Storytelling*, Lincoln: University of Nebraska Press.

MARIE-LAURE RYAN

MODERNIST NARRATIVE

'They've changed everything now...we used to think there was a beginning and a middle and an end', Thomas Hardy remarked, discussing recent fiction with Virginia Woolf in 1926 (Woolf 1985: 97). Later critics have confirmed his judgement, concluding that by the mid-1920s the narrative conventions of the Victorian and Edwardian periods had been thoroughly challenged and reshaped. As Hardy's remark suggests, this modernising or 'modernist' challenge generally affected form and structure more than subject (*see* NARRATIVE STRUCTURE; NARRATIVE TECHNIQUES). Modernist *authors were concerned with subjects including exile, the ethics of empire, the anonymity of urban life, shifting *gender relations and attitudes to sex, along with other new areas of twentieth century experience. But it is the new forms found for this experience which distinguish modernist writers from contemporaries who often shared similar concerns, but continued to express them in more conservative styles. Comparable renovations of structure and style appear in contemporary poetry, and in other art forms such as painting and *music (*see* NARRATIVE IN POETRY; PICTORIAL NARRATIVITY). Modernist innovations introduced by the writers discussed below, mostly anglophone, can also be compared with contemporary developments in the work of authors such as Marcel Proust, André Gide, Thomas Mann, Robert Musil, and Franz Kafka.

Consciousness and perception

Origins of modernist innovation can be retraced to the turn of the century. Its beginnings might even be located more exactly: between Joseph Conrad's *The Nigger of the 'Narcissus'* (1897) and the novella he wrote two years later, *Heart of Darkness*. In his Preface to the former, Conrad still emphasises conventionally realistic narrative potentials (*see* REALIST NOVEL), stressing 'the power of the written word . . . before all, to make you *see*' and to offer a 'glimpse of truth'. But in *Heart of Darkness*, his *narrator Marlow doubtfully asks his *audience 'Do you see . . . ? Do you see the story? Do you see anything?' Worrying that 'it is impossible to convey the life-sensation', Marlow tells his listeners with confidence only that 'you see me, whom you know' (Conrad 1995: 50). Such doubts typify modernism's epistemological uncertainties, and its scepticism of conventional *realism – of the possibility of reliably communicating 'life-sensation' or *'truth' independent of its subjective construction by an individual observer. Unlike the omniscient narratives of much Victorian writing – appropriate in an age more attached to the idea of an omniscient God – modernist fiction habitually mediates accounts of a perceived world through the idiosyncratic outlook of an individual perceiver (*see* NARRATIVE SITUATIONS; PERSPECTIVE; POINT OF VIEW (LITERARY)). Conrad himself continued to use a narrator in this way in later fiction such as *Lord Jim* (1900) and *Chance* (1913), as did his one-time collaborator Ford Madox Ford in *The Good Soldier* (1914). Reflecting admiration for what he called Conrad's use of a 'responsible intervening first-person singular', Henry James developed

a comparable use of certain characters as 'intense *perceivers*' – focalizers – to provide a 'structural centre' for early-twentieth century novels such as *The Ambassadors* (1903) James (1914: 275; 1962: 71, 85) (*see* FOCALIZATION; PERSON).

Authors early in the new century continued to develop tactics for reflecting the perception and consciousness of the first-person singular, also extending their use of symbolism, infusing thought and *emotion into the scene described (*see* THOUGHT AND CONSCIOUSNESS REPRESENTATION (LITERATURE)). Besides sustained authorial reports of his *characters' thoughts, D. H. Lawrence used *free indirect discourse extensively to represent their consciousnesses in *The Rainbow* (1915) and *Women in Love* (1921). Another, more decisive step – freer of the mediating *voice of the author/ narrator retained by free indirect discourse – appeared early in Dorothy Richardson's *Pilgrimage* sequence (1915–1967), in a stream of consciousness style presenting inner thoughts with the supposedly chaotic, associative immediacy of their actual occurrence (*see* STREAM OF CONSCIOUSNESS AND INTERIOR MONOLOGUE). Alternated with free indirect discourse and other inner registers, this kind of writing developed furthest in James Joyce's *Ulysses* (1922), though it was idiosyncratically extended to represent disturbed consciousnesses by William Faulkner in *The Sound and the Fury* (1929), and later used for similar purposes by Malcolm Lowry and Jean Rhys. Virginia Woolf employed comparable tactics of interior monologue in novels such as *Mrs Dalloway* (1925) and *To the Lighthouse* (1927), though she emphasised in her diary her particular reliance on the more conventional form of *oratio obliqua*, i.e., indirect discourse (*see* SPEECH REPRESENTATION). Woolf aptly summed up modernism's new commitment to focalization within character consciousness, as well as the preferences of her own writing, when she demanded in her essay 'Modern Fiction' (1919) that authors should 'look within' and 'examine . . . the mind'.

Temporality

'Modern Fiction' indicated another phase of modernist priorities in claiming that 'life is not a series . . . symmetrically arranged' (Woolf 1966: 106). In her diary, Woolf likewise renounced the 'appalling narrative business of the realist' in proceeding chronologically through a series of carefully arranged events, resolving to 'read Proust' and move 'backwards and forwards' instead (Woolf 1985: 138). Increasingly focalized within individual consciousness, modernist narrative came to rely more on what Woolf called in *Orlando* (1928) 'time in the mind' rather than 'time on the clock' (Woolf 1975: 69) (*see* TIME AND NARRATIVE; TEMPORAL ORDERING). Novels such as *The Sound and the Fury*, *Women in Love*, and *Mrs Dalloway* sometimes express explicit hostility to clockwork chronology. More generally, the 'nightmare' of World War I greatly diminished Victorian faith in progress, undermining conventional chronological development as a structuring basis for fiction, in favour of emphases on *memory and the significant moment, or 'moment of being', as Woolf called it (*see* EPIPHANY). Woolf, Joyce, Proust, and Lewis Grassic Gibbon all used their fiction to revivify memories of pre-war experience, often contrasted painfully with postwar life (*see* IRONY). Even for earlier modernists, the 'time in the mind' of memory offered an engaging freedom to move backwards as well as forwards. Such movement was facilitated by Conrad's and Ford's ostensibly oral narrators, free to present *events in the order of their recollection, rather than necessarily of their supposed occurrence – making *Lord Jim*, for example, as Conrad remarked in his 1917 Preface, 'a free and wandering tale' (Conrad 1971: 7). Joyce, Woolf, Faulkner, and Lowry similarly employed characters' memories to stitch into narratives of present experience – often of only a single day of consciousness – broad histories of past events.

Sources and values

Though new emphases on subjectivity and temporality developed progressively in early-twentieth-century fiction, they often did so independently of strong mutual influence among the authors concerned. James, Conrad, and Ford admired each other's fiction, but later modernists were often unacquainted, or unimpressed by each other's work. Unlike smaller, organised movements at the time, such as Futurism or Vorticism, modernism is a critical construct – a recognition by later commentators of a collective disposition in contemporary art and writing. The absence of much mutual influence among its creators encourages consideration of other sources for their shared priorities, in the broader thinking and theories of

their age (*see* PHILOSOPHY AND NARRATIVE). Several contemporary thinkers present themselves readily as potential influences. Friedrich Nietzsche emphasised the uncertainty of cognition and the constructed, all-too-human nature of facts and truths (*see* GENEALOGY; TRUTH). Sigmund Freud developed the kind of deeper interest in individual consciousness modernist narrative displays (*see* PSYCHOANALYSIS AND NARRATIVE). Henri Bergson and Albert Einstein, too, stressed the restrictive or artificial nature of clockwork temporality in ways Wyndham Lewis described as crucial influences on his contemporaries in *Time and Western Man* (1927).

Yet Freud's work in *The Interpretation of Dreams* (1899), for example, was almost simultaneous with the interest in 'dream-sensation' and in exploring inner reaches of the self in *Heart of Darkness*, and hardly available as an antecedent or influence for Conrad's writing. Contemporary theories and thinking are on the whole better understood in parallel with modernist narrative and its innovations, not as their cause: as comparable reactions, in another idiom, against new pressures experienced throughout the modern age. The deeper, irrational spaces of selfhood opened up by Freud's theories offered some escape from constraints imposed by rationalised, reifying forces of industry and urbanisation. Bergson's thinking, or Einstein's, likewise resisted – or seemed to – a temporality increasingly institutionalised around *travel, technology, and communications, or shaped by the 'time is money', production-line ethos of F. W. Taylor and Henry Ford. In resisting these pressures – summarised by Lawrence in *Women in Love*, and in identical terms by Georg Lukács in 'Reification and the Consciousness of the Proletariat' (1921) – modernist authors 'modernised' the novel in style and form, but generally, like Romantic writers before them, and like many contemporary thinkers, in reaction against the rationalising forces of modernity itself.

Modernist authors' free, imaginative reshaping, at the level of the aesthetic, of forces which they apparently believed could not be resisted in fact, in actual history, contributed to the negative judgements of their work which were sometimes expressed by later critics. Modernism has regularly been charged with elitism: with deliberately complicating and aestheticising the novel, as an art form, in reaction to a period when cinema, newspapers, and popular entertainment threatened to open narrative further than ever to mass consumption (*see* CULTURAL STUDIES APPROACHES TO NARRATIVE; FILM NARRATIVE). Additionally, critics such as Lukács, in his later writing, suggest that modernism's inward focalization and anachronous temporality are primarily forms of escapism; ways of evading history, political responsibility, and the immediate stresses of the contemporary world. To other commentators – Fredric Jameson, for example, or Theodor Adorno – the same innovations seem more worthwhile, offering utopian or imaginative compensation for qualities modern life itself had come to lack (*see* MARXIST APPROACHES TO NARRATIVE; SOCIOLOGICAL APPROACHES TO LITERARY NARRATIVE).

Art and language

Most commentators nevertheless agree on the general point Stephen Spender made in *The Struggle of the Modern* (1963): that for good or ill, modernism was forced to 'invent a new literature' in response to the needs of an age which was 'unprecedented, and outside all the conventions of past literature and art' (Spender 1963: x). The same need was emphasised in comments made by many modernists themselves, including Wyndham Lewis, T. S. Eliot, Woolf, and Lawrence. This need, and contemporary authors' awareness of it, often extended beyond commentary and critical writing to figure as a subject of their fiction itself, directly or indirectly. Aware of the necessity, and the difficulty, of shaping new artistic forms out of an anarchic contemporary history, modernist novelists were more than usually disposed to make art and its strategies – their own included – a central issue in their fiction (*see* EKPHRASIS; INTERMEDIALITY). In *To the Lighthouse*, for example, a character describes her artist's brush as one of the last available antidotes to a disorderly post-war world, and her comments have an immediate as well as a general relevance: split into three sections, her painting offers a figural analogue for the tripartite novel in which she appears. Other modernist novels – *Women in Love*, or Wyndham Lewis's *Tarr* (1918) – develop comparable self-consciousness, or self-reflexiveness, through their extended references to visual art and painting (*see* REFLEXIVITY).

The title of James Joyce's *A Portrait of the Artist as a Young Man* (1916) suggests a similar strategy, but the novel itself shows literary self-consciousness focusing instead, naturally enough, not on painting but on the medium of *fiction – on words and language. Their role and nature are often discussed by the novel's central figure; many factors encouraged this kind of linguistic self-consciousness in Joyce's novel and in the work of other modernist authors. Experience of empire, or exile, engaged several writers in sharp encounters with cultural difference, the arbitrariness of language systems, and their complicities with political power. Epistemological doubts and declining faith in a knowable world inevitably pressured any language which attempted to make it known. An age of expanding commerce and advertising created new anxieties about words and images as means of manipulation, rather than straightforward representation (*see* ADVERTISEMENTS). Women saw a need to reshape language in order to express more fully the particularities of female consciousness, long subordinated to the priorities of male vision and writing (*see* FEMINIST NARRATOLOGY). Many modernist authors – Lawrence, Woolf, Dorothy Richardson, Gertrude Stein, and Ernest Hemingway, in particular – both commented explicitly on relations between word and world and experimented with new forms of them throughout their fiction.

The concerns of *Portrait* were furthest extended by Joyce himself, initially in his protracted parody – not only of Homer's *Odyssey* – in *Ulysses*. Carefully reflecting the geography and city life of 1904 Dublin, *Ulysses* is still in part a realist novel, but its stylistic idiosyncrasies focus attention strongly on its own medium, and also, through parodic imitation, on the language of contemporary journalism, advertising, and *science. Interests in language figured more exclusively in Joyce's 'Work in Progress' in the 1920s and 1930s, eventually published as *Finnegans Wake* in 1939. In a way, this most challenging narrative experiment extended to new limits modernism's determination to look within the mind, creating a kind of dream language, articulating a stream of *un*consciousness. But Joyce's playful, inexhaustible, linguistic invention focuses attention, above all, on the written word, rather than its powers to 'make you *see*' or to reflect lived experience (*see* MIMESIS; REFERENCE). As *Finnegans Wake* itself suggests, Joyce's later writing is primarily just that: 'graphique', writing for itself, and not 'por daguerre'; not resembling daguerreotype, *photography, or any form of direct representation (Joyce 1971: 339).

As Samuel Beckett suggested in the 1920s, in this phase Joyce's 'writing is not *about* something; *it is that something itself*' (Beckett *et al.* 1972: 14).

Literary and critical consequences

Modernist narrative's growing preoccupation with language, form, and technique in the 1920s and 1930s had several consequences for later ages. In one way, through the work of Beckett and another Irish intermediary, Flann O'Brien, it led forward towards the 'age of fiction' Alain Robbe-Grillet defined when discussing his own work in connection with the *nouveau roman*: one in which 'invention and imagination may finally become the subject of the book' (Robbe-Grillet 1965: 46, 63). As he predicted, towards the end of the twentieth century a postmodern age grew familiar with writing about writing and writers, and with cognate concerns about fictionality, text, imagination, and the projection or reflection of worlds (*see* POSTMODERN NARRATIVE). In another way, modernist innovation, its complexities, and its formal self-consciousness helped to initiate newly serious, systematic forms of criticism, eventually leading towards the contemporary narrative theory whose scale and nature the present encyclopedia demonstrates. Writing in the 1880s, Henry James complained that very little serious criticism had been directed on fiction, encouraging a vague feeling that 'a novel is a novel, as a pudding is a pudding, and that your only business with it could be to swallow it' (James 1957: 24). This conclusion may scarcely have offered just desserts to Victorian readers, or to Victorian novelists, but the latter could fairly be said to be *less* interested than modernist successors in claiming their work as art, or in examining its nature, either within their novels, or beyond them. Like James, both Woolf and Lawrence added to the self-consciousness of their fiction by writing extensively about narrative form and technique in essays and commentaries: Woolf's 'Modern Fiction' and 'Mr Bennett and Mrs Brown' (1924) were particularly dismissive, like James, of Victorian or Edwardian predecessors. This commentary was matched by growing numbers of critical studies of recent fiction, in the 1920s, by authors including Percy Lubbock, Elizabeth Drew, Edith Wharton, Gerald Bullett, Edwin Muir, and John Carruthers. Much of this material celebrated or explained the new seriousness and complexity recent writing had brought to the novel – Lubbock, in particular, extolling the kind of artistic developments in the novel form initiated by James.

This expansion in critical interest, however, did not lead directly to the development of recent narrative theory. For most of the 1930s, 1940s, and 1950s, New Criticism focused attention on poetry and its local rhetorical and linguistic devices, rather than the larger-scale issues of form and construction more central to narrative analysis. Significantly, however, when narrative theory emerged strongly in the 1960s and 1970s, it was to modernist narrative that it most often turned for its examples, or as the object of its analyses (*see* STRUCTURALIST NARRATOLOGY). In an introduction to his influential *Narrative Discourse* (1972), Gérard Genette hesitates between defining his work as a long critical study of Marcel Proust, or instead as an outright work of narrative theory which merely uses Proust as its principal example. The analytic categories established in *Narrative Discourse* were at any rate closely configured around the areas of temporality and focalization on which modernist innovation concentrated, as described above. As Genette confirmed, of course, analysis of such areas is essential to the understanding of any narrative. Yet in developing more sophisticated relations between story and discourse – strikingly emphasising, as Genette puts it, 'narrating' over 'what it tells' – it was modernist fiction which first made this necessity inescapably apparent to readers and critics in the twentieth century (Genette 1980: 156) (*see* STORY-DISCOURSE DISTINCTION). Modernism ensured that the novel could no longer be treated as 'pudding', as a stodgy subsidiary of other literary *genres; rather, it was a form requiring new critical courses, or discourses, to be followed for its proper understanding. Modernist fiction reflected and resulted from a period whose historical stresses and accompanying epistemological anxieties enforced new, deeper interrogations of 'the power of the word' and of the ways it shapes and constrains constructions of the world in narrative. For later generations, its innovations remain not only a unique artistic achievement, but also a uniquely productive challenge for narrative analysis.

SEE ALSO: novel, the

References and further reading

Beckett, Samuel, *et al.* (1972 [1929]) *Our Exagmination Round His Factification for Incamination of Work in Progress*, London: Faber.

Bradbury, Malcolm, and James McFarlane (eds) (1991 [1976]) *Modernism 1890–1930*, Harmondsworth: Penguin.

Conrad, Joseph (1971) *Lord Jim*, Harmondsworth: Penguin.

—— (1995) *Heart of Darkness*, Harmondsworth: Penguin.

Eysteinsson, Astradur (1991) *The Concept of Modernism*, Ithaca, NY: Cornell University Press.

Genette, Gérard (1980 [1972]) *Narrative Discourse*, trans. Jane E. Lewin, Oxford: Blackwell.

James, Henry (1914) *Notes on Novelists: with Some Other Notes*, London: Dent.

—— (1957) *The House of Fiction: Essays on the Novel*, ed. Leon Edel, London: Rupert Hart-Davis.

—— (1962) *The Art of the Novel: Critical Prefaces*, London: Charles Scribner's Sons.

Joyce, James (1971 [1939]) *Finnegans Wake*, London: Faber.

Robbe-Grillet, Alain (1965) *Snapshots and Towards a New Novel*, trans. Barbara Wright, London: Calder and Boyars.

Spender, Stephen (1963) *The Struggle of the Modern*, London: Hamish Hamilton.

Stevenson, Randall (1998) *Modernist Fiction*, revised edition, London: Longman.

Quinones, Ricardo (1985) *Mapping Literary Modernism: Time And Development*, Princeton, NJ: Princeton University Press.

Woolf, Virginia (1966) *Collected Essays*, ed. Leonard Woolf, vol. 2, London: Hogarth.

—— (1975) *Orlando*, Harmondsworth: Penguin.

—— (1985) *A Writer's Diary: Being Extracts from the Diary of Virginia Woolf*, ed. Leonard Woolf, London: Triad.

RANDALL STEVENSON

MOLECULAR NARRATIVES

Just as molecules exhibit properties not displayed by the separate atoms that go into their composition, molecular narratives recount sequences of *events that no single cause serves to explain (*see* CAUSALITY). For example, accounts of complex historical sequences like the decline and fall of the Roman empire can be conceived as a chain of more basic narratives, but there is no single causal principle whose scope ranges over each of the 'atomic' narratives linked together in the chain. *See* ATOMIC AND MOLECULAR NARRATIVES.

MONTAGE

The term 'montage', at the broadest level, refers to the art of editing film. More narrowly, it refers to the set of editing techniques associated with the Soviet Montage filmmakers of the 1920s. These techniques emphasise dynamic and occasionally discontinuous juxtapositions.

Even within the Montage school, there were debates about the proper techniques and functions of editing. Pudovkin theorised montage as a tool for increasing the clarity and emotional effectiveness of *film narratives (*see* EMOTION AND NARRATIVE). He argued that the individual *shot has no significance in the cinema. The shot's significance is created by the editing, as shots are put together to build a *scene or sequence (1949: xiv).

Eisenstein criticised the approach of Pudovkin, charging that he treated shots as if they were bricks to be laid end to end. He offered an alternative, based on the concept of the dialectic: two conflicting images should collide, forcing the spectator to create a synthesis in his or her mind (1977: 37). Eisenstein proposed five different types of montage: metric montage (the lengths of shots are varied according to a mathematical pattern), rhythmic montage (the pattern takes into account movements within shots), tonal montage (editing is based on the dominant emotional qualities of shots), overtonal montage (both the dominant and subordinate tonal qualities are considered), and intellectual montage (juxtapositions cause the synthesis of intellectual concepts) (1977: 72–83).

The move to Socialist Realism brought an end to the Montage movement in the Soviet Union, but its ideas influenced cinema worldwide. In the 1930s, Slavko Vorkapich created montage sequences for Hollywood films. Similar to a *summary, the Hollywood montage sequence often compresses a series of *events into a short *time. Vorkapich softened the explicitly didactic montage techniques to allow them to serve more conventional storytelling ends.

Whereas most montage theorists located the essence of cinema in editing, the realist theorist Bazin located it in cinema's photographic capacity to capture reality in all its ambiguity. He criticised montage as an artificial and manipulative construction of reality, and advocated a style based in deep-focus cinematography and long-takes. Still, montage techniques remained influential, even among Bazin's disciples in the French New Wave, such as Jean-Luc Godard. In the 1960s, Godard's discontinuous montage techniques were taken to be a critique of Hollywood's smooth, transparent style. This re-politicisation of montage was short-lived, as New Wave editing techniques were quickly assimilated into the mainstream, eventually appearing in commercials and music videos.

Although montage is primarily associated with film, its aesthetic of discontinuous juxtapositions has affected other *media, such as literature and *photography (see INTERMEDIALITY).

SEE ALSO: realism, theories of; reality effect; visual narrativity

References and further reading

Bazin, André (1967) *What Is Cinema?*, vol. 1, trans. Hugh Gray, Berkeley: University of California Press.
Bordwell, David (1993) *The Cinema of Eisenstein*, Cambridge, Mass.: Harvard University Press.
Eisenstein, Sergei (1977) *Film Form*, trans. and ed. Jay Leyda, New York: Harcourt Brace.
Kevles, Barbara (1965) 'Slavko Vorkapich on Film as a Visual Language and as a Form of Art', *Film Culture*, 38, 1–46.
Pudovkin, Vsevolod (1949) *Film Technique and Film Acting*, trans. and ed. Ivor Montagu, New York: Bonanza Books.

PATRICK KEATING

MOOD (GENETTE)

Mood refers either to the type of discourse used by the *narrator (Todorov 1966) or to 'the regulation of narrative information' (Genette 1980). Genette's definition, which focuses on the type and amount of information conveyed in a text, has become the dominant one, with *distance and *perspective being the two chief regulatory modalities. The *narration can provide the reader with more or fewer details and in a more or less direct way (ranging from scenic representation of events/ speech to highly condensed summary; see SUMMARY AND SCENE), thus positioning itself at a shorter or greater distance from what it tells. The narrative can also regulate the information by choosing a particular perspective (ranging from an omniscient *point of view to the limited *focalization of a character). Genette has offered a vivid *metaphor to illustrate mood: the closer the viewer to a picture, the more precise the view; the less obstructed the viewer's vantage-point on the picture, the broader the view.

SEE ALSO: diegesis; mimesis; speech representation

References and further reading

Genette, Gérard (1980) *Narrative Discourse: An Essay in Method*, trans. J. E. Lewin, Ithaca: Cornell University Press.
Todorov, Tzvetan (1966) 'Les catégories du récit littéraire', *Communications*, 8, 125–51.

DAN SHEN

MOTIF

A motif is the concrete realisation of a fixed abstract idea, often spanning a complete *narrative unit. Motifs such as 'pilgrimage', 'murder', 'Cinderella', or 'crossroads' retain their paradigmatic identity across a wide variety of participants, actions, and settings. At the same time the motif is a 'moveable stock device' that appears in many periods and *genres. The content dimension of a motif comprises *character ('*doppelganger*', 'amazon') and action ('quest', 'marriage'), locality ('paradise', 'Gothic ruin'), and objects ('sword', 'rose'), temporal phases ('spring', 'night'), and dispositions ('madness', 'illness'). A motif usually builds around a nuclear action sequence which can take different forms and cover more than a single *event. Plot-intensive motifs stand at the centre of the logic of action (see ACTION THEORY), while less intensive motifs such as 'rose' or 'spring' remain peripheral and do not significantly affect a text's *narrative progression or *plot. The term 'motifeme' (Doležel 1972) is frequently used to refer to the specific deep-structural narrative function of a motif.

Owing to the inherently protean character of motifs and the mutability of their realisations they are notoriously difficult to identify and classify (Sollors 1993). However, on the basis of criteria such as 'level of abstraction' and 'preciseness of character and action', it is possible to distinguish motifs from other moveable stock devices such as 'themes' and 'plot kernels' (*Stoff*) (Frenzel 1974; Sollors 1993; Würzbach 1993) (see THEMATIC APPROACHES TO NARRATIVE). For instance, with regard to the relation between characters and their actions, the motif of 'death of both lovers' is more specific than the theme of 'love', but less specific than the plot-kernel 'Romeo and Juliet', which incorporates motifs such as 'family feud', 'combat', 'secret marriage', 'helper/adviser', 'poisoning', and 'misunderstanding'. Less specific motifs such as 'madness' and 'spring' may in fact equally well be categorised as themes. Motifs of graphic concreteness, such as the stereotypical 'rose' or motif-charged spaces such as 'crossroads' cannot, however, be understood as themes or plot kernels, although they may acquire symbolic force by being charged with additional stereotypical meaning.

*Folklore studies have been mainly concerned with the paradigmatic dimension of motifs, i.e., classification and cataloguing as well as the charting of distributions. As the central component of a *tale type* (Uther 2004), the motif is an important tool for establishing and ordering a corpus of texts. In literary studies, motif-oriented projects have tended to focus on the interpretation, combination, and variability of motifs, either in texts of individual *authors or of a literary tradition, and attention has also been paid to intratextual repetition patterns such as *leitmotifs (Trommler 1995; Daemmrich 1997). In *cultural studies, the wide distribution of a motif is generally seen as an anthropologically significant illustration of particular cultural forces within a certain context or period.

SEE ALSO: ethnographic approaches to narrative; function (Propp)

References and further reading

Daemmrich, Ingrid (1997) *Enigmatic Bliss: The Paradise Motif in Literature*, New York: Lang.
Doležel, Lubomír (1972) 'From Motifemes to Motifs', *Poetics*, 4, 55–90.
Frenzel, Elisabeth (1974) *Stoff- und Motivgeschichte*, Berlin: Schmidt.
Sollors, Werner (ed.) (1993) *Thematic Criticism*, Cambridge, Mass.: Harvard University Press.
Trommler, Frank (ed.) (1995) *Thematics Reconsidered*, Amsterdam: Rodopi.
Uther, Hans-Jörg (ed.) (2004) *New Types of International Folktales*, Helsinki: Academia Scientiarum Fennica.
Würzbach, Natascha (1993) 'Theorie und Praxis des Motivbegriffs', *Jahrbuch für Volksliedforschung*, 39, 64–89.

NATASCHA WÜRZBACH

MULTI-PATH NARRATIVE

A work of *fiction or video/film where the *audience or reader at specific points has to choose between branching alternatives in the text is sometimes called a multi-path narrative. Also known as 'interactive narrative', *'interactive fiction', hyperfiction, or 'branching narrative', these texts are not structured in a linear sequence from beginning to end, but allow exploration of a labyrinth constructed by one or more *authors (*see* ERGODIC LITERATURE). Such works can be found in many *media, from printed works (e.g., 'Choose-your-own-adventure' *detective books), to digital video installations, all the way to computer-based hypertexts or games where the user must select one among several branches in order to reach a goal or ending (*see* COMPUTER GAMES AND NARRATIVE; DIGITAL NARRATIVE). Some dramatic works, such as Ayn Rand's play *Night of January 16th* (1936), exhibit the same structure (*see* DRAMA AND NARRATIVE). Rand's play is about a trial where real members of the audience are picked out to be the jury. The play has two endings, depending on the jury's verdict.

There are three main types of multi-path narratives: works that branch only once (but sometimes in three or more prongs), often in way that reflects a moral choice or dilemma; works that present themselves as solvable puzzles or games where the user has to find the one right path among many misleading ones; and the fragmented work, where there is no right or wrong path, but where readers, lost in the labyrinth, have to construct narrative meaning as best they can.

A distinction should also be made between real and metaphorical narrative *labyrinths*. Texts such as John Fowles' *The Magus* and several of Borges' *short stories constitute metaphorical labyrinths, whereas real labyrinths – i.e., genuine multi-path narratives – are ones that contain actual, material bifurcations in the text. The best-known example of a literal fictional labyrinth is Michael Joyce's digital hypertext *Afternoon, a story* (1987), where the reader is presented with a *modernist collection of fragments, linked together in a hypertext labyrinth. In *Afternoon*, the main character is trying to gather information about his son and estranged wife, whom he may or may not have seen become victims of a car accident that same morning.

Afternoon gave rise to a whole digital *genre of fragmentary hyperfictions in the early nineties. The success of Joyce's hypertext in the academic community, as well as the huge popular success of its contemporary, the computer game *Myst* (Rand and Miller 1993), which also contained forking paths to be explored, was primarily due to its technical innovation and conceptual uniqueness.

But it remains to be seen whether this genre can continue to renew itself as a literary form.

The term 'multi-path narrative' also raises the critical question of whether these works are in fact *narratives, instead of artistic or playful games or experiments that *use* narrative fragments and devices, along with other mechanisms, for their own non- or para-narrative purposes.

SEE ALSO: narrative, games, and play

References and further reading

Fowles, John (1966) *The Magus*, London: Jonathan Cape Ltd.
Joyce, Michael (1987) *Afternoon, a story* (computer software), Cambridge, Mass.: Eastgate Systems.
Miller, Rand and Robyn Miller (1993) *Myst*, Novato, CA: Brøderbund.
Rand, Ayn (1936) *Night of January 16ᵗʰ*, New York: Longmans, Green and Co.

ESPEN AARSETH

MULTI-PLOT NARRATIVE

A narrative that follows the parallel destinies of a large cast of *characters, cutting a slice in the history of the *storyworld in breadth as well as in length. New *plot lines are initiated when intersecting destinies create new personal relationships, new goals, and new plans of *action, which interact in various ways with the previously establish plot lines. This interaction makes it very difficult to isolate discrete strands of plot in the entangled network of relations represented by the narrative as a whole. The principle of the multi-plot narrative was first theorised by André Gide and explored in his novel *The Counterfeiters* (1925). Today the most visible manifestation of the form is the *television soap opera. *See* NARRATIVE STRUCTURE (also: SERIAL FORM).

MUSIC AND NARRATIVE

'Music' and 'narrative' belong to different categories: while music is a medium, narrative is a 'transmedial' semiotic structure that can be realised in many *media (*see* SEMIOTICS; INTERMEDIALITY). Among the potentially narrative media, music – as opposed to, e.g., print-mediated fiction – would certainly not be regarded as the most natural. The categorical difference between medium and semiotic structure does not, however, preclude points of contact between music and narrative. These contacts are best described in terms of *intermediality theory.

'Music and narrative' can in fact refer to several distinct intermedial practices. Adapting the ternary categorisation devised by Steven Paul Scher (1982), these practices can be subsumed under the following headings: (1) the 'plurimedial' combination of music *and* a non-musical narrative medium, (2) the presence of, or reference to, music and musicality *in* a non-musical narrative medium, and (3) the occurrence of narratives and *narrativity *in* music. In the two latter cases the link between music and narrative can be the result of 'transmediality' or – in some cases – of 'intermedial transposition' or 'intermedial reference'. The scholarly discourses that deal with these variants of contact between music and narrative comprise intermediality theory, musicology, and narratology. While intermediality theory describes the forms and functions of contacts between music and other media in general terms, concrete definitions of musical phenomena and 'musicality' must be contributed by musicology. (Unfortunately, however, many musicologists are reticent in providing definitions that might be used beyond the confines of their discipline.) Similarly, narratology is the core discipline that must be consulted for workable definitions of *narrative and narrativity, even if much remains to be done to create a general (and generally accepted) theory of narrativity. There is as yet no consensus on the true extension of narrative, and *film and drama theory have only recently been accepted as parts of the project of a transmedially oriented *postclassical narratology.

In this entry, narrative will be conceived of in a broad sense, namely as a cognitive frame that can inform a plurality of signifying practices in order to meaningfully represent, and make sense of, temporal experience (Wolf 2002, 2003) (*see* COGNITIVE NARRATOLOGY; NARRATIVE AS COGNITIVE INSTRUMENT; TIME IN NARRATIVE). Narrativity is in addition considered to be a gradable quality whose constituents ('narratemes' [Prince]) and characteristic features can best be illustrated with verbal stories (be they factual or fictional) as prototypical narratives. But narrativity is, of course, by no means restricted to such stories. Key features include the general traits of meaningfulness, *experientiality, and representationality; more specifically, narrativity presupposes anthropomorphic *characters as promoters and experiencers of multiphase *actions that unfold in time, are causally interrelated, and develop towards some teleological outcome (*see* CAUSALITY; CLOSURE). Moreover, narratives typically build up some sort of *suspense and contain a 'point' which contributes to their *tellability.

While the basic features of narrative can be argued to have a high degree of transcultural and transhistorical constancy, conceptions of music seem to be much more dependent on historical and cultural parameters, at least as soon as one goes beyond the general feature of music as organised human-generated sound. Among the widely accepted typical traits of music is its tendency toward self-referentiality and, more generally, its pervading lack of 'hetero-referentiality'. As narrative is by definition representational and therefore hetero-referential, this restricts the possibilities of contact between music and narrative(s) considerably (*see* MIMESIS; REFERENCE).

Plurimedial combinations of music with non-musical narrative media

The simplest form of contact between music and narrative is the plurimedial combination of music with some other, more typically narrative medium that serves as a transmitter of narrativity in the medial composite. This is the case in vocal music, such as the *lied* or the song cycle (combinations of music and poetry), in musical *drama (notably in *opera, operetta, and musical), and in plays that make use of diegetic and non-diegetic music (e.g., in the form of songs and instrumental music in nineteenth-century melodrama). If film is also regarded as a narrative medium, both the silent film, which was usually performed with musical accompaniment, and the sound film, which characteristically comprises film music, must also count as plurimedial combinations that link music with narrative (*see* SOUNDTRACK).

Music and musicality in non-musical narrative media

The occurrence of elements suggesting music or musicality in non-musical narrative media is less uncommon than one would be inclined to think. This is because certain phenomena are frequently regarded as 'musical', although they are really 'transmedial' and not necessarily specific to music. Nevertheless their employment often provides an easy way to evoke the idea of music. These phenomena include the emphasis on sound and rhythm, which music shares with poetry, or devices such as *polyphony, 'contrapuntal' structures of similarities and dissimilarities, and the development of themes and 'variations', which can all be found in music as well as in *novels, drama, or film (*see* LEITMOTIF). As is the case with all transmedial phenomena, seeing correspondences across medial boundaries is here predominantly the result of particular interpretive perspectives. Often enough, these perspectives lead to hackneyed or thoughtless *metaphors and jargon ('the musicality of Shakespeare's dramatic poetry' etc.), yet they can also reveal enlightening relations between narrative and music. Thus, Raymond Queneau's ninety-nine *narrative versions of the same banal event which form *Exercices de style* is a *tour de force* of the transmedial device of variation. Yet, owing to its usual anchorage in music, 'variation' can here also be considered a form of contact between music and narrative, even if there is no evidence that a reference to music is part of the signification of the book. In this case becoming aware of the analogy with music as a medium that is often considered an essentially formal one can enhance the appreciation of the author's formal bravura.

A second way in which music or musicality can occur in other, typically narrative media would be through intermedial transposition. Because of the lack of hetero-referentiality of music (in particular instrumental music), transpositions of musical works into non-musical narrative media remain a mere theoretical possibility. It is moreover restricted to hybrid musical forms such as the opera, which can in principle be transposed into a novel or drama.

A much more common form of music occurring in another, narrative medium is intermedial reference. The simplest variant, explicit reference or *thematisation, occurs whenever, e.g., in film, drama, or narrative fiction, a musical composition is verbally described, a composer and his or her life are mentioned, or musical aesthetics are discussed.

More elaborate possibilities exist in the field of implicit references, which can be illustrated with fictional examples referring to music. A still rather basic option is the suggestion of music by partial *quotation of a musico-verbal composite such as a song. When a text quotes, or even just alludes to, the verbal text of a well-known song, the accompanying music may become present at least for some readers' inner ears.

A second option is the evocation of musical effects in the reader, e.g., the mood of a specific composition or the feelings of harmony, unrest, etc. elicited by it. This can be achieved through a *description of the visual or narrative analogies which the listening process triggers in the mind of a character or of the *narrator (as opposed to the technical discussion of a musical composition, a device which would border on the 'thematisation' of music).

The third and most challenging option of implicitly referring to music is the creation of some sort of formal analogy either by adapting a narrative text to the structure of a particular musical form or composition (resulting in 'structural analogies'; see NARRATIVE STRUCTURE), or by shaping the narrative signifiers in such a manner that their acoustic potential is foregrounded in what has been called 'word music' (Scher 1982). However, such forms of 'musicalising fiction' as well as the aforementioned musical evocations always require some explicit thematisation in order to be decipherable as intermedial references. These thematisations can take the form of a simple musical title for a text, or of the foregrounding of music in discussions among fictional characters. The distance between literature and music explains why verbal experiments with the formal imitation of music have always been marginal phenomena. Yet after some isolated experiments in Romantic and post-Romantic literature (such as Ludwig Tieck's *Die verkehrte Welt* or Thomas De Quincey's 'Dream Fugue'), 'musicalising' tendencies have become more outspoken since modernism (witness, e.g., Thomas Mann's *Tonio Kröger* and *Der Zauberberg*, James Joyce's 'Sirens' episode in *Ulysses*, Virginia Woolf's 'The String Quartet', and Aldous Huxley's *Point Counter Point*; see MODERNIST NARRATIVE). These tendencies continue well into postmodernism, with Anthony Burgess's *Napoleon Symphony*, Nancy Huston's *Les Variations Goldberg*, and, most recently, Gabriel Josipovici's *Goldberg: Variations* as outstanding examples (see POSTMODERN NARRATIVE).

Narrative and narrativity in music

Among the variants of the reverse case, namely the occurrence of narrative and narrativity in music, the transposition of originally non-musical narratives into a *hybrid genre such as the musical or the opera is a relatively unproblematic form. Verdi's *Macbeth*, Mozart's *Le Nozze di Figaro* (an operatic version of Beaumarchais's *Le mariage de Figaro*), or Richard Meale's transposition of Patrick White's Australian 'national epic', the novel *Voss*, into an opera, all belong to this category (see EPIC; NOVEL, THE). In these cases the transparency of the intermedial relation resides in the fact that the respective narratives are recognisable in the non-musical, i.e., verbal, component of the operas. This form of 'narrative and music' is basically a variant of plurimedial combination whose specificity resides in the genetic link to a non-musical narrative. If an opera based on a play incorporates entire stretches of *dialogue from the original, the device of reference through partial 'reproduction' is also involved.

Other relations between music and narrative involving 'pure' music (i.e., music without words) are difficult to categorise and are moreover problematic owing to the fact that music resists narrative's referential and representational dimensions. Nevertheless, musical appropriations of narratives and narrativity have been attempted both in musical practice and in musicological discourse. The best-known examples of these appropriations can be found in the domain of nineteenth- and early-twentieth-century programme music and *symphonische Dichtung* (symphonic poems). In some cases, where a relation to a pre-existing narrative is suggested, as in Liszt's *Dante Symphony*, which refers to the *Divina Commedia*, one can speak of borderline cases lying somewhere between partial intermedial transpositions and intermedial reference. In other cases, where a narrative programme has been invented for the purpose, as in the five episodes from a fictitious artist's life in Berlioz's *Symphonie fantastique*, it is safe to speak of an intermedial reference to an imaginary narrative script.

A ground-breaking example of the latter variant is Beethoven's sixth symphony ('The Pastoral Symphony'), which is often regarded as the first major piece of symphonic programme music. In this work, Beethoven uses several variants of narrative reference, the most obvious being the rudimentary narrative programme in the titles of the individual movements ('Awakening of joyful sentiments on arrival in the country', 'Scene at a brook', etc.). These explicit references are 'fleshed out' by implicit references in the music itself, in particular by attempts at musically imitating acoustic phenomena (such as rustic *dances, birdsong, wind, flashes of lightning and thunder) and by evoking emotional developments such as when the agitation of the thunderstorm is followed by a calm idyllic scene suggesting the grateful sentiments of anonymous experiencers. All this is chronologically and in part even causally ordered and follows a trajectory which, after encountering certain obstacles and 'problems', concludes in a calm and blissful closure, constituting a variant of Beethoven's famous motto *per aspera ad astra*, which obviously possesses considerable narrative potential in itself (*see* CONFLICT; PLOT; TEMPORAL ORDERING).

Following and in fact intensifying Beethoven's cautious attempts at narrativising 'absolute music' (*see* NARRATIVISATION), nineteenth-century critics such as Adolf Berhard Marx and Alexandre Oulibicheff approached instrumental music as actual narratives. Later examples of similar narrative 'readings' can be found in Arnold Schering's and Heinrich Schenker's critical work of the 1930s (see Burnham 1995), as well as in Theodor Adorno's 'novelistic' interpretation of Mahler's symphonies. In the past few decades musical narrativity has again found considerable attention in musicology. This development was mainly triggered by Anthony Newcomb's controversial essay 'Schumann and Late-Eighteenth-Century Narrative Strategies'. In this essay, which met fierce criticism by John Neubauer, Lawrence Kramer, and others, Newcomb tries to apply elements of the narratology of Vladimir Propp, Paul Ricoeur, and others to instrumental music and argues that the impression of narrativity in Schumann's music stems from his deviation from conventions of 'musical plots'.

This discussion of the narrativisation of music raises two crucial questions: To what extent can instrumental music fulfil the narrative claims made in programmatic titles or musicological readings? And can music be a narrative medium at all? (The latter question is clearly a special case of the question of whether music can have extramusical meaning.) The scepticism voiced by Nattiez and others seems to be largely justified, as the medial constraints imposed on music (particularly instrumental music) distinctly set it apart from typical narratives in many respects. The lack of precise hetero-referentiality prevents music from telling stories with concrete settings, characters, and *events, and the impossibility of indicating fictionality or other modes of reality (such as *virtuality or potentiality) prevents it from being able to differentiate between levels of reality (*see* FICTION, THEORIES OF; MODALITY). The same is true of temporal levels and any musical indications of past, present, and future scenarios. In addition, music cannot generate intersubjectively shared mental pictures and other forms of imagination that would transcend a strictly personal quality. It is therefore unable to produce the effects of 'aesthetic illusion' as an impression of being re-centred in a *possible world, a frequent effect created by genuine narrative media (*see* IMMERSION). Rather than letting its signs represent some pre-existing hetero-referential story, the principle of organisation of musical signs is almost exclusively intramusical and self-referential. This leads to a propensity to 'verbatim' repetitions, which creates an additional structural discrepancy between music and the linear, usually non-repetitive development of narratives.

Yet indubitably music also possesses crucial qualities which are typical of narrativity. Among these qualities is, above all, the temporality of musical progression, which includes the potential of teleology. In addition, there is the possibility of suggesting experientiality. Through different *'voices' or instruments and their combination, juxtaposition, or opposition music can evoke something like individual 'characters' (through individual themes but also through the voices of polyphonic compositions); it can also suggest 'events', conflicts, and the overcoming of obstacles indicated by, for instance, surprising developments, sudden rests, and climactic progressions. Further, music can create suspense by disharmonious passages or excursions into foreign keys which before coming to harmonious resolutions or returning to the home key. In some cases music can even transcend its typical nonreferentiality, particularly through what has been called 'aural mimicry' (Abbate 1991: 33). All in all it can in fact be claimed that music, in spite of its medial constraints, has the potential of becoming an 'aural ideogram of experience' (Orlov 1981: 137) and thus possesses some isomorphy with typical features of narratives.

However, all these similarities and isomorphisms are restricted to general formal elements. They act like clues that have the potential to elicit a narrative response but are in any case no more than empty slots which must be filled by the recipients with concrete settings, characters, and events on the basis of experience, imagination, and above all the readiness to apply a narrative frame in the first place. Obviously, the range of individual variation is much broader in the perception of music than in other, more typically narrative media and in many cases borders on the arbitrary, in particular if some preconditions are not fulfilled. Among these are a) a certain extension of the musical composition, which should be long enough to permit the impression of a narrative trajectory; b) a relatively low degree of 'verbatim' repetition and schematic fulfilment of a musical form; c) a high degree of unexpected 'dramatic' tension, contrast, and deviation from pre-established patterns (Micznik 2001); and d) the existence of structures that enable the listener to imagine an 'action' and 'characters'. Yet even if all of these preconditions are fulfilled, one must be aware of the fact that music cannot compel a narrative reading with the same urgency as, for instance, a *short story. The recipient's inclination to narrativise or not to narrativise music, and the cultural context which conditions such inclinations, are therefore factors that bear as decisively on narrative 'readings' of music as do compositional details. The importance of these factors also explains why the major narrativisations of instrumental music had their inception in the nineteenth-century. It was in this century that large-scale narrativisations of subjects like 'natural history', biology, *historiography, *philosophy, and *psychoanalysis were attempted (see McClary 1997), and the narrativisation of instrumental music followed as a matter of course. At the same time the growing importance of the sonata form with its opposition of two themes and different keys and its ternary structure, which was easily assimilable to an Aristotelian model of *narrative progression, invited the narrativisation of compositional *genres that employed this form, notably the symphony and the solo concerto.

In sum, music can be assumed to participate in narrativity as a transmedial means of organising signs – although with many restrictions. Any narrative 'reading' of a musical composition relies on the presence of narrative clues in the music itself, but at the same time it is also strongly dependent on the cooperation of the listener, whose interpretive strategy is in turn conditioned by cultural factors. In view of what has been said one can certainly not claim that musical compositions, let alone instrumental music or music in general, simply are narrative. Nevertheless, given the right type of composition (a long nineteenth-century symphony, say, as opposed to a short twentieth-century dodecaphonous piece), music can elicit a quasi-narrative response. 'Music and narrative' thus appear to be strange, but not entirely incompatible, bedfellows.

SEE ALSO: pictorial narrativity

References and further reading

Abbate, Carolyn (1991) *Unsung Voices: Opera and Musical Narrative in the Nineteenth-Century*, Princeton: Princeton University Press.

Adorno, Theodor (1960) *Mahler: Eine musikalische Physiognomik*, Frankfurt: Suhrkamp.

Brown, Calvin S. (1987 [1948]) *Music and Literature: A Comparison of the Arts*, Hanover: University Press of New England.

Burnham, Scott (1995) *Beethoven Hero*, Princeton: Princeton University Press.

Kramer, Lawrence (1991) 'Musical Narratology: A Theoretical Outline', *Indiana Theory Review*, 12, 141–62.

McClary, Susan (1997) 'The Impromptu That Trod on a Loaf: or How Music Tells Stories', *Narrative* 5, 20–35.

Micznik, Vera (2001) 'Music and Narrative Revisited: Degrees of Narrativity in Beethoven and Mahler', *Journal of the Royal Musical Association*, 126, 193–249.

Nattiez, Jean-Jacques (1990) 'Can One Speak of Narrativity in Music?', *Journal of the Royal Musical Association*, 115.2, 240–57.

Neubauer, John (1997) 'Tales of Hoffmann and Others on Narrativization of Instrumental Music', in Ulla-Britta Lagerroth, Hans Lund, and Erik Hedling (eds) *Interart Poetics: Essays on the Interrelations of the Arts and Media*, Amsterdam: Rodopi.

Newcomb, Anthony (1987) 'Schumann and Late Eighteenth-Century Narrative Strategies', *19th-Century Music*, 11, 164–74.

Orlov, Henry (1981) 'Toward a Semiotics of Music', in Wendy Steiner (ed.) *The Sign in Music and Literature*, Austin: University of Texas Press.

Prince, Gerald (1999) 'Revisiting Narrativity', in Walter Grünzweig and Andreas Solbach (eds) *Grenzüberschreitungen: Narratologie im Kontext/Transcending Boundaries: Narratology in Context*, Tübingen: Narr.

Scher, Steven Paul (1982) 'Literature and Music', in Jean-Pierre Barricelli and Joseph Gibaldi (eds) *Interrelations of Literature*, New York: MLA.

Wolf, Werner (1999) *The Musicalization of Fiction: A Study in the Theory and History of Intermediality*, Amsterdam: Rodopi.

—— (2002) 'Das Problem der Narrativität in Literatur, bildender Kunst und Musik: Ein Beitrag zu einer intermedialen Erzähltheorie', in Ansgar Nünning and

Vera Nünning (eds) *Erzähltheorie transgenerisch, intermedial, interdisziplinär*, Trier: WVT.
—— (2003) 'Narrative and Narrativity: A Narratological Reconceptualization and Its Applicability to the Visual Arts', *Word & Image*, 19, 180–97.

WERNER WOLF

MYTH: THEMATIC APPROACHES

A myth is a *narrative with a supernatural element, that has been told over and over again with variations. It has an unusually strong potential for meaning and an unusually strong potential for emotional impact (*see* EMOTION AND NARRATIVE).

Myth as narrative implies both mythic protagonists as well as *actions (*see* CHARACTER). For instance, the labyrinth, for all its symbolic or *archetypal resonance, is not a myth in and of itself; it enters the realm of myth when it becomes the locus of the actions of such mythic protagonists as Dedalus, Theseus, Ariadne, and the Minotaur.

A myth, in the original sense of the term, is a narrative with a supernatural element. Thus the myth of Don Juan brings together the story of a seducer of women with a statue who miraculously comes to life; in the case of the myth of Oedipus, the narrative could not proceed without the pronouncements of the Delphic oracle. Flaubert's *Madame Bovary* may seem to constitute a figure of mythic fascination, but the narrative lacks a supernatural element and can hardly be called a myth. Oscar Wilde's *The Picture of Dorian Gray*, by contrast, creates a modern myth, as does Robert Louis Stevenson's *The Strange Case of Doctor Jekyll and Mr. Hyde*, since in both cases there is a supernatural element that is linked with the narrative in a highly memorable way. This supernatural element is often linked with religious belief, as in the myth of the Fall in Christianity. For religious believers such a myth is true, literally or symbolically; for those considering the myth from outside it is not, although it may be considered meaningful and significant in other ways. The term 'myth' has been extended in recent times to designate something that is not true (for example, the myth of American invulnerability) or ideas and beliefs that need to be looked at critically (for example, myths of masculinity) (*see* TRUTH).

A myth, since it is told and retold in various ways, is often known in several forms or variant versions. This is especially true of *oral cultures, where constant retelling promotes original variants, and less so in cultures in which a written version may tend to preserve one particular version of the myth to the detriment of others (*see* NARRATIVE VERSIONS). But even in the literary tradition there is a pronounced tendency to retell myths in significantly different ways. Thus Faust is damned in Marlowe's play *Doctor Faustus* (as he was in the original *Faustbuch*), but in Goethe's *Faust, Part II* he is saved.

Myths have a strong potential for meaning, but this meaning is not directly imposed as it would be in the case of *allegory. Controversy has raged over the nature of this meaning, with some, like Roland Barthes in his *Mythologies*, insisting on the ideological function of myth as reinforcing the symbolic order and its social conventions, and others (such as Joseph Campbell) stressing myth's subversion of the symbolic order, by means of which it encourages people to live more deeply and more creatively (*see* IDEOLOGY AND NARRATIVE). This latter function is what C. G. Jung called 'compensation', the result of the collective unconscious providing an antidote to one-sided cultural prejudices and attitudes. It seems plausible to assume that a myth could operate in both ways simultaneously. Thus the myth of the wife who saves her husband from death, as represented in Euripides' drama *Alcestis*, could pander to the patriarchal prejudice that a man's life is worth more than a woman's; but it could also reveal a specifically feminine form of heroism ignored or marginalised by the culture, by establishing Alcestis as the female counterpart of the male *hero Herakles (*see* GENDER STUDIES). In similar fashion, in the myth of Savitri in India the story of the heroine's outwitting the god of death Yama in order to save her husband's life could reinforce the ideology of female subordination but also could subvert that ideology through its compensatory depiction of a determined and courageous trickster heroine.

The history of psychoanalytic interpretation of myth, starting with Freud's interpretation of the Oedipus myth, is rich and varied (*see* PSYCHO-ANALYSIS AND NARRATIVE). Jungian psychology has been particularly fascinated by the compensatory function of myth, and focuses often on the analogies between *dream imagery and mythology.

Emotional impact may be said to be characteristic of the effect of myths, and so purely intellectual analyses of myth in terms of meaning (such as those of Claude Lévi-Strauss) may seem not entirely satisfying (*see* MYTHEME; STRUCTUR-ALIST NARRATOLOGY). Myth, as an archaic and pre-conceptual mode of thought based on story rather than on idea, is 'emotional thinking' in both a positive and negative sense. One only comes to appreciate the power of myth when this emotional impact is factored into the equation. For example, the myth of Tristan and Iseult, which flourished at the court of Eleanor of Aquitaine and her daughters in the eleventh and twelfth centuries, expressed an ideal of romantic love 'stronger than death' that resonates emotionally in modern culture, as in Wagner's *opera *Tristan und Isolde.*

Are *fairy tales and *folktales also myths? This vexing question cannot be resolved definitively, but the general definition of myth given above would seem to apply to these forms of narrative as well. For instance, as regards potential for meaning, Marie-Louise von Franz has demonstrated that fairy tales constitute a veritable compendium of archetypal meaning. Jack Zipes has argued that fairy tales, regardless of their ultimate origin, have been subject to a process of mythicisation, and so have become myths in their own right.

Myths frequently function as pretexts (in Genette's term, hypotexts). Thus the *plot of Euripides' drama *Alcestis* is based on the myth of Alcestis as retold with original variations, and Carlos Fuentes' *novella *Aura* owes something to the pretext provided by the myth of Cephalus and Procris in Ovid's *Metamorphoses.*

SEE ALSO: intertextuality; myth: theoretical approaches

References and further reading

Barthes, Roland (1973) *Mythologies*, trans. Annette Lavers, New York: Noonday.
Coupe, Laurence (2000) *Myths*, New York: Bantam Doubleday.
Doniger, Wendy (1995) *Other People's Myths: The Cave of Echoes*, Chicago: University of Chicago Press.
Edmunds, Lowell (ed.) (1990) *Approaches to Greek Myth*, Baltimore: Johns Hopkins University Press.
Eliade, Mircea (1963) *Myth and Reality*, New York: Harper & Row.
von Franz, Marie-Louise (1997) *Archetypal Patterns in Fairy Tales*, Toronto: Inner City.
Lévi-Strauss, Claude (1978) *Myth and Meaning: Cracking the Code of Culture*, Toronto: University of Toronto Press.
Segal, Robert A. (1990) *Joseph Campbell, An Introduction*, New York: Mentor.
——(1999) *Theorizing About Myth*, Amherst: University of Massachusetts Press.
Walker, Steven F. (2001) *Jung and the Jungians on Myth*, London: Routledge.
Warner, Marina (1994) *Six Myths of Our Time*, New York: Vintage.
Zipes, Jack (1994) *Myth as Fairy Tale*, Lexington, Kentucky: The University Press of Kentucky.

STEVEN F. WALKER

MYTH: THEORETICAL APPROACHES

Theories of myth are scarcely a modern invention. They go all the way back to the pre-Socratics. But only since the second half of the nineteenth-century have theories purported to be scientific, for only since then have there existed the professional disciplines that have sought to provide truly scientific theories: the social sciences, of which anthropology, psychology, and *sociology have contributed the most (*see* ETHNOGRAPHIC APPROACHES TO NARRATIVE; PSYCHOLOGICAL APPROACHES TO NARRATIVE). Some social-scientific theories may have earlier counterparts (see Feldman and Richardson 1972), but earlier theorising was largely speculative rather than empirical. Even modern theories from literature, religious studies, and *philosophy utilise the data from the social sciences.

To study myth is to apply to it one or more theories from one or more disciplines. Theories are accounts of some larger domain, of which myth is a subset. For example, anthropological theories of myth are theories of culture as a whole, of which myth is considered an instance. Psychological theories are theories of the mind, of which myth is considered an expression. There are no theories of myth itself, for there is no discipline of myth in itself. Myth is not like literature, which, so it has or had traditionally been claimed, must be studied as *literature* rather than as something else (*see* FORMALISM).

What unites the study of myth across the disciplines are the questions asked: what is the origin, the function, and the subject matter of myth? Theories differ not only in their answers to these questions but also in the questions they answer. Some theories concentrate on the origin; others, on the function; still others, on the subject matter.

Myth as primitive science

Modern theorising about myth begins above all with the Victorian English anthropologist E. B. Tylor (1832–1917). For Tylor, myth originates and functions to explain *events in the physical world. Myth is the 'primitive' counterpart to *science, which is exclusively modern. For Tylor, there is no 'primitive science' and no 'modern myth'. Indeed, for him both terms are self-contradictory. By science, Tylor means natural, not social, science. The events explained by myth are ones like the rising and setting of the sun, though also human events like birth and death. Excluded are social events like marriage and war. For Tylor, the payoff of myth is wholly intellectual: knowledge of the world. For the Scottish-born classicist and anthropologist J. G. Frazer (1854–1941), whose theory is otherwise much like Tylor's, the payoff is practical: control over the world. Explanation is a means to control, which involves the ritualistic enactment of myth.

For both Tylor and Frazer, myth and science cover the same range of phenomena. Both are meant literally rather than symbolically. The difference is in the explanations themselves. Myth, a part of religion, attributes events to the decisions of gods (see THEOLOGY AND NARRATIVE). Science attributes events to impersonal processes. Because both myth and science offer direct explanations of events, one cannot stack myth atop science. For example, in myth a rain god collects water in buckets and then dumps the buckets on a chosen spot below. The god acts in place of meteorological processes (see NARRATIVE EXPLANATIONS). Myth and science are therefore not merely redundant but also incompatible. Because Tylor and Frazer equate modern with scientific, moderns must abandon myth for science, the authority of which is never challenged. Myth, while rational, stems from the less critical thinking of 'primitives'.

Tylor and Frazer epitomise the nineteenth-century view of myth: the view that myth is incompatible with science. In the twentieth-century the aim has been to make myth possible for moderns, yet still without questioning the authority of science. Tylor and Frazer have been berated by their twentieth-century successors for pitting myth against science and thereby precluding modern myths, for subsuming myth under religion and thereby precluding secular myths, for deeming the function of myth proto-scientific, for reading myth literally, and for deeming myth false (see TRUTH). Only at the end of the twentieth century, with the emergence of postmodernism, has the deference to science heretofore assumed been questioned (see MASTER NARRATIVE; POSTMODERN NARRATIVE).

One twentieth-century rejoinder to Tylor and Frazer has been to take the function of myth as other than explanation or control, in which case myth and science do not overlap. Another twentieth-century rejoinder has been to read myth other than literally, in which case myth does not even cover the same domain as science. More radically, both the proto-scientific function and the literal meaning of myth have been spurned. Most radical has been the postmodern transformation of explanation into mere story.

Myth as other than explanatory or controlling in function

The most influential reinterpreters of the *function* of myth have been Bronislaw Malinowski, Claude Lévi-Strauss, and Mircea Eliade. It is not clear whether for Malinowski (1884–1942), the Polish-born anthropologist, moderns as well as primitives have myth. It is clear that for him primitives have science as well as myth, so that myth cannot be the primitive counterpart to modern science. Primitives use science to explain and moreover to control the physical world. They use myth to reconcile themselves to aspects of the world that cannot be controlled.

Myth reconciles humans to the travails of life by rooting those travails in the primordial actions of gods or humans. Humans die because a god or human once did something that intentionally or inadvertently brought mortality permanently into the world. In tracing back the origin of a phenomenon, myth does explain it – this contrary to Malinowski's continual dismissal of Tylor – but explanation is only a means to an end, which is stoic acceptance of what cannot be altered.

Where for Tylor and Frazer myth deals with physical phenomena, for Malinowski it deals equally with social phenomena like customs and *laws. Myth still functions to reconcile humans to the unpleasantries of life, but here to unpleasantries that, far from unalterable, can be cast off. Myth spurs acceptance of the impositions of society by tracing them, too, back to a hoary past, thereby conferring on them the clout of tradition. Myths say, Do this because this has always been done. For example, in England fox hunting is defended on the grounds that it has always been part of rural life. A myth would show how old the practice is. In the case of physical phenomena, the beneficiary of myth is the individual. In the case of social phenomena, it is society itself. If it turns out that for Malinowski moderns do not have myth, what they have in place of myths of social phenomena is *ideology.

At first glance the French *structuralist anthropologist Claude Lévi-Strauss (b. 1908) seems a throwback to Tylor. For Lévi-Strauss, just like Tylor, deems myth a wholly primitive, yet rigorously intellectual, enterprise. Lévi-Strauss denounces non-intellectualists like Malinowski as vigorously as Malinowski denounces intellectualists like Tylor. Yet Lévi-Strauss in fact castigates Tylor for assuming that 'primitives' create myth rather than science because they think less critically than moderns. For Lévi-Strauss, primitives think as rigorously as moderns, just differently.

Primitive, or mythic, thinking is concrete. Modern thinking is abstract. Primitive thinking focuses on the observable, sensory, qualitative aspects of phenomena rather than, like modern thinking, on the unobservable, non-sensory, quantitative ones. Yet myth for Lévi-Strauss is no less scientific than modern science. It is simply part of the 'science of the concrete' rather than part of the science of the abstract. Myth *is* primitive science, but not inferior science.

Myth is an instance of thinking *per se*, modern and primitive alike, because it classifies phenomena. According to Lévi-Strauss, all humans think in the form of classifications, specifically pairs of oppositions, and project them onto the world. Many cultural phenomena express oppositions. Myth is distinctive in resolving or, more precisely, tempering oppositions. Myth tempers a contradiction by providing either a mediating middle term or an analogous, but more easily resolved, contradiction. Either tactic narrows and thereby alleviates the contradiction.

Like the contradictions expressed in other phenomena, those expressed in myth are apparently reducible to the fundamental contradiction between 'nature' and 'culture'. Humans experience themselves as at once animal-like and civilised. This split stems from the projection onto the world of the oppositional structure of the mind. By diminishing that opposition, myth overcomes a logical conundrum.

In calling his approach to myth *'structuralist', Lévi-Strauss means to be distinguishing it from 'narrative' approaches, which adhere to the *plot of myth. Lévi-Strauss locates the meaning of myth not in the plot but in the structure. The plot is that event A leads to event B, which leads to event C. The structure, which is identical with the expression and diminution of contradictions, is either that events A and B constitute an opposition mediated by event C or that events A and B are as opposed to each other as events C and D, an analogous opposition, are opposed (*see* MYTHEME).

Lévi-Strauss confines himself to primitive myths, but other structuralists analyse modern myths. The French semiotician Roland Barthes (1915–1980) takes as myths various cultural artefacts and shows how they serve to justify the bourgeois outlook of post-World War II France (*see* SEMIOTICS). The function of myth here is not intellectual but ideological. Myth has nothing to do with natural science, primitive or modern. Where Lévi-Strauss largely analyses myths independent of their social context – the grand exception is his analysis of the myth of Asdiwal – others inspired by him have tied myths to their contexts. For the Lévi-Straussian French classicists Jean-Pierre Vernant, Marcel Detienne, Pierre Vidal-Naquet, and Nicole Loraux, the relationship between myth and society is much more malleable and ironic than it is for Malinowski or even Barthes. Myth can as readily challenge as bolster existing ideology.

Just as for Malinowski, so for Mircea Eliade (1907–1986), the Romanian-born historian of religions, myth explains the origin of both social and physical phenomena by attributing them to the hoary acts of gods – for Eliade, never of humans. And just as for Malinowski, for Eliade explanation is only a means to an end, which is return to the *time of the myth, the time of the origin of whatever phenomenon it explains. In this 'primordial time' gods resided on earth, as in 'the Lord God['s] walking in the garden [of Eden] of the cool of the day' (Genesis 3:8). The return to primordial time reverses the everyday separation from gods, a separation that is equivalent to the fall, and is regenerative spiritually. The ultimate function of myth is providing proximity to gods, one or more.

Eliade ventures beyond the other respondents to Tylor and Frazer in proclaiming myth more than merely primitive. He cites modern *novels, plays, and *films that express a yearning to escape from the everyday world into another, often earlier one (*see* DRAMA AND NARRATIVE). If even professedly atheistic moderns harbour what he thereby labels myths, then myth must be universal. The figures in modern myths are humans, but humans raised so high above ordinary mortals as to become virtual gods. When 'lost' in a book, play, or movie, one forgets where one is and imagines oneself in the setting of the work, thereby encountering modern gods (*see* IMMERSION).

Myth as other than literal in meaning

The most prominent reinterpreters of the meaning rather than the function of myth have been the German New Testament scholar Rudolf Bultmann (1884–1976) and the German-born philosopher Hans Jonas (1903–1993). While they limit themselves to their specialties, Christianity and Gnosticism, they employ an existentialist theory of myth in general.

Bultmann acknowledges that, read literally, myth is exactly what Tylor and Frazer say it is: a prescientific explanation of the physical world, one incompatible with science. But unlike Malinowski and Eliade as well as Tylor and Frazer, Bultmann proceeds to read myth symbolically. In his excruciatingly misleading phrase, he 'demythologises' myth, which means not eliminating, or 'demythicising', myth but on the contrary extricating its true, symbolic subject matter. Once demythologised, myth is no longer about the external world in itself but is instead about the place of human beings in that world. To seek evidence of an actual worldwide flood, while dismissing the miraculous notion of an ark harbouring all species, would be to *demythicise* the Noah myth. To interpret the flood as a symbolic statement of the precariousness of human life is to *demythologise* the myth.

Demythologised, myth ceases to be purely primitive, as for Tylor and Frazer, and becomes universal, as for Eliade. Myth ceases to be false, as for Tylor and Frazer, and becomes true. Where Eliade invokes the existence of modern myths as *ipso facto* evidence of the compatibility of myth with science, Bultmann actually tries to reconcile myth with science. Where Eliade claims that moderns have myths of their own, Bultmann claims that moderns can retain traditional, overtly religious myths.

In translating the meaning of myth into terms acceptable to moderns, Bultmann sidesteps the issue of why moderns, even if they can have myth, need it. Since Bultmann takes the meaning of myth from philosophy, he can hardly maintain that the meaning of myth is untranslatable into non-mythic terms, the way, among others, the religious philosopher Paul Ricoeur does. Unanswered, then, is the question of the function of myth.

For Bultmann, the demythologised New Testament contrasts the alienation from the world felt by those who have not yet found God to the at-homeness in the world felt by those who have found God. For Jonas, demythologised Gnosticism pits the alienation from the physical world presently felt by Gnostics against the at-homeness in the immaterial world that they anticipate. But where Bultmann wants to bridge the divide between Christianity and modernity, Jonas acknowledges the divide between Gnosticism and modernity. In Gnosticism the state of alienation is temporary. In modern secular existentialism alienation is permanent: alienation *is* the human condition, not a fall from it. Like Bultmann, Jonas bypasses the question of the function of myth and confines himself to the meaning.

Myth as both other than explanatory or controlling in function and other than literal in meaning

The most radical departures from Tylor have transformed both the function and the meaning of myth. The most influential theorists here have been the Austrian psychoanalyst Sigmund Freud (1856–1939) and the Swiss psychiatrist C. G. Jung (1875–1961) (*see* PSYCHOANALYSIS AND NARRATIVE). For both, the subject matter of myth is the unconscious, and the function of myth is to express the unconscious. Myth involves the projection of the unconscious onto the external world, but the projection must be recognised and thereby reclaimed. Myth must be disentangled from the world.

Because the unconscious for Freud is composed of repressed sexual and aggressive drives, myth functions to release those drives, but in a disguised, symbolic, vicarious way, so that the creator and the user of a myth never confront its meaning and thereby their own nature. Myth serves simultaneously to reveal and to hide its unconscious contents. The classical Freudian study of myths by Otto Rank (1884–1939), who eventually broke with Freud, sees male *hero myths as providing a disguised, symbolic, vicarious fulfilment of, above all, Oedipal drives. Myth here serves neurotic adult males fixated at their Oedipal stage.

Contemporary Freudians like the American Jacob Arlow (b. 1912) take myth positively rather than negatively. For them, myth helps to solve the problems of growing up rather than to perpetuate them, is progressive rather than regressive, and abets adjustment to society and the outer world rather than childish flight from both. Myth serves less to vent repressed drives than to sublimate them. Myth serves everyone, not only neurotics.

Jung and Jungians have taken myth positively from the outset. For them, the unconscious expressed in myth is not the Freudian repository of imprisoned, anti-social drives but a storehouse of innately unconscious 'archetypes' (*see* ARCHE-TYPAL PATTERNS), or sides of the personality, that have simply never had an opportunity at being realised. Myth is one means of encountering this Jungian, or 'collective', unconscious. For Jungians, as for contemporary Freudians, the function of myth is growth rather than, as for classical Freudians, release. But for Jungians growth means less adjustment to the outer world, as for contemporary Freudians, than cultivation of the 'inner world'. The payoff is self-realisation. Some Jungians and Jungian-oriented theorists like the American Joseph Campbell (1904–1987) so tout myth that it becomes a panacea for all humanity's problems. Jung himself, however, never goes this far. For him, myth works best as part of therapy.

For Jungians, as for Freudians, myth is to be read symbolically rather than literally, but not because its meaning has intentionally been disguised. Rather, the unconscious speaks a language of its own. Interpretation is less like breaking the Enigma code and more like deciphering the Rosetta stone. Contemporary Jungians like the American archetypal psychologist James Hillman (b. 1926) seek to rectify what they consider the monotheistic orientation of Jung's psychology and in turn his approach to myth.

Recent theories of myth

The most notable recent theories of myth have been variations on myth taken as primitive science, theoretical and applied. Cognitivists led by the French-born anthropologist Pascal Boyer analyse the mental processes that shape religious and mythic thinking – processes far more rigorous and precise than, for Tylor, the scientific-like sequence of observation, analogy, and generalisation. Cognitivists investigate the constraints on religious explanations rather than, like Tylor, the explanations themselves. But then for cognitivists the subject matter of myth is the mind rather than, as for Tylor, the world.

The German classicist Walter Burkert (b. 1931) and the French-born literary critic René Girard (b. 1923) have revived the theory that ties myth to ritual. Where for Frazer and his English follower Lord Raglan (1885–1964) myth is the *script for the ritualistic killing of the king, whose death and replacement magically ensure the rebirth of crops, for Burkert myth reinforces the ritual that commemorates the past hunting of animals. The function of myth is not physical but psychological and social: to cope with the guilt and anxiety that members of society feel toward their own aggression, and to unite society by turning that aggression onto outsiders.

Where for Frazer and Raglan the king is heroic because he is willing to die for the sake of the community, for Girard the hero, who can range from the most marginal person to royalty, is killed as a scapegoat for the violence endemic to society. Rather than directing the ritualistic killing, as for Frazer and Raglan, myth for Girard arises afterwards to cover it up by making the victim first a criminal and then a hero. The function of myth is social: to preserve the ethos of sociability by hiding not only the killing but, more deeply, the violence inherent in society. While reviving the nineteenth-century theories of Tylor and Frazer, Boyer, Burkert, and Girard all retain the twentieth-century focus of myth on humans, not the world.

SEE ALSO: myth: thematic approaches; folklore; narrative as cognitive instrument; oral cultures and narrative

References and further reading

Arlow, Jacob A. (1961) 'Ego Psychology and the Study of Mythology', *Journal of the American Psychoanalytic Association*, 9, 371–93.

Barthes, Roland (1972) *Mythologies*, trans. Annette Lavers, New York: Hill and Wang.

Boyer, Pascal (2001) *Religion Explained*, New York: Basic Books.

Bultmann, Rudolf (1953 [1941]) 'New Testament and Mythology', in Hans-Werner Bartsch (ed.) *Kerygma and Myth*, vol. 1, trans. Reginald H. Fuller, London: SPCK.

Burkert, Walter (1996) *Creation of the Sacred*, Cambridge, Mass.: Harvard University Press.

Campbell, Joseph (1949) *The Hero with a Thousand Faces*, New York: Pantheon Books.

Eliade, Mircea (1968) *The Sacred and the Profane*, trans. Willard R. Trask, New York: Harvest Books.

Feldman, Burton, and Robert D. Richardson (1972) *The Rise of Modern Mythology, 1680–1860*, Bloomington: Indiana University Press.

Frazer, James George (1911–1915) *The Golden Bough*, 12 vols, London: Macmillan.

Girard, René (1972) *Violence and the Sacred*, trans. Patrick Gregory, London: Athlone Press.

Hillman, James (1975) *Re-Visioning Psychology*, New York: Harper and Row.

Jung, C. G. (1968) *The Archetypes and the Collective Unconscious*, in *Collected Works*, vol. IX, part 1, ed. Sir Herbert Read *et al.* trans. R. F. C. Hull *et al.* Princeton: Princeton University Press.

Lévi-Strauss, Claude (1958 [1955]) 'The Structural Study of Myth', trans. Claire Jacobson and Brooke Grundfest Schoepf, in Thomas A. Sebeok (ed.) *Myth*, Bloomington: Indiana University Press.

Malinowski, Bronislaw (1926) *Myth in Primitive Psychology*, London: Kegan Paul.

Raglan, Lord (1936) *The Hero*, London: Methuen.

Rank, Otto (1914) *The Myth of the Birth of the Hero*, trans. F. Robbins and Smith Ely Jelliffe, New York: Journal of Nervous and Mental Disease Publishing.

Segal, Robert A. (1999) *Theorizing about Myth*, Amherst: University of Massachusetts Press.

Tylor, Edward Burnett (1871) *Primitive Culture*, 2 vols, London: Murray.

ROBERT A. SEGAL

MYTHEME

Providing an important precedent for *structuralist narratology, the anthropologist Claude Lévi-Strauss coined the term 'mytheme' in his effort to use linguistics as a 'pilot-science' for the study of myths (*see* LINGUISTIC APPROACHES TO NARRATIVE). Formed in parallel with *phoneme*, a term used by Troubetzkoi, Saussure, and Jakobson to designate sound differences that are meaningful to speakers of a language, *mytheme* refers to basic units of mythological discourse whose significance stems from their relations to other such units (*see* NARRATIVE UNITS). Hence, as detailed in Lévi-Strauss's (1986 [1955]) influential account of the Oedipus myth, structural analysis of a myth requires segmenting the text into mythemes, located at various points along the syntagmatic chain of the discourse, and then grouping those constituent units into paradigmatic classes. The meaning of a myth derives from the (analogical, contrastive, etc.) deep-structural relations between the classes of mythemes into which it can be analysed. However, arguing that the French structuralists often misconstrued the linguistic models that they adapted for their own purposes, Pavel (1989) disputes the supposed parallelism between phonemes and mythemes.

SEE ALSO: function (Propp); semiotics; myth: theoretical approaches

References and further reading

Lévi-Strauss, Claude (1986 [1955]) 'The Structural Study of Myth', trans. Claire Jacobson and Brooke Grundfest Schoepf, in Hazard Adams and Leroy Searle (eds) *Critical Theory Since 1965*, Tallahassee: University Presses of Florida.

Pavel, Thomas G. (1989) *The Feud of Language: A History of Structuralist Thought*, trans. Linda Jordan and Thomas G. Pavel, Oxford: Blackwell.

DAVID HERMAN

N

NAMING IN NARRATIVE

In narrative contexts, naming involves the use of singular terms, a class of designators or referring expressions functioning like individual constants in a proposition, to label an entity or set of entities in a *storyworld or any of its subdomains. Naming practices are meant to ensure the identification of the furniture of the storyworld and the continuity of *reference to a given entity throughout the *narration (*see* EXISTENT).

The terms used for naming can be classified into proper names (or letters or numbers), pronouns and demonstratives, and definite descriptions (*see* DESCRIPTION). While proper names are the major naming device in literature, they are not indispensable. A story with two or three *characters can make do with pronouns, and *novels have been written in which all characters are designated by definite descriptions. In autodiegetic narratives, such as Dostoevskii's *Notes from Underground*, the narrator-character's name may never be mentioned, or occur just once in a *quotation from an *address by another character (*see* NARRATOR). Different *authors show clear preference for particular kinds of naming devices – for example, definite description in Zola and proper names in Flaubert. The contrastive use of names and definite descriptions may partition the personnel of a narrative into distinct groups, and may have focussing and *thematic reasons and implications. In Kafka's *The Trial*, for example, persons with whom the main character has personal relations are referred to by names, while officials are referred to by expressions designating their roles, such as 'the judge'.

A text-grammatical perspective on singular terms examines how they form extended anaphoric chains creating discourse coherence and intelligibility. This phenomenon has been studied in detail by Catherine Emmott (1997), who analyses chains such as a man → the man → John → he → the singer, etc. A semantic approach studies the role of names in establishing a storyworld's cast of characters and how they enable readers to answer questions such as: who is there, how many are there, who is who, who did or was such and such, and is it (still) the same individual? (*see* NARRATIVE SEMANTICS). Cognitively viewed, singular terms are names of mental files we keep on characters or an anchor for our construction of mental models of them (*see* COGNITIVE NARRATOLOGY; NARRATIVE COMPREHENSION; SITUATION MODEL). In the course of the narrative text, relations of co-reference, temporary or permanent, are established between different singular terms.

Inside a storyworld, proper names act as rigid designators, picking out the same individual regardless of any transformations s/he may undergo, and a character's true identity is equated with his or her baptismal name. Many literary narratives are concerned with baptismal name-giving, distortion of names leading to doubt whether it is still the same individual, confusion of names and their bearers, refusal to mention one's name or to have a name, quest for one's original name, assumed and changed names, and expressions mistaken for names and leading to false beliefs about the existence of a corresponding name bearer. A character in a narrative may bear the name of a fictional individual from an earlier work or that of an actual person (*see* INTERTEXTUALITY; POSTMODERN REWRITES). This leads to questions of sameness or counterparthood across worlds between the name bearers (*see* POSSIBLE-WORLDS THEORY).

References and further reading

Corblin, Francis (1983) 'Les désignateurs dans les romans', *Poétique*, 54, 195–212.

Emmott, Catherine (1997) *Narrative Comprehension: A Discourse Perspective*, Oxford: Oxford University Press.

Lamping, Dieter (1983) *Der Name in der Erzählung*, Bonn: Bouvier.

Nesslroth, Peter (1996) 'Naming Names in Telling Tales', Calin-Andrei Mihailescu and Walid Hamarneh (eds) *Fiction Updated*, Toronto: University of Toronto Press.

Nicole, Eugène (1983) 'L'Onomastique littéraire', *Poétique*, 54, 233–53.

URI MARGOLIN

NARRATEE

Narratee, a coinage of classical, *structuralist narratology, designates the addressee to whom a *narrator tells his/her tale. The narratee, like his/her counterpart the narrator, is integral to a communication model of narrative (*see* COMMUNICATION IN NARRATIVE; FUNCTION (JAKOBSON); NARRATIVE TRANSMISSION). This model is based on a strict non-crossable ontological separation between the double, two-partner transaction: an 'external' one between the 'real' *author and 'real' reader (e.g., respectively, Austen and anyone reading her novels) (*see* AUDIENCE); an 'internal' transaction between the narrator and the narratee, who are part of the *fiction but not necessarily part of the fictional world (where the *characters are), being one level above it (Rimmon-Kenan 1983: 91–94; *see* DIEGESIS; EMBEDDING; STORYWORLD). The double act of communication envisaged by the structuralist multilevel model of *narration entails that narrators and narratees *always* occupy the same level of narration (Genette 1980 [1972]). Thus in embedded narratives (e.g. Shelley's *Frankenstein*), not only are there multiple narrators and narratees who change roles (Walton, initially, as narrator, his sister as narratee in the frame story; then Victor Frankenstein as narrator, Walton his narratee; then the monster as narrator, Victor his narratee), but at each level the roles are fixed (the monster addresses Victor, *his* narratee, not Walton, Victor's narratee). The change in roles carries *rhetorical effects, creating *distance or sympathy (e.g. toward the monster).

Some strands of *postclassical narratology, which do not subscribe to the strict communication model of narrative, may omit the term 'narratee' altogether (Abbott 2002: 187–97) or may use it as a convenient synonym for auditor, disregarding the strict ontological and hierarchical implications explained above ('insofar as a text is posited to address a reader [or narratee]') (Fludernik 1996: 340). Other postclassical strands focus not on ideal *reader constructs, but on an empirical study of communication and literary response (*see* RECEPTION THEORY). Such work examines the relation between narrators and real as opposed to ideal readers (Bortolussi and Dixon 2003: 66–69); by implication, it either understands the narratee as synonymous with a listener, or has no need for the concept at all. It also denies, in effect, the validity of the non-crossable ontological boundaries of the communication model outlined in structuralist narratology.

Narratees can be ranged along a scale of more or less detailed characterisation: from total absence (Maupassant, 'The Necklace'), through minimal characterisation (the out-of-town customer of Whitey in Lardner's 'Haircut'), to fuller characterisation (Victor as the monster's narratee).

References and further reading

Abbott, Porter H. (2002) *The Cambridge Introduction to Narrative*, Cambridge: Cambridge University Press.

Bortolussi, Marisa, and Peter Dixon (2003) *Psychonarratology*, Cambridge: Cambridge University Press.

Fludernik, Monika (1996) *Towards a 'Natural' Narratology*, London: Routledge.

Genette, Gérard (1980 [1972]) *Narrative Discourse: An Essay in Method*, trans. Jane E. Lewin, Oxford: Blackwell.

Prince, Gerald (1973) 'Introduction a l'etude du narrataire', *Poetique*, 14, 178–96.

—— (1982) *Narratology: The Form and Functioning of Narrative*, Berlin: Mouton.

Rimmon-Kenan, Shlomith (1983) *Narrative Fiction: Contemporary Poetics*, London: Methuen.

NILLI DIENGOTT

NARRATING (GENETTE)

In Genette's terminology, *the narrating* refers to the producing narrative action and, by extension, the whole of the real or fictional situation in which that action takes place (Genette 1980: 27). The term thus designates one category in Genette's trichotomous classification of narrative: (1) story, (2) discourse, and (3) narrating. With written narratives, the real process of narrating is the *author's writing process, which lies beyond the narrative, but could fruitfully become a part of narratological study through combining intrinsic criticism with extrinsic criticism (Shen 2001). In oral *narration, by contrast, the *audience has direct access to the real narrating process of the storyteller. The storyteller's tone, *gestures, facial expressions etc. interact with his/her words, serving an important affective function. Whatever the storyteller does during the process of narrating may directly bear on the audience's response to the narrative.

The process of fictitious narrating is not accessible to the reader unless reported either by the narrator himself or herself or by a higher-level narrator. These two cases are exemplified in Conrad's *Heart of Darkness* when, on the one hand, Marlow as embedded first-person narrator recounts his own narratorial activity as follows: 'When you have to attend to things of that sort ... the reality, I tell you – fades ..., "Try to be civil, Marlow", growled a voice, and I knew there was at least one listener awake beside myself' (49); and when, on the other hand, the frame narrator reports: '[Marlow] was silent for a while .... He paused again as if reflecting, then added ... ' (39). Not surprisingly, in narrative fiction, where only the verbal signs are accessible to the reader, the fictive narrating has no other way to present itself except through being reported. And when it becomes an object of narration, it either becomes part of the story (when narrated by a higher-level narrator) or part of the discourse (see STORY-DISCOURSE DISTINCTION). Generally speaking, apart from the issue of temporal orientation (whether the narrating is retrospective, simultaneous, or prospective in relation to the narrated *events; see TIME IN NARRATIVE), there is no necessity for the narrating to be an explicit element of a narrative. When the fictive narrating is not mentioned as such it is usually 'considered to have no duration' (Genette 1980: 222; see also Shen 2001). In the case of extra-heterodiegetic narration, if the narrator is a depersonalised narrative instance, readers can only get access to the words reported via a 'disembodied' voice. If readers try to look behind the words for the narrating process, they will only find the writer's writing hand.

Since the real process of narrating lies beyond the written narrative and the fictitious process is not accessible unless narrated, many narratologists have refrained from making narrating a separate category in their classification of the dimensions of written narrative.

SEE ALSO: communication in narrative; narrative transmission

References and further reading

Conrad, Joseph (1981 [1899]) *Heart of Darkness*, Harmondsworth: Penguin.
Genette, Gérard (1980) *Narrative Discourse: An Essay in Method*, trans. J. E. Lewin, Ithaca: Cornell University Press.
Shen, Dan (2001) 'Narrative, Reality, and Narrator as Construct: Reflections on Genette's "Narrating"', *Narrative*, 9, 123–29.

DAN SHEN

NARRATING-I

The *narrator in a first-person narrative; specifically, in retrospective first-person *narration, the older self who recounts the experiences undergone by the earlier 'experiencing-I'. *See* NARRATIVE SITUATIONS (also PERSON; TIME IN NARRATIVE).

NARRATION

'Narration' can be synonymous with *'narrative' when referring to individual narrated texts, as for example in the narration or narrative of a life (*see* LIFE STORY). But in most analytic discussion of narrative, narration is more closely synonymous with *'narrating' or the *production* of narrative, and thus is subsumed within the larger category of narrative. Genette, for example, identifies narration as one of the three levels of narrative, along with story (*histoire*) and narrative discourse (*récit*) (*see* STORY-DISCOURSE DISTINCTION). However, opinions vary regarding the application of the term, ranging from a tight restriction to unquoted verbal narration by a *narrator to usage that is so broad as to encompass the entirety of narrative discourse.

Even in its narrowest sense, narration is a complex subject, containing within it a great number of narratological concerns: prolepsis, analepsis (*see* TEMPORAL ORDERING), *point of view, *voice, *suspense and surprise, *distance, omniscience, and others too numerous to take up here. Early classifications of the kinds of narration relied on distinctions of *tense and grammatical *person. These classifications persist in popular usage (as in, for example, past tense third-person narration), but in analytic usage they have been widely found to be inadequate and replaced with a number of more useful, though still debatable, systems of classification.

Narration can also be a formal attribute of augmented reflexive attention in fiction, particularly as *thematised in *modernist and *postmodernist fiction. A considerable body of later-twentieth-century commentary on narrative has drawn attention to the ways in which, in certain texts, narration can absorb a great deal of the reader's or *audience's attention, often at the expense of the story itself (see REFLEXIVITY).

Verbal narration, quotation, monologue, and interior monologue

The term 'narration' has been traditionally restricted to the verbal (oral or written) production of narrative by a *narrator (Cohn; Genette; Prince). At times, the term has been further reduced from a global to a local concept by distinguishing it from *quotation or monologue, which are set off in some way by quotation marks and/or by phrases like 'he said' and 'she said' (see SPEECH REPRESENTATION). The argument for this position turns on the fact that quotation, insofar as it occurs within the story, is more mimetic than diegetic, in that it is *directly* presented rather than *indirectly* represented through the narration (see DIEGESIS; MIMESIS). Bal, in addition to stressing narration's difference from 'embedded texts' like dialogues and monologues, draws attention to those numerous segments of almost any 'narrative' text (e.g. segments involving *description or *metanarrative comment) that do not participate in the narration of the story.

Discussion of narration and quotation has also been impacted by the common confusion between William James's concept of 'stream of consciousness' and Edouard Dujardin's term 'interior monologue' (see STREAM OF CONSCIOUSNESS AND INTERIOR MONOLOGUE; THOUGHT AND CONSCIOUSNESS REPRESENTATION (LITERATURE)). The former is meant as a description of the moment-by-moment flow and texture of consciousness, the latter as a method of representing it. For James, however, the stream of consciousness includes more than language and therefore more than can be directly represented in a monologue. Moreover, as Cohn points out, the term 'interior monologue' itself has been used to designate two very different things with two very different modes of narrative production, the one a technique of 'presenting a character's consciousness by direct quotation of his thoughts in a surrounding narrative context' and the other 'a narrative *genre* constituted in its entirety by the silent self-communion of a fictional mind' (15) (see GENRE THEORY IN NARRATIVE STUDIES). Thus Joyce deploys frequent passages of interior monologue in *Ulysses*, but with the exception of the 'Penelope' chapter these passages are contained within and mediated by narration in the third-person. Dujardin's *Les lauriers sont coupés*, by contrast, is interior monologue in its entirety and therefore essentially 'direct' first-person discourse. As Cohn points out, where the genre is a comparatively recent development, the technique is a natural outgrowth of a long tradition of representing consciousness by quotation within third-person narration.

The validity, or at least usefulness, of the distinction between quotation and narration is complicated by the fact that narration can be and frequently is found embedded within monologues or quoted discourse, and much of this 'embedded narration' conveys events of the story within which the quotation occurs (see EMBEDDING; FRAMED NARRATIVES). Correlatively, entire *novels narrated in the first-person are in essence long quotations. The tension involved in maintaining the distinction between quotation and narration can be seen in a narrative like *Heart of Darkness* in which, within a few pages, the anonymous third-person narrator who begins the narration in effect hands over the discourse to a character, Marlow, whose words, though technically being quoted, narrate the rest of the novel with few interruptions. The distinction between narration and quotation is made even more difficult by the very common novelistic practice of *free indirect discourse, which as Cohn observes occupies 'a position astride narration and quotation' (14), fusing as it does third-person narration with the language, intonation, and manner of a *character within the narrative (see DUAL-VOICE HYPOTHESIS). One could argue, however, that in written texts there is in fact no direct discourse, since, as Banfield contends, even quotation is mediated by conventions that separate it from oral discourse.

Whether for these reasons or others or simply to expand the framework for investigating the production of narrative, recent studies of narration have broadened the focus of inquiry to the point where *narration* no longer strictly denotes narrative production by a narrator.

Classification by tense

Narrative is generally understood as presenting *events that have already happened by the *time of the narration (either actual, as in historical narrative, or invented, as in *fiction) (*see* HISTORIO-GRAPHY). Narration, in other words, is understood to mediate a story, either true or fictional, that in some way precedes the narrative. For this reason, narration is rendered most commonly in the past tense ('Margaret picked up the scissors and ran at her accuser'). Not infrequently, however, novelists have deployed the present tense to narrate action in the past. Usually referred to as the 'historical present', this move is thought to heighten the immediacy and dramatic impact of the narration ('Margaret picks up the scissors and runs at her accuser'). Casparis argues that such narration altogether, throwing the stress on perception: 'Plot, character development, logical causal framework are relinquished in favour of the act of perceiving' (74). The device is also common in narration that occurs naturally in the ordinary course of conversation ('So I'm heading for the train station when suddenly this thunderstorm comes out of nowhere'; *see* CONVERSATIONAL STORYTELLING; NATURAL NARRATOLOGY).

Narration in an actual, rather than a historical, present raises the issue of when what we read or witness is no longer narration but rather the unfolding of events as they happen. Cohn (1978) and Fludernik (1996) both note that one cannot at the same time live a story and narrate it. Whether one agrees with this or not, art forms like role-playing games, theatrical improv, or 'happenings' would all appear to be as unmediated as life itself and therefore not examples of narration until rendered in retrospect (*see* DRAMA AND NARRATIVE; NARRATIVE, GAMES, AND PLAY). 'Current report' – the present-tense reporting of events as they happen (sports, on-the-scene news; *see* SPORTS BROADCAST) – even though a mediated presentation, would also appear to be so tied to the unfolding of events as (arguably) not to qualify as

a form of narration. Use of the non-historical present tense or 'narrative present' (Cohn 1978; Stanzel 1984) in fiction is often difficult to distinguish from the historical present and requires sufficient cues to be understood as one or the other. Narrative present in the first-person ('I pick up the scissors and run at my accuser') conceivably qualifies as 'monologue' or 'interior monologue', but again much depends on the context to indicate how it is to be read. In sum, present-tense narration is multi-functional and can substitute 'for *all* tenses except the present perfect and the future' (Fludernik 1996: 254).

Reacting to narrative theory's traditional bias toward the 'past-factive-completive triplet' and the increasing proliferation of event-representational texts of other kinds, Margolin has used the tense-aspect-modality (TAM) approach to try to sharpen theoretical discriminations between kinds of narration on the basis of temporal features and 'reality status'. For Margolin, any adequate analysis of narration in one of the three commonly recognisable types – in his terms, *retrospective* narration (past), *concurrent* narration (present), and *prospective* narration (future) – requires further discrimination of a multitude of potential meaningful differences within these types depending on whether the action is completed or in progress and whether the world invoked is 'actual, non-actual, hypothetical, indeterminate, counterfactual, wished for, ordered into being' (143; *see* MODALITY). Naturally, the probabilities of one or the other of these modal variants depends to some degree on the temporal position of the event in relation to the narration (e.g., the ratio of actual to non-actual modalities is usually higher in retronarration than in concurrent or prospective narration).

Classification by person; homodiegetic and heterodiegetic narration; reliability

In addition to classification by tense, kinds of narration have traditionally been discriminated according to the grammatical person of the narrating voice. Far and away the commonest types are first- and third-person narration, with second-person narration forming a comparatively small, though growing body of texts. As the basis of a useful system of classification, grammatical person is fraught with difficulty, beginning with the fact that third-person narration is so frequently contained within narration identified as first-person. Even in most, and possibly all, *autobiographies in which the authorial subject explicitly and frequently refers to himself or herself in the first-person, third-person narration tends to predominate (*see* AUTHOR). Yet customarily all that has been necessary to classify a text as first-person narration has been its delivery by a character who belongs in some way, however peripherally, to the diegesis or world of the story, regardless of how infrequent the instances of self-reference.

In an effort to improve on the inadequacy of classifications based solely on grammatical person, Stanzel developed a comprehensive complex paradigm of the kinds of narration according to their degree of *'mediacy' (*see* NARRATIVE SITUATIONS). All elements of the paradigm fall within three major modes of narration: first-person narration (internal to the story), authorial narration (external to the story), and 'figural' narration (conveyed largely through the unspoken perceptions of a character operating as a 'reflector'). Genette similarly promoted a distinction between homodiegetic and heterodiegetic narration, the one emanating from a character inside the diegesis, the other from a voice or character outside the diegesis. But Genette did not adopt the concept of an unspeaking narrator, developing instead the subsidiary concept of *focalization in place of Stanzel's reflector-mediated figural narration. Another notable reaction to the inadequacy of a system based on grammatical person is Booth's stress on the *reliability of the narrator. An author's strategic choices, for example, of 'dramatised' or 'undramatised' narrators, of 'observer narrators' or 'narrator agents', affect the narration's degree of emotional and perspectival distance from the action and hence the reliability of the views embedded in the narration (*see* EMOTION IN NARRATIVE; PERSPECTIVE).

Locating second-person narration in any comprehensive scheme of classification has also been problematic. Grammatical second-person is an implicit concomitant of narration in the imperative and instructional modes. Yet second-person narration is also arguably a subcategory of third-person narration, the narrating voice turning its attention toward what is most likely the reader (though some might argue for an implicit *narratee, or addressee, as both recipient and object of the discourse) (*see* ADDRESS). Conversely, the personal relationship implicit in the address to the reader brings with it the aura of a speaking subject: that is, a first-person behind the voice. Finally, the effect whereby second-person narration can extend the world of the narrative out into the world of the reader – i.e., incorporate the reader into the diegesis – makes it fundamentally asymmetrical with first- and third-person narration. For more on the complexities of second-person narration see Fludernik (1994; cf. McInerney 1984).

Narration in non-verbal media

For those who would limit the use of 'narration' to the production of narrative by a narrator, stories presented in drama, *film, and other non-verbal *media are non-narrational. Though works in these media often contain narrators, either as characters who address the audience or in film through *voice-over technique, such verbal narration is rarely sustained, most of the represented action being freighted by performers and other visual and aural elements. Yet the term 'narration' has been widely applied to non-verbal media, even static pictorial media like paintings (*see* PICTORIAL NARRATIVITY; VISUAL NARRATIVITY). In the discourse on film especially, narration can be a very broad concept, referring at times to the combined effects of all the elements, verbal and non-verbal, that generate the narrative as it unfolds (*see* SOUNDTRACK). Bordwell, for example, includes within the concept of narration both *sjuzhet and style, a combination that is close to what in Anglo-American narratological thought is referred to as 'narrative discourse'.

The issue of whether or not narration should be limited to narration by a narrator or, more broadly, to narration in verbal media relates intimately to the effort to distinguish telling from showing or presenting from representing (*see* SHOWING VS. TELLING). These in turn are rooted in ambiguities in the classical distinction between diegesis and mimesis, first introduced by Plato in *The Republic* as the difference between telling a story (as in *epic poetry) and performing it (as in drama; *see* MODE). Shortly thereafter, Aristotle in *The Poetics* subsumed Plato's distinction within a single, much broader, concept of mimesis that encompassed the subcategories of telling and performing. Whether following Aristotle's lead or not, mimetic theories of narration have stressed that narration can be a matter of *performance and can draw as much on visual as on aural or written elements. It was a short step from this to argue, as Pudovkin did in an early and influential treatise on film, that the camera lens is essentially the eye of an 'invisible observer' who visually narrates the film.

Contesting the idea of an invisible observer, film theorists like Branigan and Bordwell have further broadened and complicated the whole discussion by including within the concept of narration, not only formal narrational elements of mimesis and diegesis, but also the *agency of the spectator. While Branigan insists on the distinction between narrative discourse (the complete textual system as object) and narration (the implied or explicit activity of a subject in grasping elements of that system), he nonetheless greatly extends the direction Stanzel took when he introduced the idea of unspoken narration. Branigan's complex understanding of narration allows for multiple kinds of knowing, including the shifting understandings of both characters and spectators. In Bordwell's 'constructivist' account, narration is the process of eliciting the spectator's construction of the film by a complex stream of cues designed to trigger schemata that pre-exist in the spectator's consciousness (see SCRIPTS AND SCHEMATA). Encompassing and transcending not only voice-over but also the information produced by the camera eye, this is narration without a narrator. Indeed, on this view, a narrator is simply another among a multitude of schemata that may or may not be cued by the narration.

Foregrounding narration

In much twentieth-century fiction, narration itself has become a point of focus and in the process has tended to keep the reader from an *immersion in the story untroubled by questions regarding its transmission (see NARRATIVE TRANSMISSION). Though this development is one of the common signatures of modernist and postmodernist fiction, it can be found in earlier narratives like Sterne's *Life and Opinions of Tristram Shandy* (1759–1767) and Diderot's *Jacques le fataliste et son maître* (1796). The twentieth-century increase of novels using versions of the narrative present (Fludernik 1996: 251) would appear to be a part of this switch in focus, drawing attention, as Casparis argues, to the on-going production of the narrative.

This shift of focus has been frequently seen to reflect a crisis of epistemology in which doubt is cast on the capacity of narrative to represent a reality outside the prison-house of a narrator's subjectivity and language. A more radical version of the crisis is the existentialist tenet that stories exist only in the mind and nowhere in external reality. The idea there are no 'true stories' existing outside our constructing imaginations was powerfully developed in Sartre's *Nausea* (1938). Narration's displacement of story as an object of readerly attention is also developed in Brooks's reading of *Heart of Darkness* as a text in which 'the impossibility of original story, the need to retell, places emphasis of the tale on the plane of narration itself' (262). Where Brooks locates this shift in a *modernist* exhaustion of narrative possibility, Hutcheon and McHale, following the lead of Barthes, stress the way *postmodern* texts extend an invitation to the reader to participate actively in the world-making process of narration (see POSSIBLE-WORLDS THEORY; READER-RESPONSE THEORY; STORY-WORLD). The optional and transposable lexia of some forms of hypertext fiction (see DIGITAL NARRRATIVE) can be seen as variants of this trend. The collaborative products of *interactive fiction would seem to carry this process even further, yet they also raise again the question discussed above: whether or not 'narration' is an appropriate term for projects (like role-playing games and theatrical improv) that invent themselves as they go along.

SEE ALSO: evolution of narrative forms; modernist narrative; novel, the; postmoderrn narrative

References and further reading

Bal, Mieke (1998) *Narratology: Introduction to the Theory of Narrative*, Toronto: University of Toronto Press.

Banfield, Ann (1982) *Unspeakable Sentences: Representation and Narration in the Language of Fiction*, Boston: Routledge & Kegan Paul.

Booth, Wayne (1983) *The Rhetoric of Fiction*, 2nd ed., Chicago: University of Chicago Press.

Bordwell, David (1985) *Narration in the Fiction Film*, Madison, WI: University of Wisconsin Press.

Branigan, Edward (1984) *Point of View in the Cinema: A Theory of Narration and Subjectivity in Classical Film*, New York: Mouton.

Brooks, Peter (1985) *Reading for the Plot: Design and Intention in Narrative*, New York: Vintage.

Casparis, Christian Paul (1975) *Tense without Time: The Present Tense in Narration*, Schweizer Anglistiche Arbeiten, vol. 84, Bern: Francke Verlag.

Cohn, Dorrit (1978) *Transparent Minds: Narrative Modes for Presenting Consciousness in Fiction*, Princeton: Princeton University Press.

Fludernik, Monika (1993) *The Fictions of Language and the Languages of Fiction*, London: Routledge.

——(1994) (ed.) *Style*, 28.3 (Special Issue on 'Second-Person Narrative').

——(1996) *Towards a 'Natural' Narratology*, London: Routledge.

Genette, Gérard (1980) *Narrative Discourse: An Essay in Method*, trans. Jane E. Lewin, Ithaca, NY: Cornell University Press.

Hutcheon, Linda (1984) *Narcissistic Narrative: The Metafictional Paradox*, New York: Methuen.

Margolin, Uri (1999) 'Of What Is Past, Is Passing, or to Come: Temporality, Aspectuality, Modality, and the Nature of Literary Narrative', in David Herman (ed.) *Narratologies: New Perspectives on Narrative Analysis*, Columbus: Ohio State University Press.

McInerney, Jay (1984) *Bright Lights, Big City*, New York: Vintage Books.

Stanzel, F. K. (1984) *A Theory of Narrative*, trans. Charlotte Goedsche, Cambridge: Cambridge University Press.

H. PORTER ABBOTT

NARRATIVE

Though interest in the phenomenon that forms the topic of this Encyclopedia dates back to a couple of millennia, both in Western and non-Western cultures, it is only in the past fifty years that the concept of narrative has emerged as an autonomous object of inquiry. From Aristotle to Vladimir Propp and from Percy Lubbock to Wayne Booth, the critics and philosophers who are regarded today as the pioneers of narrative theory were not concerned with narrative proper but with particular literary *genres, such as *epic poetry, *drama, the *folktale, the *novel or more generally *fiction, short for 'narrative literary fiction'. It was the legacy of French structuralism, more particularly of Roland Barthes and Claude Bremond, to have emancipated narrative from literature and from fiction, and to have recognised it as a *semiotic phenomenon that transcends disciplines and *media (*see* STRUCTURALIST NARRATOLOGY).

Contemporary uses of the term narrative

No sooner had narrative come of age as a theoretical concept than it began to invade fields as diverse as *historiography, *medicine, *law, *psychoanalysis, and *ethnography (*see* NARRATIVE TURN IN THE HUMANITIES). This territorial expansion was accompanied by a semantic broadening that liberated narrative not only from literary forms, but also from any kind of textual support. A decisive influence on the current uses of narrative was Jean-François Lyotard's concept of 'Grand Narrative' (*see* MASTER NARRATIVE), as outlined in *The Postmodern Condition*. Lyotard contrasts a 'narrative' type of knowledge, typical of ancient societies, where *truth is guaranteed by the special status of the storyteller within the community, with a *scientific type in which *authors are supposed to provide proof of their claims. But scientific discourse is unable to guarantee its own validity, since it rejects authority. During the nineteenth-century, science sought legitimation in what Lyotard calls 'Grand Narratives': sweeping explanations that present scientific knowledge as the instrument of the historical self-realisation of an allegorical *hero variously named Reason, Freedom, the State, or the Human Spirit (*see* ALLEGORY). Three features distinguish 'Grand Narratives' from the little stories that we exchange in daily life: they concern abstract entities rather than concrete individuals (*see* CHARACTER; EXISTENT); they may exist as collective beliefs rather than as the message of particular texts; and they inherit the foundational role of *myth with respect to society rather than being told for their *anecdotal or entertainment value. Little stories and Grand Narratives share a temporal dimension, but while the former simply recount historical (or pseudo-historical) *events, the latter deal directly with a capitalised History. The tacit existence of the Grand Narratives, as well as their explanatory and abstract nature, paved the way toward the 'Narratives of Race, Class, and Gender' or the 'Narratives of Identity' of contemporary cultural studies (*see* CULTURAL STUDIES APPROACHES TO NARRATIVE; NARRATIVE EXPLANATION).

The increasing popularity of the term 'narrative' also reflects the epistemological crisis of contemporary culture. 'Narrative' is what is left when belief in the possibility of knowledge is eroded. The frequently heard phrase 'the narratives of science', popular in the new field of science studies, carries the implication that scientific discourse does not reflect but covertly constructs reality, does not discover truths but fabricates them according to the rules of its own game in a process disturbingly comparable to the overt working of narrative fiction. Calling a discourse 'a narrative' or 'a story' in order to question its claim to truth thus amounts to equating narrative with fiction (*see* PANFICTIONALITY).

In cognitive science and *Artificial Intelligence, narrative tends to be associated with sense-making and problem-solving activities. For instance, the AI developer Kerstin Dautenhahn calls a robot a 'storytelling agent' when, acting on the basis of its memories of past experiences, which are called its *autobiography, the robot performs a sequence of actions leading toward a goal (Dautenhahn and Coles 2001). The assimilation of *memory to autobiography, also popular in psychology (*see* PSYCHOLOGICAL APPROACHES TO NARRATIVE), expresses the idea that living one's life and reflecting upon it is like writing one's *life story: a continuous act of self-creation that involves at every moment choices, responsibilities, re-evaluations, and the addition of new chapters to the book-in-progress.

What is narrative theory to do about this metaphorical or metonymic assimilation of the concept of narrative with ideas which would have been labelled 'belief', 'interpretation', 'attitude', 'rationalisation', 'value', *'ideology', 'behaviour', 'plan', 'memory' or simply 'content' a generation ago (*see* METAPHOR; METONYMY)? Should we design a definition that acts like a semantic police, excluding all 'illegitimate' uses of the term 'narrative', but also endangering its theoretical vitality, or should we bow to current fashion, and work out a definition that accepts all current interpretations, at the price of losing some crucial distinction between narrative and other forms or products of mental activity? A compromise between these two possibilities is to regard narrative as a fuzzy set defined at the centre by a solid core of properties, but accepting various degrees of membership, depending on which properties a candidate displays (*see* MODE). The fuzzy-set hypothesis will account for the fact that certain texts will be unanimously recognised as narratives, such as *fairy tales or *conversational stories about personal experience, while others will encounter limited acceptance: *postmodern novels, *computer games, or historical studies of cultural issues, such as Michel Foucault's *History of Sexuality*.

Describing versus defining narrative

Inquiry into the nature of narrative can take two forms. The first, aiming at a description, asks: what does narrative *do* for human beings; the second, aiming at a definition, tries to capture the distinctive features of narrative.

Here are some examples of the type of observations produced by the descriptive approach: narrative is a fundamental way of organising human experience and a tool for constructing models of reality (Herman 2002; *see* NARRATIVE AS COGNITIVE INSTRUMENT); narrative allows human beings to come to terms with the temporality of their existence (Ricoeur 1984–1988; *see* TIME IN NARRATIVE); narrative is a particular mode of thinking, the mode that relates to the concrete and particular as opposed to the abstract and general (Bruner, who distinguishes 'narrative' and 'scientific' thinking); narrative creates and transmits cultural traditions, and builds the values and beliefs that define cultural *identities; narrative is a vehicle of dominant ideologies and an instrument of power (Foucault 1978; *see* DISCOURSE ANALYSIS (FOUCAULT); IDEOLOGY AND NARRATIVE); narrative is an instrument of self-creation; narrative is a repository of practical knowledge, especially in *oral cultures (this view reminds us of the etymology of the word 'narrative', the Latin verb *gnare*, 'to know'); narrative is a mold in which we shape and preserve memories; narrative, in its fictional form, widens our mental universe beyond the actual and the familiar and provides a playfield for thought experiments (Schaeffer 1999); narrative is an inexhaustible and varied source of *education and entertainment; narrative is a mirror in which we discover what it means to be human.

While descriptive observations such as these can live in peace with each other, definitional approaches tend to provide conflicting views of the nature of narrative, since different scholars will single out different features as constitutive of *narrativity. The following dilemmas illustrate some of the more contentious points.

(1) Does narrative vary according to culture and historical period, or do the fundamental conditions of narrativity constitute cognitive universals (*see* NARRATIVE UNIVERSALS)? That narrative was slow to emerge as a theoretical concept, and only enjoys recognition within academic culture, seems to speak in favour of a relativistic approach, but the culture-specific feature could be the awareness of the concept, rather than the properties that define it. The relativistic approach raises the problem of comparability: if narrative takes radically different forms in every culture, where is the common

denominator that justifies the labelling of these forms as narrative? If one opts for the culture-universal approach, the obvious differences between the narratives of different periods and cultures are a matter of thematic filling in and of variations on a common basic structure. Similarly, the *epic plot and the dramatic *plot can be seen in Western cultures as different realisations of a common scheme.

(2) Does narrative presuppose a verbal act of *narration by an anthropomorphic creature called a *narrator, or can a story be told without the mediation of a narratorial consciousness? Gerald Prince (2003: 58) defines narrative as the representation of real or fictive events by one or more narrators to one or more *narratees. The opposite position is represented by the film scholar David Bordwell, who argues that film narration does not require a narratorial figure (*see* NO-NARRATOR THEORY). Some scholars have attempted to reconcile the narrator-based definition with the possibility of non-verbal narration by analysing drama and movie as presupposing the utterance of a narratorial figure, even when the film or the play does not make use of *voice-over narration (Chatman 1990).

(3) Can the feature of narrativity be isolated as a layer or dimension of meaning, or is it a global effect toward which every element of the text makes a contribution? The first position makes it legitimate to divide the text into narrative parts that move the plot forward and non-narrative parts where time stands still, such as digressions, philosophical considerations, or the moral of a *fable (*see* STORY-DISCOURSE DISTINCTION). But this analysis runs into difficulties in the case of descriptions: while extensive *descriptions can be skipped without causing the reader to lose track of the plot, *characters, and settings could not be identified without descriptive statements (*see* SPACE IN NARRATIVE). If the purpose of narrative is to evoke not just a sequence of events but the worlds in which these events take place (*see* STORY-WORLD), then descriptions cannot be excluded from the narrative layer, and the distinction between narrative and non-narrative elements is blurred. Literary theorists, who generally adhere to the dogma of the inseparability of form and content, tend to favour the second possibility: narrativity as a global effect. Among them is the critic Philip Sturgess, who writes: 'Narrativity is the enabling force of narrative, a force that is present at every point in the narrative' (29). The inevitable consequence of this position is that narrativity becomes indistinguishable from aesthetic teleology, or, as Sturgess puts it, from the consistency with which the text uses its devices (36). Since aesthetic teleology is unique to each text, so is narrativity, and it becomes undefinable.

(4) Is narrativity a matter of form or a matter of content? The proponents of narrativity as form (*see* REALISM, THEORIES OF) radicalise the ideas of Hayden White, who argues that a given sequence of historical events can be represented either as an unstructured list (*annals), as a *chronicle obeying certain principles of unity but lacking a comprehensive explanatory principle, or as a fully formed plot (= narrative), in which events are organised according to a global teleology. But if historical events can be made into stories as well as into something else (for instance into diplomacy textbooks relying on historical examples), doesn't narrative require specific types of raw materials? Can one turn Einstein's famous equation, $E = MC^2$, into a story without adding anything to it? One way to resolve the dilemma of form vs. content is to invoke the linguist Louis Hjelmslev's distinction between form and substance, a distinction that applies to both the content plane and the expression plane of a text, i.e. to signifieds and signifiers. Narrativity in this perspective would reside on the content plane, not on the expression plane, but it would consist of both a certain form (expressed by concepts such as plot, *story arc, or *Freytag's triangle) and a certain substance (characters, settings, events, but not general laws or abstract concepts).

(5) Should a definition of narrative give equal status to all works of literary fiction, or should it regard certain types of postmodern novels (and films) as marginal? In other words, does an avant-garde text that refers to characters, settings, and events, but refuses to organise these contents into a determinate story expand the meaning of narrative, making it historically variable, or does it simply demonstrate the separability of the concepts of 'literature', 'narrative', and 'fiction'?

(6) Does narrative require both discourse and story, signifier and signified, or can it exist as free floating representation, independently of any textual realisation? Is the phrase 'untold story', so dear to tabloids, an oxymoron or can the mind hold a narrative without words, as when we

memorise the plot of a novel, or when we tell our friends: I have a great story to tell you?

Story as cognitive construct

The answer to this last question – the most crucial to a definition of narrative, since it asks what it is made of – lies in a technical distinction between 'narrative' and 'story', even though English dictionaries present these terms as synonymous. (This is why up to now this entry has used them interchangeably.) Representing a common view among narratologists, H. Porter Abbott reserves the term 'narrative' for the combination of story and discourse and defines its two components as follows: 'story is an event or sequence of events (the *action*), and narrative discourse is those events as represented' (2002: 16). Narrative, in this view, is the textual actualisation of story, while story is narrative in a virtual form. If we conceive representation as medium-free, this definition does not limit narrativity to verbal texts nor to narratorial *speech acts. But the two components of narrative play asymmetrical roles, since discourse is defined in terms of its ability to represent that which constitutes story. This means that only story can be defined in autonomous terms. Ever since the Russian formalists made a distinction between 'fabula' and 'sjuzhet' (i.e. story and discourse), the standard narratological position has regarded stories as 'sequences of events', but this characterisation ignores the fact that events are not in themselves stories but rather the raw material out of which stories are made. So what is story, if, as Hayden White has convincingly argued, it is not a type of thing found in the world (as *existents and events are) nor a textual representation of this type of thing (as discourse is)?

Story, like narrative discourse, is a representation, but unlike discourse it is not a representation encoded in material signs. Story is a mental image, a cognitive construct that concerns certain types of entities and relations between these entities (*see* COGNITIVE NARRATOLOGY). Narrative may be a combination of story and discourse, but it is its ability to evoke stories in the mind that distinguishes narrative discourse from other *text-types. Here is tentative definition of the cognitive construct that narratologists call 'story':

1   The mental representation of story involves the construction of the mental image of a world populated with individuated agents (characters) and objects. (Spatial dimension.)
2   This world must undergo not fully predictable changes of state that are caused by non-habitual physical events: either accidents ('happenings') or deliberate actions by intelligent agents. (Temporal dimension.)
3   In addition to being linked to physical states by causal relations, the physical events must be associated with mental states and events (goals, plans, *emotions). This network of connections gives events coherence, motivation, *closure, and intelligibility and turns them into a plot. (Logical, mental and formal dimension; *see* CAUSALITY; STORY SCHEMATA AND CAUSAL STRUCTURE.)

This definition presents narrative as a type of text able to evoke a certain type of image in the mind of the recipient. But, as mentioned above, it does not take a text to inspire the construction of such an image: we may form stories in our mind as a response to life itself. For instance, if I observe a fight on the subway, I will construct in my mind the story of the fight, in order to tell it to my family when I get home. The narrative potential of life can be accounted for by making a distinction between 'being a narrative', and 'possessing narrativity'. The property of 'being' a narrative can be predicated of any semiotic object, whatever the medium, produced with the intent to create a response involving the construction of a story. More precisely, it is the receiver's recognition of this intent that leads to the judgment that a given semiotic object is a narrative (*see* INTENTIONALITY; PRAGMATICS), even though we can never be sure if sender and receiver have the same story in mind. 'Possessing narrativity', on the other hand, means being able to inspire a narrative response, whether or not the text, if there is one, was intended to be processed that way, and whether or not an author designs the stimuli.

The principles that make up the present definition are hard and fast rules that specify minimal conditions. One of the conditions appears however more controversial than the others: does a story have to involve non-habitual events, or can it concern fully routine actions? Should this condition be replaced with a preference rule? This dilemma points to an area where *narrativity (the product of minimal conditions) is particularly difficult to disentangle from *tellability (an issue better described by preference rules), but if the border between narrativity and tellability is sometimes fuzzy, there are nevertheless principles that fall clearly on one side or the other.

By loosening some of the conditions of the above definition, we can account for narrative forms exhibiting less cohesion than canonical stories, such as *diaries, *annals and *chronicles, as well as for the extensions of the term 'narrative' mentioned at the beginning of this entry. The flouting of condition 3 explains for instance the narrative deficiency of some postmodern novels: while they create a world, populate it with characters, and make something happen (though they often take liberties with condition 2), these novels do not allow the reader to reconstruct the network that motivates the actions of characters and binds the events into an intelligible and determinate sequence (see INDETERMINACY). But they compensate for the subversion of story with an extraordinary inventiveness on the level of discourse. The lifting of condition 1 describes the 'Grand Narratives' and their relatives. These constructs are not about individuated beings but about collective entities, and they display general laws rather than a concrete world to the imagination. But they retain a temporal dimension, and they provide global explanations of history. Condition 2 is the hardest to ignore, but its lifting occurs when we speak of 'the narrative of white superiority', or of 'the narrative of the vitality of the Soviet system'. What happens here is that the label narrative has been *metonymically transferred from the stories propagated by colonialist literature or party-controlled media to the a-temporal propositions that form their ideological message. The label remains attached to the ideological statement even after its emancipation from particular stories.

SEE ALSO: ancient theories of narrative (non-Western); ancient theories of narrative (Western)

References and further reading

Abbott, H. Porter (2002) *The Cambridge Introduction to Narrative*, Cambridge: Cambridge University Press.
Barthes, Roland (1977 [1966]) 'Introduction to the Structural Analysis of Narratives', in *Image Music Text*, trans. Stephen Heath, New York: Hill and Wang.
Bordwell, David (1985) *Narration in the Fiction Film*, Madison: University of Wisconsin Press.
Bruner, Jerome (1986) *Actual Minds, Possible Worlds*, Cambridge, Mass.: Harvard University Press.
Bremond, Claude (1973) *Logique du récit*, Paris: Seuil.
Chatman, Seymour (1990) *Coming to Terms: The Rhetoric of Fiction and Film*, Ithaca: Cornell University Press.
Dautenhahn, Kerstin, and Steven J. Coles (2001) 'Narrative Intelligence from the Bottom Up: A Computational Framework for the Study of Story-Telling in Autonomous Agents', *Journal of Artificial Societies and Social Simulation* 4.1, http://jasss.soc.surrey.ac.uk/4/1/1.html
Foucault, Michel (1978) *The History of Sexuality*, trans. Robert Hurley, New York: Random House.
Herman, David (2002) *Story Logic: Problems and Possibilities of Narrative*, Lincoln: University of Nebraska Press.
Hjelmslev, Louis (1961) *Prolegomena to a Theory of Language*, trans. Francis J. Whitfield, Madison: University of Wisconsin Press.
Lyotard, Jean-François (1984 [1979]) *The Postmodern Condition: A Report on Knowledge*, trans. Geoff Bennington and Brian Massumi, Minneapolis: University of Minnesota Press.
Prince, Gerald (2003) *A Dictionary of Narratology*, Lincoln: University of Nebraska Press.
Ricoeur, Paul (1984–1988) *Time and Narrative*, 3 vols., trans. Kathleen McLaughlin and Paul Pellauer, Chicago: University of Chicago Press.
Ryan, Marie-Laure (2004) 'Introduction', in Marie-Laure Ryan (ed.) *Narrative across Media: The Languages of Storytelling*, Lincoln: University of Nebraska Press.
Schaeffer, Jean-Marie (1999) *Pourquoi la fiction?*, Paris: Seuil.
Sturgess, Philip (1992) *Narrativity: Theory and Practice*, Oxford: Clarendon Press.
White, Hayden (1981) 'The Value of Narrativity in the Representation of History', in W. J. T. Mitchell (ed.) *On Narrative*, Chicago: University of Chicago Press.

MARIE-LAURE RYAN

NARRATIVE AS ARGUMENT

To the extent that argument is about something it depends upon a context, a cause, and an occasion (see CAUSALITY). The purposive character of argument is most obvious in the progressive structure of public discourse: argument is variously persuasive, performative, or in the lexicon of law it constitutes an action or more technically a cause of action (see PERFORMATIVITY). The relation of narrative to argument is thus variable and depends amongst other things upon rhetorical *genre and the topic of *address. At a formal level, narrative governs argument in that arrangement, the ordering or internal progression of a discourse, depends upon a *narrative structure in which a premise is elaborated, developed, proved, or refuted. Narrative as arrangement is in this sense intrinsic to logic as well as to dialectic and rhetoric. In

Aristotelian terms, logical proof and probable argument both depend upon conceptual progression understood as the discursive trajectory from premise to conclusion. At a less formal level, narrative or the juristic *narration of the facts is a key element in the practices of persuasion and proof. Narrative is intrinsic to persuasion in the sense of effective appeal to the *audience. The topics or places of argument (*loci communes*) thus provide a guide to the types of narrative that will appeal to specific classes of audience. Without narrative, the rhetoricians were fond of declaring, argument would be nothing.

SEE ALSO: apology; law and narrative; narrative progression; rhetorical approaches to narrative

References and further reading

Bhabha, Homi (ed.) (1990) *Nation and Narration*, London: Routledge.
Cope, Edward (ed.) (1877) *The Rhetoric of Aristotle*, Cambridge: Cambridge University Press.

PETER GOODRICH

NARRATIVE AS COGNITIVE INSTRUMENT

People incorporate stories into a wide array of practices, using narrative to carry out spontaneous conversations, produce and interpret literary texts, make sense of news reports in a variety of *media (*see* JOURNALISM), create and assess medical case histories (*see* MEDICINE AND NARRATIVE), and provide testimony in court (*see* COURTROOM NARRATIVE). In this sense, stories function as a powerful tool for thinking, i.e., a cognitive instrument used as an organisational and problem-solving strategy in many contexts. Study of this 'tool function' of narrative thus complements other approaches developed under the auspices of *cognitive narratology, which seeks to map relationships between *narrative structures and modes of intelligent activity. Instead of focusing on how people make sense of stories – e.g., on the processing strategies used to update mental models of situations and *events traced over the course of a fictional narrative (*see* NARRATIVE COMPREHENSION; SITUATION MODEL) – research on narrative as a cognitive instrument highlights how stories support or enhance intelligence itself. In contexts

of *conversational storytelling, for example, narrative provides an environment for important sense-making activities (Herman 2003a; Ochs and Capps 2001), enabling tellers and interpreters to construct and jointly evaluate conceptual models of states, occurrences, and *existents located in particular regions of experience; to create overarching spatiotemporal links between those regions; and to 'inhabit' the regions in various ways by adopting relatively distant or intimate (and relatively fixed or variable) *perspectives on narrated environments (*see* DEIXIS; FOCALIZATION; IMMERSION; SIMULATION AND NARRATIVE). Further, narrative affords a basis for ascribing roles to agents within such conceptually modelled *storyworld – agents whose activities as *characters can thus be situated within networks of beliefs, desires, and intentions.

Research by Danto (1985), Mink (1978), and Bruner (1991) bolsters the claim that narrative provides essential support for cognition. Focusing on *narrative explanations of *actions and events, Danto suggests that narrative accounts of happenings are needed to bridge the gap between general world-knowledge (e.g., that water freezes at zero degrees centigrade) and knowledge of how something in particular unfolded as part of the history of (a fragment of) the world (e.g., that a frozen patch of water caused me to slip and fall down yesterday) (1985: 238). Analogously, Mink distinguishes between the brute particularity of experience and the theoretical understanding of occurrences as instances of abstract schemata, positioning narrative between these extremes (1978: 132; *see* SCRIPTS AND SCHEMATA). For Mink, furthermore, narrative alone can identify aspects of the world in a way that makes constant and necessary reference to their location in some process of development (146). Meanwhile, Bruner characterises stories as a 'symbolic system' supporting a particular domain of knowledge, i.e., the domain of social beliefs and procedures (versus domains associated with the behaviours of physical objects, for example) (1991: 21). More than just identifying key properties of narrative, Bruner's account suggests ways of mapping those properties onto forms of cognition enabled or organised by stories. For example, narratives display 'hermeneutic composability'; occurrences must be interpreted in light of larger configurations of events (i.e., *plots), whereas building up an understanding of the larger configurations in turn requires making sense of individual events (*see* HERMENEUTICS). Analogously, humans construe particular behaviours of social actors by situating them in a wider context of assumptions about *identity, while also using the specific behaviours to monitor the validity of those same interpretive frames.

Although its original formulation predates the body of research just mentioned, the 'activity theory' developed by the early twentieth century Soviet psychologist Lev Vygotsky (1978; cf. Wertsch 1998) has come to have an especially vital influence on the many fields concerned with cognitive functions of narrative, from *sociolinguistics, *discourse analysis, and *ethnography to *psychology, *education, and media studies (see, e.g., Lyle 2000; Rowe *et al.* 2002). For Vygotsky, intelligence needs to be re-described in terms of modes of activity within given environments; cognition itself is thus 'de-localised', i.e., spread across all the components of activities viewed as systems at once exhibiting and enabling intelligent behaviour. Such components can be non-human as well as human, material as well as mental (cf. Hutchins 1995); interactions among these elements make the system as a whole intelligent and, reciprocally, confer knowledge-generating properties on each component, including human ones. A key concern for cognitive narratologists is thus to specify how *narratively organised* systems of activity – systems that range from the practice of conversational storytelling to the performance of ceremonies such as eulogies – both embody and enable socially distributed cognition.

Literary narratives also help constitute such intelligent systems. For example, *framed narratives (e.g., Wordsworth's *The Ruined Cottage*, Conrad's *Heart of Darkness*) at once stage and facilitate the process of shared thinking about past events. The framed events may be more or less remote from the here-and-now of a framing communicative event that is itself structured as an act of *narration. In such contexts, narrative *embedding contributes to the formation of intelligent systems which propagate experiential frames – specifically, the experiences of character-narrators – across *time and *space (Herman 2003b; *see* EXPERIENTIALITY; NARRATOR). The resulting system affords opportunities for distributing intelligence not provided by other less richly differentiated narrative structures. In a story that does not make use of narrative embedding there

will be no framing narratorial act, and no reference to situations and events making up the framed narrative. In turn, the gestalt formed by *the relations among* these and other components (including the tellers and interlocutors located at different narrative levels, as well as the interpreters of the framed narrative as a whole) will lose definition, decreasing the system's ability to generate knowledge about multiple experiential frames. In other words, there will be a net decrease in the capacity of the system to communicate representations originating from sources potentially quite widely separated in space and time. Narrative embedding thus increases the distributional reach of a framed tale, enhancing the overall power of the knowledge-generating system to which it contributes.

References and further reading

Bruner, Jerome (1991) 'The Narrative Construction of Reality', *Critical Inquiry*, 18, 1–21.

Danto, Arthur (1985) *Narration and Knowledge*, NY: Columbia University Press.

Herman, David (2003a) 'Stories as a Tool for Thinking', in David Herman (ed.) *Narrative Theory and the Cognitive Sciences*, Stanford, CA: CSLI Publications.

—— (2003b) 'Regrounding Narratology: The Study of Narratively Organized Systems for Thinking', in Jan Christoph Meister, Tom Kindt, and Hans-Harald Müller (eds) *What is Narratology? Questions and Answers Regarding the Status of a Theory*, Berlin: de Gruyter.

Hutchins, Edwin (1995) 'How a Cockpit Remembers Its Speeds', *Cognitive Science*, 19, 265–88.

Lyle, Sue (2000) 'Narrative Understanding: Developing a Theoretical Context for Understanding How Children Make Meaning in a Classroom Setting', *Journal of Curriculum Studies*, 32.1, 45–63.

Mink, Louis O. (1978) 'Narrative Form as a Cognitive Instrument', in Robert H. Canary and Henry Kozicki (eds) *The Writing of History: Literary Form and Historical Understanding*, Madison: University of Wisconsin Press.

Ochs, Elinor, and Lisa Capps (2001) *Living Narrative: Creating Lives in Everyday Storytelling*, Cambridge, Mass.: Harvard University Press.

Rowe, Shawn, James Wertsch, and Tatyana Kosyaeva (2002) 'Linking Little Narratives to Big Ones: Narrative and Public Memory in History Museums', *Culture and Psychology*, 8, 96–112.

Vygotsky, Lev S. (1978) *Mind in Society: The Development of Higher Psychological Processes*, trans. and eds., Michael Cole, Vera John-Steiner, Sylvia Scribner, Ellen Souberman, Cambridge, Mass.: Harvard University Press.

Wertsch, James (1998) *Mind as Action*, New York: Oxford University Press.

DAVID HERMAN

NARRATIVE COMPREHENSION

Narrative comprehension is a highly inter-disciplinary area of study in which researchers from linguistics, literary studies, *Artificial Intelligence, and psychology aim to understand how readers create cognitive representations of *narratives (*see* COGNITIVE NARRATOLOGY; LINGUISTIC APPROACHES TO NARRATIVE; PSYCHOLOGICAL APPROACHES TO NARRATIVE). These cognitive representations are mental stores of information. They account for how readers shift their perceptions from the 'here and now' of everyday experience to the world of a story (*see* DEIXIS; SPACE IN NARRATIVE). Furthermore, they explain how readers mentally keep track of their knowledge and beliefs about all aspects of a story, including *characters, relations between characters, places, *time, *events, causal relations, the motivations for characters' *actions, and *plot (*see* CAUSALITY).

A major objective of those studying narrative comprehension is to understand the nature of reading. In literary studies, the mental processes involved in converting texts into rich and complex cognitive representations are often taken for granted. However, from a linguistic and psychological point of view, there is a significant amount still to be learned about the way in which readers move from perceiving mere strings of words on the pages of books to the sensation of being so immersed in different worlds that they feel as if they are witnessing events and experiencing the *emotions of characters (*see* IMMERSION; PHENOMENOLOGY OF NARRATIVE). These worlds have been called 'narrative worlds', 'text worlds', and *'storyworlds' by different researchers (Gerrig 1993, Werth 1999, and Herman 2002 respectively).

Reading can be accounted for by examining the general knowledge that readers bring to a text and the inferences that readers make using this knowledge (*see* SCRIPTS AND SCHEMATA). Early work by researchers in cognitive science examined the comprehension of 'laboratory texts' which frequently consisted of just a few sentences. This research demonstrated how inferences could enable readers to comprehend such sentences – for example, by recognising unstated but implied causal links between the sentences (e.g. Charniak 1972) – but its usefulness was limited by the fact that it did not use the kind of texts that people normally read. Much of the more recent research on comprehension, as described below, has moved on to explore the cognitive effort required to read 'real texts', such as *novels, *short stories, and newspaper articles. These real texts present information that is specific to a particular story and hence require readers to form 'text-specific' cognitive representations (Emmott 1997), such as stores of information about particular characters. These 'text-specific' cognitive representations can be complex since, in full-length stories, information about the narrative world accumulates and changes, requiring readers to store their knowledge and update their cognitive representations accordingly.

The study of narrative comprehension covers a number of key areas:

(1) *Knowledge of specific worlds* – Researchers provide models of how readers keep track of all major aspects of narratives, including how they collect information and make inferences about: (i) major and minor characters, including their relevant characteristics in the main narrative and in flashbacks; (ii) groupings of characters in particular contexts and the social relations between characters; (iii) place and time; (iv) *perspectives and possible worlds; (v) causal links between events; (vi) *plot (see Ryan 1991; Duchan *et al.* 1995; Emmott 1997, 2003; Goldman *et al.* 1999; Herman 2002; Werth 1999; *see* TEXT-WORLD APPROACH TO NARRATIVE; SITUATION MODEL; FOCALIZATION; POINT OF VIEW (LITERARY); POSSIBLE-WORLDS THEORY).

(2) *Thematic meaning* – Researchers investigate the way in which readers extract the key themes of narratives (Louwerse and van Peer 2002; *see* THEMATIC APPROACHES TO NARRATIVE).

(3) *Emotion* – Cognitive scientists have tended to focus primarily on the information content of narratives, but the emotional responses of readers are crucial and as yet under-researched. Topics of study include the interest levels of readers, their empathy with characters, and the nature of suspense (Gerrig 1993; *see* SUSPENSE AND SURPRISE).

(4) *Genres and types of world* – Different genres may make different demands on readers in terms of constructing narrative worlds, particularly those which challenge our everyday assumptions, such as the worlds of *science fiction and *postmodern narratives (Herman 2002). Some researchers argue that readers need different processing mechanisms for literary and non-literary texts (Zwaan 1993; László 1999).

(5) *Immersion in narrative worlds* – Researchers study how readers become 'transported' into narrative worlds and how their reading can affect their perception of the real world (Gerrig 1993).

(6) *Linguistic features of narratives* – Readers interpret specific linguistic items in narratives, such as *reference items, negatives, action verbs, and *metaphors, by using their knowledge and making inferences (*see* DISCOURSE ANALYSIS (LINGUISTICS)). Research on the processing of linguistic items in narrative is crucial for the development of linguistic and psychological theories that adequately reflect the nature of the texts that people read (Duchan *et al.* 1995; Emmott 1997; Goldman *et al.* 1999; Herman 2002; Werth 1999).

(7) *Readers* – Researchers in Psychology and the Empirical Study of Literature test the responses of readers (*see* READER-RESPONSE THEORY; RECEPTION THEORY). This work includes examining the general processes of reading and the study of readers of different ages, *genders, nationalities, etc. (Goldman *et al.* 1999; László 1999; Zwaan 1993).

References and further reading

Charniak, Eugene (1972) *Towards a Model of Children's Story Comprehension*, Ph.D. thesis, Cambridge: MIT Press.

Duchan, Judith F., Gail A. Bruder, and Lynne E. Hewitt (eds) (1995) *Deixis in Narrative: A Cognitive Science Perspective*, Hillsdale, N.J.: Lawrence Erlbaum.

Emmott, Catherine (1997) *Narrative Comprehension: A Discourse Perspective*, Oxford: Oxford University Press.

—— (2003) 'Reading for Pleasure: A Cognitive Poetic Analysis of "Twists in the Tale" and Other Plot Reversals in Narrative Texts', in Joanna Gavins and Gerard Steen (eds) *Cognitive Poetics in Practice*, London: Routledge.

Gerrig, Richard J. (1993) *Experiencing Narrative Worlds: On the Psychological Activities of Reading*, New Haven: Yale University Press.

Goldman, Susan R., Arthur, C. Graesser, and Paul van den Broek (eds) (1999) *Narrative Comprehension, Causality, and Coherence: Essays in Honor of Tom Trabasso*, Mahwah: Lawrence Erlbaum.

Herman, David (2002) *Story Logic: Problems and Possibilities of Narrative*, Lincoln: University of Nebraska Press.

László, János (1999) *Cognition and Representation in Literature: The Psychology of Literary Narratives*, Budapest: Akadémiai Kiadó.

Louwerse, Max, and Willie van Peer (2002) *Thematics: Interdisciplinary Perspectives*, Amsterdam: Benjamins.

Ryan, Marie-Laure (1991) *Possible Worlds, Artificial Intelligence and Narrative Theory*, Bloomington: Indiana University Press.

Werth, Paul N. (1999) *Text Worlds: Representing Conceptual Space in Discourse*, London: Longman.

Zwaan, Rolf. A. (1993) *Aspects of Literary Comprehension*, Amsterdam: Benjamins.

CATHERINE EMMOTT

NARRATIVE DISORDERS

Narrative disorders are states of impairment experienced by individuals with focal brain damage affecting discrete regions of the human neural network that enables the generation of narrative. Fundamental components of this network include (1) the amygdalo-hippocampal system, where episodic and autobiographic *memories are initially arranged (*see* AUTOBIOGRAPHY); (2) the left peri-Sylvian region where language is formulated; and (3) the frontal cortices and their subcortical connections, where individual entities and *events are organised into narratively structured sequences, whether fictional (imagined) or non-fictional (*see* EXISTENT; FICTION, THEORIES OF). Studies employing functional imaging in normal volunteers and clinical reports assessing alterations in cognition in individuals who have suffered focal brain injuries provide a convergent view of how the brain narratively organises experience.

Four types of 'dysnarrativia' will be described here. The first two types appear in individuals with global amnesia – loss of the ability to form new memories due to bilateral brain damage restricted to the amygdalo-hippocampal system. In recounting their autobiographic experience, most amnestic individuals exhibit *'arrested narration'*: they are able to frame a coherent *life story leading up to their injury but not beyond, though this narrative may be 30 years out of date. A smaller group of amnestic individuals show *unbounded narration*. These individuals develop confabulation, restlessly fabricating narratives that purport to describe recent events in their lives but actually have little or no relationship to genuine occurrences. Usually these individuals have suffered, in addition to amygdalo-hippocampal system damage producing amnesia, additional injury to frontal lobe structures that are responsible for monitoring the veracity of responses and inhibiting inaccurate replies (*see* TRUTH). A third type of dysnarrativia appears in individuals with bilateral damage to the ventromedial frontal lobe. These individuals have intact access to autobiographic memories, but fail to construct and explore internal 'as-if' narrative scenarios. Accordingly, they demonstrate *'under-narration'*, often an impairment that often results in disastrous financial and social consequences. A fourth form of dysnarrativia appears in individuals who have injury to the dorsolateral and mesial frontal cortices. These individuals are impaired in high-level cognitive programs that extract meaning from ongoing experience, organise the mind's mental contents coherently, and elaborate plans for sequenced action. Their behavioural repertoire is reduced and they become apathetic. They are unable to state (and likely fail to generate internally) a narrative account of their experiences, wishes, and actions, although they are fully cognisant of their visual, auditory, and tactile surround. These patients experience *'denarration'*, aware but failing to organise experience in an action-generating temporal frame. Individuals with brain injuries in other sectors may lose their linguistic, mathematic, syllogistic, visuospatial, memory, or kinesthetic competencies and still be recognisably the same persons. Humans who have lost the ability to construct narrative, however, have lost their selves.

SEE ALSO: biological foundations of narrative; identity and narrative; narrative as cognitive instrument; narrative psychology; time in narrative

References and further reading

Damasio, Antonio (1994) *Descartes's Error: Emotion, Reason and the Human Brain*, New York: G.P. Putnam's Sons.

Sacks, Oliver (1985) *The Man Who Mistook His Wife for a Hat and Other Clinical Tales*, New York: Summit Books.

Saver, Jeffrey L., and Antonio R. Damasio (1991) 'Preserved Access and Processing of Social Knowledge in a Patient with Acquired Sociopathy due to Ventromedial Frontal Damage', *Neuropsychologia*, 29, 1241–249.

Turner, Mark (1996) *The Literary Mind*, New York: Oxford University Press.

Young, Kay, and Jeffrey L. Saver (2001) 'The Neurology of Narrative', *Substance*, 30, 72–84.

KAY YOUNG AND JEFFREY SAVER

NARRATIVE DYNAMICS

Narrative dynamics is a perspective that views narrative as a progressively unfolding, interconnected system of elements rather than as a succession of discrete *events. Peter Brooks, for example, criticises Russian formalist and *structuralist accounts of narrative that limit themselves to distinguishing between the chronology of the story (fabula) and that of its presentation in the text (sjuzhet) (*see* FORMALISM; STORY-DISCOURSE DISTINCTION; TEMPORAL ORDERING). A more dynamic approach insists on the strongly connected or mutually entailing features of the events of a narrative. Most theorists would probably agree that a dynamic approach to narrative is a laudatory objective; however, they tend to disagree about where the dynamism should be located or how it should be described. Many theorists of *plot, including E. M. Forster, Paul Ricoeur, and Brooks, find in plot an embracing concept for the design and intention of narrative or the intelligible whole that governs a succession of events in a story; in this conception, plot makes events into a *narrative. Brooks further identifies endings as of primary importance to the dynamic shaping of narrative: the end, as it were, 'writes' the beginning and shapes the middle; in narrating, everything is transformed by the structuring presence of the end, by the meaning the events acquire when viewed from the vantage point of the end (1984: 22). Edward Said, who expresses an equally dynamic conception of narrative, argues instead that it is the choice of beginning that determines in advance the sequence that will then unfold.

Non-plot-based ordering principles can also provide an organising line or governing pattern that animates the narrative. Avant-garde writers have developed a number of alternative methods of narrative production, including alphabetical, numerological, and thematic progressions that develop unconventional narrative sequences (*see* NARRATIVE UNITS; THEMATIC APPROACHES TO NARRATIVE). Still more radical forms of text generation were developed by the authors of the *nouveau roman* and the *Tel Quel* novel; in these experiments a small group of words, *images, or objects would generate an entire narrative (see Hayman 1987; Richardson 2005).

*Reception theory has also often stressed the dynamic nature of the reader's encounter with the text. Wolfgang Iser observes that the literary text is replete with gaps of information that the reader must fill to make sense of the work (*see* GAPPING); these hypothetical constructs are then shown to be in need of further modification by subsequent textual units (*see* NARRATIVE UNITS), with the act of reading being construed as a dynamic process that always involves anticipation and retrospection.

SEE ALSO: narrative progression; reader-response theory

References and further reading

Brooks, Peter (1984) *Reading for the Plot: Design and Intention in Narrative*, Cambridge, Mass.: Harvard University Press.

Hayman, David (1987) *Re-Forming the Narrative: Towards a Mechanics of Modernist Fiction*, Ithaca: Cornell University Press.

Iser, Wolfgang (1972) 'The Reading Process: A Phenomenological Approach', *New Literary History*, 3, 279–99.

Richardson, Brian (ed.) (2002) *Narrative Dynamics*, Columbus: Ohio State University Press.

—— (2005) 'Beyond the Poetics of Plot: From *Ulysses* to Postmodern Narrative Progressions', in James Phelan and Peter Rabinowitz (eds) *A Companion to Narrative Theory*, Oxford: Blackwell.

Shklovskii, Viktor (1990) 'The Relationship between Devices of Plot Construction and General Devices of Style', in *Theory of Prose*, trans. Benjamin Sher, Elmwood Park IL: Dalkey Archive Press.

BRIAN RICHARDSON

NARRATIVE EXPLANATION

Historical theorists have dealt with the question of how narrative provides a mode of explanation from two perspectives. One is to focus on the components of (historical) narrative and ask what explanatory narrative strategies can be found there. The other is to ask oneself in what way a historical narrative, when taken as a *whole*, can be said to explain the past.

Within the framework of the first set of premises a historical narrative is seen as a series of statements about states of affairs of the past, a series in which each statement is causally linked to the one preceding it and to the one following it (*see* CAUSALITY). The explanatory force of narrative then depends on the *truth of all the individual causal claims linking together the chain of what one might call the narrative's 'argument'. As was pointed out by Haskell Fain, the problem with this model is that it does not explain what guides the selection of the individual components of the narrative whole. For example, in a narrative about Napoleon the historian should avoid moving from

an account of Napoleon's plans for an invasion of England to a neuro-physiological account of what went on in the Emperor's mind, even though these two things can be causally related. A factor comes therefore into play in the writing of (explanatory) narrative for which the model does not account. Put differently, the requirement that its individual units must be causally related may be a necessary but not a sufficient condition for satisfactory narrative explanation.

The second approach, as proposed by William Dray, argues that our puzzlement about what happened in human life is often best resolved by telling a story explaining *how* it could come about. For example, when explaining the French Revolution the historian will enumerate facts about the intellectual climate of the time, about the institutional shortcomings of the French *ancien regime*, about social friction and conflict, about a temporary economic setback in the years preceding the revolution etc., without being expected to expound the causal relationship between all these things. In other words, explanatory value lies in the pattern of these elements, not in their *causal* interaction. In short, this is an explanation of *how* something could come about, not *why* something did come about.

SEE ALSO: atomic and molecular narratives; historiography

References and further reading

Danto, Arthur C. (1985) *Narration and Knowledge*, New York: Columbia University Press.

Dray, William (1970) *Laws and Explanation in History*, Oxford: Oxford University Press.

Fain, Haskell (1970) *Between Philosophy and History*, Princeton: Princeton University Press.

FRANK ANKERSMIT

NARRATIVE, GAMES, AND PLAY

A form of activity found in all human cultures, as well as among some animals, game-playing is generally associated with the following features: players engage in it for the sake of pleasure; it stands outside ordinary (practical) life; it is originally not connected with material interests; it takes place in its own *time and *space, and it tends to promote the formation of social groupings (Huizinga 1955). Game-playing comes in two forms, which Plato called *ludus* (a technical term with a more narrow meaning than its etymological relative *ludic*, which refers to all kinds of playing) and *paidia*. *Ludus*, a category best exemplified by board games and sports games, is defined by pre-existing rules that players agree to observe; these rules specify a goal and the allowed means to attain that goal. According to Bernard Suits, the latter type of rules consist of setting unnecessary obstacles toward the achievement of the goal: games overwhelmingly prefer less efficient to more efficient means. The attainment of the goal, regarded as 'winning', is invested by the players with a positive value, which turns *ludus* into a competition between players, or between the player and the game rules. In contrast to *ludus*, the informal activity of *paidia* allows players to make (and break) their own rules, and it does not present a computable outcome; examples of *paidia* are playground activities, the use of toys, non-serious behaviours such as teasing, and the transgression of social rules found in carnival festivities.

Games and narrative interact with each other in two types of phenomena, each of which may foreground either *ludus* or *paidia*.

1 Narrative games – games that use narrative scripts.
2 Playful narratives – narratives that use game features.

(1) Narrative games foregrounding *paidia*. No ludic activity gives more prominence to narrative than the games of make-believe through which children invent imaginary worlds and create a story by impersonating characters within these worlds (*see* CHILDREN'S STORYTELLING). Kendall Walton regards make-believe as the fundamental world-making activity, and he uses the concept as the cornerstone of a phenomenological theory of *fiction. Games of make-believe are classical examples of *paidia*: participants make up the world-defining rules on the fly, for instance by deciding that a stump in the real world counts as a bear in the fictional world; the rules can be modified in the course of the game; the game is open-ended, rather than leading to a predefined goal; and there are usually no winners nor losers. The *narrativity of games of make-believe is not provided by a predefined script, but emerges during play from the collaborative activity of the participants. As players impersonate *characters and perform *actions in their name, they 'write' the

*life story of these imaginary individuals, as well as the history of the fictional world (*see* STORYWORLD).

(2) Narrative games foregrounding *ludus*. According to the French sociologist Roger Caillois, games that you either win or lose do not create fictional worlds, and consequently do not present a narrative dimension. While the abstract character of most board games and sports games seems to verify Caillois' observation, the advent of computer technology initiated a spectacular reconciliation of competitive *ludus* and narrativity. What makes *computer games unique among games is their ability to locate problem-solving activities in a sensorially rich, evolving fictional world that stimulates both strategic thinking and the imagination. In a quest-type game, for instance, players are invited to impersonate an avatar whose adventures in the fictional world are partly scripted by the code (generally as a sequence of obstacles to overcome), partly created by the player's actions.

While make-believe and some computer games involve the mimetic enactment of a story by the participants, there are numerous games that rely on the transmission or production of a diegetic text (*see* MODE) with optional narrative content: riddles, jump-rope rhymes, mad-lib party games, *tall tale contests, and games built around *nursery rhymes. Most of these games fall in the twilight zone between *ludus* and *paidia*.

(3) Playful narratives foregrounding *paidia*. We think of the spirit of play – the dynamic creation and subversion of rules – as typical of *postmodern narratives: wasn't it Derrida, one of the patron saints of the movement, who regarded language as a free play of signifiers unhindered by ties to an extra-linguistic reality, and who advocated decentred structures where elements constantly exchange their place with other members of the system, like children playing musical chairs? But *paidia* is also a major force in the earliest stages of the *novel. We find it in the ironic condemnation of the *novel voiced in *Don Quixote*, in the blank pages, digressions, and narratorial self-consciousness of *Tristram Shandy*, in the authorial intrusions of Diderot's *Jacques the Fataliste* (*see* COMMENTARY; METANARRATIVE COMMENT), and in the illusion-breaking footnotes of Jean Paul Richter's rococo novels. In postmodernism, *paidia* becomes self-reference (*see* REFLEXIVITY), paradox, *metalepsis, the carnivalesque, placing facts under erasure, the wandering of fictional characters from

one narrative world to another, treating *identities like disposable garments, and stepping in and out of roles. Through *paidia*, authors play with words, with literary *genres, with established literary conventions, with the concept of representation (*see* MIMESIS), and with fictional levels (*see* EMBEDDING), without subjecting themselves to rigid constraints and without voluntarily limiting their freedom.

(4) Playful narratives foregrounding *ludus*. Most older forms of verbal art were language games characterised by freely chosen formal patterns such as rhyme, meter, alliteration, repetitions, oppositions, double meanings, acrostics, and anagrams. Though the rules that defined these patterns served aesthetic purposes, they constituted unnecessary obstacles to the expression of meaning, especially of narrative meaning. The text was more the solution of a problem than a means of access to a fictional world. These priorities changed when the development of the novel as a wide-open prose form shifted the focus of attention from the *author's virtuosity in handling rules to the world projected by the text. But the spirit of language games was revived in the mid-twentieth century, when the *Oulipo movement developed an aesthetics based on the observance of extremely strict constraints, such as the lipogram (avoiding certain letters) or the palindrome (strings of letters that read identically from left to right or right to left). Georges Perec wrote for instance an entire novel, *La Disparition*, without using the letter *e*. Another manifestation of this ambition to reconcile narrative worlds and formal rules is the adoption by novelists of the structures of existing board or card games, for instance Italo Calvino's use of the Tarot game in *The Castle of Crossed Destinies*.

The competitive dimension of *ludus* conflicts with the disinterested nature of aesthetic contemplation, and is therefore absent from literary narratives. This marks the distinction between genuine narrative games and playful narratives.

SEE ALSO: postmodern narrative; sports broadcasts

References and further reading

Caillois, Roger (1961) *Men, Play and Games*, trans. Meyer Burach, New York: Free Press.
Derrida, Jacques (1970) 'Structure, Sign and Play in the Discourse of the Human Sciences', in Richard Macksey and Eugenio Donato (eds) *The Languages of Criticism and the Sciences of Man*, Baltimore: Johns Hopkins University Press.
Huizinga, Johan (1955) *Homo Ludens: A Study of the Play Element in Culture*, Boston: Beacon Press.
Juul, Jesper (2004) *Half-Real: Video Games between Real Rules and Fictional Worlds*, Ph. D. dissertation, IT University, Copenhagen.
Motte, Warren (1995) *Playtexts: Ludics in Contemporary Literature*, Lincoln: University of Nebraska Press.
Ryan, Marie-Laure (2001) *Narrative as Virtual Reality: Immersion and Interactivity in Literature and Electronic Media*, Baltimore: Johns Hopkins University Press.
Suits, Bernard (1978) *The Grasshopper: Games, Life and Utopia*, Toronto: University of Toronto Press.
Sutton-Smith, Brian (1997) *The Ambiguity of Play*, Cambridge, Mass.: Harvard University Press.
Walton, Kendall (1990) *Mimesis as Make-Believe: On the Foundations of the Representational Arts*, Cambridge, Mass.: Harvard University Press.

MARIE-LAURE RYAN

NARRATIVE IN POETRY

Poetry has been relatively neglected in recent narrative theory, apart from the Homeric poems and a few other exceptions, and even these tend to be treated as though they were essentially prose fictions. This is doubly surprising, since so many poems of all *genres and traditions possess a *narrative aspect or dimension, just as, conversely, many of the world's most valued literary narratives are poems, perhaps a majority of them if one takes oral literature into account (*see* ORAL CULTURES AND NARRATIVE). This neglect can be traced to the early-twentieth-century devaluation of narrative in poetry, leading to a sharp division of labour between academic poetry criticism, which devotes scant attention to narrative, and narrative criticism and theory, which slights poetry. However, longer narrative forms are currently undergoing a revival in 'postmodernist' poetry, so the time may be ripe for narrative theory to revisit this area.

As a field of inquiry, 'narrative in poetry' encompasses several distinguishable phenomena, among them.

(1) Continuous narrative poems. Under this heading fall poems in the *epic tradition, broadly construed to include 'primary' epics (i.e., those emerging in the context of oral literature: the Homeric poems, *Beowulf*, the *Kalevala*, etc.), 'secondary' literary epics (e.g., Virgil's *Aeneid*, Milton's *Paradise Lost*), and medieval and Renaissance verse *romances (e.g., Chrétien de Troyes, Ariosto, Spenser), as well as mock-epic poems; folk-ballads

and their literary imitations (e.g, Coleridge's *The Rime of the Ancient Mariner*) (*see* BALLAD; MEDIEVAL NARRATIVE); 'novels in verse' (e.g., Pushkin's *Eugene Onegin*, Browning's *The Ring and the Book*); and narrative *autobiographies in verse (e.g., Wordsworth's *The Prelude*), among other genres. Most if not all of the 'classic' issues of narratology arise in these poems, including *orality, *fictionality, *author and *audience, *narrator and *narratee, monologism and *dialogism, *diegesis and *mimesis, the *story-discourse distinction, *exposition and *description, episode and digression, *embedding, multi-plot narrative, characterisation, etc. (*see* CHARACTER).

(2) Quasi-narrative sequences, e.g., Renaissance sonnet-sequences (Petrarch, Shakespeare, etc.). Here issues of *narrativisation, *gapping- and gap-filling are particularly acute.

(3) Implicit *narrative situations of lyric poems. A lyric poem typically projects a persona who 'utters' the poem (a 'lyric I') and/or an experiencer who undergoes the experience evoked by it, and it typically implies a *narrative situation for the act of utterance and/or experience (Wolf 1998). Obvious examples are *dramatic monologues (e.g., Browning's 'My Last Duchess'), but many if not all lyric poems invite some degree of narrativisation, involving more or less complex gap-filling and inference.

(4) Narrative materials 'folded into' basically lyric poems, e.g., the *myths and 'micro-narratives' incorporated in Pindaric odes. Here the poetics of allusion come into play (*see* INTERTEXTUALITY), but also analogical structuring, internal duplication and *mise en abyme*, etc.

Over time, the locus of *narrativity in poetry has shifted away from epic. Moribund by the nineteenth century, narrative poetry in the epic tradition was replaced by verse autobiography and 'novels in verse' (*see* NOVEL, THE), and increasingly by non-narrative long poems, of which the model was Whitman's *Leaves of Grass*. This latter phenomenon reflected the sweeping 'lyricisation' that overtook all poetic genres in the nineteenth- and twentieth-centuries, creating a situation where, for the first time in Western literary history, the short lyric poem came to be accepted as poetry's universal norm. Modernist poetics of the *'image' interdicted narrative in poetry, and in place of continuous narrative and quasi-narrative sequences there arose such typically modernist alternatives as the long collage-poem (e.g., Eliot's *The Waste Land*, Pound's *Cantos*),

the 'modern poetic sequence' (Rosenthal and Gall 1983), and the 'serial poem' (Conte 1991), all of them based on the non-narrative accumulation of small lyrical building-blocks. Continuous narrative survived in marginalized and obsolescent forms (e.g., the 'epics' of E. A. Robinson and Stephen Vincent Benet, the verse novels of Robert Penn Warren, the balladry of Robert Service, etc.), while implicit narrative continued to thrive in the 'epiphanic' lyric poem that dominates the contemporary scene (*see* EPIPHANY).

Modernist-era criticism and theory followed the practitioners' lead. Criticism and analysis of poetry came to focus on verbal ambiguity and figuration, especially *metaphor (in the New Critical tradition), or on the 'poetry of grammar' (in the Formalist/Jakobsonian tradition) (*see* FORMALISM). Excluded from poetry analysis, narrative was left to specialists in prose fiction, with rare exceptions (e.g., Bakhtin's recourse to *Onegin* in developing his theory of the dialogical novel).

Reacting against the modernist interdiction of narrative, contemporary postmodernist poetry has sought to revive continuous narrative (Perloff 1985). To do so, it has resorted to such strategies as adapting conventions from popular *genre fiction (e.g., the Western in Dorn's *Gunslinger*, *science fiction in Turner's *The New World*, *soap opera in Seth's *The Golden Gate*), and rewriting pre-modernist narrative poems in a mode of pastiche or parody (e.g., *The Odyssey* in Walcott's *Omeros*, *The Divine Comedy* in Merrill's *The Changing Light at Sandover*, *Onegin* in Hejinian's *Oxota*) (McHale 2000). Some postmodernist poets (e.g., Ashbery in *Flow Chart* and *Girls on the Run*) practice what might be called 'weak narrativity', evoking narrative coherence while simultaneously undermining confidence in it through irrelevance, *indeterminacy, and deliberately incompetent storytelling (McHale 2001).

With postmodernist poets setting the pace in this way, it seems high time for narratologists to reclaim poetry for narrative theory. Of the many theoretical problems of narrative in poetry that remain ill-understood and deserve systematic attention, three stand out.

(1) World-building. Do narrative poems project fictional worlds in the same way prose fictions do, and if not, how do poetry's worlds differ? (For a promising start in this area, see Wolf 1998; *see* POSSIBLE-WORLDS THEORY; TEXT-WORLD APPROACH TO NARRATIVE).

(2) The counterpoint of narrative and verse-form. How does the unfolding of story in narrative poems relate to the formal articulation of poetry into stanzas, lines, metrical feet, etc.? e.g., how does narrative interact with Spenserian stanza-form, or with the enjambed blank verse of *Paradise Lost*?

(3) The relation between narrative and figuration. Granted the special affinity between poetry and figuration, what relations obtain between narrative logic and the logic of poetic metaphor?

SEE ALSO: modernist narrative; postmodern narrative

References and further reading

Conte, Joseph (1991) *Unending Design: The Forms of Postmodern Poetry*, Ithaca: Cornell University Press.
McHale, Brian (2000) 'Telling Stories Again: On the Replenishment of Narrative in the Postmodernist Long Poem', *Yearbook of English Studies*, 30, 250–62.
—— (2001) 'Weak Narrativity: The Case of Avant-Garde Narrative Poetry', *Narrative*, 9.2, 161–67.
Perloff, Marjorie (1985) *The Dance of the Intellect: Studies in the Poetry of the Pound Tradition*, Cambridge: Cambridge University Press.
Rosenthal, M. L., and Sally M. Gall (1983) *The Modern Poetics Sequence: The Genius of Modern Poetry*, New York: Oxford University Press.
Wolf, Werner (1998) 'Aesthetic Illusion in Lyric Poetry?', *Poetica*, 30.3–4, 251–89.

BRIAN McHALE

NARRATIVE INTELLIGENCE

The field of study called Narrative Intelligence (NI) arose at the intersection of *Artificial Intelligence; literary theory; *media theory and practice (especially as related to *narrative), and user interface and interaction design. A radically *interdisciplinary subfield of its contributing fields, NI inspires critical reflection and hybridisation of theories and practices from previously separate disciplines to formulate new topics and methods for the analysis and design of computational narrative systems and computationally informed narratological frameworks. While we can see forbearers of NI in early experiments in *computational approaches to narrative in artificial intelligence (Schank and Riesbeck 1981), NI as a mode of computational narrative theory and design began in 1990 in a reading group at the Massachusetts Institute of Technology Media Laboratory (Davis and Travers 2003).

NI addresses a variety of research questions: (1) *narrative as computational content*, in story understanding, story generation, and case-based reasoning, in interactive forms of *fiction, *drama, and cinema, as well as in *computer games, and in systems that support and capture human story-telling (*see* INTERACTIVE FICTION; FILM NARRATIVE); (2) *narrative as computational interface* (Don 1992), in narratively structured computational interfaces, i.e., interfaces to computer programs that use agents embodied as *characters to aid in navigation or provide explanations, or that use narrative forms to structure the interaction between the machine and the user; (3) *narrative as mode of design*, in the interaction design techniques of personas, scenarios, storyboards, and embodied role-playing methods sometimes referred to as 'bodystorming'; and (4) *narrative as cognitive strategy*, i.e., as an organising principle for human and computational perception, reasoning, and *memory (*see* NARRATIVE AS COGNITIVE INSTRUMENT).

Important to NI methodology, given its roots in constructivist views of meaning making (Reddy 1979), is the integration of theory and practice – i.e., of theory and artefact design. NI's research methodology is to construct artefacts in order to (de)construct theories and to construct theories in order to (de)construct artefacts. As a result, the NI group at MIT and later NI researchers produce technological artefacts that hybridise narrative theory and computational narrative practice, such as a program-debugging interface that uses storyboards consisting of *conflicts between animated characters (Travers and Davis 1993) and interactive automatic video documentary systems (Domike *et al.* 2003).

NI continues to grow as a field and was identified in the 2003 report of the National Research Council Committee on Information Technology and Creativity as one of the most promising directions for interdisciplinary research and innovation connecting the humanistic and technical disciplines.

SEE ALSO: cognitive narratology; digital narrative; narrative turn in the humanities

References and further reading

Davis, Marc, and Michael Travers (2003) 'A Brief Overview of the Narrative Intelligence Reading Group', in Michael Mateas and Phoebe Senger (eds) *Narrative Intelligence*, Amsterdam: John Benjamins.

Domike, Steffi, Michael Mateas, and Paul Vanouse (2003) 'The Recombinant History Apparatus Presents Terminal Time', in Michael Mateas and Phoebe Senger (eds) *Narrative Intelligence*, Amsterdam: John Benjamins.

Don, Abbe (1992) 'Narrative and the Interface', in Brenda Laurel (ed.) *The Art of Human Computer Interface Design*, Reading, MA: Addison-Wesley.

National Research Council Committee on Information Technology and Creativity (2003) 'Narrative Intelligence', in William J. Mitchell, Alan S. Inouye, and Marjory S. Blumenthal (eds) *Beyond Productivity: Information, Technology, Innovation, and Creativity*, Washington, DC: National Academies Press.

Reddy, Michael (1979) 'The Conduit Metaphor: A Case of Frame Conflict in Our Language about Language', in Andrew Ortony (ed.) *Metaphor and Thought*, New York: Cambridge University Press.

Schank, Roger C., and Charles Riesbeck (1981) *Inside Computer Understanding: Five Programs Plus Miniatures*, New Jersey: Lawrence Erlbaum.

Travers, Michael, and Marc Davis (1993) 'Programming with Characters', in Wayne D. Gray *et al.* (eds) *Proceedings of the First International Conference on Intelligent User Interfaces*, New York: ACM Press.

MARC DAVIS

NARRATIVE LEVELS

The notion of narrative levels identifies and differentiates the multiple narrating acts that make up most narratives (*see* NARRATION). The most widely followed model is that of Genette, in which the first, or outermost, level is the extradiegetic, at which an extradiegetic *narrator recounts the entire narrative. Narrating acts depicted within that narrative are intradiegetic, narrating acts embedded within those are metadiegetic, then tetradiegetic, pentadiegetic, and so on. *See* EMBEDDING; FRAMED NARRATIVE (ALSO: DIEGESIS; NARRATIVE TRANSMISSION).

NARRATIVE PROGRESSION

The term 'narrative progression' identifies the movement of narrative as the synthesis of two dynamic systems, one governing a narrative's internal logic as it unfolds from beginning through middle to end, and the other governing the developing interests and responses of the *audience to that unfolding. Aristotle (350 BCE) laid the foundation for the concept in his definition of tragedy as an imitation of an action that (a) is whole, complete, and of a certain magnitude and that (b) arouses pity and fear and leads to the purgation of those *emotions (*see* ANCIENT THEORIES OF NARRATIVE (WESTERN); CATHARSIS). Crane (1952) built on this foundation a concept of *plot as a synthesis of particular elements of *action, *character, and thought endowed with a power to affect an audience's emotions and opinions in a particular way (*see* THOUGHT AND CONSCIOUSNESS REPRESENTATION (LITERATURE)). Phelan (1989) renovated Crane's construction by shifting the term from plot to progression, by putting greater emphasis on the temporal dynamics of narrative movement, and by identifying basic mechanisms underlying that movement and categorising broad areas of readerly interest and response (*see* READER-RESPONSE THEORY).

Phelan proposes that progressions can be generated and developed through instabilities or tensions (*see* CONFLICT). Instabilities are unsettled matters involving elements of story, typically characters and their situations, while tensions are unsettled matters involving elements of discourse such as unequal knowledge among *authors, *narrators, and audiences (as in mysteries) or matters of different values and perceptions (as in narratives with unreliable narrators) (*see* NARRATION; RELIABILITY; STORY-DISCOURSE DISTINCTION). Narratives typically proceed by the introduction and complication of instabilities and/or tensions, and they conclude by resolving at least some of the instabilities and tensions (narratives that resist *closure will leave more instabilities and tensions unresolved than those that seek strong closure). As audiences follow the movement of instabilities and tensions, they engage in many kinds of responses: judging characters, developing hopes, desires, and expectations for them, and constructing tentative hypotheses about the overall shape and direction of the narrative.

Further, audiences develop interests and responses of three broad kinds, each related to a particular component of the narrative: mimetic, thematic, and synthetic (*see* MIMESIS; THEMATIC APPROACHES TO NARRATIVE). Responses to the mimetic component involve an audience's interest in the characters as possible people and in the narrative world as like our own (*see* STORYWORLD). Responses to the thematic component involve an interest in the ideational function of the characters and in the cultural, ideological, philosophical, or *ethical issues being addressed by the narrative (*see* IDEOLOGY AND NARRATIVE). Responses to the synthetic component involve an audience's interest in and attention to the characters and to the larger narrative as artificial constructs; *metafiction foregrounds the synthetic component. Different narratives establish different relationships among these three components. Mimetic interests dominate some narratives, some by thematic, and others by synthetic, but developments in the progression can generate new relations among those interests. In most realistic narratives, for example, the audience has a tacit awareness of the synthetic while it focuses on the mimetic and the thematic components (*see* REALIST NOVEL), but, as metafiction since *Don Quixote* has taught us, that tacit awareness can always be converted into something explicit. More generally, to give an account of a narrative's progression is to give an account of its design and its effects, one that can underlie analyses of particular *narrative techniques and of broader issues such as narrative ethics.

SEE ALSO: narrative dynamics; rhetorical approaches to narrative

References and further reading

Aristotle (1989 [350 BCE]) *Poetics*, trans. S. H. Butcher, New York: Hill and Wang.

Brooks, Peter (1984) *Reading for the Plot: Design and Intention in Narrative*, New York: Knopf.

Crane, Ronald S. (1952) 'The Concept of Plot and the Plot of Tom Jones', in Crane (ed.) *Critics and Criticism*, Chicago: University of Chicago Press.

Phelan, James (1989) *Reading People, Reading Plots: Character, Progression, and the Interpretation of Narrative*, Chicago: University of Chicago Press.

—— (1996) *Narrative as Rhetoric*, Columbus: Ohio State University Press.

Rabinowitz, Peter J. (1998) *Before Reading: Narrative Conventions and the Politics of Interpretation*, Columbus: Ohio State University Press.

Richter, David H. (1975) *Fable's End: Completeness and Closure in Rhetorical Fiction*, Chicago: University of Chicago Press.

Sacks, Sheldon (1966) *Fiction and the Shape of Belief*, Berkeley: University of California Press.

JAMES PHELAN

NARRATIVE PSYCHOLOGY

Narrative psychology can perhaps best be characterised as an approach towards the study of psychological phenomena which is strongly informed by the philosophical theories of *phenomenology and existentialism.

Central to a narrative psychological approach is the development of a phenomenological understanding of the unique 'order of meaning' constitutive of human consciousness (see Crossley 2000a; Polkinghorne 1988). One of the main features of this 'order of meaning' is the experience of *time and temporality. An understanding of temporality associated with the human realm of meaning is entirely different from that encountered in the natural sciences. This is because the human realm of meaning it is not related to a 'thing' or a 'substance' but to an 'activity'. Everything experienced by human beings is made meaningful, understood, and interpreted in relation to the primary dimension of 'activity' which incorporates both 'time' and 'sequence'. In order to define and interpret 'what' exactly has happened on any particular occasion, the sequence of *events is of extreme importance (*see* TEMPORAL ORDERING). Hence, a valid portrayal of the experience of selfhood necessitates an understanding of the inextricable connection between temporality and *identity. (See Ricoeur [1984–1988] for an extended investigation of narrative temporality.)

Another important related feature of the 'order of meaning' characteristic of human consciousness is that of 'relationships' and 'connections' (Polkinghorne 1988: 4). Along with other organisms such as cats and dogs we share what can be characterised as a 'perceptual openness' to the world in which our sensory apparatus and brain structures operate to present us with a basic experience of the objects and activities going on around us. But a characteristic feature of our human realm of meaning is that we go way beyond this rudimentary perceptual level of experience as we interpret the events around us in terms of connections and relationships. When we ask ourselves the question, 'what does this mean?' we are asking ourselves (or others) *how* something is related or connected to something or someone else; i.e. we are concerned with the connections or relationships among events that constitute their meaning (*see* CAUSALITY).

It is in accordance with such basic principles of temporality and connection that numerous authors such as MacIntyre (1981), Carr (1986), and Sarbin (1986) originally put forward the idea that human psychology has an essentially narrative structure. Sarbin, for instance, proposed what he called the 'narratory principle'; this is the idea that human beings think, perceive, imagine, interact, and make moral choices according to *narrative structures. In this way, Sarbin treated narrative as the 'organising principle for human action'. From this perspective, the concept of narrative could be used to help account for the observation that human beings always seek to *impose structure* on the flow of experience.

The work of philosopher Charles Taylor (1989) is important in expanding on such psychological understandings of the relationship between self and temporality, especially in the way such phenomena link ultimately and inextricably to issues of morality. It is Taylor's main contention that concepts of self and morality are fundamentally intertwined – we are selves only in that certain issues matter for us. What I am as a self, my identity, is essentially defined by the way things have significance for me. To ask what I am in abstraction from self-interpretation makes no sense (Taylor 1989: 34). Moreover, my self-interpretation can only be defined in relation to other people, through an 'interchange of speakers'. I cannot be a self on my own but only in relation to certain 'interlocutors' who are crucial to my language of self-understanding. In this sense, the self is constituted through 'webs of interlocution' in a 'defining community' (Taylor 1989: 39). This connection between our sense of morality and sense of self, according to Taylor, means that one of our basic aspirations is the need to feel connected with what we see as 'good' or of crucial importance to us and our community. We have certain fundamental values which lead us to basic questions such as 'what kind of life is worth living?'; 'What constitutes a rich, meaningful life, as against an empty, meaningless one?' (Taylor 1989: 42). Visions of 'the good' are articulated by and for people within particular communities through language and symbolic systems such as custom and ritual which reverberate with knowledge of connections and relationships across the generations.

One of the central premises of a narrative psychological approach, then, is the existence of an essential and fundamental link between experiences of self, temporality, relationships with others, and morality. We have a sense of who we are through a sense of where we stand in relation to 'the good'. Hence, connections between notions of 'the good', understandings of the self, the kinds of stories and narratives through which we make sense of our lives, and conceptions of society, evolve together in 'loose packages' (Taylor 1989: 105).

Originally, the narrative psychological approach was formulated as an alternative to dominant quantitative approaches which, in their attempt to numerically categorise experience through quantification and statistical procedures, failed radically to incorporate or address these hermeneutic dimensions of experience and thus lost any sense of the 'lived' nature of human reality and identity (*see* SOCIOLOGY AND NARRATIVE). However, in the light of concerns regarding the linguistic reductionism of some contemporary social constructionist approaches and the tendency to 'lose' all sense of 'self' as a lived psychological reality, it has more recently been argued that a narrative psychological approach comprises a useful tool which enables us to recapture the way in which selves and identities are grounded in 'cultural' forms of language and sense-making, whilst simultaneously maintaining a sense of the 'internal', 'coherent', and 'personal' nature of self-experience (Crossley 2000b). This humanistic commitment to preserving an appreciation of 'internal' lived reality can be linked to research on traumatising experiences such as childhood sexual abuse and serious illnesses, in relation to which many narrative approaches have developed (see Crossley 2000a).

SEE ALSO: ethical turn; master narrative; narrative as cognitive instrument; positioning; trauma theory

References and further reading

Carr, David (1986) *Time, Narrative and History*, Bloomington: Indiana University Press.
Crossley, Michele L. (2000a) *Introducing Narrative Psychology: Self, Trauma and the Construction of Meaning*, Milton Keynes: Open University Press.
——(2000b) 'Narrative Psychology, Trauma And The Study Of Self/Identity', *Theory and Psychology*, 10.4, 503–22.
MacIntyre, Alistair (1981) *After Virtue*, Notre Dame: Notre Dame University Press.
Polkinghorne, Donald P. (1988) *Narrative Knowing and the Human Sciences*, Albany: State University of New York Press.
Ricoeur, Paul (1984–1988) *Time and Narrative*, 3 vols., trans. Kathleen McLaughlin and David Pellauer (vol. 3 trans. Kathleen Blamey and David Pellauer), Chicago: University of Chicago Press.

Sarbin, Theodore R. (ed.) (1986) *Narrative Psychology: The Storied Nature of Human Conduct*, New York: Praeger.

Taylor, Charles (1989) *Sources of the Self: The Making of Modern Identity*, Cambridge: Cambridge University Press.

MICHELE L. CROSSLEY

NARRATIVE SEMANTICS

The concept of 'narrative semantics' depends on whether there is something distinct about how the forms and constituent structure of a narrative as an identifiable piece of language are interpreted and, thereby, assigned meanings relative to some world (in semantics, this world is known as a model; *see* POSSIBLE-WORLDS THEORY). Lexical semantics, for example, is a legitimate pursuit because both the form and the constituent structure of a word contribute to its interpretation; e.g., the meaning of *incredible* is determined by the structure of the word as *in + credible*, not as *incred + ible*. Analogously, 'narrative semantics' requires that there be something about narrative *per se* that evokes distinctly narrative meaning. The status of narrative semantics, however, is much more difficult to establish than that of lexical semantics.

For the purposes of this discussion, narrative may be defined as a particular kind of linguistic signal that codes participants and eventualities in temporal-causal relationships, subjected to conditions on viewpoint and speaker source (*see* CAUSALITY; CHARACTER; FOCALIZATION; NARRATION; NARRATIVE SITUATIONS; PERSPECTIVE; TEMPORAL ORDERING). (Other kinds of semiotic signals can also be narratively organised; hence the existence of narrative across *media.) Narrative is unlike other extended discourse, such as a list or *description (although it may include description). In a narrative, as in any informational system, only the signal is conveyed; hearers and receivers respond to the complexity of the signal by means of a set of interpretive conventions for that signal (Moles 1968). Thus, rather than being a property of the signal itself or of the conventions themselves, narrative semantics is a function of the linkage of interpretive conventions with the narrative signal as the interpreter develops a model of the narrated situations and *events (*see* SITUATION MODEL).

Semantic interpretations of stories allow hearers and receivers to construct narratively structured models (sometimes called *storyworld). Narrative semantic analysis lies in the delineation of the interpretive conditions that link narratively organised signals to narrative models – in the same way that lexical semantic analysis determines the interpretive conditions that link words as sound-form signals to their referents (*see* REFERENCE). The utility of the signal-convention link in narrative semantic analysis and the viability of narrative semantics itself can be explored via the function of *time in narrative; special versions of default temporal interpretation apply when a narrative is the linguistic signal.

Consider the beginning of Raymond Carver's *Fat* (1989: 64):

> I am sitting over coffee and cigarettes at my friend Rita's and I am telling her about it.
> Here is what I tell her.
> It is late on a slow Wednesday when Herb seats the fat man at my station.
> This fat man is the fattest person I have ever seen . . .

Carver's use of the present *tense not only matches the ethos of his struggling, working-class characters, but also appositely illustrates, on the one hand, the clear break between narrative coding and narrative interpretation, and, on the other, the distinctions between assertion, reference, and speaking times that must often be factored into narrative temporal interpretation. In this narrative, the present tense codes past time since the events recounted have already happened, yet are being reasserted in the present. Moreover, the tenses are embedded in a complex web of cross-references, often subsuming the reference times for other tenses.

A rough temporal map of the above excerpt might be given as follows:

> Narrator asserts NOW (to you?) that a speaker WAS THEN at Rita's and AT THAT TIME told her something – which narrator NOW re-asserts (to you?) and the character asserts THEN to Rita – as having happened (even) BEFORE NOW AND BEFORE the telling at Rita's about a man whose properties TRANSCEND TIME as far as the character's experience goes.

As this analysis suggests, in first-person narration a *narrator's speech time may or may not be coterminous with the reference time of speech events reported in the narrative (*see* PERSON; SPEECH REPRESENTATION). If it is coterminous, as in simultaneous or concurrent narration, then the presentative *here is* functions as a deictic expression that codes the link between the *narrator and the speaker and reaches outside the narrative at the same time it is inside the storyworld (*see* DEIXIS). If it is not coterminous, then the presentative is relative to the reference time set by the previous propositions, and is interpretable more as 'here was what I told her'. This simple example shows that interpreters have to actively construct the time of a narrative by determining whether or not assertion, reference, and speaking times are aligned in a given stretch of the discourse. Moreover, semantic analysis of the passage reveals the linkage of a special signal and a special interpretive convention.

More generally, this example suggests several important procedural lessons for the semantic analysis of narrative:

(1) *Narrative semantic analysis should focus on the linkage between signal and meaning; analysis of the signal or convention in isolation is not sufficient.* There can be linguistic or other semiotic signals that are non-narrative-interpretable (e.g., sequences of events that cannot be understood as narratives) and narrative interpretations of signals lacking full-fledged narrative organisation (as in the interpretation of a *photograph or still *image as a 'pregnant moment', i.e., as part of an overarching narrative not literally conveyed by the image itself; *see* PICTORIAL NARRATIVITY). As in other domains of semantic analysis, therefore, analysis of narrative would do well to focus on the mutual link between signal and convention.

(2) *Narrative semantic analysis via macrostructures is not necessarily the best strategy.* As a piece of language that seems 'bigger than' a word or sentence, a narrative would also seem to require a 'bigger semantics'. This intuition partly grounds the various accounts of narrative meaning via macrostructures, such as *scripts, scenes, scenarios, and *frames. But, in principle, there is nothing necessary about macrostructures for narrative, and their purported effects on meaning may be analysed satisfactorily below the macro-level, even if sometimes motivated by a (properly defined) macro-level. The signal-convention links in narrative might be explained through the usual techniques of lexical and propositional analysis (Frawley, Murray, and Smith 2003). Indeed, the

easy move to macro-units can be quite misleading. For one thing, many *narrative structures are not semantic at all, but syntactic – i.e., they concern the formal structural organisation of narrative information, not what the narrative is about. Much of what can be found in *story grammars, for example, does not yield any new kind of truth determination (*see* TRUTH), but instead accounts for cross-propositional, structural linkages, such as those pertaining to cause-effect relations, information focus, and combinatory patterning of *narrative units. And even if there are semantic macrostructures that anchor narratives at a high level – e.g., narrative situations or modes of perspective taking – it can be argued that the macrostructures identified to date do their essential semantic work at the micro-level.

In short, macrostructural approaches have mainly concerned themselves with aspects of narrative structure, not narrative meaning. But this does not rule out that a coherent *semantic* analysis of macrostructures might in principle enhance the project of narrative semantics.

(3) *'Cognitive-first' accounts in narrative semantics need to be approached with caution.* In some approaches to narrative theory (e.g., *cognitive narratology), a natural move is to take the cognitive as a first principle. However, if narrative semantics indeed constitutes a regular form of semantic analysis, appeals to an essentially cognitive approach to narrative are presumptive and potentially misleading. Cognitive-first accounts prematurely resort to the cognitive – before any structure is worked out – in the same way that intrinsically cognitive approaches to linguistic structure often substitute intuitions about general conceptual structure for analysis of specific linguistic structure. This move can obscure the exact nature of the link between linguistic signals and interpretive conventions that generates meaning.

The limitations of such cognitive-first approaches need to be considered vis-à-vis two strands of recent research on narrative. On the one hand, some theorists argue narratives should be studied from a cognitive perspective because they require awareness of other minds and reference to mental states (Margolin 2003; Palmer 2004; *see* THOUGHT AND CONSCIOUSNESS REPRESENTATION (LITERATURE)). Because narrators and characters act and speak with respect to other characters' beliefs, not just their behaviour, it would appear that narrative semantics requires reference to the mental to satisfy truth. On the other hand, Leonard Talmy (2000) has argued that narrative itself forms a basic pattern-forming cognitive system bearing on sequences experienced through time. Functioning 'to connect and integrate certain components of conscious content over time into a coherent ideational structure' (419), this system is in Talmy's account domain-general, i.e., operative across multiple cognitive domains (420; 446–81). From this perspective, narrative is a system for structuring any time-based pattern into a resource for consciousness (Fireman, McVay, and Flanagan 2003; *see* NARRATIVE AS COGNITIVE INSTRUMENT). Future research needs to determine whether semantic analysis provides independent support for viewing narrative under these two profiles – as a structure triggering cognitive representations and processes, and as a mode of representation giving structure to cognition itself – or whether it suggests an altogether different picture of how narratives mean.

SEE ALSO: discourse analysis (linguistics); linguistic approaches to narrative; semiotics

References and further reading

Carver, Raymond (1989) 'Fat', in *Where I'm Calling From*, New York: Vintage.

Fireman, Gary, Ted McVay, and Owen Flanagan (eds) (2003) *Narrative and Consciousness*, Oxford: Oxford University Press.

Frawley, William (1992) *Linguistics Semantics*, Hillsdale, NJ: Lawrence Erlbaum.

——, John Murray and Raoul Smith (2003) 'Semantics and Narrative in Therapeutic Discourse', in David Herman (ed.) *Narrative Theory and the Cognitive Sciences*, Stanford, CA: CSLI Publications.

Margolin, Uri (2003) 'Cognitive Science, the Thinking Mind, and Literary Narrative', in David Herman (ed.) *Narrative Theory and the Cognitive Sciences*, Stanford, CA: CSLI Publications.

Moles, Abraham (1968) *Information Theory and Esthetic Perception*, Urbana: University of Illinois Press.

Palmer, Alan (2004) *Fictional Minds*, Lincoln: University of Nebraska Press.

Talmy, Leonard (2000) 'A Cognitive Framework for Narrative Structure', in *Toward a Cognitive Semantics*, vol. 2, Cambridge, Mass.: MIT Press.

WILLIAM FRAWLEY AND DAVID HERMAN

NARRATIVE SITUATIONS

The theory of narrative situations addresses the *narrator's relationship to the process, subject, and *pragmatics of narrative communication, especially his/her authority, the degree of his/her involvement in the story, and the extent of his/her knowledge about narrated *events. Although primarily associated with the work of Austrian narratologist Franz Stanzel, all theories of narrative situations are closely related to earlier 'point of view' models such as the ones proposed by Percy Lubbock, Norman Friedman, and Boris Uspenskii (*see* PERSPECTIVE; POINT OF VIEW (LITERARY)). Growing out of a dissatisfaction with style, content, and genre-oriented approaches to fiction, Stanzel's model radically reduces the infinite variety of narrative forms to three 'theoretically ideal' types: 'first-person', 'authorial', and 'figural' storytelling (*see* PERSON). Two of these categories also identify types of narrators (first-person narrator, authorial narrator); all three of them are realised in major *genres of Western literary narrative (first-person, authorial, and figural *novels). Briefly summarised, the basic definitions of Stanzel's three types are as follows:

(1) The first-person narrative situation is one in which the narrator (often a mature *'narrating-I') tells an autobiographical story about events happening to an earlier self, the younger 'experiencing-I' (example: Defoe's *Moll Flanders*). Typically, first-person narrators are restricted to a personal, subjective, and limited point of view, they have no direct access to events they did not witness in person, and they have no way of knowing for certain what went on in the minds of other characters. Readers often treat first-person narratives as yet-to-be-validated testimony of uncertain *reliability. Typical sub-genres of first-person narration are fictional *autobiographies and *skaz narratives.

(2) The authorial narrative situation is characterised by a highly audible and visible narrator who tells a story cast in the third-person (example: Hardy's *Tess of the D'Urbervilles*). An authorial narrator sees the story from the ontological position of an outsider, that is, a position of absolute authority which allows her/him to know everything about events and *characters, including their thoughts and unconscious motives (*see* THOUGHT AND CONSCIOUSNESS REPRESENTATION (LITERATURE)). Authorial narrators speak directly to their addressees (*see* NARRATEE), freely comment on action and characters, engage in philosophical reflection, and interrupt the course of the action by presenting detailed *descriptions. Typical authorial

genres are eighteenth- and nineteenth-century *novels of social criticism (*see* REALIST NOVEL).

(3) A figural narrative situation presents the story's events as seen through the eyes of a 'reflector' character (also called 'internal focalizer' or 'figural medium'). The narrator – technically, a 'covert' incarnation of the authorial narrator – is a largely inconspicuous presenter, silent arranger, and recorder (some theorists even posit that figural texts are 'narratorless'; *see* NO-NARRATOR THEORY). Like authorial narratives, figural narratives are third-person texts, but unlike authorial texts they use little or no *exposition, avoid description, and offer a more or less direct display of a character's mind, however associative or distortive the resulting picture might be. Typical sub-genres are 'slice-of-life' and *stream of consciousness stories, often associated with twentieth century literary impressionism and modernism (example: Joyce's *Portrait of the Artist*; *see* MODERNIST NARRATIVE).

In *Theory of Narrative* (1984 [1979]), Stanzel reconceptualises the narrative situations as aggregate products of three underlying features: 'person' (based on a first-person/third-person continuum), 'mode' (based on a narrator-reflector continuum), and 'perspective' (based on an omniscience-limited point of view continuum). In this model, the narrative situations occupy three segments of a 'typological circle', each buffered by segments representing transitional forms. As Stanzel points out, the circular design not only provides an infinite number of points on which to locate paradigmatic, transitional, and theoretically possible forms but, what is more, any position on the circle is also directly indicative of the degree of deviation from the norm of the relevant standard case.

While some critics (e.g. Lanser 1981) have found fault with Stanzel's notion of ideal types, preferring a strictly combinatorial distinctive-features approach, and others have questioned the continuum of the 'perspective' scale (Cohn 1981), it is generally accepted that narrative situations provide a synthesis that is absent in purely feature-oriented approaches. Indeed, following Cohn's (1981) thoughtful review-article, in which she stressed the heuristic gain of Stanzel's synthesis, Genette himself (1988 [1983]) produced a combinatorial table correlating features of 'person' and *focalization in order to distinguish six narrative situations. Inspired by the point of view oriented work of Boris Uspenskii, Roger Fowler's (1996 [1986]) model is also predicated on features like accessibility of characters' minds and first- vs. third-person pronominal references. Although Fowler's account is noteworthy because of the way it draws on Halliday's functional linguistics to rethink narrative situations, the nomenclature used – 'External type A', 'Internal type B' etc. – has not proved popular. (Nevertheless, see Simpson [1993] for a spirited attempt to build on Fowler's categories.) Perhaps the most explicit and detailed structuralist account of narrative situations and their 'distinctive traits' has been submitted by Lintvelt (1981). Freely mixing Genettean and Stanzelian terms, Lintvelt distinguishes five main types: (1.1) heterodiegetic-authorial (= Stanzel's authorial), (1.2) heterodiegetic-actorial (= Stanzel's figural), (1.3) heterodiegetic-neutral (an intermediate position on Stanzel's circle, corresponding to 'the camera' in Friedman 1955), (2.1) homodiegetic-authorial (intrusive first-person), (2.2) homodiegetic-actorial (unintrusive first-person). While Lintvelt's study is not an easily accessible text a useful summary sketch of the model can be found in *Poétique* (35.2, 1978).

More recently, narrative situations have also been understood as cognitive 'frames' containing 'default' instantiations that predict presupposition-based inferences (Jahn 1997; *see* FRAME THEORY). On this view, assuming or attributing a narrative situation is an interpretive strategy which can be employed to make sense of textual gaps and *indeterminacies (*see* GAPPING), or to 'narrativise' texts whose narrative status is uncertain (*see* NARRATIVISATION). Indeed, it is the continuing inductive potential of the narrative situations that turns them into powerful tools of analysis in disciplines such as *natural narratology, *cognitive narratology, and *cultural studies approaches to narrative.

References and further reading

Cohn, Dorrit (1981) 'The Encirclement of Narrative', *Poetics Today*, 2.2, 157–82.

Fowler, Roger (1996 [1986]) *Linguistic Criticism*, Oxford: Oxford University Press.

Friedman, Norman (1955) 'Point of View in Fiction: The Development of a Critical Concept', *PMLA*, 70, 1160–84.

Genette, Gérard (1980 [1972]) *Narrative Discourse: An Essay in Method*, trans. Jane E. Lewin, Ithaca: Cornell University Press.

—— (1988 [1983]) *Narrative Discourse Revisited*, trans. Jane E. Lewin, Ithaca: Cornell University Press.

Jahn, Manfred (1997) 'Frames, Preferences, and the Reading of Third-person Narratives: Towards a Cognitive Narratology', *Poetics Today*, 18.4, 441–68.

Lanser, Susan Sniader (1981) *The Narrative Act: Point of View in Fiction*, Princeton: Princeton University Press.

Lintvelt, Jaap (1981) *Essai de typologie narrative: Le 'point de vue'*, Paris: Corti.

Stanzel, Franz (1984 [1979]) *A Theory of Narrative*, trans. Charlotte Goedsche, Cambridge: Cambridge University Press.

Simpson, Paul (1993) *Language, Ideology and Point of View*, London: Routledge.

MANFRED JAHN

NARRATIVE SPEED

In Genettean narratology, the relation between 'story time' (the duration of *events on the level of action) and 'discourse time' (the time it takes to recount the events). Storytelling slows down when action is presented scenically and speeds up in summary. *See* SUMMARY AND SCENE (also: STORY-DISCOURSE DISTINCTION).

NARRATIVE STRUCTURE

Narrative structure may be regarded as relating exclusively to story or as relating also to the discourse that presents that story (*see* STORY-DISCOURSE DISTINCTION). In the former (and narrower) sense, the term 'narrative structure' is understood as referring to the (structured) relationship of narrative *events within a story. This understanding has produced some celebrated models of narrative grammar (Propp 1968 [1928]; Lévi-Strauss 1963 [1958]; Greimas 1983 [1966]; Bremond 1973; Prince 1973; *see* STORY GRAMMARS). In the latter (and broader) sense, the term is understood as referring to the structure of narrative communication itself, conceived of as involving both a story (the *what* of narrative, or *fabula) and a discourse (the *how* of narrative, or *sjuzhet) that transmits that story from a range of real, implied, and inferred senders (*author, *implied author, *narrator) to a corresponding range of real, implied, and inferred addressees (reader, implied reader, *narratee; *see* COMMUNICATION IN NARRATIVE; READER CONSTRUCTS). In this understanding, a discussion of narrative structure properly involves the entire set of analytical and hermeneutic implications arising from the foundational distinction between story and discourse. The study of 'narrative structure' is thus seen (Chatman 1978; O'Neill 1994; also Prince 1987: 93) as essentially coterminous with the enterprise of narratology itself (*see* STRUCTURALIST NARRATOLOGY), subsuming all aspects of the interactive relationship of narrative agents, including such issues as *narration, *focalization, and *speech representation.

In the present entry, the term will be taken in this broader sense, but with a reduced range of application, focussing on processes of patterning in narrative fiction resulting from the discursive arrangeability of narrative events. In this understanding, since every story is wholly dependent upon (and only reconstructable from) the set of discursive acts that produce it, a discussion of narrative structure is necessarily concerned with issues relating to the discursive presentation of narrative events. While the story-discourse distinction is of particular importance for the analysis of literary narrative fiction (the *novel, *novella, and *short story), it holds in principle for all forms of narrative, including non-literary, non-fictional, and non-verbal forms. The terms 'discourse' and 'discursive acts' should thus be understood as denoting any set of presentational strategies, in any medium, employed to transmit a story (*see* MEDIA AND NARRATIVE).

Structuring narratives: epic, tragedy, novel

It is appropriate to situate a discussion of structure in narrative fiction in the context of two normative generic predecessors, *epic and tragedy (*see* DRAMA AND NARRATIVE; GENRE THEORY IN NARRATIVE STUDIES). Aristotle's *Poetics* saw the two as similar in structure: both have clearly defined beginnings and ends, and both have middle parts consisting of a number of related episodes, the number normally much greater in epic (*see* NARRATIVE UNITS). Epic is less immediate, in that it is by nature diegetic, overtly narrated; tragedy is more immediate, in that it is mimetic, its presentational strategy involving the *audience being 'shown' the ostensibly unmediated action rather than merely being told about it (*see* DIEGESIS; MIMESIS). Epic is thus looser and indefinitely extensible in structure, while tragedy is more concentrated and focused. The action of the epic may be either simple and straightforward or, for greater narrative interest, it may be complicated by a variety of recognition scenes and reversals of direction. Epic has at least one significant operational advantage over tragedy, in that it allows simultaneous events to be presented consecutively.

Tragedy and epic normally both centre on a single protagonist, but Aristotle advises against any attempt in either case to present the events of a whole life from beginning to end, recommending instead that a particularly significant sequence of those events should be selected for more concentrated focus. Similarly, he pointed to the strategic advantage of Homer's plunging the audience at once into the thick of the action, thus at once both seizing attention and creating curiosity about what prior events might have led to that pass. Aristotle's successors were particularly struck by this latter recommendation and eventually raised it to the status of a prescriptive structural principle, Horace being the first to state specifically that epic narrative should ideally begin *in medias res. The analeptic principle of ordering (involving the use of flashbacks, often of considerable length) subsequently became the central convention of epic structure, as in Milton's *Paradise Lost*.

The modern novel clearly inherits several of the structural characteristics of the classical epic: notably its potentially episodic structure, its balance of indefinite extensibility and formal concentration, its balancing of diegetic and mimetic potential, and, above all, its flexibility as regards the *temporal ordering of narrated events. By the eighteenth-century the novel was coming to be seen as the modern epic, and the in medias res principle duly became one of its standard elements. It even occurs in such a concentrated literary form as the short story: an often cited modern example is Katherine Mansfield's short story 'A Dill Pickle' (1920), which begins 'And then, after six years, she saw him again'.

Aristotle observed that the action of every tragedy may be visualised as the tying and untying of a knot, and this image of an initial process of dramatic complication succeeded and reversed by a process of complementary resolution has echoed powerfully through the centuries (*see* PLOT). Its best-known modern formulation is in the diagrammatic representation known as *Freytag's triangle, long accepted as a normative concept for dramatic structure, in which Freytag illustrates symmetrical processes of rising and falling

action through phases he designates as *exposition, complication, climax, reversal, and catastrophe (1908 [1863]: 114–15). The structural pattern identified here is common also in the novel, with an initial state of equilibrium being disturbed by an external force of some kind, the disorder increasing until it is halted and reversed by another force, which in time leads to the establishment of a new state of equilibrium (*see* CONFLICT). It need hardly be said that the presence or absence of such a pattern is nowadays a matter of description rather than prescription. Literary narrative of at least the past four centuries has shown itself increasingly hostile to normative notions of structure. One of its primary characteristics, indeed, from *Don Quixote* and *Tristram Shandy* onwards, has been its overt willingness to transgress prescriptive structural dogma (*see* QUIXOTIC NOVEL).

Simple and complex stories

Evidently, the originary model of the narrative account *per se* is chronologically linear, beginning at the beginning ('once upon a time') and proceeding in orderly fashion through a middle of greater or lesser length to an end. This is the shared model of *conversational storytelling, children's narratives, folk narratives, newspaper reports, accounts of sports events, witness statements, and historical accounts (*see* CHILDREN'S STORYTELLING; COURTROOM NARRATIVE; FOLKTALE; JOURNALISM; SPORTS BROADCAST). Unsurprisingly, it is also the model of many literary narratives, including especially the medieval *romance and its down-market successor the *picaresque novel (*see* MEDIEVAL NARRATIVE). It continues to be the model for much popular fiction, including *romance novels, adventure stories, school stories, sea stories, war stories, westerns, and so on. In its simplest form, the model is both linear and additive, involving stories in which a single protagonist (or group of protagonists) sets out to achieve a particular end, encounters in the process an indefinite number of obstacles and opponents (*see* ACTANT), overcomes them with varying degrees of difficulty and possibly with the assistance of a helper or helpers, and duly achieves the desired end (Propp 1968 [1928]; Greimas 1983 [1966]). The simple story can readily be extended and ramified by merely adding to the number and nature of the obstacles to be overcome and the number and nature of the opponents to be vanquished. It can also be made increasingly less simple by the introduction of a variety of *retardatory, misdirectional, and complicating factors: the protagonist may initially attempt to attain a false end, ostensible helpers and opponents may switch roles, obstacles apparently overcome may present themselves again in exacerbated form, and so on.

In principle, however, all of these increasing ramifications can still be accommodated under the rubric of the simple story, as long as the story's primary characteristic continues to be its linear and additive properties. More complex stories replace this characteristic by others. A complex story may thus typically consist of two interconnected simple stories – or 'storylines', to employ Rimmon-Kenan's term, who observes that in *King Lear*, for example, one can distinguish the storyline involving Lear and his daughters from the one concerning Gloucester and his sons, while their intersection constitutes a significant factor in the overall story (2002 [1983]: 16). The same observation holds equally well for *Don Quixote*, where the protagonist's story continually intersects with that of Sancho Panza; for Thomas Mann's *Buddenbrooks*, where the story of the Buddenbrook family's decline is reflected in that of a rival family's complementary rise; and for innumerable other novels of world literature. The points at which these individual storylines intersect with each other, reflect each other, or set each other off, is of course less a function of story than of the narrative discourse that presents it. The most important and most effective means of elaborating and enriching narratives, that is to say, is not by making the story itself more complex but by complicating and elaborating its discursive presentation.

Parallel and multi-plot narratives

Flaunted elaboration of narrative structuration is a prominent feature of (post)modernist novels, many of which challenge their readers to unravel sophisticated structural complexities. One of the challenges facing the reader of Beckett's *Molloy*, for example, is to decide whether that novel is more productively read as a single narrative or as two parallel narratives, namely, Molloy's search for his mother and Moran's search for Molloy (*see* MODERNIST NARRATIVE; POSTMODERN NARRATIVE).

Parallel narratives more easily identifiable as such are a common feature of the Victorian three-volume novel and of its modern institutional successor, the *television mini-series (see* SERIAL FORM). True to their terminological label, parallel narratives do not intersect, or at most they do so only incidentally or as a component element of a curtain-call closural strategy. Any one of them could in principle be deleted without affecting the structural integrity of any other. As the miniseries industry repeatedly demonstrates, each overall narrative (*Upstairs Downstairs, Coronation Street, EastEnders*) is in principle extensible at will by the complementary removal of old and addition of new characters, contributing to new parallel constituent narratives. The modern popularity and profitability of 'prequels' ensure that this extensibility is bi-directional, transgressing beginnings (*Star Wars*) as well as evading *closure (Abbott 2002: 53).

Parallel narratives, however unrelated their individual concerns may appear to be, nonetheless serve at least by implication both as mutual commentaries and as sources of potential mutual enrichment (*see* COMMENTARY; METANARRATIVE COMMENT). A text composed of a number of individual parallel narratives in principle creates a fictional world whose textural richness increases in proportion to the number of individual narratives included. *Molloy* is fascinating not least in that its manipulative textual strategies ensure its readers' continued uncertainty regarding the extent and the degree to which the two stories, Molloy's and Moran's, should or should not be regarded as mutual commentaries.

Parallel narratives may be regarded as a subset of multi-plot narratives, for the latter may or may not include examples of the former among its constituent stories (*see* PLOT TYPES). Multi-plot narratives have traditionally tended to be ample in scope (*War and Peace, The Forsyth Saga, Coronation Street*) and evocative of whole societies or sectors of a society. They may contain only parallel narratives or only non-parallel narratives or a combination of both. They frequently also include embedded narratives (*see* EMBEDDING). Many narratives have several narrators, whether following one another sequentially or with one narrator's account embedded in that of another. Faulkner's *The Sound and the Fury* provides an example of sequential narrators, where readers' understanding of the narrative grows only gradually out of their efforts to reconcile a series of partially conflicting accounts by a succession of separate and to a greater or lesser degree overtly unreliable narrators (*see* RELIABILITY). Conrad's *Heart of Darkness* and Emily Brontë's *Wuthering Heights* provide interesting examples of embedded narratives. Usually the relationship between such nested narratives is ostensibly quite clear, with the embedded narrative playing a clearly subsidiary role, simply providing one more item of narrative material for the larger narrative in which it is embedded. Thus in many prerealist texts (such as *Don Quixote*) many of the embedded narratives could be deleted without any significant damage to the structural integrity of the embedding narrative. In *Heart of Darkness*, however, we find a reversal of this power relationship, where the character Marlow's account of his adventures in Africa, though presented in the form of an embedded narrative, is clearly much more important than the embedding narrative in which it is contained and which essentially serves only as a frame for it (*see* FRAMED NARRATIVE).

Wuthering Heights provides a particularly interesting example of multiple embedded narratives, Mr. Lockwood's framing narrative embedding a lengthy oral narrative in several instalments by Nelly Dean as well as a written narrative by Catherine Earnshaw, and Nelly's embedded narrative in turn further embedding three separate narratives, by Isabella, Heathcliff, and Zillah respectively. The reader may well wonder whether it is more important that we are reading what Isabella said, or what Nelly says she said, or what Mr. Lockwood says Nelly said she said. However we may wish as readers to decide such questions, it is clear that the relationship between nested narratives is always one of mutual relativisation: while the embedding narrative is ultimately always in a position to colour fundamentally our reception of an embedded narrative, it may itself always in turn be challenged or even displaced altogether by the narrative it embeds (O'Neill 1994: 65–66) (*see* METALEPSIS).

Modernist and postmodernist experimentation has produced numerous flamboyant examples of ostentatiously multi-plot narratives. A classic example of a (comic) multi-plot narrative is Flann O'Brien's *At Swim-Two-Birds* (1939), where intersecting narratives feature a heterogeneous cast of Dublin students and barflies, various figures from Irish mythology and fairy lore, a posse of cowboys, and an author who falls in love with one of his own characters and barely escapes the murderous

intentions of some of his other characters. John Fowles's *The French Lieutenant's Woman* (1969) has an interesting claim to belong to this category in that it has three separate endings, each of them, in their consequences, retrospectively and retroactively producing a different narrative. Italo Calvino's *If on a Winter's Night a Traveler* (1979) contains one ostensibly complete main narrative and no fewer than ten incomplete embedded narratives.

Collage, incompleteness, and other strategic disruptions

Multiplot narrative has obvious comic and parodic potential. One of its discursive modalities involves narrative collage – a term borrowed from painting and modernist poetry (Eliot's *Waste Land*, Pound's *Cantos*) to denote a text constructed wholly or partly from fragments of other texts or parodically re-employing linguistic or literary usages from other times or cultures (*see* INTERTEXTUALITY). Examples of one kind of collage include attempts like those of Alfred Döblin's *Berlin Alexanderplatz* (1929) and John Dos Passos's *U.S.A.* trilogy (1938) to evoke a panoramic portrait of Berlin and New York respectively by including snatches from newsreel documentaries, *advertisements, newspaper headlines, popular songs, and the like. Joyce's *Ulysses* (1922) served as a model for both of these experiments, but it also introduced a quite different form of narrative collage in its parodically encyclopedic attempt to make brave new use of *all* previous styles employed in the writing of English-language narrative (*see* ENCYCLOPEDIC NOVEL).

If collage is a (frequently parodic) form of narrative inclusion, incompleteness is a (frequently parodic) form of narrative exclusion. Incompleteness may sometimes be involuntary on its author's part, as in the case of Kafka's three unfinished novels, but may nonetheless quite properly be accepted by the reader as a valid component of the text's signifying practice. Such a reader will note that while *The Castle* (1926) and *Amerika* (1927) have a beginning and a middle but no end, *The Trial* (1925) has a beginning and an end but only an incomplete middle. A bravura example of a parodic *narratio interrupta* is provided by Calvino's *If on a Winter's Night a Traveler*, which, as mentioned above, boasts both a beginning and an end but each of whose ten intervening chapters is presented as itself the beginning of a new (embedded) narrative left unfinished in all ten cases.

Other (post)modernist discursive practices overtly affecting the reader's perception of narrative structure include retrogressive narrative, as in Martin Amis's *Time's Arrow* (1991), a narrative in which everything goes backwards, from end to beginning. It has been pointed out, interestingly, that the resulting narrative depends for its full effect on the reader's automatic reconstruction of the true temporal order of events (Abbott 2002: 35). Another discursive innovation is aleatory narrative, such as B. S. Johnson's novel *The Unfortunates* (1969), which consists of a box of unnumbered loose leaves, to be read in any order the reader chooses. A more sophisticated example of aleatory narrative is provided by Julio Cortázar's *Hopscotch* (1963), which consists of 155 numbered chapters of variable length. An initial 'Table of Instructions' provides readers with two suggested options: the first is to read straight through to chapter 56 in traditionally linear fashion, ending at that point and leaving ninety-nine remaining chapters and some two-hundred pages of text unread; the second is to reread chapters 1 to 56 with interspersed material from the 'expendable chapters' incorporated according to a 'recommended' order – which turns out to be unworkable, for chapters 131 and 58 involve the reader in an endless loop. The textual point of these elaborately inadequate controlling strategies is that readers will almost inevitably abandon them at some point and devise their own individual strategies of reading (*see* MULTI-PATH NARRATIVE).

Narrative structure necessarily revolves around the discursive arrangeability of real or invented *storyworld facts and events. Any story, real or invented, can be told in an indefinitely large number of ways, incorporating an indefinitely large number of discursive modifications and qualifiers. The more flaunted such discursive manipulations are, as they frequently are in literary texts, the more they may serve to remind us that all narratives, literary or otherwise, are in principle, if to varying degrees, 'fictions of discourse' (O'Neill 1994).

SEE ALSO: narrative techniques

References and further reading

Abbott, H. Porter (2002) *The Cambridge Introduction to Narrative*, Cambridge: Cambridge University Press.
Bremond, Claude (1973) *Logique du récit*, Paris: Seuil.
Chatman, Seymour (1978) *Story and Discourse: Narrative Structure in Fiction and Film*, Ithaca: Cornell University Press.
Freytag, Gustav (1908 [1863]) *Technique of the Drama*, trans. Elias J. McEwan, Chicago: Scott.
Greimas, Algirdas Julien (1983 [1966]) *Structural Semantics*, trans. Danielle McDowell, Ronald Schleifer, and Alan Velie, Lincoln: University of Nebraska Press.
Lévi-Strauss, Claude (1963 [1958]) *Structural Anthropology*, trans. Claire Jacobson and Brooke Grundfest Schoepf, New York: Basic Books.
O'Neill, Patrick (1994) *Fictions of Discourse: Reading Narrative Theory*, Toronto: University of Toronto Press.
Prince, Gerald (1973) *A Grammar of Stories*, The Hague: Mouton.
——(1987) *A Dictionary of Narratology*, Lincoln: University of Nebraska Press.
Propp, Vladimir (1968 [1928]) *Morphology of the Folktale*, trans. Laurence Scott, revised by Louis A. Wagner, Austin: University of Texas Press.
Rimmon-Kenan, Shlomith (2002 [1983]) *Narrative Fiction: Contemporary Poetics*, London: Routledge.

PATRICK O'NEILL

NARRATIVE TECHNIQUES

Narrative techniques are the devices of storytelling. Most approaches to narrative recognise the utility of a general division between a *what* and a *how* (*see* STORY-DISCOURSE DISTINCTION). The what is the domain of states, *existents (including *character), and *events; the how is the domain of technique. It is variously called the discourse or the *narration, and its main components are temporality (*see* TEMPORAL ORDERING; TIME IN NARRATIVE); *voice (who speaks?); vision or *focalization (who perceives?); and style. However, narrative technique also includes matters that overlap with but are not fully explicable in terms of textual features such as (1) a *narrator's *reliability; and (2) how a given narrative follows, flouts, or otherwise relates to conventions, especially those of its particular *genre.

Although there are discussions of technique as far back as Aristotle's *Poetics*, the intensive study of it is a twentieth-century phenomenon that begins with Henry James, and gets developed in sometimes overlapping, sometimes divergent ways through the work of the *Russian Formalists, the New Critics, the Chicago neo-Aristotelians, the *structuralist narratologists, and *postclassical narratologists. Indeed, it is with the analysis of narrative technique that narrative theory has arguably had its greatest success. This entry will focus on the work of James, Booth, Genette, and Bakhtin – and the larger critical discussions surrounding these figures – and will end with an illustrative analysis of a passage from Ishiguro's *The Remains of the Day*.

From Henry James to feminist narratology

James's theoretical contribution arises out of both his fictional narratives and his discussions of them in the Prefaces to the New York Edition of his novels (1909–1910). Employing richly metaphoric language, James offers a rationale for his developing preference for narrating through the central consciousness of a character, and, more generally, for scenic presentation over narrative summary (*see* SUMMARY AND SCENE; THOUGHT AND CONSCIOUSNESS REPRESENTATION (LITERATURE)). Critics who followed James gradually converted these preferences into abstract rules for novelistic practice: dramatic presentation – via scenes rendered from the *perspective of a character – is more objective and more artistic than summary or *commentary from a non-character *narrator; in other words, the artist must show, not tell (*see* AUTHENTICATION; SHOWING VS. TELLING).

Booth's *The Rhetoric of Fiction* (1961) argues against these rules by making a case for a different way of evaluating artistic merit. A writer, Booth shows, can be neither truly impersonal nor objective, can never avoid using rhetoric (*see* RHETORICAL APPROACHES TO NARRATIVE). Thus, judgments about technique should not be made by applying abstract rules to novelistic practice but by means-end reasoning: which technique can best serve the purposes of this narrative at this point? Booth also develops a set of influential concepts for analysing author-narrator-reader relationships (*see* AUTHOR; READER CONSTRUCTS). The *implied author, that is, the version of the real author revealed through the cumulative collection of choices made in writing the narrative, creates a narrator, who may be either dramatised (e.g., Fielding's narrator in *Tom Jones*) or undramatised (e.g., Austen's narrator in *Emma*), and who may also be either *reliable* or *unreliable* (*see* RELIABILITY). A reliable narrator is one whose reports and judgments are endorsed by the implied author, and an unreliable narrator is one whose reports

and judgements are not endorsed. Booth's concept of the implied author proved to be very controversial, with some later theorists finding it of great value and others finding that it is unnecessary (Nünning 1997). In this alternative it is the real author who creates the narrator.

Rabinowitz extends Booth's work by identifying the multiple *audiences of narrative and showing how their presence influences the implied author's (or if one prefers, author's) techniques. The audiences are the actual audience; the authorial audience, i.e., the ideal audience for whom the author is writing (equivalent to the narratological tradition calls the implied reader); the narrative audience, i.e., the one positioned within the world of the narrative and, thus, in *fiction, the one who believes in the reality of characters and events; and the ideal narrative audience, i.e., the narrator's ideal recipient (*see* READER CONSTRUCTS). Phelan notes that Prince's concept of the *narratee, the audience to whom the narrator is addressing the narration, complements rather than competes with the concepts of the narrative and ideal narrative audiences, and so should be included as part of the rhetorical model. Rabinowitz extends his work on audience in *Before Reading* (1998 [1987]), a study of the way the authorial audience's implicit understanding of narrative conventions influences both authorial choices of technique and the authorial audience's understanding of those choices.

Phelan and Martin build on Booth's work by proposing a new taxonomy of unreliable narration. They note that narrators perform three main functions – reporting, interpreting (or reading) what they report, and evaluating (or regarding) it – and that they can perform these functions reliably; reliably only up to a point; or flat-out unreliably. The three functions and the last two ways of performing them mean that there are six types of unreliability: under-reporting, under-reading, and under-regarding, misreporting, misreading, and misregarding. Booth and Phelan also propose ways of linking technique with ethics, Booth by attending to the ways in which techniques influence the nature and trajectory of readerly *desires and the 'friendships' offered by narratives, and Phelan by examining the links among the ethical situations represented in narrative, the ethics of their telling, and the ethical beliefs readers bring to their reading (*see* ETHICAL TURN).

Genette develops another set of influential concepts for analysing narrative technique. First, he notes that previous studies of *'point of view' have conflated two distinct concepts, *voice* (who speaks) and *vision* (who sees or perceives) and he proposes new ways of understanding each. With voice, Genette notes that the traditional way of distinguishing who is speaking by reference to grammatical *person is inadequate because any narrator can say 'I'; he proposes instead that we distinguish narrators according to their modes of participation in the narrated action. Narrators who participate (or did participate) in the events being narrated are *homodiegetic* and those who do (or did) not are *heterodiegetic*. With vision, Genette proposes the term 'focalization' to refer to the angle of perception, and he identifies three kinds: zero (or free) focalization, i.e., *narration from the *perspective of a heterodiegetic narrator, as in 'classical narrative' such as *Tom Jones*; internal focalization, narration from the perspective of a character; and external (or objective) focalization, narration from the perspective of a heterodiegetic narrator who never offers an inside view of the characters.

Genette's discussion of focalization has generated considerable debate and proposals for revision. Bal recommends adding the focalized (the object of perception) and the concept of 'layers of focalization' (one focalizing agent containing the perspective of another). Chatman worries that Genette's concept breaks down the distinction between story and discourse because it takes an element of discourse (vision) and assigns it both to narrators (another element of discourse) and to characters (an element of story). Consequently, Chatman recommends abandoning the term and employing two others, *filter* to refer to a character's perspective and *slant* to refer to the narrator's perspective. Later commentators such as Herman point to the necessity of including hypothetical and subjunctive focalization. Phelan proposes replacing Genette's taxonomy, which is based on the relative knowledge of narrator and character, with one that describes the possible combinations of vision and voice. He also proposes the category of 'dual focalization', in which a homodiegetic narrator perceives the perceptions of his or her former self.

Genette's work also significantly advances our understanding of techniques for handling temporal relations in narrative through his discussion of *order*, *duration*, and *frequency*. Order concerns the relation between chronological sequence and discourse sequence; discourse sequence may correspond with chronological sequence, or may deviate from it either through *analepsis* (flashback) or *prolepsis* (flashforward). Duration refers to the relations between the length of story time and the length of discourse time; for example, a period of considerable length may be narrated in a single sentence; alternatively, a narrator may devote numerous pages to a period of a few moments. Frequency refers to the relation between the number of times events occur and the number of times they are recounted. Singulative narration narrates once what occurs once; iterative narration narrates once an event that occurs many times. Repeating narration recounts multiple times an event that happens once.

Herman builds on Genette's work by noting that sometimes the order in which events occurred cannot be firmly pinned down, thus, giving rise to 'fuzzy temporality'. In a related move, Margolin demonstrates that narrative need not involve a retrospective account of definite, completed events but may also be concerned with the present and the future and with incomplete and indeterminate events (*see* INDETERMINACY; MODALITY; TENSE AND NARRATIVE).

Bakhtin's analysis of 'Discourse in the Novel' is especially relevant to considerations of voice and style. He views language as inevitably carrying ideological meaning, and views any national language not as a unified system but rather as a collection of sociolects or registers, e.g., the language of the working class, the language of the academy, each of which carries the values of its group (*see* SOCIOLINGUISTIC APPROACHES TO NARRATIVE; SPEECH REPRESENTATION). Bakhtin argues that the *novel necessarily draws upon multiple sociolects and puts them into dialogic relationships (*see* DIALOGISM; HETEROGLOSSIA; IDEOLOGY AND NARRATIVE). The dialogic relations may be expressed within the same sentence, in which case we have what Bakhtin calls double-voiced discourse (*see* DUAL-VOICE HYPOTHESIS). Moreover, different novelists will establish different dialogic relations among their novels' sociolects: some will clearly privilege one over others or use one to expose the values of others, and, in so doing, may either reinforce the hierarchy of dialogic relations in society or critique them. Other novelists such as Dostoevskii, for whom Bakhtin reserves his highest praise, may make several sociolects and their attendant ideological values equally attractive; these novelists may resolve their *plots without resolving their dialogues.

*Feminist narratologists participate in the spirit of Bakhtin's work by linking technique to ideology, though they are most concerned with ideologies of *gender and their interests extend beyond discourse itself to other elements of technique. Warhol shows that Victorian women novelists frequently constructed 'engaging' narrators who used their direct addresses to their narratees to close the distance between them and to encourage real readers to identify with those narratees, while male Victorian novelists typically constructed 'distant' narrators, who use their addresses to the narratee to emphasise the gaps between them and to keep their real readers at a distance as well (*see* ADDRESS). Lanser combines the formal emphasis of Genette's concept of voice with the ideological emphasis of Bakhtin's and analyses the different ways in which women writers construct voices with narrative authority. Case distinguishes between 'authoritative' and 'feminine narration' in the eighteenth- and nineteenth-century British novel; authoritative narrators, who may be either male or female, can shape their telling into a coherent plot, while feminine narrators, who also may be male or female, cannot. For authors, feminine narration is both a restriction and a resource.

Using the tools: narrative techniques in *The Remains of the Day*

In the following passage from Kazuo Ishiguro's *The Remains of the Day*, the butler Stevens narrates his behaviour just after giving Miss Kenton permission to take a day off in order to attend her aunt's funeral:

> I made my exit and it was not until after I had done so that it occurred to me that I had not actually offered her my condolences. I could well imagine the blow the news would be to her, her aunt having been, to all intents and purposes, like a mother to her, and I paused out in the corridor, wondering if I should go back, knock and make good my omission. But then it occurred to me that, if I were to do so, I might intrude upon her private grief. Indeed, it was

not impossible that Miss Kenton, at that very moment, and only a few feet from me, was actually crying. The thought provoked a strange feeling to rise within me, causing me to stand there hovering in the corridor for some moments. But eventually I judged it best to await another opportunity to express my sympathy and went on my way.

In James's terms this passage forms part of a scene rather than constituting a summary (later commentators would emphasise its focus on interiority; *see* THOUGHT AND CONSCIOUSNESS REPRESENTATION (LITERATURE)); Ishiguro is showing rather than telling, a technique that leads us, in Booth's and Rabinowitz's terms, to focus on how Ishiguro uses Stevens's narration indirectly to communicate to the authorial audience. In Genette's terms, Stevens is a homodiegetic narrator giving us his vision at the time of the action and his voice at the time of the telling; however, the phrases 'her aunt having been, to all intents and purposes, like a mother to her' suggest a shift to his vision at the time of the telling, as they reflect Stevens's awareness of his narratee.

The passage has a complex temporality. The temporal NOW of Stevens's narrative is 1956, though that NOW shifts as Stevens writes its different instalments on his six-day journey from Darlington Hall to the West Country where he meets Miss Kenton, now Mrs Benn (*see* DEIXIS). This passage is from the instalment he writes on the evening of Day Three, and it is part of a series of analepses during which Stevens reflects on possible 'turning points' in his relationship with Miss Kenton. The effect of these analepses is to underline how much Stevens is haunted by his past behaviour, how much his journey toward Mrs Benn is intertwined with a mental journey back through his life in search of new insights into his choices and their consequences. The progression of the analepses shows Stevens both approaching and avoiding the recognition that his commitment to dignity above all things led him to repress his feelings of love for Miss Kenton and, thus, his chance for a shared life with her (*see* NARRATIVE PROGRESSION).

Storyworld time here roughly matches discourse time: Stevens hovers in the corridor 'for some moments' and his discourse lingers over his pause for the duration of the paragraph. This duration helps identify these brief moments as a turning point, and Ishiguro goes on to use what Genette calls repeating narration to emphasise their significance. In Stevens's next instalment, he corrects his report by writing that his hovering outside Miss Kenton's door occurred on the night she told him that she was engaged to Mr Benn. Further along in his journey, Stevens can locate the turning point more accurately, but his doing so only makes it more poignant. Stevens admits that he 'had no real evidence' to conclude that Miss Kenton was crying but he goes on to admit that after he left the corridor his own mood was 'somewhat downcast'. Ishiguro's technique suggests that Stevens is projecting onto Miss Kenton his own sorrow about her engagement (*see* EMOTION IN NARRATIVE).

In discussing these effects, we have begun moving to the concerns of Booth, Rabinowitz, and Phelan with the relations among implied author, narrator, and audience. The implied Ishiguro uses several devices to signal that Stevens is under-reporting, misreporting, misreading, and misregarding. In an initial act of reliable reading, Stevens recognises that the news of Miss Kenton's aunt's death would be a 'blow' to her, but he then reports that he hesitated to intrude upon her 'private grief'. The implied Ishiguro, through the series of analepses, communicates a different reason: Stevens hesitates because he cannot bring himself to do what he has never done, namely, directly express a tender emotion toward Miss Kenton. Stevens's misreporting here is accompanied by misreading and misregarding. To pause for fear of intruding upon Miss Kenton's privacy is to misread Miss Kenton's preferences about his behaviour toward her. To pause for that reason is to misregard because it rationalises behaviour that is easier for him in the short run but not in Miss Kenton's – or ultimately his own – best interest.

Stevens reliably notes his 'strange feeling', but, in stopping short of specifying that feeling any further, he under-reports. Because the authorial audience knows Stevens does care for Miss Kenton, the juxtaposition of this report with Stevens's speculation that Miss Kenton is 'actually crying' invites us to infer that Stevens is the one either crying or near tears. His sorrow is part fellow-feeling, part unconscious recognition that he is not able to comfort her. Stevens's report that he 'judged it best to await another opportunity' to express his sorrow reinforces the misreporting

and misregarding that accompany his excuse of not wanting to intrude upon Miss Kenton's grief. The ethical dimension of the technique stems from the way it evokes both negative judgment and sympathy for Stevens, in his slow struggle to come to terms with his painful past, and from the trust and cooperation that the implied Ishiguro builds in his artful indirect communication with his audience.

Meanwhile, from a Bakhtinian perspective, all the unreliability is double-voiced, because the implied Ishiguro is ironising those utterances (*see* IRONY). That double-voicing is accompanied by another dialogic relation in the passage, that between the language of genuine emotion, which is direct and unpretentious (e.g., 'Miss Kenton... was actually crying'), and the language of formal politeness and reserve (e.g., 'strange feeling'; 'another opportunity to express my sympathy'). Ishiguro orchestrates the dialogue so that the language of formal politeness is undercut by the language of emotion: after the directness of 'actually crying' the formal diction of the last sentence indicates that Ishiguro is double-voicing Stevens's judgment about what is 'best'.

As this passage and the larger trajectory of Stevens's narration shows, he is what Case would call a 'feminine' narrator, one who records the events but not one who is responsible for shaping those events into a plot that he designs. Case notes that feminine narration is a socially constructed position, not a mode necessarily tied to the narrator's biological sex. By 1989 the ideological implications of feminine narration are not as clear as they were in the eighteenth- and nineteenth-centuries, but Case's perspective invites further analysis of the link between Stevens's mode of telling and concepts of masculinity and femininity within both *The Remains of the Day* and the culture in which it was produced.

As this brief case-study suggests, although different approaches to narrative theory have developed different tools for studying narrative technique, these tools can effectively complement each other and produce rich analyses of the multiple devices of storytelling.

SEE ALSO: film narrative; graphic presentation as expressive device; narrative situations; narrative structure; narrative transmission; stream of consciousness and interior monologue

References and further reading

Bakhtin, Mikhail (1981) 'Discourse in the Novel', in *The Dialogic Imagination*, trans. Caryl Emerson and Michael Holquist, Austin: University of Texas Press.

Bal, Mieke (1985, 1998) *Narratology: Introduction to the Theory of Narrative*, trans. Christine van Boheemen, Toronto: University of Toronto Press.

Booth, Wayne C. (1961) *The Rhetoric of Fiction*, Chicago: University of Chicago Press.

—— (1988) *The Company We Keep: An Ethics of Fiction*, Berkeley: University of California Press.

Case, Alison A. (1999) *Plotting Women: Gender and Representation in the Eighteenth- and Nineteenth-Century British Novel*, Charlottesville: University of Virginia Press.

Chatman, Seymour (1990) *Coming to Terms: The Rhetoric of Narrative in Fiction and Film*, Ithaca: Cornell University Press.

Genette, Gérard (1981) *Narrative Discourse: An Essay in Method*, trans. Jane E. Lewin, Ithaca: Cornell University Press.

Herman, David (2002) *Story Logic: Problems and Possibilities of Narrative*, Lincoln: University of Nebraska Press.

Ishiguro, Kazuo (1989) *The Remains of the Day*, New York: Knopf.

James, Henry (1986) *The Art of Criticism: Henry James on the Theory and Practice of Fiction*, eds. William Veeder and Susan M. Griffin, Chicago: University of Chicago Press.

Lanser, Susan S. (1992) *Fictions of Authority: Women Writers and Narrative Voice*, Ithaca: Cornell University Press.

Margolin, Uri (1999) 'Of What Is Past, Is Passing, or to Come: Temporality, Aspectuality, Modality, and the Nature of Literary Narrative', in David Herman (ed.) *Narratologies: New Perspectives on Narrative Analysis*, Columbus: Ohio State University Press.

Nünning, Ansgar (1997) 'Deconstructing and Reconceptualizing the "Implied Author": The Resurrection of an Anthropomorphicized Passepartout or the Obituary of a Critical Phantom?', *Anglistik*, 8.2, 95–116.

Phelan, James (2004) *Living to Tell about It: A Rhetoric and Ethics of Character Narration*, Ithaca: Cornell University Press.

——, and Mary Patricia Martin (1999) 'The Lessons of "Weymouth": Homodiegesis, Unreliability, Ethics, and *The Remains of the Day*', in David Herman (ed.) *Narratologies: New Perspectives on Narrative Analysis*, Columbus: Ohio State University Press.

Preston, Mary Elizabeth (1997) 'Homodiegetic Narration: Reliability, Self-consciousness, Ideology, and Ethics'. Unpublished dissertation, Ohio State University Press.

Rabinowitz, Peter J. (1998 [1987]) *Before Reading: Narrative Conventions and the Politics of Interpretation*, Columbus: Ohio State University Press.

—— 'Truth in Fiction: A Reexamination of Audiences', *Critical Inquiry* 4, 121–41.

Warhol, Robyn (1989) *Gendered Interventions: Narrative Discourse in the Victorian Novel*, New Brunswick: Rutgers University Press.

JAMES PHELAN AND WAYNE C. BOOTH

NARRATIVE THERAPY

Narrative therapy (NT) is a form of therapeutic practice developed and refined by Australia's Michael White and New Zealand's David Epston. NT draws on personal narratives – stories – for the specific purpose of defining psychological problems and proposing solutions (*see* CONVERSATIONAL STORYTELLING; DISCOURSE ANALYSIS (LINGUISTICS); LIFE STORY). Although narrative is always an important component of the psychotherapeutic process, NT is distinct insofar as it is the narrative or script itself that provides the elements for contemplating psychological transformation. Together, the client and helper, as the therapist is called in NT, come to understand the client's script, a process that involves reflection and action. This reflective and active process starts by encouraging helpers to recognise their own scripts, so as to insure that the helper's script does not unduly influence the clients' interpretations of their own narratives. Aware of these influences, the helper is free to facilitate client insight into their scripts and to help clients make deliberate decisions about the relevance of their narratives to their personal aspirations. NT recognises that individuals, both helpers and clients, are very much a part of a larger cultural, political, and social context that influences their narratives. The process simultaneously encourages insight into the client's individual script while remaining aware of these larger cultural influences (*see* CULTURAL STUDIES APPROACHES TO NARRATIVE; SOCIOLOGY AND NARRATIVE).

Unlike positivistic or psychoanalytic approaches, clients define the context and content of the therapeutic work (*see* PSYCHOANALYSIS AND NARRATIVE). NT has no set text and does not subscribe to one *truth. In addition, rather than relying on the skill of one expert – the therapist – who draws out the client's story in order to outline a cure, NT works closely with the client to identify and recognise the client's narrative, as the client defines it, thus paving the road to a recovery that is grounded in the client's *desire. Although traditional therapeutic practices may help inform narrative therapeutic practices, it is the clients' views of themselves, their cultural, social, and political narratives, that direct the therapeutic work in NT.

NT uses several techniques and terms that draw on postmodern theory. For example, the work starts with the helper's 'preferred description'. This approach stresses insight into the assumptions that govern the helpers' therapeutic practices based on their own personal stories. NT provides that if helpers want to learn more about their clients' stories, they must be familiar with their own.

A second key element of NT practice is curiosity, which enables clients to reveal and see their stories from multiple points of view. Through this approach, the interview is shaped as much by the client's needs, as it is directed by the helper's insight and experience. Like viewing one's life through a prism, the client can see the many ways his or her life can be interpreted (see FOCALIZATION; PERSPECTIVE).

The client's narrative is shaped by a number of social, cultural, and personal factors which form a critical component of the therapeutic narrative. Clients are encouraged to reflect narratively on the discourses that embody the cultural and political underpinnings in their personal stories and to place themselves within that broader context. For example, when a woman complains of anxiety, it is important to understand its larger relevance. If she has been unable to conceive a child for several years, leading to her anxiety, it is helpful to recognise the cultural pressures she may feel in relation to motherhood. Or, if a young man identifies himself as homosexual and is also suffering from severe depression, it is helpful to realise that his father, say a senior ranking officer in the military, strongly disapproves of any suggestion that his son's sexual identity is in question. Personal and social indicators help explain the larger context of the client's suffering and situate the specific circumstances affecting his or her life.

*Deconstructive approaches to NT initiate the process of disassembling the discourses, assumptions, and overarching socio-cultural narratives that underpin the client's stories (see MASTER NARRATIVE). Deconstruction allows clients to understand more clearly the larger context of their suffering. In our examples, the woman can understand just how powerful the cultural narrative of motherhood is and the young man can see the genesis of his father's disapproval. In turn, deconstruction positions clients to free themselves from the cultural scripts through the process of 'reconstruction' (see SCRIPTS AND SCHEMATA; IDEOLOGY AND NARRATIVE).

Reconstruction allows clients to reject the cultural, social, or even personal norms that can envelop them emotionally and to write a new story.

Indeed, the force of NT is in the power it gives to clients to rename and reclassify their suffering. Using traditional therapeutic methods, a person seeking help would pay the therapist to uncover the problems, understand them in a larger context, and develop a cure. In sharp contrast, clients in NT identify the problems, describe the stories that underlie those problems, and evaluate the usefulness of those stories to their current functioning. Once the stories are revealed and understood for what they are, they can be consciously embraced or rewritten, depending on their relevance to a person's life. For example, the woman who could not conceive a child may have viewed herself through a specific motherhood lens since her own childhood. She is now 40 years old and ready to develop a life that incorporates an older adopted child. This expands a world that appeared to have collapsed to little more than a single *identity. Similarly, the young man saw the approval he sought from his father as crucial to his mental health. But as he realised that his friends now functioned as a loving family, he could relinquish his relationship with his judgmental father and free himself of his suffering. What makes NT an exciting development in therapeutic practice is the way it can help clients free themselves from outmoded stories that once defined who they were, thereby making it possible for them to reconstruct new identities.

SEE ALSO: narrative psychology; psychological approaches to narrative

References and further reading

Alphons, Richard J. (2003) 'Living Stories, Telling Stories, Changing Stories: Experiential Use of the Relationship in Narrative Therapy', Journal of Psychotherapy Integration, 13.2, 188–210.

Carlson, Thomas D., and Martin J. Erickson (2001) 'Honoring and Privileging Personal Experience and Knowledge: Ideas for a Narrative Therapy Approach to the Training and Supervision of New Therapist', Contemporary Family Therapy, 23.2, 199–219.

Monk, Gerald, John Winslade, Kathie Crocket, and David Epston (eds) (1997) Narrative Therapy in Practice: The Archaeology of Hope, San Francisco: Jossey Bass.

Schwartz, Richard C. (1999) 'Narrative Therapy Expands and Contracts Family Therapy's Horizons', Journal of Marital and Family Therapy, vol. 25.2, 263–67.

White, Michael, and David Epston (1990) Narrative Means to Therapeutic Ends, New York: Newton.

LINDA MILLS

NARRATIVE TRANSFORMATION

In the semiotic model developed by A. J. Greimas, the concept of *narrativity designates not only a discourse type – i.e., *narrative, or the recounting of real or fictional *events – but also a form inherent to the semantic universe that underlies all discourse. Organising this narrative form is an itinerary (*parcours*) around what Greimas characterised as the *narrative transformation*, which corresponds to the syntagmatic unfolding of the difference between an initial and a subsequent state. In turn, these states are defined by a specific kind of juncture between two *actants: namely, a subject and a valuable object. For Greimas, the dichotomy of state vs. transformation enables the semantic universe to take on a *narrative structure.

Narrative transformation thus creates a mediation between two states that represent the terms of a superordinate semantic category. Since narrativity is characterised by a succession of states and transformations, the purpose of narrative grammar is to outline algorithms which capture the syntagmatic unfolding of narrative transformations (*see* STORY GRAMMARS). As an action (or realised doing), narrative transformation can be analysed into four elements (*énoncés*) which constitute the narrative algorithm. Two elements, *performance* and *competence*, are centred on doing and on the conditions necessary to its realisation. Two others, *manipulation* and *sanction*, which open and close the narrative itinerary, characterise the relations among the subject actant, the values put into play by the transformation, and the other actants that instantiate those values.

SEE ALSO: narrative semantics; semiotics; text-type approach to narrative

References and further reading

Greimas, Algirdas Julien (1983 [1966]) *Structural Semantics: An Attempt at a Method*, trans. Danielle McDowell, Ronald Schleifer, and Alan Velie, Lincoln: University of Nebraska Press.

LOUIS PANIER

NARRATIVE TRANSMISSION

Narrative transmission is the storytelling process structured between the fictional universe of the text and the reader. After Jakobson (1960) postulated the addresser/addressee relationship in communication events, narratologists focused on the multiple identities and functions of the 'addresser' pole (*author, *implied author, *narrator), the multiple identities and functions of the 'addressee' pole (reader, implied reader, *narratee) (*see* READER CONSTRUCTS), and the 'message' (story and discourse) that passes from addressers to addressees. The 'message' is comprised of a *'code' (language) and a referential 'context' (*see* REFERENCE). Narrative transmission focuses on how 'contact', the sixth element in Jakobson's model, is manifested in narrative communication, examining the code of communication within the text that signifies narrating channels, especially those dramatised within the text.

Transmission is dramatised in narrative texts, particularly in narrative fiction, at the discourse level when the narrator comments to the narratee on the writing of the text. At the intradiegetic level, transmission is dramatised by how documents such as *letters, *diaries, memoirs, and transcribed oral narrations constitute the narrative in texts structured predominately of such documents. At the extradiegetic level of such texts, the fictional editorial prefaces, notes, and afterwords serve as *paratextual markers of the transmission process that brings the intradiegetic documents into a text that has been prepared for an extradiegetic narratee and ultimately for the real reader of the literary text.

SEE ALSO: communication in narrative; function (Jakobson); reader-response theory; story-discourse distinction

References and further reading

Duyfhuizen, Bernard (1992) *Narratives of Transmission*, Rutherford, NJ: Fairleigh Dickinson University Press.
Jakobson, Roman (1960) 'Closing Statement: Linguistics and Poetics', in Thomas Sebeok (ed.) *Style in Language*, Cambridge: MIT Press.
Lanser, Susan (1981) *The Narrative Act: Point of View in Prose Fiction*, Princeton: Princeton University Press.

BERNARD DUYFHUIZEN

NARRATIVE TURN IN THE HUMANITIES

Although people have talked about and analysed stories for millennia, the institutional study of *narrative for its own sake, as opposed to the examination of individual narratives, narrative features, or correspondences between them, is a fairly recent phenomenon. Only within the last four decades or so have researchers moved away from examining the narrative attributes of a play (*see* DRAMA AND NARRATIVE), *biblical story, historiographic account, or *film, and begun looking squarely at narrative itself, asking rigorous questions not about this or that narrative or story, but about exactly what a story is, where it occurs, how it works, what it does, and for whom (*see* PRAGMATICS; RHETORICAL APPROACHES TO NARRATIVE; STRUCTURALIST NARRATOLOGY). At the same time, more, and more varied, investigators have been involved in this inquiry, from inside and outside academia and from a full range of research traditions, some of which had previously ignored or even denigrated narrative as an object of study.

One consequence of the narrative (or narrativist) turn, as this phenomenon has been called (Kreiswirth 1995), is that the study of story has been effectively dislodged from its original academic home in the humanities – in religion, *philosophy, *historiography, and literary and *cultural studies – and in the text-based varieties of its near relatives – jurisprudence, linguistics, *psychoanalysis, anthropology (*see* ETHNOGRAPHIC APPROACHES TO NARRATIVE; LAW AND NARRATIVE; LINGUISTIC APPROACHES TO NARRATIVE; THEOLOGY AND NARRATIVE). In the last decade narrative has become a significant focus of inquiry in virtually all disciplinary formations, ranging from the fine arts, the social and natural *sciences, to *media and *communication studies, to popular therapy, *medicine, and managerial studies (*see* INSTITUTIONAL NARRATIVE; NARRATIVE THERAPY). All in all, a remarkable amount of valuable work has been done, to which the current volume attests. Yet, with each shift in disciplinary orientation or research tradition, as many new questions have arisen as answers. As soon as we begin to feel secure about our findings, we learn that this or that subspecies has been forgotten, this phenomenon or characteristic overlooked or suppressed, this function or structure neglected. And this is particularly so in narrative's original disciplinary domicile – the humanities.

Narrative ubiquity

There are no doubt many reasons for our inability to catch the tale, but one certainly derives from the behaviour of story itself, seen most prominently in its narrative ubiquity – its extensive discursive promiscuity and capacity for disciplinary migration (Kreiswirth 1995). Narrative cuts across *genre, substance, form, culture, class, history – seemingly all of human thought and activity (*see* NARRATIVE UNIVERSALS). It effectively provides, as Hayden White notes, the solution to a fundamental problem of our species, 'the problem of how to translate *knowing* into *telling*, the problem of fashioning human experience into a form assimilable to structures of meaning that are generally human rather than culture-specific' (1987: 1) or, even, discipline-specific (*see* COGNITIVE NARRATOLOGY; NARRATIVE AS COGNITIVE INSTRUMENT). And, if narrative is indeed co-extensive with humanity and provides the prototypical form of common knowledge, how can any discipline or research paradigm that deals with human thought and activity – with discourse, culture, behaviour, *gender, cognition, justice, and so on, with the humanities, that is – in all good conscience neglect it? By appearing practically everywhere and assuming an enormous range of discursive functions, narrative cannot help but flaunt its inherent multi- or trans-disciplinarity; and this situation generates both its explanatory appeal and its disciplinary and definitional problems, both inside and outside the humanities and, indeed, inside and outside the walls of academia itself.

In response, one swing of the narrative turn has moved centripetally in an attempt to confront the problem of narrative ubiquity head-on through specifically trans-disciplinary approaches – whether in narratology, *semiotics, cognitive science, or communication theory. Story's uncanny multidiscursive reach and prominence have also spun the narrative turn centrifugally, as scrutiny of its workings has emanated not from global multidisciplinary perspectives but from the grass-roots perspectives of multiple disciplines, and these have ranged progressively further from story's traditional institutional home in the humanities – specifically, that is, further from literary, theological, philosophical, or cultural studies.

Narratology

Narratology, stemming from French structuralism and semiotics and working primarily between traditional humanistic disciplines, was the first rigorously formal attempt to isolate story as story and consolidate narrative ubiquity by building a heuristic pan-narrative model. Among other things, it uses insights derived from structuralism to locate what narratives and only narratives have in common, and to see these common features in terms of formal, narrative-specific rules (*see* STORY GRAMMARS). In the sunny days of structuralism (in the 1960s and 1970s) great advances were made. Researchers such as Barthes, Claude Bremond, A. J. Greimas, Tzevtan Todorov, Gérard Genette, Gerald Prince, Jonathan Culler, Mieke Bal, and Seymour Chatman separated narrating from the narrated, and went on to mark, categorise, and teach a set of critical features: *focalization, order, frequency, duration, and so on (*see* TEMPORAL ORDERING; TIME IN NARRATIVE). Some felt that story's definitional characteristics were at the point of being finally stabilised as more refined semiotic instruments were employed on progressively more texts. Others, however, began to distrust the entire enterprise itself, questioning narratology's deductive methodology, excessively formalist, text-based perspective, and hidden presuppositions, particularly those deriving from the choice of the narrative corpus itself. For one thing, apparently, many species of the genus were overlooked.

Up until the 1970s or so, narrative and narrative theory had traditionally been the province of those disciplines whose research focus and methods are reflective and critical, those disciplines that have formed an important part of the accepted core of the humanities: literary, cultural, religious, and, to a lesser extent, philosophical studies. As in narratology, researchers in these fields tend not to produce narratives, but to receive them, and their work, in essence, involves commenting analytically on that reception, looking at the determinants, operations, and semantics of narrative as a genus or at those of individual narratives (*see* NARRATIVE SEMANTICS). Indeed, Jürgen Habermas's definition of the kinds of 'cognitive interests' that define the humanities – as opposed to technical or emancipatory interests – primarily involve *hermeneutics and modes of *reception: interpretation, legitimation, and, most centrally, understanding.

Beyond narratology

The ever-widening migration of narrative theory has recently begun to populate other territories. It has become an important tool in those fields – both inside and outside the humanities – that support

the other end of the communication circuit – narrative production rather than consumption. And it has affected researchers who, as part of their modes of inquiry, tend to produce discursive narratives, in disciplines such as history and historiography, ethnography, law, medicine, and therapy. Indeed, one of the most recent spins of the narrative turn for these research areas has been a kind of advocacy movement, an attempt to re-theorise narrative in such a way as to promote or resuscitate its use within this or that field as an analytic or methodological instrument, an opportunity, apparently, to exchange outmoded or tired paradigms for fresher more current modes of inquiry. That rejuvenated ways of analysing and producing knowledge in these intellectual arenas should derive from narrative and narrative theory, research areas that have been customarily lodged almost exclusively within the humanities, says something not only about the changes in modes of inquiry in the various disciplines themselves, and about larger issues of disciplinarity and inter-disciplinarity, but also about possibilities within and between fields in the humanities.

Until relatively recently, formulating, or thinking about formulating, say, political theory, or jurisprudence – or, to go outside the humanities, medicine – in terms of narrative was not even an available option. The production and dissemination of knowledge in these fields were governed by largely scientific or quasi-scientific modes of inquiry and discourse, by non-storied forms of investigation and reportage. Story may have occasionally appeared in these contexts, but it would have been mobilised and thought of only as digression, example, or rhetorical ornament, something supplementary to the guiding armature of rational argument, and not worth commenting on.

But, in the 1990s, things radically changed. Narrative and narrative theory have travelled far and wide, colonising new terrains of thought and modes of inquiry (see Kreiswirth 1995). Serious students of, say, political science, law, history, or even medicine, seemingly cannot do without them (until recently, professional history had repressed its fundamental relationship to storied forms and narrative theory). To give a rough sense of the breadth, frequency, and duration of this disciplinary migration, it is worth examining some data. For example, in the Worldwide Political Science Abstracts database, there were 16 articles published between 1970 and 1982 with 'narrative' in the title, 35 between 1983 and 1992, and 118 between 1993 and 2004. Similarly, in the Historical Abstracts database, there were 82 articles with 'narrative' in the title from 1973–1982, 263 articles between 1983–1992, and 345 between 1994–2003; in the standard legal studies database, LegalTrac, the numbers jumped from 6 articles in the first decade, to 81 in the second, and then to 140; and, in the Medical Research database, PubMed, there were 28 articles published with 'narrative' in the title between 1973 and 1983, 133 between 1984–1993, and 429 between 1994–2003. Both inside and outside the humanities, researchers have become bullish on narrative in the last ten years. Yet, when such researchers try to catch the tale, they come to the task with a set of instruments, texts, thinkers, presuppositions, and goals entirely different from those of the narratologists (or from those of other primarily literary or cultural researchers). For example, in a reference work published in 2000 by Alun Munslow, *The Routledge Companion to Historical Studies*, the entry on 'Narrative' cites forty-three works for further reading. Not one author among the forty-three listed corresponds to those in the roster of important narratologists that were mentioned above; no Barthes, Genette, or Prince. Conversely, narratological research (or, more properly, research on fictive narratives in literature and other fields) is routinely carried out without consulting the work of F. R. Ankersmit, David Carr, Arthur Danto, William Dray, W. B. Gallie, Louis Mink, Paul Veyne, or, in some cases, even Hayden White – some of the most significant theorists of narrative truth-telling (*see* FICTION, THEORIES OF; TRUTH).

Narrative turnings

Why the acceleration in the narrative turn? And why the turning within and between the disciplines? Story's migration away from the humanities into the social or even natural sciences undoubtedly stems from a whole host of interlocking perturbations to accepted paradigms of inquiry and their dissemination: constructivist, historicist, perspectivist, and anti-foundationalist challenges to these paradigms look for replacements in less universal and more contingent forms of thought and analysis (see Kreiswirth 2000). The narrative turn encompasses more and more disciplines concerned not just with story as story but with storied forms of knowledge. As researchers

come to address narratives whose epistemic status and discursive work are securely tied to facts and referentiality (*see* REFERENCE), there is the temptation to reopen the problem of how to locate the defining features of the genus, with what instruments and in contradistinction to what other categories. Such travelling of narrative theory back and forth between the humanities and other research domains has significant consequences for all involved, and especially for the humanities themselves. Not only have new, non-humanist, disciplines capitalised on the emigration of narrative and narrative theory, this resettlement has also forced a reassessment of the native domain. For example, now cognisant of the kinds of concerns narrativist historians, medical researchers, lawyers, and political scientists have brought to the table regarding storied forms of knowledge, narratologists themselves have begun to re-examine their project. The narrative turn in the humanities has turned back upon itself.

Narrative fiction and narrative fact

Gérard Genette (apologising for his own complicity) has noted that even though narratology was envisioned to capture all narratives, in practice it ended up focussing on a particular canon (a group of fictional texts used as illustrations) and thus privileged fictional narratives, making them the implicit model for narrative in general. Similarly, Gerald Prince, also belatedly apologetic, criticises narratologists for using linguistic models that ignored semantic concerns, such as truth and reference. Hence, narratology never pondered the 'alethic potential of narrative, the relations of the narrative text with truth or falsehood, the nature of the fictional as opposed to the real, the being of narratively represented worlds' (1991: 543), and, consequently, never asked the question of what importance referentiality, truth, or truth claims might have both for those species of story that are non-fictive and for story as story, more generally.

Yet, even after noting these disturbing gaps, narratologists have not gone very far toward consulting the theories of narrative and narrative knowledge that derive from more specific disciplinary formations underwritten by a rather different set of assumptions and goals, those stemming from, say, history, anthropology, or political science, let alone those that have come to narrative from further afield, from medicine, law, or therapy. But this may not be terribly surprising; those who study story as story from within the non-humanities disciplines have tended not to wander too far from their institutional homes either.

Indeed, just as traditional narratology neglected the alethic potential of narrative, history, law, or medicine's attempt to scrutinise story qua story has, until very recently, neglected practically everything else. As much as law has embraced the immigration of narrative and narrative theory, it is still, like history, very anxious about its relationship to the states of affairs it is presenting. There is worry about who is telling what story, with what warrant, and what degree of fallibility (Gewirtz 1996). Similarly, in the manifold writings on medical narratives, the issue of story's uneasy relationship to referentiality, and to epistemic and hermeneutic values also (and necessarily) remain central. Anxieties both about the form and truth-value of first-person accounts of illness (*pathographies*) challenge their clinical and scientific efficacy (Brody 1987) (*see* NARRATION; PERSON).

Yet, at the same time, it has become clear that this migration of narrative theory outside the humanities has important consequences for both the theory itself and the intellectual territories that it has traversed. For researchers who want to rethink their formerly empirically motivated, non-storied disciplines in terms of narrative, there is, at bottom, always the troubling suspicion that when all is said and done, story may actually turn out to be its wily twin, *fable. Indeed, as Marie-Laure Ryan has stated, the root concepts of narrative and fiction seem to be 'magnetically attracted to each other' (1991: 1) and, sometimes, even further entangled with that of literature (always an additional problem in discussions of narrative in truth-telling disciplines).

Narrative and the fictive

As narrative theory's journeys back and forth within the humanities and between them and other disciplines have begun to teach us, the fictive/non-fictive distinction may be more of a problem of method and perspective than of substance or definition. Rather than see narrative as some kind of subspecies of fiction, or fiction as some kind of subspecies of narrative, or hopelessly to conflate the two, as has been too often accepted in the humanities tradition, narrative thinkers interested in *speech acts, *pragmatics, rhetoric, *discourse

analysis, and cognitive science have argued that these terms might better be seen as describing acts rather than objects, discursive processes whose determinations are constituted by a community's ways of using them, not by a text's intrinsic formal features. Mary-Louise Pratt, Thomas Leitch, Monika Fludernik, David Herman, Marie-Laure Ryan, and Michael Kearns, for example, have gone a long way toward showing that the narrative and the fictive are categories that stem not from textual objects but from the competencies and expectations of *audiences (*see* READER-RESPONSE THEORY). They are not discovered intrinsic elements but extrinsic learned behaviours, tacit rules and explanatory stances that allow the interpreter to decide what elements or patterns are required to confer story status on a given phenomenon, and then, just as importantly, how to regard and process that phenomenon (*see* NARRATIVITY).

Looked at in this way, stories are neither fictive nor non-fictive by nature. Neither their internal characteristics nor the referential status of their redacted propositions determine their underlying 'storyhood', their member in the genus narrative. Rather, stories are constituted – and derive their real-world consequences – through a pragmatic transaction, itself based on institutional presuppositions and conventions. A narrative that claims to represent actual happenings (a court deposition, or self-reported depiction of an illness) works as a communicative act – that is, as performative texts eliciting certain expectations, etc. – in exactly the same way as a fictive narrative (*novel, *joke), i.e., one that doesn't make truth claims (*see* PERFORMATIVITY). Story is received as story regardless of what use it is being put to. But, and for some disciplinary traditions this is a very large 'but', these two different kinds of tellings perform very different functions and are received and acted upon very differently in the world. The distinction holds not because one is a record of fact, of what really happened, and the other is not, but because, by certain conventions, contexts, and transactive contracts, we have learned to take one to be making claims to be a record of fact and deal with that accordingly. When, in such cases, we then judge evidence and weigh probabilities, and look for fits between this narrative and other truth-telling narratives, we are not determining its claim as story or truth (that has already been ascertained by its mode of reception), but assessing its truth *value* (see Sternberg 1987).

And, despite the fact that they have remained outside the specific study of story in the humanities, such operations are obviously an extremely important part of the establishment of narrative competence, especially since the dominant forms of story are those that make claims to report facts: common *conversational narratives, *life stories, news reports, family *anecdotes, as well as court depositions, ethnographies, historiographies, formal *biographies, illness reports, etc. (*see* COURTROOM NARRATIVE; JOURNALISM). Hence narrative theory after the narrative turn must confront fictive and non-fictive narratives (and indeed theories of narrative stemming from non-fictive disciplines) in tandem, touching as much as possible upon the range of narrative forms and the various media through which they are distributed. The narrative turn and transplantation of humanities research paradigms into alien domains, opens up conditions of acceptances and resistances that can, if handled properly, transform both the theories and the paradigms.

SEE ALSO: interdisciplinary approaches to narrative

References and further reading

Brody, Howard (1987) *Stories of Sickness*, New Haven: Yale University Press.
Fludernik, Monika (1996) *Towards a 'Natural' Narratology*, London: Routledge.
Genette, Gérard (1990) 'Fictional Narrative, Factual Narrative', *Poetics Today*, 11, 755–74.
Gewirtz, Paul (1996) 'Narrative and Rhetoric in the Law', in Peter Brooks and Paul Gewirtz (eds) *Law's Stories: Narrative and Rhetoric in the Law*, New Haven: Yale University Press.
Habermas, Jürgen (1987) *Knowledge and Human Interests*, trans. Jeremy Shapiro, Oxford: Polity Press.
Herman, David (2002) *Story Logic: Problems and Possibilities of Narrative*, Lincoln: University of Nebraska Press.
Kreiswirth, Martin (1995) 'Tell Me a Story: The Narrativist Turn in the Human Sciences', in Martin Kreiswirth and Thomas Carmichael (eds) *Constructive Criticism: The Human Sciences in the Age of Theory*, Toronto: University of Toronto Press.
—— (2000) 'Merely Telling Stories: Narrative and Knowledge in the Human Sciences', *Poetics Today*, 21, 293–318.
Munslow, Alun (2000) *The Routledge Companion to Historical Studies*, London: Routledge.
Polkinghorne, Donald (1988) *Narrative Knowing and the Human Sciences*, New York: State University of New York Press.
Prince, Gerald (1991) 'Narratology, Narrative, and Meaning', *Poetics Today*, 12, 543–52.
Ricoeur, Paul (1984–1988) *Time and Narrative*, trans. Kathleen McLaughlin and David Pellauer, 3 vols, Chicago: University of Chicago Press.
Ryan, Marie-Laure (1991) *Possible Worlds, Artificial Intelligence, and Narrative Theory*, Bloomington: Indiana University Press.
Sternberg, Meir (1987) *The Poetics of Biblical Narrative: Ideological Literature and the Drama of Reading*, Bloomington: Indiana University Press.
White, Hayden (1987) 'The Value of Narrativity in the Representation of Reality', in *The Content of the Form*, Baltimore: Johns Hopkins University Press.

MARTIN KREISWIRTH

NARRATIVE UNITS

Narratives are complex representational structures involving a multitude of elements. A certain type of combination of narrative elements is the prerequisite for the formation of the most basic *narrative unit* – a *minimal narrative. While all narrative units are composite structures, the extension of these structures varies considerably. This seems to suggest that the various types of narrative units can be easily distinguished if we systematise them top-down by decreasing degree of magnitude.

However, as Culler (1975) has pointed out, a taxonomic approach of this sort cannot explain our seemingly natural ability to identify narrative units and reach agreement on their existence regardless of theoretical definitions. Readers segment narratives into units with a specific purpose in mind. For example, while one will segment a narrative into large units such as *chapters*, another structures it into *scenes* which tend to occur at the level of paragraphs. These formal segmentations may differ in scope, but they both provide insight into a narrative's compositional structure. Meanwhile, if one seeks to distinguish representational or diegetic levels in a narrative text, one will adopt yet another approach: namely, separating out the *narrative frame* from the *embedded narrative* that it contains (*see* DIEGESIS; EMBEDDING; FRAMED NARRATIVE).

Despite such differences in methodology and purpose all attempts at defining and identifying narrative units have a common point of departure: their initial focus is on the 'how' of a narrative. Apart from information about their unique *storyworld, narratives also contain discursive *processing instructions*: in which order and segmentation was the story originally conceived and assembled, and in which manner and sequence are we supposed to reassemble and interpret it to construct a dynamic mental image of the storyworld (*see* SITUATION MODEL; TEMPORAL ORDERING)? Processing instructions can be issued either by direct *rhetorical means, or implicitly and by way of structural segmentation. Analogous to that of the *dramatic unit*, the concept of *narrative unit* is reserved for the definition of such structural features.

Some of these structural features are relatively easy to identify. Thus the segmentation of a complex narrative into *parts*, *books*, *chapters*, *acts*, *scenes*, and *paragraphs* is due to an uncontroversial notational or formal system (numbers, headers, titles, or paragraph breaks), while the identification of narrative units at the level of phrases and sentences usually employs a mix of formal, structural, and semantic criteria. Intuitively, the sentences at issue are more likely to qualify as a narrative unit if we perceive them to present a coherent piece of *action in themselves, or if they play a pivotal role in our understanding of the overall action. Barthes (1977 [1966]) and Chatman (1978) have suggested calling such essential components *nuclei* and *kernels*, respectively, and the non-essential ones *satellites* (Chatman 1978).

Structuralism in general tends to adopt a 'readerly' perspective on the question of narrative units. However, *structuralists like the early Barthes follow Propp (1968 [1928]) in developing, instead, an 'actional' stance focusing on the functional definition of narrative units. Indeed, in Propp's model, the overall narrative is composed of narrative units explicitly termed *functions*. Each of these functions represents a specific nuclear action occurring in a pre-ordained position along the overall sequence. 'Functions' are indispensable from the perspective of the overall action. This top-down approach in the functional definition of the basic narrative unit has been reformulated as an inductive model in Pavel (1985). His 'move grammar' conceives of a concrete narrative as a sequence of strategic *moves*. Each move is the outcome of an agent's attempt to realise a particular short- or long-term goal. Individual strategies clash and interact, thereby resulting in the step-by-step concretisation of a system of moves that transcends particular motivations and is manifested in the overall narrative. Unlike Proppian functions, moves can be arranged in a nonsequential or multilinear fashion.

Though firmly rooted in the structuralist tradition, Genette's influential *Narrative Discourse* (1980 [1972]) discusses the problem from yet another angle. Genette proposes four types of narrative units which are located neither on the abstract level of moves or functions, nor on the elementary level of kernels and satellites. Rather, each type is defined in terms of a temporal relation which we experience during the reading process: what is the duration of the *events narrated within a unit, and how long does it take to narrate them? In a *pause* it takes the narrative a long time to narrate very few events, if there are any; in a *scene* – ideally realised in a *dialogue – events and *narration are temporally coextensive; in a *summary* little narrative *time is used to represent a lot of event time (*see* SUMMARY AND SCENE). Finally, in an *ellipsis* – an omission of information which readers can normally compensate for by inferences – a lot of time might have elapsed in the narrated world, while none was spent on narrating any of it (*see* GAPPING). This temporal-relational definition complements Genette's functional explanation of two types of narrative unit particular to 'anachronous' narratives where the order of the events' presentation no longer coincides with that of their original succession: *analepsis* (flashback) and *prolepsis* (flashforward).

The question of how to reconcile an abstract, formal perspective on narrative units with a *hermeneutic one is as old as poetics itself. Aristotle's *Poetics* introduced the notion of the *epeisodion* as the basic mimetic construct which the *epic poet had to invent and verbalise in order to turn an abstract story or *mythos* into a concrete narration (*see* MIMESIS; PLOT). An *epeisodion* was understood not just as an insular narrative, but also as a partial manifestation of the overall *meaning* of the text. The somewhat vague contemporary notion of the *episode* could perhaps be reconceptualised accordingly, namely, as the paradigmatic narrative unit which represents a semantically coherent, yet at the same time globally functional, minimal narrative. This definition might also meet the requirements for an integrated theory of narrative units as stipulated by Culler (1975), providing an account of (1) our intuitive competence at segmenting narratives into units, (2) our culturally encoded ability to recognise typical actional sequences or *scripts within these units, and (3) the broader *semiotic and logical infrastructure in which narrative units are grounded.

SEE ALSO: events and event-types; formalism; narrative semantics; narrative structure; story-discourse distinction; story grammars

References and further reading

Aristotle (1984) *Poetics*, in Jonathan Barnes (ed.) *The Complete Works of Aristotle: The Revised Oxford Translation*, vol. 2, Princeton: Princeton University Press.

Barthes, Roland (1977 [1966]) 'Introduction to the Structural Analysis of Narrative', in *Image Music Text*, trans. Stephen Heath, New York: Hill and Wang.

Chatman, Seymour (1978) *Story and Discourse: Narrative Structure in Fiction and Film*, Ithaca: Cornell University Press.

Culler, Jonathan (1975) 'Defining Narrative Units', in Roger Fowler (ed.) *Style and Structure in Literature: Essays in the New Stylistics*, Oxford: Basil Blackwell.

Genette, Gérard (1980 [1972]) *Narrative Discourse: An Essay in Method*, trans. Jane E. Lewin, Ithaca: Cornell University Press.

—— (1988 [1983]) *Narrative Discourse Revisited*, trans. Jane E. Lewin, Ithaca: Cornell University Press.

Pavel, Thomas (1985) *The Poetics of Plot: The Case of English Renaissance Drama*, Minneapolis: University of Minnesota Press.

Propp, Vladimir (1968 [1928]) *Morphology of the Folktale*, trans. Laurence Scott, revised by Louis A. Wagner, Austin: University of Texas Press.

JAN CHRISTOPH MEISTER

NARRATIVE UNIVERSALS

In contemporary usage, based on current linguistics and cognitive science, narrative universals are features of story or discourse that recur across a greater number of genetically and areally unrelated traditions than predicted by chance (*see* STORY-DISCOURSE DISTINCTION). Two traditions are genetically unrelated if they have different origins. They are areally unrelated if they have not influenced one another in relevant respects. A feature that is found in all traditions is called an 'absolute' universal. A non-absolute universal is called 'statistical'. Statistical universals that fall into correlational patterns are called 'typological'. Note that absolute universals need not be found in every narrative, only in every narrative tradition.

Because universals are often misunderstood, it is important to note what universality does *not* entail. First, universality is not a normative concept. No work and no tradition is 'more universal' than another. Second, the existence of narrative universals does not mean that narratives are directly comprehensible cross-culturally. Works from two distinct traditions may share a vast number of universal features and still be incomprehensible to readers from the other tradition. Third, a universal feature need not arise spontaneously.

It may have to be discovered in practice by each tradition separately. Finally, a universal feature does not entail some direct biological endowment (*see* BIOLOGICAL FOUNDATIONS OF NARRATIVE). A universal may be the direct product of some genetic trait. But it may result equally from common features of the environment, from universal aspects of child rearing and development (i.e., things that happen whenever adults try to raise a child), from universal aspects of group interaction, etc.

Prior to the development of modern linguistics, anthropologically and psychologically oriented critics often sought to isolate universal principles of literature or, more often, *myth. Perhaps the most influential researchers in this early period were Jungians. Jung maintained that there is not only a personal unconscious, but also a 'collective unconscious'. The latter is shared by everyone and comprises archetypes or universal symbols (*see* ARCHETYPAL PATTERNS), such as the wise old man representing the hidden meaning of life (Jung 1959: 35). These archetypes surface, with some variations, in myth, literature, and elsewhere.

Cognitive approaches to universals contrast strikingly with Jungian approaches. First, cognitivists do not accept a collective unconscious. They do, however, accept a complex mental organisation that is innate in all humans and that partially accounts for narrative universals. This innate mental organisation is primarily a matter of structures (e.g., *memory systems) and processes (e.g., emotional response sequences; *see* EMOTION AND NARRATIVE). With only limited exceptions, mental contents (the entities organised by structures and affected by processes) are not understood as innate in cognitive science. In consequence, if the wise old man is a literary universal, it is almost certainly not an innate idea. In addition, cognitive approaches most often lead to the isolation of different universals and/or different configurations of universals from those claimed by Jungians.

Specifically, in a cognitive framework, there are narrative universals of both discourse and story. Discourse universals include logical universals (i.e., features that must be universal for logical reasons). For example, in all traditions, temporal order in the discourse is either chronological or anachronic (*see* TEMPORAL ORDERING). Discourse universals also appear to include such empirical universals as the far greater frequency of chronological ordering (as opposed to the equal frequency of chronological and anachronic ordering that would result from random distribution). This is presumably explicable by reference to processing ease, given standard cognitive organisation and the need to infer causal relations (*see* CAUSALITY).

At the story level, there are universals of scene (*see* SUMMARY AND SCENE), *character and *event. Universals of scene would include, for example, the association of lovers with birds. This may be explained by reference to the universal association of positive emotions with the bodily direction up (itself explained by such things as the association of sickness and death with bodily collapse), along with more complex cognitive processes bearing on relevance.

As to character, *heroes who strive for goals, helpers who aid heroes, and antagonists who impede heroes are all universal (*see* ACTANT; CONFLICT). There are more particular types that recur cross-culturally as well, such as the figure who cleverly manipulates other characters to reach a desired outcome. The universality of this character presumably derives from its basis in the *author's own manipulation of characters, along with cognitive principles governing identification.

Event universals are of two sorts. One is the *motif, an event or series of events that recurs across story structures. For example, the quest is a narrative motif that is found cross-culturally in different *genres, with different goals, etc. Second, there are encompassing story structures that are universal (*see* NARRATIVE STRUCTURE; PLOT TYPES). Hogan (2003) has argued that there are three such structures – romantic, heroic, and sacrificial (*see* ROMANCE). The romantic structure is a complex sequence focusing on the separation and union of lovers. The heroic structure treats the usurpation and restoration of authority within in-groups and the defence of in-groups against threats from out-groups. Finally, sacrificial stories treat communal devastation and the restoration of communal well-being through sacrifice. Hogan bases his argument on the study of a wide range of written and oral traditions.

A central part of Hogan's argument is that these structures are not necessary and sufficient conditions for stories. People can and do tell stories about any number of topics. But not all stories are 'standard cases'. More technically, not all stories are *prototypical*. In Hogan's view, the body of stories that are preserved and re-told or re-read tend to coalesce in these patterns. Put differently, authors who are composing a story and readers who are reading a story tend to begin with one of these

standard cases or prototypes tacitly in mind, then deviate from that prototype as necessary.

Hogan explains these story universals by reference to a cognitive account of emotion concepts and human emotions, considering both the aims of characters and the responses of readers (*see* READER-RESPONSE THEORY).

One noteworthy aspect of a cognitive approach to narrative universals is that it does not claim to reach final and putatively definitive conclusions. Rather, cognitive theorists stress that the study of universals is part of an ongoing research program and involves continual revision. (See the website for research in literary universals sponsored by the University of Palermo, http://litup.unipa.it.)

SEE ALSO: cognitive narratology; ethnographic approaches to narrative; psychological approaches to narrative

References and further reading

Bordwell, David (1996) 'Convention, Construction, and Cinematic Vision', in David Bordwell and Noël Carroll (eds) *Post-Theory: Reconstructing Film Studies*, Madison: University of Wisconsin Press.

Hogan, Patrick Colm (2003) *The Mind and Its Stories: Narrative Universals and Human Emotion*, Cambridge: Cambridge University Press.

Jung, C. G. (1959) *The Archetypes and the Collective Unconscious*, trans. R. F. C. Hull, New York: Bollingen.

PATRICK COLM HOGAN

NARRATIVE VERSIONS

Of central importance in *music, *film, advertising (*see* ADVERTISEMENTS), literature, philology, *folklore, anthropology, and biology, the term 'version' and its cognates, 'variant' and 'variation', overlap with *'adaptation', 'account', 'rendition', 'interpretation', and 'translation'. Broadly speaking, a narrative version takes up and alters a prior story, *novel, *epic poem, or tale. The alteration involves a renarrativisation (*see* NARRATIVISATION), which may be reflected in titles, *characters, *conflicts, *motifs, etc. (*see* PARATEXT).

In Genette's (1997 [1982]) study of 'literature in the second degree', narrative versions are construed as a species of 'transtextuality'. His taxonomy includes three classes of transtextuality: intertexts (*see* INTERTEXTUALITY), metatexts, and hypertexts. Present in a text B, a text A gives rise to an intertext; among intertexts, narrative plagiarism, acknowledged or not, is a 'version' type (Kathy Acker's *Great Expectations*, whose first chapter is titled 'Plagiarism', is an example). Two texts are metatextual versions when they 'evoke' or comment on each other without direct *reference: Nabokov's *Speak, Memory* offers a novelistic *commentary on Proust's *Recherche*. As for 'hypertexts', they are 'derived' from previous texts ('hypotexts') more substantially than most narrative commentaries yet at the same time entail thorough adulteration. Still, the hypotext is 'manifestly' present, 'legible' in the hypertextual version, as in Donald Barthelme's *Snow White*.

The last example uncovers the ties between narrative versions, retelling, and rewriting – postmodern rewriting in this case (Moraru 2001; *see* POSTMODERN REWRITES). Both narrative rewriting and version-making presuppose retelling. Indeed, the version concept suggests that a text B draws from, or somehow refers back to, a text A – to some kind of original, 'invariant' story, 'matrix', or 'arche-narrative'. Consequently, many types of postmodern and other rewriting/retelling must be considered instances of 'versions' (*see* POSTMODERN NARRATIVE). But not all versions result from the often ideologically motivated radical alterations at play in rewriting, and many rewrites present us with more than just variations on a narrative text or theme (*see* IDEOLOGY AND NARRATIVE).

'Rewriting' stresses the 'how', the *means*, the textual-cultural *mechanisms* and narrative transformations yielding a 'variant'. By contrast, 'version' emphasises the 'what', i.e., the end, the *outcome*, as well as its derived status and dependence on another narrative, which it both repeats and modifies. This narrative may be a specific text such as Kafka's *The Metamorphosis* (text A), of which Philip Roth's *The Breast* (text B) is a 'version'. Or, text A may be an unidentified text, as in oral literatures, where authorship is usually collective and anonymous (*see* ORAL CULTURES AND NARRATIVE). Thus the hundreds of *Cinderella* versions do not stem from a particular, historically identifiable 'Ur-*Cinderella*'. Yet in dealing with either case, Barbara Herrnstein Smith contends, *structuralist narratology posits an 'unsullied', 'versionless version' of a given narrative (1980: 216). She takes issue with this assumption by showing that all narrative 'prototypes' are always already versions, because even a *plot is someone's version-creating construction. Versions obtain, Herrnstein Smith further claims, not by imitating

a Platonic (arche)type but as 'transactions' in varying storytelling contexts. These transactions respond to diverse interactional and cultural pressures, and reflect the multiple interests of *authors and *audiences.

References and further reading
Chatman, Seymour (1981) 'Reply to Barbara Herrnstein Smith', *Critical Inquiry*, 7, 802–09.
Genette, Gérard (1997 [1982]) *Palimpsests: Literature in the Second Degree*, trans. Channa Newman and Claude Doubinsky, Lincoln: University of Nebraska Press.
Herrnstein Smith, Barbara (1980) 'Narrative Versions, Narrative Theories', *Critical Inquiry*, 7, 213–36.
Kroeber, Karl (1992) *Retelling/Rereading: The Fate of Storytelling in Modern Times*, New Brunswick: Rutgers University Press.
Moraru, Christian (2001) *Rewriting: Postmodern Narrative and Cultural Critique in the Age of Cloning*, Albany: State University of New York Press.

CHRISTIAN MORARU

NARRATIVISATION

Both Hayden White (1987: 1–25) and Monika Fludernik (1996: 31–35) argue that the process of narrativisation consists of giving narrative form to a discourse for the purpose of facilitating a better understanding of the represented phenomena. White uses 'narrativisation' in the sense of a transformation of historical material into the shape of a story or *plot (*see* HISTORIOGRAPHY; METAHISTORY). In the act of presenting historical reality, he argues, historiographers impose culturally pre-established stories with 'well-marked beginning, middle and end phases' (1987: 2) on their material, and in so doing, create a coherence which is absent in the raw historical data. He suggests that the 'value attached to narrativity in the representation of real events arises out of a desire to have real events display the coherence, integrity, fullness, and closure of an image of life that is and can only be imaginary' (1987: 24). Additionally, White argues that in narrativising historical material, historians follow an impulse to moralise. For him, the process of narrativisation entails moralising endings, and hence, ultimately serves the purpose of moralising judgements.

While White defines narrativisation in terms of the *author's storification or *emplotment, Fludernik uses the term to describe a reading strategy that naturalises texts (Culler 1975) by recourse to narrative schemata (*see* NATURALISATION; SCRIPTS AND SCHEMATA). Fludernik argues that in the process of narrativisation readers engage in reading texts as *narratives, i.e. as manifesting human *experientiality. Recipients then actively construct texts in terms of their alignment with experiential ('real-life') cognitive parameters. When readers are concerned with ordinary realistic texts (*see* REALIST NOVEL), the process of narrativisation is quite automatic; but when readers are confronted with difficult or even potentially unreadable texts, they consciously look for ways to recuperate them as narratives. According to Fludernik, the inconsistencies of initially odd-seeming texts cease to be worrisome when they are read as a series of *events or when they are explained as the skewed vision of a reflecting or 'registering' mind (*see* FOCALIZATION; NARRATIVE SITUATIONS; NARRATOR).

Furthermore, while White argues that the process of narrativisation in terms of plot construction affects historiographic discourse as much as it does literary narrative, Fludernik attempts to differentiate between historiography and narrative *fiction on the basis of experientiality. She suggests that prototypical historiographical accounts, which basically summarise action or event sequences and therefore lack important features of experientiality (like motivation, *emotion, and perception), approach a zero degree of narrativity. However, it is only where report usurps all potentially experiential functions of narrative that *narrativity needs to be gauged at the zero mark.

References and further reading

Culler, Jonathan (1975) *Structuralist Poetics: Structuralism, Linguistics and the Study of Literature*, London: Routledge & Kegan Paul.

Fludernik, Monika (1996) *Towards a 'Natural' Narratology*, London: Routledge.

White, Hayden (1987 [1980]) 'The Value of Narrativity in the Representation of Reality', *The Content of the Form: Narrative Discourse and Historical Representation*, Baltimore: Johns Hopkins University Press.

JAN ALBER

NARRATIVITY

Narrativity designates the quality of being *narrative, the set of properties characterising narratives and distinguishing them from non-narratives (*see* TEXT-TYPE APPROACH TO NARRATIVE). It also designates the set of optional features that make narratives more prototypically narrative-like, more immediately identified, processed, and interpreted as narratives.

In the first acceptation, narrativity is sometimes called narrativehood and it is usually considered a matter of kind (texts are narratives or they are not) though it may be considered a matter of degree (texts can fulfil all, some, or none of the distinctive conditions necessary for narrativehood). In the second acceptation, narrativity is a matter of degree: as Prince (1982: 145) put it, some narratives are more narrative than others.

The optional features influencing narrativity may be quite numerous and varied. It has been argued, for example, that the degree of narrativity of a given narrative partly depends on the extent to which that narrative constitutes an autonomous whole representing discrete, particular, positive, and interrelated situations and *events, involving a *conflict, and meaningful in terms of a human project (*see* CHARACTER; EXPERIENTIALITY). Furthermore, narrativity is affected by the amount of *commentary pertaining to the situations and events represented, their representation, or the latter's context. Finally, narrativity is a function of the *disnarrated and of the richness and diversity of so-called virtual embedded narratives, story-like constructs produced in a character's mind (*see* THOUGHT AND CONSCIOUSNESS REPRESENTATION (LITERATURE)). Some of these optional features may be contradictory, some may be (partly) redundant, and some may be more important than others. Only extensive empirical study and cross-cultural testing will determine their validity, their compatibility, and their effects (Herman 2002; Prince 1982, 1999; Ryan 1991).

Rather than or along with degrees of narrativity (and narrativehood), one may discern different *modes of narrativity. For instance, Ryan (1992) distinguished between the simple narrativity of *anecdotes or *fairy tales (where the semantic dimension of the text primarily stems from a linear *plot revolving around a single problem); the complex narrativity of Dickens or Balzac (where *narrative structures appear on both the macrotextual and the microtextual level and where semantic integration obtains between the main plot lines and the subordinate ones; *see* PLOT); the figural narrativity of lyric, *historiographic, or philosophic texts (in this case, the sender of the text or its receiver constructs a narrative by reshaping universal claims, collective entities, and abstract contexts into particular characters and events; *see* NARRATIVISATION); and the instrumental narrativity of *sermons or debates (where narrative structures appearing on the microtextual level function merely as exemplifications or clarifications of a non-narrative macrotextual level).

SEE ALSO: tellability

References and further reading

Fludernik, Monika (1996) *Towards a 'Natural' Narratology*, London: Routledge.
Herman, David (2002) *Story Logic: Problems and Possibilities of Narrative*, Lincoln: University of Nebraska Press.
Prince, Gerald (1982) *Narratology: The Form and Functioning of Narrative*, Berlin: Mouton.
—— (1999) 'Revisiting Narrativity', in Walter Grünzweig and Andreas Solbach (eds) *Grenzüberschreitungen: Narratologie in Kontext. Transcending Boundaries: Narratology in Context*, Tübingen: G. Narr Verlag.
Ryan, Marie-Laure (1991) *Possible Worlds, Artificial Intelligence and Narrative Theory*, Bloomington: Indiana University Press.
—— (1992) 'The Modes of Narrativity and Their Visual Metaphors', *Style*, 26, 368–87.

GERALD PRINCE

NARRATOR

The narrator is the agent or, in less anthropomorphic terms, the agency or 'instance' that tells or transmits everything – the *existents, states, and *events – in a narrative to a *narratee. This simple definition, which posits a strong link between the concept of narrator and *narrative itself, hides some complexities and contested issues. We begin with a look at some of those issues, move toward a brief history of (mostly) fictional narrators, and then turn to survey current ideas about the narrator.

Complexities and contested issues

Some theorists conceive of a narrator as an agent who tells a verbal *narrative and they regard narrative as requiring such a narrator; consequently, they do not include *film and *drama within the domain of narrative. Others find the essence of narrative in any transmission of existents, states, and events, and, in that way, decouple narrative

from a speaking or writing narrator – and, thus, include drama and film within the domain of narrative. Furthermore, some theorists have proposed *'no-narrator' accounts of what everyone acknowledges as one kind of narrative – effaced *narration in the heterodiegetic mode such as Hemingway employs in short stories such as 'The Killers' and 'Hills Like White Elephants'. Banfield suggests that the narration in such stories cannot be located in a distinct speaker, while Walsh suggests that it is located in the *author who dispenses with any intervening narrator figure. Ryan provides an elegant solution to most of these debates, a solution that preserves the concept of narrator but allows for degrees of what she calls 'narratorhood'. Ryan breaks the concept of narrator down into three underlying functions: the creative (the narrator's shaping of the story through the management of technique; *see* NARRATIVE TECHNIQUES), the transmissive (the narrator's mode of communication, e.g., oral or written; in language or in other signs; in one *genre rather than another), and testimonial (the narrator's assertion of the *truth of the story in its reference world; *see* POSSIBLE-WORLDS THEORY; REFERENCE). Narrators with full narratorhood perform all three functions, and, thus, become identifiable agents shaping stories in speech or in writing to an *audience. Narrators with lesser degrees of narratorhood perform only one or two functions. The effaced heterodiegetic narrator, for example, has no creative function and a minimal transmissive function.

The narrator's centrality to narrative is reflected in the concept's important position in the standard communication model of narrative (*see* COMMUNICATION IN NARRATIVE; NARRATIVE TRANSMISSION), which posits that the transmission of narrative begins with a real author who creates an *implied author who constructs a narrator who addresses a narratee; the implied author, through this construction and address, communicates with an implied reader; and the real author, through all of that, communicates with a real reader (*see* READER CONSTRUCTS). Chatman (1978) diagrams the model in this way, with the box indicating which elements of the model are parts of the narrative text, and with the parentheses suggesting that the narrator and narratee may be absent – but only in non-verbal narrative:

Real Author → | Implied Author → (Narrator) → (Narratee) → Implied Reader | → Real Reader.

When we recall that the implied author and the implied reader do not have a direct textual presence, we can see even more clearly how central the narrator of *verbal* narrative is: the entity who is the immediate source of the narrative text.

A brief history of the narrator in verbal narrative

The history of narrative is peopled with an extraordinary variety of narrators, as even a brief and unavoidably inadequate survey will show. In the early days of storytelling, most authors employed unself-conscious, undramatised narrators, whose dominant function was the testimonial. In the Bible, for example, relatively few narrators even mention themselves; instead we get such straightforward and authoritative reporting as we find in Genesis: 'In the beginning God created...', and in Job 'There was a man in the land of Uz, whose name was Job; and that man was perfect and upright...' (*see* BIBLICAL NARRATIVE). Although Homer appears to be using a different technique when he begins the *Odyssey* with 'Tell me, Muse...' that 'me' never gets characterised except through his authoritative and therefore reliable reporting (*see* RELIABILITY).

Over the centuries, however, authors of narrative fiction began to embellish the creative function and thus gave their narrators more personality. By the time of Boccaccio and Chaucer, playful dramatisation of invented narrators was found attractive, and the interplay between story and narration (the discourse) became obvious, though sometimes confusing (*see* STORY-DISCOURSE DISTINCTION). In *The Decameron* a clearly labelled and dramatised narrator, Fiammetta, takes over the telling of the radically contrasting stories, with Boccaccio hiding behind the scene. In the *Canterbury Tales*, a deliberately dramatised figure called 'Chaucer' does the telling of 'The General Prologue', with many relatively subtle clues that he's not the real author but an invented *character like the other pilgrims.

Following such wonderful inventions as well as the extraordinary tricks Cervantes played with the dramatised narrator in the two volumes of *Don Quixote* (*see* QUIXOTIC NOVEL), experiments with dramatised narrators exploded, even as many authors continued to find uses for the undramatised, unself-conscious narrator. In *Tom Jones*, Henry Fielding shows the advantages of investing a dramatised narrator, or in Ryan's terms, a narrator performing all three functions, with full authority. In *Tristram Shandy*, by contrast, Laurence Sterne explored the possibilities of the narrator with a creative function and an unauthoritative testimonial function for the development of a *plot: Sterne's narrative gets its forward movement not from the developing sequence of events but rather from the way those events provide the occasion for Tristram's often unreliable narration (*see* NARRATIVE PROGRESSION).

Through the nineteenth and into the twentieth centuries, authors continued to develop new variations of both authoritative and unauthoritative narrators. In *Middlemarch*, George Eliot created a narrator in the tradition of Fielding but one who is less overtly playful. The game playing with unauthoritative narrators became ever more intricate as authors experimented with multiple forms of unreliability in the narrator's testimonial function. Emily Brontë's *Wuthering Heights* still produces intense debate about just how much we should trust its several narrators. Charlotte Brontë's semi-autobiographical *Villette*, echoing Dickens's *David Copperfield*, is entirely told by the heroine herself. But Lucy, while ostensibly deserving as much trust as David, in fact manipulates events and conceals her feelings throughout. And even David is portrayed by Dickens as someone to be viewed with sharp critical attention. In *As I Lay Dying* William Faulkner extends Brontë's technique of multiple narrators by telling the story of the Bundren family's efforts to bury Addie through sixteen frequently unreliable narrators.

In the late nineteenth- and early twentieth-centuries, a new kind of narrator emerged as a difference of degree became a difference in kind. Since the eighteenth-century narrators had been using internal *focalization to offer inside views of characters, and in the early nineteenth-century those views began to include what George Butte has called 'deep intersubjectivity', nested representations of internal consciousness, as, for example, when Jane Austen's narrator in *Persuasion* shows us that Anne Elliot perceives Frederick Wentworth's perceptions of her sister Elizabeth's perceptions of him. In the twentieth century, authors such as Henry James, James Joyce, and Virginia Woolf created narrators who rarely spoke in their own voice from their own *perspective but instead used internal focalization to filter a character's complex perceptions, including perceptions of other characters' perceptions.

Key concepts and categories

In order to be able to do justice to this extraordinary variety, narrative theorists have developed several helpful concepts and categories. First is Wayne C. Booth's distinction between reliable and unreliable narrators, that is, between narrators whose telling conforms with the telling the implied author would do and those whose telling deviates from that the implied author would do (see DISTANCE). As Phelan and Martin point out in their re-examination of Booth's distinction, narrators typically perform three main kinds of telling, and we can locate those kinds on three different axes of communication between author and reader: reporting (on the axis of facts, characters, and events); interpreting or reading (on the axis of perception/understanding), and evaluating or regarding (on the axis of ethics). Consequently, narrators can be unreliable as reporters, interpreters, and evaluators, and they can be unreliable either by being well off the mark or by not going far enough toward the mark. Thus Phelan and Martin identify six types of unreliability: misreporting, misreading, and misregarding; under-reporting, under-reading, and under-regarding.

Second, Gérard Genette's unpacking of the term *'point of view' into the concepts of vision (who sees or perceives) and *voice (who speaks) has several important consequences. The focus on voice itself opens up a new way of conceiving the traditional categorisation of narrators according to grammatical *person. Genette points out that any narrator can say 'I', and so the difference that is supposed to be designated by the contrast between 'first-person narrator' and 'third-person narrator' is really a distinction between narrators who do (or did) participate in the events and those who do (or did) not participate. Genette calls the first kind 'homodiegetic' narrators and the second kind 'heterodiegetic' (an alternative terminology for this distinction would be 'character narrator' and 'non-character narrator'). Homodiegetic narrators who are protagonists are autodiegetic.

Genette makes further distinctions according to the narrator's location in the diegetic levels of the narrative (see DIEGESIS; EMBEDDING; FRAMED NARRATIVES; STORYWORLD). In Conrad's *Lord Jim*, for example, the level on which the heterodiegetic narrator locates both Marlow and Jim is the first diegetic level; Marlow then becomes an 'intradiegetic' narrator because his narration is contained within that of the first, heterodiegetic narrator. The novel's epigraph from Novalis, 'It is certain my conviction gains infinitely, the moment another soul will believe in it' is an extradiegetic communication, attributable either to an extradiegetic narrator, to Conrad as implied author, or for those who reject that concept, to Conrad himself (see PARATEXT). Genette's work on voice stops short of solving the problem of so-called second-person narration, in which the protagonist and the narratee are the same figure, though his work does help to articulate the problem more clearly: this narration could be either homodiegetic or heterodiegetic, depending on whether the narrator is engaged in self-address as in Jay McInerney's *Bright Lights, Big City* or whether the narrator is engaged in addressing someone else as in Italo Calvino's *If on a Winter's Night a Traveler* (see ADDRESS). In addition, Genette's distinction allows us to describe more precisely the narrator's relation to characters in such modernist *novels as Woolf's *Mrs. Dalloway*: the narration is occasionally from the narrator's vision and in the narrator's voice; sometimes from the character's vision and in the narrator's voice; sometimes from the character's vision and in the character's voice, and often, through the technique of *free indirect discourse, in some blend of the narrator's and character's vision and voice (see DUAL-VOICE HYPOTHESIS; MODERNIST NARRATIVE; SPEECH REPRESENTATION).

Third, Mikhail Bakhtin's analysis of language in society and in the novel shows that a narrator's discourse may be what he calls double-voiced. Bakhtin argues that language can be divided into subclasses according to the domains in which it is frequently used – we can, for example, recognise the language of *law, the language of the academy, the language of politics, and so on – and that each of these sociolects or registers is shot through with ideological meanings (see IDEOLOGY AND NARRATIVE). The novel characteristically juxtaposes these languages in what Bakhtin calls a *heteroglossia or *polyphony. When that juxtaposition occurs within the single utterance of a narrator, we have double-voiced narration. For example, the famous first sentence of Jane Austen's *Pride and Prejudice*, 'It is a truth universally acknowledged that a single man in possession of a good fortune must be in want of a wife' juxtaposes the register of philosophical generalisation with that of those invested in the marriage market; moreover, the sentence's movement toward the sociolect associated with the marriage market is a movement toward anti-climax and in that way undercuts the ideology associated with that sociolect. In short, the narrator's single utterance includes two voices – one that believes this universal truth and one that repudiates it – and, by ironising the first voice, establishes a hierarchical relation between them (*see* IRONY; QUOTATION THEORY). Bakhtin also notes that sometimes the narrator's languages exceed the control of their authors – often with a positive effect on the novel's polyphony.

Fourth, Elizabeth Preston distinguishes among narrators' authorial disposition, self-consciousness, and aesthetic control as a way of mapping narrators along a spectrum from naive to sophisticated. Naive narrators such as Faulkner's Benjy in *The Sound and the Fury* would have none of these qualities. Mark Twain's *Huckleberry Finn* shows an authorial disposition, when he makes reference to his act of storytelling at the beginning and end of the novel, but Huck is neither self-conscious nor in aesthetic control. Self-consciousness refers to a narrator's conscious efforts to craft the narrative for a particular effect, and aesthetic control refers to a narrator's success in achieving that effect. In *Lolita* Vladimir Nabokov's Humbert Humbert is a highly self-conscious narrator, but he is only intermittently successful in achieving aesthetic control of his narrative. Successful autobiographers who narrate from the vision and in the voice of their mature selves provide the best examples of Preston's sophisticated narrators (*see* AUTOBIOGRAPHY).

Other recent developments

In recent years, critics and theorists have explored the links between kinds of narrators and ideology and kinds of narrators and ethics (*see* ETHICAL TURN). Booth explores the *metaphor of 'books as friends' as a way to account for the ethics of reading, and narrators play a significant role in constructing the terms of any friendship. Warhol examines narrator's addresses to narratees, distinguishes between engaging and distancing narration, and links her findings to the gender of authors and their ideological projects (*see* FEMINIST NARRATOLOGY; GENDER STUDIES). Lanser links Genette's and Bakhtin's concepts of voice, thus blurring the distinction between voice as form and voice as ideology, and then examines different ways women writers have given appropriate authority to their narrative voices. Case identifies 'feminine narration' in the Eighteenth- and Nineteenth-Century British novel, by which she means narration in which the male or female narrator neither seeks nor achieves what Preston would call 'aesthetic control'. Phelan offers a detailed analysis of character narration, emphasising the way it works by indirection since one text has two agents (narrator and implied author), (at least) two audiences (narratee and authorial audience), and two purposes (the narrator's, which may be witting or unwitting, and the implied author's). He distinguishes between the character narrator's disclosure functions, which govern the communication between the implied author and the authorial audience, and narrator functions, which govern the communication between the narrator and the narratee. In the standard case of character narration, disclosure functions and narrator functions work seamlessly together, but Phelan indicates that there are many situations when an author's purpose is not compatible with a narrator's; in these cases, disclosure functions ultimately trump narrator functions.

Other important work on narrators continues to develop. DelConte proposes that we move beyond taxonomies of narrators based on the concept of voice to a taxonomy based on the relations among voice, protagonist, and narratee. Culler argues that we should jettison the concept of an 'omniscient narrator' because, on closer examination, narrators do not have true omniscience; furthermore, if we abandon the concept we can develop a more nuanced account of the different functions traditionally associated with the omniscient narrator. Nielsen contends that behind every homodiegetic narrator is an 'impersonal voice' of the fiction and that sometimes the homodiegetic narrator gives way to this voice. This proposal helps account for such puzzling cases as the intermittent disappearances of Ishmael as narrator but not as character in Herman Melville's *Moby Dick*. DelConte's, Culler's, and Nielsen's proposals are not likely to garner universal approval, but they are likely to lead to further examinations of the nature of the narrator.

In sum, the narrator is one of the most important elements of narrative, and narrative theory has had considerable success in accounting for the nature, variety, and functions of narrators. At the same time, because narrators and narratives are themselves so pervasive and so various and because authors continue to expand that variety, theories about the narrator will inevitably continue to change and develop.

SEE ALSO: film narrative; narrative situations; stream of consciousness and interior monologue

References and further reading

Bakhtin, Mikhail (1981) 'Discourse in the Novel', in *The Dialogic Imagination*, trans. Caryl Emerson, ed. Michael Holquist, Austin: University of Texas Press.

Banfield, Ann (1982) *Unspeakable Sentences: Narration and Representation in the Language of Fiction*, London: Routledge and Kegan Paul.

Booth, Wayne C. (1961) *The Rhetoric of Fiction*, Chicago: University of Chicago Press.

—— (1988) *The Company We Keep: An Ethics of Fiction*, Berkeley: University of California Press.

Butte, George (2004) *I Know That You Know That I Know*, Columbus: Ohio State University Press.

Case, Alison A. (1999) *Plotting Women: Gender and Representation in the Eighteenth- and Nineteenth-Century British Novel*, Charlottesville: University of Virginia Press.

Chatman, Seymour (1978) *Story and Discourse: Narrative Structure in Fiction and Film*, Ithaca: Cornell University Press.

Cohn, Dorrit (1978) *Transparent Minds: Narrative Modes for Representing Consciousness in Fiction*, Princeton: Princeton University Press.

Culler, Jonathan (2004) 'Omniscience', *Narrative*, 12, 22–34.

DelConte, Matthew (2003) 'Why You Can't Speak: Second Person Narration, Voice, and a New Model for Understanding Narrative', *Style*, 37.3, 204–19.

Lanser, Susan S. (1992) *Fictions of Authority: Women Writers and Narrative Voice*, Ithaca: Cornell University Press.

Nielsen, Henrik Skov (2004) 'The Impersonal Voice in First-Person Narrative Fiction', *Narrative*, 12, 133–50.

Phelan, James (1996) *Narrative as Rhetoric: Technique, Audience, Ethics, and Ideology*, Columbus: Ohio State University Press.

—— (2004) *Living to Tell about It: A Rhetoric and Ethics of Character Narration*, Ithaca: Cornell University Press.

Preston, Mary Elizabeth (1997) 'Homodiegetic Narration: Reliability, Selfconsciousness, Ideology, and Ethics'. Unpublished dissertation, Ohio State University.

Ryan, Marie-Laure (2001) 'The Narratorial Functions: Breaking down a Theoretical Primitive', *Narrative*, 9, 146–52.

Walsh, Richard (1997) 'Who Is the Narrator?', *Poetics Today*, 18, 495–514.

Warhol, Robyn (1989) *Gendered Interventions: Narrative Discourse in the Victorian Novel*, New Brunswick: Rutgers University Press.

JAMES PHELAN AND WAYNE C. BOOTH

NATIVE AMERICAN NARRATIVE

Native American narratives (henceforth NAN) are closely tied to the oral tradition (*see* ORAL CULTURES AND NARRATIVE) as it was and is practiced by indigenous peoples. Thus, *orality and the symbiotic relationship among the spoken word, the imagination, and lived experience are fundamental parts of NAN. NAN include an emphasis on communality, *humour, repetition, and circularity. These emphases are evidenced not only in theme, symbol, *character, *time, season, spiritual traditions, and *narrative structure, but also within indigenous peoples' lives (*see* THEMATIC APPROACHES TO NARRATIVE). Thus, NAN often focuses on the interconnected nature of people, the environment, and the land.

Traditional types of NAN include: creation, migration and trickster stories, tribal histories, ceremonial and non-ceremonial oratory, *dreams and visions, ritual *drama, chants, ceremonies, song, *dance, and prayer. One similarity among nearly all types of NAN within the oral tradition is their interactive nature: as a narrative is performed, there is an exchange between the speaker/ storyteller/narrator and the audience/community (*see* AUDIENCE; COMMUNICATION IN NARRATIVE; NARRATOR; PERFORMANCE). For example, audience members might participate in storytelling or oration by uttering a formulaic response or offering narrative detail at an appropriate time. Because such interactions are tribally specific, they vary by nation as do the times at which certain NAN may be recounted and the freedom with which a story, ceremony, or song might or might not be acceptably changed or adapted. Even in cases when the content or presentation style of a NAN remains constant, the message will often shift depending on the identities of the narrator and/or audience member(s), the context of the presentation, the season, etc. As such interaction suggests, then, the meaning of NAN is not fixed, but fluid.

NAN also includes a long-standing written tradition, which, in many cases, has characteristics similar to, or the same as, the oral tradition. Early forms of written NAN include pictographic records on rocks, birchbark scrolls, and hides. One of the best-known early alphabetic NAN is the Quiché Mayan book of creation, the *Pupol Vuh* – originally written in Mayan hieroglyphs and transcribed into the Roman alphabet in the sixteenth century. These earliest written narratives were often repetitive in structure, circular in theme, and, like NAN in the oral tradition, centred on Native communities.

NAN published in English are thought to originate with Mohegan missionary Samson Occum's *Sermon Preached at the Execution of Moses Paul, an Indian* (1772). Occum's sermon begins an ongoing Native literary tradition that, in late eighteenth- and nineteenth-century North America, took the form of *sermons, protest literature, tribal histories, *autobiographies, and *travel narratives. Much of this work employs the power of traditional oratory to speak out against the injustices perpetrated on indigenous nations by the dominant culture – see Occum in the eighteenth-century, William Apess (Pequot), George Copway (Anishinabe), and Sarah Winnemucca (Paiute) in the nineteenth-century, and Zitkala-Sa (Dakota), Charles Eastman (Dakota), E. Pauline Johnson (Mohawk), and Luther Standing Bear (Lakota) in the early twentieth century. Humour is often noticeably absent from early NAN, despite its importance to both past and present Native traditions. A marked exception is the work of Muscogee Creek satirist Alexander Posey, who employs biting comedy to protest political corruption and land allotment in his 'Fus Fixico Letters', first published in the 1890s (*see* SATIRIC NARRATIVE). Like Posey, most Native writers penned their own stories, but in some cases, collaborative, bi-cultural narratives were produced when white writers took part in drafting, transcribing and/or editing NAN. Arguably the most famous text in this 'as-told-to' *genre is Nicholas Black Elk's and John G. Neihardt's *Black Elk Speaks* (1932). As the tepid original reception of the Neihardt/Black Elk collaboration shows, however, NAN fell from popular favour in the 1920s and 30s.

Three of the few Native-authored *novels published in the first half of the twentieth century – Mourning Dove's *Cogewea, the Half-Blood* (1927), D'Arcy McNickle's *The Surrounded* (1930), and John Joseph Matthews' *Sundown* (1934) –illustrate another common characteristic of NAN in English: a focus on issues of *identity. In each of these texts, characters struggle to find their place as mixed-blood people caught between the often-conflicting pulls of white and tribal societies. The quest for a balanced and tribally grounded identity is also seen in Kiowa author N. Scott Momaday's Pulitzer Prize winning novel, *House Made of Dawn* (1968). Momaday's landmark text signalled the beginning of what many call the 'Native American Renaissance'. This literary renaissance, which followed an upsurge of political activism by indigenous peoples, marked a significant increase in the publication of texts by Native writers. Some of the most influential indigenous writers to arise from this 'renaissance' are Sherman Alexie (Spokane/Coeur d'Alene), Louise Erdrich (Anishinabe), Joy Harjo (Muscogee Creek), Simon Ortiz (Acoma), Leslie Marmon Silko (Laguna), Gerald Vizenor (Anishinabe), and James Welch (Blackfeet/Gros Ventre). While their texts are written, these contemporary Native writers, like their eighteenth- and nineteenth-century counterparts, employ aspects of the oral tradition in their work. In the twenty-first century, NAN illustrate the strength of both the oral tradition and indigenous cultures. Ultimately, contemporary NAN demonstrate that, despite governmental attempts to eradicate or assimilate the indigenous peoples of the Americas, Native people have survived and NAN continue to flourish.

SEE ALSO: African narrative; Australian Aboriginal narrative; Chinese narrative; ethnographic approaches to narrative; Japanese narrative; myth: thematic approaches; Sanskrit narrative

References and further reading

Cook-Lynn, Elizabeth (1996) *Why I Can't Read Wallace Stegner and Other Essays: A Tribal Voice*, Madison: University of Wisconsin Press.

Momaday, N. Scott (1970) 'The Man Made of Words', in Rupert Costo (ed.) *Indian Voices: The First Convocation of American Indian Scholars*, San Francisco: Indian Historian Press.

—— (1989 [1968]) *The House Made of Dawn*, New York: Harper.

Owens, Louis (1992) *Other Destinies: Understanding the American Indian Novel*, Norman: University of Oklahoma Press.

Ruoff, A. Lavonne Brown (1990) *American Indian Literatures: An Introduction, Bibliographic Review, and Selected Bibliography*, New York: MLA.

Vizenor, Gerald (1994) *Manifest Manners: Postindian Warriors of Survivance*, New England: Wesleyan University Press.

Womack, Craig S. (1999) *Red On Red: Native American Literary Separatism*, Minneapolis: University of Minnesota Press.

LISA TATONETTI

NATURAL NARRATOLOGY

Natural narratology as proposed by Fludernik (1996) is a cognitive project which integrates the frames and concepts of ordinary storytelling and experience into an encompassing theory of narrative. Rejecting the sequentiality and logical connectedness of *plot as the major constitutive factors of narrative, Fludernik defines *narrativity in terms of human *experientiality, that is in terms of cognitive or 'natural' parameters that are based on 'real-life' experience, on our embodiedness in the world (1996: 12–13). Furthermore, for her, narrativity is not a quality that inheres in a text but rather an attribute imposed on the text by the reader who interprets it as a narrative (thus 'narrativising' it). In Fludernik's model, the term experientiality refers to the dynamic tension between the newsworthiness of the story matter (*'tellability') and its significance for the current communicational situation ('narrative point') (Labov 1972: 366). Experientiality describes the typical quality of 'natural' narratives, i.e. stories told in spontaneous conversation (see CONVERSATIONAL STORYTELLING). In these stories, the protagonist is often faced with unusual situations and unexpected *events requiring appropriate and intelligent action. On this view, the emotional involvement with and evaluation of an experience provide cognitive anchor points for the constitution of narrativity. In the model, both plot and *narrators are optional features of narrative. However, no narrative can exist without an anthropomorphic experiencer at some narrative level. Hence, the postulated existence of a human being to whom something happens is a necessary condition of the constitution of narrativity.

Three sources have fed into Fludernik's model, particularly into her use of the controversial term 'natural': research on 'natural' narratives in the Labovian tradition of discourse analysis (see DISCOURSE ANALYSIS (LINGUISTICS)); the area of linguistics called 'natural' or cognitive linguistics (Dressler 1989); and Jonathan Culler's term *naturalisation. In Fludernik's system, 'natural' narrative is a prototype for the constitution of narrativity. More specifically, she argues that 'natural' narratives cognitively correlate with perceptual parameters of human experience; and these parameters are still in force even in more sophisticated written narratives. Second, from 'natural' linguistics, Fludernik has adopted the notion that cognitive categories are physically embodied, in the sense that humans' higher-level symbolic categories rely on schemata deriving from their embodied existence (see SCRIPTS AND SCHEMATA). Above all, natural narratology is interested in the question of how human embodiedness in the environment is reflected in categories and schemata that enter into the reading process. Third, Fludernik subsumes the experientiality of 'natural' narrative and the 'natural' parameters based on 'real-life' experience under the process of interpretation which she calls *narrativisation, that is, a reading strategy which synthesises textual inconsistencies by recourse to narrative schemata.

Within the framework of natural narratology, human experientiality – the *what* of narrative – is mediated by means of consciousness (see MEDIACY). Fludernik distinguishes between four levels of narrative transmission that are based on cognitive parameters. These levels – the *how* of narrative – refer to (I) pretextual 'real-life' schemata such as readers' real-world understanding of intentional action and goal-directedness (see ACTION THEORY; INTENTIONALITY); (II) the five macrotextual frames of narrative mediation: ACTION, TELLING, EXPERIENCING, VIEWING, and REFLECTING; (III) generic and historical schemata such as the 'satire' or *'dramatic monologue' frames (see GENRE THEORY IN NARRATIVE STUDIES; SATIRIC NARRATIVE); and (IV) the level of narrativisation that utilises elements from the first three levels in order to constitute narrativity.

Fundamental to the project of natural narratology is the idea that narratives of widely disparate forms repose on the same deep-structural core of narrativity, namely experientiality. Fludernik's approach has the advantage of avoiding the conventional restrictions of the term 'narrative' to prose and *epic verse. At the same time, she opens up the field of inquiry to oral storytelling as well as *drama, poetry, and *film (see NARRATIVE IN POETRY). Furthermore, Fludernik's redefinition of narrativity allows her to define a great number of plotless texts from the twentieth century – like Samuel Beckett's scenarios of a disembodied *voice – as narratives that fully satisfy the requirement of experientiality: such texts operate by means of a projection of consciousness without needing any action-oriented base structure (*see* ACTANT; THOUGHT AND CONSCIOUSNESS REPRESENTATION (LITERATURE)).

Critics of natural narratology have focused on the universality of Fludernik's four-level model, thus questioning whether the proposed cognitivist set-up is applicable beyond a restricted period of time (Fludernik 2003: 246–50). With regard to changes in perception introduced in the wake of the media revolution (*see* MEDIA AND NARRATIVE), Fludernik argues that new perception strategies are not likely to affect level-I related cognitive parameters. Rather, they may lead to the development of new frames on levels II and III, where they can be added to a growing inventory of generic schemata. With regard to the claim that her categories do not fit experimental texts which rely heavily upon serialisation and fragmentation (*see* SERIAL FORM) (Gibson 1997; Alber 2002), Fludernik argues that such strategies refer to the surface structure of the text rather than its deep-structural core of experientiality. Additionally, she points out that her model attempts to span a long diachronic stretch of narrative. Hence, she is more interested in finding common denominators and deep-structural continuities across a wide range of historical periods than in highlighting differences in the surface structure. Nevertheless, with regard to experimental texts where language is disembodied from speaker, context, and *reference, Fludernik's concept of narrativisation by means of human experience recedes into the background. Other critics have pointed out that Fludernik provides too little illustration of the interplay between 'natural' categories and the development of new types of *fiction. However, it is reasonable to assume that once an originally non-natural storytelling situation has become widely disseminated in fictional texts, it acquires a second-level 'naturalness' by virtue of habit, thus creating a cognitive frame on level III that readers may use. Thus, new narrative forms (like second-person narration) can become so naturalised that they are no longer perceived as 'impossible' storytelling scenarios (*see* NARRATION; PERSON).

SEE ALSO: cognitive narratology

References and further reading

Alber, Jan (2002) 'The "Moreness" or "Lessness" of "Natural" Narratology: Samuel Beckett's "Lessness" Reconsidered', *Style*, 36.1, 54–75.

Culler, Jonathan (1975) *Structuralist Poetics: Structuralism, Linguistics and the Study of Literature*, London: Routledge.

Dressler, Wolfgang (1989) *Semiotische Parameter einer textlinguistischen Natürlichkeitstheorie*, Vienna: Österreichische Akademie der Wissenschaften.

Fludernik, Monika (1996) *Towards a Natural Narratology*, London: Routledge.

——(2003) 'Natural Narratology and Cognitive Parameters', in David Herman (ed.) *Narrative Theory and the Cognitive Sciences*, Stanford, CA: CSLI Publications.

Gibson, Andrew (1997) Review of *Towards a natural narratology*, *Journal of Literary Semantics*, 26.3, 234–38.

Labov, William (1972) *Language in the Inner City: Studies in the Black English Vernacular*, Philadelphia: University of Pennsylvania Press.

JAN ALBER

NATURALISATION

Naturalisation, a concept introduced within poetics by Jonathan Culler (1975: 134–60), denotes the process of recuperating local textual inconsistencies by integrating them within a more general overarching sense-pattern. As Culler argues, in the urge to find texts uniformly meaningful, readers actively attempt to revise literal evidence in favour of larger interpretative moves aimed at 'motivating' discrepancies in convincing fashion. Culler here relies on the *Russian Formalist notion of motivation and Roland Barthes's concept of the *vraisemblable* (*see* FORMALISM; VERISIMILITUDE). As Tamar Yacobi (1981) illustrates, discrepancies in a narrative are frequently 'explained away' by recourse to a set of naturalisation principles. For instance, according to the 'genetic principle', the *author got it wrong, while, according to the 'perspectival principle', the narrator is either unreliable or the passage is focalized through a *character's erroneous perception or viewpoint (*see* FOCALIZATION; RELIABILITY). Fludernik, in *Towards a 'Natural' Narratology* (1996), has applied the concept of naturalisation to the reader's recuperation of recalcitrant texts *as narrative* (*see* NARRATIVISATION).

References and further reading

Culler, Jonathan (1975) *Structuralist Poetics: Structuralism, Linguistics and the Study of Literature*, London: Routledge.

Fludernik, Monika (1996) *Towards a 'Natural' Narratology*, London: Routledge.

Lanser, Susan Sniader (1981) *The Narrative Act: Point of View in Prose Fiction*, Princeton, NJ: Princeton University Press.

Yacobi, Tamar (1981) 'Fictional Reliability as a Communicative Problem', *Poetics Today*, 2.2, 113–26.

MONIKA FLUDERNIK

NEO-ARISTOTELIANISM

Associated with the *Chicago School of literary criticism, neo-Aristotelians such as R. S. Crane, Elder Olson, Richard McKeon, and Wayne Booth took issue with the formalist orientation of Anglo-American New Critics. Neo-Aristotelians distinguished between an *efficient* cause (= the *author), a *final* cause (= effect on readers), a *material* cause (= the language), and a *formal* cause (= the mimetic content; *see* MIMESIS). Accusing the New Critics of focusing solely on the material cause of verbal art, neo-Aristotelians sought to factor in the other causes as well, thereby laying the groundwork for recent *rhetorical approaches to narrative. *See* FORMALISM.

NO-NARRATOR THEORY

The 'no-narrator theory' holds that certain sentences of fiction do not occur in the spoken language and cannot be said to be enunciated by a *narrator, if that term is understood to denote a first *person, either covert or overt. The sentence of *free indirect discourse (FID) with a third-person *point of view is one case. Banfield argues that it cannot contain a covert narrator because if a first-person is added, a third-person point of view becomes impossible. (Cf. 'How tired she was! she realised' but not 'How tired she was whenever she helped me! she realised.') Hence FID cannot be a character's and an 'omniscient' narrator's 'dual-voices' without the notion 'narrator', originally introduced for written narratives with a *narrating *I* who is not the *author but a persona (e.g., Swift's *Gulliver*), disappearing linguistically in the character's *perspective (*see* DUAL-VOICE HYPOTHESIS).

Another such 'unspeakable sentence' is the pure narrative sentence that in French would be in the preterite (*passé simple*), which Benveniste (1971 [1966]) analyses as the *tense of the *event independent of a narrator and on which he bases his concept of *histoire* (i.e. *narration), calling it the form in which no one speaks. Hamburger's (1973 [1957]) *fiktionales Erzählen* (fictional narration) similarly excludes the first-person, which is consigned to *Aussage* (statement), as an 'imitated statement' ('*fingierte Wirklichkeitsaussage*'). Benveniste's evidence is the putative non-cooccurrence of *I* and preterite in French, but given the well-formedness and frequency of sentences like 'je naquis' ['I was born'], Banfield (1982) allows first-person *narration*, distinguishing it from first-person *discourse* narratives, e.g., *skaz*, where *I* belongs to the speaker/addressee pair (*see* COMMUNICATION IN NARRATIVE; FUNCTION (JAKOBSON)). In *skaz*, as in spoken French, the preterite is excluded. A narrator is thus not necessarily a speaker. But sentences like 'ils partirent le lendemain', Benveniste and Banfield concur, are speakerless.

Spoken sentences may lack an explicit *I*, but they are not speakerless in the relevant sense, the speaker's presence guaranteeing the possibility of *I*. But in writing, the author's relation to text differs from the speaker's to discourse. The no-narrator theory does not eliminate the author but banishes him/her outside the text, whereas the theory that every text has a narrator, Banfield notes, ascribes authorial functions such as the text's style and ordering of events to narrators, thus making authors indistinguishable from narrators. It is more enlightening to maintain as distinct the two functions. Rather than 'speaking' in a text, the author creates a fictional world out of language (*see* STORYWORLD), whether or not the language is attributed to a narrator.

Benveniste and Hamburger treat linguistic subsystems as narratorless; Banfield characterises sentences as narratorless. A text may have occasional sentences in the first-person – so-called 'authorial intrusions' – without all sentences being ascribed to this narrator.

SEE ALSO: speech representation

References and further reading

Banfield, Ann (1982) *Unspeakable Sentences: Narration and Representation in the Language of Fiction*, London: Routledge & Kegan Paul.

—— (1998) 'The Name of the Subject: The "il"', *Yale French Studies*, 93, 133–74. (Special issue on 'The Place of Maurice Blanchot', ed. Tom Pepper.)

Benveniste, Emile (1966) *Problèmes de linguistique générale*, Paris: Gallimard.

—— (1971 [1966]) *Problems in General Linguistics*, trans. Mary Elizabeth Meek, Coral Gables, FL: University of Miami Press.

Hamburger, Käte (1973 [1957]) *The Logic of Literature*, trans. Marilyn Rose, Bloomington: Indiana University Press.

—— (1977 [1957]) *Die Logik der Dictung*, Stuttgart: Klett Cotta.

Kuroda, S.-Y. (1973) 'Where Epistemology, Style and Grammar meet Literary History: A Case Study from the Japanese', in Paul Kiparsky and Stephen Anderson (eds) *A Festschrift for Morris Halle*, New York: Holt, Rinehart & Wilson.

Miller, D. A. (2003) *Jane Austen, or the Secret of Style*, Princeton: Princeton University Press.

ANN BANFIELD

NON-FICTION NOVEL

Non-fiction novels are narratives depicting actual contemporary *events and using the styles and techniques of fictional discourse (*see* FICTION, THEORIES OF; NARRATIVE TECHNIQUES). A story the *author witnessed and/or investigated is presented in *dialogues and dramatic scenes (rather than in historical summaries), from the point of view of the people involved (rather than from an objective, distant point of view), and it provides an immersive context in which the *narration of actual events is as lively as the presentation of fictional worlds (Wolfe 1973) (*see* IMMERSION; POINT OF VIEW (LITERARY); SUMMARY AND SCENE). Unlike *historical novels, non-fiction novels focus on contemporary themes and dispense with fictive story elements. Since journalistic validity is part of the author-reader contract, *authors frequently legitimise their knowledge in *paratexts or *metanarrative commentary (*see* JOURNALISM).

Truman Capote claimed to have coined the term and to have created a new literary *genre with his 'true account' *In Cold Blood* (1965). Norman Mailer divided his *The Armies of the Night* (1968) into *History as Novel* and *The Novel as History* and he subtitled *The Executioner's Song* (1979) as *A True Life Novel*. Together with *New Journalism*, a term coined by Tom Wolfe for his and other journalists' use of the same method, the non-fiction novel became part of an important movement in North American literature of the 1960s and 1970s. Addressing subjects like celebrities, subcultures, political protest, and court cases of violent crimes, this literature of fact tends to eliminate the distinction between elite art forms and popular culture.

Some critics have disputed the novelty of the non-fiction novel by pointing out various predecessors, from Defoe's *Journal of the Plague Year* (1722) to pieces of journalism originating in the 1930s. Other critics have accused non-fiction fiction authors of distorting facts and turning journalism into mere entertainment, and openly subjective reporting has been attacked as a symptom of self-display and egotism. Others again have praised the psychological depth, *rhetorical power, and literary quality of the texts. Most commentators agree that non-fiction novels are part of a reaction to social changes and their mass-media representation during the 1960s as well as to a general dissatisfaction with traditional fictional *realism (*see* REALIST NOVEL). Some stress its *metafictional character, its reliance on *postmodern fabulation, and its eradication of the boundaries between fact and fiction (*see* PANFICTIONALITY), while others, in diametrically opposed fashion, consider factualism a means of confronting perplexing reality and articulating epistemological scepticism.

The aims attributed to the non-fiction novel range from that of replacing totalising interpretation by transcriptions of naked facts (Zavarzadeh 1976), to that of universalising particular events and aspiring to larger *truths (Hollowell 1977; Hellmann 1981). The non-fiction novel is either seen as a genre of its own, characterised by overlapping sets of internal (intratextual) and external (real-world) references (Zavarzadeh 1976), or as part of the larger field of documentary realism (Sauerberg 1991).

SEE ALSO: novel, the

References and further reading

Hellmann, John (1981) *Fables of Fact*, Urbana: University of Illinois Press.

Hollowell, John (1977) *Fact and Fiction: The New Journalism and the Nonfiction Novel*, Chapel Hill: University of North Carolina Press.

Sauerberg, Lars Ole (1991) *Fact into Fiction: Documentary Realism in the Contemporary Novel*, London: Macmillan.

Weber, Ronald (1980) *The Literature of Fact*, Athens: Ohio University Press.

Wolfe, Tom (1973) *The New Journalism*, New York: Harper and Row.

Zavarzadeh, Mas'ud (1976) *The Mythopoeic Reality: The Postwar American Nonfiction Novel*, Urbana: University of Illinois Press.

FRANK ZIPFEL

NOUVEAU ROMAN

The *nouveau roman* or New Novel, which is perhaps the most important French literary phenomenon of the 1950s and 1960s, comprises the fictional works published by such writers as Nathalie Sarraute, Alain Robbe-Grillet, Michel Butor, Robert Pinget, and Claude Simon. The designation was probably adopted in 1957, after it appeared as the cover-page title of an essay by Maurice Nadeau in *Critique*. As for the works, they constituted a new kind of *fiction that rejected the methods of the *realist novel and its descendants (*see* REALISM, THEORIES OF), dismissed existentialist questions or humanistic answers, and showed little concern for socio-political problems but much interest in their own procedures (*see* NARRATIVE TECHNIQUES; REFLEXIVITY).

The New Novelists did not produce collective manifestos or portray themselves as members of a school. They even protested being grouped together and there are, indeed, significant differences between Robbe-Grillet's seeming attention to the surface of things (*The Erasers*, *The Voyeur*, *Jealousy*), Sarraute's preoccupation with psychological depths (*Portrait of a Man Unknown*, *The Planetarium*, *The Golden Fruits*) (*see* THOUGHT AND CONSCIOUSNESS REPRESENTATION (LITERATURE)), Butor's mythological elaborations (*Passing Time*, *A Change of Heart*), the *humour and linguistic verve of Pinget (*Mahu, or the Material*, *Monsieur Levert*, *The Inquisitory*), and the baroque lyricism of Simon (*The Wind*, *The Flanders Road*, *The Battle of Pharsalus*). However, the New Novelists' rejection of essentialist psychology, linear chronology (*see* TEMPORAL ORDERING), mechanistic chains of cause and effect (*see* CAUSALITY), conventional novelistic props like *character and *plot; their stress on relativity or uncertainty (*see* INDETERMINACY); and, most generally, their readiness to experiment justify their grouping under one label. Sarraute, for instance, delineates the most fugacious psychological movements without situating them firmly in well-defined beings. Simon, in *The Flanders Road*, makes it difficult to distinguish objective *time from personal time and to extract a sustained storyline. In *The Erasers* and *Jealousy*, Robbe-Grillet transforms the nature and function of *description. Pinget's *Mahu* examines the elements of which novels are made. Butor's *Passing Time* analyses and exploits the relations between the duration of the telling and the duration of the events told (*see* STORY-DISCOURSE DISTINCTION); and *A Change of Heart* studies the dimensions of second-person *narration (*see* PERSON). By focusing on the adventures of writing rather than on the writing of adventures, as Jean Ricardou once argued, the New Novelists reinvented fiction.

In the mid-1960s, the New Novel began to lose its pre-eminence. Its very success had made it less provocative. But its contribution had already been substantial. The New Novelists enriched French literature with dozens of texts notable for their redefinition of the fictional domain, their illumination of the writer's activity, and their new visions of the world. They prodded their readers to relearn how to read. Above all, they helped to liberate their successors from limiting assumptions or norms and radically changed the possibilities of fictional practice.

SEE ALSO: anti-narrative; novel, the; postmodern narrative

References and Further Reading

Britton, Celia (1992) *The Nouveau Roman: Fiction, Theory and Politics*, New York: St. Martin's Press.

Heath, Stephen (1972) *The Nouveau Roman: A Study in the Practice of Writing*, London: Elek.

Nadeau, Maurice (1957) 'Nouvelles formules pour le roman', *Critique*, 13, 707–22.

Ricardou, Jean (1971) *Pour une théorie du nouveau roman*, Paris: Seuil.

GERALD PRINCE

NOVEL, THE

The aim of this entry is to provide a brief introduction to major theories of the novel, distinguish novel from *romance, and then describe and survey the major characteristics of the novel, mentioning briefly some of its major practitioners in each age of the *genre's existence: the Renaissance (sixteenth and seventeenth centuries), the eighteenth-century, the nineteenth-century (sub-divided into romanticism and realism/naturalism) (*see* REALISM; THEORIES OF), and the twentieth century (subdivided into modernism and post-modernism) (*see* MODERNIST NARRATIVE; POST-MODERN NARRATIVE). Finally, there will be some very brief thoughts on future generic developments. The novel will be treated primarily as a Western genre, with no attempt made to incorporate, for example, indigenous Japanese (Murasaki Shikibu's eleventh-century *Tale of Genji*), Chinese (the six-teenth- century *Journey to the West*), or Arabic works (the tradition of *The Thousand and One Nights*). These rich non-Western narrative tradi-tions fall outside the scope of this brief introduc-tion (*see* ANCIENT THEORIES OF NARRATIVE (NON-WESTERN); CHINESE NARRATIVE; JAPANESE NARRA-TIVE; SANSKRIT NARRATIVE).

Theory of the novel

There are three basic approaches to the theory and history of the novel: (1) the Anglo-American the-ory of the 'rise of the novel', (2) the Classical approach embracing the 'ancient novel', and (3) Bakhtin's (1981) theory of the 'emergence of the novel'. The Anglo-American paradigm gets its name from Ian Watt's important *The Rise of the Novel* (1957), which takes for granted that the novel appeared for the first time in history in eighteenth-century England in the work of Defoe, Richardson, Fielding, and others. The authority of Watt's assumption has rarely been challenged by scholars writing within the Anglo-American lit-erary tradition, and the phrase 'the rise of the novel' is generally a code for the unquestioned belief that before Defoe all fiction was, at best, merely some sort of primitive proto-novel, prose *epic, superficial and episodic satire, and/ or romance (or anti-romance) (*see* SATIRIC NARRATIVE).

The Classical position is a recent one that has grown out of the justified dissatisfaction with the imperialistic and chauvinistic Anglo-American model. The classicists' position is simple and clear: all long fictions are, and always have been, novels; the concept of romance is spurious, an invention of those modern scholars who want to deprive the ancient world of its rightful status as the time and place of the creation of the novel in the fullest sense of the word. It is, in their view, unjust to relegate Greek and Roman fictions to

mere precursor or romance status (*see* ANCIENT THEORIES OF NARRATIVE (WESTERN)). The most extensive and persuasive articulation of this position is found in the important book by Margaret Anne Doody, *The True Story of the Novel* (1996). In the work of most of the writers in this tradition, the romance-novel distinction is simply declared invalid, leaving open the option that what was written in the centuries before the modern era is as legitimately called a novel as is the most recent postmodern novel.

The third paradigm is best described by Mikhail Bakhtin in some of the essays (dating mostly from the 1930s but only available in recent decades) included in *The Dialogic Imagination* (1981) and other writings. For Bakhtin, the romance-novel distinction (which he discusses in terms of 'two stylistic lines' of the novel) is of crucial importance. Much classical and medieval literature, particu-larly (but not exclusively) certain kinds of prose fiction, contain elements of novelistic discourse, but the novel *per se* only emerges in the unique circumstances of the European Renaissance, after the invention and diffusion of the printing press, primarily with the work of Rabelais and Cervantes (*see* MEDIEVAL NARRATIVE). There is no specific form, technique, theme, or approach to *character that makes a text a novel (*see* NARRATIVE TECHNI-QUES); rather, the distinguishing characteristics of the novel are its *heteroglossia (multiple *voices) and its *dialogism (multiple consciousnesses) (*see* POLYPHONY). After the emergence of the novel, all other more monologic genres (particularly the epic, the lyric, and *drama) become 'novelised', and dialogism is a hallmark of modern literature in general. Because the novel is the genre that is defined by a dialogic worldview, it stands as the prototype of literature in general in the modern (i.e., post-medieval) world. It is the third option, Bakhtin's thesis of the emergence of the novel in the Renaissance, that seems most justified by an informed understanding of literary history and theory.

Romance

The prototypical romance (Bakhtin's 'first stylistic line') is Heliodorus' *Ethiopian History* (third cen-tury BCE), with its noble and beautiful lovers and their trials and tribulations. Other long Greek prose fictions basically follow this adventure-based *plot model (*see* PLOT TYPES). The Latin romance – Apuleius' *Golden Ass* (second century CE) is the single primary representative – is more realistic in some ways but still maintains the basic romance adventure structure. Medieval chivalric romance, such as Chrétien de Troyes' *Erec*, Wolfram von Eschenbach's *Parzival* (both twelfth century), and Thomas Malory's *Le Morte Darthur* (fifteenth century) are the first major inheritors of the classical romance tradition. In the Renaissance, this tradition continues in the chivalric romance (Garci Rodríguez de Montalvo's chivalric *Amadís de Gaula*, 1508), and in the pastoral romance (Jorge de Montemayor's pastoral *Diana*, 1559). Cervantes (his posthumous *The Trials of Persiles and Sigismunda*, 1617), Madame de La Fayette, Samuel Richardson, and Walter Scott bridge the gap between romance and the modern novel. The romance tradition remains popular today in women's sentimental romance (*see* ROMANCE NOVEL), men's adventure fictions, and fantasy romances.

The Renaissance novel

The novel that emerges in the Renaissance is best exemplified by François Rabelais' *Pantagruel* (1532) and *Gargantua* (1534), the Spanish *picaresque novel, and Miguel de Cervantes' *Don Quixote* (1605, 1615). Rabelais' extravagant, exuberant, and subversive novel is unique and had little direct influence on the novel as a genre. However, both the picaresque and, especially, Cervantes' novel became the prototypes of the novel in general (*see* QUIXOTIC NOVEL), with direct descendants in all comic, realistic, modern, and postmodern fiction. In general, sixteenth- and seventeenth-century (aristocratic, imperial, and Catholic) Spain was the site of greater experimentation with new forms of fiction than any other in the history of Europe. Dialogued hybrid novels/dramas, romanticised historical fictions, satiric texts, and philosophic fictions coexisted with immensely popular sentimental, chivalric, and pastoral romances (*see* HYBRID GENRES; HISTORICAL NOVEL; PHILOSOPHICAL NOVEL). The first international 'bestsellers' of the modern age of print were all Spanish: *Prison of Love*, *Celestina*, *Amadís*, *Diana*, *Lazarillo* and Cervantes' works: *Don Quixote*, *Exemplary Novels*, and *Persiles*.

Outside of Spain, the sixteenth century saw little except for Rabelais in the way of novelistic production, while the seventeenth century was slow to pick up on the Spanish innovations. The century's major contributions to the development of the novel include Honoré D'Urfé's long pastoral novel *L'Astrée* (1607–1627), the works of Paul Scarron (*Comical Romance*, 1651–1657) and La Fayette (*La Princesse de Clèves*, 1678) in France; Jakob Christoffel von Grimmelshausen's *Simplicissimus* (1669) in Germany; and Aphra Behn's *Oroonoko* (1688) in England. None approximates *Lazarillo* or *Don Quixote* in originality, modernity, or influence.

The eighteenth-century

The eighteenth-century, especially in England, is the site of the first great non-Spanish novelistic tradition. After Daniel Defoe's picaresque (*Moll Flanders*, 1719) and adventure (*Robinson Crusoe*, 1722) novels open the century in England, the comic novel of this period is radically at odds with the prevailing neoclassical aesthetic of restraint and propriety. The exuberant comic novels of Henry Fielding and Laurence Sterne defy the sense of classical decorum that reigns in the theatre and in lyric poetry. Jonathan Swift's *Gulliver's Travels* (1726) combines typically eighteenth-century satiric concerns and allegorical method (*see* ALLEGORY; SATIRIC NARRATIVE). Meanwhile, the romanticised novel continues to hold sway in Richardson's hugely popular novels of female seduction and rape, and also in Charlotte Lennox's *Female Quixote* (1752). In France, Denis Diderot's *Rameau's Nephew* (1762) and *Jacques the Fatalist and His Master* (1773) share much with the English comic tradition, Lesage's *Gil Blas* (1715–1735) continues the picaresque tradition, Voltaire writes the prototypical Enlightenment satire in his *Candide* (1759), while Jean-Jacques Rousseau's *Julie* (1761) and *Emile* (1762) promote a philosophical and social agenda. In Germany, the novel takes a unique trend in the *Bildungsroman (novel of development), best exemplified in Goethe's *Wilhelm Meister's Apprenticeship* (1795–1796).

The nineteenth-century: romanticism

The nineteenth-century is, by all accounts, the great century of the novel. For the first time, the novel becomes the most popular of literary genres and the writers most talked and written about are novelists. At the beginning of the century, however, the novel is largely out of step with literature in general, insofar as romanticism is not as congenial to long fiction as it is to lyric poetry and the drama. Probably the greatest of all romantic novels is Goethe's *The Sorrows of Young Werther*, published some twenty-six years before the turn of the century, in the earliest phase of German romanticism. And the best novels of the first decades of the century, during the heyday of romanticism, are Jane Austen's neoclassic anachronisms. Probably the most genuinely romantic historical novels of the period are those of Walter Scott, Alessandro Manzoni, and Victor Hugo. The grotesque aspect of romanticism is best expressed in Mary Shelley's *Frankenstein* (1818), often considered the founding work of *science fiction. But as the realistic paradigm begins to replace the romantic one, the great novelists of the century come to the fore. Honoré de Balzac inaugurates the technique of using recurring characters in his *Human Comedy* (1829–1847), a series of some ninety romanticised realistic fictions set in contemporary Paris that purports to describe in an objective and 'scientific' manner the functioning of the complex system of society (*see* SERIAL FORM). Stendhal's novels chronicle the conflict between romantic aspirations and the need to survive in post-Napoleonian bourgeois society. In England, the work of the Brontë sisters, Charlotte, Emily, and Anne, together with that of the early Dickens, helps bridge the gap between romanticism and realism.

The nineteenth-century: realism and naturalism

The hallmark of the *realist novel is its purported goal of capturing the details and tenor of life as it is in actual reality, downplaying both traditional rhetoric and the emotional excess and exaggeration of romanticism (*see* REALEME; REALITY EFFECT). The realist novelist tends to choose subjects, characters, and themes that are most distinguished by being undistinguished, typical, representative. The novel tends toward supposedly 'objective' narrative, sometimes even approximating a journalistic style (*see* JOURNALISM; NARRATION). Later in the century, under the influence of the theories of Emile Zola, there is a turn to naturalism, an extension of the realistic program into a more activist socio-political one, with tendentious novels often claiming a scientific basis, strongly under the influence of Darwin (inheritance, nature) and

Marx (social context, nurture) (*see* IDEOLOGY AND NARRATIVE; MARXIST APPROACHES TO NARRATIVE; SCIENCE AND NARRATIVE). The subject matter becomes more sordid and graphic in nature, as themes of alcoholism, exploitation, and suffering among the lower classes move into the focus of interest. The prototype of the realist novel is Gustave Flaubert's *Madame Bovary* (1857), the story of an ordinary young woman who attempts to live her life in terms of the romantic fictions she has read (shades of Don Quixote and his chivalric romances). Virtually every nation in Europe has outstanding representatives of the realist novel, and space forbids more than a brief list of some of the most prominent: in England, William Thackeray, Charles Dickens, George Eliot, and Thomas Hardy; in France, the above-mentioned Flaubert and Zola, as well as Guy de Maupassant; in Germany, Theodor Fontane; in Portugal, José Maria de Eça de Queirós; in Russia, Nicolai Gogol, Ivan Turgenev, Leo Tolstoi, and Feodor Dostoevskii; in Spain, Leopoldo Alas, a.k.a. 'Clarín', Emilia Pardo Bazán, and Benito Pérez Galdós. In North America, the realistic tradition influences Nathaniel Hawthorne, Herman Melville, and, later in the century, Henry James; in South America, Joaquim Maria Machado de Assis, whose work not only reflects the aesthetics of realism, but also anticipates aspects of postmodernism. The nineteenth-century also sees the emergence of woman novelists interested in issues of social justice, such as Harriet Beecher Stowe, Kate Chopin, and George Sand.

The twentieth century: modernism

In the transition from the nineteenth- to the twentieth-century, a variety of alternatives to the realist-naturalist model become popular. The term 'modernism' is often employed as a general descriptor for the first half of the twentieth century. The novels written during this time offered a much wider variety of styles, themes, and techniques than the previous era: aesthetic refinement, harsh neo-realism, *stream of consciousness technique, introspection, the unconscious, linguistic play, and more. The two monumental works that dominate the aesthetics of the period are Marcel Proust's enormous *Remembrance of Things Past* (1913–1927) and James Joyce's *Ulysses* (1922), both works of dense prose and stream of consciousness technique that continue to attract readers and scholarly commentary, and that have had profound influence on the subsequent development of the genre. Again, it is not possible to offer more than a brief list of some of the major novelists of the period: in England, Joseph Conrad, E. M. Forster, D. H. Lawrence, and Virginia Woolf; in France, André Gide, Jean-Paul Sartre, Albert Camus, the bilingual Samuel Beckett, and Marguerite Yourcenar; in the German-speaking world, Thomas Mann, Franz Kafka, and Robert Musil; in Greece, Nikos Kazantzakis; in Italy, Alberto Moravia; in Russia, Mikhail Bulgakov and Boris Pasternak; in Spain, Camilo José Cela; in the United States, Edith Wharton, Willa Cather, Ernest Hemingway, F. Scott Fitzgerald, William Faulkner, John Steinbeck, Zora Neale Hurston, Ralph Ellison, and Saul Bellow.

The twentieth century: postmodernism

The second half of the twentieth century saw the rise of what is called postmodernism, which in the novel is usually expressed by self-conscious narrative and *metafiction (see REFLEXIVITY). Fantasy, absurdity, pastiche, parody, *intertextuality, inconclusiveness, and ruptures in traditional *narrative structure are also characteristic of many works of the time. Although none of these elements is new (Cervantes, Sterne, Pérez Galdós, and many others had used them all), they are more prominent in fiction-writing as a whole now than ever before. Furthermore, some novelists – Ellison, Bellow – write in the second half of the century but are closer to modernism than postmodernism, while others – Unamuno, Gide (see below) – are already metafictional much earlier in the century. More than in any previous era of fiction, the works of the postmodern age are often tied explicitly to literary theory and criticism, at times being written to illustrate the tenets of *poststructuralist, deconstructionst, *feminist, and Marxist criticism, as well as *post-colonialism, *gender studies (*queer theory), and *cultural studies (see DECONSTRUCTIVE APPROACHES TO NARRATIVE); certainly many of these works are best described in these critical terms. For the first time, the Americas – both North America and Latin America – rival, if not surpass, Europe as the locus of the best and most characteristic fictional production.

Once more, a brief list of writers is evoked in order to illustrate some of the more influential fictions of the postmodern period: in Latin America – where the enormous influence of Jorge Luis Borges, Argentina, is felt everywhere, even though he wrote only short fictions – Alejo Carpentier (Cuba), Jorge Amado (Brazil), Carlos Fuentes (Mexico), Julio Cartázar (Argentina), Mario Vargas Llosa (Peru), Gabriel García Márquez (Colombia), Clarice Lispector (Brazil), and Isabel Allende (Chile); in Canada, Margaret Atwood; in the United States, the Russian-born Vladimir Nabokov, John Barth, Thomas Pynchon, Robert Coover, Kathy Acker, and Toni Morrison.

In Europe (and the post-colonial English-speaking world), the postmodern novel has also become prominent, with a trio of names at the top of the list: the Anglo-Indian Salman Rushdie and two Italians: Italo Calvino and Umberto Eco. Others, who partake of the various aspects of postmodernism to varying degrees and often in radically different ways, include: in the Czech Republic, Milan Kundera; in England, John Fowles; in France, Michel Butor, Alain Robbe-Grillet, and Marguerite Duras; in Germany, Günter Grass; in India, Anita Desai; in South Africa, Nadine Gordimer and J. M. Coetzee; in Spain, Juan Goytisolo and Carmen Martín Gaite.

Overall, in the twentieth century, the European paradigm for the novel becomes a worldwide phenomenon, as *African, Asian, Middle Eastern, and others writing in nations without a centuries-long tradition in the genre gain prominence. Examples include: in Africa, Ousmane Sembène (Senegal), Chinua Achebe (Nigeria), Bessie Head (South Africa), Ngugi wa Thiong'o (Kenya); in Asia, Natsume Sôseki (Japan), Ba Jin, and Zhang Xianliang (China), Mishima Yukio and Oe Kenzaburo (Japan); and in the Middle East and North Africa, Samuel Joseph Agnon (Israel), Naguib Mahfouz (Egypt), Tahar Ben Jelloun (Morocco), and Abdelrahman Munif (Jordan).

At least brief mention should be made, also, of the rise to prominence of *genre fiction throughout the twentieth century. Certain sub-genres of the novel have enjoyed popularity during every period of the novel's history. In the Renaissance, the sentimental, heroic, and pastoral romances and the picaresque novel were read by everyone, and the first *romans à clef were written. In the eighteenth-century, the *Bildungsroman, the libertine novel, the *epistolary novel, and *Gothic fiction all had their vogue; while in the nineteenth-century, the novel of manners, the historical novel, the regional novel, and sentimental tales of romance reached popular heights. In the twentieth century, all these varieties of genre fiction have retained a certain interest, while three sub-genres with roots deep in the nineteenth-century matured and flourished as never before: *detective fiction (with roots in the works of Edgar Allan Poe and Arthur Conan Doyle), science fiction (with Mary Shelley, Jules Verne, and H. G. Wells as primary antecessors), and *fantasy (where special mention must be made of J. R. R. Tolkien's trilogy, *The Lord of the Rings*, 1954–1956, which has achieved 'mainstream' critical recognition, as well as a cult following and led to a series of extraordinary *films), and *horror. In addition, the twentieth century has seen the rise and/or the flourishing of the western, the political *thriller, the *non-fiction novel, the *pornographic novel, the beatnik novel, punk fiction, the graphic novel, and others (*see* CYBERPUNK FICTION; COMICS AND GRAPHIC NOVEL).

The future of the novel

The novel from Cervantes to Dostoevskii to Morrison and Rushdie has always been a protean genre, able to assume any form, incorporate and embed any other genre, feature any type of character, be written in any conceivable style, deal with any and all subjects and themes. It is difficult to believe that in its print form the novel can be radically reconceived in ways that are genuinely new. As it has grown in popularity and explored endless possibilities, the novel has become synonymous with the concept of literature. The epic is dead (except in radically modified form, such as the *Star Wars* films); lyric poetry is increasingly a minority and elitist activity; and the theatre has been marginalised by film and *television. Ask any group of people to name their favourite writer, and more than ninety per cent will name a novelist. Literature today is the novel.

But in the twenty-first century the literary enterprise itself has become problematic. Pronouncements of the death of the novel became increasingly frequent and strident as the twentieth century progressed and varieties of *visual and electronic *media became more influential (*see* DIGITAL NARRATIVE). One of the most recent schools of thought is that the computer has rendered the novel obsolete. The place of the novel will be filled by *hypertext fictions (such as Michael Joyce's *Afternoon, a story*, 1987), an interactive genre in which the reader is as responsible as the *author for the creation of the work (*see* INTERACTIVE FICTION; READER-RESPONSE THEORY; WRITERLY TEXTS). Amidst all the hype for hypertext, many forget that the glories predicted for computers in other fields – replication of human vision and language, all-purpose robots, radical revamping of basic education – have yet to be realised. Maybe hypertext or some other digital variant will become dominant, but it would not be wise to bet against the traditional print format that has proven so flexible and adaptive throughout the last half millennium or to overlook the fact that narrative is part of our biological makeup (*see* BIOLOGICAL FOUNDATIONS OF NARRATIVE). As cognitive psychologist Richard Gerrig has convincingly argued, readers of narrative fiction feel transported to another *time and place and perform the actions themselves (*see* FICTION, THEORIES OF; IMMERSION; SPACE IN NARRATIVE). Designers of hypertext narratives, interactive fictions, and other computer-mediated forms thus have much to learn from the experience of immersion in a virtual world that arises when a reader interacts imaginatively with the text of a print novel (*see* VIRTUALITY).

SEE ALSO: encyclopedic novel; nouveau roman; philosophical novel; psychological novel; roman à thèse

References and further reading

Alter, Robert (1975) *Partial Magic: The Novel as a Self-Conscious Genre*, Berkeley: University of California Press.

Bakhtin, M. M. (1981) *The Dialogic Imagination: Four Essays*, ed. by Michael Holquist, trans. by Caryl Emerson and Michael Holquist, Austin: University of Texas Press.

Brink, André (1998) *The Novel: Language and Narrative from Cervantes to Calvino*, New York: New York University Press.

Couturier, Maurice (1991) *Textual Communication: A Print-Based Theory of the Novel*, London: Routledge.

Doody, Margaret Anne (1996) *The True Story of the Novel*, New Brunswick: Rutgers University Press.

Dunn, Peter N. (1993) *Spanish Picaresque Fiction: A New Literary History*, Ithaca: Cornell University Press.

Fludernik, Monika (1996) *Towards a 'Natural' Narratology*, London: Routledge.

Gerrig, Richard J. (1993) *Experiencing Narrative Worlds: On the Psychological Activities of Reading*, New Haven: Yale University Press.

Mancing, Howard (2003) *The Cervantes Encyclopedia*, 2 vols., Westport, CT: Greenwood Press.

McKeon, Michael (1987) *The Origins of the English Novel 1600–1740*, Baltimore: Johns Hopkins University Press.

Moretti, Franco (1987) *The Way of the World: The Bildungsroman in European Culture*. London: Verso.

Radway, Janice A. (1991) *Reading the Romance: Women, Patriarchy, and Popular Literature*, Chapel Hill: University of North Carolina Press.

Reed, Walter L. (1981) *An Exemplary History of the Novel: The Quixotic versus the Picaresque*, Chicago: University of Chicago Press.

Schellinger, Paul (ed.) (1998) *Encyclopedia of the Novel*, 2 vols., Chicago: Fitzroy Dearborn.

Watt, Ian (1957) *The Rise of the Novel: Studies in Defoe, Richardson and Fielding*, Berkeley: University of California Press.

HOWARD MANCING

NOVELLA

The term 'novella' refers to a prose work, generally of medium length, depicting an unprecedented, extraordinary, or ambiguous *event. It is derived from the Latin *novella*, a diminutive of the adjective *novas*, meaning new or current. By the twelfth century the Italian *novella* described a short prose account of an unusual, new event.

At odds with an orderly, everyday world, the novella's central event reveals unexpected, irrational elements intruding from outside by chance or fate. The small cast of *characters remains secondary to the event itself. A highly concentrated, symbolic, but realistic narrative, sometimes recounted orally by a character, provides a frame and an interpretive relation to the story. A sudden change in direction leads to a surprising, but logical conclusion which resolves the central *conflict.

Critics cite Boccaccio's *Decameron* (1353) as the origin of the novella. Cervantes' *Novelas ejemplares* (1613) and Marguerite de Navarre's *Heptameron* (1558) are other early predecessors. In the three centuries after the *Decameron* appeared, more than a hundred novella collections appeared in England and Romance Europe. The form took root in Germany after Johann Wolfgang von Goethe's *Unterhaltungen deutscher Ausgewanderten* was published in 1795. The German novella boomed in the nineteenth-century with works by Heinrich von Kleist, Ludwig Tieck, E. T. A. Hoffmann, Adalbert Stifter, Annette von Droste-Hülshoff, Gottfried Keller, Theodor Storm, and Gerhart Hauptmann. With its feel for the atypical and regional, the novella may have reflected Germany's geographical and political disunity better than the *novel, a *genre which dominated in other countries. The novella evolved and tapered off in twentieth-century Germany with works by Hugo von Hofmannsthal, Franz Kafka, Stefan Zweig, Hermann Hesse, Robert Musil, Thomas Mann, Günther Grass, and Martin Walser.

Germany also produced the novella's leading critics, beginning with Christoph Martin Wieland, followed by Friedrich and August Wilhelm Schlegel. Most often cited is Goethe's rhetorical question to Eckermann on 29 January 1827: 'What is a novella other than an unheard-of event that has actually taken place?' Ludwig Tieck emphasised the *Wendepunkt* or unexpected turning point. Paul Heyse's *Falkentheorie*, inspired by a falcon in the *Decameron*, identified a unifying symbol or distinctive silhouette in the novella. Following E. K. Bennett's *A History of the German Novella* (1934), attention to the genre peaked in the second half of the twentieth century with critical works by Walter Pabst (1953), Johannes Klein (1960), Benno von Wiese (1962), Karl Konrad Polheim (1965), Frank Ryder (1971), John Ellis (1974), Martin Swales (1977), Josef Kunz (1977), J. H. E. Paine (1979), Roger Paulin (1985), and Henry H. H. Remak (1996).

Novella *authors from other countries include: Great Britain (Conrad, Kipling, Conan Doyle), France (Merimée, Balzac, Gautier, Maupassant), the United States (Poe, James, Crane, Chopin, Wharton, plus many southern writers), and Russia (Gogol, Turgenev, Tolstoi, and Chekhov).

References and further reading

Paulin, Roger (1985) *The Brief Compass: The Nineteenth-Century German Novella*, Oxford: Clarendon Press.

Swales, Martin (1977) *The German Novella*, Princeton: Princeton University Press.

Weing, Siegfried (1994) *The German Novella: Two Centuries of Criticism*, Columbia, SC: Camden House.

MARGARET McCARTHY

NURSERY RHYME

Nursery rhyme is a collective term for an oral tradition of verse recited or sung to and by young children (*see* ORALITY). 'Mother Goose Rhymes' (the title of an influential collection published in 1781) comprise nonsense jingles, character rhymes, *performative verse accompanying games, counting-out formulas, riddles, rhyming alphabets, tongue twisters, nursery prayers, and lullabies, many of which date from the eighteenth- and nineteenth-centuries. Verified sources include broadside *ballads, folksongs, street cries, adult riddles, and political slander, which – because of the attractiveness of their rhymes, rhythm, and rudimentary *plot – were preserved in the nursery, frequently in a truncated or transmogrified form. Cognitive studies have highlighted the beneficial effect of nursery rhymes on children's linguistic development through their repetitive phoneme patterns and multisensory stimuli. Using Bettelheim's theory of the *fairy tale, psychoanalytical approaches seek to show how nursery rhymes offer children a way to live out forbidden *desires while containing them in a tight poetic form (*see* PSYCHOANALYSIS AND NARRATIVE).

SEE ALSO: children's stories (narratives written for children); music and narrative; narrative, games, and play; narrative in poetry; simple forms

References and further reading

Opie, Iona, and Peter Opie (eds) (1995 [1951]) *The Oxford Dictionary of Nursery Rhymes*, Oxford: Oxford University Press.

Rollin, Lucy (1992) *Cradle and All: A Cultural and Psychoanalytic Reading of Nursery Rhymes*, Jackson: University Press of Mississippi.

EVA MÜELLER-ZETTELMANN

O

OBITUARY

The obituary offers an appraisal of a life in the form of a brief *biography – published in the print *media, on the worldwide web, and on *television. It is important to note the appraisal factor, for it is this element which distinguishes an obituary from a standard news story about death. While the intent of the latter is to supply an account of a deceased person's life, often with information also on the circumstances of death, the obituary provides an assessment of its subject's character, achievements, and effect on society. This is frequently demonstrated through the use of *anecdote. It is possible to trace the emergence of the obituary in the press to *The Gentleman's Magazine* of eighteenth-century Britain and to the American colonial newspapers. Early nineteenth-century obituary style often employed ornate prose and eulogistic expression, in conjunction with a tendency to moralise about the stoicism of the subject. Hume (2000: 39) has noted that American obituaries of that era offered comfort on the nature of death and the promise of immortality for the virtuous. Later in the nineteenth-century, notably in the major British newspapers, graphic death-bed description became common.

Though such intrusive *journalism eventually grew unfashionable, realistic representation emerged in another form during the latter part of the twentieth century. Obituary practice shifted towards publication of a more candid review, on the premise that if people were not saints when alive, neither should they so be judged when dead (Whitman 1980: xiv). The aim is to capture life, with all its flaws, rather than death. According to Massingberd (1996: viii) that is best achieved through anonymous authorship. In Britain, *The Times* (founded 1785) and *The Daily Telegraph* (founded 1855) have unshakeably subscribed to that view by maintaining a policy of unsigned obituaries. In obituary composition at large, marked contrasts of style and practice are apparent. The American preference is typified by contemporaneous publication, adherence to conventional news reporting style, inclusion of date, place and cause of death, liberal use of direct *quotation, and a detailed list of surviving family. The British approach is often more languid, ignoring in many instances the time factor along with place and cause of death, adopting a reflective and occasionally ironic tone (*see* IRONY), supplying the barest essentials of surviving family, and entertaining the reader with wit, whimsy, and shafted observation. A growing interest in obituary scholarship has led to the establishment of the International Association of Obituarists, based in Dallas. It organises conferences and seminars, as well as workshops for writers new to the obituary craft.

SEE ALSO: life story

References and further reading

Fergusson, James (2000) 'Death and The Press', in Stephen Glover (ed.) *The Penguin Book of Journalism: Secrets of the Press*, London: Penguin.
Hume, Janice (2000) *Obituaries in American Culture*, Jackson, MS: University Press of Mississippi.
International Association of Obituarists: http://www.obitpage.com
Massingberd, Hugh (ed.) (1996) *The Daily Telegraph Book of Obituaries: A Celebration of Eccentric Lives*, Basingstoke: Pan.
Whitman, Alden (1980) *Come to Judgment*, New York: The Viking Press.

NIGEL STARCK

OPERA

If narrative is viewed as rhetoric – as the telling of a story by someone to someone for some purpose and on some occasion (to use James Phelan's definition) – then opera as staged, performed narrative can be seen as the embodied telling of a story by a phalanx of performers and producers for a live *audience on a public occasion in a social setting (see PERFORMANCE). Operatic narratives are 'told', therefore, through what Keir Elam calls their dramatic texts – the verbal/dramatic libretto and the musical score – and their performance texts – the production that at one and the same time interprets, visualises, and brings to aural and physical life those dramatic texts. In a sense, opera 'shows' even as it 'tells' (see SHOWING VS. TELLING).

Dramatised narrative may lack prose fiction's *descriptions of people and places, its explications, its narrative *point of view, and its easy ability to shift time and place, but it offers instead direct visual and aural presentation of people and places, enacted action and interaction as explanation, and a strikingly vivid sense of *time in the here and now. In short, it depicts as it narrates. To all this, however, opera adds *music. Like stories, music is central to human ordering, shaping, and meaning-making needs. As a narrative dimension of opera, music speaks directly to the audience, not to the *characters in the story. Only in what are called 'phenomenal songs' or instances of 'diegetic music' – self-consciously sung pieces like *ballads, serenades, toasts, lullabies – do characters share our ears and hear the music we in the audience enjoy (see DIEGESIS). As a dimension of operatic narrative, music can reinforce or contradict, support or undermine the message of the dramatic and verbal story we see and hear on stage – as Richard Wagner's famous use of the musical *leitmotif made evident. In *The Ring of the Nibelung*, when Sieglinde wonders where her father could be, the music tells the audience, but not her, that he is in Valhalla.

Music clearly adds another level of *narration and consequently complicates narratological models; therefore they have had to be adapted (not simply adopted) for use in operatic studies. Carolyn Abbate has been in the forefront of this new research. She does not use narrative as an analogy in the way that it has so often been deployed since the nineteenth-century; her interest is not in music as it proceeds through time toward *closure and, en route, generates expectations, tensions, and resolutions. For Abbate, music itself is not narrative, even if it can be described in narrative terms. Instead, she has theorised what she calls 'moments of diegesis' that function as narration in that they are disruptive and charged with a sense of distance and difference. The distance comes from the fact that the audience hears a message 'across' or against the sensual matter of the *voices we are listening to; the difference lies in the fact that these are uncanny moments of non-congruence between the words and the music in an opera, moments where narration is seen as lying.

Opera's artifice is manifest (and audible) in its sung nature, but the critical distancing that this would imply is subverted by the emotional engagement demanded by the music (see EMOTION AND NARRATIVE). The multiple musical/visual/dramatic/verbal dimensions of operatic narrative, expertly analysed by Jean-Jacques Nattiez, contribute to both the obvious complexity and the less obvious simplicity of opera's telling and showing. The narrative concision and compression demanded by the fact that it takes so much longer to sing than to say (or read) a line of text result in a libretto whose story is very focused but also, often, quite unsubtle. We are allowed a glimpse of the *desires and anxieties of a community and a culture (and not only of a creative team), as these stories work to construct as well as reflect both public and personal values. As is evident in the work of literary scholars who have turned their attention to operatic narrative, including Sander Gilman, Herbert Lindenberger, David Levin, Linda Hutcheon (in collaboration with Michael Hutcheon), and Marc Weiner, operatic narratives can be as resistant as they can be complacent. *Gender and *post-colonial studies have brought the ideological implications of operatic narrative into the forefront; significant contributions have been made along these lines by Susan McClary, Ralph Locke, and other musicologists (cf. Brett, Wood, and Thomas 1994).

SEE ALSO: drama and narrative; ideology and narrative; intermediality

References and further reading

Abbate, Carolyn (1991) *Unsung Voices: Opera and Musical Narrative in the Nineteenth-Century*, Princeton: Princeton University Press.

Brett, Philip, Elizabeth Wood, and Gary C. Thomas (eds) (1994) *Queering the Pitch: the New Gay and Lesbian Musicology*, London: Routledge.

Elam, Keir (1980) *The Semiotics of Theatre and Drama*, London: Routledge.

Gilman, Sander L. (1988) *Disease and Representation: Images of Illness from Madness to AIDS*, Ithaca: Cornell University Press.

Hutcheon, Linda, and Michael Hutcheon (1996) *Opera: Desire, Disease, Death*, Lincoln: University of Nebraska Press.

Levin, David (1998) *Richard Wagner, Fritz Lang, and the Nibelungen: The Dramaturgy of Disavowal*, Princeton: Princeton University Press.

Lindenberger, Herbert (1984) *Opera: The Extravagant Art*, Ithaca: Cornell University Press.

Locke, Ralph P. (2000) 'Exoticism and Orientalism in Music: Problems for the Worldly Critic', in Paul Bové (ed.) *Edward Said and the Work of the Critic: Speaking Truth to Power*, Durham, NC: Duke University Press.

McClary, Susan (1991) *Feminine Endings: Music, Gender, and Sexuality*, Minneapolis: University of Minnesota Press.

Nattiez, Jean-Jacques (1990) *Music and Discourse: Toward a Semiology of Music*, trans. Carolyn Abbate, Princeton: Princeton University Press.

Phelan, James (1996) *Narrative as Rhetoric: Technique, Audiences, Ethics, Ideology*, Columbus: Ohio State University Press.

Weiner, Marc (1995) *Wagner and the Anti-Semitic Imagination*, Lincoln: University of Nebraska Press.

LINDA AND MICHAEL HUTCHEON

ORAL CULTURES AND NARRATIVE

Narrative is fundamental to oral societies. Not only does it perform the usual functions of entertainment and instruction, it has also come to be seen as being foundational to the neotic processes – the means of acquiring, accumulating, storing, and retrieving knowledge – of these societies.

Milman Parry's discovery in the 1920s that the major characteristic features of Homer's poetry derive from the poet's immersion in an oral culture and the constraints imposed by the medium of *orality upon narrative led to a sustained scholarly interest in the narrative and noetic processes of oral cultures (*see* MEDIA AND NARRATIVE). From his philological studies of the Homeric *epics, Parry found that the oral medium of composition imposed certain narrative tropes and techniques which repeatedly feature in Homer's poetry (*see* NARRATIVE TECHNIQUES; ORAL-FORMULAIC THEORY). In short, since the medium was oral, the poet had to depend extensively on formulas, standardised

themes, epithets, stock *characters, and so on and these were 'copiously' repeated because they served as mnemonic aids (*see* MEMORY). These findings from studies of the Greek epics were confirmed and extended by Albert Lord, Parry's protégé and collaborator, in his own studies of contemporary oral poetry from the Balkans. The conclusion drawn from these studies was that oral conditions of production determine to a large degree the shape of narrative.

From the publication of Lord's foundational research (1960), a series of other studies appeared in quick succession which extended these findings beyond a 'literary' interest in the figuration of narrative in oral societies to questions of *orality and culture, consciousness and cognition, and the nature of the human mind in general (*see* COGNITIVE NARRATOLOGY; ETHNOGRAPHIC APPROACHES TO NARRATIVE; PSYCHOLOGICAL APPROACHES TO NARRATIVE). Prominent among these studies were Marshall McLuhan's *The Guttenberg Galaxy* (1962), Jack Goody and Ian Watt's *The Consequences of Literacy* (1963), and Eric Havelock's *Preface to Plato* (1963), all of which focused on the revolutionary changes that came with the discovery of the alphabet and the introduction of writing in western society. This new direction was consolidated by a reordering of intellectual interest beyond narrative to the contrasts between orality and literacy. Thus began the orality-literacy divide which soon spread across the various disciplines of the social sciences and the humanities.

Perhaps the one scholar whose work has come to be almost universally identified with the question of oral societies and literacy is Walter Ong, whose book *Orality and Literacy: The Technologizing of the Word* (1982) was not only concerned with empirical identifications of the features of orality but also sought to provide a philosophical basis for the distinctions between primary orality – referring to societies which have known no writing at all – and literacy. Ong's argument, foreshadowed in his earlier books such as *The Presence of the Word* (1976) and *Interfaces of the Word* (1977), is that the contrasts between orality and literacy rest on a basic sensory distinction between sound and sight. Speech, he claims, is oriented toward *time while writing is oriented towards *space. Sound exists in time and exists only for so long and is gone, irretrievably lost, while the objects of sight can be 'arrested' in time and made *repeatedly* present, because they exist in space (Ong 1976: 40). From these sensory differences and the philosophical categories of time and space that he constructs around them, Ong argues that the limitation of words to sound alone determines the modes of thought and expression available to oral cultures.

How then do oral people think, how do they store the knowledge produced, and how do they recall? Addressing these questions, Ong sets out the psychodynamics of orality and the ways in which writing restructures consciousness. Building on the findings of previous scholars who had conducted similar investigations in these domains, he concludes that thought and expression in oral cultures is additive rather than subordinative, aggregative rather than analytic, situational rather than abstract, empathetic and participatory rather than objectively distanced, marked by 'copious' repetitions, and so on (1982: 31–77).

The formulary structures which Parry and Lord found to be characteristic of oral narratives had thus been extensively reconceptualised and seen to be dependent on the structures of cognition and consciousness on which oral cultures are founded. From the ways in which narratives are structured in oral societies, intellectual inquiry had shifted to the ways in which an oral consciousness structures thought and expression as a whole. Indeed, the focus of research had returned (employing a different vocabulary) to the earlier, more fanciful formulations of cognitionists such as Levy-Bruhl (1910) and later structuralists such as Lévi-Strauss (1966), who claimed to have uncovered the very logic of the mental processes of oral peoples and the constitutive elements of their thinking (*see* STRUCTURALIST NARRATOLOGY).

However, the binary framing of investigations of oral cultures in relation to writing has caused unease among several scholars. Emevwo Biakolo (1999), for instance, has questioned the philosophical foundations of these contrastive approaches, advocating instead critical studies that examine oral societies and narratives in terms of their own individuality and specificity rather than producing grand teleological narratives of orality and oral cultures in general.

References and further reading

Biakolo, Emevwo (1999) 'On the Theoretical Foundations of Orality and Literacy', *Research in African Literatures*, 30.2, 42–65.

Goody, Jack, and Ian Watt (1963) 'The Consequences of Literacy', *Contemporary Studies in Society and History*, 5, 304–45.

Havelock, Eric (1963) *Preface to Plato*, Cambridge, Mass.: Harvard University Press.

Lévi-Strauss, Claude (1966) *The Savage Mind*, Chicago: University of Chicago Press.

Levy-Bruhl, Lucien (1985 [1910]) *How Natives Think*, trans. Lilian Clarke, Princeton: Princeton University Press.

Lord, Albert Bates (1960) *The Singer of Tales*, Cambridge, Mass: Harvard University Press.

McLuhan, Marshall (1962) *The Guttenberg Galaxy*, Toronto: University of Toronto Press.

Ong, Walter (1967) *The Presence of the Word: Some Prolegomena for Cultural and Religious History*, New Haven: Yale University Press.

—— (1977) *Interfaces of the Word: Studies in the Evolution of Consciousness and Culture*, Ithaca: Cornell University Press.

—— (1982) *Orality and Literacy: The Technologizing of the Word*, London: Methuen.

Parry, Milman (1971) *The Collected Papers of Milman Parry*, ed. Adam Parry, Oxford: Oxford University Press.

HARRY GARUBA

ORAL-FORMULAIC THEORY

Oral-formulaic theory explains the composition and transmission of oral and oral-derived narratives in terms of formulaic phraseology, typical scenes or themes, and standard story-patterns, all of which provide a performer with ready-made structural units that aid the composition of narrative in *performance (*see* NARRATIVE UNITS; ORAL CULTURES AND NARRATIVE; ORALITY). Influenced in part by Matija Murko's accounts of South Slavic *epic singers as well as by philological studies linking Homeric phraseology and meter, Milman Parry – one of oral-formulaic theory's two founding pioneers – sought to illustrate the role of oral-traditional structures in Homeric epic through analogous features in living traditions, with South Slavic epic serving as the initial comparative analogue. Parry's fieldwork in 1933–1935 with his student and co-worker Albert Lord revealed that repeated formulas and formulaic structures in Homeric epic, such as the noun-epithet phrases 'much enduring divine Odysseus' and 'goddess grey-eyed Athena', paralleled formulaic diction in South Slavic epic. This comparative approach was further developed by Lord in the highly influential *Singer of Tales* (1960), which elaborated on the concepts of the theme (e.g., 'arming of a hero') and story pattern (e.g., 'return song') and extended the analogy beyond Ancient Greek to include other traditions, such as Old English and Old French.

While the method proved very useful in identifying building blocks of oral composition and developing the concept of 'multiforms' to explain the variation that occurs in narrative from one performance to the next, it remained for later scholars to examine the wider implications of orality for a broader range of *genres and cultural traditions. The work of John Miles Foley has been especially influential in advancing such studies. Shifting emphasis from composition to reception and drawing from a wide range of theoretical approaches such as *reception theory and ethnopoetics (*see* ETHNOGRAPHIC APPROACHES TO NARRATIVE), Foley has demonstrated that the traditional formulaic idiom provides far more than a utilitarian mnemonic device. Rather, oral forms persist even in manuscript texts because of their capacity to encode context and enhance meaning for *audiences attuned to traditional associations. Having grown far beyond its original configuration, oral-formulaic theory has significantly enhanced studies in such diverse fields as anthropology, *folklore, literary studies, and art history.

References and further reading

Foley, John Miles (1985) *Oral-Formulaic Theory and Research: An Introduction and Annotated Bibliography*, New York: Garland, http://www.oraltradition.org
—— (1988) *The Theory of Oral Composition: History and Methodology*, Bloomington: Indiana University Press.
—— (1991) *Immanent Art: From Structure to Meaning in Traditional Oral Epic*, Bloomington: Indiana University Press.
—— (1995) *The Singer of Tales in Performance*, Bloomington: Indiana University Press.
Lord, Albert Bates (1960) *The Singer of Tales*, Cambridge, Mass.: Harvard University Press.
MacKay, E. A. (1995) 'Narrative Tradition in Early Greek Oral Poetry and Vase Painting', *Oral Tradition*, 10, 282–303.
Parry, Adam (ed.) (1971) *The Making of Homeric Verse: The Collected Papers of Milman Parry*, Oxford: Clarendon Press.
Renoir, Alain (1988) *A Key to Old Poems: The Oral-Formulaic Approach in the Interpretation of West-Germanic Verse*, University Park: Pennsylvania State University Press.

LORI ANN GARNER

ORAL HISTORY

Oral history represents an *interdisciplinary effort to record and preserve the narratives of individuals, groups, and communities. Historians since Thucydides have obtained information by interviewing those who participated in *events. As early as the 1890s, ethnographers made recordings of stories and songs on wax cylinders, and during the 1930s the New Deal's Works Progress Administration (WPA) commissioned an extensive interviewing project with former slaves, immigrants, farmers, labourers, and others struggling to survive the Depression. The systematic collection and archival preservation of tape-recorded oral history interviews began in 1948 when Allan Nevins founded Columbia University's Oral History Research Office. Since then, oral history projects have spread worldwide, boosted by the availability of portable, inexpensive recording equipment. The tapes and transcripts of these interviews are generally transcribed and deposited in libraries and archives, with an increasing number posted on Internet websites.

The term 'oral history' derived from a *New Yorker* article in 1942 about a Greenwich Village bohemian, Joseph Gould, who professed to be writing 'An Oral History of Our Time'. Gould envisioned supplanting the formal history of kings and presidents with an informal history of the 'shirt-sleeved multitude', but the first oral history archives in the United States focused instead on government officials, military officers, business leaders, and other elites. In Europe, oral history projects were directed mostly by social historians who sought to record the working class. By the 1970s, oral historians in general had shifted to interviewing 'from the bottom up', seeking out those who previously had been omitted from the historical narrative. The methodology adjusted to either category, from shop floor workers to top corporate executives. Oral history techniques were also used outside of academia by people conducting interviews with family and community members. Government agencies have sponsored official oral history programs, from national parks to military operations. Nations newly emerged from colonial rule, or which underwent social and political revolutions, regarded their official archives as reflections of the old regime and have encouraged the recording of citizens' personal memories of oppression and liberation (*see* POST-COLONIALISM AND NARRATIVE).

Oral history interviewing requires well-prepared interviewers who frame questions that will provide chronological context to assist in recall and to encourage *narrators to speak freely (*see* CON-VERSATIONAL STORYTELLING; MEMORY). Interviewees usually sign legal releases that establish copyright and define how and when the interview can be opened for research and dissemination. As distinguished from quantitative interviews that social and behavioural scientists conduct with questionnaires, and from unrecorded participant observation fieldwork, oral history interviews generally involve qualitative, open-ended, and specific questions tailored for each participant.

Conversational, and by definition in the vernacular, oral history has demonstrated broad appeal. The radio interviewer Studs Terkel popularised oral history in a series of books, one of which, *Working* (1974), was dramatised as *The American Clock* (1980) by the playwright Arthur Miller. Oral history has further been incorporated into children's books (*see* CHILDREN'S STORIES (NARRATIVES WRITTEN FOR CHILDREN)), documentary *films, museum exhibits, and *radio programs. In each case, the interviews allow for a variety of *voices and *perspectives that can provide balanced presentations. As a teaching device, oral history has been adopted by many secondary school teachers through the *Foxfire* programs in which students conducted interviews to produce student magazines, and in undergraduate and graduate education (*see* EDUCATION AND NARRATIVE).

Yet oral history continues to encounter scepticism from those who question the validity of memory or who suspect the narrators' motives. Critics regard oral history as a subjective source, usually collected well after the events described had occurred. Names and dates are easily forgotten, and sequences are sometimes confused and conflated. Yet individuals' long-term memory can remain surprisingly resilient even when short-term memories lapse. Gerontologists have theorised that older people go through a life review process, evaluating their successes and disappointments. Giving a life review interview can therefore have therapeutic value (*see* LIFE STORY; NARRATIVE THERAPY). Oral historians have also observed the phenomenon of whole communities getting a story 'wrong' by placing people and events in an erroneous context, and rearranging the past to make it more relevant for the present. Scholars have concluded that such collective subjectivity reveals much about the community's self-identification (*see* IDENTITY AND NARRATIVE).

Oral history has been faulted for being more *anecdotal than analytical, and oral historians have been accused of accepting uncritically the stories that informants tell them. Indeed, people naturally recount events anecdotally, in small self-contained stories that illuminate and instruct. Yet in telling their stories, narrators tend to provide their own explanations and analysis, making sense of events in hindsight and drawing conclusions that might not have been as obvious when the events occurred (*see* NARRATIVE AS COGNITIVE INSTRUMENT; NARRATIVE EXPLANATION). Interviews often confound rather than confirm interviewers' assumptions, and their full meaning may not be immediately apparent. An interview might well be interpreted differently by future researchers than by the interviewer. Inconsistencies between the oral and written record require scholarly analysis to determine which version most accurately reflects the events described (*see* NARRATIVE VERSIONS).

When oral historians first began transcribing recorded interviews, some projects omitted the questions and presented the text as an uninterrupted narrative. That practice was abandoned when oral history became widely seen as a collaborative process that involves an interviewer who steers the *narration through questions, challenges assertions, and refers to significant issues that might otherwise be overlooked. Rather than become intrusive, however, interviewers attempt to remain neutral and not interject their own opinions into the dialogue. Despite these efforts, narrators frequently shape their answers to fit what they think the questioner wants. During one of the WPA's interviews with former slaves, an elderly African American woman gave a far more benign account of slavery to a white woman interviewer than she did to a second interviewer who was African American. Differences in *gender, age, race, and ethnicity must be taken into consideration, but they are not impenetrable barriers to conducting a useful interview.

Oral historians have also found that in any group or *institution, interviews with secondary figures on the periphery can be as important as those who were principal players. People at the centre of events will recount their own accomplishments, but those on the boundaries often provide a broader perspective and can make comparisons between the key figures. Perceptions vary widely and also shape what is remembered. Imprecise or mistaken perceptions will produce misconstrued memories. Second-hand information is more susceptible to distortion, while direct involvement tends to fix more lasting memories. A single interview will record only a single perspective and cannot be comprehensive. Oral historians therefore seek to compile a range of interviews that will reflect differing points of view.

SEE ALSO: ethnographic approaches to narrative; historiography; journalism; oral cultures and narrative; sociolinguistic approaches to narrative

References and further reading

Davidson, James West, and Mark Lytle (1981) *After the Fact: American Historians and Their Methods*, New York: Knopf.
Frisch, Michael (1990) *A Shared Authority: Essays on the Craft and Meaning of Oral History and Public History*, Albany: State University of New York Press.
Gluck, Sherna Berger, and Daphne Patai (eds) (1991) *Women's Words: The Feminist Practice of Oral History*, New York: Routledge.
Grele, Ronald J. (ed.) (1991) *Envelopes of Sound: The Art of Oral History*, New York: Praeger.
Hoffman, Alice M., and Howard S. Hoffman (1991) *Archives of Memory: A Soldier Recalls World War II*, Lexington: University Press of Kentucky.
Perks, Robert, and Alistair Thomson (eds) (1998) *The Oral History Reader* London: Routledge.
Ritchie, Donald A. (2003) *Doing Oral History: A Practical Guide*, New York: Oxford University Press.

DONALD A. RITCHIE

ORALITY

The representation of the spoken language in literary works reflects the evolution of the relationship between orality and literacy, and oral and written cultures in general. Medieval storytellers and poets often read their written texts aloud to an *audience (see MEDIEVAL NARRATIVE). This practice, whose consequences Zumthor describes as *vocalité*, proved influential even into the sixteenth century. In this period of transition between oral and literate culture, oral features were probably not consciously employed by writers, but entered their works as 'oral residues' (Ong 1982), as habits of thought and expression typical of (predominantly) oral cultures. In the course of the establishment of print culture and the spread of

both literacy and the practice of silent reading, writers took a more deliberate approach to orality. Hence, orality in modern literary narratives (as well as in plays and poems) is not an authentic representation of the spoken word but a product of writing; it is a feigned or pseudo-orality (*see* SPEECH REPRESENTATION).

Since spoken and written language differ from each other in degree rather than in kind, Tannen has suggested that one should not attempt to distinguish between oral and written elements as such, but concentrate on the communicative situation and the strategies conventionally associated with speaking and writing. Koch and Österreicher not only differentiate between the various *media – conversation, formal speech, *letter, article, etc., – in which a discourse is realised phonically or graphically, they also distinguish between two principal codes or languages ('oral and written conceptions' in their terminology): the 'language of immediacy', which is marked by dynamic development, tentativeness, simplicity, and lack of planning, and 'the language of distance', which is characterised by stasis, coherence, complexity, and planning. While these two 'languages' are theoretically abstract polar opposites on the continuum of discourse styles, they can be used to assess the specific 'oral' or 'written' quality of any given discourse token. From this linguistic perspective, orality in modern literature is realised graphically and is normally read silently by a solitary reader. Speeches, *dialogues, and oral storytelling (*see* SKAZ) result from written strategies and are fixed and pre-planned. They may, however, create an illusion of spoken language and remind readers of the spontaneity and dynamics that often, though not always, accompany face-to-face interactions.

In modern narrative literature orality has various important functions. Writers employ it to create an impression of their characters' language use, dialogue behaviours, and storytelling practices. Other writers draw upon the oral traditions and *oral history of regions and ethnic groups and depict *conflicts between oral and written cultures. Still others use orality to increase the *polyphony of their works, enliven their texts with 'oral' interactions between the *narrator and reader or between the characters, and invent situations which allow them to evaluate the contrasting characteristics of oral and written cultures.

SEE ALSO: address; discourse analysis (linguistics); oral cultures and narratives; oral-formulaic theory; voice

References and further reading

Goetsch, Paul (1985) 'Fingierte Mündlichkeit in der Erzählkunst entwickelter Schriftkulturen', *Poetica*, 17, 202–18.
—— (2003) *The Oral and the Written in Nineteenth-Century British Fiction*, Frankfurt: Peter Lang.
Koch, Peter, and Wulf Österreicher (1985) 'Sprache der Nähe – Sprache der Distanz: Mündlichkeit und Schriftlichkeit im Spannungsfeld von Theorie und Sprachgeschichte', *Romanistisches Jahrbuch*, 36, 15–43.
Ong, Walter J. (1982) *Orality and Literacy: The Technologizing of the Word*, London: Methuen.
Tannen, Deborah (ed.) (1982) *Spoken and Written Language: Exploring Orality and Literacy*, Norwood, NJ: Ablex Publications.
Zumthor, Paul (1987) *La lettre et la voix: De la 'littérature' médiévale*, Paris: Seuil.

PAUL GOETSCH

ORGANISATIONS AND NARRATIVE

Whereas institution (e.g., the practice of medicine) is a category that encompasses any social group which has a continued existence over *time, organisation (e.g., the American Medical Association) is a subtype of institution with defined membership, boundaries, and legal responsibilities. In both organisations and institutions narrative has two major functions: the continuation of the life of the group, and the facilitation of its daily work. *See* INSTITUTIONAL NARRATIVE.

OULIPO (*OUVROIR DE LITTÉRATURE POTENTIELLE*)

The *Ouvroir de Littérature Potentielle* ('Workshop of Potential Literature'), or 'Oulipo' for short, is a group of writers and mathematicians based in Paris. Founded in 1960 by Raymond Queneau and François Le Lionnais, the Oulipo originally included ten members, today its membership numbers thirty-three. Vibrantly active in its fifth decade, the Oulipo undoubtedly holds the record of longevity for literary groups. Adopting the notion of formal rigour as its guiding doctrine, the Oulipo's activity can be divided into two categories: first, the identification and rehabilitation of old – indeed sometimes ancient – literary forms;

second, the elaboration of new forms. In the area of narrative, the Oulipo was inspired by Raymond Queneau, both by his theoretical writings and by the example of his many novels. Queneau deplored the fact that many novelists drive their *characters across an indeterminate narrative landscape, like a gaggle of geese (*see* NOVEL, THE). He argued instead for strict organisation, and the application of structural principles that leave nothing to chance.

As the members of the Oulipo put those ideas into practice over the years, a variety of narrative forms resulted from their experiments. One might point toward Italo Calvino's *If on a winter's night a traveler*, for instance, which relies upon A. J. Greimas's semiotic squares for its organisation (*see* SEMIOTICS). Jacques Roubaud's three *Hortense* novels borrow and deploy the combinatoric structure of the sestina. Jacques Jouet's *Fins* plays on the strict permutation of the numbers one through six in order to afford narrative shape. One might also mention works by Marcel Bénabou, Harry Mathews, Anne Garreta, Paul Fournel, and Hervé Le Tellier. Perhaps the most eloquent example of Oulipian narrative practice is that of Georges Perec. His *La Disparition* is a 312-page novel written without the letter E. As strange as it may sound, the 'lipogram' (a text eschewing a letter or letters of the alphabet) is in fact an ancient literary form, attested as early as the sixth century before the Common Era. Perec's text turns form to theme, moreover. It is structured like a detective novel whose central conceit is the disappearance of the E from the alphabet (*see* DETECTIVE FICTION). Far from being a mere exercise in literary acrobatics, *La Disparition* reads so easily that several critics, in its early reviews, failed to notice anything amiss. *La Vie mode d'emploi*, a compendious 700-page novel, puts two systems of formal constraint into play. The first uses a classic chess problem, the 'Knight's Tour', to order the sequence of ninety-nine chapters in the book. The second is based on an exceedingly arcane mathematical figure called the 'orthogonal Latin bi-square order 10'. Briefly described, that algorithm allows the symmetrical distribution and permutation of sets of forty-two constitutive elements in each chapter. Yet astonishingly enough, *La Vie mode d'emploi* is also a very accessible text that has attracted a broad and diverse readership since its initial publication in 1978. It may also be considered as the most exemplary model of Oulipian narrative theory and practice to date.

SEE ALSO: narrative, games, and play; postmodern narrative

References and further reading

Mathews, Harry, and Alastair Brothchie (eds) (1998) *Oulipo Compendium*, London: Atlas Press.

Motte, Warren (ed.) (1998) *Oulipo: A Primer of Potential Literature*, trans. Warren Motte, Normal, IL: Dalkey Archive Press.

Oulipo (1973) *La Littérature potentielle: Créations, recréations, récréations*, Paris: Gallimard.

—— (1981) *Atlas de littérature potentielle*, Paris: Gallimard.

WARREN MOTTE

P

PALIMPSEST

Originally, a reusable canvas or writing scroll containing several layers of pictures or texts. Typically, scratching the surface of a palimpsest exposes part of an earlier picture or text. In Genettean poetics, the term is used to refer to a 'layered' text which builds on, parodies, alludes to, contains traces of, or otherwise contains an earlier text. *See* INTERTEXTUALITY.

PANFICTIONALITY

The doctrine of panfictionality is the predominantly postmodern rejection of the traditional distinction between *fiction and non-fiction in favour of a model that regards all texts, and consequently all *narrative texts, as fictional (Ryan 1997). This rejection is based on two main arguments:

The linguistic argument. Saussurian linguistics describes language as a self-enclosed, self-organising system whose categories are defined by purely differential relations rather than by positive relations to an external referent (*see* REFERENCE). Language consequently creates its own world, as does fiction, rather than reflecting the structure of the world. *Counter-argument*: the categories of language may shape our representation of reality, but it does not follow from the arbitrariness of linguistic signs that language creates reality in the literal sense of 'causing to exist'. It only does so in its fictional use.

The historiographic argument. The work of Hayden White has stressed that *narrativity is the product of an act of interpretation rather than being the sort of thing that is found in the world (*see* HISTORIOGRAPHY). The *emplotment of history, which imposes on the text structures similar to those found in literary texts, is therefore the result of a fictionalisation of raw facts. *Counter-argument*: The similarities between the *plot structures of fiction and history can be explained by postulating the existence of narrative cognitive models wired into the human mind, models which impart coherence and intelligibility to imagined as well as to observed and reconstructed *events (*see* NARRATIVE AS COGNITIVE INSTRUMENT).

The doctrine of panfictionality has both negative and positive implications. On the negative side, it is epistemologically irresponsible. The argument known as 'Taking the Holocaust Test' (Doležel 1999) asks how a model that regards reality as a textual creation can justify the rejection of texts that claim that the Holocaust never happened. In a Panfictionalist model, all texts are equally valid, since all have the power of creating *truth. In a model that maintains a distinction between fiction and non-fiction, fictional texts create their own world by means of their declarations, but non-fictional texts share a common text-external reference world. This common referent places them in competition against each other, and forces them to substantiate their claims against those of other texts.

On the positive side, the doctrine of panfictionality shook narrative theory out of the complacency with which it has long approached *non-fiction. If rhetorical devices produce meaning in fiction, so do they in non-fiction (*see* NARRATIVE TECHNIQUES; RHETORICAL APPROACHES TO NARRATIVE). Until the doctrine of panfictionality came along, non-fictional *genres of discourse enjoyed an illicit immunity from textual or semiotic forms of investigation (*see* SEMIOTICS). We are now better aware that texts of non-fiction display an image distinct from their reference world, and that the construction of this image deserves consideration.

Panfictionality has important consequences for narrative practice. Werner Wolf argues that adherence to the doctrine is incompatible with the phenomenon of aesthetic illusion. The members of a culture that regards the world as text and as fiction will consider it theoretically naive to pretend belief in the autonomous, text-independent existence of a fictional world. Panfictionality thus explains the aversion of *postmodern narrative to *immersion, and its predilection for illusion-breaking devices.

References and further reading

Doležel, Lubomír (1999) 'Fictional and Historical Narrative: Meeting the Postmodernist Challenge', in David Herman (ed.) *Narratologies: New Perspectives on Narrative Analysis*, Columbus: Ohio State University Press.

Ryan, Marie-Laure (1997) 'Postmodernism and the Doctrine of Panfictionality', *Narrative*, 5.2, 165–87.

de Saussure, Ferdinand (1966), *Course in General Linguistics*, trans. Wade Baskin, New York: McGraw Hill.

White, Hayden (1987) *The Content of the Form: Narrative Discourse and Historical Representation*, Baltimore: Johns Hopkins University Press.

Wolf, Werner (1993) *Ästhetische Illusion und Illusionbrechung in der Erzählkunst*, Tübingen: Max Niemeyer Verlag.

MARIE-LAURE RYAN

PARABLE

A parable presents an *anecdote that is meant to be understood as a *metaphor for a moral or spiritual aspect of life, in particular good behaviour. The prototypical parable is a small group of stories by Jesus Christ, such as the parables of the sower, the lost sheep, and the workers in the vineyard (*see* BIBLICAL NARRATIVE). The story that is told by the *narrator functions as a concrete source domain that invites comparison with a target domain that remains implicit. Thus, the parable of the sower only narrates the actions of a farmer who sows his seed in four different places, and tells the consequences of those actions. The story itself does not contain the corresponding target domain, which has to do with the different ways in which people can receive the message about the kingdom of God. The explication of the target domain often follows as a separate text and is considered to be an extrinsic comment on the meaning of the parable (*see* METANARRATIVE COMMENT).

The fact that the story only makes *reference to the source domain explains why parable is comparable to *allegory and *fable. However, the difference is that allegory is not followed by a separate explication, and fables are often followed by an extremely brief moral. Another feature that distinguishes parable from allegory is that allegories are not specifically morally and spiritually targeted, whereas parables (and fables) are. One important distinction between parable and fable is that *characters in fables are typically non-human creatures or even inanimate things. In contrast, parables, tend to focus on human actions, though this is not necessarily the case. Some parables are more general metaphorical comparisons. One well-known group deals with the nature of the Kingdom of Heaven, which is compared with, for instance, a mustard seed. In such cases, the narrative character of parable is considerably weakened. In spite of this possible extension into more general metaphorical comparison, however, parable is as a rule more specific and dynamic than any extended metaphorical comparison with a didactic function, as when electricity is compared with the flow of water (*see* DIDACTIC NARRATIVE). This is precisely because parable is typically *narrative. Moreover, parable is not just generally didactic but also often has an inspirational purpose and a spiritual target.

The prototypical parable belongs to the domain of religion. The rationale for speaking in parables is explained by Jesus to his disciples in Matthew 13, Mark 4, and Luke 8: 'The knowledge of the secrets of the kingdom of God has been given to you, but to others I speak in parables, so that "though seeing, they may not see; though hearing, they may not understand"' (Luke 8). However, parables are also found in other domains, such as *philosophy and related areas: Plato's parable of the cave is a famous example. In literature, the Christian parables have been an important source for imitation and parody. But parable has also been practised as an art form in its own right (see, e.g., Kafka's *The Trial*). Parables have also had an effect on common language use, some well-known idioms and proverbs deriving straight from the classic texts, such as 'the blind leading the blind', or 'the last will be the first'.

SEE ALSO: sermon; theology and narrative

References and further reading

Kafka, Franz (1998) *The Trial*, trans. Breon Mitchell, New York: Schocken.
Naveh, Gila Safran (2000) *Biblical Parables and their Modern Re-creations: From 'Apples of Gold in Silver Settings' to 'Imperial Messages'*, Albany: State University of New York Press.

GERARD STEEN

PARALEPSIS AND PARALIPSIS

In Genettean narratology, two ways of violating the default narrative style for a given text – either by 'saying too much' (paralepsis) or by 'saying too little' (paralipsis). *See* ALTERATION.

PARATEXT

Every book contains the text of at least one work; but, if the text is to be accessible, the book must include additional textual matter, which Genette has usefully dubbed the 'paratext'. The ensemble of materials involved in the paratext is variable, and any attempted at a general listing must remain open-ended. Taking *novels as an example, however, any of the following would belong to their paratext: titles and subtitles (of chapters, sections, and volumes as well as the whole work), epigraphs, dedications, prefaces, afterwords, running heads, the copyright page, and all jacket copy. Genette further distinguishes between these paratextual materials adjacent to a text (the 'peritext') and those subsequent to it (the 'epitext'), in which the author comments on the work directly or indirectly, officially or unofficially – as for instance in interviews, correspondence, or journal entries. Although the term has come into wide usage in recent years, in English-language criticism so far most paratextual investigation has focused on the study of titles (e.g., Ferry 1996).

References and further reading

Ferry, Anne (1996) *The Title to the Poem*, Stanford: Stanford University Press.
Genette, Gérard (1988 [1987]) 'The Proustian Paratexte', trans. Amy G. McIntosh, *SubStance*, 56, 63–77.
——(1997 [1987]) *Paratexts: Thresholds of Interpretation*, trans. Jane E. Lewin, Cambridge: Cambridge University Press.

DAVID GORMAN

PARODY

An ironic *quotation of one text by another; a more or less openly mocking recontextualisation of a prior text by a later one. In the terminology of Gérard Genette, parody results when a hypertext comically de-valorises the hypotext it parodically transforms. Parodic effects often involve dissonance, as when a 'high' or elevated style is used to narrate banal or quotidian *events. *See* INTERTEXTUALITY; IRONY (also: NARRATIVE VERSIONS).

PARTICIPATORY NARRATIVE

A narrative whose script is only partly predefined, allowing recipients to impersonate active *characters in a fictional world, and through their *agency, to contribute to the real-time production of the *plot. This mode is found in staged happenings, 'improv' theater, pencil-and-paper role-playing games (e.g., 'Dungeons and Dragons'), and *computer games. *See* DIGITAL NARRATIVITY; NARRATIVE, GAMES, AND PLAY.

PASTICHE

A *quotation or 'sampling' of one text by another – in Genette's terms, a quotation of a hypotext by a hypertext – but without any of the ironic, mocking, or more broadly evaluative forms of recontextualisation associated with parody. For Fredric Jameson, the movement from modernism to postmodernism correlates with a shift from parody to pastiche as the dominant mode of *intertextuality. *See* IRONY; POSTMODERN NARRATIVE (ALSO: NARRATIVE VERSIONS).

PERFORMANCE

Performance is a mode of communicative display, in which the performer assumes responsibility to an *audience for a display of communicative virtuosity, highlighting the way in which the act of discursive production is accomplished, above and beyond the additional multiple functions the communicative act may serve (*see* COMMUNICATION IN NARRATIVE). In narrative performance, the act of *narration itself is framed as display: objectified, lifted out to a degree from its contextual – including cotextual – surroundings, and opened up to interpretive and evaluative scrutiny by an audience both in terms of its intrinsic qualities and its associational resonances. Storytelling is thus a mode of publication, in the root sense of making a narrative accessible to a public.

In addition to designating a mode of communicative display, the term 'performance' may also be used to label the *event in which performance and other forms of communicative display characteristically occur. In anthropological usage, those scheduled, bounded, programmed, participatory events in which the symbols and values of a society are embodied and enacted before an audience – such as ritual, festival, *spectacle, theater, concert – are often termed 'cultural performances' (*see* DRAMA AND NARRATIVE; ETHNOGRAPHIC APPROACHES TO NARRATIVE; OPERA).

The specific *semiotic means by which the storyteller may key the performance frame – that is, send the metacommunicative message 'I'm on, look at me, see how well and effectively I express myself' – are historically and cross-culturally variable. Some keying devices, however, such as special formulae (e.g., 'Once upon a time...'), formal devices (e.g., parallelism, metrical patterning), figurative language (e.g., *metaphor, simile), appeals to tradition as the standard of reference for the performer's accountability (e.g., 'The old people say...'), special registers (e.g., archaic language), even disclaimers of performance (e.g., 'I'm not really a storyteller, but...') recur with impressive frequency in the narrative performance repertoires of the world's peoples (*see* NARRATIVE UNIVERSALS).

The collaborative participation of an audience is an integral component of performance as an interactional accomplishment. From the point of view of the audience, the act of narration on the part of the performer is laid open to evaluation for the way it is done, for the relative skill, effectiveness, appropriateness, or correctness of the performer's display. Insofar as evaluation opens the way to engagement with and appreciation of the intrinsic qualities of the act of expression and the performer's virtuosity, performance is an invitation to the enhancement of experience. Performance is affecting; one of its central qualities is the capacity to 'move' an audience through the arousal and fulfilment of formal expectations – getting the audience into the 'groove' – as well as through the evocative power of resonant associations. At the same time, performance is fraught with risk, insofar as it is shadowed by the spectre of failure, of being – or being judged to be – incompetent or by eliciting affective responses that are otherwise problematic, as when female performers are cast simultaneously as objects of *desire and as morally compromised (*see* GENDER STUDIES).

The performance forms of a society tend to be among the most markedly textualised, generically regimented, memorable, and repeatable forms of discourse in its communicative economy (*see* GENRE THEORY IN NARRATIVE STUDIES; MEMORY). Likewise, performance forms tend to be among the most consciously traditionalised in a community's communicative repertoire, which is to say that they are understood and constructed as part of an extended succession of intertextually linked reiterations (*see* INTERTEXTUALITY). In one influential conception of performance, developed by Richard Schechner, performance means 'never for the first time', which locates its essence in the decontextualisation and recontextualisation of discourse, with special emphasis on the latter. At the same time, no performance can ever be perfectly replicated, ideologies to the contrary notwithstanding (*see* IDEOLOGY AND NARRATIVE); performance always manifests an emergent dimension. The dynamic interplay between the ready-made and the emergent, between tradition and creativity, must be discovered empirically in the close analysis of situated performances.

The interpretive process of evaluation invokes an intertextual field in its own right, constituted by the past performances that provide a standard for the comparative assessment of the performance now on view. A performer is thus accountable to past performances, however the standards and measures of accountability may be construed in particular cultural and historical milieux. The alignment of performance to past performances demands calibration of the intertextual relationship between them. Taking responsibility for correct doing may impel a performer to close replication of past performance in an enactment of traditional authority, while distancing of a performance from established precedent may foreground the distinctiveness of present exigencies. Indeed, ideologies of performance – and of genre – characteristically foreground and valorise particular regimens of calibration.

Performance, like any other metacommunicative frame, is labile. The analysis of narrative performance demands attention to how texts may be rekeyed from performance to another interpretive frame, or how performance may be variably calibrated vis-à-vis the other multiple functions that a given narrative may serve, either within the course of a single utterance or across successive iterations (*see* FRAME THEORY; FUNCTION ((JAKOBSON))). Understandably, analyses of narrative performance have tended to centre on forms and instances of apparent or assumed full performance. Scholars tend to seek out and record the star performers and favour the most fully artful texts. But we lose something by this privileging of full performance just as we do by taking any rendition of an artfully organised text as performance. Approaching performance in terms of the dynamics of recontextualisation opens the way to a recognition of alternative and shifting frames available for the recontextualisation of texts. Successive reiterations, even of texts for which performance is the expected, preferred, or publicly foregrounded mode of presentation, may be variously framed: reported, rehearsed, demonstrated, translated, relayed, quoted, summarised, or parodied, to suggest but a few of the intertextual possibilities (*see* QUOTATION THEORY). Here again, a focus on the calibration of the intertextual gaps between successive reiterations of a text in the dialogic history of performance illuminates the discursive foundations of socio-historical continuity.

SEE ALSO: communication studies and narrative; conversational storytelling; dialogism; discourse analysis (linguistics)

References and further reading

Bauman, Richard (1977) *Verbal Art as Performance*, Prospect Heights, IL: Waveland.
——(1986) *Story, Performance, and Event: Contextual Studies of Oral Narrative*, Cambridge: Cambridge University Press.
——, and Charles L. Briggs (1990) 'Poetics and Performance as Critical Perspectives on Language and Social Life', *Annual Review of Anthropology*, 19, 59–88.
Briggs, Charles L. (1988) *Competence in Performance: The Creativity of Tradition in Mexicano Verbal Art*, Philadelphia: University of Pennsylvania Press.
Duranti, Alessandro, and Donald Brenneis (eds) (1986) *TEXT* 6.3 (Special issue on 'The Audience as Co-Author').
Keane, Webb (1997) *Signs of Recognition: Powers and Hazards of Representation in an Indonesian Society*, Berkeley: University of California Press.
Sawin, Patricia (2002) 'Performance at the Nexus of Gender, Power, and Desire', *Journal of American Folklore*, 115, 28–61.
Schechner, Richard (1985) *Between Theater and Anthropology*, Philadelphia: University of Pennsylvania Press.
Stoeltje, Beverly J., and Richard Bauman (1988) 'The Semiotics of Folkloric Performance', in Thomas A. Sebeok and Jean Umiker-Sebeok (eds) *The Semiotic Web 1987*, Berlin: Mouton deGruyter.

RICHARD BAUMAN

PERFORMATIVITY

The concept of performativity derives from the distinction made by J. L. Austin between two types of utterance, constative and performative; constative utterances report or describe (*see* DESCRIPTION), while performative utterances constitute actions in themselves. Examples of performative utterances include bets ('I bet you . . .'), promises, and apologies; such utterances accomplish the actions that they name. The philosopher Judith Butler adopted Austin's theory to account for the historical production of gender. For Butler, performativity requires the 'citation' of conventional practices; a person's gender repeats a pre-existing mode of being. Butler's thinking has inspired many scholars working in the fields of *gender studies and *queer theory. For narratologists, the theory of performativity can illuminate such topics as (1) the effects of *narration on the *narratee, especially insofar as every narrative repeats the techniques of preceding narratives, and (2) storytelling's cultural function of manufacturing and disseminating knowledge.

SEE ALSO: intertextuality; pragmatics; speech act theory

References and further reading

Austin, J. L. (1962) *How to Do Things with Words*, Cambridge, Mass.: Harvard University Press.

Butler, Judith (1990) *Gender Trouble: Feminism and the Subversion of Identity*, New York: Routledge.
——(1997) *Excitable Speech: A Politics of the Performative*, New York: Routledge.
Searle, John (1969) *Speech Acts: An Essay in the Philosophy of Language*, Cambridge: Cambridge University Press.

MATTHEW BELL

PERSON

According to Roman Jakobson, 'Person [as a grammatical category] characterises the participants of the narrated event with reference to the participants of the speech event [= the *narration]. Thus, first-person signals the identity of a participant in the narrated event with the performer of the speech event [= *narrator], and the second-person, the identity with the actual or potential undergoer [= *narratee] of the speech event' (134). In the same vein, the third-person is a participant of the narrated event who is not identical with either narrator or narratee.

In first- and second-person narratives, one of the participants in the narrated system, that is, one of those spoken of as agent or experiencer, is also the originator or recipient, respectively, of the relevant narration. Robinson Crusoe is thus both the *hero and teller of his story; Delmont is both the hero and addressee of the story of his change of heart in Butor's novel of the same title (French original, *La modification*; see ADDRESS; COMMUNICATION IN NARRATIVE). Since the narrative communication here is, at least in part, about one of its own participants, such narratives can be termed *homocommunicative* (Fludernik 1994). In third-person narratives, such as Fielding's *Tom Jones*, the communication is about another (others) who is (are) not part of the narrative transaction, and such narratives can be termed *heterocommunicative*. In first- and second-person narratives the same individual fulfils two roles: one in the narrated system and one in the system of narration. When the two systems are anchored at different points in *time (past or future narration), as in Robinson Crusoe's memoirs or the past-tense, second-person (= 'you did') sections of Christa Wolf's novel *Patterns of Childhood* (*Kindheitsmuster*), the 'I' and 'you' of current narration may also have very different kinds or degrees of knowledge than their counterparts in the domain of the narrated. In homocommunicative narration, teller (I) and addressee (you) positions are textually marked, so that signs of narration and of the narrated alike occur in the text. In third-person narration, on the other hand, signs of narration are optional: the narrator may remain an anonymous, impersonal voice, never referring to himself as an 'I', and the narratee may equally remain textually unmarked, never being addressed as a 'you'.

Classifying narratives as homocommunicative is usually understood to mean that they are the story of the narrator's or narratee's own experiences. True, but not entirely. In most homocommunicative narratives narrator or narratee are participants in *some* of the narrated *events only. Whether a first-person narrative is autodiegetic (narrator as protagonist) or homodiegetic (narrator as minor *character or witness), some or even most of the narrated events, respectively, will concern a third party (*see* DIEGESIS). And the same applies to second-person narratives. Crusoe has Man Friday, and Delmont both a wife in France and a mistress in Italy. A third-person or heterodiegetic narrative, on the other hand, is exclusively the story of individuals who are not participants in the current speech event. The result is an asymmetry, whereby homocommunicative narratives contain narration in the third-person as well, while heterocommunicative ones do not contain narration in the first or second-person. While homocommunicative narratives must contain by definition some first- or second-person narration, the proportion between it and third-person narration is text-specific and highly variable. In addition to first-, second-, and third-person narratives in the singular, there is also a plural variety of each, examples being, respectively, John Barth's *Sabbatical*, passages in Jean Thibaudeau's *Une ceremonie royale*, and George Perec's *Les choses*. Some experimental narratives, such as Monique Wittig's *L'Opoponax* are in the impersonal 'one' mode. Stories with multiple narrators (Faulkner's *The Sound and the Fury*) as well as *epistolary novels (Rousseau's *La nouvelle Héloïse*) entail multiple deictic and pronominal shifts (*see* DEIXIS). A person referred to as 'I' in one section, may thus become a 'he' in another. Unclear shifts of speaker may lead to *indeterminacy as to who is speaking and about whom, and to resultant unclarity as to co-reference between, say, the narrated 'he' of one section and the narrated 'I' of another (*see* REFERENCE).

Each person variety of narration has its own possibilities and restrictions. In third-person narratives (*Tom Jones*) the narrating *voice may have access to characters' minds (*see* THOUGHT AND CONSCIOUSNESS REPRESENTATION (LITERATURE)); the narrator may also roam freely in *space and *time and be present at different places simultaneously. If anonymous, this voice is equated with the voice of *truth as regards information and judgement alike (*see* AUTHENTICATION). Third-person, past-tense (preterit) omniscient narration by an anonymous voice has often been regarded as the prototype of fictional narration. In first-person narrative (*Crusoe, Moll Flanders*) the teller is individuated, and his or her vision considered subjective. Such a teller normally has access to their own mind only, and the completeness or *reliability of any information or judgement they provide can be questioned. Second-person narration (*Change of Heart*) may sound unnatural: why tell someone his/her own *life story? Various local motivations can be offered: reminding, accusing, or self-address, with the 'you' being the speaker's alter ego. Such a 'you' can enter a dialogue with the narrator. The 'you' form can also function as invitation for the reader to assume imaginatively the narrated role.

'We' narratives (*Sabbatical* or Pierre Silvain's *Les eoliennes*) occupy an unstable position between the poles of first-person and second/third-person narration. The speaker is an individual member of a group, making statements about its collective actions and possibly its self-image as a collective subject. Not being the group's spokesman, though, he or she can only speak about the group, not for it. Claims about a group's mental states or *actions combine uneasily the narrator's own immediate self-knowledge with inferences about the minds of other members. It is also difficult to sustain a narrative entirely on the collective level, especially when mental functioning is concerned. There are a few narratives written entirely in the 'one' form, which is initially unspecified for person, number, and *gender. This usage has a strong depersonalising effect, as well as the overtone of the universal, the anybody. Brooke-Rose, for her part, has argued that the impersonal form of narration is the most elementary or basic position, from which all others are derived through different optional specifications.

Finally, in some first-person narratives the narrator refers to certain phases of his or her narrated, past self as 'you' or 's/he' or even 'one'.

An example is Carlos Fuentes' *The Death of Artemio Cruz*, with its alternating 'I', 'you' and 'he' passages. This usage is technically an instance of transferred or displaced person deixis, where the textual speaker refers to his or her narrated self by a personal pronoun which is inappropriate for the current speech situation. Here too various local motivations can be provided.

SEE ALSO: narrative situations; speech representation

References and further reading

Brooke-Rose, Christine (1981) *A Rhetoric of the Unreal*, Cambridge: Cambridge University Press.
Fludernik, Monika (ed.) (1994) *Style* 28.3 (Special issue on 'Second-person Narrative').
Jakobson, Roman (1971) 'Shifters, Verbal Categories, and the Russian Verb', *Selected Writings*, vol. 2, The Hague: Mouton.
Margolin, Uri (2000) 'Telling in the Plural: From Grammar to Ideology', *Poetics Today*, 21.3, 591–618.
Tamir, Nomi (1976) 'Personal Narration and its Linguistic Foundation', *PTL*, 1, 403–29.

URI MARGOLIN

PERSPECTIVE

Originally, perspective was a term used in physiology, natural *science (optics), and studies of *visual art, and in these contexts it often referred to visual phenomena such as distortion, selection, and obstruction (Gombrich 1980). Philosophical uses of the concept tend to be more metaphorical, describing general cognitive processes and proposing a theory of perspectivism according to which our knowledge of the world is inevitably partial and limited by the individual perspective from which it is perceived (Guillén 1971; *see* METAPHOR). Both the visual and the cognitive aspects of the term have been adopted by literary critics and narrative theorists, and in recent reconceptualisations, 'perspective' tends to be restricted to the subjective worldviews of *characters and *narrators. Rather than merely signifying the way a story is told (as in 'narrative perspective') terms such as 'perspective' and 'perspective structure' are now increasingly used to refer to a high-level semantic component of narratives, namely the totality of the world- and belief-models embraced by the fictional individuals of the *storyworld (*see* NARRATIVE SEMANTICS;

POSSIBLE-WORLDS THEORY; TEXT-WORLD APPROACH TO NARRATIVE). The following survey traces and discusses the three major narratological uses of 'perspective' in more detail.

(1) In *structuralist narratology as well as more recent work in narrative theory inspired by structuralist approaches, 'perspective' usually designates stylistic facets of narrative discourse (*see* STORY-DISCOURSE DISTINCTION). Closely related to the term *'point of view', it bridges aspects of *narration and *focalization but is prone to overlooking crucial differences at the level of *narrative transmission. In recent years narratology has coined a number of more specific terms such as narrative *voice (referring to aspects of narratorial discourse) and 'external' and 'internal' focalization (referring to narratorial and character-based viewpoints, respectively) to describe these basic elements more accurately.

(2) As has been demonstrated in constructivist approaches to narrative (Nünning 2000), a more productive way of using the concept of perspective is to apply it to the description of narrators and characters, instances that had largely been reduced to bare 'functions' or *'actants' in earlier structuralist accounts (Rimmon-Kenan 1989: 164; *see* FUNCTION (PROPP)). With recourse to Pfister's (1988 [1977]) definition of perspective in the theory of *drama and paying due attention to the term's cognitive dimension, Nünning (1989) reconceptualised perspective as a character's or narrator's subjective worldview. The factors that determine a character's worldview are his/her knowledge and abilities, psychological disposition, system of norms and values, belief sets, attitudes, motivations, needs and intentions as well as his/her sex, *gender, sexuality, ethnic *identity, and the general economic, political, social, and cultural conditions under which s/he lives. Because of the 'pseudoreality that characters have for the reader' (Ryan 1991: 21), the reader projects onto them everything s/he knows about real persons and the aspects that determine his or her individual view of the world. On the basis of textual data and by attributing personality structures to characters, the reader construes the various character-based perspectives inherent in a text. In addition, by attributing psychological, emotional, cultural, social, and ideological features to the narrating voice, readers can also construe a narratorial perspective (*see* EMOTION AND NARRATIVE; IDEOLOGY AND NARRATIVE). The reconstruction of a narrator's

perspective, however, is only possible in the case of narrators who appear as overtly speaking agents and thus invite the reader to perceive them as human-like persons with individual worldviews (*see* AGENCY).

(3) The sum of a text's perspectival relationships makes up its 'perspective structure', a term originally coined as a category for the interpretation of dramatic texts (Pfister 1988 [1977]) and later adapted for the analysis of narrative texts (Nünning 1989). The main interpretive strategy for establishing a text's perspective structure is to analyse the contrast-and-correspondence relationships obtaining between the individual perspectives. Many textual properties, stylistic features, and *narrative techniques contribute to the construction of a cognitive model of a text's perspective structure (Surkamp 2003): (a) the selection (the number and diversification) of perspectives; (b) the degree of homogeneity between perspectives; (c) the degree of authority and *reliability granted to each fictional individual (*see* AUTHENTICATION); (d) the degree to which a particular perspective is foregrounded or backgrounded; (e) the degree to which a personalised narrator exhibits an individual perspective and/or controls the character-based perspectives (especially in an 'authorial' *narrative situation); (f) the question of whether or not there is a hierarchy among the perspectives resulting from narrative *embedding or framing (*see* FRAMED NARRATIVE).

On the basis of these criteria, different types of perspective structure can be classified according to the degree to which the individual perspectives overlap, differ, or converge. If the perspectives can be integrated into a unified worldview or if a single point of view is privileged, the narrative text has a 'closed' perspective structure (*see* CLOSURE). If the perspectives contrast and contradict each other and if there are unresolved differences between conflicting world-models, the perspective structure of the text remains 'open' (*see* INDETERMINACY). In the latter case, the absence of any prefabricated solutions or of an authoritative, dominating perspective reveals a plurality of conflicting moral and ideological views which are granted equal validity within the text, a scenario typically characterising what Bakhtin terms *polyphony or *heteroglossia.

The semantic concept of perspective structure allows for a correlation between the structural properties of narrative texts and their cultural implications, thus opening up promising areas of investigation for *cultural studies approaches to narrative. For example, the shift to more open and non-hierarchical perspective structures that occurred in English novels between the late Victorian period and Modernism can be shown to reflect a worldview of epistemological scepticism as well as changing attitudes toward gender and imperialism (Surkamp 2003).

SEE ALSO: cognitive narratology; psychological approaches to narrative

References and further reading

Gombrich, Ernst H. (1980) 'Standards of Truth: The Arrested Image and the Moving Eye', *Critical Inquiry*, 7, 237–73.

Guillén, Claudio (1971) 'On the Concept and Metaphor of Perspective', in Claudio Guillén, *Literature as System: Essays towards the Theory of Literary History*, Princeton: Princeton University Press.

Nünning, Ansgar (1989) *Grundzüge eines kommunikationstheoretischen Modells der erzählerischen Vermittlung: Die Funktionen der Erzählinstanz in den Romanen George Eliots*, Trier: WVT.

——(2000) 'On the Perspective Structure of Narrative Texts: Steps Towards a Constructivist Narratology', in Willi van Peer and Seymour Chatman (eds) *New Perspectives on Narrative Perspective*, Albany: State University of New York Press.

Pfister, Manfred (1988 [1977]) *The Theory and Analysis of Drama*, trans. John Halliday, Cambridge: Cambridge University Press.

Rimmon-Kenan, Shlomith (1989) 'How the Model Neglects the Medium: Linguistics, Language, and the Crisis of Narratology', *The Journal of Narrative Technique*, 19.1, 157–66.

Ryan, Marie-Laure (1991) *Possible Worlds, Artificial Intelligence, and Narrative Theory*, Bloomington: Indiana University Press.

Surkamp, Carola (2003) *Die Perspektivenstruktur narrativer Texte: Zu ihrer Theorie und Geschichte im englischen Roman zwischen Viktorianismus und Moderne*, Trier: WVT.

CAROLA SURKAMP

PHENOMENOLOGY OF NARRATIVE

Phenomenology describes formal essentials in the appearance of intentional objects (*see* INTENTIONALITY). Applied to narrative it describes what qualifies texts as *narratives. One feature widely recognised as essential by phenomenologists is resolve: a narrative purports to resolve the *actions it relates. Actions are resolved when the projections representing them are satisfied in a mutual accommodation, one appreciated as supporting a joint meaning for the actions narrated.

This description of narrative suggests to many an analogy that might address issues of personal *identity. The resolution of conflicting actions seems as essential for achieving personality as it is for achieving *narrativity (*see* NARRATIVE THERAPY). Accordingly, phenomenological research into the character of narrative action has often sought to throw light on personal *agency. Ricoeur and Kermode, for example, compared the temporal logic of narrative projections with that of the projections we make of our own actions. Tilley paralleled types of *plot lines with existential expectations in different cultures. MacIntyre put storytelling at the heart of moral agency. Wilkes marked the edges of personhood at the ability to give meaning to one's action in terms of a story.

Basing a rigorous account of personal identity on the *logic of narrative continues to be difficult, however. Two problems persist. (1) With phenomenologists tending to morph into postmodernists, their emphasis on the multiplicity of narratives determining the character of any individual's actions has made them back away from claiming to provide a standard identity account. If no one story has hegemony over any other, no single story can provide an individual's identity. (2) There are two ways to relate personal experience and narrative: either experience has narrative meaning as we perceive it (Carr 1986; Kerby 1991) or it bears only the narrative meaning we impose on it (White 1981). These give us very different takes on the question of personal identity. If actions and *events can only be perceived as narratively structured, our experiences are narratives apart from any narrative abilities we may exert. If, on the other hand, they figure in our awareness before we impose narrative significance upon them, our experience has no essential narrative meaning.

These two problems are related. The claim that humans impose narratives on pre-existing actions and events can be used to buttress the claim that no one story can identify a person, and vice versa. This fault line between what might be termed 'narrative realism' and 'narrative constructivism' divides phenomenologists who apply descriptions of narrative to the question of personal identity.

SEE ALSO: closure; ethical turn; master narrative; narrative as cognitive instrument; tellability

References and further reading

Carr, David (1986) *Time, Narrative and History*, Bloomington: Indiana University Press.
Kerby, Anthony (1991) *Narrative and the Self*, Bloomington: Indiana University Press.
Kermode, Frank (1966) *The Sense of an Ending*, London: Oxford University Press.
MacIntyre, Alasdair (1984) *After Virtue*, Notre Dame: University of Notre Dame Press.
Ricoeur, Paul (1984–88) *Time and Narrative*, 3 vols., trans. Kathleen McLaughlin and David Pellauer (vol. 3 trans. Kathleen Blamey and David Pellauer), Chicago: University of Chicago Press.
Tilley, Allen (1992) *Plot Snakes and the Dynamics of Narrative Experience*, Gainsville: University Press of Florida.
White, Hayden (1981) 'The Value of Narrativity in the Representation of Reality', in W. J. T. Mitchell (ed.) *On Narrative*, Chicago: University of Chicago Press.
Wilkes, K. V. (1988) *Real People: Personal Identity without Thought Experiments*, Oxford: Clarendon Press.

RICHARD C. PRUST

PHILOSOPHICAL NOVEL

Although all novels are philosophical in the sense that they are informed by a particular view of, or philosophy about, the world, however implicit, some very general strands or tendencies in the philosophical novel or the 'novel of ideas' can be identified.

One strand is the anatomy, which, according to Northrop Frye (1957), is one of the four types of prose fiction, together with the *novel, the *romance, and the confession (*see* CONFESSIONAL NARRATIVE). The anatomy is characterised by exuberant displays of learning, a strong interest in ideas and mental attitudes (*see* THOUGHT AND CONSCIOUSNESS REPRESENTATION (LITERATURE)), the use of *characters as mouthpieces for abstract theories, and a satirical attitude towards the pedantry of philosophers (*see* THEMATIC APPROACHES TO NARRATIVE). The narrative is usually very loose-jointed and occasionally features symposium settings. Examples include François Rabelais' *Gargantua and Pantagruel* (1532–1552), Jonathan Swift's *Gulliver's Travels* (1726), Voltaire's *Candide* (1759), Samuel Johnson's *Rasselas* (1759), and the novels of Thomas Love Peacock. The influence of the anatomy is also felt in novels which explicitly present or discuss philosophical positions in an exploratory, satirical, self-conscious, and playful manner (e.g., Cervantes' *Don Quixote* (1605), Lawrence Sterne's *Tristram Shandy* (1759), Herman Melville's *Moby Dick* (1851), James Joyce's *Ulysses* (1922), Umberto Eco's *The Name of the Rose* (1980), and a number of Iris Murdoch's novels; *see* SATIRIC NARRATIVE). *Science fiction such as Philip K. Dick's *Do Androids Dream of Electric Sheep?* (1968) often plays in interesting ways with epistemological and ontological issues such as *identity, the nature of the mind, and our knowledge of other minds. Some philosophical fictions aimed at the popular reading market (e.g., Robert M. Pirsig's *Zen and the Art of Motorcycle Maintenance* (1974) and Jostein Gaarder's *Sophie's World* (1995)) have been surprisingly successful.

Another strand consists of novels which are deeply engaged with problems of philosophy, politics, and morality and which often advance a particular philosophical position. Sometimes this is not made explicit as, for example, when the *plot is used to illustrate a particular ethical dilemma (*see* ETHICAL TURN). This sort of novel is particularly characteristic of the Continental European rather than the English or American tradition (for example, the German novel from Goethe to Thomas Mann). It is often connected with wide, popular philosophical movements that express the *Zeitgeist* such as nihilism in the nineteenth-century Russian novel (Ivan Turgenev and Fyodor Dostoevsky) and existentialism in the twentieth-century French novel (Jean-Paul Sartre and Albert Camus). The relationship between Sartre's fictional and philosophical works is particularly close (see Prince 1968). Some writers such as D. H. Lawrence use their novels to convey a very personal and idiosyncratic philosophy that does not fit into these categories.

Finally, in the *roman à thèse or 'thesis novel', philosophical influences can often shade into political and social philosophies resulting in didactic and polemical approaches to issues of social reform (*see* DIDACTIC NARRATIVE). Examples include Harriet Beecher Stowe's *Uncle Tom's Cabin* (1852), the naturalist novels of Emile Zola, and the 'condition of England' novels of Benjamin Disraeli and Charles Dickens (*Hard Times* (1854)) (*see* REALIST NOVEL).

SEE ALSO: philosophy and narrative

References and further reading

Frye, Northrop (1957) *The Anatomy of Criticism*, Princeton: Princeton University Press.

Prince, Gerald (1968) *Métaphysique et technique dans l'œuvre romanesque de Sartre*, Geneva: Droz.

ALAN PALMER

PHILOSOPHY AND NARRATIVE

In considering the relationships between philosophy and narrative, two lines of discussion appear to be inevitable. The one, more predictable, follows the significance of philosophy in literary narrative and narrative theory, and the other, perhaps more unexpected, the role of narrative as a constitutive part of philosophy. This entry will proceed along both of these lines and will locate some of their key intersections.

To begin with a strong claim, throughout its history, starting with the earliest available sources and proceeding to our own time, philosophy has been indissociable from the relationships between philosophy and narrative. These relationships extend from the role of narrative in philosophical discourse to the role of narrative in the history of philosophy or in placing philosophical inquiry in the context of human history.

The earliest surviving text of Western philosophy, Anaximander's fragment, gives a narrative of justice, applied on a cosmological scale of all existing things: '. . . the source from which existing things derive their existence is also that to which they return at their destruction, according to necessity; for they give justice and make reparation to one another for their injustice, according to the arrangement of Time' (Freeman 1990: 19). Parmenides went even further and offered the fundamentals of philosophical and specifically dialectical reasoning in a narrative poem (*see* NARRATIVE IN POETRY), thus setting into operation a narrative machine of philosophy that has continued its work ever since (Freeman 1990: 41–46). Plato's narratives – for example, his allegorical narrative (following Parmenides) of the progress of the chariot of the soul in *Phaedrus* – are crucial to his works and also to the subsequent history of philosophy (*see* ALLEGORY; PARABLE). Commenting in connection with this tale that it is easy for Socrates 'to make up tales' (275b) while pursuing philosophical argument, Phaedrus himself brings narrative and philosophy together in the very

figure of Socrates as a storyteller. Further, the critique of writing versus speech and thought in *Phaedrus*, made famous by Derrida's work, is also presented by Plato through an allegorical narrative (274c–275b). Both narratives are essential intertexts for Derrida's *Dissemination*, which brings together Plato and Hegel, via Mallarmé's and Sollers's narratives, irreducibly intermixing literature, narrative, and philosophy and thus radically rethinking the relationships among them.

Aristotle, however, appears to have been the first to bring narrative and philosophy together analytically when in chapter 9 of *Poetics* he argued that poetry, specifically the narrative poetry of *drama, is more philosophical than history, by virtue of its dealing with the universal rather than with historical particulars (*see* ANCIENT THEORIES OF NARRATIVE (WESTERN); HISTORIOGRAPHY). *Poetics* thus offered a *philosophy* of narrative that sees literary narrative itself as fundamentally philosophical. It both pinpointed a feature of literary practice crucial to the history of literature from the Greeks to our own time and established the possibility for theoretical investigation of the relationships among philosophy, history, and narrative – a mode of inquiry that extends to our own time and reaches across several disciplines. Drawing on the Aristotelian understanding of poetry (in the broad sense) as philosophical, one can trace philosophical dimensions of narrative in the texts of Greek and Roman literature, through the rise of the modern *novel with Cervantes' *Don Quixote*, through the works of Stendhal, Tolstoi, and Dostoevskii, through the *modernist texts of Proust, Joyce, Musil, Faulkner, and Beckett, to the *postmodern narratives of Nabokov and Pynchon. Such literary works often engage with explicitly philosophical investigations, pursued either by means of literary techniques or else thematically, as in Tolstoi's discussion of the nature of history in *War and Peace* or in Proust's and Musil's incorporation of 'phenomenological' methods of presentation into their novels (*see* NARRATIVE TECHNIQUES; THEMATIC APPROACHES TO NARRATIVE). These aspects of literary practice have led to a philosophically oriented study of narrative literature. One finds this approach in the work of most major twentieth-century critics who worked on narrative, such as Benjamin, Bakhtin, Blanchot, Barthes, and de Man, among many others.

At the same time, the work of these critics reflects the reciprocity of the relationships among literature, philosophy, history, and narrative, and in the process reveals the constitutive (rather than auxiliary) roles of both *narrative* and *history* in philosophical inquiry itself. In the history of this problematic, the work of Hegel has a special significance. Hegel went further than Aristotle or anyone before him in understanding the more complex – mutually entangled and mutually inhibiting – relationships between narrative and philosophy. Hegel was able to do so in part because he argued history to be a fundamental component of philosophy; for Hegel, philosophical concepts inevitably carry within them the history of their emergence, which also entails at least an implicit field of narratives associated with these concepts. Hegel's argument was taken up and critically extended by literature and philosophy of the twentieth century. Beyond the literary works mentioned above, one can think of such developments as Blanchot's analysis of literature and narrative ('narrative voice'; *see* VOICE); Foucault's rethinking of the project of historiography; Deleuze and Guattari's work on capitalism and *psychoanalysis; Jacques Derrida's analysis of 'writing' as the efficacious dynamics of language; de Man's work on allegory and *irony; and Lyotard's framework for understanding postmodernity as incredulity toward metanarratives. Extending and radicalising the program set into operation by Hegel, these theories irreducibly involve the relationships among literature, philosophy, and history – relationships which, from the pre-Socratics on, narrative has helped to establish and continues to enrich.

References and further reading

Aristotle (1984 [4th century BCE]) *Poetics*, trans. Ingram Bywater, in Jonathan Barnes (ed.) *The Complete Works of Aristotle*, vol. 2, Princeton: Princeton University Press.
Blanchot, Maurice (1993 [1969]) *The Infinite Conversation*, trans. Susan Hanson, Minneapolis: University of Minnesota Press.
Deleuze, Gilles, and Felix Guattari (1993 [1980]) *Thousand Plateaus*, trans. Brian Massumi, Minneapolis: University of Minnesota Press.
Derrida, Jacques (1980 [1972]) *Dissemination*, trans. Barbara Johnson, Chicago: University of Chicago Press.
——(1975 [1967]) *Of Grammatology*, trans. Gayatri C. Spivak, Baltimore: Johns Hopkins University Press.
Foucault, Michel (1994 [1966]) *The Order of Things*, New York: Vintage.
Freeman, Kathleen (1990) *Ancilla to Pre-Socratic Philosophers*, Cambridge, Mass.: Harvard University Press.
Hegel, Georg Wilhelm Friedrich (1977 [1807]) *The Phenomenology of Spirit*, trans. A. V. Miller, Oxford: Oxford University Press.
Lyotard, Jean-François (1984 [1979]) *The Postmodern Condition: A Report on Knowledge*, trans. Geoff Bennington and Brian Massumi, Minneapolis: University of Minnesota Press.
de Man, Paul (1996) *Aesthetic Ideology*, Minneapolis: University of Minnesota Press.
Nietzsche, Friedrich (1969 [1888]) *On the Genealogy of Morals and Ecce Homo*, trans. Walter Kaufmann, New York: Vintage.
Plato (1989 [5th century BCE]) *Phaedrus*, trans. Reginald Hackforth, in Edith Hamilton and Huntington Cairns (eds) *The Collected Dialogues of Plato*, Princeton: Princeton University Press.

ARKADY PLOTNITSKY

PHOTOGRAPHS

Photographs differ from other visual representations of an isolated moment in two ways that are crucial to viewers' interpretations. First, the photograph is not only an icon (like all forms of visual representation it resembles its referent) but also an index (it attests to the past existence in our world of a referent of which it is the emanation) (*see* REFERENCE; SEMIOTICS). As a result, as Barthes perceives, we can read in photographs what was ('this has been') and also what will have been or will be (this 'is going to die') (1981: 96). In other words, any photograph of a living being can be read as evidence of the elements that constitute a *minimal narrative: an initial state and an *event that changes it. Second, the polysemy of all visual representation – viewers are sometimes unable to determine even what object or objects are depicted (*see* EXISTENT) – is increased in the case of the photograph. On the one hand the photograph itself, Barthes argues, is a 'continuous message' that comes to us uninterpreted by the brush or pencil marks that already partition a drawing or painting into discrete units and thereby guide what viewers see (1977: 17–20, 43). On the other hand, viewers of photographs, particularly in response to photographs of people or places with which they feel some connection, as Hirsch's analysis of viewing family photographs suggests, project preconceptions that shape what they see.

While art historians typically explore visual art's iconographic illustration of known stories,

Barthes's, Hirsch's, and others' theoretical positions suggest that photographs, even more than other visual representations of a single scene (*see* SCENE (CINEMATIC); SUMMARY AND SCENE), lend themselves to being interpreted as an event in a number of different stories. Any visual representation of an isolated moment, it has been argued, as long as it includes an indication of the present, prior, or subsequent presence of a human or anthropomorphic being, can be read as a 'compressed discourse' (*see* STORY-DISCOURSE DISTINCTION): a single-scene representation that viewers interpret as implying – through depicted associative or indexical values – a story or several different stories (Kafalenos 1996). Telling family history in response to photographs produces stories with varying degrees of historical accuracy and has been shown both to constitute and to change familial relationships (Hirsch 1997). It is also a form of *ekphrasis (the re-representation in words of a visual representation). Examples of ekphrasis in literature *narrativise visually depicted moments often enough, as Heffernan's analysis shows, to suggest that interpreting an isolated moment by considering the events it could cause, or be caused by, is common cognitive practice. Examining photographs by Cindy Sherman, Sonesson notes that depicted indications of whole classes of often trivial action schemata imply temporality (*see* SCRIPTS AND SCHEMATA; TIME IN NARRATIVE). Further, Sonesson argues, several of the features that have been thought to enhance *narrativity are displayed at least as effectively through visual as through verbal representation: external rather than internal events, actions rather than happenings, events involving an agent and a patient, even *disnarrated elements, since images in a series (e.g., *comics) can lead viewers to understand what is happening in one scene in a way that a later scene indicates retrospectively to have been inaccurate.

When words are placed in conjunction with the polysemous image, Barthes (1977: 38–41) proposes, the words function either as 'anchorage' – identifying elements of the depicted scene and guiding interpretations toward one rather than other possible meanings – or, less commonly in the case of the fixed image (as opposed to *film), as 'relay': image and words are complementary elements in a higher-level message that neither alone conveys. Similarly, Kibédi Varga argues that in image-word combinations images are freed from verbal dominance only when the words refuse to describe the images (e.g., the titles of Magritte's paintings) or when images are presented as a series, in which case words are sometimes indispensable and functional and sometimes merely ornamental.

Analysing types of photonarratives (series of photographs, usually with words; *see* CINÉROMAN), Baetens distinguishes between traditional ones in which the words generally dominate and more experimental ones in which the images sometimes dominate. In order to problematise the presence of (even ekphrastic) images in verbal texts, by presenting an ensemble in which the two media 'play antagonistic roles', Robbe-Grillet (1983: 39) published during the 1970s several collaborative narratives, including four photonarratives containing texts he wrote and photographs by David Hamilton (in three) and Irina Ionesco (in the fourth). W. G. Sebald's novels that contain (sometimes 'found') photographs similarly force readers to consider not only how but also whether images and words are related. In addition, Sebald's novels illustrate, through characters' responses to photographs in the narrative world (*see* STORYWORLD), interrelations between photographs, *memory, and storytelling (Long 2003).

Visiting a photographic exhibit in an art gallery, viewers are free to wander at will, each 'narrating' a story in response to the set of photographs by selecting the sequence of the viewing while the 'author' of the exhibit controls content by deciding what will be displayed (Green 1990). Responding to Marie-Françoise Plissart and Benoît Peeters's famous photonarrative *Right of Inspection*, composed of photographs without a parallel verbal text, Derrida determines that because the viewer must choose the path to take through the images, and because the *metalepsis in this photonarrative – in which photographs are *embedded within photographs – increases each image's polysemy, the story does not precede the discourse each viewer/reader narrates. Concluding his commentary with reference to Barthes's insistence on the photograph's necessarily real referent placed before the lens, Derrida suggests that if an art of photography exists it can be seen in this photonarrative's photographed frames that are themselves framed, which, without suspending reference, indefinitely defer the perceptible referent.

SEE ALSO: cognitive narratology; deconstructive approaches to narrative; image and narrative;

indeterminacy; intermediality; media and narrative; pictorial narrativity; postmodern narrative; visual narrativity

References and further reading

Baetens, Jan (2001) 'Going to Heaven: A Missing Link in the History of Photonarrative?', Journal of Narrative Theory, 31.1, 87–105.

Barthes, Roland (1977) Image, Music, Text, trans. Stephen Heath, New York: Hill and Wang.

——(1981) Camera Lucida, trans. Richard Howard, New York: Hill and Wang.

Derrida, Jacques (1998) 'Lecture', trans. David Wills, in Right of Inspection: Photographs by Marie-Françoise Plissart, New York: The Monacelli Press.

Green, Jennifer M. (1990) 'Stories in an Exhibition: Narrative and Nineteenth-Century Photographic Documentary', Journal of Narrative Technique, 20.2, 147–66.

Heffernan, James A. W. (1991) 'Ekphrasis and Representation', New Literary History, 22, 297–316.

Hirsch, Marianne (1997) Family Frames: Photography, Narrative, and Postmemory, Cambridge, Mass.: Harvard University Press.

Kafalenos, Emma (1996) 'Implications of Narrative in Painting and Photography', New Novel Review, 3.2, 54–64.

Kibédi Varga, Áron (1989) 'Criteria for Describing Word-and-Image Relations', Poetics Today, 10, 31–53.

Long, J. J. (2003) 'History, Narrative, and Photography in W. G. Sebald's Die Ausgewanderten', Modern Language Review, 98.1, 117–37.

Robbe-Grillet, Alain (1983) 'Images and Text: A Dialogue', trans. Karlis Racevskis, in Generative Literature and Generative Art: New Essays, Fredericton, NB: York Press.

Sonesson, Göran (1997) 'Mute Narratives: New Issues in the Study of Pictorial Texts', in Ulla-Britta Lagerroth, Hans Lund, and Erik Hedling (eds) Interart Poetics: Essays on the Interrelations of the Arts and Media, Amsterdam: Rodopi.

EMMA KAFALENOS

PICARESQUE NOVEL

The picaresque *novel is the story of a pícaro (sometimes translated as rogue); most characteristically, it is the satiric autobiographical narrative of an orphaned youth who must make his way in the world (see AUTOBIOGRAPHY; LIFE STORY; NARRATION; SATIRIC NARRATIVE). A uniquely flexible and inclusive *genre, the picaresque novel features a variety of protagonists: not only underprivileged adolescents, but also mature men and women, characters of higher social station, or even animals. Its structures can be more or less digressive, with various kinds of embedded stories, dramatic works, and poetry (see EMBEDDING; FRAMED NARRATIVE; NARRATIVE STRUCTURE), and its length, tone, and themes vary considerably. It is, literally, a protean genre. As opposed to the chivalric, pastoral, and sentimental fictional genres, all of which are more *romance than novel, the picaresque may legitimately be considered the first consistently novelistic genre of European letters.

The first, most original, most influential, and best of the picaresque novels is the anonymous satiric short novel Lazarillo de Tormes (1554), a brilliant satire and the first fictional autobiography in European literature. Mateo Alemán's digressive and doctrinal, two-part Guzmán de Alfarache (1599, 1604), often called simply El Pícaro, was in its age the most influential work of the genre. Francisco de Quevedo's extravagant and linguistically brilliant Vida del Buscón (Life of the Swindler, 1626) is generally considered to be the third canonical picaresque novel. In the wake of the extremely popular Guzmán, picaresque fiction was the dominant Spanish fictional genre in the early decades of the seventeenth century. The last great exemplar of the genre, and one of the best, is Estebanillo González (1646), the semi-historical, perhaps (at least partially) legitimately autobiographical, story of a dwarf and court jester.

Lazarillo, Guzmán, and many of the other works of the Spanish genre were translated and read throughout Europe. *Adaptations, sequels, and imitations of the Spanish picaresque novels are to be found at the headwaters of every European national tradition of the novel. Among the major works directly inspired by the Spanish picaresque tradition are Johann Jakob Christoffel von Grimmelshausen's Simplicissimus (1669), Alain-René Lesage's Gil Blas (1715, 1724, 1735), and Daniel Defoe's Moll Flanders (1722), all fundamental early fictions in their national literatures. In more modern times, works like Mark Twain's Huckleberry Finn (1885), Saul Bellow's The Adventures of Augie March (1953), Thomas Mann's Adventures of Felix Krull, Confidence Man (1954), and Luis Zapata's Adonis García, A Picaresque Novel (1979) all relate back to foundational works of the picaresque tradition. There is no way to exaggerate the importance of the Spanish picaresque tradition in the formation, history, and practice of the novel.

SEE ALSO: Bildungsroman; hero

References and further reading

Bjornson, Richard (1977) *The Picaresque Hero in European Fiction*, Madison: University of Wisconsin Press.

Cabo Aseguinolaza, Fernando (1992) *El concepto del género y la literatura picaresca*, Santiago de Compostela: Universidad de Santiago de Compostela.

Dunn, Peter N. (1993) *Spanish Picaresque Fiction: A New Literary History*, Ithaca: Cornell University Press.

Maiorino, Giancarlo (ed.) (1996) *The Picaresque: Tradition and Displacement*, Minneapolis: University of Minnesota Press.

Rico, Francisco (1983) *The Picaresque Novel and Point of View*, trans. Charles Davis with Harry Sieber, Cambridge: Cambridge University Press.

HOWARD MANCING

PICTORIAL NARRATIVITY

Although the most typical realisation of 'narrative' as a fundamental cognitive macro-frame is probably verbal stories, narrative is basically medium-independent or 'transmedial' (*see* INTERMEDIALITY). It consequently does not come as a surprise that *narrativity as the defining quality of *narrative has been attributed to a number of *media and *genres, verbal and otherwise, and also to the visual arts (*see* VISUAL NARRATIVITY).

No one would doubt that pictures can tell stories, especially in view of artworks such as Greek and Roman historical or mythological friezes, the *biblia pauperum* displayed in the stained glass windows of Gothic cathedrals, or the representation of 'dream time stories' in *Australian Aboriginal art. We should also remember the role pictograms play as a means of communicating stories and even in the formation of writing. Thus, intuitively, hardly anyone will find fault with the scholarly description of pictures as narratives or *istorie*, which, after all, has been a received notion in art history at least since the days of Alberti. Yet, as G. E. Lessing already made clear in his *Laokoon*, in spite of the long-established tradition of speaking of 'narrative pictures' the pictorial medium offers considerable resistance to narrativity. This becomes particularly clear if narrativity is conceived of in terms of a plurality of prototypical features, as exemplified by verbal stories (*see* MUSIC AND NARRATIVE).

The disregard for the inherently problematic notion of pictorial narrativity has led scholars such as Steiner to criticise the common 'art-historical usage of the term 'narrative painting' as 'very loose' (1988: 8). This criticism seems especially justified if the narrative potential of *all* pictures is indiscriminately taken for granted. The fact of the matter is that this potential varies widely (and can be zero) and largely depends on genre and *mode of visualisation. Thus, totally abstract art cannot be narrative because representationality is a major characteristic of narratives. If, in assessing the narrative potential of pictures, one concentrates on purely pictorial representations of possible worlds (*see* POSSIBLE-WORLDS THEORY), thereby excluding hybrid media such as the comic strip, two distinctions are especially relevant. Following Kibédi Varga these are, first, two main 'genres', namely single pictures vs. series of pictures, and, second, a differentiation of sub-genres according to the criterion of the presence of one phase or action vs. several phases or *plot strands (*see* NARRATIVE STRUCTURE). Thus, a picture series can be dedicated to one plot or – less commonly – to several parallel plots (resulting in *mono-strand* or *poly-strand picture series*). In an analogous way, a single picture can represent one or more than one phase of a narrative (resulting in *single monophase* or *single polyphase* pictures, respectively).

Among single pictures the polyphase picture (as exemplified by Bosch's triptych *The Haywagon*, whose left part simultaneously recounts three episodes from the book of Genesis) has been abandoned in Western art over the past few centuries, although only gradually so, as Fowler emphasises. This fall from favour was due to the rise of an illusionist aesthetics according to which a picture should imitate only what could be perceived from one particular point of view and point in *time (*see* PERSPECTIVE; POINT OF VIEW (CINEMATIC)). Since the Renaissance this has left the single monophase picture together with the mono-strand picture series (the pluri-strand variant being relatively rare, too) as the most frequent types of potentially narrative pictures. The following sections will therefore use these two types as points of departure for a discussion of general issues of pictorial narrativity.

Narrativity in single monophase pictures

There are single monophase pictures whose narrativity seems indisputable because they contain intermedial references to, or are even detailed transpositions of, scenes of well-known (verbal) narratives. A case in point is John Everett Millais's famous pre-Raphaelite painting *Ophelia*, which visualises the moment just before Ophelia drowns, as narrated by Queen Gertrude in *Hamlet* (IV.vii). Yet, if this reference to a literary story were the only trigger for the beholder to apply the frame 'narrative', the narrativity of such pictures would be parasitically dependent on something that lies outside themselves, namely on stories that are derived from another medium and whose identification would frequently be difficult without the captions beneath the pictures.

However, pictures, including the single monophase picture, also possess genuinely pictorial means of conveying elements of narrativity, such as 'tell-tale' objects, 'atmosphere, light, texture, and spatial relations' (Thomas 2000: 98) – devices that are encountered with particular frequency in Victorian paintings. Another of these devices is the activation of the beholder's general world knowledge and narrative competence (*see* SCRIPTS AND SCHEMATA). In Millais's example the unusualness of the scene, its *tellability, as well as its experiential quality and a suggestion of temporality are conducive to this sort of activation (*see* EXPERIENTIALITY; TIME IN NARRATIVE). A young woman floating in full dress on a brook with flowers in her hand and parted lips as if she were singing is sufficiently unusual to arrest our attention and invites us to make sense of the scene, thereby inciting us to construct an explanatory narrative (*see* NARRATIVE EXPLANATION). Moreover, the flowers depicted by Millais, like countless other objects and situations that create expectations and imply temporality in other pictures, strongly suggest a temporal dimension: there is a bunch of them in the girl's right hand, some have dropped onto the water, and some have been carried by a current to the right of the lower end of her skirt, which indicates that she has been floating on the water for some time. Her clothes, which have kept her afloat, in spite of her amazing carelessness, will presumably not do so for long. Thus, the *character in the picture is caught in a particular moment which, according to our knowledge of narratives and the world, must be preceded by certain causes and may be followed by her death. By inciting such projections the painting arguably displays a central feature of narratives, namely, the meaningful change of a situation.

In pictures with more than one character, what could be described as 'syntactic' or coherence-creating elements of narrativity, e.g., *causality and chronology, can be suggested by other means. Of special importance is body language, such as emotionally charged facial expression or *gestures, in particular when this has a visible effect on other characters (*see* EMOTION AND NARRATIVE). Other devices include the use of symbols or the representation of texts that contain clues about the general meaning of the picture as well as the past or the future of the depicted moment.

However, in connection with such 'pregnant moments' (Lessing), the narrative limits of the single picture come into focus. The most obvious one is the fact that what is depicted is not an actual change of a situation and thus a temporal *event as is typical of narratives, but only the *suggestion* of a change which the viewer is required to *infer*. Consequently, a number of elements remain uncertain which in verbal narratives would be much clearer: the exact nature of the preceding and following state, the causal and teleological implications of the depicted 'pregnant moment' and hence part of its tellability, but also its suspenseful quality (suspense being a vital component of many narratives; *see* SUSPENSE AND SURPRISE). Without the Shakespearean reference it would, for instance, not be evident how in Millais's painting the girl came to float on the water and whether she is about to drown or will eventually be rescued. With its narrative vagueness Millais's painting is typical of many other single pictures: if they are read as potential narratives, they inevitably present gaps of meaning, since essential narrative features are absent or cannot be recognised (*see* GAPPING; INDETERMINACY). The meaningfulness of such pictures thus often remains obscure, if not connected with a narrative outside themselves. In addition, without intermedial allusions a single picture can hardly avoid ambiguities about the exact position of the represented 'pregnant moment' within a narrative.

The reasons for the narrative 'deficiencies' of single pictures derive not only from this specific 'genre' but in part also from the limitations of the pictorial medium as a whole. For instance, pictures by themselves cannot actually represent spoken language, neither as an extradiegetic narratorial *voice nor as a part of diegetic worlds (*see* STORYWORLD). (In verbal narratives *speech representation contributes considerably to meaningful coherence). Nor can pictures transmit, owing to their concentration on visible surfaces, characters' psychological motivations and goals that go beyond simple physiognomic or pathognomic (emotion-related) information. Principles of causality and teleology can therefore be only inferred. In sum, a single picture can never actually *represent* a narrative but at best *metonymically *point to* a story.

Narrativity in picture series

Some of the problems with narrativity that occur in the single picture do not apply to picture series, although others persist, as William Hogarth's well-known *A Rake's Progress* demonstrates (see also Wolf 2003). Even at first glance this sequence of eight plates overtly invites the application of the frame 'narrative' (*see* NARRATIVISATION) because of its serial nature. In other words, picture series like Hogarth's use the convention of 'reading' spatial juxtaposition as an index of chronological sequence and thus imply a crucial narrative feature (*see* SPACE IN NARRATIVE; TEMPORAL ORDERING). Yet, since not all picture series are narratives (for instance, most *allegories of the four seasons are not narrative), further stimuli or manifest features of typical stories are necessary to confirm the choice of the narrative frame: the plates must be representational rather than abstract, and they must depict not merely static *'existents' (e.g., landscapes) but dynamic, temporal events which, in order to open the road to typical narrative experientiality, must involve characters. In addition, picture series frequently use titles as further stimuli of narrativity: in *A Rake's Progress* the reference to Bunyan's allegorical story *The Pilgrim's Progress* and its suggestion of a *biography indicate narrative as the most appropriate interpretive frame.

Like many other picture series, *A Rake's Progress* not only provides the 'building blocks' of typical narratives, notably distinct and recognisable characters (such as Hogarth's 'villain' Rakewell) and a multiphase *action, but also facilitates the application of the frame 'narrative' by creating narrative coherence in a variety of ways. A device of major importance is the use of the written word. As is the case with single pictures, language can appear not only in *paratexts (captions) but also in the plates themselves, e.g., in represented letter texts, pamphlets, or inscriptions. In addition to clarifying relations within one plate and to pointing beyond its boundaries, the use of language in the picture series can also establish coherence and meaning for the whole sequence. Generally, the inclusion of the written word enables painter and beholder to compensate for the actual absence of (spoken) language from pictorial representation. Thus, the representation of texts can identify elements of the depicted world (e.g., Sarah Young's name), explain reactions (as does the visible part of a letter of loan rejection for Rakewell's downcast look), and function as a substitute for authorial comments (*see* COMMENTARY). The combination of pictures with words that makes up for the narrative 'deficiencies' of the pictorial medium has been felt to be so successful that its systematic use has led to the emergence of the comic strip as a major narrative medium (*see* COMICS AND GRAPHIC NOVEL; IMAGE AND NARRATIVE).

However, the picture series also possesses purely medium-specific, pictorial means of eliciting narrativity. For instance, it can use the same devices as the single picture, such as indexical facial expressions and gestures. Yet generally, and not surprisingly, the picture series by far surpasses single pictures in its ability to represent an action that unfolds in time and points to preceding causes and future developments. The inference of causal relations is facilitated here by the Western convention of 'reading' individual as well as subsequent pictures from left to right. Further means of creating narrative meaning are ironic mirrorings of the central scene in secondary actions and iconographic, 'intramedial' references (*see* IRONY). An example of ironic mirroring is the image of a couple of dogs in the background of the wedding scene, laying bare the base motivation for the marriage. As for iconographic reference, it is illustrated by the last plate, where a group composed of the agonising Rakewell and his weeping beloved recalls Christ's deposition from the cross and critically comments on the rake's non-Christian life.

A sophisticated, self-referential device that creates coherence and meaning both within and between plates is the use of pictures within pictures (*see* METALEPSIS; REFLEXIVITY). This technique of the *mise en abyme* is used by Hogarth in plate three, for instance, where a map entitled 'totus mundus' is set on fire. This replaces an authorial comment which would foreshadow the disastrous progress of the rake's life and criticise the moral state of the world. The use of allegories and symbols, already a narrative device in the single picture, is another means of interlinking the plates of a picture series, as is the case with the repeated reference to fire in *A Rake's Progress*: in Hogarth's work this symbol, together with the reference to Nero in plate three (as a further *mise en abyme*), indicates the moralising theme of (self-)destruction. A particularly efficient way of suggesting the unity of the series is the depiction of recurrent characters, whose identity is recognisable in their shape, physiognomy, or mode of dress. Perhaps the most important way of establishing narrative coherence by purely painterly means is – again as in the single picture – the anchoring of the sequence of plates in the viewers' general world knowledge and cognitive scripts (*see* STORY SCHEMATA AND CAUSAL STRUCTURE). It is indeed due to a familiar script that we understand what happens to Rakewell in Hogarth's 'Gambling House Scene', where his heavy loss of money is the reason for his visible despair, as well as for his imprisonment in the following plate.

All these devices explain how the individual plates of a picture series such as *A Rake's Progress* can in fact be read as a meaningful narrative. In Hogarth's case it is the story of a middle-class man who after his father's death escapes from a miserly life (plate (1) to one of excessive luxury (2) and debauch (3); is disloyal to a woman who really cares for him and even intercedes for him when he is threatened with being arrested (4); marries for purely financial reasons (5); yet, owing to his extravagance involving gambling (6), is imprisoned (7) and ends up in a mental asylum (8)).

Hogarth's picture series is exemplary in the extent of its realisation of the narrative potential of the pictorial medium. *A Rake's Progress* provides essential narrative 'building blocks' and, in typical narrative fashion, links them to one another as well as to external contexts. Thus, a story emerges from the frozen moments of eight pictures that transforms spatial views of possible worlds into consecutive *chronotopes, includes causal connections among them, and is propelled by a clear (in this case downward) teleology. This teleology is exploited for a moral point and, thanks to the spectacular nature of the rake's fall, also ensures the didactic *tellability* of the narrative (*see* DIDACTIC NARRATIVE). Finally, the series displays the typical narrative qualities of representationality, experientiality, and meaningfulness and moreover permits the beholder to enter into a state of aesthetic illusion (*see* IMMERSION).

Yet the strong narrativity of *A Rake's Progress*, which is enhanced by the fictionality of a story that Hogarth can thus freely rearrange according to a meaningful scheme (*see* FICTION, THEORIES OF), should not conceal the fact that the pictorial medium here, as in similar cases, also imposes limits. This applies first and foremost to the gaps and areas of indeterminacy between individual plates, which create problems with elements of narrative 'syntax', such as exact chronology (e.g., the indication of the time that has elapsed between the depicted scenes), but also causality and teleology. Such areas of indeterminacy can hardly be avoided, except sometimes by resorting to verbal paratexts (for instance, why precisely is Rakewell transferred from a prison to a mental asylum?). The lack of narrative precision that is typical of the pictorial medium also applies to a species of causal relations, namely the motivations of characters (thus, one can only guess why Rakewell does not marry his beloved Sarah), as well as to the distinction between unique and iterative actions. Last but not least, even a serial use of the pictorial medium can barely indicate 'disnarrated elements' (*see* DISNARRATED, THE), as it cannot represent detailed alternative developments and characters' thought-worlds that eventually are not realised in the story (*see* THOUGHT AND CONSCIOUSNESS REPRESENTATION (LITERATURE)). As a result, the suspense and the eventfulness which in verbal narratives often characterise such possibilities and the choices leading to their non-realisation get lost.

Pictorial narrativity reconsidered

As our examples have shown, the pictorial medium has problems with narrativity and requires a 'reader' who is much more active in (re-)constructing a narrative than would be necessary in verbal texts. This is even true of the apparently most natural narrative form of painting, the picture series. Yet the limitations of the pictorial medium do not prevent it from realising various degrees of narrativity: it comes relatively close to typical narratives in picture series, some of which can be called genuinely narrative, while a single picture can at best be termed indexically narrative. Yet, even if the interpretive frame 'narrative' only marginally fits single pictures, it can nevertheless enhance our 'reading' of them.

However, just as not all language use is narrative, not all pictures are narrative (this applies not only to still lives but also to pictures implying a temporal dimension such as chronologically ordered meteorological maps for the same region, or representations of clocks or vehicles that suggest motion and thus temporality). Of course, assessing the narrativity of individual cases depends very much on one's concept of narrativity in the first place. In view of the many media that can participate in narrativity the best conception is arguably one that permits degrees of narrativity. This not only allows the critic to differentiate between media (e.g., verbal literature and *film as media with high narrative potentials as opposed to music with a low potential) but also between different genres inside individual (macro-)media: within verbal literature, the *novel has a greater potential for narrativity than lyric poetry and in this resembles the picture series, whose potential is clearly greater than that of single pictures. Yet, whatever conceptualisation is chosen, the potential narrativity of pictures remains undisputed.

SEE ALSO: mimesis; photographs; reference; semiotics

References and further reading

Brilliant, Richard (1984) *Visual Narratives: Storytelling in Etruscan and Roman Art*, Ithaca, NY: Cornell University Press.
Dieterle, Bernard (1988) *Erzählte Bilder: Zum narrativen Umgang mit Gemälden*, Marburg: Hitzeroth.
Fowler, Alastair (2003) *Renaissance Realism: Narrative Images in Literature and Art*, Oxford: Oxford University Press.
Kemp, Wolfgang (1989) 'Ellipsen, Analepsen, Gleichzeitigkeiten: Schwierige Aufgaben für die Bilderzählung', in Wolfgang Kemp (ed.) *Der Text des Bildes: Möglichkeiten und Mittel eigenständiger Bilderzählung*, Munich: edition text + kritik.
Kibédi Varga, Áron (1990) 'Visuelle Argumentation und visuelle Narrativität', in Wolfgang Harms (ed.) *Text und Bild, Bild und Text: DFG-Symposion 1988*, Stuttgart: Metzler.
Kunzle, David (1973) *History of the Comic Strip*, Berkeley: University of California Press.
Lessing, Gotthold Ephraim (1984 [1766]) *Laocoon: An Essay on the Limits of Painting and Poetry*, trans. Edward Allen McCormick, Baltimore: Johns Hopkins University Press.
Ryan, Marie-Laure (1992) 'The Modes of Narrativity and Their Visual Metaphors', *Style*, 26, 368–87.
Schaeffer, Jean-Marie (2002) 'Narration visuelle et interprétation', in Mireille Ribière and Jan Baetens (eds) *Time, Narrative and the Fixed Image/Temps, narration et image fixe*, Amsterdam: Rodopi.
Sonesson, Göran (1997) 'Mute Narratives: New Issues in the Study of Pictorial Texts', in Ulla-Britta Lagerroth, Hans Lund, and Erik Hedling (eds) *Interart Poetics: Essays on the Interrelations of the Arts and Media*, Amsterdam: Rodopi.
Steiner, Wendy (1988) *Pictures of Romance: Form against Context in Painting and Literature*, Chicago: University of Chicago Press.
Thomas, Julia (2000) *Victorian Narrative Painting*, London: Tate Publishing.
Wolf, Werner (2003) 'Narrative and Narrativity: A Narratological Reconceptualization and Its Applicability to the Visual Arts', *Word & Image*, 19, 180–97.
——(2004) '"Cross the Border – Close that Gap": Towards an Intermedial Narratology', *EJES*, 8.1 ('Beyond Narratology'), 81–103.

WERNER WOLF

PLOT

Despite its apparent simplicity of reference, *plot* is one of the most elusive terms in narrative theory. Narrative theorists have used the term to refer to a variety of different phenomena. Many key definitions of *narrative hinge on the aspect of temporal sequentiality, and the repeated attempts to redefine the parameters of plot reflect both the centrality and the complexity of the temporal dimension of narrative (*see* TIME IN NARRATIVE).

Many basic definitions and interpretations of plot from the first half of the twentieth century (including those from structuralism) either define it in relation to the concept of story, or even treat it synonymously with story (*see* STORY-DISCOURSE DISTINCTION; STRUCTURALIST NARRATOLOGY). The term has also been used as a convenient English translation for the *Russian Formalist concept sjuzhet. In the *poststructuralist period, narrative theory substantially expanded the frontiers of the concept: plot has been explored as an act of gender construction, as a sense-making operation or mental configuration, as a force which affects the reader as a narrative unfolds, and as the interplay of virtual and actual narrative worlds.

Plot in relation to story

Many theories of plot have one thing in common: they see plot as different from story, the basic chronology of *events, out of which something more complex, plot, is constructed. The constructedness of plot in comparison to story is already evident in the fact that one can speak of 'telling a story', but not of 'telling a plot'. The developmental history of plot models reflects the increasing recognition that plot lies in the telling and in the understanding of a narrative's story.

Theories of plot can be differentiated from each other in terms of precisely how they see plot as being different from story. In classical literary theory, Aristotle's concept of *mythos* formulates plot as the conversion of the bare bones of story into a tightly structured aesthetic unit with a beginning, middle and an end (*see* ANCIENT THEORIES OF NARRATIVE (WESTERN); NARRATIVE UNITS). E. M. Forster defined plot as consisting in the creation (and also the suspenseful suppression) of causal connections between the individual events that constitute the chronology of the story (*see* CAUSALITY; SUSPENSE AND SURPRISE; TEMPORAL ORDERING). For Forster plot is superior to story, with an emphasis on causality as opposed to mere chronology: 'The king died and then the queen died' is a story. 'The king died, and then the queen died of grief' is a plot (Forster 1990 [1927]: 87). By contrast, the Russian Formalists Tomashevskii and Shklovskii focused on the sjuzhet's rearrangement of the linear sequence of the fabula and the resulting subversion of the causal-linear structures of the chronological pattern.

Many structuralist plot models did not focus on plot's transmutation of story but tried to map the grammar or *langue* of plot by uncovering recurrent patterns in the stories told in a corpus of narratives (*see* STORY GRAMMARS). This form of plot analysis, taking its lead from Saussurian linguistics, essentially attempted to reduce a number of narrative texts to a minimal pattern by summarising their stories and comparing them with each other. In this method of plot analysis, variation is backgrounded and similarities are paramount. Todorov (1977 [1971]: 110), for example, sees the construction of story summaries as the prerequisite to the study of plot. Propp's theory of the Russian *folktale* was the first of many such models; Propp discovered basic recurrent patterns across a corpus of folktales which he saw conforming to a maximum of thirty-one 'functions' (character-bound types of *action*), as well as seven 'spheres of action' involving eight character roles (*see* ACTANT; FUNCTION (PROPP)). A different variant of the story-condensification method was practised by the anthropologist Lévi-Strauss in his analysis of the structure of the Oedipus myth, which he reconfigured in terms of binary oppositions (*see* ETHNOGRAPHIC APPROACHES TO NARRATIVE; MYTHEME). In a different, less story-oriented approach, Bremond attempted to map the dynamic pattern underlying plot by seeing it as comprising the virtual courses of events which may be desired or striven for by characters, but which may never actually occur in the *storyworld*. Bremond's approach is notable because it considers the role of *alternative courses of events* as part of plot. Bremond expresses his conception of plot in terms of a 'network of possibilities' and maps this as a three-phased (triadic) branching model which encompasses an initial situation and both the actualisation and non-actualisation of the next stage in the narrative.

Other studies produced a variety of genre-based plot models based both on story and more complex understandings of plot (*see* GENRE THEORY IN NARRATIVE STUDIES). Crane distinguishes between different types of subject matter which he calls plots of action, *character*, and *thought* (1952: 620). Frye (1957: 162ff.) identifies four 'generic plots' in his 'theory of myths': comedy, *romance*, tragedy, and irony/satire (*see* IRONY; MYTH: THEMATIC APPROACHES; PLOT TYPES; SATIRIC NARRATIVE).

The story-discourse distinction (itself based on the Russian Formalists' distinction between fabula and sjuzhet) is also part of the theory of plot, since sjuzhet can and has been translated either as 'discourse' or 'plot'. Chatman defines plot as 'story-as-discoursed': 'The events in the story are turned into a plot by its discourse, the modus of presentation' (1978: 43). Sternberg's study of the effect on the reader of different ways of presenting expositional information in the narrative, and Genette's influential theory of *order* and anachrony, which studies a narrative's deviation from story order, are also closely related to the concept of plot (*see* EXPOSITION).

Many of these models were later subject to criticisms which reflected the sense that plot, and indeed the spirit of *narrativity*, had managed to evade the systematic but reductive grid that structuralism had set up. Brooks and Ricoeur are both critical of structuralist models for their static naming of parts and 'their failure to engage the movement and dynamic of narrative' (Brooks 1992 [1984]: 20; *see* NARRATIVE DYNAMICS): 'to know all the roles – *is not yet to know any plot whatsoever*' (Ricoeur 1984–88; vol 1: 43). New departures in plot theory led to a reconfiguration of the term in a variety of theoretical directions: *cognitive, *feminist, philosophical, psychoanalytic, ethical, and ontological (*see* ETHICAL TURN; PHILOSOPHY AND NARRATIVE; POSSIBLE-WORLDS THEORY; PSYCHO-ANALYSIS AND NARRRATIVE).

Plot as gender construction

The feminist analysis of plot is primarily concerned with the (stereotypical) allocation and limitation of roles in narrative fiction due to a protagonist's gender. In the history of narrative fiction, gender discrimination was long practiced because major roles and key plot types were reserved for male characters. The historical diversification of plot types for women, which occurred in the early twentieth century, reflected the watershed of female emancipation. In studying eighteenth-century fiction, Miller (using a distinction first made by Greimas) distinguishes between 'euphoric' and 'dysphoric' texts: on the one hand the heroine's course in life can follow a trajectory of ascent in society with final integration, or on the other hand the heroine may die in the flower of youth. DuPlessis (1985) differentiates between the female protagonist as *'hero', in which she is an inde-pendent agent in her own 'quest plot', and as 'heroine', in which she is constrained within a love or 'romance' plot (*see* AGENCY). Hirsch (1989: 59) observes that pre-twentieth century heroines 'have a plot only insofar as it leads them to their eventual and inevitable marriages'. Feminist plot analysis also involved the deductive evaluation of plot absences as well as presences. Hirsch (1989) charts the development of the 'mother/daughter plot' in fiction, focusing on the striking absence of mother/daughter relationships in pre-twentieth century fiction.

Plot as mental configuration

Ricoeur and Brooks both see plot as the product of an act of mental construction (*see* NARRATIVE COMPREHENSION; PSYCHOLOGICAL APPROACHES TO NARRATIVE). Ricoeur separates out the sense-making activity brought to plots by using the related term *'emplotment', which for him refers to 'the dynamic character of the configurating operation' (Ricoeur 1984–88; vol 1: 65). For Brooks plot is not localisable as a single definition but has many manifestations. His psychoanalytic model comprehends plot as a force which drives the reader and which he calls 'narrative desire' or 'textual erotics' (*see* DESIRE). Brooks describes the

readerly desire aroused prior to the consummation of *closure as 'the *anticipation of retrospection*' (23). Ultimately, however, the reader's narrative desire for definitive closure is frustrated by the recognition that the 'mastertext is not available, [so that] we are condemned to the reading of erroneous plots' (142) (*see* MASTER NARRATIVE).

Cognitive approaches to plot centre on the understanding that plot and the mental operation of emplotment involve the attempt to make sense of a larger, unorganised entity by imposing some kind of reductive and selective explicative system of order on it. This view of plot as a mapping operation involving cognitive, temporal, and spatial aspects is stressed by Brooks (1992 [1984]: 11–12), who enumerates four semantic divisions of plot: the 'measured area of land', the 'ground plan' or 'diagram', the 'series of events consisting of an outline of the action of a narrative or drama' and the 'secret plan to accomplish a hostile or illegal purpose'. Beer implies a similar understanding of plot as referring to the 'organizing principles of [. . .] thinking' (1983: 47). In her specific investi-gation the concept of plot refers to the 'evolu-tionary metaphor' contained in Darwin's theory and its impact on man's hitherto anthropocentric conception of life. Other more recent approaches to plot as a system of explanation focus on the varied configurations of the explanatory systems of chance and causality (*see* NARRATIVE AS COGNITIVE INSTRUMENT; NARRATIVE EXPLANATION).

From a *historiographical position, White equates the term plot with narrative closure and thus views it as an ideological strategy which can be used to impose an artificial or literary structure on chronologies of events (*see* IDEOLOGY AND NARRATIVE). He is sceptical of plot in the Aristotelian sense, precisely because of its imposi-tion of a rigid and limited structure on the larger flow of events and time.

Plot and the narrative dynamics of progression and tellability

Other recent models have perceived plot as a dynamic structure which exists before closure creates the kind of rigid configuration focused on by White. This approach sees plot as the open, fluid, and dynamic patterning of events, precisely because, seen from a pre-closure position, plot is still moving towards the final organising telos of the narrative.

In his concept of *narrative progression, Phelan proposes a *rhetorical model which sees plot as a movement with a particular affective power on the reader (*see* AUDIENCE; READER-RESPONSE THEORY). Studying a narrative's progression involves investigating 'how authors generate, sustain, develop, and resolve readers' interests in narrative' (1989: 15). Phelan focuses on how a narrative's design, particularly its ending, is determined by its beginning and middle. The understanding of plot involved in the concept of progression concerns the interplay between the representation of character and the resolution of 'instabilities' in the story, and their effect on the reader's own judgement and the 'experiential dynamics' of the narrative. Narrative progression therefore concerns the process by which narratives are 'developing wholes' (15) moving towards closure. However, as Phelan shows, only some narratives reach a state of 'completeness' in their ultimate overall design, because, in addition to coming to a point of closure, they also resolve the instabilities they have created.

Applying *possible-worlds theory to narrative fiction, Ryan (1991) proposes understanding plot as the aggregate of a number of different worlds (domains) represented in the text: these worlds consist primarily of events projected within the subjective worlds of characters' minds (*see* TEXT-WORLD APPROACH TO NARRATIVE). A radical extension of Bremond's original idea of plot as a 'network of possibilities', Ryan's approach substantially revises the traditional structuralist conceptions of plot either as a story summary or as the discourse's rearrangement of story. Plot in this definition is the interaction of virtual and actual worlds (*see* MODALITY; VIRTUALITY). The 'private' worlds of characters (constituted by their wishes, knowledge, intentions, and obligations) can deviate from or be in *conflict with the 'reality' of the textual actual world (TAW), thereby generating *tellability – the stuff of interesting narrative and absorbing plots. Ryan's concept of the 'diversification principle' refers to tellable narratives with an ontologically pluralistic event structure, in which conflict is generated by clashes between alternate possible worlds; by contrast, uninteresting plots lack diversification into actual and virtual worlds.

The above range of applications and interpretations show that plot can never be arrested in one clear and stable definition. The plurality of plot theories and definitions reveals the sheer impossibility of isolating the essential nature of plot due to the intricate dynamics of the temporal dimension of narrative. 'Plot' itself is thus too complex to be satisfactorily enclosed or 'plotted' by one definition.

SEE ALSO: narrative structure; narrative techniques

References and further reading

Beer, Gillian (1983) *Darwin's Plots: Evolutionary Narrative in Darwin, George Eliot and Nineteenth-Century Fiction*, London: Routledge & Kegan Paul.

Bremond, Claude (1980 [1966]) 'The Logic of Narrative Possibilities', *New Literary History*, 11, 387–411.

Brooks, Peter (1992 [1984]) *Reading for the Plot: Design and Intention in Narrative*, Cambridge, Mass.: Harvard University Press.

Chatman, Seymour (1978) *Story and Discourse: Narrative Structure in Fiction and Film*, Ithaca: Cornell University Press.

Crane, R. S. (1952) 'The Concept of Plot and the Plot of *Tom Jones*', in R. S. Crane (ed.) *Critics and Criticism*, Chicago: University of Chicago Press.

DuPlessis, Rachel Blau (1985) *Writing Beyond the Ending: Narrative Strategies of Twentieth-Century Women Writers*, Bloomington: Indiana University Press.

Forster, E. M. (1990 [1927]) *Aspects of the Novel*, Harmondsworth: Penguin.

Frye, Northrop (1957) *Anatomy of Criticism: Four Essays*, Princeton: Princeton University Press.

Hirsch, Marianne (1989) *The Mother/Daughter Plot: Narrative, Psychoanalysis, Feminism*, Bloomington: Indiana University Press.

Lévi-Strauss, Claude (1963 [1958]) *Structural Anthropology*, trans. Claire Jacobson and Brooke Grundfest Schoepf, Harmondsworth: Penguin.

Miller, Nancy K (1980) *The Heroine's Text: Readings in the French and English Novel, 1722–1782*, New York: Columbia University Press.

Phelan, James (1989) *Reading People, Reading Plots: Character, Progression, and the Interpretation of Narrative*, Chicago: University of Chicago Press.

Propp, Vladimir (1968 [1928]) *Morphology of the Folktale*, trans. Laurence Scott, revised by Louis A. Wagner, Austin: University of Texas Press.

Ricoeur, Paul (1984–1988) *Time and Narrative*, 3 vols, trans. K. McLaughlin and D. Pellauer, Chicago: University of Chicago Press.

Ryan, Marie-Laure (1991) *Possible Worlds, Artificial Intelligence and Narrative Theory*, Bloomington: Indiana University Press.

Sternberg, Meir (1978) *Expositional Modes and Temporal Ordering in Fiction*, Baltimore: Johns Hopkins University Press.

Todorov, Tzvetan (1977 [1971]) *The Poetics of Prose*, trans. Richard Howard, Ithaca, NY: Cornell University Press.

White, Hayden (1980) 'The Value of Narrativity in the Representation of Reality', in W. J. T. Mitchell (ed.) *On Narrative*, Chicago: University of Chicago Press.

HILARY P. DANNENBERG

PLOT TYPES

Theories of *plot have almost invariably produced categorisations of plot. Often the understanding of 'plot' used in the concept of 'plot type' has more to do with the story that a narrative tells than with more complex conceptualisations of plot. Consequently, the study of plot types often focuses on the basic scheme of *events in a narrative. Plot categorisations can have either a *thematic or a structural focus, or combine both these aspects. Plot types range from the definition of fundamental patterns occurring in narrative to distinctions which divide narrative texts into sub-genres (*see* GENRE THEORY IN NARRATIVE STUDIES; TEXT-TYPE APPROACH TO NARRATIVE). The identification of plot types also overlaps with the question of *narrative structure, but the latter tends to focus more exclusively on basic techniques of narrative construction without considering thematic patterns (*see* NARRATIVE TECHNIQUES).

A simple example of a plot type is Bremond's distinction between two types of narrative movement: improvement and deterioration; Bremond describes narrative as having a cyclical pattern which alternates between these two types. A more complex example is Propp's isolation of thirty-one functions or character acts in the Russian *folktale (*see* FUNCTION (PROPP)).

Genre-based categories of plot are widespread in narrative theory: Crane defines plot types according to the narrative's subject matter, distinguishing between plots of *action, *character, and *thought. Frye's archetypal theory of *myths distinguishes between four 'generic plots' – comedy, *romance, tragedy, and irony/satire – which he sees as being fundamental narrative categories over and above literary genres (*see* ARCHETYPAL PATTERNS; IRONY; SATIRIC NARRATIVE). Todorov and Eco both use the question of repeated formulae, i.e., whether a narrative rigidly conforms to a plot type, to make a fundamental distinction between popular and high forms of narrative. Whereas popular fiction, for example the *detective story, relies on the repetition of a basic plot formula, the classics of

high literature each deviate in an original way from any previous set formula. For Eco (1981 [1979]: 160) repetition in a genre with a formulaic plot gives the reader pleasure because it allows him 'to recognize something he has already seen and of which he has grown fond'. The structure of this type of plot, Eco concludes, leads the reader to 'imaginative laziness'; it 'creates escape by narrating, not the Unknown, but the Already Known'.

Feminist criticism has identified a plethora of plot types which focus on the life trajectories and roles of female characters in narrative fiction (*see* FEMINIST NARRATOLOGY; GENDER STUDIES; LIFE STORY). One fundamental distinction is between the 'quest plot' and the 'romance plot'. The quest plot involves a 'progressive, goal-oriented search with stages, obstacles and "battles"' (DuPlessis 1985: 200) and has been used more frequently in the depiction of male characters than in the portrayal of females. In the 'romance plot', meanwhile, the role of the female character is completely subordinated to the *telos* of love and marriage (*see* ROMANCE NOVEL). Abel charts how the 'maternal subplot' and the 'plot of female bonding' gradually emerge to take their place in narrative fiction alongside the more traditional 'plot of heterosexual love'. Gutenberg offers the most comprehensive feminist survey of plot types to date, mapping variants of the romance plot (courtship plot, seduction plot, wedlock plot), the quest plot (social and spiritual quest, initiation plot, *coming-out plot, limit plot), and the family plot (generation plot, mother-daughter plot, sister plot, group plot, friendship plot) (*see* FAMILY CHRONICLE).

Brooks' psychoanalytical approach to plot also produces a Freudian array of plot types (*see* PSYCHOANALYSIS AND NARRATIVE). He shows how individual texts can be read as the battleground of different systems of signification. Thus, in Dickens' *Great Expectations*, 'official' or 'censoring' plots stand over 'repressed' plots, with the result that 'Pip has misread the plot of his life' (1992 [1984]: 130).

Ryan's (1991) definition of plot as the product of *conflicts between the various private worlds of the character domains and the actual state of affairs in the narrative world (the textual actual world or TAW) leads to a new typology of plot defined according to the specific dynamics of *conflict (*see* POSSIBLE-WORLDS THEORY). Key forms of conflict within Ryan's typology are: the conflict between the different private worlds of a single character's domain (e.g., between the Wish-world of their *desires and the moral standards of their Obligation-world); a conflict between the TAW and private world of a character, which can produce a quest plot; a difference between the Obligation-world of a character and the TAW, producing a situation of moral conflict; and conflicts and inconsistencies between the Knowledge-world of characters and the TAW, which can lead to information deficits and can generate various plots involving error (tragedy), enigma (mystery stories), and deceit (comedies, *fairy tales, spy stories).

A more recent trend in the study of plot types has been to trace the development of more specific plots in narrative fiction. Bueler investigates the 'tested woman plot', and Dannenberg charts the varied forms of 'the coincidence plot'.

References and further reading

Abel, Elizabeth (1983) 'Narrative Structure(s) and Female Development: The Case of *Mrs Dalloway*', in Elizabeth Abel, Marianne Hirsch, and Elizabeth Langland (eds) *The Voyage In: Fictions of Female Development*, Hanover, NH: University Press of New England.

Bremond, Claude (1970) 'Morphology of the French Folktale', *Semiotica*, 2, 247–76.

Brooks, Peter (1992 [1984]) *Reading for the Plot: Design and Intention in Narrative*, Cambridge, Mass.: Harvard University Press.

Bueler, Lois E. (2001) *The Tested Woman Plot: Women's Choices, Men's Judgment, and the Shaping of Stories*, Columbus, Ohio: Ohio State University Press.

Crane, R. S. (1952) 'The Concept of Plot and the Plot of *Tom Jones*', in R. S. Crane (ed.) *Critics and Criticism*, Chicago: University of Chicago Press.

Dannenberg, Hilary P. (2004) 'A Poetics of Coincidence in Narrative Fiction', *Poetics Today*, 25.3, 399–436.

DuPlessis, Rachel Blau (1985) *Writing Beyond the Ending: Narrative Strategies of Twentieth-Century Women Writers*, Bloomington: Indiana University Press.

Eco, Umberto (1981 [1979]) *The Role of the Reader: Explorations in the Semiotics of Texts*, London: Hutchinson.

Frye, Northrop (1957) *Anatomy of Criticism: Four Essays*, Princeton: Princeton University Press.

Gutenberg, Andrea (2000) *Mögliche Welten: Plot und Sinnstiftung im englischen Frauenroman*, Heidelberg: Winter.

Propp, Vladimir (1968 [1928]) *Morphology of the Folktale*, trans. Laurence Scott, revised by Louis A. Wagner, Austin: University of Texas Press.

Ryan, Marie-Laure (1991) *Possible Worlds, Artificial Intelligence and Narrative Theory*, Bloomington: Indiana University Press.

Todorov, Tzvetan (1977 [1971]) *The Poetics of Prose*, trans. R. Howard, Ithaca, NY: Cornell University Press.

HILARY P. DANNENBERG

POINT

That which must be conveyed to an *audience to ensure the success of a communicative act. In narrative, point contributes to *tellability. The concept is particularly useful in those narrative *genres that concentrate interest in a specific moment or formula, such as the punch line of a *joke or the moral of a *fable. In literary narrative, by contrast, points of interest are generally varied and distributed throughout the text. *See* CONVERSATIONAL STORYTELLING.

POINT OF ATTACK

The *event chosen to initiate the *action line of a story. There are three main options: (1) a story beginning *ab ovo* typically begins with the birth of the protagonist; (2) for a beginning *in medias res, the point of attack is set close to the climax of the action; (3) for a beginning *in ultimas res*, the point of attack occurs near the end. *See* EXPOSITION (also: EPIC; FREYTAG'S TRIANGLE).

POINT OF VIEW (CINEMATIC)

At the simplest level, point of view (POV) refers to the representation of what a *character sees, as in a POV *shot. More abstractly, it can refer to the attitudes and tendencies of a cinematic *narrator. Theorists concerned with the first category usually centre their arguments on cinema-specific techniques, such as editing; theorists concerned with the second usually connect their arguments to more general narratological approaches.

Branigan has offered the most detailed analysis of POV, in its narrow sense. A POV structure typically employs two shots. The first shot (Branigan calls it the 'point/glance' shot) shows a character looking at something off screen. The second shot (the 'point/object' shot) shows an object photographed from roughly the point in *space represented in the first shot (*see* EXISTENT). The point/glance shot cues the spectator to comprehend the point/object shot as the representation of the character's visual POV. The point/object shot is often called the 'POV shot'. This basic structure can be varied in several ways: the point/object shot can appear before the point/glance shot, the point/object shot can be sandwiched between two point/glance shots, and so on.

According to Bordwell and Thompson, the POV technique is a subset of a more general technique, the eyeline match. An eyeline match uses a glance to connect two spaces, but it is not necessary for the camera to be close to the glance's point of view in the object shot. The eyeline match is common in the shot/reverse-shot technique, which alternates between two speakers during a *dialogue scene.

These mainstream editing techniques are subjected to a rigorous analysis in the psychoanalytic 'suture' theory (see PSYCHOANALYSIS AND NARRATIVE). According to Dayan, the spectator's first response upon seeing any film *image is pleasure in the image's unity and presence. Soon, the viewer becomes aware of the frame, and the initial pleasure is replaced by an anxious awareness of absence, as the spectator realises that his or her view is necessarily incomplete. The view has been framed by another ('the Absent One'). Next, the film cuts to a shot showing a character looking. This produces two effects. First, the new image shows the previously absent space, allowing the illusion of presence to (momentarily) return. The film has opened a gap and stitched it back together (see GAPPING). This process is similar to a process described in certain Lacanian theories of the subject, as the subject is formed in the constant oscillation between the Imaginary order's sense of plenitude and the Symbolic order's permanent sense of loss (see Silverman 1983, Ch. 5). Second, the view that had been assigned to the Absent One is now reassigned to a fictional character, the character looking in the second shot. The awareness of a framing enunciator gives way to an absorption in the *fiction (see IMMERSION). Since *ideology works by passing itself as natural, this self-effacing editing technique allows the film to do its ideological work.

Carroll (1988) has criticised suture theory, arguing that the experience of spectatorship simply does not correspond to suture theory's descriptions: do spectators really undergo emotional shifts from delight to anxiety and back again while watching a dialogue scene? Carroll (1996 [1993]) offers a different explanation, drawing on evolutionary psychology. Humans have an innate

tendency to be curious about what another person is looking at. The point/glance shot automatically invites curiosity, which is then fulfilled by the point/object shot. The result is that spectators around the world can comprehend a POV structure with little training. Given Hollywood's desire to reach a mass audience, it is no surprise that it relies on such an easy-to-understand technique.

Suture theory introduces a distinction between the POV of a character, and the POV of an enunciating figure, similar to a narrator. Similar distinctions are discussed by theorists who draw on the more general insights of narratology. Wilson argues that film scholars can appeal to the notion of the *implied author (or implied filmmaker) to explain the feeling that the spectator's access to a film is guided by a figure not represented in the fiction. However, he argues that the idea of a cinematic narrator is usually incoherent. Being a visual medium, the cinema does not, in the standard case, *tell* its stories (see MODE). Some theorists solve this problem by suggesting that the images we see are understood as the perceptions of an invisible witness, this witness being analogous to a narrator. Wilson rejects this option, on the grounds that we usually regard our visual access to the film's world as direct, not mediated (see NO-NARRATOR THEORY). He concludes that we already have sufficient terms (epistemic *distance, *reliability, and authority) to describe cinematic POV without appealing to the concept of the narrator.

Bordwell goes farther, dispensing with the implied author, as well as the narrator. Most of the characteristics we would normally attribute to the implied author or narrator could simply be attributed to the *narration itself (1985: 61–62). By contrast, Chatman insists that the concept of a *narrative, resting on the *story-discourse distinction, logically requires a narrator. His own analysis of narrative POV involves two terms, slant and filter. 'Slant' refers to the attitudes of the narrator, while 'filter' refers to the mediating functions of a character's mental state.

SEE ALSO: film narrative; focalization; point of view (literary)

References and further reading

Bordwell, David (1985) *Narration in the Fiction Film*, Madison: University of Wisconsin Press.
——, and Kristin Thompson (2001) *Film Art: An Introduction*, 6th ed., New York: McGraw-Hill.

Branigan, Edward (1984) *Point of View in the Cinema*, New York: Mouton.

Carroll, Noël (1988) *Mystifying Movies: Fads and Fallacies in Contemporary Film Theory*, New York: Columbia University Press.

——(1996 [1993]) 'Toward a Theory of Point-of-View Editing: Communication, Emotion, and the Movies', in *Theorizing the Moving Image*, New York: Cambridge University Press.

Chatman, Seymour (1990) *Coming to Terms: The Rhetoric of Narrative in Fiction and Film*, Ithaca: Cornell University Press.

Dayan, Daniel (1976 [1974]) 'The Tutor-Code of Classical Cinema', in Bill Nichols (ed.) *Movies and Methods*, vol. 1, Berkeley: University of California Press.

Silverman, Kaja (1983) *The Subject of Semiotics*, New York: Oxford University Press.

Wilson, George M. (1986) *Narration in Light: Studies in Cinematic Point of View*, Baltimore: Johns Hopkins University Press.

PATRICK KEATING

POINT OF VIEW (LITERARY)

Few narrative features have been discussed as extensively as point of view – the physical, *psychological, and ideological position in terms of which narrated situations and *events are presented (*see* IDEOLOGY AND NARRATIVE), the *perspective through which they are filtered – and few have been associated with as rich a terminology (from central intelligence, vision, and *focalization to filter and slant).

There is general agreement that the filtering or perceiving entity, the holder of point of view, the focalizer can be situated in the *diegesis or out of it. In the former case, akin to Chatman's 'filter', the point of view emanates from a character (the reflector, central intelligence, or central consciousness so valued by Henry James) or from some non-anthropomorphic *existent (e.g., a camera). In the latter case, akin to Chatman's 'slant', the point of view emanates from a (more or less omniscient, more or less perceptually restricted) *narrator. In both cases, as Herman argued, the point of view can be hypothetical rather than actual, yielding that which *might* be perceived from a certain perspective.

There is considerably less agreement as to the differences between point of view and *narration. Genette's separation of *mood from *voice, focalizer from narrator, the question 'who sees?' from the question 'who speaks?' has been very influential. Yet many narratologists take point of view to involve a narrating agent as well as a focalizing one. More generally, though the source of point of view ('who sees') arguably constitutes a necessary and sufficient determinant of it, typologies often invoke factors that pertain not only to the (nature and position of the) focalizer but also to the kind and quantity of information provided ('what is seen' and 'how much is seen') or, even more expansively, to the relations between the narrator and the act of narrating, the action narrated, and the *narratee. After all, the narrator's authority as a communicator depends on his or her confidence, *reliability, and skill. Besides, s/he may give more or less information about the action and do it more or less explicitly, objectively, or approvingly. Finally, his or her contact with the narratee may prove direct or indirect, formal or informal, respectful or scornful (see Lanser 1981).

Several typologies of point of view and typological accounts of narrative based on it have been put forward. For example, Pouillon proposes a tripartite classification: (1) vision from behind (the point of view is that of an omniscient narrator who tells more than any and all of the characters know, as in Thomas Hardy's *Tess of the D'Urbervilles*); (2) vision with (the point of view is that of a character – as in Henry James' *The Ambassadors* – or that of several different characters, as in Henry James' *The Golden Bowl*, and the narrator tells only what they know); (3) vision from without (events are viewed from the outside, as in Ernest Hemingway's 'Hills Like White Elephants', and the narrator tells less than the characters know). Norman Friedman offers an eight-term classification, in order of narratorial prominence: (1) editorial omniscience (third-person narration with an intrusive omniscient narrator: *Tess of the D'Urbervilles*) (*see* PERSON); (2) neutral omniscience (third-person narration with an impersonal, non-intrusive omniscient narrator: Aldous Huxley's *Point Counterpoint*); (3) 'I' as witness (the action is viewed from the periphery by a narrator who is also a secondary character: F. Scott Fitzgerald's *The Great Gatsby*); (4) 'I' as protagonist (the action is viewed from the centre, by a narrator who is also the main character: Charles Dickens' *Great Expectations*); (5) multiple selective omniscience (third-person narration with several characters as focalizers: *The Golden Bowl*); (6) selective omniscience (third-person narration with one character as focalizer: *The Ambassadors*); (7) the dramatic mode (third-person narration and vision from without: 'Hills Like White Elephants');

(8) the camera (the action 'just happens' before a neutral recorder and is transmitted by it seemingly without organisation or selection). Stanzel distinguishes between three basic types of *narrative situations: the authorial one (characterised by third-person omniscient narration: *Tess of the D'Urbervilles*), the personal or figural one (characterised by third-person narration and vision with: *The Ambassadors*), and the first-person one (e.g., *Great Expectations*).

One of the most expansive accounts of point of view is Boris Uspenskii's. He argues that it manifests itself on four distinct levels – ideological, phraseological, spatiotemporal, psychological – and he makes a fundamental distinction on each level according to whether the focalizer is inside or outside the diegesis and whether the information provided results from an inner view or an outer one. As for the most famous (recent) account, perhaps it is that of Genette, who distinguishes between zero focalization (akin to third-person omniscient narration), external focalization ('Hills Like White Elephants'), and internal focalization, which itself can be fixed (analogous to selective omniscience), variable (analogous to multiple selective omniscience), or multiple (the same events are presented more than once, each time through a different character: Wilkie Collins' *The Moonstone*).

Many other distinctions can be made. For instance, in what may be called compound point of view, a given set of elements can be perceived simultaneously – and identically or differently – by more than one focalizer. At other times, the text does not specify the entity operating as focalizer. One might then speak of unspecified point of view. At other times still, it is impossible to determine which one of two or more specific entities the action is filtered through. One might then speak of undecidable point of view (*see* INDETERMINACY).

Of course, a single narrative can feature several different types of point of view. Indeed, one focalizer can yield to another focalizer within the space of a few words and one type of point of view can give way to another one within a single sentence. The study of the ways in which cognition and *emotion, interpretation and response are affected by the exploitation of distinct points of view constitutes one of the most important tasks of narratology.

SEE ALSO: alteration; cognitive narratology; point of view (cinematic)

References and further reading

Chatman, Seymour (1990) *Coming to Terms: The Rhetoric of Narrative in Fiction and Film*, Ithaca: Cornell University Press.

Friedman, Norman (1955) 'Point of View in Fiction: The Development of a Critical Concept', *PMLA*, 70, 1160–84.

Genette, Gérard (1980 [1972]) *Narrative Discourse: An Essay in Method*, trans. Jane E. Lewin, Ithaca: Cornell University Press.

Herman, David (2002) *Story Logic: Problems and Possibilities of Narrative*, Lincoln: University of Nebraska Press.

Lanser, Susan Sniader (1981) *The Narrative Act: Point of View in Fiction*, Princeton: Princeton University Press.

Lubbock, Percy (1921) *The Craft of Fiction*, London: Jonathan Cape.

Pouillon, Jean (1946) *Temps et roman*, Paris: Gallimard.

Stanzel, Franz (1984 [1979]) *A Theory of Narrative*, trans. Charlotte Goedsche, Cambridge: Cambridge University Press.

Uspenskii, Boris (1973 [1970]) *A Poetics of Composition: The Structure of the Artistic Text and Typology of a Compositional Form*, trans. Valentina Zavarin and Susan Wittig, Berkeley: University of California Press.

GERALD PRINCE

POLYPHONY

That which is polyphonic is literally 'many-voiced'. As employed in narrative theory, the term 'polyphony' derives from the work of Mikhail Bakhtin and describes texts or utterances in which more than one *voice can be heard. Bakhtin's most extended discussion of narrative polyphony comes in his study of Dostoevskii (Bakhtin 1984), whom he sees as the creator of the polyphonic *novel. In Dostoevskii's novels, Bakhtin identifies a plurality of independent and equally valid voices which are not subordinated to any single authorial hierarchy (*see* AUTHOR). This allows a free play between *character consciousnesses and points of view in which the judgements of the *narrator are afforded no special privilege and the narrator counts merely as one voice in a *dialogue of many (*see* DIALOGISM; POINT OF VIEW (LITERARY)). By contrast, the monologic novel subjects all discourse to the unifying authority of the narrating instance.

Bakhtin's notion of polyphony is at least partly contiguous with his broader concept of *heteroglossia (many-tongued-ness). For Bakhtin, all utterances are multivoiced, 'filled with dialogic overtones' (Bakhtin 1986: 92), and 'overpopulated' with the meanings and intentions of others (*see* INTENTIONALITY). At any given historical moment, language is 'heteroglot from top to bottom', a seething site of social and ideological differences (1981: 291) (*see* IDEOLOGY AND NARRATIVE). Furthermore, all utterances are fundamentally responsive, a link in a wider dialogic chain (1986: 69). It is hard, in this light, to see how Bakhtin can sustain a notion of monologic discourse at all, especially since, elsewhere in his work, he insists that 'even direct authorial speech is filled with recognised words of others' (1986: 115). In *Discourse in the Novel*, he characterises the novel as a *genre that makes deliberate, artistic use of heteroglossia, organising a plethora of voices, idioms, and sociolects into a structured system (1981: 262). In *From the Prehistory of Novelistic Discourse*, Bakhtin concedes that monoglossia is an essentially relative concept, because there can be no 'single' language that is not shot through with, and in constant dialogue with, the discourse of others (1981: 66). In the same essay, Bakhtin also identifies polyphonic features in classical and *medieval texts, while claiming that the tension between unifying and decentralising tendencies became particularly acute in the seventeenth century (1981: 67).

The contiguity between polyphony and heteroglossia in Bakhtin's view of narrative is particularly important in *Discourse in the Novel*. Here, Bakhtin sees the direct discourse of characters as just one among many forms of polyphony in the novel (*see* SPEECH REPRESENTATION). The reverberations of a character's voice extend considerably beyond his or her direct utterances. They infect the narratorial idiom, constituting clearly identifiable 'character zones' in which the voices of narrator and character appear to be in implicit dialogue (*see* FREE INDIRECT DISCOURSE). Analysing a series of passages from Dickens's *Little Dorrit*, Bakhtin further shows how the narrator's idiom is itself always already many-voiced, or polyphonic.

References and further reading

Bakhtin, Mikhail (1981) *The Dialogic Imagination*, ed. Michael Holquist, trans. Caryl Emerson and Michael Holquist, Austin: University of Texas Press.
——(1984) *Problems of Dostoevsky's Poetics*, trans. Caryl Emerson, Minneapolis: University of Minnesota Press.
——(1986) *Speech Genres and Other Late Essays*, trans. Vern W. McGee, Austin: University of Texas Press.
Kristeva, Julia (1980) 'Word, Dialogue, and Novel', in *Desire in Language*, trans. Leon S. Roudiez, New York: Columbia University Press.
Todorov, Tzvetan (1984) *Mikhail Bakhtin: The Dialogical Principle*, trans. Wlad Godzich, Minneapolis: University of Minnesota Press.

RICHARD ACZEL

PORNOGRAPHIC NARRATIVE

Pornography derives from the Greek *pornographos*, or 'writing about prostitutes', but in modern usage it refers to both written and pictorial depictions of sexual activity. There is a distinction between pornographic and erotic works, and a rule of thumb for the difference is that pornography depicts sexuality as transgressively obscene, whereas eroticism less aggressively integrates sex with the *emotion of love. In terms of narrative the difference largely turns on the degree to which it depicts genitalia explicitly or implicitly, the latter more characteristically erotic, the former more pornographic. Thus, Radclyffe Hall's *The Well of Loneliness* (1928) is about sexual love, but the foregrounding of love eclipses the imagery of sex to such an extent that the work is distinctly erotic. Pauline Réages *Story of O* (1954), conversely, so foregrounds the physique of sexuality and its transgressive drives that it is distinctly pornographic. The long-standing categories of 'hard' and 'soft' core pornography help to designate degrees of transgression. Both categories reflect genre writing: soft core minimises transgression, while hard core maximises it (*see* GENRE FICTION).

There is also a mode of aesthetic pornography that works of considerable narrative sophistication employ to combine transgressive sexuality with literary art. D. H. Lawrence's *Lady Chatterley's Lover* (1928) is a classic of this form, where the narrative 'sophistication' consists of Lawrence's conspicuous use of obscene language and descriptions of sexual acts. In both instances Lawrence's narrative attempts to de-toxify itself by foregrounding its 'obscenity' so as to dissipate its murky association with what he called the 'dirty little secret' of sex. Specifically, he consistently described sex in 'natural' – as distinct from 'civilised' – settings, and he undertook sanitising the word *fuck* by repetition and by contextualising it in the intimate English midlands of his gamekeeper protagonist. James Joyce's *Ulysses* (1922) was not only a bold experiment with time, language, and *stream of consciousness; it was also instrumental in reconceiving the literary possibilities of erotic narrative. Including *motifs such as male and female masturbation, female exhibitionism, impotence, adultery, voyeurism, and perverse sexual fantasies, the novel had a substantial pornographic dimension, and in bringing pornography and modernist technique together in one *narrative structure it validated a symbiotic relationship between the aesthetic and the obscene (*see* MODERNIST NARRATIVE; NARRATIVE TECHNIQUES).

Prior to Joyce and Lawrence there were instances of pornographic narrative in European literature – e.g., Pietro Aretino's *Dialogues* (1530), John Cleland's *Fanny Hill* (1750), Guillaume Apollinaire's *The Debauched Hospodar* (1905), among others – but only the Marquis de Sade had attempted a synthesis of pornography and seriously novelistic narrative (e.g., *Justine*, 1791). Following Joyce and Lawrence, pornography took its uneasy but distinctive place even in mainstream narrative. Georges Bataille's study *Eroticism* and his novel *Story of the Eye* (1928) have been influential especially in France, where he was succeeded by such writers as Jean Genet (e.g., *Our Lady of the Flowers*, 1963) and Pauline Réage. But in general pornography in serious narrative functions as an occasional rhetoric in the manner of *Ulysses*, rather than as an exclusive style.

SEE ALSO: desire; gender studies

References and further reading

Bataille, Georges (1962) *Eroticism*, trans. Mary Dalwood, London: John Calder.
Ginzburg, Ralph (1958) *An Unhurried View of Erotica*, New York: Helmsman.
Griffin, Susan (1981) *Pornography and Silence*, New York: Harper and Row.
Marcus, Steven (1966) *The Other Victorians*, New York/London: Basic Books.
Michelson, Peter (1993) *Speaking the Unspeakable*, Albany: State University of New York Press.
Peckham, Morse (1969) *Art and Pornography*, New York/London: Basic Books.
Perkins, Michael (1977) *The Secret Record*, New York: William Morrow.

PETER MICHELSON

POSITIONING

Positioning has become an influential construct in the analysis of oral narratives, allowing researchers to explore how humans make sense of themselves and construct their (and others') *identities (*see* CONVERSATIONAL STORYTELLING). In proximity but also in contrast to role-theoretical constructs, notions of footing and framing (Goffman 1981 and Tannen 1993), schema- and script-theoretical concepts, Burke's dramatism, and concepts of stance and indexicality, positioning builds on *metaphors of place to characterise the subjective sense of location, suggesting that notions of 'self' and 'identity' entail 'being in place' (*see* FRAME THEORY; SCRIPTS AND SCHEMATA; SPACE IN NARRATIVE).

Current discussions of the concept of positioning draw on two different interpretations. The more traditional view, which strongly influenced the development of this concept and showed its relevance for theorising identity, self, and subjectivity, explains positions as grounded in *master narratives (also variably called plotlines, master *plots, dominant discourses, or simply cultural texts) which are viewed as providing the social locations where subjects are positioned (Hollway 1984; Davies and Harré 1990; Harré and van Langenhove 1999). In this line of reasoning, subjects maintain a quasi-agentive status inasmuch as master narratives are construed as inherently contradictory and in competition with one another, so that subjects are forced to choose: they (agentively) pick a position among those available. According to this view, positions are resources that subjects can choose, and when practiced for a while they become repertoires that can be drawn on in narrative constructions of self and others.

An alternative view elaborates on Butler's (1990) view of performing identities in acts of 'self-marking' (*see* PERFORMATIVITY). This view is more concerned with self-reflection, self-criticism, and *agency (all ultimately orientated toward *self-revision*). It draws a line between the being-positioned orientation with its relatively strong, determining underpinning and a more agentive notion of the subject as positioning itself. In contexts of self-positioning, the discursive resources or repertoires are not always and already given but rather are constructed in a more bottom-up and performative fashion, and they can generate counter-narratives. The analysis of how speakers actively position themselves in talk – in particular in their stories – starts from the assumption that the orderliness of story-talk is situationally and interactively accomplished (*see* COMMUNICATION IN NARRATIVE; DISCOURSE ANALYSIS (LINGUISTICS)). Taking narratives as situated and performed actions, positioning has a two-way orientation. On the one hand, it orients how *characters are situated in space and *time in the *storyworld, positioning the characters vis-à-vis one another as relational story-agents. On the other hand, it simultaneously affects how the teller designs the story in order to define a social location for himself or herself in the act of telling a narrative to an *audience.

References and further reading

Butler, Judith (1990) 'Performative Acts and Gender Constitution: An Essay in Phenomenology and Feminist Theory', in Sue-Ellen Case (ed.) *Performing Feminisms: Feminist Critical Theory and Theater*, Baltimore: Johns Hopkins University Press.

Davies, Bronwyn, and Rom Harré (1990) 'Positioning: The Social Construction of Selves', *Journal for the Theory of Social Behaviour*, 20, 43–63.

Goffman, Erving (1981) *Forms of Talk*, Philadelphia: University of Pennsylvania Press.

Harré, Rom, and Luk van Langenhove (1999) *Positioning Theory: Moral Contexts of Intentional Action*, Oxford: Blackwell.

Hollway, Wendy (1984) 'Gender Difference and the Production of Subjectivity', in Julian Henriques, Wendy Hollway, Cathy Urwin, Couze Venn, and Valerie Walkerdine (eds) *Changing the Subject: Psychology, Social Regulation and Subjectivity*, London: Methuen.

Tannen, Deborah (ed.) (1993) *Framing in Discourse*, Oxford: Oxford University Press.

MICHAEL BAMBERG

POSSIBLE-WORLDS THEORY

The theory of possible worlds (henceforth PW), a modern adaptation of a Leibnizian concept, was originally developed by philosophers of the analytic school (Kripke, Lewis, Rescher, Hintikka) as a means to solve problems in formal semantics. In the 1970s a group of literary scholars familiar with structuralist methods (Eco, Pavel, Doležel) discovered the explanatory power of the PW model for narrative and literary theory, especially (but not exclusively) for the areas discussed below. Critics of the PW approach to narrative (Ronen 1994) have argued that literary worlds are not the PWs of

semantic logic in any rigorous technical sense; but this objection ignores the heuristic value of cross-disciplinary metaphorical transfers. Philosophers themselves have invited the analogy by comparing PWs to 'the book on' or 'the story of' a world.

The basis of the theory is the set-theoretical idea that reality – the sum of the imaginable – is a universe composed of a plurality of distinct elements. This universe is hierarchically structured by the opposition of one well-designated element, which functions as the centre of the system, to all the other members of the set. The resulting structure is known as 'modal system', or M-model (Kripke 1963; *see* MODALITY). The central element is commonly interpreted as 'the actual world', and the satellites as merely possible worlds. For a world to be possible it must be linked to the centre by a so-called 'accessibility relation'. The boundary between possible and impossible worlds depends on the particular interpretation given to the notion of accessibility. The most common interpretation associates possibility with logical laws; every world that respects the principles of non-contradiction and the excluded middle is a PW. More controversial is the problem of the nature of the property that designates one world as actual. Two theories of actuality stand out among the various proposals. The first, proposed by Lewis, regards the concept of actual world as an indexical notion whose *reference varies with the speaker. According to Lewis, 'the actual world' means 'the world where I am located', and all PWs are actually from the point of view of their inhabitants (*see* DEIXIS). The other theory, defended by Rescher, states that the actual world differs in ontological status from merely possible ones in that this world alone presents an autonomous existence. All other worlds are the product of a mental activity, such as dreaming, imagining, foretelling, promising, or storytelling.

The primary logical purpose of this model is to formulate the semantics of the modal operators of necessity and possibility. A proposition asserting the possibility of a state of affairs p is true when it is verified in at least one of the worlds of the system; a proposition asserting the necessity of p must be true in all the worlds; and a proposition asserting impossibility must be false in all of them. The model has also been found useful for the formulation of the truth conditions of counterfactuals and for the characterisation of the distinction between intension and extension (or sense and reference).

Possible worlds and the semantics of fiction

Before the advent of PW theory it was almost sacrilegious to mention the issue of *truth in relation to literary works. Recourse to the notion of PW makes it possible to talk about the truth of the propositions asserted in fictional texts without reducing these texts to a representation of reality (*see* FICTION, THEORIES OF). In a work like *Doktor Faustus* by Thomas Mann, for instance, we are invited to give equal credence within the fictional world to the musicological discussions and to the conversation of the hero with the devil. But as Pavel has argued, we are also entitled to regard the musicological discussions as potentially accurate information about the real world: readers occasionally use fiction as a source of knowledge. Fictional propositions can thus be evaluated in different reference worlds. While they may be true or false of worlds that exist independently of the text in which they appear, they are automatically true of their own fictional world by virtue of a convention that grants declarative (or performative) force to fictional statements: unless its narrator is judged unreliable (*see* RELIABILITY), the fictional text gives imaginative existence to worlds, objects, and states of affairs by simply describing them (*see* EXISTENT). In creating what is objectively a non-actual PW, the fictional text establishes a new actual world which imposes its laws on the reader and determines its own horizon of possibilities.

In a key article, Lewis proposed to extend his pioneering analysis of counterfactuals to the problem of the truth of statements made about (rather than found in) fiction. According to Lewis, a counterfactual statement of the form 'if p had been the case then q would have been the case' is true for an evaluator if the PWs in which both p and q are true are closer, on balance, to the actual world than the worlds in which p is true and q is false. A statement referring to a fictional world may be compared to an 'if p then q' statement in which the text specifies p and the reader provides q as an interpretation of p. The statement 'Emma Bovary was unable to distinguish fiction from reality' translates as: 'if all the facts stated by Flaubert's text about Emma Bovary were true then it would be true that she was unable to distinguish fiction from reality'. This analogy enables Lewis to formulate the truth conditions for statements about fiction in the following terms: a sentence of the form 'in the fiction f, p' is true when some world where f is told as known fact and p is true differs less, on balance, from the actual world than does any world where f is told as known fact and p is not true.

This analysis entails a principle which has come to be recognised as fundamental to the phenomenology of reading. Variously described as 'the principle of minimal departure' (Ryan 1991), the 'reality principle' (Walton 1990), and the 'principle of mutual belief' (Walton again), the principle states that when readers construct fictional worlds, they fill in the gaps (*see* GAPPING; READER-RESPONSE THEORY) in the text by assuming the similarity of the fictional world to their own experiential reality. This model can only be overruled by the text itself; thus, if a text mentions a blue deer, the reader will imagine an animal that resembles her idea of real deer in all respects other than the colour. The statement 'deer have four legs' will be true of this fictional world, but the statement 'deer have a single horn, and it is made of pearl' will be false, unless specified by the text.

The principle of minimal departure presupposes that fictional worlds, like the PWs postulated by philosophers, are ontologically complete entities: every proposition p is either true or false in these worlds. To the reader's imagination, undecidable propositions are a matter of missing information, not of ontological deficiency. This view is not unanimously endorsed by theorists. The main dissenter is Doležel, who regards incompleteness as the distinctive feature of fictional existence. He argues that by filling the gaps, the reader would reduce the ontological diversity found in fictional worlds to a uniform structure, namely the structure of the complete, Carnapian world. Doležel further believes that a filling of gaps would neutralise the effect of the strategies of showing and hiding that regulate the disclosure of narrative information – strategies which determine the 'texture' of the text and its degree of informational saturation. It is not insignificant, for instance, that visual information and the surname of the hero are suppressed in Kafka's *The Trial*. This raises the question of the location of gaps: are they part of the texture of the text, or do they belong to the fictional world itself? One way or another, however, gaps can only be apprehended against a full background: the incomplete texture of the text compared to the completeness of the fictional world for the proponents of minimal departure; the incompleteness of the fictional world compared to the fullness of the real world if gaps belong to the ontological fabric of the fictional world.

Whereas Doležel regards the imaginative domain projected by fiction as less than a complete PW, Ryan argues that this domain encompasses not just one world but an entire modal system. In contrast to modes of expression that refer to the non-actual in a hypothetical mode, such as *if ... then* statements, fiction includes both factual and nonfactual statements. The former outline a textual actual world (TAW), while the latter allude to the virtualities of the fictional system. The contrast actual/non-actual is thus reinscribed within the textual universe. Author and reader engage in an act of make-believe by which they relocate themselves as *narrator and *narratee in TAW. This imaginative relocation results in a reorganisation of the modal system around a new centre. Through the concept of playful recentring this proposal reconciles the indexical theory of actuality proposed by Lewis with Rescher's absolutist view. From the point of view of the 'actual actual world' the worlds of fiction are discourse-created non-actual possible worlds, populated by incompletely specified individuals; but to the reader immersed in the text the TAW is imaginatively real, and the characters are ontologically complete human beings.

Possible worlds and narrative semantics

As a model for *narrative semantics, PW theory is applicable to both fiction and non-fiction. The need for a semantic model that recognises different propositional modalities was recognised in the early seventies by Todorov and Bremond. Both insisted on the importance of hypothetical *events for the understanding of the behaviour of *characters. Every intent-driven *action, for instance, aims at preventing a possible state of affairs, thus making it forever counterfactual, and at actualising another state. To capture the logic of action, narrative semantics should therefore consider both the factual events of the TAW and the virtual events contemplated by characters. The mental representations of characters can be conceived as the PWs of a modal system. Eco describes the narrative text as a 'machine for producing PWs' (1984: 246). He has in mind the following three types of worlds.

1   The PW imagined and asserted by the *author, which consists of all the states presented as actual by the *fabula.
2   The possible sub-worlds that are imagined, believed, wished (etc.) by the characters.

3   The possible sub-worlds that the reader imagines, believes, wishes (etc.) in the course of reading, and that the fabula either actualises or 'counterfactualises' by taking another fork.

The worlds of type 2 are formally described by PW theorists as sets of propositions governed by modal operators, or predicates of propositional attitude (Eco, Vaina, Doležel). These predicates distinguish various domains of mental activity: worlds of beliefs (the epistemic system), of obligations (the deontic system), of *desires (the axiological system), and of actively pursued goals and plans. The propositional content of these private worlds enters into a system of compatibilities which defines the relations of antagonism or cooperation between the characters, as well as the points of *conflict in the narrative universe. The relation between *hero and villain can for instance be characterised as pursuing p versus pursuing ~p. Ryan further divides the private worlds of characters into representations of existing material or mental worlds (beliefs), static model-worlds, which capture how the actual world should or will be (obligations, desires, predictions), dynamic model-worlds, or intention-worlds, which project courses of events leading to goal states (the active plans of characters), and fantasy worlds which outline new systems of reality, complete with their own actual and possible worlds (dreams, hallucinations, acts of imagination, fictions-within-fictions). Whenever a proposition in a belief or model world becomes unsatisfied in the actual world, the narrative universe falls into a state of conflict. The general goal of characters is to resolve conflict by aligning all of their private worlds with the TAW. An action, event, or property is narratively relevant (rather than purely descriptive) when it affects, through a causal chain, the relations among the worlds of the system. The *plot of the narrative text captures the movement of individual worlds in the global narrative universe. It does not end when all conflicts are resolved, for conflict is a permanent state of any universe, but when all the remaining conflicts cease to be productive because their experiencer is no longer willing or able to take steps toward their resolution.

Narrative-worlds typology and genre theory

As already mentioned, the logical interpretation of possibility is not the only conceivable one.

A typology of narrative worlds can be obtained by narrowing down the criteria of possibility and by varying the notion of accessibility relations. In a broad sense, possibility depends not only on logical principles but also on physical laws and material causality. Following this interpretation, narrative worlds can be classified as realistic (*see* REALISM, THEORIES OF) or *fantastic, depending on whether or not the events they relate could physically occur in the real world. Maître, for example, distinguishes four types of narratives: (1) Works involving largely accurate reference to actual historical events (true fiction [*see* NON-FICTION NOVEL], creative non-fiction, or *roman à clefs). (2) Works dealing with imaginary states of affairs which could be actual (strongly realistic texts). (3) Works in which there is an oscillation between could-be-actual and could-never-be-actual (Todorov's conception of the fantastic). (4) Works dealing with states of affairs which could never be actual (Todorov's marvellous). This typology can be refined by introducing other criteria of compossibility: a world can be declared accessible from AW if it presents a common geography or history; if it is populated by the same natural species; if it is in the same stage of technological progress; if its human inventory includes the population of AW; if it may be reached without time travel, etc. Every genre defined by its content can be described through a particular set of broken and preserved relations, true fiction breaking the fewest, and nonsense verse the most. But one set of values for accessibility relations is not always sufficient to classify a textual world. Narratives may present what Pavel calls a dual or a layered ontology. In this case the domain of the actual is split into sharply distinct domains obeying distinct laws, such as the sacred and the profane, the realm of the gods and the realm of humans, or the knowable and the unknowable. The lines that divide narrative worlds may be cultural and ideological as well as strictly ontological. The deontic system can for instance describe a world (real or fictional) in which some beliefs are obligatory, others permitted, and yet others forbidden.

Poetics of postmodern narrative

Though the idea of a centred system of reality is contrary to its ideology, the *postmodern imagination has found in the concepts of PW theory a productive plaything for its games of subversion and self-reflexivity (*see* REFLEXIVITY). McHale characterises the transition from modernism to postmodernism as a switch from epistemological to ontological concerns (*see* MODERNIST NARRATIVE). Whereas modernism was haunted by the question 'What can I know about myself and about the world?', postmodernism asks more radically: 'What is a world?' 'What makes a world real?' 'Is there a difference in mode of existence between textual worlds and the world(s) I live in, or are all worlds created by language?' The ontological inquiry of postmodern literature takes a variety of forms: (1) Challenging the classical ontological model through branching plots (*see* MULTI-PATH NARRATIVE) that lead to plural actual worlds, or through the blurring of the distinction between actuality and possibility – no world in the system assuming the role of ontological centre. (2) *Thematisation of the origin of narrative worlds in mental processes and questioning of the relation creator-creature. (3) Exploitation of the relation of transworld identity through the migration of characters from one narrative universe to another. (4) Extension of the principle of minimal departure to textual worlds through postmodern rewrites (the world of the rewrite being construed as the closest possible to the world of the original). (5) Blocking of the principle of minimal departure through the creation of impossible objects, inconsistent geographies, and radically incomplete beings. (6) Recursive applications of the gesture of recentring through the Chinese box effect of fictions within fictions (*see* EMBEDDING). (7) Entangling of diegetic levels, *trompe-l'oeil* effects, play with world boundaries, and what McHale calls 'strange loops': repeated shifts into higher narrative levels which eventually lead back to the original level (*see* METALEPSIS). (8) Subversion of the hierarchy of accessibility relations, through the creation of hybrid worlds situated at the same time very close and very far from experiential reality (*magical realism). (9) Fascination with the scenarios of *counterfactual history and creation of fictional universes in which the real and the possible exchange places. (In such worlds characters may ask: 'What would have happened if Hitler had not won the war?') (10) Multi-stranded or parallel plots that play simultaneously in separate ontological domains, such as reality and computer-generated virtual worlds.

SEE ALSO: text-world approach to narrative

References and further reading

Doležel, Lubomír (1998) *Heterocosmica: Fiction and Possible Worlds*, Baltimore: Johns Hopkins University Press.

Eco, Umberto (1984) *The Role of the Reader: Explorations in the Semiotics of Texts*, Bloomington: Indiana University Press.

Kripke, Saul (1963) 'Semantical Considerations on Modal Logic', *Acta Philosophica Fennica*, 16, 83–94.

Lewis, David (1978) 'Truth in Fiction', *American Philosophical Quarterly*, 1, 37–46.

Maître, Doreen (1983) *Literature and Possible Worlds*, Middlesex: Middlesex Polytechnic Press.

McHale, Brian (1987) *Postmodernist Fiction*, New York: Methuen.

Pavel, Thomas G. (1986) *Fictional Worlds*, Cambridge, Mass.: Harvard University Press.

Rescher, Nicholas (1979) 'The Ontology of the Possible', in M. Loux (ed.) *The Possible and the Actual: Readings in the Metaphysics of Modality*, Ithaca: Cornell University Press.

Ronen, Ruth (1994) *Possible Worlds in Literary Theory*, Cambridge: Cambridge University Press.

Ryan, Marie-Laure (1991) *Possible Worlds, Artificial Intelligence, and Narrative Theory*, Bloomington: Indiana University Press.

Vaina, Lucia (1977) 'Les Mondes possibles du texte', *Versus*, 17, 3–13.

Walton, Kendall (1990) *Mimesis as Make-Believe: On the Foundations of the Representational Arts*, Cambridge, Mass.: Harvard University Press.

MARIE-LAURE RYAN

POSTCLASSICAL NARRATOLOGY

In his introduction to the essay collection *Narratologies* (1999), David Herman proposes the term 'postclassical narratology' in order to group the various efforts to transcend 'classical' structuralist narratology, which has been reproached for its scientificity, anthropomorphism, disregard for context, and gender-blindness. Herman implies that these mistakes are most often avoided in postclassical narratology, but he insists that the prefix 'post' does not quite signify a clean break with structuralism, whose many achievements are often worked into the new analyses (*see* STRUCTURALIST NARRATOLOGY). Further, postclassical narratology should not be confused with *poststructuralist approaches to narrative, since it is much wider in scope.

Without attempting to be exhaustive, Herman identifies six new angles on narrative: the *feminist; the *linguistic; the *cognitive; the philosophical (informed by *possible-worlds theory); the *rhetorical; and the *postmodern (*see* PHILOSOPHY AND NARRATIVE). In a more encompassing treatment of the new developments in which he takes up Herman's overall term, Ansgar Nünning (2003) lists no less than eight categories. He subsumes feminist narratology under the heading of contextualist, *thematic and ideological approaches (*see* IDEOLOGY AND NARRATIVE); adds a separate category for transgeneric and transmedial studies (*see* INTERMEDIALITY; MEDIA AND NARRATIVE); extends and details Herman's other perspectives, e.g., by combining the postmodern and poststructuralist approaches; and conceives of a mixed final category in which he places such diverse theories as cyberage narratology (Marie-Laure Ryan 2001) and psychonarratology (Bortolussi and Dixon 2003). Classical narratology may not have been without its variants (such as story narratology as opposed to discourse narratology; *see* STORY-DISCOURSE DISTINCTION), but the enormous proliferation of new approaches indicates that narratology is far less of a unified field than it used to be in the heyday of structuralism.

This situation has not prevented critics from sketching the general developments that have taken place. In the introduction to *Narratologies*, Herman (1999: 8, 16) summarises the differences between the old and new forms of the discipline by pointing to the growing importance for analysis of the context, both of the text and of the reader/critic. In his survey of the differences, Nünning (2003) confirms and details the shift from text to context. Whereas structuralism was intent on coming up with a general theory of narrative, postclassical narratology prefers to consider the circumstances that make every act of reading different (*see* READER-RESPONSE THEORY). From cognition to ethics to ideology: all aspects related to reading assume pride of place in the research on narrative. The reader has become so important that the concrete concerns of individuals and their broader social and cultural backgrounds may now be felt to influence narrative theory. This politically oriented development both widens the scope of narratology and enhances its relevance. Contrary to the bulk of structuralist narratology, which was mostly geared to ahistorical universals (*see* NARRATIVE UNIVERSALS), postclassical narratology is usefully setup for diachronic study because of its deep-rooted sense of relativism. Its understanding of narrative as a many-sided phenomenon also turns the new narratology into an *interdisciplinary endeavour, which may stretch as far as empirical psychology and anthropology (*see* ETH-NOGRAPHIC APPROACHES TO NARRATIVE).

While the present overview does not readily incorporate the important branch of possible-worlds narratology, which is more text-oriented than contextualist, it clearly indicates a common sense of purpose. Yet the postclassical research program must be checked for its own ideological bias. Although the distinction between classical and postclassical narratology itself forms part of a narrative about the history of the discipline, and could therefore theoretically suffer from a wish to rehype this arguably outmoded branch of the humanities, the sheer volume and variety of con-tributions dealing with narrative and aspiring to go beyond structuralism doubtlessly warrant the sug-gestion of a new phase of narrative research. If the term 'postclassical' has the connotation of sophis-tication, then that is a welcome bonus for a field that holds the promise of true interdisciplinarity. The identification of structuralism as the classical age of narratology might be contested, especially by empirically oriented scholars, who have always rejected the lack of testing typical of the structur-alist endeavour. Also, the emphasis on structural-ism might obscure prestructuralist achievements in what are now called postclassical directions, such as the work by M. M. Bakhtin. However, since the majority of postclassical narratologists has clearly been schooled in structuralism, its function as a reference point cannot be denied.

SEE ALSO: cognitive narratology; cultural studies approaches to narrative; deconstructive approaches to narrative; ethical turn; historiographic narratology; narrative turn in the humanities; psychological approaches to narrative

References and further reading

Bakhtin, M. M. (1981) *The Dialogic Imagination*, ed. Michael Holquist, trans. Caryl Emerson and Michael Holquist, Austin: University of Texas Press.

Bortolussi, Marisa, and Peter Dixon (2003) *Psychonarra-tology: Foundations for the Empirical Study of Literary Response*, Cambridge: Cambridge University Press.

Darby, David (2001) 'Form and Context: An Essay on the History of Narratology', *Poetics Today*, 22, 829–52.

Fludernik, Monika (2000) 'Beyond Structuralism in Narratology: Recent Developments and New Hor-izons in Narrative Theory', *Anglistik*, 11, 83–96.

Herman, David (1999) 'Introduction', in David Herman (ed.) *Narratologies: New Perspectives on Narrative Analysis*, Columbus: Ohio State University Press.

Herman, Luce and Bart Vervaeck (2005) *Handbook of Narrative Analysis*, Lincoln: University of Nebraska Press.

Kafalenos, Emma (ed.) (2001) *Narrative* 9.2 (special issue on 'Contemporary Narratology').

Nünning, Ansgar (2003) 'Narratology or Narratologies? Taking Stock of Recent Developments, Critique and Modest Proposals for Future Usages of the Term', in Tom Kindt and Hans-Harald Müller (eds) *What is Narratology?*, Berlin: De Gruyter.

Rimmon-Kenan (2002) 'Towards ...: Afterthoughts, Almost Twenty Years Later', in *Narrative Fiction: Contemporary Poetics*, 2nd edition, New York: Routledge.

Ryan, Marie-Laure (2001) *Narrative as Virtual Reality: Immersion and Interactivity in Literature and Electronic Media*, Baltimore: Johns Hopkins Uni-versity Press.

LUC HERMAN AND BART VERVAECK

POST-COLONIALISM AND NARRATIVE

The way in which the much-debated concept of post-colonialism is understood depends (at least in part) on the particular 'narrative' or explanatory scheme – historical, cultural, or theoretical – which it is seen as embodying. Among such 'narratives' of post-colonialism, four are worth briefly mentioning.

(1) The simplest historical narrative, where post-colonialism refers to the period after the dissolution of the European colonial empires, is simultaneously unobjectionable and unsatisfactory. It is unobjec-tionable because, by and large, colonialism ended in the period from the late 1950s to the early 1970s; it is unsatisfactory because (a) it is a process which is still not universally accomplished, and (b) the formal independence achieved ignores the continued pre-sence of neo-colonialist or imperialist methods of control and economic exploitation.

(2) If that narrative is too 'prematurely cele-bratory', as Anne McClintock has argued, there is another which would require less universal achievement, but still be reasonably optimistic. In this version, becoming *post*-colonial would involve getting past colonialism's own narratives and ideologies (*see* IDEOLOGY AND NARRATIVE). For Jacques Derrida, poststructuralism involves mov-ing beyond the theoretical assumptions or frame-works of structuralism but at the same time recognising that structuralism is not thereby com-pletely eradicated as presence or effect (*see* POST-STRUCTURALIST APPROACHES TO NARRATIVE). In the

same way, across the colonised world, writers, intellectuals, activists, and others began to break free of the constraints of ideological narratives – for instance of Western superiority and non-Western inferiority – without necessarily even the achievement of formal independence which marks the other sort of post-colonialism, and also without the need to believe that the impact of colonialism was dissipated. This process of what the exiled Kenyan writer and critic Ngugi wa Thiong'o famously called 'Decolonising the Mind' constitutes a very different way of becoming post-colonial.

(3) The third, and still partially optimistic, narrative would begin from the acknowledgement that post-colonialism is precisely not an achieved state or condition – quite the reverse – and that therefore the struggle to remove imperialist domination globally must continue. (Although this narrative of post-colonialism as an anticipatory mode is forced to recognise that formal decolonisation did not necessarily get anyone very far in terms of real liberation, it does at least assert the value of continued resistance.)

(4) A very different and altogether less positive view of post-colonialism has gained a certain fashionable notoriety in recent years. Historian Arif Dirlik argues that post-colonialism marks the onset of historical amnesia, when people forget the effects of colonialism. (As we shall see shortly in relation to post-colonial narratives, this is a most remarkable claim.) Dirlik also states that post-colonialism only begins with the arrival of Third World intellectuals in the first world, and, perhaps worst of all, that post-colonialism constitutes the cultural logic of late or multinational capitalism (here stealing Fredric Jameson's definition of postmodernism; *see* POSTMODERN NARRATIVE).

Dirlik's narrative has been roundly rebutted by Stuart Hall and others, but continues to circulate as an easy stick with which to beat post-colonialism. Regardless of academic infighting, however, post-colonialism as a narrative of the ways in which over 80% of the world, formerly, recently, or still colonised by Europe, has struggled to free itself is clearly of enormous importance.

The politics of post-colonial narrative

The fundamental importance of narrative in this area is highlighted by Edward Said's classic essay 'Permission to Narrate' (Said 1994). Focusing on the case of Palestine, Said identifies the disastrous consequences of the refusal by Israel and its allies to allow the legitimacy of a narrative of the Palestinian people. These consequences obtain not merely at the cultural, aesthetic, or ideological level, but also, and in some ways more decisively, at the political and the national, manifested in loss of *identity, cultural coherence, and international support; loss of land; the ongoing simultaneous corralling and dispersal of the population; and daily vulnerability to Israeli state aggression.

In many ways, the global importance of narrative has been at the heart of Said's work at least since *Orientalism* with its epoch-making analysis of the impact of Western narratives of the East – as, for instance, backward, uncivilised, chaotic – in terms of their legitimation of colonial control and economic exploitation. The phrase which Said takes from Marx – 'They cannot represent themselves; they must be represented' – as a kind of *leitmotif for his work is another example of the refusal of 'permission to narrate': here, Western representations of both the West and East take the place of an East supposedly incapable of telling its own story. If *Orientalism* concentrates rather on the power of the West to produce narratives, Said's *Culture and Imperialism*, with its contrapuntal insistence on 'overlapping territories, intertwined histories', notes both the extensive power of the Western narratives (in this case the European *novel) and the emergence of counter-hegemonic *voices and forces. The crucial phase or moment in this context is then that process (identified as post-colonialism point 2 above, i.e., as the second broad 'narrative' of post-colonialism) when the colonised break free of Western narratives or ideologies and represent or narrate themselves, for themselves and for others.

The constitutive power of the Western narratives against which these emergent voices pit themselves should not be underestimated. Said, for example, claims that 'imperialism and the novel fortified each other to such a degree that it is impossible, I would argue, to read one without in some way dealing with the other'. This synergy helps to account not only for the hold of 'political' narratives over colonised cultures, as well as their ability to disseminate beyond the realm of the political, but also for the aesthetic influence of the Western *novel form over cultural producers. For a post-colonial novelist like Chinua Achebe, the dominant narrative modes of Western *historiography and the European novel form were simultaneously to be resisted. In a manner which still might be called contrapuntal – though with a different inflection from Said's original meaning – a double process is under way here: on the one hand, the opposing or deconstructing of Western narratives (*see* DECONSTRUCTIVE APPROACHES TO NARRATIVE); on the other, the articulation or reconstruction of indigenous history, culture, and identity. Especially – though by no means exclusively – in the phase of anti-colonial struggle, the urgency of the situation gives the production of narrative a particular clarity of purpose – which is not always, or even usually, the case with literature. The political needs to mobilise cultural resources – including narratives of all forms – as part of the fight for liberation was well understood by activists and theorists such as Amilcar Cabral and Frantz Fanon. For Fanon, it came as no surprise that in the Algerian War of Independence the French colonisers systematically arrested the traditional storytellers. More importantly, however, as he says (Fanon 1967): 'A nation which is born of the people's concerted action and which embodies the real aspirations of the people while changing the state cannot exist save in the expression of exceptionally rich forms of culture'.

There is, however, a certain sense in which to talk about 'Western narratives' may be partly misleading. For Said, Western representations of other cultures tend to emphasise the static and undeveloping or non-progressive nature of those cultures, and that singular, unchanging image Said categorises as a 'vision'. Against vision, Said posits narrative as a mode which actively embraces history, and the possibility of change. (This opposition of vision and narrative as, respectively, closed and open forms has strong affinities with Mikhail Bakhtin's opposition between monologism and *dialogism.) In such a perspective, the articulation of indigenous narratives is shown, once again, to be a significant moment in the process of becoming post-colonial.

The important connection Fanon makes between culture and nation has been given an added twist in recent years, with the analysis of nation not – in the terms of its own ideological self-representation – as something simply, naturally 'there', but, on the contrary, as something laboriously constructed, imagined, and narrated. If this introduces a certain sense of artificiality into the proceedings, then that is compounded in the post-colonial context by the fact that all these processes are both chronologically compacted and made somewhat arbitrary by the procedures of colonial cartography. How do you narrate and celebrate a nation which has been created, as for instance in the case of Nigeria, by simultaneously lumping together and splitting apart large ethnic groups, populations of Christian, animist, and Muslim believers, major linguistic communities, etc? There is the additional problem that the dominant narratives of nationhood – those which the European nations typically told themselves about their ethnic purity, their age-old connection to the land, their cultural homogeneity, and the like – were harder to apply in the post-colonial context. The fact that such narratives were often flagrantly mythic did nothing to diminish their power. The relation of post-colonial *narration and post-colonial nation is variable: on the one hand, there are explicit political projects such as that of Ngugi wa Thiong'o, who offers a very particular revisionist history of his people across the twentieth century in a series of novels; on the other, there is the assertion, made by the Marxist critic Fredric Jameson, that *all* Third World narratives, whether knowingly or not, are unavoidably *allegories of the nation.

If the nation provides one particularly fruitful nexus of historical reconstruction and textual elaboration, the post-colonial field has produced – and continues to produce – other frameworks. Some of these frameworks or topics are particularly oriented towards the production of novelistic narratives; others are more analytic academic constructs. Some are self-evident, such as the narratives of anti-colonial resistance; others, such as Paul Gilroy's *Black Atlantic*, are less obvious, but have provided the impetus for a great range of subsequent work. An example of yet another kind of post-colonial narrative is Sukdev Sandhu's *London Calling*, which aims to write the story of London as told by its black writers from the eighteenth-century to the present day. Elements of this are well-known, but the attempt to articulate them as one narrative in this way has not previously been made.

As recently as the mid-1990s, a work as weighty as the 1800-page, two-volume *Routledge Encyclopedia of Post-Colonial Literatures in English* could assert that empire was marginal to the English novel. Published the previous year, Said's *Culture and Imperialism* makes precisely the opposite point: 'Without empire … there is no European novel as we know it'. An analogous claim regarding the contemporary situation might be that without post-colonialism there is no Anglophone novel as we know it. The *Routledge Encyclopedia* contributor's assertion is that the major nineteenth-century novelists and their works were somehow independent of the fact of colonialism; major world writers in English in the second half of the twentieth century were, however, clearly not independent of the fact of post-colonialism. The awarding of the Nobel Prize for Literature to Wole Soyinka, Derek Walcott, Nadine Gordimer, and J. M. Coetzee, and the Booker Prize to Salman Rushdie (twice), Coetzee (twice), Ben Okri, Gordimer, Margaret Atwood, Peter Carey, V. S. Naipaul, and Keri Hulme, signals the recognition (belated, but growing) of the stature of post-colonial literature, particularly narrative. At the same time, there is the dangerous parallel process by which the recognised and lauded few are transformed into an instant post-colonial literary canon, diminishing or obliterating a proper appreciation of other writers.

Narrative: forms, themes

Another notable aspect of post-colonial fiction is the variety of novelistic forms adopted. Despite a residual racism in certain quarters, which would see representational *realism as the form appropriate to 'lesser' or emergent groups of writers – as in earlier periods with women's writing and working-class writing – post-colonial narrative embraces everything from the deliberate simplicity of a reformulated oral tradition to the postmodernism of Rushdie (*see* ORAL CULTURES AND NARRATIVE; POSTMODERN NARRATIVE). What is particularly noticeable is just how many post-colonial writers break the boundaries of realism. This may take the form of very simple subversion of the mundane 'real', as in the number of African novels and films which straightforwardly assume the unproblematic co-presence of the spirit world and the material (*see* AFRICAN NARRATIVE). It may also involve the kind of 'unreal' temporal shifts seen in Caryl Phillips' *Crossing the River*, where, in an otherwise realistic novel, two brothers and a sister sold into slavery in the eighteenth-century somehow live respectively in the early nineteenth-century, the late nineteenth-century, and the mid-twentieth century (*see* TEMPORAL ORDERING; TIME IN NARRATIVE). Similar time slips occur in Phillips' next novel *The Nature of Blood* and Bharati Mukherjee's *The Holder of the World*, while Vikram Chandra's *Red Earth and Pouring Rain* combines the time shifts and the reality of the mythical/supernatural (*see* MYTH: THEMATIC APPROACHES).

Given the variety of continents, countries, and cultures subsumed within post-colonialism, any summary of the nature of narrative within such a formation is bound to be highly speculative. Schematically, one could suggest a number of successive periods or moments operating as themes or topoi (*see* THEMATIC APPROACHES TO NARRATIVE). These would include: the recovery of the (colonial or pre-colonial) past; the anti-colonial struggle; hopes for the future in the newly independent nation; post-colonial disillusionment; and moving the nation forward. Although there is an obvious linear chronology to this, it does not imply that writers simply deal with a topic and move on to the next in a quest for the theme of the moment. Questions of historical *memory, for instance, are repeatedly returned to and invoked as centrally important. Since, however, not all post-colonial societies pass through all of these phases, and since – even if such phases were part of their society's emergence into post-colonialism – not all writers choose to concern themselves with, for example, the messy business of politics, such a model needs to be applied with great sensitivity.

The question of the political is indeed a vexed one. For example, for certain critics, other cultural producers, and even the President of his native Senegal (the Negritude poet Léopold Sédar Senghor), it is the failing of someone like Ousmane Sembene that he will not relinquish his political concerns and radical stance, whereas for Sembene it is precisely the fidelity to his people, their history and politics which provides the justification for his work as novelist and filmmaker. (Senghor told Sembene to 'mind his own business' and stop involving himself in political matters. Sembene took no notice.) Again, it is worth remembering that if for someone like Sembene post-colonial politics is unavoidable for ethical reasons (*see* ETHICAL TURN), for Fredric Jameson it is quite simply unavoidable: the realities of post-colonial societies means that politics cannot be merely an (unfashionable) aesthetic option, and that their narratives have an inescapable political resonance.

Narrative and resistance

Sembene declares himself 'very sympathetic to those who "refuse"' and the notion of refusal lies at the heart of one particular narrative of post-colonial theoretical or textual production. Focusing on 'ideological orientation' rather than historical period, Mishra and Hodge identify two main forms of post-colonialism: oppositional and complicit. The former is composed of those who 'refuse', in Sembene's terms; the latter constitutes the – for some – shocking assertion that post-colonial writers could indeed be on the same side as the West in ideological or political terms. The paradigmatic figure here is V. S. Naipaul, for many in the West the very best post-colonial novelist. However, even for a temperate critic like Said, Naipaul is 'a renegade', 'a scavenger' harvesting half-truths about other cultures; someone so deeply imbued with Western attitudes that no space remains for any sympathy for the non-West; a writer drawing on the Western tradition of the (supposedly) dispassionate observer to produce narratives whose ideological bias threatens the literary qualities which even his detractors acknowledge.

Beyond the question of the complicity of individual *authors, the problem of the ideological impact of the West goes to the very foundations of post-colonial narrative production. *Marxist and feminist work, especially in the 1980s on the political implications of the history of cultural forms, highlighted, for example, the growth of the novel as part of the development of European bourgeois society, and inescapably bound up with the assumptions and attitudes of that society (*see* FEMINIST NARRATOLOGY; GENDER STUDIES). As a result, numbers of post-colonial novelists and critics have insisted on the importance of indigenous forms of narrative, both oral and written, in order to minimise any sense of ideological contamination from the cultures which colonised and exploited them. Nativist or cultural nationalist attempts to return to the supposed authenticity of pre-colonial cultural forms are both well-documented and widespread in the post-colonial world. For many, however, they are based on fundamentally flawed assumptions: that the pre-colonial culture was somehow pure or authentic, and that such a return is in any way possible. However, just as, in Said's view, the larger narrative is one of 'overlapping territories, intertwined histories', so the very forms in which such a narrative might be constituted are subject to the mixing and hybridising which is the global destiny of the post-colonial world (*see* HYBRID GENRES; HYBRIDITY). The same argument is staged yet again at the level of the theories advanced for the

analysis of narrative. Theory as an essentially Western construct, thus theory as a weapon in the armoury of the West in its assertion of superiority – such perspectives produce calls for the articulation of indigenous literary or cultural theories, or for the development of a 'Black aesthetic'.

If disavowing any ideological complicity on the basis of the use of the novel as an imported Western *genre appears difficult, this task becomes almost impossible when the narrative format is the *film. If one actually accepts the argument about the determining ideological effect of a Western cultural form, then appeals to indigenous modes of *drama or ritual performance can do little to offset the idea of cinema as *the* Western-produced genre, born at the high point of rapid European colonial expansion, massively dependent on (Western) technology and capital investment, bringing with it an even worse ideological package than the novel. Much depends, of course, on whether the allegedly compromised ideological origins of different narrative *media, modes, and techniques are seen as ultimately determining – rather in the same way as an earlier generation of feminists saw language as 'man-made' and therefore excluding or oppressing women. The alternative view, that language and narrative forms are in fact available for oppositional, even revolutionary, appropriation, fortunately still has its advocates among post-colonial cultural producers.

SEE ALSO: cultural studies approaches to narrative; narrative techniques; sociological approaches to literary narrative

References and further reading

Ashcroft, Bill, Gareth Griffiths, and Helen Tiffin (1989) *The Empire Writes Back*, London: Routledge.

Benson, Eugene, and L. W. Connolly (eds) (1994) *Encyclopedia of Post-Colonial Literatures in English*, London: Routledge.

Boehmer, Elleke (1995) *Colonial and Post-colonial Literature*, Oxford: Oxford University Press.

Childs, Peter, and Patrick Williams (1996) *Introduction to Post-Colonial Theory*, Hemel Hempstead: Prentice Hall.

Dirlik, Arif (1994) 'The Post-Colonial Aura: Third World Criticism in the Age of Global Capitalism', *Critical Inquiry*, 20, 328–56.

Fanon, Frantz (1967) *The Wretched of the Earth*, trans. Constance Farrington, Harmondsworth: Penguin.

Forsdick, Charles, and David Murphy (eds) (2003) *Francophone Post-colonial Studies*, London: Arnold.

Gadjigo, Samba, Ralph H. Falkingham, Thomas Cassirer, and Reinhard Sander (eds) (1993) *Ousmane*

Sembene: Dialogues with Critics and Writers, Amherst: University of Massachusetts Press.

Jameson, Fredric (1986) 'Third World Literature in the Era of Multinational Capitalism', *Social Text*, 15, 65–88.

McClintock, Anne (1993) 'The Angel of Progress', in Williams and Chrisman (eds) *Colonial Discourse and Post-Colonial Theory*, Hemel Hempstead: Harvester Wheatsheaf.

Mishra, Vijay, and Bob Hodge (1993) 'What is Post(-)colonialism?', in Williams and Chrisman (eds) *Colonial Discourse and Post-Colonial Theory*, Hemel Hempstead: Harvester Wheatsheaf.

Ngugi wa Thiong'o (1986) *Decolonising the Mind*, London: Heinemann.

Said, Edward (1993) *Culture and Imperialism*, London: Chatto.

——(1994) *The Politics of Dispossession*, London: Vintage.

Sandhu, Sukdev (2003) *London Calling*, London: HarperCollins.

Williams, Patrick, and Laura Chrisman (eds) (1993) *Colonial Discourse and Post-Colonial Theory*, Hemel Hempstead: Harvester Wheatsheaf.

PATRICK WILLIAMS

POSTMODERN NARRATIVE

Nothing about postmodernism is uncontroversial. Whether it is a period, a movement, or a general 'condition' of culture, how broadly or narrowly it is distributed around the world, when it began and whether it has ended, even whether it happened at all, are all matters of dispute (see, e.g., Bertens 1995 and Calinescu 1987). The prefix *post*- identifies postmodernism as chronologically subsequent to modernism (*see* MODERNIST NARRATIVE), thereby placing it in the second half of the twentieth century, but its exact relationship to modernism is as hotly contested as anything else about it. If there is little consensus about what it is, nevertheless postmodernism is used as a counter in a wide variety of contemporary language games, including the language game of narrative theory. A preliminary distinction needs to be drawn between theories of postmodern narrative and postmodern theories of narrative – that is, between theories that seek to account for the poetics of narratives identified as postmodern, and general theories of narrative based on ideas native to the postmodern period (and more properly characterised as *poststructuralist theories of narrative) (Gibson 1996). The present essay will focus on the poetics of postmodern narrative, and in particular on the repertoire of strategies and devices by means of which postmodern narrative reflects on ontological questions (questions of being). Such questions include, what is a world? How many worlds are there, of what kinds, constituted in what ways? How do they differ, and what happens when they interact or collide? What is the mode of existence of a text, on the one hand, and of the fictional world (or worlds) it projects, on the other? How are such fictional worlds made, and how can they be unmade? What are the consequences of the making, unmaking and proliferation of fictional worlds for the way we think about, and live in, the real world?

Theories of postmodernism

General theories of postmodernism abound, and it would be impossible to review them all here. Two of the most influential of these theories, one based in the history of consciousness, the other in economic history, have special relevance to narrative. The first is Lyotard's theory that postmodernism reflects incredulity toward the *master narratives of progress, enlightenment, and human liberation that served to legitimate modern culture (*see* SCIENCE AND NARRATIVE). Sceptical of such 'grand narratives', postmodernism instead values the self-legitimating 'little' narratives of local groups, limited *institutions, and subcultural enclaves. Lyotard's theory helps explain both the paradoxical *anti-narrative impulse in some postmodern narrative, and the countervailing proliferation of stories and anecdotes in everything from Latin-American *magical realist novels to *television talk-shows. The other relevant general theory is Jameson's *Marxist account of postmodernism as the 'cultural logic of late capitalism'. According to Jameson, postmodernism in the cultural sphere (including narrative forms such as film and prose fiction) reflects the late capitalist mode of production in the economic sphere. Jameson inventories the constitutive features of postmodernism: the 'depthlessness' of a culture based on simulation and the circulation of *images; the weakening of a sense of history; 'schizophrenic' disjointedness and an intensified form of collage; a new experience of the sublime, identified with technology instead of nature; and a new experience of architectural *space, or what Jameson calls 'hyperspace'.

Influential as they have been, such 'high' theories don't provide a direct bridge to actual narrative practice. Jameson comes closer to doing so than Lyotard; but closer still is Jencks, an architecture critic largely responsible for the currency of the term 'postmodernism' in his own field. According to Jencks, postmodernism in architecture is characterised by 'double-coding'. Postmodern buildings communicate on two different levels, to two different constituencies: on one level, through their modernist structural techniques and in-group ironies, they communicate with a minority constituency of architects and connoisseurs; on another, they reach a broader public of consumers through their allusions to familiar historical styles of architecture. Jencks saw analogies to architectural double-coding in the postmodern novels of John Barth and Umberto Eco, simultaneously popular (especially Eco's) and avantgarde. However, it was left to Hutcheon to develop Jencks's double-coding idea into a full-fledged theory of postmodern narrative, which she identifies with the *genre she dubs *historiographic metafiction. Historiographic metafictions such as John Fowles's *The French Lieutenant's Woman*, Eco's *The Name of the Rose*, E. L. Doctorow's *Ragtime*, D. M. Thomas's *The White Hotel*, and Salman Rushdie's *Midnight's Children* narrate versions of history in legible, reader-friendly ways yet at the same time reflect critically and ironically on historical reconstruction itself (*see* HISTORIOGRAPHY).

Common to many of these accounts (including Jameson's, Jencks's, and Hutcheon's) is the assumption of postmodernism's belatedness, its 'post-'ness. Where modernists sought to 'make it new', postmodernists rummage through the cultural attic of past devices, styles, genres, and texts, recycling them in the modes of parody, pastiche, recontextualisation, and revision (as in Kathy Acker's subversive rewritings of literary classics and Angela Carter's revisionist *fairy tales, or, in the sphere of popular culture, the proliferation of Hollywood remakes, 'tribute' albums, and 'retro' fashions) (*see* INTERTEXTUALITY; NARRATIVE VERSIONS; POSTMODERN REWRITES). Critics sceptical of the 'myth of the postmodernist breakthrough' observe that postmodernism's most characteristic features, such as metafictional self-reflection, are hardly 'innovative', since most if not all of them can be found in narratives from earlier periods (*see* METAFICTION; REFLEXIVITY). Most damning of all,

postmodernism is accused of uncritically replicating modernist aesthetic values such as *irony, difficulty, self-consciousness, etc., while pretending to have superseded modernism.

Ontological poetics

While recycling is undoubtedly a feature of postmodern narrative, the charge of belatedness can be answered by appealing to the concept of the dominant (*see* FUNCTION (JAKOBSON)). Literary-historical change rarely involves the wholesale replacement of outmoded features and values by new ones, but more typically involves a reshuffling of existing features in the light of a new dominant function. Responding to changes in the world at large (such as the onset of late capitalism, in Jameson's terms) as well as the internal dynamics of literary history, dominants shift; what had formerly been foregrounded recedes to the background, while background elements advance to the foreground. Thus modernist features certainly do persist in postmodern narratives, but subject to a different dominant: where modernist narrative had been oriented toward investigating issues of perception and cognition, *perspective, the subjective experience of *time, the circulation and reliability of knowledge, etc., postmodern narrative is oriented differently, toward issues of fictionality, modes of being and the differences among them, the nature and plurality of worlds, how such worlds are made and unmade, etc. (*see* FICTION, THEORIES OF; POSSIBLE-WORLDS THEORY; TEXT-WORLD APPROACH TO NARRATIVE). In other words, postmodern narrative reflects an ontological dominant where modernist narrative reflected an epistemological one.

Postmodern narratives probe ontological issues by deploying a repertoire of characteristic devices and strategies (McHale 1987, anticipated by Fokkema 1984). First, there are strategies for pluralizing the fictional world itself; secondly, strategies for laying bare the ways in which fictional worlds are made, or in which they *fail* to be made; thirdly, strategies for driving a wedge between text and world, splitting them apart and pitting them one against the other; and fourth, strategies for exposing to view the ultimate ontological grounding of fictional worlds – their grounding, on the one hand, in the material reality of the book, and on the other hand in the material activity of an *author.

All narratives produce multiple possible worlds – potential states of affairs, subjective realities, etc. – but these are normally subordinated to a single actual world (see MODALITY). Postmodern narratives, by contrast, actualise multiple worlds, juxtaposing them and exploring the tensions between them. Weaker forms of ontological pluralism are achieved in conspiracy narratives, with their paranoid suspicions about another order of things behind the visible one (e.g., Don DeLillo's novels, Eco's *Foucault's Pendulum*). Stronger forms juxtapose a recognisably real world with an adjacent fantastic world (e.g., Carlos Fuentes's *Aura*, Julio Cortázar's *House Taken Over*) or mingle naturalistic and supernatural elements (as in magical realist narratives), or they juxtapose the world of the living with the 'world to come', exploring the ultimate ontological frontier between life and death (e.g., Pynchon's *Gravity's Rainbow*, Alastair Gray's *Lanark*, James Merrill's long narrative poem, *The Changing Light at Sandover*). If one were to collapse such a multiworld structure onto a single plane, the result would be a paradoxical 'heterotopia', where fragments of many worlds mingle in an impossible space, such as we find in Italo Calvino's *Invisible Cities*, or in the centreless, chaotic 'Zone' of *Gravity's Rainbow*.

Plurality of worlds in postmodern narrative is often achieved by exploiting the conventions of various popular novelistic genres (see NOVEL, THE): *science fiction, with its literal juxtapositions of present and future, of one planet and another; the *fantastic, with its intrusions of other worlds into the fabric of this one; and historical fiction, with its complex mingling of the factual and the overtly fictional (see HISTORICAL NOVEL). Such genres are compatible with postmodernism's ontological dominant. By contrast, when postmodern narratives adapt the conventions of *detective fiction, a profoundly epistemological genre, they typically do so 'against the grain', subverting the genre's norms: mysteries go unsolved, detectives fail to perform their roles, ratiocination itself is discredited, and the case becomes metaphysical (e.g., Eco's *The Name of the Rose*, Paul Auster's *New York Trilogy*) (Merivale and Sweeney 1999). Plurality of worlds in postmodernist novels is sometimes signalled by the presence of a character who has 'migrated' from another fictional universe (e.g., Nabokov's Lolita in Gilbert Sorrentino's *Imaginative Qualities of Actual Things*). Alternatively, it may be signalled by the abrupt, shattering irruption into the primary world

of a being from another world, such as the angels of *Gravity's Rainbow* or the aliens of television's *The X-Files*, or by the opening of a kind of 'window' or 'portal' from one world onto another, such as the mirrors of Angela Carter's *The Infernal Desire Machines of Dr. Hoffman* or the ubiquitous television screens of DeLillo's *White Noise* and Pynchon's *Vineland*.

While some postmodernist fictions provoke ontological reflection by projecting a plurality of worlds, others do so by troubling the very processes by which fictional worlds are constructed. One means of troubling the world-building process, and thereby exposing it to scrutiny, involves projecting a state of affairs in the fictional world and then rescinding it or contradicting it or otherwise placing it 'under erasure'. Placing parts of the world under erasure is a strategy common to the *nouveaux romanciers* (Alain Gobbe-Grillet, Jean Ricardou, Claude Simon) and the American surfictionists (Ronald Sukenick, Steve Katz, Clarence Major), among others (see NOUVEAU ROMAN; SURFICTION). Robert Coover, in stories such as 'The Babysitter' and *The Elevator*, produces multiple, mutually contradictory narrative sequences, actualising the 'garden of forking paths' structure that Borges once speculated about.

A related strategy involves distributing different parts of a world, or different worlds, over a number of narrative levels, one inset or embedded or nested inside the other like Chinese boxes or Russian Matrushka dolls, as in Barth's short story 'Menelaiad' (see EMBEDDING; FRAMED NARRATIVE). Inset micro-worlds are narratologically dependent upon, and consequently ontologically 'weaker' than, the framing worlds in which they are inset, and opportunities for paradox abound, including *trompe l'oeil* effects (one level mistaken for another) and 'strange loops' or *metalepses, when narrative sequences spill over from one level to higher or lower levels (and sometimes back again). The *nouveaux romanciers*, as well as Sorrentino in *Mulligan Stew* and Calvino in *If on a Winter's Night a Traveler*, intensively exploit such opportunities. Another conspicuous narratological paradox that postmodern narratives regularly exploit is *mise en abyme*, the mirroring or duplication at a lower (embedded) narrative level of the higher-level world in which the duplicate is embedded. Familiar from the play-within-the-play structure of *Hamlet*, *mise en abyme* is ubiquitous in postmodern narrative, from the novels-within-the-novel of *If on a*

Winter's Night a Traveler to the structure of the abbey library in Eco's *The Name of the Rose*, which duplicates in miniature the novel's medieval universe.

If one focus of postmodern ontological reflection is the fictional world and its construction, another focus is the language of the fictional text. Some postmodern novels subject figurative language to particularly intense scrutiny and pressure, laying bare the unsettled relationship between the figurative and the literal. This is the approach, for instance, of García Márquez's magic realist novels *One Hundred Years of Solitude* and *The Autumn of the Patriarch*, in which surrealist imagery sometimes functions metaphorically, but at other times reflects the fantastic realities that are such conspicuous features of these narrative worlds. *Gravity's Rainbow* is riddled with overgrown similes and *metaphors that create their own finely textured micro-worlds, temporarily eclipsing the novel's primary world. Another postmodern approach to the fictional text involves opening up a rift or gap between the level of text and the level of world, dissolving their normally close interdependence and thereby impeding the reader's progress from 'word' to 'world'. This is accomplished in some cases by means of intense stylisation (e.g., Guy Davenport, William Gass), in others by cliché and deliberate infelicity (e.g., Donald Barthelme, Kathy Acker), in still others by chance (e.g., William Burroughs' cut-up and fold-in techniques) or by mechanical text-generating procedures, as in the texts of the *Oulipo writers (Raymond Queneau, Georges Perec, Calvino, Harry Mathews, and others). In every case, the object is to heighten language's palpability or its opacity, or in other words, to foreground those qualities that make language a potential object of attention in its own right, independently of any world that it might happen to project.

The entire edifice of the fictional text ultimately rests, in one sense, on the ontological foundation of its material support – the page, lines of type, the book as object – and in another sense on its origins in the activities, in real time and space, of a real author. Postmodern novels systematically trouble their own groundings, in both these senses – on the one hand, by foregrounding the materiality of the text instead of effacing it, as would normally be the case in novels; on the other hand, by making the author's problematic presence 'behind' the text an issue in the text itself. Examples of the first type of un-grounding

include narratives distributed between a 'main' text and its annotations, as in Nabokov's *Pale Fire* or David Foster Wallace's *Infinite Jest*, and the shaped 'concrete prose' found in the novels of Raymond Federman and Christine Brooke-Rose, or in Mark Danielewski's *House of Leaves*. Examples of problematising authorship include the recurrent postmodern *topos* of the writer at his or her desk writing the text at hand (Sukenick calls this the 'truth of the page'), and the simulated 'death of the author' rehearsed throughout Beckett's fiction and in Federman's *The Voice in the Closet*.

Cybertext

Some observers have thought that by the beginning of the new millennium postmodern narrative had run its course and exhausted itself, but others see it as renewing and even fulfilling itself through its affiliation with the new digital *media. Emerging in the 1980s, hypertext, i.e., textual or other informational media distributed in blocks and joined by electronic links, was championed as the actualisation and even vindication of poststructuralist theory (Landow 1997). Hypertext narrative, in particular, seemed destined to become the medium that postmodern narrative had been anticipating all along – literal gardens of forking paths! The hype outstripped the accomplishment, however, and first-generation hypertext narratives such as Michael Joyce's *Afternoon* and Stuart Moulthrop's *Victory Garden* appear in retrospect much less postmodern than they seemed at the time, and not even as fully hypertextual as contemporaneous print novels such as Milorad Pavič's *Dictionary of the Khazars*. Digital mediation does not inevitably entail reflection on ontological questions, and first-generation hypertext novels seem animated much more by epistemological concerns than by ontological ones. If postmodern print narrative is to achieve its digital fulfilment anywhere, it is more likely to be elsewhere in the range of digital forms that constitute Aarseth's umbrella category of 'cybertext', including MUDs (multiple-user domains), MOOs (object-oriented MUDs), *simulation games, and other approximations of the dream of virtual reality (Ryan 2001). Are digital media the apotheosis of postmodern narrative, or the end of narrative as we know it? Neither, probably, nothing about postmodernism is certain, but the utopian and apocalyptic scenarios are probably both exaggerated.

SEE ALSO: computer games and narrative; digital narrative

References and further reading

Aarseth, Espen J. (1997) *Cybertext: Perspectives on Ergodic Literature*, Baltimore: Johns Hopkins University Press.

Bertens, Hans (1995) *The Idea of the Postmodern: A History*, London: Routledge.

Calinescu, Matei (1987) *Five Faces of Modernity: Modernism, Avant-Garde, Decadence, Kitsch, Postmodernism*, Durham: Duke University Press.

Fokkema, Douwe W. (1984) *Literary History, Modernism, and Postmodernism*, Amsterdam: John Benjamins.

Gibson, Andrew (1996) *Towards a Postmodern Theory of Narrative*, Edinburgh: Edinburgh University Press.

Hutcheon, Linda (1988) *A Poetics of Postmodernism: History, Theory, Fiction*, New York: Routledge.

Jameson, Fredric (1991) *Postmodernism, or, The Cultural Logic of Late Capitalism*, Durham: Duke University Press.

Jencks, Charles (1986) *What is Postmodernism?*, London: Academy Editions.

Landow, George P. (1997) *Hypertext 2.0*, Baltimore: Johns Hopkins University Press.

Lyotard, Jean-Francois (1984) *The Postmodern Condition: A Report on Knowledge*, Minneapolis: University of Minnesota Press.

McHale, Brian (1987) *Postmodernist Fiction*, London: Methuen.

Merivale, Patricia, and Susan Elizabeth Sweeney (1999) *Detecting Texts: The Metaphysical Detective Story from Poe to Postmodernism*, Philadelphia: University of Pennsylvania Press.

Ryan, Marie-Laure (2001) *Narrative as Virtual Reality: Immersion and Interactivity in Literature and Electronic Media*, Baltimore: Johns Hopkins University Press.

BRIAN McHALE

POSTMODERN REWRITES

According to Pfister (1991), postmodern *intertextuality is not just 'one device among others'; rather, it is used as a 'central constructional principle' (214), thereby becoming a culturally dominant tool. *Postmodern narrative and artefacts in general are heavily intertextual since postmodern representation typically entails, and flaunts, a textual 'reprise' (Moraru forthcoming). That is, setting out to describe an object or narrate an *event (*see* EXISTENT), postmodern narrative simultaneously recollects, remembers, gathers together (collage-like and otherwise), and brings before us texts and representations of other objects and events.

Within postmodern intertextuality, critics have identified the particular practice of postmodern rewriting and, resulting from it, the postmodern rewrite. Postmodern rewrites take to another level intertextuality and its subsets as inventoried by Genette and others. A complex form, the postmodern rewrite may incorporate allusions to a previous work, *ironies, pastiches, etc., but it usually deploys, rather conspicuously, an elaborate diegetic parallel to a prior text, which oftentimes is also of narrative nature (Moraru 2001: 19) (*see* ALLEGORY). In other words, key here is the act of intentional renarrativisation (*see* INTENTIONALITY; NARRATIVISATION). As a *postmodern* act, this renarrativisation, or, retelling, differs from traditional imitation or replica in that it goes beyond simply rehashing, and paying homage to, its 'model'. In fact, numerous – if not all – postmodern rewrites erode this 'model' and its underpinning ideologies while critiquing the very social context within which the dialogue of the rewrite and the rewritten occurs. To put it otherwise, the rewrite reworks not only a text from the past – a form – but also cultural formations, i.e., the values underlying that text.

While usually suffused with intertextuality and its self-reflexive subcategory, *metafiction, not every postmodern narrative is a rewrite. Nevertheless, the number and significance of postmodern rewrites across literatures and narrative traditions are remarkable. A few examples: E. L. Doctorow's *Ragtime*, which rewrites Heinrich von Kleist's *Michael Kohlhaas*; Robert Coover's *The Public Burning*, a rewriting of Horatio Alger's novels; Charles Johnson's *Middle Passage*, which redoes Melville's *Moby-Dick* and *Benito Cereno*; John Updike's *Roger's version*, Kathy Acker's *Blood and Guts in High School*, Bharati Mukherjee's *The Holder of the World*, Maryse Condé's *I, Tituba, Black Witch of Salem*, all of which rework Hawthorne's *Scarlet Letter*; J. M. Coetzee's *Foe*, a rewriting of Defoe's *Robinson Crusoe*; Leonardo Sciascia's *Candido*, a postmodern retelling of Voltaire's *Candide*.

SEE ALSO: adaptation; metanarrative commentary; mise en abyme; narrative versions; palimpsest; reflexivity; surfiction

References and further reading

Calinescu, Matei (1997) 'Rewriting', in Hans Bertens and Douwe Fokkema (eds) *International Postmodernism: Theory and Literary Practice*, Amsterdam/Philadelphia: John Benjamins.

Cornis-Pope, Marcel (2001) *Narrative Innovation and Cultural Rewriting in the Cold War Era and After*, New York: Palgrave.

Cowart, David (1993) *Literary Symbiosis: The Reconfigured Text in Twentieth-Century Writing*, Athens: The University of Georgia Press.

Doležel, Lubomír (1998) 'Epilogue. Fictional Words in Transduction: Postmodernist Rewrites', *Heterocosmica: Fictional and Possible Worlds*, Baltimore: Johns Hopkins University Press.

Moraru, Christian (2001) *Rewriting: Postmodern Narrative and Cultural Critique in the Age of Cloning*, Albany: State University of New York Press.

——(Forthcoming) *Memorious Discourse: Reprise and Representation in Postmodern Theory and Narrative*.

Pfister, Manfred (1991) 'How Postmodern Is Intertextuality?', in Heinrich F. Plett (ed.) *Intertextuality*, Berlin: Walter de Gruyter.

CHRISTIAN MORARU

POSTSTRUCTURALIST APPROACHES TO NARRATIVE

In the second half of the 1960s, some structuralist theorists, many of whom contributed to the French literary journal *Tel Quel*, came to broaden and relativise structuralist approaches to narrative texts (*see* STRUCTURALIST NARRATOLOGY). In general, this shift implies that a narrative is no longer reduced to one abstract and supposedly universal deep structure, and that a text is no longer regarded as a self-contained structure but rather as an open and multi-stranded texture linked with the extra-textual context (*see* INTERTEXTUALITY; NARRATIVE STRUCTURE). Thus, both text and context are viewed from a different angle than the one prevalent in classical structuralism. The classical search for textual coherence is replaced by an investigation of the ways in which the text leaves things undecided, open, and even contradictory (*see* INDETERMINACY). Dynamics, multiplicity, *polyphony, and boundary transgression are the keywords, replacing the structuralist preferences for static and homogeneous structures, clearly identifiable narrating *voices (*see* NARRATOR), and clear-cut boundaries.

In this respect, poststructuralism is similar to the *deconstructive approach exemplified by the work of Jacques Derrida. Indeed, Derrida's deconstructive approach can be viewed as the central influence on poststructuralist narrative analysis. Other important influences are the works of late structuralists such as Barthes and Kristeva; the ideological analyses of Foucault and Lyotard (*see* DISCOURSE ANALYSIS (FOUCAULT)); the psychoanalytical readings of Lacan; and the psychosocial investigations by Deleuze and Guattari.

With the shift to poststructuralism's open-ended view of texts, the *narrativity and literariness of the text no longer occupy the centre of attention. They are replaced by the more general concept of textuality, regarded as the cross-point of various texts. This means that there is no single integrated poststructuralist narratology comparable to Gérard Genette's embracing structuralist systematisation. In the analysis of contexts in which particular narratives are situated, special attention is paid not only to the corporeal and the unconscious, the latter seen as a form of language, but also to the ideological patterns that infuse narratives (*see* IDEOLOGY AND NARRATIVE).

This shift is exemplified in the work of Roland Barthes. In 1966 he published a classic structuralist analysis of the narrative text (Barthes 1977a), starting from the idea that the narrative form is universal and that it is based on one single abstract deep structure, consisting of functions and indices (*see* FUNCTION (PROPP); NARRATIVE UNITS). On the higher level of *narration, Barthes admits the importance of the narrating and reading subject, but it is not until 1970 (Barthes 1974) that he explicitly states that so-called deep-structures are in fact the work of the reader. In this readerly view of narrative structures, every story and every reading entails its own structure (*see* READERLY TEXT, WRITERLY TEXT (BARTHES)). The latter is no longer studied as a combination of minimal units such as functions and indices, but rather as a texture, a weave of five *codes that the reader uses to process the text. These codes interact and refer to the extra-textual context, thereby opening up the closed system of the text, and letting in the reader's *desire and ideology. From 1970 onward, Barthes develops this link between text and desire, stating that narratives are *metaphors for bodily longings and that reading is a form of pleasure-seeking which responds to the text's seductive way of telling.

The incorporation of human desire in narrative theory highlights an ambiguity in the poststructuralist view on language. On the one hand, language is regarded as an impersonal and pre-existent realm enforcing itself upon its user, who is reduced to a mere instrument. This is reflected in Barthes' slogan (1977b) about the death of the *author and in Michel Foucault's (1970) view of 'man' as a recent and expiring invention, a mere construction of a certain type of discourse. On the other hand, the subject's desire is recognised as the prime source and drive behind the use of language (*see* PSYCHOANALYSIS AND NARRATIVE).

The connection between text and body is a recurrent theme in poststructuralist approaches to narrative texts. It reflects the move from a strictly linguistic view of the text to a broader view on language and corporeality. As such, it is influenced by Jacques Lacan's famous dictum that the unconscious is structured like a language. Lacan (1977) starts from Freud's assertion that the unconscious operates via the processes of condensation (combining elements from different semantic fields) and displacement (moving between elements from the same field); he then equates condensation with the linguistic process of metaphor and displacement with that of *metonymy. The desire underlying narratives is a constant interplay between these two processes, which form the basis of the Lacanian approach to narrative, refining the idea that such a narrative is a metaphor for the body of the writer and the reader. A comparable view of the text as a metaphoric body can be found in the work of Gilles Deleuze and Félix Guattari (1983), who relate the signifying processes of texts to the productive dynamics of a so-called body-without-organs; and in the work of Julia Kristeva (1984), who uses the concept of *chora* (intimately linked to the feminine and maternal body) as a bridge between the preverbal bodily drives (forming the basis of the so-called genotext) and the verbal structures of representation (making up the so-called phenotext). Signification arises in the interaction between these two levels.

Kristeva associates these processes with the feminine and masculine ways of signifying, linking the preverbal to the feminine and the linguistic to the masculine. This ties in with the notion of *écriture féminine*, and, more generally, with the typically poststructuralist concern for the ideological patterning of signifying processes, as witnessed by the work of Foucault. Concomitantly, ideology can be seen to be patterned like a story, or, in the influential account of Jean-François Lyotard (1986), like a *master narrative, an implicit frame providing meaning and orientation vis-à-vis so-called self-evident concepts such as man and reason. Once more, this broad, open, and contextualised view of narrative as a signifying process moves away from technical forms of narratological analysis à la Genette.

SEE ALSO: feminist narratology; gender studies; genealogy; narrative dynamics; postclassical narratology; postmodern narrative; reader-response theory

References and further reading

Barthes, Roland (1974) *S/Z: An Essay*, trans. Richard Miller, New York: Hill and Wang.
——(1977a) 'Introduction to the Structural Analysis of Narratives', in Stephen Heath (ed.) *Image-Music-Text*, Glasgow: Fontana/Collins.
——(1977b) 'The Death of the Author', in Stephen Heath (ed.) *Image-Music-Text*, Glasgow: Fontana/Collins.
Deleuze, Gilles, and Félix Guattari (1983) *Anti-Oedipus: Capitalism and Schizophrenia*, trans. Robert Hurley, Mark Seem, and Helen R. Lane, Minneapolis: University of Minnesota Press.
Foucault, Michel (1970) *The Order of Things: An Archaeology of the Human Sciences*, trans. not specified, London: Routledge.
Kristeva, Julia (1984) *Revolution in Poetic Language*, trans. Margaret Waller, New York: Columbia University Press.
Lacan, Jacques (1977) *Écrits: A Selection*, trans. Alan Sheridan, New York: W.W. Norton.
Lyotard, Jean-François (1986) *The Postmodern Condition: A Report on Knowledge*, trans. Geoff Bennington and Brian Massumi, Manchester: Manchester University Press.

LUC HERMAN AND BART VERVAECK

PRAGMATICS

When talking about the pragmatics of narrative, it is important to realise that pragmatics was not developed from inside linguistics, but rather was based on thoughts originating in related fields, such as *philosophy, *sociology, the theory of interactions, etc. Linguists were alerted to pragmatics only through the aporias that arose within their strictly limited field of view. Similarly, literary studies did not 'discover' pragmatics by itself; philosophers, literary theorists, and pragmaticists developed approaches to the study of texts as related to human users simultaneously. The purpose of these endeavours was to make sense of the fact that language does not always obey the strictures of the grammarians. Indeed, the linguistic structure of a text has, in many cases, very little to do with what the text 'does', or with how a text is produced and consumed by the users of language. Pragmatics may be defined broadly as 'the study of the use of language in human communication, as determined by the conditions of society' (Mey 2001: 6). Applying this definition to literary, in particular narrative, communication, we may say that narrative pragmatics is concerned with the user's role in the societal production and consumption of narrative.

Speech act theory and the Principle of Cooperation

Early approaches to literary pragmatics (often called 'text linguistics') took their point of departure in certain concepts that had been developed in linguistics mainly in order to cope with the needs of grammatical description. A text was thought of as a hierarchically structured complex of sentences, just like the sentence itself was considered a hierarchically structured unit of 'phrases' (noun phrases, verb phrases, etc.). 'Grammars of narrative' were proposed in parallel with the sentential grammar developed by Chomsky and his school (see, e.g., van Dijk 1972; *see* LINGUISTIC APPROACHES TO NARRATIVE; STORY GRAMMARS).

Later efforts were spurred on by the achievements of philosophers and pragmaticists such as Austin and Searle, who developed a theory of *'speech acts', that is, utterances that 'did' something in addition to being merely 'uttered'. The idea that utterances had a 'performative', not just a 'constative' value (originally due to Austin 1962) gave rise to classifications of speech acts into categories such as assertions, questions, orders, apologies, and so on (*see* PERFORMATIVITY). It was suggested that one could look at a text as if it were a gigantic macro-speech act which subsumed all sorts of individual acts, each expressed in some hierarchically ordered, linguistically recognisable form. This approach failed for several reasons. For one thing, it was not easy to explain the exact relationships between the different acts making up the text; there was also the problem of specifying hierarchical constraints given the essentially linear, and often unpredictable, nature of narrative 'speech acting'. But the idea that the sentences of a

narrative were conjoined in deeper ways than just being strung together on the surface ('concatenated' in Chomskyan parlance) had taken hold. Similarly, the notion that language 'performed', 'did' something, led to the interesting hypothesis that in narrative, certain sentences were 'doable', or 'speakable', but others not (Banfield 1982; *see* NO-NARRATOR THEORY).

Perhaps the most important insight into the nature of narrative as one way of 'doing things with words' was due, again, not to a linguist, but rather to a philosopher, H. Paul Grice, who took the ideas developed by Austin (1962) and Searle (1969) several steps further. In order to explain the regularity of human conversations and their mostly successful outcomes, Grice postulated the Principle of Cooperation (or 'Cooperative Principle'), stipulating that every person's contribution to a conversation should be commensurate to its purpose (including the aims and motives of the participants). He suggested four Conversational Maxims regulating our cooperative handling of conversational information: making it sufficient ('the maxim of quantity'), true ('quality'), relevant ('relation') and orderly ('manner'). Any infringement of these maxims should be interpreted (assuming the general idea of conversation as cooperation) as *implying* an additional meaning. For instance, breaking ('flouting') a maxim imparts a message that, although not explicitly mentioned, nevertheless is understood. Grice's famous example is that of a professor writing a recommendation for a student, consisting of a statement about the student's attendance in class and his correct English spelling – clearly irrelevant matters in the context – and thus implying that there must be a reason for the professor's unwillingness to cooperate: the student does not deserve a 'real' recommendation (Grice 1989: 30). Grice's notion of 'implicature' is of the utmost importance when it comes to explaining how *authors and readers go about 'co-creating' a literary narrative, as will be shown below.

Production and consumption

A common model of production and consumption in Western societies goes like this: A producer delivers a product to the market; the consumer pays the market price, acquires the product, and starts consuming it. After the transaction is concluded, producer and consumer part ways, never to meet again except in special cases (foreseen by the laws regulating trade in our society), such as inferior product quality or unsatisfactory handling of the financial aspects of the purchase. This relationship is purely linear and unidirectional; the deal, once consummated, cannot be reversed (barring special circumstances such as return or repossession of the product). One may be tempted to apply this simple model to the production and consumption of literary works: the author is the producer of some literary text, while the reader is a consumer who happens to be 'in the market' for a particular literary product (*see* AUDIENCE; READER CONSTRUCTS). Once the book is bought, the reader is free to do whatever he or she wants to do with it: take it home and place it on the shelf in the living room, possibly read it, or maybe even throw it in the trash – or at somebody, literally or metaphorically.

In reality, things do not happen quite like that. Buying a book is not like acquiring a piece of kitchenware or furniture. One does not just bring a *book* back from the bookstore: one takes home an *author*, inviting him or her into the privacy of one's quarters. The author, on the other hand, does not just make a living by producing reams of printed paper (granted, there are those that do), but has a message for the reader as a person. And this is, eventually, why books are bought and sold: not because they are indispensable for our material existence, but because they represent a personal communication from an author to a potential readership – a communication which, in order to be successful, will have to follow certain rules (*see* COMMUNICATION IN NARRATIVE). Such rules fall within the purview of pragmatic approaches to narrative.

Authorship and readership: rules and regulations

The process of writing has been likened to a technique of '*se-duction*': a writer takes a reader by the hand, *se*-parating him of her from the drudgery of everyday life and intro-*ducing* him or her to a new world, of which the writer is the creator and main 'authority' (Mey 2000). The reader will have to accept this seductive move and follow the author into the labyrinth of the latter's choice in order to participate properly in the literary exercise, even if it should involve meeting a Minotaur or two. The reader takes the narrative relay out of the hands

of the author: 'the author is dead, long live the reader', to paraphrase Barthes (1977; *see* READER-RESPONSE THEORY).

Marie-Laure Ryan (2001) envisions this reader participation along a twofold dimension: that of 'interactivity' (in which the reader manipulates the text) and that of *immersion (where the reader seamlessly identifies himself or herself with the text). In the immersive mode, the reader is not just a spectator on the virtual scene: the 'role of the reader' is that of an 'active participant in the process of creating the fictional space' (Mey 1994: 155; *see* STORYWORLD), and the immersed reader becomes a *'voice' in the text (see below). The reader is not only 'present at the creation' of the text; he or she is indeed its 'creator' (Barthes 1977).

Pragmatically, the success of the *narration thus not only depends on the author of the story, but to a high degree also on the reader. But there is more. In the process of creating the text, the reader, too, is created anew, reborn in the text's image. This interactivity is not just happening on the level of the text; it also involves the self, on a deeper level. 'This book changed my life' is therefore not just a trite expression we employ in the case of what we register as an exceptional reading experience: it is true for all reading and for all use and perusal of texts (Mey 1994: 155).

The dialectics of narration

A dialectic situation of interaction occurs when the interacting parties influence each other in such a way that the outcome of what one party does is a determining condition for the other's ability to operate. When speaking or writing, one is always engaged in some communication (informing our partner about some *event, apologising for inflicted injuries or insults, promising services, telling a story, and so on). In this activity, one crucially depends on the other's presence and cooperation, not only for the legitimacy of our speech acts (including those involved in narration; see below), but indeed for their very viability. Conversely, our fellow interactants depend crucially on who we think they are, and they will represent themselves to us in such a way as to be good storytelling partners. The way we see ourselves and our partners, and how they see themselves and us, is essential (*see* IDENTITY AND NARRATIVE). There is 'no narration without (self- and other-)representation', to vary an old slogan (*see* POSITIONING).

Pragmatically speaking, any text, and in particular a narrative text, is the result of what Bakhtin has called 'the meeting of two subjects' (1994: 107) – the two subjects being the author and the reader. The author is by definition conscious of his/her role in creating the 'fictional space' mentioned earlier. However, the reader's consciousness is just as essential in co-creating the fictional universe where the narration takes place. For Bakhtin, the reader is the (co-)creator of the text: it is in the dialogue between author and reader that the text, as a dialectic creation, emerges (*see* DIALOGISM).

But how do author and reader navigate the fictional space? For a reader, it is not enough to identify with the author passively; the reader must *consciously* adopt the co-creator role, assigned by the textual dialectics. Conversely, the author must *consciously* alert the reader to the signposts and other 'indexes' placed in the narrative space to enable the navigation process. In some older *novels, mainly those written in the eighteenth and nineteenth centuries (*see* REALIST NOVEL), the author often appears on the scene in person, apostrophising the reader and telling him or her what to do, what to feel, what not to object to, which disbeliefs to suspend, and so on (*see* COMMENTARY). The nineteenth-century British writer Anthony Trollope was a master of such 'persuasion-cum-connivance'.

In other cases, the co-creativity that is needed to make the narrative enterprise succeed, while less obvious, is (perhaps for that reason) considerably more effective. Notorious instances of successful 'reader deception' are found in the Argentine writer Julio Cortázar's work, as in the novella *Historia con migalas* (*A Story of Spiders*, 1985). Here, the author consciously leads the reader down a 'garden path' of narration (cf. Jahn 1999), along which the two female protagonists by default are assumed to be a male-female couple. Only in the story's very last sentence do they literally remove their morphological protection, along with their seductive veils (see Mey 1992; the trick is pulled off successfully only in the Spanish original).

The pragmatics of voice in narration

(1) Vocalisation. Vocalisation is a powerful way of creating and maintaining the fictional space, with the willing help and indispensable assistance from the readership, and of 'orchestrating' the dialectics of co-creativity between author and reader. Taken by itself, the term may be translated as 'giving a voice', 'making vocal' (or 'heard', depending on the perspective). In the context of narrative pragmatics, vocalisation means 'giving a voice to a character in the story', making the *character speak.

We are more or less familiar with the phenomenon from the simple fact of narrative *dialogue. Whenever a conversation is included in the story, we hear the voices of the characters discussing current events or other matters of interest. In situations like these, the attribution of voices is done in a straightforward manner, more or less as it happens in a play: the replies are put into the mouths of the characters, given 'voice' through the unique assignment of a familiar role name, and are often accompanied by linguistic 'signposts' such as 'he said', 'she laughed', 'he cried', and so on (called 'parentheticals').

(2) Voice and focus. Vocalisation is an intricate process, inasmuch as it not only gives 'voice' to a character in the strict sense of speaking one's part, but because it affords information about the character's *perspective or point of view (*see* FOCALIZATION; POINT OF VIEW (LITERARY)). What the voice indicates is not just the character as such (by naming the person; *see* NAMING IN NARRATIVE), but the viewpoint from which the character sees the other characters, and indeed the world. In this wider sense, voices range over the entire fictional space they create: 'Utterances belong to their speakers (or writers) only in the least interesting, purely physiological sense; but as successful communication, they always belong to (at least) two people, the speaker and his or her listener', as Morson and Emerson say (1990: 129).

Vocalisation always implies focalization, a focusing on the characters' placement in the fictional universe (Mey 2000: 148). In Bal's (1985) words, focalization is 'the relation between the elements presented [in narration] and the vision through which they are presented' (100). This vision and these relations are not open to direct inspection by the reader's naked eye, because they are mediated through the voice of the *narrator (Mey 2000: ch. 8.4); consequently, telling and seeing are orthogonal to (rather than parallel with) one another.

(3) The pitfalls of voice. In the absence of obvious 'signposts' and especially when we are dealing with an unspoken thought or an 'unspeakable sentence' (Banfield 1982), we may be

unsure whose 'voice' we are hearing (*see* THOUGHT AND CONSCIOUSNESS REPRESENTATION (LITERATURE)). This is where pragmatics comes to the rescue: a sentence, in order to be speakable, must have a speaking subject, says Banfield (1982) – not just a sentential subject, but one authoring the utterance that is placed in a context in which certain utterances are speakable by certain persons. Successful vocalisation at the author end is matched on the part of the reader by successful revocalisation: the reader co-creates the part of the fictional universe in which the utterance is spoken, and attributes the voices unambiguously to the focalizing narrator or characters.

Voices may sound in harmony, or they may clash. A voice that is not in accordance with what the reader knows about the character will jar, not sound right; we do not feel it is the voice of the character but perhaps the voice of the intrusive narrator, trying to disguise himself as a character – or even, as in the case of Trollope, as the author (*see* AUTHENTICATION; RELIABILITY). Other clashes are often explained in terms of 'poetic license', as when animals are attributed 'vocalisations' that are not in keeping with their animal status (in *Anna Karenina*, for instance, we encounter quoted thoughts ascribed to the bird-dog Laska). In other cases, the reader is confused, as when voices speak 'out of order', having access to material which is strictly not accessible given the characters' background, or maybe even false (cf Mey 2000: ch. 6). Such 'clashes' may be intentional, as when a comic effect is obtained by letting characters adopt modes of speech that are not commensurate with the speech proper to the events narrated, as in the Monty Python movie *Life of Brian*, in which Brian, hanging on the cross, intones 'Always look on the bright side of life'.

The scope of pragmatics

The role of the user has served to guide this entry's reflections on the ways readers and authors participate in the common endeavour of creating a narrative text. The dialogue of authors and readers is, in short, a dialogue of users. This 'dialectics of dialogue' explains the co-creative role of author and reader in establishing the narrative object, the story.

But dialogue does not happen *in vacuo*; it is 'a dialogue of social forces perceived not only in their static co-existence, but also as a dialogue of different times, epochs and days, a dialogue that is forever dying, living, being born: co-existence and becoming are fused into an indissoluble, concrete *multi-speeched* unity . . .' (Bakhtin 1992: 365; emphasis added). Voices in narrative are anchored in the 'multispeeched' plurality of discourse; this multivocality represents the dialectic relations between different societal forces (*see* DISCOURSE ANALYSIS (FOUCAULT); HETEROGLOSSIA). If it is true that texts, and in particular narratives, only come into existence as human texts through an actual engagement by a human user (as already stated by Roman Ingarden in 1931), then the pragmatics of texts, in particular of narratives, is anchored in such user engagement. Conversely, the user is engaged only insofar as he or she is able to follow, and recreate, the text supplied by the author. Among the voices of the text, the reader, too, has one; but also this vocalisation is subject to the same societal conditions that surround the author. The narrative dialogue thus presupposes a wider context than the actual narration: 'interactive narrativity', far from being confined to recent developments in cognitive technology and computerised interaction (Ryan 2001), is the sociosemiotic and pragmatic basis of all narratives.

SEE ALSO: discourse analysis (linguistics); sociolinguistic approaches to narrative

References and further reading

Austin, John L. (1962) *How to Do Things with Words*, Oxford: Oxford University Press.
Bakhtin, Mikhail M. (1992 [1975]) 'Discourse in the Novel', in *The Dialogic Imagination*, ed. Michael Holquist, trans. Caryl Emerson and Michael Holquist, Austin: University of Texas Press.
——(1994 [1986]) *Speech Genres and Other Late Essays*, trans. Vern McGee, Austin: University of Texas Press.
Bal, Mieke (1985 [1980]) *Narratology: Introduction to the Theory of Narrative*, Toronto: University of Toronto Press.
Banfield, Ann (1982) *Unspeakable Sentences*, London: Routledge.
Barthes, Roland (1977) *Image Music Text,*, trans. Stephen Heath, London: Fontana.
van Dijk, Teun A. (1972) *Some Aspects of Text Grammars*, The Hague: Mouton.
Grice, H. Paul (1989) *Studies in the Way of Words*, Cambridge, Mass.: Harvard University Press.
Ingarden, Roman (1973 [1931]) *The Literary Work of Art*, trans. George G. Grabowicz, Evanston: Northwestern University Press.
Jahn, Manfred (1999) '"Speak, friend, and enter": Garden Paths, Artificial Intelligence, and Cognitive

Narratology', in David Herman (ed.) *Narratologies: New Perspectives on Narrative Analysis*, Columbus: Ohio State University Press.

Mey, Jacob L. (1992) 'Pragmatic Gardens and their Magic', *Poetics*, 20.2, 233–45.

—— (1994) 'Edifying Archie or: How to fool the Reader', in Herman Parret (ed.) *Pretending to Communicate*, Berlin: de Gruyter.

—— (2000) *When Voices Clash: A Study in Literary Pragmatics*, Berlin: de Gruyter.

—— (2001) *Pragmatics: An Introduction*, Oxford: Blackwell.

Morson, Gary S., and Caryl Emerson (1990) *Mikhail Bakhtin: The Creation of a Prosaics*, Stanford: Stanford University Press.

Ryan, Marie-Laure (2001) *Narrative as Virtual Reality: Immersion and Interactivity in Literature and Electronic Media*, Baltimore: Johns Hopkins University Press.

Searle, John R. (1969) *Speech Acts: An Essay in the Philosophy of Language*. Cambridge: Cambridge University Press.

JACOB L. MEY

PRISON NARRATIVES

A prison narrative is an account of life in prison by a prisoner, or a representation of prison life by those wishing to illuminate incarceration or employ its metaphoric impact. Depictions of rogues in the eighteenth-century Newgate calendar popularised criminals in Britain. The fictional representations of prison, as seen in the Newgate novels of the nineteenth-century, opened debate about social conditions. More recent accounts of prison life range from collections of poems and *letters to *fiction and *non-fiction, autobiographical excerpts, pieces of investigative *journalism (as seen in the prisoner-written *Angolite Magazine*), *films, *television series, and documentaries. Prisoners' autobiographical reflections may be written, spoken, drawn, painted, tattooed, sung, filmed, etc. (*see* AUTOBIOGRAPHY; MEDIA AND NARRATIVE).

Topics within prison narratives vary from *descriptions of physical and psychological effects within the cells, cellblocks, communal spaces, prison yards, and 'the hole' of solitary confinements to the everyday round of life within the bars, fences, and walls. Herein we see regimented schedules, discussions of quality and kinds of food, practice or restriction of religious freedom. We find sexuality challenged and subverted, observe guard, administrator, and gang hierarchies. Inmates detail work assignments such as chain gangs, laundry, custodial

duty, and light industry. They compile their experiences of and losses of educational opportunities such as writing workshops, arts courses, college courses, self-help meetings, etc. They make accounts of unjust incarceration, describe experiences with the *law; make confessions (*see* CONFESSIONAL NARRATIVE), reveal struggles with addictions, and tell of crimes committed by and against them during imprisonment. Inmates describe riots, fires, and other violence within the prison. They depict loneliness, loss, and despair and note their dreams for release, for family, and for return to 'the world'. They also speak of transcendence and self-discovery while inside. (For recent collections of prison narratives, see Chevigny 1999; Franklin 1998; Lamb 2003.)

Prison isolates the offender from the community, and simultaneously concentrates the inmates in hierarchically organised institutions whose social structure is mirrored in their architecture. From stone-towered, walled enclaves, to campus-like reformatories, to dungeon-like rooms of solitary confinement, to prefab modular facilities, these institutions, whether state-run public prisons or private, for-profit facilities, provide the settings for narratives that answer the panoptic *gaze the guard tower has trained on the celled prisoners. Such narratives voice the prisoners' reaction to the disciplinary powers of the modern penitentiary (see Foucault 1979).

One sub-genre of prison narrative is the prisoner-of-war narrative wherein *diaries, letters, memoirs, and films figure heavily in informing about capture, confinement, torture, resilience, and the fate of soldiers in wartime. Political prisoner narratives usually detail not only the politicised nature of the crime against a state but also testify to the observed lives of 'ordinary' criminals. Testimonials by those who have been captured, beaten, or raped by soldiers or police also figure as a type of prisoner narrative, although institutionalisation may not appear in the stories. Captivity narratives told by slaves, captured settlers, or dragooned sailors also speak of detainment and coercions with or without the traditionally regimented confine of cellblocks or brigs (*see* SLAVE NARRATIVE).

Recent analyses have taken *ethnographic and critical discourse analytical approaches to prisoners' worldviews and their agentive self-positionings (see Cardozo-Freeman and Delormé 1984; O'Connor 2000) (*see* DISCOURSE ANALYSIS (FOUCAULT); DISCOURSE ANALYSIS (LINGUISTICS); POSITIONING).

Audiotaped *life story narratives of prisoners detail events that form part of the everyday discourse of prisoners, but that are seldom accessed by others. Such formerly silent voices present prison narratives within the frame of a social construction of both the self and society. For example, a male maximum security prisoner described the lasting effect of having been stabbed in his cell while he slept one night:

> I'm not scared of a knife. I would never run from a man with a knife. But, uh, just the thought of laying in your bed, in a, in a helpless position, you know, with your back turned, you know, and somebody over you. I don't care what he got, a knife, a stick, or whatever. You in a helpless position. There's nothing you could do for yourself. I don't ever want that to happen again. If I can help it, it won't happen again.
>
> (O'Connor 2000: 104)

This narrative shows the dangers inmates themselves face from predators inside the prisons. The story also indicates a reaching out for understanding in the *narrator's shift from a first-person *perspective in the interview to one that simultaneously addresses the image of his past, vulnerable self (*see* FOCALIZATION; NARRATION; PERSON). It also invites the listener to join in his fear: 'You in a helpless position'; 'There's nothing you could do for yourself'. Prison narratives, in their *reflexivity, bring new understandings to the narrators themselves, as well as to those who read, hear, or view their stories.

The sex-segregated world of prisoners, the over-incarceration of the poor and of minorities, the connections among poverty, addiction, unemployment, politics, disease, crime, and violence intertwine as layers underpinning prison narratives as discourse about power and *identity. Whether narratives tell of death-row accounts and stories of prisoners dying from AIDS, or whether first-time offenders describe their inaugural walk in a yard guarded by armed officers in towers as they pass muscled, tattooed, racially segregated, and staring cons, the narratives of prisoners speak to the non-incarcerated from within the silencing that is imprisonment. Thus, they challenge the power Foucault suggests that prisons and other such institutions assert.

SEE ALSO: Holocaust narrative; institutional narrative; narrative therapy

References and further reading

Abbott, Jack Henry (1991 [1981]) *In the Belly of the Beast: Letters from Prison*, NY: Random House.
Abu-Jamal, Mumia (1996) *Live From Death Row*, NY: Avon.
Cardozo-Freeman, Inez, with Eugene Delormé (1984) *The Joint: Language and Culture in a Maximum Security Prison*, Springfield, IL: Charles C. Thomas.
Chevigny, Belle (1999) *Doing Time: 25 Years of Prison Writing*, NY: Arcade.
Foucault, Michel (1979) *Discipline and Punish: The Birth of the Prison*, trans. Alan Sheridan, New York: Vintage Books.
Franklin, Bruce (1998) *Prison Writing in 20th Century America*, NY: Penguin.
Fludernik Monika. (1999) 'Carceral Topography: Spatiality, Liminality, and Corporality in the Literary Prison', *Textual Practice*, 13.1, 43–77.
Jackson, George (1970) *Soledad Brother: The Prison Letters of George Jackson*, NY: Coward-McCann.
John, Juliet (1998) *Cult Criminals: The Newgate Novels*, London: Routledge/Thoemmes Press.
Lamb, Wally, and the Women of York Correctional Institute (2003) *Couldn't Keep It to Myself: Testimonies of Our Imprisoned Sisters*, NY: HarperCollins.
Malcolm X with Alex Haley (1973 [1965]) *The Autobiography of Malcolm X*, NY: Ballantine.
O'Connor, Patricia E. (2000) *Speaking of Crime: Narratives of Prisoners*, Lincoln: University of Nebraska Press.
O'Hare, Kate Richards (1923) *In Prison*, NY: Knopf.
Solzhenitsyn Aleksandr I. (1974) *The Gulag Archipelago 1918–1956*, trans. Thomas P. Whitney, NY: Harper.

PATRICIA O'CONNOR

PROLEPSIS

Anticipation of a future episode that results in a non-chronological presentation of *events; a flashforward. Prolepses reset the narrative clock by jumping to a new 'narrative now'. *See* TEMPORAL ORDERING.

PROSPECTIVE NARRATION

A story about future *events; for instance, a prophetic story. *See* TIME IN NARRATIVE (also: NARRATION; TEMPORAL ORDERING).

PSYCHOANALYSIS AND NARRATIVE

When Freud clarified and developed what he called the scientific practice of psychoanalysis he worked almost exclusively with narrative productions. As a medical doctor Freud was concerned with the biological and psychological problems that patients presented to him (*see* MEDICINE AND NARRATIVE). All of his case studies describe patients who were unable to live what was considered a normal life. As a writer, Freud would present his patient as a non-normative narrative case and as a doctor he would 'cure' his patient by means of working through various resistances and anxieties to help his patient write a new narrative account of his or her life (*see* NARRATIVE THERAPY).

Freud's discovery of a narrative cure for neurotic symptoms began with a story that Freud heard in 1893 from a German colleague, Joseph Breuer, who had worked with Bertha Papenheim to relieve hysterical symptoms through talking and remembering. Freud and Breuer 'named' Bertha 'Anna O' in the collection on hysteria they published in 1895. Breuer, following earlier practices, used hypnosis to relieve hysterical paralysis of the body. Bertha suffered from multiple sites of paralysis and was helped considerably by Breuer. Later, working with his own patients, Freud discovered that hypnosis was not necessary. Painful symptoms could be removed if, through attention to the recovery of *memory, a patient could remember repressed memories of the past (*see* TRAUMA THEORY). New transformative life narratives thus involved an emotional reworking of memory.

Psychoanalysis as a discipline involves a pact between two people where one person, the patient, tells his story and the other person, the analyst, calls attention to, among other things, breaks, empty spaces, shifts in affect, and contradictions in the narrative. As the analyst asks for more information about the relationship among the *events narrated, the patient is motivated to remember more about his or her *life story. The psychoanalytic process thus is one that works both to interpret a narrative and to rewrite it as a response to the increase in understanding that the psychoanalytic dialogue seeks. Freud at times imagined psychoanalysis as a practice in the narrative recovery of memory. At other times, however, Freud felt that the *'truth' of his patient's recovered memory was not a real event in the past, but a fantasy. Thus while classical Freudian psychoanalytic practice will often insist upon seeking the truth of the past, recovered by memory, contradictions in Freudian theory itself suggest that recovered memory may contain not the truth of the historical past, but rather some other kind of verbal structure (such as fantasy) important to a psychoanalytic cure, but not factually true.

Jacques Lacan, working with *structuralist theory in France, began to read and interpret Freud with an eye to linguistic practice. For Lacan the work of psychoanalysis was essentially a work of words. And for Lacan, psychoanalytic narratives did not recover and record the historical past. Instead, they created the past by placing signifiers linked to the past within the linguistic context of the signifiers of the present. Lacan argued that psychoanalysis misunderstood the causal relation between the past and the present (*see* CAUSALITY). The past did not in some simple way lead to a meaningful present. Instead the present creates the past. Thus, for example, the sexual experimentation of children may be initiated as pleasurable and biologically playful event. It is not, in its initial 'real experience', freighted with anxiety. It is only later, in the context of some cultural law, that the past acquires its meaning. Sexual play thus becomes immoral and a threat to self-respect when it is placed in the context of western adult thought. *Events for Lacan are not meaningful in terms of some 'natural' universal biological experience. Instead events achieve meaning only in relation to some arbitrary symbolic order that is haphazardly generated by a culture responding (often neurotically or psychotically) to its own series of ideological contexts and historical encounters (*see* IDEOLOGY AND NARRATIVE).

Lacan's thought was highly influential in French and American academia where structuralist and *poststructuralist ideas offered numerous opportunities for understanding literature and literary production. The relation between narrative and psychoanalysis soon developed two very different paradigms as it came to reflect two different professional communities working with their own particular vocabularies and systems of beliefs. On the one hand, a literary scholar might read Freud as essentially a mythologist of great narrative accomplishment (*see* MYTH: THEMATIC APPROACHES; MYTH: THEORETICAL APPROACHES). On the other hand, an analyst might read literature as some version of an oedipal drama whose key elements are those nodes of oedipal *conflict given particular intelligibility by Freud and his followers.

Recent work on the relations between psychoanalysis and narrative gives particular attention to questions concepts shared by both disciplines. Contemporary psychoanalytic accounts of memory, for example, suggest that early memory can never be faithfully recorded or reported. Children perhaps have particular experiences, but these early preverbal experiences are usually not recorded in that part of the brain that structures memory in terms of verbal categories. Memory of this sort is implicit; it is a memory in the body and in characteristic forms of affective repetition. The brain does not verbally or visually remember early experience and this means that recovered memory cannot be faithfully represented. It is instead made meaningful in many different ways by a narrative responding to a number of very different verbal and historical contexts.

Concepts that have emerged as particularly important in this broader perspective on narrative and psychoanalysis include the phenomena of trauma, repetition, *plot, fantasy, *desire, representation, resistance, and working through. Early western autobiographical narratives such as Augustine's *Confessions* and Rousseau's *Confessions* highlight the importance of *emotion in narrative production (*see* AUTOBIOGRAPHY; CONFESSIONAL NARRATIVE). These early narratives suggest that emotion works as an essential binding mechanism for giving meaning to events. If narratives are essential forms for human knowing, the writing and rewriting of narratives involves a labour performed upon the material of emotion. Meaning emerges not naturally from events in themselves, but in the discovery of relationships between events. It is from this perspective that political theory, psychoanalytic theory, and the numerous postmodernist theories that connect them strive to understand the origin and the consequences of narrative productions and interpretations.

SEE ALSO: narrative psychology; psychological approaches to narrative

References and further reading

Brooks, Peter (1984) *Reading for the Plot: Design and Intention in Narrative*, New York: Random House.
Butler, Judith (1997) *The Psychic Life of Power*, Stanford: Stanford University Press.
Caruth, Cathy (1996) *Unclaimed Experience: Trauma, Narrative, and History*, Baltimore: Johns Hopkins University Press.
Davis, Robert Con (ed.) (1983) *Lacan and Narration: The Psychoanalytic Difference in Narrative Theory*, Baltimore: Johns Hopkins University Press.
Gregg, Gary S. (1991) *Self-representation: Life Narrative Studies in Identity and Ideology*, New York: Greenwood Press.
Hacking, Ian (1995) *Rewriting the Soul: Multiple Personality and the Sciences of Memory*, Princeton: Princeton University Press.
Modell, Arnold (1993) *The Private Self*, Cambridge, Mass.: Harvard University Press.
Runyan, William M. (1982) *Life Histories and Psychobiography: Explorations in Theory and Method*, New York: Oxford University Press.
Schafer, Roy (1981) *Narrative Actions in Psychoanalysis*, Worcester, MA: Clark University Press.

MARSHALL ALCORN

PSYCHOLOGICAL APPROACHES TO NARRATIVE

The diversity of psychological approaches to narrative mirrors the diversity within the field of psychology. Researchers in cognitive psychology have largely concerned themselves with the basic processes that underlie people's ability to read or hear a story and form a coherent representation of that story. Within developmental psychology, researchers have most often attempted to understand how children achieve adult competence, with respect both to understanding and generating narratives (*see* CHILDREN'S STORIES (NARRATIVES WRITTEN FOR CHILDREN); CHILDREN'S STORYTELLING). Developmental research also takes a lifespan approach and uses narratives as a way to gather evidence about the vicissitudes of individual lives. Finally, theorists have suggested that people use narratives as a vehicle for thought (*see* NARRATIVE AS COGNITIVE INSTRUMENT). That perspective on narrative also provides a context in which researchers can assess the impact narrative has on everyday life.

The cognitive psychology of narrative

The goal of most theories within cognitive psychology has been to specify the interplay between processes and representations in narrative understanding. Processes are mental operations. For narrative understanding, a range of processes play a role, from those that allow individuals to decode the perceptual input (e.g., speech or text), to syntactical analyses of phrase- and sentence-level structures in the text, to inference generation. Those processes give rise to various types of representations some of which are relatively short-lived (such as the representations of the exact wording of a text) whereas others remain accessible for a longer period (such as the meaning of a text).

Research in cognitive psychology has also particularly focused on the way that pre-existing representations in *memory guide individuals' experiences of new narratives. For example, people use prior knowledge to disambiguate and reconstruct narratives in line with cultural expectations. In addition, memory structures – usually called schemas – allow people to supplement texts with information from memory (*see* SCRIPTS AND SCHEMATA). In that way, the typical elements of scenes and *events (for example, a 'waiter' and 'ordering') become accessible once the general topic (a restaurant) is introduced within a narrative. Furthermore, people are likely to draw inferences to fill certain gaps in a text (e.g., if characters begin to eat, readers would likely draw the inference that it was the waiter who brought the food) (*see* GAPPING; PRAGMATICS; READER-RESPONSE THEORY). However, theorists recognised early on that people cannot encode all the inferences that are possible for any given scene – text representations could easily be cluttered with trivial inferences (e.g., the waiter has a spleen). For that reason, researchers have attempted to define what types of inferences people typically encode as they experience narratives. The bulk of that research has focused on automatic inferences – those types of inferences people are obliged to make without conscious intervention.

However, the major theoretical positions developed as explanations for automatic inferences have resonance beyond that realm. In particular, theories can be differentiated as to whether they propose that narrative understanding requires special mental processes. The general issue is whether narrative understanding (as a set of processes) embodies specific goals that readers and addresses might have (*see* AUDIENCE; NARRATEE; READER CONSTRUCTS). Explanation-based theories of narrative understanding argue in favour of narrative-specific processes (e.g., Graesser, Singer, and Trabasso 1994). This class of theories suggests that readers are always driven to explain why narratives mention certain *actions, events, and states. By contrast, memory-based theories suggest that narrative processing engages the same processes that are at work in non-narrative circumstances (O'Brien, Lorch, and Myers 1998).

Perhaps the most important critique of both types of theories is that they are too narrow in their focus: The theories make the tacit assumption that each text contains a unique meaning at which any competent reader would arrive. This assumption provides a clear mismatch with analyses of narrative understanding from other disciplines. For example, using simple experimental texts, researchers have provided evidence that narrative understanding gives rise to causal networks that represent the relationships between the causes and consequences of events in a story (e.g., Trabasso and van den Broek 1985) (*see* CAUSALITY; STORY SCHEMATA AND CAUSAL STRUCTURE). Some story events form the main causal chain of the story whereas others are causal dead ends. When asked to recall stories, readers typically provide information from the main causal chain rather than the causal dead ends.

Those types of experiments, however, ignore the types of causal ambiguity present in most complex narratives. Readers must often decide what causal forces are at work. Presumably, those decisions will often be informed by the *point of view the *narrator takes on narrative events. However, the study of what has been called psychonarratology is in its relative infancy (Dixon and Bortolussi 2003). From the perspective of psychonarratology, traditional cognitive psychological theories have been incomplete, most obviously, because they underestimate the range of activities in which people must engage as they experience complex narratives. Yet, as the theories expand to become more inclusive the major theoretical divide remains relevant: the enduring question is whether narrative processing is subsumed by ordinary processes or requires special processes of its own.

The advent of cognitive neuroscience holds out the promise that the brain itself might provide evidence to decide among different theoretical accounts of narrative processing (Gernsbacher and Kaschak 2003). Since pioneering research in the nineteenth-century by Paul Broca, researchers have localised most critical language functions to the left hemisphere of the brain. For example, damage to portions of the left frontal and temporal lobes will leave an individual unable to produce meaningful or grammatical language. Thus, the left hemisphere plays a critical role in many important aspects of narrative processing such as syntactic parsing. Historically, researchers believed that the right hemisphere subserved limited functions in language processing that related to the integration of information. In fact, recent data argue that it is precisely the integrative function of the right hemisphere that makes it critical for narrative processing. Specifically, brain-imaging studies using functional MRI suggest that the right hemisphere plays a role in the representation of coherent discourse. Innovations in brain imaging should allow researchers to improve their understanding of the relationship, with respect to patterns of activity in the brain, of narrative experiences to other types of experiences.

The development of narrative competence

Research on the development of narrative competence has focused on both the comprehension and generation of stories (*see* COMPUTATIONAL APPROACHES TO NARRATIVE; NARRATIVE COMPREHENSION). For both activities, narrative competence depends on children's development of both memory and language skills. For example, early in their lives, children do not have the memory skills that enable them to piece together the meaning of the stories they hear. Part of what is missing is the schematic world knowledge that facilitates adult comprehension. Children, for example, must have sufficient experience in restaurants before they can make the types of inferences that are routine for adults. In addition, children must learn the norms for different *genres and different story structures (*see* NARRATIVE STRUCTURE).

The literature on the development of narrative comprehension has put particular emphasis on the assessment of individual differences. Researchers have largely been concerned with explaining differences among children who come to read with varying levels of skill. The research goal is to find ways to ameliorate difficulties with comprehension. Some individual difference analyses have focused on variability in cognitive resources such as working memory (e.g., Seigneuric, Ehrlich, Oakhill, and Yuill 2000). Working memory is defined as a memory system that enables people to temporarily store and manipulate information. With respect to reading, research generally suggests that students who have more working memory capacity are able to understand and integrate texts more fully. Other approaches to individual differences have focused on more social aspects of the development of narrative comprehension (van

Kleeck, Stahl, and Bauer 2003). For example, parents spend varying amounts of time with their children engaging in reading and other narrative-based activities. Researchers have assessed the impact of the quantity and the quality of those activities on children's progress toward complex modes of narrative comprehension.

Social factors also play a large role in the development of children's ability to tell coherent narratives. For example, researchers have studied the similarities in narrative styles between parents and children with respect to such aspects as cohesion, coherence, and elaborative detail (Peterson and Roberts 2003). Work of this sort supports the contention that exposure to well-formed narratives can have a positive impact on children's more general cognitive development. For example, successful interventions have been implemented in which parents were encouraged to devote more conversational time to narratives and prompt longer narratives from their preschool children (Peterson, Jesso, and McCabe 1999). Children whose parents engaged in these activities showed greater narrative development and vocabulary improvement as compared to their peers whose parents did not. However, not all social experiences are beneficial to children's narrative development. In some cases there is a clash between cultural norms of storytelling and those that dominate classroom practice (Heath 1983) (*see* SOCIOLINGUISTIC APPROACHES TO NARRATIVE). For example, from classroom observations Michaels (1991) observed that middle-class white children and working-class African American children had assimilated different cultural norms for storytelling. The white children typically used a 'topic-centred' style in which each story focused on a single event with a beginning, middle, and end. The African American children typically used a 'topic-associating' style in which each story consisted of several thematically linked *anecdotes that together made an implicit point. In Michaels' analysis, those children who used the 'topic-associating' stule had their abilities 'dismantled' by teachers who insisted on the 'topic-centred' norm.

For many researchers, the content of the narratives people generate provides important information about development across the life span. Psychologists often elicit narratives as a means to assess people's general sense of *identity and well-being. For example, developmental psychologists often monitor individuals' social development by evaluating the quality of their early attachment relationships with their parents. The quality of attachment is often revealed through the content of the stories that people tell – both as children and later into life. Similarly, clinical psychologists often elicit narratives to gather evidence about the adjustment problems of their clients. Researchers have demonstrated that people's narratives capture both the causes and consequences of their distress – as well as changes over time (*see* NARRATIVE THERAPY).

Narratives often play a critical role in the way that people provide information about themselves. For that reason, researchers have also tried to document the development of skills through which people become capable of formulating coherent *life stories. To begin, the ability to tell a life story requires the more general development of storytelling abilities. However, the ability to tell a life story also requires an ability to organise autobiographical memories into a coherent whole (*see* AUTOBIOGRAPHY). Habermas and Bluck (2000) argued that the successful production of a life story requires the mastery of four types of coherence. First, life stories must be temporally coherent – people must recall or reconstruct life events so that they unfold in an orderly fashion over time (*see* TEMPORAL ORDERING; TIME IN NARRATIVE). Second, life stories must cohere with the cultural concept of *biography – people need sufficient experience of a culture to know how lives are narrated within that culture. Third, life stories must be causally coherent – people need to be able to give an account of their life that explains continuity and change. Finally, life stories must be thematically coherent – people must be able to articulate the major ideas around which their experiences have been organised (*see* THEMATIC APPROACHES TO NARRATIVE). Based on this set of requirements, Habermas and Bluck suggested that the requisite skills are not in place until adolescence; that is the period in which people begin to understand their life in terms of a coherent narrative (*see* ADOLESCENT NARRATIVE).

Narrative thought and narrative impact

The literature on life stories meshes with another important idea that has been the subject of scrutiny within psychology – the proposal that human thought is fundamentally structured around stories (Bruner 1986; Sarbin 1986; *see* NARRATIVE

PSYCHOLOGY). Bruner, for example, contrasted a paradigmatic mode of thought with a narrative mode of thought. On Bruner's account, people engage the paradigmatic mode when they reason about mathematical or scientific matters whereas the narrative mode subsumes all the other situations (*see* SCIENCE AND NARRATIVE): people use narratives as a means to understand the causes and consequences of life events. (In fact, Bruner scolded researchers for focusing most of their attention on understanding the relatively infrequent paradigmatic mode, because of its connection to academic chores.)

A core claim of this view that narrative undergirds thought is that people encode and access life experiences – both those they experience and those they witness – as stories. Schank and Abelson (1995) developed this argument as an extension of their earlier work on memory structures. On this view, people interpret their current experiences by retrieving from memory past stories that share structural similarities. By constructing a comparison set of past stories, people can generate appropriate expectations of how events might unfold in time. This comparison set of stories enables people to note immediately when expectations fail – to begin to forge explanations for those failures.

The theory that thought is constituted or assisted by narrative also partially explains why narratives may have such persuasive impact. People do not learn from stories because they have points or morals; those conclusions have little influence in isolation. Rather, people learn from stories because the stories present a coherent argument in favour of a conclusion (*see* NARRATIVE AS ARGUMENT). New experiences remind us of old experiences with similar narrative structures; causes lead inevitably to consequences.

Narratives may also have particular impact because of phenomenological aspects of narrative experiences (Gerrig 1993). When people become sufficiently immersed in narratives, that *immersion appears to inhibit the ordinary impulse to take exception to persuasive content embedded within stories. To demonstrate such an effect, Green and Brock (2000) created a measurement device for narrative transport. In their experiments, those individuals who reported themselves to have been most transported to the world of a narrative also showed the greatest change in beliefs in a direction consistent with the story. Analyses of narrative impact support the contention that stories embody a special relationship with thought (Green, Strange, and Brock 2002).

The various psychological approaches to narrative all indicate how important narrative is as an element of human experience. Cognitive psychologists wish to understand how words become worlds (*see* STORYWORLD); they trace the course of information processing that enables people to leave the here and now to venture to novel realms. Developmental psychologists wish to understand how people acquire the memory and language abilities that allow them to undertake those journeys. They also examine life stories as primary evidence about people's evolving views of the lives they lead. Finally, researchers who take their cue from theorists such as Bruner and Sarbin are guided by the overarching notion that narrative is intrinsic to thought. That proposal helps explain why stories exert such force in everyday lives.

SEE ALSO: cognitive narratology; phenomenology of narrative; situation model; story grammars

References and further reading

Bruner, Jerome (1986) *Actual Minds, Possible Worlds*, Cambridge, Mass.: Harvard University Press.

Dixon, Peter, and Marisa Bortolussi (2003) *Psychonarratology*, Cambridge: Cambridge University Press.

Gernsbacher, Morton Ann, and Michael P. Kaschak (2003) 'Neuroimaging Studies of Language Production and Comprehension', *Annual Review of Psychology*, 54, 91–114.

Gerrig, Richard J. (1993) *Experiencing Narrative Worlds*, New Haven: Yale University Press.

Graesser, Arthur C., Murray Singer, and Tom Trabasso (1994) 'Constructing Inferences During Narrative Text Comprehension', *Psychological Review*, 101, 371–95.

Green, Melanie C., and Timothy C. Brock (2000) 'The Role of Transportation in the Persuasiveness of Public Narratives', *Journal of Personality & Social Psychology*, 79, 701–21.

Green, Melanie C., Jeffrey J. Strange, and Timothy C. Brock (eds) (2002) *Narrative Impact: Social and Cognitive Foundations*, Mahwah, NJ: Erlbaum.

Habermas, Tilmann, and Susan Bluck (2000) 'Getting a Life: The Emergence of the Life Story in Adolescence', *Psychological Bulletin*, 126, 748–69.

Heath, Shirley Brice (1983) *Ways with Words: Language, Life, and Work in Communities and Classrooms*, Cambridge: Cambridge University Press.

van Kleeck, Anne, Steven A. Stahl, and Eurydice B. Bauer (eds) (2003) *On Reading Books to Children: Parents and Teachers*, Mahwah, NJ: Erlbaum.

Michaels, Sarah (1991) 'The Dismantling of Narrative', in Allyssa McCabe and Carole Peterson (eds) *Developing Narrative Structure*, Hillsdale, NJ: Erlbaum.

O'Brien, Edward J., Robert F. Lorch, Jr., and Jerome L. Myers (eds) (1998) *Discourse Processes*, 26.2–3 (special issue on 'Memory-based Text Processing').

Peterson, Carole, Beulah Jesso, and Allyssa McCabe (1999) 'Encouraging Narratives in Preschoolers: An Intervention Study', *Journal of Child Language*, 26, 49–67.

Peterson, Carole, and Christy Roberts (2003) 'Like Mother, Like Daughter: Similarities in Narrative Style', *Developmental Psychology*, 39, 551–62.

Sarbin, Theodore (ed.) (1986) *Narrative Psychology: The Storied Nature of Human Conduct*, New York: Praeger.

Schank, Roger, and Robert P. Abelson (1995) 'Knowledge and Memory: The Real Story', in Robert S. Wyer, Jr. (ed.) *Advances in Social Cognition*, vol. 8, Hillsdale, NJ: Erlbaum.

Seigneuric, Alix, Marie-France Ehrlich, Jane V. Oakhill, and Nicola M. Yuill (2000) 'Working Memory Resources and Children's Reading Comprehension', *Reading & Writing*, 13, 81–103.

Trabasso, Tom, and Paul van den Broek (1985) 'Causal Thinking and the Representation of Narrative Events', *Journal of Memory and Language*, 24, 612–30.

RICHARD J. GERRIG

PSYCHOLOGICAL NOVEL

In the broadest sense, all novels, 'popular' as well as 'serious', are psychological novels because, in order to follow the *plot, the reader must be able to construct plausible hypotheses about the thought processes and consciousnesses of the *characters. More specifically, the term can be applied to the tendency of the nineteenth-century omniscient *narrator to delve extensively into characters' minds and to follow the development of their personalities over a long period. Stendhal, George Eliot, and Tolstoi are good examples. Fludernik even locates the beginnings of what she calls the 'consciousness novel' as early as Aphra Behn in the seventeenth century.

In a narrower sense, the term describes novels which present in detail the inner workings of fictional minds at the expense of *action and plot. Typically, there is an intense focus on the consciousness of a single character through which the events of the *storyworld are experienced. This character may be presented in a third-person or heterodiegetic narration or may be the narrator of a first-person or homodiegetic narration (*see* NARRATION; NARRATIVE SITUATIONS). By contrast, novels in which action predominates over character are characteristic of *genre fiction such as the *thriller, whodunit, or romantic novel (*see* NOVEL, THE; ROMANCE).

Within this narrow sense, the term 'psychological novel' is particularly associated with two separate historical developments: the work of Gustave Flaubert and Henry James in the latter half of the nineteenth and the beginning of the twentieth century, which is characterised by figural (as opposed to authorial) narration, internal *focalization, the reflector character, and *free indirect discourse; and the *modernist novel of the early twentieth century, for example James Joyce's *Ulysses* and Virginia Woolf's *To the Lighthouse*, which is now famously associated with the concepts of *stream of consciousness and interior monologue. Many of the later novels that are influenced by these two styles can be described as psychological novels.

Some of the assumptions behind the narrow sense of the term have been questioned. Rimmon-Kenan endorses Henry James' view that character and action are interdependent: character determines action; action illustrates character. Fludernik has put the representation of *experientiality rather than the description of *events at the heart of her definition of *narrative. Palmer argues that reading all types of novels (including 'serious', 'popular', and genre fiction) requires an understanding of what he calls the whole of the social mind in action.

SEE ALSO: thought and consciousness representation (literature)

References and further reading

Auerbach, Erich (1953) *Mimesis: The Representation of Reality in Western Literature*, trans. W. R. Trask, Princeton: Princeton University Press.

Cohn, Dorrit (1978) *Transparent Minds: Narrative Modes for Presenting Consciousness in Fiction*, Princeton: Princeton University Press.

Fludernik, Monika (1996) *Towards a 'Natural' Narratology*, London: Routledge.

Lodge, David (1990) *After Bakhtin: Essays on Fiction and Criticism*, London: Routledge.

Palmer, Alan (2004) *Fictional Minds*. Lincoln: University of Nebraska Press.

Poulet, Georges (1955) 'The Circle and the Centre: Reality and *Madame Bovary*', *Western Review*, 29, 245–60.

Rimmon-Kenan, Shlomith (1983) *Narrative Fiction: Contemporary Poetics*, London: Routledge.

Stanzel, Franz (1984) *A Theory of Narrative*, trans. C. Goedsche, Cambridge: Cambridge University Press.

ALAN PALMER

PSYCHONARRATION

Dorrit Cohn's term for a *narrator's analytic and summarising report of a *character's mental events and processes. Psychonarration is related in its subject matter to 'interior monologue', indirect discourse, and *free indirect discourse, but it differs in its mode of presentation. *See* THOUGHT AND CONSCIOUSNESS REPRESENTATION (LITERATURE).

Q

QUEER THEORY

In the early 1990s, queer theory emerged out of several existing areas of scholarly interest, including lesbian and gay studies, *gender studies, and *poststructuralist accounts of *identity. Teresa de Lauretis coined the term 'queer theory' in 1991 to displace the gender division codified in 'lesbian and gay studies', establishing a category to provide common ground for these (and other) increasingly divergent fields. Critics embraced the term 'queer' in an attempt to channel its inherent power (as hate speech) toward philosophical inquiries into such epistemologically nebulous topics as sexual and affective ambivalence, linguistic failure, excess, and the limits of the body. Because many of its first practitioners had already made major contributions to the study of narrative (de Lauretis, Miller, Sedgwick), and because so many of its exponents have addressed narrative texts, queer theory has overlapped with narrative theory from its inception.

What perhaps most distinguishes queer theory, paradoxically, is its resistance to the production of determinate identities, including its own (Berlant and Warner 1995; Butler 1993; Edelman 1995); noting its historical roots and philosophical affiliations, however, yields a fuller understanding of this mercurial subject. It arrived on the heels of the lesbian and gay studies movement of the 1980s, reinvigorating that discipline with the defiance of 'queer' and the ambition of 'theory'. As de Lauretis framed the new discourse, it aspired to transgress the orthodoxies of intellectual organisation, to inaugurate new forms of community, and to recognise multiple kinds of difference (notably those of gender and race). It developed

out of several major academic dispositions that immediately preceded or were contemporaneous with it, many of which – including deconstruction, *psychoanalysis, and the broad rubric 'identity politics' – had already adopted 'difference' as a watchword (see DECONSTRUCTIVE APPROACHES TO NARRATIVE). Its appearance also represented an extension of the various types of homosexual-rights activism that preceded it (homophile, gay-liberationist, lesbian-feminist), and it came into being, significantly, after an embattled decade for gay rights in the U.S., during which widespread paranoia about AIDS worked in tandem with homophobic forces in the judiciary (e.g., the Supreme Court's 1986 *Bowers vs. Hardwick* decision, which upheld anti-sodomy legislation) and among public policy-makers (e.g., the National Endowment for the Arts controversy of 1989–1990). This climate of state-sponsored repression of homosexuality sparked highly visible responses, especially in the form of AIDS activism, which garnered frequent attention in the news media through the second half of the 1980s; simultaneously, academic work began increasingly to reflect concerns about representations of homosexuality and AIDS.

In the following years, 'queer theory' became a subject of intense fascination and scrutiny in the academy, and the discourse it named only expanded in range and complexity as critics pursued various projects under its aegis, including many that bear directly on narrative theory. For queer theorists, the intellectual and political potentials of this theory lie in its capacity to express newfound discontinuities within the sex-gender-sexuality system (Sedgwick 1993), to resignify apparently stable terms of identity (Butler 1993), and to anticipate an inchoate, perverse future (Berlant and Warner 1995). Particularly in its development of strategies for narrative analysis, queer theory has sought innovative modes of interrogation, aiming not simply to identify certain *authors and texts as queer, but also to engage in queer readings of canonical or ostensibly heterosexual texts, a practice often called 'queering' a text. Hence, one major strand of queer theory examines the complicated sexual dynamics at work in traditional narrative genres, such as prose fiction and the classical Hollywood cinema (see FILM NARRATIVE).

Its greatest value for narratology, moreover, may rest in its reimagination of the relationship between *narrative structure and sexuality. Queer readings of narrative texts may attend to characterisation in order to locate, for example, homosexual *characters or behaviours, but they are more often interested in showing how characters frustrate expectations of sexual identity. The legacy of *structuralist narratology tends to identify the traditional linear *plot with normative heterosexuality, particularly in the marriage plot, which equates the 'happiness' of its ending with a heterosexual consummation that promises patriarchal succession (see PLOT TYPES). In contrast, narrative analysis informed by queer theory often explores the ways that narrative structures can depart from such traditional principles of plot coherence and *closure. Queer analysts of narrative sometimes emphasise how certain plots move not in accordance with heterosexual rhythms or toward procreative ends, but instead in accordance with the less predictable vicissitudes of nonnormative sexual practices or toward less secure futures; hence, such readings might illustrate not only the eccentric kinds of sexuality that appear thematically in narrative texts (e.g., narcissism, fetishism, anal eroticism), but also how these expressions of *desire allegorise narrative movement (see ALLEGORY).

A short list of queer theorists whose work bears importantly on narrative would include Butler (1993), Edelman (1995, 1998), Miller (1992), Roof (1996), and Sedgwick (1993, 1997), all of whom have developed readings of narratives that emphasise these texts' queer visions of the world or perverse reading pleasures. Many scholars have also produced queer readings of classic texts of narratology (e.g., Miller 1992 and Roof 1996), demonstrating in the process how existing scholarship on narrative suppresses and/or enables queer

readings. Queer theory effectively expands the terrain of narrative theory not because it enumerates variously sexualised authors and characters, but rather because it provides alternative models of narrative structure and notes the queerness already registered in the classic models of structuralist narratology.

SEE ALSO: coming-out story; thematic approaches to narrative

References and further reading

Berlant, Lauren, and Michael Warner (1995) 'What Does Queer Theory Teach Us about X', PMLA, 110.3, 343–49.
Butler, Judith (1993) Bodies That Matter: On the Discursive Limits of "Sex", New York: Routledge.
Edelman, Lee (1995) 'Queer Theory: Unstating Desire', GLQ: A Journal of Lesbian and Gay Studies, 2.4, 343–46.
—— (1998) 'The Future Is Kid Stuff: Queer Theory, Disidentification, and the Death Drive', Narrative, 6, 18–30.
Fuss, Diana (ed.) (1991) Inside/out: Lesbian Theories, Gay Theories, New York: Routledge.
Jagose, Annamarie (1996) Queer Theory: An Introduction, New York: New York University Press.
de Lauretis, Teresa (ed.) (1991) 'Queer Theory: Lesbian and Gay Sexualities: An Introduction', Differences: A Journal of Feminist Cultural Studies, 3.2, iii–xviii.
Miller, D. A. (1992) Bringing Out Roland Barthes, Berkeley: University of California Press.
Roof, Judith (1996) Come As You Are: Sexuality and Narrative, New York: Columbia University Press.
Sedgwick, Eve Kosofsky (1993) Tendencies, Durham: Duke University Press.
—— (ed.) (1997) Novel Gazing: Queer Readings in Fiction, Durham: Duke University Press.
Warner, Michael (ed.) (1993) Fear of a Queer Planet: Queer Politics and Social Theory, Minneapolis: University of Minnesota Press.

MATTHEW BELL

QUIXOTIC NOVEL

Critics and theorists as different as José Ortega y Gasset, Lionel Trilling, Harry Levin, and Harold Bloom have all proposed that Don Quixote (1605, 1615) is the prototype of the *novel in general. We may call 'Quixotic' any novel that bears some degree of intertextual relationship to Don Quixote (see INTERTEXTUALITY). In fact, one can categorise novels as more or less 'quixotic' by assigning them positions along the following scale. First, there are the literal sequels, the continuations of the story of Don Quixote and Sancho Panza or their literal reincarnations (*see* SERIAL FORM). Second, we have texts featuring the namesakes of Don Quixote, novels in which the protagonist is explicitly identified, usually in the title, as a kind of Don Quixote figure. Third, there are novels whose protagonist is explicitly (either within the text or in paratextual authorial statements) linked to Don Quixote (*see* COMMENTARY; PARATEXT). Fourth, there is the category of all those novels whose protagonist duplicates (or at least approximates) *Don Quixote*'s basic premise of a fantasy or alternative reality inspired by books (or *film, *television, or other *media), and/or who, like Don Quixote, consciously chooses to imitate ideal models from these media. And finally, in just a short extension of the previous category, we can consider all those novels in which the protagonist is dissatisfied with his or her life and circumstances and attempts to change them in some way – in other words, just about every novel ever written. In a very real sense, to be a novel is to be a quixotic novel.

Linguist Noam Chomsky has proposed that, in a certain (deep) sense, there is only one human language – with very many (surface) variations. It is significant that leading spokespersons of every major generation of novelists explicitly trace their origins back to Cervantes: the comic novelists of the eighteenth-century (Diderot, Fielding, Lesage, Lennox, Sterne); the *realist novelists of the nineteenth-century (Dickens, Dostoevsky, Eliot, Flaubert, Melville, Pérez Galdós); the modern novelists of the early-to-mid-twentieth century (Bellow, Bulgakov, Carpentier, Faulkner, Fitzgerald, Hesse, Martín-Santos; *see* MODERNIST NARRATIVE); and the *postmodern novelists (e.g., *authors of *metafictions) of the contemporary era (Acker, Auster, Barth, Coover, Fowles, Fuentes, García Márquez, Rushdie). Perhaps the novel, like language itself, is an example of a theme and variations: all novels are but variations on the theme(s) of *Don Quixote*.

SEE ALSO: hero; thematic approaches to narrative

References and further reading

Gilman, Stephen (1989) *The Novel According to Cervantes*, Berkeley: University of California Press.

Levin, Harry (1970) 'The Quixotic Principle: Cervantes and Other Novelists', *Harvard English Studies*, 1, 45–66.

López Navia, Santiago Alfonso (1996) *La ficción autorial en el* Quijote *y en sus continuaciones e imitaciones*, Madrid: Universidad Europea de Madrid-CEES Ediciones.

Mancing, Howard (2003) *The Cervantes Encyclopedia*, 2 vols., Westport, CT: Greenwood Press.

Martínez Bonati, Félix (1992) Don Quixote and the Poetics of the Novel, trans. Dian Fox in collaboration with the author, Ithaca: Cornell University Press.

Welsh, Alexander (1981) *Reflections on the Hero as Quixote*, Princeton: Princeton University Press.

Ziolkowski, Eric J. (1991) *The Sanctification of Don Quixote: From Hidalgo to Priest*, University Park: Pennsylvania State University Press.

HOWARD MANCING

QUOTATION THEORY

Quotation theory analyses the functions and effects of *embedding somebody's discourse in a given discourse. Using Sternberg's terms, quotation involves a 'quoter', who provides a discoursal 'frame', and a 'quotee', whose discourse constitutes a quotational 'inset'. An inset is either a self-quotation or a quotation of somebody else's utterance ('autographic' vs. 'allographic quotation', according to Genette 1997: 151). Transition from frame to inset usually involves a clause of 'attributive discourse' identifying the quotee and a set of bracketing quotation marks (in some oral speech situations, speakers use a quotational *gesture). Although quotation is usually understood to be 'direct quotation', quotation theory considers all types of *speech representation, including the *'free indirect' and 'indirect' styles, which are deictically and/or syntactically subordinate to the framing discourse (*see* DEIXIS). While the inset's degree of accuracy or 'mimetic quality' (*see* MIMESIS) can range from vague approximation to verbatim reproduction, quotation rarely if ever presents an identical copy of the original utterance (e.g., mispronunciations and slips are usually filtered out) – in fact, the 'copy theory' of quotation amounts to what some theorists claim is a 'direct discourse fallacy'. In practice, the requirement of accuracy varies from *text-type to text-type but usually recedes behind the pragmatic demand to quote only as accurately as necessary (*see* PRAGMATICS).

Quotation theory puts particular emphasis on the relationship between quoters and quotees and the mechanisms of mutual value assignments. Generally, the quoter's discourse is enriched by including a memorable thought, and quotation in turn ensures the quotee's continuing reputation. The quoter's attitudinal stance toward the inset may range from 'wholly consonant' or 'empathetic' via 'neutral' to 'wholly dissonant' (*irony and unreliable *narration are well-attested effects of dissonant quotation; *see* RELIABILITY). Although often invoking the authority of the quotee, the quoter actually assumes a position of power which allows him or her to manipulate the inset by adaptation, modification, omission, etc. However, as Mikhail Bakhtin has pointed out, the quotee's discourse can also enter into a 'dialogic' relationship with the quoter's discourse, and even contradict and subvert the dominant discourse against the quoter's manifest intentions (*see* DIALOGISM; INTENTIONALITY; POLYPHONY), a fact which is of particular interest when the participants involved are *narrator and *character, respectively. Within the framework of *intertextuality, all discourses, including a quoter's framing discourse, are always already quotational in nature. Quotational conventions and value assignments play a major role in the discourses of *law and other *institutions (typical catchphrases are 'hearsay evidence',

'plagiarism', 'citation index', etc.). They also inform literary *genres such as *cento* (patchwork), *montage, parody, and pastiche. The misrepresentation and misinterpretation ('misprision') of paternal discourses has been studied by Bloom (1975), and an influential model of gender-specific 'citationality' has been proposed by Butler (1997).

SEE ALSO: discourse analysis (linguistics); framed narrative; frame theory; performativity

References and further reading

Bloom, Harold (1975) *A Map of Misreading*, New York: Oxford University Press.
Butler, Judith (1997) *Excitable Speech: A Politics of the Performative*, New York: Routledge.
Cohn, Dorrit (1978) *Transparent Minds*, Princeton: Princeton University Press.
Genette, Gérard (1997 [1987]) *Paratexts: Thresholds of Interpretation*, trans. Jane E. Lewin, Cambridge: Cambridge University Press.
Sternberg, Meir (1982) 'Proteus in Quotation-Land: Mimesis and the Forms of Reported Discourse', *Poetics Today*, 3.2, 107–56.

MANFRED JAHN

R

RADIO NARRATIVE

As the first home-based electronic medium available in the U.S., radio played a significant role in constructing a national sense of what it meant to be 'American'. The heyday for radio narrative coincided with the years of the Great Depression in the 1930s and the years of World War II and its aftermath in the 1940s, but even after the introduction of *television, serialised half-hour radio dramas remained popular in the U.S. through the 1950s. Britain and the Commonwealth countries continued to produce a limited number of radio serials and radio plays throughout the twentieth century (*see* SERIAL FORM).

Radio relies absolutely on the medium of sound to convey the action of its stories. Whatever the specific *genre – period *drama, contemporary *romance, western adventure, *science fiction, *horror, comedy, *detective fiction – radio narrative is constructed from four elements: speech (external *narration and character *dialogue); *music (both diegetic [integral to a scene, as when a character plays a harmonica] and non-diegetic ['background' or 'theme' music]); pure sound (diegetic and non-diegetic 'sound effects'); and silence (*see* DIEGESIS). These elements are combined in relationships of both reinforcement and contrast that help advance *plot and develop themes.

The potential effects of radio narrative are achieved primarily through suggestion. Individual listeners construct images of and feelings about characters, settings, and actions based on aural cues, such as expressive music (ominous strings, up-tempo horns), iconic sounds (a creaking door, chirping crickets), particular vocal qualities (barked orders, a passionate whisper), or stereotypical speech styles (heavy accents, non-standard syntax) (*see* SPEECH REPRESENTATION). This basic feature of radio allows for an extreme fluidity and flexibility in narrative construction – literally anything imaginable can happen to anyone, anywhere, at any time – but it demands active *audience participation. Clarity and logic are especially important to radio narrative, as are an intensification of drama and a high level of condensation. Half-hour narratives typically follow a single, formulaic plot line and work toward producing a single effect. Longer radio plays can be more sophisticated in their plots but still are constrained by the ability of listeners to follow the pace and complexity of the narration, remember and distinguish the voices of multiple characters, and remain actively engaged over a longer period of time.

The microphone constitutes the 'aural fixed point' of a radio narrative, meaning that it represents the position of the audience in relation to all the sound cues. Thus, radio narrative creates a sense of spatial relationships and *mise-en-scène* – in other words, a 'soundscape' – by manipulating the distance between the microphone and performers, music, or sound effects (*see* DEIXIS; SPACE IN NARRATIVE). The relative closeness of individual actors to the microphone, along with the volume of their speech, creates a sense of background and foreground, as well as a distinction between formal or public speech and intimate or interior speech. Actors can move between these positions, creating aural equivalents of zooms, close-ups, and wide-angle film shots (*see* FILM NARRATIVE). Moreover, voices, sounds, or music can be manipulated to create special effects, such as a 'hollow' quality to indicate a memory or flashback (*see* TEMPORAL ORDERING).

SEE ALSO: intermediality; media and narrative; orality; soundtrack

References and further reading

Arnheim, Rudolph (1936, rpt. 1971) *Radio*, New York: Arno.

Crook, Tim (1999) *Radio Drama: Theory and Practice*, London: Routledge.

Hilmes, Michelle (1997) *Radio Voices: American Broadcasting 1922–1952*, Minneapolis: University of Minnesota Press.

CHADWICK ALLEN

READER ADDRESS

A type of narratorial act in which a *narrator makes a direct appeal to the reader, by way of forms such as 'you', 'dear reader', and their counterparts in languages other than English. *See* ADDRESS (also: AUDIENCE; NARRATEE).

READER CONSTRUCTS

Reader-oriented approaches to narrative texts assume that these (like all texts) acquire meaning through an interaction between text and reader. However, the actual mental processes in reading are neither observable nor completely accessible to introspection (*see*, however, PSYCHOLOGICAL APPROACHES TO NARRATIVE), and there will always remain a distance between the particular reading experiences of individual readers and the theoretical abstractions and generalisations based on such particularised experiences. Theorists are therefore compelled to work with theoretical constructs when talking about a text's effects on, and the activities of, 'the reader'. Potential reading effects are in most cases inferred from analyses of textual features, and critics frequently generalise by introspecting their own reading experience and then projecting hypotheses onto other readers. It may therefore be unavoidable that reader constructs tend to be ambiguously placed between text-internal and text-external domains, and that the boundaries between different constructs tend to be fluid.

Since the 1970s, a great number of reader constructs have emerged in the context of *reader-response theories, though only a few can be sketched here. These constructs should not be confused with the fictive reader, or *narratee, i.e., the reader addressed more or less overtly by a narrator and thus serving as a text-internal agent of communication, with whom the real reader may or may not share traits and attitudes.

*Authors apparently write with a reader construct in mind, an idealised image of a readership putting into effect authorial *intentions. This intended, or ideal, reader will play the role s/he is invited to play (the 'mock reader' described by Gibson), decoding textual information according to what the author has strategically planned on the basis of shared *codes (Eco's 'model reader'). The intended reader will also, at least for the duration of the reading process, accept the attitudes and beliefs demanded by the text (and thus act as the 'authorial audience', in the terminology of Rabinowitz), even if these attitudes and beliefs contradict his or her real-life dispositions (i.e., his or her characteristics as the 'actual audience'). Apart from personally interviewing the author, the only way of formulating such reader constructs is to infer them from the text.

Probably the most widely used of all constructs in reader-oriented criticism is the 'implied reader' introduced by Wolfgang Iser. This particular reader image is construed as a counterpart to the *implied author, an entity situated in the text, and 'in no way to be identified with any real reader' (Iser 1978: 34). Critics of the 'implied reader' concept have pointed out that it is basically synonymous with authorial intention, and that scholars have simply used it as a catch-all for what they hold to be the sum of a text's meaning. Often enough, the implied reader camouflages the questionable attempt to elevate a subjective reading experience to a uniquely 'correct' reading.

Within the framework of stylistics, Michael Riffaterre coined the term 'superreader' (also termed 'arch-reader' and '*archilecteur*'), which is simply a collection of responses to particular passages of a text by real readers, among them students, translators, and interpreters of that text. Riffaterre's method is to abstract from the content-level of such responses, concentrating on the mere fact that an item has aroused readers' attention and may therefore be stylistically relevant. He thus collects evidence for a stylistic skeleton-structure of a text, which he believes can be described objectively. Although applied to poetry by Riffaterre, the superreader is also a convenient tool for narrative analysis, especially in the classroom, where it may be used to help assess the group's reactions to a text.

Stanley Fish, in his 'affective stylistics', speaks of an 'informed reader', a construct indebted to the structuralist concept of (linguistic) competence which also informs Jonathan Culler's 'competent reader' (see STRUCTURALIST NARRATOLOGY). Fish maintains that a text's effects are best realised by a reader knowledgeable about its cultural and linguistic contexts, and that on the basis of such knowledge the critic can, by a drastically slowed-down reading, trace what really happens (or happened) in a text's reception. Although this procedure may not capture actual reading processes, most students of literary narrative indeed try to be informed readers when they add to their understanding of a text by relating it to contextual information. In his later writings, Fish views the reader as more strongly immersed in an institutional context – the interpretive community that imposes a priori constraints on how a text may be understood (see INSTITUTIONAL NARRATIVE).

Norman N. Holland proposes a bipartite reader construct based on psychoanalytic theory (see PSYCHOANALYSIS AND NARRATIVE). It consists of the 'analogising reader', who relates to a text by unconsciously transforming the fantasy (drives, fears, wishes, etc.) it offers to his or her own fantasy, and the 'intellecting reader', who – at the same time – fends off the fantasies s/he finds too disturbing to admit. In this approach, the meaning of a text depends primarily on the conditions of the reader's psychological make-up.

It may appear counter-intuitive that the empirical reader, who is the subject of much empirical testing as well as theorising in cognitive-psychological research on discourse processing, should also be a construct. However, in empirical test set-ups conforming to the stricter standards of the natural sciences, the number of parameters tested is usually so small that it is difficult to apply the findings to real-life reading situations. Historical empirical readers can at any rate only be reconstructed from written evidence. Hence it seems that, for the foreseeable future, reading-oriented narratologists will have to be content with relatively speculative constructs when describing the effects of narrative on the reader.

SEE ALSO: narrative comprehension; phenomenology of narrative; rhetorical approaches to narrative

References and further reading

Culler, Jonathan (1975) Structuralist Poetics: Structuralism, Linguistics, and the Study of Literature, London: Routledge and Kegan Paul.

Gerrig, Richard J. (1993) Experiencing Narrative Worlds: On the Psychological Activities of Reading, New Haven: Yale University Press.

Eco, Umberto (1979) The Role of the Reader: Explorations in the Semiotics of Texts, Bloomington: Indiana University Press.

Fish, Stanley (1980) Is There a Text in This Class? The Authority of Interpretive Communities, Cambridge, Mass.: Harvard University Press.

Gibson, Walker (1950) 'Authors, Speakers, Readers, and Mock Readers', College English, 11, 265–69 (rpt in Tompkins 1980).

Holland, Norman N. (1968) The Dynamics of Literary Response, New York: Oxford University Press.

——(1975) 5 Readers Reading, New York: Oxford University Press.

Iser, Wolfgang (1978) The Act of Reading: A Theory of Aesthetic Response, Baltimore: Johns Hopkins University Press.

Rabinowitz, Peter J. (1987) Before Reading: Narrative Conventions and the Politics of Interpretation, Ithaca: Cornell University Press.

Riffaterre, Michael (1959) 'Criteria for Style Analysis', Word, 15, 154–74.

——(1966) 'Describing Poetic Structures: Two Approaches to Baudelaire's "Les Chats"', Yale French Studies, 36, 200–42.

Tompkins, Jane P. (ed.) (1980) Reader-Response Criticism: From Formalism to Poststructuralism, Baltimore: Johns Hopkins University Press.

RALF SCHNEIDER

READERLY TEXT, WRITERLY TEXT (BARTHES)

The notion of readerly text (or readerly narrative) (texte lisible) was introduced for the first time into the vocabulary of literary theory by Roland Barthes in S/Z (1974 [1970]). Designed to be a close reading of Sarrasine, a short *novella written by Honoré de Balzac for his Contes philosophiques, one chapter of Barthes's book defines a new theoretical paradigm which opposes the notion of readerly text to the writerly text (texte scriptible). Barthes's idea emerged from a specific context – i.e., the intellectual circles of Paris and particularly the writers and theorists of the *Tel Quel Group, for whom the larger notion of textuality had become a central theoretical and critical concern. Seeking to reinflect his earlier, structuralist investigations with a poststructuralist conception of the value and 'individuality' of literary texts (*see* POSTSTUCTURALIST APPROACHES TO NARRATIVE; STRUCTURALIST NARRATOLOGY), Barthes devotes the first section of his book to defining the concepts that turn a passively 'consuming' reader into an active 'producer' (*see* READER-RESPONSE THEORY).

The notions of readerly and writerly texts were part of Barthes's attempt to free the reader from the constraints and limitations which academic institutions tend to impose on the 'consumption' of literary texts, particularly by linking the meaning of a text to the intention of its *author and/or to the historical and cultural contexts of its production (*see* INTENTIONALITY). For Barthes, the *readerly* text represents the values which a 'classical' reader will seek in a literary text: linearity of the narrative, transparency of meaning, and continuity of *plot. The readerly text contains the 'countervalue' of the writerly text because it is a 'closed-off' text which leaves no room for the meaning-constructing 'practices' of the 'writerly' reader. By contrast, Barthes sought to develop a model capable of unravelling the hidden *codes inscribed in any given text, basing his approach neither on *science nor on *ideology, but rather on a new 'practice' of reading and writing. The idea of the writerly text grew out of that approach; it is a text which allows readers to produce a 'plurality' of meanings which goes beyond the logical or *psychological construction of the text (*see* INDETERMINACY). The writerly text thus calls into question and deconstructs literary norms and conventions, unravelling the codes of literature to produce a *sui generis*, 'ideal' text.

Barthes's concepts of the readerly and writerly have had a major impact in literary criticism and also in hypertext theory and practices (*see* DIGITAL NARRATIVE). For example, the idea of the writerly text afforded hypertext theorists like Landow strategies for characterising the role of the user vis-à-vis *multi-path narratives. Other theorists, however, have noted that the concept of the readerly is more compatible with *narrativity than is the notion of the writerly (cf. Ryan 2001).

References and further reading

Barthes, Roland (1974) *S/Z*, trans. Richard Howard, New York: Hill and Wang.
Landow, George P. (1992) *Hypertext: The Convergence of Contemporary Critical Theory and Technology*, Baltimore: Johns Hopkins University Press.
Ryan, Marie-Laure (2001) *Narrative as Virtual Reality: Immersion and Interactivity in Literature and Electronic Media*, Baltimore: Johns Hopkins University Press.

REDA BENSMAIA

READER-RESPONSE THEORY

Reader-oriented approaches to literature were developed in the 1970s by American and European scholars in reaction to what were perceived as the overly text-centred theories of New Criticism and Formalism. The term 'reader-response theory' covers a wide variety of schools, though sometimes it is applied exclusively to North American contributions. The common denominator of modern reader-oriented theories – grounded in such diverse theoretical frameworks as, e.g., *hermeneutics, stylistics, *semiotics, and *psychoanalysis – is that they investigate the reader's contribution to the meaning of a narrative (and, in fact, any text), assuming an interaction to take place between them. These approaches differ greatly in several respects: in whether they assign the decisive role to the text or to the reader; in the process models on which they base their descriptions of the interaction between text and reader; and in the importance they attribute to cultural context. Many reader-response theories have also developed specific *reader constructs.

Considerations of the effects of literature on readers (or viewers, or listeners) date back to classical poetics, arguably originating in Aristotle's concept of **catharsis'. Even philosophies hostile to literature – such as Plato's dismissal of poets from the ideal state as well as the standard rationale of censorship throughout literary history – have been based on the assumption that literature profoundly affects readers. Among the precursors of modern reader-response theory are, for instance, I. A. Richards' emotive theory from the 1920s (*see* EMOTION AND NARRATIVE) and Louise Rosenblatt's transactional theory, first proposed in the 1930s. But it was in the 1970s that major changes in attitudes towards hierarchy and authority in the Western world gave rise to new demands that readers' activities be investigated instead of authorial intentions or the allegedly a-historical aesthetic value of texts (*see* FORMALISM; INTENTIONALITY). Roland Barthes even claimed, in

'The Death of the Author', that the *author must die for the reader to be born.

Stanley Fish developed his 'affective stylistics' in reaction to Wimsatt and Beardsley's 'affective fallacy' and the attempts of stylisticians such as Michael Riffaterre to examine textual features without regard for what they mean to readers. Fish maintains that literary understanding rests in the dynamics of the reading experience. To him, what makes a work meaningful is that the succession of textual units urges the reader to continually establish and dismiss interpretations, adopt attitudes as well as discard them, etc. Later, however, Fish renounced this almost behaviouristic characterisation of the power of textual stimuli over the reader.

In Germany, the work of the Constance School was based on the principles of hermeneutics (in the case of Hans Robert Jauss) and on the *phenomenology of Edmund Husserl and Roman Ingarden (in the case of Wolfgang Iser). While Jauss concentrated on literary history (see RECEPTION THEORY), Iser focused on the reader's contribution to the meaning of a text and made an attempt to account both for the mental activities responsible for the construction of meaning and for the constraints on meaning production pre-structured by the text. Reading a narrative is seen as a dynamic set of mental processes in which past information is continually related to current understanding and hypotheses about future information, and in which gaps left by the text are filled, so that its *indeterminacy is removed (see GAPPING; SCRIPTS AND SCHEMATA).

Umberto Eco's work on reading response epitomises the contribution of semiotics and its sensitivity to contextual conditions of meaning production. Narrative understanding is conceived as dependent on *codes of signification shared by authors and readers. Authors to some extent predetermine the role of the reader by strategic encoding of information. Jonathan Culler, whose writings cover aspects of structuralism, semiotics, and deconstruction (see DECONSTRUCTIVE APPROACHES TO NARRATIVE), also views the readers' attempts at meaning construction as governed, and thus limited, by constraints which are imposed by the codes of a cultural community. Similarly, in his later work, Stanley Fish sees every reading of a text as determined, albeit unconsciously, by the reader's membership in an 'interpretive community'.

Norman N. Holland established reader-oriented research within the framework of psychoanalytic criticism, taking emotional and unconscious aspects of literary meaning construction into account. According to this approach, a text has meaning for the reader insofar as he or she can project his or her own (unconscious) fears and *desires onto the text in a way that makes them manageable. Unlike many other allegedly reader-oriented approaches, Holland puts his theory to the test in detailed investigations of empirical readers' responses to stories, in which he finds that readings correspond to the readers' individual psychological set-up, their 'identity themes' (see IDENTITY AND NARRATIVE).

While many reader-response theories proposed rather vague concepts of the readers' actual processes of understanding, since the 1980s reader-oriented study has profited from the theories and empirical findings of cognitive psychology and research in discourse processing (see PSYCHOLOGICAL APPROACHES TO NARRATIVE). In this framework, the mental activities of the reading process are described with the help of more detailed models of text understanding in general and of narrative understanding in particular (see NARRATIVE COMPREHENSION; SITUATION MODEL). Although the diverse methods and findings of these studies forbid straightforward application to instances of 'natural' literary reception, attempts to synthesise such findings (e.g., Gerrig 1993; Dixon and Bortolussi 2003) have strongly contributed to the reader-oriented aspects of *cognitive narratology.

Unfortunately, despite the obvious interest of critics in the conditions of meaning for different readers, reader-response approaches have time and again been used to rule out multiple readings, to enshrine certain literary values, and to support aesthetic hierarchies such as high vs. low culture so that innovative texts that overstrain a wide audience's competences are accredited high value, whereas those that fulfil expectations are judged as minor or 'popular'.

SEE ALSO: audience; pragmatics

References and further reading

Culler, Jonathan (1981) *The Pursuit of Signs: Semiotics, Literature, Deconstruction*, Ithaca: Cornell University Press.

Dixon, Peter, and Marisa Bortolussi (2003) *Psychonarratology: Foundations for the Empirical Study of*

Literary Response, Cambridge: Cambridge University Press.

Eco, Umberto (1979) *The Role of the Reader: Explorations in the Semiotics of Texts*, Bloomington: Indiana University Press.

Fish, Stanley (1980) *Is There a Text in This Class? The Authority of Interpretive Communities*, Cambridge, Mass.: Harvard University Press.

Gerrig, Richard J. (1993) *Experiencing Narrative Worlds: On the Psychological Activities of Reading*, New Haven: Yale University Press.

Holland, Norman N. (1968) *The Dynamics of Literary Response*, New York: Oxford University Press.

——(1975) *5 Readers Reading*, London: Yale University Press.

Holub, Robert C. (1984) *Reception Theory: A Critical Introduction*, London: Methuen.

Iser, Wolfgang (1978) *The Act of Reading: A Theory of Aesthetic Response*, Baltimore: Johns Hopkins University Press.

Suleiman, Susan R., and Inge Crosman (eds) (1980) *The Reader in the Text: Essays on Audience and Interpretation*, Princeton: Princeton University Press.

Tompkins, Jane P. (ed.) (1980) *Reader-Response Criticism: From Formalism to Poststructuralism*, Baltimore: Johns Hopkins University Press.

RALF SCHNEIDER

REALEME

This term, analogous to the structuralist linguists' 'phoneme', 'morpheme', etc., was proposed by the *Tel Aviv cultural theorist Even-Zohar to designate 'items of reality' that a semiotic system recognises and admits to its repertoire. Not everything that is observable in the world is admissible in a given semiotic system, but rather only those that are 'semioticised' in that system. No discourse ever represents reality in the 'raw', relying instead on a preselection from the universe of potentially representable realities. Realemes form organised repertoires, which differ from culture to culture, and even from one genre or register to another in the same culture. Thus, French advertising texts avoid direct reference to children – children are not 'realemes' in that register – as becomes clear when such texts are contrasted with equivalent texts in Dutch translation, where children do appear (*see* ADVERTISEMENTS). Narrative *realism is an effect achieved sometimes by conformity to realeme repertoires, sometimes by their deliberate violation (Jakobson 1971 [1921]).

SEE ALSO: realist novel; reality effect; semiotics; structuralist narratology

References and further reading

Even-Zohar, Itamar (1990 [1980]) '"Reality" and Realemes in Narrative', *Poetics Today*, 11.1: 207–18.

Jakobson, Roman (1971 [1921]) 'On Realism in Art', in Ladislav Matejka and Krystyna Pomorska (eds) *Readings in Russian Poetics: Formalist and Structuralist Views*, Cambridge: MIT Press.

BRIAN McHALE

REALISM, THEORIES OF

Philosophical realism is a position affirming the real existence of an entity or a group of entities, including common sense objects of perception such as a tree, theoretically constructed entities such as a magnetic field, or abstract entities such as *truth (*see* EXISTENT). Realism in the literary or visual arts refers to an effect produced by a text or a visual *image, whereby these artistic modes are construed as being able to reflect and reproduce aspects of the real world (*see* REALITY EFFECT). Realism in narrative contexts refers to the capacity of narrative to portray people engaged in action-oriented situations (*see* ACTION THEORY).

These meanings of realism, divided disciplinarily, appear also to be divided conceptually, as they present fundamentally different conceptions of realism. The principal one concerns the ontological status of the object represented or perceived (*see* MODALITY); the other deals with the realm of effects produced by artistic and narrative modes of expression. Since Plato, however, the question of representation (immediate as opposed to indirect, demonstrated by the difference between the bed made by the carpenter and the one fabricated by the painter) has been tied to the nature of the object thereby produced. Counter to the apparent disciplinary divide between theories of realism, the question of representation has been recognised as both fundamentally philosophical and as carrying a range of implications for art. Varieties of the realist position in *philosophy can thus be shown to converge with aspects of realism in literary and art theory.

This convergence is also relevant to the study of realism in *narrative. In connection with narrative the meaning of realism can take both directions, referring to narrative as object or as *mode. It can refer to the objective existence of a specific narrative competence identified in human beings independent of differences of culture or inclination (see NARRATIVE UNIVERSALS), or it can refer to the transparency and naturalness of narrative modes in transmitting *events. Approaching the question of the realism of narrative in its full intricacy hence requires a consideration of notions that are tied to realism in various disciplinary contexts.

Realist positions and their convergence

To map the realist position, the following three realist claims can be distinguished (see Pettit 1991):

(1) Discourses with realist commitments posit their own distinct entities. For instance, *psychological discourse posits mental states, scientific discourse posits physical entities (such as heat) and unobservable theoretical entities (such as electrons; see SCIENCE AND NARRATIVE), and *Marxist discourse posits ideological superstructures (see IDEOLOGY AND NARRATIVE). These distinct entities are irreducible to entities posited by other discourses.

In connection with art and its realistic effects, this realist claim converges with the idea of a correlation between distinct modes of representation and the concrete settings evoked by these modes. For instance, a naturalist *genre of writing, such as Zola's, produces a picture of lower-class life; the use of linear geometry posits a distinct three-dimensional *space; the use of fragmented, emotive discourse posits mental entities such as the inner thoughts of *characters; radical metaphorical discourse (as in Surrealist poetry) posits impossible objects (see METAPHOR; SURREALIST NARRATIVE). The distinct entities posited by one mode of representation are irreducible to those posited by other modes.

(2) Epistemic states, such as belief dispositions, do not influence the objective existence and properties of states of affairs. For example, for a modal realist a future possible state of the universe (see POSSIBLE-WORLDS THEORY) exists objectively, even if he/she is ignorant of how to predict possible states of affairs from the actual one.

In connection with art and its realistic effects, this realist claim would refer to the unvarying correspondence between certain texts or compositions and their objects, regardless of the reader's or observer's beliefs or epistemic disposition. *Verisimilitude, as a predominant form of correspondence, makes the reader/observer 'see' the object in the text or picture either because he/she is deceived into doing so or just because of the facile recogni-

tion the artwork allows. The observer sees the grief on the Madonna's face in the *Pieta* because her grief is objectively there, written on the face of the painted image (see PICTORIAL NARRATIVITY). This is the case even if the observer is fundamentally an atheist in belief, or a disbeliever in the power of art, or just suffering from a headache that prevents her from seeing the image clearly. Likewise, the inner thoughts of Mrs. Ramsay in *To the Lighthouse* are made knowable to the reader even if he/she knows nothing about *free indirect discourse, or misses the point of how those thoughts contribute to the narrative unfolding, or holds the view that human thoughts are in principle inaccessible to others.

(3) Entities, held to exist realistically, do so even if the substantive claims of the discourse referring to them are erroneous. Thus the chemical composition of water exists objectively regardless of whether experts in the field of chemistry present this composition in an accurate formula.

In the context of art, a realistic mode of representation can be considered effective even if the model guaranteeing *verisimilitude turns out to be wrong or deceptive (based on illusion). From Alberti to Gombrich, linear perspective is attributed absolute realism although inquiry into its visual bases has proven that its geometry cannot produce an accurate image of visual fields (Panowsky 1991 [1927]; Ronen 2002). The minute *description of everyday, common objects is taken to produce realistic effects although this mode of description can also be recruited to portray the most fantastic reality (which has given rise to the somewhat paradoxical notion of *magical realism).

Realism: a question of epistemic/representational mode

How can one decide which theory, among equally valid ones, is true? How is a story most naturally told? How is the inner world of a character/figure visually or textually transmitted? These questions do not just indicate the convergence of philosophical theories of realism with the ones that aestheticians and narrative theorists produce, but also reveal that the problem of realism raises questions regarding the mode and structure of representation no less than questions regarding the existence of the object represented. Can facts and truth be independent of language, mind, and mode of signification? This question comes up in both philosophy and art, and in both disciplinary frameworks it concerns the vehicles of representation that make the world accessible to us no less than the ontology of the part of reality being represented. The coalescence of ontological with epistemic concerns holds both for philosophical and literary views of realism. In the context of narrative this coalescence can be demonstrated in a notion implicit in many narrative theories, that *events make a narrative only when rendered as story, that is, that a narrative mode of rendering narrativises its content (*see* NARRATIVISATION).

A typical realist is concerned with the extent to which modes of theorising and representing can be trusted regarding the distinct entities they posit. Most philosophers indeed argue that realism amounts to more than just a metaphysical position about the objective existence of reality (Devitt 1991); rather, it can be couched in valid terms only when it is identified with a set of epistemic consequences regarding such topics as truth, *reference, etc. Realism is often qualified in epistemic terms, as a limit on human error for instance, by claiming that under optimal epistemic conditions of inquiry, there is no reason to assume a possible incompatibility between the existence of entities and what we know about them (Putnam 1990).

Epistemic concerns are paramount in the context of art and narrative since often the stability of objective reality, or of a generally accepted picture of reality, outside representation, is not questioned. Realistic effects of storytelling hence rely either on the use of modes assigned absolute effectiveness (descriptions are generally taken to add realism to narrative) or on the use of modes given to cultural-historical modification but appropriate for a worldview (the master-representative of the latter view is Auerbach and his notion of *mimesis).

Theories of realism can hence be mapped according to the element to which the role of mediating reality is assigned. What is known as naive realism attributes objective validity to sense perception in transmitting information about the world; modal realists trust modal operators in transmitting information about possible realities; scientific realists assign to modes of scientific inquiry the capability of discovering entities that objectively exist; realists within the philosophy of language believe language obeys a mechanism of meaning-production independent of linguistic contingencies because they trust meaning-theories to describe this mechanism accurately; realism

within aesthetics means that art can represent parts of reality by employing a variety of artistic modes transparent/verisimilar enough not to interfere with the reality represented.

Thus realism is a position that attributes to the object or state of affairs represented a status independent of representation itself, because the mode of representation is considered the only one appropriate to the task. Realism in art refers to art's capacity to raise in its recipient a sense of approximating the true nature of the represented object by means of the appropriate representational modes.

The paradox of transparency

Realism assumes that mode of representation is tied so intimately to a represented entity that the former goes unmarked, and indeed a central issue raised regarding realism relates to the efficiency of representation itself. A realistic effect in art as well as a realist position in philosophy assumes a non-problematic relation between a set of signs and things in the world, as signs refer to objects that belong to another order without being noticed as different or as not wholly congruent with the things represented (*see* SEMIOTICS). The similarity between sign and represented content is addressed by realists through a series of concepts like transparency, verisimilitude, naturalness, iconicity, resemblance, correspondence, and so forth.

It was shown above that despite what seems like realism's exclusive commitment to the existence of represented entities, there is no way of separating the entity represented from the mode of representing it. This inseparability, however, results in a paradox since realism relies on transparency and verisimilitude for its effect and efficiency, whereas in principle the represented object and the mode of representation cannot be totally reduced one to the other. Transparency is always conditioned and limited; yet transparency stipulates the very possibility of realism. This paradoxical nature of transparent representation characterises the dilemma around the problem of realism. The paradox of realism can be found in accounts of the success of theories in physics and in interpretations of the success of a meticulously drawn self-portrait.

This paradox explains why discussions of realism in various disciplines actually aim at the endless array of cases where representation includes more than the object represented or subtracts something from it. While transparency in representation is shown through the similarity between sign and its represented content, the effect produced in the recipient (life-likeness or illusion of reality in the case of art, trustworthiness in the case of science) has to be accounted for by overcoming the irreducible distance between mode and object, the two participants in the dualistic domain of realist representation. The paradoxical nature of realism manifests itself when, despite stressing the dependence of realism on transparent signification, literary-artistic realists as well as philosophical realists formulate problems that arise from the irreducibility of sign to represented content – in order to prove that this content is unaffected by the materiality and lacunae in the mode of signification.

Realism and narrative

Realism in relation to narrative can refer to two different things: (1) The naturalness of narrative representation of events and actions; (2) the distinct existence of a cognitive or cross-cultural narrative competence (see COGNITIVE NARRATOLOGY). While the first version of realism stresses narrative's representational transparency, the second stresses the innateness or universality of narrative competence, i.e., its ontological status.

Realism vis-à-vis the narrative mode typically relates to the transparency of the narrative recounting of facts, of causal relations, and of action (see CAUSALITY). The naturalness of narrative for these representational purposes is complemented by securing other modes of representation, like description, for other purposes (e.g., for creating a world of objects around human action) (Hamon 1991). Models of narrative often distinguish narrative modes according to one dominant criterion: that of the facile deducibility of narrated content. For instance, impersonal language is more transparent than the personal language of an individuated *narrator; the interpretive involvement of a third-person heterodiegetic narrator interferes with deducibility more than comments made in first-person because of the authority of the narrator (Doležel 1998; see AUTHENTICATION); iterative narrative modes interfere with transparency because they can result in grouping events irrespective of their 'real' succession (Genette 1988; see NARRATIVE TECHNIQUES). The demand for

transparency is as overriding and paradoxical as in other contexts of realism: narrative is a natural form for particular contents because the realism of this content depends on its remaining unaffected by *narrativity.

Against the idea of a natural compatibility (transparency) between the narrative mode and a specific set of entities (particulars, not universals; time-based events, not exclusively timeless properties, etc.; see TIME IN NARRATIVE), an objection can be raised. It can be argued that narrative modes are partially indifferent to narrated content on two counts: first, narrative content can be inferred from many types of representation, including the most subjective, personal, intensely interpretive account; that is, transparency cannot work as a prevailing criterion in correlating narrated content with natural narrative rendering. Second, the naturalness of narrative rendering is applicable to any content; the supposedly natural compatibility between narrative and distinct entities like events and actions has to be revised since Einstein's concept of relativity can be rendered as story, and narrative content can be rendered by means of non-narrative modes. Thus entities constructed by narrative discourse are not as distinct as realism in narrative theory may assume. Many modes of rendering can be described as narrative in the broad sense and applied to a wide variety of contents, from sports commentaries (see SPORTS BROADCAST), through *epic poetry, to a scientific report. The distinct set of entities that suits narrative naturally is hence to be defined in very broad terms, as reflected in the wide range of fields to which narrative conceptualisations have been imported (see INTERDISCIPLINARY APPROACHES TO NARRATIVE; NARRATIVE TURN IN THE HUMANITIES).

A second objection to the naturalness of narrative arises from attempts to stress the belletristic nature of narrative discourse. In other words, it is the literary rendering of narrative that makes things, both actual and fictional look real. Thus the grammatical past used in narrative (both historical and fictional) and third-person *narration signify creation, the order of a literary domain of plausibility. Narrative introduces nothing of the naturalisable but an ambiguous form located between sincerity and falsehood (Barthes 1968). Narrative puts forward fabrication more than a naturalised reality (see FICTION, THEORIES OF; NATURALISATION).

Both objections can be met if beyond defining narrative in formal terms (as pointing to a distinct set of necessary action-oriented properties that enable the rendering of material as story), the overall purpose of narrative is theoretically grounded. Thus conceptualising narrative in terms of a meaning organisation may motivate the structuring of narrative *plot more than the mere presence of particulars engaged in action (*see* NARRATIVE STRUCTURE). Similarly, psychoanalysts have suggested that narrative is an imaginary organisation of every fantasmatic material that aims to camouflage the true, unconscious question every particular fantasy posits: 'what does the other want of me?' Such suggestions hint at the distinctness of narrative and hence at the limits of narrative rendering.

The attempt to naturalise narrative forms to the point of utmost transparency is linked to the notion of narrative as a natural competence transcending cultural varieties of world-organisation. Narrative is fundamental to human ways of representation and as such is cross-cultural and transhistorical.

Against this realist view of narrative as independent of modes of belief or of cultural dispositions, one might object that narrative is man-made, fabricated for specific interests. People from distant cultures may not find the narrative mode as natural to decipher as we assume it to be because narrative forms, even if born with human history itself, are not innate; their cultural origins cannot be denied. Thus, even if narrative is a widespread way of manipulating the facts of history, one can point to other, non-narrative ways of organising facts in either history or fiction (see White 1987; *see* METAHISTORY). There is nothing more innate, or of a deeper cognitive reality, in narrative, than in other ways of reporting events. Whether narrative is seen as a universal pattern transcending cultural differences, whether narrative is taken to be a basic mode among others at the disposal of all known cultures, or whether narrative is taken to be a widely shared convention of the Western world – it is apparent that a realist position toward narrative is not easy to sustain.

The realism of narrative manifests the same paradoxical character as one finds in realism at large. The naturalness of narrative modes depends on their transparency yet also on the irreducibility of these very modes. The universality of narrative competence depends on its being sufficiently widespread, yet, in order not to lose the specificity of narrative vis-à-vis other modes of meaning organisation, narrative has to be restricted in accordance with what may turn out to be culture-dependent coordinates.

Realism, narrative, and truth

Linking the naturalness of narrative to its universal status may appear to be supported by narrative's indifference to reference and to truth value. Fictional and factual content lend themselves equally well to narrative modes of representation. We can, says Peter Lamarque, read all narratives as fictional, as pretending to have a truth-telling power; we then direct our attention to the literariness of narrative. While many literary readers of narrative realism will endorse this indifference to fact and truth and claim that narrativity is an overall quality of discursive practices, a different position can be defended from a philosophical point of view. Lamarque himself opposes the idea that philosophers, scientists, historians, and novelists equally fictionalise reality through storytelling and points at the importance of differentiating between types of commitment to truth and reference. Furthermore, when narrative introduces discrepancies with the real world (in the form of omniscient narration or of *fantastic elements), these may facilitate the reader's acquaintance with fictional truths but compromise the realism of narrative (see Walton 1990). The realism of narrative is hence stipulated, according to such views, by different degrees of commitment to referents and to truth in different kinds of narratives.

The correspondence between narrative representations and human action is difficult to prove. Yet, even if naturalness is objected to, this does not lead necessarily to a view of realism in narrative as a purely conventional matter. Even if one rejects the idea that the status of a reality is independent of the modes of its presentation and representation, the problem of realism is not resolved by opting for the view that realism amounts to no more than a familiarity with a given mode of representing or structuring a set of beliefs. Conventions cannot explain the unequally realistic effects achieved by a Vermeer and a Van Gogh; conventions cannot account for the shared sense of realism left by a meticulous description of everyday objects, a description that serves no meaningful purpose (see Jakobson 1962), or for the fact that 'the photographs in *Time* magazine seem more "realistic" to us than Egyptian wall drawings in the "frontal eye" style' (see Carroll 1999). The issue of realism involves not only the changing modes of representing but also the irreducible presence of an object.

SEE ALSO: realeme; realist novel

References and further reading

Barthes, Roland (1968) *Writing Degree Zero*, trans. Annette Lavers and Colin Smith, New York: Hill and Wang.
Carroll, Noël (1999) *Philosophy of Art*, London: Routledge.
Devitt, Michael (1991) *Realism and Truth*, Oxford: Blackwell.
Doležel, Lubomir (1998) *Heterocosmica: Fiction and Possible Worlds*, Baltimore: Johns Hopkins University Press.
Fried, Michael (1987) *Realism, Writing, Disfiguration*, Chicago: Chicago University Press.
Genette, Gérard (1988) *Narrative Discourse Revisited*, Ithaca NY: Cornell University Press.
Gombrich, Ernst, and Didier Eribon (1993) *Looking for Answers: Conversations on Art and Science*, New York: Harry N. Abrams.
Hamon, Philippe (ed.) (1991) *La déscription littéraire: Anthologie de texts théoriques et critiques*, Paris: Macula.
Jakobson, Roman (1962) 'On Realism in Art', trans. Karol Magassy, in Ladislav Matejka and Krystyna Pomorska (eds) *Readings in Russian Poetics*, Ann Arbor: University of Michigan Press.
Lamarque, Peter (1990) 'Narrative and Invention: The Limits of Fictionality', in Christopher Nash (ed.) *Narrative in Culture*, London: Routledge.
Panowsky, Erwin (1991 [1927]) *Perspective as Symbolic Form*, trans. Christopher S. Wood, New York: Zone Books.
Pettit, Philip (1991) 'Realism and Response-Dependence', *Mind*, 100, 587–626.
Putnam, Hilary (1990) *Realism with a Human Face*, Cambridge, Mass.: Harvard University Press.
Ronen, Ruth (2002) *Representing the Real*, Amsterdam: Rodopi.
Walton, Kendall L. (1990) *Mimesis as Make-Believe: On the Foundations of the Representational Arts*, Cambridge, Mass.: Harvard University Press.
White, Hayden (1987) *The Content of the Form*, Baltimore: Johns Hopkins University Press.

RUTH RONEN

REALIST NOVEL

A realist novel is one which appears to provide an accurate, objective, and confident description or authentic impression of reality. This semiotic effect, which rests on the assumption that language is an undistorted mirror of, or transparent window on, the 'real', is based on a set of literary conventions for producing a lifelike illusion (for a variety of perspectives that deeply problematise the notion of the realist novel, *see* FICTION, THEORIES OF; MIMESIS; NATURALISATION; POSSIBLE-WORLDS THEORY; REALEME; REALISM, THEORIES OF; REALITY EFFECT; SEMIOTICS; VERISIMILITUDE).

From a historical perspective, the term 'realist novel' was famously linked by Watt (1957) to the rise of the *novel in the eighteenth-century (for example, Daniel Defoe). The core use of the term relates to the nineteenth-century 'classic realist' novel (Jane Austen, Stendhal, Honoré de Balzac, George Eliot, Lev Tolstoi, Gustave Flaubert, and Mark Twain), although Lodge (1990) and Levine (1981) argue that these novelists were, in general, much less naively realist about the problems of representation than has commonly been supposed. An emphasis on *character rather than *plot led to the psychological realism of Henry James (*see* PSYCHOLOGICAL NOVEL). Naturalism is a submode of realism which relates, in particular, to such late-nineteenth-century and early-twentieth century writers as Emile Zola, Thomas Hardy, George Gissing, Theodore Dreiser, and Sinclair Lewis. Realism, and especially psychological realism, was an important element in the twentieth-century novel (for example, Arnold Bennett and Graham Greene; *see* MODERNIST NARRATIVE).

With regard to the story (*see* STORY-DISCOURSE DISTINCTION), realist novels typically comprise a detailed and unsentimental description of the domestic life of the middle and lower classes. The events described are ordinary, plausible, and generally in accordance with natural laws and behavioural expectations. The tendency to examine individuals within the complexities of group life often resulted in analyses of societal change, for example industrialisation, and the promotion of social reform. Naturalist novels purport to explain issues such as miserable living conditions in terms of contemporary physical and social sciences, particularly evolutionary theory, *sociology, and psychology. These behaviour models tend to be used in a rather deterministic and mechanistic manner and so often portray characters as passive victims of their environment.

With regard to the discourse, the realist novel is generally associated with the omniscient *narrator.

SEE ALSO: focalization; magical realism; narration

References and further reading

Auerbach, Erich (1953) *Mimesis: The Representation of Reality in Western Literature*, trans. Willard R. Trask, Princeton: Princeton University Press.
Levine, George (1981) *The Realistic Imagination: English Fiction from Frankenstein to Lady Chatterley*, Chicago: Chicago University Press.
Lodge, David (1990) *After Bakhtin: Essays on Fiction and Criticism*, London: Routledge.
Lukács, Georg (1964) *Realism in Our Time: Literature and the Class Struggle*, trans. John and Necke Mander, New York: Harper.
McKeon, Michael (1987) *The Origins of the English Novel 1600 to 1740*, Baltimore: Johns Hopkins University Press.
—— (ed.) (2000) *Theory of the Novel: A Historical Approach*, Baltimore: Johns Hopkins University Press.
Moretti, Franco (1998) *Atlas of the European Novel 1800 to 1900*, London: Verso.
Watt, Ian (1957) *The Rise of the Novel*, London: Hogarth.

ALAN PALMER

REALITY EFFECT

The notion of the 'reality effect' (*effet de réel*) was introduced by Roland Barthes in an article published in the journal *Communications* in 1968. Barthes was led to this idea by the observation that in most (if not all) 'classical' literary texts, one comes across certain descriptive details which seem to have no logical, narratological, or aesthetic necessity (*see* DESCRIPTION). For Barthes, when the *narrator of Flaubert's 'A Simple Heart' notes that in the room occupied by Madame Aubain 'an old piano supported, *under a barometer*, a pyramidal heap of boxes and cartons', the specific evocation of the 'barometer' indicates first and foremost that the description is 'true to life' (*see* REALISM, THEORIES OF; VERISIMILITUDE). Hence, what the reader of *realist novels takes for a reproduction of 'real things' is no more than a *rhetorical effect associated with a specific *genre.

The power of the 'reality effect' stems primarily from a complex of signs which stimulates the reader to transform reality into a 'naturalised' *storyworld. According to Barthes this operation of *naturalisation is achieved through a radical historical shift from an 'ancient mode of verisimilitude' to a 'new verisimilitude' which emerges with the advent of realism in literature. Before the realist sea change, one tended to consider things 'only in relation to what is known of them by those who read or hear'; by contrast, the realist mode functionalises 'all details, to produce strong structures and *to justify no notation by the mere guarantee of "reality"*' (Barthes 1986 [1968]: 147). For Barthes, each time a signifier is obscured 'to the advantage of the referent alone' (148), the 'reality effect' is produced as a phenomenon which is 'the basis of that unavowed verisimilitude which forms the aesthetic of all standard works of modernity' (148). The concept of the reality effect is thus a powerful analytical tool, throwing light on how fictional narratives can promulgate a sense of the real through the strategic, code-based use of verisimilar details.

SEE ALSO: semiotics

References and further reading

Barthes, Roland (1968) 'L'Effet de Réel', *Communications*, 11, 84–89.
——(1986 [1968]) 'The Reality Effect', in *The Rustle of Language*, trans. Richard Howard, New York: Hill and Wang.

REDA BENSMAIA

RECEPTION THEORY

It would make sense to subsume under the term 'reception theory' all possible approaches to cultural artefacts focusing on the conditions, processes, and effects that control their reading, viewing, or auditing. However, the term is usually applied in a more limited sense to the reader-oriented approach developed by the Constance School in the late 1960s and early 1970s, including the work of Hans Robert Jauss, Wolfgang Iser, and other German scholars (in a more restricted sense the term often refers to Jauss exclusively). Definition is not helped by the fact that the German term *Rezeptionsästhetik* ('reception aesthetics') is variably applied to the general approach of the Constance School, to individual approaches within that school, or to a wider range of approaches, including those of formalists and structuralists (*see* FORMALISM; STRUCTURALIST NARRATOLOGY).

Jauss approaches literary history from the reader's point of view. Most prominent in his theory is the concept of the reader's *'horizon of expectations' (*Erwartungshorizont*), a hermeneutic concept which Jauss adapts from the philosopher Hans-Georg Gadamer (*see* HERMENEUTICS). Hermeneutic theory holds that human beings always understand the world – and, by analogy, literary works – in the context of their individual, historically specific position in life. Consequently literary texts (and, more specifically, literary narratives) do not retain a fixed value or elicit uniform responses across generations, but are always understood according to what the changing horizons of the readers' expectations will allow.

Jauss believes that subjective horizons of expectation can be objectified through a formal analysis of a text's *genre markers, its use of literary conventions, and its linguistic features. A given work, then, can either conform to the audience's horizon of expectations or go against it. Beyond stating that simple fact, Jauss introduces a criterion of aesthetic evaluation: In the case of a congruency between the audience's expectations and the formal characteristics of a text, the work fails to add to the state of the art and consequently belongs to middlebrow literature. In the case of a violation of expectations, an 'adequate' horizon of expectations that would allow general appreciation of a work's aesthetic merits has not yet emerged. This may, however, happen at a later time – as can be observed with many avant-garde literary narratives. Jauss himself cites Flaubert's *Madame Bovary* as an example, a *novel which caused a major scandal when it was published in 1856. Flaubert's innovative use of *free indirect discourse left contemporary readers with the impression that the text was too reticent in its condemnation of the heroine's adultery and thus seemed to be supporting immoral behaviour. Later generations, however, appreciated Flaubert's stylistic experiment as a major innovation of the novelistic genre. Thus, the greater the 'aesthetic distance' between the horizons of expectations and the aesthetic characteristics of a work, the more aesthetically valuable it may eventually be deemed to be.

Critics of this approach have contended that horizons of expectations are neither as homogeneous as Jauss assumes nor exclusively determined by intra-literary factors only. It has also been remarked that the concept of aesthetic distance associates Jauss with the very formalist stance he was writing against.

SEE ALSO: reader-response theory

References and further reading

Holub, Robert C. (1984) *Reception Theory: A Critical Introduction*, London: Methuen.

Jauss, Hans-Robert (1982) *Toward an Aesthetic of Reception*, trans. Timothy Bahti, Minneapolis: University of Minnesota Press.

—— (1985) 'The Identity of the Poetic Text in the Changing Horizon of Understanding', in Mario J. Valdés and Owen Miller (eds) *The Identity of the Literary Text*, Toronto: University of Toronto Press.

RALF SCHNEIDER

REFERENCE

Reference can be defined as a relation between an expression (= referring expression) and an entity (= referent), such that on one or more occasions of use (= referring act) a token of the expression picks out or stands for this entity (*see* EXISTENT). The expression is used by someone to identify the entity for someone else in a specific situation, so that the referring act consists of at least sender, object, receiver, and context. In the study of imaginative literature, reference is considered as relative to a *storyworld rather than restricted to actuality (*see* MODALITY; POSSIBLE-WORLDS THEORY). Conversely, while singular terms with actual-world referents, such as *Napoleon*, have their designation codified in our cultural encyclopedia, for fictional *characters or places this designation is defined by the text in which the terms are introduced. And it is indeed characters and places which form the primary referents of literary *narrative (*see* NAMING IN NARRATIVE).

The overall reference system of a work of *fiction is multilevel. (1) The *author selects and deploys referring expressions throughout the text in order to achieve readerly effects such as ironic superiority or *suspense and surprise (*see* IRONY). An author may also first endow expressions with referential force and then withdraw it, thereby cancelling the evoked storyworld and leaving us with a pure play of signifiers (*see* DENARRATION).

(2) The narrated domain consists of a sequence of dynamic situations, such that characters acquire and lose properties and names over the course of the *action; hence there can be constant variation in the expressions which refer to them. Miss X thus turns into Mrs. Y, and the person who is the director of the company at one point is no longer director at a later point. And the same goes for characters' knowledge and beliefs about what expressions refer to themselves or to other characters in any story state. (3) Insofar as a story is told in retrospect, the narrator can know from the beginning of the narrative act which expressions refer to which character and when, thus providing a higher-level, 'olympian' system of reference (see NARRATION). The narrator, and only s/he can thus refer to an infant as 'the future general'. (4) Quotational contexts such as *focalization, indirect discourse, and *free indirect discourse further complicate the picture because their references, and the knowledge or belief they reflect, may stem from either character or *narrator (see QUOTATION THEORY). Is it quoter or quoted who refers to someone as 'this genius'? The fact/belief divide in the storyworld as a whole is largely defined by issues of reference – for example, what terms actually apply to a character in a given situation and which according to co-agents' beliefs, or what individual is actually picked out by a given expression and which according to their beliefs.

Different expressions may co-refer, that is, pick out the same individual in a given situation or throughout, but this may not be known to some or all of the characters or to the reader until very late. Successive or competing hypothetical attempts to establish co-reference between 'the murderer' and a particular proper name define the nature of the whodunit mystery *genre, resolved through a final factual equation (see DETECTIVE FICTION). Systematically undecided relations of co-reference, which are not resolved by story's end, give rise to ambiguous or indeterminate storyworld (see INDETERMINACY).

References and further reading

Margolin, Uri (1991) 'Reference, Coreference, Referring, and the Dual Structure of Literary Narrative', *Poetics Today*, 12, 517–42.

Whiteside, Anna, and Michael Issacharoff (eds) (1987) *On Referring in Literature*, Bloomington: Indiana University Press.

URI MARGOLIN

REFLECTOR

A point of view *character; a character through whose eyes the action is presented. *See* FOCALIZATION; NARRATIVE SITUATIONS.

REFLEXIVITY

As the perennial counterweight to the mimetic impulse of narrative, i.e., its tendency to be viewed as an imitative art (*see* MIMESIS), reflexivity or textual self-consciousness makes the storytelling itself part of the story told. From Homer to Angela Carter, from *Don Quixote* and *Tristram Shandy* to *The French Lieutenant's Woman* and *Midnight's Children*, narratives have foregrounded the conventions of storytelling and have bared, indeed flaunted, their constructed nature. In so doing, they have constituted their own first interpretive *commentary – often earning the wrath of pre-empted literary critics who have then declared, time and again, the 'death of the novel' from the disease of solipsistic self-obsession (*see* NOVEL, THE).

In both overt and covert ways, *metafiction (as this kind of reflexivity is referred to in the novel and *short story form) calls attention to its narrative and linguistic nature, reminding its readers that stories are made up of words and are born of other stories (*see* INTERTEXTUALITY; NARRATIVE VERSIONS). This is obviously why parody is such a major mode of what Gérard Genette calls writing 'in the second degree'. But so too is the *mise en abyme*, the microcosmic mirroring of the story within the story that André Gide loved so much and that Maxine Hong Kingston used so effectively in the opening chapters of *The Woman Warrior*, where the training of the warrior becomes the training of the writer. *Allegories like this of the act of reading and writing abound and not only in the work of a postmodern writer like John Barth; in some stories, such as Flann O'Brien's *At Swim-Two-Birds*, *characters even discover that they are created characters. At the obvious end of the spectrum, *narrators address readers directly (the 'Dear Reader' of eighteenth-century and *postmodern fiction; *see* ADDRESS). At the other, more subtle, end, riddles, anagrams, and puns are embedded in order to call attention to the linguistic identity of narratives, just as certain popular models, such as the *detective or *fantasy tale, are borrowed to point to narrative's manipulation of *time, *space, *plot, and, of course, readers (*see* AUDIENCE; NARRATEE; READER CONSTRUCTS).

Over the centuries, but especially in the 1970s when the debates raged (c.f. Graff 1973), reflexivity's multitudinous enemies have declared that reflexivity severs or even denies the link between art and life that had been so carefully and satisfyingly forged by *realist narrative. But even Aristotle saw *diegesis or storytelling as part of mimesis. The direct link that reflexive narrative makes with life is through imaginative processes of storytelling and world-creating, processes arguably as important as courting and marriage, wars and diplomacy. Indeed, narrative is central to our ordering and shaping needs as human beings (Bruner 1991; *see* NARRATIVE AS COGNITIVE INSTRUMENT). That those needs take culturally specific forms has been made self-reflexively evident in the politicised metafictions written from *gender studies, *post-colonial, and *queer perspectives.

Reflexivity is obviously a structural issue for narrative, as many have shown (e.g., Scholes, Alter, and Rose); but it also results in a hermeneutic paradox for readers who are forced to acknowledge the artifice of what they are reading, while at the same time becoming active co-creators of the meaning of the work. Indeed, reflexive narratives make overt demands for intellectual and affective engagement comparable in scope and intensity to any other in life (Hutcheon). Reflexivity offers, in fact, a kind of mimesis of process; it is process made visible. The pleasure of telling stories becomes part of the shared pleasure of reading.

Reflexivity is not only a quality of written and read narratives, however. From Shakespeare's *Hamlet* to Luigi Pirandello's *Six Characters in Search of an Author* to the plays of Tom Stoppard, we are reminded of its history on the dramatic stage (*see* DRAMA AND NARRATIVE). Richard Strauss's *Capriccio* and John Corigliano's *The Ghosts of Versailles* have continued a long tradition of *operas about operas. The *films of Jean-Luc Godard or Spike Jonze's *Adaptation* are the reflexive cinematic equivalent of those convex mirrors in the paintings of Memling and Quentin Metsys that reflect the scene being painted (*see* PICTORIAL NARRATIVITY). As reflections upon the fact that stories are ordered constructs in language, *images, or *music, metanarratives are as old as narrative itself. The obsession with textual self-revelation is not new to modernist poetry or postmodern novels. Rather, fascination with the process has always been inseparable from the product.

SEE ALSO: autofiction; historiographic metafiction; metanarrative comment; modernist narrative; reader-response theory

References and further reading

Alter, Robert (1975) *Partial Magic: The Novel as a Self-Conscious Genre*, Berkeley: University of California Press.

Barth, John (1967) 'The Literature of Exhaustion', *Atlantic*, 220.2, 29–34.

—— (1980) 'The Literature of Replenishment: Postmodernist Fiction', *Atlantic*, 245.1, 65–71.

Bruner, Jerome (1991) 'The Narrative Construction of Reality', *Critical Inquiry*, 18, 1–21.

Genette, Gérard (1997) *Palimpsests: Literature in the Second Degree*, trans. Channa Newman and Claude Doubinsky, Lincoln: University of Nebraska Press.

Graff, Gerald (1973) 'The Myth of the Postmodernist Breakthrough', *Tri-Quarterly*, 26, 383–417.

Hutcheon, Linda (1984) *Narcissistic Narrative: The Metafictional Paradox*, London and New York: Methuen.

Martin, Wallace (1986) *Recent Theories of Narrative*, Ithaca: Cornell University Press.

Rose, Margaret A. (1979) *Parody/Meta-fiction*, London: Croom Helm.

Scholes, Robert (1967) *The Fabulators*, New York: Oxford University Press.

—— (1970) 'Metafiction', *Iowa Review*, 1, 100–115.

LINDA HUTCHEON

RELIABILITY

Ever since Wayne C. Booth first proposed the unreliable *narrator as a concept, the degree of (un)reliability that a given narrator exhibits has been one of the key questions explored by *rhetorical approaches to narrative. Booth's well-known formulation has become the canonised definition of the term 'unreliable narrator': 'I have called a narrator *reliable* when he speaks for or acts in accordance with the norms of the work (which is to say the implied author's norms), *unreliable* when he does not'. According to the majority of critics who have followed in Booth's footsteps the distinction between reliable and unreliable narrators is based on the degree and kind of *distance that separates the values, tastes, and moral judgements of a given narrator from the norms of the *implied author of the text. The general effect of unreliable narration consists in redirecting the reader's attention from the level of the story to the discourse level occupied by the speaker, and in foregrounding peculiarities of the narrator's psychology (*see* STORY-DISCOURSE DISTINCTION). There may be a number of different reasons for unreliability, including the narrator's limited knowledge, personal involvement, and problematic value-scheme (Rimmon-Kenan 2002 [1983]), and there are standard types of unreliable narrators such as the madman, the naive narrator, the hypocrite, the pervert, the morally debased narrator, the picaro, the liar, the trickster, and the clown (Riggan 1981; *see* PICARESQUE NARRATIVE).

Scrutinising Booth's definitions, a number of commentators have pointed out that the norms and values of the implied author are often very difficult to determine. Booth also leaves it open whether unreliability is primarily a matter of misrepresenting the *events or facts of the story or whether it results from the narrator's deficient understanding, dubious judgements, or flawed interpretations. One can therefore distinguish between 'factual' unreliability associated with a fallible narrator (a narrator whose rendering of the story the reader has reasons to suspect), and 'normative' unreliability characterising an untrustworthy narrator whose judgements and comments do not accord with conventional notions of sound judgement. As Olson (2003) has pointed out, these two types of unreliability elicit markedly different responses in readers. Distinguishing three axes of unreliability (the axis of facts/events, the axis of values/judgements, and the axis of knowledge/perception), Phelan and Martin (1999) arrive at six basic kinds of unreliability: misreporting, misevaluating (or misregarding), misreading, underreporting, under-regarding, and under-reading.

Focussing on the interactivity between textual modes of representation and readers' choices in constructing narrative worlds, some theorists (e.g., Yacobi 1981, 2001; Nünning 1998) have proposed a reader-centred and cognitive approach to unreliable narration which relocates unreliability in the interaction of text and reader (*see* READER-RESPONSE THEORY). Unreliability, on this view, is the result of an interpretive strategy that naturalises textual anomalies by projecting an unreliable narrator figure (*see* COGNITIVE NARRATOLOGY; NATURALISATION; NATURAL NARRATOLOGY). A number of empirical frames of reference and literary models function as standard modes of naturalisation by means of which readers as well as critics account for contradictions both within a text and between the fictional world-model of the text and empirical world models of readers. Textual indicators of unreliability include such features as internal inconsistencies, conflicts between story and discourse, multiperspectival accounts of the same event, and verbal idiosyncrasies (Wall 1994; Nünning 1998) (*see* PERSPECTIVE). In their attempt to gauge a narrator's degree of unreliability readers also draw on such extra-textual frames of reference as norms, cultural models, world-knowledge, personality theory, and standards of (e.g., psychological) normality. Narrators who violate agreed-upon moral and ethical norms or the standards that a given culture holds to be constitutive of normal psychological behaviour are generally taken to be unreliable (*see* ETHICAL TURN). Developing an approach that complements this cognitive turn in the theory of unreliable narration, Zerweck (2001: 151) has called for a 'second fundamental paradigm shift, one toward greater historicity and cultural awareness'. Since the cultural frames of norms and values are also subject to historical change, the whole notion of (un)reliability needs to be seen in the context of broader cultural developments (Nünning 2004; *see* CULTURAL STUDIES APPROACHES TO NARRATIVE).

Other theorists (e.g., Olson 2003; Phelan 2004) have criticised the cognitive approach for overstating the role of the reader at the expense of the author's *agency and the textual markers of unreliability, emphasising that practically all commentators have accepted that unreliability is predicated on at least three factors – the reader, the personalised narrator, and textual markers. However, accounts of unreliable narration still differ significantly with regard to the respective degree of importance they attribute to each of these three factors, and there is an ongoing debate about whether unreliability is a property of first-person narrators only, or whether it can also be attributed to third-person narrators (Yacobi 2001; *see* NARRATIVE SITUATIONS; PERSON).

References and further reading

Booth, Wayne C. (1983 [1961]) *The Rhetoric of Fiction*, Chicago: University of Chicago Press.
Chatman, Seymour (1990) *Coming to Terms*, Ithaca: Cornell University Press.

Nünning, Ansgar (ed.) (1998) *Unreliable Narration: Studien zur Theorie und Praxis unglaubwürdigen Erzählens in der englischsprachigen Erzählliteratur*, Trier: WVT.

Nünning, Vera (2004) 'Unreliable Narration and the Historical Variability of Values and Norms: *The Vicar of Wakefield* as Test-case for a Cultural-Historical Narratology', *Style*, 38.

Olson, Greta (2003) 'Reconsidering Unreliability: Fallible and Untrustworthy Narrators', *Narrative*, 11.1, 93–109.

Phelan, James (2004) *Living to Tell About It: A Rhetoric and Ethics of Character Narration*, Ithaca, NY: Cornell University Press.

——, and Mary Patricia Martin (1999) 'The Lessons of "Weymouth": Homodiegesis, Unreliability, Ethics and *The Remains of the Day*', in David Herman (ed.) *Narratologies: New Perspectives on Narrative Analysis*, Columbus: Ohio State University Press.

Riggan, William (1981) *Picaros, Madmen, Naifs, and Clowns: The Unreliable First-Person Narrator*, Norman, OK: University of Oklahoma Press.

Rimmon-Kenan, Shlomith (2002 [1983]) *Narrative Fiction: Contemporary Poetics*, London: Methuen.

Wall, Kathleen (1994) '*The Remains of the Day* and Its Challenges to Theories of Unreliable Narration', *Journal of Narrative Technique*, 24, 18–42.

Yacobi, Tamar (1981) 'Fictional Reliability as a Communicative Problem', *Poetics Today*, 2, 113–26.

—— (2001) 'Package Deals in Fictional Narrative: The Case of the Narrator's Unreliability', *Narrative*, 9, 223–29.

Zerweck, Bruno (2001) 'Historicizing Unreliable Narration: Unreliability and Cultural Discourse in Narrative Fiction', *Style*, 35.1, 151–78.

ANSGAR NÜNNING

REMEDIATION

Remediation, a concept developed by Jay David Bolter and Richard Grusin (1999), describes the way in which *media (particularly but not exclusively digital media) refashion other media forms (*see* DIGITAL NARRATIVE). Not a theory of narrative *per se*, remediation nonetheless has interesting implications for narrative theory.

Remediation maintains that what is new about new digital media is the extent to which they borrow from, pay homage to, critique, and refashion their predecessors, principally *television, *film, photography, and painting, but also print (*see* PHOTOGRAPHS; PICTORIAL NARRATIVITY). Video and *computer games remediate cinematic narrative by styling themselves as 'interactive movies', incorporating *narrative techniques standardly used in Hollywood cinema. Virtual reality remediates film as well as perspective painting. Digital photography remediates the analogue photograph. The Internet absorbs and refashions almost every previous visual and textual medium, including television, film, *radio, and print. Furthermore, the concept of remediation holds that older media can remediate newer ones within the same media economy. Traditional Hollywood cinema attempts to retain its influential cultural status by employing computer graphics in otherwise conventional films, by creating films entirely with computer animation, or by replacing the logic of linear narrative with more iterative, game-like narrative logic (*see* NARRATIVE, GAMES, AND PLAY). Television is making use, more and more, of information boxes, scrolling text, and windowed or split screens, and when it does TV screens look increasingly like pages of the World Wide Web.

Remediation identifies two distinct, contradictory visual styles or logics of mediation at the end of the twentieth century: 'transparent immediacy', in which the goal of a medium is to erase or eliminate the signs of mediation – epitomised most powerfully in virtual reality or photorealistic computer graphics; and 'hypermediacy', in which a medium multiplies and makes explicit signs of mediation – epitomised in the windowed and fragmented visual style of DVDs, the PC's desktop, or the Internet. Although these two logics of mediation obey contradictory imperatives, they are the necessary halves of a double logic of remediation, in which mediation is simultaneously multiplied and erased.

This double logic did not begin with the introduction of digital media; the same process recurs throughout the last several hundred years of western visual representation (*see* VISUAL NARRATIVITY). Transparent immediacy has been the predominant style of mediation throughout the history of realistic visual arts like painting, photography, and narrative cinema, as well as in the *realist novel. Hypermediacy, too, has a history in visual arts like altarpieces, collage, and photomontage, as well as in experimental forms of prose narrative, *drama, and poetry. Remediation operates across a spectrum from transparent immediacy to hypermediacy. At one extreme is what the contemporary entertainment industry calls repurposing (Holtzman 1997; Levinson 1997), in which a 'property' in one medium is reused in another, as when the characters from a children's movie are re-purposed as cartoon characters or action figures. At the end of the twentieth century, the expression of transparent immediacy in conventional Hollywood narrative film was evident in the upsurge of film versions of classic or contemporary *novels, almost none of which contain overt reference to the novels on which they are based outside of the credit section, which is not part of the narrative body (*see* ADAPTATION; NARRATIVE VERSIONS).

Just as cinematic narratives remediate earlier media like prose fiction, so for the past two decades or more film has remediated newer media like computer and video games. Early films like *Tron* (1982), *Joysticks* (1983), and *The Last Starfighter* (1984) reflected society's concerns about the effects of video games on young people. More recent films have tried to capitalise on popular games by translating them into cinematic narratives, including among others *Super Mario Brothers* (1993), *Street Fighter* (1994), *Mortal Kombat* (1995), *Final Fantasy* (2001), *Lara Croft Tomb Raider* (2001), and *Resident Evil* (2002). Other films like *The Matrix* (1999), *Crouching Tiger, Hidden Dragon* (2000), *XXX* (2002), and the most recent Bond films have targeted game-playing spectators by employing game-like visual effects, camera angles, and action sequences. Most interesting for cinema studies scholars, however, is the way in which some more recent films like *Groundhog Day* (1993), *Lola Rennt* (1998), *ExistenZ* (1999), and *Femme Fatale* (2003) have begun to experiment with iterative, game-like narrative logics instead of more conventional linear narratives (*see* TEMPORAL ORDERING; TIME IN NARRATIVE).

Whereas video games are remediated by film, the opposite is also true. At the start of the twenty-first century the *semiotics of video game screen space have become increasingly conventionalised in the incorporation of 'cinematics', letter-boxed narrative segments introducing a game's various levels of play. It is now customary in almost every game (even animated games with no connection to previously released films) to employ a semiotic distinction between the full-screen visual space of the video game and the widescreen (letter-boxed) visual space of the cinematics, where the space of play is the full-screen space of the TV monitor, but the space of narrative spectatorship is the widescreen space of the letter-boxed film. The remediation of cinematic narratives by computer and video games ranges from the transparent to the explicitly self-conscious. The most transparent remediations involve the design and release of games based on successful films, like the James Bond, Star Wars, or Harry Potter franchises. Less transparent are games like the 'Grand Theft Auto' series, which has been marketed like a film, including cinema-style promotional billboards and the release of CD *soundtracks for each game. Most hypermediated are games like *Enter the Matrix*, which makes available to the player who wins the game more than an hour of unreleased cinematic sequences that supplement the narrative of *The Matrix Reloaded*, the second film of the Wachowski brothers' trilogy.

The concept of remediation is not explicitly addressed to questions of narrative theory, but designed to account for the visual *genealogy of contemporary digital media. Nonetheless in laying out the double logic through which digital media remediate other media forms, remediation proves to be a suggestive concept for making sense of the interrelations among various forms of narrative, whether within a single medium or across different media forms (*see* INTERMEDIALITY).

SEE ALSO: hybridity; intertextuality; mediacy; multi-path narrative

References and further reading

Bolter, Jay David and Grusin, Richard (1999) *Remediation: Understanding New Media*, Cambridge, Mass.: MIT Press.

Hayles, N. Katherine (2002) *Writing Machines*, Cambridge, Mass.: MIT Press.

Holtzman, Steven (1997) *Digital Mosaics: The Aesthetics of Cyberspace*, NY: Simon & Schuster.

Johnson, Steven (1997) *Interface Culture: How New Technology Transforms the Way We Create and Communicate*, San Francisco: Harper.

Latour, Bruno (1993) *We Have Never Been Modern*, Cambridge, Mass.: Harvard University Press.

Levinson, Paul (1997) *The Soft Edge: A Natural History and Future of the Information Revolution*, London: Routledge.

Manovich, Lev (2001) *The Language of New Media*, Cambridge, Mass.: MIT Press.

McLuhan, Marshall (1964; rpt. 1994) *Understanding Media: The Extensions of Man*, Cambridge, Mass.: MIT Press.

Mitchell, William J. (1994) *The Reconfigured Eye: Visual Truth in the Post-Photographic Era*, Cambridge, Mass.: MIT Press.

RICHARD GRUSIN

REPURPOSING

The term 'repurposing' is used to describe the practice of adopting a narrative for a number of different purposes – for example, Disney's creation of an animated *film, a *soundtrack, a Broadway musical, a Saturday morning cartoon, and a complete line of children's products from the *fairy tale *Beauty and the Beast. See* MEDIA AND NARRATIVE; REMEDIATION (ALSO: NARRATIVE VERSIONS).

RETARDATORY DEVICES

As the mode of thought and representation by which we mediate and negotiate human temporality, *narrative puts into play not only the *time of the story, but the time it takes for the reader to form a comprehensive and definitive mental image of the story (*see* STORY-DISCOURSE DISTINCTION). Retardatory devices refer to various techniques for delaying *closure (*see* NARRATIVE TECHNIQUES). They contribute to our sense of narrative dynamics by suspending, partially unveiling, and momentarily blocking the answers to the questions that propel a narrative forward (*see* NARRATIVE DYNAMICS). These devices imply a spatio-temporal metaphor. By suggesting that there is a goal to reach, but one that will not be attained through the fastest route, they retard our perception of the narrated whole. Further, as techniques for keeping a narrative in suspension, retardatory devices are part of what Barthes calls the *hermeneutic code (*see* CODES FOR READING).

Retardatory devices are as old as narrative itself. For example, *fairy tales use triplication as retardation: the eldest son tries and fails, the second son tries and fails, the third son tries and succeeds. In *epic poetry, the *hero may have to visit various locations and pass dangerous tests before returning home or facing his opponent in the decisive confrontation. In fact, with its string of episodes, epic poetry makes retardation into its basic structuring principle.

Retardatory devices typical of *realist narratives include snares, equivocations, false replies, and jammed answers. Snares are misleading answers; for example, they present multiple causes for the narrative enigma, but purposefully omit the one cause that would explain it (*see* CAUSALITY). Equivocations mix snares with partial solutions. They depend on a double understanding: the

discourse highlights a set of connotations, yet another set indicating the solution of the enigma is also possible, but it is downplayed. False replies are deliberate errors, acknowledged as such by the discourse, while jamming the answer consists of declaring the enigma unresolvable. Both devices delay *narrative progression by emphasising the difficulty of reaching the end.

Twentieth-century literature developed a wariness of teleological form and the imposition of endings. In *modernist fiction, consequently, retardatory devices no longer serve the gradual exposition of *'truth' but function as ways of exploring the conditions of narrative meaning. Prominent among these devices are techniques of breaking up the 'organic' historical totality of narrative and techniques of creating the effect of simultaneity (*see* SPATIAL FORM). The achronological and fragmented presentation of *events requires that the reader engage in temporal reordering and make inferences about missing narrative links (*see* GAPPING; TEMPORAL ORDERING). Focalizing the same events from different *perspectives of many characters (*see* FOCALIZATION), using multiple *narrators to retell the same events, or presenting the meandering consciousness of various characters as they confront reality delay our understanding of how the multiple perspectives and narratives relate to each other in a temporal sequence (*see* THOUGHT AND CONSCIOUSNESS REPRESENTATION (LITERATURE)). Yet as the notion of temporality remains relevant for organising experience, these devices highlight the disjunctions between private and public conceptualisations of *time.

In *postmodernist fiction retardatory devices include repetition and experimental typographies. Repetition may consist, for example, of the reiteration of almost identical scenes that nevertheless contradict each other without the reader being able to evaluate the reality of any version (*see* SUMMARY AND SCENE). Experimental typographies play with conventional ways of presenting temporality by, for example, breaking up different narrative strands in separate areas of the page so that readers may follow a variety of temporal itineraries (*see* GRAPHIC PRESENTATION AS EXPRESSIVE DEVICE). Postmodern fiction multiplies the number of retardatory devices in order to make readers lose sight of the end as a goal; the narrative process itself becomes the destination. Also, these devices emphasise various notions of time as products of socio-cultural (including narrative) 'ideologies'.

SEE ALSO: ideology and narrative; plot; suspense and surprise

References and further reading

Barthes, Roland (1974) *S/Z*, trans. Richard Miller, New York: Noonday.
Brooks, Peter (1984) *Reading for the Plot*, Cambridge, Mass.: Harvard University Press.
Heise, Ursula (1997) *Chronoschisms: Time, Narrative, and Postmodernism*, Cambridge: Cambridge University Press.
McHale, Brian (1987) *Postmodernist Fiction*, New York: Methuen.

HETA PYRHÖNEN

RETROSPECTIVE NARRATION

A story about past *events – the default case of storytelling, as opposed to the less common cases of 'prospective' and 'simultaneous' *narration. *See* TIME IN NARRATIVE.

RHETORICAL APPROACHES TO NARRATIVE

Rhetorical approaches conceive of narrative as an art of communication, and they typically have one of two major emphases: (1) on the language of the narrative text, particularly the logic of its patterns; (2) on narrative as an interaction between an *author and an *audience through the medium of a text for some purpose. The two emphases are of course not mutually exclusive: those who analyse the linguistic patterns of the text typically consider the consequences of that analysis for the overall communication, and those who emphasise the communication typically pay attention to the linguistic patterns. Indeed, since most analyses of narrative involve some attention to linguistic patterns and overall communication, rhetorical considerations are central to contemporary narrative studies. *Deconstructive approaches to narrative, for instance, are often fundamentally rhetorical in their attention to language. Seymour Chatman's communication model of narrative, which traces the transmission of the narrative text from

real author, *implied author, and *narrator (as senders) to *narratee, implied audience, and real audience (as recipients) has been widely adopted (*see* READER CONSTRUCTS). More generally, rhetorical approaches have some overlap with narratology and its offshoots, including *feminist and *postclassical narratology (*see* STRUCTURALIST NARRATOLOGY).

Rhetoric itself continues to be a vital discipline, and both older rhetorical models such as Kenneth Burke's pentad of act, agent, *agency, scene, and purpose and newer work such as that on feminist rhetoric have had some influence on narrative studies. But some approaches to rhetoric have been more influential within narrative studies than others, and some approaches to narrative are more thoroughly rhetorical than others. Consequently, this entry will focus on the two most prominent developments in this area: (a) Mikhail Bakhtin's *dialogism; and (b) neo-Aristotelian or *Chicago School criticism.

Mikhail Bakhtin's dialogism

Bakhtin was part of a circle of Russian scholars that met between 1918 and 1929, a group that also included Pavel Medvedev and Valentin Voloshinov, two scholars whose books are sometimes attributed to Bakhtin. Bakhtin's work was not widely noticed in the West until the early 1980s when new translations of *The Dialogic Imagination* and *Problems of Dostoevsky's Poetics* appeared, and when literary criticism and theory, having moved beyond the orthodoxies of the New Criticism, began to pay increasing attention to the ideological dimensions of literature (*see* FORMALISM). Bakhtin's rhetorical approach is rooted in his conception of language, a conception that differs markedly from the structuralist view articulated by Ferdinand de Saussure.

One of the key distinctions in Saussurean linguistics is that between *langue* and *parole*, between, that is, the formal, abstract system of language, and language in use. For Saussure, *langue* makes *parole* possible, and parole leads to diachronic change in *langue*. For Bakhtin, there is no *langue* because *parole* is too diverse to be adequately captured by any single, abstract system. That diversity is a function not just of the range of semantic forms and syntactic structures used by speakers but also of the relation between language and *ideology. In Bakhtin's view, every utterance conveys both a semantic and an ideological meaning, because every utterance carries both a content and a set of values associated with the diction and syntax of that utterance. No one speaker fully owns his or her utterance because the words of the utterance have been used by others and carry with them the marks of their previous uses. Consequently, Bakhtin regards any one language, say, English, as composed of an almost countless number of social dialects or mini-languages (or, in one meaning of the term, registers), each one shot through with ideology. For example, we could identify the language of the *law, the language of the street, the language of the academy, the language of the popular media, and so on. Furthermore, a given society will often establish a hierarchy among its social dialects, with some more officially sanctioned and, thus, more authoritative than others. For Bakhtin, the task of establishing oneself as a mature speaker involves establishing one's relation to existing authoritative discourses by adopting what he calls internally persuasive discourses, ones which the individual values regardless of their place in the societal hierarchy.

Bakhtin argues that the *novel is the highest form of literary art because it most effectively puts the multiple dialects of a society in dialogue with each other. This dialogue may occur through a sequential juxtaposition of dialects or through what Bakhtin calls 'double-voiced discourse', the use of more than one dialect within a single utterance. Some novels will orchestrate what Bakhtin calls the *heteroglossia or the *polyphony of these dialects so that one emerges as superior to the others. Other novels, such as those of Dostoevskii, which Bakhtin values above all others, orchestrate the polyphony so that no single dialect, and, thus, no single ideological position, emerges triumphant. Bakhtin's preference for the unresolved dialogue points to his underlying assumption that dialogism constitutes the essence of the novel. *Characters are important less for their personalities than for their alignments with one or more of the novel's dialects. Similarly, for Bakhtin, *plot is a means of showing how the *conflicts among the novel's dialects will develop and resolve themselves or remain open-ended.

Although contemporary narrative studies have not generally adopted Bakhtin's view of the essence of the novel or extended that view to *narrative itself, Bakhtin's influence on the study of narrative rhetoric has been extensive. His analyses of double-voiced discourse in Dickens and Turgenev provide a model that has been widely adopted, and his ideas about the link between language and ideology have influenced efforts to define the concept of *voice. Furthermore, his work has highlighted the multiple discourse *genres that have been employed within fictional and non-fictional narrative: *letters, *diaries, oral testimony, *skaz, heterodiegetic *narration, *free indirect discourse, and so on.

To illustrate briefly: viewed from Bakhtin's perspective, the famous first sentence of Jane Austen's *Pride and Prejudice*, 'It is a truth universally acknowledged that a single man in possession of a good fortune must be in want of a wife' is a double-voiced discourse that points to and takes a stand on the ideological conflict between those, who, like Mrs Bennet, firmly believe in this truth, and those who, like the narrator and Elizabeth Bennet, regard this truth with scepticism and playfulness. One could then extend the Bakhtinian analysis in two main ways: (1) by seeing the novel as a complex dialogue among these and other discourses such as those of Mr. Collins, Lady Catherine, and Darcy, a dialogue that reveals Austen's values and attitudes about social class, gender relations, public and private behaviour, and marriage; (2) by examining how Austen's ideologically inflected discourse influences our judgements of the characters and their situations and of the culminating marriage of Elizabeth and Darcy.

Chicago School rhetorical critics would take this second alternative. They see Bakhtin's emphasis on the ideological dimensions of narrative discourse as adding something distinctive to our understanding of narrative communication, but they stop short of adopting Bakhtin's assumption that dialogism is the essence of the novel.

Wayne C. Booth and Chicago School criticism

From the perspective of rhetoric, the key figure in the Chicago School or neo-Aristotelian movement was Wayne C. Booth, a member of the second generation of such critics. In the 1930s R. S. Crane led a movement at the University of Chicago to shift literary study from philology to interpretation by taking Aristotle's method in the *Poetics* and extending it to kinds of literature that

Aristotle never dreamed of. The method has (a) an interpretive moment, during which the critic seeks to reason back from the effects of a work to the causes of those effects in the elements of its construction; and (b) a moment of poetics, during which the critic uses the interpretation as a step toward articulating the principles underlying other works of the same general class. Crane's 'The Concept of Plot and the Plot of *Tom Jones*' brilliantly exemplifies the method, as Crane seeks to identify both the key elements of Fielding's plotting that produce the audience's sense of comic pleasure and the principles underlying Fielding's construction. Those principles reveal plot itself to be a synthesis of character, *action, and thought designed to affect the audience's emotions in a particular way (*see* THOUGHT AND CONSCIOUSNESS REPRESENTATION (LITERATURE)).

Booth, a student of Crane's in the late 1940s, shifts the emphasis of the neo-Aristotelian approach from poetics to rhetoric by realising a potential within both Aristotle's *Poetics* and the work of the first generation. (Other prominent figures of the second generation, particularly Sheldon Sacks and Ralph W. Rader, continued to work on poetics.) Although Aristotle conceived of rhetoric and poetics as distinct arts, his definition of tragedy in the *Poetics* has a strong rhetorical component. The definition emphasises not just the plot of tragedy but also the effect of that plot on an audience: tragedy is an imitation of an action that arouses pity and fear and leads to the *catharsis of those emotions. The neo-Aristotelians took this dimension of Aristotle's thought as the basis for linking form and emotive effect (*see* EMOTION AND NARRATIVE).

Although this conception of form underlies Booth's analysis in *The Rhetoric of Fiction* (1961), that analysis also ends up conceiving of the novel – and by extension, narrative – as a thoroughly rhetorical act. Booth's project is to investigate the conditions under which the use of overt rhetoric in a novel, e.g., a narrator's *commentary on the action, would be effective or ineffective. He argues that we cannot answer the question by reference to such abstract rules as 'show, don't tell' (*see* SHOWING VS. TELLING), but instead must consider whether a particular use of overt rhetoric contributes to or detracts from the novel's achievement of its purpose. Booth generalises this argument by noting that any technique will generate some effects and not others and that a technique that is effective

for one purpose may be detrimental for another (*see* NARRATIVE TECHNIQUES). Consequently, the novelist cannot choose *whether* to employ rhetoric but only *how* to employ it – in overt commentary, in the withholding of commentary, in the use of a secondary character, a subplot, and so on.

The Rhetoric of Fiction also analyses the relations among authors, narrators, and audiences, and, along the way, introduces concepts that continue to be influential for the analysis of narrative discourse, particularly the *implied author and the unreliable narrator (*see* RELIABILITY). The implied author is the version of himself or herself that the actual author constructs through the total set of rhetorical choices that go into the narrative. The implied author may either endorse the narrator's account and evaluation of the events or may establish *distance from the narrator's account and evaluation. The endorsement yields reliable narration, and the establishment of distance yields unreliable narration. Reliable narration forms the basis for one kind of relationship among author, narrator, and audience, while unreliable narration forms the basis for another. The reliable irony of the first sentence of *Pride and Prejudice* establishes a bond between implied author and narrator, on one side, and the implied audience that understands the irony on the other. Furthermore, part of the pleasure Austen offers her reader involves the interaction with this playful but always reliable narratorial guide to the actions of the characters. By contrast, the unreliable narration of, for example, Whitey the barber in Ring Lardner's 'Haircut' establishes a bond between the implied author and the audience at the expense of Whitey, whose moral obtuseness adds to the chilling effect of the story he tells about cruelty and murder in an American small town.

Booth's attention to the overall quality of the relations among authors, narrators, and readers leads to his *ethical turn within the larger rhetorical conception of narrative. In *The Company We Keep* (1988), Booth emphasises the ways in which the rhetorical construction of a narrative affects its audience's *desires and, thus, implicitly influences that audience to desire some things rather than others. More generally, he develops the metaphor of books as friends, who, in their multiple relations to us, can be either beneficial or harmful. Booth's attention to ethics also shows another dimension of his privileging of rhetoric over poetics, as he values 'co-duction', the effort to establish agreement about interpretation and ethics, more highly than the agreement itself.

The third generation

Students of Booth, Sacks, and Rader such as David Richter, Mary Doyle Springer, and Harry Shaw, have continued to investigate both the poetics and the rhetoric of narrative, but this entry will focus on the rhetorically-oriented work of Peter J. Rabinowitz and James Phelan. Rabinowitz has developed an influential model of audiences, distinguishing among (a) the flesh and blood audience, each reader in his or her own commonness and idiosyncrasy; (b) the authorial audience, the ideal reader who understands the implied author's communication, including, in fictional narrative, the message that the characters and events are invented (this audience corresponds to what narratology calls the implied reader); (c) the narrative audience, the role readers take on when they enter the narrative world and adopt its assumptions, including a belief in the reality of the characters and events (see STORYWORLD); and (d) the ideal narrative audience, the hypothetical listener/reader who perfectly understands the narrator's communication as the narrator intends it. In 'Haircut', for example, the authorial audience recognises Whitey's unreliability and its consequences for Lardner's communication; the narrative audience, like the customer to whom Whitey addresses his tale, believes in the reality of Lardner's characters; and the ideal narrative audience is the hypothetical customer who would share Whitey's interpretation and evaluation of the story. Phelan has supplemented Rabinowitz's model by distinguishing more clearly between the narrative audience and the narratee, defining the former as the observer role within the fiction, and the latter as the audience addressed by the narrator. In 'Haircut', then, Whitey's customer is the narratee, while the narrative audience, though not directly addressed, also hears Whitey telling his story to the customer.

Rabinowitz has extended his work on audience in *Before Reading*, a study of the tacit conventions that govern readers' interpretations and evaluations of narrative. Rabinowitz identifies four sets of such conventions, corresponding to four kinds of readerly activities: deciding which textual details are most important (Rules of Notice); assigning larger meanings to those details (Rules of Significance); attending to a narrative's developing shape (Rules of Configuration); and finding larger patterns that provide unity to the text (Rules of Coherence). Rabinowitz also demonstrates, through the analysis of some misreadings and some processes of canon formation, that readers' own ideological commitments often significantly influence the way they apply the conventions.

Phelan has emphasised the multiple layers of rhetorical communication, first, in *Reading People, Reading Plots*, where he builds on Crane's concept of plot to develop the concept of *narrative progression (the fusion of a text's internal dynamics and the authorial audience's responses to those dynamics) (see NARRATIVE DYNAMICS). In addition, he identifies three different components of character that also correspond to three different kinds of readerly interest: the mimetic (character as possible person), thematic (character as representing one or more ideas), and synthetic (character as an artificial construct that has a role in the narrative's design; see MIMESIS; THEMATIC APPROACHES TO NARRATIVE). Thus, for example, Lardner's Whitey's mimetic function consists of his identity as the town barber and the more specific traits that Lardner gives him, especially garrulousness, a desire to be 'one of the guys', and moral obtuseness. His thematic function consists in his representativeness, both as a spokesperson for the town to the visiting customer and as an inhabitant of the general American small town; thus, Lardner suggests that Whitey's moral obtuseness is not his alone but something typical of small town America. Whitey's synthetic function consists of his role as the unreliable observer narrator, one of the chief means by which Lardner dramatises his thematic concern with the viciousness beneath the placid surface of small town American life.

In *Narrative as Rhetoric* Phelan proposes a rhetorical definition of narrative: somebody telling somebody else on some occasion and for some purposes that something happened. In working with this definition, he emphasises the multiple layers of rhetorical communication, especially the cognitive, emotive, and ethical. Phelan often takes the concepts of narratology and demonstrates their usefulness for a rhetorical rather than a structuralist approach to narrative. To take one example, he offers an account of what he calls 'paradoxical paralipsis', a narrative technique in which a naive narrator tells a retrospective story about losing his or her naiveté (see ALTERATION). Although the technique defies naturalistic probability – the paradox arises because the loss of naiveté occurs before the narrator tells the tale – it is often rhetorically effective because it allows the audience to experience the full force of the perspective-altering event (*see* FOCALIZATION; PERSPECTIVE). In this way, paradoxical paralipsis reveals that, within character narration, the implied author's communication to the authorial audience, governed by what Phelan calls disclosure functions, and the narrator's communication to the narratee, governed by narrator functions, may occasionally conflict, and that, when they do, the disclosure functions will trump the narrator functions. In *Living to Tell about It*, Phelan builds on this distinction between narrator functions and disclosure functions in a study of character narration that links its rhetorical dynamics to their ethical consequences.

The history of narrative theory shows that no single approach to narrative has dominated the field, and our current interest in *interdisciplinary approaches and in narrative's varied relations to culture makes it unlikely that the situation will change any time soon (*see* CULTURAL STUDIES APPROACHES TO NARRATIVE). Nevertheless, because rhetorical approaches, regardless of their specific emphases, are ultimately concerned with the how, the what, and the why of narrative, we can expect them to continue to play a central role in the field.

SEE ALSO: communication in narrative; communication studies and narrative; discourse analysis (linguistics); dual-voice hypothesis

References and further reading

Bakhtin, Mikhail (1981) 'Discourse in the Novel', in *The Dialogic Imagination*, ed. Michael Holquist, trans. Michael Holquist and Caryl Emerson, Austin: University of Texas Press.
—— (1985) *Problems of Dostoevsky's Poetics*, trans. and ed. Caryl Emerson, Minneapolis: University of Minnesota Press.
Booth, Wayne C. (1961) *The Rhetoric of Fiction*, Chicago: University of Chicago Press.
—— (1988) *The Company We Keep: An Ethics of Fiction*, Berkeley: University of California Press.
Crane, R. S. (ed.) (1953) *Critics and Criticism, Ancient and Modern*, Chicago: University of Chicago Press.
Kearns, Michael S. (1999) *Rhetorical Narratology*, Lincoln: University of Nebraska Press.
Phelan, James (1996) *Narrative as Rhetoric: Technique, Audience, Ethics, and Ideology*, Columbus: Ohio State University Press.
—— (2004) *Living to Tell about It: A Rhetoric and Ethics of Character Narration*, Ithaca, NY: University Press.
Rabinowitz, Peter J. (1977) 'Truth in Fiction: A Re-examination of Audiences', *Critical Inquiry*, 4, 121–41.
—— (1998 [1987]) *Before Reading: Narrative Conventions and the Politics of Interpretation*, Columbus: Ohio State University Press.
Rader, Ralph W. (1973) 'Defoe, Richardson, Joyce, and the Concept of Form in the Novel', in William Matthews and Ralph W. Rader (eds) *Autobiography, Biography, and the Novel*, Los Angeles: William Andrews Clark Memorial Library, University of California.
Richter, David H. (1974) *Fable's End: Completeness and Closure in Rhetorical Fiction*, Chicago: University of Chicago Press.
Sacks, Sheldon (1966) *Fiction and the Shape of Belief: A Study of Henry Fielding with Glances at Swift, Johnson and Richardson*, Berkeley: University of California Press.
Shaw, Harry (1983) *The Forms of Historical Fiction: Walter Scott and His Successors*, Ithaca: Cornell University Press.
Springer, Mary Doyle (1975) *Forms of the Modern Novella*, Chicago: University of Chicago Press.

JAMES PHELAN

RIDDLE

A literary and *folklore form consisting of a question and an answer, which must be subtly hinted at in the question to make the riddle solvable. The enigmatic character of the riddle resides in the ambiguity of the descriptive elements contained in the question. To solve the riddle is to identify the referent. Though not in themselves a narrative *genre, riddles are often used narratively as tests presented to the *hero as part of a quest. *See* JOKE; NARRATIVE, GAMES, AND PLAY.

RING-COMPOSITION

Ring-composition designates a structuring device in which a *narrative unit is framed symmetrically by repeated material, such as a word or group of words, a *motif, or a narrative sequence. The term refers to both simple framing structures with single repeated elements surrounding a central core in an a-x-a' scheme and to more elaborate chiastic structures in which multiple narrative elements are repeated in inverse order, following an a-b-c-c'-b'-a' pattern. The term 'ring-composition' itself became widespread, especially in classical studies, following Willem A. A. van Otterlo's structural analyses of ancient Greek texts in the 1940s. Related, often synonymous, terms include envelope pattern (Bartlett 1935: 9–29), framing, chiasmus, and ring structure (*see* FRAMED NARRATIVE).

Often understood as a feature of oral narrative, ring-composition has been identified in a wide range of oral traditions, such as South Slavic *epic (Lord 1986: 54–64), African epic, and Scottish and English *ballads (Buchan 1972: 94–144; *see* AFRICAN NARRATIVE). The structuring device has also been well-documented in texts that derive in some way from an oral tradition, including Old English narrative verse, the ancient Greek *Iliad* (Whitman 1958: 249–84), the Middle English *Sir Gawain and the Green Knight*, the Old French *Chanson de Roland*, the Middle High German *Nibelungenlied*, and the Gospels. Though extensive examinations of ring-composition have tended to focus on such oral and oral-derived narratives, a small number of studies such as Kay Davis's analysis of Ezra Pound's *Cantos* (1984: 41–59) attest to the presence of these structures in modern texts more dependent upon writing and literacy.

Generally operating in tandem with other structuring and rhetorical devices (*see* NARRATIVE TECHNIQUES), ring-composition has been shown to serve a number of significant narrative functions, both pragmatic and artistic: it provides a mnemonic aid during composition in oral *performance (*see* ORAL-FORMULAIC THEORY); it navigates into and out of digressions embedded within the main *plot, as Ward Parks (1988) has shown for Homeric and Old English epic; it underscores the importance of the narrative core enclosed by the ring or system of concentric rings; it serves as an organising principle for an entire narrative, as John D. Niles has demonstrated for the Old English *Beowulf*, which opens and closes with mirroring funeral episodes; and, in the case of oral narrative, it integrates *audience responses and other distractions in performance while maintaining control of the overall narrative structure, as Okpewho has observed in African epic (1979: 194–201).

SEE ALSO: embedding; narrative in poetry; narrative structure; oral cultures and narrative; orality

References and further reading

Bartlett, Adeline Courtney (1935) *The Larger Rhetorical Patterns in Anglo-Saxon Poetry*, New York: Columbia University Press.

Buchan, David (1972) *The Ballad and the Folk*, London: Routledge and Kegan Paul.

Davis, Kay (1984) *Fugue and Fresco: Structures in Pound's Cantos, Orono*, Maine: National Poetry Foundation.

Lord, Albert B. (1986) 'The Merging of Two Worlds: Oral and Written Poetry as Carriers of Ancient Values', in John Miles Foley (ed.) *Oral Tradition in Literature*, Columbia: University of Missouri Press.

Niles, John D. (1979) 'Ring Composition and the Structure of *Beowulf*', *PMLA*, 94, 924–35.

Okpewho, Isidore (1979) *The Epic in Africa: Toward a Poetics of the Oral Performance*, New York: Columbia University Press.

Parks, Ward (1988) 'Ring Structure and Narrative Embedding in Homer and *Beowulf*', *Neuphilologische Mitteilungen*, 89, 237–51.

Whitman, Cedric H. (1958) *Homer and the Homeric Tradition*, Cambridge, Mass.: Harvard University Press.

LORI ANN GARNER

ROMAN À CLEF

The novel styled roman à clef disguises real people and events – or is reputed to do so –under the guise of fictional ones. It follows that its true meaning cannot be fully apprehended unless one is in possession of a 'key' which may be either secret or more or less public. For a novel to be truly *à clef*, the key has to be both intentional on the author's part and decipherable to the reader, or at least to some readers. There is a wide range between pure personal *allegory, where every fictional name merely stands in for a real one (frequently hinting at it by anagram, assonance, or a measured series of dashes or asterisks), and the occasional *character whose role or manner suggests a real-life analogue.

Many romans à clef are indeed hardly disguised; in a satirical writing or a scandalous revelation it would be counter-productive for such transfers not to be perceived. *Les Amours de Zéokinizul* (1746), attributed to Claude Crébillon, is an obvious take-off by anagram on Louis XV (Louis Quinze), especially since Crébillon's own name on the title page is scrambled as Krinelbol. When Liza Haywood publishes *The Fortunate Foundlings: being the genuine history of Colonel M——rs, and his sister, Madam du P——y, the issue of the Hon. Ch——es M——rs, son of the late Duke of R——l——d* (London, 1744), the key is furnished by the title itself for any reader able to fill in a few blanks; in the text, the characters have other names, the Duke of Rutland for example being called Dorilaus.

Many novels, from the seventeenth century on, have been reputed to be *à clef* though the supposed key, or its authenticity, could not be demonstrated. In a sense almost any novel can be made out to be one, given that absence of a key can never be proven. All kinds of admixtures being possible, in practice the roman à clef is less a distinct *genre than a set of techniques aimed at creating a particular kind of *reality effect, variously shared with other fictional categories.

SEE ALSO: fiction, theories of; naming in narrative; novel, the; realeme

References and further reading

Drujon, Fernand (1888) *Les Livres à clef*, Paris: Rouveyre.
Schneider, Georg (1951) *Die Schlüsselliteratur*, Stuttgart: Hiersemann.
Stewart, Philip (2000) 'Le roman à clefs à l'époque des Lumières', in Pierre Popovic and Érik Vigneault (eds) *Les Dérèglements de l'art*, Montréal: Presses de l'Université de Montréal.

PHILIP STEWART

ROMAN À THÈSE

Susan Suleiman defines the roman à thèse or 'ideological novel' as a *didactic, *realist novel seeking to demonstrate the validity of a political, philosophical, or religious doctrine. Suleiman analyses novels by Bourget, Barrès, and Malraux, all writers with strong social and political convictions (other examples are Beecher Stowe's *Uncle Tom's Cabin*, Dickens's *Hard Times*, and Lawrence's *Lady Chatterley's Lover*, targeting slavery, utilitarianism, and prudery). The roman à thèse uses rhetorical devices which create sufficient linguistic redundancy to eliminate ambiguity and *indeterminacy (*see* RHETORICAL APPROACHES TO NARRATIVE). The *plot (usually a variety of the *Bildungsroman) develops an exemplary *conflict and is resolved in transparent *closure. The text's implied value-system is often supported by explicit narratorial *commentary as well as by reflections of an authoritative character. However, Suleiman has also shown that the roman à thèse can be fruitfully read against the grain as it is often torn between its intended univocity and the *polyphony of *perspectives required by *realism. Macherey, who, following Bakhtin, claims that the form of the novel itself, always involving a multitude of positions and perspectives, undermines any attempt at conveying a systematically coherent ideological vision, has proposed similar considerations.

SEE ALSO: ideology and narrative; novel, the

References and further reading

Macherey, Pierre (1990) *A quoi pense la littérature?*, Paris: Presses universitaires.
Suleiman, Susan Rubin (1983) *Authoritarian Fictions: The Ideological Novel as a Literary Genre*, New York: Columbia University Press.

LIESBETH KORTHALS ALTES

ROMANCE

The term 'romance' is understood in two ways: as a historical narrative *genre, and as a transhistorical literary *mode surpassing the formal elements of generic romance (see Parker 1979). In the first instance, romance developed in Europe during the 1100s as a form of *fantastic narrative poetry articulating the chivalric values of the aristocracy. In the second, the structures and thematic concerns of the original genre are employed in diverse literary forms such as lyric, *drama, *epic, and the *novel. *Motifs such as the love *conflict, the quest for honour, the idealised or magical setting, and the episodic wandering structure are common to both genre and mode. The Arthurian romances of Chrétien de Troyes (late 1100s) are instances of the original romance genre, while *science fiction and *fantasy novels of the late 1900s exemplify the broader interpretation of romance.

Generally, romance is a narrative with an episodic *plot structured by the protagonist's quest for love and honour within an idealised, imaginative, often mythical setting (*see* MYTH: THEMATIC APPROACHES). During the quest, the romance *hero or heroine confronts tests of sincerity and *identity. The literary origin of the term comes from twelfth century France, where the word *romance* denoted a secular verse tale of love and adventure in the vernacular, featuring knightly aristocrats who demonstrate chivalric definitions of honour in combat and courtesy in love. Initially, chivalric romance evolved in Europe during the medieval period as a *hybrid genre incorporating elements of Old French and Germanic battle epics, *fairy tale and *folklore (most notably, Breton tales of King Arthur), treatises on courtly love, and Christian devotional writing (see MEDIEVAL NARRATIVE). In the Arthurian romances of Chrétien de Troyes, for example, the importance of courtesy to women and the predominance of single combat distinguish these tales from their immediate ancestors, the chansons de geste (e.g., *The Song of Roland*, ca 1000), although both genres deal with aristocratic self-definition and feats of arms. In addition to the chivalric romance, the allegorical romance also enjoyed great influence during the High Middle Ages (e.g., de Lorris' and de Meun's *Roman de la Rose*, composed between 1230 and 1280; see ALLEGORY).

In the Renaissance, the revival of classical learning brought a renewed European knowledge of Hellenistic-era Greek and Latin prose tales of *travel, kidnapping, and adventure. These so-called 'Greek romances' (e.g., Heliodorus's *Aethiopica*, third century) intersperse episodes of adventure with pastoral love interludes set within a *locus amoenus* or ideal natural environment. Inspired by Hellenistic models, Renaissance writers combined features of medieval chivalric romance, classical epic, and pastoral to produce the heroic romance such as Ariosto's *Orlando Furioso* (1516) and Spenser's *The Faerie Queene* (1590). Vernacular prose romances such as Madeleine de Scudéry's *Le Grand Cyrus* (1653) increasingly emphasised the feelings of the heroine and the theme of lovers versus society, while the test of honour through combat, a staple of medieval chivalric romance, faded in significance. Pastoral settings in which elegant and cultured shepherds demonstrated courtly manners and ethical discrimination reflected the changing role of the aristocracy and the idealisation of a lost rural life. Yet middle-class Protestant writers such as John Milton in *Paradise Lost* (1667) and John Bunyan in *Pilgrim's Progress* (1675) frequently employed the combat motifs of medieval romance as *metaphors for the emotional and spiritual trials of the wayfaring Christian.

Miguel de Cervantes' *Don Quixote* (1605) is a parodic farewell to the chivalric romance genre even as it carries romance themes into the future in the form of the modern European novel: namely, interest in interiority, emotional states, the conflict between the individual and society, and the imagining of other worlds beyond prosaic reality (see PSYCHOLOGICAL NOVEL; QUIXOTIC NOVEL). Cervantes represents the ideals of chivalry as incompatible with an increasingly disenchanted and materialistic society. The *Gothic romance novel (e.g., Walpole's *The Castle of Otranto*, 1764) departs from the *realist novel of manners because of its dual emphases on idealised imaginative settings and the supernatural. The *historical novels of Sir Walter Scott (e.g., *Ivanhoe*, 1819) combine the chivalric and Gothic aspects of previous romance incarnations with a detailed, realist descriptive style to epitomise the historical romance (see DESCRIPTION). Meanwhile, the fairy tale and supernatural elements of earlier romance incarnations anticipate the imaginative worlds of late-twentieth-century science fiction and fantasy genres, which also share the traditional romance themes of the quest for identity and the testing of the protagonist's honour (e.g., the *Star Wars* *films).

In the twentieth century, the romance mode has received sustained critical analysis. Northrop Frye claims that romance is 'the structural core of all fiction' and 'man's vision of his life as a quest' (Frye 1976: 15). With this capacious definition, Frye identifies core transhistorical elements of romance. These include the hero's quest for identity through a descent into a figurative underworld and a corresponding ascent to self-recognition and erotic wish-fulfilment. Fredric Jameson, in his *Marxist materialist approach to genre analysis, modifies Frye's idealist, mythic concept by charting romance's ascendance in transitional historical moments when one mode of production is struggling to transform or replace another. Thus romance has a tendency to be either nostalgic or *utopian, but rarely deals with the present. At its medieval beginnings, romance clearly articulated the aristocratic ideology of chivalry for a privileged *audience, but Frye, Jameson, and others have noted how romance frequently illustrates wishful alternatives to social and historical realities.

The subversive pleasures of popular romance may be 'hijacked', in Frye's terms, to serve the interests of the ruling order, but from its earliest days, romance has been seen as morally dangerous for weak minds. Since the seventeenth century, critics and readers have identified a dialectical relationship between romance, associated with idealism, magic, *emotion, fantasy, and the libido, and realist fiction, associated with empiricism, *science, reason, and self-control (McKeon 1987; see REALIST NOVEL). In the early 1800s, the perceived imaginative freedom of the romance mode especially appealed to the poets Keats and Wordsworth, who used romance motifs extensively to express politically and culturally subversive themes. The success of mass-market *romance novels among female readers of the late twentieth century has simultaneously attracted sociological attention, *feminist analysis, and public condemnation. Almost from its inception, romance has struggled for critical respect and prestige from cultural and moral authorities, but this lack of respect has never affected its enduring popularity.

SEE ALSO: ideology and narrative; sociological approaches to literary narrative

References and further reading

Auerbach, Erich (1953) *Mimesis*, trans. Willard Trask, Princeton: Princeton University Press.

Frye, Northrop (1976) *The Secular Scripture*, Cambridge, Mass.: Harvard University Press.

Jameson, Fredric (1981) *The Political Unconscious: Narrative as a Socially Symbolic Act*, Ithaca: Cornell University Press.

McKeon, Michael (1987) *The Origins of the English Novel 1600–1740*, Baltimore: Johns Hopkins University Press.

Parker, Patricia (1979) *Inescapable Romance: Studies in the Poetics of a Mode*, Princeton: Princeton University Press.

Vinaver, Eugene (1971) *The Rise of Romance*, New York: Oxford University Press.

SUE P. STARKE

ROMANCE NOVEL

The romance novel is a type of formulaic fiction told primarily from a woman's point of view (see FOCALIZATION; GENRE FICTION; POINT OF VIEW (LITERARY)), where the *plot focuses on the development of a romantic relationship between two people that is resolved happily. The *genre has grown enormously since the 1970s, accounting for 54.5% of all popular paperback fiction sold in North America in 2001, with a reader base that, while almost exclusively female, is quite diverse in marital status, age, and level of education (Romance Writers of America 2003). Romances from the 1980s on include the use of both historical

and modern settings, varying degrees of approval of extra-marital sex, varying degrees of sexual explicitness, a wide range of markets targeted (young adult through adult), and increasing crossover into *science fiction/fantasy, mystery (see DETECTIVE FICTION), and western fields. However, ethnic minority characters are seriously under-represented and novels about homosexual relationships are rare (see QUEER THEORY).

While often scorned by literary critics, romance novels have become a serious topic of study for other researchers, especially those in popular culture and feminist criticism (see CULTURAL STUDIES APPROACHES TO NARRATIVE; FEMINIST NARRATOLOGY). There is an ongoing debate as to whether romances are empowering or disempowering for their readers. Arguments for disempowerment (e.g., Russ 1972) are based on claims that romances ratify the values of a patriarchal society; the *hero has complete power over the heroine, who finds happiness only by subordinating her *desires to his. In contrast, some critics see even the more conservative romances as covertly subversive (e.g., Modleski 1982; Radway 1991). They point out that the plot centres on feminine development and supports a feminine worldview extolling emotional commitment. In addition, because the hero ultimately accepts the heroine's expressions of anger at his insensitive and controlling behaviour, these critics claim that romances cause readers to feel that their own frustrations with partners have been validated and assuaged. However, the critics in question also express concern that readers will content themselves with their vicarious triumph in the romance and not be motivated to change their real lives. Finally, complete supporters of the romance novel (e.g., Thurston 1987) find at least the more modern ones unambiguously empowering, since an increasing number of heroines hold powerful positions in satisfying careers, show overt pleasure in their own sexuality, and choose lovers who appreciate their sexual confidence and support their professional aspirations.

SEE ALSO: gender studies; novel, the; reader-response theory; romance; sociological approaches to literary narrative

References and further reading

Modleski, Tania (1982) *Loving with a Vengeance: Mass-Produced Fantasies for Women*, New York: Routledge.

Radway, Janice A. (1991) *Reading the Romance: Women, Patriarchy, and Popular Literature*, Chapel Hill: The University of North Carolina Press.

Ramsdell, Kristin (1999) *Romance Fiction: A Guide to the Genre*, Englewood, CO: Libraries Unlimited, Inc.

Romance Writers of America (2003) Industry Statistics, http://www.rwanational.org/statistics.stm

Russ, Joanna (1972) 'What Can a Heroine Do? Or Why Women Can't Write', in Susan Koppelman Cornillon (ed.) *Images of Women in Fiction: Feminist Perspectives*, Bowling Green: Bowling Green University Popular Press.

Thurston, Carol (1987) *The Romance Revolution: Erotic Novels for Women and the Quest for a New Sexual Identity*, Urbana: University of Illinois Press.

MARY ELLEN RYDER

RUSSIAN FORMALISM

Based in Moscow and Saint Petersburg during the second and third decades of the twentieth century, the Russian Formalist movement profoundly influenced the evolution of modern-day narrative theory. Formalists such as Boris Eikhenbaum, Roman Jakobson, Vladimir Propp, Viktor Shklovskii, Boris Tomashevskii, and Iurii Tynianov took the decisive step of uncoupling theories of *narrative from theories of the *novel. Specific studies that have proved particularly consequential for narrative theory include Shklovskii's research on *plot, which outlines the *story-discourse distinction; Tomashevskii's distinction between 'bound' (plot-relevant) and 'free' (non-plot-relevant) *motifs, which anticipated Barthes's nuclei and catalysers, and Chatman's kernels and satellites; and Propp's development of the idea of invariant *functions attaching to variable dramatis personae in stories. *See* FORMALISM; STRUCTURALIST NARRATOLOGY (ALSO: ACTANT; NARRATIVE UNITS).

S

SANSKRIT NARRATIVE

South Asia has an age-old and multiform narrative tradition both in the vernacular languages and in Sanskrit, the dominant literary language of India. Some of these texts, as well as Indian literary theory as a whole, include strong non-narrative features.

We find fragments of narratives in the oldest Sanskrit texts, i.e., in the sacred verses of the *Veda* (1200–1000 BC), as well as short prose narratives on mythological subjects in the commentaries of Vedic verses (the *Brāhmaṇas*, 1000–700 BC; *see* MYTH: THEMATIC APPROACHES). But the golden age of Sanskrit narrative began in the first centuries BC with the two great *epics *Mahābhārata* and *Rāmāyaṇa*. The first in particular incorporated many earlier *folktales and minor epics, such as the story of Nala, embedded within its main *plot. It became an influential example of the technique of framing (*see* EMBEDDING; FRAMED NARRATIVE), a structure which has remained very popular in Indian narrative. Collections of *fables and *fairy tales, the oldest of which were compiled approximately in the same period as the epics, were almost invariably constructed in this way, the most sophisticated texts making use of five or six levels of embedding.

The two great epics also served as inventories of narrative *motifs for subsequent Sanskrit literature. Individual episodes of the *Mahābhārata* and the main plot of the *Rāmāyaṇa* have given rise to retellings in the form of *drama, court epic and *short stories (*see* NARRATIVE VERSIONS). This recycling of old material is another typical feature of Sanskrit literature. As A. K. Ramanujan and others have shown, many Indian texts do not have sharp boundaries or an autonomous existence but should be recognised instead as participating in a continuous process of storytelling (Ramanujan 1989: 203). Because of its respect for tradition and its continuous dialogue with the past, Sanskrit literature displays an unusually high degree of *intertextuality. Narrative motifs may remain constant, but every different context gives them a new interpretation.

In the so-called classical era of Sanskrit literature (third century to ninth century AD), the simplest narrative form was a 'story' (in Sanskrit *kathā* or *ākhyāna*). The stories were collected into cycles with a more or less methodical system of frames. Some of these cycles, like the many versions of *Pañchatantra*, were originally *didactic in purpose, teaching wise conduct and worldly wisdom. Others placed greater emphasis on entertainment. The oldest and probably the most extensive text of this group, called *The Great Story* (*Bṛhatkathā*), has been lost, but like the two classical epics it lived on as an inventory of good stories and a model for later reworkings, the most famous of which is *The Ocean of Stories* (*Kathāsaritsāgara*, 1066–1081), by Kashmirian Somadeva. In the didactic collections the majority of the stories are animal fables, the approach is semi-realistic, and the usual form is a mixture of simple narrative prose and gnomic (aphoristic) verse. In the entertainment group the fairy story and the *romance are the predominating story types and the action often takes place in the sphere of the *fantastic. These works are usually written in verse or in ornate prose.

Another *genre of narrative, the court epic (*mahākāvya*), was far more complicated and stylised than the *kathā* genre and enjoyed a higher literary prestige. By the eighth and ninth centuries court epics had lost most of the features that normally define a *narrative. Plot and characterisation (*see* CHARACTER) had both been buried deep under long poetical *descriptions and technical bravura. The rarely used genre of the prose *novel developed along the same lines. An early work by Daṇḍin, The Adventures of Ten Princes (*Daśakumāracarita*, seventh century), is a *picaresque novel that shows affinity with the more realistic Sanskrit dramas of the same age, but the successors of Daṇḍin chose to cultivate original and elaborate diction at the expense of plot and dramatic action. The genre of mythological narrative called *purāṇa* ('ancient history') had more in common with folk traditions than with literary conventions of the court, but because of their length and their theological preoccupations the *purāṇas* are no less static in character (*see* THEOLOGY AND NARRATIVE). The two epics and the *purāṇas* were nevertheless the most widely distributed types of Sanskrit narrative, for they were regularly recited at the festivities of the Hindu community.

Classical Indian literary theory was quite subtle and versatile but like all other premodern literary theories it did not treat narrative as a separate field of study, its two main concerns being the theory of poetic figures and the nature of the aesthetic experience. The emphasis of theoretical texts on the prosodic and semantic aspects of single expressions and the predilection of *authors for witty *metaphors and intricate descriptions favoured narratives with a decidedly low degree of *'narrativity'. The action and the plot were looked upon as secondary elements which should not be paid excessive attention, for fear of disturbing the aesthetic attitude that is called for by literary works. However, the theory of drama described in the standard textbook of dramaturgy, *Nāṭyaśāstra* (fifth century AD), stressed characterisation, the unity of the plot, and its principles of construction. A main action should be supported by a subsidiary one and developed through five phases, in which an objective (*kārya*) is attained after *conflicts and frustrations which build up *suspense. Many of the simpler Sanskrit narratives can be said to follow this scheme.

SEE ALSO: African narrative; ancient theories of narrative (non-Western); Australian Aboriginal narrative; Chinese narrative; Japanese narrative; narrative structure; Native American narrative

References and further reading

Chadwick, Hector Munro, and Nora Kershaw Chadwick (1936) 'Early Indian Literature', in *Growth of Literature*, vol. 2, Cambridge: Cambridge University Press.
Gerow, Edwin (1977) *Indian Poetics*, Wiesbaden: Harrassowitz.
Lienhardt, Siegfried (1984) *A History of Classical Poetry: Sanskrit – Pali – Prakrit*, Wiesbaden: Harrassowitz.
Mangels, Annette (1994) *Zur Erzählungstechnik im Mahābhārata*, Hamburg: Verlag Dr. Kovac.
Ramanujan, Attipat Krishnaswami (1989) 'Where Mirrors are Windows: Toward an Anthology of Reflections', *History of Religions*, 28.3, 187–216.
Shackle, Christopher, and Rupert Snell (eds) (1992) *The Indian Narrative: Perspectives and Patterns*, Wiesbaden: Harrassowitz.
Warder, A. K. (1972–1992) *Indian Kavya Literature*, 6 Vols, Delhi: Motilal Banarsidass.

VIRPI HÄMEEN-ANTTILA

SATIRIC NARRATIVE

'Satire' designates not only a *genre, a class of literature with a distinct repertory of conventions, but also a *mode, that is, a tone and an attitude. However fine-tuned, the satiric mode is always aggressive, being angry, sarcastic, or indignant in motivation, derisive, vituperative, or slanderous in intent as well as sceptical, questioning, and unbelieving in its stance (*see* INTENTIONALITY; NARRATIVE AS ARGUMENT). The hostility of satirists is directed at discernible historical particulars, i.e., at historically authentic personages and professions, issues and institutions, events and affairs. Major practitioners, such as Dryden, Pope, Swift, Byron, and Orwell, have insisted that personal *reference in satire is not only desirable but inevitable. The polygeneric status of satire is reflected in Isaac Casaubon's 1605 etymology of the word *satire* itself, which he derived not from Greek *satyros*, satyr play, but from Latin *satura*, a peppery collection of heterogeneous parts – a recipe potentially available to all genres but defying generic definition, producing satirical texts rather than satires.

Satiric *narration is often, therefore, an incidental element in narrative texts. The most obvious case in point is the *picaresque novel, which affords its *author many an opportunity for lambasting the rampant corruptions of the contemporary scene (as in Smollett's *Roderick Random*, 1748), even if it is mediated through the eyes of a scoundrel (as in Defoe's *Moll Flanders*,

1722). Similarly, many novels by Dickens, especially *Oliver Twist* (1837–1838) and *Hard Times* (1854), are studded with images of individual and social monstrosities which satirise the oppressive uses resulting from Victorian attitudes and institutions. But the satirical spirit may inhabit whole genres, too. The most obvious is *utopian fiction. Both More's prototypical *Utopia* (1516) and Morris's socialist *fantasy *News from Nowhere* (1890) juxtapose the vision of a seemingly ideal alternative world with the satiric scene of a disorderly society riddled with political and social evils. Another genre lending itself to satirical purposes is *allegory: Swift's *Tale of a Tub* (1704) is a religious allegory showing a world inhabited by villains and dunces; *Gulliver's Travels* (1726) is a political allegory containing a satirical *travel narrative of Everyman's journeys into the history of contemporary English politics and *science; and Orwell's beast *fable *Animal Farm* (1945) is a discordant allegory of the Russian revolution and the subsequent disintegration of its ideals under Stalin.

Throughout its history, satire has also shown a particular affiliation with narrative verse genres (*see* NARRATIVE IN POETRY). The impulse to speak in aggressive verses manifests itself in a number of paradigmatic texts of English literature – e.g., Butler's *Hudibras* (1662–1680), a satire of civil war and religious schism in Commonwealth England; Pope's mock-epic *The Dunciad* (1728; 1743), a virulent retort to the 'fools and scoundrels' that had annoyed the poet for years; and Byron's *epic satire *Don Juan* (1819–1824), which in a 'rehearsal of the past' displays its animus against almost all objects of the poet's scorn.

References and further reading

Elkin, P. K. (1973) *The Augustan Defence of Satire*, Oxford: Clarendon Press.
Elliott, Robert C. (1960) *The Power of Satire*, Princeton, NJ: Princeton University Press.
Griffin, Dustin (1994) *Satire: A Critical Reintroduction*, Lexington: University Press of Kentucky.
Nokes, David (1987) *Raillery and Rage: A Study of Eighteenth-Century Satire*, Brighton: Harvester Press.
Rosenheim, Edward W. (1963) *Swift and the Satirist's Art*, Chicago: University of Chicago Press.

JOSEF HERMANN REAL

SCENE (CINEMATIC)

A scene can be defined in two broad ways: (1) as a *unit* of narrative made up of all or part of a narrated *event (*see* NARRATIVE UNITS); (2) as a representational *mode* in which the duration of the event and the duration of its representation are assumed to be equal (*see* STORY-DISCOURSE DISTINCTION; TIME IN NARRATIVE). Genette's work on written narrative has strongly influenced understandings of scene taken in the second sense. However, it is difficult to use Genette's approach to analyse narratives presented in *media such as *drama and movies, because audio-visual media represent temporal processes directly, rather than by means of language. Thus, whereas Genette contrasts scene with other representational modes such as *summary, in which the duration of discourse time is shorter than that of story time, *film narratives are characterised by a built-in equivalence between the narrated time and the time of narration, whereby scene becomes the standard mode of representation. Nonetheless, summary effects can be achieved in film by compressing sequences of events through ellipses, as for instance in *Citizen Kane*, where several years of narrative time are represented in approximately two minutes of screen time.

For his part, Metz (1974: 129) draws on the understanding of scenes as narrative units when he defines a film scene as a segment of a film narrative occurring in a single *space and in continuous time.

References and further reading

Genette, Gérard (1980 [1972]) *Narrative Comprehension: An Essay in Method*, trans. Jane E. Lewin, Ithaca: Cornell University Press.
Metz, Christian (1974) *Film Language*, trans. Michael Taylor, New York: Oxford University Press.

MICHAEL NEWMAN AND DAVID HERMAN

SCHEMATA

Deriving from work in cognitive psychology and from *Artificial Intelligence research, the term 'schemata' is used more or less interchangeably with *frames and refers to knowledge representations of relatively static objects and relations, in contrast with the representations of dynamic (or temporal) processes known as *scripts. Whereas scripts generate expectations about how particular sequences of *events are supposed to unfold, schemata create expectations about how domains of experience are likely to be structured at a particular moment in *time. *See* COGNITIVE NARRATOLOGY; PSYCHOLOGICAL APPROACHES TO NARRATIVE (ALSO: STORY SCHEMATA AND CAUSAL STRUCTURE).

SCIENCE AND NARRATIVE

This entry begins from the assumption that the culture of modernity and then postmodernity are inconceivable apart from the relationships between *narrative and science. The first section provides an introduction to the subject of narrative and science by reviewing some specific examples of the relationships between them. Section 2 offers an explication of the relationships between narrative and science in modernity and postmodernity. Sections 3 and 4 then consider the significance of the relationships between narrative and science in current discussions in literary studies and in the history of science, respectively. In the context of my discussion, the terms *narrative* and, later on, *modern* and *postmodern narrative* (*see* MODERNIST NARRATIVE), will be used broadly, referring to storytelling wherever and in whatever *media it occurs, rather than in a sense denoting certain types of literary works.

Between science and narrative

Albert Einstein's contemporaries, scientists and lay readers alike, were not surprised to find a fair amount of storytelling in his popular accounts of relativity, such as his famous discussion of moving trains and the clocks inside moving along with them (Einstein 1977). Nor were the readers of many other accounts of mathematics and science, before and after Einstein, surprised by similar uses of narrative, or other illustrative means, such as pictures or *metaphors (*see* PICTORIAL NARRATIVITY). It is not that most of Einstein's readers saw narrative and scientific thinking and practice as fundamentally related. Rather, they saw storytelling as an auxiliary means to illustrate scientific ideas to the general public or sometimes scientists, while assuming science to be fundamentally different and, at least in principle, separable from narrative and the other 'illustrative' means just

mentioned. Thus the deeper relationships between science and narrative remained unperceived.

The situation becomes more complicated when narratives appear in more technical works, such as the famous story of a cat, now known as Schrödinger's cat, in Erwin Schrödinger's thought experiment in his 1935 article, 'The Present Situation in Quantum Mechanics' (Schrödinger 1993). The cat is placed in a box where a radioactive decay (a probabilistic event) may or may not take place, thus triggering or not one mechanism or another that would kill the cat, who accordingly has a fifty per cent chance of surviving the ordeal. We close the box and then open it a few hours after the emission has or has not taken place. It is possible to argue that, if one treats the whole arrangement as a quantum system, quantum mechanics would predict a fifty per cent chance of finding the cat in either condition, dead or alive, *after* the box is opened. On the other hand, the cat should be in a definite state of being dead or alive immediately upon the occurrence or non-occurrence of the emission. This appears to be a paradoxical state of affairs, which is a matter of considerable debate and part of the continuing controversy surrounding quantum mechanics and its interpretation.

Schrödinger's choice of his thought experiment might have helped to focus attention on the subtle quantum problem in question, and the story has had a great popular appeal, usually unrelated to the essence of the physics involved. Ironically, however, the story and this particular instance of storytelling do not capture the deeper relationships between narrative and science mentioned above.

Yet thought experiments often centrally involve narrative, as suggested by Einstein's articles, technical and popular, and also by the work of Galileo, Einstein's primary precursor in his use of this powerful theoretical tool. Galileo tells the story of loading a ship with all manner of living creatures (in turn perhaps alluding to the story of Noah's ark). He then invites his readers to enact the experiment, at least as a thought experiment, and to contemplate the fact that they would not observe any difference between the ship and the world around them standing still or uniformly moving. Unlike the story of Schrödinger's cat, in this case the narrative *is* science, rather than merely serving to illustrate key scientific concepts, insofar as this particular aspect of modern physics and indeed the very idea of motion, which grounds all physics, cannot be conveyed without a narrative. 'Something moves' is a narrative! Accordingly, every time something begins to move a narrative begins, and, conversely, every time there is a narrative something begins to move or at least stands still (which still requires the idea of motion), as Vladimir Propp taught us (Propp 1968 [1928]).

Schrödinger's article, too, brings together physics and narrative, suggesting that narrative has a fundamentally constitutive role in scientific thinking and argument (*see* NARRATIVE AS ARGUMENT; NARRATIVE AS COGNITIVE INSTRUMENT). It also tells what Jean-François Lyotard calls a 'grand narrative', 'metanarrative', or *master narrative (see my exposition below). The metanarrative in question is that of the history of physics and its classical ideal, plus that of the revolution (or what we sometimes call, following Thomas Kuhn, a paradigm change), brought about by quantum mechanics, which fundamentally put the classical ideal into question. In contrast with classical physics, in quantum mechanics, no narrative account of the behaviour of quantum objects, such as electrons and photons, is *ultimately* possible, although such accounts can provisionally be used in scientific practice or elsewhere (Bohr 1987). It is the possibility of offering such an account (at least in principle) that defines the classical ideal in physics and in other sciences; the loss of that possibility for narrative was lamented by Schrödinger and by Einstein, neither of whom accepted quantum theory as the ultimate account of nature. They both wanted a narrative of physical behaviour at the ultimate level.

In our own, postmodern context, we are no longer surprised to find (and are willing to confront) such fundamental, reciprocal relationships between narrative and science, which have by now been the subject of many discussions in several fields. Arguably the most prominent among these discussions have taken place in the history and sociology of science and in literary and cultural studies, to be considered below. One can, however, make an even stronger claim. Our culture, beginning at least with modernity (which may be defined by two key cultural junctures, the Renaissance and then the Enlightenment) is inconceivable apart from the relationships between science and narrative.

Reciprocally, these relationships brought both categories, narrative and science, into new levels of mutual elucidation and also of mutual questioning.

This questioning is not solely due to the nearly uncontainable and diverging proliferation of scientific fields, subfields, and projects, or narrative practices, although this is an important factor. The difficulty often arises even from within a single denomination, be it a given science or other field, or a given project. In fact, it is no longer possible unconditionally and once and for all to define either narrative or science, useful and indeed necessary as such definitions may be. Nor it is possible to relate, conceptually or historically, narrative and science in a single, fully determinable way. Instead, we must navigate a complex and equivocal conceptual and historical space where such definitions or relations find their proper but inevitably limited place.

For example, was Lucretius's *De rerum natura* a narrative or at least a philosophical account of science, which *could have been* at some point presented by a narrative? There is no easy answer to this question, leaving aside the question, hardly any easier, whether Lucretius's work itself could be contained by the rubric of 'narrative', or 'literature'. It is, however, difficult and in a certain sense impossible to argue that what Lucretius presents (e.g., Democritean atomism) is physics in the modern mathematical-experimental sense (Serres 1983). Is it then not science at all, but, say, *philosophy? It would not be easy to make this claim either, given that for a long time science was referred to as 'natural philosophy'. A more complex and stratified argument needs to be made.

Recent investigations have taught us that *myth, religion, *theology, philosophy, everyday life, and the narratives that all of these domains involve are intermixed in a more complex way than was widely recognised in the time of Copernicus, Kepler, Descartes, Galileo, Newton, Leibniz, or even Einstein. In this sense, Einstein's stories of the trains and the clocks in his account of relativity, or the life and culture behind these stories, have a deep significance for his thinking and for the broader history of relativity (Galison 2003). However, it cannot therefore be assumed that the complexity of the relations between science and narrative reduces the significance and disciplinary independence of specific, e.g., mathematical-experimental, features of modern science. Yet the recent rethinking of science does make it difficult to justify unequivocal one-dimensional narratives of the history of modern science that dominated the subject for so long – for example, those of its gradual or discontinuous break with theology or philosophy (or narrative) or the previous state of science itself, or, conversely, those historical narratives in which such separation never occurs.

Narrative, science, and knowledge, modern and postmodern

In *The Postmodern Condition* (1984 [1979]), Lyotard lays the groundwork for the argument for the essential significance of the relationships between narrative and science in the culture of modernity and postmodernity. According to Lyotard, both modernity and postmodernity are defined by the role of narrative in them, and by their attitude toward metanarratives in general and toward certain types of metanarratives which Lyotard calls grand narratives. Beyond their metanarrative function (in relation to other or even all narratives operative in a given culture), grand narratives are presumed to uniquely comprehend or in practice govern a culture or even a whole civilisation. Lyotard's central example is the grand narrative of the Enlightenment and the progress of knowledge, largely enabled by the advancement of modern science and industrial technology, which thus brings narrative (as grand narrative) and science together in defining modernity.

This narrative may also be seen, in terms of literary narrative *genres, as an *epic narrative, on the model of Virgil's *Aeneid*: the Enlightenment, most especially through science, becomes the *hero of the story and establishes the new empire, the empire of modernity. Against modernity's trust and investment in its grand narratives, postmodernity is defined by 'the incredulity toward metanarratives' and, especially, toward grand narratives that function as such metanarratives (Lyotard 1984 [1979], xxiv). At bottom, however, modernity, too, harbours a suspicion concerning its grand narratives. The difference between the modern and the postmodern perspectives lies is in their response to the loss of belief in the efficacy of such narratives, and, correlatively, in the capacity of our knowledge to comprehend, even in principle, the ultimate constitution of nature, mind, or society. The first response, defining the modern, is a nostalgia for this loss, in effect a nostalgia for the impossible. The second, defining the postmodern, is the affirmation of this loss and the welcoming of new and expanded spaces of narrative or knowledge that result from this loss (Lyotard 1984: 81).

Our contemporary culture still contains both attitudes and may be defined by the *conflict between them.

Modernity and postmodernity are, thus, equally defined by the character of the knowledge they practice, or theorise, and by the transformation of this character from modernity to postmodernity in industrialised and, by the time of postmodernity, computerised societies. 'The postmodern condition' of Lyotard's title is thus made possible by new information technologies, which have also changed the *pragmatics and legitimation of knowledge in general and in science in particular, including the role of narrative (vs. grand narrative) in these domains. Lyotard argues further that, contrary to most views and ideologies of scientific knowledge, science has always been at least partly para-logical in its argumentation (*see* IDEOLOGY AND NARRATIVE). That is, science uses not just logical but also rhetorical, political, and other means of persuasion (*see* RHETORICAL APPROACHES TO NARRATIVE). Postmodernity came to accept and deploy paralogy in its cognitive and scientific practices, but without surrendering scientific knowledge and practice to the rule of grand narratives of the Enlightenment. Reciprocally, these two different concepts and practices of science differently shape the dominant concepts and uses of narrative in the contexts of modernity and postmodernity; modernism is marked by a reliance on grand narratives involving science, whereas a hallmark of postmodernism is the way it traffics in a multiplicity of narratives or forms of cognition in general.

Postmodern epistemology may be seen as inaugurated by twentieth-century mathematics and science, on the one hand, and philosophy, literature, and art, on the other. The postmodern information technology and computerisation of knowledge in the second half of the twentieth century enable and necessitate the deployment of the new paradigm of knowledge, narrative, scientific, and other, these developments thus changing the nature of the legitimation of knowledge. Early-twentieth-century mathematics and science, such as quantum theory, on the one hand, and art and literature, and specifically narrative literature, from Joyce to the *digital narrative of hypertexts, on the other hand, provide the paradigm itself.

Postmodern epistemology is radical by virtue of its anti-realist and a-causal character (*see* CAUSALITY; REALISM, THEORIES OF). In particular, it entails a new, radical concept of chance, emerging across the landscape of postmodernity. In the traditional view of chance, chance is reducible, at least in principle, to some underlying though perhaps unknown necessity, often accompanied by a corresponding (grand) narrative. By contrast, in the postmodern view, an assumption of the ultimate necessity underlying chance is, by definition, impossible. Chance becomes irreducible to any necessity, knowable or unknowable. More fundamentally, this epistemology is defined by allowing for and even requiring something that cannot, even in principle, be known and yet is also given an essential role in shaping what can be known. The lack of realism and causality at the ultimate level is an automatic consequence, suggesting that an incontrollable plurality is at the heart of the postmodern. By contrast, the appeal to controllable pluralities can be viewed as modern, insofar as they are mastered by modern paradigms – scientific, such as those of classical physics, or cultural, such as those defined by grand narratives. By the same token, such master narratives would also, at least in principle, govern our cognitive, ethical, or political practices (*see* ETHICAL TURN). The postmodernist view does not erase the significance of narrative in science, philosophy, or elsewhere, but complicates its applicability, especially by suspending grand narratives.

Narrative, literature, and science

Many recent studies of the relationships among literature, narrative, and science proceed by investigating the paradigmatic significance of literary narratives for postmodernist conceptions of knowledge and culture, and of the reciprocal traffic between postmodernist literature and new science, and, more recently, new technologies, especially digital and virtual technologies. These connections acquire even greater richness and significance when considered against the background of similar connections between classical science, such as Newtonian physics, and literature and narratives of modernity, from Kepler and Galileo to Maxwell and Darwin. The significance of literary narratives is also apparent in most founding theoretical texts, such as Lyotard's writing on postmodernism, Deleuze's engagement with modern mathematics and modernist literature, or Derrida's interpretations of Joyce, Kafka, and Blanchot (Derrida 1991). Among more overtly postmodernist literary

narratives especially prominent in this context are those of Thomas Pynchon, Don DeLillo, and, in the realm of *drama, Tom Stoppard; these texts are especially notable for their connections to quantum physics and chaos theory (*see* ENCYCLOPEDIC NOVEL). The significance of the interactions between literature, narrative, and science in this postmodernist context can, however, be traced back to earlier twentieth-century literature and even before.

Of course, the relationships among literature, narrative, and science cannot be restricted to the contexts associated with modernity and postmodernity; yet the relationships in question acquire a new significance in the modern and postmodern epochs. Whether one speaks of John Milton's imperative to 'justify the ways of God to men' in the post-Copernican, modern world in *Paradise Lost*; or William Blake's visionary confrontation with Newton in his great narrative poems; or Mary Shelley's exploration of ethical dilemmas of science in *Frankenstein*; or George Eliot's engagement with Darwin's theory of evolution, in all these works one faces the problematic of modernity as both narrative and scientific modernity. Literary studies almost inevitably reflect this problematic in one way or another, even when they do not deal expressly with the relationships between literature, narrative, and science.

Histories and narratives of science, old and new

Most examples of the relationships between narrative and science mentioned earlier in this entry could be discussed from the perspective of the relationships between modernity and postmodernity. Consider Kepler's narrative of the Earth created by God as a beautiful ship to follow. Kepler implies a mathematical inscription, the trajectory of a circle or (in a modification that would complicate Kepler's argument but not dissuade him) an ellipse around the sun and its light, physical and divine. Countering the theological objections to the Copernican view, Kepler's narrative reinstates a theological grounding to the Copernican system. Making, in Galileo's words, nature a book written in the language of mathematics, the mathematical harmonies involved are themselves part of this theological determination, from Kepler or Copernicus (or Plato and Pythagoras) to Newton to Einstein to modern and postmodern relativistic cosmologies. The latter offer us the latest example of conceptual and cultural interactions between science and narrative in modern or postmodern physics. Kepler's narrative is only one among many indices of the profound connections, both epistemological and narrative, between 'the Copernican (r)evolution' and theology and its narratives – connections that have been extensively considered in recent investigations in the history of science, including so-called constructivist science studies (Latour 1999).

Especially significant among these developments are projects involving *gender studies in history and philosophy of science, most prominently biology and *medicine (Fox Keller and Longino 1996). As this work suggests, theological and grand narratives are gendered or, more specifically, patriarchal (or phallogocentric), and they functioned as such in shaping modernity. Modern biology and the theory of evolution have been especially prominently discussed in this context. Indeed, the theory of evolution is one of the great areas of contestation when it comes to debates about the relations between science and narrative – debates whose epistemological, ethical, cultural, and political dimensions gender theorists have helped illuminate.

SEE ALSO: cultural studies approaches to narrative

References and further reading

Bohr, Niels (1987) 'Discussion with Einstein', in The Philosophical Writings of Niels Bohr, vol. 2, Woodbridge, CT: Ox Bow Press.
Derrida, Jacques (1991) Acts of Literature, New York: Routledge.
Einstein, Albert (1977) Relativity: The Special and the General Theory, New York: Random House.
Fox Keller, Evelyn and Helen Longino (eds) (1996) Feminism and Science, Oxford: Oxford University Press.
Galison, Peter (2003) Einstein's Clocks, Poincare's Maps: Empires of Time, New York: W. W. Norton.
Gould, Stephen Jay (2002) The Structure of Evolutionary Theory, Cambridge, Mass.: Harvard University Press.
Kuhn, Thomas (1996) The Structure of Scientific Revolutions, Chicago: University of Chicago Press.
Lakatos, Imre (1987) Proofs and Refutations, Cambridge: Cambridge University Press.
Latour, Bruno (1999) Pandora's Hope: Essays on the Reality of Science Studies, Cambridge, Mass.: Harvard University Press.
Lyotard, Jean-François (1984 [1979]) The Postmodern Condition: A Report on Knowledge, trans. Geoff Bennington and Brian Massumi, Minneapolis: University of Minnesota Press.
Propp, Vladimir (1968 [1928]) Morphology of the Folktale, trans. Laurence Scott, revised by Louis A. Wagner. Austin: University of Texas Press.
Schrödinger, Erwin (1993) 'The Present Situation in Quantum Mechanics', trans. J. D. Trimmer, in John A. Wheeler and Wojciech H. Zurek (eds) Quantum Theory and Measurement, Princeton: Princeton University Press.
Serres, Michel (1983) Hermes: Literature, Science, Philosophy, Baltimore: Johns Hopkins University Press.

ARKADY PLOTNITSKY

SCIENCE FICTION

Science fiction, a term popularised in the 1940s, has come to refer to a form of *genre fiction characterised by the narration of imaginative and speculative alternative worlds. Though typically set in the future or in space, sf (usually abbreviated in lower case) also encompasses narratives of *counterfactual history, *virtuality, and an extreme *defamiliarisation of contemporary society. The defamiliarising technique has been seen as central to the sf blend of rationalised plausibility with startling innovation, which Suvin (1979) termed 'cognitive estrangement'.

Largely a twentieth-century and current genre, sf has its roots in the mass literacy, industrialisation, urbanisation, and scientism of nineteenth-century Europe. Some (Aldiss and Wingrove 1986) have dated the *Gothic novel – in particular Frankenstein (1818) – as the precursor of sf, with further parentage claimed for *utopian and *didactic fiction. The genre developed as a *short story or serialised narrative form in France (Jules Verne) and Britain (H. G. Wells), and became massively popularised by the 'pulp' magazines in the eastern U.S. in the 1920s and 1930s (see SERIAL FORM). Sf has since become one of the most widely read and global forms of genre fiction, and has expanded into cinema and TV, as well as informing semi-narrative forms such as computer-supported action games, and influencing art and architecture, design, public ethics debates, and governmental social policy (see COMPUTER GAMES AND NARRATIVE; FILM NARRATIVE; TELEVISION).

Sf writing in the so-called 'golden age' of the 1940s and 1950s tended to emphasise technological progress and was generally positive about innovations and social change. The values conveyed emblematically, thematically, or directly out of the mouths of *characters were either liberal and progressive or, by contrast, focused on an extreme libertarianism and the freedom of the individual. Later social sf tends to be darker, moving into *dystopian visions and the nightmarish landscapes of inner space. The genre has generated a multiplicity of sub-genres and movements, ranging from the outer space and physics of 'hard sf' to the 'New Wave' of stylistically experimental narratives; from the *cyberpunk adventures in techno-capitalism of computer junkies to the feminist dystopias satirising gender oppression (see GENDER STUDIES); from the 'splatter fiction' narratives of film to more cerebral social and political allegories; from the galactic sweep of 'space opera' to exercises in philosophical 'speculative cosmology' (see PHILOSOPHY AND NARRATIVE).

Throughout its history, sf has retained a sense that the short story format is its prototypical essence. Even novelised sf narratives exhibit short story features and organisation (see NOVEL, THE). Science fictional *plots tend to centre on problem-resolution patterns, manifested in a similar way as *detective fiction (alongside which the genre developed) and action *thrillers. Characterisation tends not to follow the psychologised pattern of post-Romantic narratives; instead, characters tend to be ciphers or types, more similar to the tokens of medieval *romance and *allegory (H. G. Wells referred to his own work as 'scientific romance'). Technological and social innovations form the rich background to the imagined world, and it is often one of these aspects or gadgets that operates as a mechanical plot device to engineer a climactic, explosive, or revelatory ending.

In the second half of the twentieth century, a kind of feedback loop emerged in which some sf narratives became more cinematic in *perspective and pacing, and more experimental writing developed in imitation not of *modernist or *postmodernist literature but of movie techniques. At the same time, non-sf fiction writers were more likely to draw on sf features (as in postmodernist and *magical realist narratives), and sf narratives began to demonstrate a more self-reflexive and allusive style in relation to the sf tradition. A sudden popularity of Mars novels just prior to the millennium, for example, looked back to early sf with an elegiac blend of nostalgia and retro-futurism.

Sf in general derives its narrative progression from its manifestly rationalist and progressive *ideology. Even in narratives where technological mishap threatens extinction or destruction, the solution is always sought and usually found in scientific knowledge and reasoning. The scientific technique of observation and deduction places scientists, action-men, idiosyncratic mavericks, or those with special telepathic abilities in the roles of dynamic protagonists. Expert knowledge or adaptable skills in the alternate fictionalised society are the key values for the sf *hero, who must overcome some adversarial, social, or alien conundrum in order to reach a resolution. Sf narratives have a strong sense of an ending (often apocalyptically, or by narrowly averting catastrophe), even if, occasionally, climaxes gesture towards an ineffable mysticism. Such gestures toward the transcendental are not anti-rationalist or supernatural, however, but constitute a technique in sf for illustrating how incredibly advanced the portrayed technology is from the perspective of the contemporary reader.

This blend of rationalism and transcendentalism manifests itself in a concern for explanatory (pseudo-)scientific plausibility. Innovations are almost always made plausible by narratorial or character explanation (see NARRATION; NARRATIVE EXPLANATION), or by a demonstration of the working mechanism to the reader (Stockwell 2000). This *realism in *narrative technique is what distinguishes sf from *fantasy (Roberts 2000). At the same time, sf has been claimed as a symbolist mode (Delany 1977), in the sense that it represents our world in alternate form, rather than reproducing it directly. Corresponding with the sf blend of scientific rationalism and literary artifice, we could say that sf is symbolist in function but realist in technique.

SEE ALSO: fantastic, the; plot types; possible-worlds theory; science and narrative

References and further reading

Aldiss, Brian, and David Wingrove (1986) Trillion Year Spree: The History of Science Fiction, London: Gollancz.

Clute, John, and Peter Nicholls (eds) (1993) The Encyclopedia of Science Fiction, London: Orbit.

Delany, Samuel (1977) The Jewel-Hinged Jaw: Notes on the Language of Science Fiction, Elizabethtown, NY: Dragon Press.

James, Edward (1994) Science Fiction in the 20th Century, Oxford: Oxford University Press.

Malmgren, Carl (1991) *Worlds Apart: Narratology of Science Fiction*, Bloomington: Indiana University Press.

Roberts, Adam (2000) *Science Fiction*, London: Routledge.

Stockwell, Peter (2000) *The Poetics of Science Fiction*, London: Longman.

Suvin, Darko (1979) *Metamorphoses of Science Fiction: On the Poetics and History of a Literary Genre*, New Haven, CT: Yale University Press.

Wolmark, Jenny (1994) *Aliens and Others: Science Fiction, Feminism and Postmodernism*, Brighton: Harvester Press.

PETER STOCKWELL

SCREENPLAY

The screenplay (script, scenario) functions as the framework text from which motion-picture, *television, and digital-media narratives are produced (*see* FILM NARRATIVE; DIGITAL NARRATIVE). Screenplays developed out of the single-page scenario used in the early silent-film era and in the course of film history became indispensable to the planning and execution of film production. Occasionally preceded by a narrative synopsis and/or treatment, the screenplay proper is divided into *dialogue and scene text. The latter consists of scene headings, character and scene descriptions, and, optionally, technical cues (specifying dissolves, camera movement, etc.). Working scripts are usually loosely bound, with a single page roughly equalling one minute of screen (i.e., discourse) time (*see* STORY-DISCOURSE DISTINCTION; TIME IN NARRATIVE). Screenplays are primarily written as professional 'blueprints' for the film's director, cast, and crew, but, increasingly, edited versions have been published for a general readership.

Situated at the interface between literature and film, the screenplay has to utilise a verbal system to prefigure an audiovisual one (*see* INTERMEDIALITY; MEDIA AND NARRATIVE). The task of the screenwriter, consequently, is to write 'visually' and to suggest elements of editing and *montage (Pudovkin 1928). Assumptions about the screenplay's subordination to cinematographic form have occasionally been challenged, however. Eisenstein (1929), for instance, objects to overly 'technical' scripts and calls instead for an emotional literary manifestation which is positioned halfway between the film's initial concept and its realisation by the director. Balász (1945) sees the screenplay as combining a functional purpose with a literariness clearly distinct from that of the *novel and that of the written stage play (*see* DRAMA AND NARRATIVE). Pasolini (1965) notes the structural duality inherent in film scripts and emphasises the collaboration required from the reader to complete imaginatively what has only been alluded to (*see* GAPPING; PRAGMATICS).

While these views stress the screenplay's centrality, attention should also be paid to its instability and transitoriness. Unlike a stage play, the film script is realised only once in a fixed recording and cannot profit from multiple *performances and interpretations. In industrialised film production, the screenplay is regarded as a piece of property subject to revisions beyond the original screenwriter's control. Irrespective of market conditions, the transformation from script to screen is usually dominated by the director, to whom film 'authorship' is conventionally ascribed (*see* AUTHOR). As Sternberg (1997) has shown, however, a great number of macro- and microstructural elements, ranging from costume and body language to colour schemes and filmic *narrators, can be prefigured in the script. Although a director significantly shapes a film, it is the screenplay which not only determines the film's story but, to a considerable extent, also anticipates its 'discourse', i.e., its concrete cinematic presentation.

References and further reading

Balász, Béla (1970 [1945]) *Theory of the Film: Character and Growth of a New Art*, trans. Edith Bone, New York: Dover.

Eisenstein, Sergei (1988 [1929]) 'The Form of the Script', in *Selected Works*, vol. 1, trans. Richard Taylor, Bloomington: Indiana University Press.

Pasolini, Pier Paolo (1986 [1965]) 'The Screenplay as a "Structure that Wants to Be Another Structure"', *American Journal of Semiotics*, 4.1–2, 53–72.

Pudovkin, Vsevolod I. (1933 [1928]) *Film Technique*, trans. Ivor Montagu, London: George Newnes.

Sternberg, Claudia (1997) *Written for the Screen: The American Motion-Picture Screenplay as Text*, Tübingen: Stauffenburg.

CLAUDIA STERNBERG

SCRIPTS AND SCHEMATA

These practically synonymous terms are associated with schema theory, a sub-discipline of cognitive science which has its origins in the Gestalt psychology of the 1920s and 1930s. Schema theory's basic assertion is that all new experiences are understood by means of comparison to a stereotypical model, based on similar experiences and held in *memory. New experience is evaluated in terms of its conformity to, or deviation from, that model or 'schema' (pl. 'schemata').

The development of research on *Artificial Intelligence (AI) in the 1970s instigated the greatest expansion of interest in schema theory. AI researchers quickly realised that any computer designed to replicate human cognition would need access to a vast store of knowledge and experience. Just how this knowledge store would be organised and deployed presented AI scientists with a considerable problem. The most promising solution to this problem, the knowledge 'frame', was suggested first by Marvin Minsky (1963; see FRAME THEORY). Minsky's work was later developed in a highly influential investigation into knowledge 'scripts' by Roger Schank and Robert Abelson (1977) (see also Rumelhart 1975 and 1980).

Schank and Abelson (1977: 61–66) detail three different types of script: 'situational', 'personal', and 'instrumental'. Situational scripts contain our knowledge of what to expect in everyday situations, such as going to a restaurant (the RESTAURANT script), taking the bus, or going to a football match. Personal scripts tend to have *character roles which people adopt as the occasion arises, and include such examples as JEALOUS SPOUSE, FLIRT, and so on. Some examples of instrumental scripts are LIGHTING A CIGARETTE, STARTING A CAR, BUTTERING BREAD, and any other *action which requires knowledge of how to achieve a particular physical objective.

More recently, schema theory has been adopted as a means of analysing literary texts, most notably by Guy Cook (1994) (see also Cockcroft 2003, Culpeper 2001, and Semino 1997). Cook proposes a shift in focus in literary theory, from analysis restricted to textual structure to a consideration of the interaction between the text and the reader's knowledge of the world. He attempts to define literariness as the process by which a text presents such a challenge to the reader's expectations that he or she is forced to abandon established schemata in favour of new, 'refreshed' ones. Cook further argues that the schema 'disruption' and 'refreshment' caused by literary texts differs from the effects of other often textually deviant discourse, such as advertising (see ADVERTISEMENTS).

He claims that advertising relies on the shared worldview of its *audience which it actively seeks to reinforce rather than disrupt.

SEE ALSO: cognitive narratology; humour studies and narrative; narrative comprehension; psychological approaches to narrative; situation model; story schemata and causal structure

References and further reading

Cockcroft, Robert (2003) *Rhetorical Affect in Early Modern Writing: Renaissance Passions Reconsidered*, London: Palgrave.

Cook, Guy (1994) *Discourse and Literature*, Oxford: Oxford University Press.

Culpeper, Jonathan, (2001) *Language and Characterisation: People in Plays and Other Texts*, London: Longman.

Minsky, Marvin (1963) 'Steps Toward Artificial Intelligence', in Edward Feigenbaum and Julian Feldman (eds) *Computers and Thought*, New York: McGraw-Hill.

Schank, Roger, and Abelson, Robert (1977) *Scripts, Plans, Goals, and Understanding: An Inquiry into Human Knowledge Structures*, Hillsdale: Lawrence Erlbaum.

Rumelhart, David (1975) 'Notes on a Schema for Stories', in Daniel Bobrow and Allan Collins (eds) *Representation and Understanding*, New York: Academic Press.

——(1980) 'Schemata: the Building Blocks of Cognition', in Rand Spiro, Bertram Bruce, and William Brewer (eds) *Theoretical Issues in Reading Comprehension: Perspectives from Cognitive Psychology, Linguistics, Artificial Intelligence and Education*, Hillsdale: Lawrence Erlbaum.

Semino, Elena (1997) *Language and World Creation in Poems and Other Texts*, London: Longman.

JOANNA GAVINS

SECONDARY ORALITY

Marshall McLuhan's and Walter Ong's term for the cultural changes and renewed importance of oral forms of narrative brought about by the development of *media of long-distance communication such as *radio, *television, and the telephone. These diffusers of talk challenged the supremacy of print as a source of information, and created new forms of *oral storytelling, such as radio and television news, personal confessions on call-in talk shows, and real-time *narration through cell phones. See ORAL CULTURES AND NARRATIVE.

SECOND-PERSON NARRATION

A story in which the protagonist is referred to by the pronoun *you*. Second-person stories can be homodiegetic (protagonist and *narrator being identical) or heterodiegetic (protagonist and narrator being different). *See* PERSON.

SEMIOTICS

Semiotics (from Greek *semeion* = 'sign') is the study of the production, transmission, reception, interpretation, reaction to, and storage of significations and meanings via signs, regardless of whether the transference of information involves signs in nature (e.g., animals marking their territory); human speech, writing, or non-linguistic sign production; or creative sign use in artistic and scientific work.

Semiotic activity is a prerequisite for maintaining life. It goes on all the time as information processing within the body, and as a reading of the signs in the environment (e.g., the hunter following the tracks of an animal). Animals, as well as humans, have a basic semiotic competence, i.e., they interpret signs in their environment and they communicate with each other by means of signs, often called signals. Humankind, however, is the only species that has developed language and is able to invent an infinite number of sign systems (clothing, road signs, the 'language' of chemistry, etc.). Hence, the scope of semiotics ranges from biosemiotics, the study of the sign behaviour of organisms, plants and animals, to the poetic use of language and to questions of representation (or the lack thereof) in the arts. The scope of semiotics is, of course, wider than that of narrative; nevertheless, *narrative, conceived as the transformation of states of affairs by means of *action, plays a central role within semiotics because signs in general are produced, whether intentionally or unintentionally, in order to determine changes in the environment of sign producer and sign interpreter.

Precursors of modern semiotics

As a science, semiotics comes from antiquity. It had four primary sources. The first is *medicine, e.g., the reading of symptoms (Hippocrates and Galen). This reading consists of a hypothetical inference 'If red spots of a certain kind are present, then the patient has measles'. One concludes from the observation of the symptoms the presence of the disease as a whole, and one interprets the sign as the cause and the illness as the effect, or vice-versa (*see* CAUSALITY). Even today symptomatology is sometimes called semiotics. The roots of semiotics in medicine are important because they point to the fact that semiotics is not restricted to intentionally produced signs created by humans (*see* INTENTIONALITY). The three additional sources of semiotics are divination, *philosophy, and philology and rhetoric (*see* RHETORICAL APPROACHES TO NARRATIVE).

Even though it was later excluded from serious studies, divination, like the reading of medical symptoms, is an effort to interpret signs in order to predict the future. Philosophy's investigations concerning the relationship between the surrounding world, the senses, and the formation of concepts, as well as its exploration of the relations of signs to thought are, in fact, deeply semiotic. Plato's discussion of signs in *Cratylos*, and Aristotle's studies of logic and epistemology are foundational, but problems of a semiotic nature were also studied by the stoics and other philosophical schools in antiquity (*see* ANCIENT THEORIES OF NARRATIVE (WESTERN)).

In the domain of the semiotic study of literature, Aristotle's *Poetics* represents a major landmark. He divides *drama into six elements, which can also be used in the description of other *genres with minor modifications: *plot (*mythos*), *characters (*ethe*), deliberative thought (*dianoia*) (*see* THOUGHT AND CONSCIOUSNESS REPRESENTATION (LITERATURE)), words (*lexis*), *music (*melos*), and the visual (*opsis*) (*see* SPECTACLE; VISUAL NARRATIVITY). He distinguishes different types of plot and proposes a formal definition of story by dividing it into a beginning, middle, and end (*see* NARRATIVE UNITS). He further stresses the importance of the reversal of the *hero's fortune (*peripeteia*) – in tragedy from good to bad, in comedy from bad to good – and of the relation between reversal and recognition (*anagnorisis*; *see* PLOT TYPES). As even this synoptic overview suggests, twentieth-century narratology has been deeply influenced by Aristotle.

Reflections on signification and meaning continued in the late antiquity and in the Middle Ages. In *De doctrina christiana*, Saint Augustine (354–430) makes a distinction between natural ('smoke' as a sign of fire) and conventional signs (the English word 'woman' used to refer to a person of a certain gender and age group, in contrast with the use of the French word 'femme' to refer to the same kind of human being). More generally, scholastic philosophers discussed the nature of representation and debated the respective merits of the doctrines of *realism and nominalism. From the Renaissance to the present, most philosophers have been preoccupied with semiotic problems. Some of the names that stand out in this domain are Locke, Poinsot, Kant, Leibniz, and Cassirer.

Semiotics in the twentieth century

At the turn of the century, one of the foundational works of modern linguistics, Ferdinand de Saussure's *Course in General Linguistics* (published posthumously in 1916 by his students), had a decisive influence on European semiotics. Saussure analysed language as a system of signs, that is to say, as a self-enclosed network of similarities and differences between discrete elements. This conception of language as a system allowed him to study the combination of elements on different levels such as phonology, syntax, and semantics (*see* NARRATIVE SEMANTICS). To Saussure, language was only one, albeit very important, kind of semiotic system among others, and he defined the future science of semiotics (or semiology, as he called it) as the study of the life of signs in society. Given Saussure's awareness of the multiplicity and diversity of sign systems, it is ironic that linguistics was later regarded by his structuralist disciples as a model science for the study of signs (*see* LINGUISTIC APPROACHES TO NARRATIVE; STRUCTURALIST NARRATOLOGY).

At about the same time, the American philosopher, mathematician, and logician C. S. Peirce wrote important studies on signs and meaning. For Peirce, the subject-matter of semiotics is 'semiosis', the production, transmission, and interpretation of signs. And while Saussure focused on the internal analysis of semiotic systems, Peirce focused on the use of signs, on their *reference to objects, and on the different modes of the representation of the object by the sign. He distinguishes 'iconic' signs, based on a relation of similarity, 'indexical' signs, based on contiguity or causality (*see* DEIXIS), and 'symbolic' signs, based on convention. Most signs, however, have iconic, indexical, and also symbolic features. Whereas Saussure conceives the sign as a dyadic relation between signifier and signified (a view that excludes the referent), Peirce understands signification as a triadic relation between sign-vehicle, object and 'interpretant'. He defines this latter term as the interpretation of the sign through a feeling, an effort or action, a habitual reaction, or another sign.

Twentieth-century semiotics of literature began with Russian Formalism in a period that extended from 1915 to about 1932 (*see* FORMALISM). The most prominent members of this school include Jakobson, Vinokur, Bogatyrev, Shklovskii, Tynianov, Eikhenbaum, and Tomashevskii. Russian Formalism attacked the major forms of nineteenth-century positivist scholarship, such as *historicism, biographism, and psychologism. At the same time it promoted the *intrinsic study of poetic form*, assuming that the true subject-matter of literary studies was the analysis of the poetic and rhetorical devices that make literature different from other discourses. Though the Formalists were mainly concerned with poetry, verse, and imagery, one work of this school made a pathbreaking contribution to narratology. In *Morphology of the Folktale* (1968 [1928]), Vladimir Propp analysed a hundred Russian folktales, abstracting from them 31 'functions', i.e., minimal plot units related to the hero and other characters, such as villainy, fight, victory, flight, marriage, etc. Propp showed that although individual tales may leave out some of the functions, all tales share a number of functions and retain their sequential order (*see* DRAMATIC SITUATIONS; FUNCTION (PROPP)).

In the mid twenties, important semiotic work was accomplished by a group known as the *Prague Linguistic Circle*. Founded in 1926 by Mathesius and Jakobson, the Prague circle included among its members Mukařovský, Trubetskoi, Bogatyrev, Wellek, and Vodička. It was dissolved by the Communist regime in 1948, but reopened in 1990. Foregrounding the communicative process, Prague Structuralism views the text as plurifunctional and its aesthetic dimension as one of its many social functions. The distinction between different discourses is conceived as dependent on which elements and structures are foregrounded (*see* FOREGROUNDING). In this perspective, literary history becomes again a major subject of research, and semiotics acquires a diachronic as well as synchronic profile.

Like Russian Formalism, the Anglo-American school of New Criticism, from the 1920s onwards (Eliot, Richards, Brooks, Ransom, Wimsatt, Beardsley, Wellek), was a reaction against positivist and impressionistic criticism. New Criticism concentrated its efforts on the intrinsic study of individual texts, mainly lyric poetry, because it believed in the autonomy of literature. The text was seen as an organic unity created by a balance of opposed forces. Rejecting the belief that poetry communicates an insight that is independent of its poetic form, New Criticism proclaimed paraphrase to be heretical. Although New Criticism did not focus on the study of narrative in particular, Cleanth Brooks's several studies of the narratives of William Faulkner should be mentioned in this context.

The 1950s and 1960s saw the flourishing of French Structuralism and with it an intensification of interest in semiotic models and methods. Structuralist theory combined influences from Saussure, Russian Formalism, Prague Structuralism, Danish Glossematics, *phenomenology, Marxism (*see* MARXIST APPROACHES TO NARRATIVE), and *psychoanalysis. Within anthropology, Lévi-Strauss studied the myths of South American Indians as systems of oppositions, transformations, and mediations (*see* ETHNOGRAPHIC APPROACHES TO NARRATIVE; MYTH: THEORETICAL APPROACHES), and thus he contributed much to narratology. Althusser studied Marx from a structuralist point of view, and Lacan used insights from structuralist linguistics, but also from Hegel, in his version of psychoanalysis. French Structuralism, which explicitly acknowledged that it belonged to semiotics, also made strong contributions to the study of literature, and especially to the study of narrative, through the work of Barthes, Greimas, Todorov, and Genette.

Two Greimasian models of narrative structure

Greimas attempted to revise and simplify Propp's functions. His best-known contributions to narrative studies are inspired by his study of Propp, namely, the notion of the semiotic square, and the *actant model. According to Greimas, it is fruitful to distinguish three textual levels. Level one is the level of semantic deep structure and its basic oppositions and combinations. Level two is the level of surface structures, of agents and actions. These two levels are called the semio-narrative structures. The third level consists of discursive structures, that is, of elements such as *space, *time, and characters, as well as imagery. The semiotic square belongs to semantic deep structure and represents basic semantic elements arranged

by contrary and contradictory oppositions:

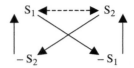

S_1 may be 'femininity' and S_2, its contrary opposition, 'masculinity'. The specification of the contradictory oppositions, $-S_1$ and $-S_2$ (i.e., S_1 and S_2 negated) is open for interpretation. S negated is everything that is not S, and it thus needs specification in concrete analyses. As this model suggests, if the contradictory oppositions are given a sensible interpretation, this allows the interpreter to grasp basic oppositions and their transformations within the narrative text (*see* NARRATIVE TRANSFORMATION). The following example by Greimas should give the reader an idea of how to use the model:

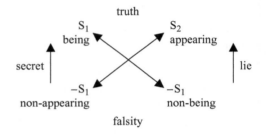

truth = being + appearing

falsity = non-appearing + non-being

secret = being + non-appearing

lie = appearing + non-being

The above investment of the square may be illustrated on the level of action by a traditional story of an incognito prince clad as peasant (i.e., secret = being + non-appearing) who kills a monster and cuts its head off to free the princess. The princess recognises him as her saviour, they talk, but he falls asleep from his wounds. An evil knight steals the monster's head and forces the princess to follow him to her father, the king. Although the princess protests, the king is at the point of giving her to him in marriage because of his proof that he has killed the monster (i.e., lie = appearing + non-being). However, the prince recovers and he also claims the bride. Because he can show the tongue from the monster's head, his story is accepted (i.e., truth = being + appearing), while the evil knight's story is revealed as a fraud (i.e., lie = non-being + appearing). The knight is executed, and the prince is accepted as son-in-law, but not until it is revealed that he is not a peasant, but a prince (i.e., from secret = being + non-appearing to true identity = being + appearing).

Finally, the square may be used to illustrate Aristotle's idea of *peripeteia*. In most cases, but not always, tragedy will represent the transformation of a state of happiness into one of unhappiness through destructive action (e.g., King Lear divides his kingdom and gives it to his daughters), while the action of comedy normally evolves in the other direction (e.g., the beautiful and virtuous slave girl loved unhappily by the young upper-class lover whose father forbids such marriage is really part of a rich family, having been abducted in infancy):

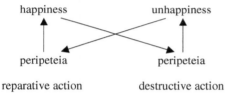

happiness   unhappiness

peripeteia   peripeteia

reparative action   destructive action

Greimas's other well-known contribution to the semiotics of narrative is the actant model:

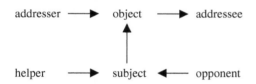

addresser ⟶ object ⟶ addressee

helper ⟶ subject ⟵ opponent

This model, created to analyse *folktales, is useful because it gives a static representation of the tale's main *conflicts and transformations: The upper axis is called axis of communication because an object is transferred from addresser to addressee (e.g., the king gives the princess to the soldier). The axis between subject and object is the axis of *desire, or fear (e.g., the soldier desires the princess). The lower axis is called the axis of conflict. The opponent, who may be (a part of) the addresser, or may act on his behalf, fights the subject who is assisted by the helper whose powers or magical objects eventually make the subject victorious.

Other recent trends

Structuralism's ambition was, in the words of the Danish linguist Louis Hjelmslev, to find the system behind the process, both with regard to individual texts and with regard to genres and discourses. From the 1970s onward French structuralism was challenged by the so-called poststructuralism, associated with theorists such as the later Barthes, Derrida, Foucault, and Kristeva (*see* POSTSTRUC-TURALIST APPROACHES TO NARRATIVE). These scholars were opposed to what they considered the formal and 'closed' nature of the structuralist project. They were more interested in following the unpredictable play of the signifiers in the production of meaning. Together structuralism and poststructuralism covers a considerable part of the general semiotic enterprise, i.e., study of the production and reception of signs. Unfortunately, there was little cooperation and no synthesis.

The Moscow-Tartu school of semiotics (Lotman, Ivanov, Segal, Revzin, Toporov, and others) attempted to strike a balance between the study of codes and the study of the signifying process. The school was founded in 1964 in Tartu, Estonia. This school builds on the work of Russian Formalism and Prague structuralism, but also on French structuralism, cybernetics, and system theory. Language is the primary modelling system on which other systems such as literature, religion, and *folklore, called secondary modelling systems, are founded. According to Lotman, the poetic text communicates information that rests on a multiplicity of *codes and interrelationships of elements on different levels. Lotman views the artistic text as the setting into motion of a constellation of linguistic codes. But texts must also be understood in their cultural and historical contexts. Culture is understood as a large and dynamic network of sign systems, but the relations among the different subsystems are always evolving, and their stability is always threatened. There are, furthermore, significant variations in the relative stability and coherence of different cultures and subcultures. These variations depend on, among other things, whether cultures are oriented toward codes or toward texts, and whether they turn toward myth or toward *science.

Saussurian linguistics dominated twentieth-century European semiotics until the sixties. At this time, the other major figure in contemporary semiotics, C. S. Peirce, started to play a more important role for semiotics, for instance in the work of Umberto Eco. The appeal of Peirce's theory of signs is due to its dynamism, generality, and to the fact that the object of the sign is included in the attempt to explain the processes of signification. According to its advocates, Peircean semiotics overcomes the limitations of French structuralism by complementing its synchronic emphasis with a diachronic emphasis. Peircean semiotics is mostly focused on general questions concerning sign production and sign interpretation. However, Johansen (2002) discusses the relevance for the study of literature and the arts of Peirce's division of signs into (1) qualisigns, sinsigns and legisigns, (2) iconic, indexical, and symbolic signs; and (3) rhemes (propositional functions), dicents (propositions), and arguments. This last division may prove particularly fruitful for research on narrative.

Since the publication of work by Lakoff and Johnson (1980, 1999) and Fauconnier and Turner (2002), cognitive semantics has become a major force in the study of language and literature. Cognitive semantics sees itself as a part of cognitive science in general, i.e., of the interdisciplinary field created by the collaboration between branches of psychology, neuroscience, computer science, philosophy, linguistics, and *Artificial Intelligence (cf. Ryan 1991) (see BIOLOGICAL FOUNDATIONS OF NARRATIVE; COGNITIVE NARRATOLOGY; COMPUTATIONAL APPROACHES TO NARRATIVE). Cognitive semantics has, however, so much in common with structuralist approaches to the study of meaning (historically, the work of Jakobson provides a link) that it certainly belongs to the family of sign studies that make up semiotics. The axiom of cognitive semantics is that our mind is embodied. Hence, our understanding is both shaped and mediated by basic physical experiences. This postulate is important to the study of signification in two ways. First, since our experiences involve movements, contact/avoidance of contact, and changes, narratives, or proto-narratives, are involved in our simplest performances. The analysis of scripts, e.g., the analysis of visiting a restaurant given by Abelson and Schank (1977), may be mentioned as a cognitive approach to analysing actions and narrative. Analogously, scripts such as 'eating at a restaurant' are interaction patterns that facilitate our daily life, and provide a basis for analysing both actions and their representation in literary and other narratives (Abelson and Schank 1977; see SCRIPTS AND SCHEMATA). Furthermore, mental phenomena and abstract objects are comprehended by drawing analogies inspired by our embodied experiences, this is to say, by creating *metaphors. This means that the study of narrative and metaphor are central to cognitive semantics.

References and further reading

Abelson, Robert P., and Roger C. Schank (1977) *Scripts, Plans, Goals and Understanding: An Inquiry into Human Knowledge Structures*, Hillsdale, NJ: Lawrence Erlbaum.

Aristotle (1927 [ca. 330 BCE]) *The Poetics*, trans. W. Hamilton Fife, Cambridge, Mass.: Harvard University Press.

Augustine (1952 [397–426 CE]) *On Christian Doctrine*, trans. J. F. Shaw, in *Augustine: Great Books of the Western World*, vol. 18., ed. Robert Maynard, Chicago: William Benton.

Fauconnier, Gilles, and Mark Turner (2002) *The Way We Think*, New York: Basic Books.

Greimas, Algirdas Julien (1983 [1966]) *Structural Semantics*, trans. Danielle McDowell, Ronald Schleifer, and Alan Velie, Lincoln: University of Nebraska Press.

—— (1987 [1970]) *On Meaning: Selected Writings in Semiotic Theory*, trans. Paul J. Perron and Frank H. Collins, Minneapolis: University of Minnesota Press.

Jakobson, Roman (1960) 'Linguistics and Poetics', in Thomas A. Sebeok (ed.) *Style in Language*, Cambridge, Mass.: MIT Press.

Jameson, Fredric (1981) *The Political Unconscious: Narrative as a Socially Symbolic Act*, London: Methuen.

Johansen, Jørgen Dines (2002) *Literary Discourse: A Semiotic-Pragmatic Approach to Literature*, Toronto: University of Toronto Press.

Lakoff, George (1987) *Women, Fire, and Dangerous Things: What Categories Reveal about the Mind*, Chicago: University of Chicago Press.

—— (1999) *Philosophy in the Flesh*, New York: Basic Books.

——, and Mark Johnson (1980) *Metaphors We Live By*, Chicago: University of Chicago Press.

Lemon, Lee T., and Marion J. Reis (eds) (1965) *Russian Formalist Criticism*, Lincoln: University of Nebraska Press.

Lévi-Strauss, Claude (1963 [1958]) *Structural Anthropology*, trans. Claire Jacobson and Brooke Grundfest Schoepf, New York: Basic Books.

Lotman, Iurii, and Boris Uspenskii (1978 [1971]) 'On the Semiotic Mechanism of Culture', *New Literary History*, 9.2, 211–31.

Peirce, Charles Sanders (1931–1958) *Collected Papers of Charles Sanders Peirce*, 8 vols., eds. Charles Hartshorne, Paul Weiss, and A. W. Burks, Cambridge, Mass.: Harvard University Press.

Propp, Vladimir (1968 [1928]) *Morphology of the Folktale*, trans. Laurence Scott, revised by Louis A. Wagner, Austin: University of Texas Press.

Ryan, Marie-Laure (1991) *Possible Worlds, Artificial Intelligence and Narrative Theory*, Bloomington: Indiana University Press.

JØRGEN DINES JOHANSEN

SERIAL FORM

The origins of the serial form lie in the nineteenth-century, when the works of *authors such as Charles Dickens and George Eliot were published serially in periodicals prior to being published as *novels. Nowadays the serial form is perhaps most often associated with *television although it also occurs in a range of *media including novels, *radio, comic books, newspaper comic strips, cinema (in *film series such as *The Matrix* and *The Lord of the Rings*), and *computer games (*see* COMICS AND GRAPHIC NOVELS).

Serial form refers to the segmentation of a narrative into instalments that are released sequentially with, usually, a time lapse between the release of one instalment and the next. Unlike episodic series, in which each episode is self-contained and storylines do not continue across episodes, each instalment of a serial is part of a continuing narrative that is not concluded until the end of the series. Some long-running serial forms, such as *soap opera, maintain open-ended narratives indefinitely and some storylines remain unresolved even when the serial itself comes to an end (*see* CLOSURE).

Serials have distinctive formats in which narrative works at the levels both of individual instalments and of the serial as a whole. Because serials must maintain the interest of readers across hiatuses, they prioritise enigma over resolution until the concluding instalment. The narrative progresses through a succession of complications, *plot twists, concealments, and false leads, and each instalment except the final one concludes with a cliffhanger event (*see* PLOT TYPES). The hiatuses between instalments also necessitate modes of repetition to remind readers of where the previous instalment left the story. In television serials, this is done in one of two ways: each episode may begin with a pre-titles sequence that reiterates the latest climactic story *events; or, as happens in soap operas, *characters repeatedly discuss events that have occurred in the previous episode.

With the exception of soap operas, long-running serial forms usually move between and/or combine the narrative forms of the serial with those of the episodic series, in which each episode is self-contained and its storyline is resolved. *The X-Files* consists of both stand-alone episodes and episodes that form part of a narrative that continues across the series as a whole. *ER* episodes weave together multiple storylines, some of which are ongoing and others of which begin and end within a single episode. Film and novel series similarly produce instalments composed of both self-contained and on-going storylines. Such combinations, described by Robin Nelson as 'flex-inarratives', are increasingly superseding both the continuing serial form and the episodic series.

SEE ALSO: audience; reception theory

References and further reading
Eco, Umberto (1990) *The Limits of Interpretation*, Bloomington: Indiana University Press.
Feuer, Jane (1986) 'Narrative Form in American Network Television', in Colin McCabe (ed.) *High Theory/Low Culture: Analysing Popular Television and Film*, Manchester: Manchester University Press.
Kozloff, Sarah (1994) 'Narrative Theory and Television', in Robert C. Allen (ed.) *Channels of Discourse, Reassembled*, London: Routledge.
Nelson, Robin (1997) *TV Drama in Transition: Forms, Values and Cultural Change*, Basingstoke: Macmillan.

SARA GWENLLIAN JONES

SERMON

Historically the sermon has been viewed as a type of religious discourse, usually taking place in the setting of communal worship. This broad definition has been qualified (there are, for example, exegetical, hortatory, doctrinal, and proselytising sermons), but in general the sermon has typically taken the form of a structured argument or *exposition (*see* NARRATIVE AS ARGUMENT). Narrative elements, however, have long been a feature of the inventional repertoire of the preachers delivering sermons. For instance, in Christian sermons stories have appeared chiefly either as narrated examples from scripture or as *anecdotal illustrations from life or history – normally set within the sermon's overall argument.

Since the 1970s, under the influence of contemporary narrative theory and because of disappointment with overly rationalistic, propositional sermons (typically numbered 'points' with subheadings plus application), North American Christian homiletics (i.e., the study of preaching) has sought to develop narrative or story sermon models that touch not only on narrative's role in invention, but also on the way narrative can shape rhetorical arrangement (*see* RHETORICAL APPROACHES TO NARRATIVE). Thus, sermons can range from primarily narrated elaborations of a single story from the scriptures ('Biblical storytelling-' or 'Biblical narrative-preaching'), to a juxtaposition of two or more longer stories which may be either Biblical or contemporary (the more generic 'story-' or 'narrative-preaching'), to narrative models which 'plot' the sequence of both narrative and non-narrative sermon elements in *time (in accordance with a logic of *conflict, complication, reversal, and denouement) rather than 'constructing' a sermon propositionally in *space (as in a numbered outline; *see* PLOT). Still other theoreticians, though not advocating narrative/story sermons *per se*, use narrative theory to explore structural and rhetorical relations between Biblical texts and sermons.

Some students of preaching, however, recognise that the rise of these sermon models is not altogether novel. Henry Mitchell, for example, argues that many of these sermon *genres have been a staple of African-American preaching for some time – and may actually have some of their roots in pre-Christian West African religious practices. Indeed, what these 'new' models of sermons bear witness to is this: much of the appeal of narrative for preaching derives not just from the narrative form of so many beloved scripture texts, but also from what Stephen Crites has called 'the narrative quality of experience' itself.

SEE ALSO: Biblical narrative; narrative structure; theology and narrative

References and further reading

Buttrick, David (1987) *Homiletic: Moves and Structures*, Philadelphia: Fortress Press.
Campbell, Charles (1997) *Preaching Jesus: New Directions for Homiletics in Hans Frei's Postliberal Theology*, Grand Rapids: Eerdmans Publishing Co.
Crites, Stephen (1971) 'The Narrative Quality of Experience', *Journal of the American Academy of Religion*, 39, 291–311.
Long, Thomas (1989) *Preaching and the Literary Forms of the Bible*, Philadelphia: Fortress Press.
Lowry, Eugene L. (2001) *The Homiletical Plot: The Sermon as Narrative Art Form*, Louisville: Westminster John Knox Press.
Mitchell, Henry (1990) *Black Preaching: The Recovery of a Powerful Art*, Nashville: Abingdon Press.
Steimle, Edmund A., Morris J. Niedenthal, and Charles L. Rice (1980) *Preaching the Story*, Philadelphia: Fortress Press.

DAVID SCHNASA JACOBSEN

SHORT STORY

The ancestor of the short story is the verbal or pictorial representation of a significant *event (*see* PICTORIAL NARRATIVITY). For making the account memorable, for detaching it from facts and housing it in the imagination, certain strategies developed: focus on a single, paradigmatic event or pattern of events; primacy of one human (or substitute-human) agent (*see* AGENCY; CHARACTER); and a modulated tension, at every point, between suspended outcome and imminent *closure (*see* SUSPENSE AND SURPRISE). These remain the defining characteristics of a type of fictional prose narrative longer than the *anecdote and shorter than the *novella. Ian Reid offers a useful taxonomy of short narrative forms that prefigure or parallel the short story proper (*see* SIMPLE FORMS): e.g., *fables, *parables, *folktales, *ballads, and detachable segments of sagas, *epics, and compendia like the Bible (*see* BIBLICAL NARRATIVE) and the *Satyricon*.

Some histories of the *genre start with the framed tales of Giovanni Boccaccio's *The Decameron* (c.1350) (*see* FRAMED NARRATIVE), or with the stylised vernacular stories of mid-sixteenth century China (*see* CHINESE NARRATIVE). However, the term 'short story' is usually reserved for the short prose genre coming into focus and currency in Europe and America in the early nineteenth-century. Three factors contributed to the rise of this specialised genre: first, the adaptation of Romantic aesthetics to regional material, endowing realistic detail with immanent meaning, as in Nathaniel Hawthorne's 'Young Goodman Brown' (1835); second, the spread of commercial periodicals and 'gift book' anthologies, providing a renewable market for consumable narratives; and third, the advocacy and example of Washington Irving and, especially, Edgar Allan Poe. In practice and in theory, Poe argued that the short prose tale must be conceived in terms of a 'single effect', such as the terror generated in 'The Fall of the House of Usher' (1839). This effect must be achieved with the utmost economy and concentration of means, and must be evoked, with the help of the reader's imagination, within the span of a 'single sitting'. Poe elevated the status of the short story as an art form. His credo of making every word count was widely accepted, notably by two late nineteenth-century realists, Guy de Maupassant, who brought a sharply ironic focus to the genre (*see* IRONY), and Anton Chekhov, who focused attention on telling details.

Practitioners have had a prominent role in shaping the discourse of short story criticism in English. During the first two thirds of the twentieth century, three were especially important. James Joyce highlighted the *epiphany, an interior moment of insight or understanding toward which the entire story moved, as illustrated in 'The Dead' (1914). Ernest Hemingway, in stories like *Indian Camp* (1925), used highly charged images and actions to suggest an emotional subtext and an unstated narrative that the reader must infer, as one gauges the iceberg from its visible tip (*see* EMOTION AND NARRATIVE). And Frank O'Connor argued that the short story historically flourishes among 'submerged populations' in unsettled social climates (e.g., the USA, Ireland, Russia, and South America), because it is suited to express the subjective experience of marginalised individuals such as Akaky Akakievich in Nikolai Gogol's 'The Overcoat' (1842). Taken together, these theories shaped the Modernist view of the short story as a sojourn within the extraordinary consciousness of an ordinary character, unfolding through the cumulative effect of meaningful imagery rather than through the linear logic of goal-directed *action, and leading to a deepening of perception rather than to a resolution of problems (*see* MODERNIST NARRATIVE; THOUGHT AND CONSCIOUSNESS REPRESENTATION (LITERATURE)).

In the last third of the twentieth century, theories of the short story revisited Poe's distinction between the tale and the *novel, debating whether it was a difference of kind, as he had insisted, or of degree, as might be inferred, for example, from the traits it shared with the Impressionist novel. Structuralist approaches to genre, especially those of the Russian Formalists Boris Eikhenbaum and Vladimir Propp, the German taxonomist Helmut Bonheim, and the American text-grammarian Gerald Prince, suggested that the short story could be reduced to a predictable set of slots or a minimal story kernel (*see* FORMALISM; MINIMAL NARRATIVE; STRUCTURALIST NARRATOLOGY). *Reader-response theories of the short story noted the effects of brevity on strategies of comprehension. Imminent closure allowed for the balancing of linear sequence with spatial design, for the reliance on networked imagery, and for the structuring of meaning even in *antinarrative experiments like Jorge Luis Borges's 'The Garden of Forking Paths' (1942) or Robert Coover's 'The Babysitter' (1969). *Postmodern short stories could suppress or deny an articulated *plot, while defining anew what was gained or lost in a critical moment.

Beginning around the 1980s, short fiction theory branched again. On the one hand, it responded to *cultural studies. Both within and outside of the academy, stories functioned as socially derived artefacts, easily sampled by nationality, class, ethnicity, or other categories. The spare, working-class fiction of Raymond Carver was an example, as were the cross-cultural stories of Chinua Achebe or Sandra Cisneros. On the other hand, short-story theory overlapped with psychology (*see* PSYCHOLOGICAL APPROACHES TO NARRATIVE). New models emerged from text-processing studies, *story grammars, theories of goal-outcome plans, and research on *scripts and schemata. According to some researchers, the most enduring feature of the short story is its link with a basic scenario: engagement with the environment, interaction or *conflict, and a helpful or harmful result. At the beginning of the twenty-first century, at the interface of cognitive and literary theory, the short story has been studied, for example, as a structured sequence of affects or as a series of shorter, putative stories embedded in the narrative (*see* EMBEDDING).

Regardless of approach, theorists of the short story must take into account the small scale (readable between meals), cognitive unity (single or concentrated effect), and communal significance that have authorised, shaped, and preserved the genre of the short story from its ancient precursors to its modern-day variants around the world.

References and further reading

Brewer, William F., and E. H. Lichtenstein (1982) 'Stories Are to Entertain: A Structural-Affect Theory of Stories', *Journal of Pragmatics*, 6, 473–86.

Hanson, Clare (1985) *Short Stories and Short Fictions, 1880–1980*, London: Macmillan.

Lohafer, Susan (2003) *Reading for Storyness*, Baltimore: Johns Hopkins University Press.

May, Charles E. (ed.) (1994) *The New Short Story Theories*, Athens: Ohio University Press.

O'Connor, Frank (1985 [1963]) *The Lonely Voice: A Study of the Short Story*, New York: Harper and Row.

Reid, Ian (1977) *The Short Story*, London: Methuen.

SUSAN LOHAFER

SHOT

A shot is a single continuous image in a *film. Though it is possible to film a scene in one shot, most mainstream films form scenes by cutting together several shots (establishing shots, close-ups; *see* SCENE (CINEMATIC)). In the 1920s, Soviet *montage filmmaker Pudovkin compared the shot to a word and argued that the shot had no significance until it was combined with other shots in editing. Later, Bazin criticised montage techniques and promoted the realist virtues of deep-focus cinematography (*see* REALISM, THEORIES OF). Critics began to appreciate *mise-en-scène* (staging, set design) and cinematography (camera movement, framing) as means of creating significance within a shot. Drawing on *semiotics, Metz shifted the focus back to the question of how shots are combined. He argued that the shot was the minimum unit of cinematic grammar, though he suggested that the shot was more like a statement than a word (*see* STORY GRAMMARS). Bordwell criticised Metz by pointing out that narrative *action, *time, and *point of view can be manipulated within a shot. A shot can consequently cover several distinct scenes and *narrative units.

References and further reading

Bazin, André (1967) *What Is Cinema?*, Vol. 1, trans. Hugh Gray, Berkeley: University of California Press.

Bordwell, David (2004) 'NeoStructuralist Narratology and the Functions of Filmic Story-telling', in Marie-Laure Ryan (ed.) *Narrative Across Media: The Languages of Story-telling*, Lincoln: University of Nebraska Press.

Metz, Christian (1991 [1968]) *Film Language*, trans. Michael Taylor, Chicago: University of Chicago Press.

Pudovkin, Vsevolod (1949 [1928]) *Film Technique and Film Acting*, trans. Ivor Montagu, New York: Bonanza Books.

PATRICK KEATING

SHOWING VS. TELLING

The terms showing and telling refer to a difference in presentation: showing is a relatively unmediated enactment or dramatisation of events, while telling is a mediated report on them (*see* MEDIACY). The distinction is a modern recasting of the opposition, going back to Plato, between *mimesis (or imitation) and *diegesis (or *narration). In its modern form, it developed in the late 19th and early 20th centuries, in the wake of Henry James and especially Percy Lubbock. Buried beneath this apparently straightforward duality lies a series of parallel distinctions, including the distinctions between scene and panorama (Lubbock 1947 [1921]), between scene and summary (*see* SUMMARY AND SCENE), between perspectivism and aperspectivism (Stanzel 1984 [1979]), between dramatisation and *description, and between objectivity and partiality. It is also possible to frame the distinction in terms of self-consciousness: a reflector-character who is unaware of the narrative act may serve as a medium for showing; but telling requires a teller who is aware of the act he or she is performing (Stanzel 1984 [1979]: 147), even if he or she is naive about its effects. Alternatively, the distinction can be framed in terms of the direction of the implied reader's attention: according to Lubbock, showing points the reader toward the story while telling points the reader toward the storyteller (*see* READER CONSTRUCTS). Since showing and telling can be also understood in terms of inference and statement (Friedman 1955), it is possible to recast the distinction yet again in terms of the activities required of the *audience: telling, at least when it is reliable, demands less complicated judgements on the reader's part (*see* RELIABILITY).

Lubbock is primarily responsible for converting this pair of descriptive terms into an evaluative hierarchy. Using Henry James's fiction (especially the late novels) as his touchstone, he promoted showing (especially using the expedient of reflector-characters) as the superior mode (*see* FOCALIZATION). This hierarchical view was generally supported by the New Critics. Wayne Booth, however, starting from the assumption that different artistic purposes require different rhetorical techniques, argued that it was futile to see the difference as a difference in value, since each manner of presentation has its own particular rhetorical strengths (*see* NARRATIVE TECHNIQUES; RHETORICAL APPROACHES TO NARRATIVE). Genette attacked the hierarchy more radically, erasing the distinction by pointing out that narrative is by its very nature always telling, and that in narrative, showing is therefore always an illusion. Especially in its hierarchical form, the showing/telling distinction remains more vigorous today in handbooks for creative writers than in works of narrative theory.

SEE ALSO: mode

References and further reading

Booth, Wayne C. (1961) *The Rhetoric of Fiction*, Chicago: University of Chicago Press.
Friedman, Norman (1955) 'Point of View in Fiction: The Development of a Critical Concept', *PMLA*, 70, 1160–84.
Genette, Gérard (1980) *Narrative Discourse: An Essay in Method*, trans. Jane E. Lewin, Ithaca: Cornell University Press.
Lubbock, Percy (1947 [1921]) *The Craft of Fiction*, New York: Peter Smith.
Stanzel, Franz Karl (1984 [1979]) *A Theory of Narrative*, trans. Charlotte Goedsche, Cambridge: Cambridge University Press.

PETER J. RABINOWITZ

SIMPLE FORMS

The term 'simple forms' translates the title of the book *Einfache Formen* by André Jolles (1930), a work which has not been published in English. Since the forms in question are culture-specific discourse frames, some of them have no exact English equivalent. Jolles conceives simple forms as forms that develop spontaneously in ordinary communicative contexts without conscious poetic crafting. Referring to Hamann, Herder, and especially Jakob Grimm's concept of 'nature poetry', he sets as his goal the description of the evolution from language to literature by exploring those forms that have been neglected by the aesthetic and historical branches of 'literary science' (*Literaturwissenschaft*) and left to other disciplines, such as *folklore (Volkskunde)*, which at the time of his writing were not considered worthy of inclusion in literary studies.

Jolles's catalogue of simple forms comprises both canonical narrative *genres, and forms of questionable or lesser *narrativity. The following list limits itself to the strongly narrative forms, leaving out riddle, proverb, and *Kasus*, a form derived from legal cases.

(1) *Legende* (*legend): the term first occurs in the mid-thirteenth century, designating the lives of the saints. The legend is not interested in the historical representation of a life but only in its value as a model of Christian life (*see* ALLEGORY; DIDACTIC NARRATIVE; LIFE STORY). This value is measured by the power of the saint to perform miracles. Today, only record-breaking athletes become the subjects of legends.

(2) Contrasting with *Legende* (literally, 'to be read'), *Sage* refers to an oral tradition addressing significant events, persons, or places, as well as themes pertaining to family, tribe, and blood relationships (*see* ORAL CULTURES AND NARRATIVE). As 'saga' it may assume the English meaning of heroic *epic (*see* HERO).

(3) *Mythe* (myth) is related to oracle in that it tells a *truth (*Wahrsagung*) endowed with a predictive force. It provides an answer to a question that humans ask about the world surrounding them. According to Jolles, myth contrasts with knowledge (*Erkenntnis*), as 'mythos' contrasts with 'logos' (*see* MYTH: THEORETICAL APPROACHES).

(4) *Memorabile* (memorability, a Latin adaptation of the Greek *apomnemoneuma*) is a form used by Antisthenes to describe Socrates' personality as he remembered him in specific situations. *Apomnemoneuma* also describes the method used by the evangelists to remember Jesus in the context of contemporary events. The trademark of *Memorabile* is the use of concrete details to guarantee the authenticity of reported facts (*see* REALITY EFFECT).

(5) *Märchen* (*fairy tale): following Jakob Grimm, Jolles contrasts the spontaneous simple form of the fairy tale with the elaborate art form of the *novella. The appeal of the fairy tale resides in its reliance on a 'naive moral' that reflects the way we feel the real world should be. Denying the tragic character of life, and free to create its own laws, the fairy tale represents the supernatural in a way that appears, paradoxically, totally natural (*see* FANTASTIC, THE).

(6) The *Witz* (*joke) is a form that systematically subverts the restrictions of language, logic, and ethics in order to serve two functions: (1) to show inadequacies in reasoning by repeating the same element but reversing its value (plus becoming minus and vice versa); and (2) to free the mind from inhibitions, thereby creating a liberating

experience. In the world of the comical, the dissolution of rules becomes a constructive force.

Jolles regarded his set of simple forms as a complete system which established a middle ground between language and literary art. His exploration of these forms proved to be an important stepping-stone toward the current extension of narrative studies beyond literature.

SEE ALSO: text-type approach to narrative

References and further reading

Jolles, André (1972 [1930]) *Einfache Formen: Legende, Sage, Mythe, Rätsel, Spruch, Kasus, Memorabile, Märchen, Witz*, Tübingen: Niemeyer.
Koch, Walter A. (ed.) (1994) *Simple Forms: An Encyclopedia of Simple Text-Types in Lore and Literature*, Bochum: Brockmeyer.

SIGRID MAYER

SIMULATION AND NARRATIVE

Sean Cubitt defines *simulation* as a copy without a source, an imitation that has lost its original (Cubitt 2001: 46). This definition originates in Plato's strong feeling of repugnance toward 'imitative poetry' and the painter's art, of which he said 'this is that weakness of the human mind on which the art of conjuring and of deceiving by light and shadow and other ingenious devices imposes, having an effect on us like magic' (*The Republic*, Book X). Simulation theory was born of Plato's complaint, inspiring Nietzsche to describe our understanding of reality as a *fable, as something we can never hope to grasp, and Baudrillard to postulate a (political) philosophy of simulation which is the cornerstone of postmodernism (*see* POSTMODERN NARRATIVE). However, Baudrillard's theory focuses on static representations and neglects the notion of process (Ryan 2001: 62–63).

Simulators are often mechanisms (usually run by computers) that are designed to represent a simplified version of the operations of a complex system, such as an aircraft, and were initially used primarily for training. Plato saw *narrative itself as an abhorrent simulation, but today the concepts of simulation and narrative are often located at opposing ends of the spectrum. This opposition is most evident in the nascent field of computer game theory (*see* COMPUTER GAMES AND NARRATIVE).

In the 1980s and 90s, academic discussions of *interactive fiction focused on the formal principles that govern hypertext and computer games with hypertext structures. The newer ludology approach, promoted by Espen Aarseth (among others), focuses on the kinds of computer games mostly ignored by narratological theorists, the games that remediate not just movies or television shows, but all games, including games of chance, puzzles, and what have come to be known as simulation games (*see* NARRATIVE, GAMES, AND PLAY; REMEDIATION). Examples include *puzzle* games such as *Tetris* and *Pac-Man*, in which the logic exercises are the end in themselves and not the means to an end (as they are in more narratively based adventure or role-playing games), and genuine *simulation games* such as *Microsoft's Flight Simulator, Warcraft, SimCity, Civilization*, and *Age of Empires*.

Chris Crawford, designer of such wargames as *Eastern Time* (1941), *Tanktics* (1978), and *Excalibur* (1983), wrote *The Art of Computer Game Design* (1983), which included a taxonomy of computer game *genres which is based on game structure. Crawford drew a sharp distinction between simulations and games. Originally, the word *simulation* only applied to 'serious attempts to accurately represent a real phenomenon in another, more malleable form' (Crawford 1984: 8) for purposes such as training. A game is a simplified and often stylised representation of a phenomenon, designed to entertain.

At first the distinction Crawford drew between simulations and games was more or less maintained by referring to games that were abstracted versions of simulations. Simulation games started out as fly and drive simulators designed to train military personnel. In fact, the military and the gaming industry often join forces now to design training simulators that then get turned into games. Microsoft's *Flight Simulator* (1995) is probably the best known game in the fly or drive simulation genre. The term 'simulation' has also come to include strategy wargames that mimic historic battles, such as *American Civil War: From Sumter to Appomattox* (1996) and many others. Simulations also include sports games, such as racing games that allow you to adjust tire pressure, spoiler drag, etc., and *Soccer Manager* (1992), where you make the same decisions a soccer manager would make, right down to the catering. In other words, just about anything can be simulated for a simulation game, even a civil process like a court investigation.

When Will Wright created *SimCity* (1989), possibly the first game to be referred to in the industry as a *sim* (short for *simulation game*), he was inspired by board wargames with hex grids such as *Panzer Blitz*, *Global War*, and *Sniper*, which are strategy games. However, the rules for these games were so elaborate that it was difficult, if not impossible, for a player to keep a mental model of the entire simulation game in his or her head (*see* SITUATION MODEL).

Players of Wright's computer simulation games such as *The Sims* are aided in this modelling process by a simple *metaphor that the designers put forward to help the player get an initial grasp of the game. So *SimCity* is likened to a train set and *The Sims* (2000) to a dollhouse. However, as the player develops a better understanding of the game dynamics, he or she will discover that this initial metaphor is not all that accurate, and that there is a more complex underlying metaphor that can only be grasped as the game is being played – e.g., 'gardening' for *SimCity*.

Crawford refers to mental models as the philosophical core, as well as the *raison d'être*, of the historical game. He argues that every form of historical examination has biases built into it; hence computer games are not evidence in themselves, but they are prisms through which we can look at the evidence. Players also carry mental models in their heads, and those models can change according to circumstances. For example, Microsoft was pressured to remove the player's ability to fly between New York's Twin Towers and even crash into them in *Flight Simulator*, after the Twin Towers were destroyed in just that way by terrorists on 11 September 2001. But during the 1991 war on Iraq players demanded that flight simulator companies sell add-on Iraq war scenario disks to already existing flight simulator games (Dunnigan 1992: 249). Clearly, simulation games are not just about competing against other players, or a computer, at computation (though this describes most puzzle games). Simulation games are also about the mental models of a simulation in the player's head. The player's models and the designer's models can come into conflict with each other. The playing out of these simulation games results in simulation narratives (Ryan 2001: 110–14).

A simulation narrative is a system that produces a story, or a narrative trace, as it runs, as opposed to a text that represents events that have already taken place – really or fictionally (Ryan 2001: 62–65). Such systems have the power of producing many stories because of unreliability built into the system: either as a result of the *Artificial Intelligence built into it, or by being connected to a fluctuating variable in the real world, or because of the unpredictable reactions of other players. Examples of simulation narratives range from *Eliza*, the dialogue system programmed by Joseph Weissbaum in 1966 to simulate a therapy session with a Rogerian therapist, to board wargames, to modern simulation games. Cubitt likewise describes Disney's Main Street, USA, and the town of Celebration (where Disney employees try to live out the Main Street, USA, fantasy) as simulations.

SEE ALSO: digital narrative

References and further reading

Aarseth, Espen J. (1997) *Cybertext: Perspectives on Ergodic Literature*, Baltimore and London: Johns Hopkins University Press.
—— editorials in www.gamestudies.org, especially vols. 1 and 2 (accessed 22 July 2004).
Baudrillard, Jean (1994 [1981]) *Simulacra and Simulation*, trans. Sheila Glaser, Ann Arbor: University of Michigan Press.
Crawford, Chris (1984) *The Art of Computer Game Design*, New York: McGraw Hill.
Cubitt, Sean (2001) *Simulation and Social Theory*, London: Sage.
Dunnigan, James (1992) *The Complete Wargames Handbook: How to Play, Design and Find Them*, San Jose: Quill.
Eskelinen, Markku (2001) 'The Gaming Situation', www.gamestudies.org, 1.1 (accessed 22 July 2004).
Pearce, Celia (2002) 'Sims, Battlebots, Cellular Automata, God and *Go*: A Conversation with Will Wright', www.gamestudies.org, 2.1 (accessed 22 July 2004).
Ryan, Marie-Laure (2001) *Narrative as Virtual Reality: Immersion and Interactivity in Literature and Electronic Media*, Baltimore: Johns Hopkins University Press.

ALISON McMAHAN

SIMULTANEOUS NARRATION

Also referred to as 'real-time' or 'concurrent' *narration, a narrative mode in which the telling coincides with the events told – as in Greek drama teichoscopy (literally, 'telling from the wall'), Coetzee's *Waiting for the Barbarians*, *sports broadcasts, blow-by-blow accounts given during cell-phone conversations, etc. *See* TIME AND NARRATIVE.

SITUATION MODEL

Situation model is a term used by cognitive psychologists to denote mental representations of states of affairs described in texts. The term was introduced by van Dijk and Kintsch (1983) and is similar to the notion of mental models (re)introduced by Johnson-Laird (1983). When we read a story, we combine ideas derived from the text with our background knowledge and experience into a coherent mental representation of the described situation. The construction of a situation model is an iterative process in which the reader continuously updates the representation with each incoming clause.

Situation models are updated along several dimensions: the *time and location (*see* SPACE IN NARRATIVE), the focal entity (entities) of the situation (*see* CHARACTER; EXISTENT), and the causal motivational relations between the current situation and the previous situation(s) (*see* CAUSALITY). Empirical evidence suggests that readers are sensitive to changes on each of these dimensions (Zwaan and Radvansky 1998). Thus, for example, a shift in story time (e.g., as denoted by 'an hour later') leads to a momentary slow-down in reading, presumably because the reader is updating his or her situation model. The same occurs when the story focus shifts from one protagonist to another or when a new goal is introduced. Thus, the reader continuously shifts focus as new *events in the situation are being described.

The human cognitive system can hold only a limited amount of information active in working *memory at any given moment in time. Therefore, it is important which older information is kept in an active state and which is transferred to long-term memory. Various linguistic cues inform the reader what information is important to keep active. An example of a lexical cue is: 'They found this bird in the backyard'. The use of 'this' (rather than 'a') causes readers to expect to hear more about the bird and thus keep it active in memory (Gernsbacher and Shroyer 1989). An example of a syntactic cue is a cleft sentence, such as 'It was Bill who entered the room'. Other information does not require linguistic cues, but is intrinsically important and thus kept active. For example,

compare 'The swimmer saw seaweed when she looked down' to 'The swimmer saw a shark when she looked down'. The reader is far more likely to keep the shark active in memory than he or she is to keep the seaweed active. Thus, several factors influence the updating process as the reader progresses through the story.

Situation models are distinct from mental representations of the text itself, that is, of its exact wording or of the explicitly stated semantic content. Although there is evidence that representations of the text itself are also constructed in memory, these representations are usually short-lived. The reader tends to forget the exact wording very quickly (Kintsch, Welsch, Schmalhofer, and Zimny 1990), except in the case of poetry or song lyrics, where metre, rhyme, rhythm, and melody provide memory cues (Rubin 1995). The reader also tends to forget which information was explicitly stated in the text and which information was inferred (Kintsch *et al.* 1990). In contrast, the situation model is rather resistant to decay. The general consensus is that the construction of a coherent situation model is the modal goal of comprehension.

Recent theories take the notion of situation models one step further. It is not enough simply to assume that readers construct mental representations of the situations being described in narratives because it is not clear why this would be a useful activity to engage in. Reading narratives is best understood as the vicarious experience of the described situation (Barsalou 1999; Duchan, Bruder, and Hewitt 1995; Gerrig 1993; Zwaan 1999). This may seem obvious intuitively. However, empirical evidence is needed to substantiate this claim. It is supported by evidence from several areas of research, most notably cognitive neuroscience and cognitive psychology. Brain imaging experiments have shown that if people are presented with a word denoting a tool, a part of the motor cortex becomes active that overlaps with an area active when the tool is actually being used. Analogously, certain animal words activate the visual cortex (see Martin, Ungerleider, and Haxby 2000 for an overview). This evidence suggests that reading a word is recreating an experience with the referent.

Cognitive reaction-time studies on narrative comprehension show that people behave as if they are in the *storyworld (*see* IMMERSION). Ongoing events are more active in the reader's mind than past events, physically close objects are more active than more distant objects, present object features, such as colours, are more active than absent colours, visible objects are more active than occluded objects, objects in front of the immersed experiencer are more active than objects behind him/her (see Zwaan 2004 for an overview).

All these findings are consistent with one idea. Comprehending a story amounts to a vicarious experience of the described situation. The verbal input activates traces from experience that are used in a mental simulation of the described events. This simulation can be so strong that it interferes with performing actions. Thus, when reading a sentence about someone opening a drawer (which involves moving the hand towards the body), it is relatively difficult to at the same time move your own hand away from your body (Glenberg and Kaschak 2002).

SEE ALSO: cognitive narratology; deixis; mental mapping of narrative; narrative comprehension; psychological approaches to narrative; scripts and schemata; story schemata and causal structure

References and further reading

Barsalou, Lawrence W. (1999) 'Perceptual Symbol Systems', *Behavioral and Brain Sciences*, 22, 577–609.

van Dijk, Teun A., and Walter Kintsch (1983) *Strategies of Discourse Comprehension*, New York: Academic Press.

Duchan, Judith F., Gail A. Bruder, and Lynne E. Hewitt (eds) (1995) *Deixis in Narrative: A Cognitive Science Perspective*, Hillsdale, NJ: Lawrence Erlbaum.

Gerrig, Richard J. (1993) *Experiencing Narrative Worlds*, New Haven, CT: Yale University Press.

Gernsbacher, Morton Ann, and Susan Shroyer (1989) 'The Cataphoric Use of the Indefinite *this* in Spoken Narratives', *Memory & Cognition*, 17, 536–40.

Glenberg, Arthur M., and Michael P. Kaschak (2002) 'Grounding Language in Action', *Psychonomic Bulletin & Review*, 9, 558–65.

Johnson-Laird, Philip N. (1983) *Mental Models: Towards a Cognitive Science of Language, Inference, and Consciousness*, Cambridge, Mass.: Harvard University Press.

Kintsch, Walter, David Welsch, Franz Schmalhofer, and Susan Zimny (1990) 'Sentence Memory: A Theoretical Analysis', *Journal of Memory and Language*, 29, 133–59.

Martin, Alex, Leslie Ungerleider, and James V. Haxby (2000) 'Category-specificity and the Brain: The Sensory-motor Model of Semantic Representations of Objects', in Michael S. Gazzaniga (ed.) *The New Cognitive Neurosciences*, Cambridge, Mass.: MIT Press.

Rubin, David C. (1995) *Memory in Oral Traditions: The Cognitive Psychology of Epic, Ballads, and Counting-out Rhymes*, New York: Oxford University Press.

Zwaan, Rolf A. (1999) 'Situation Models: The Mental Leap into Imagined Worlds', *Current Directions in Psychological Science*, 8, 15–18.

—— (2004) 'The Immersed Experiencer: Toward an Embodied Theory of Language Comprehension', in Brian H. Ross (ed.), *The Psychology of Learning and Motivation*, Vol. 44 (pp. 35–62). New York: Academic Press.

——, and Gabriel A. Radvansky (1998) 'Situation Models in Language Comprehension and Memory', *Psychological Bulletin*, 123, 162–85.

ROLF A. ZWAAN

SJUZHET

A term used by Russian Formalists to denote the way in which a narrative text presents (or cues readers to reconstruct) a chronological sequence of situations and *events. In the account developed in Seymour Chatman's influential book *Story and Discourse* (1978), the sjuzhet is the 'discourse' level of narrative, i.e., the narrative 'how' encoding the narrative 'what', which in formalist terminology is called the fabula. *See* STORY-DISCOURSE DISTINCTION (also: FORMALISM; STRUCTURALIST NARRATOLOGY; TEMPORAL ORDERING).

SKAZ

As Erlich (1981 [1965]) notes, *skaz* (from the Russian *skazat*, 'to tell') is a key term of Russian Formalist stylistics without an English equivalent (*see* FORMALISM). The title of Eikhenbaum's (1962 [1918]) *The Illusion of Skaz* captures its sense: a literary style imitating oral monologue, including, Erlich says, its 'articulation, mimicry and sound gestures'. Titunik (1973) calls it *narration with features of the *speech act; Trahan (1982) the written reproduction of oral narration (*see* CONVERSATIONAL STORYTELLING). Indications of the *narrator's pronunciation, especially departures from standard pronunciation, dialectal forms, slang, the second-person, and constructions reserved for spoken language, mark its mimetic *orality (*see* MIMESIS; PERSON; SPEECH REPRESENTATION).

First identified by the Russian Formalists perhaps because the form was widespread in Eastern European literature, e.g., in Gogol and Leskov, *skaz* often appears where literate and non-literate traditions coexist (*see* ORAL CULTURES AND NARRATIVE). Other examples are Sholom Aleichem's stories in Yiddish, the 'Cyclops' episode of Joyce's *Ulysses*, Mark Twain's *Huckleberry Finn*, Ring Lardner's 'Haircut', Faulkner's first version of *Spotted Horses*, and J. D. Salinger's *Catcher in the Rye*.

Banfield (1982) treats *skaz* as a first-person narrative which is a form of Benveniste's *discour* and reserves the term 'first-person narration' for narratives such as Proust's, Dickens' *David Copperfield*, or Emily Brontë's *Wuthering Heights*, which she analyses as examples of his *narration* (*see* NARRATIVE SITUATIONS; TENSE AND NARRATIVE). As discourse or imitated *performance, *skaz* contains a story-internal second-person, the narrator's potential interlocutor, the Sholom Aleichem who is the *audience for Tevye the milkman. In Erlich's definition of *skaz* as a narrative manner focussing on the 'personal "tone" of the fictional narrator', 'personal' should be understood as mimetic of performance, like the dramatic impersonation of a character's speaking *voice that Plato invokes in *Republic* 3. *Skaz*, mentioned in Bakhtin (1981), was no doubt among Bakhtin's (1986) speech *genres. McLean (1985), rejecting an exclusively oral conception of *skaz*, extends it to phenomena like *free indirect discourse (FID) – Eikhenbaum (1982 [1919]) did use it for Gogol's style in *The Overcoat*, whose narrator is presented as writing the story. But this leaves no distinct term for the attested style imitating a first-person's fictionally speaking voice and not, like FID, representing the linguistically subjective form of a third-person's thought or speech (*see* THOUGHT AND CONSCIOUSNESS REPRESENTATION (LITERATURE)). It is telling that while syntactic indications of subjectivity like exclamations occur in FID, not even FID representing speech (Banfield's 'represented speech'), contextually distinct but syntactically indistinguishable from FID representing thought (Banfield's 'represented thought'), can show the signs of pronunciation.

SEE ALSO: dramatic monologue

References and further reading

Banfield, Ann (1982) *Unspeakable Sentences: Narration and Representation in the Language of Fiction*, London: Routledge & Kegan Paul.

Bakhtin, M. M. (1981) *The Dialogic Imagination*, ed. Michael Holquist, trans. Caryl Emerson and Michael Holquist, Austin: University of Texas Press.
—— (1986) *Speech Genres and Other Late Essays*, ed. Caryl Emerson and Michael Holquist, trans. Vern W. McGee, Austin: University of Texas Press.
Eikhenbaum, Boris (1982 [1919]) 'How Gogol's "Overcoat" is Made', trans. John Fred Beebe and Elizabeth W. Trahan, in Elizabeth Trahan (ed.) *Gogol's 'Overcoat': An Anthology of Critical Essays*, Ann Arbor: Ardis.
—— (1962 [1918]) 'Illjuzija skaza', in *Skvoz' literatur*, 'S-Gravenhage: Mouton, 1962.
Erlich, Victor (1981 [1965]) *Russian Formalism: History-Doctrine*, New Haven: Yale University Press.
McLean, Hugh (1985) 'Skaz', *Handbook of Russian Literature*, New Haven: Yale University Press.
Titunik, I.R. (1973) 'The Formal Method and the Sociological Method (M.M. Bakhtin, P.N. Medvedev, V.N. Voloshinov) in Russian Theory and the Study of Literature', in V.N. Voloshinov (au.) *Marxism and the Philosophy of Language*, trans. Ladislav Matejka and I. R. Titunik, New York: Seminar Press.
Trahan, Elizabeth (ed.) (1982) *Gogol's 'Overcoat': An Anthology of Critical Essays*, New York: Ardis.
Vinogradov, Victor (1926) 'Problema skaza v stilistike', *Poètika*, 1, 24–40.

ANN BANFIELD

SLASH FICTION

Slash fiction is *fiction written by fans which describes sexual encounters between *television or *film characters of the same sex (*see* CHARACTER). It first appeared in the late 1960s and early 1970s, in response to the cult *science fiction series *Star Trek*, and took its name from the 'slash' juncture used in the expression 'Kirk/Spock' ('K/S') describing stories presenting scenes of sexual intimacy between these two characters. In pre-Internet days, slash fiction was mostly written by heterosexual female fans, pulished in print form and distributed at fan conventions or through subscription mailing lists. With the expansion of the Internet in the mid-1990s, slash moved online, together with much of fandom itself, and its popularity has increased accordingly. Like all *genres, slash is continually evolving and today the term is widely used to describe female/female ('F/F') homoerotic fan fiction as well as male/male. Purists, however, insist that slash refers only to the latter.

Although slash fiction accrues both to television series and to films of various genres, it is markedly more prevalent around science fiction, *horror, and *fantasy television series such as *Star Trek, The X-Files, Xena: Warrior Princess*, or *Buffy the Vampire Slayer* (*see* SERIAL FORM). Such series share characteristics that make them unusually open to imaginative interpretations and interventions. They are set in fantastical worlds, populated by exotic cultures, and governed by logics different from those of our own world (*see* POSSIBLE-WORLDS THEORY). At once anti-realist, semantically rich, and incomplete, they present dynamic alternate realities that engage the imaginations of fans and support their creative interpretations, interventions, and reworkings (*see* GAPPING; REALISM, THEORIES OF).

Studies of slash have usually considered it alongside other creative fan practices such as fan art, *music, videos, and other types of fan fiction. Slash has been theorised as a form of resistant reading, in which fans rework elements of the text in ways that reflect their own interests, needs, and *desires (*see* READER-RESPONSE THEORY). Penley proposes that slash originated as a 'guerrilla erotics', a means by which women took texts in which female characters were peripheral and countered this lack by reworking male characters and their relationships in terms of homoerotic desire and romance. Contemporary slash, on the other hand, mostly reworks series that *do* contain strong central female characters and slash fiction exists alongside a range of other types of erotic fan fiction.

SEE ALSO: gender studies; queer theory

References and further reading

Bacon-Smith, Camille (1992) *Enterprising Women: Television Fandom and the Creation of a Popular Myth*, Philadelphia, PA: University of Pennsylvania Press.
Brooker, Will (2002) *Using the Force: Creativity, Community and Star Wars Fans*, New York: Continuum.
Caldwell, John Thornton (1995) *Televisuality: Style, Crisis and Authority in American TV*, New Brunswick, NJ: Rutgers University Press.
Jenkins, Henry (1992) *Textual Poachers: Television Fans and Participatory Culture*, New York: Routledge.
Jones, Sara Gwenllian (2002) 'The Sex Lives of Cult Television Characters', *Screen*, 43.1, 79–90.
——, and Roberta E. Pearson (eds) (2004) *Cult Television*, Minneapolis: University of Minnesota Press.
Penley, Constance (1997) *NASA/Trek: Popular Science and Sex in America*, London: Verso.

SARA GWENLLIAN JONES

SLAVE NARRATIVE

Slave narrative is an American literary *genre of autobiographical accounts narrated and either written or dictated by ex-slaves about plantation life as a slave, escape, and freedom (*see* AUTOBIOGRAPHY). A highly conventionalised genre, its status as literature was long disputed, but the literary merits of its most famous examples such as Frederick Douglass's *Narrative of the Life of Frederick Douglass, an American Slave* (1845) and Harriet Jacobs's *Incidents in the Life of a Slave Girl* (1861) and the powerful influence of slave narratives on the development of African American fiction are widely recognised today. Generally sponsored by abolitionist groups, slave narratives have as their stated aim the exposure of the cruelty of slavery, and they forcefully propagate its abolition. The genre's characteristics include prefatory or appended authenticating material (*see* PARATEXT), a homodiegetic *narrator who speaks as an 'unlettered' slave (to minimise the distance between narrating- and experiencing-I), a journey from South to North culminating in an escape from slavery, an achievement of freedom both externally and internally, often indicated by a change of name (*see* NAMING IN NARRATIVE). Its themes include the deprivation of bodily necessities such as food, clothing and shelter, the denial of spiritual needs such as instruction and religious guidance, physical brutality, economic exploitation of the slave, sexual exploitation of slave women (particularly in narratives written by women), and the destruction of families (especially the separation of black families and the corruption of white ones). The role of *gender in shaping the experiences of men and women under slavery and in constructing the self-representation of the writers is particularly illuminated by a comparison of Jacobs's and Douglass's narratives.

While its peak of popularity was from the 1840s to the 1860s, the earliest slave narrative to be published was the *Narrative of the Uncommon Suffering & Surprizing Deliverance of Briton Hammon* (1760), a captivity narrative. Olaudah Equiano's narrative of African freedom, European and American enslavement, religious conversion, and worldwide travels, first published in 1789 in London, established the genre pattern. Douglass's narrative of achieving freedom and manhood and Jacobs's tale of resistance, seven-year concealment in a small garret, and eventual escape are particularly representative. The publication of their narratives put both writers at risk of recapture and necessitated subsequent flight and the eventual purchase of their freedom. The narratives of Henry Bibb and William Wells Brown integrate folkloric material such as trickster *motifs (*see* FOLKLORE). One of the most widely read novels of the mid-nineteenth-century, Harriet Beecher Stowe's *Uncle Tom's Cabin* (1852), was based on narratives of escaped slaves. After emancipation the narrative genre of 'slave memoirs' became prominent. About 6000 slave narratives have been collected (Olney 1985: 148), including written accounts, transcriptions, and oral accounts such as those collected by the Works Projects Administration (WPA) in the 1930s (*see* ORAL HISTORY).

As first-hand testimonies of slavery, slave narratives made authenticity their highest priority. Fictionality was minimised through devices such as testimonials by white friends or sponsors, the inclusion of documentary texts (bills of sale, notices of auctions, *letters, excerpts from newspapers or legal texts, legal certificates), the various inscriptions of self and authorship such as signatures, *photographs, or engraved portrait on the cover, the claim of authorship in the title (tagged 'written by himself'), the standard beginning 'I was born', and a poetic epigraph (Olney 1985: 151–53) (*see* AUTHOR; REALITY EFFECT). Stepto (1979) has elaborated on the various degrees of integration of *voices and authenticating strategies in the development of the genre, drawing a line from early narratives to Booker T. Washington's *Up From Slavery* (1901). The dual voice of experiencing and narrating self is characteristic of this genre, exemplified in Douglass's image of his feet having been 'so cracked with the frost' that the gashes will hold the writing pen. Direct reader *address is commonly used, and the writing is self-reflexive (*see* REFLEXIVITY), particularly since the acquisition of literacy is closely bound up with the desire and achievement of freedom. The genre shares stylistic and structural elements with the adventure story (focus on rescue and escape), the *picaresque novel (*narration in retrospect, linear episodic structure, a narrator of obscure origin and outcast status, the use of deception and trickery for survival), and the sentimental *novel (characterisation, style, appeal to readers' sentiments, and conventions of decorum; *see* CHARACTER; NARRATIVE STRUCTURE; NARRATIVE TECHNIQUES; TEMPORAL ORDERING; TIME IN NARRATIVE). Andrews (1986) has pointed out the affinities of the genre to the jeremiad, particularly in the case of Douglass' narrative.

Slave narratives were long considered popular literature or were solely read as historical documents since they were considered sensationalist propaganda manipulated by abolitionists. The authenticity of the narratives was often questioned because they were sometimes mediated by white amanuenses due to the illiteracy of many ex-slaves. Frederick Douglass, a well-known abolitionist orator, was accused of lying and of never having been a slave. Jacobs' narrative, published under the pseudonym Linda Brent, was long considered to have been written by its editor, anti-slavery writer Lydia Maria Childs. However, Yellin (1985) has convincingly demonstrated Jacobs' authorship based on Jacobs' letters. Sometimes called 'black message in a white envelope', slave narratives raise the issue of narrative control by white editors and black subjects of narration. This has profoundly influenced so-called neo-slave narratives by contemporary African American writers such as Toni Morrison, Ishmael Reed, Sherley Ann Williams, Charles Johnson, and Ernest Gaines.

SEE ALSO: confessional narrative; identity and narrative

References and further reading

Andrews, William L. (1986) *To Tell a Free Story: The First Century of Afro-American Autobiography, 1760–1865*, Urbana: University of Illinois Press.

Carby, Hazel (1987) *Reconstructing Womanhood: The Emergence of the Afro-American Woman Novelist*, New York: Oxford University Press.

Davis, Charles T., and Henry Louis Gates, Jr. (eds) (1985) *The Slave's Narrative*, New York: Oxford University Press.

McDowell, Deborah E., and Arnold Rampersad (eds) (1989) *Slavery and the Literary Imagination*, Baltimore: Johns Hopkins University Press.

Nichols, Charles H. (1963) *Many Thousand Gone: The Ex-Slaves' Account of Their Bondage and Freedom*, Bloomington: Indiana University Press.

Olney, James (1985) ' "I was born": Slave Narratives, Their Status as Autobiography, and as Literature', in Davis and Gates (1985) *The Slave's Narrative*, New York: Oxford University Press.

Rushdy, Ashraf H. A. (1999) *Neo-Slave Narratives: Studies in the Social Logic of a Literary Form*, New York: Oxford University Press.

Sekora, John, and Darwin T. Turner (eds) (1982) *The Art of the Slave Narrative*, Macomb: Western Illinois University Press.

Stepto, Robert B. (1979) *From Behind the Veil: A Study of Afro-American Narrative*, Urbana: University of Illinois Press.

Yellin, Jean Fagan (1985) 'Text and Contexts of Harriet *Jacobs's Incidents in the Life of a Slave Girl: Written by Herself*', in Davis and Gates (1985) *The Slave's Narrative*, New York, Oxford University Press.

ESTHER FRITSCH

SOAP OPERA

Soap opera originated as a *genre of long-running *radio drama serial in the 1930s but is today better known as a *television genre. It is characterised by melodramatic content, multiple storylines, dialogue-driven *plots, cliffhanger episode endings, and a distinctively open-ended narrative form. *See* SERIAL FORM.

SOCIOLINGUISTIC APPROACHES TO NARRATIVE

The turn to narrative within the social sciences and humanities has led to proliferating research initiatives and numerous advances in many areas (*see* NARRATIVE TURN IN THE HUMANITIES). Within sociolinguistics, these have in turn created diverse, inter- or multidisciplinary approaches to narrative. Since Labov's pathbreaking work (1972; also Labov and Waletzky 1967) on *narrative structure, sociolinguists and discourse analysts have focused particular attention on natural narrative, particularly the kind that relates the teller's personal past experiences (*see* DISCOURSE ANALYSIS (LINGUISTICS); NATURAL NARRATOLOGY).

The typical environments in which such stories are audio- and/or videotaped for analytical purposes are a) research interviews and b) conversations (*see* CONVERSATIONAL STORYTELLING). In the 1970s and 1980s, the investigation of natural narratives was mainly focused on the social and cultural variability of their ways of telling. The concepts of evaluation (Labov and Waletzky 1967), i.e., the means by which a storyteller signals the point of his or her story, and *tellability (a story's point, or worthiness of telling) were most influential in this type of inquiry. The main aim was to determine the correlation between choices that mark the teller's subjectivity and the teller's social or cultural group. The point of departure for such studies was that both narrative structure and the devices used to signal a story's tellability (mostly captured by the notion of evaluation) were universal but subject to all kinds of variation (social, cultural, situational).

Empirical analyses of narrative in a range of interactional contexts (both informal and *institutional) have since attested to the context-sensitivity of narratives in various respects: e.g., the number and types of poetic patterns in their formal organisation; the degree and roles of *audience participation in their telling; the selection of particular kinds of *events and topics as tellable; the language choices used for marking tellability (Polanyi 1985; Johnstone 1990; Georgakopoulou 1997); and the ways in which children are socialised into storytelling (*see* CHILDREN'S STORYTELLING). Researchers have also richly documented the roles of narrative in establishing and maintaining structures within the social order, including relations of inequality and control (*see* DISCOURSE ANALYSIS (FOUCAULT); SOCIOLOGY AND NARRATIVE).

From the 1990s onwards, as sociolinguists have worked to complement variationist and distributional studies with dynamic, discourse-oriented, and contextualised views of language use, narrative approaches have accordingly been shifting towards more situated and local explorations of the relationships between stories and the occasions on which they are told. In this respect, it is currently accepted that the construction of social and cultural *identities in the course of storytelling is a process with multiple, contingent meanings that cannot always or in a straightforward way be attributed to larger processes and norms that pertain outside the here and now of the storytelling situation. Current-day analyses thus tend to focus on how storytellers on-the-spot bring about, position, and/or perform aspects of their selves during particular storytelling occasions (*see* PERFORMATIVITY; POSITIONING).

One strand within this paradigm shift pays specific attention to the sequential properties of narrative: what relationships it bears with its surrounding talk; how it gets introduced in it and how it is exited from; how meanings and events are co-authored between storytelling participants, including the researcher and the researched in interview situations (*see* COMMUNICATION IN NARRATIVE). Other theorists have focused on a wide range of possible kinds of storytelling events, including stories about the future; stories that do not have a main teller but are systematically co-constructed; stories whose events are known to the teller and (part of the) audience; stories that are significantly complemented by their surrounding talk and are as such fragmented or elliptical; stories in multiple modalities (not just verbal but also *visual) and diverse *media.

The canonical narrative in sociolinguistic research

The main approaches to narrative in socio-linguistics, as outlined above, have been intimately linked with the definitions of *narrative that have had wide currency and in turn with the types of narratives on which the scholarship has focused. In this respect, Labov's study of personal narratives undoubtedly set the tone for subsequent research. In his model, narratives of personal experience were defined as one method of recapitulating past experience by matching a verbal sequence of clauses to the sequence of events which had actu-ally occurred (Labov 1972: 360). In addition, Labov defined a *minimal narrative as a sequence of two or more clauses which are *temporally ordered. One of the main assumptions in Labov's model is that of a direct correspondence (or referential relationship) between actual and nar-rativised (i.e., told) *events (see NARRATIVISATION; REFERENCE).

This assumption is largely traceable to the two-tier conceptualisation of natural narrative (within *structuralist narratology) as 'narrated events' in the *storyworld or *diegesis and 'narrative events' in the here-and-now of the narrative discourse (see STORY-DISCOURSE DISTINCTION). Researchers have studied the strategies by which tellers create vary-ing degrees of distance or affinity between the two. In turn, this salient distinction between told (past) and telling (current) has led to the privileging of certain types of narrative as a focus of inquiry. At issue are narratives featuring a coherent temporal progression of events located in a past time and place and that have a beginning, middle, and end. It is granted that they may be reordered or manipulated for rhetorical and other purposes, but fundamentally storytellers are expected to employ various strategies in order to present a structured and coherent account. They are also expected to use various rhetorical means in order to convey to their *audience the point of their story, as well as

their *perspective on the events related (Ochs and Capps 2001: 57).

In this type of story, the teller appears to have ownership of and privileged experiential access to the events narrated; this creates a rather sharp distinction between teller and audience, at the same time granting privileged telling rights to the teller. In terms of structure, stories of personal experience about past events tend to be (or are assumed to be) largely monologic and sustained (i.e., floor-holding) *narrations, which build up to a climax (high point) that is subsequ-ently resolved. Bounded sequentiality, teleology, and teller-centred *experientiality: these pivotal aspects of what can be called the canonical narrative in sociolinguistics are all in the good company of stories studied in narratological approaches that can be traced back to Aristotle's Poetics (see ANCIENT THEORIES OF NARRATIVE (WESTERN)).

The canonical status of these sorts of narratives was first questioned by analysts of naturally occurring conversational environments of story-telling between intimates. For instance, Goodwin's (1990) study of the stories of African-American female adolescents brought to the fore stories that involved telling on an absent third party and in turn generated stories of future confrontations between members of the peer-group (see GOSSIP). More generally, it has become apparent that per-sonal past-experience stories may be far from the norm in conversations between intimates; their frequency in Labovian and post-Labovian studies was intimately linked with their context of occurrence (e.g., relationships between inter-viewer and interviewee, the fact that they were elicited, etc.).

Narrative and socio-cultural variability

As shown above, the definitions of narrative in sociolinguistics are in agreement with structuralist notions of narrative and as such tend to be based on textual criteria. At the same time, approaches have been informed by *psychological and anthropological definitions of narrative as a pri-vileged mode for sense-making and self-construc-tion (see ETHNOGRAPHIC APPROACHES TO NARRATIVE). According to these studies, narrative is a central if not primary means by which to articulate experience and discursively (re)con-stitute reality. As such, it affords tellers with unique positionings and generates unique sensibilities. This foundational ontological role accorded to narrative has made it one of the prime candidates for an investigation of social and cultural variability with respect to its construction.

In this investigation, narrative has undergone scrutiny both in terms of how it is organised (how events hang together in a more or less coherent whole) and of how it displays the teller's subjective and affective stances vis-à-vis both the events related and his or her audiences (*see* EMOTION AND NARRATIVE). Since narrative organisation is also a matter of subjective selection and interpretation, analysts have found it hard to keep the two separate. Taking their cue, however, from the Labovian distinction between complicating action and evaluation, researchers have invariably attempted to tease apart the sequential arrangements of events from the teller's more or less explicitly articulated involvement in them. The task seemed to be, in the first instance, to identify the devices for signalling narrative organisation and/or the teller's subjectivity and, subsequently, to link those with socio-cultural identities and norms on one hand and situational factors (e.g., relations between storytelling participants) on the other hand. The methodological rationale for establishing such more or less straightforward associations between text and context was provided by variationist sociolinguistics in the context of which Labov developed his approach to narrative analysis. Within this framework, the choice of a language form or structure over another is not haphazard but systematic; what is more, it presents patterned variability.

In Labov's own work, increased use of external evaluation was proposed as a marker of middle-class educated speakers whereas internal evaluation seemed to be favoured more among working-class black storytellers in the inner city. Outlining a more ambitious program for research, Polanyi (1985) constructed a cultural grammar (i.e., a list of values and attitudes) for North American stories by analysing evaluation in a corpus of stories, arguing that what stories can be about is to a significant extent culturally constrained. Similarly, Johnstone (1990) found that stories in Middle America revolved around socio-culturally sanctioned *plots and points, but at the same time displayed gendered differences in terms of their themes and ways of telling (e.g., women's stories were trouble stories and stories of embarrassment, while men's stories

focused on activities with other men; women's stories included more reported speech than men's, etc.) (*see* FEMINIST NARRATOLOGY; GENDER STUDIES; SPEECH REPRESENTATION; THEMATIC APPROACHES TO NARRATIVE).

Other post-Labovian studies also reported differences in storytelling, particularly between Americans and non-Americans, and specifically with regard to evaluative (cf. involvement, *performance) devices, including use of the historical present (*see* TENSE AND NARRATIVE), repetition, and reported speech. An influential study in this respect has been Chafe's (1980) edited volume on the retellings by members of different cultures of a silent film, known as the Pear Stories. Such studies have been valuable for putting the study of natural narrative firmly on the map and shedding light on the cultural specificity of its uses and functions. They do however display a tendency to create unproblematic and simplistic associations between language choices and cultural groupings; the latter are at times presented as undifferentiated wholes.

Another strand of research into the cultural aspects of natural narrative is traceable to the ethnography of communication. Two main assumptions here have been that language use is permeated by socio-cultural forces (see Saville-Troike 1989) and that narrative, in particular, is centrally situated within cultural practices. Hymes's (1981) ethnopoetic analysis of *Native American narratives attested to rhythmic, poetic patterns in narrative organisation, shaped in accordance with a community's sense of sacred and 'magic' numbers (e.g., twos and fours or threes and fives). These patterns are assumed to structure every level of the narrative text, starting from lines (low-level unit) and extending to higher-level groupings of lines (e.g., stanzas, verses). Hymes has argued that such narrative patterning is universal but that it has receded from the narratives of more literate, urbanised cultures (*see* NARRATIVE UNIVERSALS; ORAL CULTURES AND NARRATIVE). Additionally, local circumstances determine principles of grouping and cultural norms dictate preferred patterns. Form, content, and prosody are strongly interacting components in the identification of such poetic units (*see* NARRATIVE UNITS).

One of the benefits of ethnopoetic research was that it demonstrated the verbal artistry involved in the shaping of non-literary stories. These artful qualities of oral stories were also highlighted by another ethnographer of communication, Richard Bauman (1986). Bauman's analysis of Texans' stories called attention to an array of devices (e.g., use of repetition, characters' direct or reported speech and *dialogues, the historical present, imagery, details, ellipsis, paralinguistic devices such as intonational variation, etc.) by means of which storytellers perform rather than just relate their stories; drawing on culturally appropriate ways of telling a good story, they exploit poetic and creative means for displaying to their audiences communicative skill and efficiency.

By drawing attention to the cultural specificity of ways of telling a story, ethnography of communication also brought to the fore the significance of narrative as an agent of enculturation. Various studies have examined the ways in which culturally bound narrative norms interact with children's school performance and transition to literacy. The aim of such studies has been to explore the relationships between classroom practices and home cultures and at the same time to encourage the former to be aware of and sensitive to the latter, so that children can make the transition to school-based literacy more easily.

A case in point is Heath's (1983) study of the storytelling styles of two adjacent North American communities, one working-class white and the other working-class African American. Heath identified in these communities distinct sets of practices used to socialise children into storytelling, each linked with different ways of speaking (e.g., modes of participation, attitudes toward the relationship between fact and *fiction, etc.) and presenting different implications for a transition to school-based literacy (see EDUCATION AND NARRATIVE). Michaels (1981) specifically related children's storytelling styles to classroom definitions of narrative. She found that the stories of white middle-class speakers presented a Labovian structure and explicit evaluation; they also appeared to be highly coordinated with teacher's talk. In contrast to such 'topic-centred' narratives, the 'topic-associating' narratives of working-class African American pupils exhibited topic shifts through prosodic signalling and implicit – non-lexicalised – evaluation that was based on rhythmic patterns, parallelism, and repetition. Although not focused on educational settings, Scollon and Scollon's work (1981) drew attention to cases of marginalisation on account of differences in narrative styles. Their study suggested that the stories of

Athabaskans in an Alaskan community were treated as cryptic and opaque by North Americans as a result of their implicit, community-bound ways of telling.

Such studies have documented the encoding of ideological and power relationships in narrative (see IDEOLOGY AND NARRATIVE). More evidence for the role of narrative as a political activity and a site of ideological conflicts has come from studies of storytelling in institutional contexts, particularly in court (see, e.g., Briggs 1996; see COURTROOM NARRATIVE; INSTITUTIONAL NARRATIVE). This research has shown how certain narrative accounts are deemed to be appropriate, while those who depart from the expectations and rules of telling in a given context are less successful (credible, convincing). Not only are there constraints on the sayability and hearability of certain stories, but what is more tellers have differential access to resources and styles that have been institutionally legitimated.

Although a lot of the above work is based on ethnography, it too is at times characterised by a simplistic identification of both narrative styles and cultural categories: the multiplicity and varying relevance of both in different contexts seem to be glossed over and the potential for indirect connections between the two is not always explored. Finally, theorists working in these traditions have not drawn enough attention to intricate processes of resistance to, negotiation with, and contestation of cultural and narrative meanings.

Narrative as talk-in-social interaction

Moving away from normative associations between language use and socio-cultural groupings, analysts have increasingly come to view narrative as a situated practice, the meanings of which are locally occasioned and contingent. In a similar vein, the sorts of identities that storytellers construct are intimately linked with the roles of the participants in the storytelling situation and their relationships with them. These premises force attention to the local interactional environment of a story, in the sense of prior and upcoming talk. As Sacks (1974), among others, has pointed out, stories arise in or are prompted by the ongoing course of an interactional occasion. As such, their design and constructional features are locally occasioned and interactionally achieved.

Emphasis on narrative as an interactional activity and a locally accomplished project allows researchers to avoid privileging certain kinds of stories at the expense of others; it also breaks away from a longstanding tradition of treating narrative as a 'monologic' or self-contained discourse unit. Although it is still important to identify a structure in narratives, this structure is seen as emerging through the teller's actions and the audience's negotiated process, rather than as a finished product that can be postulated a priori (Goodwin 1984). By the same token, evaluation is productively linked with processes of piecing together, assessing, and negotiating multiple perspectives. In other words, the formal organisation of a story serves to place participants in and help concretise a social organisation (see Goodwin 1990).

Focus on the interactional properties of stories has brought to the fore a range of possibilities for the tellers' self-presentation that have to do with moment-by-moment alignments or mis-alignments with their interlocutors. It has been shown (e.g., Schiffrin 1996) that tellers can split into many personae or selves (e.g., as characters in the narrated events, as reporters of other characters' speech, as tellers in the narrative events, etc.) in order to align and position themselves differentially to participants, to diffuse or maximise their responsibility for and *agency within the events related, and to adapt their stories to local interactional business (e.g., illustrating a point, winning an argument, etc.).

The emphasis on the situated meanings of stories is increasingly pushing into the centre of sociolinguistic concern a multitude of forms of stories and a range of storytelling events (e.g., reports on their daily activities that family members exchange round the family dinner table [Ochs and Capps 2001]; stories on talk shows and radio phone-ins; stories arising in doctor-patient interactions, etc.; see MEDICINE AND NARRATIVE) that depart from the canonical case of personal experience stories elicited in research interviews, thus enriching and broadening the scope of inquiry. Nonetheless, a difficult balance remains to be struck between interactionist work that attends to the micro-level of storytelling and work that can illuminate the capacity of stories for shaping social arenas and larger discursive projects that go beyond the here-and-now of their occasion of telling. Connections between the micro- and macro-levels are difficult to establish, not just for sociolinguistic approaches to narrative but for narrative studies in general.

SEE ALSO: communication studies and narrative; interdisciplinary approaches to narrative

References and further reading

Bauman, Richard (1986) Story, Performance and Event: Contextual Studies of Oral Narrative, Cambridge: Cambridge University Press.

Briggs, Charles (ed.) (1996) Disorderly Discourse: Narrative, Conflict, and Inequality, Oxford: Oxford University Press.

Chafe, Wallace (ed.) (1980) The Pear Stories: Cognitive, Cultural and Linguistic Aspects of Narrative Production, Norwood, NJ: Ablex.

Georgakopoulou, Alexandra (1997) Narrative Performances: A Study of Modern Greek Storytelling, Amsterdam: John Benjamins.

Goodwin, Charles (1984) 'Notes on Story Structure and the Organization of Participation', in J. Maxwell Atkinson and John Heritage (eds) Structures of Social Action, Cambridge: Cambridge University Press.

Goodwin, Marjorie H. (1990) He-Said-She-Said: Talk as Social Organization among Black Children, Bloomington: Indiana University Press.

Heath, Shirley B. (1983) Ways with Words, Cambridge: Cambridge University Press.

Hymes, Dell (1981) 'In Vain I Tried to Tell You': Essays in Native American Ethnopoetics, Philadelphia: University of Pennsylvania Press.

Johnstone, Barbara (1990) Stories, Community and Place: Narratives from Middle America, Bloomington: Indiana University Press.

Labov, William (1972) 'The Transformation of Experience in Narrative Syntax', in Language in the Inner City, Philadelphia: University of Pennsylvania Press.

——, and Joshua Waletzky (1967) 'Narrative Analysis: Oral Versions of Personal Experience', in June Helm (ed.) Essays on the Verbal and Visual Arts, Seattle: University of Washington Press.

Michaels, Sarah (1981) '"Sharing Time": Children's Narrative Styles and Differential Access to Literacy', Language in Society, 10, 423–42.

Ochs, Elinor, and Lisa Capps (2001) Living Narrative: Creating Lives in Everyday Story-telling, Cambridge, Mass.: Harvard University Press.

Polanyi, Livia (1985) Telling the American Story, Norwood, NJ: Ablex.

Sacks, Harvey (1974) 'An Analysis of the Course of a Joke's Telling', in Richard Bauman and Joel Sherzer (eds) Explorations in the Ethnography of Speaking, Cambridge: Cambridge University Press.

Saville-Troike, Muriel (1989) The Ethnography of Communication: An Introduction, Oxford: Blackwell.

Schiffrin, Deborah (1996) 'Narrative as Self-portrait: Sociolinguistic Constructions of Identity', Language in Society, 25, 167–203.

Scollon, Ronald, and Suzanne Scollon (1981) Narrative, Literacy and Face in Interethnic Communication, Norwood, NJ: Ablex.

ALEXANDRA GEORGAKOPOULOU

SOCIOLOGICAL APPROACHES TO LITERARY NARRATIVE

The complex interweaving of literary texts and their social contexts has been studied throughout the twentieth century, but it was only during the last third of the twentieth century that a socio-logical approach to narrative began to claim its autonomy within literary studies and assume names like 'the sociology of literature', 'socio-logical poetics', or 'literary sociology'. Academics became convinced that (comparative) criticism should be organised according to a sociological model. This approach fostered a variety of research topics ranging from the relationship between literature and *ideology, the social origins of literary *genres, the social embedding of themes, and the sociological conditions underlying literary evolution (*see* EVOLUTION OF NARRATIVE FORMS). Those topics continue to inspire academics, but they are in general no longer perceived as part of 'literary sociology' because of a significant change in scope and perspective.

Roughly speaking, the history of the sociology of narrative can be subdivided into three stages. In the first stage Georg Lukács, Mikhail Bakhtin, Bertolt Brecht, Walter Benjamin, and Theodor W. Adorno were looking for a blueprint of a Marxist (dialectical) theory of culture that investigated the mediating factors between modern society, on the one hand, and the literary text on the other (*see* MARXIST APPROACHES TO NARRATIVE). The rela-tionship was not conceived as a mere mirror effect (as in the official arts politics in the Soviet Union). Instead, these theorists focused on mediating semantic constructions ('Visions of the world', 'ideologies', or 'the collective consciousness') that bore traces of conflicts in capitalist society and at the same time produced semantic oppositions on the textual level. Although many Marxists agreed with this general position, they differed very strongly on the way in which literary works could be evaluated as influenced by and commenting upon modern culture. The debate concerning *realism and modernism abundantly proves this. In the eyes of Lukács and his followers, modernism was a backward step in comparison with the realist diagnosis of problems with modernity, and was considered a kind of retreat from the complexity of modern culture (*see* MODERNIST NARRATIVE). For their part, modernist authors such as Bertolt Brecht and theoreticians such as Walter Benjamin

and Theodor Adorno conceived of modernism as a powerful critique of modern society because of its ability to resist – through the use of experimental *narrative techniques – the dominant ideologies and worldviews in modern society (Bloch *et al.* 1994).

During the second stage of the development of a sociology of (literary) narrative, a stage which coincides with the academic institutionalisation of the research domain, the insights of earlier theor-ists were extended by scholars like Erich Köhler, Peter Bürger, Lucien Goldmann, Pierre Macherey, Peter V. Zima, Terry Eagleton, and Fredric Jameson. This stage significantly differs from the first stage because of the strong literary-theoretical self-consciousness of the commentators in ques-tion. Marxist sociology underwent a linguistic turn; it reacted against the older, hermeneutical approach, and it was enriched by a discourse-analytical point of view (Zima 1985; Macherey 1966; Jameson 1981) (*see* DISCOURSE ANALYSIS (FOUCAULT); HERMENEUTICS; SEMIOTICS).

A third, post-Marxist stage started in the late 1980s. Inspired by *poststructuralist French philosophy to an unprecedented degree, the literary-sociological focus was transformed into an investigation of social identities (*see* IDENTITY AND NARRATIVE). Pierre Bourdieu's field theory, for instance, no longer zooms in on parameters such as class or social ideology, but attempts to examine the aesthetic dispositions that are at the basis of the art producers' social identity. Other, post- or non-Marxist theories testify to the same philosophical sources and concentrate, more than they used to, on questions regarding the constructions of identity that dominate cultural (and therefore also literary) life. Cultural studies, New Historicism, post-colonial and *gender studies all seek to understand literary phenomena as symptoms of social conflicts and power mechanisms involving gender, race, sexuality, and the hierarchy of high and low forms of culture (*see* CULTURAL STUDIES APPROACHES TO NARRATIVE; POST-COLONIALISM AND NARRATIVE).

Modernity and narrativisation

During the first two stages of its history, literary sociology largely coincided with theories of the *novel. This rather one-sided perspective stemmed from the close relationship between this genre and the cultural-sociological developments in the

Western world since the Renaissance period, as it was perceived by literary sociologists. One of the most important contributions of the aforementioned Marxist theorists to literary theory as a whole lies in the description and interpretation of novelistic narrative strategies in general and of the vicissitudes of the Western subject in a fragmented modern society in particular (*see* AGENCY). The starting-point of this historical '*métarécit*' (*see* MASTER NARRATIVE) is the observation that the novel no longer constitutes a narrative paradigm like the others (comedy, tragedy, *'romance'*, '*chanson de geste*', melodrama, etc.). The latter are genres in the real sense of the word: fictional forms based on canonised rules and structured by the ideological visions of a specific social group. The novel, on the contrary, is no longer the prerogative of a certain class or social group; it has no fixed structure, but rather consists of a series of operations and procedures absorbing the ideological stories of the previous genres and social groups.

This is especially clear in the evolution of the *'hero'* concept: from a *character that possessed unchangeable *a priori* qualities (bravery, saintliness, loyalty, sense of sacrifice), the hero evolved in the direction of a searching individual who is confronted with a world in which no universally valid value systems exist. In modernity, religious or *ethical values gradually lose their normative importance: on the one hand, the values' status becomes relative (because of the functional differentiation of social groups and a concomitant disintegration of the cultural system into specialised subsystems); on the other hand, those values no longer occupy a dominant position in a world that is governed by money and exchange value. With its fragmentation of social relationships and systems of sense-making, modernity in this view constitutes the most important meaning horizon for the novel; it is a cultural condition which is felt to be problematic by the characters.

According to the dominant story in literary sociology, the literary confrontation with modernity gained momentum in the post-romantic period. In Balzac's realism, for example, literature helps to reveal the truth about modernity. Lukács argues that the Balzacian novel stages a miniature version of modernity's cultural revolution. Cultural revolutions are historical moments of rupture in which coexisting cultural patterns (for instance, an agrarian, premodern pattern of culture and a mercantile, modern pattern of culture) conflict with each other and make their way to the centre of political and social life. The great *realist novels are pervaded by impulses from contradictory cultural traditions and can be seen as a discursive battlefield in which the great moments of cultural history claim their part by means of the different representatives in the character system of the novel (*see* CONFLICT).

More generally, according to Lukács, Adorno, and Goldmann, great novels manage to bring to life the general and the typical, by means of putting particular characters on stage. Nevertheless, they agree that this does not hold for all manifestations of the modern novel. In the nineteenth-century, the novel progressively becomes less of a direct 'sociological' instrument and the problematic hero changes; from now on, she or he seems to be assailed by a process of mental and behavioural disintegration. Subjects that almost frantically look for a solid subject position in an evermore complex society take centre stage. In high modernism this results in a staging of isolated and even disintegrated or fragmented subjects (*see* THOUGHT AND CONSCIOUSNESS REPRESENTATION (LITERATURE)). Jameson, for example, extensively discusses the transition from realism to modernism and takes the modernist refusal of manifest political diagnoses and broader sociological perspectives as his starting point. He argues that the relation between literature and social codes changes thoroughly after the turn of the century. The political, in his view, is no longer visible in the high modernist texts, but has become a kind of political unconscious; modernist novels symptomatically express the repressed social and social-psychological conflicts by which modern individuals are beset. However, according to most late-twentieth-century literary sociologists, ideological criticism is still at work in these texts, even if it has moved underground, because the novel testifies to the *condition humaine* under capitalism. The quest for *truth, which was typical of realist novelists, is continued in a more modest form, namely in the pursuit of a 'truthful' reconstruction of 'authentic inner experiences'. Modernists create an empire of authentic subjective experiences, because they seem to believe that this strategy can counter the disenchanted, rationalised market society. In that sense, they strive for a utopian compensation for the decline of subjectivity in the fragmented modern world (*see* UTOPIAN AND DYSTOPIAN FICTION).

From a hermeneutic to a discourse-analytic approach

Adorno, Lukács, and Goldmann never hesitated to buttress their hypotheses with meticulous textual analyses, but what is lacking in their work is the insight, which derives from French structuralist and poststructuralist approaches, that texts (or, more generally, discourses) shape consciousness (*see* STRUCTURALIST NARRATOLOGY). For contemporary literary sociologists (especially Macherey, Zima, and Jameson), the Hegelian-Marxist gambit of earlier literary sociology – the idea that consciousness reflects a world that exists independently of the mind – is unacceptable. The external world that is dealt with in literature is pervaded by linguistic mechanisms and can only be discussed as part of a 'sociolinguistic' situation (Zima 1985) (*see* SOCIO-LINGUISTIC APPROACHES TO NARRATIVE). Therefore, it no longer pays to confine literary sociology to the study of the ideological, consciousness-shaping contents that operate in a specific text; rather, these texts should be read as intertextual nodes that process and aesthetically transform ideological discourses (*see* INTERTEXTUALITY).

The sociologically oriented theorist who is most successful in examining narratives as ideologically inflected textual constructs is perhaps Fredric Jameson. Working within the framework of Lacanian epistemology, Jameson sharply delineates the object of study in his political criticism. Abandoning the traditional concerns of Marxist literary sociology – the discovery of extralinguistic referents (which are represented as stable and knowable) or (pre-existing) ideological *codes – Jameson's work focuses on the reconstruction of the semantic conditions of possibility that lie at the basis of narrative texts.

For Jameson, every individual literary expression must be considered as a construction that is fundamentally marked by its textuality. For that reason, literary criticism is, in Jameson's opinion, nothing but an attempt to describe art's implicit reaction to its environment; it is nothing but 'the unmasking of cultural artefacts as socially symbolic acts' (1981: 20). The symbolic *speech acts of literary *authors have to be taken as strategies that attempt to express the ineffable in a certain cultural constellation. Even when the socio-historical context does not manifestly take the shape of a text or a linguistic utterance, it is still safe to assume that it will answer to the logic and means of expression afforded by language: 'history is not a text, not a narrative, master or otherwise, but [...] it is inaccessible to us except in textual form' (1981: 35). In other words, the impact of the political (the socio-historical reality) presents itself as an unconscious as well as a textual influence; it finds its expression in literature as a subtext. Jameson's analysis of Balzac's *La Vieille Fille*, for instance, demonstrates how the plot lines develop according to a Greimasian semiotic square. The four semantic components clearly involve political connotations and the relations between them reveal important historical tensions (e.g., aristocratic powerlessness versus bourgeois energy). The political subtext inevitably escapes consciousness and can only be reconstructed through meticulous analysis of 'its narrativization in the political unconscious' (Jameson 1981: 35) (*see* NARRATIVISATION). A trace of Lacanian epistemology is immediately recognisable: the unconscious is structured like a language. The political unconscious – the traumatic, problematic reality – cannot be known directly, but one can try to get to know the pressure of reality through linguistic symptoms. Just as a psychological trauma leaves its traces in the patient's discourse on the couch, social and political traumata leave their traces in the narratives circulating within a culture (*see* PSYCHOANALYSIS AND NARRATIVE; TRAUMA THEORY).

From a semantic to a pragmatic approach

The tendency to consider literary sociology as one of the major 'pilot disciplines' in literary studies started in the sixties and persisted until the early eighties. Since that time, however, several of the leading authorities have diagnosed literary criticism as suffering from sociology fatigue. This waning of interest is not unrelated to the evolution within (sociologically inspired) cultural theory. Using Marxist criticism for inspiration, literary sociology in its heyday thought it could describe literary phenomena from the historical perspective of bourgeois modernity. It situated literature against the background of the process of modernisation and its carrier, the bourgeoisie. But however important the theoretical insights of the above-mentioned theorists, the modernisation process can no longer function as the sole referent for a study of contemporary cultural products. The problem of modernity has become increasingly complex, as the many debates surrounding the idea of postmodernity illustrate.

In the light of recent developments within the social sciences, it comes as no surprise to see that literary scholars are now finding it more and more difficult to thematise the relationship between literature and society. In recent years, therefore, terms like 'literary sociology' and 'the sociology of literature' have lost much of their self-evident character. The central problems of literary sociology are still taken up by literary theorists, albeit in a more secretive or subcutaneous manner. The name is silently dropped, but the research issues are more alive than ever and continue to steer the literary-critical agenda of comparative literature. Some literary sociologists such as Fredric Jameson and Peter Bürger underwent a 'cultural turn' by changing their focus from semantic to pragmatic issues (*see* PRAGMATICS). Less attention is paid to methods of textual analysis, while the complex interweaving of cultural and social tendencies is foregrounded. Literature is seen within a broad perspective, including issues of cultural identity and the everyday practices of postmodern subjects, or the influence of media society and information technology (*see* MEDIA AND NARRATIVE).

The problem encountered by literary sociology – and also by a variety of other culturally oriented approaches to narrative – is that modernity has in effect caught up with itself. 'Bourgeois society' can no longer be looked at as a monolithic concept, which is one of the reasons why Marxist literary sociology underwent a crisis. The inability to establish an adequate Marxist discourse is undoubtedly related to the crisis of the concept of 'class'. A multiplicity of 'subject positions' (class, race, sex, nationality, and generation) has functioned as the starting point of cultural theory since the 1990s. Of crucial importance in this theoretical evolution is the sociological fact that today's urbanised citizens, as the German sociologist Ulrich Beck has noted, live in an individualised society; they identify less and less with the disciplinary and hierarchical collectivising institutions of the past (such as religious institutions, moral authorities, political parties, socio-economic class, or neighbourhoods) and more and more with so-called peer groups (frequently conceptualised through the notions of subculture and lifestyle) (*see* INSTITUTIONAL NARRATIVE; SOCIOLOGY AND NARRATIVE).

Indeed, the majority of contemporary studies (as well as the studies by the English *éminence grise* Raymond Williams, who anticipated the new developments at an early stage) start from the insight that the collective consciousness cannot be analysed as an isolated element, because it is rather articulated in and through micro-sociological everyday practices. In a certain sense, the earlier, semantically oriented text interpretations remain loyal to the concepts of Marx, Durkheim, Weber, and American functionalism because they implicitly conceive of culture as the result of an ideal activity: the manipulation of ideals or the output of value-judgements by producers of culture. Following Michel Foucault's *philosophy, Norbert Elias's sociogenetic research, the work of development psychologists such as Jean Piaget, and the sociology of symbolic interactionism, the more recent sociology of culture and literature calls the origin of such values into question. For Pierre Bourdieu, for instance, a cultural product is primarily a strategic object; it is brought into play in order to confirm a certain social identity and, at the same time, to react against a competing identity.

For Bourdieu, a specific cultural product can only be understood when the analysis is based in a structure of conflicting practices. In a number of articles dating from the late sixties and the early seventies, but especially in *Les Règles de l'art* (1992), Bourdieu shows that art is not so much a cultural heritage of valuable products as a practice of different groups that aim to realise specific attitudes toward and perspectives on art. In contrast with earlier sociological approaches to narrative, the analysis does not primarily deal with the textual structure of the work of art, but concentrates explicitly on the strategies of writers as social agents. Within this perspective, the concept of intertextuality is reformulated as a sociological phenomenon. Narratives have to be evaluated as strategies to obtain a solid position within the literary intertext, the 'space of works'. They try to transcend canonised works of art and use, at the same time, innovative works or manifestos to revolutionise the aesthetic practices of a specific literary community. Moreover, the entire artistic community conflicts with other social groups. Writers identify themselves with their cultural role as 'literati' and distinguish themselves from nonwriters through their knowledge of the materialised culture (the literary canon) and through the skills that they have acquired in their education and upbringing. Starting from this general view of artisthood, Bourdieu arrives at a specific view of literary works. From this perspective, narratives can be read as testimonies to an aesthetic ideology. In his analysis of Flaubert's *L'Education sentimentale*, for instance, Bourdieu shows that the protagonist's development is marked by a growing separation from utilitarian values and a tendency towards 'useless' aesthetic practices.

Apart from the Bourdian approach, there are many other literary theories in which the literary-sociological legacy can be felt. The focus on the cultural construction of identity influenced a number of subdomains within contemporary literary studies, namely gender studies, post-colonial studies, and cultural studies. While hermeneutic and discourse-analytic literary sociology mainly investigated the influence of the capitalist conditions of subjectivity in the text, the emphasis has now shifted to the subject-constituting influence of literature and culture. Stephen Greenblatt formulates this reorientation as follows: 'Something happens to objects, beliefs, and practices when they are represented, reimagined, and performed in literary texts, something often unpredictable and disturbing. That "something" is the sign of both the power of art and of the embeddedness of culture in the contingencies of history' (1990: 231). Nevertheless, this reorientation does not mean that the Marxist legacy has completely withered away. On the contrary, the theoretical apparatus of the aforementioned forms of cultural studies often introduce neo-Marxist concepts such as hegemony, modernity, and subjectivisation. Post-Marxist literary theory does, however, differ from the traditional literary-sociological approach in that it starts from the Foucauldian observation that subjects are not only influenced by macro-sociological evolutions (e.g., class conflicts), but also by micro-sociological mechanisms like disciplining, moral pressure, and taste-building or discrimination. Adapted to narratives, this kind of reorientation explores the rules of identity formation that can explain *characters, conflicting cultural discourses underlying textual *motifs, or plotlines that evolve according to power conflicts in the micro-sociological sphere (*see* PLOT). In short, this kind of narrative analysis seems less interested in historical master narratives than in the space of everyday practices.

SEE ALSO: sociology and narrative

References and further reading

Adorno, Theodor W. (1974) *Noten zur Literatur*, Frankfurt am Main: Suhrkamp.
Bloch, Ernst, Theodor Adorno, and Georg Lukács (1994) *Aesthetics and Politics*, trans. Ronald Taylor, London: Verso.
Bourdieu, Pierre (1992) *Les Règles de l'art: Genèse et structure du champ littéraire*, Seuil: Paris.
Bürger, Peter (1974) *Theorie der Avantgarde*, Frankfurt am Main: Suhrkamp.
Eagleton, Terry (1976) *Criticism and Ideology: A Study in Marxist Literary Theory*, London: NLB.
Goldmann, Lucien (1964) *Pour une sociologie du roman*, Gallimard: Paris.
Greenblatt, Stephen (1990) 'Culture', in Frank Lentricchia and Thomas McLaughlin (eds) *Critical Terms for Literary Study*, Chicago: University of Chicago Press.
Jameson, Fredric (1981) *The Political Unconscious: Narrative as a Socially Symbolic Act*, Ithaca: Cornell University Press.
Keunen, Bart, and Bart Eeckhout (eds) (2001) *Literature and Society: The Function of Literary Sociology in Comparative Literature*, Brussels/Bern: Peter Lang/PIE.
Köhler, Erich (1982) *Literatursoziologische Perspektiven: Gesammelte Aufsätze*, Heidelberg: Winter.
Macherey, Pierre (1966) *Pour une théorie de la production littéraire*, Paris: Maspéro.
Williams, Raymond (1977) *Marxism and Literature*, Oxford: Oxford University Press.
Zima, Peter V. (1985) *Manuel de sociocritique*, Paris: Picard.

BART KEUNEN

SOCIOLOGY AND NARRATIVE

Narrative sociology is grounded in the recognition that stories are a fundamental part of personal and collective human experience. Sociologists study narrative to discern the underlying patterns and practices that shape human experience and our interpretation of the social world. *Narrative structures and storytelling activities are enduring, evolving, and revealing. They are central aspects of communication, which is the foundation of social life; human experience and communicative action are represented by the use of stories and accounts, as well as interpreted through them.

Narrative structures exist in and derive from social settings and cultural configurations. They outline the themes that are most available for understanding and interpreting our experiences.

By studying narratives, sociologists can uncover these structures and examine how they vary or persist within certain time-frames. For example, acceptable narrative structures of racial and *gender expectations shape our interpretations of experience and the way we explain our own lives. The stories we tell, and the way we relate our accounts, reveal underlying beliefs and expectations of which we may not be fully aware, yet which shape our behaviours, interactions, and realities. Narrative structures can be shaped in turn by human *agency, as members of society redefine and transform acceptable practices over time.

Similarities and differences exist among the narrative practices of various social groups and social locations. These continuities and contrasts may be structural, cultural, or experiential and they represent particular historical, social, and/or geographical locations (see ETHNOGRAPHIC APPROACHES TO NARRATIVE). Comparative analysis provides insights into continuity and change over time. Knowledge about the availability, influence, and use of diverse narrative structures in different situations sheds light on how the practice of representation shapes and is shaped by social realities.

The value of narrative research has not always been recognised in the field of sociology and has been the subject of some debate. The relevant issues are reflected in the micro/macro, qualitative/quantitative divides that have concerned sociologists for decades. As Maines (2001: 164–65) notes, a full recognition of narrative's importance in studying social life has been obscured by sociology's quest for recognition as a scientific discipline. The quest for precise, quantitative, rational knowledge about human experience has been highly valued by many sociologists. This knowledge is ideally derived from the standardised gathering of large collections of individual data which are sorted by category into small units that can be described and counted; such units are then recombined and rendered into aggregated data in a manner that provides predictability and generalisability for social science, but sometimes gives an under-nuanced representation of social reality.

In contrast, the richness and ambiguity represented by large samples of narrative data may be characterised as unwieldy, hard to quantify and compare, providing little generalisability or predictive value, and therefore unscientific. These limitations have led more scientific-minded sociologists to dismiss the validity, reliability, and overall value of narrative data. Narrative sociologists, on the other hand, consider such complex data to be important sources of knowledge about human experience. The early classic work by Thomas and Znaniecki represents this split. Their study, which included a large segment of rich narrative data representing immigrant life, was critiqued in terms of measurement and precision, reflecting sociology's scientific aspirations at the time. Similar debates continue about the status of the data collected by narrative sociologists, yet a recent longitudinal study of married couples by Holmberg, Orbuch, and Veroff has demonstrated that narrative analysis of large data sets is both possible and productive.

The use of narrative data has enriched sociological knowledge in many substantive areas, including research on the family, religion, the *law, sexuality, illness and *medicine, gender, race, social movements, *identity, and social roles. Narrative research has made important contributions to historical sociology, particularly in the areas of agency, collective *memory, causal analysis of *events (see CAUSALITY), and cultural change. The impact of narrative on sociological research includes recognition of the narrative nature of the interview process negotiated by its participants, leading to new methods of data collection and analysis. Categorising the structures, forms, and content of the narrative data, as well as its functions and representations, has expanded the repertoire of sociological analysis.

Sociologists study written texts, including *biography and *autobiography, both as individual accounts and as representations of the social practices and narrative structures of their historical and social locations. The practice of auto-ethnography has brought new insights into the creation of accounts, the representation of *perspectives, and the nature of intersubjectivity. Just as sociologists study narratives, they also produce narratives in their representations of research findings, in their writing about the research process, in their use of *reflexivity, and in writing about writing. In effect, narrative sociologists see storied activity as fundamental to social life: a vital link between social thought, identity, and communicative action.

SEE ALSO: cultural studies approaches to narrative; discourse analysis (linguistics); life story;

science and narrative; sociological approaches
to literary narrative

References and further reading

Davis, Joseph E. (ed.) (2002) *Stories of Change: Narrative and Social Movements*, Albany: State University of New York Press.
DeVault, Marjorie L. (1999) *Liberating Method: Feminism and Social Research*, Philadelphia: Temple University Press.
Ewick, Patricia, and Susan Silbey (2003) 'Narrating Social Structure: Stories of Resistance to Legal Authority', *American Journal of Sociology*, 6, 1328–72.
Gubrium, Jaber E., and James A. Holstein (1997) *The New Language of Qualitative Method*, NY: Oxford University Press.
Holmberg, Diane, Terri L. Orbuch, and Joseph Veroff (2004) *Thrice-Told Tales: Married Couples Tell Their Stories*, Mahwah, N.J.: Lawrence Erlbaum.
Maines, David (1993) 'Narrative's Moment and Sociology's Phenomena: Toward a Narrative Sociology', *Sociological Quarterly*, 34, 17–38.
—— (2001) *The Faultline of Consciousness: A View of Interactionism in Sociology*, Hawthorne, NY: Aldine de Gruyter.
Orbuch, Terri (1997) 'People's Accounts Count: The Sociology of Accounts', *Annual Review of Sociology*, 23, 455–78.
Reissman, Catherine Kohler (1993) *Narrative Analysis*, Newbury Park, CA: Sage.
Richardson, Laurel (1997) *Fields of Play: Constructing an Academic Life*, New Brunswick, NJ: Rutgers University Press.
Somers, Margaret R. (1994) 'The Narrative Constitution of Identity: A Relational and Network Approach', *Theory and Society*, 23, 605–49.
Thomas, W.I., and Florian Znaniecki (1918–1920) *The Polish Peasant in Europe and America*, Boston: Badger.

LINDA J. MORRISON

SOUNDTRACK

The term 'soundtrack' refers to the audible component of a *film. The soundtrack of a film may comprise the speech of *characters (*see* SPEECH REPRESENTATION), the sound of depicted events, ambient sound, the voice of a *voice-over narrator, and, perhaps most notably, *music. For reasons of space this article is restricted to the role of soundtrack music in fiction film. It is perhaps obvious how the other elements of a soundtrack can contribute to the narrative in a fiction film, but less obvious how music can do so.

A distinction of utmost importance is that between *diegetic* and *non-diegetic* music. Diegetic music has its source in the story being presented on screen, whereas non-diegetic music does not; diegetic music is that which may naturally be understood as occurring in the story, whereas non-diegetic music must be understood as being somehow imposed from without (*see* DIEGESIS; STORY-DISCOURSE DISTINCTION). Non-diegetic music is the paradigm of film music. Such non-diegetic music is of two main kinds, which might be labelled *composed* and *appropriated*; the former is music explicitly written for a film, the latter is pre-existing music that is adapted and arranged by the filmmaker.

Non-diegetic film music presents something of a puzzle to the theorist, having no naturalistic basis in the scene it accompanies, and appearing to come out of nowhere. Such music has a number of artistic functions, the most commonly noted of which are: creating and defusing of tension, creating atmosphere or mood, aiding achievement of continuity, characterising of characters, foreshadowing of events, amplifying the inherent *emotion of a scene, and commenting on the action. Some of these functions, clearly, are narrative ones, and the music involved can be labelled *narrative film music. In such cases, the music makes a difference in the narrative; in other words, something in the story is made fictional by the soundtrack music, and the music must thus be understood as in the service of, and ascribable to, the film's cinematic *narrator or presenter. In other cases non-diegetic music is heard as significant yet not narrative, that is, not such as to make something fictional in the film. Such music, which can be labelled *additive* film music, is generally a vehicle of *commentary on a film's fictional world, rather than a device for delineating that world; additive music must thus be ascribed directly to the implied filmmaker or *author. Some films with notable use of additive music are *Mouchette*, *Badlands*, and *A Clockwork Orange*.

The extent to which soundtrack music is attended to by moviegoers, even professional ones, and the extent to which it needs to be registered in order to function effectively, remain matters of controversy among theorists of film.

SEE ALSO: narration; storyworld

References and further reading

Brown, Royal S. (1994) *Undertones and Overtones: Reading Film Music*, Berkeley: University of California Press.

Buhler, James, Caryl Flinn, and David Neumeyer (eds) (2000) *Music and Cinema*, Hanover: University Press of New England.

Carroll, Noël (1990) *Mystifying Movies*, New York: Columbia University Press.

Chatman, Seymour (1990) *Coming to Terms: The Rhetoric of Narrative in Fiction and Film*, Ithaca: Cornell University Press.

Chion, Michel (1995) *La Musique au cinéma*, Paris: Fayard.

Gorbman, Claudia (1987) *Unheard Melodies: Narrative Film Music*, Bloomington: Indiana University Press.

Kalinak, Kathryn (1992) *Settling the Score: Music and the Classical Hollywood Film*, Madison: University of Wisconsin Press.

Kivy, Peter (1997) 'Music and the Movies: a Philosophical Enquiry', in Richard Allen and Murray Smith (eds) *Film Theory and Philosophy*, Oxford: Oxford University Press.

Levinson, Jerrold (1996) 'Film Music and Narrative Agency', in David Bordwell and Noël Carroll (eds) *Post-Theory: Reconstructing Film Studies*, Madison: University of Wisconsin Press.

JERROLD LEVINSON

SPACE IN NARRATIVE

In narrative theory, consideration of space got off to a slow start mainly for two reasons. One was that Gotthold Ephraim Lessing's characterisation of narrative literature as a 'temporal' art (as opposed to 'spatial' arts like painting and sculpture) seemed too evident to be seriously interrogated. The second reason was that space in narratives – especially pre-nineteenth-century ones – often seemed to have no other function than to supply a general background setting, something to be taken for granted rather than requiring attention, far less essential than the temporal directedness ('teleology') of the *plot.

The apparent – though ultimately misleading – imbalance of *time and space in narrative can be demonstrated in a variety of ways. It is space, not temporal sequence, which can be radically minimised without any obvious loss in 'narrativehood' (Gerald Prince). A story cannot have too much of temporal sequentiality, but it does grind to a halt when overloaded with spatial *description (cf Georges Perec's short 'story' *Still Life/Style Leaf*). *Minimal stories often do without indications of

space altogether, yet always retain a kernel of temporal order. Thus in E.M. Forster's famous 'The king died, and then the queen died of grief' no concrete setting is mentioned and the text can be fully understood on the simple presupposition that the characters must have lived and died 'somewhere'. Similarly, a stage can be left wholly bare in a theatre without significantly detracting from the *audience's understanding of the enacted *events. By contrast, radical subversion of temporal sequence, such as follows from 'achrony' and related techniques of *temporal ordering, not only crucially weakens narrative coherence but usually also triggers elaborate attempts at reintroducing temporal order via a strategy of *naturalisation.

Although the foregoing evidence may appear to confirm the intuition that space is less important than time in narrative, there is a 'spatial turn' in narrative theory whose pre-history can be traced along four major way stations. (1) Disregarding Lessing's dictum, many descriptions of narrative style, organisation, and structure (*see* NARRATIVE STRUCTURE), notably those articulated by Henry James at the beginning of the twentieth century, employ the images of spatial arts, especially painting and architecture (e.g., James's 'House of Fiction' *metaphor). (2) In a much-noted essay Joseph Frank (1963 [1948]) discussed 'major works of modern literature' – by Flaubert, Proust, and Joyce – whose practice of juxtaposing simultaneous events created what he termed a *spatial form. (3) In a pathbreaking essay on *chronotopes (literally, 'timespaces'), Mikhail Bakhtin (1981 [1938–1973]) argued that time and space were best treated as an inseparable complex of parameters, with time supplying 'the fourth dimension of space' as in Einstein's theory of relativity (Zoran 1984). (4) In the nineteen-forties and fifties, the French philosophers Maurice Merleau-Ponty (1962 [1945]) and Gaston Bachelard (1994 [1957]) offered a liberating theorisation of 'lived space', a concept specifically addressing space within the framework of literature and human perception.

Today, critics and narrative theorists alike have come to recognise that features of narrative space are far more relevant than might be expected given Lessing's original pronouncement. Indeed, a great number of staple critical terms – *foregrounding, *gapping, *isotopy, centre, liminality, margin, migration, transgression, transition, etc. – are spatial metaphors easily illustrated by referring to spatial *existents in narrative texts. Moreover, there is a remarkable number of space-oriented narrative *genres, as is testified by the following entries in this Encyclopedia: *cyberpunk fiction, *eco-narrative, *fantasy, *Gothic novel, *historical novel, *Holocaust narrative, *prison narratives, *romance, *science fiction, *slave narrative, *travel narrative, *utopian and dystopian fiction. Perhaps the best indication of a new spatial focus in narrative studies is the sheer size of Bauer and Fokkema (1990) – the five-volume proceedings of a conference on 'Space and Boundaries'.

Defining narrative space

At its most basic level, narrative space is the environment in which story-internal *characters move about and live. Narrative space is characterised by a complex of parameters: (1) by the boundaries that separate it from coordinate, superordinate, and subordinate spaces, (2) by the objects which it contains, (3) by the living conditions which it provides, and (4) by the temporal dimension to which it is bound. Narrative space in this sense includes landscapes as well as friendly or inimical conditions (including climatic and atmospheric ones), and it is never simply 'the north of England', 'Dublin', or 'a kingdom', but 'the north of England at the beginning of the nineteenth-century', 'Dublin on 16 June 1904', and 'many and many a year ago, in a kingdom by the sea' (as in Charlotte Brontë's *Shirley*, James Joyce's *Ulysses*, and Edgar Allan Poe's *Annabel Lee*, respectively). Also useful is Ronen's distinction between 'framed' and 'framing' spaces, and her technical definition of 'setting' as the current base-level spatial frame, equivalent to the space represented on a theatrical stage ('the actual immediate surrounding of an object, a character or an event', as Ronen puts it [1986: 423]; *see* DRAMA AND NARRATIVE). If the base-level setting is a room, for instance, it is usually conceived of as being part of a set of framing spaces – a house, a city, a country, a continent, etc. Many systematic distinctions can be derived on the basis of these stipulations – zones of decreasing/increasing sharpness, foreground and background spaces, open and closed spaces, accessible and inaccessible spaces, close and distant spaces, actual and imaginary spaces, static and dynamic spaces, etc. Moreover, three types of spatial organisation within narrative worlds might be distinguished: (1) texts containing contiguous subspaces, where characters freely move from one space

to the next, (2) texts with discontinuous, ontologically distinct spaces that allow communication in exceptional circumstances only (Lewis Carroll's *Alice in Wonderland*, C.S. Lewis's *The Chronicles of Narnia*), (3) texts with ontologically distinct spaces that do not allow communication, except through *metalepsis (e.g., texts with embedded fictions; *see* EMBEDDING).

Just as the *story-discourse distinction supplies the narratological underpinnings of the concepts of 'story time' and 'discourse time', so, Chatman (1978: 96 ff) argues, it is profitable to distinguish between 'story space' and 'discourse space'. Story space refers to the immediate spatial environment containing an action episode (more globally also the range or amplitude of environments across all episodes), while discourse space denotes the *narrator's current environment (more globally also all environments framing the narrator's activities, including the act of storytelling or writing itself). For instance, favourite modern discourse spaces include hospitals and psychiatric wards, as in J. D. Salinger's *The Catcher in the Rye* and Günter Grass's *The Tin Drum*.

On a lower level of abstraction, the terms 'story-HERE' and 'discourse-HERE' denote the current 'points of origin' in story space and discourse space, respectively. Story-HERE is the zero point in story space determining the use of deictic expressions such as 'here', 'there', 'left', 'right', etc., often closely shadowing the physical location and point of view of a story-internal character (*see* DEIXIS; POINT OF VIEW (LITERARY)). Discourse-HERE, on the other hand, is the current point of orientation in discourse space, equivalent to the current physical location and vantage point of the narrator. Story-HERE and discourse-HERE, in conjunction with story-NOW and discourse-NOW, identify a narrative text's 'deictic centres', i.e., the origin(s) of its spatio-temporal coordinate system(s). Many of the insights worked out in the approaches to be surveyed in greater detail below stress this perspectival aspect of space (*see* PERSPECTIVE); for the same reason, representation and perception of fictional space is closely related to *focalization.

Finally, the intricate correspondence between objects and spaces and the spatial nature of the text itself are well worth theoretical notice. A house is an object in a larger (superordinate, framing) environment, but for its inhabitants it is part of their living space. A human body is an object in space, too, but in a possible narrative world where a drug allows characters to shrink to the size of a bacterium, it becomes a space for exploration, quest, and adventure, as in the *science fiction film *Fantastic Voyage* (1966). Similarly, the architecture of hypertext, as described by navigational maps, is a special type of textual space, and navigating hypertext, just as reading fiction itself, is often likened to a journey (*see* DIGITAL NARRATIVE; METANARRATIVE COMMENT).

Representations of space: scenic presentation, depiction, description

Although the following distinctions are not universally used, it makes terminological sense to say that (1) on the theatrical stage, space is 'scenically presented' (*see* SUMMARY AND SCENE), (2) in pictures and *film it is 'depicted' (*see* PICTORIAL NARRATIVITY), and (3) in verbal narratives, it is 'described' (Chatman 1978). More obviously than in the other modes of representation, spatial description is relative to either observers (i.e., narrators or characters) or intrinsically oriented objects (Ryan 2003: 217). Moreover, as Stanzel (1984 [1979]: ch. 5.2) points out, space in a *novel is distinct from space in the visual arts because description relies on *gapping and audience cooperation to accomplish its task (*see* READER-RESPONSE THEORY). Describing the interior of a room to the smallest discernible detail is practically impossible, whereas the 'full' presentation of a room on a stage is unproblematic (at least in principle), as is a similarly plenitudinous depiction in the *media of picture and film. In verbal narrative, however, spatial features are usually invoked by tracing the visible boundaries and referring to obstructions and typical or characteristic objects. At the same time, deictic expressions such as 'here', 'there', etc., serve as strategic cues inviting the reader to transpose to the scene of action and to picture the setting imaginatively, often adopting the position of a hypothetical observer or an 'internal focalizer' (*see* IMMERSION).

Another media-related difference is that once a setting has been established verbal description tends to be parsimonious with respect to static or 'durative' spatial properties. While filmic depiction is continually refreshed at the rate of 24 times per second, verbal description simply 'continues to apply' until an explicit update is required by a change in conditions (Ronen 1986: 424). Interestingly,

filmic depiction can be effectively reductive in just this way, demonstrating the functional family resemblance between the modes of representation. Consider the stock establishing *shot of an office building in a soap opera. As with all filmic depiction, it contains an almost infinite amount of information validating the proverbial truism that a picture tells more than a thousand words. Yet the relevant information transmitted exactly amounts to what the verbal description in the film's script succinctly (and in proper Bakhtinian style) expresses as 'Cut to: Exterior. Day. The Ewing Oil office complex' (*see* SCREENPLAY).

Approaches to space

One of the most influential impulses for the spatial turn in narrative studies has come from the philosophical field of *phenomenology, and it was studies like Maurice Merleau-Ponty's *The Phenomenology of Perception* (1962 [1945]) and Gaston Bachelard's *The Poetics of Space* (1994 [1957]) which offered the first groundbreaking modelling of the human interface of space. The central concept developed within phenomenological studies is the notion of 'lived space' (*espace vécu*), the humanly embodied counterpart of the three-dimensional, empty, and basically unoriented spaces of physics and geometry. Lived space is deictically oriented space as perceived and talked about in everyday life. The term itself indicates that human (or 'natural') conceptions of space always include a subject who is affected by (and in turn affects) space, a subject who experiences and reacts to space in a bodily way, a subject who 'feels' space through existential living conditions, mood, and atmosphere. It is in the framework of these subject-oriented interrelations that spatial descriptions acquire the rich semantics they have both in real life and in narrative texts. Hoffmann's (1978) voluminous study of British and American novels offers a complex typology of such experiential spaces, including *fantastic, grotesque, uncanny, visionary, and mythic spaces (*see* MYTH: THEORETICAL APPROACHES).

Approaching the matter from a literary-historical perspective, critics have mainly commented on the uneven distribution of 'perspectival' and 'aperspectival' representations of space (Stanzel 1984 [1979]: ch. 5.2). In early narrative texts, space is often reduced to a mere backdrop or stage design whose relevant features are largely assumed to be known even if the setting itself is as crucial as the *locus amoenus* in medieval and romantic literature or indicative of the social status of characters as in the novels of Jane Austen. It is not until the rise of the *realist novel that detailed description of spatial elements becomes a functional feature of narrative discourse. The trimmings of space become more relevant still in movements such as literary impressionism and psychological realism until, at the beginning of the twentieth century, the pauses of narratorial description are largely replaced by perceptions of space shown from the *perspective of an internal focalizer (*see* PSYCHOLOGICAL NOVEL; SHOWING VS. TELLING; THOUGHT AND CONSCIOUSNESS REPRESENTATION (LITERATURE)). While aperspectival representation remains indeterminate in the sense that 'the interior of a room is never depicted in such a way that a graphic sketch can be made of it, even if the reader is given a more or less complete inventory of the objects in the room' (Stanzel 1984 [1979]: 120), *authors such as Gustave Flaubert and Henry James, and later the rest of the modernists, used highly perspectivised representations of spatial objects and spatial relations (*see* MODERNIST NARRATIVE). As Stanzel points out, however, the self-conscious turn characteristic of postmodernism seems to revert to a variant of aperspectivism as exhibited, for example, in William Burrough's *The Naked Lunch* and John Barth's *Lost in the Funhouse* (*see* POSTMODERN NARRATIVE). A similar tendency can be observed in more recent representations of cyber- and virtual spaces.

Pursuing a structuralist-semiotic approach, Iurii Lotman has persuasively shown that spatial oppositions such as near/far, high/low, front/back, etc., are usually correlated with judgmental values such as good/bad, familiar/strange, valuable/worthless, and so on (*see* SEMIOTICS). The metaphorical and emotive potential inherent in this conjunction of spaces and values has led theorists to speak of the semantic charging (or 'semanticisation') of space (Pfister 1988: 257; *see* EMOTION AND NARRATIVE). Other semioticians have tried to push this insight further and to analyse spatial opposites such as city/country, civilisation/nature, public space/private space, house/garden, and so on, as emotionally laden cultural constructs (van Baak 1983; Hess-Lüttich *et al.* 1998). As van Baak points out, any cultural definition of lived space means, first of all, that space is variable and subject to change even if its dimensions remain physically constant. Cultural appreciation of the city/country

distinction, for instance, has repeatedly changed over the centuries and is likely to change again given appropriate circumstances. What makes the research conducted by van Baak and other space semioticians so fruitful is that it lends itself to far-ranging extrapolation, allowing the researcher to address the larger issues of cultural habits and change itself.

The relevance of space categories is even more evident in the investigations conducted within the frameworks of *gender studies, cultural studies, and post-colonial studies (*see* CULTURAL STUDIES APPROACHES TO NARRATIVE; MARXIST APPROACHES TO NARRATIVE; POST-COLONIALISM AND NARRATIVE), in which ethnic, racial, gendered, and class-based segmentations and perceptions of space play a major part (McDowell and Sharp 1997; Higonnet and Templeton 1994). One only has to think of spaces like ghettos, colonies, the Diaspora, or indeed 'the house in Victorian England' (as a place of female consignment) to see the relevance of space within these studies.

Space and its natural-language representations have also attracted considerable interest in the empirical and *Artificial Intelligence branches of cognitive studies. Working in this tradition, Duchan *et al.* (1995) have surveyed spatial cues in narrative texts from several perspectives, including making concrete (if speculative) proposals on how to code the internal representations involved. Pursuing a more professedly narratological orientation, Ryan's (2003) project of a 'literary cartography' explores the strategies of reconstructing maps of fictional worlds involving readers of varying literary competence. Based on an informal experiment in which students were asked to draw a map of the setting of Gabriel García Márquez's *Chronicle of a Death Foretold*, Ryan offers a close analysis of textual cues and corresponding mapping actions and of the relationship between cognitive maps and more encompassing mental models of narrative structure. Above all, what Ryan's investigation demonstrates is that a dedicated model of narrative space and space representation deserves to be made a standard component of *postclassical narratology.

SEE ALSO: cognitive narratology; mental mapping of narrative; situation model

References and further reading

van Baak, Jan Joost (1983) *The Place of Space in Narration: A Semiotic Approach to the Problem of Literary Space*, Amsterdam: Rodopi.

Bachelard, Gaston (1994 [1957]) *The Poetics of Space: The Classic Look at How We Experience Intimate Places*, trans. Maria Jolas, Boston: Beacon Press.

Bakhtin, Mikhail (1981 [1938–1973] 'Forms of Time and the Chronotope in the Novel', *The Dialogic Imagination: Four Essays by M. M. Bakhtin*, ed. Michael Holquist, trans. Michael Holquist and Caryl Emerson, Austin: University of Texas Press.

Bauer, Roger, and Douwe Fokkema (eds) (1990) *Space and Boundaries/Espace et Frontières: Proceedings of the XIIth Congress of the International Comparative Literature Association*, München: iudicum.

Chatman, Seymour (1978) *Story and Discourse: Narrative Structure in Fiction and Film*, Ithaca: Cornell University Press.

Duchan, Judith F., Gail A. Bruder, and Lynne E. Hewitt (eds) (1995) *Deixis in Narrative: A Cognitive Science Perspective*, Hillsdale, NJ: Erlbaum.

Frank, Joseph (1963) 'Spatial Form in Modern Literature', in *The Widening Gyre: Crisis and Mastery in Modern Literature*, New Brunswick: Rutgers University Press.

Hess-Lüttich, Ernest W. B., Jürgen E. Müller, and Aart van Zoest (eds) (1998) *Signs & Space: An International Conference on the Semiotics of Space and Culture in Amsterdam*, Tübingen: Narr.

Higonnet, Margaret R., and Joan Templeton (eds) (1994) *Reconfigured Spheres: Feminist Explorations of Literary Space*, Amherst: University of Massachusetts Press.

Hoffmann, Gerhard (1978) *Raum, Situation, erzählte Wirklichkeit: Poetologische und historische Studien zum englischen und amerikanischen Roman*, Stuttgart: Metzler.

Lotman Iurii (1977 [1973]) *The Structure of the Artistic Text*, trans. Gail Lenhoff and Ronald Vroon, Ann Arbor: University of Michigan, Department of Slavic Languages and Literatures.

McDowell, Linda, and Joanne P. Sharp (1997) *Space, Gender, Knowledge: Feminist Readings*, London: Arnold.

Merleau-Ponty, Maurice (1962 [1945]) *The Phenomenology of Perception*, trans. Colin Smith, London: Routledge & Kegan Paul.

Pfister, Manfred (1988) *The Theory and Analysis of Drama*, trans. John Halliday, Cambridge: Cambridge University Press.

Ronen, Ruth (1986) 'Space in Fiction', *Poetics Today*, 7.3, 421–38.

Ryan, Marie-Laure (2003) 'Cognitive Maps and the Construction of Narrative Space', in David Herman (ed.) *Narrative Theory and the Cognitive Sciences*, Stanford, CA: CSLI Publications.

Stanzel, Franz K. (1984 [1979]) *A Theory of Narrative*, trans. Charlotte Goedsche, Cambridge: Cambridge University Press.

Zoran, Gabriel (1984) 'Towards a Theory of Space in Narrative', *Poetics Today*, 5, 309–35.

SABINE BUCHHOLZ AND MANFRED JAHN

SPATIAL FORM

Spatial form is a mode of *narrative structure that foregrounds *thematic rather than chronological or causal principles of order (*see* CAUSALITY). In this sense 'spatial' is not a referential category but a structural *metaphor. This metaphoric spatiality, moreover, is a tendency rather than an absolute: given the fundamental sequentiality of the reading process and of language itself, and given the centrality of temporal concepts in conventional ways of conceiving the world, *temporal ordering clearly cannot be eliminated. However, spatial-form texts seek to de-emphasise or obscure temporality via parataxis, fragmentation, *montage, and multiple plots (*see* PLOT; PLOT TYPES) – or by simply omitting temporal references. More generally, *event and plot are de-emphasised in favour of a synchronic 'field', portrait (especially the representation of consciousness), or encyclopedic inventory (*see* ENCYCLOPEDIC NOVEL). Despite its disjunctive organisation, spatial form possesses an underlying coherence based on thematic analogies (Sternberg 1978: 154) and associative cross-references, but this coherence must be established by the reader.

The concept was initially formulated by Joseph Frank, who stressed its importance in modernist poetry (Pound, Eliot) and fiction (Joyce, Proust, Djuna Barnes) (*see* MODERNIST NARRATIVE). Critiquing Lessing's differentiation of spatial and temporal arts, Frank argued that modernist texts sought to approximate the effects of the spatial arts by using juxtaposition to foster the 'secondary illusion' (Kestner: 1978: 19) of simultaneity. The alternating focus of Flaubert's county fair scene in *Madame Bovary* provides, for Frank, a small-scale instance of spatial form, but a more substantial and sustained example would be the four disjunct sections of Faulkner's *The Sound and the Fury*, each with a different narrator and a different temporal locus. Frank's formulation recognises the crucial role of the reader in synthesising, by 'reflexive reference', the disparate elements of spatial-form narratives. He employed this term as a structural metaphor, but it has also been misleadingly applied to *ekphrasis (*see* INTERMEDIALITY).

Although the flexibility of spatial form was particularly well-suited to the modernist focus on consciousness, perception, and feeling (*see* THOUGHT AND CONSCIOUSNESS REPRESENTATION (LITERATURE)), versions of this type of organisation have been identified as early as Apuleius. The most recent development of spatial form is hypertext, as Landow and Bolter have shown, but by replacing the fixed reading order of traditional narrative with a series of choices, hypertext narratives have put even greater demands on readers to identify schemas of coherence (*see* DIGITAL NARRATIVE; MULTI-PATH NARRATIVE).

SEE ALSO: space in narrative; time in narrative

References and further reading

Bolter, Jay David (2000) *Writing Space: Computers, Hypertext, and the Remediation of Print*, Mahwah, NJ: Lawrence Erlbaum.
Frank, Joseph (1991 [1945]) 'Spatial Form in Modern Literature', in *The Idea of Spatial Form*, New Brunswick, NJ: Rutgers University Press.
Ireland, Ken (2001) *The Sequential Dynamics of Narrative: Energies at the Margins of Fiction*, London: Associated University Press.
Kestner, Joseph (1978) *Spatiality and the Novel*, Detroit: Wayne State University Press.
Landow, George (1997) *Hypertext 2.0*, Baltimore: Johns Hopkins University Press.
Smitten, Jeff, and Ann Daghistany (eds) (1981) *Spatial Form in Narrative*, Ithaca: Cornell University Press.
Sternberg, Meir (1978) *Expositional Modes and Temporal Ordering in Fiction*, Baltimore: Johns Hopkins University Press.

DAVID J. MICKELSEN

SPECTACLE

The term 'spectacle' (lat. *spectaculum*: play; *spectare*: to watch) signifies an object of curiosity or a dramatic public display, mostly linked to entertainment and sensation. In aesthetic theory, spectacle was considered an inferior element as early as in Aristotle's *Poetics* (Poetics 4.4.).

While in the sixteenth and seventeenth centuries Montaigne and Pascal explained the *desire for diversion from a socio-psychological perspective, in the discourse of Enlightenment such desire was attacked as neglect of the individual's obligation to perfect the self. The conflict between entertainment and the 'historic mission' of perfection emerges again with the arrival of cinema and is elaborated in Adorno's critique of the 'culture industry', which sought to use aesthetic identification and pleasure to affirm the status quo in the social order. In the 1960s, Debord also discusses spectacle – which 'aims at nothing other than itself' – as the defining element of modern society.

Although Habermas dates a shift in the mode of perception from (public) reasoning to (private) consumption as early as the nineteenth-century, this shift becomes accentuated with the appearance of *television. Postman considers diversion the message of this medium and, bringing together McLuhan and Adorno, states: technology is *ideology. With the advent of digital media, diversion and spectacle gain new attention in many regards (*see* DIGITAL NARRATIVE; MEDIA AND NARRATIVE). A number of critics (e.g., Sven Birkerts) attributed to the electronic media as such a decline of reading skills. Meanwhile, proponents of electronic writing (such as Robert Coover) argued that the multimedial Web threatened to reduce the substance of non-linear *narration to surface spectacle (*see* INTERMEDIALITY; MULTI-PATH NARRATIVE). Since the bi-directionality of digital media allows, indeed often requires, active participation of the reader/visitor/user on the physical level, the *audience is no longer inclined to contemplate or even concentrate in the process of perception. While in print media and electronic media, including cinema and television (*see* FILM NARRATIVE), the spectacle (car chases, extravagantly staged panoramas, highly stylised designs) usually remains a component of the story; in digital media technical effects (especially if the user is interactively involved in their appearance) take precedence over narrative interest. Flash animations, for instance, often avoid cinematographic language and narrative intention, in order to foreground the computer's graphic power and the programmer's virtuosity.

This fascination with technology is reminiscent of early filmic experimentation (e.g., Hans Richter's *Vormittagsspuk*) as well as of the extensive use of digital effects in cinema towards the end of the twentieth century (*Star Wars, The Matrix*). The emphasis on technical effects over content leads to an aesthetics of the sensual and signifies 'a shift away from prior modes of spectator experience based on symbolic concerns (and "interpretative models") towards recipients who are seeking intensities of direct sensual stimulation' (Darley 2000). This poetics of sensation can be discussed critically with respect to the culture industry (now hiding behind interactivity) and kitsch (as surrender to the object instead of critical distance from it). It can also be seen within the tradition of formal aesthetics, which favoured a presentational over a representational rhetoric and aimed to free the visual sign from its meaning-bearing role (*see* FORMALISM). It can be argued that whenever the purpose of the digital code is not to represent meaning but to display itself as such, this code becomes the modern equivalent of the pure visual. The display of technology becomes an even stronger *anti-narrative force than the *mise en spectacle* of the visual.

SEE ALSO: visual narrativity

References and further reading

Darley, Andrew (2000) *Visual Digital Culture: Surface Play and Spectacle in New Media Genres*, London: Routledge.
Debord, Guy (1977) *Society of Spectacle*, Detroit: Black and Red Books.
Manovich, Lev (2001) *The Language of New Media*, Cambridge, Mass.: MIT Press.

ROBERTO SIMANOWSKI

SPEECH ACT THEORY

Speech act theory is a branch of ordinary language *philosophy that originated in the 1950s in Austin's *How to Do Things with Words* and continued most prominently in the work of Searle. Austin begins by undermining the widespread philosophical assumption that a 'statement' can only describe a situation or state a fact, and that it must be either true or false (*see* TRUTH). Coining the term 'constative' for such true/false utterances, he provisionally contrasts them with a radically different kind of speech, the 'performative', in which by saying something (for instance, saying 'I do' during a wedding ceremony), the speaker performs an act (*see* ACTION THEORY). Performatives are neither true nor false, although (since the person saying 'I do' may not be eligible for marriage) they do have a parallel quality designated by the distinction happy/unhappy (or felicitous/infelicitous). Finding the constative/performative distinction difficult to maintain, however, Austin soon abandons it in favour of a more nuanced three-levelled distinction: utterances are simultaneously locutionary, illocutionary, and perlocutionary acts. The locutionary refers to an utterance's meaning in the strict semantic sense; the illocutionary refers to what Austin calls the 'force' of the utterance, the action it aims to

perform (e.g., promising, warning, betting); the perlocutionary refers to the utterance's effect on its *audience. As a locutionary act, speaking the words 'This car can hit 120 miles an hour' has a particular meaning, a particular sense and *reference. These words, however, could be used to perform different illocutionary acts: warning about driving dangers, for instance, or boasting about automotive power. Persuading someone to watch the speedometer or to push the gas pedal to the floor are perlocutionary acts, which – regardless of the speaker's intentions (*see* INTENTIONALITY) – might or might not result from the illocutionary acts of warning or boasting. Austin believed that his concentration on illocutionary acts, acts closely tied to context and convention, was the key contribution of speech act theory.

Austin's work was refined by Searle, who applied speech act theory to a number of enduring philosophical questions, and by Grice, who argued that conversation is regulated by the cooperative principle and its four maxims of quantity ('Make your contribution as informative as [but no more informative than] is required'), quality ('Try to make your contribution one that is true'), relation ('Be relevant'), and manner ('Be perspicuous') (Grice 1975: 45-46; *see* PRAGMATICS). Grice shows how utterances remain meaningful, through what he terms 'implicature', even when a maxim is 'flouted' by a participant. If, for example, I write a single-sentence letter of recommendation saying 'Student X showed up for class', a reader can determine, from my extreme violation of the maxim of quantity, that X is not a good candidate for graduate school.

Austin explicitly sidestepped literary speech acts, but literary scholars have nonetheless seized on his distinctions. Some simply used one or another of his terms (not always in the ways he meant them) as part of a larger, more eclectic project. The notion of the performative, for instance, has been taken up by critics as different as Lyotard and Butler (*see* PERFORMATIVITY). But more complete versions of speech act theory have entered narrative studies, in at least two distinct ways.

First, some critics have used Austin's categories as an interpretive tool, often by analysing speech acts within the diegetic world (*see* DIEGESIS; STORYWORLD). Eaton, for instance, uses a key speech-act observation – that the same words can be used with different illocutionary forces – to argue that James's *The Turn of the Screw* is intentionally ambiguous. Second, critics have used speech act theory to explore the nature of literary discourse itself. Speech act theory has not provided definitive answers – but it has offered new ways of thinking about old problems, such as the logical status of *fiction and the role of authorial intention (*see* AUTHOR). Thus, for instance, critics have debated whether fiction is (1) not an illocutionary act at all (Beardsley); (2) a flawed or incomplete kind of illocutionary act parasitic on real-life illocutionary acts (Searle claims that writing narrative fiction is pretending to perform a serious illocutionary act); or (3) a particular illocutionary act on its own (Ohmann, for instance, sees the illocutionary force of fiction as mimetic (*see* MIMESIS), whereas Genette offers a definition of narrative fiction as a special kind of declarative through which an author posits fictional objects, with the perlocutionary effect of getting readers to imagine a state of affairs). Similarly, speech act theory's distinction among locutionary, illocutionary, and perlocutionary acts has allowed critics to distinguish different levels of intention which are relevant for answering different kinds of questions.

Pratt has probably provided the most influential work on the status of literature as a speech act. She studies literature generally rather than fiction alone, disputing the Russian Formalists' and New Critics' belief that literary discourse is a particular 'kind of language', and arguing instead that it is a particular 'use' of language (Pratt xiii; *see* FORMALISM). More specifically, Pratt argues that literature is a special type of utterance, a display text – a text that calls on the audience to consider events or situations that are tellable (contrary to expectations or otherwise worthy of attention; *see* TELLABILITY). Literary works, however, are not autonomous or self-contained, rather, like all other speech acts, they work in a context. The specific context for literature is institutional: the reader knows, for instance, that the work has survived review through some socially sanctioned process. This extra-textual knowledge allows readers to assume that Grice's cooperative principle is hyperprotected, which in turn means that readers will regard violations of the principle as intentional floutings rather than as indications of authorial incompetence. Thus, for example, when readers encounter a *narrator who offers contradictory accounts of the same event, they assume that the inconsistency signals the narrator's unreliability, not the author's incompetence (*see* NATURALISATION; RELIABILITY).

SEE ALSO: reader constructs; reader-response theory

References and further reading

Austin, John L. (1975 [1962]) *How to Do Things With Words*, ed. J. O. Urmson and Marina Sbisa, Cambridge, Mass.: Harvard University Press.

Beardsley, Monroe C. (1973) 'The Concept of Literature', in Frank Brady, John Palmer, and Martin Price (eds) *Literary Theory and Structure: Essays in Honor of William K. Wismatt*, New Haven: Yale University Press.

Butler, Judith (1993) *Bodies that Matter: On the Discursive Limits of 'Sex'*, London: Routledge.

Eaton, Marcia A. (1983) 'James's Turn of the Speech-Act', *British Journal of Aesthetics*, 23, 333–45.

Genette, Gérard (1993 [1991]) *Fiction and Diction*, trans. Catherine Porter, Ithaca: Cornell University Press.

Grice, Paul H. (1975) 'Logic and Conversation', in Peter Cole and Jerry L. Morgan (eds) *Syntax and Semantics, Volume III: Speech Acts*, New York: Academic Press.

Kearns, Michael (1999) *Rhetorical Narratology*, Lincoln: University of Nebraska Press.

Lyotard, Jean-Francois (1984) *The Postmodern Condition: A Report on Knowledge*, trans. Geoff Bennington and Brian Massumi, Minneapolis: University of Minnesota Press.

Ohmann, Richard (1971) 'Speech Acts and the Definition of Literature', *Philosophy and Rhetoric*, 4, 1-19.

Pratt, Mary Louise (1977) *Toward a Speech Act Theory of Literary Discourse*, Bloomington: Indiana University Press.

Searle, John (1969) *Speech Acts: An Essay in the Philosophy of Language*, Cambridge: Cambridge University Press.

—— (1979) *Expression and Meaning: Studies in the Theory of Speech Acts*, Cambridge: Cambridge University Press.

PETER J. RABINOWITZ

SPEECH REPRESENTATION

Speech and *thought representation are important areas of research in both linguistics and narratology. Thus, drawing distinctions among direct speech (or discourse), indirect speech, *free indirect discourse, the narrative report of speech (or thought) acts or content paraphrase constitutes a linguistic problem in its own right and has been the subject of extensive analysis by grammarians and linguists (e.g., Short, Semino, and Wynne 1999). On the other hand, the forms and functions of speech and thought representation have always been a central issue in literary and narrative studies. In its structuralist phase, narrative theory (i.e., narratology) was particularly interested in the formal differentiations between indirect and free indirect discourse and in the so-called dual-voice phenomenon (see below; *see* STRUCTURALIST NARRATOLOGY).

The importance of speech representation in narrative had been acknowledged as early as Plato's *Republic* III (292D–294E), in which Socrates distinguishes between *narration (*diegesis*) and speeches (*mimesis*), thus separating the *genre of poetry (in which the *author speaks in his own *voice) from the *epic (in which *diegesis, the narrator's speech act, and *mimesis, the *characters' discourse, are mixed). Besides giving rise to generic differentiations, the mimesis/diegesis distinction has come to stand for the fictional representation of pure vs. mediated figural discourse, i.e., the representation of protagonists' words in unmediated direct speech (mimesis) vs. their mediated and shifted manifestations (in indirect speech, free indirect discourse, and speech report) within the narrator's diegetic discourse. Even more misleadingly, the mimesis/diegesis dichotomy is sometimes regarded as an antecedent of Benveniste's and later Genette's/Chatman's *histoire* vs. *discours* opposition. This is misleading because Genette's term *diégèse* does not refer to the narrator's speech act (as in Plato) but to the story that is being told, i.e., the *histoire*; and *discours* corresponds precisely with what Plato calls diegesis, the *narrator's act of narration (*see* STORY-DISCOURSE DISTINCTION).

In the Platonic (Socratic) distinction between diegesis (narrative) and mimesis (rendering of characters' speech) the leading characteristic – narratologically speaking – is that of narrative *level*: protagonists' utterances which are (apparently) quoted verbatim open a subordinate level of discourse on which embedded narration can be produced – a story within a story (*see* EMBEDDING). Protagonists' discourse is *quoted* and *framed*: each act of narration can serve as a frame for an embedded act of narration (*see* FRAMED NARRATIVE; FRAME THEORY; QUOTATION THEORY).

Since characters' speech acts are part of the *plot of a narrative and consist of words, the mimesis of speech, as Genette noted (1980 [1972]: 164, 169), is the only type of perfect mimesis available (the medium of representation is identical to the object of representation – words repeat words). Besides embedding and framing, speech representation therefore additionally involves a factor of authenticity and *realism. Not only does the quotation of an utterance in language seem to be a near-perfect reproduction of the original speech act; the linguistic representation of language in addition allows the imitation of speech peculiarities such as dialectal, sociolectal, and idiolectal variants (*see* SOCIOLINGUISTIC APPROACHES TO NARRATIVE). It therefore significantly affects the production of *reality effects in (narrative) texts.

Genette's thesis of a one-to-one correspondence between quoted language and its original source does, however, require some important qualifications. Thus, in literary language, the speech acts are all invented – there cannot be verbatim repetition of non-existent prior discourse. Nor does direct discourse in narrative fiction operate as an impersonation since – in contrast with Plato's dramatic model – no visible actor utters it. On the contrary, direct speech in narrative texts is best characterised as a rhetorical strategy on the part of the narrator, employed to enhance the *performativity value of the narrative (Wolfson 1982; *see* PERFORMANCE; RHETORICAL APPROACHES TO NARRATIVE). Written language cannot ever hope to reproduce oral language; the most realistically written passage of direct speech is always a stylisation of uttered discourse (as transcriptions of tape recordings document) (*see* ORALITY). Moreover, in the evocation of dialect and sociolect, literary discourse employs numerous devices of repetition, exaggeration, selection, and condensation which serve to typify the representation (Fludernik 1993: ch. 9). A quoted passage of characters' discourse supposed to sound genuine will therefore selectively focus on features of oral discourse, dialect, etc. that make the passage into a verisimilar evocation of an exclamation, a Cockney diatribe, or a request uttered by a working-class person. Such features foreground the *alterity of the quoted speakers' language and therefore institute a linguistic norm represented by the narrator's register and style. A comparison with transcripts of conversation shows that such passages of pseudo-orality are linguistically lopsided towards exaggerating a few prominent features of conversational discourse, dialect, or sociolect, and that they neglect other features. Paradoxically, an over-detailed copy of the speech act actually detracts from the overall effect of realism by making the representation too complicated, too obscure, or too laborious for easy reading comprehension. In fact, it is only in *oral* narrative that a speech act could hope to be mimed with anything close to perfection, and even here – as one can observe in conversational narrative – speech representations are geared towards producing an effect of vivacity, exaggerating specific features and downplaying other authentic aspects of the original utterance acts (*see* CONVERSATIONAL STORYTELLING).

The handling of direct speech, of quotation, is therefore a much more complicated matter than is usually assumed. It combines aspects of style, of narrative authority and manipulation, authenticity claims, and propositional veracity. In some contexts, such as the reporting of utterances in court or in the non-tabloid press, there is an understanding that reports should be near-verbatim repetitions of the original utterance (*see* COURTROOM NARRATIVE; JOURNALISM); in other *text-types and in the oral language, however, such faithfulness is neither possible nor indeed expected or practised.

Speech representation in narrative does not exclusively occur in the representation of characters' utterances; the discourse of the narrator, if conceived of as a pseudo-oral type of utterance, builds on the same strategies of the evocation of authentic speech which we already noted for the *dialogue of characters. The pseudo-orality of narratorial reporting, especially in *skaz narration, invokes a situation of communication between narrator and *narratee; the reader seems to be overhearing an actual speech act. Such narratives clearly depart from the traditional realist formula in which a more or less stylistically neutral discourse of the narrator in standard English (French, German, etc.) is opposed to the quoted characters' utterances in lower-class idiom, dialect, idiolectal variants, and colloquial diction (*see* REALIST NOVEL). The systematic difference between the narrator's and the characters' language in fact makes it possible to distinguish echoes of characters' discourse in the narrative. Narratologists and stylisticians have been extremely interested in such a 'mixing' of narrators' and characters' languages or styles (*see* DIALOGISM; HETEROGLOSSIA). From the adoption of single words or phrases that can obviously be traced to the characters' discourse (citation), to larger borrowings from figural language in what F. K. Stanzel has called *Ansteckung* ('infection'), this mixing of idioms and styles reaches its climax in free indirect discourse where, according to the *dual-voice hypothesis, the narrators and the characters 'speak together' in *polyphony.

Traditionally, a complete formal (i.e., grammatical) symmetry is expected to exist between speech representation and thought representation (but see below and Palmer 2004). The terminology, especially for thought representation, is inconsistent. The following table mentions only the most current terms. For a fuller treatment see Palmer's entry in this Encyclopedia (*see* THOUGHT AND CONSCIOUSNESS REPRESENTATION (LITERATURE)).

Comments on the table

(1) Scale. The categories below are not to be seen as absolutely distinct but as a scale of forms situated

Basic category and examples	Speech representation	Thought representation
quoted and unquoted direct discourse *'Hey, I love you'*	direct/quoted speech	interior monologue (Cohn: quoted/unquoted monologue) (Short: [free] direct thought)
free indirect discourse *Hey, he loved her*	free indirect speech	free indirect thought (Cohn: narrated monologue)
indirect discourse *He said/thought he loved her*	indirect speech	indirect thought?
narrative report of discourse/ content summary	speech report (Short: narrative report of speech acts) *He finally took courage and proposed to her*	psychonarration (Short: narrative report of thought acts) *His heart beat pit a pat. He suddenly realised he was in love with her*

on a cline from syntactic independence through semi-independence to complete syntactic integration (McHale 1978; Fludernik 1993: ch. 5). Overlaps and undecidable cases abound.

(2) Some critics make a distinction between 'quoted' and 'unquoted' (better perhaps: 'framed' and 'unframed') direct discourse. In speech representation this distinguishes between passages of direct speech introduced or structurally framed by inquit phrases and tags (*He raised his glass and shouted; Josie noted; she gleefully suggested*) and unintroduced passages (*He raised his glass. 'A la liberté!' They drank*). The distinction is more significant for thought representation since passages of free direct thought and unquoted interior monologues like Molly Bloom's soliloquy in James Joyce's *Ulysses* convey quite specific literary effects (Cohn 1978; Short *et al.*, 1999).

(3) Some critics (Short *et al.* 1999) also distinguish between various versions of the narrative report of speech acts. Where the reported discourse is extremely long (an address or *sermon), the summary can either be quite detailed (*Mr. Jardin expressed his sincere gratitude for the ambassador's visit and went on to articulate the Ministry's willingness to come to an early agreement ...*) or extremely condensed (*After a speech of welcome in which a promise of cooperation was given, the party transferred to the conference rooms ...*).

(4) Two major imbalances between the two columns can be noted. The first concerns the category of indirect thought. At least in English, this is frequently indistinguishable from psycho-narration: e.g., *He thought she was in love with him* can be read both as 'He said to himself, She is in love with me' and as 'He started to believe she was in love with him'. In the first case, as indirect discourse, the wording supposedly captures a verbal thought act that reproduces the propositional content of the 'original'; in the second case only a *description of the sentiments or utterance is intended; it need not relate to a propositional content but renders the illocutionary force of the utterance. As a consequence, the viability of having a category of indirect thought is suspect. (Cohn, Fludernik, Short, and Palmer elide it.)

Secondly, some critics include an additional category called narrated or (free indirect) perception (Brinton 1980) on the scale. This type of sentence combines the description of a character's perceptions with the free indirect rendering of his/her impressions: *She looked out into the garden. The butterflies were hovering over the hedges, and the little brook was snuggling warmly in the sunshine.* The second sentence can be read as the character's impressions of the scene.

Formal criteria: syntax and vocabulary

As already indicated, the scale of forms of speech and thought representations operates from syntactic freedom to syntactic dependence and integration. It additionally spans a range from maximal to minimal expressivity.

Syntactic (in)dependence describes the extent to which the clause rendering the reported speech is part of a syntagm introducing or signalling a speech act. Thus all *verba dicendi* framing or introducing the report correlate with syntactic dependence. (Compare: *He said that Bill had killed the pig* and *He said: 'Bill killed the pig'. He said* by itself is impossible; *verba dicendi* are transitive verbs requiring a complement.) An intermediate form between the introductory inquit phrase and unintroduced discourse representation is taken up by the parenthetical: '*Lets go', he shouted, draining his glass.* Banfield (1982) distinguished between direct discourse parentheticals as above and so-called 'narrative' parentheticals, which occur in free indirect discourse: *That was the height of independence, she felt.* Even if there is no narrative parenthetical, the referential and temporal alignment with the surrounding narratorial discourse in free indirect discourse constitutes a form of dependence: *Sally stamped her feet. She hated Jimmy's arrogance!* Although free indirect discourse is syntactically free in the sense of having no inquits or *verba dicendi* in a syntactic frame structure, the free indirect discourse phrase – like indirect discourse – continues to 'shift' *tense and pronominal *reference in accordance with the surrounding narrative discourse, traditionally in third-person past tense. Note that temporal concordance and referential alignment inevitably disappear from view in first-person present-tense narratives (*see* NARRATIVE SITUATIONS; PERSON; TIME AND NARRATIVE).

Expressive markers and characters' *deixis are most prominently displayed in direct discourse: 'Wow, what a nice kitty! O, *how cute* she is! Kitty, kitty do you want to be tickled on your tummy? Here we are, that's nice, isn't it?' In this passage, we find the deictics *here* and *you*; there are additionally exclamatory clauses, questions, tag questions (*isn't it*), interjections (*wow, o*), and lexical markers of expressivity (*kitty; tummy; cute*). In an indirect discourse rendering or in speech report, these as a rule cannot be preserved. By contrast, one of the key features of free indirect discourse consists precisely in the deployment of expressive markers and deictics. A free indirect discourse rendering of the above speech could therefore look as follows: 'Laura approached the kitten. Wow, what a nice kitty *that was. O,* and how cute she *was*! Kitty, kitty, *did kitty* want to be tickled on *its* tummy? Here we *were*, that *was* nice, *wasn't* it?' The tenses and pronouns are aligned with the surrounding third-person past-tense narrative, but the lexical, syntactic, and deictic items continue to relate to the reported speaker's (Laura's) here and now. Idiomatic phrases also frequently serve as expressive markers and may remain unshifted. (Compare the 'we' in the phrase 'Here we are' above, or the preservation of *you know* in free indirect discourse.) Although indirect speech is supposed to be untainted by characters' expressivity, there are in fact numerous cases of such mimicry by the narratorial discourse (for examples see Fludernik 1993: ch. 4). There is, therefore, no continuous increase of expressive markers as one moves toward the direct discourse end of the scale nor an absolute decrease as one moves toward speech report and psychonarration.

This mixture of temporal and referential alignment with syntactic independence on the one hand and the prominence of expressivity signals on the other which invoke the characters' language has given rise to the dual-voice hypothesis of free indirect discourse. In the wake of Roy Pascal (1977), who coined the term, Stanzel and others have assumed that in free indirect discourse, two 'voices' can be heard simultaneously, especially in ironic passages of free indirect discourse as in Jane Austen's work (*see* IRONY). If one assumes that there is a clear authorial voice elsewhere in the text, such an effect of two voices in competition can easily arise. From a factual, grammatical point of view, however, this doubling of voices has been rejected by the *no-narrator school of narratologists, whose most prominent representative is Ann Banfield.

There is as yet little known about the early history of speech and thought representation. One needs to take into account the diversity of grammatical possibilities in different languages (e.g.,

German has an independent form of indirect discourse with subjunctive verbs; Japanese does not usually express the category person and eschews finite verbs). The most thoroughly researched area has been free indirect discourse, which has several key studies devoted to it (Bally 1912; Banfield 1982; Pascal 1977; Steinberg 1971), and which has also been examined in the context of other forms of speech and thought representation (Cohn 1978; Fludernik 1993; Sternberg 1991; Voloshinov 1986 [1929]). Whatever the proportions between direct and indirect discourse in the various genres, free indirect discourse in modern European languages can now be traced to first occurrences in the *chansons de geste*, the medieval *romances, and to the saints' legends of the twelfth to the fourteenth centuries (*see* MEDIEVAL NARRATIVE). (It has supposedly even been found in ancient Greek texts.) Later, it appears in fits and starts in sixteenth-century texts, and from the end of the seventeenth-century becomes increasingly important as a technique of speech representation, with thought representation at first lagging behind but almost displacing speech representation in the late nineteenth-century. It is therefore not quite correct to say that free indirect discourse was invented in the late eighteenth-century, though this is when its more extensive use for the portrayal of mental processes became a significant factor from the *Gothic novel onward.

The functions of the different forms of speech and thought representation are diverse and text- and genre-specific. On the whole, indirect discourse tends to be more factual, brief, and content-oriented whereas free indirect discourse is noted for its liveliness, evocation of realistic effect, and ironic potential. Although direct speech in the realist novel significantly enhances the *verisimilitude of the story, earlier instances of characters' monologic utterances, especially for the representation of thought, were extremely stylised and artificial. A comparison of dramatic and narrative speech representation is an important, but as yet unaccomplished, task for narratological research.

SEE ALSO: drama and narrative; speech act theory; sociolinguistic approaches to narrative; stream of consciousness and interior monologue

References and further reading

Bally, Charles (1912) 'Le style indirect libre en français moderne I, II', *Germanisch-Romanische Monatsschrift*, 4, 549–56, 597–606.

Banfield, Ann (1982) *Unspeakable Sentences: Narration and Representation in the Language of Fiction*, Boston: Routledge and Kegan Paul.

Brinton, Laurel (1980) ' "Represented Perception": A Study in Narrative Style', *Poetics*, 9, 363–81.

Cohn, Dorrit (1978) *Transparent Minds: Narrative Modes for Presenting Consciousness in Fiction*, Princeton, NJ: Princeton University Press.

Fludernik, Monika (1993) *The Fictions of Language and the Languages of Fiction: The Linguistic Representation of Speech and Consciousness*, London: Routledge.

Genette, Gérard (1980 [1972]) *Narrative Discourse. An Essay in Method*, trans. Jane E. Lewin, Ithaca, NY: Cornell University Press.

Harweg, Roland (1968) *Pronomina und Textkonstitution*, Munich: Fink.

McHale, Brian (1978) 'Free Indirect Discourse: A Survey of Recent Accounts', *Poetics and Theory of Literature (PTL)*, 3, 249–87.

Palmer, Alan (2004) *Fictional Minds*, Lincoln, NE: Nebraska University Press.

Pascal, Roy (1977) *The Dual Voice: Free Indirect Speech and its Functioning in the Nineteenth-Century European Novel*, Manchester: Manchester University Press.

Short, Michael, Elena Semino, and Martin Wynne (1999) 'Reading Reports: Discourse Presentation in a Corpus of Narratives with Special Reference to News Reports', in Hans-Jürgen Diller and G. Stratmann (eds) *English via Various Media*, Heidelberg: Winter.

Stanzel, Franz Karl (1959) 'Episches Praeteritum, erlebte Rede, historisches Praesens', *Deutsche Vierteljahrsschrift für Literaturwissenschaft und Geistesgeschichte*, 33, 1–12.

—— (1984 [1979]) *A Theory of Narrative*, trans. Charlotte Goedsche, Cambridge: Cambridge University Press.

Steinberg, Günter (1971) *Erlebte Rede: Ihre Eigenart und ihre Formen in neuerer deutscher, französischer und englischer Erzählliteratur*, Göppingen: Alfred Kümmerle.

Sternberg, Meir (1991) 'How Indirect Discourse Means: Syntax, Semantics, Poetics, Pragmatics', in Roger D. Sell (ed.) *Literary Pragmatics*, London: Routledge.

Voloshinov, V. N. (1986 [1929]) *Marxism and the Philosophy of Language*, trans. Ladislav Matejka and I.R. Titunik, Cambridge, Mass.: Harvard University Press.

Wolfson, Nessa (1982) *CHP: The Conversational Historical Present in American English*, Dordrecht: Foris.

MONIKA FLUDERNIK

SPORTS BROADCAST

Sports broadcasts provide reports of sporting events over radio or *television. Such reports were part of early radio broadcasting (e.g., the 1921 heavyweight title fight between Dempsey and Carpentier was carried 'from ringside'). They are now included in most news programmes, and they constitute the exclusive materials of specialised cable channels like ESPN and Eurosport.

Not all sports broadcasts have a *narrative structure. The ones that do fall under two main categories:

1   The *summary*: Originating in a studio, the summary has the form of a posterior narrative (*see* NARRATION; TIME IN NARRATIVE). That is, it involves a retrospective viewpoint; the announcers know the outcome of the event, and they can select and organise the facts according to that knowledge. Answering the question 'who won?', the summary usually includes the result of the contest, a commentary, and (on television) the replay of moments of that contest regarded as noteworthy ('highlights').

2   The *live broadcast*: Originating at the location where the sporting event is occurring, the live broadcast has the form of a simultaneous narrative. That is, the announcers report what is happening; they describe the event and comment upon it, but without knowing how it will end (i.e., 'who will win'). Media theorists have pointed to the constructedness of this type of report. They have argued that live broadcasts are not genuine simultaneous narratives, since event time and broadcast time no longer coincide when the report is interrupted by commercials and such items as taped interviews and profiles of the athletes (Kozloff 1987: 66). Similarly, they have explained that the frequent replays make the singulative narrative of the contest into a repeating narrative, as parts of the event are shown several times – from different angles, at different speeds, and with a different commentary. Finally, they have insisted on the role of the broadcaster as an interpreter who, even though he/she does not know the whole story, seeks to impose narrative coherence on the contest by 'activating a script', e.g., by tentatively characterising a game still in progress as a 'Come-From-Behind Victory' or an 'Inevitable Collapse' (Ryan 1993: 145).

Whether they take the form of the summary or the live report, sports broadcasts, in most cases, are also components in two larger narratives: the history of sports broadcasting as a *media genre, and the story of the longer competition (e.g., the lea- gue, the cup, the tournament) of which the contests they are transmitting constitute individual episodes (Kinkema and Harris 1998: 33).

SEE ALSO: narrative techniques; narrative units

References and further reading

Kinkema, Kathleen M., and Janet C. Harris (1998) 'MediaSport Studies: Key Research and Emerging Issues', in Lawrence A. Wenner (ed.) *MediaSport*, New York: Routledge.

Kozloff, Sarah Ruth (1987) 'Narrative Theory and Tele- vision', in Robert C. Allen (ed.) *Channels of Discourse*, Chapel Hill: University of North Carolina Press.

Ryan, Marie-Laure (1993) 'Narrative in Real Time: Chronicle, Mimesis and Plot in the Baseball Broad- cast', *Narrative*, 1.2, 138–55.

PHILIPPE CARRARD

STORY ARC

The term 'story arc' is used primarily by non- scholar production and fan communities as a way to reduce narrative analysis to a ritualised movement broadly appropriating the structure of *Freytag's triangle. In an even more simplified sense, the term refers to the narrative flow from equilibrium to action-driven climax to new equili- brium. In serialised forms (*see* SERIAL NARRATIVE) like *television and comic book (*see* COMICS AND GRAPHIC NOVEL), the story arc describes shorter narrative cycles within the overall structure, mini- series within the main series. In interactive games (*see* COMPUTER GAMES AND NARRATIVE), the story arc outlines the near- and long-term goals that keep players motivated to confront the challenges arising during game play. In postclassical Holly- wood *film narrative, the term has commonly been used as shorthand to analyse the succession of narrative jolts so important to *spectacle-driven cinema. Often compared to roller coasters, blockbuster action films are expected to present an escalating progression of story arcs, moving the *audience from one visceral 'payoff' to the next. Films with insufficiently robust story arcs, even documentaries, are thought to be less likely to succeed with contemporary audiences. Screen- writers' adoption of Joseph Campell's concepts of the 'mythic question' and the *hero's journey

popularised the use of the term 'story arc' and its corollary, the *character arc.

SEE ALSO: conflict; narrative structure; tellability

References and further reading

Bordwell, David (1985) *Narration in the Fiction Film*, Madison: University of Wisconsin Press.

Campbell, Joseph (1949) *The Hero With a Thousand Faces*, Princeton: Princeton University Press.

McKee, Robert (1997) *Story: Substance, Structure, Style and the Principles of Screenwriting*, New York: Harper Collins.

PETER LUNENFELD

STORY GRAMMARS

An approach popular in the late 1970s and early 1980s, narrative grammars were an attempt to exp- and Noam Chomsky's linguistic theory, generative- transformational grammar, from the sentential to the textual level. Of all the natural language *text- types proposed by theorists (such as narrative, *description, argumentation, and instruction), nar- rative has been the only one to inspire descriptions cast in the form of a Chomsky grammar, arguably because it is the only text-type sufficiently well- structured and sufficiently well-defined to justify such an approach.

The distinctive feature of Chomsky's linguistic model is the claim that natural language can be described by a grammar consisting of two com- ponents: (1) a set of context-free generative rules that produce abstract schemata, the so-called 'deep structure' of sentences; and (b) a set of context- sensitive transformational rules that map these deep structures upon actual, or surface, sentence structure without affecting meaning. The context- free component of the grammar is a formal system made up of the following elements: a start symbol (S, for sentence); a set of non-terminal symbols (syntactic categories such as verb phrase and noun phrase); a set of terminal symbols (the words of the language), and a set of rules of the form $A \rightarrow B$, where A is a non-terminal symbol, and B can consist of any string of symbols within the model. The rule $A \rightarrow B + C$ reads 'rewrite A as B' and it can be visually represented as

$$A \\ / \ \backslash \\ B \ C$$

The rewrite rules of Chomsky's grammar produce an infinite number of different sentence structures, as well as structures of infinite complexity – a complexity that far exceeds the processing abilities of the human mind. As for the transformational rules, they are formulated in terms of the four possible types of operations that can affect strings of symbols: deletion, insertion, permutation, and replacement. An example of a context-sensitive transformational rule would be: $A + B \rightarrow A + D$, which reads as: replace B with D when it follows A. Although Chomsky believed at one time that the context-sensitive rules of transformations are an integral part of the speaker's linguistic competence – they account for instance for the intuition that passive and active sentences convey the same propositional content – there is no evidence that natural languages present features that cannot be generated by a context-free grammar. In other words, the context-sensitive component of the grammar may be formally superfluous.

The visual representation of the generative process produces a type of diagram known in graph theory as a tree. A tree is a hierarchical structure, dominated by a root-node (the start symbol), and precluding circuits: there is only one possible route between any two nodes. By diagramming sentences as trees, Chomsky made a major cognitive claim. Tree-diagrams are important structures in computer science because they can be much more easily generated and searched than graphs that allow circuits (known as networks). If the brain is a computer, Chomsky's model makes the prediction that natural languages are easy to process, and it supports the view that linguistic competence is an innate mental faculty.

Adaptations of the model to narrative are driven by similar ambitions of cognitive relevance. By describing narrative in terms of rewrite rules that produce structured story schemata (*see* STORY SCHEMATA AND CAUSAL STRUCTURE), story grammars represent an attempt at formalising the 'narrative competence' that enables people to produce narratives, to interpret texts narratively, and to judge whether or not a given text constitutes a well-formed story. Story grammars have been proposed by psychologists (Rumelhart; Mandler and Johnson; Stein), text grammarians (van Dijk), folklorists (Colby), and narratologists (Prince; Pavel).

As an example of what a story grammar looks like, here is an adaptation of Mandler and Johnson's grammar for the *genre of *fable (Ryan 1991; the terminal symbols are in italics; in a concrete story, they are replaced by language strings, but this replacement cannot be formalised by rules):

Fable → Story + *Moral*
Story → Setting + Event structure
Setting → State
Event structure → Episode
Episode → Beginning CAUSE Development CAUSE Ending
Beginning → *Event*
Development → Complex reaction CAUSE Goal path
Complex reaction → Simple reaction CAUSE Goal
Simple reaction → *Internal event*
Goal → *State*
Goal → *Internal state*
Goal path → Attempt CAUSE outcome
Attempt → *Event*
Outcome → *Event*
Ending → *Event*
Ending → *State*
(+ and CAUSE are connectors)

This grammar was used to predict the incidence of recall of various parts of the text (*see* MEMORY). According to Mandler and Johnson (1977), the most frequently remembered elements were setting, followed by beginnings, outcomes, and attempts. In other narrative applications, grammars have been used to model causal structures (Stein 1982), the minimal conditions of *narrativity and the complexity of stories (Prince 1973), and the spreading of *conflict in a narrative universe (Pavel 1985). Tree diagrams also provide efficient visualisations of the hierarchy of goals and subgoals in plans (Ryan 1991).

While some story grammars are entirely formulated in terms of context-free rules, others use transformations. Following the early Chomsky, Prince (1982) proposes so-called generalised transformations that operate on several independently generated narrative strings. Generalised transformations are responsible for structures involving conjoining, alternation, and *embedding of semi-autonomous stories (*see* PLOT TYPES). On the other hand, phenomena responsible for the distinction between story and discourse such as *gapping and chronological reordering can be accounted for by classical transformations operating on a single string (*see* STORY-DISCOURSE DISTINCTION; TEMPORAL ORDERING).

After the mid-1980s, story grammars fell out of favour. This was due in part to the inherent limitations of the tree diagram: for instance, because every node must be connected to a single parent (otherwise two paths would merge), a given element can receive only one function, in conflict with the principle of *tellability that recommends functional polyvalence. Furthermore, because branches cannot intersect, a tree will subsume entire plans of actions under one node, and it would be very difficult, if not impossible, to model the dynamic revision of plans performed by *characters, as they counteract the *actions of other characters. Another factor in the disappearance of story grammars was the rise of models more flexible or more complex than the tree (and therefore intellectually more appealing), such as the rhizomes of Deleuze and Guattari, a type of structure allowing growth in every direction rather than at the end of branches exclusively, and the neural networks of cognitive science, decentred, non-hierarchical systems of connections that constantly reorganise themselves by reassessing the relative weight of their component nodes. Yet if the brain is a neural network, a network is a forest that contains many tree-shaped subgraphs, and while no set of tree-producing rules can offer a complete mapping of story, this does not mean that structural grammars and arborescent diagrams cannot illuminate major aspects of narrative understanding.

SEE ALSO: cognitive narratology; computational approaches to narrative; linguistic approaches to narrative

References and further reading

Chomsky, Noam (1965) *Aspects of the Theory of Syntax*, Cambridge, Mass.: MIT Press.
Colby, Benjamin (1973) 'A Partial Grammar of Eskimo Folktales', *American Anthropologist*, 75, 645–62.
Deleuze, Gilles, and Félix Guattari (1987) *A Thousand Plateaus: Capitalism and Schizophrenia*, trans. Brian Massumi, Minneapolis: University of Minnesota Press.
van Dijk, Teun A. (1972) *Some Aspects of Text Grammars*, The Hague: Mouton.
Mandler, Jean M., and Nancy Johnson (1977) 'Remembrance of Things Parsed: Story Structure and Recall', *Cognitive Psychology*, 9, 111–51.
Pavel, Thomas (1985) *The Poetics of Plot: The Case of English Renaissance Drama*, Minneapolis: University of Minnesota Press.
Prince, Gerald (1973) *A Grammar of Stories*, The Hague: Mouton.
—— (1982) *Narratology*, The Hague: Mouton.
Rumelhart, David E. (1975) 'Notes on a Schema for Stories', in Daniel G. Bobrow and Allan Collins (eds) *Representation and Understanding: Studies in Cognitive Science*, New York: Academic Press.
Ryan, Marie-Laure (1991) *Possible Worlds, Artificial Intelligence and Narrative Theory*, Bloomington, Indiana University Press.
Stein, Nancy L. (1982) 'What's a Story: Interpreting the Interpretations of Story Grammars', *Discourse Processes*, 5.3–5, 319–35.

MARIE-LAURE RYAN

STORY-DISCOURSE DISTINCTION

The distinction between story and discourse (in French, between *histoire* and *discours*) was first put forth by the French narratologist Todorov in 1966, and has been widely adopted by narratologists. *Story*, in simplest terms, is *what* is told, whereas *discourse* refers to 'how' the story is transmitted (Chatman 1978). *Discourse* in classical (Genettean) narratology mainly comprises three aspects: tense (order, duration, and frequency), mood (forms and degrees of narrative representation; *see* MODALITY), and voice (the way in which the *narrating itself is implicated in the narrative). The story-discourse distinction corresponds to the structuralist distinction between signified and signifier, and the traditional distinction between content and style/form/expression, subject matter and treatment, or matter and manner (*see* STRUCTURALIST NARRATOLOGY). But as distinct from the other distinctions, the story-discourse distinction is exclusively applicable to narratives. The same goes for the Russian Formalists' distinction between fabula (the basic story stuff) and sjuzhet (the story as actually told in artistic presentation and arrangement). Rather than referring to content in general, *story* refers specifically to the narrated *events (*actions and happenings) and *existents (*characters and setting), and *discourse* to the rearrangement or treatment of the events and existents on the level of presentation.

According to Phelan, a fictional story has three components: the mimetic, the synthetic, and the thematic (*see* MIMESIS; THEMATIC APPROACHES TO NARRATIVE). The fictional writer creates a story to convey certain themes. A sequence of story events, as opposed to a sequence of real happenings, is an artificial construct, hence 'synthetic'. But the sequence of story events has a mimetic function (*see* MIMESIS). To some narratologists, 'story' designates the narrated events, abstracted from their disposition in the text and reconstructed in their chronological order, together with the participants in these events (Rimmon-Kenan 1983: 3). This view, which sees story entirely as a matter of the reader's inference and construction from the text or discourse, highlights the story's synthetic component and neglects to a certain extent its mimetic component. Because the story has a mimetic component, it can be taken as a non-textual given, as independent of the presentation in discourse (see Shen 2002). This separability of story from discourse is a prerequisite for the discussion of unreliable *narration (*see* RELIABILITY). A narration is regarded as unreliable precisely because the reader has come to the conclusion that things are not or cannot be as the discourse represents them, a judgement almost always based on the reader's world knowledge. Behind the veil of the unreliable discourse that often denies the reader the possibility of reconstructing the 'factual' story, the narrative implies the existence of the 'factual' version of the story.

Summarising various narratological views on the autonomy of the story, Rimmon-Kenan (1983: 7) observes that story is an abstraction from the following three aspects of discourse: (1) the specific style of the text in question (e.g., Henry James's late style or Faulkner's imitation of Southern dialect and rhythm), (2) the language in which the text is written (English, French, Hebrew), and (3) the medium or sign-system (words, cinematic *shots, *gestures; *see* MEDIA AND NARRATIVE; SEMIOTICS). But if we are to take account of different media consistently, the first aspect can be extended to cover the creative style of the writer, playwright/director, or film-director/producer etc., and the second may also be expanded to accommodate different cultures' preferences for expressing things in another medium (e.g., different ways of expressive miming or dancing; *see* DANCE AND NARRATIVE). Not surprisingly, Rimmon-Kenan's second aspect (English, French, etc.) does not fall within the purview of narratologists, who usually take the different languages for granted. Moreover, narratologists also tend to overlook the first aspect in Rimmon-Kenan's list, i.e., matters of verbal style (in terms of choices of lexis, syntax, cohesion, phonology, graphology etc.). This may be due to (a) narratologists' concern with techniques shared by different media, (b) their focus on the relation between story events and their rearrangement, and (c) a metaphorical, rather than literal, use of linguistic models (Rimmon-Kenan 1989; Shen 2005; *see* LINGUISTIC APPROACHES TO NARRATIVE).

The distinction between story and discourse will collapse when the mimetic component of the story is subverted, as in certain *postmodern narratives or in the case of *metalepsis (Genette 1980: 234–37). In order to gain a fuller picture of this issue, we need to examine the *author, the text (work), and the reader (*see* READER CONSTRUCTS), respectively. As regards the author, the story-discourse distinction becomes irrelevant when he or she only intends to play a non-mimetic narration game or language game, as with the inconsistent chronology in Robbe-Grillet's *La Jalousie* (see Robbe-Grillet 1965: 154). As for the text, the distinction will break down when it neither contains nor implies a story separable from the discourse. In terms of readers, it all depends on whether they are still trying to find out 'what really happened'. For a reader who, reading against the grain of Robbe-Grillet's anti-chronological chronology, attempts to reconstruct the 'real' sequence of events, the story-discourse distinction remains intact on a subjective level (Shen 2003). Even if the story is mimetic, the distinction between story and discourse may lose its pertinence when a discourse choice leads to a change in the fictional reality, or when one element belongs at the same time both to the level of story and to that of discourse (see Shen 2002).

SEE ALSO: narrative techniques; narrative versions; space in narrative; temporal ordering; time in narrative

References and further reading

Chatman, Seymour (1978) *Story and Discourse: Narrative Structure in Fiction and Film*, Ithaca: Cornell University Press.

Genette, Gérard (1980) *Narrative Discourse: An Essay in Method*, trans. J. E. Lewin, Ithaca: Cornell University Press.

Phelan, James (1989) *Reading People, Reading Plots*, Chicago: University of Chicago Press.

Rimmon-Kenan, Shlomith (1983) *Narrative Fiction: Contemporary Poetics*, London: Methuen.

Rimmon-Kenan (1989) 'How the Model Neglects the Medium', *The Journal of Narrative Technique*, 19, 157–66.

Robbe-Grillet, Alain (1965 [1963]) *For a New Novel: Essays on Fiction*, trans. Richard Howard, New York: Grove Press.

Shen, Dan (2002) 'Defence and Challenge: Reflections on the Relation Between Story and Discourse', *Narrative*, 10, 422–43.

—— (2003) 'What Do Temporal Antinomies Do to the Story-Discourse Distinction? – A Reply to Brian Richardson's Response', *Narrative*, 11, 237–41.

—— (2005) 'What Narratology and Stylistics Can Do for Each Other', in James Phelan and Peter Rabinowitz (eds) *The Blackwell Companion to Narrative Theory*, Oxford: Blackwell.

Todorov, Tzvetan (1966) 'Les catégories du récit littéraire', *Communications*, 8, 125–51.

DAN SHEN

STORY SCHEMATA AND CAUSAL STRUCTURE

Stories, in general, are perceived to be a unique form of discourse, having consistent, identifiable structures. Their distinctive content and organisation can be described in terms of internal structures called schemata (Bartlett 1932). These story schemata are described by a set of rules, whose internalisation can be compared to the internalisation of language rules – in short, to a grammar (*see* STORY GRAMMARS). Such schemata bear on the types of content that unfold in stories and the ways in which these content components are causally related to one another. By using a discourse analysis based on units consisting of 'story categories' (*see* NARRATIVE UNITS), several investigators have constructed a set of working hypotheses about the types of rules that are used to understand and produce stories (Mandler and Johnson 1977; Rumelhart 1975; Stein and Glenn 1979; Stein and Trabasso 1982).

These sets of rules or 'story grammars' are relational in nature, specifying not only the content of different types of clauses, but also the ways in which one clause is related to each of the other clauses. Thus, the rules outlined in the story grammars can be used to assess whether a writer has been audience-friendly in creating a 'well-formed' story or whether the author has created a text that omits or obscures central units of a story, making comprehension difficult. Story grammars are different from the sentence grammars proposed by Chomsky and his colleagues. Whereas Chomskian grammars allow for a test of the well-formedness of a sentence, story grammars allow for a test of the well-formedness – and comprehensibility – of an entire narrative text.

According to two of the story grammar models (Mandler and Johnson 1977; Stein and Glenn 1979), the central higher-order unit of a story is an *episode* and includes seven categories: setting, initiating *event, internal response, goal, attempt, consequence, and reaction. Each category can include one or more clauses. The *setting* introduces a specific animate protagonist and contains information referring to the physical, social, or temporal context of the story (*see* SPACE IN NARRATIVE; TIME IN NARRATIVE). The *initiating event* marks some change in the protagonist's environment. The *internal response*'s major function is to evoke an *emotion or belief in the protagonist. The *goal* describes the protagonist's desire to achieve a goal or change of state, which motivates the protagonist to carry out an *attempt*, a set of overt *actions in the service of the goal. The attempt results in a *consequence*, signifying whether the protagonist succeeded in attaining the goal. The final type of information in a story is a *reaction*. Three types of information can be classified as reactions: (1) the protagonist's emotional and cognitive responses to goal attainment or failure; (2) future consequences that occur as a result of goal attainment or failure; and (3) a moral, summarising what the character learned from achieving or pursuing a goal.

The knowledge that people acquire about stories, in the form of a story schema, guides them during the comprehension or production process (*see* NARRATIVE COMPREHENSION). Using a story schema allows a person to set up expectations about the types of information that should occur in a story and the types of logical/causal connections that should link the components of a story. When an incoming story text violates expectations about proper story sequence, comprehenders will use their story schema to construct a representation that corresponds more to the expected sequence than to the actual content and sequence that has been heard or read. The story schema allows elaboration on the incoming content so that the mental representation is more coherent than the actual story text that was heard or read.

Indeed, prior knowledge and expectations about stories greatly influence and predict *memory for stories, even when a deliberate attempt is made to retain a verbatim account of incoming story information (Stein and Trabasso 1982). When a presented story text does not match the expected sequence of events, the ability to accurately represent the text decreases significantly. The time necessary to process and encode the text increases, as does confabulation, or the inventing of information never presented in the text (Stein and Trabasso 1982). Thus, if incoming story information contains several violations of expectation, in terms of readers' knowledge about well-structured stories, the story may need to be repeated several times before an accurate representation is retained.

A story schema also contains information about ideal types of causal structure that should link the components of a story (*see* CAUSALITY). Trabasso *et al.*, (1984) have demonstrated that both narrative understanding and memory of narrated events are directly proportional to the number of causally active clauses used in the text. In other words, a causal chain can be formed from the beginning to the end of a well-structured story. The number of story clauses that lie on the causal chain predicts memory for the story. Additionally, the number of causal connections a given clause has to other clauses predicts whether that clause will be remembered.

Story schemata can be acquired in two ways: by listening to or reading stories, and by understanding intentional action that gets carried out in everyday social interaction (*see* INTENTIONALITY). Acquisition starts almost as soon as children begin to understand and use language (Stein and Albro 1997). Much of story knowledge is organised around the desire to achieve and promote personally significant goals, the obstacles that preclude goal attainment, and plans that overcome obstacles to goal attainment. Thus, goals are central organising components of the story schema. By the age of three, children have acquired a rich repertoire of knowledge about different types of stories. They use this knowledge to recount their memories and evaluations of events, emotions, desires, actions, and outcomes, especially those pertaining to the maintenance of personally meaningful goals. Both children and adults use their knowledge of stories to create fantasies, participate in arguments, and plan for future interaction (Stein and Albro 2001). They are then able to build a deeper understanding of more complicated stories as their knowledge of obstacles and plans for overcoming obstacles increases.

SEE ALSO: children's storytelling; discourse analysis (linguistics); psychological approaches to narrative

References and further reading

Bartlett, F. C. (1932) *Remembering: A Study in Experimental and Social Psychology*, London: Cambridge University Press.
Mandler, Jean M., and Nancy Johnson (1977) 'Remembrance of Things Parsed: Story Structure and Recall', *Cognitive Psychology*, 9, 111–51.
Propp, Vladimir (1968 [1928]) *Morphology of the Folktale*, trans. Laurence Scott, revised by Louis A. Wagner, Austin: University of Texas Press.
Rumelhart, David E. (1975) 'Notes on a Schema for Stories', in Daniel G. Bobrow and Allan Collins (eds) *Representation and Understanding: Studies in Cognitive Science*, New York: Academic Press.
Stein, Nancy L., and Elizabeth R. Albro (1997) 'The Emergence of Narrative Understanding: Evidence for Rapid Learning in Personally Relevant Contexts', *Contemporary Issues in Education*, 60, 83–98.
——, (2001) 'The Origins and Nature of Arguments: Studies in Conflict Understanding, Emotion, and Negotiation', *Discourse Processes*, 32.2–3, 113–33.
——, and Christine G. Glenn (1979) 'An Analysis of Story Comprehension in Elementary School Children', in Roy O. Freedle (ed.) *New Directions in Discourse Processing*, Norwood, NJ: Ablex.
——, and Thomas Trabasso (1982) 'What's in a Story: An Approach to Comprehension and Instruction', in Robert Glaser (ed.) *Advances in Instructional Psychology*, vol. 2, Hillsdale, NJ: Lawrence Erlbaum.
Trabasso, Thomas, Tom Secco, and Paul van den Broek (1984) 'Causal Cohesion and Story Coherence', in Heinz Mandl, Nancy L. Stein, and Thomas Trabasso (eds) *Learning and Comprehension of Text*, Hillsdale, NJ: Lawrence Erlbaum.

NANCY L. STEIN AND VALERIE I. KISSEL

STORYWORLD

In research on natural language processing, the terms *mental model* (Johnson-Laird 1983) and *discourse model* (Webber 1979) are used to refer to non-linguistic representations of the situation(s) described by a sentence or set of sentences, i.e., a discourse (Stevenson 1996; *see* SITUATION MODEL). Models of this sort are global mental representations enabling language users to draw inferences about items and occurrences either explicitly mentioned or else implicitly evoked in a discourse. Storyworlds, in turn, can be defined as the class of discourse models used for understanding narratively organised discourse in particular. In this sense, narrative comprehension requires reconstructing storyworlds on the basis of textual cues and the inferences that they make possible (Herman 2002).

Storyworlds are thus mental models of who did what to and with whom, when, where, why, and in what fashion in the world to which interpreters relocate (Ryan 1991) as they work to comprehend a narrative. Like Jahn's (1997) cognitive frames and Emmott's contextual frames (1997), storyworlds function in both a top-down and a bottom-up way during narrative comprehension. Top-down, they provide the presuppositions guiding readers to assume that fast food restaurants and electron microscopes are not components of the world of Proust's *Recherche*. But, bottom-up, a given story-world is also subject to being updated, revised, or even abandoned in favour of another with the accretion of textual cues, as when the reader of a text featuring an unreliable homodiegetic narrator gradually realises that the storyworld is not at all the way its teller says it is (*see* RELIABILITY).

More generally, when compared with cognate narratological terms such as *fabula* or *story*, *storyworld* better captures what might be called the ecology of narrative interpretation. In trying to make sense of a narrative, interpreters attempt to reconstruct not just what happened but also the surrounding context or environment embedding storyworld *existents, their attributes, and the *actions and *events in which they are involved. Indeed, the grounding of stories in storyworlds goes a long way towards explaining narratives' immersiveness, their ability to 'transport' inter-preters into places and times that they must occupy for the purposes of narrative comprehension. Interpreters do not merely reconstruct a sequence of events and a set of existents, but imaginatively (emotionally, viscerally) inhabit a world in which things matter, agitate, exalt, repulse, provide grounds for laughter and grief, and so on – both for narrative participants and for interpreters of the story. More than reconstructed timelines and inventories of existents, then, storyworlds are mentally and emotionally projected environments in which interpreters are called upon to live out complex blends of cognitive and imaginative response.

SEE ALSO: cognitive narratology; deixis; discourse analysis (linguistics); emotion and narrative; immersion; narrative comprehension; story-discourse distinction

References and further reading

Emmott, Catherine (1997) *Narrative Comprehension: A Discourse Perspective*, Oxford: Oxford University Press.
Gerrig, Richard J. (1993) *Experiencing Narrative Worlds: On the Psychological Activities of Reading*, New Haven: Yale University Press.
Herman, David (2002) *Story Logic: Problems and Possibilities of Narrative*, Lincoln: University of Nebraska Press.
Jahn, Manfred (1997) 'Frames, Preferences, and the Reading of Third-Person Narratives: Towards a Cognitive Narratology', *Poetics Today*, 18, 441–68.
Johnson-Laird, Phillip N. (1983) *Mental Models: Towards a Cognitive Science of Language, Inference, and Consciousness*, Cambridge, Mass.: Harvard University Press.
Ryan, Marie-Laure (1991) *Possible Worlds, Artificial Intelligence and Narrative Theory*, Bloomington: Indiana University Press.
Stevenson, Rosemary J. (1996) 'Mental Models, Propositions, and the Comprehension of Pronouns', in Jane Oakhill and Alan Garnham (eds) *Mental Models in Cognitive Science*, East Sussex: Psychology Press.
Webber, Bonnie Lynn (1979) *A Formal Approach to Discourse Anaphora*, New York: Garland.

DAVID HERMAN

STREAM OF CONSCIOUSNESS AND INTERIOR MONOLOGUE

The two terms 'stream of consciousness' and 'interior monologue' have different origins but have now become inextricably linked. 'Stream of consciousness' was first used by the psychologist William James (brother of the novelist Henry James) in *Principles of Psychology* (1890). It is thought that 'interior monologue' was probably first used to describe James Joyce's *Ulysses* (1922). Although the formal or theoretical definitions for these terms vary widely, the ostensive or practical definitions are very precise. Apart from occasional references to earlier novelists (for example, Edouard Dujardin), theorists define the phrases in relation to the *modernist novels of Joyce, Virginia Woolf, William Faulkner, and Dorothy Richardson. The examples used to illustrate the terms are invariably taken from *Ulysses* or, less often, from Woolf's *To the Lighthouse* (1927) or *Mrs. Dalloway* (1925).

Some of the theoretical definitions describe the types of fictional thought that occur in the minds of *characters in the story or fabula (*see*

STORY-DISCOURSE DISTINCTION; THOUGHT AND CONSCIOUSNESS REPRESENTATION (LITERATURE)). Although most emphasise the random, associative, illogical, and seemingly ungrammatical free flow of thought, others mention more controlled and directed thought; non-conscious, but also conscious thought; verbal, but also non-verbal thought. Some specify cognition only, while others include various combinations of cognition, perception, sensations, and *emotions.

Confusingly though, other theoretical definitions refer to a completely separate issue: the techniques of thought and consciousness presentation in the discourse or sjuzhet. Most definitions stress an apparently unmediated presentation in the mode of free direct thought. However, this can be misleading. Many illustrative passages contain a dense mixture, often in equal proportions, of surface description of the physical *storyworld and of all three modes of thought presentation: thought report, free indirect thought, and direct thought. For example:

> Made him feel a bit peckish (*thought report*). The coals were reddening (*surface description*). Another slice of bread and butter: three, four: right (*free direct thought*). She didn't like her plate full (*free indirect thought*).
>
> (*Ulysses*)

There is no clear consensus on the relationship between the two terms in question. Some theorists use the terms interchangeably. Others regard one as a particular type or subset of the other. Some attach different and separate meanings to each. Perhaps the most common distinction is this. Stream of consciousness describes the thought itself and/or the presentation of thought in the sort of third-person passage which is illustrated above and which is characteristic of Woolf and the early episodes in *Ulysses*. Interior monologue (or what Cohn terms the 'autonomous monologue') describes the long, continuous, first-person passages or whole texts that contain uninterrupted, unmediated free direct thought such as 'Penelope' (Molly Bloom's famous monologue in the last episode of *Ulysses*) or the first three sections of Faulkner's *The Sound and the Fury* (1929). For example:

> I suppose she was pious because no man would look at her twice I hope Ill never be like her a wonder she didn't want us to cover our faces.
>
> (*Ulysses*)

SEE ALSO: dramatic monologue; free indirect discourse; mediacy; psychological novel; speech representation

References and further reading

Bickerton, Derek (1967) 'Modes of Interior Monologue: a Formal Definition', *Modern Language Quarterly*, 28, 229–39.

Chatman, Seymour (1978) *Story and Discourse: Narrative Structure in Fiction and Film*, Ithaca: Cornell University Press.

Cohn, Dorrit (1978) *Transparent Minds: Narrative Modes for Presenting Consciousness in Fiction*, Princeton: Princeton University Press.

Dujardin, Edouard (1991 [1887]) *The Bays are Sere and Interior Monologue*, trans. Anthony Suter, London: Libris.

Fludernik, Monika (1996) *Towards a 'Natural' Narratology*, London: Routledge.

Friedman, Melvin (1955) *Stream of Consciousness: A Study of Literary Method*, New Haven: Yale University Press.

Lodge, David (1990) *After Bakhtin: Essays on Fiction and Criticism*, London: Routledge.

ALAN PALMER

STRUCTURALIST NARRATOLOGY

The French term *narratologie* (formed in parallel with *biology*, *sociology*, etc. to denote 'the study of narrative') was coined by Tzvetan Todorov in his 1969 book *Grammaire du 'Décaméron'*. As suggested by the circumstances of its baptism, narratology originated as an outgrowth of structuralist literary and cultural theory in France – more specifically, of the structuralist attempt to use Saussurean linguistics as a 'pilot-science' for studying cultural phenomena of all sorts (Dosse 1996: 59–66; *see* LINGUISTIC APPROACHES TO NARRATIVE). Structuralists like the early Roland Barthes (1972 [1957]) had sought to describe and explain diverse forms of cultural expression (*advertisements, *photographs, museum exhibits, wrestling matches) as rule-governed signifying practices or 'languages' in their own right (Culler 1975). Narratologists such as Gérard Genette, Algirdas Julien Greimas, and Todorov participated in the same structuralist revolution, viewing particular stories as individual 'narrative messages' supported by a shared semiotic system whose constituents and combinatory principles it was the task of narratological analysis to bring to light.

The roots of the structuralist approach can be traced back to the early twentieth century, when Russian Formalist literary theorists laid important groundwork for narratological research (*see* FORMALISM). For example, in distinguishing between 'bound' (or plot-relevant) and 'free' (or non-plot-relevant) motifs, Boris Tomashevskii (1965 [1925]) anticipated the distinction between 'nuclei' and 'catalysers' set out by Roland Barthes in his 'Introduction to the Structural Analysis of Narratives' (Barthes 1977 [1966]). Likewise Viktor Shklovskii's early work on *plot as a structuring device prefigured what became one of the grounding assumptions of structuralist narratology: namely, the *story-discourse distinction (see the materials assembled in Shklovskii 1990). The most important precedent, however, was furnished by Vladimir Propp's pathbreaking *Morphology of the Folktale* (1968 [1928]), whose first English translation appeared in 1958. Propp abstracted 31 functions, or character actions defined in terms of their significance for the plot, from a corpus of Russian *folktales; he also specified rules for their distribution in a given tale (*see* ACTION THEORY; CHARACTER; FUNCTION (PROPP)). In turn, as discussed in more detail below, Claude Lévi-Strauss (1986 [1955]) built on Propp's work to formulate a 'deep-structural' analysis of *myth; the result was a proto-narratological account of *'mythemes' and their distributional patterns in the Oedipus myth.

Just as the narratologists adapted and synthesised the ideas of earlier scholars to elaborate a systematic approach to the study of stories, current-day theories of narrative remain influenced by the many notable achievements of structuralist narratology, which generated a host of terms and concepts that have become foundational within contemporary narrative studies – from *actant, anachrony, and *focalization, to homodiegetic *narrator, iterative *narration, and *metalepsis. Since these and other specific contributions from narratology are treated elsewhere in this Encyclopedia, the present overview focuses instead on the broader contexts and conceptual underpinnings of the narratological initiative as a whole. For this purpose, Barthes' programmatic 'Introduction' can be used as a touchstone; viewed in context, Barthes' essay helps illuminate the *object*, *methods*, and overall *aims* of structuralist narratology as an investigative framework. But by the same token, the following discussion touches only intermittently upon what Barthes could not have

foreseen, i.e., the legacy (better, legacies) of narratology under the structuralist dispensation. At issue are *postclassical developments that build on classical, structuralist notions of *narrative but enrich narrative theory with ideas that were either developed after the heyday of structuralism, incubated in other disciplines, or adapted from other subdomains within the study of literature and culture (Herman 1999; *see* INTERDISCIPLINARY APPROACHES TO NARRATIVE).

The object of narratology: narrative versus narratives

From the start Barthes's 'Introduction' underscored that, far from being a school or method of literary criticism – i.e., a way of interpreting novels and other specifically literary narratives – narratology aimed to be a transmedial investigation of stories of all kinds, *natural as well as artful, verbal (spoken or written) as well as image-based, painted as well as filmed (cf. Herman 2004) (*see* INTERMEDIALITY; MEDIA AND NARRATIVE). It also aimed to be transcultural and transgeneric, investigating everything from *legends and *fables to *epics and tragedies (*see* GENRE THEORY IN NARRATIVE STUDIES). *Ethnographic and *sociological impulses, reflecting the linguistic, anthropological, and folkloristic bases for structuralist analysis of narrative (*see* FOLKLORE), reveal themselves when Barthes writes: 'All classes, all human groups, have their narratives, enjoyment of which is very often shared by men with different, even opposing, cultural backgrounds' (Barthes 1977 [1966]: 79).

Barthes goes on to suggest that a common, more or less implicit model of narrative explains people's ability to recognise or interpret so many diverse productions and types of artefacts as stories; the same model allows them to compare an *anecdote with a *novel or an *opera with an epic. Narratology's *raison d'être* is to develop an explicit characterisation of the model underlying people's intuitive knowledge about stories, in effect providing an account of what constitutes humans' narrative competence. To invoke the stark opposition used by Barthes: either a narrative is 'merely a rambling collection of events', and thus unamenable to description in terms of rule-governed patterns, or else 'it shares with other narratives a common structure which is open to analysis', no matter how difficult it might be to formulate an adequate account of the structure in question. Hence, having conferred on linguistics the status of 'founding model' (Barthes 1977 [1966]: 82), Barthes identifies for the narratologist the same object of inquiry that (*mutatis mutandis*) Ferdinand de Saussure (1959 [1916]) had specified for the linguist: the system (*la langue*) from which the infinity of narrative messages (*la parole*) derives and on the basis of which they can be understood as stories in the first place.

In targeting 'narrative *langue*' rather than 'narrative *parole*' as the focus of investigation, the narratologists were therefore acceding to a more general Saussurean-structuralist imperative. For Saussure as for the structuralists who adopted his ideas in an effort to develop a generalised science of the sign (*see* SEMIOTICS), the priority was to discover the properties characterising sign-systems viewed as *codes, not those attaching to the individual constellations of signs made possible and intelligible by the codes in question. Analogously, structuralist narratologists targeted the supra- or transtextual code in terms of which story recipients are able to identify narratively organised discourse and interpret it as such.

Narratological method: linguistics as model and metaphor

Narratologists like the early Barthes used structuralist linguistics not just to identify their object of analysis, but also to elaborate their method of inquiry. (Indeed, given the structuralist heritage of narratology, in this case the method arguably determined the profile of the object being analysed, not the other way around.) Before the birth of narratology proper, a key methodological precedent had been provided by Lévi-Strauss (1986 [1955]), who sought to improve on Propp's approach by shifting from the notion of '*functions' to that of '*mythemes', or 'gross constituent units' of *myth, which he patterned after Troubetzkoi's, Saussure's, and Jakobson's understanding of phonemes. In the method outlined by Lévi-Strauss, structural analysis of a myth required segmenting the text into mythemes and then grouping those constituent units into paradigmatic classes, whose members may in fact be dispersed at various points along the syntagmatic chain of the discourse. Hence, in parallel with the structuralist distinction between *parole* and *langue*, the 'telling' of a myth can be opposed to its 'understanding', which

depends on reconstituting the structural code that lies beneath the myth's surface manifestation in spoken or written words, *images, etc. More specifically, the semantic interpretation or meaning of a myth, Lévi-Strauss proposed, derives from the (analogical, contrastive, etc.) deep-structural relations between the classes of mythemes into which it can be analysed.

As structural analysis of narrative moved from the pre-narratological to the narratological phase, the adaptation of structuralist-linguistic concepts and methods was to prove both enabling and constraining. (See Pavel 1989 for a wide-ranging critique of structuralist appropriations of ideas from linguistics.) On the positive side, the example of linguistics did provide narratology with a productive new vantage-point on stories, as well as affording terms and categories that were fruitful for subsequent research on narrative. To return to Barthes' 'Introduction', the linguistic paradigm furnished Barthes with what he characterised as the 'decisive' concept of the 'level of description' (Barthes 1977 [1966]: 85–88). Imported from grammatical theory, this idea suggests that a narrative is not merely a 'simple sum of propositions' but rather a complex structure that can be analysed into hierarchical levels – in the same way that a natural-language utterance can be analysed at the level of its syntactic, its morphological, or its phonological representation. Building on then-recent proposals to divide narrative into the levels of 'story' and 'discourse', Barthes himself distinguishes three levels of description: at the lowest or most granular level are *functions* (in Propp's and Bremond's sense of the term); then *actions* (in the sense used by Greimas in his work on actants); and finally *narration (which is 'roughly the level of "discourse" in Todorov').

Using the linguistic theories of Emile Benveniste to draw a further distinction between horizontal or 'distributional' relations between units at the same level and vertical or 'integrational' relations between units at different levels (*see* NARRATIVE UNITS), Barthes went on to advance a number of propositions that proved consequential for later work in narrative theory. Specifically, Barthes suggested that:

1   distributional functions can be subdivided into nuclei (or 'cardinal functions') and catalysers, which Chatman (1978) renamed 'kernels' and 'satellites' (roughly, *events that

cannot be deleted from a paraphrase of a narrative without altering the story itself versus events that can be safely deleted);

2 integrational functions can be characterised as character-marking or atmosphere-establishing 'indices', serving not to advance the action but rather to indicate some enduring feature of the *storyworld (a character's malice, a house's *Gothic qualities);

3 indices themselves can be parsed into 'indices proper' and 'informants', with informants serving to locate *existents in *time and *space;

4 a generic typology can be set up on the basis of a continuum stretching from heavily functional (or action-oriented) to heavily indicial (or 'psychological') narratives;

5 the basic unit of 'narrative syntax' is the *sequence* (a small group of functions that is assigned a generic heading such as 'struggle' or 'betrayal' and thereby made sense of in terms of humans' stereotypical knowledge of the world) (cf. Herman 2002: 85–113; *see* SCRIPTS AND SCHEMATA);

6 analysing *characters in terms of interiorised, psychological essences rather than their pertinence for the unfolding action carries with it ideological as well as methodological assumptions that the structuralists wished to dispel (*see* IDEOLOGY AND NARRATIVE);

7 the profile of the *narrator can be reconstructed on the basis of signs immanent to the narrative itself, in contradistinction to the profile of the *author;

8 the production and interpretation of stories is premised on a particular type of communicative situation, which can be distinguished from those of argument, exhortation, insult, and so on (*see* COMMUNICATION IN NARRATIVE; SOCIO-LINGUISTIC APPROACHES TO NARRATIVE; TEXT-TYPE APPROACH TO NARRATIVE).

Yet structuralist narratology was also limited by the linguistic models it treated as paradigmatic. Ironically, the narratologists embraced structuralist linguistics as their pilot-science just when its deficiencies were becoming apparent in the domain of linguistic theory itself (cf. Herman 2001). The limitations of the Saussurean paradigm were thrown into relief, on the one hand, by emergent formal (e.g., generative-grammatical) models for analysing language structure. On the other hand, powerful tools were being developed in the wake of

Ludwig Wittgenstein, J. L. Austin, H. P. Grice, John Searle, and other post-Saussurean language theorists interested in how contexts of language use bear on the production and interpretation of socially situated utterances (*see* PRAGMATICS; SPEECH ACT THEORY). These theorists began to question what they viewed as counter-productive modes of abstraction and idealisation in both structuralist linguistics and the Chomskyean paradigm that displaced it. Research along these lines led to the realisation that certain features of the linguistic system – implicatures, discourse anaphora, protocols for turn-taking in conversation, etc., – emerge only at the level beyond the sentence (*see* DISCOURSE ANALYSIS (LINGUISTICS)).

Accordingly, Barthes reveals the limits of structuralist narratology when he remarks that 'a narrative is a long sentence, just as every constative sentence is in a way the rough outline of a short narrative', suggesting that one finds in narrative, 'expanded and transformed proportionately, the principal verbal categories: tenses, aspects, moods, persons' (Barthes 1977 [1966]: 84). Other early narratologists shared with Barthes the assumption that all the categories pertaining to sentence-level grammar could be unproblematically scaled up to the discourse level, without compromising the descriptive or explanatory power of the grammatical machinery involved. Todorov's 1969 study of Boccaccio's *Decameron* borrowed categories from traditional grammars to compare narrated entities and agents with nouns, actions and events with verbs, and properties with adjectives (Todorov 1969). Genette (1980 [1972]) drew on the same grammatical paradigm in using tense, mood, and voice to characterise the relations between the narrated world (*see* STORYWORLD), the narrative in terms of which it is presented, and the *narrating that enables the presentation. Meanwhile, in his effort to refine Propp's plot-based approach to character, Greimas (1983 [1966]) turned to the syntactic theories of the linguist Lucien Tesnière. In fact, Greimas' use of the term *'actant' itself derives from Tesnière's work on the grammar of noun phrases and other sentence-level constituents.

Whatever the limitations imposed by the early narratologists' reliance on models that predate state-of-the-art research on discourse-level phenomena, their self-conscious emulation of linguistic theory has proven to be productive for narrative theory in its postclassical phase. Soon after the publication of the founding documents of the narratological initiative (e.g., the essays by Barthes, Bremond, Todorov, Greimas, and others assembled in the special issue of *Communications* that appeared in 1966), narrative theorists began to explore methodological questions stemming from the use of linguistics as a paradigm for narrative analysis (Prince 1973; Culler 1975). Ever since, metatheoretical inquiry into the relations between linguistic and narratological models has become a basic research activity, a gesture in part constitutive of the field (cf. Herman 2002).

The aims of narratology: description versus interpretation or evaluation

The narratologists' appropriation of ideas and methods from structuralist linguistics not only determined their object of inquiry, but also shaped the aims of the narratological enterprise itself. As noted by Culler, 'linguistics is not hermeneutic' (Culler 1975: 31): linguistic analysis seeks to provide not interpretations of particular utterances, but rather a general account of the conditions of possibility for the production and processing of grammatically acceptable forms and sequences. Similarly, narratologists argued that the structural analysis of narrative should not be viewed as a handmaiden to interpretation. The proper goal of narratology, rather, was to characterise narrative *langue* so that 'the infinite number of narratives' could be 'described' and 'classified' (Barthes 1977 [1966]: 82). The aims of narratology were, in other words, fundamentally descriptive instead of interpretive. Structural analysis of stories concerned itself not with *what* narratively organised sign systems mean but rather with *how* they mean, and more specifically with how they mean *as* narratives.

By the same token, the descriptive focus that narratology adopted from linguistics meant that normative or 'axiological' criticism – in the sense of the evaluation of some narratives as better or worse than others – fell outside the narratological domain. The narratologists adhered to Jakobson's (1960) distinction between poetics and criticism; in privileging the code of narrative over particular stories supported by that code, they pursued narrative poetics, not narrative criticism. The critic engages in serial readings of individual stories; the narratologist studies what allows a constellation of verbal or other signs to be construed as a narrative in the first place.

In this respect, the narratologists again took inspiration from linguistics. Linguists do not evaluate the aesthetic success or failure of verbal productions, even though such productions might be deemed 'good' or 'bad' on the basis of extra-linguistic standards used to confer social prestige on particular dialectal variants, speech styles, etc. Instead, they examine how the linguistic system licenses a range of possible forms, exploring what processes lead to their construction and patterns of use. In the same way, and also because of their conception of narrative as a transgeneric phenomenon inhabiting both 'high' and 'low' artefacts and contexts, narratologists eschewed the use of 'good', 'bad', and cognate evaluative terms to characterise stories. In turn, the structuralists' focus on narrative *langue* has led theorists to emphasise the factors that systematically prompt people to include a given text or discourse in the category 'narrative', as well as the factors correlated with the *narrativity of a text or discourse, i.e., the degree to which it is amenable to being processed *as* a narrative (*see* NARRATIVISATION; TELLABILITY). As suggested by narratologically inflected scholarship on ludic, often bizarre *postmodern fictional experiments (e.g., McHale 1987), identifying the factors that conspire to produce a low-narrativity narrative is not the same thing as denying that text the status of story or labelling it as 'inferior' to other, higher-narrativity narratives.

However, a number of postclassical approaches, including those concerned with the rhetoric of narrative (*see* RHETORICAL APPROACHES TO NARRATIVE), the role of narrative in the formation of *identity, and the relations between narrative and *gender or *ideology, have challenged the structuralist emphasis on description over interpretation and evaluation. For scholars working in these areas, though the theorist may make structural features of narrative a focus of investigation, he or she will also frame interpretations of what a given story implies about the nature of identity or assess the extent to which a work of fiction contests or affirms surrounding ideological forces. In effect, scholarship along these lines draws a fuzzy rather than a binarised distinction between narrative poetics and narrative criticism, using but not limiting itself to the tools of structuralist narratology.

References and further reading

Barthes, Roland (1972 [1957]) *Mythologies*, trans. Annette Lavers, New York: Hill and Wang.

—— (1977 [1966]) 'Introduction to the Structural Analysis of Narratives', in *Image Music Text*, trans. Stephen Heath, New York: Hill and Wang. (Originally published in *Communications*, 8, 1–27.)

Chatman, Seymour (1978) *Story and Discourse: Narrative Structure in Fiction and Film*, Ithaca: Cornell University Press.

Communications 8 (1966) (Special issue on 'Recherches sémiologiques: L'Analyse structurale du récit').

Culler, Jonathan (1975) *Structuralist Poetics: Structuralism, Linguistics, and the Study of Literature*, Ithaca: Cornell University Press.

Dosse, François (1996) *History of Structuralism*, vol. 1, trans. Deborah Glassman, Minneapolis: University of Minnesota Press.

Genette, Gérard (1980 [1972]) *Narrative Discourse: An Essay in Method*, trans. Jane E. Lewin, Ithaca: Cornell University Press.

Greimas, Algirdas Julien (1983 [1966]) *Structural Semantics: An Attempt at a Method*, trans. Danielle McDowell, Ronald Schleifer, and Alan Velie, Lincoln: University of Nebraska Press.

Herman, David (1999) 'Introduction', in David Herman (ed.) *Narratologies: New Perspectives on Narrative Analysis*, Columbus: Ohio State University Press.

—— (2001) 'Sciences of the Text', *Postmodern Culture*, http://www.iath.virginia.edu/pmc/text-only/issue.501/11.3herman.txt

—— (2002) *Story Logic: Problems and Possibilities of Narrative*, Lincoln: University of Nebraska Press.

—— (2004) 'Toward a Transmedial Narratology', in Marie-Laure Ryan (ed.) *Narrative across Media: The Languages of Story-telling*, Lincoln: University of Nebraska Press.

Jakobson, Roman (1960) 'Closing Statement: Linguistics and Poetics', in Thomas A. Sebeok (ed.) *Style in Language*, Cambridge: MIT Press.

Lévi-Strauss, Claude (1986 [1955]) 'The Structural Study of Myth', trans. Claire Jacobson and Brooke Grundfest Schoepf, in Hazard Adams and Leroy Searle (eds) *Critical Theory Since 1965*, Tallahassee: UP of Florida.

McHale, Brian (1987) *Postmodernist Fiction*, London: Methuen.

Pavel, Thomas G. (1989) *The Feud of Language: A History of Structuralist Thought*, trans. Trans. Linda Jordan and Thomas G. Pavel, Oxford: Blackwell.

Prince, Gerald (1973) *A Grammar of Stories*, The Hague: Mouton.

—— (1995) 'Narratology', in Raman Selden (ed.) *The Cambridge History of Literary Criticism*, vol. 8., Cambridge: Cambridge University Press.

Propp, Vladimir (1968 [1928]) *Morphology of the Folktale*, trans. Laurence Scott, revised by Louis A. Wagner, Austin: University of Texas Press.

de Saussure, Ferdinand (1959 [1916]) *Course in General Linguistics*, ed. Charles Bally and Albert Sechehaye, in collaboration with Albert Riedlinger, trans. Wade Baskin, New York: The Philosophical Library.

Shklovskii, Viktor (1990) *Theory of Prose*, trans. Benjamin Sher, Elmwood Park, IL: Dalkey Archive Press.

Todorov, Tzvetan (1969) *Grammaire du 'Décaméron'*, The Hague: Mouton.

Tomashevskii, Boris (1965 [1925]) 'Thematics', in Lee T. Lemon and Marion J. Reis (eds) *Russian Formalist Criticism*, Lincoln: University of Nebraska Press.

DAVID HERMAN

SUMMARY AND SCENE

In narrative theory, *summary* refers to a concentrated report of *events by the *narrator, while *scene* denotes a detailed rendering of events which focuses on *characters' experiences and/or employs extensive stretches of *dialogue. As *narrative techniques, summary and scene belong to the 'telling' and 'showing' modes of narrative representation respectively (*see* SHOWING VS. TELLING), the term *scene* being used in analogy with *drama. Due to the influence of Henry James and then of Percy Lubbock, scene was privileged over summary until Lubbock's prescriptive view was finally superseded by Gérard Genette's descriptive analysis of summary and scene as equally valid increments of narrative speed.

Genette (1980 [1972]: 86–112) subsumes the traditional distinction between summary and scene under his concept of 'duration', which concerns the relation between discourse time and story time (*see* STORY-DISCOURSE DISTINCTION; TIME IN NARRATIVE). Duration in its turn represents one of the three subcategories of tense, which Genette uses not in its grammatical sense, but with reference to a narrative's chronological structure. In written narratives, duration is somewhat difficult to define because it is based on a complex temporal-spatial relationship, i.e., the relation between the time the events are supposed to take up in the story and the textual space (as measured in lines, paragraphs, pages, or chapters) which is dedicated to their *narration. The measure yielded by this relationship is speed, with constancy of pace (i.e., an even ratio of story time to discourse time) representing the theoretical norm. Summary or concentration is typically characterised by speed-up (acceleration), i.e., an episode's discourse time is considerably shorter than its story time, while in scene the two are conventionally regarded as being congruent. Adding ellipsis (or the complete omission of an event from the narration) and the descriptive pause to summary and scene (*see* DESCRIPTION), Genette arrives at a four-partite scale which ranges from maximum to minimum speed: in the case of ellipsis, zero textual space corresponds to some story duration, while in the case of the descriptive pause there is some stretch of text, but no time passes on the level of story. It follows that speed is fixed in the case of scene (where there is isochrony, i.e., a congruence between discourse time and story time), zero in the case of pause, infinite in the case of ellipsis, and (variably) accelerated in the case of summary.

As Genette indicates, the conventional pattern in narrative fiction up to the end of the nineteenth-century was the alternating use of summary and scene, with summary providing the transition between passages featuring detailed scenic presentation. The fact that changes of speed usually indicate the relative importance of events is explicitly stated in the famous opening chapter of book II of Henry Fielding's *Tom Jones* (1749), where the narrator declares his intention not to 'keep even pace with time', but instead to use summary, ellipses, and scenic presentation as required by the (non-)significance of his subject-matter.

SEE ALSO: scene (cinematic)

References and further reading

Bonheim, Helmut (1982) *The Narrative Modes: Techniques of the Short Story*, Cambridge: Brewer.
Genette, Gérard (1980 [1972]) *Narrative Discourse. An Essay in Method*, trans. Jane E. Lewin, Ithaca: Cornell University Press.
—— (1988 [1983]) *Narrative Discourse Revisited*, trans. Jane E. Lewin, Ithaca: Cornell University Press.
Rimmon-Kenan, Shlomith (1983) *Narrative Fiction: Contemporary Poetics*, London: Methuen.

MARTIN LÖSCHNIGG

SURFICTION

A term modelled on 'surrealism' (*see* SURREALIST NARRATIVE), 'surfiction' was coined by French-born American novelist Raymond Federman (b. 1928) as an alternative to 'experimental fiction'. Federman's underlying assumption, shared with some poststructuralists, is that reality itself is fictional, in the sense of being constructed through discourse (*see* FICTION, THEORIES OF). Surfiction's function is to expose this fictionality of reality, making surfiction a paradoxical form of *realism; but it also aspires to project alternatives to 'received' reality. Sukenick, a novelist/theorist who uses Federman's term, though with certain reservations, emphasises instead the spontaneous and improvisational aspect of surfictional writing, and its incorporation of the writer's actual situation and process ('the truth of the page'). Related to *metafiction and the French *nouveau roman*, surfiction is often treated as the name for a group of American postmodernist novelists, including Steve Katz, Clarence Major, George Chambers, Jonathan Baumbach, Ursule Molinaro, and others, associated with Federman and Sukenick in the Fiction Collective, an alternative publishing enterprise devoted to avant-garde fiction, founded in 1974.

SEE ALSO: historiographic metafiction; panfictionality; postmodern narrative; poststructuralist approaches to narrative

References and further reading

Federman, Raymond (1975) 'Surfiction – Four Propositions in Form of an Introduction', in *Surfiction: Fiction Now ... and Tomorrow*, Chicago: Swallow Press.
Sukenick, Ronald (1985) *In Form: Digressions on the Act of Fiction*, Carbondale and Edwardsville: Southern Illinois University Press.

BRIAN McHALE

SURREALIST NARRATIVE

Surrealism was a communist art movement which arose in Paris at the end of World War I. Rejecting the rationalism and bourgeois values which claimed to represent the world, the surrealists sought to re-engage the human spirit with its immediate tangible reality first by destroying and negating those values and then by replacing them with writing, *images, objects, and events that accessed the real unconscious mind, and blurred such literary distinctions as lyric and *narrative.

Centring around André Breton, Tristan Tzara, Louis Aragon, Paul Eluard, and Francis Picabia, the first surrealist activities were in experimental writing. The production of surrealist images quickly expanded to graphic art, the plastic arts, *performance, and *music, and surrealism became enormously influential in the 1920s and 1930s in

Europe, spreading to Latin America and the U.S., where it relocated to New York at the start of the World War II. Though the ideology and explicit politics of the movement were largely sidelined, the surrealist technique has remained as one of the most influential forms especially in poetry, *film, and contemporary graphic and installation art, as well as in advertising and in comedy performance (*see* ADVERTISEMENTS).

The surrealist technique was concerned with denying the rationalist authority of *authors and individual egotism (whose products were scorned as 'literature'). By contrast, 'poetry' was writing that evaded these determinants of form and structure. So the surrealists engaged in 'automatic' writing, in which free word-association and hypnotic states were used, 'collage' in which found fragments were reassembled for their accidental value, and 'chainpoems' where lines were contributed by different writers. Accounts of dreams, delusions, hysterical outbursts, and the ravings of psychotics were transcribed, and the surrealists valued *fairy tales, the *fantastic, *myths, and particularly *Gothic novels as offering direct access to the immediacy of experience.

For these reasons, form was less important than the force of the surrealist image, and surrealist writing makes little distinction between lyric and narrative. Breton rejected the bourgeois *novel as a form that represented reality (and thus distorted it through capitalist values). However, narrative writing did appear regularly in the journal *La Revolution Surréaliste* and in other surrealist works, where it claims to *create* reality for the reader. In surrealist narrative, writers are researchers in the unconscious, and the 'poetry' is the landscape which readers are then invited to explore as a means of engaging with their own pre-rationalist mind.

SEE ALSO: dream narrative; psychoanalysis and narrative

References and further reading

Brandon, Ruth (1999) *Surreal Lives: The Surrealists 1917–1945*, London: Macmillan.
Breton, André (1972) *Manifestoes of Surrealism*, trans. Richard Seaver and Helen R. Lane, Ann Arbor: University of Michigan Press.
Gascoyne, David (1970) *A Short Survey of Surrealism*, London: Frank Cass.
Matthews, J. H. (1976) *Towards a Poetics of Surrealism*, New York: Syracuse University Press.
Richardson, Michael (ed.) (1993) *The Dedalus Book of Surrealism: The Identity of Things*, Sawtry, UK: Dedalus.
—— (ed.) (1994) *The Dedalus Book of Surrealism 2: The Myth of the World*, Sawtry, UK: Dedalus.

PETER STOCKWELL

SUSPENSE AND SURPRISE

Suspense, an effect which results from our temporal-affective *immersion in a narrative, describes our tension-filled *desire to know its outcome. Suspense cuts across *genres and literary historical periods, although it is often associated with *realism and popular genres. It is to be distinguished from both anticipation and (structural) tension, for not everything drawing us through a story counts as an element of suspense. Similarly, surprise results from immersion: readers experience an *emotion of surprise when, in Prince's definition, their expectations about what is going to happen are violated by what in fact does happen. Although the interplay of suspense and surprise traditionally constitutes a feature of good plotting, they are not necessarily linked to each other (*see* PLOT).

Suspense engages our emotions through anxious uncertainty. It relies on a structured *horizon of expectations that incorporates a double temporal perspective: readers are made aware of the various ways in which past *events can restrict both immediate and long-range events (*see* TIME IN NARRATIVE). Suspense therefore depends on our ability to envision events and project possible scripts for *action based on the desires, plans, and goals of *characters (*see* SCRIPTS AND SCHEMATA). The intensity of suspense is inversely proportional to the range of possibilities. Suspense is heightened when a situation or an event enables us to chart the future into diverging, but reasonably computable outcomes. Its climax begins when narrative possibilities are reduced to clear-cut binaries such as success or failure. This quality suggests that our interest in the fate of characters contributes to the experience of suspense. Typically, when a likable character is in danger, readers hope for a favourable outcome. Carroll links suspense not only with probability but also with morality, arguing that, in popular fictions at least, suspense raises two logically opposed outcomes: one is morally correct but unlikely, while the other is evil and likely. Suspense need not, however, be tied to morality as, for example, Patricia High-smith's Tom Ripley novels suggest by making readers fear for an amoral criminal. Suspense may be created with any device that allows the projection of possible narrative paths while simultaneously constraining the horizon of possibilities, such as foreshadowing, prediction, flashforward, and dramatic *irony (see TEMPORAL ORDERING).

Ryan distinguishes among four types, based on the focus of suspense. *What suspense* spotlights the imminent resolution of a binary alternative that involves emotional engagement with the fate of a *hero(ine) and a desire for a positive outcome for him or her. Given that the orienting question is 'what will happen next', this type involves readers in the unfolding of the action and the *perspective of the hero(ine). An enigma generates *how and why suspense*: readers must find out the cause of an already established event (see CAUSALITY). Because the focus is on the prehistory of a known state, suspense concerns curiosity for the solution of a problem. This type suggests multiple possibilities converging toward the known goal. Yet once the narrative has jumped backward in time and started moving toward this goal, readers may experience suspense on the level of the individual episodes. *Who suspense* limits the number of solutions to the number of suspects. Typical of the *detective story, it relies on the intellectual satisfaction of solving a problem. A limit case is *metasuspense* involving a point of view external to the textual world (see POINT OF VIEW (LITERARY)). The dynamics of storytelling replace the dynamics of storytime: metasuspense concerns our curiosity about how the *author will tie all the narrative strands together and give the text narrative form (see NARRATIVE STRUCTURE; STORY-DISCOURSE DISTINCTION).

An intriguing aspect of fictional suspense is its resiliency: why does suspense persist over multiple readings or viewings, waning only gradually? This phenomenon is known as 'anomalous suspense' (Carroll 1996; Gerrig 1996), because suspense ought to evaporate once uncertainty is removed. Carroll explains repeated suspense by invoking two cognitive phenomena. First, given that the availability of beliefs is subject to variation and intensification, in multiple readings or viewings readers push their knowledge and beliefs about the outcome of the story into the background of consciousness. Second, in *fiction propositions are contemplated but not asserted. Emotional responses, however, are not sensitive to this distinction between asserted and unasserted propositions. In (repeated) fictional suspense, readers contemplate the unasserted proposition that a hero(ine) is in danger, and the intensity of this contemplation generates the emotional response of anxiety. Imagination makes the state of affairs temporarily present and true, and from the perspective of the present, the future has not yet happened.

A narrative may create surprise without suspense as when a bomb of which we know nothing suddenly explodes and, conversely, relieve suspense without surprise when, for example, an event takes place that is fully foreseeable, but not certain to occur. Also, surprise comes into play only at the moment when suspense is resolved. An aesthetically and emotionally effective surprise plays on anticipation: what in fact happens violates expectations, yet is well grounded in what happened earlier. As a matter of illuminating insight, the surprise effect plays on semantic possibilities as well as on notions of probability and plausibility. By making readers retrospectively review and revise their expectations, it includes a metalevel perspective that invites readers to consider how the effect was achieved.

The challenge in creating the surprise effect is the difficulty of coming up with, for example, a hidden truth or guilty knowledge whose disclosure will not seem anticlimactic compared to the speculative possibilities the preceding situations permit. Following Irwin, we may distinguish two broad types of surprise. Exhaustable surprise is tied to a definitive resolution of the narrative, while inexhaustible surprise is tied to repeatable solutions that conserve, by endlessly refiguring, the narrative's central enigma. The latter characterises narratives that, like a Möbius strip, offer self-reflexive descriptions of their own workings (see REFLEXIVITY).

SEE ALSO: narrative dynamics; narrative progression; psychological approaches to narrative

References and further reading

Carroll, Noël (1990) *The Philosophy of Horror or Paradoxes of the Heart*, New York: Routledge.
—— (1996) 'The Paradox of Suspense', in Vorderer, Wulff, and Friedrichsen (eds) *Suspense: Conceptualizations, Theoretical Analyses, and Empirical Explorations*, Mahwah, N.J.: Lawrence Erlbaum.
Gerrig, Richard J. (1996) 'The Resiliency of Suspense', in Vorderer, Wulff, and Friedrichsen (eds) *Suspense: Conceptualizations, Theoretical Analyses, and*

Empirical Explorations, Mahwah, N.J.: Lawrence Erlbaum.

Irwin, John T. (1994) *The Mystery to a Solution*, Baltimore: Johns Hopkins University Press.

Prince, Gerald (1987) *A Dictionary of Narratology*, Lincoln: University of Nebraska Press.

Ryan, Marie-Laure (2001) *Narrative as Virtual Reality*, Baltimore: Johns Hopkins University Press.

Vorderer, Peter, Hans J. Wulff, and Mike Friedrichsen (eds) (1996) *Suspense: Conceptualizations, Theoretical Analyses, and Empirical Explorations*, Mahwah, N.J.: Lawrence Erlbaum.

HETA PYRHÖNEN

SYLLEPSIS

In Genettean narratology, a form of presentation which prefers *thematic, spatial, or associational linkage over chronological arrangement. *See* TEMPORAL ORDERING (also: SPATIAL FORM).

T

TABLOID NARRATIVE

The term 'tabloid' strictly refers only to certain half-broadsheet size newspapers, but it has come to define a particular kind of formulaic, colourful narrative related to, but somewhat distinct from, standard styles of *journalism.

In the United States, tabloid style began in the 'Penny Press' of the 1830s, whose writers drew on the formulaic conventions of broadsheets and *ballads to produce 'human interest' news that focused on dramatic, personal tales of crime and mayhem, frequently with an implied or overt moral. It developed further in the 'yellow journalism' of the late nineteenth-century, as publishers competed for rising numbers of literate but unsophisticated readers. Avoiding the euphemisms and distanced style of elite newspapers, these writers painted lurid word pictures of crime victims and scandalous events. True 'tabloids' emerged in Britain during the first decade of the twentieth century, and in the United States in the 1920s. Entertainingly sensational, they were written in the idioms of the people, as William Randolph Hearst proudly declared when launching the American *Daily Mirror* in 1924 (Bird 1992).

Tabloid style is not dependent on content; tabloids may cover the same topics as mainstream journalism, although typically more briefly (see Bird 2002). Tabloid narrative eschews the 'inverted pyramid' format of modern journalism, preferring to lead with a 'teasing' introduction, followed by the complete tale, laid out concisely. The style has changed little since the 1920s, and allowing for local idiomatic differences, it is similar across the English-speaking world, whether in weekly 'supermarket tabloids' or more news-oriented dailies. Adjectives abound; stories are 'amazing', 'baffling', 'untold', or 'incredible'. Particular story types call for familiar words: Heroes are 'spunky', or 'gutsy'; a male celebrity may have a 'gal-pal' or 'cutie', whereas females will have 'boy toys' or 'hunks'. Small children are 'tots', dogs are 'pooches', husbands are 'hubbies', and unsavoury types are 'creeps' or 'sickos'. The use of stock clichés produces a short-hand style that invites readers into the tabloid assumptions of good and bad, appropriate and non-appropriate. Reporters combine and recombine information in familiar patterns (*see* PLOT TYPES), giving tabloids their distinctive flavour of titillating novelty delivered with soothing predictability. Standard interview practice is to ask questions requiring a yes or no answer; the question then becomes the quote, producing interview subjects who are consistently 'shocked', 'flabbergasted', and 'bowled over'.

While narrative style is similar across various types of tabloid, there is wide variation in how these tabloid types are perceived. U.S. weeklies range from those featuring sensational but verifiable celebrity and political *gossip to those filled with fictional tales of alien abductions. More respectable tabloids, such as the *National Enquirer*, sometimes launch stories into the mainstream press, although they are still perceived as disreputable. Readers enjoy the personality-driven stories, applying them to their own lives, while not necessarily believing every word. The essentially fictional titles, such as the *Weekly World News*, are widely regarded as comic diversions, although some readers find even the most bizarre stories credible (Bird 1992). British dailies have a heavier emphasis on both explicit sex and hard news, told in tabloid style and appealing to their more consciously working-class readers.

In recent years, tabloid style has become the focus of widespread unease among journalism critics; the word 'tabloidisation' has come to connote a decline in journalistic discourse, whether in *television or print (Sparks and Tulloch 2000).

SEE ALSO: audience; media and narrative

References and further reading

Bird, S. Elizabeth (1992) *For Enquiring Minds: A Cultural Study of Supermarket Tabloids*, Knoxville: University of Tennessee Press.
—— (2002) 'Taking it Personally: Supermarket Tabloids after September 11', in Barbie Zelizer and Stuart Allen (eds) *Journalism after September 11*, London: Routledge.
Sparks, Colin, and John Tulloch (eds) (2000) *Tabloid Tales*, New York: Rowman & Littlefield.

S. ELIZABETH BIRD

TALL TALE

The tall tale plays with one of the most fundamental typological principles in the classification of narrative, namely, *truth. It derives its interpretive effect from being framed as a purportedly true narrative of personal experience in which the circumstances of the narrated event are stretched by degrees to the point that they challenge or exceed the limits of credibility (*see* FICTION, THEORIES OF). Although it is widely defined as a tale of extravagant lying and hyperbole, the tall tale relies as much on ludicrous imagery, circumstantial detail, and strategic understatement as it does on exaggeration.

The tall tale is a characteristically male genre, at home among men who are separated from settled, domestic milieux: hunters, fishermen, seamen, cowboys, loggers, frontiersmen. The telling of tall tales occurs in two principal contexts: (1) esoteric settings, such as 'the liars' bench' in the general store or other settings of male sociability, in which participants are attuned to the expressive dynamics of tall tales and relish the virtuosity of skilled raconteurs; and (2) exoteric settings, as between frontier people and greenhorns or locals and tourists, in which tall tales become a means of putting on outsiders or neophytes by playing upon their naiveté, ignorance, or gullibility.

While some tall tales still current in oral tradition may be traced back to classical antiquity and to European antecedents (such as those attached to Baron Münchhausen), the tall tale has been especially prized in the United States, even claimed as a distinctively American *genre. The American penchant for tall tales has been variously attributed to the scale, abundance, and wildness of the American landscape, a concomitant tendency to create and celebrate larger-than-life *heroes, and the impulse of frontiersmen to repudiate the canons of gentility by playing to the stereotypes and anxieties of effete outsiders.

SEE ALSO: ethnographic approaches to narrative; gender studies; legend; orality; simple forms

References and further reading

Bauman, Richard (1986) *Story, Performance, and Event: Contextual Studies of Oral Narrative*, Cambridge: Cambridge University Press.
Boatright, Mody (1949) 'The Art of Tall Lying', *Southwest Review*, 33, 357–62.
Brown, Carolyn S. (1987) *The Tall Tale in American Folklore and Literature*, Knoxville: University of Tennessee Press.
Cothran, Kay L. (1974) 'Talking Trash in the Okefenokee Swamp Rim, Georgia', *Journal of American Folklore*, 87, 340–56.
Henningsen, Gustav (1965) 'The Art of Perpendicular Lying', *Journal of the Folklore Institute*, 2, 180–219.

RICHARD BAUMAN

TEL AVIV SCHOOL OF NARRATIVE POETICS

Since the mid-1960s, many of the leading contributors to narrative theory in Israel have been associated with the Department of Poetics and Comparative Literature at Tel Aviv University and its affiliated research centre, the Porter Institute for Poetics and Semiotics. Founded in 1966–1967 by Benjamin Hrushovski (who later Hebraized his name to Harshav), the new department provided an institutional home for structuralist-oriented research in literary theory and poetics, including narrative poetics (*see* STRUCTURALIST NARRATOLOGY). This entry briefly outlines the history of the Tel Aviv school's contribution to narrative theory, traces the school's intellectual genealogy, and identifies three of its distinctive characteristics: its unified theory of the literary text, its precocious emphasis on the reading process, and its functionalist orientation.

Research in the first decade of the Tel Aviv circle's existence, much of it published in *Ha-Sifrut* (*Literature*), the Hebrew-language journal founded by Harshav in 1968, focused largely, though not exclusively, on Hebrew literature, including *biblical narrative (Perry and Sternberg, subsequently extended and developed in Sternberg 1985). The group began to make an impact internationally from the mid-1970's, with the founding in 1975 of the Israeli Institute for Poetics and Semiotics (renamed the Porter Institute in 1977) and the launching of two English-language journals, the short-lived *PTL* (1976–1979) and its successor, *Poetics Today*, founded in 1979. In the same year, the Porter Institute hosted a major international conference on Narrative Theory and Poetics of Fiction, which provided material for three influential special issues of *Poetics Today* in 1980–1981. While *Poetics Today* has remained an important outlet for research on narrative, many of the original Tel Aviv narratologists have moved on to other fields, with the conspicuous exception of Sternberg. Apart from the 'core' first-generation group of Harshav, Sternberg, Perry, and Even-Zohar (*see* REALEME), second-generation Tel Aviv scholars who have contributed to narrative theory include Ziva Ben-Porat, Uri Margolin, Ruth Ronen, Nomi Tamir-Ghez, Tamar Yacobi, and Gabriel Zoran. Others whose work has occasionally intersected with Tel Aviv school narrative theory include Ruth Amossy, Shlomith Rimmon-Kenan, Ellen Spolsky, and the authors of the present entry.

The intellectual sources of Tel Aviv narratology are diverse. Its cornerstone is Russian Formalist poetics of prose, especially the fundamental distinction between fabula and sjuzhet (*see* FORMALISM; STORY-DISCOURSE DISTINCTION) and the notion of motivation. The Tel Aviv narratologists supplement this basic Formalist apparatus with a model of the reading process derived from the Polish phenomenologist Ingarden (*see* PHENOMENOLOGY OF NARRATIVE), especially his concepts of the reader's concretisation of the literary work and of pockets of *indeterminacy in the world of the literary work. From the former concept they derive their own notion of the (re)constructed level of the text, while from the latter they elaborate an entire poetics of gaps and gap-filling (*see* GAPPING). Other sources are the New Critics'

attention to *spatial form, analogies, and patterns of recurrence, and Booth's rhetoric of fiction (*see* RHETORICAL APPROACHES TO NARRATIVE), with its distinction between *narrator and *implied author and its apparatus of narratorial unreliability (*see* RELIABILITY). Conspicuously absent from the Tel Aviv tradition is analysis of story-functions in the Propp-Bremond-Greimas line (*see* FUNCTION (PROPP)). Despite certain similarities of orientation, neither French structuralist narratology nor the *reader-response approach of the Constance school are true antecedents of the Tel Aviv school, which should more correctly be seen as an independent, parallel development.

Synthesising multiple traditions of twentieth-century narrative theory, the Tel Aviv school nevertheless displays several distinctive features. First, its narrative theory is not free-standing, but rather inscribed within a more general, unified theory of the literary text, for which Harshav is mainly responsible. This unified theory treats all literary texts, of whatever *genre, as semantic continua where units of meaning are integrated by being linked up into patterns, sometimes according to intra-literary models (e.g., rhyme, analogy), sometimes by reference to reality-like templates or frames (*see* FRAME THEORY; NARRATIVE UNITS; SCRIPTS AND SCHEMATA). Such frames belong to one or more fields of *reference, which may be external to the text (i.e., bodies of 'real-world' knowledge) or internal to it. A literary text is defined as a text possessing at least one internal field of reference. Narrative patterning appears in this light as just one among a range of possible forms of semantic integration (*see* NARRATIVE SEMANTICS).

Distinctive, too, or at least somewhat ahead of its time, is the Tel Aviv narratologists' insistence on the central role of the reading process. Emphasis falls on the reader's activity of framing and pattern-making; on gaps as invitations to readerly problem-solving; on the reader's ongoing hypothesising and retrospective revision of hypotheses; on effects of primacy ('first impressions') and recency; and on the lingering, cumulative influence even of rejected interpretations (see, e.g., Perry 1979; Perry and Sternberg 1986; Sternberg 1978 and 1985). By contrast with theories of reading such as Fish's, based on arbitrarily constituted interpretive communities, the Tel Aviv theory posits a more parsimonious model, whereby the reader brings to the text only as much 'worldly' knowledge, and only as many predispositions, expectations, etc., as are strictly necessary to 'operate' the text. This amounts to treating the reading-process as a *metonymy of text-structure, and vice versa.

Finally, Tel Aviv narratology is distinguished by its functionalist orientation, which transforms its Formalist heritage and structuralist affinities. Instead of merely describing forms, the Tel Aviv narratologists explore their motivation; indeed, forms exist for them only in the light of their functions. This functionalist orientation is already discernible in the earliest publications of the school, such as Golomb's account, strongly influenced by Bakhtin, of *dual-voice or (in Tel Aviv terminology) 'combined' discourse, where linguistic criteria for distinguishing dual voice are subordinated to functional criteria. The school's functionalism becomes fully explicit in the later work of Sternberg, where this 'anti-formalist' approach is generalised into a 'Proteus Principle' of many-to-many correspondence between linguistic forms and their functions: 'in different contexts...the same form may fulfil different functions *and* different forms the same function' (Sternberg 1982: 148) (*see* QUOTATION THEORY). Sternberg identifies three types of narrative interest, or master functions: suspense, which is future-oriented and involves the reader's prospection; curiosity, which is past-oriented, and involves the reader's awareness of specific gaps in the narrative; and surprise, which involves the dynamics of recognition, hinging on one or more gaps whose existence the reader only discovers belatedly (*see* NARRATIVE DYNAMICS; SUSPENSE AND SURPRISE). Sternberg (1992: 529) defines *narrativity in functionalist terms as the play of these three master functions, suspense, curiosity and surprise, and redefines *narrative as a text where such play dominates.

SEE ALSO: Chicago School, the

References and further reading

Golomb, Harai (1968) 'Combined Speech – A Major Technique in the Prose of S. J. Agnon: Its Use in the Story "A Different Face"', *Ha-Sifrut*, 1, 251–62. [In Hebrew.]

Hrushovski [Harshav], Benjamin (1988 [1976]) 'Theory of the Literary Text and the Structure of Non-Narrative Fiction: In the First Episode of *War and Peace*', *Poetics Today*, 9.3, 635–66.

Perry, Menakhem (1979) 'Literary Dynamics: How the Order of a Text Creates Its Meaning [with an Analysis of Faulkner's "A Rose for Emily"]', *Poetics Today*, 1.1/2, 35–64, 311–61.

——, and Meir Sternberg (1986 [1968]) 'The King Through Ironic Eyes: Biblical Narrative and the Literary Reading Process', *Poetics Today*, 7.2, 275–322.

Sternberg, Meir (1978) *Expositional Modes and Temporal Ordering in Fiction*, Baltimore: Johns Hopkins University Press.

—— (1985) *The Poetics of Biblical Narrative: Ideological Literature and the Drama of Reading*, Bloomington: Indiana University Press.

—— (1982) 'Proteus in Quotation-Land: Mimesis and the Forms of Reported Discourse', *Poetics Today*, 3.2, 107–56.

—— (1992) 'Telling in Time (II): Chronology, Teleology, Narrativity', *Poetics Today*, 13.3, 463–541.

Zoran, Gabriel (1984) 'Towards a Theory of Space in Narrative', *Poetics Today*, 5.2, 309–35. (Expanded book version published in Hebrew, 1997.)

BRIAN McHALE AND MOSHE RON

TEL QUEL

Tel Quel (TQ) was an avant-garde quarterly review founded by a group of very young writers around Philippe Sollers and edited by Seuil in Paris. Published from 1960 to 1982, the journal's main sources of inspiration were the works of Marx (read through Althusser), Freud (interpreted through Lacan), Foucault, *feminism, and later Maoism. Its aim was the achievement of social revolution through *écriture* and 'thought' (*see* DISCOURSE ANALYSIS (FOUCAULT); ÉCRITURE FÉMININE; MARXIST APPROACHES TO NARRATIVE). With many of its key collaborators – Kristeva, Todorov, Barthes, Derrida, and Lacan – linked to academia, TQ contributed significantly to the diffusion of the latest theories of the text, ranging from generative linguistics to *semiotics and 'semanalyse' (Kristeva's theory of the materiality of the sign and of the relationship between language and body of the speaking or writing subject). The contribution of Kristeva has been decisive: her eclectic elaboration of the notion of *intertextuality (inspired by Bakhtin), of Saumjan's mathematical language theory, and of Saussure's work on anagrams set the model for TQ's attitude toward reading and writing – textual elements could be freely combined, liberating them from constraints of linearity and submission to sense. With the growing impact of *psychoanalysis, the suspect notion of the subject was reintroduced (*see* IDENTITY AND NARRATIVE). Ricardou, the other 'terrorist' theoretician of both the *nouveau roman* and Tel Quel, worked out the notion of textual *générateurs*, whose aleatory procedures unleashed the plays of meaning celebrated by TQ.

TQ rediscovered de Sade, Lautréamont, Mallarmé, Valéry, Roussel, and Joyce, proposing a new canon privileging transgressive, reflexive, and combinatorial writing – hence their close association with Bataille, *nouveau roman* authors, and experimental poets such as Françis Ponge and Denis Roche (*see* TRANSGRESSIVE FICTIONS). After a short common trajectory, the members of TQ distanced themselves from the *nouveau roman*, whose exponents were, in their view, too complicitous with the *ideology of representation and expression. Instead, TQ writers such as Sollers (*Nombres*) or Ricardou (*La prise de Constantinople*) advocated an empty 'écriture' from which meaning and subjectivity were wholly evacuated. In their view, reading does not lead to any other reality than the space of the page, to no other experience than that of the free play of language (*see* REFLEXIVITY). The radicalness of this project ironically turned the *(anti-)narrative writing of Tel Quel into rather predictable *allegory. The appeal of their literary work has been less lasting than their theoretical reflections, and less influential than the writings of the *nouveau roman* novelists or the more playful American *surfiction authors.

SEE ALSO: deconstructive approaches to narrative; novel, the; Oulipo; postmodern narrative; poststructuralist approaches to narrative

References and further reading

Ffrench, Patrick (1995) *The Time of Theory: A History of Tel Quel (1960–1983)*, Oxford: Clarendon Press.
Kauppi, Niilo (1994) *The Making of an Avant-Garde: Tel Quel*, Berlin: Mouton.
Kristeva, Julia (1980) *Desire in Language: A Semiotic Approach to Literature and Art*, Oxford: Blackwell.
van der Poel, Ieme (1992) *Une révolution de la pensée: Maoïsme et féminisme à travers Tel Quel, Les Temps Modernes et Esprit*, Amsterdam: Rodopi.

LIESBETH KORTHALS ALTES

TELEVISION

In order to consider the characteristics of television narrative, we must look at television as a medium and the ways in which its various aspects, from production to *reception, condition its narrative *codes. This entry focuses on U.S. television, which has, through its dominance of the global television market, long exerted a powerful influence on the nature and development of television in other nations and can reasonably be considered a global trendsetting model.

Television is multifaceted, ubiquitous, and prolific – qualities that make it notoriously difficult to address in its totality. It exists as an industry, a set of technologies (of production, delivery, and reception), as content, and as the begetter of a peculiar demographic – the 'television audience' (*see* AUDIENCE). It has dynamic relationships with other *media, both in its *remediation of other media forms (such as cinema) and in the extension of some of its own fictions into multimedia franchises like those around cult series such as *Star Trek* and *The X-Files* (*see* FILM NARRATIVE). It delivers content around the clock – a ceaseless organised procession of sequences and sets of sequences, the experience of which Raymond Williams describes as television's 'flow' and which consists not only of programmes but also of the commercial breaks (*see* ADVERTISEMENTS), trailers, and announcements that intersect them.

Television's 'flow' is not seamless, however. It must accommodate interruptions, both within its own programming and in the context of its reception in domestic environments where distractions are likely to occur. As Jane Feuer has argued, 'it would be more accurate to say that television is constituted by a dialectic of segmentation and flow' (1983: 15). Both operations are integral to the organisation of television content, to its constant rhythm of acts, climaxes, breaks, and episodes and their structured procession within the macro-narrative of the television schedule (*see* NARRATIVE STRUCTURE; NARRATIVE UNITS). The evolution of television's many and various narrative forms reflects these dual imperatives, most notably in the medium's adoption and adaptation of modes of serialisation (*see* SERIAL FORM), which enact patterns of continuity and discontinuity ideally suited to television's necessary interplay of flow and interruption.

Cultural evolution of the TV medium

Television is a dynamic and evolving medium, unusually sensitive to technological and economic developments. Television scholars commonly divide its history to date into two eras, each of which demonstrates the interrelatedness of industry, technologies, consumer contexts, and content (see Collins 1992; Reeves, Rodgers, and Epstein 1996). The first era, referred to as the network era or 'TVI', covers the period from the 1940s to the 1970s during which the American television industry was dominated by three major television networks (CBS, NBC, and ABC). The first two decades of the network era are often nostalgically described as television's 'Golden Age' – a period of innocence dominated by a 'quality programming' philosophy that had not yet been undermined by the pressures of commercialism. Most of television's major formats originated during this early phase, including the single play, episodic drama series, continuing serials (including soap opera), situation comedies, variety shows, game shows, and factual programmes. The 'Golden Era' produced landmark series such as *I Love Lucy* and *The Phil Silver Show* and its live broadcast television plays launched the careers of stars such as Jack Lemmon, Rod Steiger, and Grace Kelly.

By the mid-1950s, however, the Golden Era was coming to an end, superseded by formulaic programme-making that applied the Fordist logics of the mass-market to television, mass producing television fare for a mass audience. Output became crudely ratings-driven, organised around the repetition of narrative and production formulae in 'cookie-cutter' programmes which aimed simply to attract the largest possible share of a 'family' television audience perceived as more-or-less homogenous in its tastes, values, and interests – a philosophy that earned later network era television the derisory epithet of 'lowest common denominator' television.

In the 1970s, deregulation ended the virtual monopoly of the three major networks and ushered in the post-network or 'TVII' era of multichannel cable, satellite, and digital television that we know today. The fractured character of television in the post-network era has been further underlined by the development of auxiliary television technologies such as VCRs, DVD players, video games consoles (*see* COMPUTER GAMES AND NARRATIVE), and remote control handsets that allow viewers to effortlessly switch from channel to channel. In response to these developments, the television industry radically revised its understanding of its public. The pursuit of raw ratings was, for the most part, abandoned in favour of strategies for attracting coalition audiences which consist of the 'quality demographics' most valued by advertisers: population groups with expendable income and identifiable interests that allow targeted advertising. As Jim Collins observes, the audience is 'no longer regarded as a homogenous mass but rather as an amalgamation of microcultural groups stratified by age, gender, race, and geographic location' (342).

In the post-network era, *genre serves the triple function of standardising production, 'branding' a channel or a series, and hailing an audience. Commercial channels such as the *History Channel*, the *Sci-Fi Channel*, and *MTV* define and market themselves entirely in terms of genre, catering to niche audiences and delivering them to advertisers. Genre series proliferate on all channels and genre hybridity has become commonplace as a means of maximising a series' appeal to different demographic groups (*see* GENRE FICTION; GENRE THEORY IN FILM STUDIES; GENRE THEORY IN NARRATIVE STUDIES; HYBRID GENRES). *Buffy the Vampire Slayer*, for example, combines the generic conventions of *horror, the high school drama, *romance, and martial arts movies, thus addressing itself to male and female viewers in their teens, 20s, and 30s, as well as to several subcultures, fandoms, as well as a range of other special interest groups and taste groups. In many long-running drama serials, genre hybridity operates alongside a range of postmodernist devices such as bricolage, self-referentiality, and *irony, which together work to form multifaceted programmes characterised by their simultaneous address to diverse demographic groups and by their openness to processes of interpretation, re-articulation, and remediation that extend and prolong their circulation (*see* POSTMODERN NARRATIVE; REFLEXIVITY).

Along with the shift from mass marketing to niche marketing there has occurred a further progression towards the subsuming of the specificity of 'television' under a wider transmedial entertainment industry of which the production, distribution, and composition of television programmes are only one part. Successful television drama serials such as *Star Trek* or *The X-Files* originate in but are not limited to television; rather, they have become franchises that extend across a range of media (movies, novelisations, computer games, and so on; *see* ADAPTATION) and spin-off products (such as action figures, models, collectors' cards, and posters). Their status as transmedial fictions is centred upon the storytelling potential of the narrative world rather than any single form of its expression, production, or *narrativisation. It raises new and interesting questions about the construction and circulation of commercial fictions across different media, the generation and interrelationship of different narrative forms within a single commercial fiction phenomenon, and the various modes of viewer/consumer engagement with its diverse yet interconnected manifestations.

Types and forms of television narrative

This section will focus on fictional television narratives but, even with this restriction, the characteristics of television and its narratives defy final and singular definitions. This is because, as Sarah Kozloff points out, narrative codes on television change over time and because the medium offers such a variety of types of texts that generalisations are of limited value (93) (*see* TEXT-TYPE APPROACH TO NARRATIVE). Furthermore, television's narrative codes are often not specific to television but rather reflect its mongrel origins and myriad borrowings from a range of other media and cultural forms such as theater (*see* DRAMA), cinema, *radio, music hall, the *novel, magazines, *comic books, and, most recently, computer games. Yet in television's appropriations and reworkings of narrative forms developed in other media, its own distinctive character, purposes, and progressions become manifest. By looking at some of the major narrative forms of television drama, we can discern some of the forces that contour and drive their configurations and developments in a dynamic and ever-changing medium.

(1) *The single drama or television play*: The single drama is the television version of a theatrical play. During the so-called 'Golden Era' of 1940s and 1950s American television, the single play was a popular format and plays were performed and broadcast live in anthology series such as NBC's *Philco Television Playhouse* and CBS's rival *Studio One*. Like theatrical plays, they were self-contained texts arranged into acts, used stage sets, and were *character and dialogue-driven rather than action driven (*see* DIALOGUE IN THE NOVEL). Their popularity waned in the U.S. in the late 1950s as audience tastes changed to filmed productions that owed more to the influence of cinema than to theater.

(2) *The mini-series*: Hybrids of the single drama and the continuing serial forms, mini-series tell their stories in instalments across a limited number of episodes (usually between four and twelve). Often described as 'television novels', they explore *characters, situations, and *events in more depth than the single drama and present more defined structures of beginning, middle, and end than do longer continuing serials. Parallels with the novel are underlined by the fact that miniseries are often television adaptations of novels, Alex Haley's *Roots* being one notable example.

(3) *The episodic series*: Episodic series consist of self-contained episodes. With the exception of occasional two-part specials, their storylines do not continue from one episode to the next. Progress occurs only within single episodes and not across the series as a whole. Continuity is provided by the use of the same set of major characters in each episode, but the characters do not develop and make no mention of events that have occurred in previous episodes.

This formulaic play of repetition and novelty is clearly apparent in murder-mystery episodic series such as *Columbo*, *Murder, She Wrote*, and *Diagnosis Murder* (*see* DETECTIVE FICTION). In each of these series, every episode begins in the same way: with a murder that occurs in a context that ensures that the series' regular protagonist will be drawn into the investigation. A range of suspects and motives is presented as the protagonist delves deeper into the circumstances surrounding the murder and the story proceeds. Every episode concludes with the apprehension of the murderer, following a denouement in which the evidence is reprised and all the loose ends are tied up. The appeal of such formulaic series lies in their combination of the syntagmatic predictability of the narrative and the paradigmatic variations of secondary characters, settings, and story events. The audience anticipates and is reassured by the familiar procession of the narrative towards its predictable resolution, while each episode's introduction of new paradigmatic elements provides just enough novelty to maintain viewer interest (Eco 1994) (*see* SUSPENSE AND SURPRISE).

(4) *The continuing serial*: Unlike the episodic series, the continuing serial continues its storylines across episodes. The narrative progresses from episode to episode and characters learn, develop, and have memories. Individual episodes do not work towards their own narrative resolution but

rather progress through a series of mini-climaxes towards a cliffhanger episode ending intended to create enough anticipatory interest in viewers to ensure that they will return to find out what happens in the next episode. Storylines multiply as the serial progresses and final resolution is deferred until the final episode of the serial. Within this format, soap operas are a special category of continuing serial, presenting open-ended narratives in which final resolution is endlessly deferred.

(5) *The flexi-narrative*: Flexi-narratives dominate among the prestigious long-running drama series that are the centrepieces of evening schedules and the frequent recipients of Emmy awards. Series such as *ER*, *The X-Files*, *NYPD Blue*, and *The Sopranos* combine high production values with flexi-narrative formats which share narrative characteristics of both the episodic series and the continuing serial (see Nelson 1997). The flexi-narrative form emerged in the early 1980s with the groundbreaking police series *Hill Street Blues*. Its development was, in part, a response to the important industry practice of syndication, through which television channels purchase the right to broadcast a particular series for a specified period of time. Syndicated series are produced in seasons of (usually) twenty-two episodes. In order to maximise profits through standardisation of production, a successful syndicated series will usually consist of five seasons' worth of episodes, although unsuccessful series are cancelled after just one or two seasons while the most successful may extend to as many as eight or nine. In their entirety, such series usually consist of more than a hundred hours of screen-time and are in production and first-run distribution for many years.

There are two types of flexi-narrative. The type developed for *Hill Street Blues*, which is also the narrative form of series such as *ER*, *Homicide*, and *NYPD Blue*, entails the interweaving of both self-contained and continuing narratives within every episode. Each episode contains at least two storylines that begin, develop, and are resolved within that same episode. In addition, it also includes several storylines that continue from previous episodes and go on into future ones. As with the episodic series, every episode presents a new set of secondary characters whose presence in the series is limited only to that episode and its self-contained storylines. At the same time, the series' primary characters are involved both in self-contained and continuing storylines, their engagement in the latter providing continuity, progression, and some suspense across multiple episodes. As in the continuing serial, storylines proliferate and final resolution is deferred until the concluding episode of the serial as a whole.

The second type of flexi-narrative occurs in series such as *The X-Files* and *Star Trek: Deep Space Nine* and involves a strategy of shifting between 'standalone' episodes that are self-contained and 'narrative arc' episodes that form part of and help advance a continuing narrative (*see* STORY ARC). By shifting back and forth between episodic series and continuing serial formats, the series remains open to new viewers who have come late to it, and for whom standalone episodes form an accessible point of entry, whilst maintaining the interest and loyalty of regular viewers invested in the gradual unfolding of the much longer continuing narrative. In an interesting variation of this format, *The X-Files* also adopts the narrative logics of the conspiracy theories that constitute its core subject matter and in which the resolution of one narrative thread is often revealed as the beginning of another as conspiracy leads to conspiracy.

Interactive television

During the 1990s, television's primacy as a home entertainment technology has increasingly been challenged by the personal computer and the Internet (*see* DIGITAL NARRATIVE). Computers compete with television both on tangible and ideological levels. The personal computer has already appropriated one of television's auxiliary functions, functioning as a platform for viewing films, and even television series, on integrated DVD players. Its technologies – most notably the Internet – offer a range of entertainment alternatives to television, as well as informational alternatives such as news websites. Documentaries and dramas are available online for downloading, while Web TV sites offer 'television' without television. 'Internet TV' services such as Microsoft's *MSN.TV* offer limited and user-friendly Internet access via television sets rather than computers and mark the encroachment of computer companies into the television industry's territory.

At the same time, the marketing of computer and other digital technologies has taken a stage further the notion of 'consumer choice' that dominates the globalised, late capitalist media world. 'Interactivity' is emphasised as a means to 'a more powerful sense of user engagement with media texts, a more independent relation to sources of knowledge, individualised media use, and greater user choice' (Lister *et al.*, 2003: 19). Television companies have responded to the challenge of interactivity by seeking ways of offering viewers some crude means of limited participatory engagement with some programmes. Viewers are encouraged to send in emails to live broadcasts, some of which are read out on air to create the impression of a dialogue between the presenters and the audience. Reality TV shows, such as *Big Brother*, invite viewers to intervene in the text by voting for contestants after each episode and thereby influence the unfolding narrative and outcome of the series. The BBC's experimental series *Fightbox* works through a symbiosis of computer and television as viewers construct characters and devise strategies on computers, using a programme downloaded from the BBC website, and become players in a multiplayer computer game hosted on television. In these examples, television programmes are, in a limited way, forsaking their traditional linear and circular narrative forms in favour of the forking-path narrative form of computer games and hypertexts (*see* MULTI-PATH NARRATIVE).

Underlying such tentative innovations is the possibility of a future convergence of television and computer technologies. The process of experimentation in this direction, already underway, is situated as much in the translation or marriage of narrative forms across media as it is in the competing technologies of television and computer. It represents, perhaps, the opening movement of a 'TVIII' era in which reformulations of television industry, technologies, audience, usage, and content are again reflecting the medium's characteristic qualities of continuity and change.

SEE ALSO: interactive fiction

References and further reading

Collins, Jim (1992) 'Postmodernism and Television', in Robert C. Allen (ed.) *Channels of Discourse, Reassembled*, London: Routledge.
Eco, Umberto (1994) *The Limits of Interpretation*, Bloomington: Indiana University Press.
Ellis, John (1992) *Visible Fictions*, London: Routledge and Kegan Paul.
Fiske, John (1987) *Television Culture*, London: Methuen.
Feuer, Jane (1983) 'The Concept of Live Television: Ontology as Ideology', in E. Ann Kaplan (ed.) *Regarding Television: Critical Approaches – An Anthology*, Frederick, MD: University Publications of America.
—— (1986) 'Narrative Form in American Network Television', in Colin McCabe (ed.) *High Theory/Low Culture: Analyzing Popular Television and Film*, Manchester: Manchester University Press.
Fight Box, http://www.bbcfightbox.co.uk
Gregory, Chris (2000) *Star Trek: Parallel Narratives*, Basingstoke and London: Macmillan.
Jancovich, Mark, and James Lyons (eds) (2003) *Quality Popular Television: Cult TV, the Industry and Fans*, London: British Film Institute.
Kozloff, Sarah (1992) 'Narrative Theory and Television', in Robert C. Allen (ed.) *Channels of Discourse, Reassembled*, London: Routledge.
Lister, Martin, Jon Dovey, Seth Giddings, Iain Grant, and Keiran Kelly (eds) (2003) *New Media: A Critical Introduction*, London: Routledge.
Nelson, Robin (1997) *TV Drama in Transition: Forms, Values and Cultural Change*, Basingstoke: Macmillan.
Reeves, Jimmy L., Mark C. Rodgers, and Michael Epstein (1996) 'Rewriting Popularity: The Cult Files', in David Lavery, Angela Hague, and Marla Cartwright (eds) *Deny All Knowledge: Reading The X-Files*, London: Faber and Faber.
Williams, Raymond (1975) *Television: Technology and Cultural Form*, New York: Schocken Books.

SARA GWENLLIAN JONES

TELLABILITY

As William Labov observes, the worst reaction that a storyteller can elicit is a 'so what?' response from the *audience. Labov develops the concept of tellability to capture the features of the story that protect storytellers from this humiliation. Tellability is a quality that makes stories inherently worth telling, independently of their textualisation. It contrasts with *narrativity, a property found in all texts interpretable as stories, whether they elicit a 'so what' or a 'wow' reaction. But the two concepts are often hard to disentangle, and some scholars regard tellability as a condition of narrativity (Bruner 1991). The concept of tellability presupposes that stories exist in a virtual state in the mind of the storyteller, before they are actualised as texts in the storytelling (or writing) performance – a view that challenges the literary dogma of the inseparability of form and content. It is an intuitive sense of tellability that makes people say, 'I have a great story to tell you', even though the story only exists at this point as a mental construct. Labov observes that a poor performance can ruin a tellable story; conversely, a brilliant performance of mediocre narrative material can enthral the audience. Whereas popular literature invests heavily in the tellability of *plots, high literature often prefers to make art out of the not-tellable (*see* UNNARRATABLE), thereby following in the footsteps of Flaubert, who claimed that *Madame Bovary* was 'a novel about nothing'.

The study of what makes a narrative successful involves two components: the rhetorical, or performantial component (*see* RHETORICAL APPROACHES TO NARRATIVE; PERFORMANCE), which focuses on the discourse features through which *narrators display *storyworld in a way that invites audiences to respond emotionally, intellectually, or aesthetically (*see* EMOTION AND NARRATIVE); and the tellability component, which focuses on the discourse-independent features that predict such responses. Tellability involves a wide variety of principles: context-specific and context-free; culture-relative and universal; semantic and *pragmatic. Moreover, tellability can be concentrated in a single, precisely identifiable feature – the point of the text, such as the punch line or the piece of information wanted by the hearer – or it can be the effect of properties that operate throughout the narrative, structuring interest in the story as a sequence of peaks and valleys.

A typical case of context-specific tellability is a text that relies on the newsworthiness, that is, unusual character or expectation-defying nature of its information. As Mary Louise Pratt has shown, the normally trivial story 'Bill went to the bank today' becomes a fascinating piece of news if Bill is known to the speaker and hearer as an old miser who keeps his money in a sock. But extraordinary events work better in factual than in fictional narrative, because they are too easy to make up. Some stories have to be true to be tellable at all. The story of the hiker who amputated his arm to free himself from a rock jam in a Utah canyon is too sensationalist for 'serious' literary fiction, at least in its raw form, but it made headlines in the press as an authentic report of facts. On the other hand, it is far too restrained to make it as a *joke, a *tall tale, or a *thriller.

The dependency of tellability on cultural factors is illustrated by a French recipe for bestsellers that recommends the following ingredients: religion, sex, aristocracy, and mystery. According to this formula – which of course should be taken tongue in cheek –, the ultimate in tellability is achieved in the story: 'My God, said the Duchess, I am pregnant. Who done it?' In a list of themes of 'absolute interest', the *Artificial Intelligence researcher Roger Schank mentions, alongside themes that capture universal human preoccupations (death, danger, sex), narrative topics more typical of Western capitalist societies, such as power or large amounts of money.

Whether universal or culture-specific, a list of popular themes deals with the substance of content. But the form of content also plays a major role in tellability. By far the most important formal requirement on the level of *plot is the existence at some point of *conflict between the *desires, knowledge, or obligations of different *characters, or between those of one character and the state of affairs of the storyworld, though conflict is so fundamental to stories that it could be regarded as a condition of narrativity and not merely of tellability. Internal relations of parallelism and opposition and sudden turns in the fortunes of characters also provide efficient devices of plot construction. Tellability demands a certain degree of semantic complexity, and complexity derives in part from functional polyvalence. In *Oedipus Rex*, for instance, the marriage of Oedipus to Jocasta complicates the plot by functioning simultaneously as the satisfaction of a desire, as the fulfilment of a prediction, as the violation of an interdiction, and, through this violation, as ground for punishment.

Another form of semantic complexity that contributes to tellability is a narrative's ability to deploy a rich field of *virtualities. Ryan (1991) argues that some *events make better stories than others because they project a wider variety of forking paths on the narrative map. Even though the story can follow only one path, the understanding of these events involves a consideration of the 'virtual narratives' of the unrealised sequences that branch out of the event. All things being equal, a story in which a character conceives a plan to solve a problem and carries out this plan successfully with the help of other characters should be less interesting than a story that involves temporary failure, deceit, treason, violation, broken promises, erroneous beliefs, and goals achieved in unexpected ways, because these types of events generate a more complex field of unrealised possibilities: the character's plan versus the outcome in the case of failure; the character's beliefs versus the narrative facts in the case of error; the agent's intent versus the victim's reconstruction of this intent in the case of deceit; or the agent's construction of the intended victim's construction of his intent versus the intended victim's actual construction, in the case of unsuccessful deceit. This last example suggests however the limits of semantic complexity as factor of tellability: these limits are coextensive with the boundaries of the interpreter's processing ability.

SEE ALSO: Artificial Intelligence and narrative; cognitive narratology; discourse analysis (linguistics); possible-worlds theory

References and further reading

Bruner, Jerome (1991) 'The Narrative Construction of Reality', *Critical Inquiry*, 18, 1–21.
Labov, William (1972) *Language in the Inner City*, University Park: University of Pennsylvania Press.
Pratt, Mary Louise (1977) *Toward a Speech Act Theory of Literary Discourse*, Bloomington: Indiana University Press.
Prince, Gerald (1983) 'Narrative Pragmatics, Message, and Point', *Poetics*, 12, 527–36.
Ryan, Marie-Laure (1991) *Possible Worlds, Artificial Intelligence, and Narrative Theory*, Bloomington: Indiana University Press.
Schank, Roger (1978) 'Interestingness: Controlling Inferences', Research Report 145, Yale University Department of Computer Science.
Wilensky, Robert (1983) 'Story Grammars versus Story Points', *Behavioral and Brain Sciences*, 6, 579–623.

MARIE-LAURE RYAN

TEMPORAL ORDERING

Temporal ordering involves the relationship between *events in the story (fabula) of the represented world, and their arrangement in the discourse (sjuzhet) which articulates them (see STORY-DISCOURSE DISTINCTION; STORYWORLD). These valuable distinctions, Englished by Chatman, stem from Russian Formalist critics in the 1920s (see FORMALISM). When the reader reconstitutes the chronological sequence in which events supposedly occurred, differences often appear in the order of the discourse. These anachronies (Genette's term) or chronological deviations may be divided into three broad types: analepsis, prolepsis, and co-occurrence. Most generally, questions about ordering seek to establish the position in *time of particular events relative to others, and to assess the significance of that positioning as regards choices of *perspective, turning-points of *plot, narratorial priorities, aesthetic effects, and differences between expectation and realisation (see NARRATIVE TECHNIQUES; NARRATOR; SUSPENSE AND SURPRISE).

Analepsis, Genette's relatively neutral designation, is preferred to the more ambiguous 'flashback', with its cinematic and psychological associations (see FILM NARRATIVE). It signals the retrospective evocation of an event, and may be internal (within the main narrative), external (pre-narrative), mixed or overlapping (prior to but continuing into the main narrative). An initial place in an *exposition may not mean being first in order of occurrence: classical *epic employs a dramatic technique of *in medias res, before reverting to an account of antecedent events. Objective types of anachrony, such as a detached report of external events, may be separated from subjective types, such as a character's internalised record of events in stream of consciousness fiction (see STREAM OF CONSCIOUSNESS AND INTERIOR MONOLOGUE; THOUGHT AND CONSCIOUSNESS REPRESENTATION (LITERATURE)).

Analepsis can take two main forms: homodiegetic analepsis creates a jump in time along sequences of events involving the same character and within the same plotline; heterodiegetic analepsis jumps to a different plotline. Analepsis can also vary in the distance between two moments (portée), and in the extent of its duration (i.e., how long the *narration departs from what is perceived as the narrative now). Informational gaps or ellipses, as, for instance, in *detective fiction, may range from explicit to unmarked, and be filled in later by analepsis, with extended accounts or factual summaries (see GAPPING).

Less common than analepsis, its polar twin is prolepsis, or 'flashforward'. Allusions to future events may be within (internal), beyond the temporal bounds of the fiction (external), or quasi-proleptic (Prince's 'hypothetical narrative'), when a narrator or *character, as in the first (Victorian) ending to Fowles's *The French Lieutenant's Woman*, imagines possible futures, which the novel does not actualise. With autobiographical and first-person fiction, the narrator already knows the order of events, and prolepsis serves to indicate how one incident leads to another, or to underline future relevance (see AUTOBIOGRAPHY; PERSON). In some anachronies, temporal indications may be so vague and indeterminate as to verge on achrony (*see* INDETERMINACY). A related form, syllepsis, dispenses altogether with chronology in favour of thematic, spatial, or associational linkage (*see* SPATIAL FORM).

Whereas implicit types of prolepsis lack details of expected placement, explicit types give clear advance notice, as with chapter-end announcements of documents awaiting in a new chapter; also, with rare exceptions (e.g., Sterne's allusion in *Tristram Shandy* to a non-existent volume 20), explicit types are internal. In scale, prolepsis can range from anticipatory hints, or false clues (Genette's 'leurres'), to extended episodes, which may partially duplicate later events.

The third broad type of anachrony, co-occurrence, subdivides into parallel and simultaneous phases. Typesetting conventions and consecutive page layout mean that a parallel phase is placed after a given sequence, though on the level of events the reader is meant to assume that the phase occurs parallel with it (*see* GRAPHIC PRESENTATION AS EXPRESSIVE DEVICE). Thus, the action reverts from the point in time reached at the end of a previous sequence, with the narrator providing background, suggesting unsuspected analogies and contrasts among characters already introduced, rather than advancing events. A simultaneous phase occurs where the start of a sequence coincides with the end of a previous sequence, but it features different characters or plotline. Often, by switch of focus, the phase increases suspense by fastening upon another, sometimes less vital line of action, while implying that the central narrative line continues, though unremarked upon, 'offstage'.

Whereas fabula/sjuzhet have restricted application, the terms *linear/nonlinear* span both narrative and extra-narrative experience. Historically, epic and *picaresque, *Bildungsroman and serial publication may be contrasted with non-linear types such as Arthurian *romance cycles and *framed narratives, the 'time-shift' novel of Conrad, and hypertext fiction (*see* DIGITAL NARRATIVE; SERIAL FORM). Proponents of linear form, or prochronologists, whose most prominent representative is Sternberg, argue that theory has been geared to disorder, that critics have ignored the virtues of plot coherence, intelligibility, and memorability, and devalued omniscient narration and historytelling. Linear narrative, it is claimed, may potentially be more subtle than the open ruptures of anachrony.

Anachronophiles, by contrast, refute 'natural' parallels between life and art, citing the free association and fusion of time-planes in the human *memory, foregrounding significant personal values rather than objective causal links, and emphasising the psychological or aesthetic qualities of non-linearity. For Russian Formalists, non-linear narrative illustrates *defamiliarisation, by refreshing the reader's powers of perception. While Trollope and Fontane exemplify linear ordering, *modernists such as Woolf and Faulkner thematically exploit chronological deviations. Within the linear category, chronology dominates in *chronicles, *annals, and *diaries, *causality in descriptive tales and portraits (*see* DESCRIPTION), and logic in *sermons and literary essays. Within the non-linear category, 'dis-orderly' arrangements may be termed *order transforms*. Ireland (2001) identifies some fifteen different types.

SEE ALSO: narrative structure; tense and narrative

References and further reading

Bal, Mieke (1985) *Narratology: Introduction to the Theory of Narrative*, Toronto: University of Toronto Press.

Chatman, Seymour (1978) *Story and Discourse: Narrative Structure in Fiction and Film*, Ithaca: Cornell University Press.

Fludernik, Monika (1993) *The Fictions of Language and the Languages of Fiction*, London: Routledge.

Genette, Gérard (1980) *Narrative Discourse: An Essay in Method*, trans. Jane E. Lewin, Ithaca: Cornell University Press.

Ireland, Ken (2001) *The Sequential Dynamics of Narrative: Energies at the Margins of Fiction*, Cranbury, NJ: Associated University Presses.

Prince, Gerald (1982) *Narratology: The Form and Functioning of Narrative*, Berlin: Mouton.

Rimmon-Kenan, Shlomith (1983) *Narrative Fiction: Contemporary Poetics*, London: Methuen.

Sternberg, Meir (1990) 'Telling in Time (I)', *Poetics Today*, 11, 901–48.

Toolan, Michael J. (1988) *Narrative: A Critical Linguistic Introduction*, London: Routledge.

KEN IRELAND

TENSE AND NARRATIVE

If narrative recounts past *events, tense, it is assumed, grammaticalises events' temporal relations by marking verbs referring to them as 'past', 'present', or 'future', understood by reference to the deictic *now* of the *speech act. Tense is accordingly standardly treated as deictic (e.g., see Reichenbach, 1947; *see* DEIXIS). But *narrativity also involves establishing sequential order via the logical relations 'earlier than' and 'later than' of the philosopher McTaggart's (1988 [1927]) B series, different from past, present, and future, McTaggart's A series (*see* TEMPORAL ORDERING). Comrie's (1986) objection that, beyond past time *reference, 'chronological sequencing' is not exclusively part of past tense meaning can be accommodated by adopting Russell's (1914) formulation of B series 'time-relations among events' to include 'simultaneous with' and not just 'earlier or later than'. The preterite thus establishes *either* chronological order or simultaneity – compare 'I opened the door and stepped out' with 'I sat and ate'; context and a verb's lexical meaning govern the interpretative choice between sequentiality and simultaneity.

Russell (1988) observes that past, present, and future 'correlate' with earlier and later than because both series show the same ordering, but complains that Indo-European languages offer no way to express solely B-series relations, i.e., pure *diegesis, because verbs have tenses. Russell's conception of *time is called *tenseless* in recent philosophical discussions of time. But Indo-European's deficiency disappears if the B series is characterised as *non-deictic* rather than *tenseless* and the possibility of non-deictic tenses entertained, e.g., the French preterite. The verb of Russell's B-series proposition 'It rained at time *t*', which translates the A series 'It was raining yesterday', should be in the preterite.

The possibility of non-deictic tenses is implicitly found in Benveniste (1971 [1966]), Hamburger (1973 [1957]), and Weinrich (1964) and explicitly in Banfield (1982, 2000). Two distinct temporal systems are posited, one deictic and centred on the speech act and the other non-deictic and narrative. Benveniste's (1971 [1966]) well-known distinction between *discours* (discourse or communication) and *histoire* (history or narration) takes the French preterite or historical past (*passé simple*), almost exclusively written in modern French, as the defining tense of *narration, which excludes the present and future, while discourse excludes the preterite. Hamburger (1973 [1957]) similarly distinguishes *Aussage* (discourse/statement) and *fiktionales Erzählen* (fictional narration). (Benveniste's examples include *fiction and non-fiction.) Weinrich (1964) likewise differentiates two tense systems, one conversational, i.e., discourse, and the other narrative. Only in discourse are tenses like present and past cotemporal with deictics like *now* and *yesterday*, respectively; narration 'translates' them into non-deictic temporal adverbs, e.g., *later* and *the previous day*. Benveniste observes that the French preterite is incompatible with temporal deictics. Banfield (2000) similarly treats the narrative present as non-deictic. Evidence that it is distinct from the present of discourse is its invariable inflection with -*s* in some dialects: 'So this guy/these guys hangs one on me/them, and I/they goes out like a light.'

Hamburger first described a narrative phenomenon, also *exclusively written*, where a past tense is cotemporal with present and future deictics, e.g., 'tomorrow was Monday', calling it the 'epic preterite'. Stanzel (1959) restricts it to *free indirect discourse (FID). This is a deictic preterite, but not, like the preterite of discourse, cotemporal with past deictics. Bronzwaer (1970) believes that Weinrich's assigning the preterite exclusively to narration ignores the epic preterite. But his claim fails to note that, while phenomena covered by tense and narrative are cross-linguistic, similarly named and historically related tenses do not necessarily have the same function across languages. German expresses the past tense cotemporal with *now* by the preterite. English does so either by past progressive (for non-statives such as 'it was raining now'; 'she was knowing it now' is ungrammatical) or by the preterite ('she knew it now'). But French uses the imperfect for this purpose, i.e., that anomalous imperfect Bally (1912) takes as signalling FID in French (*elle le savait maintenant*) and whose peculiarity consists in its cotemporality with a present deictic. It thus contrasts sharply with the French preterite, which is incompatible with FID. So Barthes (1967 [1953]) identifies the preterite and 'the third-person of the novel', by which he means FID, as two separate 'narrative signs' of novelistic writing. The French imperfect has other functions – e.g., the habitual, which quantifies events, i.e., indicates an unspecified number of repetitions. The English preterite occurs both as a discourse tense, with past deictics, and as a narrative tense, without deictics, in addition to its 'epic preterite' function, with present deictics. Hence, it is the presence or absence of deictics and their temporal status which indicates the English preterite's function, whereas tense alone marks the French preterite as exclusively narrative.

SEE ALSO: no-narrator theory

References and further reading

Bally, Charles (1912) 'Le style indirect libre en francais moderne', *Germanisch-Romanische Monatsschrift*, 4, 549–56, 597–606.

Banfield, Ann (1982) *Unspeakable Sentences: Narration and Representation in the Language of Fiction*, London: Routledge & Kegan Paul.

—— (2000) 'Tragic Time: The Problem of the Future in Cambridge Philosophy and *To the Lighthouse*', *Modernism/Modernity*, 7.1, 43–75.

Barthes, Roland (1967 [1953]) *Writing Degree Zero*, trans. Annette Lavers and Colin Smith, New York: Hill and Wang.

Benveniste, Emile (1966) *Problèmes de linguistique générale*, Paris: Gallimard.

—— (1971 [1966]) *Problems in General Linguistics*, trans. Mary Elizabeth Meek, Coral Gables, FL: University of Miami Press.

Bronzwaer, W. J. M. (1970) *Tense in the Novel: An Investigation of Some Potentialities of Linguistic Criticism*, Groningen: Wolters-Noordhoff.

Comrie, Bernard (1986) 'Tense and Time Reference: From Meaning to Interpretation in the Chronological Structure of a Text', *Journal of Literary Semantics*, 15.1, 12–22.

Hamburger, Käte (1973 [1957]) *Die Logik der Dichtung*, Stuttgart: Klett Cotta.

—— (1993 [1957]) *The Logic of Literature*, trans. Marilyn Rose, Bloomington: Indiana University Press.

McTaggart, John McTaggert Ellis (1988 [1927]) *The Nature of Existence*, vol. 2, Cambridge: Cambridge University Press.

Reichenbach, Hans (1947) *Elements of Symbolic Logic*, London: Collier-Macmillan.

Russell, Bertrand (1914) *Our Knowledge of the External World*, London: George Allen & Unwin.

—— (1988) *Language, Mind and Matter, 1919–26*, *The Collected Papers of Bertrand Russell*, vol. 9, ed. Richard A. Rempel *et al.*, London: George Allen & Unwin.

Stanzel, Franz (1959) 'Episches Praeteritum, Erlebte Rede, Historisches Praesens', *Deutsche Vierteljahrsschrift für Literaturwissenschaft und Geistesgeschichte*, 33, 1–12.

Weinrich, Harald (1964) *Tempus: Besprochene und erzählte Welt*, Stuttgart: Verlag W. Kohlhammer GmbH.

ANN BANFIELD

TESTIMONIO

The term 'testimonio' refers to a non-fiction narrative depicting the living conditions and political struggles of subaltern groups that emerged in the second half of the twentieth century in Latin America in the context of the new social movements that demanded civil rights for minorities, ethnic groups, women, gays and others (*see* FICTION, THEORIES OF). A *testimonio* is often an oral narrative of illiterate people solicited and edited by mainstream intellectuals (*see* ORALITY). Two well-known texts are *I, Rigoberta Menchú* and *Here's to You, Jesusa!*. *Testimonio* has affinities with confessions, ethnography, *autobiography, *oral history, *journalism, and human rights reports (*see* CONFESSIONAL NARRATIVE; ETHNOGRAPHIC APPROACHES TO NARRATIVE; SLAVE NARRATIVE).

Early *testimonio* literature, including Menchú's text, claimed to offer a voice to the voiceless. This, however, was achieved only by suppressing its own rhetorical strategies and the historical contexts that circumscribed its production and reception. The informant was often presented as someone who could speak on behalf of a whole collectivity. The mediating role of the interviewer and the editing process were not examined critically. Finally, not enough attention was given to reading as a historically determined practice. Nonetheless, from the subaltern perspective, *testimonio* has been a tool for empowerment.

References and further reading

Arias, Arturo (ed.) (2001) *The Rigoberta Menchú Controversy*, Minneapolis: University of Minnesota Press.

Guggelberger, George (ed.) (1996) *The Real Thing*, Durham: Duke University Press.

Menchú, Rigoberta (1984) *I Rigoberta Menchú*, London: Verso.

Poniatowska, Elena (2001) *Here's to You, Jesusa!*, New York: Farrar, Straus and Giroux.

LUIS FERNANDO RESTREPO

TEXT-TYPE APPROACH TO NARRATIVE

Text-type approaches to narrative have been developed both within literary studies and within linguistics, albeit with different concerns. The notion of text-type has been proposed as a principle of abstraction and classification, an analytical category that aims at capturing structural, functional, and other conventionalised patterns of usage in narrative. In this sense, it sheds light on commonalities and differences amongst the wide range of texts that *narrative can subsume; it can also be an effective means for setting outer boundaries between narrative and other (non-narrative) types of text. How far the boundaries of narrative can be extended has been a contentious point in the literature, particularly with regard to certain *genres, such as historical writing, *drama, poetry, and paintings (*see* NARRATIVE IN POETRY; PICTORIAL NARRATIVITY). Agreement has also not been reached on which text-types narrative can be set apart from, nor on the exact criteria of classification. Nonetheless, studies seem to converge on the fundamental status of narrative in distinctions drawn between types of text. The boundaries of narrative have mostly been determined in terms of text-internal criteria (i.e., form and content) and at the expense of text-external (i.e., functional, socio-cultural) criteria. This has resulted in classifications that do not account for the historical and situated flux of narrative genres as social practices (*see* DISCOURSE ANALYSIS (FOUCAULT); SOCIOLINGUISTIC APPROACHES TO NARRATIVE).

Within the text-type approach, because different levels of analysis need to be kept apart and analytic categories applied recursively, there has been a proliferation of terminology. From the level of entire classes of texts (text-types) one moves to the intermediate level of genres (sometimes used interchangeably with 'discourse types') and to lower levels of parts of specific texts (e.g., segments of *description or *exposition in a narrative text, which have been a particular concern within literary studies). The latter are frequently described as *'modes' of discourse, a term that can also refer to rhetorical stances and metafunctions or metagenres (*see* RHETORICAL APPROACHES TO NARRATIVE).

To tease narrative apart from other text-types requires definitional criteria. The least controversial of these is the principle of the *temporal ordering of *events. Chatman (1990: 9) put this more specifically as the criterion of double chronology: for a text to qualify as narrative, it has to entail movement through time not only externally (i.e., through its telling, cf. discourse time) but also internally (through the duration of the sequence of events that constitute its *plot, cf. story time) (*see* STORY-DISCOURSE DISTINCTION; TIME IN NARRATIVE). To this, a principle of orientation toward human or human-like agents can be added; this principle is another way of capturing Fludernik's (1996) suggestion that narrative is

centrally – indeed, definitionally – concerned with *experientiality. This makes some stories more prototypically narrative than others. At the same time, text-type approaches have on occasion bridged (rather than emphasised) the gulf between genres that had been thought of as unconnected or as not belonging to narrative proper (see, e.g., Chatman's 1990 study of fictional as well as *film narrative and Fludernik's 1996 integrative approach linking natural and literary narrative; *see* NATURAL NARRATOLOGY).

Despite the recognition that narrative encompasses a huge variety of genres, it tends to be presented as a homogeneous category and relationships between narrative genres have not been systematically explored. The main preoccupation has been less with exploring intra-narrative connections and more with establishing which text-types narrative can be set apart from. These have in different studies included description, argument/argumentation, exposition (e.g., Chatman 1990; Longacre 1976; Werlich 1976), explanation, instruction (e.g., Werlich 1976), and non-narratively organised conversation. Some scholars elaborating these distinctions have avoided indicating the relative importance or pervasiveness of each text-type. However, other scholars working in a variety of fields (e.g., *education, film and *media studies, art history, biblical studies, and *psychology) have not only drawn a distinction between narrative and non-narrative, but also advocated the fundamental status of narrative (*see* BIBLICAL NARRATIVE). The primacy of narrative has also been postulated in text-linguistic research where narrative constitutes a pre-or metagenre that cannot be put on the same level as 'ordinary' genres (Swales 1990); it has also been argued to have a 'basic' status amongst the different text-types, as it has the 'potential to realise the widest array of discourse types' (Virtanen 1992: 306). For example, we can tell a story to put forth an argument, but the metafunction of narrating cannot be performed by argumentative texts (*see* NARRATIVE AS ARGUMENT).

Attempts to separate narrative from other 'modes' of discourse (in the sense of metafunction or metagenre) have as a rule been based on an ontogenetic and historical preference for narrative, rather than textual criteria *per se* (see e.g., Bruner's 1986 distinction between narrative and logico-semantic or analytical modes). In such approaches, narrative is seen as a universal and archetypal category (*see* NARRATIVE UNIVERSALS; ARCHETYPAL

PATTERNS), central to the constitution of human experience. Moving from such an all-encompassing or essentialist view of narrative to specific analyses of textual or functional features is not straightforward; similarly, narrative is presented as a deceptively homogeneous category and its internal variation gets obscured.

Genre approaches within linguistics and literary studies have recently been informed by new conceptions of genre which acknowledge its dynamic nature and socio-cultural embeddedness and resist setting up frameworks that attempt to delimit different types of text solely on the basis of abstract textual criteria. Text-type research could productively draw on such advances. One possibility would be to explore narrative as a dynamic conglomeration of more or less prototypical textual, functional, and contextual parameters. Another legitimate extension of text-type research would involve the study of narrative as a metagenre on the basis of a dynamically and interpretatively defined property of *narrativity (cf. Fludernik 1996; Ryan 1991). This could serve as a point of entry into a consideration of the sorts of resources that participants attend to or deliberately ignore in the making of discourse (Georgakopoulou and Goutsos 2000: 70). In this respect, conventional associations between narrative and non-narrative modes in particular communities and cases of hybridisation and intermingling of modes would be particularly interesting to explore.

SEE ALSO: discourse analysis (linguistics); hybrid genres; linguistic approaches to narrative

References and further reading

Bruner, Jerome (1986) *Actual Minds, Possible Worlds*, Cambridge, Mass.: Harvard University Press.
Chatman, Seymour (1990) *Coming to Terms: The Rhetoric of Narrative in Fiction and Film*, Ithaca: Cornell University Press.
Fludernik, Monika (1996) *Towards a 'Natural' Narratology*, London: Routledge.
Georgakopoulou, Alexandra, and Dionysis Goutsos (2000) 'Revisiting Discourse Boundaries: The Narrative and Non-narrative Modes', *TEXT*, 20, 63–82.
Longacre, Robert E. (1976) *An Anatomy of Speech Notions*, Lisse: Peter de Ridder.
Ryan, Marie-Laure (1991) *Possible Worlds, Artificial Intelligence and Narrative Theory*, Bloomington: Indiana University Press.
Swales, John (1990) *Genre Analysis*, Cambridge: Cambridge University Press.
Virtanen, Tuija (1992) 'Issues of Text-Typology: Narrative – a "Basic" Type of Text?', *Text*, 12, 293–310.
Werlich, Egon (1976) *A Text Grammar of English*, Heidelberg: Quelle and Meyer.

ALEXANDRA GEORGAKOPOULOU

TEXT-WORLD APPROACH TO NARRATIVE

Text-world approaches to narrative are based on the notion that human beings process and understand fictional discourse by constructing detailed mental representations of it in their minds (*see* SITUATION MODEL). Such approaches draw their main theoretical and methodological influences from a range of cognitive-scientific disciplines, including cognitive psychology and cognitive linguistics (*see* COGNITIVE NARRATOLOGY; PSYCHOLOGICAL APPROACHES TO NARRATIVE). Although the basic concept of text-worlds also overlaps with that of *possible-worlds theory, the central aim of text-world approaches to narrative is to provide an accurate account of how human beings experience narrative worlds in all their cognitive and psychological complexity.

Chief amongst text-world frameworks is Text World Theory, originally devised by Paul Werth (1994, 1995a, 1995b, 1999). Werth divides both fictional and non-fictional discourse into three main conceptual levels. The first of these, the 'discourse world', corresponds with the actual world and is inhabited by participants engaged in a language event. The discourse world also contains all the objects and elements immediately manifest to the participants and, crucially, all the personal knowledge and experience they bring with them to the discourse. All of these elements have the potential to affect the way a discourse is produced and understood. Which of them will be needed by the participants in order to understand the discourse at hand will be determined by the text itself. In Text World Theory terms, this is known as the 'principle of text-drivenness'.

As the participants in the discourse world communicate, they construct mental representations or 'text worlds' in their minds. These worlds are as richly detailed as the real world from which they spring. Text worlds are made up of 'world-building elements', which define the spatial and temporal boundaries of the world, and 'function-advancing propositions', which, in narrative texts, can be seen to propel the story forwards (*see* PLOT;

SPACE IN NARRATIVE; TIME IN NARRATIVE). Any variation of the basic parameters of the *text* world will result in the construction of a new world. In Werth's framework, these worlds are known as 'sub-worlds'. Sub-worlds may be created for a number of reasons and can be seen to exist at a level which is in some way conceptually removed from the discourse participants (*see* DEIXIS). Narrative features which trigger sub-worlds include *speech representation, *thought and consciousness representation, flashes forwards and backwards in *time, instances of *modality, and the use of conditional constructions and hypotheticality.

SEE ALSO: mental mapping of narrative; storyworld

References and further reading

Gavins, Joanna (2003) 'Too Much Blague? An Exploration of the Text Worlds of Donald Barthelme's *Snow White*', in Joanna Gavins and Gerard Steen (eds) *Cognitive Poetics in Practice*, London: Routledge.
Hidalgo Downing, Laura (2000) *Negation, Text Worlds and Discourse: The Pragmatics of Fiction*, Stanford: Ablex.
Werth, Paul (1994) 'Extended Metaphor: A Text World Account', *Language and Literature*, 3.2, 79–103.
—— (1995a) 'How to Build a World (in a Lot Less than Six Days and Using Only What's in Your Head)', in Keith Green (ed.) *New Essays on Deixis: Discourse, Narrative, Literature*, Amsterdam: Rodopi.
—— (1995b) ' "World Enough and Time": Deictic Space and the Interpretation of Prose', in Peter Verdonk and Jean Jacques Weber (eds) *Twentieth Century Fiction: From Text to Context*, London: Routledge.
—— (1999) *Text Worlds: Representing Conceptual Space in Discourse*, London: Longman.

JOANNA GAVINS

THEMATIC APPROACHES TO NARRATIVE

Thematic approaches share the notion that theme expresses what a narrative is about, but differ in their conception of its status and functions. Many see theme as having a triple linkage: with itself, with literature, and with the world. It thus has a referential function in providing an interpretation of human experience and of the world (*see* REFERENCE). Two broad types of approach may be distinguished. Syntagmatic study focuses on a single text or a group of closely related texts to which a structure of meaning is assigned (intrinsic interpretation). Paradigmatic study focuses on recurring content in various, ostensibly unconnected works.

Stoffgeschichte (thematology) represents paradigmatic study. It traces the tracks of a *Stoff* and its transformations in the contexts of the history of ideas and of transnational literatures. It works with three related concepts: *Stoff* (subject matter), *motif, and theme. *Stoff* refers to a stereotyped *plot schema (*see* PLOT TYPES; SCRIPTS AND SCHEMATA), while motif designates a smaller substance unit, a building block (*see* NARRATIVE UNITS). As an element of '*Gehalt*' (ideational content), theme expresses various ideas and concepts that a *Stoff* with its specific motif configuration can be taken to illustrate (Frenzel). The organisation of the motifs of a *Stoff* may, for example, be situation-bound (father-son *conflict) or character-bound (Prometheus; *see* CHARACTER). Thanks to its ready-made nature, a *Stoff* functions as a fruitful locus of comparison by bringing out the particular character of a work in the context of a *Stoff*'s history. Comparison demonstrates the role *Stoffe* play in artistic creation by showing how *authors balance originality against tradition, which itself is linked to the history of ideas.

Narrative thematics is a *plot-oriented approach with roots in *formalism and structuralism. Formalist analysis reduced narratives to their smallest, indispensable thematic elements, motifs, in order to analyse *narrative structure. Tomashevskii distinguished bound motifs, which are logically essential to narrative action and its causal-chronological coherence, from free motifs, which remain logically inessential to it. Also, motifs can either be static, designating a state, or dynamic, designating an *event. Propp defined specific acts (motifs) in terms of their significance for the course of the action in which they appear (*see* FUNCTION (PROPP)). Structuralism added to this analysis a system of semantic parameters that specifies the intentional status of an *action (voluntary or involuntary) and its phase of actualisation (projected, in process, or completed; *see* STRUCTURALIST NARRATOLOGY). Narrative thematics systematises these findings.

According to Ryan, in assigning a motif to a narrative theme we determine the motif's precise narrative meaning in a plot. Narrative themes may be organised hierarchically, moving from single ones to thematic sequences and, ultimately, to plot schemata. Moreover, they have at least three functions. At the elementary level, narrative themes enable readers to link motifs (such as *events and incidents) to more general and abstract categories of meaning. As narrative themes describe primarily the interaction of agents, they indicate what kinds of actions, intentions, and results the particular motifs instantiate (for example, 'deception', 'vengeance', and 'violated interdiction'). The individual motifs link with one another, forming sequences of various lengths, made up of specific sets of actions by agents. Thinking of plot as a series of action sequences brings out the second function of narrative themes. They help readers sketch the plot's semantic skeleton by indicating its strategic points, which describe those events, actions, intentions, and results of action that keep it moving and that are indispensable for understanding the totality it forms. Hence, narrative themes show how the separate motifs form thematic and often stereotyped sequences composed of various motif configurations. The third function of narrative themes lies in their synthesising capacity: they may be used as shorthand expressions for the abstract plot schemata subtending narratives. Such thematic conceptualisations of whole narrative patterns may take the form of an adage (killing two birds with one stone), a typical situation (a man torn between two women), or a character's name (Oedipus). The assignment of narrative themes is thought to be less subject to variation than the assignment of other types of themes, for it mainly involves comprehension of the relationships between plot elements.

The New Critics, proponents of syntagmatic study, argued that theme unifies and resolves a text's paradoxes, ironies, and ambiguities (see IRONY). Theme is defined as an abstract idea or concept that is extractable from a text and relatable to coded human experiences of other texts and of reality. Thus it functions as a mediator between *fiction and reality. This relationship is analogical: themes are fictive instances of a class of certain situations, characters, and behaviours that resemble their real counterparts in a consubstantial way (Chatman 1983). Theme expresses virtual reference that is actualised only when we have in mind a specific cognitive teleology of either the work or of our reading of it (Brinker 1993). Themes confront readers with philosophical, moral, theological, and other such questions that call for contemplation without supplying definite answers. Thus theme, unlike thesis, makes no claims and cannot be called true or false (see TRUTH).

Hermeneutic thematics, finally, stresses how themes help readers organise texts according to conceptual frames (*see* FRAME THEORY), creating unity and coherence. Theme is a semantic and hermeneutic 'device' for selecting, specifying, and organising the meanings a text puts into play. As theme insists on the meanings it demarcates, it demonstrates how meaning results from thematic interpretation. Further, not only does theme choose and particularise meanings but it also abstracts, generalises, and expands them by connecting a text to other fictional and factual texts exhibiting the same theme. It thus has a double status. Because motifs instantiate a theme, the theme can be said to be in, or immanent to, a text. But because theme links motifs to general and abstract frameworks, it is also outside the text. Theme is simultaneously intra- and extra-textual. Hermeneutic thematics emphasises, however, that a theme need not unify the whole text; it suffices if it unifies a significant subset of its components.

SEE ALSO: hermeneutics; thematisation

References and further reading

Beardsley, Monroe C. (1958) *Aesthetics: Problems in the Philosophy of Criticism*, Indianapolis: Hackett.

Bremond, Claude (1993) 'Concept and Theme', in Werner Sollors (ed.) *The Return of Thematic Criticism*, Cambridge, Mass.: Harvard University Press.

——, Joshua Landy and Thomas Pavel (eds) (1995) *Thematics: New Approaches*, New York: State University of New York Press.

Brinker, Menachem (1993) 'Theme and Interpretation', in Werner Sollors (ed.) *The Return of Thematic Criticism*, Cambridge, Mass.: Harvard University Press.

Chatman, Seymour (1983) 'On the Notion of Theme in Narrative', in John Fisher (ed.) *Essays on Aesthetics: Perspectives on the Work of Monroe C. Beardsley*, Philadelphia: Temple University Press.

Frenzel, Elizabeth (1966) *Stoff- und Motivgeschichte*, Berlin: Erich Schmidt.

Propp, Vladimir (1968 [1928]) *Morphology of the Folktale*, trans. Laurence Scott, revised by Louis A. Wagner, Austin: University of Texas Press.

Ryan, Marie-Laure (1993) 'In Search of the Narrative Theme', in Werner Sollors (ed.) *The Return of Thematic Criticism*, Cambridge, Mass.: Harvard University Press.

Tomashevskii, Boris (1965) 'Thematics', in Lee T. Lemon and Marion J. Reis (eds and trans.) *Russian Formalist Criticism: Four Essays*, Lincoln: University of Nebraska Press.

HETA PYRHÖNEN

THEMATISATION

Thematisation refers to either writing or interpreting texts in the light of given themes. As a compositional, author-centred activity, it alludes to artistic creation as an artist's conscious effort of balancing originality against acknowledged tradition (*see* AUTHOR). In *reader-response criticism, it brings together textual clues (such as *motifs, topoi, stereotyped narrative sequences), the reader's thematising attention, and the thematic operations guiding this attention. These operations include the reader's positing a theme in a text; suppressing a postulated theme if the text does not sufficiently support its elaboration; composing a number of already identified themes into a complex theme, or decomposing a complex theme into simpler ones. Generalisation substitutes a more abstract label for a number of concrete themes, while specification narrows a general thematic designation to address a specific one.

Text-oriented thematisation holds that texts supply clues about the themes readers should pay attention to. Consequently, some themes are weightier than others in a text's totality. However, explicit themes may be less important than implicit ones. A theme is taken to unify a large or conspicuous or important portion of textual components, relative to a specific descriptive interpretation of its language and world. In *reader-oriented thematisation* it suffices for a reader to see a theme in a text for the theme to be there. Because any theme is or can become important, the idea of a thematic hierarchy in a text is rejected. Thus thematisation may serve as a tool of textual and cultural symptomatology, for marginal themes are taken to reveal the text's *ideology.

SEE ALSO: thematic approaches to narrative

References and further reading

Bremond, Claude (1988) 'En lisant un fable', *Communications*, 47, 41–62.
———, and Thomas Pavel (1995) 'The End of an Anathema', in Claude Bremond, Joshua Landy, and Thomas Pavel (eds) *Thematics: New Approaches*, New York: State University of New York Press.
Pavel, Thomas (1993) 'Thematics and Historical Evidence', in Werner Sollors (ed.) *The Return of Thematic Criticism*, Cambridge, Mass.: Harvard University Press.

HETA PYRHÖNEN

THEOLOGY AND NARRATIVE

In the mid-twentieth century, several lines of inquiry that sought to link theology and narrative took shape under the name of 'narrative theology'. This movement is found on both sides of the Atlantic, but the motivations are different: the narrative theology developed by Anglo-American writers was a result of their new awareness of the theological importance of storytelling; the narrative theology that emerged in the German-speaking countries, on the other hand, originated in criticism of a theology that had become mired in abstract theorising.

In 1941, the American theologian H. Richard Niebuhr pointed out that the majority of the fundamental Christian convictions are anchored in a narrative system – the books of the Bible (*see* BIBLICAL NARRATIVE). While many previous theological thinkers had noticed that most of what the Bible has to say is communicated in the form of a story, Niebuhr was the first to give serious thought to the significance of this fact for theology.

The term 'narrative theology' (German: '*Narrative Theologie*') as understood in the German-speaking countries was coined by the linguist Harald Weinrich (1973) and the theologian Johann Baptist Metz (1973). Their primary intent was to reassert the long-denied crucial theological importance of *narration. With this move they aimed to reground the hermeneutic methods of theology in the domain of human experience (*see* HERMENEUTICS): just as people use stories to encapsulate and make sense of events in their lives, scriptural traditions are themselves narrative-based sense-making strategies and need to be interpreted as such. Meanwhile, the rise of the concept of story among Anglo-American theologians led to the development of what is known as 'story theology', of which the Methodist theology of Stanley Hauerwas is a prime example (e.g., Hauerwas 1997).

The theological uses of the concept of narrative cover a number of very different phenomena. For a start, the word *narrative* can refer to the basic *narrative structure found in the Bible. Narrative is the literary form of the vast majority of biblical texts. In order to do justice to this fact, it is important for theologians to develop a theory of Biblical *narrativity and to integrate issues of narrative theory (or narratology) into their theological research. Seen in this way, narrative theology might be described as having a twofold purpose. It must recognise and accept the narrative nature of its data and then subject that narrative quality to a detailed theoretical analysis. The result would be a theology that is both passively informed by narrative theory and able to employ it actively.

In a broader sense, *narrative* can also be understood as referring to the practical use of narration in Christianity (understood as a community bound together by narrative and *memory). Insofar as it takes the form of a practical paradigm for understanding life itself, the notion of *experientiality provides a comprehensive background against which theological statements can be interpreted. Narratives constitute a basic level from which convictions and theological positions are abstracted. One of the most prominent definitions of this kind of narrative theology can be found in the work of Michael Goldberg (1982: 35ff.). Goldberg believes that the central idea of narrative theology resides in locating the roots of all convictions in narrative, whether or not these convictions are religious. As a consequence, the most serious of disputes will frequently stem from competing narrative representations. In this line of thought, the first duty of the narrative theologian is to give due recognition to the linguistic structures that are involved in portraying the interlocking relations between persons and *events in stories (*see* CHARACTER). In these relations we find the source and foundation of religious convictions. The only way to properly illuminate, explain, and transform the deep-seated religious convictions that contribute to a community's sense of *identity is to give sufficient consideration to the narrative structure of the stories that form the cultural heritage of that community.

Finally, it is possible to use the term 'narrative' to refer to the function of narration within the critical study of theology. From the very beginning, narrative theology has had an important place in Judaism – the narration of the miraculous deeds performed by God to rescue his people not only represents a basic principle but also the very nucleus of the entire Judaic tradition. Jesus himself, and his disciples after him, passed on his theology by narrating, narrating again, and narrating adaptively. Insofar as the ultimate source of revelation is to be found above all in a narrative (as opposed to legislative) theology, some narrative theologians have drawn the conclusion that narration is not a mere method but in fact the primary

mode of theology itself, the proper form that theology should take. The efforts of this kind of narrative theology are directed at preventing the language of theology from being ossified into rational argumentation and reduced to mental abstractions, for dissecting and simplifying religious belief in this way inevitably means that much of our lived experience of faith is lost.

Because of these very different conceptions of the territory covered by the term 'narrative', it has not yet been possible for a consensus to form about the role that narrative should play in theology. The term 'narrative theology' should consequently be seen less as a name for a unified and coherent theory than as a collective label for a number of diverse theological concepts of narrative, most of which are scattered across short essays, isolated critical notes, and interim proposals that make no claim to definitiveness. Nonetheless, even the most vociferous critics of the term 'narrative theology' acknowledge that the motivation that underlies the movement is legitimate, and that it has given new life to the discipline.

SEE ALSO: interdisciplinary approaches to narrative; narrative turn in the humanities; sermon

References and further reading

Frei, Hans W. (1993) *Theology and Narrative: Selected Essays*, ed. George Hunsinger and William C. Placher, Oxford: Oxford University Press.

Goldberg, Michael (1982) *Theology and Narrative: A Critical Introduction*, Nashville: Abingdon.

Hauerwas, Stanley, and L. Gregory Jones (eds) (1997) *Why Narrative? Readings in Narrative Theology*, Eugene, Or.: Wipf and Stock.

Metz, Johann Baptist (1973) 'Kleine Apologie des Erzählens', *Concilium*, 9, 334–41.

Niebuhr, H. Richard (1941) *The Meaning of Revelation*, New York: Macmillan.

Ritschl, Dietrich, and Hugh O. Jones (1976) '*Story' als Rohmaterial der Theologie*, Munich: Kaiser.

Sandler, Willibald (2002) 'Christentum als große Erzählung: Anstöße für eine narrative Theologie', in Peter Tschnuggnall (ed.) *Religion – Literatur – Künste: Ein Dialog*, Anif and Salzburg: Müller-Speiser.

Stegner, William Richard (1989) *Narrative Theology in Early Jewish Christianity*, Louisville, Ky.: John Knox Press.

Stroup, George W. (1981) *The Promise of Narrative Theology: Recovering the Gospel in the Church*, Atlanta: John Knox Press.

Weinrich, Harald (1973) 'Narrative Theologie', *Concilium*, 9, 329–34.

ANJA CORNILS

THIRD-PERSON NARRATION

A story in which the *narrator does not take part as an acting *character, hence one in which all pronominal references to the characters are restricted to third-person forms (i.e., *he*, *she*, *it*, *they*). According to F. K. Stanzel, there are two major subtypes: 'authorial' narratives and 'figural' narratives. *See* NARRATIVE SITUATIONS; PERSON (also: NARRATION).

THOUGHT AND CONSCIOUSNESS REPRESENTATION (FILM)

The *image and sound recording devices of *film provide experiences that seem to be directly witnessed by the spectator rather than narrated. Unlike verbal narrative, film has no problem presenting speech that is unmediated by *narrators, and the medium makes no sharp distinctions between third-person *narration and *character experiences (*see* NARRATIVE SITUATIONS; PERSON; SPEECH REPRESENTATION). The mental states and goals of other people will often be inferred from non-verbal clues, like facial expressions, actions, and the world that surrounds them. That a character attends to something may for instance be indicated through a *shot of the character's eyes and glance direction, followed by a shot of the object that has caught his or her attention (shot glance followed by shot object). However, the character's focus of attention might just as well be inferred from more general clues.

People do not normally regard what they see (or hear) in real life or on a film screen as taking place in somebody's mind: they typically project these experiences onto the surfaces of the distal object world. We cannot be directly conscious of the way in which our eyes and brains are processing light and sound (the proximal processes); we take our mental representations as being an exterior reality rather than inner representations. If therefore a film wants to cue viewers into experiencing, 'feeling', something as 'inner' mental states, it somehow needs to block the normal projection of the experiences onto an exterior world so that the perceptions are felt as mental *events. This process demands a redefinition of the reality status of what is seen (*see* MODALITY). The redefinition of reality status can be brought about either perceptually by presenting deviant images and/or sounds; or

cognitively by blocking the transformation of perceptions into *actions, as in films about ghosts – whose behaviour cannot be influenced by normal actions. Thus, only those aspects of consciousness that have a deviant reality status are felt as 'inner' and 'mental'.

Experiencing a given phenomenon as real or unreal (mental) is, however, no reliable indication of its objective reality status. The feelings and *emotions that signal the degree of reality of images and scenes are developed in order to enable us to tell whether or not (and how) we may physically interact with the phenomena. Emotions express action readiness. Just as hate or love indicates action readiness for violent or caring behaviour, so different feelings signal the action or inaction type that a given situation affords. A still in a film is experienced as less 'real', more 'action-blocking', and thus more mental than moving images irrespective of whether it is realistic or not. A foggy landscape or a dark cityscape with blinking neon signs may be experienced as if it existed in a dream or in a subjective vision. Such *spaces are not necessarily less real than a sunlit landscape, but we feel that it is more difficult to act in them.

A number of film techniques for evoking subjective experiences rely on the innate mechanisms that have evolved to distinguish dreams, memories, or sensory distortions caused by such states as drunkenness or concussions from undistorted online experiences. Visual distortions may consist of altered proportions between figures and spaces (an effect which can be obtained by the use of wide-angle lenses), of surrealistic transformations of colours (*see* SURREALIST NARRATIVE), or of the sudden replacement of coloured images by black-and-white ones. *Time may be shown in slow-motion or frozen to a still. The dream sequence in Hitchcock's *Vertigo* alters the perception of depth by synchronising camera movement with change of focal length, so that the space expands (*see* DREAM NARRATIVE).

A precondition for experiencing a film sequence as a portrayal of an exterior reality is that it shows some living individuals who can see that world and who regard it as a goal for actions. In a vague sense the diegetic world represents these living beings' consciousness (*see* DIEGESIS; STORYWORLD). But if a world is visually described without any individuals who focus on it the viewer will tend to experience this world as a mental phenomenon. As a consequence documentaries that do not comment upon the images through *voice-over narration or descriptive sequences in fiction films will be experienced as lyrical and mental, even if they provide super-realist representations. Art films such as those made by Marguerite Duras create an atmosphere of inner life either by making visual *'descriptions' without any focalizing character or by bleaching out all processes in the world so it is difficult to distinguish still from eventless space (*see* FOCALIZATION). Films portraying sublime experiences may have focalizing characters, but the world that they perceive often has qualities or proportions that block the possibility of relating to this world through action, such as vistas of remote mountains, visions of the cosmos, or supernatural beings.

Words spoken in normal conversation belong experientially to intersubjective space. To provide words with a 'feel' of existing in inner mental space, film may for instance dissolve realistic modality synthesis (i.e., the synthesis of the information from different senses) or dissolve temporal unity by means of a voice-over that is not anchored visually in the film. It may come from a time-space other than the one being shown on the screen, or if it comes from the same time-space, it may be acoustically distorted with respect to volume, distance, or spatial ambience, or a character may speak without lip movement. All these devices impede the normal fusion of sound, vision, and movement. The realist-objective experience can also be transformed into a mental one by severely limiting the field of vision to that of a character's point of view (POV) (*see* POINT OF VIEW (CINEMATIC)).

Many scenes that are experienced as mental phenomena are based on associative networks that would be impossible in external worlds. In the mind, spatial or temporal distances do not exist, and elements are organised by similarity or contrast, rather than according to temporal or spatial contiguity. This applies to memories as well as to pure creations of the imagination. In a film, these associative networks may be represented through double exposures, through the superposition of multiple layers that represent different time-spaces, or through *montage sequences of objects linked by metaphorical relations (*see* METAPHOR). Narratives that have a strongly scrambled temporal order will likewise tend to be experienced as representations of mental processes (*see* TEMPORAL ORDERING).

SEE ALSO: scene (cinematic); soundtrack; thought and consciousness representation (literature)

References and further reading

Bordwell, David (1985) *Narration in the Fiction Film*, Madison: University of Wisconsin Press.

Branigan, Edward (1984) *Point of View in the Cinema: A Theory of Narration and Subjectivity in Classical Film*, Berlin: Mouton.

Grodal, Torben (1997) *Moving Pictures: A New Theory of Film Genres, Feelings, and Cognition*, Oxford: Oxford University Press.

—— (2000) 'Subjectivity, Realism and Narrative Structures in Film', in Ib Bondebjerg (ed.) *Moving Images, Culture and the Mind*, Luton: University of Luton Press.

TORBEN GRODAL

THOUGHT AND CONSCIOUSNESS REPRESENTATION (LITERATURE)

When the *narrators of *novels present direct to readers the contents of *characters' minds, they are doing what cannot be done in real life. We cannot look into the minds of other people in the actual world in the way that, as readers, we look into the minds of people in a fictional *storyworld. This highly artificial device of direct access is considered by Cohn and others to be a distinctive feature of fictional narrative: it is what distinguishes it, for example, from historical narrative (*see* FICTION, THEORIES OF; HISTORIOGRAPHY). It is also a very visible mark of the omniscient narrator of fiction. Classical narrative theory considers thought and consciousness representation in terms of what may be called the speech category approach. Characters' thoughts are analysed by using the same categories that are used to analyse characters' speech (*see* SPEECH REPRESENTATION). Many of the discussions of thought presentation in narrative theory are included in, or added onto, discussions of speech presentation, and Cohn's *Transparent Minds* (1978) was until recently the only full-length study solely devoted to thought presentation (see Palmer 2004). However, there are several concerns about the validity of the speech category approach. Many recent *postclassical and cognitivist accounts take a more holistic approach to the subject and show that there is a good deal more to the presentation of fictional minds than has yet been revealed within traditional narratology (*see* COGNITIVE NARRATOLOGY).

The speech category approach

There are several different models for the speech categories or modes which use a variety of names for their elements, but they are all, in essence, derived from this basic three term model.

1 Direct thought is the narrative convention that allows the narrator to present a verbal transcription that passes as the reproduction of the actual thoughts of a character. For example: 'She thought, "Where am I?" '
2 Thought report is the presentation of characters' thoughts in the narrator's discourse. It can range from the equivalent of indirect speech (for example: 'She wondered where she was') to highly condensed summary (for example: 'She thought of Paris').
3 Free indirect thought is most simply described as a combination of the other two categories. It combines the subjectivity and language of the character, as in direct thought, with the presentation of the narrator, as in thought report. For example: 'She stopped. Where the hell was she?' The second sentence is free indirect thought because it presents the subjectivity of the character (the narrator knows where the character is) and the language of the character ('Where the hell'), but in the third-person ('she') and past tense ('was') of the narrator's discourse.

McHale's (1978) widely adopted seven-point scale relates to the three-mode model in the following way:

Diegetic summary	> thought report
Less purely diegetic summary	>
Indirect content-paraphrase	>
Indirect discourse	>
Free indirect discourse	> free indirect thought
Direct discourse	> direct thought
Free direct discourse	>

Direct thought is considered to be the most mimetic and the least mediated category (*see* MIMESIS; MEDIACY). It can be used only for the part of the fictional mind known as inner speech, the highly verbalised flow of self-conscious thought. Thought report is the most diegetic and the most mediated category (*see* DIEGESIS). It is suitable for presenting all areas of the mind, including inner speech. The status of free indirect thought with regard to mimesis and mediacy is disputed. It is very suitable for inner speech, and some theorists think that it can also be used to represent some other areas of the mind such as long-held beliefs and attitudes. In practice, the three modes are usually found in combination with each other in an intricate and dense patchwork of effects. For example:

> She was most forcibly struck (*thought report*). The truth of his representation there was no denying (ambiguous between *thought report* and *free indirect thought*?). She felt it at her heart (*thought report*). How could she have been so brutal, so cruel to Miss Bates! – How could she have exposed herself to such ill opinion in anyone she valued! And how suffer him to leave her without saying one word of gratitude, of concurrence, of common kindness! (*free indirect thought*). Time did not compose her. As she reflected more, she seemed but to feel it more (*thought report*).
>
> (Jane Austen, *Emma*)

There is a consensus on the historical development of the speech categories. Fiction during the eighteenth-century and into the nineteenth-century gave shallow inside views mainly by way of thought report in the form of very short explanations of motivation. It also used occasional direct thought in the form of rhetorical, rational, logical, deliberate, and often vocal soliloquy (see, for example, Henry Fielding, Stendhal, and Honoré de Balzac). Free indirect thought became increasingly popular in the nineteenth-century as the novel began to focus more closely on the internal mental life of characters (Jane Austen, Gustave Flaubert, and Henry James). The twentieth century was characterised by varying combinations of the three modes. In the early part of the twentieth century, modernist writers such as James Joyce (in *Ulysses*) and Virginia Woolf developed the often illogical, associative, and spontaneous submode of free direct thought, in which quotation marks and tags (such as 'She thought') are not used (*see* MODERNIST NARRATIVE). Free indirect thought was very common (Joyce in *Portrait*, Franz Kafka), while thought report was the predominant mode of formal conservatives such as Evelyn Waugh. Although the speech category approach is generally used on third-person or *heterodiegetic narration, Cohn applies the approach very informatively to first-person or homodiegetic *narration (*see* NARRATIVE SITUATIONS; PERSON).

Direct thought

This mode is also known as quoted monologue and private speech (and free direct thought is also identified with *stream of consciousness and interior monologue). Narrators frequently draw attention to the artificiality of this device (for example, Walter Scott and Leo Tolstoi). It is significant that many novels do not reflect characters' idiosyncratic spoken speech patterns in direct thought for fear of sounding silly. This conservatism emphasises the artificial quality, not only of formal soliloquy, but also of standard direct thought and even of free direct thought.

Thought report

Thought report is the most flexible and the most versatile category. It is also known as psycho-narration, narratised speech, internal analysis, narratorial analysis, omniscient description, and submerged speech.

Cohn (1978) has made an influential distinction between what she calls dissonant and consonant thought report. In dissonant thought report, the prominent or overt narrator is emphatically distanced from the character's consciousness and language. Explorations of psychic depth present and evaluate the inner life that the character is occasionally unwilling or unable to see. The narrator often makes confident ethical judgments. Dissonant thought report is characteristic of the intrusive narrator of authorial narrative (for example, Balzac) (see NARRATIVE TECHNIQUES). In consonant thought report, which is characteristic of figural narrative (for example, Henry James and Joyce in *Portrait*), the effaced or covert narrator readily fuses with the narrated consciousness. The narrator tends not to make general statements, indulge in speculative or explanatory *commentary, employs analytical and conceptual terms, or use cognitive and ethical privilege. The language of the narrator is often coloured by the idiom of the character. Such 'coloured' thought report verges on free indirect thought and often lapses into it.

Thought report has a large number of functions, many of which are unique to this mode. It can be used to present:

- a variety of mental events including inner speech, perceptions, sensations, *emotions, visual images, memories, imaginings, attention, mood,

visions, and dreams (see DREAM NARRATIVE; EMOTION IN NARRATIVE);
- a character's thoughts as mental action (for example: 'She decided to walk');
- the mental causal network behind behaviour which includes motives, intentions, and reasons for *action (see CAUSALITY; INTENTIONALITY);
- what the character does not know about his or her mental functioning and sometimes does not wish to know (for example: 'Jane would not admit to herself that she looked rather dumpy'), a technique which is particularly significant in the context of motives and intentions;
- latent states of mind such as attitudes, judgments, evaluations, beliefs, skills, knowledge, character traits, tendencies of thought, intellect, *desires, and the Freudian unconscious (see PSYCHOANALYSIS AND NARRATIVE);
- constructions of character in which thought report regularly shades imperceptibly into characterisation and the creation of personality, allowing the reader to link the present thoughts of the character with earlier judgments and hypotheses regarding that character and to predict the future course of the narrative;
- summaries, as it is the most flexible mode in temporal terms, of inner developments over a long period of *time using a panoramic view or telescopic perspective (see SUMMARY AND SCENE);
- expansions or elaborations of mental instants of particular significance, a technique which is very popular in the modern novel (Marcel Proust onwards);
- combinations of *descriptions of thought processes with surface descriptions of the physical storyworld;
- intermental or group, joint, or shared thought;
- the expression of a consensus, a shared view within a particular social group; and
- interpretation, analysis, commentary, and judgment.

Most of these functions illustrate the ability of thought report to link the thought processes of individual characters to their environment, and thereby demonstrate in very concrete and specific ways the social and active nature of thought as mental functioning. It is in thought report that the narrator is able to show explicitly how characters' minds operate in a social and physical context.

Several of these functions have been given very little attention within traditional narrative theory.

Free indirect thought

*Free indirect discourse (that is, referring to both speech and thought) is also known as free indirect style, *le style indirect libre, erlebte Rede*, narrated monologue, represented speech and thought, dual voice, substitutionary speech, narrated speech and thought, immediate speech, and simple indirect thought. Significantly, the term 'free indirect speech' is regularly used to refer to thought as well as speech. The length of this list of terms shows the extent of the hold that this technique has exercised over narrative theory. In addition, there is a sub-category known as free indirect perception or narrated perception. In the sentence, 'He sat on the bench while the train pulled away', the second clause looks initially like a description by the narrator of the surface of the physical storyworld, but it can also be read as the character's perception of the physical event (*see* FOCALIZATION; POINT OF VIEW (LITERARY)). Free indirect thought and coloured thought report are both examples of Mikhail Bakhtin's notion of double-voiced discourse (*see* DIALOGISM; HETEROGLOSSIA; POLYPHONY).

Examples of free indirect thought often share ambiguous grey areas with:

- free indirect speech, when it is not clear whether a character's speech or thoughts are being presented;
- surface narration, as in free indirect perception; and
- thought report, as in consonant, coloured thought report (see example above).

Neumann (1986) has suggested that occurrences of free indirect discourse should be regarded as definite, almost definite, or indefinite, depending on the degree of ambiguity.

The precise nature of free indirect discourse has been the subject of a lengthy, technical, and fiercely contested narratological debate for a number of years. Some theorists, notably Banfield (1982), argue that free indirect discourse occurs if and only if a set of certain well-defined grammatical features is present. Others such as McHale (1983) dispute that precise linguistic criteria can be used in this way and suggest that it is a 'fuzzy' concept. In particular, it is heavily dependent on the interpretive decisions of readers which are often intuitively based on the context of the surrounding sentences. Discussions of the nature of free indirect thought sometimes tend to move away from fictional minds and into wider issues. For example, disagreements on the *dual-voice hypothesis (that sentences of free indirect discourse contain the voices of both the narrator and the character) are part of a wider controversy over the *no-narrator theory.

A number of virtues are claimed for free indirect thought, all of which are illustrated in the above example. Its use avoids a monotonous procession of tags. Its characteristic ambiguity can result in interesting and complex confusions over shifting points of view. The relationship between the two voices of narrator and character can cause the well-recognised effects of *irony and empathy. It often has a key role to play when the narrator wishes to create an apparently seamless interweaving of various types of thought presentation. Finally, it has an immediacy that is very suitable for use in situations of tension, crisis, upheaval, turmoil, spiritual searching, and inward struggle (*see* CONFLICT).

Narrative theorists hold free indirect thought in very high regard. It is sometimes described as distinctively, strictly and even exclusively literary, despite the fact that it is regularly found in non-literary contexts such as oral storytelling and minutes of meetings (*see* CONVERSATIONAL STORY-TELLING), and sub-literary contexts such as Mills and Boon romances. The concept has become so fashionable that, as Fludernik (1993) and Jahn (1992) have pointed out, the term is sometimes inappropriately used to describe perfectly straightforward examples of thought report.

Concerns with, and objections to, the speech category approach

Leech and Short (1981) warn that the discourse effects produced by the thought categories are different from those produced by the speech categories, because the norm for speech is direct speech, while the norm for thought is thought report. Cohn (1978) argues that, as the speech category approach carries too far the correspondence between speech and thought, it tends to leave non-verbal consciousness out of account. She stresses that, because thought report is not primarily a method for presenting mental language, it is the most neglected of the basic techniques. In Fludernik's view (1993), both the traditional three-mode model and the seven-point scale are hopelessly inadequate to the empirical evidence. They are unable to deal with the functional differences between the representation of speech and of consciousness because, as Leech and Short say, the discourse effects of speech and thought representations are entirely incompatible. Fludernik (1993) also refers to one of the assumptions behind the approach as the direct discourse fallacy: the mistaken belief that direct discourse is a primary source from which indirect quotation can be derived. Palmer (2002) draws attention to the following problems with the speech category account: the privileging of direct thought and free indirect thought over thought report; the overestimation of the verbal component in thought; the neglect of narrators' thought report of events such as emotions and states of mind such as beliefs, intentions, purposes, and dispositions; the privileging of some novels over others and some scenes in novels over others; and the view of characters' minds as a private, passive flow of consciousness, not as purposive, engaged, social interaction.

It may be that narrative theory has been concerned for too long primarily with the privacy of consciousness and that an emphasis on the social nature of thought would form an informative and suggestive perspective on fictional minds. What is required for the future is a holistic view of the whole of the social mind in action in narrative fiction.

Postclassical and cognitivist approaches

Within postclassical narratology, a number of scholars are now probing the nature of fictional minds within two related conceptual frameworks. One is *possible-worlds theory, which regards the fictional text as a set of instructions according to which the storyworld is recovered and reassembled. The other, derived from cognitive science, studies how various cognitive frames and scripts which are made up of real-world, stereotypical knowledge are applied to the reading process (see FRAME THEORY; NARRATIVE COMPREHENSION; PSYCHOLOGICAL APPROACHES TO NARRATIVE; SCRIPTS AND SCHEMATA).

For example, Fludernik (1996) has used cognitive frames to support her concept of a *natural narratology. Specifically, by making *experientiality central to her definition of narrative, she has recontextualised the whole concept of *narrative by basing it on the notion of consciousness. Ryan (1991) argues that the reader constructs fictional minds through what she calls embedded narratives (see EMBEDDING; FRAMED NARRATIVE). The set of a character's various perceptual and conceptual viewpoints, ideological worldviews (see IDEOLOGY AND NARRATIVE), and plans for the future can be considered as individual narratives which are embedded within the whole narrative that comprises the fictional text. Jahn has applied cognitive frame theory to such issues as Stanzel's three narrative situations, free indirect discourse, and focalization. Margolin (2003) has illuminated the relationship between cognitive science, fictional minds and various aspects of literary narrative, in particular by examining the role of the narrator in terms of the mental functioning of a thinking mind.

Palmer (2004) argues that the constructions of the minds of fictional characters by narrators and readers are central to our understanding of how novels work because fictional narrative is, in essence, the recounting of characters' mental functioning. He suggests that one of the key cognitive frames for comprehending texts enables the reader to create a continuing consciousness out of the isolated passages of text that relate to a particular character. Such a cognitive approach shows that, for example, the distinction between descriptions of thought and descriptions of action is not as clearcut as narrative theorists have assumed. Also, the intermental nature of fictional minds raises a number of fascinating issues related to the socially situated or distributed nature of much of our cognition, action and even *identity. Finally, the cognitive approach highlights the role of the reader in constructing characters' embedded narratives by means of a series of provisional conjectures and hypotheses about their mental functioning, and shows how readers read *plots as the interaction of those embedded narratives (see READER-RESPONSE THEORY).

SEE ALSO: mindscreen; mind-style; thought and consciousness representation (film)

References and further reading

Banfield, Ann (1982) *Unspeakable Sentences: Narration and Representation in the Language of Fiction*, London: Routledge.

Chatman, Seymour (1978) *Story and Discourse: Narrative Structure in Fiction and Film*, Ithaca: Cornell University Press.

Cohn, Dorrit (1978) *Transparent Minds: Narrative Modes for Presenting Consciousness in Fiction*, Princeton: Princeton University Press.

Fludernik, Monika (1993) *The Fictions of Language and the Languages of Fiction: The Linguistic Representation of Speech and Consciousness*, London: Routledge.

—— (1996) *Towards a 'Natural' Narratology*, London: Routledge.

Jahn, Manfred (1992) 'Contextualizing Represented Speech and Thought', *Journal of Pragmatics*, 17, 347–67.

Leech, Geoffrey, and Michael Short (1981) *Style in Fiction: a Linguistic Introduction to English Fictional Prose*, London: Longman.

McHale, Brian (1978) 'Free Indirect Discourse: A Survey of Recent Accounts', *PTL, a Journal for Descriptive Poetics and Theory of Literature*, 3, 249–87.

—— (1983) 'Unspeakable Sentences, Unnatural Acts: Linguistics and Poetics Revisited', *Poetics Today*, 4.1, 17–45.

Margolin, Uri (2003) 'Cognitive Science, the Thinking Mind, and Literary Narrative', in David Herman (ed.) *Narrative Theory and the Cognitive Sciences*, Stanford, CA: CSLI Publications.

Neumann, Anne Waldron (1986) 'Characterization and Comment in *Pride and Prejudice*: Free Indirect Discourse and "Double Voiced" Verbs of Speaking, Thinking and Feeling', *Style*, 20.3, 364–94.

Palmer, Alan (2002) 'The Construction of Fictional Minds', *Narrative*, 10.1, 28–46.

—— (2004) *Fictional Minds*, Lincoln: University of Nebraska Press.

Ryan, Marie-Laure (1991) *Possible Worlds, Artificial Intelligence, and Narrative Theory*, Bloomington: Indiana University Press.

Stanzel, Franz (1984 [1979]) *A Theory of Narrative*, trans. Charlotte Goedsche, Cambridge: Cambridge University Press.

ALAN PALMER

THRILLER

The 'thriller' is probably the most ubiquitous and successful *genre of narrative in modern times. The term designates a catholic embrace of a wide range of narrative sub-genres including the police procedural, spy stories, hard-boiled fiction, *noir*, adventure narratives, ratiocinative tales, Golden Age whodunits, the cozy, hard-boiled *detective stories, gangster *films, crime fiction, sensation *novels, action *films, and so forth. Some readers may be absolutely committed to one of the thriller's sub-genres to the exclusion of the others; some readers might range across them all. However, expansive analyses strongly suggest that what characterises all thriller narratives is a broad and accommodating framework of conspiracy.

Palmer (1978) argues that the conspiracy in thrillers always has a political complexion in that the genre is a constant refraction of paranoid fears that have existed since the near-simultaneous inception of industrial capitalism and the thriller genre. Anchoring the thriller genre in a specific time and place in this way can be problematic; others therefore suggest that conspiracy in the thriller is even more deeply ingrained, psychologically and historically. The occasional American marketing designation of the general thriller genre as 'mystery' constitutes good practice in this sense since it represents the common cognitive activities of problem solving and knowledge seeking which are featured in various ways in thriller narratives.

As a genre, the thriller is to be considered less a tangible formula for narrative than as a bundle of expectations harboured by readers about the quality of interaction that a text will facilitate for them (Cobley 2000). This is important: as Roland Barthes (1974), in particular, has emphasised in his discussion of the 'hermeneutic code' in *narration (*see* CODES FOR READING), knowledge accumulation and problem solving are components of *narrative in general. These are precisely the cognitive activities that are foregrounded in the generic expectations which characterise the thriller genre. They provide structure whilst facilitating an enormous wealth of variation and change.

Even though the thriller cannot be reduced to a set of restricted, immutable features, nevertheless it has been seen by some as a type of narrative that originated at a definite time (the 1840s), with a specific author (Edgar Allan Poe), and a specialised type of procedure ('ratiocination' or puzzling). Other commentators suggest that the origins of the thriller are more deep-rooted than this and reflected in its overlap with many other narrative genres, some of which were later incorporated as more or less definite sub-genres of the thriller. Among these are Newgate confessionals (memoirs of criminals putatively composed as they awaited execution; *see* CONFESSIONAL NARRATIVE); adventure stories; ratiocinative tales; memoirs of police; sensation novels; and hard-boiled narratives. All of these genres are, themselves, multiply determined – by pre-literate genres as well as closer literary relatives such as *romance, *Gothic novel, and *Bildungsroman. They are also determined by outgrowths of other narrative genres: for example, chapbook tales of criminality predated *The Newgate Calendar*; *The Odyssey* of Homer came before the adventure story; Gothic narratives came before the sensation novel, and so on.

The potency of the thriller is perhaps indicated by the way that it has become a staple of narrative in *media such as print, *comic books, films, *radio and *television formats (for example, series and serials), videogames, and other interactive computer media (*see* COMPUTER GAMES AND NARRATIVE; SERIAL FORM).

References and further reading

Barthes, Roland (1974) *S/Z*, trans. Richard Howard, New York: Hill and Wang.
Cobley, Paul (2000) *The American Thriller: Generic Innovation and Social Change in the 1970s*, London: Palgrave.
Eco, Umberto, and Sebeok, Thomas A. (1983) *The Sign of Three: Dupin, Holmes, Peirce*, Bloomington: Indiana University Press.
Knight, Stephen (1980) *Form and Ideology in Crime Fiction*, London: Macmillan.
Palmer, Jerry (1978) *Thrillers: Genesis and Structure of a Popular Genre*, London: Arnold.

PAUL COBLEY

TIME IN NARRATIVE

The relationship between narrative and temporality has been one of the most popular research areas in narrative theory. Indeed, the analysis of *tense, i.e., temporal verbal inflection, in narrative texts can be argued to have initiated narratological study at the turn of the twentieth century when the narrative and linguistic uses of the French *imparfait* past in the context of *free indirect discourse were discovered by Adolf Tobler and Charles Bally.

When it comes to a relationship between temporality and narrative three major perspectives need to be distinguished: (a) the general, philosophical aspect of temporality and its significance for the story and discourse level; (b) the relationship between the story and discourse levels (*see* STORY-DISCOURSE DISTINCTION); and (c) the grammatical and morphological devices (tense markers) and their significance for the discourse and story level.

Perspective (a) is a largely philosophical question that has been discussed in reference to Saint Augustine through Bergson to Paul Ricoeur;

perspective (c) represents a linguistic and stylistic inquiry. Perspectives (b) and (c) have traditionally had a significant status in narratology. Thus, in parallel with work by Culler and Adams, Paul Ricoeur's and Hayden White's notions of configurality and story structure correlate with important narratological insights into narrative teleology and *causality. Perspective (c) includes questions of the so-called 'epic preterite', the use of the present tense, the future tense, and even the conditional as a main narrative tense, the dynamics of tense shifts, and the metaphorical use of tense in narrative (compare Weinrich's theories, as well as work on the historical present tense). The deployment of tense is particularly important in the discussions about the difference between literary and non-literary, fictional and non-fictional, *narrative and non-narrative texts (*see* FICTION, THEORIES OF; TEXT-TYPE APPROACH TO NARRATIVE). The use of tense in conversation, newspapers, or instructional prose both determines the interpretation of what these tenses signify in literary and particularly narrative prose, and provides a foil against which specific literary, fictional, or narrative manifestations need to be measured. An extremely under-researched area is the use of tense in (narrative) poetry outside the medieval period (*see* MEDIEVAL NARRATIVE; NARRATIVE IN POETRY).

Temporality, story, and discourse

This entry focuses mainly on perspective (b), the temporal relationship between the story and discourse levels of narrative, first analysed by Günther Müller in 1948. Müller distinguished between *Erzählzeit* (narrating time, text time, or discourse time) and *erzählte Zeit* (narrated time or story time). Discourse time is measured in words or pages of text or in the hours of reading time, whereas story time represents the temporal duration and chronology of the underlying *plot. The distinction becomes useful when one contrasts the uniform progression of story time, which is modelled on our everyday notions of clock and calendar time, with the fits and starts, pauses and speed-ups encountered on the discourse level of narratives. Thus, many traditional *novels end with a chapter that summarises the *hero's life after the conclusion of the main events of the story, treating twenty years in three pages, whereas in previous sections a single day was awarded several chapters and some 100 pages of text. The relationship between story and discourse time therefore ties in with the general selectivity of narrative discourse: life cannot be told exhaustively (*Tristram Shandy* documents the absurdity of the attempt to do this), and narrative therefore has to concentrate on the choice of significant episodes that establish a configuration and meaning for the text.

The distinction between these two levels of temporality ties in with the axiomatic narratological dichotomy between *story* and *discourse* (Chatman 1978), earlier noted in a variety of similar binary oppositions (story versus plot – E.M. Forster; *fabula* versus *sjuzhet* – Shklovskii; *histoire* versus *discours* – Benveniste). This binary opposition of story versus discourse moreover determines the way narratology treats the concept of *chronology*. It is usually assumed that the *story* level of a narrative, i.e., the sequence of events reconstructed from the surface level of the linguistic medium, can be viewed as having a chronological order, whereas on the *discourse* level (the sequence of words on the page that constitutes the text) several reshufflings take place to produce a number of *anachronies*, as Genette calls them, i.e., flashbacks, flashforwards (*see* TEMPORAL ORDERING). The study of these two temporal orders enshrined in story and discourse inevitably leads to the analysis of chronological distortions on the surface level of the narrative text, and therefore comes to connect the study of temporal levels with the surface-structure analysis of tense in narrative. This connection is particularly strong because anachronies are frequently signalled by means of tense shifts.

The importance of Genette's model

Genette, in his pathbreaking study *Narrative Discourse*, added a third constitutive level of narrative texts, the level of *narration, or of the production of the discourse and its communicative strategies. In his model the discourse level is therefore further split into *narration* (the telling or writing process) and the *text* as its linguistic product. Müller's *Erzählzeit* (narrating time) can then be said to refer to the level of *narration* rather than to the textual surface structure. It has even been argued that Müller's *Erzählzeit* should in fact be conceptualised as *reading time* rather than as the number of pages of text in relation to the temporal duration represented on the story level. (This would involve the addition of the reception level as a fourth temporal plane.)

Genette's detailed analyses of temporal relationships, which cover three chapters in *Narrative Discourse*, are concerned with the concepts of order (chronological reshuffling), speed (duration), and frequency as major subcategories of what Genette calls *tense* (in the triad of *tense*, *voice* and *mood*). With respect to *speed*, Genette tackles the problem of selection and emphasis. He notes four types of speed: ellipsis (non-narration of story elements; *see* GAPPING), summary (abbreviated representation of story *events), scene (the seemingly one-to-one relation of event time and discourse time, as in the pseudo-tape recording of characters' *dialogue), and pause (descriptive dwelling on a point in time in which action does not move forward) (*see* SUMMARY AND SCENE). Recently, narratologists have added *stretch* as a fifth category – text time exceeds event time, as in filmic slow-motion (see Chatman 1978: 72–73; *see* FILM NARRATIVE). *Frequency*, on the other hand, concerns temporal iteration and condensation in relation to the singularity and identity of events. When characters knock on a door once or several times, this can be represented once or a number of times. Thus, a single knock can recur with symbolic frequency in the textual version, just as a series of knocks may be condensed into a single representative instance in the narrative discourse. (The best-known examples of these two cases are, on the one hand, the centipede in Robbe-Grillet's novel *La jalousie* whose crushing, as most critics believe, occurred only once although the scene is described several times in the text; and, on the other, Proust's extended representation of one typical gathering at the Guermantes which replaces a series of such soirées on the plot level.)

Genette, besides distinguishing order, duration, and frequency in his chapters on tense, also includes a section called 'Time of the Narrating' in his chapter on voice; here he discusses the relation between the time of narrating and the time of the story. Narration most traditionally is subsequent to the events it relates (retrospective narration), but predictive discourse is situated prior to the events, and narration and story can also stand in a relation of simultaneity and interpolation. Note that the term 'anterior narration' is applied to extended passages or entire texts; if only short segments of a narrative are predictive they would have to be treated under the category of prolepsis.

Simultaneous narration in real life occurs most frequently in sports reporting (Ryan 1993; *see* SPORTS BROADCAST). In the late twentieth century simultaneous narratives (frequently written in the present tense) have generally become very common. Genette's 'intercalated' narration, perhaps better called 'narrative in instalments', refers to *epistolary and *diary discourse in which the narrating and the experiencing alternate – the acts of narration are inserted into the flow of experience which gives rise to the story that these interpolated acts of telling produce. This most complex type of the temporality of narration remains under-researched (but see Margolin 1999: 150–53; Margolin also provides invaluable information on experiments with odd tenses and verbal moods like the subjunctive). In particular, like simultaneous narration, intercalated narration often lacks the teleology and story configuration that are frequently considered to be necessary constituents of *narrativity.

Other approaches to time and narrative

Returning to perspectives (a) and (c), one will have to consider the relationship between time and narrative additionally under the aspects of chronology, temporality, and sequentiality. We are all tempted to see time as an objective, measurable, and unambiguous category that can be pictured as a dotted line progressing from past to future. However, narrative temporality makes apparent the complex interrelationship of different types, or orders, of temporality. Thus, on the story level temporality is conceptualised in the common sense 'objective' manner that we all take for granted. On the discourse level, with the reading or viewing of narrative discourse, however, a cognitive order of temporality is instituted which is based, not on sequentiality or chronology, but on holistic structures of *narrative comprehension. Adams (1996), in the wake of earlier work by Jonathan Culler and Philip Sturgess (1992), has documented this dynamic interrelation of the process of narration and narrative comprehension. Narrative comprehension crucially correlates with teleology, with the story producing (and being produced by) the stringencies of teleological design. Oedipus, these critics argue, needs to kill his father and marry his mother in order for the omen to become true; when delving into his past he does not recover any previous truths; the story design determines what he finds in the past. It is a foregone conclusion that, once he has heard about the omen, he will discover that he is guilty (*see* LOGIC OF NARRATIVE).

In these proposals, as also in Ricoeur's magisterial three volumes of *Time and Narrative* (1984–1988), the understanding of temporality becomes increasingly divorced from objective or scientific notions of time and moves towards more psychological, subjective, and contextually malleable conceptions of temporality. (These developments are particularly clear in the work of Henri Bergson; see his concept of *durée* for the subjective meaning of temporality and note also the distinction between clock time vs. mind time.) Instead of a continuous uniform band of time that extends into infinity, time – like post-Einsteinian *space – becomes warped, discontinuous, four-dimensional. Reading time embraces not only the number of hours spent turning the pages of a book; it additionally comprises the expectations and interpretative moves of the reader, the factor of suspense (*see* SUSPENSE AND SURPRISE), the computing of alternative outcomes or developments, and the emotional consummation of narrative *closure (*see* EMOTION AND NARRATIVE). These aspects of narrative *reception straddle the merely temporal quality of the reading process in the same way that the experience of time in *memory, or even in everyday perceptions of lived temporality, is entangled with the emotional impact on the individual psyche. The cognitive order of the reading process is therefore closer to the *experience* of time than to the notion of clock time extending uniformly from past into future.

These observations link with the narratological proposals presented in Monika Fludernik's *Towards a 'Natural' narratology* (1996). In this study the definition of narrativity (traditionally based on the plot) has been replaced by a conception of representation *of*, and *by means of*, consciousness. Fludernik's model defines narrativity as based on *experientiality. This redefinition of narrative as rendering not necessarily a plot but a character's or *narrator's experiential reality was influenced by insights from conversational narratives in which the point of the story is not merely 'what happened' but, especially, what the experience meant to the narrator and what he or she wanted to convey with it (*see* CONVERSATIONAL STORYTELLING).

From a further perspective, narrative temporality moreover significantly interacts with indexicality.

A real-world *speech act of narration, as described in early narratological studies by William Labov and Marie Louise Pratt, is uttered at a specific point in time and retrospectively evaluates the narrative experience as both significant (as having *tellability) and topical (as displaying narrative point). Whereas empirical time is conceived of as a continuum with each point of reference yielding a view both back into the past and forward into the future, what complicates matters in fictional narrative is the determination of a focal point of reference. In conversation, the deictic reference point of *I* speaking *now* determines that my past will be past in relation to the point of speaking (*see* DEIXIS). The major difference in relation to fiction is that in fiction the speaker of the text is taken to be the narrator whose *I* (if there is an *I*) does not necessarily belong to the here-and-now of the historical *author or the contemporary reader. The deictic properties involved in the act of narration, therefore, do *not* coincide with the deixis appertaining to the situation of writing or reading conceived as a present communicative scenario. Since there is no face-to-face communication in fiction, the temporal deixis involved in literary narrative depends on Bühler's *Deixis am Phantasma*, i.e., on a deictic anchoring point divorced from that of the real reader and frequently of the real author as well. (Perhaps one can best translate the term as 'virtual' deixis (*see* VIRTUALITY). See Bühler (1990 [1934]) and Duchan *et al.* (1995) for a theoretical update.) As a consequence, the pastness of the traditional past-tense narrative signifies a kind of unspecified past whose relation to the present moment of reading is one of distancing rather than of precise location. A dating of fictional events except in the *historical novel is fairly rare, and in *epics and *fairy tales the past acquires an almost mythic quality that is quite distinct from the prosaic deictic past in historiographic texts (*see* HISTORIOGRAPHY; MYTH: THEMATIC APPROACHES). In the wake of Hamburger, it has become common to use the term 'epic preterite' for the past tense in fictional narrative. In this usage, the terms *epic* and *preterite* are conceived of as oxymoronic: fictional narrative employs a non-deictic, and therefore epic, preterite whose function is that of foregrounding the *fictionality* of the text, not its preterital temporal location in relation to the here and now of the author/reader.

From a narratological perspective, a few further points should be noted. The most important of these concerns the notion of real deixis in fictional texts. First-person narratives, deictically speaking, have a deictic past tense in relation to the moment of utterance/writing of the teller figure, the first-person narrator. However, not all first-person novels or *short stories nowadays also have a determinable teller figure or indeed a determinable moment of speaking (*see* NARRATIVE SITUATIONS; PERSON). A great number of twentieth-century texts in the first-person format are written in the reflector mode, as Stanzel calls it; they concentrate on the *I*'s experiences without evaluating them from the perspective of a teller who retrospectively views his or her former life and ensures narrative closure. As examples one can mention J.M. Coetzee's *Waiting for the Barbarians* (1980), the short fiction of Ernest Gaines, Margaret Atwood's *Surfacing* (1972), or Eva Figes's *Ghosts* (1988).

As a consequence, one can argue that the basic dichotomy is not that between first- and third-person texts but between teller and reflector mode narratives. Texts that have a prominent teller figure employ the preterite as a deictic signalling of pastness in relation to the time of the teller figure's writing or speaking. Narratives in the reflector mode do not have a teller figure and therefore the past tense has no deictic anchoring in relation to an extradiegetic present. It is anchored instead in the consciousness of the reflector character, and in relation to this deictic centre the epic preterite signals simultaneity with the figural consciousness. In reflector mode texts the preterite therefore has no deictic meaning of pastness.

The *epic preterite* proper (as defined by Hamburger and Stanzel), i.e., the simultaneity of here-and-now deixis and the preterite tense, can occur in either first- or third-person contexts, but the phenomenon is confined to those passages that have incipient reflector mode properties, whose deictic centre has moved from the teller figure to the experiencing self or character who begins to function as a reflector character and therefore establishes a deictic centre. The epic preterite proper is to be distinguished from what is also called the *narrative past tense* which denotes the past tense as the regular tense in narrative clauses, which has become a marker of fictionality. The narrative past tense may refer to a real past in *historical novels, but usually signifies an unspecified past and can even be used for future events in utopias and *science fiction texts located in the deictic future of the contemporary author and reader (*see* UTOPIAN AND DYSTOPIAN FICTION).

The label *narrative past tense* was chosen advisedly in parallel to the *narrative present tense* (Fludernik 1996: ch. 6). When all narrative clauses are kept in the present tense, but the events do not occur in the here-and-now of the narrator's discourse, the present tense loses its natural deictic quality. Like the narrative past and the epic preterite, the narrative present can be argued to connote fictionality. Another way of describing this phenomenon of 'fictionality' would be to compare it to Weinrich's *tense metaphor*. According to Weinrich, the juxtaposition of non-contiguous tense forms gives rise to metaphorical interpretations of such tense shifts. The narrative present, thus, can be interpreted as a *metaphor for fictional distancing.

SEE ALSO: narrative psychology; speech representation; thought and consciousness representation (literature)

References and further reading

Adams, Jon K. (1996) *Narrative Explanation: A Pragmatic Theory of Discourse*, Frankfurt: Lang.

Bühler, Karl (1990 [1934]) *Theory of Language: The Representational Function of Language*, trans. Donald Fraser Goodwin, Amsterdam: John Benjamins.

Casparis, Christian Paul (1975) *Tense Without Time: The Present Tense in Narration*, Berne: Francke.

Chatman, Seymour (1978) *Story and Discourse: Narrative Structure in Fiction and Film*, Ithaca, NY: Cornell University Press.

Duchan, Judith, Gail Bruder, and Lynne E. Hewitt (eds) (1995) *Deixis in Narrative: A Cognitive Science Perspective*, Hillsdale, NJ: Erlbaum.

Fleischman, Suzanne (1998) 'Tense in Narrative', in Paul E. Schellinger (ed.) *Encyclopedia of the Novel*, Chicago: Fitzroy Dearborn.

Fludernik, Monika (1993) *The Fictions of Language and the Languages of Fiction: The Linguistic Representation of Speech and Consciousness*, London: Routledge.

—— (1996) *Towards a 'Natural' Narratology*, London: Routledge.

—— (2003) 'Chronology, Time, Tense and Experientiality in Narrative', *Language and Literature*, 12.2, 117–34.

Genette, Gérard (1980 [1972]) *Narrative Discourse. An Essay in Method*, trans. Jane E. Lewin, Ithaca, NY: Cornell University Press.

Hamburger, Käte (1993 [1957]) *The Logic of Literature*, trans. Marilynn J. Rose, Bloomington: Indiana University Press.

Margolin, Uri (1999) 'Of What Is Past, Is Passing, or to Come: Temporality, Aspectuality, Modality and the Nature of Literary Narrative', in David Herman (ed.) *Narratologies: New Perspectives on Narrative Analysis*, Columbus, OH: Ohio State University Press.

Müller, Günther (1968 [1948]) 'Erzählzeit und erzählte Zeit', in *Morphologische Poetik: Gesammelte Aufsätze*, Tübingen: Niemeyer.

Ricoeur, Paul (1984–1988) *Time and Narrative*, trans. Kathleen McLaughlin and David Pellauer, 3 vols., Chicago: Chicago University Press.

Ryan, Marie-Laure (1993) 'Narrative in Real Time: Chronicle, Mimesis and Plot in the Baseball Broadcast', *Narrative*, 1.2, 138–55.

Stanzel, Franz K. (1959) 'Episches Praeteritum, erlebte Rede, historisches Praesens', *Deutsche Vierteljahrsschrift*, 33, 1–12.

Sturgess, Philip J. M. (1992) *Narrativity: Theory and Practice*, Oxford: Clarendon Press.

Weinrich, Harald (1985 [1971]) *Tempus: Besprochene und erzählte Welt*, Stuttgart: Kohlhammer.

MONIKA FLUDERNIK

TRANSFICTIONALITY

Two (or more) texts exhibit a transfictional relation when they share elements such as characters, imaginary locations, or fictional worlds. Transfictionality may be considered as a branch of *intertextuality, but it usually conceals this intertextual link because it neither quotes nor acknowledges its sources. Instead, it uses the source text's setting and/or inhabitants as if they existed independently.

Transfictionality puts into question the *closure of texts and calls for a multidisciplinary approach combining *possible-worlds theory and theories of *fiction, on the one hand, and *pragmatics and sociology of literature, on the other (*see* SOCIOLOGICAL APPROACHES TO LITERARY NARRATIVE). The possible-worlds/fiction perspective insists on accessibility between fictional realms and on the ambiguous relationship between their respective components. The relation between Sherlock Holmes in Conan Doyle's stories and Holmes in, say, Michael Dibdin's pastiche *The Last Sherlock Holmes Story* is obviously stronger than simple homonymy, but many readers will probably refuse to construe it as a strict identity, since this would entail that the latter's adventures would become part of the former's 'authentic' *biography. The solution here may be to consider transfictional versions as counterparts, i.e., as inhabitants of distinct possible worlds, bearing close relationship to their original, even though it might seem counterintuitive to assign original and version to separate worlds. One may also wonder what degree of resemblance is necessary for such a counterpart relationship to hold. How many – and which – properties of the original can be modified, added or deleted in the version without the latter being considered an altogether different entity instead of a counterpart (or 'immigrant', to borrow Terence Parsons' (1980) notion)?

The pragmatic-sociological approach puts stress on contextual and institutional factors such as authorship or the distinction between literary and mass-media fiction. These factors strongly influence any assessment of transfictionality. Clearly, a purely semantic approach is not sufficient for explaining the (in)compatibility of transfictional versions. Major modifications in a character's attitude or behaviour are likely to be accepted as new twists when they are made by the original *author, whereas faithful versions, when written by somebody else, will probably be taken as apocryphal. The situation in mass-media fiction is quite different, insofar as authorial considerations do not weight as much as they do in literature proper; hence the phenomenon of extensive circulation of characters between *television series, movies (*see* FILM NARRATIVE), *comics, and so forth.

SEE ALSO: character; narrative versions; postmodern rewrites; remediation

References and further reading

Doležel, Lubomír (1998) *Heterocosmica: Fiction and Possible Worlds*, Baltimore: Johns Hopkins University Press.

Genette, Gérard (1997 [1982]) *Palimpsests: Literature in the Second Degree*, trans. Channa Newman and Claude Doubinsky, Lincoln: University of Nebraska Press.

Margolin, Uri (1996) 'Characters and Their Versions', in Calin-Andrei Mihailescu and Walid Hamarneh (eds) *Fiction Updated: Theories of Fictionality, Narratology, and Poetics*, Toronto: University of Toronto Press.

Parsons, Terence (1980) *Nonexistent Objects*, New Haven: Yale University Press.

Saint-Gelais, Richard (2001) 'La fiction à travers l'intertexte: Pour une théorie de la transfictionnalité', in Alexandre Gefen and René Audet (eds) *Frontières de la fiction*, Quebec City: Nota bene.

—— (2002) 'La fiction hors-cadre', in Jean-François Chassay and Bertrand Gervais (eds) *Les lieux de l'imaginaire*, Montreal: Liber.

—— (2003), 'Énigme et transfictionnalité: Un arpentage du réseau *Edwin Drood*', *La Licorne*, 64, 211–228.

RICHARD SAINT-GELAIS

TRANSFOCALIZATION AND TRANSVOCALISATION

In Genettean poetics, two ways of creating a new text from an old text, either (a) by changing the old text's type of *focalization or (b) by changing its *narrative situation. For instance, a narrative using internal focalization through character A can be *transfocalized* into one that uses focalization through character B. On the other hand, a first-person *narration can be *transvocalized* into a third-person narration or vice versa. *See* INTERTEXTUALITY; NARRATIVE VERSIONS (also: REMEDIATION).

TRANSGRESSIVE FICTIONS

During the last decades of the twentieth century, literary production was divided into two distinct realms: (1) general (or 'mainstream') literature, which respects the limits imposed by 'reality', that is, the limits imposed by considering the world in its historical and socio-psychological dimensions; and (2) imaginary literatures (*fantasy, *the fantastic, *science fiction, *magical realism, *metafiction), which overstep those limits, operating under their own sets of rules. Some *fictions however are located in the nebulous area between these two domains. They will be discussed here as *transgressive fictions*. The transgression may affect either the level of story (world order) or the level of discourse (narrative rules; *see* STORY-DISCOURSE DISTINCTION).

(1) Transgressing the world order begins with the violation of temporal laws. *Narration is connected to *time at both the story and discourse levels (cf. Genette 1980 [1972]). In transgressive fictions, however, the past takes on different forms, leading to 'uchronias', an effect based upon postulates such as 'Hitler won the second world war' (Dick, *The Man in the High Castle*, 1962; *see* COUNTERFACTUAL HISTORY), or to fictions mixing authentic data with authorial fantasies (Levi, *Le Rêve de Confucius*, 1989). Time travel, initiated by Wells, is exploited not only in science fiction (Gerrold, *The Man who Folded Himself*, 1973), but also in mainstream literature (Coupry, *Le Rire du Pharaon*, 1984). Moreover, the very substance of time is submitted to dissolution, explosion, circular paradoxes, and other aporias.

The dislocation of time leads to the transgression of other natural laws governing our universe, both physical and biological. According to the scientific imagination of his or her time and to the scientific speciality taken into consideration, an *author can deal with existential problems through a considerable variety of *metaphors. In some cases, transgression can be explained rationally (Matheson, *The Shrinking Man*, 1956), while in others it is imposed as a given fact (Kafka, *Die Verwandlung*, 1916).

Transgressive fictions may introduce the supernatural. To do so they often refer to *myths that are connected to the unconscious, inviting exploration by the author (*see* PSYCHOANALYSIS AND NARRATIVE). While Western literature has been permeated with Greco-Roman myths for centuries, transgressive fictions actively engage in the transformation or distortion of the magic and symbols provided by these myths (Silverberg, *The Man in the Maze*, 1969). Other traditions also play a role, such as Jewish myths (Germain, *Tobie des marais*, 1998), Christian myths (Vian, *L'Arrache-coeur*, 1953), and Buddhist myths (Tristan, *Le Singe égal du ciel*, 1972).

The disruption of everyday reality makes it possible to create another world which responds not to natural laws, but to principles specific to the text (cf. Ryan 1991). In such a world, removed from physical and/or organic constraints, transgression may cast social behaviour in a different light (Orwell, *Animal Farm*, 1945). Strange universes may also be created by putting symptoms of mental disease into a concrete form (Berthelot, *La Ville au fond de l'œil*, 1986; *see* THOUGHT AND CONSCIOUSNESS REPRESENTATION (LITERATURE)).

(2) The transgression of narrative rules begins with the rejection of the conventions of pre-existing literary *genres. Hence, a *novel presenting the typical features of a space *opera (adventures on a foreign planet, space battles, stereotyped *characters, etc.) cannot be considered a transgressive fiction as long as it continues to operate within the boundaries of this genre. Transgressive fictions hover on borderline areas rather than fitting into a well-defined literary genre.

In their attempt to subvert narrative conventions, many authors incorporate the theme of art into their fictions (*see* EKPHRASIS). Since art is a form of representation, and since representation is never an exact copy of reality, it inevitably involves a distortion of the represented that borders on transgression. These problems have been approached in such various domains as painting (Haddad,

L'Ami argentin, 1999), sculpture (Brussolo, *Le Syndrome du scaphandrier*, 1991), theater (Pieyre de Mandiargues, *Le Deuil des roses*, 1983), *music (Ligny, *La Mort peut danser*, 1994), and architecture (Petit, *Architecte des glaces*, 1991), a novel that twists the creation process of the architect (*see* DRAMA AND NARRATIVE; PICTORIAL NARRATIVITY).

One way of denaturalising narrative is to put a story in a more or less realistic frame of reference and then to introduce a troublesome factor into the text. By contradicting narrative laws at story and/or discourse level (*see* METALEPSIS), this unconventional element may disturb standard representations, thereby progressively and dramatically challenging the reader's perception of reality (Dick, *Time Out of Joint*, 1959; Banks, *The Bridge*, 1986).

A further step in this direction is a more general subversion of narrative conventions, especially of those that involve the postulation of an individuated narrator or narrative *voice. Unable to attribute a source to the discourse, the reader is left in doubt as to whether or not the narration is reliable (*see* RELIABILITY). Some authors, considering that reality defies all portrayal, take the very principle of *fiction as a narrative topic (Priest, *The Affirmation*, 1981), while others create fictions that undermine themselves as fictions in their pursuit of an unattainable reality (Bologne, *Requiem pour un ange tombé du nid*, 2001; *see* HISTORIOGRAPHIC METAFICTION; METAFICTION). Yet others mix contradictory reports about the same events to highlight the fictional nature of text (Tristan, *Stéphanie Phanistée*, 1997), or employ discursive modes other than narration, as in Haddad's *L'Univers* (2000), a work composed as a dictionary with each entry revealing a different aspect of the story (*see* HYBRID GENRES).

Finally, literary language itself can act as a transgressive factor, whether authors invent words (Queneau, *Zazie dans le métro*, 1958), employ a poetic style that blurs the boundary between reality and phantasm (Gracq, *Au château d'Argol*, 1958), adopt unusual turns of phrase or rhythms (Beckett, *Molloy*, 1951), or orchestrate astonishing verbal disruptions (Burroughs, *Naked Lunch*, 1959).

Although contemporary culture continues to adhere, for commercial reasons, to a distinction between mainstream and experimental literature, transgressive fictions inhabit a grey area where the conventional dividing lines of literary genres are constantly subverted.

SEE ALSO: possible-worlds theory; postmodern narrative; reflexivity

References and further reading

Barets, Stan (1994) *Le Science-Fictionnaire*, Paris: Denoël.
Berthelot, Francis (2003) 'Les Fictions transgressives depuis 1990', *Iris*, 24, 45–57.
Genette, Gérard (1980 [1972]) *Narrative Discourse: An Essay in Method*, trans. Jane E. Lewin, Ithaca: Cornell University Press.
McHale, Brian (1987) *Postmodernist Fiction*, New York: Methuen.
Ryan, Marie-Laure (1991) *Possible Worlds, Artificial Intelligence and Narrative Theory*, Bloomington: Indiana University Press.
Schaeffer, Jean-Marie (1989) *Qu'est-ce qu'un genre littéraire?*, Paris: Seuil.
Todorov, Tzvetan (1975 [1970]) *The Fantastic: A Structural Approach to a Literary Genre*, trans. Richard Howard, Ithaca, New York: Cornell University Press.
Valéry, Francis (2000) *Passeport pour les étoiles*, Paris: Gallimard.

FRANCIS BERTHELOT

TRAUMA THEORY

Trauma, from the ancient Greek root *traumat*, means 'wound' and has been used for centuries in English and other European languages to designate a physical wounding of the body. 'Trauma theory', however, began to develop only in the late nineteenth-century; it can traced back to efforts by medical doctors in France and Central Europe, most notably Jean-Martin Charcot, Pierre Janet, Sigmund Freud, and Josef Breuer, to understand extreme psychic disturbances (at the time usually diagnosed as 'hysteria') of their (mainly female) patients. Trauma theory is of interest to narrative theorists because trauma has been perceived as an aberration of *memory which affects the individual's ability to recount *events in an ordinary fashion – to create a narrative of personal experience. Technical definitions of trauma, case studies of traumatised individuals, objections to standard accounts of trauma, and the particularly productive nature of trauma theory for analysts of literary narrative will be reviewed below.

Definition and mechanisms of trauma

The psychological use of the term 'trauma' confusingly refers to both the forces or mechanism that cause a psychic disorder and the resulting psychic state. In 1980 the American Psychiatric Association included a diagnosis of 'Posttraumatic Stress Disorder' (PTSD) in the third edition of the *Diagnostic and Statistical Manual* (DSM-III) to designate the development of symptoms such as amnesia, dissociation, dysphoria, flashbacks, hallucinations, hyperarousal, intrusion, nightmares, numbing, social withdrawal, and suicidal preoccupation in response to horrific events like natural disasters, combat, rape, and torture. Official acknowledgment of the similar symptomology of victims of quite different experiences and of a malady based on the structure of response to an event rather than on the event itself has had numerous (positive) therapeutic and sociological consequences (see Herman 1997; *see* SOCIOLOGY AND NARRATIVE). Nonetheless, the original description of the causal traumatic occurrence in the DSM-III as 'outside the range of usual human experiences' was quickly challenged, and the phrase was dropped in the DSM-IV (1994).

The issue of *causality remains a vexed one for the professional community. The same event will not necessarily affect exposed individuals similarly, though certain conditions like extreme exhaustion, being taken by surprise or being trapped, or previous traumatisation seem to increase the likelihood of developing PTSD. Severity of the disease is frequently worse when the violence is of human design and long-term. 'Disorders of Extreme Stress Not Otherwise Specified' (DESNOS) refers to cases where abuse and subsequent response to the abuse are chronic. The initial presentation may involve symptoms like physical discomfort, insomnia, and general anxiety or depression, not as recognisably related to trauma as are amnesia and flashbacks. DESNOS seems to develop when events conspire to compromise the fundamental sense of self and relational trust at critical developmental periods (Ford and Kidd 1998; *see* IDENTITY AND NARRATIVE). Other terms proposed for the effects of prolonged exposure to stressors include 'complex PTSD' (Herman 1997: 120–22) and 'insidious trauma' (Root 1996: 374–75). The task force for DSM-V is considering the official recognition of the diagnosis of DESNOS or of some other term for chronic PTSD.

The exact mechanism of infliction of trauma is still debated. While Freud thought of both a repression and a dissociation as relevant, Janet and many contemporary researchers think of dissociation as the most appropriate model. Cathy Caruth describes trauma as a gap, 'missed' or 'unclaimed' experience of the threat of death (1995, 1996). Confronted with danger, the ordinary human response involves a complex, integrated set of physical and mental reactions to prepare the individual for *action. Feelings of extreme helplessness – that no action is possible or of avail – tend to overwhelm this preparation. Longlasting changes in physiological arousal, *emotion, cognition, and memory may occur, and normally integrated functions may be severed from one another. Thus there may be memory of the event without emotion or there may be intense emotion, vigilance, and irritability without memory of the event (Herman 1997: 34).

The physiological basis for disturbances of memory storage and therefore narrative functioning are explained by Bessel van der Kolk and Onno van der Hart (1995). Severe or prolonged stress can affect the hippocampal localisation system (which normally allows memories to be placed in their proper context in *time and place), creating 'context-free fearful associations', that is to say, 'amnesia for the specifics of traumatic experiences but not for the feelings associated with them'. The experience of feeling extreme terror 'cannot be organised on a linguistic level, and this failure to arrange the memory in words and symbols leaves it to be organised on a somatosensory or iconic level' (1995: 172). Furthermore, the intense autonomic activation at the time of the traumatic event can 'teach' the alarm bell of the central nervous system, the locus coeruleus, to go off under any situation that resembles the initial event. The locus coeruleus secretes noradrenaline, and with repetition endogenous opioids, which, in turn, 'dampen perception of pain, physical as well as psychological. These neurotransmitters...affect the hippocampus, the amygdala, and the frontal lobes, where stress-induced neurochemical alterations affect the interpretation of incoming stimuli further in the direction of "emergency" and fight-or-flight responses' (1995: 173).

Traumatic memory vs. narrative memory

Because PTSD appears to be caused by an inability of the individual to integrate atrocities into consciousness, there is almost universal agreement that in order for the traumatised individual to go on with life more smoothly, some kind of transformation of the initial imprinting of the experience has to take place. Van der Kolk and van der Hart maintain that contemporary neurobiology and decades of clinical experience bear out the original understanding of trauma treatment by Janet as the need to create a story of the trauma that can be truly heard, not just repeated by the individual and communicated to others (1995: 175). 'Traumatic memory', van der Kolk and van der Hart explain, is not adaptive, comes unbidden, is often accompanied by overwhelming affect, and is not addressed to anybody. For these reasons, some have proposed that it should not be considered a type of 'memory' at all. More accurate descriptive terms include 'traumatic re-enactment' and 'traumatic recall'. Janet used the phrase *idées fixes* (fixed ideas). 'Ordinary memory' or 'narrative memory', in contrast, is *narrative in form, integrates experiences into existing mental schemas, is accompanied by modulated affect, and can be adapted to the circumstances of the telling.

Treatment and case studies

Clinical treatment for trauma can be characterised as involving a kind of transformation of traumatic memory into narrative memory (van der Kolk and van der Hart 1995: 160–63). Exactly how this is accomplished, however, remains somewhat of a mystery even to practitioners. It appears in part that because the infliction of the trauma involves an inability to act, the taking of action in the form of narrating a story has a therapeutic function for the patient (*see* NARRATIVE THERAPY). However, since patients frequently display phobias for anything connected with the traumatic event, Dori Laub and others stress the importance of a sympathetic listener to promote the individual's ability to revisit the traumatic event and create a narrative about it (Felman and Laub 1992: 57–92). On the one hand, treatment of trauma by creating an appropriate story should be seen as consonant with the general belief of Freud and psychoanalysis in the 'talking cure' and the development of psychotherapy as a 'narrative science'. On the other, this understanding is anti-Freudian in that the stories that require transformation by trauma victims may need to be taken quite literally and not be interpreted as distortions caused by *desires, wishes, and repressions.

Case studies aid in understanding the nature of traumatic memory and therefore the ways in which stories of trauma might need to be transformed. Janet repeatedly cited the case of his patient Irène who had lost her mother to illness after 60 days of caring for her. Irène had total amnesia for the night of her mother's death and for the funeral, though she could 'say' her mother had died since people told her so over and over again; she did not feel sad, because she did not believe what she had been told. And yet, when positioned at a certain angle to a bed (similar to the physical set-up of the room in which she had taken care of her mother), Irène would re-enact all the events of that night in a trancelike state. This re-enactment was immutable and would take several hours. Through hypnotism and conversation, Janet was able to bring Irène to the point where she could feel sadness and tell of her mother's death in numerous versions, depending on her *audience (summarised in van der Kolk and van der Hart 1995: 160–63).

Contemporary psychotherapist Jodie Wigren shares the case study of Hugh, who had to have a leg amputated in the aftermath of a hunting accident. His initial explanations about what had happened to him always focused on memories of hearing the gunshot and falling to the ground. Diagnosing incomplete grief reaction, the therapist used passive muscle relaxation and guided imagery to help Hugh talk more about what his legs meant to him and to help him grieve. It came out that Hugh's father was an abusive alcoholic and that the son's growing strength and eventual ability to 'stand up' to his father and protect his mother were important psychological milestones for him as an adolescent. When these discoveries proved to offer only temporary relief to Hugh, the therapist probed further and realised that what was obvious to her and to anyone meeting Hugh, was not obvious to him: although Hugh could technically see that he had only one leg, psychologically speaking he had not yet undergone the amputation. Inspired by Kingsbury's observation that 'patients often stop their traumatic nightmares just before the action which is truly intolerable for them' (paraphrased in Wigren 1994: 420), the therapist helped Hugh to narrate the as yet untold conclusion to his story. It was only after talking about the hospital, multiple surgeries, his fears that he might lose his prosthesis or, worse, even more of his leg, that he began to show longer lasting signs of recovery like dealing with a family crisis and resuming some of his social roles (417–20). Wigren concludes from this and other case studies that the goal of trauma treatment must be to help the patient create complete stories, which 'segment experience, link action and characters, identify affect and make meaning, or sense' (422; *see* NARRATIVE AS COGNITIVE INSTRUMENT). She warns of the importance of the therapist not completing these tasks herself (as she initially did by adding the segment of amputation to Hugh's story for him).

Refinements and objections to the standard account of trauma

Numerous and varied objections have been raised against aspects of this outline of the relationship of narrative, memory, and trauma. Philosopher Susan Brison protests Caruth's characterisation of the infliction of the trauma as a 'missing' of the experience of the threat of death. She observes a slippage in Caruth's logic between an individual's lack of preparedness for this threat and a missing of the experience altogether. While this may describe the experience of some survivors, Brison suggests that 'at least in the case of a single traumatic event, the event is typically experienced at the time and remembered from that time, although the full emotional impact of the trauma takes time to absorb and work through' (2002: 32).

Roberta Culbertson, Kali Tal, and Caruth have separately voiced concerns about the truth value of the healing narrative of the trauma that is created afterward (*see* TRUTH). Culbertson points out that 'narrative, as simply an accounting in time of events in time, limits what can be told, indeed making the truth of body recall appear unintelligible and false, because too disjointed and without context' (1995: 191). What the body, especially the body of a young child may register during an assault, may not in fact have narrative content, she suggests. And yet the physical body does store memories. Tal reminds us that all textual representations, literary, visual, and oral, are mediated by language and therefore cannot have the impact of the traumatic experience (1996: 15). Caruth similarly speaks of the narrative as a 'deformation' since its creation involves 'the loss, precisely, of the event's essential incomprehensibility, the force of its affront to understanding' (1995: 154).

Many contemporary social critics have raised concerns about the process of transforming traumatic memory into narrative memory not because it may deform the trauma, but because it may in fact invent the infliction of one (see Leys 2000: 18, 81, 306; on the danger of therapists contributing to this process, see Herman 1997 [1992]: 180). Objecting to the presumed therapeutic value of remembering altogether, Ruth Leys claims a mischaracterisation of the work of Pierre Janet by van der Kolk, van der Hart, Herman, and even Janet himself, citing case studies in which Janet cured his patients, including Irène, not only by helping them create narratives of the traumatic events, but also by transforming and often excising those very memories (2000: 105–16). For Janet, Leys concludes, 'narrated recollection was insufficient for the cure' (116). Whether or not Leys' characterisation of Janet's beliefs is accurate, many contemporary psychotherapists observe that the talking cure is inadequate and possibly even counter-productive for patients with chronic PTSD or DESNOS (Ford and Kidd 1998: 744, 755).

Arguing for the significance of cultural differences and of multiple minority statuses (*gender, race, and class) for certain groups like poor African American women, Maria P. Root points out that our current descriptions of trauma are actually based on experience with a very narrow range of types of events and patients. She pleads for 'willingness to hear about traumatic events that have not been medicalised or legitimised by the diagnostic system' due to lack of ethnocultural sensitivity in data collection and treatment (1996: 382). Patrick J. Bracken argues for the importance of history and culture even more broadly than Root, suggesting that PTSD should be considered 'the product not of trauma in itself, but of trauma and culture acting together. PTSD is thus the product of a particular cultural situation', not an inherent disease of homo sapiens (2001: 742). These objections are important in terms of the narrative we create about trauma theory itself: is it a universal phenomenon that was only recently recognised or one that is highly inflected by specificities of history and culture? While original theorists like Freud would have claimed the former, more and more critics today would argue for the latter.

Trauma theory and the theory of literary narrative

Trauma theory has had particular resonance for literary scholars. Inspired by the notion that trauma itself is inaccessible and immutable and

specifically by Charlotte Delbo's idea of 'deep memory', Lawrence Langer has used the kind of close reading usually reserved for literary narrative to analyse the structure of personal storytelling in video testimony given by *Holocaust survivors (1991). Similarly focusing on notions of unspeakability and incomprehensibility, Caruth has reread Freud, Lacan, Kant, Kleist, and Duras/Resnais through the framework of trauma theory (1996).

Marianne Hirsch has proposed the term 'postmemory' to characterise the experience of 'those who grow up dominated by narratives that preceded their birth, whose own belated stories are evacuated by the stories of the previous generation shaped by traumatic events that can be neither understood nor recreated' (1997: 22). She has used this concept to analyse unusual *genres like Art Spiegelman's 'commix' Maus I and II and *photographs and installations by artists such as Christian Boltanski (see COMICS AND GRAPHIC NOVEL).

Expanding Laub's notion of multiple levels of witnessing to trauma (Felman and Laub 1992: 75–76), Irene Kacandes has proposed a schema of circuits of literary witnessing to analyse novels of/as trauma (2001: 89–140). Working outward from the depiction of a *character who is unable to witness to a traumatic event to characters who are unable to serve as witnesses for each other to the act of reading a novel depicting these failures of witnessing, Kacandes proposes that the text itself can mimic symptoms such as amnesia through ellipses or flashbacks through anachronies and repetitions (see TEMPORAL ORDERING). When a reader makes the connection between such textual features and trauma she is engaged in literary-historical witnessing to the trauma of the text.

SEE ALSO: medicine and narrative; narrative psychology; psychoanalysis and narrative; psychological approaches to narrative

References and further reading

Bracken, Patrick J. (2001) 'Postmodernity and Post-traumatic Stress Disorder', Social Science & Medicine, 53, 733–43.
Brison, Susan J. (2002) Aftermath: Violence and the Remaking of a Self, Princeton: Princeton University Press.
Caruth, Cathy (ed.) (1995) Trauma: Explorations in Memory, Baltimore: Johns Hopkins University Press.

Caruth, Cathy (ed.) (1996) *Unclaimed Experience: Trauma, Narrative, and History*, Baltimore: Johns Hopkins University Press.

Culbertson, Roberta (1995) 'Embodied Memory, Transcendence, and Telling: Recounting Trauma, Re-Establishing the Self', *New Literary History*, 26.1, 169–95.

DSM-III (1980) *Diagnostic and Statistical Manual of Mental Disorders*, 3rd ed, Washington, DC: American Psychiatric Association.

DSM-IV (1994) *Diagnostic and Statistical Manual of Mental Disorders*, 4th ed, Washington, DC: American Psychiatric Association.

Felman, Shoshana, and Dori Laub (1992) *Testimony: Crises of Witnessing in Literature, Psychoanalysis, and History*, New York: Routledge.

Ford, Julian D., and Phyllis Kidd (1998) 'Early Childhood Trauma and Disorders of Extreme Stress as Predictors of Treatment Outcome with Chronic Posttraumatic Stress Disorder', *Journal of Traumatic Stress*, 11.4, 743–61.

Herman, Judith Lewis (1997 [1992]) *Trauma and Recovery: The Aftermath of Violence – from Domestic Abuse to Political Terror*, New York: Basic Books.

Hirsch, Marianne (1997) *Family Frames: Photography, Narrative, and Postmemory*, Cambridge, Mass.: Harvard University Press.

Kacandes, Irene (2001) *Talk Fiction: Literature and the Talk Explosion*, Lincoln: University of Nebraska Press.

van der Kolk, B. A., and Onno van der Hart (1995 [1991]) 'The Intrusive Past: The Flexibility of Memory and the Engraving of Trauma', in Caruth (1995: 158–82).

Langer, Lawrence (1991) *Holocaust Testimonies: The Ruins of Memory*, New Haven: Yale University Press.

Leys, Ruth (2000) *Trauma: A Genealogy*, Chicago: University of Chicago Press.

Root, Maria P (1996) 'Women of Colour and Traumatic Stress in "Domestic Captivity": Gender and Race as Disempowering Statuses', in Anthony J. Marsella, Matthew J. Friedman, Ellen T. Gerrity, and Raymond V. Scurfield (eds) *Ethnocultural Aspects of Posttraumatic Stress Disorder: Issues, Research, and Clinical Applications*, Washington, DC: American Psychological Assocation.

Tal, Kali (1996) *Worlds of Hurt: Reading the Literatures of Trauma*, Cambridge: Cambridge University Press.

Wigren, Jodie (1994) 'Narrative Completion in Treatment of Trauma', *Psychotherapy*, 31.3, 415–23.

IRENE KACANDES

TRAVEL NARRATIVE

Travel, an out-of-the-ordinary experience and occasion for observations and encounters, has provided stimulus and material for narrative since ancient times. Encouraging linear and episodic *narration, travel forms the basic *plot of such types of literary narrative as the *epic, the quest *romance, the *picaresque novel, the *utopian novel and *science fiction, the adventure novel, the Robinsonade, and the *Bildungsroman. Much of this literature draws on another ancient and prolific form of travel narrative: the travelogue or travel account (also travel writing), which claims and/or is read in the belief that the text is non-fiction, i.e., that the journey recorded actually took place and is presented, in an autobiographical manner, by the travellers themselves (*see* AUTOBIOGRAPHY; FICTION, THEORIES OF). Such records vary in the degree to which they are focused on the travelled world or on the travelling subject, but they inevitably reveal both the culture-specific and the individual patterns of perception and knowledge which every traveller brings to the experience of a journey.

Fictional stories about travel, most importantly *novels, are told in both the first- and the third-*person. They often utilise travel to project foreign or alternative, even fantastical, worlds. Travel in a novel also frequently provides a scenario in which the protagonist's spiritual, sentimental, or other kind of inner 'journey' can be developed or symbolically mirrored (*see* ALLEGORY). Examples abound, including instances as varied as Thomas More's *Utopia*, John Bunyan's *The Pilgrim's Progress*, Jonathan Swift's *Gulliver's Travels*, Laurence Sterne's *A Sentimental Journey*, and Virginia Woolf's *The Voyage Out*.

The *genre of the travelogue encompasses accounts of the pilgrimage, mercantile travel, early-modern discovery and colonisation, the great scientific voyages of the eighteenth-century, the Grand Tour, picturesque and romantic touring, domestic travel, tourist trips, missionary and exploratory travel of the imperial age, and, with growing significance since the late nineteenth-century, journeys undertaken for the sake of self-exploration, escape from civilisation, or simply writing about travel; the latter have been particularly encouraged by *postmodernist self-reflexivity and given rise to work with a high degree of meta- and *intertextuality (Bruce Chatwin, Paul Theroux, Jonathan Raban) (*see* METANARRATIVE COMMENT; REFLEXIVITY).

Like the fictional travel narrative, with which it is closely connected (Adams 1983; Batten 1978), the travelogue is a constructed narrative: it reconstructs a journey from greater or smaller temporal distance (retrospective account vs. the more immediate journal or letter), thus translating travel experience into a travel plot. In some varieties, the travel-narrator's persona is also notably dramatised. At the same time, however, the travelogue is defined by a basic actuality or factuality (von Martels 1994). Thus, it has not only been studied in literary criticism, but also considered as source material in geography, history, and anthropology (*see* ETHNOGRAPHIC APPROACHES TO NARRATIVE; HISTORIOGRAPHY). Increasingly during the 1990s and early 2000s, travel writing has become of major interest to various approaches in the field of *cultural studies, e.g., *discourse analysis (Foucault), imagology, New Historicism, *post-colonial studies, and *gender studies. In this area of cultural narratology, travelogues have been analysed – often along with travel fiction – for their projection of culture-specific discourses (e.g., orientalist or imperialist), their constructions of *alterity and self-identities, their imagings of countries and peoples, or as phenomena of inter-culturality (*see* CULTURAL STUDIES APPROACHES TO NARRATIVE; IDENTITY AND NARRATIVE). Particular attention has been attracted by early-modern voyages to the 'new' world (Hulme 1986; Fuller 1995) and the varieties of British imperial travel (Pratt 1992; Youngs 1994). The circumstances and qualities of women's travel and travel writing form another area of vivid critical debate sparked by the pioneering studies of Foster (1990) and Mills (1991).

With respect to *narrative technique, there appears to be no watertight distinction between travel fiction and travelogues. However, travelogues are almost exclusively narrated in the first-person: the *narrator and the travelling persona are accordingly fused, and by autobiographical contract the reader of a travelogue also assumes that the narrator-traveller is basically identical to the *author. Nevertheless it is important to distinguish between author, narrating-I, and experiencing-I, since the views voiced by the narrating-I might not be fully identical with those of the 'real' author, and the narrator may also, just like any first-person narrator, create a certain *distance from him or herself as traveller, as in the writings of Mary Kingsley or Bruce Chatwin. Furthermore, the travelogue is a more *hybrid genre than the novel with a travel plot. Its generic definition requires a basic narrative structure, but it makes ample use of non-narrative modes of presentation. In different proportions, which depend on period as much as the type of travel depicted, narrative report will be intermingled with lengthy *description, *exposition, and 'apodemic elements', i.e., passages of prescription, suggestion, and advice related to travel and travelling. Many travelogues also include statistics and other collections of empirical data, advice of the guidebook-type, the occasional poem, or illustrations and *photographs. Crossovers with the essay, the *letter, reportage, the sketch, *anecdote, and treatise are frequent, and just as varied is the intention of travelogues to inform, instruct, and delight (*see* INTENTIONALITY).

References and further reading

Adams, Percy G. (1983) *Travel Literature and the Evolution of the Novel*, Lexington: University of Kentucky Press.

Batten, Charles L. (1978) *Pleasurable Instruction: Form and Convention in 18th-Century Travel Literature*, Berkeley: University of California Press.

Foster, Shirley (1990) *Across New Worlds: Nineteenth-Century Women Travellers and Their Writings*, New York: Harvester/Wheatsheaf.

Fuller, Mary C. (1995) *Voyages in Print: English Travel to America, 1576–1624*, Cambridge: Cambridge University Press.

Hulme, Peter (1986) *Colonial Encounters: Europe and the Native Caribbean, 1492–1797*, London: Methuen.

——, and Tim Youngs (eds) (2002) *The Cambridge Companion to Travel Writing*, Cambridge: Cambridge University Press.

Korte, Barbara (2000) *English Travel Writing: From Pilgrimages to Post-colonial Explorations*, Basingstoke: Macmillan.

Lawrence, Karen R. (1994) *Penelope Voyages: Woman and Travel in the British Literary Tradition*, Ithaca NY: Cornell University Press.

von Martels, Zweder (ed.) (1994) *Travel Fact and Travel Fiction: Studies on Fiction, Literary Tradition, Scholarly Discovery and Observation in Travel Writing*, Leiden: Brill.

Mills, Sara (1991) *Discourses of Difference: An Analysis of Women's Travel Writing and Colonialism*, London: Routledge.

Pratt, Mary Louise (1992) *Imperial Eyes: Travel Writing and Transculturation*, London: Routledge.

Youngs, Tim (1994) *Travellers in Africa: British Travelogues, 1850–1900*, Manchester: Manchester University Press.

BARBARA KORTE

TREBLING/TRIPLICATION

The triple repetition of an action-sequence, as found for instance in a *fairy tale recounting the failure of two brothers and the success of the third at fulfilling a certain task. Trebling functions narratively as a *retardatory device that temporarily frustrates, and thereby heightens, the reader's desire to know what will happen. *See* NARRATIVE STRUCTURE; NARRATIVE TECHNIQUES.

TRUTH

Truth has hardly been a major topic in narrative theory. How could it be, when most literary theorists seem allergic to the very idea of truth? The source of the allergy (felt all across the humanities) lies in poststructuralism, with its across-the-board scepticism about cognitive values or aspirations, and its particular hostility to grand metaphysical pieties of the kind often associated with the term 'truth' (e.g., Smith 2000; *see* MASTER NARRATIVE; POSTSTRUCTURALIST APPROACHES TO NARRATIVE). Even those who find the claims of poststructural theory mostly overblown, however, should grant that, on the subject of truth, they represent a justifiable reaction against a tendency traditional in the humanities to speak in precisely such grand, pious terms about 'literary truth'. Such truth, inaccessible to merely empirical inquiry, is held to be embodied in poetry, *fiction, and other literary modes; it is diffuse in its essence, since the truth that, say, a *novel can convey is expressed by the work as a whole rather than by any of its component sentences. The impasse between mysticism on the one hand and dogmatic scepticism on the other leaves open-minded inquirers in the field of narrative facing two questions. Can the notion of truth be rehabilitated? Can it play any useful role in the study of narrative?

Literary theorists who wish to rehabilitate truth should look to contemporary analytic *philosophy, where discussion of the concept flourishes (see Dasenbrock 2000 for pioneering work in this direction). What these philosophers have done is to 'deflate' the concept to one degree or another. They simply ignore the metaphysical assumption that all particular truths must add up to one grand Truth-with-a-capital-T about the universe, thus preempting the poststructuralist critique, and concentrate instead on the function of terms like 'true' and 'false' in workaday thought and conversation. Some philosophers have followed the deflationist route all the way, denying that truth serves any purpose beyond a metalinguistic one: they hold that an assertion '*P*' is synonymous with the assertion 'It

is true that *P*', and therefore that the whole use of the truth-predicate ('It is true that...') is to characterise certain assertions in certain way. Other philosophers have maintained that truth, even on the most prosaic interpretation, remains a substantial notion, central to linguistic and intellectual activity in a way that requires explanation rather than elimination (cf. Blackburn and Simmons 1999). Attempts to explain the concept frequently preserve vestiges of what had been the standard theories of truth – the correspondence, coherence, and pragmatist accounts – which find themselves largely relegated to a pedagogical role in contemporary philosophy. (That they still hold interest in other fields is attested by their use in Ryan 1998 to generate a taxonomy of literary *genres.)

One would think that truth would be an important concept in the study of factual narrative, but this remains a conjecture, since narrative theorists have so far largely ignored non-fiction (*see* NON-FICTION NOVEL). Although Hayden White might be cited as a counter-example, what he has done is largely to assimilate factual discourse to fiction. His major claim is that both are constructed – that narrative of any type exhibits linguistic and structural patterning (*see* EMPLOTMENT; METAHISTORY; NARRATIVITY). While there is a genuine insight here, many literary theorists have been eager to draw the conclusion – strongly opposed by many historians – that the purported 'truth' of, e.g., historical narrative is fabricated (*see* HISTORIOGRAPHY). The inference is false, however: there is no incompatibility between discourse having the property of being constructed and that of being true. As Bernard Williams has emphasised in an excellent discussion of White, to deny that facts pre-exist their linguistic expression does not mean that there are no facts at all (2002, ch. 10). Louis Mink brought out the real issue here, in what was unfortunately his sole discussion of it (1987 [1978]): what needs working out is the relationship between the concepts of narrative and truth. White's view that it is purely a matter of convention remains unsatisfying (*see* REALISM, THEORIES OF).

In work on fictional narrative, meanwhile, the concept of truth has made only rare appearances. The misleading title of Riffaterre's *Fictional Truth* (1990) provides an example. He begins by defining fiction as false discourse, rendering the notion of truth irrelevant to his discussion, the actual subject of which is the appearance of truth or *vraisemblance* (*verisimilitude) in fiction. A more sophisticated case is that of Lamarque and Olsen's *Truth, Fiction and Literature* (1994), because the authors do not simply discount the idea that truth is a concept relevant to literature in many ways. However, they advocate what they call a 'no-truth' theory of literature, which consists in denying that the concept is essential to the explanation of fictional narrative or any other literary form. More than anyone else it was Doležel who advocated the significance of truth for literary theory, not only in his account of fiction in terms of *possible-worlds theory, but also in his analysis – conceptually distinct – of how the 'truth' (i.e., the facts) of a fictional narrative is a function of the 'authenticity' (i.e., the *reliability) of its *narrator (1980).

SEE ALSO: authentication; reference

References and further reading

Blackburn, Simon, and Keith Simmons (ed.) (1999) *Truth*, Oxford: Oxford University Press.

Dasenbrock, Reed Way (2000) *Truth and Consequences: Intentions, Conventions, and the New Thematics*, University Park: Pennsylvania State University Press.

Doležel, Lubomír (1980) 'Truth and Authenticity in Narrative', *Poetics Today*, 1.3, 7–25.

Lamarque, Peter, and Stein Haugom Olsen (1994) *Truth, Fiction and Literature*, Oxford: Clarendon Press.

Mink, Louis O. (1987 [1978]) 'Narrative Form as a Cognitive Instrument', in *Historical Understanding*, Ithaca: Cornell University Press.

Riffaterre, Michael (1990) *Fictional Truth*, Baltimore: Johns Hopkins University Press.

Ryan, Marie-Laure (1998) 'Truth Without Scare Quotes: Post-Sokalian Genre Theory', *New Literary History*, 29, 811–30.

Smith, Barbara Herrnstein (2000) 'Netting Truth', *PMLA*, 115, 1089–95.

White, Hayden (1973) *Metahistory: The Historical Imagination in Nineteenth-Century Europe*, Baltimore: Johns Hopkins University Press.

Williams, Bernard (2002) *Truth and Truthfulness: An Essay in Genealogy*, Princeton: Princeton University Press.

DAVID GORMAN

U

UNNARRATABLE, THE

Although Gerald Prince defines the 'narratable' as that which is worthy of being told, 'unnarratable' is more than an antonym. Following Prince's definition, *events may be unnarratable because they are too boring to be mentioned (for instance, a *narrator might not detail tooth-brushing or shoelace-tying). Such events 'go without saying'.

More interestingly, some unnarratable events cannot or should not be told, because of manners, taboo, or literary convention. For example, bodily functions such as excretion or copulation are unnarratable in Victorian fiction; when a Modernist *novel such as James Joyce's *Ulysses* puts them into words, the category of the unnarratable stretches along with the *genre (*see* MODERNIST NARRATIVE). Unnarratable events may come into narratives through allusion, euphemism, or *metonymy, or they may be known by their results.

Certain genres use 'unnarration', as distinct from 'disnarration'. In disnarration, a speaker tells an audience what will not be included in the narrative, naming what is not to be told. In unnarration, a speaker claims the inadequacy of language to represent an event (e.g., 'Words cannot express how she felt'). Unnarration cues readers to participate imaginatively in co-creating the narrative.

SEE ALSO: denarration; disnarrated, the

References and further reading
Prince, Gerald (1987) *A Dictionary of Narratology*, Lincoln: University of Nebraska Press.

ROBYN WARHOL

UNRELIABLE NARRATION

Introduced in Wayne C. Booth's *Rhetoric of Fiction* (1961), the term describes the discourse of an untrustworthy *narrator who misrepresents or misevaluates characters and events. Often creating a humorous effect, unreliable narration is frequently found in *jokes, *irony, *satire, and parody. By contrast, non-humorous unreliable narration can emphasise biased *perspective, limited knowledge, or serious character flaws. *See* RELIABILITY.

URBAN LEGEND

Jan Brunvand (1981) popularised the term 'urban legend'; it refers to the sub-genre of *legend that Richard Dorson associated with the modern, urban environment and defined as 'the story which never happened told for true' (1959: 249). Frequently framed as having happened to a friend of a friend (or 'FOF'), these traditional narratives and synopses of narratives – alternatively referred to by legend scholars as *contemporary legends*, *modern legends*, *rumour legends*, *belief legends*, and *emergent legends* and by the popular press as *urban myths* – are communicated informally in conversational settings ranging from the adolescent sleep-over to the professional boardroom. They are also disseminated through print and broadcast *journalism, over e-mail, by means of fax and photocopier, and as moments in or the subject of *novels, *short stories, *television programs, and movies (*see* FILM NARRATIVE). Urban legends are a multicultural and international form of narrative. Common themes include murder and/or violence (*The Slasher Under the Car*) or narrowly escaped violence (*The Hook*), sex and scandal (*The Stuck Couple*), food contamination (*Kentucky Fried Rat*), disease (*Welcome to the World of AIDS*), the illegal harvesting of body parts (*The Kidney Heist* and *The Baby-parts Story*), accidents and embarrassing situations (*The Exploding Toilet*), mistrust of modern technology (*The Microwaved Pet*), as well as such topics as satanic panics, UFO abduction reports, government bureaucracy and cover-up, suppressed inventions, and hidden images in movies and advertising.

SEE ALSO: anecdote; conversational storytelling; ethnographic approaches to narrative; folklore; genre theory in narrative studies; simple forms

References and further reading

Brunvand, Jan (1981) *The Vanishing Hitchhiker*, New York: W. W. Norton & Co.
Campion-Vincent, Veronique (1990) 'The Baby-Parts Story: A New Latin American Legend', *Western Folklore*, 49, 9–25.
Dorson, Richard (1959) *American Folklore*, Chicago: The University of Chicago Press.
Fine, Gary Alan (1992) *Manufacturing Tales: Sex and Money in Contemporary Legends*, Knoxville: The University of Tennessee Press.

CATHY LYNN PRESTON

UTOPIAN AND DYSTOPIAN FICTION

Utopian thought attempts to envision a society in which the various social, political, and economic ills of the real world have been solved, leaving an ideal realm of justice and tranquillity. All *fiction, by projecting a world that is different from the real, physical one, has a potential utopian component. Indeed, the attempt to imagine a world better than our own has long been recognised as one of the crucial functions of all literature. Thus, Sir Philip Sidney, in his *Defence of Poetry* (1579–1580), argues that imaginative writing is superior to history and other forms of non-fiction because the natural world is 'brazen', while 'the poets only deliver a golden'. Nevertheless, some works of literature are more specifically dedicated to the projection of utopian visions than are others. There is, in fact, an entire tradition of utopian fiction that attempts to envision ideal societies, generally far removed from the *author's world either temporally or geographically. Meanwhile, beginning especially in the twentieth century, this tradition has given rise to a dystopian counter-tradition that tends to be highly sceptical of utopian visions.

The tradition of utopian fiction dates back at least as far as the ancient Greeks, who produced a number of utopian works, the most important of which is Plato's *Republic* (380–370 BC), especially in terms of its influence on later utopian writers. The most fundamental political principle of Plato's ideal republic is that it is ruled by an enlightened elite of specially trained, philosophically minded thinkers, known as the Guardians. This elitism, of course, would be abhorrent to many in the modern world, as is Plato's tendency to argue that individual freedom should be sacrificed in the interest of greater happiness for all. This early work thus already indicates the potentially problematic nature of all programmatic utopian visions.

The next major contribution to the tradition of utopian fiction was Sir Thomas More's *Utopia* (1516), the book that gave the tradition its name. More's utopia is more concrete than Plato's in that his ideal society is located in an actual physical setting (an island off the coast of South America), even though the Greek word utopia literally means 'no place'. More, by describing the visit of a European (Raphael Hythloday) to the island, also gives his work a more narrative bent than Plato's, helping to establish a generic model for future writers of utopian fiction (*see* GENRE THEORY IN NARRATIVE STUDIES). More's book also makes clear the important satirical component that resides in almost all utopian fiction in that his ideal society is quite specifically set against his own present-day England as a way of criticising the ills of that real-world society (*see* SATIRIC NARRATIVE).

Other utopian works, such as Tommaso Campanella's *The City of the Sun* (1602–1623) and Francis Bacon's *New Atlantis* (1627) followed soon after More's, but the tradition of utopian fiction received a special boost from the Eighteenth-century onward, when humanist faith in the potential of *science and of human beings in general led to a widespread growth in notions that an ideal society, based on the principles of the Enlightenment, could literally be established. These more modern utopian visions culminated in the late nineteenth and early twentieth centuries, when a spate of utopian fictions, often inspired by socialist ideals, appeared. These centrally included

Edward Bellamy's *Looking Backward* (1888), William Morris's *News From Nowhere* (1890), and H. G. Wells's *A Modern Utopia* (1905).

Utopian fictions continued to appear throughout the twentieth century, though these more modern fictions were often informed by a complexity and scepticism that tended to make the line between utopia and dystopia rather unclear, though the thin line between utopia and dystopia had already been emphasised in earlier works such as Book IV of Jonathan Swift's *Gulliver's Travels* (1726). Thus, a crucial modern 'utopian' fiction such as B. F. Skinner's *Walden Two* (1948), clearly intended as a serious exploration of the possibilities of behavioural psychology to produce citizens suited for life in an idealised society, strikes many as a nightmare vision of brainwashing and social control. Some modern works, such as Marge Piercy's *Woman on the Edge of Time* (1976), include both utopian and dystopian visions of the future, though others, such as Ernest Callenbach's *Ecotopia* and Ursula K. Le Guin's *The Dispossessed* (1974), have attempted more legitimately utopian visions, often inspired by the ideals of the oppositional political movements of the 1960s. In addition, twentieth-century thinkers such as Ernst Bloch continued to explore the potential of utopian thought and to emphasise the utopian potential of fiction and other cultural products.

Still, imaginative visions of ideal societies in the twentieth century took a general turn toward the dystopian and toward a suspicion that, if 'ideal' societies could be established at all, this establishment would lead to stagnation, tyranny, and the suppression of dissent. The tradition of dystopian fiction remains dominated by three founding texts that have helped to set the standards for all other dystopian works. These include Yevgeny Zamyatin's *We* (1924), Aldous Huxley's *Brave New World* (1932), and George Orwell's *Nineteen Eighty-Four* (1949). Zamyatin's book is concerned with the dystopian potential of Soviet socialist utopianism, Huxley's with the dystopian potential of capitalist consumerism, and Orwell's with the potential for totalitarian oppression that he finds in both communism and capitalism. Subsequent dystopian works were often specifically aimed either at communism or capitalism, though Western imaginative fiction in particular tended to take a general dystopian turn in the second half of the twentieth century, perhaps due to a diminished utopian imagination that some critics have associated with the era of postmodernism (*see* POSTMODERN NARRATIVE). For example, the *cyber-punk science fiction of writers such as William Gibson tends to see a relatively bleak future, in comparison with the utopian visions and technological optimism that had informed many earlier works of science fiction.

SEE ALSO: dystopian fiction; eco-narrative; Marxist approaches to narrative; science fiction; sociological approaches to literary narrative

References and further reading

Bloch, Ernst (1996 [1954–1959]) *The Principle of Hope*, 3 vols., trans. Neville Plaice, Stephen Plaice, and Paul Knight, Cambridge, Mass.: MIT Press.

Booker, M. Keith (1994) *The Dystopian Impulse in Modern Literature: Fiction as Social Criticism*, Westport, CT: Greenwood Press.

—— (1994) *Dystopian Literature: A Theory and Research Guide*, Westport, CT: Greenwood Press.

—— (2002) *The Post-Utopian Imagination: American Culture in the Long 1950s*, Westport, CT: Greenwood Press.

Elliott, Robert C. (1970) *The Shape of Utopia: Studies in a Literary Genre*, Chicago: University of Chicago Press.

Jameson, Fredric (1991) *Postmodernism, or, The Cultural Logic of Late Capitalism*, Durham, NC: Duke University Press.

Kumar, Krishan (1987) *Utopia and Anti-Utopia in Modern Times*, Oxford: Blackwell.

Moylan, Tom (1986) *Demand the Impossible: Science Fiction and the Utopian Imagination*, New York: Methuen.

Rabkin, Eric S., Martin H. Greenberg, and Joseph D. Olander (eds) (1983) *No Place Else: Explorations in Utopian and Dystopian Fiction*, Carbondale: Southern Illinois University Press.

Ruppert, Peter (1986) *Reader in a Strange Land: The Activity of Reading Literary Utopias*, Athens: University of Georgia Press.

M. KEITH BOOKER

V

VERISIMILITUDE

The term 'verisimilitude' literally means 'truth-to-life' or 'lifelikeness'; but in the narratological context, the term translates the French '*vraisemblance*', a concept adapted by the structuralists from seventeenth-century French classicist poetics. Genette defines a verisimilar narrative as one 'where the actions answer . . . to a body of maxims accepted as true by the public to which the narrative is addressed' (2001 [1968]: 242). Verisimilitude is the effect of *realism achieved when states and behaviours in the narrative generally conform to its readers' *ideology and/or model of the world. Related concepts are motivation (in the Russian Formalist tradition; *see* FORMALISM) and *naturalisation. Culler (1975) elaborates five levels of verisimilitude, including conformity to general cultural models and to genre-specific conventions (*see* GENRE FICTION), while Sternberg (1983) critiques the formalist and structuralist approaches, subsuming verisimilitude under the 'quasi-mimetic mode' of motivation as opposed to the aesthetic or rhetorical mode.

SEE ALSO: mimesis; reality effect; structuralist narratology

References and further reading

Culler, Jonathan (1975) 'Convention and Naturalization', in *Structuralist Poetics: Structuralism, Linguistics and the Study of Literature*, London: Routledge and Kegan Paul.
Genette, Gérard (2001 [1968]) '*Vraisemblance* and Motivation', trans. David Gorman, *Narrative* 9.3, 239–58.
Sternberg, Meir (1983) 'Mimesis and Motivation: The Two Faces of Fictional Coherence', in Joseph P. Strelka (ed.) *Literary Criticism and Philosophy*, University Park: Pennsylvania State University Press.

BRIAN McHALE

VIRTUALITY

The importance of the concept of virtuality for literature and narrative has been recognised since antiquity. In Aristotle's *Poetics* (section 5.5) we read: 'The function of the poet is not to say what *has* happened, but to say the kind of things that *would* happen, i.e., what is possible in accordance with probability and necessity.' The philosophical concept of the virtual entertains close relations with the possible. In scholastic Latin, *virtualis* designates 'what is in the power (*virtus*) of the force.' The classical example of virtuality is the presence of the oak in the acorn. This conception of the virtual, which opposes it to the actual, may be called the virtual as potential. In the eighteenth-century, when the image projected by a mirror became known as a virtual image, the term developed an association with the fictive and the non-existent. Exploiting the ideas of fake and illusion associated with the mirror image, the more recent usage associates the virtual with that which *passes as* something other than what it is. Virtual Reality technology, for instance, uses the electronic signals of the computer to create the illusion of the presence of a three-dimensional world. This second sense constructs an opposition between the virtual and the real.

The 'fake' interpretation of the virtual presents obvious affinities with the concept of *fiction. The feature of inauthenticity describes not only the unreal character of the reference worlds created by fiction (*see* POSSIBLE-WORLDS THEORY; REFERENCE), but also, as John Searle has suggested, the logical status of fictional discourse itself. Insofar as the speech acts that construct fictional worlds are not serious, but pretended assertions, fiction can be described as a virtual report of facts (*see* SPEECH ACT THEORY).

The virtual as potential has various applications in literary theory. It lies at the core of the conception of the text developed by the phenomenology of reading (*see* READER-RESPONSE THEORY). Roman Ingarden conceives the literary work of art as an incomplete entity which must be concretised by the reader into an aesthetic object. This concretisation requires of the reader a filling in of *gaps and places of *indeterminacy (Iser 1980). Since every reader completes the text on the basis of a different life experience and internalised knowledge, texts unfold into a variety of mental images. For the French philosopher Pierre Lévy, the inherent virtuality of the text resides in this one-to-many relation, which constitutes the polar opposite of models assuming a deterministic extraction of meaning.

The semantics of *plot offers a more narrowly narrative manifestation of the virtual as potential. Far from being limited to what actually happened, plots interweave a factual sequence of objectively happening events with virtual scripts produced in the minds of *characters by activities such as dreaming, imagining, planning, wishing, promising, or fearing (*see* THOUGHT AND CONSCIOUSNESS REPRESENTATION (LITERATURE)). A fundamental cognitive operation, the contemplation of virtual scripts is essential both to the strategic thinking of characters and to the interpreter's rationalisation of the characters' behaviour. As G. H. von Wright has shown, an agent who plans an *action to solve a problem must calculate what will happen if he or she performs the action, and what would happen if events ran their course without intervention. The interpreter who evaluates the success of the action must not only re-construe these two courses of *events, but also compare them to the actual outcome. In narrative as well as in life, action necessarily virtualises one of the scripts of its logical structure: the sequence to be prevented in the case of success, the agent's plan in the case of failure.

In the temporal progression of narrative (*see* NARRATIVE PROGRESSION), the virtual takes two forms: the still possible, which corresponds to forking paths that lead from the present or the future into a more remote future, and the counterfactual, which corresponds to forking paths that branch out of the trajectory of the actual at some point in the past, and consequently missed their chance of actualisation. We may think of the possible as the live (or active) virtual, and of the counterfactual as its fossilised form. As narrative moves along its timeline, the possible is turned into

either the actual (i.e., historical) or the counterfactual; but, as the work of Claude Bremond has shown, every new event opens its own field of possibilities.

The dynamics of the Aristotelian plot, with its characteristic rise and fall in tension, rest on a careful management of the virtual field (*see* FREYTAG'S TRIANGLE; SUSPENSE AND SURPRISE). The level of tension is minimal during the *exposition, when the range of the possible is so wide that the interpreter cannot form projections. The complication heightens the tension by narrowing down this field to a finite number of possibilities. Now the interpreter can look into the future, and sees several reasonably well-defined paths. The action climaxes when the field is reduced to two paths leading in opposite directions, but though the destinations are visible, the exact itinerary must be hidden from the interpreter; otherwise the plot would not be able to generate surprise. The pruning of one of these paths during the denouement results in a fall of tension, for tension cannot survive the disappearance of the active form of the virtual.

Yet the resolution of narrative *conflict does not mean the end of the contemplation of the virtual. Even after the possible has been exhausted by the actualisation of a certain course of action, the interpreter revisits mentally the paths that have fallen into the domain of the counterfactual, so as to assess the ethical or strategic decisions of the characters, as well as the aesthetic decisions of the *author. In this mode of evaluation, narrative acquires significance against a background of virtual stories that never made it into actuality.

SEE ALSO: counterfactual history

References and further reading

Aristotle (1996) *Poetics*, trans. Malcolm Heath, London: Penguin.
Bremond, Claude (1973) *Logique du récit*, Paris: Seuil.
Ingarden, Roman (1973) *The Literary Work of Art: An Investigation on the Borderlines of Ontology, Logic, and the Theory of Literature*, trans. George Grabowicz, Evanston: Northwestern University Press.
Iser, Wolfgang (1980) 'The Reading Process', in Jane P. Tomkins (ed.) *Reader-Response Criticism: From Formalism to Poststructuralism*, Baltimore: Johns Hopkins University Press.
Lévy, Pierre (1998) *Becoming Virtual: Reality in the Digital Age*, trans. Robert Bonono, New York: Plenum Trade.

Ryan, Marie-Laure (1991) *Possible Worlds, Artificial Intelligence, and Narrative Theory*, Bloomington: Indiana University Press.
——(2001) *Narrative as Virtual Reality: Immersion and Interactivity in Literature and Electronic Media*, Baltimore: Johns Hopkins University Press.
Searle, John (1975) 'The Logical Status of Fictional Discourse', *New Literary History*, 6, 319–32.
von Wright, Georg Hendrik (1967) 'The Logic of Action: A Sketch', in Nicholas Rescher (ed.) *The Logic of Decision and Action*, Pittsburgh: University of Pittsburgh Press.

MARIE-LAURE RYAN

VISUAL NARRATIVITY

The question of visual narrative falls into two components: First, what is a written image, hence, how can it be read? Second, how can (graphic) images narrate? The former concerns the visual dimension of narrative, the latter the narrativity proper to, or possible in, visual images (*see* IMAGE AND NARRATIVE). For both questions, a definition of *narrativity is presupposed, as well as a reflection on what an image is (Mitchell 1985). After what Mitchell (1994) called 'the pictorial turn' many literary scholars began to analyse visual artefacts such as paintings, prints, and *films (*see* PICTORIAL NARRATIVITY). This development requires reflection on the two questions above, which underlie such *interdisciplinary endeavours. This entry first addresses appearances of visuality in verbal narrative under the heading of *figurations*. Second, I turn to figuration's counterpart, the narrative aspects of visual depiction, i.e., the narrativity of images. This mode of visual narrativity is examined primarily through the concept of *focalization. The last section focuses on the cultural-political implications of the resistance that investigations of visual narrativity have encountered. As a whole, the entry aims to relativise, perhaps even undermine, the distinctions usually maintained between the two *media of text and image (*see* INTERMEDIALITY).

Visuality in literary narrative

In narrative texts an effective means of visualisation is generally considered to be *metaphor, which can cause something 'to be seen' in a way not revealed by the literal meaning, but only accessible through *visualisation. Furthermore, *space represented in narrative is very often depicted through visual images and the representation of viewing positions. In *novels, *narrators describe what they see or what they saw when they were younger, and this gives a particular importance to the subject of the *gaze, which narratologists refer to as the focalizer. But, in a doubling over of this visualisation, that which is described is not necessarily a space or a vision but may consist of a visual representation itself: an image, a painting (Proust, Shakespeare's *Lucrece*), an engraving, or a *photograph (Sebald). If the depiction does not exist as an actual artwork, such a visual narrative is called an *ekphrasis (Mitchell 1994: ch. 5). On other occasions, the visualisation is not doubled over, but is rather underlined or intensified. The thing seen is described as visually framed, as if it were seen in a picture frame, or through a magnifying glass or a telescope, or as a projection from a magic lantern, or the framing of a shot seen through the lens of a camera (*see* FRAME THEORY). These are ways in which narratives can generate their narrative thrust, even their *plots, by means of visualisations. Thus, the suicide in Shakespeare's narrative poem *Lucrece* is brought about by the visual description of a painting, non-existent but seen by Lucrece as well as the visualising reader. Visuality, thus, rivals action-generated *events for dominance over the plot structure. We can call this plot-generating aspect of visuality *figuration*.

Figuration is a visualising strategy of the narrative text, but it remains an effect of language. Written or oral narratives, after all, work within the medium of language. If we take into account this self-evident fact, then each visual image in narrative is first of all a verbal image, and refers only indirectly, at the level of its meaning, to the visual images of other categories. Thus we could say that metaphors are verbal images of mental images, while descriptions are verbal images of perceptual images, e.g., the description of Rouen in *Madame Bovary*. Both mental images and the perceptual images are capable in turn of referring to *graphic images, which are visible, but only by means of a chain of mediations. The optic dimension is often interposed, less as an image than as the medium for an image, in order to underline even more insistently the fact that these images are, after all, the products of language.

In this way, the study of visuality in narrative constitutes the counterpart to the study of the discursive, specifically narrative aspects – that is the narrative, rhetorical, and propositional aspects – of images in visual art (*see* RHETORICAL APPROACHES TO NARRATIVE). The question 'how to read visually' (Scarry 1998) complements the question 'how to look narratively' (Steiner 1988). In their complementarity these two fields of study suggest modes of understanding within a culture of exchange and interaction between the two 'sister arts.' They position themselves within the growing domain of the parallel study of text and image as a form of interdisciplinary narratology.

In the study of narrative, a renewed interest in visual aspects has grown out of the realisation that subjectivity is formed by a perpetual adjustment of images passing before the subject who, as focalizer, makes them into a whole that is comprehensible because it is continuous. Having a certain continuity in one's thought depends, at a level that is more subliminal than it is conscious, on having a certain continuity in one's images.

But continuity is not the same thing as coherence. This distinction is another source of interest that informs work on visual narrativity. In such very different texts and images – both historically and sociologically – as modern novels, the ancient and incomplete fragments that make up the Hebrew Bible (*see* BIBLICAL NARRATIVE), and Rembrandt's paintings, one constantly comes up against that which eludes the coherence of these artefacts. One's attention is systematically arrested by the detail that seems out of place, the contradiction that tears open the work, the monstrous element that reveals the flaws and the disparities and, because it provokes astonishment, offers a source of never-ending possibilities for the understanding of these works. Such experiences lead to considerations of those dimensions of literature that classical narratology has tended to consider marginal (*see* POSTCLASSICAL NARRATOLOGY). At issue, specifically, are aspects of literary narrative that afford structures of meaning besides those grounded in linear plots (*see* NARRATIVE STRUCTURE).

The narrativity of visual images

In the second area, that of the narrativity of images, a long tradition of iconographic reading has trained viewers, including art historians, to consider images as illustrations of classical texts. The founder of contemporary iconographic reading, Erwin Panofsky, developed a 'thicker' method, meant to account for the visual equivalent of the history of mentalities. He called this method 'iconology' and iconographic reading was a preparatory procedure for it. But his followers have largely relied on iconography, thus making specifically visual narrativity all but invisible. According to iconographic practice, the images would then be judged adequate or less adequate in their rendering of the text, or rather the text's dogmatic interpretation by church officials or religious orders.

Scholars knowledgeable in both literary and visual analysis have produced more complex readings of visual imagery, in particular in the wake of the second feminist wave (e.g., Mulvey 1975; Silverman 1983; *see* GENDER STUDIES). There, the spectatorial attitudes encouraged or discouraged by the visual representation became a focus of attention. The position of the viewer endorsing visuality as a mode of reading can shift back and forth and in variable degrees from textual focalizer to erotic voyeur. It is worth examining how these two interact. But in order to avoid terminological confusion, methodological eclecticism, and a failure to investigate the ideological underpinnings of frameworks for studying visual narrativity, it is imperative that we first assess the visual status of the narrative focalizer. Arguably, this concept offers a way to acknowledge the ontological gap between literary and visual imagery without reifying it.

The concept of focalization pertains to narrative as a discursive genre, but also yields insights into discourse itself as a semiotic system (*see* SEMIOTICS). In fact, it relates those two aspects, the narrative represented and its representation, by acting as the *perspective that directs the representation of the events (or fabula) that is verbalised in the text by the narrator (*see* STORY-DISCOURSE DISTINCTION). Although its basis in the notion of perspective *seems* to make its transposition to the realm of the visual simple, such a transposition is not unproblematic. In order to make the concept operational for visual art, it helps to be aware of the following considerations.

(1) In narrative discourse, focalization is the direct *content* of the linguistic signifiers. In visual art, it would be the direct content of visual signifiers like lines, dots, light and dark, and composition. In both cases, focalization *is already an interpretation*, a subjectivised content. What we see is before our mind's eye, already interpreted.

(2) In narrative there is an external focalizer distinguished in function, not identity, from the narrator. This external focalizer can embed an internal, diegetic focalizer (e.g., 'He saw that she noticed her mother's embarrassment', a second-degree *embedding), just as an external narrator can 'cite' a *character. For the analysis of narrative, this relation of embedding is crucial. In visual art, the same distinction between external and internal focalizer holds, but this distinction is not always easy to point out. For example, in Rembrandt's etching of Joseph and Potiphar's wife, the external focalizer, with whose view the spectator is asked to identify but from which the spectator's view remains distinct, embeds the internal Joseph-focalizer. As the internal focalizer, the focalization of Joseph is entirely contingent upon the fantasy of this external focalizer, which I identify with Potiphar. We can see the same structure of focalization in the Biblical story of Susanna and the Elders, so often depicted in visual art, where young Daniel is practically 'produced' by the focalization of the Elders (Bal 1991, ch. 4).

(3) In narrative, the fabula or *diegesis is mediated, or even produced, by the focalizers. Similarly, using the concept in analysing visual art implies that the event represented has the status of the focalized object produced by focalizers. In the case of a diegetic focalizer, the 'reality'-status of the different objects represented is variable and contingent upon their relation to the focalizer.

(4) Thus, the same object or event can be differently interpreted according to different focalizers. The ways in which these different interpretations are suggested to the reader or viewer are medium-bound, but the principle of meaning-production is the same for verbal and visual art. In Flaubert's *Madame Bovary*, the heroine's eyes are variably dark, black, blue, and grey, according to the internal focalizer with whom we watch her. The words conveying these incompatible descriptions do not themselves betray the difference between them. Flaubert could simply have been careless. But in order to make sense of the work as it is, only the hypothesis of different focalizers can account for these differences. Similarly, in the Joseph etching one object, the woman's body, is represented in two different, incompatible ways, according to the two different focalizers, one of whom is internal (Joseph) and one hinging between internal and external. The lines composing the body do not themselves betray the difficulty – the

body could have been simply 'ugly' or poorly etched – but the hypothesis of two different focalizers makes visible the rabbit-or-duck problem underlying this mistake or 'ugliness.'

(5) In narrative discourse, the identification of the external focalizer with an internal one can produce a discursive conflation often called *free indirect discourse. The identification between the external focalizer of visual images with an internal focalizer represented *in* the image can similarly give rise to such a conflation. This conflation would then strengthen the appeal to identification. But nevertheless, the conflation is still on the level of the representational work itself, the pictorial text.

The dynamics of focalization at work in every visual image that contains traces of the representational labour, as seen and interpreted by the viewer, since it is precisely in those traces that the work becomes narrativised. In principle all works contain such traces, but some display these more openly than others.

The stakes of visual narrativity

Why is the cross-over between visuality and narrativity important as an area of study? There are many cultural situations in which images are called upon to do the work of narrative. Anthropologist Johannes Fabian devoted a study to a body of paintings made in Zaire in which the artist presented his work as 'The History of Zaire as Painted and Told by Tshibumba Kanda Matulu.' The prelude to the study is a dialogue in which the artist tells the story of his story. His paintings offer an alternative history to the official one, and image a more adequate medium to tell it in. Imaging is taken up as a language the authorities cannot quite understand. The narrativity of images, then, becomes a secret code, a subcultural language that facilitates the production of subversive narratives.

If, in such cases, political *agency requires the deployment of imagery to be able to tell stories, this is so because the official political authorities rely on linguistic narrative to instil in their citizens the 'proper' stories. The law before which the telling of forbidden stories will be punished is largely verbal, as is the practice of jurisdiction (*see* LAW AND NARRATIVE). Visual narrative, in such circumstances, is a counter-discourse (*see* MASTER NARRATIVE). But this antagonism is, in the end, untenable. Although legal practice continues to have more difficulty dealing with contested visual material than with written texts, the distinction between language and imagery as two (formally) different media for storytelling has never been easy, and is, for that reason, replete with ideological and political meaning.

The political implications of the belief in a strong ontological difference, even opposition, between the two media becomes especially clear in the face of cultural objects that cannot be isolated as either verbal or visual. Film scholars routinely contend with the inextricable mixture of images and narrative (and sound) that constitutes their object of study. Films do not only consist of images as well as texts (and, of course, sound; see SOUND-TRACK). As is most obvious in silent films, the moving image itself is a narrative object that is nevertheless completely visual (Verhoeff 2002). Whereas some film scholars tend to privilege the visuality of their objects, others resist this polarisation between image and story, as when Kaja Silverman draws on *psychoanalysis to study the *narrative dynamics of the film image. Such work suggests how coming fully to terms with visual narrativity – in film but also in other artefacts – can reveal structures of meaning that dominant ideologies within a given culture may have driven underground.

As Mitchell has pointed out, the issue of the relationship between text and image, and hence between modes of narrativity in textual and visual representation, is not simply a question of media; it is also a question of *interests*. Besides being a formal issue, the division between the two modes is also an issue of 'the forms that sociability and subjectivity take, . . . the kinds of individuals and institutions formed by a culture' (Mitchell 1994: 3). People who fear that *television and the computer have made the novel obsolete hold a very different view of social life than those who study the forms of narrativity that emerge with the hypertextual organisation of the Internet (Ryan 2001). These forms can no longer be cast as either textual or visual; hence, if the Internet makes anything obsolete, it is the divide itself, and the protectionist attitudes toward visual or literary 'purity.'

Because of the clumsiness of the division between words and images, many scholars have been seeking alternative analytic concepts to account more adequately for artefacts that manifest visual narrativity. Morse (1998) deploys the concept of the performative to analyse the news qua visual narrative (see JOURNALISM; PERFORMATIVITY). She needs that concept in order to account for the (virtual) relation between speaker and addressee, or narrator and *narratee. This allows her to focus on the way narrative turns on the relation between narrator and narratee to do its work. Thus, narrativity is shifted from the events in the image to the event *of* the image: the pragmatic effect of verbal-cum-visual storytelling (see PRAGMATICS).

In the recently developed interdisciplinary field of study called 'cultural memory', visual narrativity is a prominent concern. For instance, Hirsch discusses how family snapshots help shape subjects through the narratives they tell. *Memory, like dreams, operates largely by means of the kind of visualisations that Mitchell would call mental images; at the same time, we tend to see memory as profoundly narrative, since it plots the temporality of our lives (see TIME IN NARRATIVE). And when Hirsch develops the concept of *postmemory* to describe memories, often visual ones, transmitted by parents to their children who conceive of the stories as their own memories, both the narrativity and the visuality of those memories is key to their functioning. Narrativity and visuality do not always harmoniously cooperate in memory, however. The specific branch of memory studies devoted to (collective) *trauma theorises the tensions, even the incompatibility, between the two (Alphen 1997). Whereas the non-traumatised subject can have narrative memories, the traumatised subject is instead assaulted from the outside of consciousness by visual and other sense-based images that do not coalesce into memories because they lack the attribute of narrativity.

Visual narrativity is culturally pervasive, not least because reading itself requires constant *visualisation. Accordingly, it is not the novel that is obsolete, but the idea that narrative and imagery are *essentially* different cultural expressions. This 'visual essentialism', along with the literary elitism that is its counterpart, only encourages the repressions that constitute intrapsychic, interpsychic or cultural, and political forms of censorship. Narrative and image need each other as much as cultures need both of them.

SEE ALSO: point of view (cinematic); point of view (literary)

References and further reading

van Alphen, Ernst (1997) *Caught by History: Holocaust Effects in Contemporary Art, Literature, and Theory*, Stanford: Stanford University Press.

Bal, Mieke (1991) *Reading 'Rembrandt': Beyond the Word-Image Opposition*, New York: Cambridge University Press.

——(1996) *Double Exposures: The Subject of Cultural Analysis*, New York: Routledge.

——(1997) *The Mottled Screen: Reading Proust Visually*, trans. Anna-Louise Milne, Stanford: Stanford University Press.

Fabian, Johannes (1996) *Remembering the Present: Painting and Popular History in Zaire*, Berkeley: University of California Press.

Hirsch, Marianne (1997) *Family Frames: Photography, Narrative, and Postmemory*, Cambridge, Mass.: Harvard University Press.

Mitchell, W. J. T. (1985) *Iconology: Image, Text, Ideology*, Chicago: University of Chicago Press.

——(1994) *Picture Theory*, Chicago: University of Chicago Press.

Morse, Margaret (1998) *Virtualities: Television, Media Art, and Cyber-culture*, Bloomington: Indiana University Press.

Mulvey, Laura (1975) 'Visual Pleasure and Narrative Cinema', *Screen*, 16.3, 6–18.

Panofsky, Erwin (1955) *Meaning in the Visual Arts*, Harmondsworth: Penguin.

Ryan, Marie-Laure (2001) *Narrative as Virtual Reality: Immersion and Interactivity in Literature and Electronic Media*, Baltimore: Johns Hopkins University Press.

Scarry, Elaine (1998) *Dreaming by the Book*, New York: Farrar, Strauss and Giroux.

Silverman, Kaja (1983) *The Subject of Semiotics*, New York: Oxford University Press.

Steiner, Wendy (1988) *Pictures of Romance: Form Against Context in Painting and Literature*, Chicago: University of Chicago Press.

Verhoeff, Nanna (2002) 'Narrativity', in *After the Beginning: Westerns Before 1915*, Utrecht: Institute for (Re)presentation and Media.

MIEKE BAL

VISUALISATION

Converging evidence from cognitive and neuro-psychological studies shows that visualisation (imaging) while reading has cognitive and affective consequences that are keyed to the interconnected variables of reader and text. Standardised questionnaires and personal interviews indicate that some individuals habitually visualise in reading and other activities, while others visualise little and deploy a more verbal style of response. The distinction between visualisers and non-visualisers is experimentally important, as some researchers demonstrate that visualisation has an effect only when the subjects are distinguished from one another based on questionnaires about the vividness of their imagery and how frequently they use it. Readers also differ in their beliefs as to whether visualisation is an appropriate reading strategy. William Gass, for example, argues that visualising over-specifies the verbal information that a literary text provides and thus violates the artistic integrity of the work (*see* MEDIA AND NARRATIVE). Although a propensity to visualise was linked to *gender in the early 1880s, when the eminent scientist Sir Francis Galton reported from a small sampling that women and children visualise more frequently and vividly than educated British male scientists and intellectuals, his analyses are now understood to reflect gender, racial, and class biases. Nonetheless, research on this variable and other individual differences continues (Esrock 1994; Richardson 1999).

Researchers have explored the cognitive effects of imaging for numerous kinds of verbal terms, ranging from isolated words in a list to tightly organised *narratives. Experiments consistently show that subjects recall words that are more concrete than abstract when the items are presented in a list. On the basis of these findings, Paivio suggests that the literature of writers like Shakespeare and Coleridge is best comprehended and appreciated when readers visualise. He holds that symbolic, verbal images that are visualised can serve as prototypes in *memory, which can assist the reader in textual recollection and manipulation.

However, when individual sentences are placed within paragraphs, the imagery effects are less robust than with isolated words and sentences. Marschark and Hunt show that readers who visualise are better able to recall information from loosely organised prose and suggest that visual imagery provides a coherence that is otherwise lacking. By contrast, when the verbal material has a tighter organisation, they find that the visualisation strategy does not increase performance. Their data do not imply, however, that visualising has no effects for narrative reading, as some units within narratives might have less tightly organised structures than others (*see* NARRATIVE UNITS), and visualisation might serve other purposes than the ones tested above. Denis, for example, demonstrates the mnemonic efficacy of visualising in the reading of prose when the subjects are distinguished as high or low imagers by their scores on Marks' Vividness of Visual Imagery Questionnaire. Other experiments show that visualisation enhances the reader's comprehension of narratives that involve the manipulation and recall of spatial and geographical information, as would be conveyed in *travel narratives (Denis et al. 2001) (see NARRATIVE COMPREHENSION; SPACE IN NARRATIVE). For a reader of Dante's *Inferno*, with its numerous and individualised topographies, visualisation would likely prove a helpful reading strategy, and Yates conjectures that it may have been an organising principle for the *author, inspired by ancient memory systems. As Collins demonstrates in an analysis of a poem by William Carlos Williams, visualisation can also help a reader or listener understand obscure verbal descriptions by placing the reader in a familiar visual *perspective.

For the reading of narrative, the most important aspects of visualisation are likely not the cognitive but the emotional effects (see EMOTION AND NARRATIVE). Experiments using narratives indicate that imaging is linked in different ways to such factors as the reader's level of interest and empathy (see Paivio and Sadowski 2001). Denis suggests that imaging might serve as a kind of pleasure taking. For some readers, visualising is a necessary or preferred means of identifying with characters or becoming emotionally involved with a narrative reality (see IMMERSION; STORYWORLD). Such findings are not surprising, as visual images have long been thought to have affective powers related to their content *per se*, as with *archetypal, mystical, and cosmological images, or to personal and cultural associations, as discussed by psychoanalysts and cultural theorists (see PSYCHOANALYSIS AND NARRATIVE; CULTURAL STUDIES APPROACHES TO NARRATIVE). Nonetheless, there is less empirical work on the emotional than on the cognitive dimension of visualisation and language.

Experiments concerning the effects of visualisation are integral to an effort to understand the representational nature of imagery, that is, the means by which visual images are stored and retrieved. The question of which representational model will prevail is significant to narrative studies because some models accommodate a greater range of visualisation effects than others (see Paivio 1983; Kosslyn 1994; Denis et al., 2001). Our understanding of how visualisation functions in the reading of narrative will be deepened by future research that integrates empirical experiments with literary and cultural scholarship.

SEE ALSO: biological foundations of narrative; cognitive narratology; ekphrasis; graphic presentation as expressive device; image and narrative; mental mapping of narrative; psychological approaches to narrative; reader-response theory; situation model

References and further reading
Collins, Christopher (1991) *Poetics of the Mind's Eye*, Philadelphia: University of Pennsylvania Press.
Denis, Michel (1984) 'Imagery and Prose', *TEXT*, 4, 381–401.
——, Robert H. Logie, Cesare Cornoldi, Manuel De Vega, and Johannes Engelkamp (eds) (2001) *Imagery, Language and Visuo-Spatial Thinking*, East Sussex: Psychology Press.
Esrock, Ellen (1994) *The Reader's Eye: Visual Imaging and Reader Response*, Baltimore: Johns Hopkins University Press.
Fleckenstein, Kristie S., Linda T. Calendrillo, and Demetrice A. Worley (eds) (2002) *Language and Image in the Reading-Writing Classroom: Teaching Vision*, Mahwah: Lawrence Erlbaum.
Galton, Sir Francis (1883) *Inquiries into Human Faculty and Its Development*, London: Macmillan.
Kosslyn, Stephen M. (1994) *Image and Brain: The Resolution of the Imagery Debate*, Cambridge, Mass.: Harvard University Press.
Marschark, Mark, and R. Reed Hunt (1989) 'A Reexamination of the Role of Imagery in Learning and Memory', *Journal of Experimental Psychology: Learning, Memory, and Cognition*, 15, 710–20.
Paivio, Allan (1983) 'The Mind's Eye in Arts and Science', *Poetics*, 12, 1–18.
——, and Mark Sadowski (2001) *Imagery and Text*, Mahwah: Lawrence Erlbaum.
Richardson, John T. E. (1999) *Imagery*, East Sussex: Psychology Press.
Schwenger, Peter (1999) *Fantasm and Fiction: On Textual Envisioning*, Stanford: Stanford University Press.
Yates, Frances A. (1966) *The Art of Memory*, Chicago: University of Chicago Press.

ELLEN ESROCK

VOICE

Voice is an umbrella term for the field of questions relating to the speech acts of the *narrator, ranging from *narrative situation to narratorial idiom (see SPEECH ACT THEORY; SPEECH REPRESENTATION). The narratological sense of the term was introduced by Gérard Genette (1980) in connection with the question 'who speaks?' in a narrative text, as opposed to the question of 'who sees?' or 'whose perspective orients the text?' (*see* FOCALIZATION; PERSPECTIVE). Genette answers the question of 'who speaks?' with a typology of narrators (auto-, extra-, hetero-, homo-, intra-diegetic narrator), and further extends the discussion of voice to the question of where the narrator speaks from (narrative level) (*see* EMBEDDING; FRAMED NARRATIVE), and when the narrator speaks ('time of the narrating') (*see* TEMPORAL ORDERING; TIME IN NARRATIVE). Although Genette does not consider 'how' the narrator speaks, the qualitative aspect of voice, embracing questions of register, idiom, and tone, historically precedes the more limited narratological use of the term and remains central to the analysis of narratorial speech acts. It also makes more motivated use of the voice-metaphor. Today, most narrative theorists would recognise, with Mikhail Bakhtin, that narrative texts are made up of a constellation of different, and sometimes even competing, voices (*see* POLYPHONY), although there is far less agreement as to the status of these voices in ontological and metaphorical terms.

A significant move towards a qualitative conception of voice in narratology was made by Seymour Chatman (1978), who attempted to categorise narrative voices in terms of their audibility. Chatman offered a scale of vocal audibility going from extreme overtness (explicit narratorial self-mention) to scarcely perceptible covertness. The limitation of such a scale is that the central criterion for overtness and covertness remains the speaker's relationship to the discourse spoken (i.e., the position, level and time from which the story is told), and not the quality of the discourse itself. Distinctive idiomatic traits – from readily identifiable sociolects to highly ornate narrative styles – are not seen as indicators of voice (*see* SOCIOLINGUISTIC APPROACHES TO NARRATIVE). Indeed, some theorists have even gone on to equate extreme narratorial covertness with an absence of voice (*see* NO-NARRATOR THEORY). Thus Monika Fludernik has claimed that in pure reflector mode narrative it is impossible to identify any narrative voice at all (Fludernik 1993: 443) (*see* NARRATIVE SITUATIONS). Such a claim is consistent with a narratological view of voice as a narratorial function rather than effect, but it remains peculiarly counter-intuitive to think of reflector-mode narratives by flamboyant stylists such as Flaubert, Conrad, Dostoevskii, or James as devoid of voice.

Outside of *structuralist narratology, narrative voice has more generally been viewed as an aspect of stylistics (*see* DISCOURSE ANALYSIS (LINGUISTICS); LINGUISTIC APPROACHES TO NARRATIVE). Indeed, when literary critics write of, say, the Dickensian or Conradian voice, the term 'voice' is related primarily to the *author rather than the narrator, and would appear to be more or less co-terminous with style. In more ideologically oriented criticism, the voice *metaphor has also accrued political connotations, with *vox* figuring above all as a medium of political representation, a means of being heard (*see* IDEOLOGY AND NARRATIVE). In this way, it has been customary to speak of marginal, suppressed, subversive, or even silenced voices in narrative fiction. Particularly important here was is the work on narrative voice in post-colonial and feminist literary studies (Lanser 1992) (*see* FEMINIST NARRATOLOGY; GENDER STUDIES; POST-COLONIALISM AND NARRATIVE).

Much of the politicised stylistics of narrative voice takes its bearings from the work of Bakhtin, who conceived of all utterances as 'overpopulated' with the voices of others. For Bakhtin, a key characteristic of the *modernist novel after Dostoevskii is the incorporation of a diversity of voices and styles of social discourse which are not subjected to the authority of a single authorial idiom. In the prose of Dostoevskii, Bakhtin also identified what he called double-voiced discourse, where an author adopts the discourse of another for his or her own purposes. Double-voiced discourse can be 'uni-directional', where the direction or intentions of the original discourse are maintained, as in stylisation (*see* INTENTIONALITY); 'vari-directional', where another's discourse is used for purposes contrary to its own; and 'active' or 'reflected', where another's discourse is seen to act upon that of the author, usually in the form of a 'hidden polemic' (Bakhtin, 1984: 185–99). The idea of a double or 'dual' voice has also been particularly significant in the study of *free indirect discourse in narrative fiction (Fludernik 1993; Pascal 1977) (*see* DUAL-VOICE HYPOTHESIS).

Perhaps the most sustained challenge to the very notion of identifying voices in narrative texts has come from *poststructuralist narrative theory and deconstruction (*see* DECONSTRUCTIVE APPROACHES TO NARRATIVE). For deconstruction, voice has always been associated with the privileging of speech over writing and the 'metaphysics of presence' (Gibson 1996: 146). The very notion of voice, it is argued, represents a hankering after the chimera of individual origin, self-presence, and authority. One might, however, argue (with Bakhtin) that voice is a much more slippery concept. If all utterances are always already polyphonic, quotational, and composite (*see* QUOTATION THEORY), voice can never be unproblematically returned to a single, unified speaker. One might do better to think of voices less as given qualities present within texts, and more as constructs of the readers who interpret these texts (*see* READER-RESPONSE THEORY). Literary works are perhaps best seen as acts of complex ventriloquism, where the ultimate ventriloquist is the reader.

References and further reading

Aczel, Richard (1998) 'Hearing Voices in Narrative Texts', *New Literary History*, 29.3, 467–500.
Bakhtin, Mikhail (1981) *The Dialogic Imagination*, ed. Michael Holquist, trans. Caryl Emerson and Michael Holquist, Austin: University of Texas Press.
—— (1984) *Problems of Dostoevsky's Poetics*, trans. Caryl Emerson, Minneapolis: University of Minnesota Press.
—— (1986) *Speech Genres and Other Late Essays*, trans. Vern W. McGee, Austin: University of Texas Press.
Cohen, Ralph (ed.) (2001) *New Literary History*, 32.3 (special issue on 'Voice and Human Experience').
Chatman, Seymour (1978) *Story and Discourse: Narrative Structure in Fiction and Film*, Ithaca: Cornell University Press.
Fludernik, Monika (1993) *The Fictions of Language and the Languages of Fiction*, London: Routledge.
Genette, Gérard (1980) *Narrative Discourse: An Essay in Method*, trans. Jane E. Lewin, Ithaca: Cornell University Press.
Gibson, Andrew (1996) *Towards a Postmodern Theory of Narrative*, Edinburgh: Edinburgh University Press.
Lanser, Susan Sniader (1992) *Fictions of Auhority: Women Writers and Narrative Voice*, Ithaca: Cornell University Press.
Pascal, Roy (1977) *The Dual Voice: Free Indirect Speech and its Functioning in the Nineteenth Century European Novel*, Manchester: Manchester University Press.

RICHARD ACZEL

VOICE-OVER NARRATION

Voice-over *narration is a technique commonly used in *film and *television of having oral statements, conveying any portion of a narrative, spoken by an unseen speaker situated in a *space and *time other than that simultaneously being shown by the *images on the screen. The term is often shortened to 'voice-over' or even abbreviated as 'v.o.'. Sometimes the term is used more casually, to refer to any situation of non-synchronous speech, such as voice-off (when the speaker is temporarily out of frame), or instances of interior monologue (when the speaker may be on the screen but his or her lips are not moving as viewers are given access to his or her thoughts; *see* THOUGHT AND CONSCIOUSNESS REPRESENTATION (FILM)). It is preferable, however, to restrict the use of this term to storytelling situations.

Voice-over narration is indebted to the use of lecturers and intertitles during the silent era, and to the example of *radio dramas in the 1930s. Evidence indicates that in the United States it was first used in short newsreels in 1930. The use of such narration has remained a staple of non-fiction film and television, from news broadcasts to feature documentaries.

Voice-over *narrators can be divided into those who inhabit the narrative world (homodiegetic, or first-person narrators), and those who speak from outside the confines of the story (heterodiegetic, or third-person; *see* NARRATIVE SITUATIONS; PERSON). First-person voice-over is often used to provide a *character's interpretation of his or her own story, as in the films *About a Boy* and *Apocalypse Now* or the television series *The Wonder Years*. Film noirs and *adaptations of *novels are particularly likely to use this device.

Third-person voice-over narration is common not only in documentary formats, but in *epics and semi-documentaries. Many critics have objected to the use of third-person voice-over narration, claiming that the voice (historically nearly always belonging to a deep-voiced white male) speaks from a position of overweening ideological authority, making him a 'voice-of-God' and restricting any alternate interpretation of the visual images (*see* IDEOLOGY AND NARRATIVE). Kozloff (1984) argues that this is more a matter of scripting and casting than inherent to the technique itself.

Voice-over narration can be used creatively and effectively to provide *exposition or to offer intimacy, *irony, or the complication of a limited or unreliable narrator (*see* RELIABILITY). Filmmakers have used this device in a number of intriguing ways: to allow the dead to speak (*Sunset Boulevard*); to create multiple storytellers (*All About Eve*), to analyse characters' foibles from a scientific standpoint (*Mon oncle d'Amérique*). Feminist theorists have seen emphasis on the *voice as a more positive avenue for exploration than the objectifying, 'male gaze' of the camera.

SEE ALSO: focalization; framed narrative; gaze; gender studies

References and further reading

Chatman, Seymour (1999) 'New Direction in Voice-Narrated Cinema', in David Herman (ed.) *Narratologies: New Perspective on Narrative Analysis*, Columbus: Ohio State University Press.

Fink, Guido (1982) 'From Showing to Telling: Off-Screen Narration in the American Cinema', *Letterature d'America*, 3.12, 5–37.

Kozloff, Sarah (1984) 'Humanizing "The voice of God": Narration in *The Naked City*', *Cinema Journal*, 23.4, 41–53.

——(1988) *Invisible Storytellers: Voice-over Narration in American Fiction Film*, Berkeley: University of California Press.

Nichols, Bill (1983) 'The Voice of Documentary', *Film Quarterly*, 36.3, 17–30.

Youdelman, Jeffrey (1982) 'Narration, Invention and History: A Documentary Dilemma', *Cineaste*, 12.2, 8–15.

SARAH KOZLOFF

WRITERLY TEXT

Coined by Roland Barthes, the term 'writerly text' refers to a text which is made up of a 'galaxy of signifiers' and requires an active reader who co-produces the plurality of its meanings. Barthes opposes the writerly text to the readerly text, which is characterised by narrative linearity, transparency of meaning, and continuity of *plot. *See* READERLY TEXT, WRITERLY TEXT (BARTHES); READER-RESPONSE THEORY.

Index

Note: Page numbers in **bold** refer to key discussions. Titles of entries contained in the Encyclopedia are listed in SMALL CAPS. Except in cases where there are sub-headings, page numbers for Encyclopedia entries are listed first in bold and separated by a semi-colon from other relevant page references.

The coeditors gratefully acknowledge the assistance of Dörte Bonhagen, Sabine Buchholz, and Maren Kiwitt in compiling this index.

FILM NARRATIVE (ctd.)
  SCENE (CINEMATIC); SCREENPLAY; SHOT;
  VOICE-OVER NARRATION
film noir, 203, 636
film script, 65, 227, **520**. *See also* SCREENPLAY
filter (Chatman), 174, 176, 372, **441–2**. *See also*
  FOCALIZATION; PERSPECTIVE; POINT OF VIEW
  (LITERARY); slant
Finnegans Wake, 126, 319
FIRST-PERSON NARRATION, **173**; 6, 155, 399, 340–2,
  364, 396, 399, 423, 536, 603, 611, 636. *See also*
  HOMODIEGETIC NARRATION; NARRATION;
  NARRATIVE SITUATIONS
Fish, S., 29–30, 67, 483, 485
Fisher, W. R., 44, **76–7**
Fitzgerald, F. S., 258, 260, 313, 442
Fitzpatrick, P., 274
fixed focalization, **174**, 176. *See also*
  FOCALIZATION; multiple focalization;
  NARRATIVE TECHNIQUES; PERSPECTIVE; POINT
  OF VIEW (CINEMATIC); POINT OF VIEW
  (LITERARY); variable focalization
Flanagan, O., 364
flashback, 39, 72, 172, 186, 372, 383, 591,
  609, 615, 618. *See also* ANALEPSIS;
  TEMPORAL ORDERING
flashforward, 79, 171, 372, 383, 468, 591, 609.
  See also PROLEPSIS; TEMPORAL ORDERING
Flaubert, G., 236, 263, 284, 314, 329, 401, 447,
  475, 491–3, 548, 554–5, 590, 603, 631, 635
Flaubert's Parrot, 216
flexinarrative, 527, 588. *See also* SERIAL FORM;
  TELEVISION
flow (R. Williams), 585. *See also* TELEVISION
Fludernik, M., 70, 92, 120, 127, **155**, 305, 341,
  381, **386–7**, **394–5**, 474–5, 561, 595, 606, 610, 635
focal character, 173–7
FOCALIZATION
  and cognitive narratology, 69
  and cultural studies approaches, 92
  embedding of, 134–5
  and film/visual narrative, 251, 630–1
  and the gaze, 194
  and indeterminacy, 241
  and magic realism, 282
  main discussion of, 173–7
  and modernist narrative, 317, 319, 320
  and mood (Genette), 173, 322
  and narrative techniques, 370, 372

and the narrator, 389
and perspective, 424
and transfocalization, 613
vs. voice, 370, 372, 465–6. *See also*
  PERSPECTIVE; POINT OF VIEW (CINEMATIC);
  POINT OF VIEW (LITERARY)
Fokkelman, J., 41
Fokkema, D. W., 457, 552
Foley, J. M., 178, 411
FOLKLORE, **177–9**; 39, 126, 160, 323, 385,
  507, 531. *See also* anthropology;
  ETHNOGRAPHIC APPROACHES TO NARRATIVE;
  FOLKTALE; interviews; ORAL HISTORY
folktale, **179–80**; 1, 83, 125, 157, 177, 182,
  191, 200, 212, 258, 299, 436, 523, 525, 572.
  See also FAIRY TALE
Ford, F. M., 317–18
FOREGROUNDING, **180**; 523
foreshadowing. *See* PROLEPSIS; TEMPORAL
  ORDERING
formal intermedial imitation, 255. *See also*
  INTERMEDIALITY
FORMALISM, **180–5**; 98, 110, 257, 523–5
formula, 34, 67–8, 176, 199–200, 439–40, 560
Fornara, C. W., 21
Forster, E. M., 13, 58, 183, 353, 402, **436**, 609
Foucault, M., **34**, 84, **112–14**, 143, 198, 215, 288,
  345, 427, 461–2, 468, 547
found manuscript, 188
Fowler, D., 139
Fowler, R., 278–9, 311, **313–14**, 365
Fowles, J., 119, 176, 323, 369, 457, 591
Fox Keller, E., 518
fractals, 182
fractured narrative, 586
fragmentation, 35, 196, 323, 395, 555
frame story, 134, 338. *See also* Chinese-box
  structures; diegetic levels; EMBEDDING;
  FRAMED NARRATIVE; NARRATIVE LEVELS;
  NARRATIVE TRANSMISSION; transmission
FRAME THEORY, **185–6**. *See also*
  metacommunication; phenomenology;
  SCRIPTS AND SCHEMATA
framebreaking, 24. *See also* frames
FRAMED NARRATIVE, **186–8**; 338, 350. *See also*
  frames; frame story; framing devices
frames
  and codes for reading, 67
  and cognitive narratology, 69–71

motivation (ctd.)
and narrativisation, 387
and plot, 347
as revealed through embedded narratives, 135
and situation models, 534
and theories of communication, 77
and theories of emotion, 137
and verisimilitude, 627. *See also* agent;
    CHARACTER; goals; INTENTIONALITY; plans
Moulton, C., 139
move grammar, 383. *See also* events; EVENTS
    AND EVENT-TYPES; goals; grammar; plans;
    STORY GRAMMARS
moveable stock device, 322. *See also*
    ORAL-FORMULAIC THEORY
movie, 65, 120, 123, **168–72**, 224, 227, 239,
    289–90, 315, 346, 497, 513, 519, 586, 623.
    See also ADAPTATION; ANIMATED FILM;
    CINÉROMAN; FILM NARRATIVE; GENRE THEORY
    IN FILM STUDIES; INTERMEDIALITY; MEDIA AND
    NARRATIVE; MINDSCREEN; MONTAGE; POINT OF
    VIEW (CINEMATIC); SCENE (CINEMATIC);
    SCREENPLAY; SHOT; VOICE-OVER NARRATION
Mrs. Dalloway, 52, 174, 317–18, 390, 570
MTV, 6
MUD, 459
Mukařovský, J., 121, 180, 523
Mukherjee, B., 454, 460
Müller, G., **608–9**
multiculturalism, 107, 142, 147, **228**, 282, 623.
    See also cultural and historical narratology;
    CULTURAL STUDIES APPROACHES TO
    NARRATIVE; HYBRIDITY; POST-COLONIALISM
    AND NARRATIVE
multimediality, 126, 161, 237, 254, 256, 291,
    556, 585. *See also* composite media;
    INTERMEDIALITY; MEDIA AND NARRATIVE;
    plurimediality; remediation
MULTI-PATH NARRATIVE, **323–4**; 484. *See also*
    COMPUTER GAMES AND NARRATIVE; ERGODIC
    LITERATURE; digital media; DIGITAL
    NARRATIVE; HYPERTEXT; interactivity;
    MULTI-PLOT NARRATIVE; PARTICIPATORY
    NARRATIVE
multiperspectivism, 78, 92, 174, 208, 214,
    277, 496
multiple focalization, 174, 176. *See also* fixed
    focalization; FOCALIZATION; NARRATIVE
    TECHNIQUES; PERSPECTIVE; POINT OF VIEW

(CINEMATIC); POINT OF VIEW (LITERARY);
    variable focalization
multiple narrators, 176, 338, 359, 389, 422.
    See also co-narration; NARRATION;
    NARRATOR
multiple realities, 186
MULTI-PLOT NARRATIVE, **324**; 357, **368–9**.
    See also MULTI-PATH NARRATIVE; NARRATIVE
    STRUCTURE; PLOT; PLOT-TYPES
Mulvey, L., 194, 630
Mumby, D., 76–7
Murray, J., 27, 81, 108–9, 237
MUSIC AND NARRATIVE, **324–9**; 171, 250, 255,
    276, 408, 487, 550. *See also* diegetic vs.
    non-diegetic music; MEDIA AND NARRATIVE;
    musicalisation of fiction; OPERA; RADIO
    NARRATIVE; SOUNDTRACK
musical, 200, 326. *See also* DRAMA AND
    NARRATIVE; OPERA
musicalisation of fiction, 255, 276, 326. *See also*
    INTERMEDIALITY; MUSIC AND NARRATIVE
Musil, R., 263, 317, 402, 404, 427
must-have-thought style, 217
'My Last Duchess', 124, 356
mystery (enigma), 103, 314, 440, 590. *See also*
    CODES FOR READING; SUSPENSE AND SURPRISE
mystery story, **199**, 314, 440, 494, 508,
    587, 607. *See also* DETECTIVE FICTION;
    GENRE FICTION; police procedural; spy story;
    THRILLER
mystery plays, 120
myth criticism. *See* ARCHETYPAL PATTERNS;
    archetype; MYTH: THEMATIC APPROACHES;
    MYTH: THEORETICAL APPROACHES
MYTH: THEMATIC APPROACHES, **329–30**; 20, 26, 31,
    77, 88, 126, 160, 165, 178, 265, 274, 384,
    614. *See also* ARCHETYPAL PATTERNS; MYTH:
    THEORETICAL APPROACHES; NARRATIVE
    UNIVERSALS
MYTH: THEORETICAL APPROACHES, **330–35**; **439**,
    572–3; 203, 257, 344. *See also* anthropology;
    ETHNOGRAPHIC APPROACHES TO NARRATIVE;
    MYTH: THEMATIC APPROACHES; MYTHEME;
    Oedipal complex; PSYCHOANALYSIS AND
    NARRATIVE; RELIGION; SCIENCE AND
    NARRATIVE; THEOLOGY AND NARRATIVE;
    STRUCTURALIST NARRATOLOGY
MYTHEME, **335**; 257, 573. *See also*
    STRUCTURALIST NARRATOLOGY

poststructuralism. *See* DECONSTRUCTIVE
APPROACHES TO NARRATIVE; POSTSTRUCTURALIST
APPROACHES TO NARRATIVE
POSTSTRUCTURALIST APPROACHES TO NARRATIVE
and autobiography, 35
and autofiction, 37
and closure, 66
and *écriture féminine*, 131
and feminist narratology, 161
and gender studies, 196
and intentionality, 248–9
and intertextuality, 258–9
and the law, 273
main discussion of, 461–2
and post-colonial narratives, 451
and postmodern narrative, 456, 459
and psychoanalytic approaches, 469
and sociological approaches, 544, 546
and surfiction, 577
and theories of plot, 435
and theories of truth, 621
and voice, 635
and the writerly text (Barthes), 483. *See also*
DECONSTRUCTIVE APPROACHES TO NARRATIVE;
POSTCLASSICAL NARRATOLOGY
Pouillon, J., 173, 442
Pound, E., 357, 369, 505, 555
power
and agency, 9–10, 91, 132
in cases of supernatural causality, 51
in courtroom narrative, 86–7
and critical discourse analysis, 115
of cultural narratives, 406, 453
in cyberpunk fiction, 93
ethical approaches to, 143
ethnographic approaches to, 146, 149–50
Foucault's critique of, 112–13, 345, 467
and gossip, 207
and institutional narratives, 243, 245–6
and Marxist approaches to narrative, 315
and master narratives, 317–18
micro- and macrosociological approaches
to, 548
in penitentiaries, 467–8
of quoter vs. quotee, 480
and representations of alterity, 13
and sociolinguistic approaches to
narrative, 542, 544. *See also*
DISCOURSE ANALYSIS (FOUCAULT);

disempowerment; empowerment;
inequality; New Historicism
Powers, R., 138
PRAGMATICS, **462–7**; 67, 143, 149, **164–5**, 198,
262, 278, 308, 364, 381, 479, **546–7**, 613,
632. *See also* CAUSALITY; Cooperative
Principle; DISCOURSE ANALYSIS (LINGUISTICS);
GAPPING; LINGUISTIC APPROACHES
TO NARRATIVE; implicature; SPEECH
ACT THEORY
Prague Linguistic Circle, 180, **523**
Pratt, M. L., 12, 193, 381, **558**, 590, 611
preaching. *See* gospel; homiletics; PARABLE;
SERMON; THEOLOGY AND NARRATIVE
predictive discourse, 609
preface, **75**, 84, **185–6**, 188, 267,
377, **419**
preference rules, 67, **69–70**, 347.
See also COGNITIVE NARRATOLOGY;
EVENTS AND EVENT-TYPES
prefiguration, 91, 168
pregnant moment, 292, 305, 316, 363, **432**.
See also IMAGE AND NARRATIVE; painting;
PHOTOGRAPHS; PICTORIAL NARRATIVITY
prequel, 242, 368
prescriptivism
in Bakhtin's theory of the novel, 213
in genre theory, 202
and Lubbock's novelistic theory, 576
in theories of narrative stucture, 367
in travel narratives, 620. *See also* normativity;
norms
present tense, 21, 56, 106–7, 215, **341**, 362, 561,
608, 610. *See also* NARRATION; past tense;
TENSE AND NARRATIVE
pre-Socratics, 330, 427
Preston, M. E., 391
presymbolic communication, 131
pretence, 60–1, **165**, 238, 265. *See also* FICTION,
THEORIES OF; SPEECH ACT THEORY
pretext, 11, 34, 81, 229, 256, 261, 330, 394
Pride and Prejudice, 102, 390, 501–2
primacy effect, 70, 282, 528, 583, 595.
See also NARRATIVE DYNAMICS;
recency effect
priming, 238
Prince, G., 2, 30, 100, 106, 118–19, 120, 126,
151, 154, 162, 177, 217, 241, 305, 312, 324,
346, 366, **380**, 387, 529, 551, 565, 623